Lady Mary Wortley Montagu

FRONTISPIECE. Mary Wortley Montagu by Jonathan Richardson, painted about
1726. Reproduced by kind permission of the Earl of Harrowby

Lady Mary Wortley Montagu

ISOBEL GRUNDY

OXFORD
UNIVERSITY PRESS

OXFORD

UNIVERSITY PRESS

Great Clarendon Street, Oxford OX2 6DP

Oxford University Press is a department of the University of Oxford.
It furthers the University's objective of excellence in research, scholarship,
and education by publishing worldwide in

Oxford New York

Athens Auckland Bangkok Bogotá Buenos Aires Calcutta
Cape Town Chennai Dar es Salaam Delhi Florence Hong Kong Istanbul
Karachi Kuala Lumpur Madrid Melbourne Mexico City Mumbai
Nairobi Paris São Paulo Singapore Taipei Tokyo Toronto Warsaw

with associated companies in Berlin Ibadan

Oxford is a registered trade mark of Oxford University Press
in the UK and in certain other countries

Published in the United States
by Oxford University Press Inc., New York

92wor/ 3095312

First published 1999

British Library Cataloguing in Publication Data

Data available

Library of Congress Cataloging in Publication Data
Grundy, Isobel.
Lady Mary Wortley Montagu / Isobel Grundy.
pm.
Includes bibliographical references (p.).
1. Montagu, Mary Wortley, Lady, 1689–1762. 2. Women and literature—Great Britain—History—
18th century. 3. English letters—Women authors—History and criticism. 4. English letters—
18th century—History and criticism. 5. Women authors, English—18th century—Biography.
6. Diplomats' spouses—Great Britain—Biography. I. Title.
PR3604.Z5G78 1999 823'.5—dc21 98-48471

ISBN 0–19–811289–0

3 5 7 9 10 8 6 4 2

Typeset in Fournier
by Jayvee, Trivandrum, India
Printed in Great Britain
on acid-free paper by
Biddles Ltd,
Guildford and King's Lynn

To the Memory of Robert Halsband

and of

my parents
died 1997

ACKNOWLEDGEMENTS

MY first debt, acknowledged in the dedication, is to Robert Halsband, who taught me about Lady Mary and about research, and was unfailingly generous in the teaching process. Before him, Kirstie Morrison had introduced me to Lady Mary. Other people have worked and written on her and her life, without whom this book would have far more shortcomings than it has: Valerie Rumbold, Lois Kathleen Mahaffey, Emily Morse Symonds, Lady Louisa Stuart. To all of these I am deeply grateful.

My second debt is to libraries and library systems. Where would this book be without the British Library, the Bodleian, the University of Alberta Libraries, and many more? Staff at a dozen County Archives have been far-sighted enough to bend their own regulations about how many manuscripts could be ordered at a time, once they saw me thumbing speedily through piles of loose sheets. Staff at Italian libraries have remained courageous and optimistic in the face of language barriers. People in the past, alive and dead, have initiated and maintained these libraries with vision and with funds; may others continue to do so.

My third debt is to individuals who have helped. These include owners of manuscripts, owners of expertise and special knowledge, helpers of many kinds. The following list undoubtedly has glaring omissions, people whose names I have lost during my years of work. I am grateful to those forgotten ones, and to my parents (the only people to read a draft of the work from beginning to end), and to the following: Giuseppina Bertolek-Lucini, Patrizia Bettella, Michael Bosson, Robin Brackenbury, Joan Brumlik, William Buist-Wells, Ann Burling, Pamela Clark, The Revd Clive Cohen, Carolyn Creed, John Comyn, David Falconer, Helena Fracchia, Christine Gerrard, Bruno Gialluca, Germaine Greer, John Grundy, John Guinness, Frances Harris, the Right Honourable the Earl of Harrowby, Chantel Lavoie, Michael Londry, Maynard Mack, Jane Magrath, James E. May, David McLean, James McLaverty, Sara Heller Mendelson, Ann Messenger, Michael Moss, Antoin E. Murphy, Elizabeth Murray, Janet Orr, David Parker, Sir Michael and Lady Partridge, Ruth Perry, Richard Quaintance, Nasrin Rahimieh, Prue Raper, Jonathan and Sarah Raper, Jeremy Rex-Parkes,

Betty Rizzo, Andrea Rusnock, Mary Sampson, Betsy Sargent, Diana Scarisbrick, Rusty Shteir, Charles Siegel, Francis Sitwell, Andrew S. Skinner, Christina Sommerfeldt, Nora Foster Stovel, Konrad Suchanek, Helen Tasker-Poland, Jan Piet Teding van Berkhout, Pam and Norman Thorne, Massimo Verdicchio, Jane Waley, Keith Wikeley, Arnot Wilson, Carol Gibson Wood, Susan Wright, David Yaxley.

I.M.G.

July 1997

CONTENTS

❧

LIST OF ILLUSTRATIONS

❧

FRONTISPIECE

Mary Wortley Montagu by Jonathan Richardson, painted about 1726

PLATES: BETWEEN PAGES 328 AND 329

MAPS

ABBREVIATIONS

Ad. MSS   Admiralty MSS, Public Record Office, Kew
b.   born
Bod.   Bodleian Library, Oxford
BL   British Library
BL Eg. MSS   British Library, Egerton MSS
CB   MWM, Commonplace-Book, Fisher Library, University of
               Sydney
CL   MWM, *Complete Letters*, ed. Robert Halsband (Oxford, 1965–7)
CUL   Cambridge University Library
d.   died
DNB   *Dictionary of National Biography*
E&P   MWM, *Essays and Poems and Simplicity a Comedy*, ed. Robert
               Halsband and Isobel Grundy (Oxford, 1977; 1993)
ECF   *Eighteenth-Century Fiction*
ECS   *Eighteenth Century Studies*
ELN   *English Language Notes*
EWM   Edward Wortley Montagu
GEC   G. E. C[okayne], *Complete Peerage*, ed. Vicany Gibbs *et al.*
               (1910–59)
GM   *Gentleman's Magazine*
H MSS   Harrowby MSS Trust, Sandon Hall, Stafford
Hertford–Pomfret *Corr.*   *Correspondence Between Frances, Countess of Hartford,*
               (Afterwards Duchess of Somerset,) and Henrietta Louisa, Countess
               of Pomfret, between the years 1738 and 1741 (1805)
HMC   Historical Manuscripts Commission
m.   married
MWM   Lady Mary Wortley Montagu
N&Q   *Notes and Queries*
NLS   National Library of Scotland
NPG   National Portrait Gallery
POAS   *Poems on Affairs of State* (1703); *State Poems, Continued . . .*
               to . . . 1697 (1703); 4 more vols. from 5th edn., 1703–7 (Sandon
               Hall)
Pope, *Corr.* Alexander Pope, *Correspondence*, ed. George Sherburn (1956)

PRO	Public Record Office
RES	*Review of English Studies*
RW	Sir Robert Walpole
RW	MWM, *Romance Writings*, ed. Isobel Grundy (Oxford, 1996)
SB	*Studies in Bibliography*
SECC	*Studies in Eighteenth-Century Culture*
SL	MWM, *Selected Letters*, ed. Isobel Grundy (1997)
SP	State Papers
TE	Alexander Pope, *Poems*, The Twickenham Edition (London and New Haven), i. *Pastoral Poetry and An Essay on Criticism*, ed. E. Audra and Aubrey Williams (1961); ii. *The Rape of the Lock and Other Poems*, ed. Geoffrey Tillotson (1940; rev. edn., 1954); iii—i. *An Essay on Man*, ed. Maynard Mack (1950); iii— ii. *Epistles to Several Persons (Moral Essays)*, ed. F. W. Bateson (1951; rev. edn., 1961); iv. *Imitations of Horace*, ed. John Butt (1939; rev. edn., 1961); v. *The Dunciad*, ed. James Sutherland (1943, rev. edn., 1963); vi. *Minor Poems*, ed. Norman Ault and John Butt (1964)
TLS	*Times Literary Supplement*
Walpole, *Corr.*	Horace Walpole, *Correspondence*, ed. W. S. Lewis *et al.* (1937–83)
Wh MSS	Wharncliffe MSS, Sheffield Central Library

The old illusion comes over us. Here is the past and all its inhabitants miraculously sealed as in a magic tank; all we have to do is to look and to listen and to listen and to look and soon the little figures—for they are rather under life size—will begin to move and to speak, and as they move we shall arrange them in all sorts of patterns of which they were ignorant, for they thought when they were alive that they could go where they liked; and as they speak we shall read into their sayings all kinds of meanings which never struck them, for they believed when they were alive that they said straight off whatever came into their heads. But once you are in a biography all is different.

Virginia Woolf, 'I am Christina Rossetti'[1]

Scolastic Works, spiders webs.

Lady Mary Wortley Montagu,
Commonplace-Book, fo. 6

[1] 1930, in *Women and Writing*, 1979: 161–2.

INTRODUCTION

~ᴥ~

'It will have the Air of a Romance'[2]

LADY MARY WORTLEY MONTAGU is no stranger to fame or to ill fame. She has been celebrated since her own day as a letter-writer, as a traveller to the east, and as the introducer to the west of inoculation against small-pox. She has been notorious as an enemy or victim of the poet Pope. Now, belatedly, she is coming into her reputation as a writer.

She was born into the highest nobility. She was brilliant in mind and beautiful in face and body. She educated herself, since no one else would do it for her. Sooner than marry the peer's son chosen by her father, she eloped with an untitled man who later became, by his own efforts, one of the richest in the land. Long before that his appointment as British ambassador to Turkey made her the first Englishwoman to experience and report on life in a non-Christian, non-European culture: a unique literary opportunity which she grasped with both hands. Her daughter married a future Prime Minister and spread her blood-line far and wide among the English and Scottish nobility. When London life galled her, she moved abroad, and lived for twenty years in France and Italy. During those years she was accountable to no one but herself, in a manner almost unimaginable for most women of her period.

But when she herself related the story of her life and talents, she said the bad fairies found means to nullify every gift the good one gave. Most of the potential benefits of her rank came with a 'Men Only' label to them. The wealth that surrounded her in youth and age was never her own, but always her father's or husband's. Her beauty fell a prey to smallpox.

These were matters about which she said she did not care. But the way that gender restrictions applied to her high social status was nothing to the

---

[2] *E&P* 77.

way they applied to her literary ambitions. Her intellect made her hated, she said, and her emotional sensitivity made her suffer. Her hard-won education brought her far more derision or disapproval than respect. Her feelings about making her writings public were painfully conflicted.

Even to name her involves thought and compromise. As an earl's daughter she had 'Lady' attached to her Christian name, and was regularly called by that honorific first name (Lady Mary) in situations where a surname would normally be used. 'Lady Mary' sounds to most modern ears either over-deferential or pseudo-glamorous. Yet *not* to use it would be to edit out that rank and status which to her own mind and the minds of her contemporaries was a fixed part of her identity. She then married a man with two surnames, of which the more current one (at least in England) was Wortley. In reference to her literary career I shall call her Montagu, erasing her contemporaries' usage in favour of that of today's critics and literary historians. In other contexts I shall call her Lady Mary.

The most obvious facts about her, when examined, prove ambiguous or slippery. She eloped like a quintessential romantic heroine—but with a man she did not love. She respected him; she knew he would be hard to live with; she had broken off her relationship with him a dozen times. She was in love with a different man, someone who was already lost to her for reasons as unknown as himself.

Her face was ruined by smallpox—but within a few years it was *de rigueur* again for those meeting her to comment on her beauty, as if either her looks had somehow repaired themselves or those around her found it unthinkable that she should not be beautiful.

The period when Pope was her worshipper is not directly visible, but only refracted through the letters he wrote when she was safely distant and expected to remain so for the foreseeable future. The true causes why his worship turned to rancour are still mysterious, and unlikely ever to be fully explained. Fuller understanding could probably emerge not from hunting a particular moment or particular event, but only from clearer and bolder thinking about the working out of gender issues. We have made some progress in capacity to detect the hostility already immanent in the adoration. No reader today will find in Pope's letters to Lady Mary on her travels a transparent wish to please. He constructs her as a beautiful body—implicitly a nude body—while she is busy constructing herself as doing and seeing and writing. She was still constructing herself this way years later, when he was painting her as a monster.

Pope's final, full-blown, gendered hatred is extraordinary, yet it is also typical. As a highly visible, assertive, unconforming woman Lady Mary was a lightning rod for misogynist anxiety and anger. In the almost half a century from her elopement to the British expatriate campaign against her when she was an old lady in Venice, she seldom ceased to attract opprobrium. In London she lived in the limelight; the media treated her not as an aristocrat but as a celebrity.

Early in her adult life came the scandal of her (involuntary) appearance in print, accused of writing some sophisticated satires on high society which were read as attacks on the court. Next came the scandal of her support for inoculation. This first step in preventative medicine stemmed not from scientific theory or the medical establishment, but from the female folk-practices of a culture both remote and despised. The battle to naturalize the new practice in England was fought out in the press with no holds barred. Not only was this arena no place for a lady; it was no place for a woman, since antifeminist rhetoric was one of the trustiest weapons of the anti-inoculation faction. This left another indelible mark on Lady Mary's reputation.

Conspicuous as an icon, she is hidden as an agent. The extent of her inoculation activity has to be inferred from hints in pamphlets and from the way her friends' children fill the roster of early inoculees. None of the major issues of her life has left traces enough to clarify it: not the feelings surrounding her elopement, her precise role in inoculation, her most important female friendships, her quarrel with Pope, her relation to men of learning and to the Enlightenment in general, her sister's descent into madness, her middle-aged love-affair with Francesco Algarotti (and any other love-affair she *may* have had at any time), her motives for going abroad in 1739, her survival among homicidal criminals in North Italy, her extensive purchases of property there, or the factual outline (never mind the feelings) of her relationship with her errant son.

To this list can be added almost the entire story of her life as a writer— now secretly wangling herself into print, now actively self-censoring. Her published works fill five volumes: *Complete Letters*, 1965–7, *Essays and Poems*, 1977, 1993, *Romance Writings*, 1996. Her lost works would certainly outnumber these, including as they do a lifelong diary (destroyed by well-meaning relations), a dozen or more important lost correspondences (probably victims of chance or piecemeal tidying), and a 'History of [her] own Time', destroyed by herself as fast as she finished it—or so she told her potentially disapproving daughter. When in old age she said that all her works were 'consecrated to the fire for fear of being put to more ignoble uses',[3] she seems to refer to large-scale destruction.

---

[3] *CL* iii. 170.

The works missing from Montagu's record almost certainly include a number in each of the following broad categories. Firstly, topical works of political and social commentary. Reading the ephemera of the early Hanoverian period in prose and verse, I have often wondered, 'Is this hers?' (Sometimes I was not the first: her contemporaries had wondered too.) Ballads by her are much mentioned, seldom identified. She was a close friend both of Maria Skerrett, the Prime Minister's mistress (who was thought to wield real political influence) and of John, Lord Hervey, his agent in the House of Lords and watchdog at court, and one of the most prolific and effective contemporary pamphleteers. Lady Mary held strong views on topics like interest rates and workers' wages, as well as on the personal issues surrounding the politics of a patronage society. She expressed some of these opinions in her periodical the *Nonsense of Common-Sense*, 1737–8—a work which does not look like a debut. It was probably not for nothing that Skerrett burned a trunkful of Montagu's writings just before her marriage.

Secondly, love-poetry. I mean not her poems of passion (the surviving handful of which is a striking contradiction of some suppositions about Augustan style), but light lyrics capturing and often fictionalizing the fleeting moods of desire or evasion or repulse. Her papers include many such pieces, unpublished, for which no author has ever been suggested and she herself is the most likely suspect.

Thirdly, fiction. All her surviving longer fictions are either incomplete in themselves, or designed as parts of some more extended composite work. She wrote in this genre for her own amusement; her deliberately casual, even slighting terms for it have until recently been accepted at face value by critics. Drafts and fragments relating to 'Princess Docile' suggest that Montagu worked seriously at it over a period of many years. Those years would have accommodated a considerable output.

This is not the place to argue her importance as a writer, but my assumption of her stature underlies the way I have treated her here. Interest in her as an author does not detract from interest in her as a personality. Her capacity for adventure was extraordinary. It is somehow typical of her that when she made an enemy it was the leading English poet of the age, and when she got involved with a shady character it was the most formidable bandit in Brescia.

While often seeing herself (accurately) as governed by forces she could not control, she strove all her life to exercise a measure of autonomy by understanding and analysing those forces. Her thinking is strong and often highly original. She did not retain her early, idealistic concern for the underdog and rejection of social rank as a measure of worth. But on issues regarding gender she moved away from acceptance into radicalism. She not only asserted the worth of women, but mounted a clear-eyed critique of the inequities of marriage law and of attitudes to non-marital sex. In her poem 'Mrs Yonge' the man accusing the woman is also the reason—the excuse—for her 'crime'. She consistently presents seduction as an evil whose perpetrator is rewarded while its victim is punished.

Lady Mary's was a life of struggle in almost all its phases, both in the way inevitable for any woman of her time who 'attempt[ed] the pen',[4] and in a range of unpredictable ways connected with her particular, highly unusual circumstances and associates. The story of her life brings us hard up against the dominance of money matters over family relationships during this period, and the gulf separating those who had either property or access to property from those who did not. (Women fell normally, though not invariably, into the second category.) Many stories related in this book are somewhat tangential to Lady Mary Wortley Montagu the writer and intellectual; yet they shaped her life and therefore her mind. These include the stories of how her father arranged his children's marriages, how her husband made his pile in coal-mining and how he bequeathed it, how her sister became the weapon wielded by her Jacobite husband's family in their desperate fight to salvage their fortunes, and how her son scrounged and conned his living on the fringes of respectable society.

Many of these situations seem like extreme or exaggerated versions of what might be expected. The people close to Lady Mary look similarly more colourful than the norm. Her friend Sarah, Duchess of Marlborough, was (like herself) perceived as constantly engaged in quarrels. Lady Stafford (probably a lesbian) sprang from the glamorous court societies of Louis XIV and Charles II. Skerrett and Hervey became known in their different ways for sexual deviance. Lady Mary's 'sister Mar' was, it seems, literally driven mad by her role as an object of exchange between the conflicting forces of England and Scotland, Whigs and Jacobites. Lady Mary's son became a criminal; her son-in-law became a hysterically hated Prime Minister.

Ability is commoner among her friends than is conformity. Hervey and Skerrett can each claim some credit for Sir Robert Walpole's long exercise of power; James Stuart Mackenzie contributed similarly to Lord Bute's shorter innings. Algarotti, whom Lady Mary fell in love with, had real originality as a cultural theorist; so had Sir James Steuart, whom she said she loved as a literary sister, as an economic theorist. Other friends, like Marie La Vie and Wilhelmina Tichborne, came from a much lower social stratum than hers

---

[4] Finch 1903: 4.

and led unrecorded lives; yet each of these forgotten women left one witness to her special, remarkable quality.

Even if she had allowed nothing to survive, or if she had not written, Lady Mary would be an object of interest today. She touched life at many points. She crossed a field of military carnage at Peterwardein, visited the women's public baths at Sofia, and stood on the site of Troy. She waded into international disputes and attempted to solve them. She embroidered 'like an angel', creating her own designs;[5] she circulated portraits of herself among her friends; she made bread and butter, cheesecake, and her own wine; she raised poultry for profit and experimented with growing tea and spinning silk. When she turned to the study of herbs, it was not long before she was offering home-made remedies.

Historians see her lifespan as a time during which conduct-books extended their influence, and élite and middle-class women became increasingly subject to new and on the whole restrictive ideals of sensibility and domesticity. Woman was to feel, to exert a refining influence; she was not 'to know, to reason, and to act'.[6] Lady Mary lived in the shadow of these forces. Her desire for approval was very strong, and it battled perpetually with her urge to achieve: that is, to rebel. But though the internal struggle was wearing, sometimes dispiriting, the outcome was never in doubt. She saw herself as a writer; she has made the world accept her as a writer, too.

～❧～

In quoting from manuscripts I have followed spelling and have attempted to follow capitalization exactly. For the comfort of readers, however, I have supplied or supplemented inadequate punctuation, lowered raised letters (as in Mr, Mrs), and expanded the ampersand and other standard abbreviations (like wn for when and yt for that) except in the rare case where there was some reason not to. When other editors have decided differently, I have of course reproduced their printed text exactly.

When quoting eighteenth-century texts I have occasionally ignored very heavy typographical emphasis (in titles of poems, for instance, or whole passages of italic). When quoting modern editions of Montagu I have sometimes omitted the angle brackets, < >, which mark unclear readings, in cases where there can be no doubt about what the manuscript says.

For some minor deposits of manuscripts (e.g. the Murray MSS and Craigievar MSS), and for the Bute MSS (not available for consultation at the time of going to press) I have used copies in the Halsband MSS.

CL ii. 54.   [6] Samuel Johnson, *Rambler*, 25 June 1751, number 133.

English dates before 2 September 1752 are given in the Old Style (Julian calendar) then still in use there. Continental dates are given in the New Style (Gregorian calendar); dates relevant to both sides of the English Channel are given in the double form '7 Aug./27 July 1739'. Old Style is modified to the extent that January to March are counted as part of the year beginning, not the year ending.

I have normally cited Montagu's *Complete Letters* only. Her *Selected Letters* is more readily available, but double citation seemed too cumbersome.

The list of works cited covers only books, pamphlets, and articles which I have used as sources of information. It omits the many eighteenth-century works (pamphlets predominating) which are mentioned in the text without being so used, and it omits more modern works which I have used (often to my great benefit) but not cited.

I have kept to the briefest possible form both the citation of works in the notes, and their listing in Works Cited. I have given place of publication only when it is not London, and publisher only where this information has some particular interest or relevance.

1

Before 1699

❧

Roots: 'there is no Nobler descent'

MARY PIERREPONT, the future Lady Mary Wortley Montagu, sprang from two families lavishly endowed with rank, wealth, and power, as well as with ability and achievement. (During her lifetime, a period of rapid economic change, the nation's 400 or so families of this rank did very well for themselves.) The title of this chapter is a claim which Lady Mary made, with relish, when relating her life as fiction.[1] Although her father held no title at the time of her birth, he was the brother of two earls (one dead, one living); her mother was the sister of another. Her family tree was an intricate web of earldoms, baronies, and dukedoms both English and Irish. Printed records of these multifarious bloodlines are all arranged so as to identify and highlight the patrilinear succession: in her case the Pierreponts, whose proud claim it was to have arrived with William the Conqueror.[2] Biologically, of course, the patrilinear element in anyone's heritage steadily diminishes as the line is traced back, from one-half and then one-quarter, to a genetically negligible one thirty-second, one sixty-fourth, and so on. But Norman blood in the paternal line is Norman blood in the best place.

During the thirteenth century the Pierreponts became great landowners in Nottinghamshire. Henry Pierrepont, who married a daughter of the famous Bess of Hardwick, had a mansion at Thoresby by 1589. From this base the men of the family continued to accumulate land, peerages, and honours, using marriage as the vital strategy in their programme of acquisition.[3] They commanded cavalry regiments, served as Lords Lieutenant of their county, and collected and carefully bequeathed books and manuscripts. So

---

[1] 'Autobiographical romance: fragment', *E&P* 77; Burnett 1969: 141.
[2] Family and genealogical information comes, unless otherwise specified, from GEC, *DNB*, Henning 1983, Sedgwick 1970, and Namier and Brooke 1964.
[3] Higginbottom 1987: 54; Brackenbury 1992: *passim*; Staves 1990: 200.

did the men of Mary Pierrepont's mother's family, the Feildings, and the men of other immediately ancestral families. However broadly or narrowly her family is defined, it is rich in privilege and in talents. In each successive generation, male Pierreponts made marriages which gobbled up the distinguished surnames borne by their brides, incorporating into their heritage the genes, possessions, and honours of those families.

Evelyn Pierrepont, Mary's father, became in turn a member of parliament, an earl, marquess, and duke. He was an Ll.D. of his old university (Cambridge), Knight of the Garter, a Privy Councillor, Lord Lieutenant of Wiltshire, Lord Privy Seal, and one of the Regents of the kingdom during the monarch's absences. It was an impressive career, but not untypical of his family. In marrying Lady Mary Feilding, daughter of the third Earl of Denbigh, he made an alliance of connections and not without wealth. The Feildings had produced several remarkable individuals, though none yet to rank with the future novelists Henry and Sarah Fielding.[4] Evelyn Pierrepont may never have received the £6,000 dowry which his bride's brother was meant to supply (her father being dead); but in its place her stepmother, the Dowager Lady Denbigh, who had brought her up, produced £1,000 as a 'voluntary guift'.[5]

If Evelyn Pierrepont saw money as a marital priority, that was part of his inheritance. His father, Robert, had married (at the behest of 'Wise Parents' on both sides)[6] Elizabeth Evelyn, heiress of West Dean in Wiltshire; and *his* father, 'Wise' William Pierrepont of Thoresby, had married Elizabeth Harries, heiress of Tong Castle in Shropshire; and *his* father Robert Pierrepont, first Earl of Kingston, had married, at seventeen or eighteen, Gertrude Talbot, heiress of the seventh Earl of Shrewsbury.

Thus in four successive generations marriage settlements conveyed into the Pierrepont family the estates once owned by the fathers of heiresses, and multiplied blood-ties to other channels of rank and power. Each generation of Pierreponts, too, included some who did not marry: who, as uncles and aunts, left wills conveying their property back to the family's central stem. Mary Pierrepont's great-great-uncle Gervase Pierrepont, who died in 1679, earmarked in his will £10,000 with which his brothers were to get the family a dukedom.[7] Perhaps, however, 'Old Gervase' underestimated the price: it was not until 1715 that Mary's father was created Duke of Kingston, immediately after inheriting the estate of another childless Gervase, her great-uncle. The extant Pierrepont papers graphically illustrate the way a great

---

[4] Henry said he was the first of the family who could spell (*Westminster Review*, 1837: 27. 134).
[5] Marriage settlement 23 June 1687 (H MS 377; copy BL Eg. MS 3526. 6).
[6] Robert Pierrepont's memorial in West Dean church.   [7] BL Eg. MS 3517. 97–8.

family fed off its individual members, up to and including its head: how 'Heir urges heir, like wave impelling wave.'[8]

As an adult, Lady Mary Wortley Montagu professed high-minded unconcern with her family's vast estates and opulent possessions. She often took an acerbic tone about the codes of conduct subscribed to by noblemen: those of her father and those of his heir, her nephew.[9] But she took pride in other aspects of her heritage. Her forebears' intellectual gifts, for instance (and those of her husband's forebears, too), marked out her grandchildren to excel. In this context she cited the reputation of her great-grandfather William Pierrepont, who was nicknamed 'Wise',[10] and also the sharp and lively understanding of the grandmother who was hers by marriage, not by biology.

The family had produced other intellectuals as well. Wise William's brother the second Earl of Kingston delighted in hard study from his youth, qualified in both law and medicine, outraged the class feelings of his fellow peers by practising both professions even after he came into the title, and left to the College of Physicians a library valued at £4,000. Another great-great-uncle of Lady Mary, the second Earl of Denbigh, was credited by the historian Lord Clarendon with great abilities and political perception. (From Clarendon's viewpoint, but not from Lady Mary's, he exercised them on the wrong side.) Her grandfather Robert Pierrepont was (according to his memorial in West Dean church) 'LEARNED, much beyond the Gentlemen of This Age, in Languages and Arts, cheifly Mathamatical'. Her uncle the fourth Earl became patron before he was out of his teens to the satirist John Oldham.[11] Because great families married their offspring young, these preceding generations were not long gone.

For Lady Mary her forebears' politics were as inspiring as their abilities. In old age she boasted her education in the principles of 'old Whiggism', a creed which had schooled her to defend to the death a point of principle. This creed, she said, was already obsolete when she learned it, extinct in practice if not in theory among her father's Kit-Kat associates.[12] *His* Whiggism, she implies, was the decadence of *her* older, more heroic tradition. It was old Whiggism which had impelled men on both sides of her family to

[8] These transactions uncannily prefigure the uncles in Samuel Richardson's *Clarissa*, 1748–9. Cf. Staves 1990; Pope, *Second Epistle of the Second Book of Horace*, 1737: 253.

[9] *E&P* 77; *CL* ii. 65.

[10] The historian Lucy Hutchinson, William's contemporary, judged him one of parliament's 'wisest counsellors and most excellent speakers' (*CL* iii. 20, 27; Hutchinson, quoted in GEC).

[11] Clarendon 1888: viii. 245; Oldham 1987: xxxiv. For Robert Pierrepont's monument see p. 10–11, 12.

[12] *CL* iii. 277; CB MS fo. 8v. Her granddaughter Lady Louisa Stuart called her 'Whig to the teeth— Whigissima' (Stuart 1901: i. 86). Swift was a self-styled 'old Whig', but so was many an aristocratic radical.

oppose their king in the English civil war. Clarendon's Earl of Denbigh had
fought against his own father at the battle of Edgehill. Wise William and his
younger brother also sided with the parliament, against their elder brother.
(Legend said their father, the first Earl of Kingston, vowed to remain
unaligned, broke his vow in joining the royalists, and was struck down by
God's vengeance in the form of a stray cannon-ball.)

Wise William was a lifelong moderate and mediator: a peace-party leader
in 1642–3, an Anglican parliamentarian resisting the Scottish Presbyterian
model, later a moderate Cromwellian. He withdrew from public life at the
Restoration (which he had opposed) to exercise a behind-the-scenes concili-
ating influence, with only partial success. This stoic, under-rewarded greatness was just the thing to appeal to his great-granddaughter.

Many of these forefather tales must have been common family lore,
passed on to the young Pierreponts after their mother's premature death by
the women around them: their Pierrepont grandmother and aunt, and their
old nurse from the Feilding family. The doings of foremothers were probably related too. Though they were ineligible to direct regiments or councils,
they had not been behindhand in achievements or assertiveness. Though the
wives among them owned no property, many wrote out their confidently
phrased wills in their own flowing hands (unlike the men, who employed
legal copyists). They also served as executrix for other family wills. They
had strong political views. It was her Whiggism that made grandmother
Elizabeth Pierrepont her father's sole heiress, for Sir John Evelyn (a Presbyterian till the Restoration, when he conformed to the established church) cut
off his other daughter with 'Five Shillings for her Legacy' for marrying a
Tory.[13]

Several of Lady Mary's female forebears sound like proto-feminists. Lady
Elizabeth Pierrepont (not the grandmother but an unmarried great-great-
aunt) wrote to a clergyman to question the unequal retirement ages for men
and women (sixty and fifty respectively) from the duty of observing the fasts
of the Church. (The answer she received made a polite show of reluctance to
rehearse the 'Infirmities proper to that Sex', but stoutly asserted that to be
past child-bearing was, for a woman, to enter old age.)[14] Mistress Anna
Weamys dedicated her *Continuation of Sir Philip Sidney's Arcadia*, 1651, to
Lady Anne and Lady Grace Pierrepont, daughters of the lawyer-doctor-
earl: by their command, she said. Though she called herself simply 'a young
Gentlewoman', the bouquet of prefatory verses to her book called her a

[13] BL Eg. MS 3517 (wills of Lady Elizabeth and Lady Grace Pierrepont).
[14] Edward Turner to Lady Elizabeth Pierrepont, 28 Feb. 1673 [1674?] (Bod. MS Tanner 461. 45).

virago, a brave Amazon, and an inspired Minerva. F. Vaughan declaimed, 'Lay by your Needles Ladies, take the Pen, | The onely difference 'twixt you and men | . . . Since all Souls equal are, let all be heard.' Presumably these sentiments were expected to appeal to the Pierrepont dedicatees.[15]

More convincing as Amazon or virago was Lady Mary's perhaps most famous ancestor of all: the redoubtable Bess of Hardwick, who was her great-great-great-great-grandmother. (Perhaps at this level of society it would be more uncommon *not* to have Bess as an ancestor.)[16] Lady Mary makes no mention of her (nor of Weamys's *Arcadia* sequel, which had a second edition the year after her birth), but she must have known of the relationship. The Pierrepont estates in Nottinghamshire lay close to the area of Bess's mansion- and empire-building, and the dynasties founded by Bess had supplied several advantageous later intermarriages.

Mary Pierrepont was born, in April or May 1689, to a fairly peripheral position in all this worldly splendour. Her father's eldest brother, the 3rd Earl, had died seven years before, at not much more than twenty-one.[17] His second brother, the 4th Earl, in his twenties and recently married, had just ambitiously extended and adorned the family seat at Thoresby, Notts., and looked set fair to retain the earldom for his still awaited progeny. Mary's father had no need to repine at being a youngest son. Christened with his mother's family name, he was designated by his grandfather Evelyn's will as heir to the Evelyn estates—if he proved 'an Obedient and Dutifull Son' to his widowed mother. He duly married at her behest, aged twenty, the orphaned Lady Mary Feilding.[18] Mary, their firstborn, must have disappointed them by not being a boy, though not so much as the two sisters who followed. She was born not at any family seat but in London, where she was christened at St Paul's church, Covent Garden, on 26 May 1689. It was a propitious moment for Whiggism: William and Mary had recently been crowned.[19]

Of the earliest influences on this child, very little can be known. Practices in childbirth and infant care were undergoing one of their frequent

---

[15] Weamys 1994: xxii–xxiii.

[16] See Durant 1977. All her children were Cavendishes, by the second of her four husbands. Her eldest daughter, Frances, married Henry Pierrepont; their son became 1st Earl of Kingston.

[17] Her father, then aged 15, had written on his mother's behalf (she being still too grief-stricken to do so) to thank Dr Martin Lister of York for his unavailing care (18 July 1682, Bod. MS Lister 3. 204–5).

[18] The *DNB* and GEC call her about 19 at her marriage; the licence calls her about 22 (BL Eg. MS 3517. 62–3; fac. 27 June 1687; John Evelyn 1955: iv. 551).

[19] In old age MWM made a note about a classical author who 'reckons the first advantage being born in a celebrated City' (CB 9). Her parents must have been in lodgings or at some relative's house, of which there were several nearby. The coronation was 11 Apr.

revolutions, so the range of what *may* have happened to her is wide. As to childbirth, the old exclusively female occasion, managed by a midwife, was gradually giving way to something more professionalized, medicalized, and costly. Mothers-to-be had by tradition chosen half a dozen close friends and relations as gossips, or supporters with whom to shut themselves up. This they did literally: air and daylight were carefully excluded during the birth itself and the early stages of the month's lying-in. Household management devolved on someone else; husbands yielded authority to the occupying women; new mothers spent up to a fortnight in bed, and two more weeks confined indoors.[20]

Mothers seldom gave birth in bed, but sitting or kneeling, or even standing up. The midwife would at the Pierreponts' socio-economic level be a person of some standing; she might have received extensive practical training from an older midwife, who was often her mother. She would be skilled in recognizing the successive stages of labour, and entirely capable as long as the birth went normally. Occasionally, in cases of difficulty, she might call in a man whose professional title was surgeon; in real emergency he had little to offer except perhaps to save the mother by sacrificing the child.[21]

It was already fashionable to employ a male midwife, who (as supporters of the new way were never tired of reiterating) was the preferred choice of most mothers who could afford him. Men had studied anatomy both in Latin textbooks and in dissecting rooms; they alone were permitted to use the advanced technology of the forceps. For reasons of modesty they had to keep a sheet between themselves and their patients (making contact with hands but not with eyes). Because of the inevitable sheet as well as the possible forceps, they preferred women to lie prone while giving birth. The forceps undoubtedly saved some lives, of both mothers and babies, and undoubtedly killed others who might have been saved by patience and manual skill. Today the real advance represented by the new methods looks somewhat insecure. But Mary Pierrepont, born to upper-class parents in London, may well have been born new-style.[22]

New ideas were spreading, too, about how to treat the newborn infant. Till recently upper- and even middle-class babies had been starved *and* purged for several days before being handed over to a wet-nurse. Now 'godly' women of those classes were turning to the use of their own breasts. Pundits across a broad spectrum (John Tillotson, Archbishop of Canter-

---

[20] Wilson 1990*b*: 68, 71–3, 86; Wilson 1995: 25 ff.   [21] Wilson 1995: 50–3.

[22] Hugh Chamberlain, of the famous midwife family, was now doing well in London—as was his son, also Hugh, when she bore her own children (Wilson 1995: 55–6).

bury, Samuel Clarke the 'advanced' churchman, John Locke the philoso-pher, and Richard Allestree the popular conduct-book writer) were at one in arguing just at this date that mothers ought to suckle their children, and that reluctance to do so could only spring from feminine vanity. Since nursing mothers were barred from sexual intercourse, however, their perceived maternal duty might conflict with marital duty, and their husbands might well prefer the old tradition of wet-nursing. This tradition meant frequent pregnancies, for breast-feeding usually though not invariably has a contra-ceptive effect. Since Lady Mary Pierrepont, née Feilding, had four babies in three years and five months, she is very unlikely to have been breast-feeding.

Probably, therefore, young Mary was wet-nursed, and so she missed out on colostrum, the rich and protective secretions which a woman's breasts produce immediately after giving birth. Her wet-nurse would have been well into lactation. Infants 'at nurse' were usually boarded, sometimes for years, in the home of artisan or cottager foster-parents, away from the unhealthy environment of London.[23] In that case any bond formed with the biological mother would be far from a primal one, and whatever primal bond was formed would be broken without leaving any conscious trace. It is quite probable that Lady Mary Wortley Montagu's earliest, inaccessible layers of memory concerned some cottage either in the London suburbs or in the Wiltshire or Hampshire environs of West Dean. The mother whom she lost as a little girl may not have been at that time the most important person in her life; the loss may have been significant chiefly as a loss of future care and guidance.[24]

Lady Mary's father was a rake who begot numerous 'illegitimate progeny'. His own associates saw him much as she did: 'a very fine Gentle-man, of good Sense, well bred, and a Lover of the Ladies.'[25] When she read Richardson's *Sir Charles Grandison*, she found in the picture of Sir Charles's parents 'what I have heard of my Mother and seen of my Father'. This is a clue not only to her feelings about her father but also to the imagined mother in her mind. The novel presents a noblewoman who marries, for love, 'one of the handsomest men of his time', someone 'whom every-body admires'. His 'great notion of magnificence in living' soon exhausts his fortune and hers. When he has 'shew'd her every-where' he loses interest in his wife; she lives to feel that she was wrong to choose him. Her goodness is 'founded in principle': she is economical but also generous, obedient but never tame or servile. She loved her husband; she forgives him; but she implicitly judges

[23] See Fildes 1990: 81–5, 156–62 *passim*.
[24] This is how MWM's autobiography-as-romance sees it (*E&P* 77).
[25] Macky 1733 (written 1705): 75; *E&P* 10.

him. She does not subscribe to his 'riveted' notion, 'which is common to men of antient families, that daughters are but incumbrances, and that the son is to be everything'. She dies a heroic as well as a holy death: '*I have fought a good fight; I have finished my course; I have kept the faith.*'[26] Long before Richardson wrote, this was the kind of mother Lady Mary longed for. Whether or not as a three year old she was devastated by her loss, as a growing girl she felt it acutely.

꙳

This child avoided about a one-in-five chance of dying in her first year, and about a one-in-three chance of dying before she was five.[27] While her intimate life remains invisible, noteworthy events befell her family. When she was sixteen months old, on 17 September 1690, her remaining paternal uncle died.[28] Her parents became Earl and Countess of Kingston; she became Lady Mary; there was probably already a baby sister to become Lady Frances. The parents must have begun to spend much of their time at the Thoresby estate, with or without the children. Lady Evelyn, the third girl, was born on 6 September 1691, and William, Viscount Newark, the son and heir, on 21 October 1692. A month or so later the young mother died.[29] The children passed into the care of their grandmother Elizabeth Pierrepont, née Evelyn, of West Dean. She was seconded by her daughter, Gertrude, Lady Cheyne, who had a house in Chelsea near London, estates in Buckinghamshire, and no children of her own.[30]

Dean, as the family called it, was a spacious Jacobean manor house which had not been renovated and improved as Thoresby had. Lady Mary's life there between the ages of three and nine left no later trace, she said, on her memory. When she saw it again eleven years after leaving it, she did not think much of it. 'Here is nothing to be lik'd . . . every thing in [the] same Mode and fashion as [the] Days of King Arthur and the knights of the round table.' As a child, with her sisters and little brother, she would not care for mode or fashion, but would enjoy the elm grove, the Dutch gardens, parterres, terraces, straight-sided canals, and yew hedges.[31]

[26] *CL* iii. 90, *Richardson* 1972: vol. ii, letter xi, 310–13, 315.   [27] Porter 1982: 27.
[28] Suddenly, it seems: till three weeks earlier he had been involved in the surveillance and arrest of local Catholics in connection with a threat of French invasion (BL Eg. MS 3516. 68, 70, 74).
[29] PR 538, Diocesan Record Office, Notts. County Council. Narcissus Luttrell said on 8 Dec. that she was 'lately dead' (1857: ii. 636). The two youngest children were baptized at St Anne's, Soho, at two and three weeks old.
[30] Her husband, William, Viscount Cheyne, was son and nephew respectively of the writers Lady Jane and Lady Elizabeth Cavendish.
[31] *SL* 26; Olivier 1951: 254–5. In 1726 the 85 books there (some 'old Imperfect Ones', one printed in 1591) were valued at only £6 (Manvers MS 4883).

The house is gone now, except for its stable block. It stood between its park, parish church, and the village which bestrides the Wilts.—Hants border. The whole lies on the track of a Roman road, in a muddy east-west valley. Dean Hill to the south, and other surrounding hills, are outposts of the great chalk sweep of Wiltshire.

Lady Mary later emblematized the view from these hills. About a year after her return to Dean as a young adult she recalled how, 'when I took the air upon the Downs at 4 year old', she imagined that 'Salisbury Steeple', a few miles off, was running away from her efforts to reach it. It is surely the same experience which in 1757 became 'the childish desire of catching the setting Sun, which I can remember running very hard to do: a fine Thing truly if it could be caught, but experience soon shews it to be impossible'. The childhood reminiscences in her writings are all moralized in this manner, charged with a Lockean sense that the child is mother to all that is universally human in the woman. At twelve, she says, she despised tarts and cheese cakes 'as being too childish for one capable of more solid Pleasures'; at twenty she felt the same way about reading novels.[32]

There are, however, not many even of these generalized reminiscences. The question 'Was she happy at West Dean?' can be approached only with somewhat flimsy speculation. Washing (either of the children or their clothes) was probably minimal, though only a generation later a French traveller was to report in tones of surprise, 'English women and men are very clean; not a day passes by without their washing their hands, arms, faces, necks and throats in cold water, and that in winter as well as in summer.'[33] The children's clothes were tight, formal, and easy to spoil. Discipline would have been strict. Their play was probably gender specific, as Lady Mary later imagined that of her own grandchildren to be: the girls busy with 'babies' (dolls), their brother riding the poker as if it were a horse. If Bernard Mandeville can be believed, Lady Mary was probably introduced very early to female propriety: daily nagged at 'scarce three Years old . . . to hide her Leg' on pain of serious rebuke; fully conscious by six that to let it be seen was shameful.[34]

The children's 'Governess' had been their mother's 'Nurse'. She was probably therefore the Mrs Dupont to whom grandmother Pierrepont left £20 as a legacy for looking after them. Two under-nurses helped her; Mrs Pierrepont supervised them all.[35] Lady Mary generally depicts nurses as

[32] *CL* i. 112; iii. 132; ii. 484.   [33] Porter 1982: 33, 239 (quoting Cesar de Saussure).
[34] *CL* iii. 134; Bernard Mandeville, *The Fable of the Bees*, 1714, Remark C, ed. John Phillip Harth, 1970, 105, 103.
[35] The will gave the under-nurses £5 each: half the other servants' legacy. For today's pounds, multiply by at least 60 (Burney 1988: 951–2).

foolish and benighted, notably the tattling peasant nurse in her satirical tale 'Princess Docile'. This also presents a deplorable governess: 'Prudish, sanctimonious, and stupid beyond belief'. As a young adult Lady Mary sounded quite tolerant of her own governess: 'thô perfectly good and pious', she lacked 'a capacity for so great a Trust'. Later her opinion hardened: though she thought the governess was what a didactic novelist would call exemplary, she judged her influence to have been entirely baneful. It included taking 'so much pains from my Infancy to fill my Head with superstitious Tales and false notions, it was none of her Fault I am not at this day afraid of Witches and Hobgoblins, or turn'd Methodist'. Lady Mary also wrote angrily of 'the silly Prejudices of my Education [that] taught me to beleive I was to treat no body as an Inferior, and that poverty was a degree of Merit'.[36]

Elizabeth Pierrepont made her will on 2 August 1698. She left legacies to her other grandchildren but none to the nine-year-old Mary. This omission, however, may reflect not displeasure but some grand family plan. The youngest girl, christened Evelyn like her father, was marked out in the will as the Evelyn family heiress, receiving a handsome £12,000 and destined (in the event of her grandmother's death) to pass into the care of her aunt Lady Cheyne, not her father. The will decreed that aunt Cheyne should keep Evelyn with her; if Evelyn died she was left free whether or not to replace her with either Mary or Frances. Mrs Pierrepont left Frances £1,000, 'desiring her Father . . . not to give her the Less'.[37] If Evelyn died unmarried, however, *her* opulent share was to be divided equally between her sisters, and Frances's extra portion withdrawn. Money for each girl would only be forthcoming if she married with proper consent. Mrs Pierrepont left 'all my Jewells to whoever is Heir to the Family', never to be 'sold or parted with to any but the Heir'. This sounds like a context for rigid propriety rather than for vindictive favouritism. Frances may have been felt to need an equivalent for Mary's 'expectations' from her bachelor great-uncle Gervase, Lord Pierrepont of Ardglass and later of Hanslope: expectations that were to outlast Mary's undutiful elopement, but not her uncle's death in 1715.[38]

Even if not a disinheritor, Elizabeth Pierrepont remains a shadowy, intriguing figure. If she herself composed or helped compose the lengthy inscription on her husband's tomb, then she possessed not only prudence

---

[36] *RW* 108; *CL* iii. 25–6, 36; BL Eg. MS 3517; *E&P* 77.

[37] It was the same amount as their dead mother's gift from *her* grandmother, but that had supplied a missing dowry.

[38] BL Eg. MS 3517. 116–29, 153–65; see p. 74, 95; Halsband 1956: 3.

and a 'prodigious memory',[39] but also real literary aptitude and strong ambition. This monumental elegy is eccentric in style (in both verse and prose)
but strong and rich in the metaphysical manner. Robert Pierrepont's early
death, it seems, as good as robbed him of the two earldoms awaiting him. He
inherited 'Bullion VERTUES', but no opportunity to coin them into great
exploits like his ancestors'. His body passed 'Un-mutilated, Un Diseas'd'
through the perils of European travel, only to suffer, with 'Passive Valor',
the amputation of a leg at home. Since it was peacetime, this suggests he died
by accident.[40]

His wife, now his widow, receives considerable attention in this elegy. She
is 'a LADYE—(Of Whom | Though All Good might, Nothing must Here
be said, | Since—VAULTS Speake not the Living but the DEAD . . .)' A Latin
sentence declares that Robert Pierrepont's 'sorrowing relict desired him to
be mourned in no mean fashion'.[41]

It cannot have been bad for Lady Mary to have a grandmother who may
have been a poet; it might not have been bad to have a grandmother with no
mean idea of her own importance. Yet doubts remain about West Dean.
Something of her own childhood certainly went into Montagu's 'Princess
Docile', a work of her old age. Since Docile's governess is akin to Lady
Mary's, her appalling royal mother *may* carry some hint of grandmother
Pierrepont. It is not hard to imagine this passionate, imaginative, idealistic
child committing herself to some religious vow which she later re-created,
with protective irony, as the vow Docile takes 'to remain for seven years sitting cross-legged in honour of the Goddess Vishnu'. This vow, which outrages the codes of her upbringing, springs from Docile's emotional
isolation: 'she would rather belong to Vishnu, than to nobody.'

Docile's idealism has two phases: a brief religious one and the Enlightenment one which replaces it, which she never outgrows. She is eleven when
she makes the vow; and reaction to the vow provokes her passage from religion to philosophy. Lady Mary is almost never precise about the dates of her
own life, and no exact parallel should be sought for. But her tone about
grandmother Pierrepont and Aunt Cheyne is never warm. When she cites a
pattern for her own grandparental role, it is not the grandmother she lived

---

[39] Noted in her youth by her cousin John Evelyn the diarist, who at her death called her 'a most excellent,
& prudent lady' (1955: i. 557; v. 310).

[40] Body and soul are described as striving together; since the body is 'it' and the soul 'she', the dead man
appears to be called 'she' throughout.

[41] The church, where Gilbert White was to be briefly curate, has vanished, but its south aisle or Borbach
Chantry is preserved by the Redundant Churches Fund, which issues a leaflet on it. Thanks to Rosemary
Nielsen for translating. The monument cost £500 (BL Eg. MS 3526. 10).

with but her grandmother-by-marriage, Lady Denbigh.[42] Later, when she
felt warmly towards her mother's brother, William Feilding, and chillily
towards her father's sister, Lady Cheyne, she was clearly responding to their
differing reactions to her elopement.[43] But some feelings from her childhood
may have lingered too.

West Dean was moth-eaten and old-fashioned, and *may* have been emotionally bleak. But the park and the downs offered scope to run. The adults
around Mary presented belief-systems that would later have to be rejected.
In the church the Evelyn monuments were overshadowed by Robert
Pierrepont's life-size, kneeling figure: a young grandfather with naked, hefty
torso and helpful, hovering angel. His surround of text, cherubs, urns, and
heavy architectural detail dominates the east wall. What would an impres-
sionable child have made of this Baroque bravura?[44] No wonder she grew up
with a strong infusion of family pride; no wonder also if that pride were mixed
with aspirations after 'exploits' and after the intoxicating power of language.

Elizabeth Pierrepont's death, on New Year's Day 1699, divided the family.[45]
Mary, Frances, and William passed into their father's care, and moved to
Thoresby without Evelyn. The different relationships that developed
between the sisters can be guessed from the notes Lady Mary kept of letters
despatched to England from Adrianople on 1 April 1717. To Frances, now
Sister Mar, went a letter packed with exotic detail: 'Hope she 'l be glad to hear
I am wel. French Ambassadresse and Ambassador pomp. Cavalcade thro
the Town. Court to me. Description of Dress. Jew Ladys.' To Evelyn, now
Sister Gower, went something that sounds like a quintessential duty letter:
'Hope she will glad to hear we all well. Compliments.'[46]

Lady Mary's epoch-making visit to the Kit-Cat Club must have predated
her grandmother's death, since she was eight years old at the time. It would
then have been at Lord Cheyne's in Chelsea that the child was staying when
the message arrived from her father that she was to be sent forthwith to the
tavern where the club met. He had proposed her as a toast (an honour
reserved for reigning beauties), but they would not accept her name until
they had seen her. Lady Mary later presented the experience as one of intoxicating delight: to be dressed in her best, admired and made much of, to go
'from the lap of one poet, or patriot, or statesman, to the arms of another', to
have 'her health drank by every one present, and her name engraved in due
form upon the glasses'. It was a taste of applause calculated to make applause

[42] *RW* 109, 114; *CL* iii. 27.   [43] *CL* i. 172, 216, 353; ii. 31, 63, 77–8.
[44] The sculptor was John Bushnell.
[45] She was buried at Dean on 4 Jan. (Evelyn 1955: v. 310; Wh MS M 439/59).
[46] *CL* i. 325–6 n. 3, 344.

an addiction; and years later she confessed she was a flattery addict, eagerly gulping down what she felt to be doing her harm. Meanwhile she was not *only* honoured by this Whig centre of power as if she were a grown-up woman;[47] unlike any woman, she had entered it. Such delight could never happen again.

Her story presents her father as a figure of power and glamour, but it suggests (as her granddaughter Lady Louisa Stuart astutely noted) that he thought of her as something rather like a social asset, a luxury plaything. It evokes the attraction he exerted for her, but is very far from contradicting her other representation of him as 'thô naturally an honest Man . . . abandonn'd to his pleasures, and (like most of those of his Quality) did not think himselfe oblig'd to be very attentive to his children's Education'.[48] To pass into his care was to enter a sphere where she would strive for attention but not receive it, where the unattainable would be always within sight.

[47] *E&P* 8; Hunter 1831: ii. 322; Treglown and Mortimer 1981; *CL* iii. 141. Lady Mary was probably older than 8 when the club got its famous name, but not when it began. The story went that her father 'carried on the frolic . . . by having her picture painted for the club-room' (*E&P* 9); but no known portrait of her is so early. His own was done for the club in 1709. She is listed as a toast in 1712 (as Pierrepont) and 1714 (Tonson MSS, National Portrait Gallery).

[48] *E&P* 77. In his accounts, sums given to charity are smaller than those for wine, brandy, and racehorses (1711–12, Manvers MS 4265).

2

1699–June 1709

✦

Juvenilia: 'Poetry my dear my darling choice'[1]

IT would be interesting to know if Lady Mary was as much struck by the contrast between West Dean and Thoresby in early 1699 as she was when she went back to Dean in 1710. As a child she must have found Thoresby dazzling. The neighbours were all of high birth and large estates. The park had been part of Sherwood Forest when its huge oaks were young.[2] The mansion (three or four times the size of West Dean) was by William Talman, leading architect before Vanbrugh and Hawksmoor came on the scene. Completed at just the time of Lady Mary's birth, it drew on French, Italian, and Dutch models for a style quite new to England, which Talman later developed at Chatsworth.[3] Its massive central block of three bays, in stone, was flanked on each side by five more bays in brick. This imposing façade did not reveal the building's full extent as a Palladian frontage would, but, like an Oxford or Cambridge college, concealed a whole rectangle of wings on the same scale. The stone centre block, square but elaborate, might well look to a nine year old like a magnified version of grandfather Pierrepont's tomb.

Thoresby, the centre of great estates, was a complex, humming business concern; it absorbed three children and their attendants almost without noticing. Information about it comes mostly from a generation later, when the children's father died; but it was probably not much changed. Each of the senior indoor staff had his or her separate room or office. Apart from the librarian and at least one of Kingston's three chaplains, these were house-keeper, surveyor of the works, clerk of the kitchen, steward, and cook.

---

[1] 'Look round (my soul) and if you can' (Grundy 1971: 252).

[2] Sherwood declined during the seventeenth century, and the wild deer were replaced by herds in parks. In 1722 Lady Mary's father sought permission to enclose 1,217 barren acres and add them to the Thoresby park; rights of common would thus be lost (Chambers 1966: 157, 162, 164). I assume Thoresby was new to Lady Mary; but she might have visited it already.

[3] Harris 1961, 1963.

The outdoor staff included a 'surveyor of the out works' (also called the gardener), park-keeper, bailiff, 'sportsman', pheasant breeder, 'gentleman of the horses', helper in the stables, and two under-keepers.[4] The master of the house would be there in summertime (the social off-season), but absorbed by adult company. The three children seem to have been close, though the youngest, the boy, had greater status. Till December 1706 he was Viscount Newark; then their father became Marquess of Dorchester and William, overnight, became what his father had been—Earl of Kingston.[5]

Their father's houses provided what we should now regard as a splendid grounding in general culture. Though even the most elegant rooms were sparsely furnished by modern standards, a course in art history adorned the walls.[6] The guests included his Kit-Cat cronies: Congreve, Dr Samuel Garth, Addison, and Steele. Masters were employed to instruct Lady Mary in drawing (until, to her 'great mortification', her 'over eagerness' at it was thought to be harming her eyes),[7] in the Italian language, and in carving joints of meat. This last, begun 'as soon as she had bodily strength for the office', was a necessary skill for a political hostess. Lady Mary was in training to eat her own meal without ceremony, alone, in order to devote herself at dinner to ceremonious serving of guests. She practised on wooden models of 'the different joints of meat'; her carving master came three times a week. She also acquired female skills such as embroidery and cooking, and the physical arts of dancing and riding.[8]

But the centre of her education was an achievement all her own. She gave its dates and details inconsistently. She told an admiring Joseph Spence on the one hand that her 'stealing the Latin language' began from her admiring Ovid, on the other that it began from 'somebody'''s chance remark; on the one hand that she was then thirteen, on the other that she had already met her future husband and owed the thought to him. The first story has her getting and hiding her 'dictionary and grammar with all the privacy in the world', studying five or six or eight hours a day for two years in the library, 'whilst everybody else thought I was reading nothing but novels and romances'.[9] Yet at twenty she presented herself to Edward Wortley Montagu as a novice

[4] Manvers MS 4349. 46; 4883.
[5] Lady Mary retained a book with his signature of 1704: 'William Newark, his book' (Wh M MS 135).
[6] Smith 1993: 57. The London house was hung with Salvator Rosa, Raphael, and Michelangelo as well as Kneller (Manvers MS 4882).
[7] It helped, she thought, to form her elegant handwriting (*CL* iii. 24).
[8] See p. 24; *CL* iii. 23–4; i. 21–2; Lady Louisa, *E&P* 11–12; Hunter 1831: ii. 322. She later treasured her recipe book and was skilled at making bread and butter (*CL* ii. 447, 485; iii. 136).
[9] Spence 1975: 357; Spence 1966: no. 743. Passages of the Bible which Lady Mary translated into Latin as a girl survive in her commonplace-book. She did not learn Greek (CB 31 ff.; Hunter 1831: ii. 321).

needing advice and help. Later again she forgot her twenty-year-old pupillage and exaggerated her initial precocity. It is impossible to adjudicate between her stories, but the results were clear enough.

She said nothing of help from her brother's tutor. But after the thirteen-year-old William had moved on (probably with his tutor) to Trinity College, Cambridge, he mined the classics for the same sort of influence that she did. Among the proofs of diligence which he sent his father was an essay (in English, with a strong Roman flavour) arguing that honour and probity are better than riches. Lady Mary's early annotations in a set of *Poems on Affairs of State* show her already opposed to tyranny of church or state. Family tradition taught her to exult in a tyrant's fall;[10] for the moment the likeliest tyrant on her horizon was Queen Anne.

The relations of the children's lost mother kept an eye on them from a distance. In her early teens Lady Mary corresponded regularly with her eighty-year-old grandmother Denbigh; her uncle William Feilding was an intellectual stimulus and resource.

Time slipped by leaving few legible traces. But there are grounds for seeing 1704–5, the year Lady Mary turned fifteen, as some kind of watershed. She later thought of fifteen both as the usual age for girls to begin menstruating, and as the age by which childish dreams of fame ought to be extinct. At fifteen, she later said, she longed to rule as abbess over a Protestant nunnery or retired community of women. One of her two surviving albums of juvenile writing has '1704' and '1705' on its title-page and cover, and claims to have been compiled at fourteen. The other includes a couple of poems written in May 1705 about a crisis in the writer's relationship with the friend who has been her muse and inspiration.[11]

Her early writings therefore—including a poem on the golden age when 'There was no giveing Rich, nor begging poor, | In Common all enjoy'd an equall store'[12]—took shape during her own almost-golden age of freedom to think and dream. She delighted in heroic fiction; she marked with a star an account of a heroine's 'noble and solid curiosity of knowing things in their beginnings', her 'strict vigilancy to accuse and correct her selfe, if her perfections could have been capable of the least error'. These pursuits seem to have been shared as well as solitary. The real names of her sister Frances and their friend Sarah Chiswell appear in a list on the cover of one of Lady Mary's albums, among names which otherwise belong to the world of romance. Whether or not Frances or Sarah was Silvianetta or Belvidera or

[10] H MS 77. 140–9; *POAS* at Sandon Hall (ii. 34, 92, 383); *E&P* 311.
[11] *CL* iii. 27; H MSS 250, 251. 31–2; see p. 20–1. William left for Cambridge a year later.
[12] H MS 251. 25–6.

one of the others, they had some share in this imaginary world.[13] In the same volume Lady Mary listed characters from Scudéry, from Ovid's *espistles* (presumably the *Heroides* in English), from 'a Tartarian Hystory', and from innumerable plays. These might well have been read together.[14]

This vellum-covered volume throws a momentary light on the Lady Mary of 1704–5. Its 'Poems Letters Novels Songs etc' are not her first: a poem survives which she wrote at twelve. Nor do her imitations of Ovid and Virgil demonstrate command of Latin; she may have used translations. But she was already formidably well read and stylistically adept. 'Aged Monarchs of the Grove' and 'silver floods' suggest Thoresby Park, but still more they evoke Lady Mary's reading. The library is usually denominated her father's. It was the best and largest room among all Thoresby's pomp and splendour, fitted out in black leather and morocco with busts of classical philosophers. Just before his death her father, now a duke, commissioned a printed catalogue: the first to an English private collection. *Catalogus Bibliothecae Kingstonianae* numbers 1,200 manuscripts (all later destroyed by fire) and thousands of books. Its handsome ornaments depict the house, the park, and the library itself. Whether or not the duke was, as his daughter's fiction says, 'no Scholar himselfe', his books reflect a studious family. They are reading copies, not rarities; the classics and modern science are equally well represented.[15]

Perhaps women of the family accounted for the library's wealth of Madeleine de Scudéry. Lady Mary's granddaughter was to see her lifelong devotion to Scudérian romance as something frivolous, even anomalous. But not Lady Mary herself: Scudéry's works were still well respected. Lady Mary's devotion implies nothing about a women's tradition; as late as 1718 she still thought a man, Georges de Scudéry, had written them. But respect for them regularly implied recognition of their 'feminist' potential. Martha Fowke (later Sansom) 'read there with Pleasure the Empire of Women' and fed her youthful dream of finding 'a King or Prince' to marry.[16]

Lady Mary had cause to identify with Scudéry's Sapho: an orphan of noble birth, passed over for inheritance in favour of her brother, well educated by a female cousin, and a wonderful writer in verse and prose. Sapho is

[13] Biondi 1624, English trans. 1632: 12 (now at Sandon); H MS 250. Many of the romance names (including Silvianetta, from Aphra Behn's *Feigned Courtesans*, 1679) reflect Lady Mary's reading.

[14] By Beaumont and Fletcher, Dryden, Behn, Congreve, Corneille, Molière, and a dozen more.

[15] Bod. Caps. ix. 14; Pollard and Ehrman 1965: 63–75, 274; *E&P* 78. Pollard and Ehrman give different totals for the number of books (63, 75). Jean-Bernard Le Blanc thought the library a scholar's paradise (Monod-Cassidy 1941: 266–7).

[16] H MS 250; *CL* i. 440; Sansom (formerly Fowke) 1752 (written 1723): 10. Mary Delany too valued Scudéry highly (1861–2: iii. 214; iv. 335).

beautiful (though short); her black eyes 'sparkle like fire' yet combine languor with vivacity. But her wit transcends her beauty. 'The greatest wits of the world were greedy of her verses', which she is modestly chary of imparting. She dislikes marriage (which, she says, makes men into tyrants) and gets a judgement from the courts of love to justify her living happy ever after with Phaon—without marrying him.[17] If Lady Mary read in Scudéry the empire of women, she thought this empire was authorized by men.

Someone, male or female, had filled the library at Thoresby with books about queens and other female worthies, and works by the historical Sappho (translated by Anne Dacier), by Isabela Andreini, Marie Catherine d'Aulnoy, and Margaret Cavendish, Duchess of Newcastle.[18]

Lady Mary wrote her juvenilia under the sway of the later Dryden and his contemporaries (of whom Congreve and Garth were her father's friends and John Sheffield, Duke of Buckingham, was to become her own), of the slightly earlier Cowley, Behn, and Katherine Philips, and of the very latest fiction. These writers, like Matthew Prior (whom she knew by heart at this age and quoted all her life), first dawned on her consciousness as moderns. They were of her own class, or closely connected with it: living patterns for an ambitious child. For a young lady, however, they were problematic. Waller's Sacharissa is another presence in Lady Mary's early poems: her reading offered her the role of muse and idol as alternative to the role of poet.[19]

Like Lady Mary's later writings, her earliest must have been far more extensive than what now remains. But what is left holds deep interest, both for itself and as token of achievement to come.

Her topics are conventional, but she already knows how to reshape convention to her own needs. Her themes are social and moral comment on the world, romantic love and loss, and praise of country retirement. Having read a new novel consisting of letters from a heroine to a confidante, she assumes the persona of the confidante to tell *her* story, and distils the essence of a heroine's progress into the five letters of her *Indamora to Lindamira*. She challenges the published author by inviting readers to compare the two

---

[17] Scudéry 1690: x. 189–92, 197, 347–8.

[18] H MS 250; Grundy 1994a. Lady Mary eloped without any of the books she owned, but was later reunited with a copy of John Barclay, *Argenis*, trans. Kingsmill Long, 1625, in which her signature—'Ma'—joins those of her grandmother Pierrepont ('Elizabeth Evelyn her boock', in childish script) and great-grandmother: 'Jane Evelyn, 1643'.

[19] She refers in verse to poems by Halifax and Garth, inspired by Lady Sunderland and Lady Louisa Lennox. A handwriting analysis at this age calls her forceful, mature, highly imaginative yet self-disciplined, 'unusually objective and curious about the world around her', independent-minded but no rebel, eager to achieve but not ostentatious (The Graphology Business, 21 Apr. 1995). It also reads her as lacking femininity, emotion, or juvenile fun.

works.[20] Her Indamora is morally flawless and bears a charmed life amid all perils. She is also the only fictional character whose virtue Lady Mary ever rewarded. Her story ends with her happy (second) marriage.

Lady Mary tackled male experience of love with a verse-and-prose romance, 'The Adventurer', modelled on Behn's *Voyage to the Isle of Love*, 1684. On a visit to this allegorical Isle, Strephon runs the gamut of adventures: losing his one true love, being jilted by a worthless flirt, then happily two-timing a pair of mistresses. He never enters the 'Old Ruinous Palace' of marriage (where 'Discord, Strife and uneasyness' dwell), and unlike Indamora he is free at last to turn away from love towards fresh fields. 'The Adventurer' is not, like *Indamora*, consistently unworldly. Its imaginary scenes run a gamut of moods: here 'young Mourning Doves | Lament in Murmurs their unhappy Loves'; there an erotic discovery scene warms and teases; elsewhere 'Dutchesse . . . Gallops in hackney Coach'.[21]

Many of Lady Mary's shorter poems (fifteen in her first album) rehandle famous love-stories: Julius Caesar and Cleopatra, Ovid and the emperor's daughter, Alexander the Great and his two queens. Even in amatory verse she is a feminist-in-training. In imitating Virgil she swaps his gender roles: injured man and fickle woman become injured woman and fickle man (an exchange which she might have learned from Behn). In imitating Ovid, she creates a female speaker whose grief at the departure of her soldier-lover is mingled with envy of his prospective glory: 'what my Soul wou'd doe, my Fate denies, | And I can kill with nothing but my Eyes.'

Not love alone is her theme, but the whole world. Her 'tatter'd red coat begging in the street' is proud of honourable scars though others jeer at them; her 'poet waiting at the great man's door, | Haughty in rags and proudly poor, | Disdains the ignorant rich'; 'his gouty Lordship' reciprocates his disdain. This poem concludes with a pious turn towards 'Heaven's unknown and unimmagin'd bliss'. The rejection of ambition, whether for love, heaven, or rural retreat, may sound somewhat hollow when made by a female to whom public office was closed; but women poets often used it to figure the choice between public status dependent on a man, and personal integrity without one. Lady Mary attacks the venality of the great world with relish. She idealizes a park-like countryside until, with a sudden swerve towards realism, she notices its cold, floods, and 'Aukard Swains'.

Her literary ambitions were serious. She chose a fictional identity for herself, like Behn and Philips, like Cowley in *The Mistress* and Waller in his

---

[20] Pierrepont 1994; also *RW* 1–15. An earlier version was entitled 'Adventur's of Indamora'. Both stem from *The Adventures of Lindamira*, 1702, probably by Thomas Brown.

[21] H MS 250; Grundy 1971: 260–2.

Myra poems. The title-page of her earlier volume is dedicated 'to the fair hands of the beauteous Hermensilda by her most obedient Strephon'. Yet Lady Mary makes no bones about being female: in perhaps the most succinct introduction on record, she epitomiszs the content of a thousand apologetic prefaces by women writers, turning their humility into pride.

I question not but here is very many faults, but if any reasonable person considers three things they will forgive them.
1. I am a Woman
2. without any advantage of Education
3. all these was wrote by me at the age of 14.

The second album abandons Strephon. Its title-page—'The Entire Works of Clarinda. London'—firmly asserts both gender and aspiration to print. Here she transcribed most of her earlier surviving poems, with some revision, and added more to a total of twenty-seven.

The volumes reveal something about the first obstacle Lady Mary encountered in her writing career. The earlier one has had twenty pages cut out and two poems completely obliterated by heavy scribbling. On a page already almost full, she added the following, apparently confessional, lines.

> 'Twas folly made mee fondly write
> (For what [have] I to doe with Love and wit?)
> I own I tre[s]pass'd wickedly in Rhime
> But oh my Punishment exceeds my crime.
> My Folies tho' on parchment writt
> I soon might burn and then forget,
> But if I Now both burn and blot
> (By mee) the[y] cannot bee forgot.

It seems that she *did* both burn and blot; but she left enough to hint at the story, and she went on, defiantly, to compound her crime by imitating a published 'Complete Works'. 'What have I to do with love and wit?' is just rhetoric; she had to do with both.

It is not clear who punished Lady Mary, or why. Perhaps we see here the hand of the despised governess. Adults in authority may have disapproved of her writing in general, or of her writing love-poems, or of her writing to some particular individual, either male or female. Or somebody she had addressed in rhyme may have responded so as to make her reject her own work. A group of poems in the second volume concerns the beloved Hermensilda (variously spelled), who on becoming a Maid of Honour ('Attendant on the best of Queens') in London basely jettisoned her friendship with

Clarinda.[22] The Maid of Honour among Lady Mary's early friends was Jane Smith, daughter of the Speaker of the House of Commons. The friendship the poems describe is modelled on erotic or courtship relations in cavalier poetry: the Thoresby trees bear Clarinda's name 'on each Bark | With Heremenesilda's joyn'd'. Yet it sounds as if Lady Mary wrote about this relationship because of its real-life importance rather than inventing the love because the poetry needed it, as Cowley did. These poems sound less fictional than others: because two are dated (apparently 20 and 26 May 1705), because the poet calls herself Clarinda (the name on her title-page), and because she drops her usual pastoral mode to praise a London life and disparage retirement amid 'Bleak northern Groves'.

Lady Mary's feeling for Hermensilda, and the impulse to flee from society to 'some close obscure retreat', may have fed her 'favorite Scheme' for an 'English Monastery' with herself as Lady Abbess. This sounds as if she had already read Mary Astell's plan for college-like institutions for unmarried women. Astell was a High Church Tory, and was soon to publish a vigorous attack on Lady Mary's father's associates the Kit-Cats. She was a controversial model for a young girl, and nowhere more so than in her first book, which proposes havens of non-family, independent living for eligible girls as either an alternative or a prelude to marriage.[23]

If Lady Mary read Astell, the unknown circle of friends who probably read her juvenilia *may* have read Astell too. They spanned a wide social range: from Lady Mary's distant cousin Lady Henrietta Cavendish Holles, of princely Welbeck Abbey, to Sarah Chiswell of Holme Pierrepont near Nottingham, an orphan whose father had worked for the Pierreponts' father. Henrietta was a great heiress, Sarah something like a 'humble companion'. Lady Mary later retained a special devotion to both these playfellows from 'the happy days of ignorance'.[24]

The Pierrepont girls were not always at Thoresby. Their social calendar included the annual race-meeting at Nottingham.[25] They had Pierrepont cousins in the town, one of whom wrote vivaciously to Lady Mary about

[22] Docile is early duped by false professions of love from a woman (*RW* 113–21).

[23] Grundy 1971: 290; *CL* ii. 493; iii. 97; Astell, 1694 and 1697. Astell had a close friend (Lady Elizabeth Hastings) in Arlington St., and ran a school at Chelsea, where MWM's aunt and second sister lived (Perry 1986: 23, 231, 243). MWM is not, however, the 'Honourable Md Mountague' to whom Astell inscribed a copy of her *Proposal*, now BL 12314 a. 22.

[24] *CL* i. 114; accounts submitted by Sarah's father, land-agent Charles Cheswell, 1692, 1697, and 1700 (Manvers MS 4233, 4234, 4349. 67). Family MSS at Notts. Record Office generally spell the name 'Cheswell'. For his occupation see Hughes 1949: 189–99. Lady Henrietta became Lady Harley, then Lady Oxford.

[25] They may have gone to York Races too, whose distance would demand an extended visit to friends or relations. One of Lady Mary's friends, Anne Justice, lived at York.

dancing to 'a sett of fiddles' and jointly visiting some grander cousins: the
Mannerses, Dukes of Rutland, a Belvoir Castle nearby.[26] This letter was sent
to her at Holme Pierrepont: the ancient family seat, in the meadows just
south of Nottingham, where no doubt she stayed during the races.[27] It is a
square-built, castellated house in rosy, weathered brick, a century older than
Thoresby. Sarah Chiswell's brother-in-law and guardian was rector of the
church standing almost in its shadow.

This church vied with that of West Dean as a lesson in Pierrepont worldly
greatness. Its exterior had been remodelled in classical style in 1666. Its
florid monuments commemorate two Henry Pierreponts in effigy (died
1499 and 1615), and the 'illustrious Princess Gartrude', heiress-wife of the
first Earl of Kingston. She, her tomb asserts, 'hath left a memory that will
never dye'. Another monument, with Latin inscription and carving perhaps
by Grinling Gibbons, commemorates the poet John Oldham; this was
erected by his patron, William, fourth Earl of Kingston, the children's uncle.
Oldham is known today chiefly for Dryden's sombre poem on his untimely
death. Lady Mary would know that the fatal smallpox seized him at Holme
Pierrepont; and she would know him as author of *Satires upon the Jesuits*,
1681. Her uncle had shown sound political as well as literary judgment in his
choice of protégé.[28]

❦

The spring that brother William went up to Cambridge, 1706, Lady Mary's
friend Dolly Walpole (later Lady Townshend) got into trouble. She had
been drawing moral support from Lady Mary about two problems: a suitor
she favoured, whose family objected to her lack of dowry; and hostility from
her elder brother's wife. Now the loss of her lover nearly lost her her reputation, when she turned for comfort to the machiavellian and no longer
respectable Lady Wharton. This incident, says Lady Louisa Stuart, set Lady
Mary decisively against Dolly's sister-in-law Catherine Walpole. If so, Lady
Mary was still a girl when the first seed was sown for later animus against her
by Catherine's son Horace.[29]

The overture was over, the major themes of her life beginning mutedly to
sound. Retired study; the heady, risky, censorious town; the circle of friends;

[26] A. Pierrepont, n.d., H MS 77. 120–1. The Duchess of Rutland mentioned here is Catherine, daughter
of the famous Lady Rachel Russell.

[27] Holme Pierrepont had a park of 2,198 acres in 1700 (Chambers 1966: 167).

[28] Oldham left MSS at Holme at his death, which Kingston passed to his publisher (Oldham 1987: p. xxxiv
and n. 163; Pevsner 1951: 84–5).

[29] *E&P* 22–4; Plumb 1956: 124–5. Lady Mary sounded protective about Dolly, who was, however, nearly
three years older.

the promise of praise; and behind the scenes the forces mustering to direct her life without her assent.

A few years after Dolly Walpole's wobble on the tightrope of respectability, the obscurity around Lady Mary lifts again, more decisively. Her circle still included daughters of the nobility, the gentry (like the Brownlows next door in London), and those barely squeezing up into the gentry. Their social span is exemplified in her six known female correspondents for the year 1710. Mary Banks and Anne Justice (her 'dear Nanny') were the daughters of Sheffield and York attorneys. Anne married another attorney, who was later Mayor of York; and though York was a highly fashionable centre, to be its mayor was irremediably bourgeois, as can be seen in the satire on Lady Mayoresses in Mary Davys's comedy *The Northern Heiress, or The Humours of York*, 1716. Of friends a generation older than Lady Mary, Ann (Buck) Levinz was daughter of a London lawyer and wife of an MP, while Frances (Bettenson) Hewet was a gentlewoman whose husband was both a small landowner and an agent to larger landowners (like the fathers of Lady Mary and Lady Henrietta).[30] Philippa Mundy of Markeaton and Anne Wortley (of whom we shall hear more) belonged wholly and securely to the rank of gentry.

No letters now survive from Lady Mary to Ann Levinz[31] or to Mary Banks, whose attorney father had already acquired several marks of gentry status: setting up his coach, building himself a country house at Scofton (near Thoresby and nearer Worksop), and becoming a force in local politics.[32] Mary Bank's two surviving letters to Lady Mary Pierrepont provide the best available glimpse of life in Nottinghamshire. In January 1710, while kept from visiting Thoresby by 'these terrible Frosts and Snow',[33] she could send 'the Boy' twice a day if necessary with letters or packets. She wrote 'I am a Dutyfull Servant to her Majesty', which sounds like an ironical pretence of Toryism—unless it possibly refers to the Pierrepont governess. Later she sent Lady Mary rather unepiscopally gallant messages of

[30] Lady Mary shared with Hewet her interest in Delarivier Manley (*CL* i. 15–19). The Hewet estate at Shireoaks (2 miles from Worksop) was a centre of political influence; but Frances Hewet adopted an ingratiating tone to Lady Henrietta's mother, while disparaging her to Lady Mary (Higginbottom 1987: 15–16; 31 Jan. 1712 [?1711], Portland MSS, Nottingham University (Pw2.411); *c*.29 Nov. 1713, *CL* i. 202). Could any of these middle-class women have provoked MWM's later outburst about 'heartily repent[ing]' having formed unequal friendships (*CL* iii. 36)?

[31] In Jan. 1712 [?1711] Frances Hewet observed that Ann Levintz 'gos bravely on with her great belly' (Portland MSS Pw2. 411).

[32] Hunter 1869: 394. The funeral sermon for the former Mary Banks praised her 'superior Genius and education, the productions of her wit, and her condescending, gracious, obliging Temper and Carriage, putting Herself, in a manner, upon the same level with those of an inferior Rank' (John Mason, *The Good Christian's Gain by Death*, 1726, 11).

[33] The Thames was frozen for three months this winter.

adoration from Archbishop Tenison. She reported on the progress of various errands and commissions: 'Cloath' ordered from a mercer, penknives, and 'a great parcel' of pamphlets and books 'just come out', which her father gathered expressly for Lady Mary. She returned a borrowed book, and forwarded poems transcribed from the manuscripts of Mary (Molesworth) Monck, together with work by one of the Molesworth brothers. These manuscripts were rough or 'Scrawl'd'; Mary Banks, showing them without Mary Monck's knowledge, begged 'your Ladyship will keep the Sheets together'.[34]

The relationships here are complex. Tenison was a close friend of Lady Mary's cousin John Evelyn, a fellow member of the Radical enlightenment with him and Mary Monck's father, later Lord Molesworth. Lady Mary was clearly not yet acquainted with Monck (who died young before becoming a published author). But besides being favoured with an unauthorized sight of Monck's work, she was acting as ghost-writer in an Italian correspondence between Monck and Banks. She promised Banks to 'Spare a few moments' to compose an Italian letter for her to send in reply to one from Monck (and also to send a translation, so that Banks would know what she was supposed to have said). Lady Mary kept among her papers five poems either by or about Monck, and was later friendly with several of her relations. In faintly deferential terms, Mary Banks was, it seems, reporting on a kind of mostly female writing circle.[35]

Among the fathers of this group, dukes and attorneys were alike in inflicting serious emotional trauma on their children when the time came to choose a marriage partner. Among the group of friends, the courtships of Frances Hewet, Anne Justice, and Anne Levinz are undocumented. The Brownlow family offered a chilling hint that women were interchangeable. Margaret Brownlow died of smallpox just before she should have been married; ten months later her fiancé married her sister Jane instead. Mary Monck's husband George was deranged by 1712, 'now very sober' but 'by fits . . . quarrelsome and withal dangerous'.[36] Jane Smith (Hermensilda) and Sarah Chiswell never married: Sarah was probably too poor ever to have an offer. But Mary Banks, Philippa Mundy, Lady Henrietta, and the Pierreponts went through remarkably similar ordeals.

[34] H MS 77. 116–20. Mary Banks visited the Moncks at Handsworth near Sheffield (Hill 1952: 14).

[35] H MS 77. 118–19; Monck 1716; Jacob 1981: 89, 154. Robert Molesworth, son of a Dublin merchant, was ennobled the year he published his daughter's work. Another of this circle, Philippa Mundy, kept two MS poems by Monck and was connected with her by marriage (MM/12/2/17). Lady Mary also collected a poem by 'Mrs Finch', later Lady Winchilsea (H MS 81. 122–3, 143–5).

[36] The Brownlow fiancé was the future Duke of Ancaster (Cartwright 1883: 99, 137; Cust 1898; HMC 1913: viii. 258).

I am not talking here about real marriage disasters, like that of Lady Anne Vaughan, a Chelsea friend and distant relative. The piously educated Lady Anne became an heiress on her father's death in 1713; noble suitors came running. She made a careful choice (the Duke of Bolton's heir), only to be rejected (allegedly as they came out of church after the wedding), told she could never please him, and consigned to solitude.[37] Such an extreme experience was mercifully rare, but a rough ride into the haven of marriage was very common.

Mary Banks was called a jilt for her temerity in turning down one young man on grounds of his excessive drinking. Her next suitor rejected her, or rather the financial terms proposed, in a manner that outraged her father. Each of these ruptures was painful or damaging to Mary in one way or another. Of her third, successful suitor we know nothing. Lady Henrietta, another great catch financially, surprised her friends by mustering courage to defy her mother's first choice of a (literally or figuratively?) stinking prospective husband. She disliked the second choice (heir to the Earl of Oxford), but over the course of negotiations grew to like him as her mother turned against him, and defied her mother again to keep to the bargain which had been struck with him.[38]

Philippa Mundy shared with Mary and Frances a playful secret code for use in their letters, in which Paradise meant marriage for love, Hell meant marriage with reluctance and detestation, and Limbo meant marriage with indifference. Each of the three confided in the others about a Paradise whom she truly loved. But none of them expected to be able to marry her Paradise, and none of them did. Philippa was urged to be brave when hers without warning dashed her hopes by marrying someone else; Frances, characteristically, seems never to have hoped and to have greeted her loss with settled despondency; Mary's unidentified Paradise is first heard of after her father had chosen her a Hell, and last heard of not long before she eloped with her Limbo, Edward Wortley Montagu. Philippa's next suitor cannily involved her in corresponding with him about his negotiations with her parents; by this means he stole into her affections even while he was driving his bargain for her fortune.[39] The marriages of these girls were made not in heaven, nor in the romance worlds of Indamora or Strephon, but in a world of haggling, of parental decisions and compulsions, where family financial policy was the primary concern.

The passage was not quite abrupt from juvenile 'love and wit' or adolescent high spirits to the rigours of the marriage-market. However little

---

[37] *CL* ii. 439; Blunt 1906: 162–4. [38] Hill 1952: 2–14, 50; *CL* i. 202.
[39] M/M MSS, Lincoln Record Office.

Lord Dorchester (formerly Kingston) regarded his children's wishes over
choice of partner, he did not marry them early by the standards of his time
and class. But they were early acclimatized to the twice-yearly migration
with coach, servants, baggage, and anxious attention to the weather
prospects, between Nottinghamshire and London. The heavy coach, elegantly curved beneath and riding on steel springs, panelled, carved, and
gilded, with blinds fitted to its sliding glass windows, represented both a triumph of technology and an object of display.[40] Roads were improving.
Turnpike trusts were just breaking free of the control of local Justices of the
Peace. Various means were developing of contouring the surface to drain
the water off.[41]

Journey's end was an imposing house in Arlington Street, between Green
Park and St James's Square.[42] Mary and Frances probably went often to see
their sister Evelyn at Chelsea; Mary had several Chelsea friends. Their
London days began while they were still young enough to scale the garden
wall for illicit chat with the Brownlow girls next door at Lord Guilford's.
They clung with fingers and toes and enjoyed the taste of the forbidden, till
'one fatal morning down drops Miss Nelly', bruising herself in unmentionable parts.[43] This brought down the wrath of elders; they were reduced to the
tedium of visiting by coach and by the front entrance.

London had two meanings. It meant the huge swarming town (of 700,000
people, more than twenty times the size of any other in England), with coal-
polluted air and noisy, smelly, dangerous streets; and it meant the micro-
cosm of fashionable society, with its concomitant of 'public adoration'.
Formal visiting was the rule: a ritual as far away in spirit as can be imagined
from the gossip of girls over a garden wall. Chairs were still placed in a ser-
ried row around the walls, not disposed in groups. Ladies' fashions had long,
tight waists which called for well-laced stays underneath. A mantua, like a
long jacket pulled back and bunched at the hips, might be worn on top.
Gowns and petticoats swept the floor. A 'petticoat' was a skirt as well as an
under-skirt; the richly decorated outermost petticoat was often divided in
front, designed to show a broad strip of the equally decorated next one.
Hoops were just coming in. Hairstyles had become less elaborate recently:

[40] At their father's death he had three old but still high-priced vehicles: town coach, travelling coach, and
'Charriott' (Manvers MS 4882).
[41] Thrupp 1877: 42, 45–6, 49; Laugero 1995: 50–1.
[42] Only one Arlington St. ratepayer (Lord Manchester) paid more than Dorchester's £7. Lord Stair paid
£4. 10s., Lady Molesworth £2. 10s., other households 10s. Walpole's Arlington St. rent was £300 p.a. (Burnett 1969: 143). Dorchester made payments to an insurance company, overseers of the poor, surveyors of
highways, scavengers, and a watchman (BL Eg. MS 3135. 162).
[43] Unmentionable not by Lady Mary but by Dallaway, her editor in 1803, who censored her here.

beribboned reinforced 'towers' had given way to arrangements using only the natural hair, most of it drawn up and back in a bun or chignon, with loose strands or ringlets around the face to soften the effect. Dressing to attend a church service at court was a matter of high excitement and anxiety. The girls removed their watches before going into crowds, for fear of thieves.[44]

The afternoon pastimes of shopping and walking in the park permitted less formal dress than visiting; but different levels of formality demanded time for changing clothes and accessories. 'Ease' was no excuse for negligence. Lady Mary later recalled how often her pleasure in attracting notice in the Mall (in St James's Park) was 'sour'd before I slept by the Informations of my female Freinds, who seldom fail'd to tell me it was observ'd I had shew'd an inch above my shoe heels, or some other criticism of equal weight, which was construe'd affectation'. Her imaginative life, which dwelt on the slights meted out to romantic lovers, 'proudly poor' poets, and wounded soldiers, would not have helped her to endure such criticism.

Evening amusements were the theatres, the opera, or private assemblies where there might be cards (with betting) or dancing. Lady Mary later recalled dancing with other girls at a private house. She left no surviving account of the night she lost £100 at cards, though it probably joined the colourful episodes accumulating in her diary.[45] Of court occasions (the most formal of all) she attended Queen Anne's official birthday on 6 February 1711 but missed it in 1712; she writes as if the main pleasures of a court appearance are planning one's dress beforehand and then admiring the men's 'Fring'd Gloves, embrodier'd Coats, and powder'd wigs in irresistable Curl'.[46]

Lady Mary Pierrepont was little and slender, with fair skin and dark, smooth hair. Her dark, heavily fringed eyes had an arresting life and sparkle. Years later Lady Hertford (who was ten years her junior and not herself beautiful) vividly remembered her 'beauty greater than I ever saw'. These natural gifts, driven by a lively and restless mind, brought her more heartfelt flattery than her social rank alone would have done.

Since the fashionable world overlapped with the literary, some flattery took the form of verse. Years later Lady Mary told how she unmasked a suitor of one of her friends, who had tried to ingratiate himself with a verse offering, as a 'poor Plagiary' whose gift was straight out of Thomas

---

[44] The rigid, heavily embroidered and bejewelled court fashions had fossilized years before; they stayed that way for years to come (Buck 1979: 13, 17, and *passim*; *SL* i. 3).

[45] *CL* ii. 446–7; iii. 79, 171; see p. 41. Elsewhere in this house the grandmother of one of the dancers was 'screaming and crying' with the vapours.

[46] *CL* i. 115.

Randolph. (He was, she added, unlucky to be caught: selecting an out-of-fashion poet, he 'would have escap'd any one of less universal reading than my selfe'.)[47]

She was not above obliquely soliciting such compliments. To young Lord Castlecomber, English holder of an Irish peerage, she quoted from an Italian song, saying it 'might give a pritty hint for an English verse'. Castlecomber knew a challenge when he heard one, and responded with some very creditable lines calling her Orinda (a bow to her writing), and saying that despite her disdain 'I must adore, persist, and still pursue, | It is my destiny, it is her due.' These she copied into an album where she kept verses by herself and others. It is not clear whether poems she transcribed there were more precious to her than those (Mary Monck's and Anne Finch's, for instance) of which she kept loose copies. Political squibs and poems by and about other women are prominent among her early hoard, along with the tributes to herself.[48] Such collecting was perfectly acceptable for a young lady.

Young ladihood, however, was Lady Mary's veneer but not her substance, to judge from what is probably her second-earliest extant letter, written in 1709 to a friend still to be discussed: Anne Wortley or Wortley Montagu. Speculation has been rife about this friendship; Lady Mary's later involvement with Anne's brother Edward has even been read as pure displacement of her feelings for Anne.[49] In fact surviving letters throw less light on this friendship than on those of Lady Mary with Philippa or Anne Justice or Frances Hewet: almost all of these bear the heavy impress of Edward's supervision.

Anne was praised in a verse satire of 1708 for unstudied simplicity. She was, it seems, an *ingénue*. The topics of one pre-Edward letter to Lady Mary, written from London to Thoresby, are the 'great wedings upon the stock', the opera, ladies showing off their coaches and six in the park—and money transactions. Lady Mary and Lady Frances had between them overpaid some debts to Anne: gambling debts. These are nothing serious, being reckoned in shillings, not pounds; but they confirm the feeling that Anne belonged in the world of comedy, not that of romance.[50]

---

[47] Hertford–Pomfret, *Corr.* ii. 234; *CL* iii. 22.

[48] e.g. 'The Ghost' (political) and 'Amongst the writing Race of modern Witts' (*POAS* 1703: ii. 317; 1704: iii. 147–8; H MS 81. 116–17); 'Written in a Ladys Quintus Curtius, By E[dward] W[ortley] to the Lady M. Pierrepont'; 'Verses for L. M. P. address'd to the Nymph that presides over the Medicinal Waters of Acton, by E[dward] Vernon' (a brilliant young naval officer, later a famous admiral); and the poem by Castlecomber—nephew of the diarist Alice Thornton, who came into his title in Sept. 1707, m. in 1715, and d. in 1719 (H MS 255).

[49] Mahaffey 1963: 174 ff.

[50] *St James's Park*, 1708, 13. Her last figure is for 'your staks at last which was but 8 (or 9)' (dated 'Saturday March', H MS 77. 124–5).

The only extant authentic exchange between the two ('an insipid scarll' from Anne[51] and a longer fantasia on its theme from Lady Mary) catches the voice of adolescent girls, giggling and outrageous. It seems Lord Herbert, a young bachelor, had stolen the chamber-pot of the beautiful, married Lady Bridgewater as a love-token. Like other news items in Lady Mary's early letters, this may have been fabricated out of pure mischief—though pots *were* often pricey objects engraved with coats of arms.[52] Lady Mary gave her wit free rein on the notion of a chamber-pot as analogy to a Kit-Cat glass, serving the double purpose of drinking toasts and refreshing memory. (It would hold not just a paltry line of verse but a long panegyric.) But if the custom of pots as love-tokens should catch on, 'it would be terribly inconvenient to you and the rest of my beautiful Acquaintance', unable to keep a pot in the house no matter how carefully secured.[53] On the basis of these few uncensored letters Anne Wortley was perhaps immature, but she was fun.

[51] Dated 17 June [1709], perhaps wrongly since Lady Mary's reply bears the same date, though she was at Thoresby (H MS 77. 122–3).
[52] Costing £7. 11*s.* or £11. 10*s.* in the 1670s (Price 1875: 20).   [53] *SL* 3.

3

July 1709–February 1712

❦

Marriage Market: 'what price my master will put on me'[1]

ANNE WORTLEY's light-hearted voice was soon hushed. Not yet by death: that was nine months away. But only a month after the chamber-pot exchange Anne was writing out a letter not of smut and scandal but of ceremony and compliment, and she was not making it up but copying words provided by her brother. For every one of her remaining letters to Lady Mary, Edward's draft survives. Anne sometimes mangled his spelling, but faithfully transcribed his sentiments. The tone became highflown, turning on Lady Mary's transcendent attractions and her flocks of lovers. Anne dwelt on her sincere love and Lady Mary's 'inimitable maner'. In August 1709 she solemnly copied: 'You have often found that the most angry, nay, the most neglectful Air you can assume, has made as deep a wound as the kindness.' She mentioned 'the only fault you have, your inconstancy. But upon second thoughts, how can this be a fault? No, tis none and you are altogether perfect.'

Other pressing topics were Lady Mary's love of the Thoresby solitude where she now was, and her efforts to learn Latin 'without a master'. She was told 'that those shining qualities in you were design'd to adorn a Court and please a multitude and do honour to nature and that a retirement is an abuse of 'em'. Obliquely, in his sister's voice, Edward offered 'a Cambridge Doctor' (himself) to assist in Lady Mary's studies.[2] Lady Mary several times called him 'master' after they were married, *perhaps* in tender allusion to his early tutelage.[3]

No evidence survives of serious aspirants to her hand before Edward Wortley. Her father bought a fine house, Berrymead Priory at Acton near

---

[1] *CL* i. 64.   [2] H MS 77. 126–7; 15 [Aug.] 1709, H MS 77. 134–5; [19] Aug. [1709], H MS 74. 90–1.
[3] e.g. on their first wedding anniversary (*SL* 111).

London, in 1708;[4] he may have thought that time spent within reach of fashionable society would help him to get his children married. But a potential suitor for one of them received a courteous brush-off: 'haveing had lately occasion to talk seriously to my daughter of marrage, I find she is in very good earnest when she declaires against it, which I am very sorry for.'[5] Dorchester was by implication overstating the freedom of choice open to his daughters. But since they had a brother, and were no heiresses, pressure to marry was not yet acute.

According to an autobiographical romance which Lady Mary began some time after 1715, she first met 'Sebastian' (Edward Wortley Montagu) when he put in a brief, dutiful appearance at a female gathering held by a young lady whose fortune he had designs on. (Later tradition said the gathering was his sister's.) He 'did not expect much Conversation amongst a set of Romps', but was electrified by the wit and beauty of 'Laetitia' (Lady Mary), who proved herself able to sustain a riveting conversation not only on the latest play, or on English poetry, but even on the classics.[6] Though the story is openly romanticized, though Lady Mary makes herself 'then but newly enter'd into her teens', and makes Sebastian's sisters court her friendship purely for his sake, her outline is otherwise fairly accurate. Edward Wortley Montagu *did* genuinely admire her mind, and such admiration from a friend of Addison and Steele, a travelled man, an MP, was intoxicating enough.[7] He had a good mind himself, and was handsome and well spoken with it.

Edward's father was born Sidney Montagu, second son of the great naval commander Edward Montagu, Earl of Sandwich. Sidney had left his native home counties for the north to marry the heiress and take the name of the royalist Sir Francis Wortley, of the manor of Wortley just outside Sheffield. Though Sir Francis was an author (who ranks an entry in *DNB*) he was not a sensitive soul.[8] He lived long apart from his wife. Having no children by her, he made his illegitimate daughter Anne Newcomen his heiress conditionally on her future husband taking his name. He intended, if he had lived, to marry her into the Willoughby or the Berkeley family. But Lord Sandwich

---

[4] It was 'handsome, low, and regular', with lovely gardens (see p. 52). It was later in Salisbury Street. Though scheduled for restoration in 1980, it was demolished in 1984.

[5] Osborn MSS. An endorsement names the recipient as Henry Hyde, 2nd Earl of Clarendon; more likely would be his heir, Edward Hyde, a childless widower of bad character, who succeeded as 3rd Earl in 1709.

[6] *E&P* 77–81. Laetitia strongly suggests Madeleine de Scudéry's 'Sapho' (see pp. 17–18). Baptized on 13 Feb. 1678 at St Martin's in the Fields, EWM was eleven years older than MWM.

[7] EWM was friendly with Addison and Steele, who were well known to Lady Mary's father (Spence 1966: 744). He was godfather to Steele's daughter Elizabeth, and was honoured with the dedication of the collected *Tatler*, vol. ii (Rogers 1993: 216; Bond 1964: 493–4).

[8] He admired female sufferance of 'a husband as intollerably hard as harsh' ('The true character of a northerne lady . . .', quoted in Hunter 1831: ii. 318). Hunter's account of the Wortley family is ii. 299 ff.

was one of his executors, charged with Anne's protection and education, and it was Sandwich's son Sidney who married her.

Like her father's wife, Anne Newcomen was given in a marriage 'more of ambition than affection', and was in due course 'forced to demand a separation'. Sidney splendidly rebuilt for his mistress a family house about six miles from Wortley. In the year Lady Mary was born, a bill in parliament settled the maintenance for Anne's five children during her lifetime. She became a Catholic and moved abroad.[9] Her second son, Edward, 'always spoke of his father's conduct towards her with resentment and indignation'. He and his elder brother Francis were sent to Westminster School when already in their teens (unusually late), perhaps because of this family break-up. They were in time to experience the headship of the 'terrific disciplinarian' Dr Busby, on whose death Edward wrote a Latin poem. Busby made history by bringing the sons of the nobility and upper gentry to join the middle-class boys at a 'public school'; but Westminster declined steeply towards the end of his long rule.[10]

Sidney Wortley Montagu did not wrap up his maritally acquired talents in a napkin, but set about multiplying them by a lifetime of business deals, many of them shady. He bought leases on church lands at bargain-basement prices, which came his way through the good offices of his uncle Nathaniel Crew, 3rd Baron Crew and Bishop of Durham (where Sidney's brother John Montagu was Dean). Crew seems to have been an unmitigated rogue, as well as a High Tory in a Whig family.[11] Years later Lady Mary found in Lord Oxford's manuscript collection some poems highly critical of the Wortley family; she handled the discovery with proper discretion.[12]

Sidney gave his second son a good education. After Westminster came Trinity College, Cambridge (where Edward wrote a Latin poem on Christopher Wren's library), then the Middle Temple (he was called to the bar in 1699), then the Grand Tour, part of it with Addison. During his tour, in 1702, Francis Wortley died. Like Tristram Shandy in parallel circumstances, Edward found himself the heir. But he could not bank on inheriting Sidney's huge self-made assets—only the core of them, the entailed Wortley estates.

[9] At St Ellen's Well (now St Helen's, Barnsley), it was ornamented with busts of goddesses, including Diana and Astrea (Hunter 1831: ii. 319–20, 395; Henning 1983).

[10] Busby d. Aug. 1694, aged 88 (*E&P* 13; Barker and Stenning 1928: i; Carleton 1965: 13–14, 16–20, 163; H MS 81. 316–17).

[11] He was fiercely acquisitive and famous for 'political tergiversations' (*DNB*, uncharacteristically outraged; Mackenzie and Ross 1834: i, pp. lvi–lvii).

[12] EWM tried to withdraw the MS from the expected Harleian sale around 1742, but it could not be found. It apparently 'Reflected' on his grandfather Wortley, his mother, and eldest brother (*CL* ii. 342 n. 3, 354).

In 1709, when he began dictating his sister's letters, Edward was thirty-one. In Lady Mary's romance he was 'rather an Adorer than an Admirer of Learning'. As he later recalled, he was pressed to join the government under Queen Anne, but declined.[13] He was also already somewhat valetudinarian. Over the next few years he was flexing his political and business muscles. He distinguished himself in parliament in 1708 (supporting naturalization of French Huguenot immigrants) and 1710 (sponsoring a Place Bill to curb office-holding by MPs). With his father he attended meetings of the five biggest Tyneside coal-owners, at which they planned to squeeze out smaller operators and to 'adjust' the course of the River Wear. (This last put them among the type of heroically proactive landowners later celebrated in Pope's *Epistle to Burlington.*) But 'young Wortley' was not flush with money, though his father was.[14]

In Lady Mary's tale, 'Sebastian' 's meeting with her instantly deflected him from the rich woman he had his eye on; the couple came quickly to an understanding and marriage preparations moved into lawyers' hands. Perhaps this is what really happened. Although in life the hesitant, even reluctant courtship spanned more than three years, the lawyers' meeting came early on. But it proved abortive: no happy ending, but only a brief intermission.

The true story had four distinct phases, punctuated by three interruptions of a progressively more divisive kind: Anne's death, the failed legal negotiations, and a later, complete breach on emotional grounds which lasted for more than a year. At various times various helpers were involved: letters were received or carried by Lady Mary's maid, by someone unidentified but probably male, and by female friends. These unidentified people have left no recorded comment on the strange relationship they forwarded. Nor did two better-known helpers, Wortley's friend Richard Steele and his wife.[15]

With Anne Wortley's sudden death in February 1710,[16] Lady Mary lost a friend; Anne's brother lost his stalking-horse. It seems he waited a few weeks, then wrote to her in his own name. With his letter he sent a copy of *Tatler*, no. 143 (9 March 1710), by Steele: a reproof to women for hankering after consumer luxuries, so that indulgent males had gently to nudge them out of their 'Faults and Errors'.[17]

---

[13] 'In Novam Bibliothecam', H MS 81. 315; Halsband 1956: 9; *E&P* 78; Halsband MSS.

[14] Hughes 1952: 67, 178, 181, 191.

[15] *CL* i. 33, 54, 39, 74, 76. One friend was probably Lady Margaret Crighton; another was a married woman.

[16] She was said to have 'died of grief for the follys and imprudences' of her sister Catherine (an unlikely story). Buried on 23 Feb. (Clavering 1967: 69–70), she must have died around the end of the three months' Great Frost. Mary and Frances Pierrepont were at Thoresby in Jan., in London by Mar., their arrival probably set back by the exceptional weather.

[17] Steele *et al.* 1987: ii. 314. *Tatler*, no. 141, had recently advocated its own ideal of education for women; but no. 63 had attacked Astell's views on the same topic.

When this advice reached her, Lady Mary was gossiping with female correspondents, studying Italian, attending the opera (to see the *castrato* Nicolini lavishing his considerable acting talent on battle with a kind of pantomime lion). The letter provoked her to the strictly forbidden (though not uncommon) step of writing to a man. As Philippa was to do, as she herself was to censure Mary Banks for doing, she entered into independent negotiation with a suitor. She played this transgression up, not down, in her letter, dramatically terse in style. 'You are Brother to a Woman I tenderly lov'd . . . I don't injoin you to burn this Letter. I know you will. Tis the first I ever writ to one of your sex and shall be the last . . . My resolutions are seldom made, and never broken.' He did not burn it, but made a careful copy and kept both. She did not keep her resolution, but, as she observed wryly some months later, embarked on a course of making a great many and breaking them all.

In reply, Wortley opened the second phase of courtship by setting forth, more explicitly than he had done before, some views which were to become excruciatingly familiar. They were of opposite temperaments; he was 'a reasonable man'; she 'coud not seem to forget you knew how to please others as well as him'. He therefore thought 'you can never suit'; but he invited her to attempt persuading him.[18] This phase—brief but eventful, ending with lawyers—had hardly begun when the pair were severely tested by two related near-disasters. First, in April, Lady Mary went down with measles at Acton. Measles is a nasty complaint for an adult, and at this time was not infrequently fatal. But more important than her physical sufferings was the impossibility of sending illicit letters from Acton. Her suitor was anxious for her health (though he said he would welcome a total loss of her beauty, as a deterrent to her other admirers). Her silence exacerbated his anxiety.

To convey letters in this emergency he employed someone Lady Mary thought a shockingly bad risk.[19] Unpleasant consequences followed. Both fathers discovered that Lady Mary was receiving letters from Wortley, though the crucial fact of her *writing* to him remained unknown. Sidney Wortley's knowing, wrote Edward, might do him serious (presumably financial) harm, 'but that I don't value'. Lady Mary could not afford to be so insouciant. She burned the letters she had so far received, and refused to answer the latest. But someone, perhaps a maid, concocted a reply on her behalf: 'She gives her love and respects to you . . . M.P.'[20]

[18] [28 Mar. 1710], *CL* i. 22–5; H MS 74. 2–3, draft, endorsed by EWM 'To P2'.
[19] Sebastian uses an orange-woman; they were a group notorious as paid go-betweens in dubious intrigues (*E&P* 80).
[20] 17 Apr. 1710, *CL* i. 27–8; *E&P* 81.

Edward was delighted with this 'kinder' letter, until Mary indignantly disowned it, when he became aggrieved. Perhaps, like 'Sebastian', he thought she had engineered her father's discovery in order to precipitate a formal proposal, since this was, indeed, what followed. He visited Acton at least once before travelling on business to Durham. This may have been a strategic withdrawal, for his negotiations with Lord Dorchester did not go well.[21]

The sticking point was the entail. Dorchester wanted a large jointure (the income set aside for a bride in case of her husband's death). This, said Wortley, was no problem, for 'too high a rate cant be set upon you'.[22] But Dorchester also wanted everything, or almost everything, tied up for the yet-to-be-born eldest son: the family power base would be strengthened, and the future father made a kind of trustee or sitting tenant for his heir. This was common practice.[23] But Edward Wortley Montagu, speaking here for progressive Enlightenment thinking, argued that the practice was bad. Reason, not Custom, should decide. Why should an eldest son be pre-ordained to wealth, 'be he perverse, ungrateful, impious, or cruel'? Suppose a younger son were to prove a more worthy heir?

Commentators have been quick to note one kind of irony: Wortley's only son did indeed turn out perverse, ungrateful, and impious. Because in the end the marriage went ahead with no settlement, Wortley was later free to direct his immense fortune away from his son to the offspring of his deserving daughter. A further irony is that each negotiator—Dorchester the father as well as Wortley the suitor—was a younger son who had been 'promoted' at his elder brother's death. Dorchester was a peer only because his *two* elder brothers had both died; yet he seems to have felt no sense of 'there but for the grace of God'. When Wortley proposed retaining the freedom to choose his own heir from among his putative offspring, his putative father-in-law 'rejoined that he did not wish to see his grandchildren beggars'—a magnificently illogical statement from one who wanted to benefit just his eldest male grandchild at the expense of younger ones. A third irony is Wortley's later choice of his second grandson (picked, it seems, not on merit but purely on position in the family) as his heir.

Lady Mary meanwhile found her every movement spied on by her sister Frances. In early June she was packed off to the 'frightful solitude' of West

---

[21] 20 Apr.–7 May, *CL* i. 28–40.

[22] [20 Aug. 1710], *CL* i. 51. Dorchester no doubt knew that EWM was not on good terms with his father, that he had a younger brother, and could *count* on inheriting only the smaller, entailed portion of his father's property. He could not foresee that EWM would surpass his father at *making* money.

[23] See Staves 1990.

Dean. Somehow she continued to write to Wortley. She tried to convince him she was no empty-headed debutante but was worthy of his respect and confidence; she used Mary Astell's argument that it behoved a woman undertaking a lifetime's marital obedience to be 'cautious who I set for my Master'. Wortley seems to have visited West Dean, as he had visited Acton; but he found Lady Mary's present master no easier to deal with than before. It seems, indeed, that a 'treaty' with some other suitor was being discussed.[24]

In late July Wortley was offering to bypass the unbudgeable Dorchester and take Lady Mary with 'nothing'; he implied that it depended on her whether he pursued or abandoned his plan to travel, for his health, to the popular resort of Spa in Belgium. By 10 August, however, with his 'treaty' with Dorchester 'quite broke off', he departed for Spa. He relieved his feelings first by writing out his arguments about entail and marriage settlements in general, for Steele to publish in the *Tatler*. His stance was not wholly progressive, and although he thought love ought to play a larger role in marriage arrangements, Steele (or Addison) felt it necessary to modify his language on this topic, to make it warmer.

Wortley condemned the whole modern fashion of settlements which allotted a woman a fixed jointure in widowhood, replacing what he called the 'ample and generous provision . . . the third of her husband's estate' granted by the old system of dower. Women, he said, had been perfectly content with dower until profit-conscious lawyers came up with more complicated procedures. There is something in this argument; but, although it is rash to pronounce as to which system gave women a better deal in practice, the swing against dower was certainly driven in part by a feeling that widows were getting too much. Wortley waxed eloquent on the awful prospect of a mercenary woman making 'a kind of Auction for her selfe', using the first bidder as a lever to raise the bids of others, and willing to remain unmarried rather than not get the best deal.[25] Such a process, it seems, was what he feared and suspected.

Lady Mary had lost her expected sociable summer at Thoresby. But West Dean was at least 'over the Hills and far away'. She took the suspense and turmoil philosophically: literally so, for she began her rural exile by making

---

[24] [28 July, 20 Aug. 1710], *CL* i. 48, 54. Although Jill Campbell thinks Charles Jervas's picture of Lady Mary as shepherdess represents a semi-escape from social framing, this style of portrait (like modern *Country Life* portrait photos) signalled a young lady about to be married (Campbell 1994: 80; information from Martha Hamilton Philips). The portrait is dated 1710, but since Lady Mary was then out of London it may belong to 1712, and Clotworthy Skeffington's courtship.

[25] H MS 80. 130–4, 258–65; *Tatler*, nos. 199, 223, 18 July and 12 Sept. 1710; Bond 1964; Staves 1990: 112, 116, and *passim*.

an English translation of the philosopher Epictetus.[26] Epictetus, in life a slave and a cripple, was in his thinking a stoic. He believed it feasible to hold one-self mentally superior to external circumstances, keeping the soul and the self untouched by pain and ill-treatment. His doctrine held a strong appeal for feminist thinkers of Lady Mary's day, like Astell and Mary, Lady Chudleigh—and for Elizabeth Carter, his most famous translator. Lady Mary, though she later saw bodily pain as the greatest evil, continued throughout her life to seek strength at moments of difficulty in the stoicism of Epictetus. It did not always serve her well: it may have contributed to her apparent spinelessness in the face of Ugolino Palazzi.

Meanwhile, having made her translation, she was hungry for criticism and no doubt for praise. She showed her work to Gilbert Burnet, Bishop of Salisbury, who had already given generously of his time in instructing her. He was a Scot, an influential Whig writer, an admirer of her great-grandfather Wise William. The Thoresby library was well stocked with his works, and West Dean was in his diocese. His wife was also a writer and thinker, with leanings towards stoicism.[27] But neither Gilbert nor Elizabeth Burnet took a radical line on questions of gender—which fact no doubt dictated the submissive tone of the covering letter which Lady Mary sent with her work.

This letter argues forcefully for women's education. It is ignorance, she says, not learning, that makes so many women loud and pushy in their opinions; better education will teach them how much they do not know, and make them better helpmeets. She provides example as well as argument, with lavish quotation from Erasmus, in Latin. Then comes a decorous note of caution. 'I am not now arguing for an Equality for the 2 Sexes; I do not doubt God and Nature has thrown us into an Inferior Rank. We are a lower part of the Creation; we owe Obedience and Submission to the Superior Sex.' She quotes Erasmus to mobilize the authority of the Renaissance educationalists (who took a strong interest in teaching women); she turns to a more recent educationalist, Bathsua Makin, for proper feminine disclaimers.[28]

She was to come later to 'arguing for an Equality'; for the moment she needed to woo her audience. But if she already knew Astell's *Serious Proposal*, then she knew the argument that women's undeniable follies and

[26] *SL* 26; MWM 1803: i. 265–309. The Thoresby library had Epictetus in Greek and Latin, 1640, with English versions by Ellis Walker, 1695, George Stanhope, 1704, and Sir John Davies, 1670, and Politian's commentary, 1595 (*Kingstoniana*).

[27] Burnet 1897: i. 21. Mary, Lady Blayney, noted that Burnet often cited his mother and aunts as authorities (BL Add. MS 61466.186).

[28] To Burnet, 10 July [1710], *CL* i. 45. 'I do not (as some have witily done) plead for Female Preeminence. To ask too much is the way to be denied all. God hath made Man the Head . . .' (Makin 1673: A2v). Lady Mary perhaps found Erasmus in Makin's citation (23).

vices stem from 'our paying too great a deference to other Peoples Judgments, and too little to our own'.[29]

She relaxed before and after this effort of high seriousness by flippant comments to Anne Justice and Frances Hewet on the shortage of eligible men around West Dean. The local swains were a world away from the swains of romance: 'insensible of other pleasures than Hunting and drinking'. The nearest approach to intelligent society was supplied by poverty-stricken, reactionary, or aged parsons.[30] She was condemned to such society for several months.

Her relationship with Edward Wortley Montagu remained pending even now he was absent and (not by her) rejected. Its sparring quality was already established. In dispute before the marriage talks collapsed, they had entered into an 'engagement of friendship'; failing any closer tie, Wortley said, he would hold her to this undertaking for ever. He said he would write from Spa 'at least once a day while I stay and hope you will write as often'. Lady Mary was surprised that he still kept to this after breaking off negotiations; he must have supposed her father might come round.[31]

He was no sooner gone than she heard that Dorchester was planning a grand marriage for her brother. The projected financial settlement was to produce inalienable incomes for herself and Frances (to match the one that Evelyn already had from their grandmother). After this her father would no longer be free to cut her off on a whim. She wrote at once to tell Wortley the welcome news—welcome, she said, because it would enable her to remain single if she felt that Wortley was just too likely to 'confine [her] to the Country'. Yet she added that *if* his future plans were such as she wished to share— particularly if he really intended 'to travel'—then she would 'chuse you before any Match could be offered me'. She qualified this breathtaking boldness by a hint of shamefacedness, a positive denial that she spoke out of passion, and a professed intention to obey her father in everything short of actual forced marriage. But she clearly felt that these altered circumstances might make Wortley reconsider; she explicitly invited him to reapply.[32]

Once abroad, however, he had changed him mind about staying in touch. He had 'resolv'd to have a Truce . . . with business, Politicks and Love'. Without informing her, he had countermanded his request to Steele to forward letters. She, left in the country during his two-month absence, wrote at

---

[29] Astell 1697: 35–6; see p. 21.

[30] *CL* i. 42–3, 49–50; *SL* 27. They were, she noted, supporters of Sacheverell, who had caused a furore by preaching against the Revolution Settlement of 1688; Burnet had been threatened by Sacheverell supporters that spring (Holmes and Speck 1967: 79).

[31] *CL* i. 48–9; H MS 74. 82–5.

[32] She thought she was to receive £10,000—an overestimate (*CL* i. 53–4).

least six times, with growing anxiety, into the void he had created. 'I am torn with variety of Imaginations, and not one pleaseing one. I conjure you to write; I beg it of you . . . Tis impossible to expresse the pain I write in.' She addressed this letter, 'Pray send this wth care to Mr Edward Wortley Mountague wherever he is.'

It seems that politics at least got through to him at Spa, and he hastened his return on hearing that the Whig government was dissolved and elections imminent. In fact his re-election went through in his absence.[33] Once back, he grumpily informed Lady Mary that reading her letters (all but two, which were lost) had made him 'more out of humour' than he had been since talking to her father. (He was then astonished that this should make her 'angry'.) He none the less went painstakingly through her letters, answering them point by point, mostly with criticism of her character. About to leave London again for the north, he suggested that it would be best to give up corresponding. He seemed equally ready to disbelieve and contradict her whether she said she cared for him or whether she said she did not. Yet soon (while continuing his complaints) he was asking 'what I might expect to hear on a second offer of my selfe', and talking of 'clos[ing] the bargain' as if this was entirely in his own power. And she, though she lamented both his distrust and her own inconsistency, sounded still willing to be courted.[34] (Her Paradise had not yet appeared on the scene.) For at least a moment in November 1710 Wortley thought that his recurrent desire of 'seeing into her heart' had been granted.

Grudging and mutually reproachful, their correspondence staggered on after a brief lapse around the Christmas holidays. Lady Mary wrote lightheartedly to Anne Justice about the difficulty of getting a letter finished in London, between visitors and diversions and planning one's dress for the queen's birthday celebrations. She would never have written in this vein to Wortley. In February 1711 her many letters to him were dominated by his jealous complaints and suspicions, and by arrangements for some rendezvous at which they might talk privately about points of conduct too delicate to settle by letter. (Even in suggesting houses to meet at, he insulted her by calling the notoriously immoral Lady Wharton her 'friend'.)

The less he believed what she wrote, the more he wished to 'see into your heart'. He reiterated a plea made the previous autumn: 'this once try to avoid being witty and write in a style of business' or 'as you woud with an intimate friend'.[35] To him, wit was incompatible with seriousness. To her, it was her

---

[33] On 5 Oct., for Huntingdon.   [34] 24 Oct.–[c.17 Nov. 1710], *CL* i. 57, 59, 63, 67; H MS 74. 33 (draft).
[35] [c.3 Feb., 13 Feb. 1711], 4 Nov. [1710], *CL* i. 70–1, 74, 63.

signature, the tone of all her female intimacies. The more he saw of her in mixed company, the more he worried about her vivacious manner and the way she basked in admiration. He accused her of bestowing 'whispers, glances', and tête-à-tête talk on other men. He made some kind of a scene in public. He tried to get sister Frances to confirm that Lady Mary was behaving badly. His views on women were much like those of Addison and Steele, whose modern reformist journals were pronouncing female wit to be suspect as well as sexy.[36] Wortley liked a woman to be sensible but decently subordinate, bright but modest. She must not be over-fond of pleasure; nor must she call attention to herself.

After a year of corresponding with Lady Mary, he found himself a prey to passion. He was obsessed, possessive, angry at his own helplessness. He seems to have paid little attention to women previously; his letters to Addison suggest that his deepest orientation *may* have been towards men. But no degree of disapproval could dilute his desire for Lady Mary; and no amount of desire could do away with his disapproval. She was amazingly, perhaps unwarrantably, encouraging. She wrote, 'I like your conversation . . . I propose to my selfe a Happynesse in pleasing you and do not think it impossible.' But even this could not soften him. 'Had you bin so well pleas'd with my conversation', he returned, 'you would have had it long since at forty different places.' He felt that her easy manner with others was an abuse of him.[37]

She surely had him in mind many years later in creating Prince Sombre, the successful suitor of Princess Docile. Sombre is tall, well built, and morally upright, but wholly unamiable and ungracious, rigidly rational and impenetrably discreet. Unaccustomed to ladies' company, he has 'always treated them with a coldness verging on Contempt'. Naturally suspicious, he thinks 'less of pleasing . . . than of studying' his beloved, and is acutely aware that he does not please. He deludes himself that his growing passion is merely generous concern until he is 'stung to the quick' by sudden jealousy. His horror as he recognizes his own passion is like that of a 'pious Prude in love with her Stableman'. Because he cannot forgive Docile for her power over him, he *wants* to despise her and swallows false reports of her misconduct. He 'reproached himself as if for the deepest baseness, for the slightest sentiment in her favour'. Most tellingly like Lady Mary's actual suitor of many years before, Sombre seeks Docile out purposely to insult her, hoping

---

[36] 9 Feb. 1711 [10 Feb., 20 Apr. 1711], *CL* i. 72, H MS 74. 73–4, 94–5 (drafts). Addison's *Spectator*, no. 15, pub. 17 Mar. 1711, sharply contrasts the model, country-loving wife with unacceptable women. His ideal is just what EWM's letters wished for, his warnings just what EWM feared.

[37] [10, 13 Feb. 1711], *CL* i. 73–5.

by a quarrel to rid himself 'of a taste that he regarded as a blemish on his honour'. This plan backfires; his love redoubles, and with it his fury. He 'felt it as a Humiliation that she was necessary to his happiness'. He saw himself as a slave; 'his Pride would have wished to be self-sufficient.'[38]

Lady Mary offered more of a handle for criticism than her creation Docile. She had a wildness far beyond that of the *Tatler* character Jenny Bickerstaffe, whom Wortley proposed to her as a model. Jenny's crime was the venial one of buying too flashy a coach; Lady Mary, according to somebody calling himself 'Typographate' ('the Printer') lost half her annual allowance in a single gambling session at the Duke of R.'s house.

Typographate, writing to 'Zephelinda' (Pope's flighty friend Teresa Blount), took the matter lightly: 'The loss my Lady Mary Pourpoint had at play was nothing only of a hundred pounds.' Having lost this rather large 'nothing', half to a Mr Gascoigne and half to her noble host, she told Gascoigne (who was to leave next day) 'that she would send him his fivety pounds the next morning, which she did effectually. As for your Grace (says she to the latter) we being neighbours, and young [Wenches?] having not always plenty of ready money by 'em, I shall pay you as soon as I can.' Such insouciance! A couple of weeks later her father arrived in London, and the Duke of R. 'sent him word that his daughter had lost to him 50 pounds, which he desir'd he would send him. My Lord Do[r]chester answer'd that he never pay'd his daughters debts.' Typographate clearly felt the duke had acted like a cad and deserved to be snubbed; he gave no hint as to whether Dorchester, answering so glibly, had all his daughters in mind or just his daughter Mary. He must have seen her at this moment as a chip off the old block.[39]

Writing to Edward Wortley Montagu she found it necessary to construct a less worldly, more bashful self; but there is no reason to suppose she was not sincere with him. All her life she was torn between parties and privacy, the pleasures of the salon and those of the library. All her life she loved to dance and was highly susceptible to music; and even in the high musical art of the eighteenth century the bodily rhythms of dancing are still strong. Yet she deeply desired to be known for sense and reason, balance and good judgement. The rules of good breeding forbade her to declare her love without receiving a prior declaration; but also the persona of a girl in love, as figured in contemporary fiction, drama, and poetry, was unacceptable to her as a self-image.[40] A typical specimen was the heroine of Prior's 'Henry and

---

[38] *RW* 123–5.
[39] Mapledurham MS, vol. iii, dep. d. 310, fo. 122: thanks to Valerie Rumbold and Richard Williams. The duke is probably Rutland, not Richmond. For the unidentified Typographate, see Rumbold 1989: 54–5.
[40] This issue is well discussed by Salmon 1991.

Emma' (a poem which Lady Mary almost knew by heart). Emma in love is distraught, self-abasing, and irrational. When Lady Mary wrote, 'I can esteem, I can be a friend, but I don't know whether I can Love', she was describing her ideal for herself as well as, probably, the actual state of her feeling for Wortley. It was easy for her to impugn her flirting partners as 'wretches' obsessed with style, who had no claim on her serious regard—but not so easy to break with them all for ever.

By February 1711, with letters flying back and forth across London, the relationship felt very tense. Arrangements were being finalized for the marriage (the first among the Pierrepont children) of Lady Mary's under-age brother. The bride was an illegitimate heiress, Rachel Baynton, whose situation was just what Wortley's mother's had been. There was to be a private bill in parliament. Lady Mary grieved for her beloved brother, indissolubly tied to a stupid fifteen year old; Wortley pondered the financial implications. He wrote to ask Dorchester's leave to apply to him again in Lady Mary's changed circumstances; but in the event he never did this,[41] for he required her first (against all normal social convention) to persuade him that she loved him and had wholly committed herself to him.

For months he urged her to convince him. She protested that she loved no one else; she expatiated on the friendship—made up of esteem and tenderness—which she felt for him.[42] This was going very far; but for Wortley it was not enough, especially since he could not control her social contact with other men. He pined from one rare tête-à-tête to the next; yet he could not keep himself from accusing her. She was at court for the queen's birthday (a particularly splendid celebration this year, although smallpox was rife) and at the theatre, probably to see *The Man of Mode*.[43] But what was normal social activity to her, was to him an endless series of opportunities to be 'irregular as far as she coud with safety', 'acquainted with every man of fashion in town and with several of 'em too much'. In vain she tied herself in epistolary knots of self-justification. He thought she was leading on a 'new man', or even two of them: Mr D. and Mr K. The latter had been present at the birth-night and the theatre, and had serenaded her at Acton. Wortley felt sure the 'Violence' of his own 'Passion' was nothing to her.[44]

When she said she did care, when she said the men she flirted with had not enough 'understanding' to hold her interest, he berated her for insincerity.

[41] *CL* i. 30, 101.   [42] [24 Mar. 1711], *CL* i. 95–6.

[43] *British Mercury*, 6 Apr.; Avery 1960: 243. Her political views were already formed. On the birthday she dressed to display her Whig allegiance; in her diary she violently criticized Anne and her favourite Abigail Masham (*CL* i. 70–1; *E&P* 23).

[44] *CL* i. 78, 93, 100, 85.

(At the same time he was urging her to tell social white lies to her sister Frances; that apparently did not count.) Often he apologized for bullying her, yet even his apologies modulated into fresh accusations. Each of the pair frequently assured the other that he or she was glad the relationship was now closed. Lady Mary, indeed, felt freest to mention the ideas of love and marriage when she mentioned them as now relinquished. 'While I thought you lovd me, I could have liv'd with you in any place or Circumstances', she wrote at the end of April. 'Adieu. I desire you not to answer.' Wortley could not resist the last word, though it merely confirmed hers. 'Adieu, Dearest L. M. This once be assurd you will not deceive me. I expect no Answer.'[45] At last he had stilled his own wavering.

Mary and Frances had just left London; she let it go, and enjoyed what was to be her last Nottinghamshire summer with the old friends. She arrived at Thoresby numbed and apathetic, she told Philippa; but when she turned from her own affairs of the heart to those of Philippa and Mary Banks, her spirits revived. Sarah Chiswell came to stay at Thoresby; they indulged in a little flutter in the Two Million Lottery. The country was not uneventful. In July their neighbour the Duke of Newcastle was thrown from his horse and killed. It turned out that he had left as little to his wife as he could, but still suitors were drawn to the wealth of his daughter, Lady Henrietta Cavendish-Holles.[46] Rumour said that one of them was Philippa's (unidentified) Paradise. Lady Mary reassured Philippa by ruthlessly decrying the looks and talents of Henrietta: she had already advised Philippa that a highly advantageous Hell (a distasteful marriage) might be worth accepting, though this was more than she could yet persuade herself to.[47]

In autumn 1711 the sisters were still at Thoresby, riding to hounds and dancing—listlessly, said Lady Mary, without admirers to watch. Then it was winter, and still their father left them 'spending the irretreivable days of youth, in looking upon wither'd Trees and stone walls', while he and his lawyers plotted their futures. It seemed he had a Hell picked out for each of them. Lady Mary called herself 'a poor distracted Wretch of wretches'; she knew her father's choice would not be Limbo but full-blown Hell—to whose 'Fire, brimstone, Frosts and burnings' she would nevertheless succumb. Yet when writing to Frances Hewet she was still able to turn her

---

[45] [28 Apr., 2 May 1711], *CL* i. 105–6. He was then at Wortley. In Aug. he meant to stay three months longer; before those were up he decided to stay till the New Year. He wanted Addison to join him; Addison favoured taking shared lodgings in Kensington (Addison 1941: 265–6).

[46] [c.4 May, c.4 Aug. 1711, Jan. 1712], 25 Sept. [1711], *CL* i. 106–8, 114–15, 109. Prizes in this lottery were drawn 1–15 Aug. 1711. In a later one Sarah won a cheap table (*CL* i. 108, 115). For the row about Newcastle's will see Browning, 1975, 2–4.

[47] *CL* i. 114–15.

mind to politics, and the War of the Spanish Succession. Lady Frances (who unlike herself nourished a hopeless passion for an unattainable Paradise) felt their situation yet more acutely, and hinted to Philippa a longing for death. Years later Mary wrote to her, 'Don't you remember how miserable we were in the little parlor at Thorsby? We thought marrying would put us at once into possession of all we wanted.' But not marrying into Hell: that would be the acutest misery of all.[48]

It was well into February 1712 when, after weeks of suspense, they were belatedly summoned to join the London season. Lady Mary expected to go by the Great North Road via Stamford, which would give no chance of seeing Philippa *en route*. At the last moment the coachman changed his mind, and she found herself at Leicester, only a few miles from her friend but too late to arrange a meeting: a small symbolic instance of her lack of control over her destiny.

[48] *CL* i. 109–14; ii. 84; Mundy MS 11/5/29. Anne Justice m. 22 Jan. 1712.

4

February–August 1712

꧁ ꧂

Elopement: 'ran away with, without fortunes'[1]

BUMPING and swaying towards London in the massive family coach in February 1712, with their maids and their personal effects, Mary and Frances were travelling towards prospective Limbos or worse, selected by their father. Lady Evelyn's selection had been made by 'Aunt Cheyne': arrangements were almost complete for her to marry John Leveson-Gower, Baron Gower, not yet twenty-one. This marriage settlement took another expensive private Act of Parliament. His impressive family estates were a good speculation, though there was a cash-flow problem which made Lady Evelyn's £10,000 portion very welcome to his guardians. They had recently melted down family silver for sale; the dowry served to redeem other possessions in pawn.[2]

The first event of this London sojourn was a fire in Albemarle Street, just across Piccadilly from Arlington Street. A house burned down; damage was estimated at £30,000; a 'Cook Maid and Chamber Maid' jumped from a garret window 'and were dash'd to Pieces'.[3] Next week came the wedding which made Lady Evelyn into Lady Gower, or in Lady Mary's words 'put 2 people in Limbo'. The third event occurred on 3 April, when as Philippa heard from Lady Frances, 'my Sister Kingston is brought to bed of a son'. Frances— perhaps Mary too—stayed with their sister-in-law overnight and apparently all the next day.[4] The arrival of a Pierrepont heir satisfied their father's most pressing hopes for the family; but two daughters remained on his hands. He had an extra motive for wanting them gone: 'a design to marry him selfe'.[5]

---

[1] *CL* i. 123.   [2] Wordie 1982: 31, 81–2. They m. at St Anne's, Soho, early Mar. 1712.
[3] 2 Mar. (*CL* i. 118; Swift 1948: 502–3; *The Flying-Post: or, The Post-Master*, 4 Mar.). MWM continued to harbour a fear of fire (*CL* i. 372).
[4] *CL* i. 119; BL Eg. MS 3531; Mundy MS 11/5/27, 4 Apr. [1712].
[5] Lady Mary had heard this by Aug. 1712; Walpole says the bride would not have Dorchester 'unless he

Mr D. and Mr K., whom Wortley believed so favoured by Lady Mary, remain unidentified: so does a third person—her dear and charming Paradise, first heard of this spring.[6] Presumably he had the good sense and good nature which she later reckoned a lover's most essential qualities. Presumably he was good-looking; presumably he lacked money to marry on. Most probably he belonged to the small circle of the London fashionable élite (in which case Lady Mary would have continued to see him in society long after he was lost to her). Just possibly, however, he may have been some approximation to the space-travelling Prince of Venus whom Docile loves and loses:[7] an visitant from some exotic other world.

Meanwhile her father's chosen husband for her had been viewed, and unalterably classed as no mere Limbo, but Hell itself. He was Clotworthy Skeffington, of whom little is known except that he was about eight years older than Lady Mary, and heir to Viscount Massereene. Though she often talked of knuckling under, she felt she 'had rather give my hand to the Flames than to him'.[8] He was of her own kind: from a home-counties family which had been rewarded with an Irish peerage for services to the Whig cause. He sat in parliament for County Antrim; he married a year after Lady Mary eloped. It is salutary to ponder what issues unsuspected by the parties concerned—Lords Dorchester and Massereene—hung on the outcome of these marriage negotiations. No Embassy Letters could have been written by one Viscountess Massereene, formerly Lady Mary Skeffington, and probably no prose or verse analysis of the Hanoverian court. Perhaps she could have come up with other projects to enrich the literature of the English-speaking world; but it wouldn't be a safe bet.

It was in this desperate juncture of her affairs that she received out of the blue, in early June 1712, a letter from Edward Wortley Montagu. He was still in love, and he saw her slipping out of his grasp for ever. His letter came just as her spirited resistance was causing rumours that her 'Match' was 'Broke'.[9] Wortley believed that she still had power to make her father change tack and reopen negotiations with himself. 'Your relations, I am sure, whatever they threaten, will never treat you barbarously.' He reminded her, in the formal third person, that 'I admire her more than I do any one living, and that I am capable of Loving her to excess'.[10]

would marry off' his remaining daughters. He m. two years later, after, it was said, a long pursuit (*CL* i. 160; Walpole, *Corr.* xiv. 243).

[6] To Philippa, *CL* i. 121. Horace Walpole says (in a context of much unfounded gossip) that Lady Mary was courted by Richard Lowther, 2nd Viscount Lonsdale (*Corr.* xiv. 243).

[7] *RW* 124, 127–8, 130–2, 134.   [8] *CL* i. 141.

[9] Anne Howard to Burrell Massingberd, 15 June [1712], Mundy MS 2MM/b/10/3.

[10] *CL* i. 123–4, 125–6.

Thus opened the last phase of their courtship. He was still balancing the same issues as before: his passion, her disquieting volatility, the need to accept undesirable terms, her probable expensiveness. She was now clear about her own absence of passion: Paradise, indeed, was physically close at hand although out of her reach. Two weeks after Wortley had contacted her, Lady Mary's feeling that she was 'by turns raveing and stupify'd' had little to do with him and everything to do with Paradise's despair at her drift towards Hell.[11] Nevertheless, in writing to Wortley she floated new schemes for renouncing the world (i.e. renouncing Hell, though she did not use this terminology to him) in favour of an ideal, rational, rural retirement. She already knew that their union could happen only at the expense of a total break with her family; she had yet to convince him of this.

By letter the couple took up again a reprise of earlier themes: houses for secret meetings (Lady Mary's situation on the verge of marriage made her especially liable to censure), money matters, the real doubts of each as to whether the other could meet their needs. The Steeles were again pressed into service, and the Duchess of Shrewsbury, and Ludovico Casotti (Lady Mary's Italian teacher). Wortley said that the uncertain political climate (due to Queen Anne's precarious health) and his own business affairs combined to make it a bad moment for him to marry[12]—even assuming he could succeed where Lady Mary had failed, and persuade her father to rethink. She, meanwhile, sought to convince him that this was no longer an option. Striking a stoic attitude, she said there was nothing left for her but 'to behave my selfe with my fortune, in a manner to shew I do not deserve it'. She could 'see all the Misfortune of marrying where it is impossible to Love'. Yet as late as 15 July she told Philippa she was 'now going to' marry Hell (i.e. Skeffington) and that only the visible suffering of Paradise (not Wortley) had made her resist so long.[13]

The difficulties between them had not diminished. As ever, Wortley found it hard to credit what Lady Mary said: 'I am satisfy'd this affair is not so very much determind as you make it.'[14] She replied with graphic accounts of her family's persecution. In late July she decided, since 'the folly of [her] own temper' made her liable to collapse emotionally at a harsh word, to write a letter to 'the disposer of me' (her father) instead of speaking to him. This tactic failed. 'He did not think fit to answer this letter, but sent for me to him.' The immediate issue was her offer 'never to marry at all' if he would spare her Skeffington.

[11] *CL* i. 126–7.

[12] He also warned her that he would be busy for the next two months—perhaps abroad—with a 'private affair of moment' ([16 June 1712], H MS 74. 44–5).

[13] *CL* i. 124, 128–9, 133.   [14] [16 June 1712], *CL* i. 125.

He told me he was very much surpriz'd that I did not depend on his Judgment for my future happynesse, that he knew nothing I had to complain of etc., that he did not doubt I had some other fancy in my head which encourrag'd me to this disobedience, but he assur'd me if I refus'd a settlement he has provided for me, he gave me his word, whatever proposalls were made him, he would never so much as enter into a Treaty with any other; that if I founded any hopes upon his death, I should find my selfe mistaken—he never intended to leave me any thing but an Annuity of £400 . . . and at the same time commanded me to communicate my design to my Relations and ask their Advice.—

Lady Mary thought she had won. She told 'all [her] nearest Relations' that she intended to live single (presumably on her existing allowance of £200 p.a., with the prospect of doubling it at her father's death) and 'was surpriz'd at their blameing it to the greatest degree'. When she said she did not love the man chosen for her, she was called a little romantic, and told 'they found no Necessity of Loveing . . . if I consider'd this Town I should find very few women in love with their Husbands and yet a manny happy'. Although her nearest relations presumably included sympathizers like the Dowager Lady Denbigh, no one would support or abet her decision.

Nevertheless, she went back to her father (who had meanwhile done his own canvassing of the same family circle) and 'told him that I prefer'd a single life to any other, and if he pleas'd to permit me, I would take that Resolution'.[15] But Dorchester did not please. His Harlowe-like answer was that 'pleaseing him was only to be done by Obedience; that if I would disobey, I knew the consequences—he would not fail to confine me where I might repent at Leisure.'

Since he 'spoke this in a manner hinder'd my answering', she had recourse again to her pen. She wrote that

my Aversion to the Man propos'd was too great to be overcome, that I should be miserable beyond all things could be imagin'd, but I was in his hands, and he might dispose of me as he thought fit.—He was perfectly satisfy'd with this Answer, and proceeded as if I had given a willing consent.

Edward Wortley Montagu was at least easier to communicate with than this, and must have looked an increasingly attractive proposition. Dorchester knew or suspected his continuing presence in Lady Mary's life, and made a point of assuring her that he would never accept Wortley's proposals even 'if he had no other Engagements'.[16]

[15] Some weeks later she told Philippa, 'I know nothing certain but that I shall not dye an Old Maid, that's positive' (*CL* i. 150).

[16] *CL* i. 133–5. Forty years on, MWM read Richardson's *Clarissa* and relived the pain of being pressured, persecuted, and misread (*CL* iii. 90).

But her account of these transactions brought out all Wortley's indecisiveness. He wrote a long letter, burned it, and wrote another next day. This agreed that she was wise to refuse Skeffington since she disliked him so extremely—yet reminded her that her father's belief that he was 'more proper for you than I am' was founded in close knowledge of all three. Wortley was surprised and piqued that Dorchester could refuse his own abnormally generous offers and demand so little from Skeffington, whose Irish estate would rank far below an English equivalent. He felt this letter was too business oriented and nearly burned it too. Two days later he sent a note which did the next best thing to burning the former letter. If her marriage to Skeffington were to be 'broke', it ought to be done without regard to himself:

My health will not suffer me to make any great progress in a bargain now, but if you shoud be free when I return, my opinion is I shall be desirous to engage, tho perhaps not upon unreasonable terms. But my return is not to be depended on, and therefore I cannot agree you shoud dismiss the other affair on my Account.

He had just brought a secret lawsuit to a successful conclusion after three years' effort; his health was impaired by staying too long in London; he had already put off, for her sake, a journey designed to improve it. (He had in fact had a fever; Lady Mary was about to catch it.) Any demand for a sudden decision, he said, would give him 'so much pain that you must not wonder if I run away on a sudden in hopes of being easy'.[17]

It seems he was planning not just another trip to Spa, but a longer-time 'scheme' or 'plan of happynesse': a rural retirement, perhaps abroad, with a close male friend, probably Addison. This seems to account for a new theme in her letters, of shared retirement not merely in the country but abroad. The chosen place is Naples. It does not seem that Wortley had liked Naples especially when he made the Grand Tour, but perhaps it was now the goal either of his friendship scheme or his planned business trip. Lady Mary said nothing about the architectural or political identity of Naples. Although she may already have been forming friendships with foreigners like diplomats' wives, she wrote of Naples as a literal utopia, a no-place where they would form no ties but live only for each other, as if the rest of the world had ceased to exist.[18] Clearly this would mean renouncing her love of parties, dancing,

---

[17] *CL* i. 136–7.

[18] *CL* i. 282. In old age MWM jotted, 'Naples paradise before the Creation of Man' (CB 8). Non-dreamers like Burnet, Addison, and others saw it as non-Utopian, ridden by superstition and oppression. EWM and Lady Mary mooted variant plans: eloping to Spa, *en route* either to Italy or back to England (*CL* i. 153, 155, 141, 150–2, 156, 161; H MS 74. 40).

flirtation, and gossip. On the other hand, society ran on very formal lines; she often saw its routines and rituals as drudgery she would be glad to escape.

Normally, marriage would seal her fixed position in society. She would receive set visits of congratulation to usher in a predictable pattern of life: nothing would occur that the marriage contract had not foreseen and financed. Lady Mary did not hanker, like Lydia Languish, for the dramatic *mise en scène* of elopement ('ladder of ropes—conscious moon—six horses'), but she may have hankered for the unpredictability and spontaneity that elopement implied. With one part of her mind she amply recognized the gravity of marrying without the usual financial safeguards; with another, she longed to be out of it all,—'over the Hills and far away'.[19] 'Naples' was an integral part of the uncharted future she hoped to secure by marrying Edward Wortley Montagu.

On the first of August he struck for the first time a note in tune with all this. He suggested that they come to an agreement 'without troubling your family': that is, elope, with no marriage contract. She perceived the radical suggestion under his oblique phrasing, and replied the same day. 'I know not what to say. I am sure I cannot say enough to thank you for the Generosity of your proposal.' Then he wavered again; yet his very wavering made her the more eager to promise every kind of self-sacrifice. 'I abandonn all things that bear the name of pleasure but what is to be found in your companny. I give up all my Wishes, to be regulated by yours, and I resolve to have no other study but that of pleasing you.'[20] Readers of these letters have puzzled over their failure to depict the birth and growth of romantic love. But they perfectly delineate the growth of mutual psychological dependence between an emotional withholder and punisher on one hand, and an emotional volunteer and victim on the other.

But Wortley had his moments. A week and many letters after his elopement proposal, he was thanking Lady Mary for the 'firm resolutions you have taken of putting yourselfe in my power and being pleas'd with any retirement in my company'. Her latest letter ('which I coud not help kissing very often') had 'transported me by removing those doubts which I resolve shall never rise up again. I now, with the utmost pleasure, own you have convinc'd me of an esteem . . . I now declare to you that I am already, if you please, marri'd to you.' He urged her to say the same; then the ceremony would be merely 'to satisfy others'.[21]

[19] R. B. Sheridan, *The Rivals*, 1775: v. i; Lady Mary to Anne Justice [*c*.12 June 1710] (*SL* 26).
[20] *CL* i. 138, 140.   [21] [7 Aug. 1712], *CL* i. 144–5 (rough draft).

Each of them wrote tumultuous and self-contradictory letters; she was just as capable as he was of making advances and then retracting. Almost as he was declaring himself married to her, she was indignantly repudiating some judgement made of her by some of his friends: self-proclaimed experts on women who may well have been Steele and Addison. After a meeting she wrote, 'had there been a parson in the room with us, I had certainly marry'd you last night, in defiance of consquences'. But she went on, 'When I come to consider . . .' She made great promises, but like Astell's printed marriage advice they stemmed from a sense of how hard it was for marriage to be satisfactory. Her offers of self-sacrifice were 'absolutely necessary if we are to meet; and you need have no doubt but I will perform them.'[22]

These absolute promises rested on far-from-certain possibilities. Hesitantly, Lady Mary put forward provisoes of her own. She hoped he might permit her to invite the company of 'a Lady you have heard me speak of, whom [*sic*] I am sure will follow me over all the world if I please'. (This was most likely the indigent Sarah Chiswell, suitable candidate for the position of companion.) She hoped he might make her some 'Assurance of a provision if I should be so unhappy to lose you'. She admitted it was 'odd' to ask for anything at all 'when I bring you no fortune': normally the sum she brought him would dictate the income allotted to her by marriage settlement in case of widowhood. If Wortley should die, she thought her brother 'would keep me'; but (apart from the harshness of dependence) what if he were to die too, and the estate pass to 'guardians of his son'? Such men would look askance at an aunt supported out of charity.

Perhaps to counteract the impression of boldness that might be made by bargaining (as opposed to being bargained for) she renounced any claim for 'pin money', the personal allowance which was a normal item in marriage settlements, and which from Skeffington was to be £300 a year. 'I don't understand the meaning of any divided interest from a Man I willingly give my selfe to', she wrote, with just the kind of premarital unworldliness which often landed women in trouble later on. 'Money is very little to me', she later added, 'because all beyond necessarys I do not value that is to [be] purchas'd by it . . . I have in my Life known a good deal of shew, and never found my selfe the happier for it.'[23]

For most of her relations she entertained nothing but contempt: they were stupidly materialist; 'they know no happynesse but Equipage and furniture.' But there were two she respected and wished to consult: her brother (even though she felt his wife to be utterly untrustworthy), and another man,

---

[22] *CL* i. 140–2.   [23] *CL* i. 142, 153.

unnamed but probably William Feilding. He, it seemed, had stood out against the unanimous condemnation of her plan to live unmarried. He had not only understood her feelings about the Skeffington match, but had offered to mediate with her father: 'when he heard me in some passion of greife assure him it could do me no good, he went yet farther, and tenderly ask'd me if there was any other man tho' of a smaller fortune I could be happy with.' He had promised his support; he knew Wortley, and would approve.[24]

Meanwhile the Skeffington 'writeings' arrived from Ireland with some minor error, and were sent back for correction. A three weeks' reprieve seemed likely. Wortley sent a letter which swung more violently than ever before from con to pro to con. She did not value him, he wrote; her recent letters 'have implied the contrary of what you said'; she was probably planning to jilt him as she had jilted better men. 'All your letters of late have implied the contrary of what you said.' Yet he went on,

You may appoint the time and place, and I will provide a Coach, a Licence, Parson, etc. A Coach and six looks much better than a pair for such a service, but will it not be more likely to have company about it while it stands near your house?

If we shoud once be in a coach let us not say one word till we come before the parson, least we should engage in fresh disputes; but why shoud we meet at all, if we are so likely to have 'em? It is plain we shou'd not . . .

For her part, Lady Mary told Philippa,

I know not what I shall do; perhaps at last I shall do something to surprize every body . . . Limbo is better than Hell. My Adventures are very odd; I may go into Limbo if I please, but tis accompanny'd with such circumstances, my courrage will hardly come up to it, yet perhaps it may. In short I know not what will become of me.[25]

Dorchester now took the initiative. Having perhaps got wind of this scheming, he appeared at the Acton house on Monday, 11 August, and told his daughter that in one week more she was to move to West Dean. 'I am not to come from thence but to give my selfe to all that I hate.' This precipitated action. Lady Mary, scrupulously leaving Wortley free to decline, invited him to present himself after dark on Sunday 'under this Garden wall, on the road, some little distance from the summer house', and to set out for Italy straight away. The only second chance would be the brief moment between her return to London and her wedding. She left him free to choose that second chance, and to use the interval for reconsideration. She withdrew her

---

[24] *CL* i. 141, 146–7.   [25] *CL* i. 147–8, 150.

request for assurance of a jointure, assuming that 'a Man so generous to take me without a fortune' would remain generous. Again he rose to the occasion: 'I shall go to meet you with more joy than I shoud to take possession of Riches, Honour or Power; nay, then I shoud to meet you if you brought 'em along with you because I coud not so well convince you how much I value you.'[26]

⁓⁂⁓

The countdown had begun. But inconsistency and insecurity persisted. Wortley soon regressed from joy to fault-finding. He alluded persistently to 'cuckoldom', most woundingly in 'If you are likely to think of Cuckoldom, you are mad if you marry me.' He told her 'for the sake of my health I had better not be in the same bed for a time'. Then, realizing this might imply he had some sexually transmitted disease, he substituted the gallant prophecy that 'the quiet of mind I shall gain by being near you will effectually prevent my receiving any harm and do me more good than any other remedy'. Lady Mary for her part concluded her warmest love-letter to date with 'one would think this Letter were determin'd; yet I know not what I shall do.—I know if I do not venture all things to have you, I shall repent it.'[27]

Gradually, however, the two tides were turning, and the emotional current of each letter-writer setting firmly towards the other. Lady Mary yearned for feeling tempered by reason. She kept promising to be selfless, yet she thought a life with some diversion in it would be more conducive to preserving love than solitude *à deux*. But solitude at Naples might combine the best of both worlds.

If we marry, our happynesse must consist in loveing one Another. Tis principally my concern to think of the most probable method of makeing that Love Eternal . . . I am more susceptible of gratitude than any body living. You may mannage in a manner to make me passionately fond of you . . . I read over some of your first Letters, and I form romantic Scenes to my selfe of Love and Solitude. I did not believe I was capable of thinking this way, but I find tis in your power to make me think what you please.[28]

In the hustle of planning and debating, one of her letters opened like a lyrical poem on eloping: 'I tremble for what we are doing. Are you sure you will love me for ever? Shall we never repent? I fear, and I hope.' She gets a beat of gallopping horses into her first two sentences, only to check their flight in the next two, shorter ones. Her thoughts rise here to a level of

[26] [11 Aug. 1712], *CL* i. 150–2.   [27] *CL* i. 157–9.   [28] *CL* i. 154, 156, 157.

abstraction: although she conveys almost exactly the same meaning as Lady Caroline Lennox to Henry Fox when *they* were about to elope, Lady Mary's words would fit any act of emotional commitment, with or without running away.[29] At the same time, her absolutism provides a touch of self-mockery: 'Are you sure you will love me for ever?' contrasts with her sober certainty, voiced in other letters, that 'for ever' must be unsure.

Nearly thirty years later she gave the admiring Joseph Spence a glamorized or perhaps a sanitized account, subtracting seven or eight years from her age at the time. She 'had a vast number of offers . . . and the thing that kept her awake was, who to fix upon'. (This might have been almost true in 1710 or 1711, though it erases her father's power over her; but there were few who would offer to snatch her from another's grasp in 1712.) Only two desires, says Spence, were constant in her: 'to be married to somebody, and not to be married to the man her father . . . advised her to.' (Is that discreet 'advised', one wonders, Lady Mary's or Spence's?) 'The last night of the month she determined: and in the morning left the man her father had fixed upon, buying a wedding ring for her, and scuttled away and married Mr. Wortley.'[30]

This pearlily transfigures the gritty facts. Skeffington, or his father, *had* been put to the expense of 'Equipage etc.' A Mrs Smith was said to be 'busily imploy'd in providing cloths and servants for her'.[31] Dorchester spent £400 on wedding clothes. Lady Mary let it happen 'without saying any thing', but quailed at bearing the responsibility for this vain expense.[32] She began to harbour a wish that after eloping they might go straight to seek pardon and blessing from one father at least: Sidney Wortley Montagu. Scuttling away was, like everything else, harder to do than to say. Tactical detail had to be organized: how many horses to the coach, what servants, where to be married, where to go for the first night?

It was only on 16 August (the day before *the* projected day, now put forward from Monday to Sunday) that Wortley bought a special marriage licence—the only alternative to waiting three weeks for banns to be called. He bought, in fact, a licence to marry next day in London. Then on second thoughts he went back for another, of the more expensive type which allowed them to marry anywhere, at any time. The licence bore the name, seal, and permission of Thomas Tenison, Archbishop of Canterbury. Tenison was the second bishop (with Burnet) in Lady Mary's life. As recently as

---

[29] *CL* i. 159; Tillyard 1994: 27–8.   [30] Spence 1975: ii. 229.
[31] Presumably not Hermensilda (Jane Cotterell to Sir William Trumbull, 3 Sept. 1712, BL Trumbull MSS).
[32] Not in Dorchester's accounts (Manvers MSS 4265).

March he had sent her word that 'he still remembers Her, and, perhaps . . . it wou'd be more for his repose cou'd he possibly forget Her.'[33] This connection must have increased anxiety over the licence.

Lady Mary's unidentified married friend offered them her house for the first night. Lady Mary referred her acceptance to Wortley, assuring him she would have no scruples about spending it at his lodgings if he preferred. 'Let it be what it will; if I am your Wife, I shall think no place unfit for me where you are.' The same friend, who had supplied a servant to carry urgent letters from Acton, would also wait with her on a balcony, watching the road for Wortley's arrival with the elopement vehicle—something that Frances probably dared not do. 'Forgive my Instabillity,' Mary wrote. 'If I do it, Love me; if I dare not, do not hate me.—'[34]

On Sunday (the day named in the first licence and now chosen for their flight) disaster struck. Dorchester arrived at Acton, had a 'long conference' with his eldest daughter, and discovered to his fury—probably not from evidence in his possession but merely from her panic—that she was 'keeping a correspondance, etc'. Too rattled to deny it, she 'foolishly made what promises he would'. She was sent up to her room, 'whence I shall not move till early to morrow morning to go into the coach, to begin my Journey.—' So said a note written on Sunday evening 'with the utmost difficulty and danger'. At 5 a.m. next morning she 'stole from my Sister' (her bedfellow and jailer: either Lady Frances or Lady Kingston) and scribbled a note saying that nobody would be watching during the next two hours before their departure for West Dean, so that if Wortley could get there she could slip away. From six to seven she was on the balcony, 'But heaven was not so kind to bring you.'

Monday was awful. Lady Mary, in the coach barrelling westwards from London in her brother's custody, deprived of the company of her maid (whom she was made to leave behind), felt sick in body and mind, 'overcome by fateigue and misfortune'. She had not heard from Wortley all the previous day, and feared he might be ill or that 'after so much trouble about it you resolve never to think more of so unlucky a creature as I am'. But with her usual irrepressibility she began a letter to him during the first change of horses, and her mind leapt forwards to new plans. If she should be kept out of London 'till the night before my intended [wedding]', and that was not a night convenient for Wortley to carry her off, 'perhaps sicknesse may serve for a pretence to delay it 2 or 3 days'. Though full of self-blame 'for my cowardice and folly', she was not giving up yet.

[33] Mary Banks, 25 Mar. [1712], H MS 77. 116–17. For Tenison and Burnet as reformers, and their later opposition to Atterbury, see Bennett 1975: 15, 20–2, 66, 83, 109, 127.
[34] [16 Aug. 1712], *CL* i. 161, 163, 164.

She finished her letter at the inn where the party stayed overnight, some-where along the present A30 road; still ill, she went to bed early. Next morn-ing she discovered that her lover, hot on her heels, was at the same inn; if she had stayed up longer she would have seen his 'Gentleman' and learned of his presence. But he had no 'conveniency to carry me away decently', that is no coach. She apparently baulked at eloping without a servant, to be carried off literally on Wortley's horse. Once it was too late she suggested that they might actually have made a secret marriage at the inn, if only they had found each other. Before her maid's hostile stand-in was up to watch her, she scrib-bled him three successive notes, two of them on the inn's cheap, coarse writing-paper that blotted at a touch.

She reached West Dean as much a prisoner as ever, and wrote Wortley a proper letter telling how the people of the inn had seen him prowling around and suspected him of being a highwayman. She was now eaten up with anx-iety about the strength of his resolve—and of hers too. 'If possible I would do what you desire, and say No, tho' they brought a parson, but I hope we shall not be put to that hard Necessity, for I fear my own woman's weak-nesse.' Her last known letter as Lady Mary Pierrepont ended, 'Adeiu. I am entirely yours if you please.'[35]

Two days later Wortley was back in London dining with Steele, perhaps confiding in him.[36] In two days more, it seems, these lovers fled away. According to sister Frances, they were married at Salisbury. Lady Mary supplied the date in an anniversary note apparently dated 23 August 1713: 'This night last year I gave my selfe to you . . .' A hundred years later an old Lady Fremantle 'who, lived all her younger days at Dean remembered a mound near the old House where she always heard the carriage was brought that took Ly M. Pierrepont off with her husband'.[37] In the lottery of life (to use a metaphor of her own) Mary Wortley Montagu had drawn her ticket.

[35] *CL* i. 164–7.   [36] Steele 1941: 278.
[37] Mundy M/M MS 11/5, to Philippa, 15 Oct. 1712; 23 *or* 25 Aug. (*SL* 109, 505: EWM's endorsement, characteristically, confuses rather than clarifies); Wh MS M 439/37, C. J. Wall to Lord Wharncliffe, n.d.

5

August 1712–January 1715

❧

Domesticity: 'a proper matrimonial stile'[1]

Now she was Lady Mary Wortley. So her contemporaries mostly called her, ignoring the second part of the surname. Though Montagu was—outside Yorkshire—a more distinguished name than Wortley it was perhaps felt to be past history for this family.[2]

Her elopement divided public opinion. James Brydges reported fairly neutrally: when everything was 'agreed on, & ye day appointed' for her marrying Skeffington, Lady Mary had 'married herself privately' to Wortley. Others approved or violently disapproved. The never-never land of heroic romance provided images for both camps (and for Lady Mary herself). Lady Jekyll, who had aided and abetted the courtship, told Sarah, Duchess of Marlborough:

Mr Wortley is the Knight Errant that has rescued the Lady. A frolick is the last thing I shou'd have suspected him of but a lover may be allowed to act in the Spirit of his Mistris. As the lady has no fortune secured to her and the Thief a good Estate and other good qualities I hope he may be forgiven.

To Jane Cotterell he was no knight errant, and his failure to make a profit was no excuse. Taking her cue from Aunt Cheyne, she wrote that Lady Mary's

fault has indeed all the aggravations that could attend it, my Ld Dorchester being a mighty good Father, and having offered her to put this match off, if the going into Ireland was any objection to her. I only wonder amongst all her flights, she did not (in a romance) meet with some notions of Honour, as well as love, which might have been some rule against using a man of quality so basely.

---

[1] *CL* i. 168.
[2] Lady Mary at first spelled 'Mountague'; in 1711 she went over to 'Wortley' alone. She went on using it alone often, even while shifting her spelling to 'Mountagu' (1712) and 'Montagu' (after marriage).

Lady Mary's 'temper', she observed darkly, had always promised something 'extroardinary'. 'Mr Sceffington' had no doubt 'thought it not convenient to take her out of a window or from the side of a wood.' Now Dorchester had received a letter from each culprit, purportedly submissive and apologetic; but 'if they asked pardon t'was so slightly he could hardly find it out'. The fact that these letters came by the penny post caused additional offence.[3] The first olive branch was, as Lady Mary had foreseen, rejected.

Lady Frances gave out her sister's new address. It was the one Edward Wortley Montagu already used: care of the publisher Jacob Tonson in Catherine Street, the Strand. The couple began married life, that is, in the London bachelor lodgings about which he had taken an apologetic tone. Though he boasted this year of having 'by my own management made a large addition to my fortune', they had less than £800 a year to live on. It was four times Lady Mary's previous allowance, but she had so far had no living expenses. A wealthy noblewoman's wardrobe was reckoned in thousands; a lace headdress might cost £50 or £60.[4]

Catherine Street, which now links Bow Street to Aldwych, lay in a somewhat raffish area: near the theatres and the Fleet Street alleys and courts, but also near the newly finished St Paul's Cathedral and the oasis of the Temple. It was handy for the Thames, which was still the major London thoroughfare, far quicker than the cobbled, overcrowded streets.

Their establishment of servants must have been minimal, since Lady Mary apparently made country-house visits with no personal maid. A maid of all work (the least they could conceivably have employed) would have cost them only three pounds a year in wages. Next summer they had a man named John as coachman and general servant.[5] Lady Mary was soon pregnant: just under nine months were to elapse before the birth of her son. It is perhaps surprising that so touchily jealous a husband found nothing to worry him in these dates; but his certainty that he was the child's father carries conviction.

Lady Mary's first reported impressions of marriage were rapturous. To be together after all that writing and reading was apparently ecstasy. She told Lady Frances she had 'found Paradise where she expected but limbo'. Frances reported to Philippa that her sister was 'happy in her Apostacy'. Her having 'so luckily Jump'd into [Paradise] unawares' might convert the rest of them to believing that it was, after all, possible to love a second time.

---

[3] Brydges, later Duke of Chandos, to Anthony Hammond, 29 Aug. 1712 (Huntington MS; *TLS* 4 Sept. 1937); Lady Jekyll, 3 Sept. (BL Blenheim MS E.43); Jane Cottrell, 3 Sept. (BL Trumbull Papers, information from Frances Harris). MWM later used knight-errant imagery to mock other people's courtships.
[4] *CL* i. 136; iii. 257; Burnett 1969: 146.   [5] Porter 1982: 102; *CL* i. 186.

Frances, who was trying vainly to forget her own lost Paradise, sounded almost disapproving.[6]

In October the married pair travelled north on a round of visits. Probably (the dates of Lady Mary's letters are not conclusive) they went first, together, to stay with Sidney Wortley at Wharncliffe Lodge, Wortley, near Sheffield.[7] This was only forty miles beyond Thoresby, but it was most emphatically what Lady Mary had recently called West Dean: a 'new world', 'over the hills and far away'.

After moving among plains or little hills from London to just beyond Thoresby, they saw dark high moors to their left, coming closer. Then, probably skirting Sheffield without going through it, they left the high road and took to steep, rutted lanes. The horses had to hurl every ounce of weight against their collars going up, and to sit back heavily into the breeching going down lest the coach should run away.[8] The lane was so deep and narrow that they were constantly tilting as one pair of wheels or the other rose lopsidedly up the bank. The journey back, downhill, was to make Lady Mary 'so fateigu'd and sick I went strait to Bed from the Coach'.[9]

The village of Wortley is strung out along a high north–south ridge, looking westwards across a broad valley into the teeth of gales from the even higher Peak, where the snow comes early and lies till spring. Wortley Hall is set protectively back a little from the ridge, into a dip. But the Hall was un-inhabited, almost a ruin. They were heading for Wharncliffe Lodge, which Sidney Wortley had taken over from his own gamekeeper. Sir Thomas Wortley had built it early in Henry VIII's reign, on a 'crag' in the 'mydys of Wanclife', 'for his plesor to her the hartes bel'[10]—to hear, that is, no man-made instrument but the bellowing challenge of the hart or stag in the rutting season.

The lane dipped a little through Wharncliffe Chase, and there was the Lodge: looking more like a pair of low-roofed cottages than a gentleman's seat, built of rough stone, and perched like an eagle's nest at the very edge of tree-clad cliffs dropping sheer to the Rive Don 500 feet below. Lady Mary's daughter later called it 'a wretched hovel', but her youngest granddaughter, Lady Louisa Stuart, wrote of it 'wildly . . . in raptures'.[11]

---

[6] 15 Oct. [1712], Mundy MS MM/11/5.

[7] Lady Louisa Stuart thought it was MWM's only visit there in the first few years of her marriage (Hunter 1831: ii. 322).

[8] Hoping to arrange a meeting with Philippa, Lady Mary enjoyed the gesture of adult independence with which she offered to send her own coach (*CL* i. 169).

[9] *CL* i. 168. She was two months pregnant.   [10] Hunter 1831: 329.

[11] Stuart Wortley 1925: 213. Hunter mentions a town razed by Sir Thomas to make the Chase, a local memory of corpses lying thick after a 'great pestilence', an affray of 1592 involving secret oaths and a

Lady Mary, meanwhile, liked the setting. She described it in her diary with enthusiasm, though also with a slightly apologetic sense of confessing to eccentric tastes. The fashion for such wildness had not yet dawned. Years later she called the view from her belvedere at Avignon 'the most beautifull land prospect I ever saw (except Wharncliffe)'.[12] For the situation indoors, however—for her husband's father, his uncle the Dean of Durham, his brother John and sister Catherine—she could not muster the same approval. Lady Louisa Stuart relayed her diary account of the elders, from memory, to the local historian Joseph Hunter, and later smoothed it somewhat for her grandmother's *Letters and Works*, 1837. Here is her first version:

a large rough-looking old man, wearing a huge flapped hat, speaking loud, and swearing boisterously at his servants from his great chair; while dean Montagu, a venerable figure, with silver locks shadowed by a velvet cap, sits by in silence, sighing at every oath he heard, and sometimes meekly lifting up his eyes to heaven, as if asking forgiveness for his brother's offence.

Lady Louisa added that it was 'sufficiently wonderful' that 'so many people, together with their servants, could be packed into so small a space'.[13]

Lady Mary had left the existing volumes of her diary—several years of it—behind when she fled from West Dean; her sister burned them rather than risk their father's reading them. Their author was said to be 'not very well pleased' by their loss. But she agreed with her husband to preserve their courtship letters 'as memorials';[14] and she found good strong material at Wharncliffe for her new diary. The contrast with Thoresby could hardly have been more marked.

Next the couple separated for a while. He went to his uncle the dean at Durham, probably on colliery business. She went back to Nottinghamshire, not to Thoresby of course but to stay with the Whites of Wallingwells, a family of lesser gentry whose house (near that of Frances Hewet: on the site of a Benedictine nunnery) had its canal, water gardens, and 'sizable grotto'. Thomas White, head of the family (who had married the heiress of the estate), combined the roles of landowner on his own account and agent to Lord Dorchester (his distant cousin) and other local grandees. He must have been independent-minded, to harbour his patron's prodigal daughter.[15]

---

ceremonial deer's head, a ballad of a local dragon, a busy ironworks, and the view of nearby Sheffield spires and the distant cathedrals of Lincoln and York (1831: 330–2).

[12] *CL* ii. 315.

[13] Hunter 1831: ii. 320; *E&P* 20. Six servants were thought the bare minimum for a gentry family (Burnett 1969: 153).

[14] *E&P* 16, 18.

[15] Higginbottom 1987: 15–17. He had a salary from Dorchester: £100 p.a. (Manvers MS 4265).

At Wallingwells Lady Mary mobilized her arts of pleasing for her first letter as wife to husband. 'I Lament your Absence as if you was still my Lover,' she wrote; and as 'the tenderest expressions of [her] Love' looked forward to the time when their own children's noise (unlike the 'Squalling' of the youngest Whites) 'may have more charms for us than the Music of an Opera'.[16] She also likened the Whites' domestic happiness to one of those edifying *Spectators* which she had once laughed at. Mr White recalled a *Spectator* patriarch (metaphorically 'both King and Priest'), who says his two great pleasures in marriage are 'Power or Domination', and paternity: 'I am pleased to see my self . . . perpetuated.' But her epistolary cajoling had little effect; she was soon in a panic because Wortley did not reply, but seemed 'entirely forgettfull of all this part of the World'.[17]

As Christmas approached, Lady Mary made another visit on her own, this time to Hinchingbrooke just outside Huntingdon, seat of Lord Sandwich. He was head of the Montagu family. Since his heir, Lord Hinchingbrooke, had as yet no son, it was still on the cards that Wortley might one day become Earl of Sandwich and master of Hinchingbrooke. Meanwhile he was working on approaches to another cousin, Lord Halifax, about employment,[18] and to members of *her* family and 'friends' (in the contemporary sense of likely patrons), about *rapprochement* with her father. Those he spoke to included Bishop Burnet, the formidable Lady Cheyne, and Lord Pierrepont, the great-uncle from whom Lady Mary had expectations. Pierrepont thought it would be 'proper' for Dorchester to grant a reconciliation, but, maddeningly, would not suggest this himself.

In her husband's absence, Lady Mary exercised wifely practicality, noting that Huntingdon (his constituency) would demand lavish entertaining if he appeared at Christmastime. She continued to woo him with images of domesticity. Rummaging old trunks of family papers, she said, she had come on the correspondence of the first Lord Sandwich and his affectionate, managing, home-loving wife: a good example for herself. She stressed her solitude, too: her recreation had been voracious reading and writing, and pacing the terrace attended by a friendly 'Robin red breast'. This last, however, drew a startlingly harsh rejoinder, an accusation of 'having better company than the Robin, who would not have hindred you in writing. Whoever was

---

[16] *CL* i. 168–9. Patricia Spacks notes how she conveys her own longings through tales of other people (1988: 181–2).

[17] *CL* i. 170; *Spectator*, no. 500, 3 Oct. 1712.

[18] Addison had reported Halifax's high opinion of him in 1708. MWM quoted Dryden to express her wryly mixed feelings when a pregnancy of Lady Hinchingbrooke's ended in a stillbirth (*E&P* 19; Addison 1941: 118).

with you, sure your absence might have bin excus'd for a minute to tell me
of your health.'[19]

Clearly, Wortley's jealousy was something else that remained 'as if you
was still my Lover'. For the first years of his marriage, said Lady Mary, he
retained 'that sort of Passion for me, that would have made me invisible to all
but himselfe, had it been in his power'. Perhaps her Wallingwells letter had a
subtext—for Addison's fictional, Thomas White-like husband made a point
of denying that husbands need be cuckolds. And perhaps Lady Mary was still
a resisting reader of the *Spectator*, for she said her hours of solitary thought at
Hinchingbrooke would qualify her to produce a daily paper of her own, to be
called *The Meditator*.[20] Her letters of this time mention her melancholy as an
established fact, about which she will not trouble her husband.

She did not let his accusation pass, but responded more in sorrow than in
anger: 'I am alone without any Amusements' (she had already told him that
for days after his departure she had 'had no occasion of opening my mouth
to speak') 'and you write me quarrelling Letters!' She ended hers, 'Adeiu, je
suis à vous de tout mon coeur.' Her pregnancy ('the condition I am in') was
a reason to argue that cheerfulness was vital to her health. Besides, she had
staked everything on her marriage, and she wanted and needed to make it
succeed.[21]

Her fiction 'Docile' invites revisiting here. There are no grounds whatever to suppose that Lady Mary went through the marriage service in floods
of tears, like her heroine; but parallels may be uneasily suspected between
her and Docile as newly married women. Docile devotes herself

entirely to pleasing Prince Sombre, and even to loving him. She constantly presented to herself the obligation which she believed she owed him for his disinterested conduct; she sought to make the most of all his good Qualities and turn a blind
eye to his faults. Finding herself unable to force her Inclination, she exerted herself
to offer him at least the forms of tenderness . . . Her object was not that of appearing
otherwise than what she was, but that of striving to become what she wished to be.
This . . . completed the alienation of the Prince. He was too penetrating . . . to fail to
perceive the constraint she was under to conceal a sorrow which gnawed at her. He
gave the reins freely to his ill humour, sometimes in reproaches, sometimes in biting
jests, with never a single moment of Confidence, or esteem, or tenderness.[22]

Docile's marriage for gratitude followed on losing the suitor she really
loved. The elderly author Montagu surely drew on her own experience in
this account, however much she emotionally heightened it.

  [19] *CL* i. 175, 172.
  [20] *CL* i. 168, 175; *E&P* 83. Some of her collected maxims may belong to this date (CB 2 ff.).
  [21] *CL* i. 173–6.   [22] *RW* 132, 135–6.

Back at the London lodgings in the new year, 1713, she and her husband each dispensed advice by letter. Wortley told his agent on no account to drop the price of coal just because less efficient operators had failed to get their annual quota sold. Lady Mary advised Philippa on her love-life, with an ostentatious air of maturity and experience. She thought it might be unwise for Philippa to reject her 'disagreable Lover'. (In fact this was very probably the man she eventually married, Burrell Massingberd, whom she was just beginning to warm to, through the medium of illicit correspondence.) To break with one's family was no joke, Lady Mary asserted. It might become matter for regret: 'will you not try, [when] Tryal be too late, | To find your Father's Hospitable Gate . . . That Gate for ever barr'd to your Return?' Under the safeguard of words not her own but Prior's, she hinted at some shadow of regret. But she also found a poet to endorse the choice she had made, and quoted Lansdowne proclaiming that the ties of 'freind and Benefactor' are stronger than the marriage tie alone.[23]

One of the benefits of marriage was access to Wortley's literary friends. Some of her recent reading went into an ambitious piece of literary criticism: on Addison's tragedy, *Cato*, which was not yet published or performed. Her critique was 'Wrote at the Desire of Mr. Wortley', but 'suppress'd at the desire of Mr. Adison'. The latter did, however, adopt items of her advice, which 'contributed materially to the effectiveness of the play'. Her essay, which today might be judged a little too close to Ph.D.-thesis style, cites Aristotle, Euripides, Horace, Shakespeare, Dryden, Buckingham, Otway, and 'all the French critics' as well as Racine by name.[24]

The *Cato* furore may have been in Lady Mary's mind, along with the new session of parliament, as she wrote in April 1713 of London as a centre of discord. Ten days after his play opened, Addison wrote that various persons of quality assumed that their verses on it would accompany it into print. Lady Mary may have been one of these: she wrote an epilogue which flippantly punctures *Cato*'s high-mindedness (as epilogues had licence to do even to the most highflown tragedies), and which Addison chose not to have spoken or printed.[25] Acquaintance with literary men, it turned out, was no simple route to sharing their public platform.

It was good, at least, to have her husband's support in her writing projects. Two months after marriage she wrote, 'ex tempore in Company',

---

[23] *CL* i. 177, 179 (quoting Lansdowne); Hughes 1952: 192.
[24] *E&P* 62, 63. Addison took her advice to mention liberty more and to close the acts with couplets; her critique of the love interest and of the undramatic nature of stoicism were harder to deal with (Smithers 1968: 262, 271, 273).
[25] *CL* i. 180; *E&P* 180; Addison 1941: 276.

a virtue-breathing little poem which explains that 'While Thirst of Power, and desire of Fame, | In every Age is every Woman's Aim', *she* will not encourage flatterers or think herself 'Virtuous, if not grossly Lewd'. Instead she will work on the principle that 'Too near he has approach'd, who is deny'd.' In short, if a man steps out of line with a married woman, it must be her fault for encouraging him. Lady Mary transcribed the poem as 'Written . . . in a Glass Window', which may or may not have been literally true. The poem received wider exposure in time, reinforcing the obvious point that even in her vow of virtue she was angling for admiration from others besides her husband.[26]

On 22 April her sister-in-law produced her second baby, a girl, christened Frances. Lady Mary had not long to wait. She bore her son on 16 May. Her experience of pregnancy is another hidden area. Did she find her changed body a 'source of humiliation'? Just how anxious might she have been about miscarriage, or losing her baby in childbirth, or the pain and danger (either of dying or suffering permanent physical damage)? 'That part of [my life] which we pass'd together' was her later phrase for pregnancy (written to her daughter, not her son). That sounds as if the experience meant something else besides fear.[27]

Lady Louisa observes that Wortley's relations with his father made it impossible for his son to be born at Wharncliffe; but London had other advantages. The birth was neatly sandwiched between two generally admired speeches which he made in the House of Commons, 14 and 18 May, against a Treaty of Commerce with France which was seen as menacing the English woollen industry. The bill was duly defeated.[28] It was good moment to be making his mark, for by law this session had to be the last of the current parliament; a general election was in prospect.

As with Lady Mary's own birth, one wonders about the circumstances of her son's. These parents probably could not afford a male midwife. But who made up the customary team of attendant women? Lady Mary had no mother or mother-in-law. Her sisters may have been with her, but Frances would have needed permission, and might not have got it. Her sister-in-law, even if she had wanted her, would still have been lying-in herself. Perhaps some friends made themselves available during the new mother's month-long confinement in her shuttered and airless room: first alone, then receiving company amid 'white Satin Quilts and laced Pillows', answering ritual

[26] *E&P* 179; date from her note in Dodsley's *Collection* (see p. 580).
[27] BL Eg. MS 3531; Chaber 1996: 209, 214–24; *CL* ii. 492. Chaber agrees that the quoted phrase probably refers to pregnancy.
[28] Hunter 1831: ii. 321; Cartwright 1883: 334–5, 338; Lawson-Tancred 1937: 257.

enquiries and sharing the special childbirth drink of caudle.[29] She probably employed a wet-nurse, but if so she did not deposit her child at the nurse's house, but kept him with her. He was christened Edward, but his parents seem hardly to have used his name; he was at first 'the child', later 'our'—or 'your'—'son'. Nor do we know who were his godparents.[30]

His birth came towards the end of six months which seem to have been their longest uninterrupted period yet of living together. Five weeks later, soon after Lady Mary regained her freedom to move at will beyond the house, her husband was off again northwards: to Hinchingbrooke first, then to the two tiny parliamentary constituencies of Boroughbridge and Aldborough in north Yorkshire. He had been selected as candidate for Aldborough by Lord Pelham, who as Duke of Newcastle was soon to begin his forty-year reign as premier election-manager for the Whigs.[31] Here he was to battle against the rival candidates put up by Pelham's aunt, the widowed Duchess of Newcastle.

His wife saw him off, apparently expecting him back by the end of the week. She walked in the park a while, and found 'without knowing it my selfe . . . I am come home only to write to you' and spend the evening 'thinking of you, in a Manner you would call Affectation'. Her thinking made her what might now be called passive-aggressive: 'You will accuse me of Deceit when I am opening my Heart to you, and the Plainesse of expressing it will appear Artificial.' It sounds, in fact, as if there had been a quarrel. Instead of saying she could not live without him, she said she felt she could *not* say this in case he disbelieved her. She feared he would break his promise to write soon, but also that a long letter from her would 'tire you'. Her next found her 'ready to chide': he had missed the post for her by writing to a friend first.

In both her letters anxiety shadowed her marital fencing: her brother had smallpox. She wished to believe that Dr Garth has magnifying the danger in order to claim credit for a difficult cure; but he was not. Within a week Lord Kingston, not yet twenty-one, was dead. He died at Acton on the first of July 1713, with the dreadful pain, disfigurement, and stench that smallpox entails, leaving a widow in her teens and two small children. Lady Mary visited them, and heard from Lady Frances that her father 'had not seen her nor nobody'. That day inexpressibly 'sunk my Spirits'.[32] This was the first significant death of her adult years, coming hard on the heels of birth.

[29] Hervey to Griselda Murray, 1725 (Mellerstain MSS).

[30] MWM later took a strictly contractual view of the sacraments, and ascribed the duty of religious education to parents, not godparents (*CL* iii. 94).

[31] EWM was the Pelhams' second choice, after William Monson; but his Treaty of Commerce speech, his father's Yorkshire estates, and his marriage, all told in his favour (Lawson-Tancred 1937: 229, 257).

[32] BL Eg. MS 3526; *CL* i. 183–5.

William, Lord Kingston, was buried at Holme Pierrepont on 9 July.[33] It was not customary at this date for women to attend funerals, even if the family rift had allowed it. But Lady Mary had to make or get made black clothes for herself, probably in bombazine, which had a matt finish with no shine. Her measurements may still have been larger than usual after her pregnancy; but she would have to wear these clothes three months at least, until passage from deep mourning to half-mourning allowed her to change to grey. She may or may not have donned a long scarf and enveloping hood for appearing in public, leaving 'not a bit to be seen of [her]'. But whatever servants she had would certainly have to be refitted: 'for a brother's mourning all people put there [*sic*] servants in gray.'[34]

She wrote at length and bitterly in her diary. Yet she may well have felt that life was leaving her no time to mourn. Two more of her old friends were married at the end of the month: Lady Anne Vaughan and Dolly Walpole. Lady Mary later recorded her outrage at the way Anne, as Duchess of Bolton, was despised and rejected by her husband. She felt Dolly, having fallen prey to scandal, was lucky to catch Lord Townshend—though his character was haughty and violent, 'brutal in his expressions, and cruel in his disposition'. She marked the occasion by writing Dolly's early history into her new diary. Another of her earliest friends, Lady Henrietta Cavendish-Holles, was cut off from her now that Wortley was her mother's electioneering opponent.

The past was slipping, or had slipped, away. In the present, Lady Mary's brother was dead and her husband's plans had changed. He stayed away, leaving her to pack up the lodgings, organize her child and nurse and servants, and choose a house to rent in Yorkshire (near Sheffield or possibly near York) for three or four months. There were at least half a dozen candidates for her to look at.[35]

On 12 July Lady Mary arrived with the baby at Wharncliffe Lodge, finding there no letter from her husband, who was at Boroughbridge. 'While you are well and Love me,' she wrote, 'I am insensible of any Misfortune, but 'tis impossible for me to hinder makeing some Melancholy Reflections on the untimely Death of my Brother and the Manner of it.'[36] After three days (during which a letter from Wortley arrived, and the nurse charmingly put

---

[33] His father's library contained a *Funeral Poem* to his memory by Elkanah Settle, who was famed for opportunistic elegizing (*Kingstoniana*; Brown 1910).

[34] *Wentworth Papers*, 124, of the year 1710; Lady Strafford in 1712 (quoted in Buck 1979: 60–3).

[35] *E&P* 21, 22–3; Hervey on Townshend, 1728 (1931: i. 80). The houses were Bramley Grange, Attercliffe Hall, Car House, Pule Hill Hall, Dodworth (all near Wortley), and Middlethorpe Hall, or possibly a house in York itself (where Anne Justice, now Mrs Thompson, was still resident).

[36] *CL* i. 185.

it in the baby's hands as 'an Acceptable present') she found she was expected to move on to make room for another visitor: Lord Sandwich. She left the baby and nurse with Mrs Northall, the Wharncliffe housekeeper, and went down to Wallingwells (where the Whites were eager to help with house-hunting), then back to Wharncliffe.

There she had bed provided, not board. She had to do her own house-keeping, and did it seriously: when the price of meat in the village rose to an exorbitant $2\frac{1}{2}d$. a pound, 'besides cheating in the weight', she 'lost all patience' and sent the couple of miles to Sheffield for better meat at a half-penny a pound less. The snag to Wharncliffe life was its irregularity, which she could not help: she had to feed Mrs Northall, and the maids, and often 'Some Tennant or other'. On the credit side she had a little horse she liked 'mightily' when she had trained him not to kick.[37]

On 3 August, on her way to look at a house called Bank Top, her coach overturned in the lanes. Nothing daunted, she kept on inspecting possible places, mostly clustered around the village of Wortley. None of them satis-fied her. One owner meant to keep a room for himself; another had sold the furniture; another had changed her mind about renting at all. Bank Top, newly built and 'very pritty' though unfinished, had not a stick of furniture; Mr and Mrs Adams, the owners, thought that in a couple of months they might get round to installing old hangings 'of their own spinning'. Lady Mary 'could never have beleiv'd' that anyone existed who could build such a house and leave it such a mess.[38]

She was all energy and almost all good humour. Her bulletins to her hus-band breathe frequent exasperation, but also pleasure in exercising her execu-tive abilities, in the prospect of laying in coal and airing rooms, in the issues of whether to buy or hire pewter and brassware and whether or not to brew their own beer. Increasingly, though, an underlying and all-pervasive snag became palpable. She wished, like a good wife, to conform to her husband's preferences: 'I could chide you (if I could chide you at all) for not saying something positive.' Either from native indecisiveness or from pressure of other business, he wanted her to settle everything.[39] Still, he could not con-quer the habit of finding fault. When there were pros and cons (as there always were) he could be counted on consistently to oppose con to her pro, and vice versa. Their co-indecisiveness makes painful reading, and must have been even more painful to live through.

On 22 August, the day before their wedding anniversary, Lady Mary went to York to inspect Middlethorpe Hall, not quite two miles to the south.

[37] *CL* i. 186–8, 194.   [38] *CL* i. 190–5.   [39] *CL* i. 196.

This house was a phenomenon: as much an architectural wonder as Thoresby. A Sheffield ironmaster, Thomas Barlow, had built it, apparently in order to take his upward step into the gentry at a discreet distance away from his erstwhile Sheffield neighbours. He had spared no expense, producing an elegant, symmetrical, red-brick, Italianate villa, like nothing else in Yorkshire. Having completed it, he had set out with his son on his Grand Tour, a mature student aiming at cultural polish.[40]

Lady Mary had 'often heard' of Middlethorpe before Joseph Banks mentioned it as to let. Probably it won her at first sight: it was a rational as well as an aesthetic choice, being far the closest to the scene of action at Aldborough. What she said was, 'I know not what to do, because I know not which you will like best . . . why won't you give me some little hint?' But it seems Wortley favoured his home beat around Sheffield (despite its distance from Aldborough), or that he disliked the idea of his wife having access to the smart society of York. What he said was, 'you must decide, if one of us must'. Barlow's agent needed a decision on the spot; Wortley himself feared that hesitation might lose them both the options in play. Yet his 'you must decide' letter goes on, 'If you woud resolve on Mr. Barlow's, perhaps it may be as well not to engage absolutely till night'—and then again 'but that need not hinder preparing beds etc'.[41]

On this, their first wedding anniversary, Lady Mary added to the end of her letter the reassuring message that she would make the same choice of *partner* over again, 'from all Mankind'. On the choice of *lodging* she went so far as to say, 'what signifys any one place more than another for 3 or 4 months?' And, professing to read his preference from between-the-lines hints, she made the decision. She engaged for Middlethorpe, planning to stay on there herself and send the coach back to Wharncliffe for the baby, attendants, and belongings.

This did not settle it. A couple of days later she was still waiting for his 'final determination' before renting Middlethorpe; she was 'impatient to be somewhere and Indifferent where, provided you like it'. He apparently joined her there, heard there was someone else after it, and agreed to rent it as she had arranged.[42]

Nevertheless, within a hairsbreadth of achieving her own wishes, she proceeded for the second time to take an action based on her reading of his implicit signs: 'I fancy'd you look'd after me as if you repented your orders, or at least that complaisance had some share in them.' Had he indeed given a

---

[40] Worsley 1985. Now owned by Historic House Hotels.
[41] *CL* i. 186, 196; *SL* 111.   [42] *SL* 111; *CL* i. 197.

double message, or signalled retraction of his approval of Middlethorpe? In any case, Lady Mary was off again on the two-day journey back to Bank Top—only to hear that the Adamses had all of a sudden retracted their offer of letting it. Her interpretation was that Mr Adams, who professed a flatteringly high opinion of Wortley, 'would willingly do it, but his Wife won't let him, who I perceive is very arbitrary in her government'. Only Middlethorpe remained. Lady Mary, now close to Wharncliffe, went there to collect her baby son. It seems Wortley was jealous of her maternal feeling, for as September began and she headed at last for 'home' she assured him, 'I Love the Child, but after you, and because it is yours.'[43]

Wortley and his running mate, William Jessop, lost at Aldborough to the Duchess of Newcastle's candidates. (The Tories romped home in the country generally.) Next spring they entered a petition against the result, more for form's sake than in hope of getting it reversed.[44] Meanwhile, the expected three or four months at Middlethorpe stretched out to six.

Lady Mary was much alone in the stylish house she had rented: not alone as we understand it today, since she had her servants as well as her baby— but alone for all that. She writes of waiting for Wortley to come home, 'expecting every noise made by the Wind was you coming in'. The tall sash windows, new and fine as they were, would rattle in a wind, especially on the north side, where the towers of York Minster showed in the distance beyond the winter trees. The clocks ticked. Otherwise the house was very silent. Wortley's business trips often turned out longer than expected.[45] When at home, he probably went shooting in the water-meadows along the Ouse. Would Ireland have been better?

Lady Mary wrote superciliously about the social gossip of York, 'Love being as much forc'd up here as Melons'. But she gossiped busily by letter about other people's choice of partner: to Frances Hewet about Lady Henrietta Cavendish Holles, and to someone unnamed about Sir John Vanbrugh, whose presence must have been connected with work still in progress on the nearby baroque mansion of Castle Howard.

Another letter of this date defies interpretation. It is a declaration of love from a married woman, who signs herself Fidelia, to another woman, Almeria. Fidelia admits she is laying herself open to the ridicule which she herself used to heap on 'fond Expressions' between ladies, yet confesses with amazement that she now sees Almeria 'rather with a Lovers Eye then with a

---

[43] *CL* i. 197–200.
[44] Result known by 8 Sept. 1713; petition entered 5 Mar. 1714. They charged misbehaviour; but their own side evicted tenants who refused their support.
[45] e.g. H MS 74. 148–9.

Freinds'. She thinks about her constantly, dreams of her, and hopes for a return of love, although 'I blush for what I say.' Her husband Aristus, she says, has noticed her coldness and is growing jealous. She sends her letter by a messenger, and hopes for a reply. She concludes, 'I beg you burn this Letter which for the world I would not have seen by any one but your dear self.'[46]

This letter is written in an unknown, apparently female hand. If Lady Mary was not Fidelia (who does not *sound* like her), we are left to wonder whether she was Almeria—and kept the letter, as she kept addresses from men, as a memento of a conquest—or whether the letter was an exercise in fiction, like Lord Hervey's lesbian poems.[47]

In January 1714 Lady Mary was preparing to move the household to London (though they would retain the lease of Middlethorpe). A house to rent had to be found through someone else's agency, and coal and beer laid in. She had shipped the bulk of their goods by water; expecting Wortley home, she was 'surpriz'd and afflicted' at his delay. She was worried about papers he had left locked in his closet.[48] He had the key, and she dared not break it open, though she hoped he would trust her to pack the papers. She was most worried that he might have changed his mind about the move itself. In the end she did not leave for London until the end of February, having managed for nearly two months without most of her basic household possessions. Expecting to be only a month or so in London, she left her son in York with a Mrs Cromwell. But, just as their stay at Middlethorpe had lengthened, so the month in London lengthened to four.[49] Without knowing it, Lady Mary was being trained as a traveller and sojourner.

~ so ~

London life must have been awkward for her, still unforgiven by her father, even if she chose times when he was away for visiting her brother's bereaved family at Acton. A marriage was being arranged for sister Frances— perhaps secretly.[50] On her way south Lady Mary had met Philippa's brother at Leicester, and heard that Phil too would soon be married. She was eager

---

[46] 18 Oct. 1713, H MS 79. 289–90.

[47] The former Nelly Brownlow (who hurt herself falling off the wall) married a couple of weeks before MWM, and was named as an active lesbian in 1717 (John Thomlinson, BL Add. MS 22560. 43).

[48] Probably the little room to the left of the front entrance, with elegant low-relief panelling. This spring EWM and the other Tyneside coal-owners were in conflict with the keelmen over way-leaves from the mines to the water (Hughes 1952: 290).

[49] *CL* i. 202–5. Smallpox was rife in London this spring. Sarah, Duchess of Marlborough, saw two grandchildren recover from it, but her daughter Lady Bridgewater died (Harris 1991: 199).

[50] Rachel, Lady Kingston, writing to Philippa Mundy in July, did not mention it (Mundy MS M/M 11/5/38).

for the full story, quick to assure Philippa that the wife for whom her Paradise had jilted her had no attraction whatever except money, yet also inclined to urge the advantages of prudence over passion in choice of a husband. 'Whatever Romances and heat of youth impose on the minds of young people, Passion is soon sated, and a real freindship and mutual Value the only tye that makes Life pass easily on, when 2 Freinds agree . . .'[51] This *might* have been written with hopes for sister Frances; it suggests some confidence in the mutual value, the tie of friendship, between herself and her husband.

On 30 June the *Spectator*, recently revived after a lapse of two years, carried a piece by Addison about a club of widows. It rang some clever changes on the time-honoured stereotype of women draining men dry both financially and sexually; to even the balance between the sexes it purported to come from an unrepentant male fortune-hunter. Lady Mary was moved to reply: and promptly, for Addison printed her riposte on 28 July. It purports to be a letter from the president of the widows' club, detailing with verve the shortcomings of her six successive husbands. A serious point about male exploitation of women is combined with a fictional portrait of a woman turning the tables and unrepentantly pursuing her own pleasure and profit. Sold for her fortune at fourteen, she now delights in tormenting her would-be tormentors. The husbands she chooses for herself are: a total nullity, a prospective sex object (who turns out to be interested in nothing but hounds and booze), a rake who runs through all her money, a hypochondriac who takes endless nursing, and a miser who would have starved her if she had not driven him to suicide by spending £2,000 on diamonds.

Most interesting for a critic about this virtuoso performance is its remoteness from the moralizing tone usual in the *Spectator* (and widespread in Montagu's own writing). It is positively anti-didactic. It teems with instances of spoof poetic justice, but no genuine ones. Most interesting for a biographer is the Honourable Edward Waitfort, the narrator's most persistent suitor, hovering on the sidelines. He is first drawn to her by her money, his 'Esteem and Love' being wholly engrossed by himself. She responds with all kinds of bad behaviour to his complacent certainty of gaining her: she makes a show of simpering and blushing, treats him 'like a Dog for my Diversion'. When he reads her an 'insolent Lecture upon the Conduct of Women', she promptly marries someone else. She loves to prove by maltreating him that 'it was yet in my Power to give pain to a Man of Sense'. What glory it would be for her, she says, if he were to hang himself! When

---

[51] *CL* i. 207. She only learned for certain of Philippa's marriage after it had happened.

he briefly wavers towards another woman, she yet again marries another man. The essay leaves her still certain of her power over him, uncertain whether to marry him.[52]

This rewrites and transmutes her own courtship in the most extraordinary way. Wortley's persistence, his several re-entries into the field, and his tendency to lecture, are represented quite faithfully in Waitfort. The widow's malicious delight in power is nothing like Lady Mary's recorded behaviour or language, but it echoes his version of her. Did he read this essay before it was printed? Did he recognize himself? What did he think if he first read it in print? And how did Addison see this transaction in which he published his friend's wife's caricature of his friend? Another friend, Thomas Tickell, knew of Montagu's authorship, and wished he might make it public.[53] But it remained a secret until this century.

Meanwhile the prospect of sister Frances's wedding crept closer. It was two years since Frances had confided to Philippa her misery at losing her Paradise and her belief that 'ev'ry living body shou'd fear hell above all other things'.[54] Now her father had chosen for her a widower fifteen years her senior, father of a schoolboy son: John Erskine, 6th Earl of Mar. He was a Tory (though his family were Presbyterians), markedly Scottish in his speech. His portraits show him as handsome, though his body was said to be crooked. He claimed to have been long in love with Lady Frances. He was doing well under Queen Anne, as a Privy Counsellor and Secretary of State for Scotland (a post carrying a house in the Privy Garden, Whitehall), and a pension of £3,000 p.a. secured for him by Lord Oxford.[55]

But neither his circumstances nor his character would stand scrutiny. His rental income was only £261 Scots (with odd shillings). His debts and his late father's came to over £150,000 in the same currency, though he gave assurances that they could not 'touch' his estate or the money he would receive with Lady Frances.[56] Besides, as she was later to know too well, the rental from Scottish estates was by custom paid in arrears, and in kind. The initial arrears would be doubled by the haggling necessary to convert kind into cash. And Mar's character: an associate later thought it 'impossible for him

[52] *E&P* 69–74. Her idea may have come from *Female Tatler*, no. 14, which, however, is far more moralistic: Clarissa loves Cynthio; her parents marry her to Senorio; he dies; she marries Rant instead of Cynthio, is widowed again but finds she has lost her chance with Cynthio.

[53] Draft of Tickell's introduction to the last *Spectator* volume, pub. 1715 (Hodgart 1954: 369, 372–4).

[54] To Philippa, 4 Apr., 15 Oct., 31 Oct. [1712], Mundy MS M/M 11/5.

[55] Gregg 1982: 180. There may have been a personal connection that took in the Pierrepont girls: Mar was a friend of Lord Stair, at whose house Lady Mary went dancing (*CL* iii. 171).

[56] 'A breviat of the Earl of Mar's Rental', 1713 (Mar and Kellie MSS, GD 124/2/191; also 124/2/157, 160–83 *passim*, 190, 124/10/485, 124/15/1158).

even to play a fair game, or to mean but one thing at once'. A historian calls his letters 'models of ineptitude and tergiversation'.[57]

For Lord Mar the benefits of this marriage were clear: Lady Frances was a catch. Twelve years later he tried to justify his second marriage to his son by his first (who might 'repine' at the income he proposed to leave this second wife if he died). He insisted he had married to serve 'the good of the ffamilie'. He could hardly have been more open about his marrying for what he could get.[58]

On the other side, it was a strange marriage for a daughter of Evelyn Pierrepont, Marquess of Dorchester. Lady Mary thought Frances was pressured by aunt Cheyne and a Mar relative. One of Dorchester's Whig circle wrote, 'there is a good Whig *marr'd* by taking a Scotch Jacobite for her Husband'.[59] Did Dorchester miscalculate, seeing the high office and the estates, failing to note the debts?[60] His 'design to marry him selfe' made it urgent for him to dispose of his remaining single daughter.[61] But also, with Queen Anne's health in rapid decline and the succession uncertain, eminent Whigs were hedging their bets. Marlborough did this; Dorchester may have done so too. If the Elector of Hanover succeeded to the throne, well and good; but if it should be James III after all, a Scotch Jacobite son-in-law might be handy.

Lady Frances's marriage contract is a powerfully alienating document. It is a sizeable volume, full of lawyers' jargon and (to English eyes) impenetrably Scottish terms: 'All and Haill the lands of Kintilloch the lands of Kettleston with the miln lands multures and sequels thereof.' Every one of its eighty-seven pages is signed at the bottom left 'Dorchester' and at the bottom right 'Mar', with the less absolute 'F Pierrepont' tucked away below the 'Mar'. They did this signing on 13 July 1714. Wherever the scribe had made his many corrections they signed the margins too: Lady Frances wrote about a hundred times the maiden name she was about to relinquish. Her trustees were her uncle Lord Cheyne and her cousin Lord Denbigh: to them her husband was to pay regular pin-money, 'for her own proper personal expences to be used employed and bestowed as the said Lady herself shall

[57] Atterbury 1869: ii. 70 (1725); Tayler 1938: 12.

[58] By 'unforseen accident' Queen Anne died leaving his salary unpaid, and Lady Mar's portion, 'which I had designed for clearing the remaining old debts on the esteat', was diverted to London debts (Mar 1896: 176–7).

[59] *CL* i. 216; Thomas Burnet (son of the bishop) 1914: 69. Mar was related to the earls of Seaforth and Loudoun.

[60] Mar told his brother, Lord Grange, that he 'had a good dale of trust' in the 'lawer' Dorchester was employing for the marriage contract—Sir David Dalrymple, a Scot—although he was on 'tother side' (Mar MS GD 124/15/1129/1).

[61] *CL* i. 160; *E&P* 21. Dorchester's prenuptial settlement with Lady Isabella Bentinck lies cheek by jowl with his security to Mar for £8,000 (1 July, 27 July 1714, BL Eg. MS 3660. 78).

think fitt and expedient without the advice and consent of the said Earl of Mar'. Dorchester gave £8,000 (sterling) 'as her tocher and marriage portion'. Lands were set aside to pay her an annual jointure of £1,000 in case of widowhood, and to provide portions of varying amounts for varying hypothetical combinations of children, right down to 'only a daughter or daughters'. The system at least designed for her a security that her sister Mary lacked. Ten witnesses signed.[62]

The wedding took place on 20 July, soon after Philippa's. Now the three who had exchanged gossip about Paradises and Hells had all of them crossed the river of no return. Lady Mary had just left London. Her diary voiced some foreboding about her sister's fate, but coolly: she had no notion how bad it would be. Her husband stayed behind for a while, hoping to achieve a meeting with her father, who had told him to 'apply to him again when Lady F. was marry'd'. He was apparently already thinking of soliciting a post abroad. Lady Mary visited her uncle Lord Pierrepont on the way north, and promised at his earnest desire that Wortley would do the same. She also wanted him to visit her grandmother Lady Denbigh.[63]

She arrived to find Middlethorpe 'in great disorder' and her baby son distressingly feeble. He had no teeth yet; she was assured this was normal, but still 'my heart achs about him very often'. There were no maids, no cook, and hardly any writing-paper. The baby, 'allmost never out of my sight', was 'very cheerfull and full of play'. (His complaint was probably rickets, which was common in an age when fresh air was believed to be bad for the very young.) Lady Mary had heard cold bathing recommended, but feared it might be hazardous. 'Thô I am convinc'd in my reason tis both silly and wicked to set one's heart too fondly on any thing in this world,' she wrote, 'I cannot overcome my selfe so far as to think of parting with him with the resignation that I ought to do.' Perhaps these weeks taught her how 'a tender mother' must sometimes force medicine on her baby, 'thô it squalls and struggles with all its strength'.[64]

Again she was besieged with the need to make decisions. Wortley was apparently tired of Middlethorpe; she had promised him to search for another house. She loaded him with advice about the conciliatory visits he was to make on his way to join her, about the best time of day to arrive (at dinnertime, hoping to be invited to stay the night) and what to tip the servants (not too much). She had unfortunately led Lord Pierrepont to expect him sooner than would now be possible. About her son she consulted

---

[62] Mar MSS GD 124/3/83, 53, 2–3, 82, 24–37. [63] *E&P* 21; *CL* i. 208–9, 215, 227, 228.
[64] *CL* i. 208–10; Perry 1986: 143; *Nonsense of Common-sense*, no. 2 (*E&P* 112).

a doctor, who advised dipping him nine times in the cold well at nearby Water Fulford. 'Thither I carry'd him with a beating heart tother day.'[65] It seemed to do him good, and she felt confident enough to leave his next visit to the care of a servant and to accept the invitation of Lord Carlisle's daughters to spend a day with them at York races. Her father's friend Lord Wharton, they told her, was staying with them and would have called on her if he had had more time. She reported this rather wistfully; it would have been recognition of a kind.

Into this trivial daily round burst the news of Queen Anne's death, on 1 August 1714. (Wortley, in London, was probably expecting it; he may even have stayed for that reason.) Just behind it came news of Dorchester's 'prodigious proceedings': his marriage, on 2 August, to Lady Isabella Bentinck, a court beauty only one year older than Lady Mary. The latter confided to her diary the tale of Isabella's ambition, and how she jilted a younger, romantic lover to marry this eminent middle-aged rake.[66] Once married, Dorchester 'flew off' from his offer to negotiate with Wortley. The queen's death brought out mobs in York, with bonfires to burn the Pretender in effigy; it might bring civil war, or invasion through Scotland, or both.

Once Anne was dead 'all the principal men of any figure took post for London'. Middlethorpe, tall and four-square beside the road that led to the archbishop's palace, offered an obvious temptation to plunder. Lady Mary received another invitation from Carlisle's daughters, who were left unprotected while their father galloped to London on state business. They suggested she bring her child and take refuge with them at Castle Howard. ''Tis the same thing as pensioning in a Nunnery,' she assured her husband, 'for no mortal man ever enters the doors in the absence of their father.' She begged him in vain for permission or advice; she even wept over his silence; but she moved into Castle Howard. Like Thoresby, it was a mansion within a park. Its master, Carlisle, was her father's most intimate friend. His daughters, Lady Elizabeth, Lady Anne, and Lady Mary Howard, were only a little younger than herself; they were probably glad to welcome the fifteen-month-old baby. They may or may not have felt that honour or fashion required them, thus secluded, to adopt the full court mourning for a monarch whose policies they had disliked. If so, it would have been easy for Lady Mary Wortley Montagu to get out clothes made for mourning her brother. She stayed at Castle Howard till the end of the month.[67]

---

[65] *CL* 208, 211. Another treatment was the milt *straight* from a freshly butchered bullock, bound on a child's navel for 24 hours (1733, Devonshire MSS, Chatsworth: 199.1).

[66] *E&P* 31. [67] *CL* i. 213, 215–16, 219.

Edward Wortley Montagu never did come back to Middlethorpe. His star was rising with that of the Whigs: his wife stopped begging him to join her (which would mean leaving London without seeing the new king) and began begging him to exert himself, to think big, to realize his ambitions. She hoped that when the new reign brought a new parliament he would be elected, perhaps for Aldborough.[68] She provided him with character sketches of players on the political scene: Lord Pelham (future Duke of Newcastle), cousin of her friend Lady Henrietta; Lord Townshend, husband of her friend Dolly; Lord Morpeth, brother of the ladies with whom she was staying. She was alert to the indirect political influence open to women.

Her new brother-in-law, Mar, did not expect to retain his posts under George I, though he wrote to pledge allegiance. His wife believed that *if* he lost his positions he would be compensated with a pension on the 'Equivalent' fund provided by the Act of Union in 1707: she would not have to exchange, as Samuel Johnson was to put it, the rocks of Scotland for the Strand. In her relief she wrote to her sister about 'fine preparations for the Coronation, etc'.[69]

Lady Mary returned to Middlethorpe partly to sound out the potential of York as a parliamentary seat for Wortley, whose father had decided to take over Huntingdon. York news was not encouraging; previous incumbents looked sure to be re-elected. Her son was still not strong, and had swollen joints. The coachman, John, had given notice and was sticking to it. He had 'heard we intended to live in the Country' and he wanted London. Since he would be hard to replace, Lady Mary sent their horses to winter at Wharncliffe and prepared to go on living in convent style. She hoped Wortley would soon pay his respects to the new king and be free to join her. By about 6 September he was promising to come soon.[70]

It was an unsatisfactory existence, even with the resource of reading 'all Day', even with temporary company from a bland young lady visitor. The Thompsons (not the former Anne Justice's immediate relations, but a York family with strong parliamentary influence) came to Middlethorpe to visit and assured her that Wortley *could* easily have become their candidate, but had now missed the boat. She still worried about the baby. She told her husband, 'I wish to God you was as impatient to see me as I am to see you.' Since she was convinced he had lost two possible constituencies (Aldborough and York) by delay, she could not resist counselling him about the need to seize opportunity when it presented. But she could not avoid a hectoring tone.

---

[68] *CL* i. 214, 218–19.   [69] *CL* i. 218; Samuel Johnson, *London*, 1738, 10.   [70] *CL* i. 219–22.

Tis surprizing to me that you are all this while in the midst of your freinds without being sure of a place when so many insignificant creatures come in without any opposition . . . I am very sorry for your sake that you spent so much money in vain last year, and will not come in this, when you might make a more considerable figure than you could have done then.[71]

She felt he was throwing away her chances as well as his own.

On 18 September 1714 the Elector, now George I, landed in England and began distributing appointments. By the end of the month Thomas White of Wallingwells, Joseph Banks (Mary's father), and William Levinz (MP for Nottinghamshire, whose wife was Lady Mary's friend) had all offered their services to Pelham (the manager of the Whig parliamentary machine). 'Thô I am very impatient to see you,' Lady Mary began a letter late that month, 'I would not have you by hastening to come down lose any part of your Interest.' This letter sprouted into a major pep talk.

I need not enlarge upon the Advantages of Money. Every thing we see . . . puts us in remembrance of it. If it was possible to restore Liberty to your Country . . . by reduceing your selfe to a Garret, I should be pleas'd to share so glorious a poverty with you, but as the World is and will be, tis a sort of Duty to be rich, that it may be in one's power to do good, Riches being another word for Power, towards the obtaining of which the first necessary qualification is Impudence, and (as Demosthenes said of Pronunciation in Oratory) the 2nd is Impudence, and the 3rd, still, Impudence. No modest Man ever did or ever will make his Fortune . . . The Ministry is like a play at Court. There's a little door to get in, and a great Croud without, shoveing and thrusting who shall be foremost; people that knock others with their Elbows, disregard a little kick of the shinns, and still thrust heartily forwards are sure of a good place. Your modest man stands behind in the Croud, is shov'd . . . to death, and sees a 1,000 get in before him that don't make so good figure as him selfe.

Lady Mary could see what Wortley lacked, but she probably misjudged his response to such exhortation from a wife, even when softened by flattery: 'you deserve every thing, and are capable of every thing.' In fact he valued his own deserts too highly to push or shove. If he was inactive in seeking election, he hankered after something better, perhaps a government post. She maintained that 'being chose by your Country is more Honnourable than holding any place from any king', though she also hinted that once elected he might aspire even to the Speaker's chair. She later thought 'he had that Opinion of his own Merit as made him think any offer below that of Secretary of State not worth his acceptance'.[72]

[71] *CL* i. 223–5, 228.   [72] *CL* i. 226–7, 229; *E&P* 83.

Early in the courtship he had written, 'I have so high an opinion of you that I think if you were old and ugly you woud forward me in any pursuit I coud possibly have.'[73] Now she worked at forwarding him. She advised him about getting elected ('You say you hope you shall be sure else where, but you don't seem to know where, and I am afraid it will be finally no where'), and about strategy with Lord Pierrepont and Lord Dorchester, who had reneged on his financial offers. Wortley was inclined to evade subjects which Lady Mary knew must be broached. She continued to chide him for indifference about their child.

But shifts were occurring. On 1 October she wrote, 'My duty to Papa'; so they were back on speaking terms. And Wortley was negotiating for a post in the Treasury under his cousin Halifax, who was the Whigs' long-standing choice for Lord High Treasurer. That day Halifax agreed to accept the slightly less splendid title of First Lord of the Treasury.[74] When Lady Mary heard of Wortley's Treasury appointment and wrote to express her pleasure, he contradicted the news and suggested that she wanted him in the job only 'in veiw of spending mere [*sic*] money than we do'. She was 'very much vex'd', and wrote urging high-minded reasons for acceptance, as disinterestedly as 'if I was your freind and not your wife'. One difficulty was the party renown that Wortley had acquired back in 1710, with the Tories entrenched in government, for introducing a bill designed to prevent MPs from doubling as office-holders; this set him up for criticism if he were to accept office *and* seek election. Lady Mary argued that if he declined office it would never be believed he had been offered it, whereas if he held office he would have the option of resigning on principle.

On 13 October Wortley accepted a post as junior Commissioner of the Treasury, with three others including the ex-Tory Robert Walpole. His wife's opinions probably made no difference; Lord Pierrepont's may have made some. She kept her frustration for a postscript: 'I suppose this long Letter might have been spar'd, for your Resolution I dont doubt is allready taken.'[75]

Next week the king was crowned; then parliament was prorogued. Still Lady Mary was stuck in the frustrating gap between her energies and her husband's action. Female influence, she suggested, like that of her unhappy friend Lady Winchester (the former Anne Vaughan), might be a good route into parliament; perfunctorily she added, 'You should understand these things better than me.' When he began a new round of questioning about

---

[73] H MS 74. 52–3.   [74] *CL* i. 227, 228. Halifax was a poet and patron of poets.
[75] *CL* i. 228–31; *E&P* 83.

prospects at York (where she thought he had already delayed too long to recover), she was provoked so far as to suggest he could 'deposite a certain Sumn in some freind's hands, and buy some little Cornish Burrough'. This might not look too good, but it was a reliable method. It was also more or less what Wortley was to do one day, but not yet.

She even found a new area in which to prod him: the coal trade, where splits were looming in the Tyneside 'Regulation' or owners' cartel where the Wortley Montagus, father and son, were key players. And she ran through a list (unreliable, as it turned out) of ladies hoping for places in the household of Caroline of Anspach, new Princess of Wales. 'She must be a strange princesse if she can pick a favourite out of them . . . I wonder they don't think to fit to place Women about her with a little common sense.'[76] This was a delicate issue. Though Lady Mary's birth would have qualified her as a lady-in-waiting, her marriage to a commoner disqualified her, while the post of Bedchamber Woman would be beneath her. The new reign was beginning and she had no place in it; her husband seemed fixed in London, and said nothing of her joining him.

Her complaints multiplied. Wortley left her in dire need of cash, hardly ever wrote, never asked after his son, though he passed on enquiries from Burnet and Lady Denbigh. Lady Mary tartly replied that she was grateful for 'their kind enquirys after the Child, and the more because 'tis certainly neither of theirs'. Matters came to a head when the new coachman overturned the coach 'at the side of the Ditch, that twas the particular providence of God or I had undoubtedly been kill'd'. She became nervous, stayed indoors, suffered from insomnia, and ran a fever accompanied by 'prodigious' swelling of her face, which she had to have lanced. To her account of her illness Wortley replied that he hoped it was not so bad as she made out.

Once again she embarked on a manifesto letter. 'I have taken up and laid down my pen several times, very much unresolv'd in what style I ought to write to you.' Then she poured it all out:

I know very well that no body was ever teiz'd into a Likeing, and 'tis perhaps harder to revive a past one than to overcome an Aversion, but I cannot forbear any longer telling you I think you use me very unkindly. I don't say so much of your absence as I should do if you was in the Country and I in London, because I would not have you believe I am impatient to be in town when I say I am impatient to be with you. But I am very sensible I parted with you in July, and tis now the middle of November. As if this was not hardship enough you do not tell me you are sorry for it . . .

[76] *CL* i. 232–3.

She hinted that if he was 'asham'd of passions that are natural and reasonable' he might be 'proud of those that [are] shamefull and silly'; she suggested he should follow Lord Winchester's example in outright rejection instead of covert indifference; she told him she would return the next purely business letter 'enclos'd to you in blank paper'.[77]

Whatever this outburst did for her emotionally, it seems to have produced practical results. Though Wortley tried to make her feel bad by telling her that her letters had been opened and scrutinized by government spies, he rented a London house at once. This precipitated new indecisions: should she bring the child, or leave him in the country? How many horses would she need for the journey (a question asked before, when they eloped)? Where should they buy or hire horses, and where and for how long engage a coachman and postilion? Especially she wondered about the house he had taken, in Duke Street (no longer standing) to the east of St James's Park: was it on the park side, where all the houses were damp, and most urgently was it the house where a niece by marriage of Lord Halifax, Ricarda Posthuma Montagu, had died of smallpox together with her child? That house had stood empty since. 'I know tis 2 or 3 year ago, but tis gennerally said, that Infection may lodge in Blankets etc. longer than that.'[78]

Nothing was easy. Roads might be under snow, as they never were for the twice-yearly migrations of the London season. The child's nurse would not go. Lady Mary made enquiries about a replacement, but hated the idea of taking someone new to London, with no trial period first. Her present nurse wanted to keep the little boy at her own home; Mrs Thompson (*perhaps* the former Anne Justice) and 'some other good Wives of York' could keep an eye on him. Lady Mary trusted this nurse, in whose care Edward had grown from a pathetic weakling into 'as fine a Child as ever was seen, and allways merry and at play from morning till Night'. She was afraid he would catch cold or be injured on the road; he had a few teeth, but was about to teethe in earnest. On the other hand she was 'unwilling to part with him, and 'tis pity you should not be Acquainted with him'; 'I'm sure you'd be very fond of him.' To decide, she needed to know whether the rented house had a proper room for a nursery, and whether they would be returning to Middlethorpe again. There is no record of an answer from Wortley about the house. 'As to the Child,' he wrote, 'if you do wrong about him, you will have no reason to blame me, for I desire it may be as you like best.'[79]

[77] *CL* i. 234–7.

[78] The owner was Sir Charles Wager, friend of MWM's early admirer Edward Vernon. Ricarda, wife of George Montagu, died during a bad epidemic (*British Mercury*, 4 Apr. 1711).

[79] *CL* i. 238–9.

He wanted her to engage a coachman just for the journey; in London she could look for a long-term one and also for horses. He had 'too much business' for such matters; they were her province. Meanwhile she contacted Middlethorpe's owner about his future plans; she packed boxes to go by various modes of transport. Inside her packing she hid a letter (not extant) giving the full story of something involving Wortley's sister Catherine. Five days before Christmas she panicked at the news that one of the Scottish representative peers was still in the house Wortley had rented, and might mean to stay until parliament rose. Wortley suggested that in this event she could after all stay a few months more in Yorkshire; she assured him that this would not only leave her without necessaries, but would also cost money overall. She urged him to be tough with the peer, and to rent sheets if their own had not arrived.[80]

Her last, flurried letters are not all anxiety. She would wait for the full moon, 'which is absolutely necessary in so long a Journey'. She would stay one night at Wallingwells *en route*. 'I love travelling,' she wrote, 'and if I did not, I should not think any thing uneasy to come to you.' At the last moment everyone insisted on the danger to the child of this winter journey, and she left him behind. 'I would take the more care of him because if you have 20 children you may never [have] one like him, for he is very pritty, and has more apprehension than is usual at his Age.'[81] Writing this on 5 January 1714, just before setting out, she sounded happy in her marriage, with the world lying all before her, going to London to seek her fortune.

---

[80] This man, Lord Seafield, was reported as leaving for Scotland on 16 Feb. 1715 with MWM's brother-in-law Mar; where he lived in the interim is not known.

[81] *CL* i. 237–45.

6

1715

❧

High Society: 'The Winners Pleasure, and the Losers pain'[1]

JOURNEYING south, Lady Mary escaped the attentions of the great gang of highwaymen infesting Hertfordshire and Middlesex.[2] She drove into London, and the crowds swallowed her from view. How was her meeting with her husband after six months apart? We do not know. Since her marriage her day-to-day activities had been documented while she was away from him but mostly hidden while they were together. Only three of her letters to other people are known to survive from her early married years. Her invisibility becomes most regrettable in the years 1715–16, spent in London. These saw a total eclipse of the sun, another great frost (with oxen roasting on the frozen Thames), mob unrest, a military encampment in Hyde Park (after the Jacobite Rebellion), and trials and executions.[3] They saw Lady Mary's short-lived career as a courtier and the dawn of her fame as a writer. She had no idea she would be leaving for Turkey in 1716; she thought she was shaping a lifestyle to last the foreseeable future.

It seems she was so busy that she even neglected her diary. Though she captured anecdotes like the one about James Craggs (below), her granddaughter says she gave extensive treatment to nothing from 1715–16.[4] It was a heady time, a moment of expanding opportunities. So far, since her marriage, Lady Mary's first priority had been to please her husband. While he was away she had had no one to please but herself. The other people in her life—her little son, her Yorkshire servants, even most of her Yorkshire visitors, like the Listers and Thompsons—were in some way or other her subordinates or satellites. Now it was incumbent on her to please others,

---

[1] Cardelia on the cash rewards of the game of basset ('Thursday', *E&P* 196).
[2] A newspaper item, like many topical events mentioned below.
[3] John Fox in *Anecdote Library* [1822]: 49–50.
[4] She had already detailed her stepmother's story (*E&P* 30–1).

including first and foremost the new arrivals from Hanover. 'The new Court with all their Train was arriv'd before I left the Country', she wrote later; this fact must have fretted her. She had herself introduced at court as soon as she could organize the clothes.

As Elector of Hanover, George I had reigned over dominions which English people felt to be rather too small for a proper sovereign state. (He was 'Elector' because he had the right to vote for the Austrian Emperor in Vienna). Now he had the crown which his mother had so much wanted, but had missed by dying three months before her cousin Queen Anne. He had brought 'all his German Ministers and playfellows male and female' to his new capital to face the intense curiosity of his British subjects and of an already flourishing popular press. Lady Mary, in her distinctly disillusioned 'Account of the Court of George I', said that by nature he was 'an Honest Blockhead'.[5]

Of the three male Hanoverians she named, von Schlitz had acquired a sizeable fortune by managing George's treasury. This must have aroused hopes for Edward Wortley Montagu; but von Schlitz found nothing for him in England and did not stay. Wortley built a good deal on being the only one of the four junior Treasury Commissioners who knew French and so could talk to the non-English-speaking king; but George I turned out to take no interest in Treasury business.

Lady Mary made a hit with the female courtiers. She was soon writing letters to the king's mistress, Baroness von der Schulenburg. On her travels she was to correspond, no doubt by invitation, with Schulenburg, with the king's illegitimate half-sister, Madame von Kielmansegg, and with his daughter-in-law the Princess of Wales. By the princess, indeed, she 'was always . . . particularly favoured'.[6] Her mental as well as physical gifts contributed to the impression she made: each of these ladies had serious intellectual interests. (And each was to be savagely satirized by Alexander Pope.) Though Lady Louisa characterizes George I's evening gatherings as crushingly dull, there was a difference between the formal court evenings with Schulenburg and the more cultured evenings with Kielmansegg, who as Lady Darlington was to become Lady Mary's real friend.[7]

Meanwhile Lady Mary was said to be the only Englishwoman invited to these evening parties. The only English*man* so honoured was the politician

---

[5] Historians are becoming less sure of this (*E&P* 83–4, 86; Hatton 1978: 172).

[6] *CL* i. 310–12, 353, 245; Hunter 1831: ii. 322. Kielmansegg's relationship with the king was not understood: she was assumed to be his mistress. She was later Countess of Darlington, Schulenburg later Duchess of Kendal.

[7] See p. 190–1.

James Craggs the younger, 'one of the most dramatic instances of upward mobility in Augustan England', protégé of the Duke and Duchess of Marlborough and friend of Pope.[8] Lady Mary suggested that Craggs, like Marlborough before him, had reached the top by exercising his sexual charms. She was on practical-joking, semi-flirtatious terms with him, as he showed one night in an episode which says little for either's gifts as a courtier. At the foot of the great staircase of St James's Palace (what was he doing there, one wonders?), Craggs met Lady Mary slipping away early from the royal presence, and slightly light-headed with the exertions of diplomacy it had cost her to win leave to depart. She was indiscreet enough to boast 'how urgently the King had pressed her to stay longer'. At this Craggs 'snatch[ed] her up in his arms as a nurse carries a child'—hoop, pet-ticoats, train, fan, and all—'ran full speed with her up-stairs, deposited her within the ante-chamber, kissed both her hands respectfully, (still not saying a word,) and vanished'. At once the pages flung wide the doors to the inner chamber, 'and, before she had recovered her breath, she found herself again in the King's presence'. But when he and Schulenburg 'began thanking her for her obliging change of mind', she was so fluttered as to commit a second indiscretion. 'Oh Lord, sir! I have been so frightened!' she cried, and 'told his Majesty the whole story exactly as she would have told it to any one else'. This brought a royal reprimand to Craggs when he reappeared, and later a 'bitter reproach, with a round oath to enforce it' from Craggs to Lady Mary, which she felt she had fully deserved. She was 'heartily vexed' with herself.[9]

This lesson in not saying what she thought may have been salutary in dealing with Caroline of Anspach, Princess of Wales. Caroline later became patron to a range of thinkers and writers from the Revd Samuel Clarke to the thresher poet, Stephen Duck. She was also to be a key player, on account of her sharp mind and forceful personality as well as her rank, in the campaign for smallpox inoculation which Lady Mary initiated six years later. Yet Lady Mary's 'Account of the Court of George I' is hard on Caroline. Sarah, Duchess of Marlborough, was even harder: she thought the princess's 'face frightfull, her eyes very small & green like a Cat & her shape yet worse', while her clothes were only fit for 'Drolls I had seen at Bartholomew Fair when I was a girl'.[10] Lady Mary concentrated her fire on Caroline's moral qualities: her 'Low Cunning' and natural inclination to cheating, her

[8] Hunter 1831: ii. 322. She was also on terms of familiar friendship with another of the same social group, the notorious wag Giles Earle (Christie 1995: 56; _CL_ iii. 261). Craggs was favoured at court less for his undoubted ability than for his familiarity with Hanover.
[9] _E&P_ 28–9.   [10] Harris 1991: 204.

efficient manipulation of her husband the prince, the future George II. Lady Mary summed him up as ardent and sincere but stupid, looking on 'all the Men and Women he saw as Creatures he might kick or kiss for his diversion'.[11] On balance it seems most likely that the 'Account', which is otherwise hard to date, was written before Lady Mary found herself sharing with the princess the role of medical pioneer.

She noted in conclusion that the coolness already apparent between the king and the prince encouraged many ambitious people to concentrate their efforts at ingratiating themselves on either one court or the other. She herself attended both, and found scope for her gifts at each. Soon after her arrival she was reported as learning German 'to make her court to the King'.[12] Knowing German was thought to have helped some people to the court favour without which nothing could be done.[13] The court was the seat of pleasure, too, although still in mourning for Queen Anne.[14]

Lady Mary was on the road at the time of the Twelfth Night celebrations, but she would have heard about them later. As was 'customary', the king opened the gambling at court by 'throwing off' 200 guineas; that night the Princess of Wales won 600 guineas. Lotteries were all the rage as usual, and gambling was still a way of life at court, though a royal proclamation had just banned subjects from doing it on the Lord's Day. It was a way of life to which Lady Mary had already shown she was not averse.

Though she missed this royal gambling and this royal anti-gambling message, she was in time for another proclamation 'Calling a New Parliament' (on 15 January), and for the day of 'Publick Thanksgiving for his Majesty's happy and peaceable Accession' five days later, and for much of the distribution of jobs and perks. Frances Hewet's husband had just been made 'Surveyor of the Forrests, Parks, &c. on the South-side of Trent'; peers of Lady Mary's acquaintance became Custos Rotulorum for this or that county. On 29 January newspapers reported both the appointment of her uncle Lord Cheyne to an Exchequer post, and the expected inclusion of her father among a batch of dukes shortly to be created. Dr Clarke (of whom more below) became a royal Chaplain in Ordinary in March. Wortley, who

---

[11] *E&P* 93–4. Robert Walpole too judged that the princess ruled the prince 'by deceiving him' (Hervey 1931: iii. 788).

[12] Lady Loudoun, 5 Mar. 1715, Huntington MS Lo 11254. She added, 'but that won't do for he can't like any body so litle let ther mind be as large as it will.'

[13] Information from Frances Harris.

[14] Newspapers noted that mourning would be slightly relaxed on 2 Feb. There was a petition to end all mourning at Easter, and meanwhile ladies subscribed to keep a milliner and her twenty apprentices in business through this lean period. The milliner, Hannah Ludlum of Long Acre, could then afford to wait to sell the work subscribed for: an example of the female solidarity later urged by authors like Mary Ann Radcliffe and Priscilla Wakefield.

already had his position, stood as Member for Westminster (a seat which, despite its large number of freeholder voters, was controlled by the court). No one opposed him, and he was duly elected. By February the Whig landslide was complete. Wortley's father and his cousin Hinchingbrooke were duly chosen for Huntingdon. The 'Regulation' or association of five great coal-owners was just breaking up amid acrimony which focused more on Sidney Wortley than on his son.[15]

Lady Mary responded characteristically to the scramble for court patronage: she satirized it in poetry. By the end of March 1715 she had written 'Roxana Or the Drawing room', which later became the first of her 'Eclogues'. She had time just to look about her before composing it, since it mentions the prince and princess's attending a performance of John Gay's *The What D'Ye Call It*. This 'Farce, which some Prudes Scrupled to go to, on the score of the Title', opened on 23 February and was given at the Prince of Wales's command next day.[16]

Her poem's protagonist, decked out in roses, must have graced either this command performance or else the Princess's birthday, 1 March, when mourning was briefly suspended and there was a 'great Appearance of the Nobility at Court'. 'Roxana' presents the fat, fortyish, prudish, Tory Duchess of Roxburgh[17] lamenting that the princess has given a coveted court job not to her but to the artful, ensnaring Coquetilla—based on the Duchess of Shrewsbury, née Adelaide Paleotti. This Italian's marriage into the English peerage had caused some scandal; she was also a close friend of Edward Wortley Montagu, and had forwarded his courtship.[18] The poem is just as slippery as Gay's 'Tragi-Comi-Pastoral Farce' itself. Montagu's Roxana deplores the lewdness of the princess's court; but since Roxana misinterprets the play's title and wrongly supposes it to be 'filthy', her judgement is not to be trusted.[19] Her philistinism stands revealed in her objections to the play. Roxana's creator accepted the court ambience which Roxana detests; she was developing a rapport, if not with Princess Caroline, at least with some of her courtiers and protégés.[20]

[15] Hughes 1952: 194–5.

[16] The poem is dated '1714/15' (i.e. Jan.–Mar. 1715) in the copy belonging to Lord Harley, later Lord Oxford—husband of the former Lady Henrietta Cavendish-Holles (*E&P* 182; Gay 1966: 19; Avery 1960: 344).

[17] The duchess had been hauled over the coals by Manley in *New Atalantis*, 1709: ii. 240. Her husband became a Scottish representative peer about this date. Many newspapers of the time seethe with anti-Tory sentiment.

[18] Sir David Hamilton said Shrewsbury was 'forced to Marry Donna Palliotti'. Sarah Marlborough complained of her 'thrusting out her disagreeable breasts with such strange motions' (Hamilton 1975: 93, 121; Somerset 1984: 201–2; *CL* i. 75).

[19] Lady Cowper, a Whig like Lady Mary, mentioned another play this Feb. which the princess liked but the duchess thought obscene (*Diary*, 1864: 46).

[20] Many people misread the poem, including Caroline herself; but one pamphlet recognized that its topic

The Duke Street lodgings, between Whitehall and St James's Park, were less than a mile from the Wortley Montagus' previous ones along the Strand, but a world away in proximity to centres of power: to parliament, where Wortley was now a member, and to the court. In no time at all, it seemed, Lady Mary was juggling a court life, an intellectual-philosophical life, and a literary life, as well as the social life usual for a lady of her rank.

She had once said she 'never valu'd my selfe as the daughter of——, and ever dispis'd those that esteem'd me on that Account'.[21] The change of reign and change of government gave her her first chance as an adult to attempt *winning* esteem. Her ambition stands revealed in the list of those she culti- vated this year: the influential Mrs Charlotte Clayton (Bedchamber Woman to the Princess: later Lady Sundon), the brilliant, self-made young Craggs, the poets Pope and Gay, the visiting Italian polymath Antonio Conti, and so on. I shall come back to most of these. But it seems also that her idealism— what she later called 'the silly prejudices of my Education'—was still strong. Indeed, she never lost either the earnest desire to do right herself, or the habit of bringing other people's actions to the bar of ethical judgement. But in old age she based that judgement on endorsement of rigid social hier- archy, while in youth she felt she 'was to treat no body as an Inferior, and that poverty was a degree of Merit'.[22] This non-exclusiveness served her well. Her social circles in 1715–16 reflected merit even more than wealth or rank.

She does not date the stages of her ideological development, and only her fictional heroine, Docile, suggests that it began with her governess's religi- osity. Docile the infinitely malleable passes instantly from superstitious piety to Enlightenment philosophy; in Lady Mary this change (unless it related to her move to Thoresby as a child) was probably gradual. Her egali- tarian ideals were natural to ardent Christian belief (think of the Virgin Mary exulting that God 'hath put down the mighty from their seat' or of Christ's remark about the rich man and the needle's eye).[23] These ideals may have been connected with the two elderly bishops she corresponded with before her marriage, both men of social conscience: Burnet, an eminent Whig politician, opponent of pluralism and champion of the poverty- stricken lower clergy, and Tenison, who preached Nell Gwyn's and Queen Mary's funeral sermons, reproved William III for adultery, and built

was 'the Venom of a Prude' (*Moore Worms for the Learned Mr. Curll, Bookseller*, 1716, quoted in Straus 1927: 59, 241).

[21] *c.*26 July 1712 (*CL* i. 135). Duke Street no longer exists.

[22] *CL* iii. 36. Clayton, later Sundon, maintained a huge correspondence, mostly in her capacity as patron. Hervey thought she was, unusually for her station, sincerely benevolent (BL Add. MSS 20102–5, 30516; Forster Collection, Victoria and Albert Museum, F. 48 E 14; Hervey 1931: i. 67).

[23] The Magnificat (repeated every Sunday at Evensong); Matthew 19: 24.

London's first public library. Both men were Latitudinarians, ecumenicals who wished to see a liberal, progressive Church of England opening her doors to Protestants of every sect; they might have contributed towards making the young Lady Mary an egalitarian.[24]

Or her ideals may have reached their full flowering only in adult, independent life: i.e. about this time. In 1715 both Tenison and Burnet died; and Lady Mary met the more radical and heterodox churchmen Samuel Clarke, William Whiston, and John Toland.[25] She became quite closely acquainted with each of these remarkable men, though only chance remarks in her letters bear witness to the fact. She may have met them through her court attendance: there was a surprisingly intellectual element in each Hanoverian court, each supplied more by women than men. George I was linked to the world of ideas through his unacknowledged sister, Kielmansegg (later Lady Darlington); the Prince of Wales was so linked by Princess Caroline.

Thus the cut and thrust of theological dispute, and dabbling in her later favourite theory of fatalism, were pleasures Lady Mary could combine with her assault on the summits of court society. Caroline employed Charlotte Clayton, and patronized both Clarke and Whiston. Years later, exasperated amusement mingled with affection in Lady Mary's memories of Whiston's hot-headedness in debate; but she thoroughly approved of his and Clarke's 'natural religion'. She recalled with pleasure how Clarke and Clayton had striven to persuade her that she 'was a free agent', and how she had refused to be convinced. (She asked Clarke to recommend a chaplain for her husband's embassy, but he 'excus'd himselfe ... as not being acquainted with many Orthodox Divines'.)[26]

Lady Mary's only surviving letter from these months is an undated note to Clayton, who had invited her one evening when she was pre-engaged to Lady Jekyll. She clearly owed her first loyalty to Lady Jekyll, who had supported her in the difficult days of courtship; but just as clearly she hated to turn Clayton down. Fittingly for a fatalist, she hoped someone else might save her from this dilemma. 'I wish you would come and take me away.'[27]

[24] Tenison's library, in St Martin in the Fields churchyard, boasted 'the best modern books in most faculties' (William Oldys quoted in Bagford 1861: 401; Clarke and Foxcroft 1907; see p. 37; Spellman 1993). Pope was perhaps already satirizing Burnet: in what became 'Memoirs of P. P. Clerk of this Parish' (pub. 1727) and in the dedication to *Homer in a Nut-Shell*, 1715 (Pope 1986: ii. 102–5).

[25] Burnet d. 17 Mar. 1715, Tenison on 14 Dec. MWM's new intellectual contacts probably belong to 1715. Toland (see Evans 1991) was a protégé of Mary Monck's father, Lord Molesworth.

[26] *CL* i. 317, 411, 247; ii. 174–5; iii. 93; see p. 113. Clarke was an apologist for Newton; Samuel Johnson was to disapprove of him as anti-Trinitarian (Boswell 1934: iv. 416 n. 2). Conti corresponded with Malebranche, Leibnitz, and Mlle Kielmansegg, later Lady Darlington. Whiston 'had the friendship of all the eminent Whigs in London: Craggs, Addison, Steele, Robert Walpole, Jekyll, Peter King' (Gronda 1964; John Fox in *Anecdote Library* [1822]: 50).

[27] *SL* 130.

Along with the radical Anglicans, she met their new acquaintance the Abbé Antonio Conti, who was to become a friend of long-term significance. Conti, a noble Venetian and a Catholic by origin, was a cosmopolitan intellectual and a sceptic by choice. He had left his religious order in 1708, feeling himself no longer equal to the responsibility of hearing confession; like Clarke he believed in a Supreme Being but not in the Trinity as delineated by orthodox Christianity. He was still a priest only because Holy Orders were not reversible: by calling himself *abbé*, not *padre*, he signalled some detachment from Catholicism.[28] His interests embraced mathematics, medicine, and tragedy, Descartes, Newton, and Plato. He arrived in London on 22 April 1715 from Paris, to observe an eclipse of the sun. This, with an aurora borealis and a comet, made it a memorable year for those interested in scientific advance.[29]

Conti came to study science and to meet with scientists. Like Lady Mary, but without her handicap of gender, he explored the intellectual resources of London. Kielmansegg, who was already his friend, introduced him to her weekly suppers for her half-brother the king, 'where the table was fill'd with agreeable authors and People of wit and humour'. Princess Caroline received him; he was elected to the Royal Society. He expounded Newtonianism to the new monarch (which Clarke could not do because he knew no French); he acquired from Princess Caroline a manuscript of Newton's chronology of the world; he read Pope's *Rape of the Lock*; he met the poet John Sheffield, Duke of Buckingham (perhaps through Lady Mary); and he interested both noble poets in his project for tragedies on the topic of Julius Caesar.[30] Since he later translated both Montagu's poetry and Pope's *Rape*, he perhaps shared her literary as well as her philosophic circle. She chose him as recipient of her most searchingly philosophical Embassy Letters; his opinion clearly counted with her.

This friendship gratified both her intellect and her ambition, bridging the worlds of literature and fashion. Elsewhere the worlds diverged. She became close to the sisters Anne Griffith (a Maid of Honour) and Elizabeth, Lady Rich (notorious for her flighty, clueless manner).[31] Intellect was not the only weapon in Lady Mary's armoury. An anecdote presents the future George II calling on his wife, 'in a rapture ... to look how becomingly Lady Mary was dressed! "Lady Mary always dresses well," said the Princess drily,

---

[28] Badaloni 1968; Robert Shackleton to Robert Halsband, 8 Dec. 1971.
[29] Whiston became a butt of another of MWM's new circles, by using these phenomena for millenarian prophecy (Rousseau 1987: 28–9; Shackleton 1988: 214).
[30] Halsband 1956: 57; Gronda 1964; Michaud [1870–3]; *Dizionario biografico*.
[31] *CL* i. 344–5.

and returned to her cards.' Lady Louisa supposed that Lady Mary's favour at the prince's court was ended by jealousy of two different kinds: George I's and Caroline's.[32]

An even more fateful friendship was that with Alexander Pope, the rising poet of their generation. Later, Lady Mary maintained that 'the chief poet of those times' had been Addison, not Pope.[33] But her own poetry—marked by Pope, not Addison—reflects her once-different opinion. At this date Pope too was an explorer, hoping to add the world of high society to his conquests in literature. In rank he was further from Lady Mary than Conti was: an only child of elderly middle-class parents (both now around seventy), who were also Roman Catholics.[34] Not only was he excluded, as a Catholic, from full civil rights; he suffered a serious disability. Pott's disease (tuberculosis of the bone) had stopped his growth at about four foot six, and he was gradually and inexorably becoming more hump-backed. Side-effects included severely impaired sight, almost constant headache, muscle pains, and respiratory troubles. These he faced not merely with courage but with gallantry and panache; but the years 1715–16 were among his healthiest. Though his parents were still (until spring 1716) living at Binfield in Windsor Forest, he was often in London, and enjoyed mock-rakish relations with Caroline's Maids of Honour.[35]

He may not have been entirely new to Lady Mary: literary networks already connected them. Though he said he did not know her before her marriage, he had at least some distant acquaintance with her father (who had read his *Pastorals* before they were published). She was an early reader of his *Essay on Criticism*. Addison accepted revisions to his *Cato* from Pope and from her, and used Pope's prologue for the play although he did not use her epilogue.[36] Many other individuals knew both of them well enough to have been capable of bringing them together. It was in 1715–16, however, that Pope's and Lady Mary's interaction struck sparks.

Pope brought to it much complexity. Hampered in or barred from most of the usual social expressions of his masculinity, he was now, in his twenties, eager to declare himself intensely and outrageously attracted by witty women, while his *chosen* ideal of femininity was one of muted and attentive docility. He had emotional ties with the Blount sisters, Martha and Teresa; but he was coming more and more to see the soft and gentle 'Patty' as the

---

[32] *E&P* 27. In fact there were other causes.   [33] Spence 1966: 746.

[34] His one sibling, Magdalen (Pope) Rackett, daughter of his father's first marriage, was much older.

[35] Mack 1985: 153–8; Nicolson and Rousseau 1968: 7–82, esp. 25.

[36] She read the *Essay* before reading 'the ancient critics', whom she read by 1713 (Pope, *Corr.* ii. 22; TE i. 38; Spence 1966: 745; Addison [1803]: ii. 93).

type of true womanhood, and to judge and to disapprove the flirtatious, assertive Teresa. Lady Mary clearly leaned to the Teresa side of the balance, but her blend of physical attraction and intellectual challenge was unique. Her effect on him was violent and long lasting.[37]

This relationship was entwined with others. Pope was to remember their time together as shared often with Congreve, occasionally with the nobleman-poet Buckingham, and crucially with John Gay, with whom in early 1715 Pope's social life was interwoven. During Queen Anne's reign, while their political star was in the ascendancy and before Lady Mary's had risen, these two young men had been members of the Scriblerus Club, a group of like-minded literary iconoclasts and Tories, now scattered by political change. Gay had begun his London life as a silk-mercer's apprentice, and had been a domestic steward only a couple of years before this date. Lady Mary might well see herself as condescending or egalitarian in extending him the hand of friendship.

For the sake of literary friendships and literary recognition she must have been eager to condescend; and Pope would have been far too polite to reveal to her his real opinion of upper-class writers, as confided to Henry Cromwell. From anyone who wrote 'at leisure hours, and more to keep out of idleness, than to establish a reputation', his expectations were low. Such a poet might achieve 'pretty conceptions, fine metaphors' and so forth, but never 'Design, Form, Fable' (the soul of poetry), or 'exactness, or consent of parts' (its body).[38]

In April 1715 Pope was at his usual, congenial London base: the St James's lodgings of the painter Charles Jervas or Jarvis. Here Jervas housed his growing collection of old masters, and painted several of Pope's friends. Here he and Pope talked and worked at their sister arts 'While summer suns roll[ed] unperceiv'd away'. The studio was a meeting-place for the worlds of fashion and the arts, for sitters and customers. Lord Townshend and his wife (the former Dolly Walpole) lived next door. Jervas was known for painting girls (including the young Lady Mary) as shepherdesses. Lady Winchilsea had written a poem in praise of one of his society portraits.[39] Addison was now sitting to Jervas: Gay mentioned this in the same breath as he mentioned Pope's introducing him 'to a lord and two ladies'. One of those may well have been Lady Mary.[40]

---

[37] Rumbold 1989: 131. My reading of this relationship owes much to her.

[38] Pope, *Corr.* i. 109–10.

[39] Portrait of Mrs Chetwynd, whose assemblies MWM knew (TE vi. 156–9; Jervas [1740], BL C. 118.h.3 (14, 15); McGovern 1992: 102; Steele 1714: 38–9; *CL* i. 367).

[40] Sherburn 1934: 69 n. 1; Pope, *Corr.* i. 295, 288; Mack 1985: 227.

While she was becoming a friend of Jervas, Lady Mary was being painted by Sir Godfrey Kneller—who was the nearest thing to a court painter. She sat in an unusually plain gown in a sumptuous ivory fabric; the book in her hand represents either literary ambition or (inaccurately) retirement. The result has less idiosyncracy than her later portraits; but she must have liked it. Whoever paid Kneller's steep fee, it seems she had several copies made for friends.[41]

Whether or not she had met them before this, Lady Mary surely knew Pope and Gay already through their published work. Gay's *Rural Sports*, 1713, *The Fan*, 1714, and *The Shepherd's Week*, 1714, would not have passed her by. Still less would Pope's *Rape of the Lock*, 1712 and 1714, or *Windsor Forest*, 1713. She now found literary London eagerly anticipating the first instalment of Pope's already controversial Homer translation: the *Iliad* volume one.[42] On her arrival it was also anticipating the opening of Gay's *What D'Ye Call It*. In her poem about this play, Lady Mary mapped out various points in common between herself and Gay: its protagonist has, like him, failed to land a job at court; it compliments his play *and* the Princess of Wales in his very own style of tongue-in-cheek raillery.[43]

While Lady Mary was climbing at court, she also achieved terms of easy familiarity with Pope, Gay, Jervas, and the lawyer William Fortescue. Jervas's rooms were just across the park from Duke Street.[44] Despite the rainy weather (which delayed the printing of Homer),[45] for her it must have been an exciting spring. By 23 July 1715 Pope knew her well enough to boast of her visiting him to retail town gossip.[46] After she had survived smallpox, Jervas sent Pope a note on her behalf, summoning him to visit her next day 'about 5 a Clock which I suppose she meant in the Evening'. He pictured her (in dog-Latin, for fun) in a phrase that translates 'sitting with Gay, and laughing with Fortescue', or 'sitting Gayly, and laughing Fortescuvianly'.[47] The impression is of a group of clever young people fooling around, their class differences dissolved in shared fun.

---

[41] One, owned by the Marquess of Bute, in 1914–18 looked down from a drawing-room wall on to a naval hospital ward. Another went to the Duke of Rutland's family; another perhaps to Lady Buck (see p. 287 n. 3). Each of these two seems later to have been given to a granddaughter of MWM by a granddaughter of the first owner (inscription on picture: Kerslake 1977: ii. 190; Wh MS M 439/42).

[42] Pope, *Corr*. i. 273. For attacks on him at this time, see Sherburn 1934: 164–5; Guerinot 1969: 20–33.

[43] Gay's 'Letter to a Lady', pub. 20 Nov. 1714, which makes a joke of his own attempts to write a poem in Caroline's praise, evidently failed to impress her (Gay 1974: i. 7). In time MWM, like Gay, was to have her disguised compliment taken at face value and disapproved. Henry Fielding was to use this technique in *Tom Jones* for praise of Garrick's acting.

[44] Mack 1985: 227.   [45] Pope, *Corr*. i. 288.

[46] Ironically, in view of the way the 1715 Jacobite rebellion was to scar her sister's life, this gossip made fun of government fears of invasion (Pope, *Corr*. i. 309).

[47] Pope, *Corr*. i. 340.

This gloss of excitement no doubt reflected sexual attraction and social mixing. But here too a part was played by the same theologically libertine thinking, the 'fideistic scepticism', that drew Lady Mary to Whiston and Clarke, and was later to draw her to Hervey. She kept her own copy of Pope's 'Universal Prayer' (titled simply 'A Hymn'), which she made while the poem was still a deist manifesto, before Pope smoothed it into conformity with orthodox Christianity.[48] In her copy God is adored by specifically 'heathen Sage' as well as 'Christian Saint'. Fortune rules 'the world below'; Pope later limited her sway. In the early version the speaker aspires to follow conscience without thought of hell or heaven; he not only prays to be delivered from pride but adds, 'If e're the Wretched I deny'd | Do thou deny me Heaven.' Finally, Lady Mary's copy includes the stanza later suppressed:

> Can Sins of Moments claim the Rod
> of Everlasting Fires?
> Can those be Sins with Natures God
> Which Natures selfe inspires?

If Pope meant this poem to please her, she must have encouraged its heterodoxy.[49]

Pope and Gay were already masters of the arts of literary collaboration (the speciality of the Scriblerus Club) and of mixing and mocking their genres; and Gay had already written a 'town eclogue', as Swift had done before him.[50] They carried with them their poetic reputations, which were to prove enduring. They were older than Lady Mary by one year and four respectively, and they were male. For these reasons it has always been supposed that they were the leaders in the joint literary enterprise which followed, and she the disciple.

This, however, is by no means clear. Lady Mary wrote 'Roxana' before the end of March 1715. There is no evidence she knew Pope or Gay by then; indeed, her poem (with its clever and memorable use of Gay's play) may well have introduced them. It was not a new departure for her in poetic form: her juvenile albums include many dramatic monologues (most, but not all, epistles or pastorals). One has exactly 'Roxana' 's form.[51] Two manuscript

---

[48] Hervey provides an extreme example of scepticism: in 1728 he thought 'the fable of Christianity . . . so exploded in England' that upper-class men and women were afraid to confess they believed it (1931: i. 92). For 'fideistic' scepticism (which coexists with religious belief) and its descent from the Renaissance humanists to the Scriblerians, see Parnell 1994: 221–42. When Pope told Ralph Allen years later, 'I believe no man has' a copy of the Hymn, he may have been tacitly excepting one woman.

[49] TE vi. 145–50. This says her copy (H MS 255, 7–8) was made after 1740; but from its place in her MS 1715 is far more likely (Grundy 1971: 208–9).

[50] Gay, 'Araminta. A Town Eclogue', 1713; Swift, 'A Town Eclogue', 1710.

[51] Latona addresses Jupiter; her tone, however, is pathetic (H MS 250, fo. 1; Grundy 1971: 244–5).

copies of 'Roxana' survive in which it stands alone, not entitled 'Eclogue' or followed by companion eclogues. Lady Mary seems to have sent these copies to friends of her own: to Frances Hewet and the former Lady Henrietta Cavendish Holles. Clearly she was proud of this single poem; it seems Pope and Gay had no part in it. That was Joseph Spence's view when he transcribed Montagu's poems in 1741 and noted on this one: 'On the coming over of the Hanover family: soon after which the others were wrote.'[52]

It is likely that Montagu wrote a good deal of poetry in 1715; and it seems that her own unaided writing was what brought her intellectually close to these immensely talented poets of about her age, on terms much more nearly equal than the stratifications of the social system knew how to allow for. She was not their patron, as her uncle had been to Oldham; she was not, like Lady Winchilsea, a member of an older generation to be treated with condescending courtesy. She was a potential, and soon—in 1716 if not in 1715—an actual, collaborator. It may have been their heady praise that she had in mind when she later confessed that people who had 'profess'd more value for me than I was conscious of meriting' had sometimes flattered her into thinking better of them than they deserved.[53] Of her new friendships, only that with Conti was equally important.

While new friendships provided the flourishes, the ground bass of Lady Mary's life was what her wifely letters describe wherever they survive: day-to-day household management, performing personal-assistant services for her husband, and (once the winter was over) pleasure in her child's play and growth. Wortley's Treasury career did not run smoothly.[54] As early as December 1714 Halifax was rumoured to be at odds with his younger colleagues and likely to be succeeded by Robert Walpole. He died on 19 May 1715,[55] and Walpole did succeed him five months later, as First Lord of the Treasury and Chancellor of the Exchequer. Wortley entertained dislike if not hatred for Walpole, a feeling which may or may not have sprung from working with him. (It might not be irrelevant that Walpole was just now making himself seriously rich.)[56] Since Lady Mary remained

[52] Portland MSS, University of Nottingham (Pw V 517); BL Lansdowne MS 852. 184–5 (collection of Lord Oxford, Lady Henrietta's husband); Cornell MS E6004, 29–31 (Joseph Spence's transcription of poems by MWM). Horace Walpole said MWM admitted the eclogues 'were first thought of in company with Pope and Gay' (note in BL C. 117. aa. 16).

[53] See p. 104 ff.; *CL* iii. 48–9.

[54] Among his troublesome jobs was extracting from George I the £2,000 which Queen Anne had left to the poor: when this was referred to him in Oct. 1715, the official who would dispense it feared 'being torn to pieces' by desperate claimants (Bishop Smallridge to Townshend, HMC 1887: 132).

[55] His death, with Wharton's that year and Jekyll's the next, left the way open for younger Whigs—i.e. for Walpole—to reinvent the party.

[56] Plumb 1956: 207.

loyal to her old friendship with Walpole, this became something problematic between them.

There were other old friends to consider, and her relations. Many of her contemporaries were immersed in child-bearing. Lady Harley (formerly Henrietta Cavendish-Holles) lay in this spring, after bearing a daughter (the future Duchess of Portland) on her own birthday. 'Sister Mar' was pregnant for the first time. Although her husband was no longer Secretary of State for Scotland, she still lived at the house in the Privy Gardens, Whitehall. Some houses there backed on the river; it was a stone's throw from Duke Street. Since Lady Mary wrote constantly to her when they were apart, she probably saw a good deal of her this year: more than of either 'Sister Gower' or of their father. He was officially reconciled to her but, between public life and his new marriage, unlikely to have been warm. Lady Mary's widowed sister-in-law, Rachel, Lady Kingston, may have moved out of the Acton house when her new mother-in-law moved in; as a young widow she was an object of pursuit and courtship.[57]

In May 1715 Lady Mary's hopes suffered a setback when Gervase, Lord Pierrepont, died and was found not to have altered his will since 1682, before she was born. He had done the patriarchal thing for a childless uncle, and left his all to the head of the family. Dorchester, already tipped for this elevation, became Duke of Kingston on 10 August.

It is not known whether Lady Mary stayed in London for the summer off-season in 1715, or when her son was brought or fetched from Yorkshire.[58] In any case, she must have had her attention deflected from her own affairs to those of sister Mar. Rumours of a landing by the Pretender (Queen Anne's half-brother, James II's son, claimant to the throne as 'James III') had been a regular occurrence since George I's accession. Lord Mar had promised the king his loyal support in the summer of 1714, but had been dismissed from all his posts (along with most Tory office-holders). On 9 August 1715, the day after his daughter's birth, he set out on horseback for Scotland with rebellion in his heart but entirely without practical or theoretical knowledge of the art of war. He left his wife without money, and without telling her where he was going.[59] Whether or not Lady Mary's sister Frances had been allowed to attend her in childbirth two years before, it seems likely that she would have

---

[57] She had already written to Philippa about husbands assigned to her by gossip (Mundy M/M MS 11/5/35–8). She was soon to begin a notorious affair with the future Lord Scarborough (see p. 180).

[58] EWM was busy that Aug. with an appeal about a disputed way-leave (Hughes 1952: 301).

[59] The daughter, Lady Frances Erskine, must have come of age on 8 Aug. 1736 (see p. 358). The 1715 rebellion was the 'former occasion' on which Mar later said he had left his wife not knowing where he was going (Tayler 1938: 52).

chosen to be with Frances now. If she was there, the sequence of events would not have endeared her brother-in-law to her. His personal plans and personal pique were crucial causes of the first Jacobite rebellion: he was putting himself first.[60]

Ten days after this birth, news reached London that France was after all not going to support the Jacobite action. Without French aid it could not succeed; but Lord Lansdowne in London had no way of getting this news to his ally Mar in Scotland. Mar meanwhile had set up the 'Chevalier''s standard at the Braes of Mar, and made a proclamation beginning, 'Our rightful and natural King James the VIIth, by the Grace of God, who is now coming to relieve us from our oppressions . . .' Mary Banks's father no doubt spoke for his whole social group, as well as for Mar's father-in-law, when he wrote, 'some perjured Protestants, out of Resentment (because they are not in place) have Join'd the Popish Leaders, of this English Rebellion'.[61]

Mar's forces encountered those of the Duke of Argyll, the premier Whig of Scotland, at Sherrifmuir on 13 November. The battle went only marginally in Argyll's favour, but Mar proposed to him that the rebels be allowed to lay down their arms and withdraw. Argyll refused; Mar's offer was later to make Jacobites dub him traitor or 'Bobbing John'. By then his wife in London had been forced to sell everything she possessed of any value, '(which was not much)', and was destitute. Whether Lady Mary was able to help, or to get Wortley to help, is not known. Her sister hoped that Scottish friends like Lord Kinnoul might give help *secretly*, for instance with her stepson Lord Erskine's school fees.[62]

On 30 September 1715 Jacob Tonson published Sir Richard Steele's *Letter from the Earl of Mar to the King*, which juxtaposes Mar's profession of loyalty to George with his proclamation of James a year later. It adds Steele's 'Remarks on my Lord's subsequent Conduct': a measured moral judgement which admits to having formerly spent pleasant hours in Mar's company.[63] This public condemnation by a close friend of the Wortley Montagus must have caused further pain to Lady Mar. By the autumn, back in London after the respite of a stay in the country, she was sounding as depressed as in her teenage letters to Philippa Mundy: 'tis my misfortune that things shou'd happen so unluckily for me, I must bear it as patiently as

[60] He may have acted less to change the government than to further the private advantage of Robert Harley, Lord Oxford (Gregg 1982: 182; Lenman 1980: 126–8). An undated letter from his small son, about 'mama' and his baby sister, shows no awareness of his father's activities (Mar MS GD 124/15/1155.

[61] To Newcastle, 28 Oct. 1715, BL Add. MS 32,686, 69. The rebels' failure is often blamed directly on Mar's incompetence, e.g. Bennett 1975: 197.

[62] Gregg 1982: 182; Lady Mar to Grange, n.d., 18 Aug., 2 Nov. [1715], Mar MSS GD 124/15/1158.1, 2, 3.

[63] Steele 1944: 356 ff.

I can.' She wrote this to her husband's brother, Lord Grange, who in Mar's absence was acting head of the family.

Grange was a tormented and difficult man, a Holy Willie who frequented religious fortune-tellers. His spiritual diary records inward battles waged between warmth of prayer on the one hand and on the other 'sensual pleasures', 'a vain wandering carnal heart'. An unsympathetic ballad said he 'whoors with upcast eyes'. He is famous for getting rid of a wife he found inconvenient by abducting her, announcing her death, and marooning her on the lone and barely habitable isle of St Kilda.[64] Inheriting Whig views from his mother, he flirted with Jacobitism but later named his brother's treason as one of his greatest griefs: 'It was dishonourable and sinfull in him his going over to the Pretender, notwithstanding all the solemn and sacred ties he was under to the present Government.'[65] Grange was also a hard-headed Scot who cared far more for the family estates than for his English sister-in-law, whose claims on those estates conflicted with other outstanding creditors' claims. He extracted a promise from her (still in force in November 1715) not to talk to the duke her father about her difficulties until he, Grange, gave her permission. Putting her trust in Grange might have made it hard for her to trust her sister Lady Mary, or for her sister not to be impatient with her.

Just before Christmas the Pretender, after delay from contrary winds, reached Scottish soil and met Lord Mar, whom he had constituted his Commissioner there,[66] and whom he now created a duke. On 3 February 1716 the 'king' and 'duke', tacitly admitting the failure of their enterprise, sailed together for France. On Mar's arrival there his wife wrote to Grange that she, her baby daughter, and her stepson 'must all of us depend upon the Government for our maintenance'. Sure enough (thanks to her father's politics), she was rescued by the reigning monarch whom her husband had tried to dethrone. On 11 February, six days before Mar was attainted by Act of Parliament and his estates forfeited, George I granted to Lord Cheyne a thirty-year lease of the Whitehall house, at a ground-rent of £60 a year, in trust for her. Later that year came a promise under the Great Seal guaranteeing a £1,000 annuity to replace the jointure named in Lady Mar's marriage contract, together with the interest on the £10,000 set aside for her daughter, Lady Frances Erskine. The Crown, in confiscating the estates, would allow

[64] Elements in this story are unexpected. His wife had been acting as factor for his estates; her financial rather than sexual conduct seems to have sparked this awful punishment, which began in 1732.
[65] GD 124/15/1158.3; MS diary 24, 43–4 (1726–7); Grange 1843: ix. 78.
[66] 15 Nov., Mar MS GD 124/15/1153.

or compel Mar to fulfil his obligations to his wife and daughter.[67] It was worth a Hanoverian monarch's while to protect the marriage portion paid by a Whig duke.

Mar was lucky. The aftermath of the rebellion was swift government revenge. Besides estates forfeited in England and Scotland, '26 English rebels were executed, including 12 commoners, 13 gentlemen and one unrepentant Earl'.[68]

[67] BL Eg. MS 3531. 102–4; GD 124/17/647/2.   [68] Monod 1989: 327.

7

December 1715–August 1716

꠸꠸

Loss of Face: 'This fatal stroke, this unforseen distress'[1]

WHILE the Countess of Mar fought for financial survival in December 1715, Lady Mary was fighting for her life in earnest. The smallpox, which had killed her brother, which she had feared for her husband and baby, had got her at last. After a couple of weeks' incubation period, the sudden onset of severe symptoms must have frightened her badly. Her two-and-a-half-year-old son (who, like his sister later, was probably in the habit of playing about the room while she dressed or wrote her letters) would have been sent hurriedly away, with his nurse, to someone else's house. Her temperature soared to at *least* 103° fahrenheit. The sweat pouring from her did nothing to bring it down.[2] For two whole days her pulse raced, her back ached, and her head ached even worse. She was constipated; she vomited; she had a dreadful thirst.

On the third day of her illness the spots appeared, confirming what she already knew about her case. Her fever diminished, but in other respects her condition deteriorated rapidly. First a perceptible redness appeared around the roots of her hair, and within hours the heat, and itching, and pustules spread to cover almost the whole surface of her head and face, her body, and then her limbs. The spots itched; they filled with clear liquid; they went on itching. They ran together over large areas of her body. The word went out that she was 'exceedingly full'. Her whole skin, both where it was all spot and even where there was space between the spots, was so swollen that her face became literally unrecognizable. The mucous membranes of her mouth and throat, nostrils, eyes, and sexual parts, were also swollen, and terribly

---

[1] Cardelia again, on 'the Queen of Clubs thrice lost' ('Thursday', *E&P* 194).

[2] *E&P* 31; *CL* ii. 28. The high fever, inseparable from smallpox, would not have been measured: human temperature was still estimated by touch, and was thought never to exceed 96° F. (McGuigan 1937: 149–51).

painful. Breathing became difficult as her nose and throat closed up; her voice was hoarse and she had to keep spitting an unstaunchable flow of saliva.

After a week or so the watery substance in the pocks turned to thick yellow pus which smelled offensive, especially when the pocks burst, which friction from the bedclothes made impossible to avoid. Her temperature rose again in secondary or suppurative fever, bringing back with it all the familiar symptoms, as well as (perhaps) a nervous restlessness verging on delirium. If her mind was capable of grasping the fact, she would have known that she was past the worst, that she would live. A few days later the spots began to dry, and then to scab. Only the itching was worse than ever. The scabs began one by one to detach, leaving behind them reddish-brown marks which gradually bleached to ugly white dimples or pits.[3] During this process the question throbbed in her mind: how badly would she be marked?

She had the best medical attendance: Samuel Garth, Richard Mead, and John Woodward. All would have agreed with Thomas Sydenham that this, like other diseases, was 'nothing else but Nature's Endeavour to thrust forth with all her Might the Morbifick Matter'. They aimed to assist this fictional endeavour by bleeding and especially by purging, since it had been noticed that diarrhoea often accompanied the patient's 'turn' towards recovery.[4] But for the overall management of the disease there were competing treatments in vogue, the hot and the cold. The only thing common to the two treatments (as to childbirth custom) was darkness. In the one Lady Mary would have sweated through her tormented skin under layers of bedding, with the windows closed behind heavy curtains, and a roaring fire making shadows leap and flicker in the darkened room. In the other she would have shivered between carefully wetted sheets; even in December the window might have been open, the curtains shuddering in the draught. In either case the Duke Street traffic (if not hushed by snow) was probably quietened by straw spread on the cobbles, and a muffled knocker greeted the footmen calling at the door to enquire.

During the two days' crisis, around Christmas, 'the Town said she wold Die'. But as it became apparent that she was winning the battle, concern (friendly or otherwise) for her safety modulated rapidly into concern for what would happen to her looks. Those 'Ladies who know every minute of ye day, what her distemper takes, say she . . . will be very severely markt.' Some wit (perhaps one of the enviers whom *she* thought the inevitable

---

[3] This account based on *Encyclopaedia Britannica*, 11th edn., 1911.

[4] Garth and Mead, prominent Whigs, belonged to MWM's father's circle. Garth remained a friend of MWM. Mead, who wrote on the plague, 1720, and on smallpox, 1747, later fought a duel with Woodward (Pope, *Corr.* i. 442; MacMichael 1968; Sydenham 1669: 1). MWM hated being bled (*CL* i. 113–14).

concomitant of social success) said 'she was very full and yet not pitted [pitied]'. Her court career was assumed to be over, and Wortley said to be 'inconsolable for ye disappointment this gives him in ye carrier he had chalkt out of his fortunes'.[5] (Any more intimate emotion that he may have felt went unreported.) Lady Loudoun thought that with a 'pair of good Eyes' like Lady Mary's 'being mark'd is nothing', but only because complexions could be bought. This sounds double edged: Lady Loudoun had provided a forwarding address during Lady Mary's courtship, but their friendship did not endure.[6] Pope announced on 20 March in his 'Epistle to Mr. Jervas' that 'other Beauties envy *Wortley*'s Eyes'. This, even if it had been *written* before her illness, sounds like loyal optimism; but the context makes it problematic. The 'other' beauties are those as yet unborn, who will see the 'frail flow'r' of today's beauty only in so far as Jervas's painterly art can preserve it.[7] For the recipient, this compliment might only re-emphasize the present unhappy contrast between her portrait and herself.

In the event Lady Mary's 'very fine eye-lashes' succumbed to the infection and never grew back; their loss 'gave a fierceness to her eyes that impaired their beauty'. After a while the routine compliments on her looks began again; but they probably did not undo her sense of being changed.

Her recovery was variously reported on 3 and 26 January 1716, the latter the day Gay published his *Trivia, or the Art of Walking the Streets of London*. As she slowly gained strength 'under the apprehension of being totally disfigured', beyond her windows the town was gripped by a frost. With all the gusto of 1709–10, though for a shorter period, London took to the frozen Thames in a mood of carnival and metamorphosis. *Trivia*, which graphically paints a Thames ice-fair, had the advantage of appearing while a new one was actually in progress. Wortley profited from the abnormal demand for coal. But as Lady Mary emerged, transformed, from her sheltering darkness she found the snow 'painfull to the Sight'. To her, as to many of its victims, smallpox left the legacy of recurrent inflammations of the eyes.[8]

According to later family tradition, she used her closing eclogue, 'Satturday, The Small Pox', to express her own feelings while convalescent. It

---

[5] Lady Loudoun, 3 Jan., James Brydges, Lord Carnarvon (later 1st Duke of Chandos), 26 Jan. 1716 (Huntington MS LO 7417; Chandos Letter-Books (Huntington), xii. 255).

[6] Lady Loudoun, 22 Dec. 1715, Huntington MS LO 7412; *CL* i. 74, 94. Her husband was a friend of Lord Mar.

[7] Pope, TE vi. 157–9. Mahaffey thinks her danger 'discovered to Pope the depth of his regard for her'; for her he wrote 'Of her Sickness', misdating to keep the secret (TE vi. 10; Mahaffey 1963: 52–3). No evidence bears this out.

[8] *E&P* 35, 207; John Fox in *Anecdote Library* [1822], 49–50; Cheyne 1742: 176. Cosmetic ingredients and wig powder also caused inflamed eyes (Burton 1967: 316–17).

corresponds to Pope's 'Winter' in his *Pastorals* or Gay's 'Friday' in his *Shepherd's Week*, in completing the pastoral cycle with a poem about death. Montagu's closure, however, makes no mention of death itself, the terror of death, or even physical torment. Protected by a mask yet 'trembling at the light of Day', the convalescent Flavia is attended by sympathetic friends (as pastoral mourners traditionally are) and by complacently soothing physicians. It is her beauty that she mourns: that beauty which once brought her conquests and cash presents, which served her like an epic hero's strength and valour, which even 'promis'd Happyness for Years to come'. Its loss evokes from her the words and cadences typically evoked by death itself. 'Ye Operas, Circles, I no more must view! | My Toilette, Patches, all the World Adieu!'[9]

Lady Mary had lost a lot: greater beauty than Lady Hertford ever saw in any other face. But the real Lady Mary knew her beauty was not all the world.[10] Flavia is a creation finely balanced between satire, pathos, and self-representation: her complete submission to the beauty myth combines the astringency of the other eclogues with a plangent note of its own.

Besides its routine pain, terror, and loss, the smallpox brought Lady Mary one disaster all her own—and one benefit. Almost certainly it laid the foundation for her enduring fame. Her doctors were all Fellows of the Royal Society (of which her great-great-uncle was a founder member, but for which her sex rendered her ineligible). The Society had before this date received reports of the Turkish practice of 'engrafting' or inoculation (properly 'variolation') against smallpox. A Fellow of the Society, Woodward, had passed on the report of Emanuel Timoni or Timonius of Constantinople.[11] The extraordinary notion that immunity from a disease might be produced by deliberate exposure to it was a topic which might naturally arise between these learned men and their learned patient. It was an idea that was to bear fruit.

Her unique, personal disaster was this one. While she was thought to be dying, some friend to whom she had entrusted a copy of 'Roxana' showed it

---

[9] *E&P* 35, 201–4. Gay *ends*, in his 'Saturday', on poetic creation. Anne Finch used 'Flavia' for a 40-year-old woman still displaying her ruined beauty ('The Appology', 1903: 13). This was unpublished, but might be known to MWM.

[10] Hertford (wife of a man who figures in 'Tuesday'), thought MWM lucky in that beauty 'was only one of her various powers to charm' (17/6 Dec. 1740, Hertford–Pomfret, *Corr.* ii. 233–4). I do not agree with Marcia Pointon that Flavia's urge to disfigure the painting of her lost beauty constitutes a death-wish or a self-mutilation. For one thing it echoes Prior, 'When my own Face deters Me from my Glass, | And *Kneller* only shows what Celia was' ('Celia to Damon', 1941: 33; Pointon 1992: 46).

[11] English and Latin (Royal Society 1665– : no. 29 [for Jan.–Mar. 1714], 1717: 72–82). Timoni had seen no ill effects of inoculation, despite many false rumours. See Klebs 1913: 71; Grundy 1994c: 15. Constantinople is now Istanbul.

about at court. Lady Loudoun reported the fatal detail: 'the Princess has seen it.' Evidently Caroline's sense of humour, or her literary expertise, was unequal to decoding the poem's double turn and reading Roxana's condemnation as a compliment.[12] 'Poor Lady Mary will not know how to come to Court again', wrote Lady Loudoun—adding, interestingly: 'this wold put a body with a good assurance out of countenance, how will her modesty go through with it?'[13] An unexpected way out lay ahead of her. As early as 16 February Pope was arranging for Wortley to meet Sir William Trumbull, a former British Ambassador to Turkey, 'to advise about the value and profits of [the] Embassy'.[14] This opened the momentous opportunity of travelling to Turkey.

But if Lady Mary's career as courtier was set back, her career as poet was pushed on. 'Roxana' was news. Two people who purveyed word of her illness (Lord Carnarvon and Lady Loudoun) also purveyed copies of the poem. Its authorship was still supposed to be a secret, but it seems Lady Loudoun was right to feel sure it would very soon be all round town.

At some time or other, retitled 'Monday', it became the first of a set of six 'eclogues', one for each weekday. It is not clear whether the others followed in the order of their eventual names. Pope's beautiful presentation transcript is wrong in saying they were all 'Written in the Year, 1716'. At least half were probably earlier. 'Monday' was early 1715; 'Tuesday' is overtly or covertly connected with events of that year (a Mancini opera and the marriage of one of its speakers, Patch, alias Algernon Seymour, Lord Hertford); 'Thursday' was circulating by 26 January 1716, when Lady Mary was barely on her feet after smallpox.[15] 'Friday', which dwells on a pregnancy that ended in February 1716, was ready for Curll to snap up for illicit printing by about the end of that month. Only 'Wednesday' carries no clue as to a precise date; only 'Satturday' *certainly* postdates Lady Mary's smallpox. Written early in 1716, it closes a cycle which seems likely, therefore, to have been otherwise complete.

---

[12] Although 14 of the most controversial lines (including 'A Vertuous Princesse with a Court so lewd'), were probably not in the copy she saw.

[13] 3 Jan. 1716, Huntington MS LO 7417. Soon after Addison and Steele started *The Freeholder* and *Town-Talk* respectively (17 and 23 Dec. 1715) Lord Somers's mother was sent a copy of 'Roxana' and news of many more 'lampoons' ascribed rightly or wrongly to MWM: she was 'like to pay for 'em in some way or tother' (Margaret Cocks, Somers MSS, Reigate: copy in Halsband MSS). The 14 lines were absent, too, from copies MWM sent her friends.

[14] Pope, *Corr*. i. 406. At this date most diplomats saw the foreign service as a step towards high office at home (Black 1985: 67).

[15] Lady Loudoun, 7 Jan. 1716, Huntington MS MO 7419; Sherburn 1934: 204. *Hydaspes* was given in May and Sept. 1715 and May 1716 (Avery 1960: 355, 365, 402). Frances Thynne and Lord Hertford married in early Mar. 1715.

Unless Montagu's brush with death (or her exposure as a satirist) spurred her to an immediate burst of creativity, she must have been busy writing before her illness. The eclogues *look* like the fruit of collaboration between her, Pope, and Gay; but the extent of direct input from these two is questionable.[16] Pope's fair copy shows that he believed five of the six poems to be her work, and what he says about the other one, 'Friday', is inconsistent. Horace Walpole thought Pope and Gay were in on the first idea for the series; if so the idea may have sprung from 'Monday' (as 'Roxana'). Joseph Spence, a more engaged and sympathetic witness than Walpole, said 'Monday' gave the hint for the rest.[17] All six read like a woman's work: in the way they treat seduction and marriage, in the way they present female characters and predominantly female speakers, and in the way they modify standard conventions and motifs. I shall discuss them as Montagu's own work, while acknowledging that quite possibly—despite her explicit denial—more than one mind went to their shaping.

The group as a whole presents a Hobbesian world. Men (rakes, seducers, even doctors) compete with each other for dominance. Women, competitors with each other, are also the means by which men compete. Every one of these women utters some plaint about failure or disappointment sustained in the competitive arena. 'Tuesday' and 'Thursday', which are lighter than the rest, take the form of dialogues between two men and two women respectively, who strive to outdo each other, apparently in pleasure, really in kudos.[18] In 'Thursday, The Bassette Table', two ladies debate their addictions, one to cards and one to love; their competition ends in a tie. Their tastes are very similar: gambling is presented erotically, and love as highly materialistic; the competition is to be won by her who 'suffers most'. The devotee of love—the loser—was said by Walpole to be an authorial self-portrait (no evidence adduced), and the devotee of cards to be Lady Bristol, a courtier, mother of Lady Mary's future friend Lord Hervey.[19]

---

[16] MWM claimed all six as her own, in writing: both in H MS 256, and on seeing them in Dodsley's *Collection* (see pp. 107, 580). She there noted 'mine wrote at 17', a confusion of date which does not invalidate her claim. Cf. Halsband 1953: 237–50. Walpole reported her as 'owning' that the scheme was 'first thought of in company with Pope and Gay'. David Nokes supposes that Gay wrote 'Friday' and the other eclogues followed, MWM writing only 'most of' the two others pub. by Curll (Walpole, *Corr.* xiv. 292; Nokes 1995: 224–7).

[17] MWM 1977*a*; Walpole, *Corr.* xiv. 242–3 (he calls Gay's own eclogues 'far inferior'); see pp. 429–31. A copy of 'Thursday' which Pope kept, 'corrected by his own hand' with minimal variants, was printed in his *Works*, 1751, as his (vi. 56).

[18] Pope's print-style transcript of what he called Montagu's *Court Eclogs* places the two dialogues before all the single-speaker poems except the first (MWM 1977*a*). See Locke 1916 for Ombrelia.

[19] *E&P* 193–8. Lady Bristol, not yet 40, was probably now pregnant with her 20th child, 'few of whom lived to grow up' (Porter 1982: 41). She too was outraged over 'Coquetilla' 's appointment (discussed in 'Monday'); she tried hard for a court post, which eluded her until 1718 (Halsband 1973: 21–2, 34).

The debate between two young blades in 'Tuesday, St James's Coffee House' is a little harsher. Here the object of each is love—not love as personal fulfilment, but love as status symbol, notching up its score of ladies or preferably of countesses. Patch triumphs over Silliander, but his 'so important' conquest is inflected with mockery. Further mockery inheres in the context (known to the poem's original readers, lost today). Patch, the victor, married a fabulously wealthy fifteen-year-old heiress in 1715, while Silliander was still five years away from his marriage, apparently for love, to a Maid of Honour without resources.[20]

The fun of these poems lies partly in the pretence of giddy-headed delight in the accoutrements of their milieu—stays fashioned by Cosins, an erotic tableau fashioned by the woman who displays herself:

> Warm from her Bed, to me alone within,
> Her Nightgown fasten'd with a single Pin,
> Her Nightcloaths tumbled with resistless Grace
> And her bright Hair play'd careless round her Face.
> Reaching the Kettle, made her Gown unpin,
> She wore no Wastcoat, and her Shift was thin.

The privileged women in this poem enthusiastically connive in their own role as objects of exchange. 'Tuesday' offers, too, as Pope famously did in *The Rape of the Lock*, a glimpse beyond the charmed circle: while the opera-goers (the performers, the bourgeois, the lords and ladies) are variously preparing for the evening's entertainment, the bell of St James's, Piccadilly, is tolling in 'wretches' in 'tatter'd Riding hoods', for all the world as if these underclass figures had a monopoly on sin and penitence. Pope's wretches are criminals who 'hang that Jury-men may Dine'; Montagu's wretches are prostitutes—the only women whose sexual sale is stigmatized.[21]

Those of her eclogues which centre on a single speaker include the two ('Wednesday' and 'Friday') whose authorship really raises difficulty. This is the first occasion in Montagu's career for recalling how she supposedly said, 'No, Pope, no touching! For then, whatever is good for any thing will pass for yours, and the rest for mine.'[22] The monologue poems broach more delicate issues than the dialogues: 'Wednesday' and 'Friday' each presents a distinctively female and distinctly unorthodox viewpoint on a vexed gender issue. In 'Wednesday', Dancinda pleads with Strephon (who is demanding a sexual reward for his sighs and tears) to rest content with platonic affection: 'Love is a Child, and like a Child he plays.' She recapitulates their affair as

---

[20] Algernon Seymour m. Frances Thynne (b. 1699) in 1715; John Campbell m. Mary Bellenden in 1720.
[21] *E&P* 185–9; *Rape of the Lock*, i. 85.   [22] Pope 1797: ii. 332 n.

having been always extorted from her without reference to her own wishes, just like the material love-tokens which Patch and Silliander literally steal from the women they pursue. Strephon used 'ensnaring Art', Dancinda says, in first seducing her 'fond, uncautious Heart'; he promised then to rest content with friendship. Since then her love and her mental conflict have become more visible, threatening her reputation. Now he demands that she transgress her mother's maxims and soil her family honour; once she has done this she feels sure he will drop her.

Unlike the other eclogues, 'Wednesday' opens with no colourful scene-setting: no sedan chair, no card-table, no church bell ringing to service. Its perspective is inward from the start; only when speech dries up do the characters have recourse to the fan or snuffbox. At that moment, in bursts 'Made'moiselle' to warn of the imminent arrival of Dancinda's husband.

> The sighing Dame to meet her Dear prepares;
> While Strephon cursing slips down the back Stairs.

This poem has been read as if Dancinda's position, her wish for platonic affection, becomes wholly untenable when the reader learns she is married: as if only a virgin's ignorance could excuse the yearning for love without sexual demands. As Montagu herself had written, only a few years before, 'Too near he has approach'd, who is deny'd.' A feminist reading would be different. To start with, as the example of Lady Mary's personal circle shows, Dancinda cannot be assumed to have married for love, or to be receiving any emotional satisfaction or support from the husband whose approach closes the poem. She is a woman with sexual feelings, whose 'wishes' and 'burning Blushes' her lover calculatedly arouses although there is no prospect of her satisfying them without disgrace and self-hatred. The predatory, irresponsible male slips easily away, leaving the female shut up together with her unloved 'Dear'. The poet's own attitude remains ambiguous; but it is notable that Spence, who read 'Wednesday' under her tuition, as it were, took at face value the idealization of love as childish play.

It seems that Montagu received and rejected two suggestions from other people for ending this poem differently. In one, no husband appears, and Strephon achieves his desire. He completes his interrupted speech, contrasting human love (the male's for a single female) with the indiscriminate love of bull or horse (a contrast which the habits of Patch and Silliander call into question). The heroine then 'blush'd, while he put out the Light, | And all that follow'd was Eternal Night.' This ending Lady Mary kept among her papers—but not in the volume of her own authenticated verses, and not linked with this eclogue or with the series. The other rejected ending has

Dancinda *wish* that Strephon had achieved his desire instead of wasting the time in talk; Pope transcribed this in his presentation copy, and she defaced its beauty so far as to strike out his conclusion and substitute her own.[23]

This points to collaboration, but to contested collaboration, with Montagu resisting the remodelling of her unhappy, irresolute heroine (who wants the feelings of love without the action) as someone who needs a man to tell her what she *really* wants, a man to give her sex in place of love. This is the only poem of the six in which Walpole and Spence did not (on information from the author) identify the characters.

The case of 'Friday' is even more labyrinthine. Montagu's manuscript of this poem has 78 lines, of which 43 coincide word for word with a 106-line version which Gay published as his own. Gay left no claim to authorship *except* publication. Montagu made her claim twice. She copied her version into the volume which she inscribed 'all the verses and Prose in this Book were wrote by me, without the assistance of one Line from any other. Mary Wortley Montagu.' And she included it in her 'mine' in Dodsley's *Collection*. Pope's testimony is too inconsistent for his denials of her authorship to be taken at face value. In 1717, transcribing the other eclogues as hers, he omitted this one. In 1735 (at the height of his campaign against her) he told Spence that 'Friday' was 'almost wholly Gay's . . . There are only five or six lines new set in it by that lady.' He weakened this testimony by adding inaccurately, 'It was that which gave the hint and she wrote the other five eclogues to it.' Between these two dates (in 1729) he wrote a note to the *Dunciad* which is itself ambiguous, but which clearly identifies 'the true writer' of this and the other two poems published by Curll as 'a Lady of quality'.[24]

Each version of 'Friday' begins by picturing thirty-five-year-old Lydia, past her prime, lamenting 'th'Inconstancy of Man'.

> No Lovers now her morning Hours molest
> And catch her at her Toilette halfe undrest,
> The thundering Knocker wakes the street no more,
> Nor Chairs, nor Coaches, croud the silent door.

Montagu's Lydia, but not Gay's, looks out of the window as if her house is a trap or a prison (like Dancinda's).[25] In both versions the opening paragraph makes poetry out of daily life; but halfway through the paragraph Gay's

---

[23] *E&P* 189–93.

[24] *E&P* 198–200; Gay 1974: 572–3; H MS 256; Spence 1966: no. 236; Pope, TE v. 104. Gay pub. his version in his *Poems*, 1720, to which MWM subscribed. His modern editors argue that metrics prove the poem to be his. Walpole thought all six eclogues were by the same hand.

[25] I owe this point to Ann Messenger. MWM herself never used as title either 'town eclogues' (like Gay) or 'court eclogues' (like Curll).

version slips away into whimsy and fantasy, in which fashionable lapdogs, 'monkeys and mockaws' take the place of the traditional shepherdess's flock as well as of her 'perjur'd Beaus'. Already Gay's Lydia is more of an object, less of a subject, than Montagu's.

As Lydia's speech unfolds, Gay makes her dwell persistently on the way the younger Chloe has displaced her in Damon's affections. In his version she has only just learned that her rival is 'now what Lydia was before!'—that is, an object of adoration. Fearing Damon *will* marry Chloe, she comforts herself by scorning her rival's servile aptitude for marriage, and telling herself she is proudly ready to reject the rejecter. Cosmetics and her maid's flattery will carry her through.

Montagu's Lydia faces a different prospect: not that her lover may marry but that (married already) he is now veering away from her and back to his wife. It is Montagu's Lydia alone who wonders, 'To please your Wife am I unkindly us'd?' She, as his mistress, has been unsisterly towards his wife as long as she had the upper hand: 'Her Credulous Friendship, and her Stupid Ease, | Have often been my Jest in happier Days.' Now that she wants to take revenge on her lover, she hugs the thought that she, the mistress, dares do this as a wife would not. She perhaps sounds angrier than Gay's Lydia; she certainly raises questions about women's experience inside and outside marriage which Gay never broaches.

Though the overlap between the two versions is so large (they use the same words for closing as well as opening), they present entirely different stories.[26] Gay's Lydia faces the age-old, simple dilemma of being discarded for another (which Lady Mary had treated in several juvenile poems), and the social failure of remaining unmarried. Montagu's Lydia faces a sharply particularized dilemma posed by contemporary marriage practices; Montagu's poem is one of social criticism. 'A Miss for pleasure and a Wife for breed' suggests that her Lydia is discarded not so much for merely ageing as for the sake of inheritance imperatives which were unknown to ancient pastoral. The financial institution of modern marriage is the cause of her predicament, as it is of Dancinda's. And unlike Gay's Lydia but arguably like Dancinda, Montagu's is no pure figure of pathos, but has actively colluded with the system which now penalizes her.[27]

Overall, evidence suggests that 'Wednesday' and 'Friday' were created

---

[26] Montagu's Lydia, like Gay's, overestimates the durability of her beauty and power. For a slightly different comparative reading, see Messenger 1986: 84–107.

[27] Messenger notes that whereas Gay's Lydia avoids the shops out of sentiment, MWM's hates the idea of paying for things herself instead of receiving them as gifts from admirers—and that with her heartlessness she has admirable wit, courage, and clarity of self-assessment (1986: 89, 96).

not so much by collaboration as by proposition and answer, with some disagreement. It is not hard to imagine what aspects of 'Tuesday' and 'Thursday' might have been similarly co-produced and disputed. 'Monday' and 'Satturday' appear to be non-collaborative works by Montagu.[28] Such a summary puts her squarely in the position of primary author.

Her version of 'Friday' sounds, as Gay's does not, as if it were closely tailored to some real-life situation. Sure enough, Lydia, Damon, and Chloe were identified in Walpole's and Spence's notes to her poem as Mary (Hale) Coke, her lover (James, 3rd Earl of Berkeley), and Lady Berkeley. The last of these, married four or five years but not much past twenty-one, was the former Lady Louisa Lennox, whose beauty Lady Mary had celebrated in one of her juvenile poems. Mrs Coke had borne a child in 1714 which was assumed to be not her husband's but Lord Berkeley's; Lady Berkeley bore his son and heir on 13 February 1716. To complete the poem's appeal as topical scandal, Lady Berkeley had landed a post as Lady of the Bedchamber to Princess Caroline.[29] 'Friday''s scandalous potential almost matched that of 'Monday' ('Roxana'). Very likely 'Tuesday', 'Wednesday', and 'Thursday' conceal equally fascinating titbits of insider gossip, if only we could decode them.

In February 1716 there were plenty who could. And just as someone had already shown one of the poems to Princess Caroline, now someone showed three of them to the publisher Edmund Curll. Curll was a pirate, a purveyor of smut and scandal, a 'foul bird acting as scavenger for a literary battle-field'.[30] Pope, whom he already regarded as good copy or fair game, was more so than ever now, as a Catholic in the aftermath of the Jacobite uprising. The second volume of Pope's *Iliad* appeared on 24 March; on 26 March Curll published a slim octavo volume of *Court Poems*, 'Price Six-Pence'. Its contents were the poems which Montagu calls 'Thursday', 'Monday', and 'Friday', which Curll titled 'The Basset-Table. An Eclogue', 'The Drawing-Room', and 'The Toilet'. Curll issued them through James Roberts's pamphlet-shop, with his usual sharp eye to marketing. The title-page, naming no author, says that they were found in a pocketbook (or wallet) picked up in Westminster Hall (seat of the lawcourts) on the last day of Lord Winton's trial for his part in the rebellion.[31]

---

[28] Yet even the highly personal 'Satturday' bears traces of more than one mind. The refrain 'Beauty is fled, and——is no more' parallels something Pope wrote as a joke in a letter dated 15 July 1715 (*Corr.* i. 307).

[29] She was to die of smallpox just a year after Lady Mary survived it.

[30] Sherburn 1934: 161. For Curll's admission of responsibility, and W. Moy Thomas's speculation that MWM arranged it herself, see MWM 1977a: 239 and nn.

[31] Grundy 1971: 220. George Seton, Earl of Winton, was condemned to death (which, however, he escaped) on 19 Mar. Curll was later arrested for printing an unlicensed *Account* of his trial (TE v. 104). It was

Curll's newspaper advertising for his pamphlet promised a 'Preface giving some Account of the Author';[32] but his 'Advertisement' prefacing the pamphlet kept the promise only equivocally, by juggling with tantalizingly opposed theories as to who that author was. The gilded youth of St James's Coffee-House (hang-out of Patch and Silliander) judge it to be 'a Lady of Quality': i.e. Montagu, though only the *cognoscenti* would know her identity. The clientele of Button's, *the* literary coffee-house, favours Gay, asserting the likeness of 'Thursday' to his *Shepherd's Week*. Curll's chosen umpire, a Chelsea 'Gentleman of distinguish'd Merit' (i.e. Addison), asserts that the author could be none other than 'the Judicious Translator of Homer', i.e. Pope.

This was angled to arouse maximum debate and gossip; the finger was pointed at Pope, Gay, and implicitly at Lady Mary (though only Gay, who had least status, was actually named). Curll's offence was not that he blackened Lady Mary's name at court: that had been done already.[33] He did real damage to Gay, who was still hoping for court employment. Lady Mary *probably* felt the publicity to be unwelcome and demeaning. Pope took it that way, since he later presented himself as heroic defender—or at any rate avenger—of her honour. He also had a protective loyalty to Gay, and already a long score of his own to settle with Curll.[34]

His revenge as he described it went like this. Two days after *Court Poems* appeared, Bernard Lintot (a Pope ally, publisher of his Homer) invited Curll to discuss business over an evening drink. During this Pope dropped in, 'under pretence of business with Mr. Lintot'. He reprimanded Curll mildly about *Court Poems*, appeared to accept his excuse and apology, and invited him to drink to their reconciliation. Curll's drink looked like 'common sack, yet it was plain, by the pangs this unhappy stationer felt soon after, that some poisonous drug had been secretly infused therein'. The prose is the more seemly part of Pope's anonymous *Full and True Account of a Horrid and Barbarous Revenge by Poison, On the Body of Mr. Edmund Curll*, published only a few days later. Mock-heroic lines on its title-page plumb the depths of bad taste:

Oldmixon who gave Curll the poems. This was also the month that Pope and his parents left their Binfield home. Mahaffey suggests that slips in the title-page of *Court Poems* and the passage of veiled hints at authorship indicate last-minute changes in material (1963: 71).

[32] *Post Man*, 27 Mar.

[33] His text (inaccurate in many details) agrees with the early MS copies of 'Monday' in omitting 14 potentially offensive lines.

[34] He said Curll 'meant to publish' the poems as MWM's work, 'but being first threaten'd, and afterwards punish'd, for it by Mr. *Pope*' he switched to printing them as Pope's. This may or may not mean that some threat from Pope preceded publication (TE v. 104). Halsband argues that Pope wanted mainly to protect Gay and avenge himself (1953: 237–50; 1956: 54).

> So when Curll's stomach the strong drench oercame,
> (Infused in Vengeance of insulted fame)
> The Avenger sees, with a delighted eye,
> His long jaws open and his colour fly;
> The while his guts the keen emetics urge,
> Smiles on the vomit and enjoys the purge.

This extraordinary act of physical violence was no fiction. Nearly twenty years later Curll had not forgotten or forgiven his dose of 'half a Pint of Canary, antimonially prepared'.[35] Pope followed up his first pamphlet with *A Further Account of the most deplorable Condition of Mr. Edmund Curll*. This tells how, after his physical travails, Curll gradually lost his wits: first he spoke politely to customers, then he began saying his prayers, then he confessed his business frauds. Pope must have gloated over his title-page line, 'To be published Weekly': a threat to prolong the ordeal by pamphlet indefinitely, as Swift had done to the astrologer Partridge.[36]

Pope did not carry out this threat. But other repercussions continued. Oldmixon (or someone else in his name) publicly announced that he had nothing to do with the preface to *Court Poems*. Curll asserted Pope's authorship of them on the title-page of *State Poems*, 19 May (and pinned on Montagu, while omitting a few letters from her name, something else she perhaps never saw).[37] He kept reissuing *Court Poems* as Pope's (with accretions) for twenty years; the two last dates, 1726 and 1736, suggest some impish sense of anniversary. He increased the nuisance value to Pope of his first reprint by titling it *Pope's Miscellany* and printing it as an elegant little duodecimo in Elzevier type: the very style which Pope usually chose when he wanted to give his work a classic cast. Curll, in fact, dressed up his stolen goods to pass as one of Pope's specialities. Customers must have been taken in, for copies of the true and false 'Elzevirs' were sometimes bound up together.[38]

While Gay's career may have been damaged and Pope's enemies increased by this affair, Lady Mary's court prospects seem not to have been affected. The princess apparently came round after 'Roxana'; Lady Mary's stock with the king continued high (despite her smallpox scarring).[39] But in

---

[35] Curll's preface to Pope 1735: pp. vii–viii.   [36] Sherburn 1934: 169–71.

[37] *Flying Post*, 3 Apr. The salacious, name-dropping 'Ramble. Between Belinda a Demy-Prude, and Cloe a Court-Coquette' is said to be adapted from La Fontaine by 'a fam'd Female *Wit* (the Lady *W—y M—gue*'). Probably Curll teased Pope further in two pamphlets by [Oldmixon] and [Dennis], both pub. 31 May (Guerinot 1969: 41).

[38] For the true ones Pope used his other publisher, Tonson (Foxon and McLaverty 1991: 29; *Whitehall Evening Post*, 29 July 1725). One such twin binding is Bod. Don. f. 497.

[39] See p. 128. Lady Louisa says the Prince of Wales competed with the king for her loyalty even after 1718 (Hunter 1831: 322).

the long run she had not the temperament of a courtier. Her teenage vision
of poets as 'Haughty in rags and proudly poor', the episode with Craggs, her
disgust at the Prince of Wales's treatment of his inferiors, her many later
comments on the tedium and stupidity of courts, all indicate that she could
never have emulated the starry-eyed devotion to Caroline that was later
voiced by, for instance, Lady Hertford and Lady Pomfret. Gay's 'Friday'
calls a perjured courtier 'cringing'; hers calls him 'crafty'. Perhaps she saw
court life as offering more scope for action than did Gay;[40] but their distaste
for it seems to have been one more thing which these two, surprisingly, had
in common.

~~*~~

Her husband equalled or outdid her in disillusion. Before Walpole's promotion at the Treasury he too had written an essay on the politics of the
moment: 'On the State of Affairs when the King Entered'. This brief sketch
opens with narrative panache but narrows into a single-minded attack on
Walpole. Wortley sees him as duping and manipulating men of higher rank
than himself, widening the gap between Whig and Tory, damaging the
king's popularity by his bad judgement. The king and Halifax come in for
criticism too; so does the whole handling of Treasury affairs. Walpole, says
Wortley, is 'already looked upon as the chief minister', a status he owes
largely to his brother-in-law Townshend (and so implicitly to Lady Mary's
friend Dolly). Wortley regrets King William's days, when Treasury Commissioners were 'all men of great figure', not upstarts like Walpole. He
thinks the Treasury is a reliable ladder to greatness, and Walpole ought to be
kept off it. He refers indirectly to himself as the only Treasury man who is
not Walpole's creature. He is unable to 'hinder any of [Walpole's] projects',
and can only 'inform the King of his affairs'. The essay explains the rift
between Court Whigs (bad) and Country Whigs (good but unrewarded).[41]
It breaks off at the question, 'WHAT IS A COUNTRY GENTLEMAN?'[42]

   Wortley's 'State of Affairs' provides a coded account of his career so far,
as one-man, behind-the-scenes opposition to Walpole. He told Addison that
Walpole was so keen to get him out of the Treasury that he offered him, with
the king's approval, an appointment worth £3,000 a year.[43] All this helps to
explain the later persistence of his anti-Walpole stance. Where Lady Mary's
account depicts the early days of George's reign as a fluid situation driven by

---

[40] Another observation of Messenger's.
[41] The only exception, says EWM, was the favour briefly enjoyed by his close friend Sir Peter King,
whom Hervey later thought dilatory and irresolute (1931: i. 243–4).
[42] MWM 1861: i. 135–41.   [43] 29/18 July 1717 (Tickell MSS: copy in Halsband MSS).

the complex motives of a number of strong-willed individuals, his presents a closed, self-sustaining, almost totalitarian system. The actual course of events turned out to be rapid change leading to a period of stability, but not of a kind welcome to Wortley. Already the Whig junta which had guided the party in opposition was melting away, with the successive deaths of Wharton, Halifax, and Somers. Its survivors, Stanhope and Sunderland, were to break with the new men, Walpole and Townshend, during Wortley's absence in Turkey, with disastrous results for Wortley's public career.[44]

Meanwhile, he ran no risk in criticizing the government in manuscript. But by having her name (thinly concealed) bandied about in print—in low pamphlets about an infamous publisher's disgusting bodily processes— Lady Mary lost caste. Wortley, who was proud as well as disaffected, must have found all this very distasteful. It was altogether no wonder that he showed an interest in the post of ambassador to the Ottoman Porte (or Empire), whose latest war with the Republic of Venice had lasted since late 1714.[45] Previous ambassadors to Turkey who were 'men of great figure' included Lady Mary's great-great-uncle the 2nd Earl of Denbigh. Wortley declined the post at first (it would not equal £3,000 a year), but accepted when he was promised generous compensation at the end of his term of office. His appointment was announced in the newspapers in 7 April 1716, and confirmed by the Levant Company (who held the charter for trade in the area, and would part-fund the embassy) on 10 May.[46] He would replace Sir Robert Sutton, a north country associate of his. Sutton had served in Constantinople for fifteen years; Wortley committed himself to stay for five at least.[47]

The small print was still to be negotiated, but long before the Levant Company's rubber stamp was in place Lady Mary, probably still masked against the daylight, was back in administrative mode. She was mulling over decisions. Servants' liveries for the embassy: should they be plain, or laced, or laced with threads of silver? A chaplain: where could she find one sufficiently orthodox? A nursemaid for her son: a candidate from Wharncliffe must make up her mind whether she wanted the job, 'for tis necessary the child should be some time accustom'd to his maid before he goes a Journey under her Care'. All her letters, no matter how short, tell her husband, 'Your Son presents his duty.' At nearly three, he 'improves ev'ry day in his

---

[44] Holmes and Speck 1967: 34.   [45] *Dawks's News Letter*, 1 Jan. 1715.
[46] He later began to reckon the 'Usual Extrodinarys' or perquisites of the post from 30 May, and the Levant Company's pay from 13 June (Halsband MSS). It was not till 1803 that the government took this appointment out of the hands and off the payroll of the Company (Wood 1925: 538).
[47] Levant Co. to Onslow, 8 Oct. 1717, Tickell MSS.

Conversation, which begins to be very entertaining to me'. He was almost ready to be 'breeched': to make the transition from infantile—that is female—to male attire.[48]

She was still playing the obedient, invaluable wife, as she had probably done through the dizziest period of her court ambitions. She urged Wortley (while he was in Yorkshire on business in April) to take care of his health. She kept him abreast of political news: how Sir Joseph Jekyll had voted and would vote next time, how the House had divided, what was thought about the fact that Wortley (a known proponent of Place Bills) would now hold both a parliamentary seat and a diplomatic post. On this topic she added, 'You know your own affairs better than I do, and shall therefore say nothing.'

A chaplain, Mr Crosse, was engaged at £100 a year. So was a surgeon, Charles Maitland, a bachelor Scot of nearly fifty.[49] Twenty suits of livery were ordered. Sarah Chiswell was invited, but her sister and brother-in-law thought the journey too dangerous to contemplate. On 5 June George I signed the Treaty of Westminster, which brought Austria (that is, the Habsburg Empire) one step closer to joining Venice in war against Turkey. England had badly wanted to prevent this, and had been trying for at least a year to stave it off.[50] More and more it seemed that these great powers might be at war before His Britannic Majesty's ambassador could intervene.

The ambassador's credentials were signed on 2 July 1716; preparations hotted up. That month Pope wrote what was meant to be his half of a joint letter: he addressed a half-filled sheet to Lady Rich. Lady Mary was to fill the facing half of it, addressed to Lady Rich's husband, Sir Robert. If she did so, her letter is lost. Pope was crafting for her a style of flattering gallantry. He called her to observe 'how all the letters that compose these words lean forward after Lady *M*'s letters', and protested that she must not go to Constantinople without knowing the depth of his devotion.[51]

Pope put in a plea for some of her 'last Moments'—he was applying the metaphor of death to this journey to another world. He was taking it hard. His letters make it clear that her decision to travel with her husband, rather than wait at home with their child for his return, was seen as unusual: he liked to present her as a heroic wife but a negligent mother. Her sister Mar and her early friends Jane Smith (Hermensilda) and Sarah all seem to have thought

---

[48] Buck 1979: 205.

[49] The Company generally conceded to the ambassador its right to select the chaplain. Maitland was 80 when he d. at Aberdeen, 1748 (Wood 1925: 539; *Scots Magazine*, x. 102).

[50] McKay 1977: 161–3. Britain's obligation to help the Empire against Turkey had ended in late 1715 with the Third Barrier Treaty.

[51] Pope, *Corr.* i. 345–6.

she would repent her boldness. Someone wrote a poem 'On a Lady of Quality going to Turky', which used her early name of Clarinda, but stayed unprinted for nearly thirty years. Someone else wrote a pamphlet as 'E. Parker, Philomath', elaborately describing a comet appearing over Constantinople to mark the arrival of 'a British Ambassadress of marvellous Beauty, with a long Train of Attendants'.[52]

On 23 July 1716, a week before their eventual departure, Lady Mary's stepmother bore a daughter, Lady Caroline Pierrepont. Lady Mary might have thought wryly about this new and heavier disappointment of her father's wish for a son and heir, echoing her own birth twenty-seven years before. She never managed to feel sisterly towards Lady Caroline. But she was engrossed with her own future: ''twas a sort of dying to her friends and country: but 'twas travelling, 'twas going farther than most other people go, 'twas wandering, 'twas all whimsical, and charming, and so she set out with all the pleasure imaginable.' As in the days of the courtship, and 'Naples', romance supplied her model: it was because she 'had always delighted in romances and books of travels' that she was 'charmed with the thoughts of going into the East'.[53]

---

[52] *London Magazine*, Nov. 1744: 564–5; *Mr. Joanidion Fielding. His True and Faithful Account of the Strange and Miraculous Comet . . .*, Dec. 1716 (quoted in Nicolson and Rousseau 1968: 184–6).

[53] BL Eg. MS 3531; Spence 1975: 357. She may have owned the 'Persian Tales' (see p. 135).

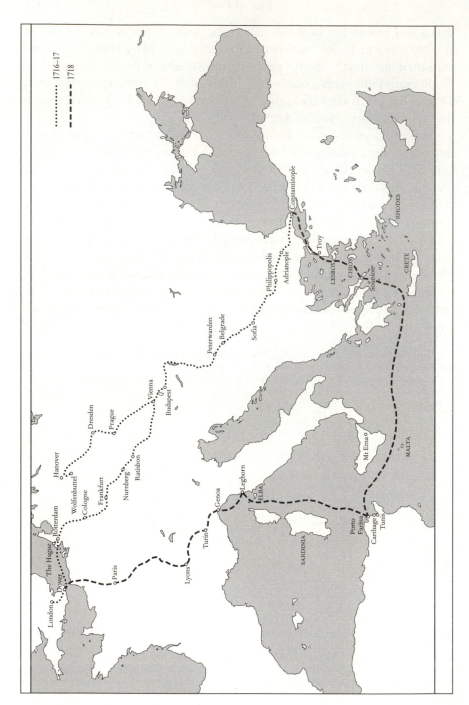

Map I. Travels 1716–18

8

August 1716–January 1717

꙰

Overland: 'having ... allmost made the tour of Europe'[1]

FRIENDS and well-wishers came to wave them off on 1 August. For travelling Lady Mary wore a riding habit, a style whose plain jacket and skirt were often seen as masculine. Pope later presented it as a matter of dispute whether or not she had set out in a black full-bottomed wig: a huge, elaborate, expensive, and exclusively male item of dress.[2]

At last their procession of heavy vehicles was on the move, carrying twenty liveried servants as well as the family party.[3] At this date there was only one bridge over the Thames. They rolled north along Whitehall to where Charing Cross stood between the Royal Mews and Northumberland House (no Trafalgar Square existed). They bowled along the Strand, through the area where their married life had begun. They passed under Temple Bar: Wren's neoclassical design of 1670, incongruously adorned with relics of executed Jacobites (which may have aroused a thought for Lord Mar in exile at Avignon). Over Fleet Bridge they rumbled and through Lud Gate, horses straining up the steep incline of Ludgate Hill, and past the great, new bulk of St Paul's. Whether they took the broader Cheapside and Poultry, or the narrower Watling Street and Cannon Street, they reached Fish Street Hill at last, and descended in the incessant stream of coaches, carts, riders, and walkers jerking to a halt and jostling on again as they threaded themselves into the needle's eye of London Bridge. Here the shops that lined the thoroughfare, built on the bridge, jutted out with each storey so that they almost met overhead, in the manner of City of London

---

[1] *CL* i. 444.

[2] *CL* i. 313, Pope, *Corr.* i. 368. Violet Stuart Wortley says, on no known evidence, that Kingston now fitted MWM out lavishly with jewels ([1948]: 38).

[3] As on earlier, more domestic journeys, the heavy baggage was going by water the whole way (Halsband 1956: 58).

houses before the Great Fire and the rebuilding. The traffic coming against
them included herded animals and towering loads of summer produce for
the feeding of London. In high summer the city must have smelt its
strongest.

St Saviour's, Southwark, guarded the south side of the bridge as Wren's
St Magnus Martyr guarded the north. Heading for Gravesend in the mouth
of the Thames, they bore eastwards. Perhaps, like Lady Mary in 1739, they
crossed Blackheath. Perhaps, like one of Lady Mary's fictional characters,
they ordered their coachman to stop 'on a rising Ground from whence it was
possible to survey that great Town', and look their last at the spires and the
masts of shipping in the Thames. They did not know when they would see
home again. They expected to spend much more time in Turkey, but much
less on the journey, than in the event they did. It seems that at this stage
they meant to cross the Alps, take ship at Leghorn, and sail through the
Mediterranean.[4]

The next day found them at Gravesend, embarking on a 'Yatcht' for the
Channel crossing. It was no doubt a less sporting vessel than Lady Mary's
word suggests. There was no wind, but the captain persuaded them to put to
sea anyhow. For two days they were becalmed; then 'the Wind blew so hard
that none of the Sailors could keep their feet'. The captain gave way to panic.
Lady Mary was 'so lucky neither to suffer from Fear or sea sickness'. She
dropped a note (not extant) to Pope to say she had survived the crossing;[5]
but she was so keen to get forward that she had the longboat put out to set
them ashore at Hellevoetsluis, where they hired 'Voitures' to get to Rotterdam faster than by water. Rotterdam had a recent history as a centre of the
republic of letters, the workplace of Pierre Bayle and Jean Le Clerc. This,
with the other Dutch towns of Hellevoetsluis and Brill, was Lady Mary's
first 'abroad'. Her recorded response was 100 per cent enthusiasm.

Brill charmed her with its neatness, but Rotterdam 'presented me a new
scene of Pleasure'. She loved the nicely paved streets, the cleanliness ('I'll
assure you I walk'd allmost all over the Town Yesterday, incognito, in my
slippers without receiving one spot of Dirt'), the crowds ('such busie faces,
all in motion'), the efficient canal transport, the splendid shops, the variety
and ingenuity of the women's hairstyles, the prevailing fondness for driving
a good bargain, the absence of 'loathsome Cripples' like those who begged
in the streets of London. Protestant Holland was probably the spur for her
brief prose essay on 'The Luxury and degeneracy of the Romans', which she
headed 'Wrote when I begun my first Travels'. So far, she reported, 'I make

⁴ 'Louisa', *RW* 74; Pope, *Corr.* i. 358, 363.   ⁵ *CL* i. 248–9; Pope, *Corr.* i. 356.

no complaints, and if I continue to like travelling as well as I do at present, I shall not repent my project.'[6]

When she wrote these words is uncertain. Almost none of the letters she despatched from her embassy travels survives, though she was an assiduous correspondent, as can be seen from her 'Heads' of the letters she actually sent from Turkey. The comments quoted on Rotterdam come from the embryo travel book, in epistolary form, which she shaped after the event: perhaps as early as some weeks, or perhaps as late as some years, afterwards. She probably based it mainly on her diary; she gets the dates wrong too often to have been transcribing actual letters written *on* those days. For this travel 'book' she selected from among the accounts she had written, and picked a small handful from among her actual correspondents (their names veiled by initials) as recipients of reconstituted letters which were meant to be read as literature. In the album the first recipient is 'dear Sister' (Frances, that is); the next were old friends of stay-at-home inclinations: Jane Smith and Sarah Chiswell.

From Rotterdam the party doubled back to the Hague, an oddity of route which may possibly mark the first change in their travel plans. For even before they set out, on 25 July by English reckoning or Old Style (which was 5 August in the New Style of the Continent), an Austrian army under Prince Eugene had almost wiped out the invading Turks at Peterwardein or Peterwaradin. This radically shifted the balance of power.[7] The embassy party was one day to hear more of this battle. Meanwhile, as soon as the news reached London and statesmen had taken stock, countermanding orders must have set out after Edward Wortley Montagu, whose time becalmed at sea would have made him easy to overtake. He then headed for Vienna.

Meanwhile, whatever the diplomatic agenda, the Dutch countryside delighted Lady Mary as much as the towns, and for the same qualities: the garden-like neatness and order, and the convenience of the 'large Canals full of Boats passing and repassing'. The Hague, like Rotterdam, reminded her of London, and set her to comparing prices in the shops. Nijmegen, set on steeply rising ground above a river, reminded her vividly of Nottingham; she told Sarah Chiswell how she had looked out over the Dutch fields and thought of the situation of Holme Pierrepont. At Nijmegen she first sounded a matched pair of favourite traveller's themes: modern improvements and religious barbarism, typified by the moving bridge on the one hand and the broad-brimmed hat and 'extrordinary antick Gestures' of a Calvinist

---

[6] *CL* i. 249–50; essay (unpub.) H MS 81. 34–5.
[7] McKay 1977: 161–2. Britain, alone in Europe, had not yet adopted Pope Gregory's modifications to Julius Caesar's calendar. British dates were therefore 11 days behind the Continent's.

preacher on the other.[8] All through Europe she celebrated the modern. Medieval or 'old built' towns left her cold.

After the United Netherlands came a succession of German princely states and merchant cities. Vienna was slightly to the south and far to the east; their immediate route lay through the still unindustrialized Rhineland. Few people today know what it is like to take a long journey at horses' pace. Moving faster than walking, more slowly than bicycling, to the rhythms of larger bodies, with no need to watch your footing, you develop an intimate acquaintance with the verges of the road. The surrounding landscape changes shape slowly, slowly, till you realize with surprise that some hill which has been your companion it seems for ever, has finally vanished behind. And none of us knows what it was like to travel in a carriage, which was draughty in the shade, stuffy in the sun, and cramped at all times. Its windows framed and curtailed the view; unlike a car, it did not go fast enough to escape its own dust. When they travelled post, each stage ended in a strange inn-yard, where sweating horses were unhitched and fresh ones backed into position, while grooms and porters shouted in unknown languages and innkeepers came bowing and scraping and offering refreshment. Where no post route existed, with systems for passing horses back and forth from the various stages, they had to slacken their pace so that the horses could keep going all day.

Nevertheless Lady Mary claims that they hoped to reach Cologne in two days from Nijmegen, a distance of at least a hundred miles, with a single set of hired horses. The first inn was 'but very indifferent'; the second (where they were forced to stop three hours short of Cologne when the horses could go no further) could muster only 'a room not at all better than a Hovel . . . where the wind came in from a thousand places'. She travelled with her own bed (a feather-bed to lie on and covers to lie under, that is, not a bedstead), but that night she slept in her clothes. For part of the night, that is: they were up at daybreak and reached Cologne about 6 a.m., in time for another three hours' sleep.

On this she felt perfectly recovered from all her fatigues, and was out sightseeing at once: incognita again, so that the handsome young Jesuit who showed her the town's single Catholic church (the seventeenth-century St Maria Himmelfahrt) amused her with free-spoken 'complements and railerys' which he would never have offered if he had known her rank. She was struck by the cost and magnificence of the altars, images, and reliquaries, but 'could not help murmuring in my heart at that profusion of pearls,

[8] *CL* i. 251–2.

Diamonds and Rubys bestow'd on the adornment of rotten teeth, dirty rags, etc.' She always mocked the apparatus of piety, especially 'the farce of Relicks': was it breaking a Commandment, she wondered, to covet St Ursula's pearl necklace, 'an Image not being certainly one's Neighbour'? As for the skulls of this saint's eleven thousand virgins, sharing the honours of her medieval church with its dazzling golden chamber (1643): since Ursula was supposedly English the only possible line to take about them was nationalistic complacency.[9]

Cologne was 'old built': Lady Mary found the wine at supper more worthy of comment than the medieval splendours outside. By the time she reached Nuremberg on the far side of Germany, another couple of hundred miles up the Rhine, she had found a pattern for her mixed responses to the various places she saw. Under absolute governments, like those of the German princelings, society was corrupted by dependence: half the potential workers were beggars instead, the towns were filthy and run down, and people of quality were 'tawder'd out' in shabby finery. The 'free Towns', self-governing societies of traders, were thriving if not luxurious, their 'shops loaded with Merchandize, and the commonalty clean and cheerful'.[10] This opinion, of course, like her general anti-Catholicism, was politically correct both by national standards and by those of the intellectual Enlightenment.

At Regensburg (which the English called Ratisbon) they joined the Danube. This town, seat of the Holy Roman Empire, where the Imperial Diet convened, was the first place they halted on their journey—because she had caught a cold, Lady Mary said. But, cold or no cold, she went sightseeing and society-seeing. Mme von Wrisberg, the Hanoverian envoy's wife, entertained her graciously, and introduced her 'to all the assemblys'. Lady Mary was impatient with the diplomatic atmosphere of long-inherited feuds and cold shoulders. 'I have not been here above a Week and yet I have heard from allmost every one of 'em the whole History of their wrongs . . . in hopes to draw me to their Party, but I think it very prudent to remain Neuter.' Since the goal of everyone's competitive striving was the title of Excellency, she proposed making the title universal; her irreverence was not well received.[11]

---

[9] *CL* i. 252–4, 255. Thomas Nugent reported sixty years later that even Catholics disbelieved this story—thought to turn on the misreading of a name, 'Undecimilla' (1778: ii. 320). The skulls were still shown in the 19th century.

[10] She reflected that sumptuary laws, which forbade dressing above one's station, would prevent many self-inflicted debt crises. She regretted, however, the lack of English-style country houses (*CL* i. 254–6, 286).

[11] *CL* i. 256–8.

After the roads, the journey by water down the Danube from Ratisbon to Vienna was a delight both aesthetically and practically. Lady Mary loved the views: the 'woods, rocks, Mountains cover'd with Vines, Fields of Corn, large Citys, and ruins of Ancient Castles', also the speed achieved by twelve oarsmen and a strong current, also the heated cabins and kitchens: 'all the conveniencys of a Palace'. At Vienna they broke their journey for more than two months, waiting on the emperor's convenience. While their son, none the worse for a month cooped up in coach or barge, had more scope for play, his father faced a challenging task. He was received the very day after his arrival by the Emperor Charles VI. Wortley was to apply his best abilities to initiating peace negotiations. The emperor was delighted that his general, Prince Eugene, had just thrashed the sultan, but continuing the war was another matter. The next step must be to wrest Belgrade from the Turks; but Europe now hoped to face them down without having to attack Belgrade.[12]

For the moment Lady Mary had to drop the role of traveller for that of ambassador's wife. She vividly described Vienna: magnificent palaces whose fronts could not be seen because they stood in such narrow streets (the *most* exquisite palaces, like the *gartenpalast* of the Reichsvizekanzler, Count von Schönborn, lay beyond the city walls), and incredibly tall houses, whose five or six storeys looked to her as if builders had made more space 'by claping one Town on the Top of another'. In these houses, amazingly, the luxuriously furnished 'Apartments of the greatest Ladys and even of the Ministers of state are divided but by a Partition from that of a Tailor or a shoe-maker'. Leaders of society hastened to invite the Wortley Montagus to dinner; the French ambassador shrewdly reported that they were studying local life on the one hand and feeding local gossip on the other. About a week after their arrival, Lord Harrold, a grand tourist whose mother had befriended Wortley during his courtship, called repeatedly without finding him free. The message that 'Being very busie that day he could not recieve me' clearly gave offence.[13]

Lady Mary had more leisure. She went to the first night of Johann Josef Fux's new opera, *Angelica vincitrice di Alcina*, composed to celebrate the recent victory over the Turks (as well as the birth of an archduke). It opened on a Sunday, which as a Protestant she found surprising. The splendid auditorium at the Favorita Palace was outdoors, and the dazzling audience was thrown into disarray by a shower. By way of contrast she went to a popular comedy, or farce, by Josef Anton Stranitzky, a 'brilliant and irresistibly

---

[12] *CL* i. 259, 271; Schaub to Townshend, 16 Sept. 1716, SP 80/33. They arrived in Vienna on 14/3 Sept.

[13] Schloss Schönbrunn was begun by Johann Bernhard Fischer von Erlach. Harrold left for Hanover in Oct. (*CL* i. 259–61; 12/23 Sept., MS at Beds. Record Office, L30/8/33/19).

comic talent from the people', in his new Kärntnertor Theatre. The language was laced with 'Styrian-Salzburg-Viennese dialect', but a lady with her provided on-the-spot translation, so that she missed none of the obscene language or the low frauds perpetrated by Jupiter and Mercury in the guise of mortals. For the climax she needed no translator: 'the 2 Sosias very fairly let down their breeches in the direct view of the Boxes, which were full of people of the first Rank that seem'd very well pleas'd with their Entertainment.'[14] She saw round the emperor's treasure-house and art gallery, and visited some of the city's many convents. She noted, too, the high prices, caused by reliance on imports and dearth of home-produced goods, which in turn she ascribed to 'the want of Genius and Industry in the people'.[15]

The high point of Lady Mary's visit, described early in the Vienna Embassy Letters, was reception at court. The requisite costume was not only formal but 'more monstrous and contrary to all common sense and reason than tis possible for you to imagine'. She addressed her embassy account of it to sister Frances (her chosen recipient for almost all her accounts of exotic clothes), and did her level best to realize it for her mind's eye. The headdress had a foundation 'about a yard high', covered in both false and natural hair, 'it being a particular beauty to have their heads too large to go into a moderate Tub . . . Their whalebone petticoats out-do ours by several yards Circumference and cover some Acres of Ground. You may easily suppose how much this extrordinary Dresse sets off and improves the natural Uglyness with which God Allmighty has been pleas'd to endow them all generally.'

Despite this robust resistance to Viennese fashion, Lady Mary was thoroughly charmed with the empress, Elisabeth Christine of Brunswick-Wolfenbüttel: with her beauty, her sweetness, her favour to her English visitor, her pregnancy, and later by her grief at the death of her previous child, five months old, long desired, and male. (Lady Mary did not hesitate to blame his death on bad management, saying he was 'kill'd by . . . weaning him in the beginning of the Winter'.) The empress's relation to George I was another point in her favour. When Lady Mary left Vienna she was charged with a message from the empress to her mother, now Duchess of Blankenburg.

She was almost equally charmed by the late emperor's widow and her teenaged daughters; she even liked the emperor's excruciatingly pious mother. She was intrigued to see the princesses at their favourite sport,

---

[14] *CL* i. 262–4; La Grange 1990: 51; Knepler 1994: 94.   [15] *CL* i. 276–9, 284.

target-shooting with precision guns at the summer palace of Schönbrunn, which 'might make as good a figure as the prize shooting in the Æneid if I could write as well as Virgil'. She was less favourably impressed by the empress's immensely formal and ceremonious drawing-room reception, which admitted no men but the emperor.[16]

Viennese conventions governing relations between the sexes—very unlike those of England—were fascinating even in somewhat lower life. Lady Mary attended assemblies, and parties given for individuals on the festival of the saint whose name they bore. She reported the novelties which struck her: ices were served, winter or summer, but gambling was prohibited. The value set on older women ('older' here meaning upwards of thirty-five or forty) delighted the not-yet-thirty-year-old traveller. She made friends with at least one woman a generation older than herself, wife of the Polish ambassador. She felt more ambivalent about the institution of *cicisbeism*, by which each married lady had an officially acknowledged lover who attended her in public, paid her an allowance, and generally took 'the troublesome part' of her husband's commerce with her off his hands. In any case, she froze off a young count who offered either to become her lover, or failing that to procure her an affair with anybody she might fancy among his circle. She disliked the general obsession with ceremony and precedence as much as she had at Ratisbon (though it favoured ambassadors and their wives), and she reported in a neutral tone the fact that Austrian women were left legally in possession of their own money on marriage, except for a dowry whose size was limited by law.[17]

If not among the Austrians, she found close friends among the cosmopolitans of Viennese society (whose greatest beauties, she said, were Hungarians). She met and liked the Venetian savant Pietro Grimani. She enjoyed that kind of 'chosen conversation compos'd of a few that one esteems' which she always reckoned 'the greatest happynesse of Life'. These people, including Spaniards of both sexes, 'were perfectly to my own taste . . . I could never pick up in any other place such a number of reasonable, agreable people. We were allmost allways together.'[18] Apart from these kindred spirits and the royal Habsburgs, her imagination was stirred by those barred from normal social exchange: court dwarves, and nuns. But whereas she dismissed the dwarves as 'little monsters as ugly as Devils . . . the refuse of Human Nature', her heart warmed to some of the nuns. She

---

[16] *CL* i. 265–9.
[17] *CL* i. 275, 269–72, 344. She remembered this count—perhaps a Count Volkra—for King Goodchild in 'Docile' (Pope, *Corr.* i. 363; *RW* 142).
[18] *CL* i. 303, 294–5. Grimani, FRS, future Doge of Venice, was a friend of Newton and of J. B. Rousseau.

reported most favourably on those of the Laurenzerinnenklöster, which, built in 1327, was among the newer foundations. Its rule was not stern and penitential but decorous and relaxed; nuns of good family had chambermaid nuns to serve them; they could receive female visitors and even play at cards by permission of the aged abbess. Even more interesting than this sweet old woman was a beautiful, intelligent young nun who claimed to be 'perfectly happy' in her lot, yet spoke of her former comrades in the world with tears in her eyes. She inspired Lady Mary with 'tender pity', with anger against the Roman Catholic Church, and with a firm conviction that there was some secret 'real' reason for her taking the veil.[19]

At Vienna, letters from England caught up with them. Lady Mary heard from several friends, including Lady Rich and Pope. He, it seemed, had formed a plan for 'the Letters I am beginning to write to you'. It seems that by moving literally as well as metaphorically out of his reach, she had supplied him with something he wished for: an opportunity for poetical devotion to a *princesse lointaine*. Her inaccessibility was part of her charm. His letters (which, unlike her replies, survive) envisage 'the most impartial Representation of a free heart, and the truest Copies you ever saw, tho'' of a very mean Original. Not a feature will be soften'd, or any advantageous Light employd to make the Ugly thing a little less hideous, but you shall find it in all respects most Horribly Like.' It must have become easier to play with the idea of his own ugliness now her bodily presence was removed: though her beauty was scarred, still he could hardly have taken such a proprietory tone while face to face with her ingrained great-lady manners, her vigorous health, and her larger size (smaller than most women, but still larger than he was). Her attitude to the court dwarves hardly boded well for her relationship with the handicapped poet. But Pope's letters, with Congreve's, were the ones she copied in full into her journal. She kept her literary contacts burnished.

Pope's first letter confesses 'Love', though hedged about with allusions, comparisons, implications. She has ruined him, he says, for the company of other people (men lack softness; other women lack 'every thing else'), and even for books. He sprinkles his letter with *risqué* allusions. Not everyone naked (in mind or body? it's hard to tell) would be 'so fine a sight as yourself and a few more'. 'The unhappy Distance at which we correspond, removes a great many ... punctillious Restrictions and Decorums.'[20]

---

[19] *CL* i. 294–5, 276–8. Maria Regina Erenberger had been abbess for sixteen years (Wiedemann 1883: 73–4).

[20] *E&P* 32; Pope, *Corr.* i. 352–3.

He asks her only seldom and perfunctorily for accounts of foreign men or manners. He wants 'what relates purely to yourself . . . your own mind, temper, and thoughts'. As first taste of the intimate, the introspective, he wants to hear from *her* how *he* behaved at their parting: 'what degree of Concern did I discover when I felt a misfortune which I hope you never will feel, That of parting from what one most esteems?' Though he wishes her to be 'surrounded with all the Enchantments and Idaeas of Romance and Poetry', this applies not so much to her travel experiences as to her relationship with her husband, whom he supposes overwhelmed with gratitude for her 'Self-neglect and Resolution' in going with him. (The idea that she might be gratifying herself does not arise.) Wortley here becomes a kind of surrogate for Pope's feeling, which by his third letter he is defining as something which 'I can't very decently own to you, much less to any other; yet what if a man has, he can't help it.' He is glad to think his letters will trouble her, like ghosts reminding her she has committed murder: 'of the man who has really sufferd by you, and whom you have robbd of the most valuable of his enjoyments, your Conversation.' She has done him injury by making him fall in love, so she now owes him something; he holds her responsible for his emotional comfort.[21]

How did she feel about his claims on her? She had words for such suitors later: they 'mourn with counterfeited Greife | And ask so boldly like a begging Theife'; they degrade women with 'the sneer of affected Admiration'.[22] Her immediate response to Pope is lost. It included an account of Viennese gallantries which her later, public version omits. The rewriting avoids sexual reportage, but suggests that 'the fine things you say to me' are all 'wit and railery'; that she would be a fool to take them seriously, but that now she is so distant she wishes and hopes his admiration is real. She must have written something close to this in fact, but his reply chooses to thank her for agreeing, not just hoping, his professions are serious. Her public answer takes up his allusion to the religious difference between them (her Anglicanism, his Catholicism) and also casually displays her knowledge of plays by Plautus, Molière, and Dryden, as well as of Jeremy Collier's attack on the stage.[23] By letter as in person, she angled for Pope's intellectual rather than his sexual admiration.

Though both British and Turkish diplomats would have preferred Wortley to head straight for Turkey, it seemed the new political situation demanded his return to Hanover (where George I was making a six-month

[21] Pope, *Corr.* i. 354, 355–7. For their epistolary relation see Spacks 1984; Rumbold 1989: 135 ff.

[22] 'An Answer to a Love Letter in Verse'; *Nonsense of Common-Sense*, 6 (*E&P* 245, 134).

[23] Pope, *Corr.* i. 383; *CL* i. 262–4.

visit) for new instructions and credentials. He was, besides, to return with a letter from the king to the emperor.[24] He and his wife left Vienna on 24/13 November to travel via Prague, Dresden, and Leipzig. The winter journey through Bohemia, Saxony, and Brunswick-Wolfenbüttel had its rigours.[25]

The Kingdom of Bohemia is the most desart of any I have seen in Germany; the Villages so poor and the post houses so miserable, clean straw and fair Water are blessings not allways to be found ... Thô I carry'd my own bed with me, I could not sometimes find a place to set it up in, and I rather chose to travel all night, as cold as it is, wrap'd up in my furs, than go into the common Stoves, which are fill'd with a mixture of all sort of ill Scents.

It took '3 nights and days, hard post travelling' from Vienna to Prague. They did not stop there, though invited by many noble families whose relations Lady Mary had met at Vienna. Dresden took another '24 hours post travelling without sleep or refreshment', the mail packet strapped behind them. It was night when they crossed the Erzgebirge, with frightful precipices down to the River Elbe. Wortley slept as they rumbled and swayed, but his wife could not.

In many places the road is so narrow that I could not discern an inch of Space between the wheels and the precipice ... I perceiv'd, by the bright light of the moon, our Postillions nodding on horseback while the Horses were on a full Gallop ... I have been told since, tis common to find the bodys of Travellers in the Elbe, but thank God that was not our Destiny.

Wortley, awoken by her shouting to the postilions (who had control of the horses if anyone had, since a coach with postilions in the saddle has no driver on the box), said that in five Alpine crossings on the Grand Tour he had seen no road so dangerous as this.[26]

Lady Mary addressed to sister Mar her public, retrospective comment on Prague and Dresden. She found Prague mostly 'old built', thinly inhabited, with only traces of 'its former Splendour' as a royal capital. She admired the cooking but derided the fashions, which were carried to even greater excess than in Vienna, rendering women invisible between their headdresses and hoop petticoats.

At Dresden (where a brother of her friend Henrietta Vernon was British

---

[24] SP 80/34; Halsband 1956: 64. In 1717 EWM made a merit of having carried this letter, and travelled overland to Constantinople instead of more comfortably by sea (to Addison, 29/18 July, Tickell MSS).

[25] SP 80/23.

[26] *CL* i. 280–2, 285–6. In 1748 Thomas Steavens found this road 'made me funk my soul out'; fifty years on, Hester Piozzi was reminded to compare notes with MWM as she passed it (Black 1992: 63; Piozzi 1989: 217).

envoy) they took time to breathe. Lady Mary met old acquaintances and made new ones. The ladies were 'genteely dress'd', civil and good-natured to foreigners, but dreadfully affected, assuming 'a little soft Lisp and a pritty pitty pat step'. Here as at Prague, one-horse sledges or traineaus, driven at speed by a gentleman with one female passenger, were objects of ostentatious display. This Protestant town was the neatest Lady Mary had seen in Germany, with new-built houses, a fine palace, and a royal collection of curiosities. She admired the use of Dresden china for the huge heating stoves which kept Germans warm in the severest cold. 'If ever I return,' she told her sister, she would defy the fashion and instal one. Technology and commerce were high on her list of interests, but so was human behaviour. She closed her account of Saxon ladies with the story of Augustus the Strong (Elector of Saxony and King of Poland) and Anna Constanze, Countess von Hoym and later von Cosel: a story which began with romance and ended with violent resentment from the countess, who claimed the king had reneged on a promise of marriage.[27]

Lady Mary relished the fortified town of Leipzig as a trading centre with a famous fair. Here at last she found pages' liveries, as well as 'Gold stuffs for my selfe'. She found Hanover small, plain, and overcrowded with English people, many of whom she knew. She admired the opera house and—despite the deep snow—the gardens at Herrenhausen. As before in London, she delighted in court attendance, in being busy and popular. George I was all affability and gave them apartments at court; they dined at his luxurious table, where the hot-house tropical fruits much impressed Lady Mary. John Clavering wrote to his sister Lady Cowper that she 'is mighty gay and airy, and occasions a great deal of discourse, since her Arrival the King has took but little Notice of any other Lady, nay even of madame Kilmanseck, which the Ladys of Hanover dont relish very well'. However, he said, it made the English 'not a little vainglorious'. Lady Mary managed a long tête-à-tête conversation with the king's nine-year-old grandson Prince Frederick Louis, and was charmed with his 'Sprightlynesse and understanding', as well as his fine blond hair, just like that of his mother, the Princess of Wales. (This courtly praise was tactically addressed to Lady Bristol, a strong Whig who had achieved her Lady of the Bedchamber post by the time Montagu created her Embassy Letters.)[28]

In England Count von Bothmer, Hanoverian Representative and friend of Lady Mary (though not of her husband), wrote to Robethon in Hanover

---

[27] *CL* i. 280, 346, 282–4, 288, 290.
[28] *CL* i. 284, 286–7, 290; Clavering, 4/15 Dec., Panshanger MSS D/EP F196, Herts. Record Office. They had 'lately' passed through Leipzig on 28 Nov., *Daily Courant* (12 Dec. 1716).

regretting that she had had such a 'penible voyage' for so short a stay, and would miss the Carnival at Hanover. He hoped she would now travel back to England, not onwards to Constantinople. Friends of hers hoped the same; 'all the World', she was told, believed she would pull out. But she said she had no thought of this: while Wortley persevered, so would she. His new royal instructions, in English and Latin, noted the changed political situation, but they told 'Our Ambassador Extraordinary' nothing whatever that he did not know before his frantic journey.[29]

Before mid-December they were off again, facing 'a terrible journey in the worst roads and weather that ever poor Travellers suffer'd' in order to carry the empress's message to her mother. The Duke and Duchess of Blankenburg (a little town on the edge of the Harz mountains) occupied a castle on top of a hill so steep that the ducal coach and six, despatched to retrieve the Wortley Montagus from a 'miserable inn', could hardly get up it. Once at the summit, however, they found affable hosts: church-going, card-playing, domestic. Lady Mary evaded church on the grounds that her German was not up to it. Though politely pressed by the duchess to stay, she left after a couple of days, bearing a maternal reply for the empress, and promising to correspond.[30]

At Dresden, where they arrived at daybreak on New Style New Year's Day, 1717, the embassy party stayed only long enough to eat and change horses before pressing on. On 7 January/27 December they re-entered Vienna, to the vivid contrast of extreme cold outdoors and Carnival amusements within. Lady Mary (in spite of a sore throat picked up on the journey) attended the Italian comedy, enjoying the scenery but despising the men in women's roles and the 'intolerable low farce without either wit or humour'. She frequented grand and crowded public balls, where the music was mixed with hunting horns 'that allmost deafen the company'. Every ball concluded, by custom, with badly danced English country dances, a restricted and repetitious selection. Her efforts to introduce new dances did not take. She had a most cordial audience of leave-taking with the imperial couple, who pressed her to revisit Vienna one day, and a more tender parting from her own chosen circle. Many tried to scare her off the journey, and her female friends had 'so much goodness for me, they cry whenever they see me'. Prince Eugene himself, conqueror in the recent campaign, spoke authoritatively of the discomforts of Hungarian habitations and the dangers

---

[29] *CL* i. 291, 287; BL Stowe MS 229. 329–30; H MS 80. 121–3.
[30] *CL* i. 289–90. Charles-Lewis Pollnitz concurred in praising the affability of the Blankenburg family (1739: i. 76–80).

of uninhabited areas. (He wanted them to wait for the Danube to thaw, and travel by water.)[31]

As well as Eugene, she met his protégé the poet Jean Baptiste Rousseau, who was exiled from France for his political satires. He had been recalled in February 1716, but was holding out for a full exoneration. At this period of her life Lady Mary may have thought the shoemaker's son Rousseau (an erotic poet as well as a satirist, called 'le premier des lyriques français') a greater man than his patron. His predicament as satirist had personal interest for her. It was in a copy of his *Œuvres* that she drafted her Catullus version beginning 'Let us live my Lesbia and Love.'[32]

Despite her illness and a twinge of alarm for the health of her 'poor infant', Lady Mary still sounded more excited than apprehensive about leaving Vienna. Memories of 'I love travelling' cling to the drama of 'Adeiu, Dear Sister . . . If I survive my Journey you shall hear from me again', and 'I think I ought to bid Adeiu to my friends with the same Solemnity as if I was going to mount a breach.' This latter she wrote to Pope, adding, 'the Weather is at present such as very few ever set out in. I am threaten'd at the same time with being froze to death, bury'd in the Snow, and taken by the Tartars.' She did not mention rape, but Pope made a good deal of that in a letter which she may or may not have received at this stage. It hinted directly at physical arousal, begged her not to pass through Hungary, and alluded to the Circassian slave he wanted Lady Mary to buy for him, a replica of her own beauty.[33]

In the real world, Wortley took further instruction from imperial ministers, received his Turkish passport, and made final decisions about their overland route. All this took three weeks. They left on 27/16 January, headed for Peterwardein or Petrovaradin (scene of Eugene's decisive victory six months before), and for Turkish-held Belgrade.[34] Well swathed in furs, with their carriages set on sled runners, they took their leave of their last European capital.

On this most gruelling leg of her journey Lady Mary seems to have kept notes in her journal, under heaven knows what unpropitious circumstances. These, padded with history-book material, later made up an Embassy Letter addressed to her sister Mar. Two days out from Vienna brought them to the former frontier town of Raab, which boasted a cathedral and military

[31] Sir Richard Vernon to Townshend, 1 Jan. 1717, SP 88/24; *CL* i. 291–2, 293–5.
[32] Michaud [1870–3]; Rousseau 1712, at Sandon Hall; *E&P* 181.
[33] *CL* i. 296–7; Pope, *Corr.* i. 363–5.
[34] Stanyan to Methuen, 27/16 Jan. 1717, SP 80/34; Halsband 1956: 66. This stage of the journey is discussed by György 1994: 105–9.

garrison, and a long history of seizure by Christian and Muslim in turn.[35] They were received with honours: 'the best house in the Town' for their billet, a guard set at the door, visits from the Austrian governor and other dignitaries, and gifts of fruit, wine, and venison. Again they refused invitations to linger.

Their route lay near the right bank of the Danube, but the snow enabled them to travel cross-country whether or not there was a road. The smooth, hissing runners were a relief from the usual jolting and rattling; the cold outside may have made it easier to bear the cramped proximity of the coach. A few more days brought them to Buda, 'through the finest plains in the world, as even as if they were pav'd, and extreme fruitfull, but for the most part desert and uncultivated, laid waste by the long war between the Turk and Emperour'. Even crueller, Lady Mary noted, was the 'civil War' between Catholic and Protestant. Once again they arrived very early at Buda, and left the same day after being entertained 'with all possible Civillity' by the Austrian governor and his wife.

Lady Mary noted with interest the tight-packed rows of Serbian houses in shanty towns beyond the walls, 'like odd fashion'd thatch'd Tents', consisting of 'one hovel above and another under ground; these are their Summer and Winter apartments.' Nothing could be sadder, she thought, 'than travelling through Hungary, refflecting on the former flourishing state of that Kingdom and seeing such a noble spot of Earth allmost uninhabited'. Due south of Buda they saw ruined Turkish towers, and forests so remote that the game birds showed no fear. Despite Prince Eugene's forebodings, the grubby villages offered 'allways . . . a warm stove and great plenty' of game. Ordered to provision this strange western expedition, the local peasants, clad in sun-cured sheepskin from head to foot, were amazed to receive 'the full worth of what we had from 'em'. They showed their gratitude in farewell gifts such as 'a dozen of fat Pheasants'.[36]

At Mohács the embassy party were shown, not for the first or last time, a historic battlefield. On crossing the frozen Danube they were made much of by an Austrian general. After traversing forests made 'very dangerous from the vast quantity of wolves that herd in them', besides exceptionally deep snow, they reached Esseg or Osijek late at night on 4 February/24 January. Lady Mary had a chance to sightsee while her husband made contact with the Ottoman Empire, composing a letter to send by courier to the Bassa or Paşa of Belgrade. This man was a replacement; they were told his predecessor

[35] Later Győr. Turkey had surrendered it the previous autumn (Horwath 1988: 36).
[36] *CL* i. 299–301; Horwath 1991.

had been assassinated two months back by his war-weary men, for permitting irregular actions against the Austrians. The new Bassa was to arrange their passage across the invisible frontier into enemy territory.[37]

Their own culture, or a culture akin to their own, had still some hospitable gestures in reserve. At the Serbian town of Bocowar or Vukovar[38] they were given a 'handsome Dinner' by the Hungarian wife, daughter, and niece of an Austrian colonel. Lady Mary found their 'conversation very polite and agreable', and described their costume for her sister; their scarlet velvet and sables, jewelled buttons, and gold-tasselled caps suggest some Turkish influence. At Peterwardein the Commandant came out to meet their party 'at the head of all the officers of the Garrison'. They were given the best rooms in the governor's house, and splendid entertainment 'by the Emperor's order'. Wortley's courier rode in from Belgrade bearing 'the Bassa's answer in a purse of scarlet Satin'; an interpreter relayed its promise of an honourable reception and its invitation 'to appoint where he would be met by the Turkish convoy'. Wortley sent the courier back to name Betsko or Beska, a village midway between Peterwardein and Belgrade.[39] They expected to wait some days at Peterwardein 'till all points are adjusted concerning our reception on the Turkish frontiers'. Lady Mary (so she said later) began writing letters. But the Bassa was now 'in such haste to see us, he dispatch'd our Coureir back . . . without suffering him to pull off his boots'.

So after two nights they set forward attended by the garrison officers, and added to them a guard of fifty grenadiers, fifty hussars, and a hundred wild Serbian troops, who looked like 'Vagabond Gypsies or stout beggars' and were indeed 'rather plunderers than soldeirs'. At the meeting place, Beska, the Bassa provided a second private army, half as big again, though he had promised an exact equivalent. An aga of the janizaries commanded this force: no wild irregulars but a unit of crack troops composed originally of Christians captured in battle.

The last topic Lady Mary found for her pen in Christian Europe was the battlefield of Peterwardein, scene of Eugene's 'last great Victory', when the Turkish cavalry fled towards Belgrade, leaving perhaps 30,000 janizaries to be slaughtered and some impaled or decapitated. An English officer wrote, 'We took no more than twenty prisoners because our men wanted their blood and massacred them all.' All this had happened almost as the Wortley Montagus left England. 'No attempt was made to bury the dead'; they must have been badly decomposed, though now, with snow lying on the ground,

---

[37] *CL* i. 301–2, 306.
[38] Horwath 1988. In 1996 Vukovar again lay in ruins (*Guardian Weekly*, 24 Mar.).
[39] *CL* i. 302–3. Horwath notes that Turkey lost Beska in the next campaign (1992: 24–6).

they no longer stank. Lady Mary's first response was emotional shock and outrage—sharpened, no doubt, by her personal acquaintance with the victor, who had been fresh from this triumph when she met him.[40] But these painful feelings quickly modulated into intellectual analysis of the human systems which permit struggle and slaughter for the sake of small spots of earth, even while fertile tracts lie unoccupied.

The marks of that Glorious bloody day are yet recent, the feild being strew'd with the Skulls and Carcases of unbury'd Men, Horses and Camels. I could not look without horror on such numbers of mangled humane bodys, and refflect on the Injustice of War, that makes murther not only necessary but meritorious.

The entrenched acceptance of such a harmful custom, she thought, plainly proved 'the irrationality of Mankind (whatever fine claims we pretend to Reason)'. In her Embassy Letters she addressed this impassioned argument to Pope.

Her six months' travelling had shown her a Europe not yet obviously more powerful than the Ottoman state she was now about to enter. She had seen much that was new and strange (most recently the Serbian priests, whose untrimmed hair and beards seemed to her like 'Indian Bramins').[41] She had rambled incognita through foreign streets, and been squeezed and frizzed unrecognizably to conform to the fashions of the imperial court. But the underlying frameworks of society had been familiar. The Europe she saw had once been largely united under the Romans; the people with whom she scraped acquaintance—the flirtatious young Jesuit, the venerable Mother Superior, the pregnant and sorrowing empress—shared her Christian background; their languages, though foreign, were Indo-European. After Beska, things would be different.

[40] *CL* i. 304–5; Horwath 1987; McKay 1977: 161–3.
[41] *CL* i. 305, 304; Hourani 1991: 137. Scholars no longer believe that 18th-century Islam was in decline (Levtzion and Voll 1987: 16).

9

February–May 1717

✦

Adrianople: 'not so unpolish'd as we represent them'[1]

ON the threshold of the unknown there was no looking back. Lady Mary's immediate concern was that the two private armies should part without any quarrel arising between them. Having struggled through deep snow to Belgrade with their twenty waggons and 500 janizaries (arriving on 5 February 1717), they found they were still not safe from quarrels. Here they heard the true story of the fate of the previous bassa, cut to pieces by the scimitars of a tumultuous mob, in the presence indeed of the religious judges, the Cadi and Mufti, but before those dignitaries had time to pass sentence. It was not for permitting skirmishes against the Austrians that he had been killed, but for restraining them. They learned too that Mustapha, his successor, had taken no action against the perpetrators, but 'affected to applaud' them, and was trying to conciliate the garrison by cash presents and licence to attack and burn poor houses. They were in fact 'under the Government of an insolent Soldiery'. One of their interpreters, a Jew, was arrested and beheaded as a suspected spy. Though they had meant to press on after one night, they found the bassa was to detain them till orders came from the sultan's court at Adrianople, which might take a month.[2]

But there were compensations. The house where they were billeted, one of the finest in Belgrade, belonged to an Islamic effendi: a gentleman-scholar, learned and free-thinking, a lover of wine, poetry, and studious retirement. Lady Mary calls him Achmet-Beg; she found him a kindred spirit, like Conti (to whom she addressed her longest account of him). Amid the brawls and murderous violence of Belgrade, in cold which kept the windows iced up inside in spite of 'a very large stove', he chose to spend 'the greatest part of his Life' amid his excellent, wide-ranging library. Their

---

[1] *CL* i. 414. [2] *CL* i. 306–7; McKay 1977: 164; Pope, *Corr.* i. 406.

shared language was probably Italian, since that appears in her Turkish-language notes. They ate their supper together every night in Turkish style: sitting on cushions, with portable trays on legs instead of a heavy fixed table. Many small dishes succeeded each other, highly spiced, and ending with the soup. Achmet-Beg 'drinks wine very freely. You cannot imagine how much he is delighted with the Liberty of converseing with me.' He would have known something of Christian ladies (Belgrade, like all the disputed towns, was ethnically mixed), but he had never met one like this one.

It was probably he who told her how, after the débâcle at Peterwardein, the camels 'far out-run the swiftest horses and brought the first news of the loss of the battle to Belgrade'. They spoke, too, of religion, of literature, and of gender. Lady Mary felt these conversations gave her an 'opertunity of knowing their Religion and morals in a more particular manner than perhaps any Christian ever did'. Achmet-Beg assured her that if she could read the Koran in the original she would find it 'the purest morality deliver'd in the very best Language': stories against it were the work of ignorant, corrupt, and prejudiced Greek Orthodox priests. He admitted that his use of wine was 'deviateing from some part of Mahomet's Law', but added that the law was not made to bind those capable of moderation, but only, wisely, the common people, whom wine would make drunk and disorderly. God would not have made vines and prohibited tasting their juice. His argument that 'all the Creatures of God were good and design'd for the use of Man' was a favourite one of her own.

She expounded the difference between the churches of Rome and England; he told her of the schisms and degeneration in Islam (whose sects he enumerated). He condemned image-worship, Mariolatry, and Transubstantiation, but 'was pleas'd to hear' about more rational forms of Christianity. She identified his position and that of his whole class as 'plain Deism', well in tune with Clarke and Whiston.

Her knowledge of the 'Persian Tales' made him suppose at first that she knew Persian. (In fact they had recently been translated into French and English.)[3] He then drew on his perfect command of Persian and Arabic to instruct her in the finer points of Arabic poetry, while himself learning to read the English alphabet and 'write a good Roman hand'.

On one topic did they have 'frequent disputes': on 'the difference of our Customs, particularly the confinements of Women. He assures me there is nothing at all in it; only, says he, we have the advantage that when our Wives

---

[3] *CL* i. 307–8, 316–19, 377, 340; H MS 80. 270–83. MWM later owned two French works by Antoine Galland sometimes called *Persian Tales*; an English trans. was advertised on 3 Feb. 1715 (Wh MS M 135).

cheat us, no body knows it.' It was said that Mohammedan men generally
spoke of women with decency, without the endless *double-entendres* beloved
by western males, though they did 'occasionally repeat some of those
common-place sarcasms on women, which are found current in every
country'. Lady Mary's Embassy Letters do not mention the harem (or
women's quarters) in Achmet-Beg's house. But before her acquaintance
with Turkish women began, her three weeks' 'intimate daily conversation'
with him laid the groundwork for her mission as defender of Islam against
Christian prejudice.[4]

After three weeks the ambassador's permission came through, and they
resumed their progress through the winter forests and the long, dark nights:
not so long as at home, since they had reached the latitude of the south of
France, but probably long enough to make them sometimes crunch over the
snow by moon or starlight. Lady Mary said the Danube was still frozen,
Wortley that it had thawed; in any case they travelled by land, staying the
nights in the 'miserable Houses' of the frontier lands. Enquiries beforehand
had assured them that the area was free from plague. Presumably their 500
escorting janizaries carried tents. Such numbers must have been a nightmare
to travel with, but they were not useless: local robbers operated in gangs
twenty strong. While some of their janizaries surrounded the ambassadorial
sledge, others scouted widely to provision the party by violent raids on
'villages so poor that only force could extort from them necessary provisions'. These were plundered even more remorselessly than on the other
side of the border. Poultry and sheep were taken 'without asking who they
belong'd to, while the wretched owners durst not put in their claim for fear
of being beaten. Lambs just fall'n, Geese and Turkeys big with Egg: all
masacre'd without distinction.' The soldiers' 'insolencies in the poor
villages' had Lady Mary in tears almost every day.

To convey her horror at these scenes of tyranny and oppression she
turned to ancient literature. It was not on grounds of its racial or religious
Otherness that she recoiled from the inhumanity of Ottoman imperial rule.
Her frame of reference remained what it had always been; she condemned
them in terms borrowed from Virgil, by appeal to the values which had
shaped her annotations to *Poems on Affairs of State* and her admiration for
Quintus Curtius. It was consistent with these values to admire the Turkish

---

[4] *CL* i. 307–8, 317; Russell 1794: i. 181. Edward Said notes that early amateur travellers welcomed 'the
Orient as a salutary *dérangement* of their European habits of mind' (1978: 150). Rousseau and Porter say they
often portrayed the exotic as more *normal* than home; that Europe at this date was self-critical, ready to learn
(1990: 12, 14). Melman sees MWM's letters as initiating a gender-specific discourse, separate from orientalism (1992: 2).

culture embodied in Achmet-Beg, while hating the military rule embodied in the janizaries.[5]

Before they had been long on the road the reassurances about the plague proved erroneous: several towns on their route were 'most violently infected'; two people died of it next door to them. Their second cook sickened, and showed the alarming symptoms of buboes. Wortley concealed the diagnosis from Lady Mary, protecting her feelings either as woman, or as mother, or as recent smallpox sufferer. They pressed on, leaving Maitland behind with the sick man, who in due course recovered.[6]

At Nis (birthplace of the Emperor Constantine) their waggoners from Belgrade were sent back 'without payment, some of their Horses lam'd and others kill'd without any satisfaction made for 'em. The poor fellows came round the House weeping and tearing their Hair and beards in the most pitifull manner without geting any thing but drubs from the insolent Soldeirs.' The English travellers did not intervene, believing that any payment they might make would be pocketed by the aga who commanded the janizaries.[7]

Four more days on mountain roads brought them to their next major Turkish city: Sofia, 'scituate in a large beautifull Plain . . . surrounded with distant mountains'. Here they visited the ruins of the sixth-century church (later a mosque) which gave the town its name. It was the first time Lady Mary mentioned Wortley sightseeing. But her more crucial excursion in Sofia was made without him. Here she hired an *araba* or Turkish coach and set out—incognita again—for a Turkish public bath. The whole experience was entrancing, beginning with the coach, which had louvres or lattices instead of glass (to shade and to conceal its female occupants), painted and gilded with flowers and mottoes, with a fringed, embroidered canopy in scarlet cloth. The baths occupied a five-domed stone building lit only through its roof. After the entrance hall came four rooms, in three of which (including the actual bath rooms) Lady Mary found the heat most uncomfortable. The fourth room, a marble interior with sulphurous steam seeping through it (Sofia's medicinal hot springs come at about 46.8°C), contained perhaps two hundred Turkish women, drinking coffee or fruit juice, embroidering, doing each other's hair—and 'in plain English, stark naked'.

Here was something farther beyond the range of Lady Mary's direct or vicarious experience than Achmet-Beg's scholarship or the janizaries' depredations. The women's beauty delighted her: the 'shineingly white' skins, with no ornament but 'their Beautiful Hair divided into many tresses

---

[5] *CL* i. 316, 310. She cites Virgil's first eclogue: Meliboeus complaining of injustice and official extortion.

[6] *CL* i. 338; 10 Apr./31 Mar., SP 97/24.   [7] *CL* i. 311.

hanging on their shoulders'. The good order, good humour, and friendliness of the naked assembly—the freedom from 'surprize or impertinent Curiosity', immodest gestures, 'disdainfull smiles or satyric whispers'—impressed her even more. So did the egalitarianism (you could hardly tell the great lady from her slave). As usual, Lady Mary was alert to what was and what was not different. The female body was *the* standard of beauty in her own culture; the Turkish women's grace and charm were what she might have expected (though their freedom from smallpox scarring, and from the red marks left by tight lacing, were unfamiliar). It was like an artist's fantasy, and Lady Mary 'had wickedness enough to wish secretly' that her friend Jervas might have been there invisible to represent it on canvas. But to find unadorned, unimproved femininity free from lewdness or narcissism or rivalry: this was a most happy denial of what her own culture had led her to expect.[8] From now on she had two separate models of the admirable in Turkish culture: the male library and this 'Women's coffee house'.[9]

Montagu's account of this scene became notorious the moment her Embassy Letters were (posthumously) printed. Most reviewers found something to blame: either barbaric Turkish nudity, or her condoning of this nudity, or her failure of delicacy in reporting it, or her failure of integrity in inventing it. Neither critics nor champions of Islamic culture were willing to admit that Turkish women practised such communal nudity. Montagu was said to be mistaken or lying: it was asserted that women at the Turkish bath kept themselves always modestly covered with a towel or wrapper. Later travelling Englishwomen endorsed her accuracy but called her tone misleading: such groups of naked women were really 'most hideous and disgusting'.[10] The scene was illustrated for a reprint of her travel letters in 1783; later a young art student named Ingres copied the passage out (in French translation); and as an old man he reverted to its inspiration.[11]

Today the debate has been reopened on a different set of premisses, with

---

[8] *CL* i. 311–15; Davis 1986: 134; *Sofia* 1960: 42, 62. Spenser, typically, uses naked women in water as an emblem of lust (*Faerie Queene*, II. xii. 62–8). 'Malice and censure of w[ome]n' in one of MWM's letter-summaries *probably* points at antifeminist travel-writers (H MS 80. 124). Dumont, for instance, heavily sexualizes Islamic women (1705: 273, 276–7).

[9] *CL* i. 312–15. London's men-only coffee-houses were centres not only for gossip but for politics—perhaps the element which MWM most coveted (Bohls 1994: 192–3; Aravamudan 1995: 81–2). Nussbaum too suggests she was envious, but more of sexual than political liberty (1995: 90–1, 138–41). For a positive view of her as anti-stereotypical see Fernea 1981.

[10] e.g. Dumont 1705: 274; Russell 1794: i. 137, 380–2; a Lady Nisbet (Wh MS M 439/3); Harriet Martineau (David 1987: 53). Thomas Tyers thought MWM 'would deserve censure' from modest English *and* Turkish women 'merely for the discovery' (1782: 42.) My colleague Nasrin Rahimieh confirms that there is nothing incredible about the women's nakedness.

[11] Ingres (1780–1867) painted *Le Bain Turc* in 1862, having made notes nearly fifty years earlier (*New Yorker*, 13 Jan. 1986; *CL*, i. 406–7).

special attention to the eroticism in Lady Mary's account, and to her declining to join the Turkish ladies, when their spokeswoman

would fain have undress'd me for the bath. I excus'd my selfe with some difficulty, they being all so earnest in perswading me. I was at last forc'd to open my skirt and shew them my stays, which satisfy'd 'em very well, for I saw they beleiv'd I was so lock'd up in that machine that it was not in my own power to open it, which contrivance they attributed to my Husband.

Montagu, once condemned for condoning nudity, has since been condemned either for not joining in (thus asserting superiority or denying womanhood) or for comparing these living bodies to Italian and English art works (thus denying their ethnicity and corporeality).[12] But if she had undressed, and the fact had got out, it would have gravely compromised both her personal reputation and her husband's political mission. Later, at a private bath, as she told Joseph Spence, she did allow the lady of the house to slip off her gown, revealing her stays.[13]

After Sofia they crossed still higher mountains under year-round snow, with ruins of Roman defences against the barbarians. Then the Turkish military road dipped downhill and joined the ancients' river Hebrus (later Maritza, then Evros). On its banks Orpheus, patron of music, had been torn to pieces by Thracian women; down its waters his head had floated, still calling on his lost Eurydice. Lady Mary's first entrance on classic ground was as horror haunted as her last sight of Christian Europe had been.[14]

Four days' travel from Sofia brought them to Philippopoli (later Plovdiv), a largely Greek city which had once received an epistle from St Paul. Its wealthiest inhabitants now kept their riches prudently hidden. Near here there occurred one last unsettling incident of misrule. Lady Mary 'happen'd to bespeak pigeons for my Supper' from one of the janizaries; he found the headman had none, and offered her the headman's head in reparation for this failing.[15]

The embassy travellers were now near their goal: not Constantinople but Adrianople (now Edirne), a hundred miles short of it, a smaller city away from the coast. The plague was supposed not to be endemic there, as at

---

[12] Leeks 1986: 31; Melman 1992: 91; Pointon 1992: 60, 64. Cf. also Bohls 1994: 187–9; Nussbaum 1995: 140–1; Campbell 1994: 79–81; and Lew 1991: 432, 445. MWM cites Titian, Guido Reni, and Milton's reminder that Adam and Eve in their first nakedness had no 'guiltie shame, dishonest shame | Of Nature's works' (*Paradise Lost*, iv. 312–20).

[13] Spence 1966: 764.

[14] For Pope she recalled or invented a near-accident beside the Hebrus, and spun a flight of fancy about her literary allegiances (see p. 200).

[15] *CL* i. 324–5. The story was judged by another traveller to be impossible, produced perhaps by misunderstanding a joke (de Tott 1784: i, pp. xxvii–xxxi).

Constantinople. Recent Turkish emperors had tended to prefer Adrianople, and that was where the court of Ahmed III was now ensconced.

The last leg of their journey was idyllic: summer after winter, flower-strewn meadows after snowdrifts and howling wolves. 'Vines grow wild on all the Hills, and the perpetual Spring they enjoy makes every thing look gay and flourishing.' They shared the road with oddly proportioned camels (led in strings of fifty or more by a man on a donkey), and clumsy black oxen or 'Buffolos' with sinister little white eyes, and red-dyed tails and forelocks. Bug-ridden smoky huts gave way to fine, stone-built 'Publick Hans or Inns'. These reminded Lady Mary of Oxford or Cambridge colleges, being formed of a hall (accommodating 300 or 400 travellers), a mosque, and a square with shops occupying its arches or cloister. Close to Adrianople the land was 'laid out in Gardens, and the Banks of the River set with Rows of Fruit trees'. Families picnicked on Persian carpets, drinking coffee to the music of pan-pipes; shepherd boys fashioned garlands of flowers for lambs, like those in ancient pastoral poetry. Greek women, 'neat and handsome', sat at their looms in the shade of trees, not veiled as they would be in town. Young Greek girls danced, following the improvisations of their leader, to music 'extreme Gay and Lively, yet with something in [it] wonderfull soft'.[16]

Turkey at this date was very far from being a third-world power (in today's usage); nor was it an 'empty' space ripe for colonization. It was an imperial nation 'in full power and pride'—and, Lady Mary decided, one of the finest countries in the world. It was not only the countryside. Even more dazzling was Adrianople, where they arrived on 24/13 March 1717, expecting to make it a part of their lives for years. It boasted the Selimiye Mosque, built in 1569–75, masterpiece of the octogenarian Selim Pasha, 'the Islamic Michelangelo'. Massive buildings were faced all over in faience, in glittering, closely patterned tiles in a style the English travellers had formerly seen only on tiny, precious art-objects. People driving or riding animals, people in black and people in jewel-encrusted gold caftans, people 'who follow the Court or Camp', loitered or hurried amid mosques, palaces, castles, aqueducts, and hamams or bath-buildings. The street scenes included women as well as men.[17]

Wortley met and took the measure of his embassy staff. He had a secretary, Mr Hefferman, who had held his post (doubled with one with the

    [16] *CL* i. 311, 331–2, 340–1, 344.
    [17] Lady Louisa Stuart in MWM 1861: i. 81; *CL* i. 309, 354; Robinson 1982: 84–5; Sözen 1987: 274–8, 285, 300, and *passim*). Coming Turkish decline was not yet perceptible. Adrianople was a centre for illumination, miniature-painting, and book-binding.

Levant Company) throughout Sir Robert Sutton's embassy.[18] His three dragomans or interpreters were probably Italians: Ottoman subjects from the Italian quarter of Constantinople. Marked out by a special eye-catching uniform which included yellow shoes, they were his 'eyes, ears, and mouth', but were liable to entertain conflicting loyalties. They were supplemented by an effendi (or priest) who came in daily for the purpose of Turkish writing, especially letters, and whom Lady Mary found useful. The chaplain was to see to the 'factory' library. The ambassador himself had to pay the wages of his bodyguard janizaries; he was never to go out without them, for a large retinue was essential 'to conform to all that rigid system of pomp and ceremony' by which success and status were measured among the diplomatic colony.[19]

With this backing Wortley was to manage Turkey's somewhat reluctant negotiations with the emperor (who had just proved his military superiority), while through the French ambassador the Turks contacted Sweden and Venice in hopes of a separate peace. He had his first audience on 11 April/31 March, with Halil Pasha, the Grand Vizier, an elderly, upright character, who had to be pressured to accept the customary presents. He had replaced an able but paranoid and xenophobic predecessor: Ali Pasha, slain at Peterwardein, who had weakened his country by executing too many rivals. Next for Wortley would come an audience with the sultan, Ahmed III, whom his predecessor, Sutton, had called 'hasty, violent and cruel, but variable and unsteady'.[20] Until recently Ottoman custom had demanded 'contempt and rudeness' in the reception of foreign ambassadors;[21] Wortley did not know how his offer of peace terms would be received. He jockeyed with the new French ambassador, Jean-Louis d'Usson, marquis de Bonnac, to present his credentials first.[22]

Wortley began building relations with Turkish officials. On 3 May he was able to report that he had twice met with the mosaip or sultan's favourite, Nevşehirli Damad Ibrahim Pasha, and sought to disabuse him of underestimating Austria's capacity to follow up its recent gains. He later claimed he had squeezed out de Bonnac as political confidant to Ibrahim—who later

---

[18] BL Add. MS 61547. 138 (BL Blenheim Papers: scribal copy of letter from EWM to Sunderland). Sutton left Turkey the month EWM arrived (SP 97. 24).

[19] Wood 1925: 538–41.

[20] Sutton 1953: 2; *CL* i. 354. The French ambassador agreed with this assessment (Schefer 1894: 134–8). A British ambassador's reception painted by Guardi about twenty years later shows an odd mixture of the two cultures' ceremonial male dress: robes and breeches, white wigs and towering turbans.

[21] Dallaway 1797: 25.

[22] De Bonnac won, presenting his costly gifts on 13/2 Apr., five days ahead of EWM, but it was a close-run thing (EWM to Paul Methuen, Secretary of State, SP 44/360/3).

still became an innovator in building friendly relations with the west. De Bonnac said Wortley negotiated 'trop froidement'; Wortley himself said he was indefatigable.[23]

⋇

He and Lady Mary were 'lodg'd in a Palace belonging to the Grand Signor' on the banks of the Hebrus. Like most Turkish houses it was of wood, not built either for durability or external beauty, but 'commodious', a quality which she always respected. It had two 'distinct parts', one for occupation by each sex, joined by a narrow passage. Each building had galleries (porches or verandas) running right round it; the ladies' building or harem, 'remov'd from sight' behind the other, turned all its windows towards the high-walled gardens. These had no flowerbeds but were planted with tall cypress trees. Baskets of flowers and marble fountains adorned the low-ceilinged, panelled, and painted rooms, 'all spread with Persian Carpets'. Built-in features took the place of furniture in the western sense. Cupboards were set into the panelling. Each end of Lady Mary's own room had a dais or 'Sopha' raised two feet, clad in richer carpeting, whose central area was raised even more, covered in scarlet gold-fringed silk, with larger and smaller cushions, lavishly ornamented. 'I shall never endure Chairs,' she wrote, 'as long as I live.' It was another travel-writers' myth that Turkish houses were miserable constructions; Lady Mary grew to like their irregularity or 'Confusion'.[24]

She chose fabrics and ordered Turkish costume, whose basics were an embroidered smock, long-sleeved, in transparent silk; a tight long-sleeved gold-and-white waistcoat; baggy pants and matching caftan in 'thin rose colour damask brocaded with silver flowers'; and over all the ferace and asmak, cloak and veil. (She detailed to her sister the buttons, belt, slippers, and head-dress.) She arranged to be painted in this costume, as a present for Frances. Jean Baptiste Vanmour did her as a small figure in an outdoor setting, her dress displayed in great detail, all but the enveloping silk 'ferigée'.[25] This last disguised her when she visited mosques, especially the

[23] Göçek 1987: 8–9; EWM's notes *c*.1746, Halsband MSS; Schefer 1894: pp. xxxiii, lxxviii, 137; BL Add. MS 61547. 138.

[24] *CL* i. 331, 341–3, 414. On the absence of furniture see Ettinghausen, in Lewis 1976: 71.

[25] *CL* i. 326–7, 397. Vanmour later did her in conversation-piece style (see p. 163). His single figure of her was formerly ascribed to Charles Philips, and owned by Robert Halsband (NPG 9061). The NPG lists too a probable single-figure copy, differing in a few costume details and in a background of Turkish cushions instead of trees. Vanmour, based at Constantinople since 1699, would have been at Adrianople with the court (Van Luttervelt 1958). Russell argued that in some ways MWM's costume was 'rather Grecian than Turkish' (1794: i. 105).

fabulous Sulaimaniye, and exchanges or shopping centres, one of which contained 365 shops. Turkish dress was preferable for visits, because the low neckline of European fashion scandalized the Turkish ladies, and they thought she was embarrassed at having to defend it. They were prudish in other things too, disapproving rather than envying western women's freedom to drink and (so they believed) indulge in extramarital love-affairs. When Lady Mary said such affairs were condemned by society, her Turkish interlocutor declined to believe her. No, no, she said: she knew that infidel customs were disgraceful; she knew that a wife who was free to exchange words and glances with another man would soon be exchanging more; she knew that Lady Mary was too sensible really to approve what she had for form's sake to defend.[26]

Lady Mary acquired a horse, 'a little white favourite that I would not part with on any terms. He prances under me with so much fire you would think that I had a great deal of courrage to dare Mount him, yet I'll assure you I never rid a Horse in my life so much at my command.' This was even better than riding in England; Lady Mary had brought her side-saddle, which as 'the first was ever seen in this part of the World' provoked 'as much wonder as the ship of Columbus . . . in America'. She repaid this wonder at a specialist exchange or bazar for 'horse furniture . . . glittering every where with Gold, rich Embrodiery and Jewels'. She tried local delicacies (botargo or tuna-roe sauce) and cosmetics: the renowned balm of Mecca. She must have had an allergy: it brought on terrible swelling, a rash, and reproaches from her husband.[27]

The welcome opportunity to take stock, to mull over, and to write up what she had seen, was affected by pressure of time. A ship was to leave Constantinople within weeks of their arrival at Adrianople; it might then be months until the next. Lady Mary had sent a letter to Pope, her most demanding correspondent, from Peterwardein back via Vienna.[28] Now, in intervals from various activities which she saved to write about later, she prepared in short order seventeen letters about her journey and her first impressions: to her sisters, her father, her friends, and promising contacts both at home and in some of the courts she had visited. Letters went to a Polish countess, a German duchess, and the Princess of Wales; to Madame Kielmansegg and Baron Bothmer (to both of whom she said she had written often); to Lady Bristol; to Lady Rich and her sister Anne Griffith,

[26] *CL* i. 354; Spence 1966: 763; *E&P* 163–4. Nussbaum thinks MWM became 'complicit in imperial designs' by 'masquerad[ing] as the Other to free her libido' (1995: 160).

[27] *CL* i. 341, 355, 369.   [28] It pleased him by some generous expressions (*CL* i. 304; Pope, *Corr.* i. 407).

Henrietta Vernon, Jane Smith, and Frances Hewet;[29] to Conti, Congreve, and Pope; to Treasury clerk Charles Chevalier, who was to deal with business matters and deliver letters to others; to Lord Cadogan, a friend and former officer of Marlborough's, who had mopped up the Jacobite rebellion and was soon to make the headlines on corruption charges.[30] She kept track of her letters by writing brief summaries, which her husband later labelled 'Heads of L. M.'s Letters From Turky'.

As the 'Heads' record, she wrote to sister Frances about her social success in Adrianople, and about 'Jew Ladys'.[31] She regaled Pope with the more literary aspects of her recent journey, and with the love-life of Turkish women,[32] and Conti with theological and cultural analysis gleaned from Achmet-Beg. For Lady Bristol she contrasted English and Turkish styles in politics (implying that Hanoverian rule was best) and in fabrics. She wrote about 'Small pox' both to her father, who was a friend of Dr Garth, and to court friends (as Sir Hans Sloane later recorded). This was her first report on inoculation. She had found it practised by both the local cultures, Turkish and Greek; and she probably found it not by chance but because she was looking. She was primed both by personal experience and by intellectual contact as an Enlightenment researcher.[33]

Some of the summaries are miniature gems, like this to Hewet: 'I like travelling. Hurryd up and down. Long Journeys, new scenes every day.' To Lady Rich, Lady Mary assumed an air of humility: 'Desire her to write. Mine will be dull.' She repeats some points, like 'Ladys free' and 'Pomp'. She was immediately and strongly impressed by the relative liberty of Turkish women, and the way it undermined (male) western complacence about the fortunate, pampered conditions of western women. A couple of weeks later she sent another batch of letters: to three more friends (Sarah Chiswell, Elizabeth West, Anne Thistlethwayte), two more relations (her grand-

[29] This, her last extant letter to Hewet, is the only actual letter to survive of all those she wrote from Turkey. She may still have been in touch with Hewet in 1732 (see p. 306 n. 3).
[30] MWM can have known nothing of this coming event: Cadogan's vindication was a defeat for Walpole (then in opposition) and a victory for her friend Craggs (Plumb 1956: 256; Hill 1989: 92; Chevallier to MWM, 4 Sept. 1717, H MS 168–9).
[31] *CL* i. xv, 344–6. Frances left England in April for six months with her exiled husband in Avignon. Jewish women sold the harem women's needlework for them. But the Jews, oppressed under Islam, often relayed to Europeans an 'inveterate and invincible dislike' of it (Peirce 1993: 141; Russell 1794: i. 227; Mantran 1982: 129, 131).
[32] An 18th-century visitor to England from Turkey thought Englishwomen more confined in their activities and financially more at their husbands' mercy than Muslim women (Abu Talib Khan, quoted in Lewis 1982: 289). In 1722 an effendi published fulminations against women's gadding about (Davis 1986: 223).
[33] *CL* i. 321 n., 326 n.; Sloane in Royal Society 1755–6: xlix. 516; Timoni in Royal Society 1717 [for 1714–16]: xxix. 72–6; see p. 102. Russell in Aleppo thought that only the Greeks used inoculation; his brother found it was also the Arabs and Bedouin (1794: ii. 317).

mother Lady Denbigh and uncle William Feilding), and another potential patron (Melusina von Schulenburg).[34]

Two more letters from Pope must have awaited Lady Mary here, both written months before, professing to hope either that she might come home without Wortley or that he himself might join or pursue her. Replying to hers from Vienna, he assures her (alluding wittily to Lockean philosophy) that in his heart her 'Idea lyes as warm, and as close, as any Idea in Christendom'. Distance, he adds, will only increase their intimacy by letter, as 'modest people . . . when they are close together, keep all decorums, but if they step a little aside, or get to the other end of a room, can untye garters or take off Shifts without scruple'. Another time, having invoked her as a departed spirit worthy to receive 'Addresses and prayers', he has great fun with a fantasy of her in her progress eastwards, shedding one Christian belief after another. He waxes steadily more *risqué*: first she will learn to sit on a Turkish sofa and fold a turban; then she will convert. He will hear how a 'Basha' (imagined as a priest)

received the fair Convert with tears of joy . . . how earnestly you joind with him in exhorting Mr Wortley to be circumcised . . . how . . . you had a Vision of Mahomet's Paradise, and happily awaked without a Soul. From which blessed instant the beautiful Body was left at full liberty to perform all the agreeable functions it was made for.

He rounded this off with a couplet on his own death for love, borrowed from Tibullus—in whom the death follows a scene of sexual bliss.

Whether she rumbled him on Tibullus, whether she was offended by this open talk of her sexuality, is as usual unknown. If she really sent Pope something like the Embassy Letter she constructed for him later, she was still hoping to join the circle of learned friends who helped with his Homer translations. She offered notes on eastern manners and eastern poetic style, especially in relation to Homer. But all this Pope seems to have ignored.[35]

Her first experience of Adrianople included a royal procession to the mosque. She duly reported the janizaries with 'vast white Feathers on their Heads', the royal gardeners as brightly clad as their own tulips, an aga of janizaries in purple and silver, the Kuzlir Aga or chief black eunuch in yellow

[34] *CL* i. 308 n., 345, 352–3. Elizabeth West, daughter of Bishop Burnet, was mother of Richard West the poet. Anne Thistlethwayte lived till 1714 at Winterslow near West Dean, then partly at Kelham near Newark, and had close links with the families of Sutton (Lord Lexington) and Manners (Duke of Rutland). She was unmarried, and was (from her will) less family oriented than the norm for her class (Daly MS 2235, Hampshire Record Office; information from the Revd Clive Cohen). The greater liberty of Turkish women was also noted by Elizabeth, Lady Craven, later Anspach (1789: 205, 233–4).

[35] EWM endorsed some of Pope's letters, not this one (Pope, *Corr.* i. 365, 383–4, 367–70; *CL* i. 331 ff.; Scodel 1991: 284). I owe the point about Tibullus to James McLaverty.

'lin'd with Sables', all preceding 'his Sublimity him selfe in Green lin'd with the Fur of a black Muscovite fox, which is suppos'd worth £1,000 Sterling, mounted on a fine Horse'. She thought the sultan handsome, graceful, and severe, especially when 'his Eyes very full and black' turned 'very attentively' on herself.

She also reported on a royal occasion she had missed: the wedding of Princess Fatma, one of the sultan's thirty daughters, which was the most lavish in the final two centuries of Ottoman rule.[36] Though Fatma was hardly thirteen she was a widow: her first husband had been Ali Pasha, the grand vizier who died at Peterwardein with most of the troops he commanded. The magnificent wedding ceremony with her second, Ibrahim (the mosaip whom Wortley claimed as a confidant), had served as national morale booster; but Ahmed III had denied his new son-in-law leave to consummate the marriage, telling him there was no room for personal gratification at this time of crisis. Men who married a sultan's daughter married into political power, but the sultan was vigilant to limit that power. They also renounced their right to other wives. Fatma's new husband was three times her age, as her former one had also been; but he was an accomplished poet and leading patron in an age of exciting developments in Turkish poetry. He sought to hasten the consummation of his marriage by an outpouring of courtship poems.[37]

In this situation of dubious import for the bride, Lady Mary (who may have heard the story with some infusion of gallant convention) discerned the germ of romance. Her account presents the first marriage as a love-match and the second, by contrast, as a painful duty. She got hold of some of Ibrahim's love-verses and experimented with their translation and imitation, beginning from a literal version (perhaps in Italian), supplied by the embassy interpreters.[38] She then introduced English poetic diction and substituted the ancient myths of English poetic convention for Arabian fable. 'The Nightingale now wanders in the Vines, | Her Passion is to seek Roses' became 'Now Philomel renews her tender strain, | Indulging all the night her pleasing Pain.' She set aside time for regular study of Turkish language and 'Oriental Learning'. The Turkish style, which was even now asserting its own identity against the hegemony of the Persian, reminded her of the biblical and the Homeric; she perceived that their eastern provenance gave them something

---

[36] *CL* i. 323–4, 321 and n. 3. For the status of sultan's daughters—who also bore the title of Sultan—see Davis 1986: 1, 14, 16–19.

[37] Fatma (1704–33) m. first Kömürcü Ali Pasha (*c.*1667–1716), then, on 9/20 Feb. 1717, the westernizer Nevşehirli Ibrahim Pasha (*c.*1666–1730) (*CL* i. 321; Schefer 1894: 135; Davies 1986: 16–18; Alderson 1956: Table XLI; *Encyclopaedia of Islam* 1995: ii. 442, 809–10; Hourani 1991: 143).

[38] Her vocabulary and grammar notes are in another hand, translation exercises in her own. She probably used Thomas Vaughan, *Grammar of the Turkish Language*, 1709 (H MS 80. 270–83; Wh MS 135).

in common. She wrestled with the paradox that a pleasing term in one language may have an exact lexical equivalent which is unacceptably 'low' in another. She greedily imbibed the pleasures of engagement, both aesthetic and scholarly, with another new world: one of poetry and manuscripts.[39]

Though her travel letters highlighted her encounters with Turkish culture and visits to Turkish ladies, she lived mostly among the thriving community of western European expatriates or 'Franks'. The British ambassador was an essential shield to merchants of the minority Christian persuasion, especially the rich ones: 'the great Quantity of Greek, French, English and Italians that are under our Protection make their court to me from Morning till Night', she wrote. In 'Satturday', her mouthpiece Flavia had bracketed beauties with monarchs and found herself dethroned forever: here Lady Mary had found an unexpected new kingdom.

She knew one or more Greek ladies: as 'interpretress', as skilled musician (who preferred the Turkish music to the Italian), and as instructor in Greek dances.[40] While her husband plotted against the French ambassador, she made a friend of his teenage bride, Madeleine-Françoise (de Biron), who had married in December 1715 and reached Turkey, heavily pregnant, in October 1716.[41] Madame de Bonnac had a zest for life, and even when bearing a baby a year she enjoyed 'forms and ceremonys'. She never stirred out without her full complement of ambassadorial trappings: 'an open Gilt chariot' (contrasting with the closed Turkish ones), two dozen footmen, gentlemen ushers, and 'a Coach full of attending Damsels yclep'd maids of Honour'. Her retinue and Lady Mary's combined drew vast crowds, all (unlike London mobs) 'silent as Death', to see the unheard-of phenomenon of '2 young Christian Ambassadresses'.[42] Much as she preferred going incognita, Lady Mary enjoyed the young Frenchwoman's company. A month after they met, Monsieur de Bonnac expressed the hope that his wife would learn the good counsels he saw Lady Mary followed in managing her life. She had been a force, he noted, in English affairs; but he added drily that he did not want her teaching his wife Latin.[43]

[39] *CL* i. 333–7, 366. The first Turkish printing press in Constantinople began work in 1729 (Lewis 1968: 33). The use of 'Philomela' as *nom de plume* by Elizabeth Singer, later Rowe, suggests that the name could shed any recollection of the myth of rape behind it.

[40] *CL* i. 338. Olaudah Equiano wrote fifty years later that the Greeks were 'in some measure, kept under by the Turks, as the Negroes are in the West Indies by white people' (1987: 124).

[41] Schefer 1894: pp. xx, xxxi, 163.

[42] *CL* i. 323–4, 333, 347. Mme de Bonnac bore a son on 7 Dec. 1716 and was 'big again' a year later (*CL* i. 372 and n. 1). An attendant retinue was a marker of male power in Turkish society (Peirce 1993: 8).

[43] De Bonnac seemed alarmed at MWM's scholarly knowledge of Virgil and Horace (13, 23 Apr. 1717: Ministère des Affaires Etrangères, Constantinople, 57. 151, 153). He was himself a student of Turkish culture (Schefer 1894: p. lxiv).

The pair had soon visited several harems. 'The Houses of the great Turkish Ladys are kept clean with as much nicety as those in Holland', Lady Mary wrote later. She was now to discover something of the complex truth behind the overheated western notion of the harem, the long-established 'obsession with the sexuality of Islamic society'. She learned that the harem rested less on sexual than on family politics; that women (veiled, of course) moved freely about the streets; and that the segregation of the sexes created a female space with its own culture and its own hierarchy, a women's network extended by rituals of female visiting.[44]

The visits she describes in most detail were made on her own except for her 'interpretress' and her woman-servant. It was a signal honour 'never given before to any Christian' to be invited 'to dine with the Grand Vizier's Lady', for eating with foreigners had till recently been unthinkable for Turks. She went in her Viennese court dress, as the most magnificent she had, but incognita—without footmen or maids of honour—in a closed Turkish coach. Met at the door 'by her black Eunuch, who help'd me out of the Coach with great Respect', she was led through several rooms, through a guard of honour composed of her hostess's finely dressed female slaves, into the presence of the lady herself and half a dozen of her friends. The serving of the dinner reminded Lady Mary of Achmet-Beg's household: many successive small courses on low tray-tables, and being pressed to eat more than she wanted. Coffee concluded the meal, and as 'a high mark of respect' two kneeling slaves perfumed her 'Hair, Cloaths, and handkercheif'. There was no pomp. Everything—the meal, the talk, the slaves' singing and dancing—was plain and artless. The grand vizier's lady, like her husband, was very religious; 'her whole expence was in charity and her Employment praying to God.'[45]

When she wrote up this occasion, Montagu used the home of this pious middle-aged woman to highlight by contrast the next she saw: that of Fatima, wife of the kâhya (who was in effect the grand vizier's superior though in name his subordinate). The 'very house confess'd the difference between an Old Devote [her first hostess was fifty] and a young Beauty'. Here there were *two* black eunuchs; the slaves were dazzlingly beautiful young girls; *four* of them served coffee and perfumed the air with incense at

[44] *CL* i. 345, 387. Peirce notes how westerners have seen harem power as the sexual power of concubines, not the family power of mothers (1993: 3, 7, 117; Russell 1794: i. 141). In MWM's letters women use the veil for social and sexual liberty; talking to Spence in 1741, she recalled Turkish women defending it as ensuring modesty and fidelity.

[45] *CL* i. 347–9; Göçek 1987: 37. A near-Deist, MWM made no distinction between Allah and Christian concepts of God.

the visit's end; to this was added the gift of a rich embroidered handkerchief. Lady Mary was enraptured by Fatima's decor, dress, and jewels, by her personal beauty of face and figure, and by her graceful yet majestic manner. In Europe everyone would have thought her 'born and bred to be a Queen, thô educated in a Country we call barbarous'. (Her mother, as Lady Mary learned later, had been a Polish woman 'taken at the Seige of Caminiec' in 1672.) The evening's entertainment was what is now called belly-dancing to a lute and guitar:

Nothing could be more artfull or more proper to raise certain Ideas, the Tunes so soft, the motions so Languishing, accompany'd with pauses and dying Eyes, halfe falling back and then recovering themselves in so artfull a Manner that I am very possitive the coldest and most rigid Prude upon Earth could not have look'd upon them without thinking of something not to be spoke of.[46]

An earlier pattern of private and public resumed its sway in Lady Mary's life. As a public person she entertained and visited harems, where the rapport established was not *only* between one woman and another, but between two states and two cultures. As a private person she sat writing in her chamber, with a storks' nest under the window symbolizing good luck, and turtle-doves in the cypresses beyond symbolizing love. Perhaps those were the doves which appear in her undated 'Verses Written in a Garden'. This deceptively simple little poem, about the doves' unabashed openness in love, makes a philosophical point: that it is wrong to divorce the ideas of Virtue and Pleasure. Separated, they produce the 'Pedant Preist, and Giddy Rake'; united, they produce a life lived according to nature: 'For Constancy is Nature too.' It was about a month after she reached Adrianople that Lady Mary's second pregnancy began (assuming it to have run to term). The baby, later Lady Bute, was born on 19 January 1718.

There is no truth in later rumours which, as Lady Louisa put it, 'would give us all the honour of descending from the Sultan Achmet'.[47] (Edward Wortley Montagu the younger liked to hint—with obvious absurdity—that *he* was sired by the sultan.) Nor can Lady Mary's pregnancy be taken as evidence about the state of the marital relationship at this time as compared with other times: apart from the element of chance, no record would survive of, for instance, any miscarriage she may have had at any date. Being

---

[46] *CL* i. 386, 349–52; Davis 1986: 162. Bridget Orr discerns in this encounter what Irigaray describes as 'admiration' or wonder at the Other (1994: 164). Some read MWM as revealing or half-revealing desire for Fatima; but the dance (by professionals) renders desire into high (and expensive) art.

[47] *E&P* 300–1; Wh MS M. 439/38. Nor is some other lover at all likely. EWM was later happy to see his daughter resemble his dead sister, Anne (*E&P* 13).

pregnant in Turkey had some advantages. A certain glory accrued to her, from the belief that 'the End of the Creation of Woman is to encrease and Multiply', that bearing children was the most important thing she could do. Lady Mary later wrote to a Frenchwoman friend that she had got tired of being despised, and thought it time to comply with the fashion and have a baby like everyone else.[48]

They were not long at Adrianople. A couple of months after their arrival, before summer could dry the river, they were making ready to leave for Constantinople. The court was packed up; the sultan had gone to join the army encamped outside the city, which he was to lead in person to battle. Lady Mary, like other ladies, had been in her *araba* to admire the camp, where the great men's tents (all in the auspicious colour of green) resembled palaces. She had watched a magnificent procession of the sultan's subjects, all in their various social groups and trades, testifying loyalty and offering financial backing for the war effort: husbandmen, millers, bakers; jewellers, mercers, furriers; and half-naked volunteers displaying their valour by piercing themselves with arrows and slashing themselves with knives—a part of the show which Lady Mary found so 'barbarous' that she left the window while it passed by. In all there were two thousand men eager to follow their monarch to war against the army of her old acquaintance Prince Eugene.

The sultan was 'resolv'd to lead his Army in Person': bad news for Wortley, who had hoped to bring him to the negotiating table without more fighting. '[H]is Highness' watched his loyal procession from the Seraglio. Lady Mary watched it from the house of an admiral's widow, who was probably the heroine of a romantic story she recounted later. This Spanish-born lady had been, long ago, on a sea voyage with her brother, 'attack'd . . . boarded and taken'—in two senses—by the Turkish admiral. As Lady Mary put it, the 'same Accident happen'd to her that happen'd to the fair Lucretia so many Years before her, but she was too good a Christian to kill her selfe as that heathenish Roman did'. Her ravisher, 'charm'd with [her] Beauty and long-suffering', freed her brother, and then, on receipt of £4,000 ransom money, offered to free her too. This faced the raped Spaniard with a hard decision. 'Her Catholic Relations, as the kindest thing they could do for her in her present Circumstances, would certainly confine her to a Nunnery for the rest of her Days. Her Infidel Lover was very handsome, very tender, fond of her, and lavish'd at her feet all the Turkish Magnificence. She answer'd him very resolutely that her Liberty was not so precious to her as

[48] *CL* i. 363, 372, 404; Davis 1986: 33.

her Honnour, that he could no way restore that but by marrying her.'
Although she suggested he should keep the ransom as dowry, he returned
it to her family. He took her with nothing, and never had another wife.
They lived happily until his death (when, since 'there is no remaining
honnourably a single woman', she remarried). Lady Mary insisted that her
friend acted not out of love, but 'wholly on principles of Honnour'.[49]

[49] *CL* i. 355–7, 408–9.

10

May 1717–July 1718

❦

Constantinople: 'Imperial City'[1]

ON the road from Adrianople to Constantinople (with five *arabas*, thirty covered waggons, and a Greek lady keeping them company) they met a succession of 'the great Spahys and their Equipages, coming out of Assia to the War'. While the spahis pitched their nightly tents, Lady Mary 'chose to lye in Houses' on this four-day summer journey. In a 'Conac, or little Seraglio' built to accommodate the sultan's harem on journeys, she was pleasurably 'surpriz'd to see the Walls almost cover'd with little distichs of Turkish verse writ with pencils'. Several of them, once translated, proved to be a credit to Turkish ladies' literary skills. Beside the sea of Marmara, they admired sights including two more creations of the architect Selim: a famous multiple-span bridge and an imperial pavilion and fountain. The most attractive of their stopping places, now a school, had once been a 'Monastery of Dervises'. The schoolmaster, with his wife and children, had their beds on platforms at the top of a cypress: Lady Mary wanted to see, and climbed halfway up to it by a ladder of steps; but when she realized she must then clamber from branch to branch she changed her mind and came down.[2]

In the evening of 8 June/28 May they saw the famous skyline ahead: 'Each gilded Crescent and each antique Spire.' The brooding dome of the Sulaimaniye, the work of Selim's maturity, crouched among its 400 lesser domes and grove of minarets. This skyline was to act as backdrop to at least three portraits of Lady Mary, blazoning her fame as a traveller.

They lived at Pera on the south bank (like most of the *corps diplomatique*), in a splendid seventeenth-century palace. Wortley's predecessor Lord Paget had contributed a chapel in the style of St George's Chapel, Windsor;

---

[1] Constantinople: from her poem 'To [William Feilding]' (*E&P* 208).
[2] Sözen 1987: 144, 146; *CL* i. 360, 361–2. Quatrains called *manis* were a female genre (Davis 1986: 145).

Wortley planned to spend £250 in furnishing. Pera, with Tophana and Galata, was divided from Constantinople proper by the Bosphorus. It was not a suburb, she said, any more than Westminster (her previous home) was a suburb of London. It was 'wholly inhabited by Frank Christians': a melting-pot where a single individual might have Greek, Italian, French, Armenian, English, Russian, and Asian blood. A dozen or more languages yelled and chattered in the streets, conjuring up the tower of Babel. The embassy palace had a terrace, a garden, a view: the 'crouded City, and Resounding Sea', and 'the distant hills of Assia, perhaps all together the most beautifull Prospect in the World'. They had Arab grooms, Russian housemaids, French, English, and German footmen, miscellaneous Greek servants, and an Italian steward. Lady Mary quickly became acquainted, no doubt through her son, with four year olds who had more languages than years, and none of them English. But the foreign diplomats dealt mostly with Greek and Armenian merchants and Jewish brokers; few (except the Venetians) made any real contact with Islamic Turks, as opposed to Christian subjects of the Turkish empire.[3]

Some of Lady Mary's female friends, like Madame de Bonnac, never crossed the water to Constantinople, partly from dislike of the concealing *asmak*, partly from fear of the watermen. But Lady Mary found the Bosphorus a delight: 'The Asian Side is cover'd with fruit trees, villages and the most delightful Landschapes in nature.' Opposite stood Constantinople on its seven hills, 'Shewing an agreeable mixture of Gardens, Pine and Cypress trees, Palaces, Mosques and publick buildings, rais'd one above another', to which she applied the 'very odd Comparison' of a skilfully ordered cabinet of china and rarities.[4]

Lady Mary at Constantinople brings to mind Virginia Woolf's hero/heroine Orlando. Despatched there as British ambassador under Charles II, the would-be writer Orlando changes sex in Constantinople. Journeying home in the early eighteenth century, she ponders the curious interdependent fooleries of being female and being male. Back in London, she cultivates authors and witnesses Pope's destructive power. Did a reading of Montagu go to fuel the creation of all this? Did Woolf have her letters in mind as she evoked the noises and smells rising 'even to the heights of Pera', 'the strident multi-coloured and barbaric population', and the immense dissimilarity of Asian mountains to the 'towns of London and Tunbridge Wells'?

When Orlando changes sex, the deities Purity, Chastity, and Modesty try

---

[3] *E&P* 207, 208; *CL* i. 362, 390, 397; Halsband 1956: 74; Mantran 1982: 129, 131.   [4] *CL* i. 397.

feebly to cover her naked form with 'a garment like a towel'. In her baggy Turkish trousers Orlando never thinks about her new sex; but sailing home, reclined under an awning, she renounces ambition for 'contemplation, solitude, love'. In Woolf's deliberately anachronistic London, under the new dome of St Paul's, Orlando harks back from the 'distraction of sex' to poetry; she repeats like a mantra, 'Addison, Dryden, Pope'. Woolf's Pope is frightening. 'Darts of malice, rage, triumph, wit, and terror . . . shot from his eyes.' Orlando learns the failings and foibles of authors, and their propensity to turn her into their patron and hostess; she feels Pope has 'run her through the body with his pen'.

Surely Lady Mary is implicated in all this: her visit to the baths, her Turkish costume, her voyage home, her quarrel with Pope. Woolf renders her idiosyncratic experience abstract and symbolic: a type both of her moment in history, and of the travails of the 'poet's heart . . . caught and tangled in a woman's body'.[5]

⤙❧⤚

Meanwhile, in 1717, the Wortley Montagus' time at Constantinople was soon interrupted. In only a couple of weeks the summer heat and the fear of plague drove them ten miles out to Belgrade Village. The embassy's country villa there, Lady Mary told Pope, 'perfectly answers the Description of the Elysian fields'. Set amid fruit trees, with 'many Shady Walks upon short grass', it enjoyed refreshing breezes from the Black Sea, which was visible some miles off. Though Lady Mary felt twinges of nostalgia for 'the Smoak and Impertinencies' of London, there was no lack of society. Her typical week, as she rehearsed it to Pope, gave a day each to reading English, reading the ancients, Turkish studies, writing, and needlework, but also one to hunting partridges and one to music and visits. Every evening Greek girls in national dress sang and danced at a fountain across the clearing. Here, she later said, she argued with a lady (nationality not given), a believer in charms and love-potions.[6]

This idyllic interlude was short; events on the military and diplomatic front brought them back to the city even before the heat eased up. According to Wortley's later, lengthy self-justification, he had written on Austrian advice, via the British ambassador in Vienna (Abraham Stanyan), to inform the emperor of current Turkish stipulations for a peace, which he judged to be much the most submissive so far. He meant to send Hefferman with

    [5] Woolf 1928: 111, 126–7, 146, 150, 184, 194; Woolf 1929: 83.
    [6] *CL* i. 365–7, 369–70. For a century the disputed sites of her house (either 'in a desolated field' or 'embosomed in the depth of the forest') remained a tourist sight (Dallaway 1797: 47; Hobhouse 1813: ii. 861).

further details in cipher. Meanwhile the emperor knew the Turks had accepted the idea of mediation by the British Crown and were well disposed towards Wortley's principle of 'Uti Possedetis': that each side should keep what it held when negotiations began. Wortley thought that threats to Austria from Spain and Sicily gave the Austrian empire every reason to desire peace with Turkey; he was 'at a Loss to Ghess' why it ignored his letters, which put peace within its grasp. He did not know that Stanyan, who wanted his job, was undermining him in Vienna; and he seemed not to realize that 'Uti Possedetis' was an invitation to grab more territory (perhaps 'Bosna' as well as Belgrade) before negotiating. Austria used his letters to impress Sicily with its strength *vis-à-vis* Turkey; it made no move to negotiate.[7]

Wortley dreamed of achieving a peace treaty by autumn 1717. But he had two shocks in store. The summer campaign proceeded; Eugene besieged Belgrade. Battle was joined in dawn fog on 16/5 August 1717, and a week later the city surrendered. Eugene left not a house standing; Achmet-Beg's fate is not known.[8]

The fall of Belgrade threw Turkey into political crisis. The new grand vizier was deposed, replaced by the basha of Cairo; behind the scenes Ibrahim began consolidating a power base.[9] Wortley's status in Turkey benefited; but to the Austrians he now looked like the man who had tried to make peace prematurely, without their new territorial gains.

He was more radically undermined by events in Britain which happened earlier but reached him later. That spring Walpole and his associates had resigned, to be replaced by Stanhope and Sunderland. Ironically in view of Wortley's dislike of Walpole, he must have looked to the new ministry like a Walpole man. On 22/12 July Joseph Addison, brand-new replacement for Methuen as Secretary of State, signed a warrant for his old friend Wortley's recall. Two months later he followed it with the most tactful letter he could contrive: the king was perfectly satisfied with Wortley's conduct, he insisted, and would offer him 'a place for life' on his return; the changed political situation called for long-established Turkey hands; also it called for two of them, and Wortley might not wish to share. The letter (endorsed by Wortley 'Reason for my being recalled') almost makes it sound as if the primary reason was his own benefit.[10]

The recall has been taken as proof that Wortley was no great shakes as

[7] Halsband 1956: 76–7. In England opinion differed widely as to whether peace would eventuate (BL Add. MS 61547. 138–9; John Thomlinson in BL Add. MS 22560. 58).

[8] Schefer 1894: p. xxiii; McKay 1977: 163–5. EWM later boasted that during the siege the sultan received medical attendance from a man primed with his private instructions: Dr Emanuel Timoni, who had reported on inoculation to the Royal Society in London.

[9] Schefer 1894: 137.   [10] Hill 1989: 90; PRO, SP 44/360/39; Addison 1941: 376–8.

ambassador, in particular that he displeased his British masters by favouring the Turks—even that this was due to his wife's remarkably pro-Islamic sentiments.[11] The truth is that he was a pawn in games being played elsewhere. Commissioned to negotiate a peace, he set his sights on peace, sharing neither the Turkish sense that peace was shameful even if expedient, nor the Austrian sense of mission about re-Christianizing Europe by conquest. His recall was decreed too soon to be based on his performance (unless on negative *forecasts* sent from Vienna the moment he left it). Of his own two detailed accounts of the matter, one (sent to Sunderland soon after his return) claims he was treated with shameful injustice while others reaped the reward for his brilliant negotiations; the other (written thirty years later) makes less of the injustice than the financial loss.[12]

One of the most painful aspects of the recall was that it operated retrospectively. According to his own account Wortley received neither the official communication nor Addison's personal letter for six months after they were written:[13] months during which he exerted himself to the utmost to secure the peace negotiations at which he meant to play a prominent and profitable role. To this end he set out with Timoni on 12 September on the ten-day journey to the sultan's camp in Philippopoli, not knowing when he would be back. Before leaving he drew up an 'Estimate of my Personal Estate being what I have to pay debts in Sept. 1717'. He expected an infusion of cash on 13 September, which, he wrote, *might* suffice 'to pay what is due to servants for wages, and carry on the whole Expenses of the family till the Quarter day in December'. He had not yet been fully reimbursed for his outlay in equipping himself for the embassy. He now had 9,600 in hand, presumably reckoned in pounds sterling but including value in kind: 'Effects' bought from Sutton, and 'wine sugar Wood Corn and other necessaries'.[14] Part of these last, from the 'Allowance for Provisions' made him by the sultan, would be surplus to his needs; it was normal practice for ambassadors to turn a cash profit by selling that part on. The embassy was an entrepreneurial concern. Meanwhile in London Addison was about to sign an order for payment to Sutton (Wortley's predecessor, and now one of his two replacements) of £1,000 for his equipage and £10 per diem expenses

---

[11] Stanyan joked that she must have shifted her affections from Prince Eugene to the Mosaip (23 June 1717, *Annals of Stair*, ii. 36).

[12] BL MS 61547. 138–43; Halsband MSS. Cf. Michael 1936: 363.

[13] The king officially informed the Levant Company of EWM's recall on 1 Oct., with formulaic expressions of praise for him. The Company were, Sir John Williams informed him, shocked and offended. They had no say in choosing a successor, but received various sweeteners instead (H MS 79. 190–1; 78. 53–5; Halsband 1956: 78).

[14] Halsband MSS.

backdated to 29 July.[15] Stanyan was the other replacement. No wonder Wortley harboured resentment and demanded compensation.

At the sultan's camp, Wortley told the mosaip Ibrahim that the emperor would settle for nothing less than Belgrade. Ibrahim agreed that, even so, Turkey must make peace. (De Bonnac reported Ibrahim's views almost identically.)[16] After three days Wortley proceeded, at the mosaip's request, to the vizier's camp near Sofia. There he 'lived some time'. Ibrahim said the vizier would agree to stomach the loss of Belgrade in the cause of peace: Wortley was to get word of this conveyed to Eugene by Hefferman.[17]

Hefferman set out 8 October. He was quarantined at Belgrade, but he sent the vizier's letter on to Vienna. There, said Wortley later, it enabled Eugene virtually to plagiarize his 'Uti Possidetis' principle and the terms he had achieved: Belgrade, Temeswar, 'with the Countries belonging', expansion in Walachia and Serbia—more than had been expected or might otherwise have been demanded. For the whole package, said Wortley, 'the German [i.e. Austrian] Ministers were altogether Indebted to me'.[18]

Turkey in turn hesitated over responding to Eugene's proposals: accepting might provoke further demands. In mid-December the vizier wrote desiring that the plenipotentiaries might meet once, but not mentioning 'Uti Possedetis'. Wortley did not yet believe in his own dismissal. The merchants had wind of it from sailors' gossip; but Hefferman wrote from Belgrade in November without saying 'one Word' of it. Even after receiving Addison's private letter, in December, Wortley assumed that any plan to drop him must now be revoked in view of 'the Great Success of my Negociations'. In order to maximize his future influence, therefore, he said he moved cautiously and gradually towards the full diplomatic agreement which he felt within his grasp.[19]

By mid-February 1718, with no reply yet from Austria, the mosaip and Reis Effendi began to fear 'another Campagne'. They came to Wortley and the Dutch ambassador for advice; they appeared ready to accept 'Uti Possedetis' in order to secure an immediate peace congress. Timoni interpreted, and wrote the report which was sent in English and Dutch to England and Holland. 'A few Days after . . . comes Mr. Hefferman.' He

---

[15] 7 Nov. 1717, SP 44/360/61–2; BL Add. MS 61547. 139. Extraordinary expenses would also be met if backed by bills in Sutton's hand. Stanyan's allowed expenses were £5 a day: up from £3 (SP 44/360/62–4; BL MS 61547. 142).

[16] They differed only in the degree of blame they assigned to Ali Pasha for Turkey's weakness (BL Add. MS 61547. 139; Schefer 1894: 139).

[17] First he and Hefferman had a private meeting with Ibrahim's confidant, the Reis Effendi or Chancellor, and his interpreter (BL MS 61547. 139).

[18] The only snag he admitted was that inexperienced Turkish ministers had trouble with the Arabic equivalent to 'Uti Posseditis' (BL MS 61547. 139).

[19] BL MS 61547. 139; Halsband 1956: 79.

brought Eugene's agreement to an early meeting (the fruit, said Wortley, of his own intelligence work); he also brought 'my Revocation'.

For Wortley the blow had fallen at the moment of triumph. The congress, he wrote, 'answer'd Expectation'. The peace which was finally signed in July 1718, advantageously for the emperor, was based on what he had negotiated in August 1717. But it was signed without him—even as he embarked for home to an ambassadorial salute sounding hollow in his ears. Not for him the large presents which Lord Paget had received at the previous Austrian–Turkish peace—and which, with his popularity, he could have hoped to top.

With dogged integrity but with unconcealed bitterness he prepared to withdraw. He wrote to Prince Eugene to ask *him* to arrange his employment at the negotiations, but received a courteous refusal.[20] He gave away or sold 'at a very low rate' his 'Horses, Liveries, Furniture, Clothes and other Necessaries'. He had almost completely equipped himself for the congress, having only another £500 to expend. All these things 'would have serv'd me for some Years had I been Continued'. He gave away his official present of tents from the sultan, as he felt he 'should', to Sutton. He had to give cash rewards to those who had served him; there was no time for the usual course of paying them with favours extracted from the host country, and he had chosen not to ask favours so long as he felt it worth ingratiating himself. His pay ceased at the arrival of Stanyan (whom in May 1718 he had to present to the grand vizier). His Allowance for Provisions was transferred to Sutton. But for the honour of himself and his country he continued to live like an Ambassador Extraordinary.

He had lost his present and his future: as ambassador and as plenipotentiary at the congress. But still it was 'unreasonable' that he should lose so much. Before the end of the year he had written a maxim-type essay 'On Fame', which notes that 'The Crosses and fatigues which every man has in Publick Assemblies make him often wish to be out of them almost at any rate. | Especially if his health is not perfect. | A man is very commonly made unfortunate by his popularity.' A companion piece on 'Losses' adds: 'If a man suffers by another man's not being reasonable this is one of the most common Accidents.'[21] This sounds like the stoicism of Epictetus, in which his wife too was later to take refuge.

❧

Lady Mary stayed behind at Pera while her husband was dancing attendance on Turkish ministers. How far she was privy to his plans and hopes cannot

---

[20] Michael 1936: 363.   [21] BL MS 61547. 140; Halsband 1956: 80; H MS 80. 126–8.

be known. Around the time of the siege, when she was four months pregnant, Timoni the part-time diplomat and early enquirer into inoculation became her family physician. It seems that her diary-keeping may have slipped during this pregnancy: she dated no Embassy Letters between 17 June 1717 and 4 January 1718. Again she was passing part of her life, in a very particular sense, 'together' with another person.

Towards New Year she enjoyed the spring-like warmth and unseasonal flowers. The only means of heating in use (a serious fire risk) was a *tandır*, a low table standing over a container of hot ashes from the cooking fire: the user sat with her feet under the table, with a carpet draped over the whole thing. But it was warm enough to sit outdoors, at a date when a year ago, in Vienna, she had been ready to die from 'Excessive cold'.

On Boxing Day she sat in her garden kiosk writing a letter in verse to her uncle William Feilding: a meditation on the seasonal cycles that bring infant buds to replace mother flowers, and one wave of conquerors to replace another. Her oriental learning flavours this poem, which celebrates spring lushness and its transience in the style of the great lyricist Mesihi. She knew as she wrote that she was soon to lose this paradise, which realized her youthful dream of pastoral retreat. About now she demanded of Congreve (a faithful correspondent) 'Why he lets P[o]p[e] make Lampoons'. She received Pope's gift of a copy of his recently published *Works*, and a letter heavily hinting that the end of *Eloisa to Abelard*, with its image of hopeless, faithful love, refers to his love for her. Reading *Eloisa* and 'Elegy to the Memory of an Unfortunate Lady', she would clearly have seen the personal allusions. In the balmy midwinter sunshine, London stood for exhausting complications, for 'Censorious Folly, noisy Party rage, | The thousand Tongues with which she must engage | Who dare have Virtue in a vicious Age.' Her aspiration after virtue echoed a poem of five years before, 'While Thirst of Power'. Then too she had looked forward to a new debut in London society. But she had then said the recipe for virtue was 'sure'; a woman had only to assert her virtue to be accepted as virtuous.[22] By now she saw active virtue as attracting no recognition, but only censure.

Three weeks later she bore her daughter, attended by a midwife whose nationality she does not mention.[23] The Turkish style of childbirth was a social, even noisy, affair, with the midwife in charge. Upper-class women might stay in bed for six days, but that was all. Lady Mary would not have

---

[22] *CL* ii. 492; i. 292, 374; *E&P* 207–10, 179; Pope, *Corr.* i. 407; Lewis 1963: 161–3; TE ii. 331–6; Rumbold 1989: 109.

[23] 19 Jan. (*CL* i. 371–4; *E&P* 206–10). The man-midwife was still an exclusively English phenomenon (Wilson 1995: 5–6).

adopted these customs, or have heard her new baby greeted with the 'Ziraleet' or cry of exultation, but she may have used the honey-and-spice ointment which was held to be good against complications.[24]

As she told her daughter drily years afterwards, 'There was a mutual necessity on us both to part at that time, and no obligation on either side.' She did not find childbirth as easy as Turkish women, but she did find it 'not halfe so mortifying here as in England'. Three weeks after it she was out repaying the visits made to her. She probably received gifts on the occasion, though they would not have matched those Mme de Bonnac had received on bearing a son and heir in Pera. Little Mary must have been christened by the chaplain, Mr Crosse; the Catholic de Bonnacs stood godparents.[25]

Soon after this, one morning's early light revealed

not very far from my House the bleeding body of a young woman, naked, only wrapp'd in a coarse sheet, with 2 wounds with a knife, one in her side and another in her Breast. She was not yet quite cold, and so surprizingly Beautifull that there were very few men in Pera that did not go to look upon her, but it was not possible for any body to know her, no woman's face being known.

It was assumed that she had been murdered on the Constantinople side, probably by a jealous husband. There must have been women who knew who she was; but no investigation ensued. Even in face of this, Lady Mary held to her position that such violence was 'extreamly rare' in Turkey, whose people were 'not naturally cruel'.[26]

By early March she resumed her visits to Turkish ladies. She later addressed her public accounts of them (as well as a sketchy one of her daughter's birth) to her sister Frances.[27] Her most distinguished hostess, Hafise Kadinfendi (whose name she misspells throughout), had been the favourite of the previous sultan, Mustafa II, and briefed her on the manners and customs of the Seraglio.[28] Hafise contrived to have her guest enter her marble-pillared room before she did, 'to avoid riseing up at my Entrance'. Her dress, her pearls, diamonds, rubies, and emeralds, and the gold of her table settings, were the acme of Arabian Nights-style luxury. Lady Mary, computing busily, reckoned her jewels to be worth £100,000 sterling, her sables £600, and her slave-girls £4,000.

---

[24] Davis 1986: 33–4, 37. Russell 1794: i. 299–302; he thought Turkish women found childbirth easy because of their use of the hot baths (i. 140).

[25] *CL* i. 380; ii. 492; Schefer 1894: p. lxix; H MS 77. 154–5.

[26] *CL* i. 407–8.   [27] Who was back in England from mid-Oct. 1717.

[28] Davis explains the seraglio's complex hierarchy, down to female clerks and cooks. The sultan's usually four kadıns (concubines, not wives) ranked after his daughters. They could not receive visitors during their sultan's lifetime. The ikbals (like them translated 'favourites') ranked next (1986: 1, 3, 6).

But the aesthetic experience was richer at the Constantinople palace of her old acquaintance Fatima, the kâhya's wife, 'in a high part of the Town', with 'the Prospect of the Sea and the Islands and the Assian Mountains'. Fatima outshone the wealthy Hafise as she had outshone the pious grand vizier's wife. Her walls were panelled in 'inlaid work of Mother of Pearl, Ivory of different Colours and olive wood, exactly like the little Boxes you have seen brought out of this Country'; her soft furnishings, different for winter and summer, each involved gold and each, too, was of exquisite workmanship. Since their previous meeting Lady Mary had learned enough Turkish for conversation. They exchanged compliments on each other's beauty, and she found Fatima 'very curious after the manners of other countrys and has not that partiality for her own, so common to little minds'.[29]

Lady Mary aimed to avoid such littleness.[30] She boasted that she was in danger of forgetting her English. She discovered that it was possible to 'quarrel, reproach, or send Letters of passion, friendship, or Civillity, or even of news, without ever inking your fingers' by means of the small objects which Turkish tradition invested with symbolic meanings. Soap, she found, meant 'I am sick with Love', and pepper 'Send me an Answer.' She took extensive notes on these emblematic objects, and packed a set of them in a little box for despatch by sea to a friend.[31]

This month, March 1718, Wortley was away, as he had been for most of the winter. He was taking his enforced leave of the sultan.[32] A warship, the *Preston*, was coming to take them home, but was not expected until July. Their recall brought Lady Mary lots of business to see to. She arranged to buy pearls from the Dutch ambassador's wife (apparently behind the Dutch ambassador's back); she debated the purchase of 'table gilt plate . . . not fine Silver but makes the same shew'. Her uncle Feilding had recently repaid her a sum of £1,550 (how she had it to lend is a mystery), and she wondered whether to take the Spanish pieces of eight and exchange them in England, or to invest them in goods—which would be worth while only if they could be taken duty-free. On this the final decision lay with Wortley; she wanted him to 'think more than once' about it. She also urged him to send her father 'a civil Letter . . . as if writ during my Lying in' three months back. People were asking her if they were going by the man-of-war, or overland instead. Wortley remained undecided till the end of June, while his wife told enquirers '(as I allways do upon your affairs) that I knew nothing of it'.[33]

[29] *CL* i. 380–7.   [30] Cf. Fernea 1981.   [31] *CL* i. 388–9; CB 17–20.

[32] He arrived at Adrianople to take leave on 23 Mar.; the new minister reached Constantinople by 1 Apr.

[33] *CL* i. 391–5.

In one sphere that did count as hers, the management of her family, she took an unprecedented step while Wortley was away; but she took it with the support of the surgeon Maitland, and probably of Timoni (though, according to Voltaire, in the teeth of disapproval from the Revd Mr Crosse). She and Maitland had already prepared themselves by study. Now she asked him to find her a 'Young Person, of a Sound Constitution', suffering from 'the best sort of the Small Pox'—i.e. a mild strain—from whom to inoculate her son. This he did, with 'a good deal of Trouble and Pains', by 18 March 1718. Lady Mary summoned the old nurse who was Constantinople's 'General surgeon' for inoculation. The nurse pricked one of the little boy's wrists with a needle, laid a tiny droplet of smallpox matter on the wrist, and mixed it with the drop of blood from the puncture. According to Maitland's later memory her needle was blunt and rusty and her hand shook; the boy screamed, although he was generally a tough little fellow. (Mme de Bonnac confirmed his reputation by calling him 'mon petit mutin de favory'.)[34]

Maitland's account, the only one extant, was written and published during vicious controversy in England, when association with an 'ignorant' old woman (or with women and with Islam in general) bid fair to 'stifle this safe and useful' new discovery 'in its Birth'. Maitland sought to make this experimental inoculation respectable by appropriating it for modern medicine: he inoculated the second arm 'with my own Instrument, and with so little Pain to him, that he did not in the least complain of it'.[35]

A dressing was applied, and removed after about twelve hours; the tiny scabs lasted three days. The child was 'confin'd to a warm chamber'; five days after the operation his mother reported him 'singing and playing and very impatient for his supper'—which would be, by order, a light vegetarian one. She was still anxious enough to 'pray God' he would go on well. A few days later he became hot and thirsty, and about a hundred spots appeared on his body, whose 'crusts' quickly dropped off and left no trace. He suffered no headache, no back pains, no inflamed mucous membranes, no vomiting or panic attacks: none of the classic symptoms of smallpox which she had herself endured. She would gladly have had her infant daughter done too; but her Armenian nurse had never had smallpox, and Lady Mary felt certain (more so than professional medics) that inoculated smallpox would be just as infectious as the natural kind.

---

[34] *CL* i. 392; *E&P* 95–6; Maitland 1722: 3–7; Voltaire 1963–93: letter 11; Mme de Bonnac, 20 Sept. 1719, H MS 74. 154–5: 'My favourite, the little rebel'. A later opponent of inoculation said that while Timoni was away with the ambassador his wife inoculated their daughter Elizabeth, who, he alleged, later d. of smallpox. His account contains inaccuracies (Haen 1759: 48 ff.).

[35] *CL* i. 392; *E&P* 95–6; Maitland 1722: 3–5, 7.

With her daughter born, her son inoculated, and her departure imminent, she must have felt she had seen all too little of Constantinople across the water, and she set out with energy to catch up. 'I ramble every day, wrap'd up in my ferigé and asmak, about Constantinople and amuse my selfe with seeing all that is curious in it.' Of Topkapi, the seraglio or seat of government, 'a Palace of prodigious extent', she took care to 'see as much . . . as is to be seen' beyond its high walls. This was not much: its treetops and white minarets decked out with gilding.[36] Of the many mosques, which she found almost interchangeable, she preferred the Sulaimaniye and the more recent Valide, called after a sultan's mother to the 'honour of our Sex'. She transcribed a Latin inscription from the pedestal of an Egyptian obelisk in the Atmeydan or hippodrome; she despaired of learning the true origin of the famous 'serpent column'; she explored the bazaars and shops; she went by water to visit the ancient city of Calcedon (later Kadiköy) on the Asian coast; she watched dervishes dancing at their monastery, and was moved by their gravity, austerity, 'Submission and mortification'. She inspected the palace built by Ali Pasha to receive his bride, Princess Fatma, and cited its mother-of-pearl panelling, with emeralds placed like nails, as the acme of all her accounts of Turkish luxury. Repeatedly in her descriptions, 'out of a true female spirit of Contradiction', she attacked the misstatements of previous western voyage-writers.[37]

She turned her mind to souvenirs to take home. She had begun a 'Collection of Greek Medals' (she dismissed the style of icons as 'monstrous') and 'bespoke a Mummy'. Vanmour painted her again. Standing before the Constantinople skyline, in a setting of Turkish decor (carpet, sofa, cushions), she holds her son by the hand in an awkward pose which *might* be designed to show off his inoculation scars. A female servant plays an ethnic musical instrument; a janizary holds out a letter. This last perhaps alludes not only to the lifeline represented by news from distant home, but to Lady Mary's travel-book-in-embryo, the future Embassy Letters. A related conversation piece of her shows shipping in the background instead of buildings; it has no letter-carrier, but Lady Mary herself holds a scroll to represent her oriental learning.[38]

[36] *CL* i. 405, 397–8. Clearly though she states this, controversy arose as soon as the letters were printed as to whether she had been inside.

[37] *CL* i. 399–403, 405, 413–14.

[38] *CL* i. 361, 364–5; NPG and archive (Vanmour discussed by Margaret Drabble in *The Middle Ground*, 1980: 215–16). The male figure shows this is not a harem (cf. DelPlato 1988: 163–78). The instrument is a *tehegour* (Pointon 1992, 70). The Constantinople background does not *prove* it was painted there, since Vanmour could no doubt work from memory. A series of six water-colours of Turks in various costumes (from the sultan downwards; only one female) has been ascribed to MWM's hand (*Antiques Roadshow*, 16 Feb. 1997; cf. p. 382). But *if* they really came from her she may have owned, not painted, them.

She visited some baths again, for a bridal reception (and what would now be called a shower) held there. The 'Beautifull Maid of about 17, very richly drest and shineing with Jewells . . . was presently reduce'd . . . to the state of nature' by thirty naked long-haired virgins. They perfumed her and walked with her in procession before an audience of two hundred or more 'she-friends, Relations and acquaintance of the 2 familys newly ally'd', who each 'saluted her with a compliment and a present, some of Jewells, others pieces of stuff, Handkerchiefs, or little Galantrys of that nature'. Again Lady Mary was delighted by the beauty and courtesy of the scene.[39]

During these last months her departure weighed on her. She had been alone a great deal between September 1717 and mid-May 1718. In June, Wortley must have been haunted by thoughts of the peace congress taking place without him.[40] In 'A Satyr', which she 'Wrote at Constantinople' in imitation of Boileau's satire ten, she conventionally anatomizes the aberrations of women in western society: female gamesters and misers, madcaps and fashion addicts, the quarrelsome, the jealous, the sickly, the learned and the political. It was not unusual for her to criticize her own sex, but unusual for her to show no trace of the sympathy evident in, say, her eclogues. This poem expresses impatience with her own culture; and it treats with profound scepticism the aspiration to give up roving and rambling and to settle down.[41]

The prospect of home included the prospect of Pope. As a literary friend he was in some ways rewarding. His assiduous letters brought her news and gossip (often of court or literary figures: Craggs, Methuen, Congreve, Garth, Buckingham). He sent her books (his own included) and reported his reverential preservation of her eclogues.[42] If he was sometimes too ardent for comfort, until the summer of 1717 she knew he must remain ardent at a distance. (He may have been equally content that his hypothetical worship ran no risk of being tested in action.)[43] Six months after her departure he had said he was raving mad over her distance and her danger, and lamented that the cloak of 'friendship' should mask 'the real truth of my heart'. In June 1717 she was still his deity; love for her had inspired him to write of Eloisa's love for Abelard; his 'faint slight, timorous' letters fell short of his 'warm

---

[39] *CL* i. 406–7.

[40] On 11 May he was still at Adrianople, hoping to leave in a few days. The talks were held under canvas; all buildings between Belgrade and Nis were destroyed (McKay 1977: 167).

[41] *E&P* 210–14.

[42] 'They lie inclosd in a Monument of Red Turkey, written in my fairest hand; the gilded Leaves are opend with no less veneration than the Pages of the Sybils; like them, lockd up & conceald from all prophane eyes' (Pope, *Corr.* i. 441–2, 470).

[43] Rumbold concurs (1989: 136, 140).

& tender' memories.[44] Even in autumn, when he knew she was coming home prematurely: 'I lye dreaming of you in Moonshiny Nights exactly in the posture of Endymion gaping for Cynthia in a Picture . . . I feel you as you draw nearer, My heart leaps at your arrival.' Yet already there is a hint of embarrassment. If she should 'at last come rolling back again' (like the moon), he will have to awaken from his dream. He writes 'as if I were drunk, the pleasure I take in *thinking* of your return transports me beyond the bounds of common Sence and decency'. This seems to suggest that common sense, decency, and sobriety might in time reassert their power.

He reopened the idea of meeting her in Italy—like a troubadour who followed a countess to Jerusalem, and expired well satisfied with a glimpse of her. Or 'our Romance' might have a happier ending, through the fair Circassian slave, her surrogate, 'as near as possible to that face, but . . . the colours a little less vivid, the eyes a little less bright'. His next surviving letter offers more of the same (though it also stresses his ill health). 'The Women here are—Women. I can't express how I long to see you, face to face, If ever you come again, I shall never be able to behave with decency . . . Come for God's sake, come Lady Mary, come quickly!'[45] Though he holds sobriety at bay, and promises (or threatens) to make an exhibition of himself for her sake, this also demotes her from the role of a female Ulysses, one who has seen cities and human life, to one who is herself the spectacle.

When she came to write up her Embassy Letters she revealed how far her feelings at the prospect of return diverged from what was expected of her. Wortley, for instance, seemed to fear she might embarrass him by expressions of joy; she assured him this was the opposite of the truth. To a correspondent she made excuses for her reluctance: 'much as I love travelling, I tremble at the inconveniencys attending so great a Journey with a numerous family and a little Infant hanging at the breast.' To Conti she risked suggesting that the Turkish habit of spending life in 'Music, Gardens, Wine, and delicate eating' might indicate a better 'notion of Life' than the race for political power and scientific knowledge: 'I had rather be a rich Effendi with all his ignorance, than Sir Isaac Newton with all his knowledge.' In general she concealed her regret and tried to console herself by alluding to her 'rambling Destiny', her habit of endeavouring to turn 'all the odd turns of my Life . . . to my Diversion'.[46] One suspects that her gender may have been more of an issue here than she admitted. Political power and scientific

---

[44] Pope, *Corr.* i. 389, 405–7. The letter from Lady Mary printed at i. 421–4 is spurious.
[45] Pope, *Corr.* i. 439–42 (italics added), 469–70. In the Embassy Letter which purports to answer this, she said 'I can hardly forbear being angry at you for rejoyceing at what displeases me so much' (*CL* i. 435).
[46] *CL* i. 394, 405, 412, 415.

knowledge were out of a woman's reach, but she could come closer to the experience of the effendi than of the scientist: the grapes were sour. In Turkey, it seems, she was remembered into the twentieth century 'as one of the most enlightened Europeans to have visited our country'.[47]

Her final sightseeing seems to have been in Saint Sophia, the former centre of Byzantine Christendom. She left two conflicting accounts: that, by persistence and submission, she got a special dispensation to visit it; and that she and a Greek friend, the Princess of Transylvania, decided to go without permission: 'to dress themselves up in men's clothes, to run the risk of it.' (Now a mosque, it was forbidden to Christians.) She told the latter tale to the admiring—perhaps credulous—Joseph Spence in 1741, setting it on her last day in Turkey. She said that being used to high heels she found it awkward walking barefoot as the holy place demanded; she was bold enough to 'steal' her slippers on again, trusting to her long masculine robes to conceal this infringement. Meanwhile she was forced to exert protective control over her friend, who rashly gave way to tears as she thought of the fallen grandeur of her people. Lady Mary was less fearful for herself (as an ambassadress) than for the princess. 'Do you consider where you are?' she hissed, 'and what a discovery in this place would cost you? . . . Methinks I see the flames already lighted. For God's sake, leave off blubbering!'[48]

Anything more would have been anticlimax. Lady Mary properly admired Saint Sophia (not defaced, but not cared for either) and got out safely. Then she sailed away.

---

[47] Turkish ambassador to Persia, Teheran, 1926. The Turkish ambassador to London in the 1930s hoped to discover more about her (Stuart Wortley [1948]: 19, 57).

[48] *CL* i. 405; Spence 1975: 357, 359–60.

11

July–October 1718

~≈~

Voyage Home: 'with regret I saw us sail swift from this Island'[1]

THE *Preston*, which anchored at Constantinople on 18 June 1718 to bring the Wortley Montagus home, was not an entirely happy ship. She was newly built, with fifty guns and a crew of 240. But the first lieutenant, a Mr Dore, had been 'confined for some time' awaiting court-martial, as Captain Robert Johnson was to inform the Admiralty once he was back in English waters. Dore, often too drunk to carry out his duties, had once burned a hole in his cabin with a candle. Another time, during a squall on the dawn watch, instead of altering course as directed he had brought the ship suddenly to: masts would have been broken and lost if the ship's Master (Walter Morrison) had not luckily been on deck and ordered the topsail and sheets (nautical parlance for ropes) to be let fly. As it was, the mainmast had been 'very dangerously Sprung'.[2] The unhappy Lt. Dore (in irons? in a locked cabin?) was an incongruous, possibly an unsuspected presence somewhere beneath Lady Mary's feet as she stood on deck gazing in rapture at the classical shores of the Mediterranean. (Was she, like Woolf's Orlando, protected by an awning?) The voyage was a high point of her travels. She was eager to gain and sorry to part with her fleeting glimpses of Sappho's island and of many other scenes of ancient story.

At 3 o'clock on 5 July, 'the Ambassador with his Retinue'—nineteen servants at least—went abroad, to a salute of eleven guns. These were not the only explosions to startle the children,[3] since a five-gun salute was then exchanged with the 'Rumney' galley. It was a day of fair weather, whose early breezes had disappointingly dropped off. They weighed anchor within

---

[1] *CL* i. 421.   [2] Halsband 1956: 87; Robert Johnson to the Admiralty, 24 Dec. 1718, Ad. MS 1/1982.
[3] Halsband 1956: 88. Violet Stuart Wortley imagines young Edward, the embassy pet, weeping as if the gates of Paradise were closing ([1948]: 57).

half an hour, to shouts and whistles, ropes thrown, ropes hauled, ropes coiled, till the tall ship was moving sluggishly through the water and the canvas spreading like heavy wings. It took them an hour and a half's sailing to reach the state prison of the Seven Towers and longer to pass the myriad splendid waterside palaces, and reach somewhere Lady Mary had not yet explored.[4]

The logs kept by the Master and the Captain charted their progress league by league, through day after day of fine weather, with 'little wind' more usual than 'moderate gales'.[5] Their first day out was spent in the Sea of Marmara, where they sighted five ships which they 'took to be Turks', and later a Frenchman. On the second day they threaded the narrow gap between Asia and Europe, variously called the Strait of Gallipoli, the Dardanelles, or the Hellespont. They anchored there long enough for the Master to take a party 'on shore to a small tour on curiosity'.

It was as if they were sailing—slowly, slowly—backwards in time, into Homer's wine-dark sea. When Lady Mary came to write this up she presented herself as constantly impelled into verse to match the poetic scenes around her. She quoted Addison, Dryden, Virgil, Lucian; she conjured the shades of Hero and Leander (the 'swimming lover and the nightly Bride'), of a Christian governor's daughter who betrayed a castle for love of a Turkish besieger, of Xerxes who bridged the Hellespont with boats, of Queen Hecuba (said to be buried nearby), of Alexander the Great and of the god Apollo. Only these last two charismatic males made her turn modernist and ironical.[6]

On their fourth evening at sea they anchored, two miles offshore, in Troy bay on the Asiatic coast of Turkey. Here had stood that great city; here the heroes had beached the keels which Helen's face had launched, and stayed for ten years of battles and glory. By Lady Mary's account the travellers made two landings in the vicinity of Troy. On the first occasion they decided the visible ruins were not old enough to have been Homer's Troy, though there was 'some pleasure in' seeing even the site of 'the greatest City in the world'. On the promontory of Sigeum they noticed a stone slab with a Greek inscription—a Trojan decree commemorating a peace treaty of 279 BC. They 'order'd this on board the Ship' to join Wortley's considerable collection of ancient marbles; it was later to make their house a place of pilgrimage for antiquaries.[7]

---

[4] *CL* i. 365, 413.   [5] Captain's log PRO Ad. 51/4296, Master's log 52/254.

[6] Alexander, she said, 'ran naked round [Achilles'] Tomb in his honnour, which, no doubt, was a great comfort to his Ghost'; Apollo listed the island of Tenedos 'in the particular of his estate when he courted Daphne'. His courtship aimed at rape (*CL* i. 416–17, 421).

[7] *CL* i. 417–18. After EWM's death his daughter gave the collection, at his wish, to his old Cambridge

The collecting impulse was baffled by an even more interesting inscription, in the very ancient script which is called *boustrophedon* because it goes backwards and forwards across the page like an ox ploughing. This was later to yield to Lord Elgin, but meanwhile Captain Johnson 'assur'd us that without having Machines made on purpose, twas impossible to bear it to the Sea Side, and when it was there his long Boat would not be large enough to hold it'. Lady Mary had to content herself with a transcription.

Fiction seemed to come to life. Gazing around her she spotted ancient topographical features and admired 'the exact Geography of Homer, whom I had in my hand' (perhaps in her parallel-text Greek and Latin edition). At the second landfall she got up at 2 a.m. for coolness, and 'hir'd an Ass (the only voiture to be had there) that I might go some miles into the Country and take a tour round the Ancient Walls, which are of a vast extent. We found the remains of a castle on a Hill and another in a valley, several broken Pillars, and 2 pedestals.' Again there were inscriptions, this time in Latin, to copy.

After the islands of Lesbos (which Scudéry called 'one of the most delectable places in the world') and Chios or Scio (a cornucopia of oranges and lemons, corn and wine, cotton and silk), they headed across the Aegean, through the strait between Euvoia and Andros, towards mainland Greece. The 'venerable' temple of Sounion, seen from offshore, was the closest Lady Mary got to Athens. Her longing 'to land on the fam'd Peloponessus' had to yield to the information that 'instead of demy Gods and heros . . . 'tis now over run by Robbers'. In her thoughts the tourist present paled before an almost unimaginable distant past, when such a journey would have offered the delights of sketching the splendid temples and prodigious, undamaged statues, of 'converseing with the most polite and most gay of humankind', and even (by an anachronism which claims her foremother for her own circle) 'drinking a dish of tea with Sappho'.[8]

For the professionals, meanwhile, the slow voyage was uneventful. The ship's logs record Cape Angelo 11 July, Cape Malopan 12 July, spiced only with desultory exchange of fire with stray Turkish ships on 12 and 13 July. All parties fired to leeward, not intending damage. Meanwhile Crete came and went on their horizon, and Lady Mary strained her eyes towards Knossos, 'the scene of Monstrous Passions'.

Two weeks out, as they neared Malta, the weather briefly changed. On 20 July the mainsail split in a squall. Undeterred, the crew 'unbent it and

college, Trinity: now on extended loan to the Fitzwilliam Museum (Classical Heritage exhibition catalogue, 1978). Trinity retains a bust of EWM, with honorific Latin inscription.

[8] *CL* i. 417–21; Scudéry 1690: x. 188: another clue that MWM's Sappho owed much to Scudéry's intellectual and feminist heroine as well as to the ghostly figure of history.

brought another too'. Next day, with 'Fresh Gales', the topsails were reefed, unreefed, and reefed again, with Mount Etna visible in the offing, 'whose Flame appears very bright in the night many Leagues off at Sea, and fills the head with a thousand Conjectures'. Late that evening hard squalls necessitated much activity with the maintopsail; towards midnight their ship 'came in with a Spanish Squadron' and exchanged the usual fire. They then caught the attention of some passing English transport ships, by means of their cannon, to learn the reason for the Spanish presence. This brief burst of activity closed on 22 July at Cape Passaro (the southernmost tip of Sicily), where the 'Foretopsail Yard being Sprung in the Slings' was unrigged and 'fisht' again.[9]

Either this was a long process, or wind was lacking as usual. It was evening on 29 July before the *Preston* anchored off Porto Farina near Tunis. The African coast, and Queen Dido's city of Carthage, were near at hand. While the *Preston* took on water, ferried by their own longboat and one from an English merchantman, the ambassadorial party went ashore. They accepted the hospitality of the British consul at Tunis; Lady Mary was eager to see 'this part of the world'. The consul's chaise set out at 9 p.m. and travelled all night. Peering in the moonlight, she observed the sandy soil to be fruitful in 'Date, olive and fig trees', with vineyards and melon fields enclosed with prickly pear. It was Ramadan: the local people who had fasted all day were grouped in 'Companys' under the trees, 'eating, singing, and danceing to their wild music'. This was the kind of adventure the Wortley Montagus could both enjoy. Soon after daybreak they spent two hours closely inspecting a massy, well-preserved aqueduct of Roman origin, which Wortley pronounced superior to those at Rome itself. In Tunis, which was built of brilliant white stone and entirely without trees or gardens, Lady Mary found the heat and glare so 'excessive' that she could hardly bear it. Writing a single letter made her 'halfe blind'. The ruins of Carthage, whither she set out after a single night's rest at the consul's, were equally hard going. She was 'halfe broil'd in the Sun, and overjoy'd to be led into one of the subterranean Apartments'—where she at once began speculating as to its original purpose.[10]

On the way to Tunis she had noted the 'natural Deformity' of the 'country people . . . not quite black, but all mulattos, and the most frightfull Creatures that can appear in a Human figure': near-naked but covered in ornamental tattoos. Lady Mary would have been familiar with the *idea* of such tattooing from Aphra Behn's *Oroonoko*, but she was more dismissive of

[9] *CL* i. 423–4; PRO Ad. 51/4296.   [10] *CL* i. 424–7, 428. The consul was Richard Lawrence.

it than Behn, finding it ugly as well as perceiving that it would have been painful. While she sheltered in the Carthaginian cellars, picking up broken bits of marble and porphyry, women flocked in 'from the Town of tents not far off' to look at her, and hospitably to offer 'milk and exquisite fruit'.

As when she met Fatima, Lady Mary was mindful that 'the gaze' is a two-way street: 'we were equally entertain'd with veiwing one another.' But she failed to muster for these North African women the appreciation of difference which the Turks had aroused. This time she saw the Other as existing not in culture but only in nature; and she saw nothing but ugliness. To Conti, the most 'scientific' of her correspondents, she reported:

Their posture in siting, the colour of their skin, their lank black Hair falling on each side their faces, their features and the shape of their Limbs, differ so little from their own country people, the Baboons, tis hard to fancy them a distinct race, and I could not help thinking there had been some ancient alliances between them.

Ideas about human–animal interbreeding were not new but classical: they had recently arisen in her mind a propos the 'monstrous passions' of Knossos.[11] To her these comments were well observed and wittily applied; to look back on them from the other side of age-long violence and agony inflicted by (mainly) white on (mainly) black 'races' must be to deplore them. She *might* not have fallen into that littleness if only she had entered the 'Town of tents' and seen its living arrangements.

On 2 August a feeble wind moved the *Preston* slowly off the coast of Africa. At 1 p.m. thirteen guns were fired, 'being his Majesties happy Accession to the Throne'. They were heading north for Leghorn or Toulon, 'where the Embassadore designs to disimbark and proceed homewards by land'. The captain meant if the wind served to put in at Naples first; but no such landing is mentioned in either the ship's logs or Lady Mary's letters. It seems this odd realization of a past romantic dream did not take place. On this lap the *Preston* spoke with two French ships and an English galley. She crept past Sardinia (4 August), Monte Christo (8 August), and Elba (9 August), to Leghorn, where Captain Johnson reported that 'the Ambassador is not yet Determin'd where to Land'. So after two days they sailed again, and in the cloudy dawn of 15 August they gained the lantern at the mouth of Genoa harbour. The prospect of the city, its buildings and gardens climbing the slope above its 'very fine bay', was striking from 'off at Sea'; yet

---

[11] *CL* i. 42, 425–7. Serious or 'scientific' likening of black people to non-human primates was to burgeon in the work of Buffon, who alleged human copulation with apes (1749–67), Edward Long (1774), and others. It coincides with the growth of the slave trade. Cf. Grundy 1993*a*: 73–86; Nussbaum 1995: 91–2; Hudson 1996: 247–64.

in Lady Mary's eyes it 'lost much of its Beauty' by comparison with Constantinople.[12]

By mid-morning they were at anchor. Wortley would rather have pressed on to Toulon, to avoid the passage of the Alps. But the moderate gale which had brought them to harbour proved short lived, and the all-too-familiar calm seemed 'like to be soe for many days'. The last six weeks had taught him just how slow a sea passage could be. They were still, by water, only a third of the way home. He decided to leave the *Preston* as soon as they could arrange their ten days' plague quarantine, 'from which no body is exempt coming from the Levant'. On the evening of 17 August, saluted by fifteen rounds from the *Preston*'s guns, the ambassador and his wife went 'on Shoar' at Genoa, leaving their children to continue by sea.[13]

They made the right decision as regards time. The *Preston*, sailing from Genoa on 22 August, took almost six months to reach port. Apart from three weeks in Port Mahon repairing a leak and ten days at Gibraltar dropping off sick crew members, her problem was 'very Terible weather'. It was not until 6 January 1719 that she finally moored at Woolwich and the much-tried Armenian nurse brought the children home.[14]

Meanwhile their parents had spent a pleasant quarantine at San Pietro d'Arena outside Genoa, in the Palladian mansion of the British envoy, Henry Molins Davenant, and his wife Frances. Lady Mary praised both Mrs Davenant, who rejoiced in 'good humour and good Company', and her house, which was 'well design'd and . . . nobly proportion'd'. (This made a contrast with Turkey, but Lady Mary did not say so.) While in quarantine they could receive visitors only under the eye of 'a noble Genoese Commission'd to see we did not touch one Another'. Once released, she plunged wholeheartedly into the life of the Genoese republic, or 'more properly . . . Aristocracy'. She reported delightly on mansions by Palladio (two of them models for Thoresby)[15] and Renaissance paintings, coolly on the churches (which looked 'mean' after St Sophia), and sceptically on the famous 'emerald' dish at St Lawrence's church—which was, indeed, later found to be fake. She approved the sumptuary laws, recently passed to curb the nobility's extravagance, and was amazed at the institution of *cicisbei* or 'tetis beys', reminiscent of Vienna. While Genoese 'virgins are all invisible, confin'd to convents', every married woman enjoyed the service and total devotion of a

[12] Lawrence to Craggs, 23/12 Aug. 1718, SP 71/27; PRO Ad. 51/4296; Johnson from Leghorn, Ad. 1/1982; *CL* i. 428.
[13] Johnson from Genoa, 21 Aug. 1718, Ad. 1/1982; Ad. 51/4296; *CL* i. 432.
[14] Johnson from Port Mahon, Lisbon, Falmouth, Downes, 28 Aug.–24 Dec. 1718, Ad. 1/1982.
[15] The Farnese and Palavicino palaces (Harris 1961: 11).

gentleman not her husband. This, Lady Mary was assured, had brought 'peace and good humour' to good society, ending 'those family Hatreds which tore their state to pieces' by keeping busy 'those young Men who were forc'd to cut one another's throats pour passer le temps'. Though the palmy days of eight or ten 'humble admirers' per lady were gone, and men 'grow more scarce and sawcy', the nature of the relationship was still not open to question: 'the husband is not to have the Impudence to suppose 'tis any other than pure platonic Friendship.'[16] Islamic society was not the only one in which it was fun to discover women wielding unexpected power.

After the quarantine it took several days to equip themselves for land travel. They they were off. Two days on fine roads brought them to Turin, gateway to the Alps and seat of government of Victor Amadeus II, ruler of the composite state called the Two Sicilies. (His dukedom of Savoy was secure, his kingdom of Sicily currently menaced by the French.) The Wortley Montagus lodged during their brief stay in the architecturally splendid Piazza Royale. They had met noble Savoyards in London: one was now in disgrace 'for some small overtures he presum'd to make to a Maid of Honnour'; the other presented them at court (in its summer quarters at Rimini). Lady Mary thought the royal family swamped in religiosity, but liked the intelligence and anglophilia of the queen (a granddaughter of Charles I of England) and 'return'd her Civillity by giving her the title of Majesty as often as I could, which perhaps she will not have the comfort of hearing many months longer'. She did her usual sightseeing, but found Turin disappointing after Genoa. As for the famous Shroud, 'I have not respect enough for the holy Handkercheif to speak long of it.'[17]

From Turin they could already see the white peaks of 'those dreadfull Alps, so much talk'd of'. Wortley had crossed and recrossed them on the Grand Tour. For Lady Mary they were not, as for so many English travellers, the first mountains she had seen; still, they were far and away the most formidable. Writing up her travels later, she indulged a small fanfare, echoing that with which she had left Vienna for Hungary. 'If I come alive to the bottom you shall hear of me.' The first day's journey, westward towards the Mont Cenis pass as far as Novalesa, was pure pleasure. Then came the moment when their chaises were 'taken to pieces and laid upon Mules', while they themselves, thickly wrapped in furs, were 'carri'd in little seats of twisted Osiers fix'd upon Poles, on men's shoulders'. There was something 'solemnly entertaining' in the 'prodigious Prospect of Mountains cover'd with Eternal Snow, Clouds hanging far below our feet, and the vast cascades

---

[16] *CL* i. 428–32.   [17] *CL* i. 432–4.

tumbling down the Rocks with a confus'd roaring'. But physical discomfort marred her enjoyment. Not all her furs could keep her warm, or keep out the 'misty rain, which falls perpetually'. After a moment to admire Lac du Mont Cenis at the head of the pass came the descent of a north slope 'so steep and slippery, 'tis surprizing to see these chairmen go so steadily as they do'. Before they reached their night's lodging two hours after dark, Lady Mary was 'halfe dead with cold'.

The rest of their alpine road was passable in their reconstructed chaises. Lady Mary noted fine vineyards, pastures, and mountain goats. But by the time they had left the mountains and entered France, she found she had been right to fear falling sick more than breaking her neck. She spent a week in bed with a fever and sore throat at 'a sorry Inn' in Lyons, bullied by doctors 'who are charm'd with a new customer'. In a room 'cram'd with the mortifying objects of Apothecarys' viols and Bottles', she read and answered a large batch of letters which had been caught at Marseilles and rerouted to Lyons. Before the doctors wanted she was up and sightseeing. She transcribed for Pope the inscriptions in which the Emperor Claudius had conferred Roman citizenship on the Lyonnais, and sketched in words the handsome buildings, Roman remains, and medieval churches. Again she found something *not* to admire: the statue of Louis XIV 'trampling upon Mankind', incongruously pompous like 'an old Beau who had a mind to be a Hero, with a Bushel of curl'd hair on his head and a gilt Truncheon in his hand'.[18]

The journey from Lyons to Paris was miserable—not only on account of her lingering illness. In every village, while fresh post-horses were led out, 'the whole town comes out to beg, with such miserable starv'd faces and thin, tatter'd Cloaths, they need no other Eloquence'. 'I think nothing so terrible as Objects of misery, except one had the God like attribute of being capable to redress them.' Twenty years later the 'pale yellow Faces wrapp'd up in Blankets' were still a vivid memory.[19] Fontainebleau was Lady Mary's first taste of 'French Magnificence', though the palace was less attractive than the park.

Paris provided a wonderful surprise. Two days after their arrival on 29/18 September, another English visitor appeared: Lady Mary's sister Mar, *en route* to join her husband at the Jacobite court. 'She as little expected to see me as I her.' The way they met, said Lady Mary, embracing repeatedly and asking after each other's adventures, was worthy of a Scudéry romance. At last, 'all Questions and answers and exclamations and compliments being

---

[18] *CL* i. 434–7.   [19] *CL* i. 438; ii. 143.

over, we agreed upon running about together and have seen Versailles, Trianon, Marli and St. Cloûd'. They duly admired the well-paved, regularly lighted streets, the art collections, the boy monarch, and his uncle the Regent.[20]

All kinds of amusements were in full swing: Lady Mary was never at a loss for occupation even in the absence of her sister (who was sitting for her portrait twice a day). The Fair of St Lawrence offered handsome, orderly booths and distastefully obscene Harlequins. The Opera at the Palais-Royal was nothing to Vanbrugh's Haymarket, and the music 'abominable grating'. (Lady Mary preferred the Italian style.) The Comédie Française, too, was architectually inferior to the new Lincoln's Inn Fields, but its expressive style of acting was a revelation: 'our best actors can be only said to speak, but these to feel.'[21]

Lady Mary disliked Frenchwomen's heavy make-up: 'these grotesque Dawbers', she said, made her long for 'my dear pritty Country women'. But Parisian social life was cosmopolitan and in many ways delightful. She met many of Mme de Bonnac's 'very considerable and numerous Family', and made herself a news exchange for the clan.[22] Conti introduced her to *savants* whom he had shown her letters: perhaps Antoine-Robert Pérelle, certainly Nicolas-François Rémond. Before leaving Turkey she had received from Rémond a fan letter which flattered her writing, dropped the names of Conti and Lord Stair (British ambassador in Paris), and proffered devotion in terms ominously akin to Pope's. She had spoiled him, he said, for other ladies' conversation, no matter how witty; he had conceived an instant devotion to her, like devotion to an ancient goddess; he gloried in letting his emotions rule his reason; and he would certainly pursue her to the East if only he were sure she had philosophy enough to perceive his beautiful soul despite his ugly body. It seems Lady Mary had not been so wary of this incense as would have been wise: in Paris he proposed to her that he should wear a ring in honour of their eternal friendship.[23]

Another circle of acquaintance may have stemmed from Jean-Baptiste Rousseau. He knew the Irish banker Richard Cantillon, who was just entering into partnership with the 'sagacious, daring ... tall, imposing, dark'

[20] *CL* i. 440–2. The duchesse d'Orléans had on the contrary complained in summer heat that the Paris streets stank unendurably, what with rotting meat and fish, and people relieving themselves (quoted in Elias 1978: 132).

[21] *CL* i. 439–42, 440 n. 4. This painting of Lady Mar is not known; she sat with her daughter to Francesco Trevisani in Rome in 1719.

[22] H MS 77. 154. Mme de Bonnac, daughter of the duc de Biron, had thirteen siblings who lived to maturity.

[23] *CL* ii. 438–40; i, pp. xv–xvi, 395–6 (Rémond, 20 Apr. 1718); Halsband 1956: 91.

Scottish financial wizard, John Law.[24] Lady Mary took a sardonic pleasure in Law's status in Paris: he 'treats their Dukes and Peers extremely de haut en bas, and is treated by them with the utmost Submission and respect'. By August 1718 Cantillon had realized that his insider knowledge could make a fortune in Law's 'Company of the West'; in November they established the Louisiana Company. This was to develop France's new North American colony in conjunction with the English South Sea Company's development of South American natural resources and the Pacific trade (which included slaves). In September 1718 the Mississippi Scheme (which with the South Sea scheme would constitute 'the first major stock market boom in Europe') was expected to benefit French, Africans, and Indians alike. While in Paris, Lady Mary wrote a stanza in praise of an unnamed entrepreneur and in her view philanthropist (probably Cantillon or his brother), who replied in spirited verse calling himself her 'faithfull Slave' and applying an investment metaphor to their friendship. Lady Mary credited him with reconciling opposed religions and bringing 'the Savage' to enjoy 'Social Tyes'. She concluded: 'The only Spot, where Nature's Sons yet claim | Their Rights, and Christian is no dreadfull Name!'[25]

Today it seems as grotesque to see philanthropy in the Mississippi and South Sea schemes as to see sound economics. But it was her mistake on the second, not on the first point, that would bring Lady Mary penalty and obloquy. With hindsight, her crowded and happy days in Paris can be seen to contain the seeds of future trouble, both through her relationship with Rémond and through that with Law and Cantillon.

All too soon she had to leave. She promised Conti to keep writing. The final sea passage was painfully exciting. After the packet boat had tossed violently all night in a storm, its master, 'considering the weakness of his Vessel, thought it prudent to remove the mail, and gave us notice of the Danger. We call'd a little fisher boat, which could hardly make up to us, while all the people on board us were crying to Heaven, and 'tis hard to imagine one's selfe in a scene of greater Horror.' Even in extremity, Lady Mary spared a smile at the mingled passions of another woman divided between concern for her immortal soul and for a lace head-dress which she was 'contriving to conceal from the custom house Officers'. Though 'the wind grew high and our little vessel crack'd', Lady Mary managed to be 'thrown' into the fishing boat without breaking her neck.[26]

[24] Carswell 1960: 7.
[25] *CL* i. 442; Murphy 1988: 70, 75, 65; *The Flying-Post; or, The Post-Master*, 18 Sept. 1718; *E&P* 215.
[26] *CL* i. 443–4.

Safely landed at Dover on 30 September, she had time to write (so she said later) to Conti and to Pope. From Pope she had just received a letter, written on September the first, which had been to Italy and back. It assured her that more than for any of her sonnets, remarks, or 'oriental learning' he longed for her 'Oriental Self'; that he expected her time in the East to have '*advanced*' her '*Back* into true nature & simplicity of manners'; that he would find her younger, more innocent, and more open. He continued daringly,

I expect to see your Soul as much thinner dressd as your Body; and that you have left off, as unwieldy & cumbersome, a great many damn'd European Habits. Without offence to your modesty be it spoken, I have a burning desire to see your Soul stark naked, for I am confident 'tis the prettiest kind of white Soul in the universe.

He added an intellectual touch: he valued her body, like 'the Diamond-Casket that held Homer's Iliads', for the wit and meaning it housed. But even this sentence so dwells on 'seeing your body', on eyes and dimples, that it does nothing to de-eroticize the whole.[27]

This time she was really offended. Pope put into the same letter his account of the two rustic lovers struck by lightning at Stanton Harcourt in Oxfordshire during his recent stay there. (The rhyming dirty joke which he—or possibly Gay—also wrote about them went to nobody but Teresa Blount.) To Lady Mary he stressed their pastoral innocence, the protective-ness of John towards his Sarah in danger, the idea that their sudden death (the greatest possible happiness next to that which they *would* have enjoyed in marriage) was Heaven's reward for their virtue—and especially the idea of Lady Mary's sentimental response. He expected her to honour them 'with a Tear from the finest eyes in the world. I know you have Tenderness; you must have it: It is the very Emanation of Good Sense & virtue: The finest minds like the finest metals, dissolve the easiest.'[28] He went straight on from pity for the dead lovers to pity for himself and his extremity of fondness. He was using this double death as 'just the topic to bring out the latent softness in which he still believed', hoping to win her to a *sentimental* friendship.[29]

Lady Mary did not co-operate. Her flippant reply has drawn shocked critical comment which mostly ignores the personal context. He had asked to see her soul stark naked; he had asked that it should be discovered weeping. It was probably not his idealization of the labouring classes which stuck

[27] Pope, *Corr.* i. 494. He could have gone further: a month later he wrote to Martha and Teresa Blount of 'those white Bums which I dye to see', begging them not to 'Scratch your backsides' in public or 'leave the company to p—ss' (i. 515–16). 'Sonnets' suggests short poems, not now known.

[28] He sent similar accounts to Caryll and Atterbury (TE vi. 197–201; *Corr.* i. 494–500).

[29] Rumbold 1989: 140–1.

in her craw so much as his idealization of marriage or of herself. Her
'Epitaph' sent in reply briskly disposes of the ideas of special providence—
'the bold Thunder found them out | (Commission'd for that end no
Doubt)'—and of ideal marriage—'A Beaten Wife and Cuckold Swain'—
and of any special favour in such a death—'Now they are happy in their
Doom | For P[ope] has wrote upon their Tomb.' In prose Lady Mary added
that she would 'rather continue to be your stupid living Humble Servant
than be celebrated by all the Pens in Europe'.[30] Although so light in touch,
her poem engages in serous ideological debate. If it was indeed written on
the spot, and met Pope in the full flush of excited anticipation, it may have
caused the first crack in their friendship. Even if it belongs with her later
reworking of her Embassy Letters, it is still an early example of her burlesque octosyllabic manner. Pope, seeking to point her towards sentiment,
may have helped her to find a voice for ballads, for political intervention, and
for personal lampoon.

Having 'regulat[ed] our March to London, bag and Baggage', the Wortley Montagus set out the day after landing. One day more brought them to
London; and on 3 October Wortley 'waited on his Majesty at Hampton-
Court', as was officially certified by James Craggs (friend of both Lady
Mary and Pope) in his new capacity as Secretary of State. Wortley's feelings
of humiliation must have been compounded by the gossip which falsely
insisted that he had come home very rich.[31] There would be no more escort
of yellow-shod dragomans, no more fifteen-gun salutes. The ambassador
and his lady were plain citizens again.

[30] *CL* i. 445–6; *E&P* 215–16. Many have thought her response a matter of class (e.g. Thomas 1994: 121–3).
Scodel notes in it the elements of satire on marriage and denial of Pope's erotic fantasies (1991: 281–4).

[31] *St James's Evening Post*, 4 Oct. 1718; SP 44/360/142; Montagu Bacon, 21 Oct. 1718, quoted in Paston
1907: 289.

12

October 1718–1720s

❧

Settling Down: 'one's own fancy upon one's own Ground'[1]

AGAIN the rapid flow of London life received and swallowed them; for the next two and a half years records are sadly lacking. Pope saw a lady's arrival in London as an occasion of self-display: 'the first week must needs be wholly employd in making New Gowns, the second in showing them, the third in seeing other people, the fourth, fifth, & so on, in Balls, plays . . .' At Belgrade Village, Lady Mary had thought of London life as a 'perpetual round' of the court, the opera, the play, of in-group hostesses' receptions, of 'hearing the same Scandal and seeing the same follies acted over and over'. Years later she recalled how 'it was hard to invite six people that would not, by cold looks or piqueing Refflections, affront one another'. London was more fraught than usual just now. The quarrel between George I and his heir was growing to an 'open international scandal'. In November the Princess of Wales bore and christened her second son; in December the 'desperate rush of business and festivity' made Addison gravely ill.[2]

Lady Mary's return called for exchange of visits with friends and family. But each of these groups presented problems. Her sister Mar, having pursued her way from Paris to 'James III' 's court-in-exile in Rome, was enmeshed in problems impenetrable to anyone outside that hothouse environment.[3] Her sister Gower, married in 1712, had had a baby almost every year ever since. (Lady Mary was probably godmother to the second daughter, Mary

---

[1] *CL* ii. 25.   [2] Pope, *Corr.* i. 505; *CL* i. 366–7; ii. 446; Smithers 1968: 414–15, 418.
[3] To some she was a tower of strength and reason, her husband's 'most important political adviser'. Lord Pitsligo counted her a hero like Lady Nithsdale, who had saved her condemned husband's life. But James Murray, riled by her Whig leanings and haughty manner, mounted a campaign of public humiliation which she felt deeply. Her husband (already playing a political double game) was away for much of 1719 on spying ventures and in prison in Milan and Geneva. The British Crown stopped her allowance that July for keeping him in touch with 'James III' 's wife, Clementina (Gregg 1982: 180, 186; Tayler 1938: 52, 61, 63, 83, 87, 147, 168–9, 192–3).

Leveson-Gower.) Her sister-in-law, Rachel, Lady Kingston, had become notorious as the mistress of Lord Lumley, later Lord Scarborough. She went on to have two sons by him, teach her Pierrepont children to call him 'Papa', and feel herself 'as good as married to him'. She was in childbed again, and he had recently come into his estate on the death of his father, when she realized *he* did not feel himself to be married to *her*. She died—of a broken heart, said her family. Lady Mary explicitly blamed Scarborough.[4]

Her father, Duke of Kingston and since 1718 Lord President of the Council, seems to have remained distant. His second marriage had produced one baby girl in its four years (the period in which his first had brought four children and his wife's death). He must still have hoped for an heir, even after his fifth daughter (and last child) was born in 1721. The king himself was this baby's godfather.[5] It seems Lady Mary was not, like her sister Gower, a summer visitor at Thoresby, for her daughter Mary did not know her grandfather. She remembered seeing him only once: a distinguished elderly stranger (tall, dignified, 'still handsome'), at whose appearance in her mother's dressing-room Lady Mary started up 'from the toilet-table with her hair about her ears', to fall on her knees and beg his blessing.[6]

When the Wortley Montagu children—one-year-old Mary 'in [her] Nurse's Arms', and Edward rising six—at last joined their parents in January 1719, the Dowager Lady Denbigh, their great-grandmother only by marriage, may have been the relative most eager to meet them. Lady Denbigh was to die at the end of this year (aged 96, Lady Mary said), keeping to the last the uncommon 'vivacity and clearness of her understanding'.[7]

New friends lay just over the horizon; meanwhile many old friends were problematic for Lady Mary. The divisions in the royal family and in the Whig party had split most of them into two antagonistic camps. Her friend Craggs was (on Addison's resignation) helping Sunderland and Stanhope to run the government; her friend Walpole was cultivating the anti-government Prince of Wales. Walpole's working partnership with Princess Caroline began this winter, though he also maintained ties with Lady Mary's correspondent the Duchess of Kendal (the erstwhile Ermengard Melusine Schulenburg). Lady Mary herself was sharply upbraided by Caroline for

---

[4] *CL* ii. 182 and n. 1; MWM 1837: ii. 236 n. Her 'slip with Lord Lumley' was 'the scandal of the town' in Oct. 1718 (Paston 1907: 290; Walpole, *Corr.* xxxiv. 258). Scarborough was warmly esteemed by the future George II and by Lord Chesterfield (Plumb 1960: 170; Chesterfield 1990: 41–2).

[5] She was b. 1 Feb. 1721 and christened a month later; her royal christening gift was a gilt basin (BL Eg. MS 3531; newspapers, 4 Mar. 1721).

[6] Manvers MS 4349, 59; *E&P* 31; Hunter 1831: ii. 322.

[7] On 8 July 1721 she was followed by Lucy, Lady Pierrepont, widow of Gervase (*CL* iii. 27; newspapers).

continuing to frequent George I's evenings after the split.[8] But she seems to have made little further use of her carefully nurtured court contacts, possibly on account of her husband's blighted career. John Hervey became her friend and circulated her poems before he was either a lord or a courtier.[9]

William Congreve was an important older friend, a Kit-Cat member who had probably held the eight-year-old Lady Mary on his lap at her very first social triumph. He was a bracingly outspoken critic of her writing, with that eagle eye for weaknesses (more beneficial in the long run than easy praise) which women could rarely command. On his death she was to express 'boundless Love'. But at this stage her friendship with him did not run smoothly. He was ageing, suffering badly with his eyes, and was the lover of Henrietta, Lady Godolphin (later Duchess of Marlborough in succession to her father). She was inclined to be possessive. Lady Mary suspected the first summer after her return that Congreve was neglecting her; later Henrietta accepted an invitation on his behalf with the remark that he was 'like all good things, hard to come at'.[10]

Conti, after a very extended visit to England, had now left. For at least a couple of years Lady Mary kept up with Madeleine-Françoise de Bonnac in Constantinople. She reported her baby daughter's beauty, and exchanged vivacities about her letter printed in the *Mercure galant* in October 1718. Mme de Bonnac teased her about this publication; Lady Mary, perhaps tongue-in-cheek, professed regret about it, and said Wortley threatened to protect his daughter from such a fate by keeping her illiterate.[11]

Pope had begged Lady Mary, before she reached England and while he was in the country, to send him a message care of Jervas 'the first minute of your arrival', so that he might 'return to the Living' to see her. He then devoted the rest of his letter to impersonal tourist description. When she did arrive, on 3 October 1718, he made no haste to London: either she sent no message or he did not respond. Had she sent him her debunking response to the lovers struck by lightning? In any case, there loomed before each of them the need to bring their relationship down from the rarefied heights of the ideal and the eroticized towards a more manageably workaday level. They had made some progress by summer 1719, when Dr Arbuthnot noted Pope's habit, when with Lady Mary, of perpetrating ghastly puns, 'for which you are so often reprimanded, & never reformd'.[12]

---

[8] Plumb 1956: 286–7; Hunter 1831: ii. 322. Addison's friendship with EWM may well have suffered over the recall.

[9] See p. 335 f.; 27 Jan. 1722 (Hervey MS 47/2. 14).

[10] *E&P* 247; Pope, *Corr.* ii. 13; *CL* ii. 58.

[11] Mme de Bonnac, 20 Sept. 1719, 28 Apr. 1720 (H MS 77. 154–7).   [12] Pope, *Corr.* i. 505–8; ii. 10.

If the Wortley Montagus ran true to form, it was Lady Mary who took on the finding and fitting of a London house. They chose one in Covent Garden (her birthplace): nos. 9–10, the Piazza, at an annual rent of £125. It now forms part of the Opera House site. Here they were closer to their first married quarters than to their more recent Westminster ones. Covent Garden was a centre for clothes shops, and home to goldsmiths, lacemen, milliners, tallow-chandlers, inventors, forgers, and gaming houses,[13] as well as to the King's Street theatre (one of London's two stages licensed for drama) and to Will's famous literary coffee-House. It was a marginal district where high and low society met, featuring in literature both as an address for upwardly mobile City types, and as a site for street football. Newspapers regularly reported duels and muggings, fires and thefts; but these were endemic all over London. In January 1725 a number of tradespeople and others were arrested for scandalous dancing in masquerade costume.[14]

The large, handsome houses were popular, too, both with the upper classes and with theatrical or artistic types. In and around the Piazza in 1720 lived the politicians George Bubb Dodington and James Craggs, Lady Mary's uncle Feilding, a relation of her friend Philippa, the actor-manager Colley Cibber, the upholsterer Thomas Arne (father of one musical and one theatrical genius), the famous man-midwife Dr Hugh Chamberlen, and the miniaturist Christian Zincke. In 1721 Wortley and Dodington paid the highest poor rates in the district. Next year both were reduced: Wortley's by more than Dodington's.[15]

Lady Mary always loved interior decorating. When writing of happy marriage she presented it as adorning a trysting-place for the beloved.[16] Now she probably found that she could, after all, endure chairs again; but she contrived a 'sopha' to display her genuine Turkish cushion-covers. She found wallpaper still all the rage.[17]

Wortley, meanwhile, lost no time in preparing his claim for payment of arrears and 'extraordinaries' due in regard to his Embassy: he submitted it on 14 November, for £8,885. 12s. 3d. and three farthings. He also drafted and redrafted lengthy, self-justifying memos.[18] He begged leave to acquaint

[13] Wh MS M 508; Buck 1979: 158; newspapers 9 Dec. 1723, 15 Feb. 1724, 6 Aug. 1723, 16 Nov. 1723, 25 Apr. 1724.

[14] Pix, *The Beau Defeated*, 1700, Acts I and IV; Gay, *Trivia*, ii. 343–56; newspapers.

[15] Poor Rate Overseers' Accounts, 1720–1, H 499–501.

[16] 'Sur la Maxime de Mr de Rochefoûcault', which maintains that marriage can be delightful as well as convenient (*E&P* 160).

[17] 197,000 yards sold in 1713 (Porter 1982: 240).

[18] BL Add. MS 61547 (Blenheim Papers), 138–42; Halsband MSS. He referred bitterly to categories of expense he was not to report (PRO SP 44/119/233; Halsband MSS). Sutton got £1,000 for his 'equipage'

Lord Sunderland 'that by whatever Error his Imperial Majestys Ministers might Possibly at any time Imagine I had been to blame, they were at last Convinced that in every part of my Conduct with respect to the Peace I had Deserv'd their Approbation and Thanks.' He rehashed everything that still rankled: how the emperor had left his letters unanswered, how he was the true architect of the peace, how he had found the rumours of his recall incredible, how he had been financially penalized. None of this, he complained, was *reasonable*. (He might have been even more irked if he had realized that Austrian–British relations were about to deteriorate, so that gratifying the emperor would no longer be a priority.) Sunderland tried to use Wortley's claims as a bargaining counter to buy his support for the Peerage Bill; but he did not know his man. Wortley both spoke and voted against the bill, to which Charlotte Clayton co-ordinated opposition. It was defeated before the year's end.[19]

There was no chance now that the embassy would prove a stepping-stone to higher things. But as long as Walpole was out of office, Wortley's parliamentary prospects as Member for Westminster looked good.[20] He kept his friend Peter King—now Lord King—informed on parliamentary divisions as he did on stock prices. In November 1718 the birth of a son to his cousin Lord Hinchingbrooke put him out of the running for an earldom.[21] Addison's death, in June 1719, was a personal *and* political loss.[22] Walpole's resumption and consolidation of power set Wortley irrevocably in opposition mode. When he spoke in the House, though the custom was to do so extempore, he used a script, with marginal notes to himself: ' 'pause for a minute'—'cough'—'look round'—'slow'—'loud', etc.'[23]

His embassy losses encouraged him to throw himself heart and soul into his coal-mining business in the north, though it was still on his father's

---

plus £10 a day for sixteen months in 1717–18; he put in a claim for 'extraordinaries' (for 'Stationer's wares', spying, and occasional relief of His Majesty's distressed subjects) of £3,649. 8*s*., besides £2,564 for his journey to Vienna (SP 44/360/61, 44/360/158, 44/360/163–4, 44/360/202, 44/360/220–1). Addison had referred Stair's claim for £1369. 10*s*. 3*d*. to the Treasury before paying it (SP/44/360/35); Lord Paget claimed and received £13,869. 3*s*.

[19] Carswell 1993: 264–5; Sedgwick 1970; Somerset 1984: 214.

[20] In 1722 EMW reverted to sitting for Huntingdon. Parliament sat for about half the year, from Nov. or Dec. Its hours were about 10 a.m. to 4 p.m., having shifted from slightly earlier ones during EWM's absence in Turkey (Sedgwick 1970: i. 3). In 1723 MWM waited for the rising of parliament (27 May) before moving to Twickenham—presumably on his account (*CL* ii. 23).

[21] Future Lord Sandwich b. 20 Dec. 1718 (Montagu folder, Halsband MSS). Hinchingbrooke was Sandwich's heir.

[22] MWM apparently drafted some lines to Addison's memory on the back of a note from Pope. She later reused them for Congreve (note now at Sandon Hall; Pope, *Corr*. ii. 22–3; Grundy 1971: 461; *E&P* 246).

[23] *Quarterly Review*, 1820: 23. 416. It is doubtful whether (as the *Quarterly* assumes) this practice shows him up as phlegmatic or stupid.

property more than on his own.[24] The physical plant of the mines—'waggon ways way-leaves staithes Utencills and Appurtenances used in working and carrying on the same'—was rapidly modernizing. Ingenious mechanisms had appeared. Filtering systems separated large lumps of coal from the small pieces and dust which would go for coke. 'Newcastle roads' or railways were so constructed that gravity took over from horses for the downhill journey to the staithe or quay, where the coal dropped through trapdoors 'with a great noise and dust into the ship's hold or keel'. The annual rent on such a track might be £1,000.[25] Underground there was still no substitute for muscle. Keeping wages down was as valuable a managerial skill as keeping prices up.[26]

The owners were a tough-nosed group: aggressive technological innovators, veterans of entrepreneurial infighting. Their business was dangerous for its workers, vital for the nation, highly profitable for only the most ruthless.[27] English coal consumption almost doubled between 1700 and 1750, despite the cartel's price-fixing.[28] Households and industries in and out of London depended absolutely on coal for fuel. So, increasingly, did the ironmasters and the Caribbean sugar colonies.[29] The Tyneside owners already knew the value of combining. A new 'Combination' or Grand Alliance—Liddell, Bowes, and Wortley—was set up on 27 June 1726 to replace the earlier 'Regulation'. This aimed to prevent new collieries opening, often by buying up land or rights to cut off river access. These men planned to extend their 'complete control' from the Tyne to include the Wear. They fixed both prices and output (which in time Wortley's mines came to dominate). Any market restiveness produced short-term price wars, then consolidation.[30]

Wortley rose to the top of the 'Newcastle trade', as one of its 'meteors'. His wealth came not from vaguely 'saving', but from intense, focused

[24] A new 'Regulation' was discussed in 1717 (EWM participating by letter) but not set up. He kept full accounts of the running of Barnsley Moor colliery (Sheffield), 1705–26, 1744, and Hutton and Benwell (Northumberland) and Burdon (Durham), 1723–5 (Hughes 1952: 210; Wh MS M 114, 115).

[25] As Mary Banks's father explained to the Commissioners for Forfeited Estates in 1719 (Hughes 1952: 154).

[26] Miners had a reputation as 'clever, but wild and lawless'. In 1801 men around the mines were paid carefully graduated wages from about 10s. a week down to less than 2s. (Wh MS M D 246d; Porter 1982: 107; *Newcastle* 1801: 494–5, 497–8; Lewis 1971: 22).

[27] They employed many boys as well as men; 600 men and boys died in explosions in Tyne and Wear coal-mines in 1812–13 (Mackenzie and Ross 1825: 92).

[28] Porter 1982: 203; Flynn with Stoker 1984: 257. The early 19th century resounded with paeans to the industry (e.g. 'Coal-Trade' chapter in *Newcastle* 1801).

[29] Lewis 1971: 15–16.

[30] There is some doubt whether EWM, as well as his father, signed this agreement in 1726 (Flynn with Stoker 1984: 258; Sweezy 1938: 24–8; Buxton 1978: 36–7; Hughes 1952: 195).

activity. Lady Mary seldom or never went with him to Tyneside, where he spent a lot of time in the next two decades; but in his absence they corresponded regularly.[31] He travelled on horseback, perhaps already measuring and recording his journey times, which improved steadily as the turnpike movement improved the roads. His northern addresses were probably his uncle's Deanery at Durham and his father's cramped and pinched household at Wharncliffe.[32]

⤜⤛

Pope was planning by January 1719 to settle in Twickenham, a fashionable, fast-growing Thames-side village just west of London. Craggs was soon to take a house there too. Early in 1719 Wortley promised Pope to bring Lady Mary there for a weekend and 'accept of the kind offer of your house'—perhaps as guests, perhaps as tenants (through Pope's good offices) of the painter Sir Godfrey Kneller, who owned the substantial nearby estate and grand house of Whitton (later Kneller) Hall. The house they rented from him was a handsome brick-built Queen Anne one (later called Savile House), in the 'back lane' across the flat outskirts of Twickenham, where cattle grazed on the common and the green. It was not far from the Thames, or from Pope's house (which he rented from Thomas Vernon). Though Lady Mary calls Savile House small, it would not seem so today, having two floors with ceilings 10 feet high, besides its attics. The two main bedrooms measured 22 by 17 feet and 18 by 14 feet, each with its closet or dressing-room; there were later said to be eight or nine other bedrooms. Throughout the 1720s and 1730s, Wortley paid around half as much again in rates as Pope.[33]

Three-way negotiations were pursued with Kneller, first about minor matters like rent and furnishings, airing and painting and panelling. Then Wortley's surveyor was dissatisfied with the fabric; Kneller's said there was nothing wrong with it that two days' work would not fix. Then Kneller backed off, saying he had found someone else who was willing to take a long lease if not actually to purchase. He threatened to delay or withdraw his offer, perhaps seeking to pressure Wortley into a longer lease than he

[31] Hughes 1952; *DNB* (under MWM); Sweezy 1938: 29. Letters from him to MWM survive from 1725, 1729, and 1734 (H MS 74. 106–11).

[32] An inventory at his father's death valued the contents of EWM's room at £11. 14s. 6d.: fire implements, bed, hangings (for bed, window, and walls), 'Eight Cutts' (almost the only pictures listed), etc. No room scored higher, though 'A Parcel of Rape Seed' in the garret was worth £14 (Wh MS M 126).

[33] Walpole, *Corr.* xxxii. 199; Pope, *Corr.* ii. 16; sale catalogues, 1853, 1860, 1868; information from Christine Turfitt (Twickenham Public Library, Local Studies room). A leaflet shows photos of the front and back of the house shortly before demolition in 1904 or 1909.

wanted. The couple did rent somewhere in Twickenham for the summer of 1719 (part of it unusually hot).[34] In August Arbuthnot was joking to Pope that Lady Mary was a greater draw to Twickenham than he was. But it may have been in 1720 that Wortley managed to rent Savile House. Two years later he bought it from Sir Godfrey, and Lady Mary embarked with gusto on 'some small alterations'. She later held that 'a Handsome convenient House with pleasant Gardens' was 'amongst the most solid Satisfactions of Life'.[35]

They were setting up a pattern of living that would last them (as life in Turkey had not) for twenty years. In Twickenham and Covent Garden the early doubling of Thoresby and Arlington Street was more modestly echoed. Amid her reading and writing, the court and the social whirl, Lady Mary became a gardener. The plot of land at Savile House measured almost 50 by about 200 yards. The house was set back from the lane (now Heath Road), leaving 130 yards for the garden behind it. She thought it small, like the house; it now accommodates forty suburban houses and gardens. The brick wall at the bottom of the garden, nine feet high, had a door leading towards Pope's house and the river.[36]

Twickenham was *the* centre for the new garden mania. Pope acquired the land for his famous garden in November 1719, and began planning his 'enchanted bowers'.[37] James Johnstone at the rather grand Orleans House employed Charles Bridgeman for landscaping. At Whitton House in one direction Lord Ilay (later Duke of Argyll) was naturalizing exotic trees and shrubs. At Richmond, in the other, self-appointed experts were competing to set their mark on the Prince of Wales's gardens. From the village itself a leading garden writer of the day, Batty Langley, commented appreciatively on many Twickenham gardens and gardeners (but not, alas, on Lady Mary).[38]

Nursery gardens lined the London–Twickenham road, which she liked to travel on horseback (presumably in daylight: her friend Lady Stafford lost £80 and a gold watch to highwaymen one night between Richmond and

---

[34] Pope reiterated his 'Concern that you should be setled in my neighborhood', badgered Sir Godfrey, and canvassed other possibilities (Pope to Burlington, Wortley to Pope, Kneller to Pope, Pope to Wortley: *Corr*. ii. 2, 6–7, 12, 38–9).

[35] Pope, *Corr*. i. 8, 9; *CL* ii. 19; iii. 15. Mahaffey, who redates or reassigns several letters in Pope's correspondence, believes they rented Savile House by late June 1719, and bought it in 1720 (1963: 147–8).

[36] Her garden and the next are now bounded by Heath Road and Gardens and Radnor Road and Gardens; Savile Road, named from the house, crosses the spot where it stood. Part of the garden wall survives. Pope's Avenue, Pope's Grove, Grotto Road, and Kneller Radio Cars are all nearby.

[37] Pope, *Corr*. ii. 18, 19, 14.

[38] The lawns at Ham House, the slopes at Marble Hill, General Bisset's amphitheatre, Thomas Vernon's wilderness, Lady Humble's former cypress walk, Peterborough's tulip-tree, and Johnstone for all-round excellence (Langley 1728: pp. vii, x, xii, 52–5, 66, 73, 81, 149).

Mortlake).[39] Hervey regarded Lady Mary as unsuitably addicted to 'the offices of a Groom and a Nursery-Maid'.[40] In the summer of 1725 she had a horse which unlike any human being since the Fall was 'without a fault'. On it she followed the royal staghounds in Richmond Park, and felt as much delighted with her new-found 'vast courrage and skill' as if she had acquired a new sense.[41]

Twickenham was Lady Mary's rural retreat, her Belgrade Village. There was at yet no bridge over the Thames anywhere nearby: only a ferry which closed down in rough weather.[42] The summer court of the Prince and Princess of Wales, at Richmond on the other bank, was therefore not so near as a map suggests, although the royal couple frequented Orleans House, and from 1723 the prince's mistress Henrietta Howard was established at Marble Hill in Twickenham.

Lady Mary also, no doubt, drank her fill of London amusements. Edward Young soon afterwards satirized '*Britannia*'s Daughters' for their delight in public places and public events:

> Assemblys, Parks, coarse feasts in City-Halls,
> Lectures, and Tryals, Plays, Committees, Balls,
> Wells, *Bedlams*, Executions, *Smithfield*-Scenes,
> And Fortune-tellers caves, and Lyons dens
>
> .   .   .   .
>
> Tumblers, and Funerals, Puppet-shews, Reviews,
> Sales, Races, Rabbets, (and still stranger!) Pews.[43]

But she had her domestic interests, indoor as well as outdoor. Her non-intellectual pursuits have been quite properly obscured by her literary ones; but they were significant and continuing aspects of her life. She embroidered, she said herself, 'like an angel', sometimes for six hours a day. When Mary Astell celebrated her as 'The Fair Clarinda' (her juvenile *nom de plume*) she touched her triumphs 'at the Park, the Court, the Play', but chose to centre on the private sphere.

> But when retir'd from Public Shew and noise,
> In silent Works her fancy she employs,
> A smiling train of Arts around her stand.

[39] Martin 1984; newspapers, 14 July 1721. In 1726, even in Nov., MWM was riding that road 'perpetually' (*CL* ii. 71).

[40] He added a crack about riding as woman-on-top (28 Oct. [1727], MS at Victoria Art Gallery, Bath). Their dispute about country vs. town, nature vs. art, green vs. multicoloured, ran for years (see p. 440).

[41] *CL* ii. 54–5. Lady Isabella Finch found her 'Ears . . . full of dust and dirt' on 'a noble Chace near 50 miles in all though not indeed end ways and we thought twas pretty fair to ride tired horses 12 miles home after the Sport was over' (1730s, Devonshire MS 219.16). The park at this date also had a flock of imported wild turkeys (McDowall, 1994: 53).

[42] Pope, *Corr.* ii. 119.   [43] *The Universal Passion*, no. 5, 1727.

Astell gives equal weight to 'the Pen, and Needle'; or rather, what with the needle's 'gay silkend Landskips', and cutting 'Flow'rs and Groves' out of paper, and singing, she seems to describe not an author with hobbies but a generally artsy woman who also dabbles in writing. As Astell's biographer observes, this emphasis is deliberate; Astell 'wished Lady Mary would stay at home more'.[44]

Lady Mary was a keen snuff-taker (an awkward habit for an embroiderer, being very apt to leave smudges). She was a serious housekeeper at a time when a French traveller found English housekeeping standards high. 'Not a week passes by but well-kept houses are washed twice in the seven days, and that from top to bottom; and even every morning most kitchens, staircase, and entrance are scrubbed.' Among her servants she had a name for 'indulgence and familiarity'.[45]

Educating her daughter (the office of 'a Nursery-Maid') was now one of her priorities. But this education remains uncharted territory, unlike that of her son. He followed his father to Westminster School, at a cost of £20 a year for boarding and five or six guineas for tuition. His date of entry is unknown. Eighteenth-century public schools took boys far earlier than those today, and mothers expected to relinquish their sons to a tutor at seven.[46] In 1720, when Edward was nearly seven, Lady Mary attended the annual Westminster English Play (a tradition only less cherished than the Latin Play, to which ladies were not admitted). Lady Mar's stepson, Thomas, Lord Erskine, was starring as Otway's sentimental heroine Monimia in *The Orphan*. Lady Mary, who liked the play, thought young Erskine 'one of the most Beautifull Figures that could be seen'. She may have been there partly to size up the school as a prospective parent.[47]

Westminster was uniquely placed to make its pupils feel they had a place in a great national history. Its buildings in Dean's Yard nestle against the glorious late-medieval abbey, which in 1720 was nearing its long-awaited completion by Hawksmoor's western towers. But those buildings were in bad shape: the Old Dormitory was derelict. Francis Atterbury as Dean of Westminster headed an appeal; Lord Burlington laid the foundation of a new dormitory in May 1722; but it took eight years to complete.[48]

[44] *CL* ii. 54; iii. 18; H MS 81. 112–13; Perry 1986: 271. MWM was later pictured with a painter's mahlstick (see p. 382).

[45] Cesar de Saussure in Porter 1982: 239; *E&P* 44.   [46] Burnett 1969: 154; Crawford 1990: 12.

[47] Erskine was 14 or 15, and had already showed his political leanings at school. Nine-year-old Tommy, Lord Dupplin (son of Jacobites, nephew of the former Lady Henrietta Cavendish-Holles), spoke the epilogue (by Prior) to *The Orphan* (HMC 1899: v. 593; *CL* ii. 401; Low 1916: 11–12).

[48] The boys wore academic dress, and revered Queen Elizabeth as their founder. Prominent old boys

Westminster boys, under Dr Robert Freind as under Busby, were an élite indeed. They were also, despite copious beatings, unruly beyond the worst fears of present-day teachers. (Lady Mary might have thought no worse of them for whipping Curll and tossing him in a blanket just before she went to Turkey.)[49] In late June 1722 a fight with lads from other schools left three people dead, one of them a sedan-chair man who sportingly but rashly came to the aid of the weaker side. Another time a wood-turner who displeased some boys was assaulted, his house damaged, and his pregnant wife frightened into a near-fatal miscarriage. Next day a hackney-coachman who attracted their ire became the centre of a 'great Fray' and had 'much ado getting off with his life'. In August 1723 two boys fought an impromptu duel with penknives; one sustained a dangerous wound, but recovered.[50] Some boys at Westminster must have learned to be victims, and some to be persecutors.

Young Edward may well have been in the school plays. Although he ran away from it more than once, he remembered Westminster fondly enough to send his son there after him. Another Edward Wortley Montagu, conceived outside legal marriage (probably by Miss Elizabeth Ashe), became a King's Scholar at Westminster in 1763, aged twelve. (Named as chief beneficiary in his father's will, he died prematurely in 1777, lost at sea on his way home from service with the East India Company to claim his inheritance.)[51]

✦

Lady Mary had time now to cultivate her talent for close friendship: a category distinct from the network of social relationships which her milieu demanded. She did not choose her intimates for sharing her opinions; but she did choose those who had strong views as well as warm hearts. One of these was Lady Harley (formerly Lady Henrietta Cavendish Holles, later Lady Oxford). The outrageous Sarah, Duchess of Marlborough, said that

included Dryden, Wren, and Locke, and from MWM's generation the Pelhams, Pulteneys, and Lord Oxford (Field 1987: 10, 21). The second master was now John Nicoll or Nicholls, the head usher Samuel Wesley the younger (Pope, *Corr.* ii. 266 n. 4; *DNB*). John Cleland, future lampooner of MWM, attended for two years from Jan. 1721 (aged 8–10).

[49] In 1717 Curll had printed (unauthorized) the *Posthumous Works* of Dr Robert South, an eminent churchman and ex-pupil. This garbled a Latin funeral oration by the then Captain of the School (information from Valerie Rumbold).

[50] Newspapers, 7 July 1722, 8, 9, and 17 Aug. 1723.

[51] Edward *said* he first ran away before he turned 11 (spring 1724). He kept a Westminster epilogue to 'Phornoro': probably Terence, *Phormio* (Curling 1954: 38, 226; Montagu MSS, folder 11.8, primary material among Halsband MSS; Barker and Stenning 1928; Carleton 1965: 24–5, 27, 155–6). A fellow OW, Sir John English Dolben, set up a memorial to EWM III.

'dear Lady Mary' was 'always very good to me'. Although Sarah quarrelled with most people and normally hated 'a Bel esprit', and although Lady Mary had a 'tender esteem' for Sarah's daughter the Duchess of Montagu, in Sarah's eyes she could do no wrong. (The Duchess of Montagu, a chip off the old block, was 'at open War' with her mother for most of her adult life. Each, said Lady Mary, could count on her never to tell tales to the other.)[52] With the 'vivacious' Lord Bathurst Lady Mary was sometimes 'well and ill ten times' in two months. She enjoyed teasing him, often by contrasting his volatility with her steadiness. Yet to her he remained constant, as he made no bones of reminding Pope after Pope had defected.[53]

Her new circles were as socially heterogeneous as those of her youth. Sarah Marlborough sometimes brought herself to endure standing hostess to a party of three *bels esprits* who could 'be in the clouds together': Lady Mary, the Countess of Darlington (formerly Kielmansegg), and Marie La Vie.[54] This is a wonderfully incongruous concatenation: the brilliant and beautiful Lady Mary, the able, ugly, semi-royal Lady Darlington, and La Vie: Huguenot refugee, governess and humble companion to a banker's wife.[55] For Lady Mary, to be in the clouds with these two was to sidestep social stratification with some panache.

In Darlington, Lady Mary saw vivacity and a taste for polite learning. Pope saw, at about this date, a caricatured Artemisia, the queen who went with Xerxes to invade Greece (with George to possess England). He wrote that she 'talks by Fits, | Of Councils, Classicks, Fathers, Wits; | Reads *Malbranche, Boyle*, and *Locke*'. He found her dirty, painted, haughty, and hugely fat: 'Her Voice theatrically loud, | And masculine her Stride.' The way Pope equates female intellect with female monstrosity gives a foretaste of the metamorphosis that was to occur, after Lady Darlington's death, in his view of Lady Mary.[56]

The redoubtable Miss La Vie had been smuggled out of France as a child (hidden under old sails and empty Bordeaux hogsheads) by her banker father when the Edict of Nantes was revoked in 1685. She reached England

---

[52] Sarah gave MWM an open invitation to stay a month with her each summer (12 Mar. [?1727], dated from ref. to Blenheim), 18 Sept. 1731 (Pierpont Morgan MSS; MWM 1861: i. 20). Sarah became very fond of MWM's daughter (*E&P* 45).

[53] *CL* ii. 53, 57, 406; *E&P* 242–4; Pope, *Corr.* iii. 134.

[54] About 1720 (Mary (Cairns), Lady Blayney, 25 Feb. 1772, BL Add. MS 61466, 163–4).

[55] La Vie might well feel cordial towards EWM: in Feb. 1708 he had offered strong support in parliament for naturalizing Huguenot immigrants.

[56] MWM kept the earliest extant copy of Pope's lampoon on the Duchess of Kendal (formerly Schulenburg), but not its pair, on her friend. Both were unpub. till 1728. Darlington's size and rouge disgusted the child Horace Walpole (Mahaffey 1970: 466–71, revising the dates given in Pope, TE vi. 48–9). For Darlington's intellectual interests see Shackleton 1988: 204.

destitute. By now she 'had read every book'—in many languages—'and a great deal of the world'; she had 'an infinite deal of wit and lively imagination'. In the summer of 1719 she played the eunuch Alexas in an amateur *All for Love* in the 'bow-window-room' at the newly occupied Blenheim Palace.[57]

Patronized by two great ladies (Darlington as well as Marlborough), La Vie was a regular at Darlington's weekly supper for her half-brother the king. George I mixed with 'agreeable authors and People of wit and humour' here, though chiefly with political climbers at the Duchess of Kendal's. If it was at Darlington's that Lady Mary attended on him, she seems to have exchanged court glamour and power for a different aspect of Hanoverian life.[58]

Marie La Vie sounds more like a stimulating acquaintance than a real friend.[59] But Lady Stafford and Maria Skerrett, Lady Mary's two closest friends of the 1720s and 1730s, were in different ways almost as much outsiders as she was.[60] Claude-Charlotte, Countess of Stafford (another friend of Darlington), was twenty years older than Lady Mary, a living link to the courts of Charles II and Louis XIV. Her father, Philibert, comte de Gramont, had served with le Grand Condé, then as an exile in England had married 'la belle' Elizabeth Hamilton. Legend said it was a shotgun wedding brought about by her brother, who later wrote up Philibert's rakish exploits in the famous *Mémoires de Gramont*.[61]

Claude-Charlotte, Lady Stafford, inherited the wit of both parents but not her mother's beauty. She and her sister were Maids of Honour to the Dauphine, and often in the Sun King's presence. They were penniless but for bequests from an aunt; Saint-Simon saw them as coquettes on the make. Claude-Charlotte met and married the much older 10th Earl of Stafford in France, separated from him, and by 1700 was the object of his hatred. When he died in 1719 she came to England to see about his estates; she travelled

[57] The cast included La Vie's pupil Malye Cairns, young Lady Charlotte McCarthy (Sarah's honorary granddaughter, later MWM's close friend Lady De La Warr), and sundry grandchildren of Sarah, who prohibited stage embraces and 'scratch'd out some of the most amorous speeches' (Harris 1991: 224–5, 258; BL Add. MS 61466. 176).

[58] R. O. Bucholz argues that the court had declined as cultural centre under Anne and was becoming staid and ineffectual under George (1993).

[59] MWM *could* have been the female 'Philosopher' who offered to sit with Miss La Vie during surgery on her face (La Vie to Sarah Marlborough, 27 Oct. 1722, BL Add. MS 61466. 143–6).

[60] Other important friends (like Lady Buck, p. 287, n. 3) remain undocumented.

[61] Hamilton m. Gramont in 1663. She was later a religious convert, penalized for links with Port Royal, a bitter enemy of Madame de Maintenon, and correspondent of Fénelon. (Her daughter Lady Stafford later owned these letters.) Besides *Memoires de Grammont*, Anthony Hamilton wrote mock fairy-tales prefiguring Voltaire's *Candide* and MWM's 'Docile' (*CL* iii. 27; Clark 1921: 22–3, 112–17, 119, 121, 167, 232–3, 256; note in Hamilton 1772: p. vi n.).

with Lord Peterborough, and gossip said they would marry.[62] Lady Stafford never did remarry; but she spent more and more of her time in England. Hervey admired her imagination and unstudied wit. As an old lady, he said, she had as much wit, fun, and humour 'as any man or woman I ever knew, with a great justness in her ways of thinking and very little reserve in her manner of giving her opinion of things and people'. Horace Walpole, who noted her strong ties with Lady Mary, thought she had the more wit of the two—especially when she was, as usual, on opium.[63]

Lady Mary said Lady Stafford 'knew me better than any body else in the world, both from her own just discernment, and my Heart being ever as open to her as my selfe'. It was partly due to this friendship that she counted herself a European (or citizen of the world), and read hugely in French. From Lady Stafford's reminiscences about her youth came local colour for the stories which Lady Mary set at Louis XIV's court. Lady Stafford still spent some of her time in Paris. She knew the son of Anne Thérèse, marquise de Lambert (*salonnière*, writer, and close associate of Fontenelle).[64]

Maria or Molly Skerrett may have been met through Lady Stafford, since her merchant father had a house only two doors away.[65] She was an *ingénue* compared to Stafford, but a few years after meeting Lady Mary she became the Prime Minister's mistress. This put her outside the pale of respectability. It also made it incumbent on her to avoid the world's notice, which she effectively did. But she, like Stafford, sounds like a nonconformist. She too had 'extreme good understanding'; she may have known Mary Astell. Once she and Lady Mary visited the dumb fortune-teller Duncan Campbell, who charged a guinea and wrote his predictions down on paper. He duly 'told their names, etc.' without their informing him. This may have been when Lady Mary asked 'that odd question? Whether Mr Wortley was the first, etc.'[66]

These two very important friendships represent two areas of deep and deplorable ignorance about Lady Mary's life: about what she did and about

[62] 3 Sept. 1719 (MS newsletter written by John Farr to Francis Thistlethwayte: McMaster University).

[63] Hervey 1931: ii. 551; Ilchester 1950: 83; Walpole, *Corr.* ix. 119.

[64] *CL* iii. 27. Stafford later shared a jokey code with her, writing from Bath about a ladle, a cucumber, and a moustache (n.d., H MS 77. 254–5, 248–9, 250–1). Publication of Mme de Lambert's works—supposedly against the author's will—began in 1727 with her defence of women; this and her *Advice from a Mother to a Son and Daughter* were both translated into English, 1729.

[65] In Stratton Street (Plumb 1960: 113). There seems no basis for Horace Walpole's idea that Molly and MWM were related.

[66] See p. 248 ff. Campbell remained dumb even when a client tested him by slamming his fingers in the door. It may have been of 'some conjuress' that MWM asked her unexplained but suggestive question (Spence 1966: 756; [Haywood], 1724, 54, 146).

how she felt. Skerrett contributed to this situation by burning a whole trunkful of letters, poems, and papers of Montagu's before she married.

Lady Mary several times told her sister how much she preferred 'a small snug set', 'some Cotterys where wit and pleasure reign', to 'the Grand Monde, which has allways had my hearty contempt'. Her 'dear Intimates' or 'Amis choisies' range from the flamboyant to the quite unknown.[67] Most were at home, like her, in the upper ranks of society, but many share with Stafford and Skerrett some whiff of the outsider. Pope (to whom she was still close, though she downplayed the friendship to her sister) prided himself on his noble connections. Hervey, career courtier, writer, and bisexual, thrived on gossip and publicity.[68] Mary Astell, although a properly modest woman, had left her home in Newcastle for the metropolis at about twenty-one, and been bold enough to make a name for herself in the literary market-place.

The friendship with Astell—across a gulf of age, rank, party loyalty, and religious faith—is remarkable, especially this stage of it. If Lady Mary met Astell before she went to Turkey, she met a woman in her forties with the exciting reputation of a published author. Astell had now published nothing for a decade. She was an elderly middle-class woman, heavily involved in piety and good works; but she was also a sparkling mind, a debater, a wit. She saw friendship as morally grounded in the helpful, unflinching criticism which friend supplies to friend. But this was a closer, warmer relationship than that may suggest. Astell's fondness was later remembered in Lady Mary's family. At some unspecified date she had a protectively anxious dream about her younger friend, apparently when she had been urging some highly personal advice and found Lady Mary unresponsive. She then begged

leave to tell my dream . . . tho my waking, most reasonable & tendrest thoughts, are it seems not worth notice . . . Methought I saw you last night wth agony of Soul, Shipwreckt, struggling for Life wth ye insulting billows indifference. I cry'd, I beg'd, but all in vain yt they wou'd take a Boat yt lay by ym & try to assist you. Not one wou'd run ye least hazard, or so much as spoil their fine clothes in your service. Whereupon I threw myself out of ye window into ye Sea, resolv'd to save . . . you.[69]

This cry of alarm speaks to a quite different level of feeling from anything recorded by anyone about most of Lady Mary's friendships.

Astell took another kind of liberty with her friend: defacing a book from her library. She borrowed Lady Mary's copy of Pierre Bayle's *Pensées*

[67] Hervey 1931: i. 86 n.; *CL* ii. 15, 44, 45.   [68] For Hervey, see p. 335 ff.
[69] Perry 1986: 139, 144. Astell had attacked the Kit-Cat Club in *Bart'lemy Fair*, 1709. Lady Louisa Stuart was probably wrong to think she addressed to MWM a poem on friendship (MWM 1837: i. 53–4; *E&P* 33; Grundy 1980: 407–10).

diverses, found his sceptical philosophy provoking, and covered the volume with closely written critical annotation. On the flyleaf she scribbled two paragraphs of critical analysis, in which somewhat perfunctory apology is quickly forgotten for righteous indignation: 'I ask pardon for scrolling [scrawling] in Your Ladyships Book. The Author is so disingenuous and inconsistent that no lover of Truth can read it without a just Indignation.' She found Bayle illiberal, anti-religious, incoherent, and in every way inferior to his antagonist Pascal, whom she strongly recommended instead. It probably did not bother Lady Mary to have her book vandalized. She wrote freely in books including her much-admired *Amelia* and a text printed in 1610.[70] She freely sprinkled personal comments through John Guillim, *A Display of Heraldrie* (4th edn, 1660).

Other female friends, though they lack Astell's fame, were clearly remarkable individuals. Lady Frances Feilding was, said Lady Mary, the only intelligent one among her fair but foolish cousins, Lord Denbigh's children. Besides maintaining her friendships with the Duchesses of Marlborough and Montagu, Lady Mary 'liv'd in much Intimacy' with another of the Marlborough circle: Charlotte (MacCarthy) West, Lady De La Warr (patron of Lewis Theobald and probably of Elizabeth Thomas). She wrote of De La Warr and Congreve as successors to Sappho and Ovid, yet no plays or poems by De La Warr are known, only an impromptu verse on Sarah Marlborough.[71] Mary Anne Cantillon, née O'Mahony, who became Lady Mary's friend on settling next door in Covent Garden in 1723, was daughter of an Irish 'wild goose' or mercenary hero, and newly married to the financial wizard Richard Cantillon. He was twenty years her senior; within six months of his death she was living with the man who became her second husband. Mary Anne was a friend of J. B. Rousseau and Montesquieu in France and Lord and Lady Hervey in England. Despite her many Jacobite connections she held Enlightenment views.[72]

Along with friendship, literary activities had pride of place in Lady Mary's life. She loved shopping for books. For someone with little private spending money, she amassed a remarkable library, including titles published in every year of her London residence. For some of these, like Gay's *Poems on Several*

---

[70] [Verville], *L'histoire veritable*, 1610, 526–37 (now, like Bayle and *Amelia*, at Sandon); Guillim owned by Janna Brandt and Michael Quam.

[71] *CL* ii. 113; BL Add. MS 61443, 164 (1719, adapted from Garth). For Theobald see p. 331; for Thomas see HMC 1901: vi. 29. Lord Sunderland's private correspondence (BL Add. MS 61654) involves his third wife's Molesworth relations, James Hammond, Cantillons, and De La Warrs—all friends of MWM.

[72] *CL* ii. 25; Murphy 1986: 198–205.

Occasions, 1720, and Pope's *Odyssey* translation, she subscribed;[73] others may have been gifts. But also she followed the advice of her relation John Evelyn: 'rummage and often . . . revisit the shops of frippery *Booksellers*.'[74] The dates of her books give some idea of her pattern of acquisition (although not all the books she bought were new). She usually wrote 'M' or 'Ma' or 'Ma W' in them, not her full name.

She acquired many books published in the first few years after her return; if she bought them new, she was keeping her ear to the ground. She followed canonical literature: Nicholas Rowe's *Lucan's Pharsalia*, 1718 (another subscription: called by Johnson 'one of the greatest productions of English poetry'); the various *Poems on Several Occasions* issued by Prior, Congreve, Lansdowne, and Parnell in 1718, 1720, 1721, and 1722 respectively; and collections of plays by Charles and Thomas Shadwell, both printed in 1720.[75] With these came lighter books: collections of poetry and letters, essays and fiction, much of it anonymous.[76] From these years her library contained two books of information: Elias Ashmole's *Antiquities of Berkshire*, 1719, and Benjamin Hoadly's controversial work on the rights of subjects and the nature of the Sacramental Test, 1718.

Lady Mary gathered French books as regularly as English ones. Here the 'canon' was represented by the *Œuvres* of J. B. Rousseau, 1723, and of Marie-Catherine Desjardins, Madame de Villedieu, 1721. In the latter Lady Mary wrote, 'plus delicat que Crebillon, plus amusant que Voltaire'. She acquired personal history and fiction (two virtually indistinguishable genres) about the French seventeenth century. She acquired travel writing: Maximilien Misson on Italy.[77] The Enlightenment supplied a volume of works by thinkers and philosophers which, although edited by Pierre Desmaiseaux, was the brainchild of Conti,[78] and *Lettres galantes et philosophiques*, 1721, by Rémond de Saint-Mard, brother of her Paris admirer.

---

[73] Both her sisters, her father, and her stepmother also subscribed to Gay, her father and her husband (5 copies) to Pope's *Odyssey*.

[74] Evelyn 1661: 64.

[75] Wh MS M 135. She had quoted Lansdowne for years before acquiring his *Poems*, 3rd edn. Her copy of Thomas Shadwell's *Dramatick Works*, 1720, has 'Anne Newnham' on the first flyleaf ('Ma' on others).

[76] Two titles are only doubtfully identifiable: a probable fiction called *Passionate Letters* or *Passionate Love-Letters*, 1719, and a probable satire called *Praise of Drunkenness*, either 1720 or 1723. *The Mirror*, 1719 (essays), *The Grove*, 1721 (poems, of which uncle Feilding took two royal-paper copies), and Martha Fowke's and William Bond's *Epistles of Clio and Strephon*, 1720, were all anonymous. Thomas Gordon set his name to *The Humourist*, 1720 (essays), as did Mary Hearne (if she really existed) to *Novels*, 1720.

[77] The ten-volume *Memoires*, 1722, of the Seigneur de Brantôme (soldier and biographer, a century dead); Mme de Lafayette's *Histoire*, 1720, of Henrietta, sister of Charles II of England; Segrais's *Nouvelles françoises*, 1722 (actually co-written with the duchesse de Montpensier); Maximilien Misson, *Voyage D'Italie*, 5th edn., 1722 (DeJean 1991: 52).

[78] Desmaizeaux (ed.), *Recueil de . . . pièces sur la philosophie*, 1720.

This small segment of Lady Mary's book acquisition reflects consistent tastes. She loved poetry, drama, fiction, and knotty thought. She felt as much at home in French as English. She had a special interest in women's work: an interest more obvious at this date in her French than English titles, since Frenchwomen—or ladies—had achieved a level of recognition as authors which was as yet beyond the dreams of Englishwomen. Her own acquaintance, as well as her own sex, compelled her special interest. Apart from John Gay, she had personal knowledge of Congreve, Rousseau, and Conti, and very likely of several others whose work appears in this random sample. To read and own the work of friends came naturally to her, as a habit shared with her father and probably her uncle Feilding.

As well as buying books and receiving them from authors, she continued to hoard up poems, both published and unpublished, in manuscript. Before her marriage she had begun both to copy such poems into a bound volume, and to amass copies just as she received them: poems by Congreve and Prior (whom she was still transcribing in the 1730s), Colley Cibber and Henry Fielding, Astell and Anne Finch, and plenty of still unattributed work which *could* be her own. A number of light-hearted, piercingly perceptive songs and ballads on love-situations, for instance, sound quite like her in style; she might have thought it too *risqué* to circulate them.

Other poems by her did circulate. Going from hand to hand, they attracted written comment (like Astell's eulogy) as well as spoken. Her friend Lady Harley (later Oxford) and her daughter each kept several. Such copies usually lacked a title and often an author's name. Titles and labels smacked of print; but lacking them helped to make copies ephemeral. Many of Lady Mary's poems that have vanished were ballads: topical, often personal. They gave short-term pleasure, and sometimes made long-term enemies.[79]

Within months of her return to England, the Duke of Buckingham named 'the Fam'd Lady *Mary*' in a ballad as a 'hopeful' successor to Nicholas Rowe as Poet Laureate. This—though not serious—shows her poetic stock was high.[80] Soon afterwards Thomas Burnet (son of the bishop) sent out 'from my Parnassus' a poem in her praise which was very soon and very persistently attributed to Pope. It begins: 'In Beauty or Wit'. Having paid tribute to her for these two properly female qualities, it recognizes others more problematic. Men, it says, may find it hard to yield to a lady in learning. Eve,

---

[79] H MS 255; H MS 81; BL Harley MSS; Portland MSS. An undocumented story has Pope commemorating in verse a female ballad-singer praised by MWM and admired by Swift and Gay (Irving 1940: 93).

[80] 'Election of a Poet Laureat In 1719'; Rowe d. 6 Dec. 1718 (Pope, 1726, 223; Portland MSS, 17. 95–6).

after all, paid heavily for tasting just one apple of knowledge: what should Lady Mary pay for having 'robbed the whole tree'?[81] She preserved a copy of this poem, ascribed to its proper author.

In 1719 George Sewell printed his 'To the Lady W—y M—e, Upon Her Poems Being Publish'd without a Name.' She would have approved his argument, if not his versification. Admirers of her eclogues, he said, knowing nothing of the author's beauty, must love the poems for themselves alone. He likened her to angels singing, or a hidden stream invisibly nurturing. 'Great Minds are Secret'; her anonymity proves her to be above the vanity of fame.[82]

But as she was praised for secrecy, glimpses of her author identity were appearing in print. Conti had not been secretive about her letters to him from Turkey, and one of them was now published in London. Her original French was accompanied by an English translation, and a title flattering both writer and recipient: *The Genuine Copy of a Letter Written from Constantinople by an English Lady . . . no less distinguish'd by her Wit than her Quality; To a Venetian Nobleman, one of the prime Virtuosi of the Age.*[83]

In September 1719 a friend in the country sent Lady Hertford (wife of 'Patch', friend of the poet Anne Finch) an unnamed poem by Lady Mary. It may well have been the one she addressed to William Feilding from Turkey. She valued this work highly: it was the only one she copied into Pope's elegant transcription of her eclogues.[84] Her uncle valued it too, and showed it about (indiscreetly, she later said) until it reached print. This it did in *A New Miscellany of Original Poems*, published 19 May 1720—through the agency either of Anthony Hammond, the *Miscellany*'s editor, or of the ubiquitous Curll, its printer. Curll falls under suspicion because that same month he issued Addison's *Scating: A Poem* as a sixpenny pamphlet including also *Mr. Pope's Verses to the Lady Mary Wortley Mountague* (i.e. 'In Beauty or Wit').

Curll was giving 'In Beauty or Wit' maximum exposure. It appeared in Hammond, in *Scating*, and in *Court Poems* (last reprinted in 1719)—always as by Pope, whose market value far exceeded Thomas Burnet's. But Curll exercised some caution over naming Lady Mary. His two new publications (both far less ungenteel than *Court Poems*) keep her name off their actual

---

[81] 5 Feb. 1719 (Halsband 1956: 99–100). Pope, TE vi. 423, lists the many attributions of it to him.

[82] Sewell 1719: 59–60, repr. 1728 in his *Posthumous Works*. He also praised the novelist Jane Barker. He pub. with Curll, who was still reprinting *Court Poems*, and had an interest in identifying MWM as well as praising her.

[83] The *Genuine Copy* was issued through James Roberts and Anne Dodd, with intent to conceal the author and/or the person issuing it (see p. 339).

[84] MWM 1977a: 52 ff. The sender, Mrs Arabella Marow, was also a friend of Elizabeth Singer Rowe (Hughes 1940: 57; Wilmot 1812: 272).

title-pages. *Scating*'s half-title supplies it (honorifically linked with those of Pope and Addison). The *Miscellany*'s title-page names the 'most Eminent Hands' on display inside: Prior, Pope, the notorious Lord Rochester, and Delarivier Manley. But Montagu's (next to Manley's) is notionally veiled by initials. The less eminent contributers Susanna Centlivre and Martha Fowke (later Sansom) do not make the title-page. Montagu's own poem is headed only 'By a Lady'.[85] But her name in full heads 'In Beauty or Wit', since that features her as lady, not as author.[86]

What she really felt about her appearance in 'Hammond's Miscellany' cannot be known. She implied (years later, sounding self-righteous) that she was displeased. In recent literary tradition anonymity had meant power rather than bashfulness. One response, however, must surely have pleased her if she knew of it. A young poet, Elizabeth Tollet, celebrated her poem in an exultant stanza: 'The *British* Muse . . . for *Pierpoint* plants immortal Bays.' This appeared in Tollet's first, anonymous volume in 1724. She was well placed to know the *Miscellany*, since her father was Hammond's colleague on the Navy Commission. It was odd of her to use Montagu's birth name, and apt of her to choose as oriental parallels for 'Pierpoint' 's spellbinding power not only Helen (who appears in the printed poem) but also Orpheus and Sappho. She could not have found these in the poem, but could have found them in the Embassy Letters. Had she read the manuscript?[87]

At the centre of Lady Mary's literary life stood Pope, still eager to flatter her mind as well as her 'Person'. Of the fifty or sixty letters which he wrote to her altogether (many of which she copied into her diary), few except the oriental extravaganzas survive. He must have kept writing to her on her return, except when she was at Twickenham. In the spring of 1720 Gay gave her a prominent role in his verse celebration of Pope's completing the *Iliad*. The translator singles out from a troop of admiring ladies one whose 'eyes' declare she is 'Wortley'. Gay exclaims, 'How art thou honour'd, number'd with her friends? | For she distinguishes the good and wise.'[88] Although

---

[85] No doubt many owners of the vol. knew enough to fill in her name, as in the BL copy.

[86] [Anthony Hammond] 1720: 95–101, 274; Addison 1720: 15. The *Miscellany* prints Rochester letters, not poems. In it Manley praises Lady Bristol; tributes to Manley, Centlivre, and Fowke are printed or mentioned; every female poet comes equipped with a passport of male approbation. A rather pedestrian 'Song. On the Lady Eleanor Montague' gives this lady MWM's former pen-name, Clarinda ([Hammond] 1720: 76–7, 191–6, 201–7, 257–71, 322–34).

[87] *CL* iii. 169; Paul Hammond 1993: 123–42; Tollet 1724. Tollet, a Tory and a Londoner, had several friends in common with MWM. She later owned a copy of *To the Imitator of . . . Horace*, 1733 (*Betley Hall*, 19 Apr. 1723, no. 195; information from Michael Londry).

[88] 'Mr. Pope's Welcome from Greece'; MWM is attended by Griselda Murray and Mary Lepell, Hervey's future bride. In a copy presumably made after *c*.1728, Gay changed 'Wortley' to 'Howard' (1974: i. 256; Spence 1966: 747, 752). The *Iliad*'s last two vols. were ready on 12 May 1720 (Mack 1985: 347).

Pope did not write 'In Beauty or Wit' (as was so often asserted); he did this
year write a short effusion expressing love and loss. He says he has perfected
his garden, but cannot enjoy it in Lady Mary's absence—'Joy . . . only dwells
where W——— casts her eyes'—and he likens himself to a deer struck to the
heart by an arrow.[89]

Pope still talked poetry with her. Though she was Addison's friend, he
must have shown her his satirical lines on Addison soon after her return. He
showed Lord Bathurst his exquisite manuscript of her eclogues; he apparently assisted her in looking through some of her past writings, which stood
the scrutiny well. They may have been reading her eclogues together, or her
actual letters to him from Turkey, or her Embassy Letters, if these were
already taking shape. But most likely she showed him some earlier work,
for he compliments Lady Mary *Pierrepont*, saying he is 'pleasd with some
Fragments of hers, as I am with Sappho's'.[90]

At some time between 1719 and 1724 Montagu wrote up her travel experiences. She may have used actual letters; she certainly used her journal.[91]
She must have relived her travels as she did this; she also expended serious
literary effort. She chose some fourteen individuals as addressees, cloaking
them with initials. (Most of them have proved identifiable today; more
would have been identifiable to contemporaries.) Ten of these also figure in
the lists of those to whom she had *actually* written from Turkey. She
excluded from her edited volumes many she had written to in fact, including
her father (who might well have disapproved), William Congreve, and
several people of influence under George I. She shared out her material,
avoiding the duplication which is natural to actual letters, but making the
content fit the recipient. To Lady Mar ('Countesse of M———' in the MS) she
allotted detailed accounts of exotic costume; the butterfly Lady Rich had her
request for a Greek slave (politely) snubbed; the Princess of Wales got a
patriotic effusion. To Pope went literary discussions and to Conti the most
'Enlightenment' letters (on the structure of the Ottoman administration, the
mixture of races at Constantinople, on classical learning and archaeology).
One recipient of five letters, Anne Thistlethwayte, was evidently a good
friend; yet nothing is known of the relationship but these fabricated
letters.[92]

The resulting Embassy Letters are an Enlightenment travel treatise, but a

---

[89] 'To Mr Gay', *CL* i. 15–16. Name expanded to WORTLEY in print (TE vi. 225–6).

[90] Pope, *Corr.* ii. 10, 22, 39; TE vi. 142–5.

[91] For instance, the Embassy Letter to Lady Mar dated 21 Nov. from Leipzig clearly incorporates passages written at Dresden, of which MWM says 'here' and 'hence' (*CL* i. 282–3).

[92] See p. 144.

relaxed and racy one.[93] Montagu is attentive to history and its visible mani-
festations in buildings and other tourist sights; but more so to technological
improvement (the heating stoves of Germany), to intellectual frameworks
and systems of government, and to the place of women in society, which the
masculine focus of other travel writers had so far rendered all but invisible.[94]
Her comparative surveys of various countries cover religion (both Christian
and Islamic variants in theology, clergy, ritual, and burial customs), legal
systems (betrothal, marriage, property inheritance, slavery, crimes and
penalties), and the culture of daily life: costume, furniture, eating habits,
pastimes, etc.

She moves easily between narrative and description, splicing in passages
of historical material from standard sources. She firmly sets the record
straight from the perversions of 'voyage' writers who traduce the
Mohammedans: who 'never fail giving you an Account of the Women, which
'tis certain they never saw, and talking very wisely of the Genius of the Men,
into whose Company they are never admitted, and very often describe
Mosques, which they dare not peep into.'[95] She delights in exploding received
ideas, and uses what she asserts to be the liberty of Turkish women as a stick
to beat English society with. She is not above self-dramatization (in the scene
on the moonlit precipice, for example, she implies that she saved her husband's life). Quoting Virgil on the banks of the Hebrus, she flatteringly
chooses a passage which Pope had just reworked in his 'Ode on St Cecilia's
Day'. But where Pope likened her to Euridice, she not only counters by likening herself to Orpheus, but asserts her claim to literary identity by a further
web of allusions. She quotes a line from Dryden—'As equal were our Souls,
so equal were our fates'—which brackets the poets Anne Killigrew and
Katherine Philips, both killed by smallpox. Lady Mary, a recent smallpox
survivor, thus equates herself at a single stroke with Orpheus *and* with two
foremothers in English poetry.[96] More than her *Spectator* essay, more than
her eclogues, these letters constituted a bid for literary laurels.

Astell, as she wrote in her preface for this work, wanted to see it in print.
But even Astell had chosen to leave some of her own work (poetry, not
prose) in the private-circulation medium of manuscript. Lady Mary
belonged, by rank and practice, to an older world which published without

---

[93] She headed her MS 'Copys of Letters'. But 'Embassy Letters', though not hers, is preferable to
'Turkish Letters', since more than half deal with Christian Europe. MWM hardly used the word 'Levant'.

[94] This may seem to deny MWM's own complaints of voyage-writers' disinformation about women; but
those writers tend towards an essentialist approach (what do other cultures reveal about women and
gender?) as opposed to her own (what do other cultures practise?).

[95] *CL* i. 368. Perhaps remembering her own rashness at St Sophia.   [96] *CL* i. 330; *SL* 150–1 and n. 3.

printing. Readers of the Embassy Letters in manuscript probably included most of those who had received her actual letters from Turkey, and many who had not. Possessing such an audience, she may not have felt like a frustrated author. Besides Astell, an anonymous hand contributed praise:

> Your Elder Sisters in the Lists of Fame
> Rose to Deserve, but not Despise a Name;
> Persist in this Distinction of Renown,
> And wear a Laurel that is All Your own;
> Still keep Conceald This Bright and Learned Store—
> For why should *Pope* and *Congreive* Write no more?[97]

This admirer (someone interested in former women writers) seems positively to approve the work's remaining unprinted.

Whether or not Lady Mary was just now writing up her travels, she chose to allude to them by wearing modified Turkish costume for the portrait of her which Pope commissioned from Kneller around New Year 1720. If not the very garments she had had made in Adrianople, they were a westernized version. Clothes in this style (more authentically Turkish than surviving ones which she is thought to have owned) feature in most portraits of her from this time. She no doubt went *en Turque* to masquerades, untroubled by the style's erotic associations. She contributed, in person and posthumously through her Letters, to the long-lasting rage for the orient.[98]

Pope masterminded this portrait. Kneller was to visit her and sketch her face in crayons; he could then transfer his sketch to canvas at his own house without bothering her again. 'This I must observe, is a manner in which they seldom draw any but Crown'd Heads; & I observe it with a secret pride & pleasure.' In the end, though, Kneller needed to make a second visit 'to take a sketch of you in your dress, if you'l give leave'. Pope asked this leave with such elaborate submissiveness as to suggest irony: 'Your Will be done! but God send it may be the same with mine!'[99]

The picture which resulted was to hang in Pope's 'Best Room Fronting the Thames' until his death, when bitter enmity had for years divided him from its sitter. A sketch for it hung in his great parlour. It shows Lady Mary reclining on her right elbow, with the fingers of her right hand to her cheek.

---

[97] MS bound into H MS 253; also in H MS 259, the 'Molesworth' copy of the Embassy Letters.

[98] Clothes at Victoria and Albert Museum and at Sandon. The frontispiece of Defoe's *Roxana*, 1724, is much in MWM's Turkish style. Turkish dress was worn by 11 of 34 people named at one 1750s masquerade (Badminton MSS, Fm T/B1/4/4; Ribeiro 1984: 221, 228–9).

[99] It may be that his concern with these sittings, and the memory of former times shared with MWM and Jervas, were the spur for an undated letter to the latter, now in Ireland. Pope seems to allude to MWM, but may have deleted her name for print (Pope, *Corr.* ii. 22–3).

She looks down and away, evading the viewer's gaze as she does in no other portrait. She is unmistakably a traveller: behind her is seen the Constantinople skyline, and behind that the 'Asian Mountains'. She wears the drop pearl earrings in which Kneller had painted her five years before, but with them clothes which reverse her earlier unobtrusiveness: her Turkish talpoche, shift, anteri (long waistcoat), heavy jewelled belt, and ermine curdee or mantle. Since Kneller had to come to her to sketch all this, it must have been her property. Though it is elegantly westernized, it is not western. The portrait recognizes no marks of smallpox: she has both eyebrows and the harder-to-fake eyelashes.[100] It is hardly surprising that Kneller should approach Jervas's style in this work: Jervas and his studio were a part of Pope's and Lady Mary's history together.[101]

Kneller did a fine job. He caught the mystery and wistfulness of Pope's idol, as well as some glimpse of the self who is legible in Montagu's writings and in the elaborately staged Vanmour painting. Pope celebrated in verse the portrait's 'happy air of Majesty and Youth', its success in catching the 'playful smiles around the dimpled mouth'. He lamented the impossibility of rendering Lady Mary's inner qualities: the learning, the wisdom, the 'Soul Divine'. In his poem her body is a perfectly fitted signifier for her soul: there is no memory of their discordance after the smallpox, or of that imposition she was later to bewail, of feminine softness on her 'haughty Soul' and ungendered mind.[102]

Another (contested) portrait of Lady Mary shows her wearing these clothes of hers again. It is unique (with its versions and copies) in that its exotic backdrop is not Constantinople, but an encampment of tents—presenting her as daring explorer rather than exotic sophisticate. It seems that this original was copied: twice at least as a portrait of Lady Townshend, the former Dorothy or Dolly Walpole.[103] These pictures, like the Embassy Letters, locate the sources of Lady Mary's fame in the recent past.

---

[100] Mack 1969: 31. Pope 'made a perfect Passion of preferring your present Face to your past'. Wycherley's Sparkish observes that 'painters don't draw the small-pox' (*The Country Wife*, 1675, III. ii; Pope, *Corr.* ii. 22–3).

[101] Painting, 37 × 48 in., owned by the Marquess of Bute. A note in the NPG archive (994) reads 'More like Jervas': often engraved. Richard Phillips, publisher of MWM's *Works*, 1803, seems to have commissioned two versions, by Caroline Watson and by Freeman. R. Sands's outline was pub. by Vernor, Wood and Sharpe in 1811, H. Cooper's more conventional engraving by Longman, 1812. All these face left, like the original. A right-facing version appeared in the *Graphic*, 21 Mar. 1891 (323). In *c*.1724 Pope had Jervas paint a similar but moonlit picture of Henrietta Howard, apparently in rebuke to MWM (now at Marble Hill).

[102] 'On Lady Mary Wortley Montagu's Portrait', TE vi. 211–12, unpub. till 1803; *CL* ii. 106.

[103] One version (sold at Christie's, 1975, as MWM by Kneller) reproduced on cover of *SL*; another at Dulwich Picture Gallery, ascribed to Jervas and identified by inscription and coat of arms as Lady Townshend. A variant picture was given to the NPG as being of MWM: now called Lady Townshend. The tents *may* be the sultan's gift to EWM (see p. 158).

13

1720 Onwards

~~❧~~

Inoculation: 'pull'd about and solicited'[1]

WHILE Lady Mary's Turkish adventures dropped behind her, new and problematic adventures awaited. Nicolas-François Rémond, Conti's friend whom she had met in Paris in 1718, had been pursuing her ever since. Like Pope, he combined begging and boldness; he slanted it towards boldness. He admired her 'manieres... si nobles et si douces'. He professed himself aston-ished to find such enlightened good sense and such dazzling imagination in a great lady; he tried to impress her with boasting about his unintellectual rakery with other women. Soon after meeting her he sent her a meditation circling round the question of whether and in what manner he loved her: was it love, or tender friendship? If he heard she had a lover he would be in despair; but then if it were possible for her as a virtuous woman to offer him the choice between her body and her heart, he would prefer her heart even to her delectable body. He cited Plato; he told her he could not live without her; he talked of her visiting Paris.[2]

Rémond wrote as an anglophile of English politics, literature, and theatre, and as a virtuoso of ancient and modern literature and the respective merits of rhyme and blank verse. He enriched Lady Mary's life in a way he could not foresee, by introducing her future friend Lady Stafford, then visiting England.[3] But all this, he said, had only one aim: to please her, which he could better do as a pedant than as a lover. But from poetry in general it was a short step to poems to her, and to the precise connotations of *je vous aime* and *i [sic] love you*.

In February 1720, more ominously, he consulted her about financial matters: his 'little tottering fortune', his needs and dreams, his dealings

---

[1] *CL* ii. 26.   [2] *CL* i. 446–7; H MS 77. 223–4.
[3] She and Peterborough reached England again on 22 Jan. 1720 (newspapers). She took a house at Mortlake.

with John Law, his losses in the Mississippi Scheme, and his desire to invest in 'vos fonds public'—the South Sea Company. She had already, it seems, told him this would not be practicable. Together with his financial aspirations, he expounded his more lover-like motives for wanting to see England and especially Twickenham.[4]

Name-dropping was integral to his epistolary style. Conti, Law, Lord and Lady Stair, and Pope (whom he longed to meet) recurred frequently. He presented himself as a libertine in both senses: sardonic, worldly, reading Propertius by his fireside, and recalling his former loves. All this might have its charm; yet by spring 1720 he was already complaining of her failure to respond to hints that she should come to Paris. He joked about the profit he might make by printing her letters; this *could* be read as verging on a threat.[5] While England was sliding towards the South Sea crash and a fearful smallpox epidemic, Lady Mary slid towards confrontation: with Rémond, and over inoculation. The most embattled phase of her life—so far—was on its way.

In May 1720, as the South Sea boom was gathering steam, Rémond arrived in London to make her 'a visit, against my will'. He found her elusive: during his first fortnight he saw her once only, at a supper party. He blamed this failure to make contact not on any intention of hers (though at that supper she spoke not a word to him), but on the dissipated lives that both were leading. He resolved to try harder. Meanwhile, walking in the park, he was surprised to meet her sister Mar. (He probably knew that Lord Mar, no longer 'James III' 's Secretary of State, was in prison in Geneva; he clearly did not know that Lady Mar was visiting England in connection with her father's battle to reclaim for her the forfeited Mar estates.) Lady Mar was on her way to church; Rémond arranged to wait at her house for her return. She was a promising avenue to her sister.[6]

Lady Mary's is the only account of what transpired between her and Rémond: an account which, confided to her sister later, does not fully elucidate her feelings at the time. He had a high opinion of his own talents (complicated, perhaps, by his having two brothers more intellectually distinguished than himself), and he professed a high opinion of hers. She said he flattered her perseveringly, took immense pains to impose on her, and claimed that 'there never was so extrodinary an attachment (or what you please to call it)' as his for her. He aimed his flattery at her writing ambitions:

⁴ H MS 77. 221; *CL* i. 448.   ⁵ *CL* i. 448–50.
⁶ *CL* ii. 1; to Alvarez, H MS 77. 227 [late May 1720]. Lord Annandale had been renting Lady Mar's Whitehall house, but had perhaps left.

he expatiated on politics and criticism, and boasted his literary connections. He cited Socrates, Boileau, Racine, Cicero, Virgil, Terence, Horace. He told her that people who had read her letters to him were astonished and impressed.

He also confided his wish for a small country retreat. He consulted her on financial management: should he invest in diamonds or stocks? She, while reiterating that 'twas impossible to make [him] happy [his] own way', began to feel that she owed him something, and that it would be magnanimous, 'a high point of Generosity', to do him a service. Her influence *may* have helped him acquire £2,000 worth of hard-to-get South Sea stock in the third subscription, opened on 15 June. Her 'very strenuous' advice, given at a time when she was already avoiding him, certainly did him a favour by causing him to sell early. He had been inclined to hold on and hope for more (like many who lost their shirts). But at her bidding he took the prudent course (like Richard Cantillon and Lord Gower), sold to Lord Stair, and made £840—about 40 per cent profit.[7] Meantime he did not learn the full extent of his Mississippi losses till he got home.

Having helped him to a windfall, Lady Mary felt she could decently press for his departure, 'which his follys made me think necessary for me'. She 'exact[ed] his Absence', although he tearfully protested that it would kill him. By early August 1720 he was back in Paris, to her immense relief; but he left his English winnings in her hands to reinvest. (When she advised the further prudence of stopping while he was ahead, he 'reply'd that twas too little to be of any value, and he would either have it double or quit'.) She yielded to his entreaties, 'and flatter'd my selfe . . . that I was doing a very heroic Action in trying to make a man's fortune thô I did not care for his addresses'.[8] With his money he left her a signed authority to invest it, acquitting her of liability if it should be lost. He then, on 4 September/24 August 1720, wrote to express doubts over the South Sea and to suggest it might be better to sell, and either buy land or keep the cash. (He also made play with the name of the late Madame Dacier, and lamented what he depicted as Lady Mary's withdrawal from their tender friendship.) But South Sea stock could not be casually bought or sold: each subscription opened on a set date, dispensed pre-booked shares, and closed on another set date. Selling did become possible when it closed, but only if a buyer could be found.

With Rémond out of the way, Lady Mary was enjoying the South Sea, sharing with Pope and other friends the exhilaration of gambling and the

---

[7] *CL* i. 451 n. 4; ii. 1; H MS 74. 447, 448, 449, 450. Gower reportedly made £64,000: a profit of 300% (Richards 1973: 6).

[8] *CL* i. 450; ii. 2; Gregg 1982: 188.

smugness of a sure thing. She no doubt agreed with Pope that it would be
'Ignominious (in this Age of Hope and Golden Mountains) not to Venture'.
'The scent of money was in the air like the breath of spring'; and because the
law had never turned its attention to the stockmarket, it was open for women
to deal in on just the same terms as men.[9] (No investor seems to have given a
moment's thought to the presence of negro slaves among the commodities
ostensibly being traded; in practice it was promises, not solid objects or
persons, which changed hands.) Though not flush with cash of her own,
Lady Mary was well placed to acquire stock. She had the ear of young
Craggs, whose father seems to have been the project's driving force. In the
third subscription she had arranged a £5,000 purchase by her sister Gower's
mother-in-law. On 18 July she staked a claim with Craggs for the coming
fourth subscription. Mary Astell, who like other pious people saw the rage
for profit as a kind of epidemic, wrote on 12 August that the Muses, or love of
fame, were out of fashion: 'we hear no more of Lady Mary Wortley's Wit,
but of her Bargains.' On the one hand opprobrium was heaped on 'female
stock-jobbers'. On the other hand someone wrote a poem to celebrate 'La:
Mary Wortley's having bought Shares in the South Sea.'[10]

That month Pope urged her to buy, the 'General discourse and private
intelligence then scatter'd about being of a great rise'. (In fact the value of
the stock had begun to slip, but eyes were still optimistically fixed to the
future.) Rémond's first letter since his return, even though it suggested
alternatives to stocks, still coyly exulted in the profit Lady Mary was going
to secure him.[11] The day of his letter (4 September in Paris, 24 August in
London) was that on which the fourth subscription opened. Lady Mary paid
out his money for stock in the presence of her sister Frances. She then sold
out fast at a small profit the moment the subscription closed; she 'thought I
had manag'd prodigious well', combining boldness with circumspection.[12]

But history was not on her side. By 19 September South Sea stock (which
in June had stood at 1050) had fallen 450 points, to the fury of investors; ten
days later its notes and bills were waste paper.[13] Megalomaniac building projects stood unfinished and deserted; lavish orders of clothes and jewels lan-
guished uncalled-for at their makers'. Bankruptcies and panic flights abroad
ensued, along with savage satirical cartoons and a parliamentary committee
of enquiry (on which Edward Wortley Montagu sat). Never in human
memory had London been so empty. Cox and Cleave, respected gold-

[9] Pope, *Corr.* ii. 33–4; Carswell 1993: 116, 119.
[10] *CL* i. 450–2; Perry 1986: 392; Carswell 1993: 55–6; H MS 81. 129.   [11] Pope, *Corr.* ii. 52; *CL* i. 453.
[12] *CL* ii. 2.   [13] Scott 1912: 417, 427–8, 429.

smiths and bankers, to whom Lady Mary had sold Rémond's stock, went bankrupt.[14]

With the stock returned on her hands and shrunk to half its value, Lady Mary wrote, 'with the Sincere Sorrow natural to have upon such an Occasion'—and, no doubt, a humiliating sense of failure—to inform Rémond of his loss and to ask if she should sell the stock or hand over £500 in cash. He did not answer her question, but sent 'a long Eloquent Oration of miserys of Another Nature'. She thought him disinterestedly careless of material gain; but she was wrong. After months of ignoring her repeated requests for instructions, he told her, in January 1721, 'that he had discover'd all my tricks, that he was convince'd I had all his money remaining untouch'd, and he would have it again or he would print all my Letters to him'. She begged him to return the letters; she begged her sister Frances (now in Paris) to reason with him; she sent back a present he had given her; she complained that the suspense was undermining her health.

In July 1721, terrified at rumours that he was coming to London, she offered to place the whole affair in the hands of a lawyer of his choice, or to submit to examination by 'any person, Man or Woman, either Lawyer, Broker, or person of Quality'. She got the broker she had used for the stock to make a statement to 'a Lawyer of Reputation and Merit', Isaac Delpeche. She suggested that Rémond should 'send a Letter of Attorney to examine my Accounts'.[15]

He must have known quite well the scale of the South Sea crash (from newspapers and from the arrival in Paris of both injured and allegedly guilty parties), and known that his loss was not Lady Mary's fault. It was not, in any real sense, she who had lost his money; but he chose to act as if it was. It was a canny if not an ethical bid to salvage something for himself from the wreck. Although, she said, she had 'attestations and wittnesses' to every step in her management,[16] she was plunged into agonies of self-blame for her own stupidity and into terror that it would come to her husband's notice. Wortley might not any longer be ragingly jealous; but his rigid sense of honour and decorum might well be dismayed to find his wife writing to a platonic admirer. And he hated the loss of money; and her money was his. Lady Mary fervently hoped that he might never know.

---

[14] *Weekly Journal or Saturday's Post*, 18 Nov. 1721; *CL* ii. 2–3. EWM made a modest South Sea profit himself (Child and Co., ledgers: 18, 1718–31, 158).

[15] *CL* ii. 2–3, 9, 10, 11. On 1 Apr. a newspaper reported: 'a certain Lady living near Covent-Garden, and of no mean Extraction or Estate', had 'mortgaged her whole Estate' in the South Sea, 'parted with every Thing valuable [and] must inevitably perish in a Goal [*sic*] if not timely relieved' (*Weekly Journal: or, British Gazetteer*). This April fool *may* point at MWM.

[16] *CL* ii. 3.

In deploying brokers and lawyers she acted like a woman of business. But her best hope of controlling Rémond lay in her contacts as a lady of fashion. Her friends (Lady Lansdowne, Griselda Murray) helped by carrying or receiving letters. Another friend, a man, entrusted by Rémond with a letter to Wortley giving his side of the sorry story, handed it over to her instead. Throughout the year 1721 she studded her letters to Lady Mar with desperate appeals. She begged her sister to reason with Rémond, and to invoke the heavy artillery of Lord Mar and Lord Stair. She got Lady Stafford to write, early in 1721. Stafford's 'long plain letter' expressed contempt too frankly to be politic;[17] but she also offered to write to the courtier duc de Villeroi, Rémond's patron. Lady Mary was ready with her own threats; but 'something to fright him' probably did not mean, as Horace Walpole supposed, a beating by hired thugs or a challenge from Mar or Stair.[18] In this patronage society, a threat to intervene between a man and his patron was something serious.

On one point she kept her head. Although by August she felt frantic enough to send Rémond all the money she had in hand, she would not do so without his 'general Acquittance in due form'. Nor, on lawyer's advice, to ensure herself against future demands, would she place it in anybody else's hands without his 'express order'. Rémond would send no such order. By 6 September Lady Mary had ceased to care about her letters. Let them be left at his mercy, if only he would send her instructions that would enable her to deposit his money with someone else. But when this message was relayed to him, his response was to demand (not by an official order, but verbally) the 'whole summ', which was 'as much in my power as it is to send a million'. She refused. Later he demanded £2,000, which would leave her seriously out of pocket, and threatened 'to print I know not what Stuff against me': also something serious to one already aware 'that the most groundless Accusation is allways of ill Consequence to a Woman'.[19]

At this crisis point, Lady Mary's dealings with Rémond vanish from sight. She must have confided in her husband, since he read and neatly endorsed Rémond's earlier letters. The later, threatening ones are not extant: probably they were handed over to a lawyer. Rémond was exorcized—more or less. His memory came back to scare her when his brother published *Lettres*

---

[17] *CL* ii. 5. Lady Mar (who returned briefly to England after spending Jan.–Sept. 1721 in Paris) was meanwhile anxiously soliciting their father about a pardon for her husband, assuring him how economically they lived (Tayler 1938: 208–9).

[18] *CL* ii. 10; note in Pope's *Works*, 1743, Lewis Walpole Library, 49. 2453.

[19] *CL* ii. 11–12, 13, 14. It was easier for men: no one minded when Lord Molesworth confessed the 'folly' of borrowing £2,000 from a woman to put in the South Sea, and losing it (HMC 1913: viii. 350).

galantes et philosophiques de madame de * * *, *suivies de son histoire*, and when
Pope conjured him up as a skeleton in her closet.[20]

꧁꧂

The later stages of this private drama ran concurrently with a public one:
that of inoculation for smallpox. Though Lady Mary had survived herself
and protected her son, the disease remained ever threatening. On her return
from Turkey she found 'a veritable smallpox war'—about treatment, not
prevention—being waged among doctors: John Woodward versus Sir Hans
Sloane and John Freind. It involved (besides a duel) a peppering of printed
salvoes, which, if she read them, would have confirmed her low opinion of
medical ethics. She took no action during a severe outbreak of the disease in
1719; her inoculation experience 'lay asleep'.[21]

In 1721 it was awakened by another serious epidemic. Early January was
unseasonably warm: violets and roses bloomed.[22] In February, in the words
of Charles Maitland (formerly surgeon on the embassy), smallpox seemed
'to go forth like a destroying Angel'. Death notices in the papers show a
steady attrition of Lady Mary's friends and connections.[23] The fear of contagion brought London social life to a virtual standstill; formal visiting gave
way to enquiry by servants (who had probably been picked in the first place
as having already had smallpox). The epidemic coincided with power struggles in the medical profession. The College of Physicians moved against
unlicensed competitors both among the rich and the poor. Apothecaries,
who served the lower classes, were charged with 'Quacking about in the
Office of Physicians'.[24]

In April 1721 smallpox was still killing people Lady Mary knew almost
every week. Between first breaking silence on her Rémond problem and

---

[20] *Lettres galantes*, see p. 195; Pope's innuendo, see p. 277. It was no doubt Pope's gloss on the story that
made MWM's descendants keep her *cris de cœur* to her sister out of print till 1837, and then segregate them in
an appendix (Grundy, 1998).

[21] Levine 1977: 11; Miller 1957: 36; Sloane 1756: 516. Sloane was about to become President of the College
of Physicians, and later that of the Royal Society. For fuller relation of MWM's inoculation work to its
context, see Grundy 1994c.

[22] *Churchman: or Loyalist's Weekly Journal*, 14 Jan. This was in violent contrast to the year before.

[23] Maitland 1722: 3. The dead included her Twickenham neighbour Craggs (16 Feb.), her 16-year-old
cousin Lady Hester Feilding (20 Feb.), the Duke of Rutland (husband to one of her friends) and two of his
daughters (18 Feb., 22 Feb., 2 Mar.), Lady Louisa Berkeley, a child whose mother (also dead of smallpox)
MWM had satirized as Lydia (3 Mar.), and Lord Irwin, who had m. Lady Anne Howard (10 Apr.).

[24] High-life competitors faced malpractice suits; low-life ones faced trouble if they prescribed without the
newly revised official *Pharmacopoeia, or London Dispensatory* (which was useless to those without Latin).
Thomas Dover, attacked by name for letting patients 'slip though his Hands into the other World', was later
vindicated with specific reference to a successful inoculation (Clark 1964: ii. 507, 511, 530–1; news items of
4, 11, 18 Mar. 1721; *Whitehall Evening-Post*, 26 Apr. 1722).

moving to Twickenham for the summer, she wrote to Maitland, who was practising in Hertford, to tell him she had decided to have her daughter inoculated. He duly presented himself to consult, but at first declined to act. He had his career in mind: for a mere surgeon to perform inoculation ('engrafting') in London under the eyes of the College of Physicians was a much graver affair than doing it in faraway Turkey. He was ready to be persuaded, but only on certain conditions: a week or two's delay until the cold, wet weather cleared up, and the invitation of two doctors to witness the procedure (who could testify, in case of accidents, that at least he had not been negligent). According to Maitland, Lady Mary in turn resisted this. However, he won her assent to attendance by three 'learned Physicians of the College . . . all Gentlemen of Honour' as witnesses. Lady Louisa Stuart says they were 'deputed by government'; if she was right, then Lady Mary had already carried the inoculation issue to the highest levels.

This time it was not hard for Maitland to find a smallpox patient—one with not-too-virulent symptoms—to provide the infected matter. The little girl was not bled or purged, in view of her invariably 'very cool, regular Diet'. The virus was 'ingrafted . . . in both Arms, after the usual Manner'. On the tenth night after this she was 'a little hot and Feverish'. An 'Ancient' neighbourhood apothecary was called to see her; next morning the pocks began to emerge, and Maitland's observers were sent for, 'one after another, to visit the young Lady'. They found her 'playing about the Room, chearful and well, with the Small Pox rais'd upon her'. The official witnesses were not alone. Friends of Lady Mary's, 'Several Ladies, and other Persons of Distinction', saw the child during the few days before she was back to normal.[25]

One of the medical observers was James Keith, who had been a fellow student with Maitland at Aberdeen but who practised near Covent Garden. Though he is also listed as a perfumer, he belonged to the College of Physicians. He had lost two sons to smallpox in 1717.[26] He was an instant convert, begging Maitland 'to lose no Time to ingraft the only Son he had left'. Four-year-old Peter Keith (born two months after his brothers' deaths) was inoculated on 11 May, and did well. Within months the story of young Mary's inoculation had crossed the ocean to Boston (which was suffering the same fearful epidemic).[27]

The tradition later current in Lady Mary's family held that not all the observers were as positive as Keith. On the contrary, they

---

[25] *E&P* 36; Maitland 1722: 9–11.   [26] They died at 8 and at $3\frac{1}{2}$ (Henderson 1934: 56–8, 141–2).
[27] Maitland 1722: 11; Henderson 1934: 58; Mather 1721.

betrayed not only such incredulity as to its success, but such an unwillingness to have it succeed, such evident rancour and malignity, that lady Mary often said, she never durst leave them alone with the child one second, lest they should do it some injury.[28]

Doctors vied with parsons and journalists in bitter media warfare over the new practice. Although Lady Mary told her sister in June 1721 that the Rémond affair was engrossing her 'as ... if my house was on Fire', she must have been finding time and energy for forwarding the rapid spread of inoculation. Many of the persons of distinction visiting three-year-old Mary were steeling themselves to inoculate some child of their own. This month 'some Physicians' made a case to the king for an experimental testing of the new process, on condemned criminals in Newgate. Behind these physicians stood the scientifically minded Caroline, Princess of Wales. As Lady Mary told it, the princess 'was her firm support and stood by her without quailing'.[29] In the heated public debate at the time, those papers and pamphlets which supported inoculation found it expedient to suppress the heavy female involvement (which would only give an opening for misogynist bile) and to mention authoritative males in their stead.

In many contemporary accounts, therefore, it was 'Wortley Montague, Esq; when Ambassador', who inoculated 'his' son, and George I who patronized the Newgate experiment. This was not wilful inaccuracy, but sound public relations.[30] The underlying facts (as related at the time by Sloane, the royal physician, but unpublished for thirty-five years) are that one of Princess Caroline's daughters had nearly died of smallpox, and that the mother, 'to secure her other children, and for the common good, begged the lives of six condemned criminals' for the experiment.[31]

Maitland was understandably nervous of performing in this largely hostile limelight. (The unheard-of innovation of inserting noxious matter into a healthy body savoured both of black magic and of impious meddling in the workings of God's Providence.) As in the case of Lady Mary's daughter, he stipulated for professional support: he refused to act at Newgate until Sloane had procured further authority from a doctor with Turkish experience, who in this respect ranked above ladies, or foreigners, or a surgeon like himself.[32]

---

[28] Lady Louisa Stuart in Hunter 1831: 322 n. 1; wording slightly altered in *E&P* 36.

[29] *CL* ii. 6; newspapers, 17 June (coinciding with news of expected Turkish military action against Christians); Lady Louisa (Hunter 1831: ii. 322: omitted from her 'Biographical Anecdotes', no doubt because of its highhandedness towards royalty).

[30] e.g. *St James's Evening Post*, 17 June 1721; Mather 1721; la Mottraye 1723: 396 (corrected in Fr. edn., 1727). A second son replaced young Mary in Harris 1722, and the *St James's Journal*, 16 Aug. 1722.

[31] Sloane 1756: 516–20: based on BL Sloane MS 4034. 28–9; French version, perhaps original, Sloane MS 3329. 34–5.

[32] Sloane 1756: 517. The doctor was Edward Tarry. Isaac Massey later accused Maitland of coffee-house

The furore preceding the Newgate experiment opened a long-running, bitter controversy. Lady Mary was an active promoter: persuading and encouraging parents, showing off her confidence in her little daughter's immunity, visiting convalescent patients. She reaped a double harvest of fulsome praise and savage excoriation. Published tributes began at once, then faltered, and only reached their peak too late for her to hear. Published attacks sounded clamorously through all the years of her direct involvement and beyond. Both were often coded rather than overt: her rank gave attackers pause, and made sympathizers loath to flaunt her involvement in such public and dirty warfare. Face-to-face hostility met her on many of her visits—blatant from her equals, covert from servants—and even in the streets she encountered people 'taught to hoot at her as an unnatural mother, who had risked the lives of her own children'.[33]

Because the royal family supported inoculation, most opposition or independent papers were against it.[34] They struck a purposely paranoiac tone, playing on prejudice not merely against the new science but also against foreigners and women. (Current military events in eastern Europe provided a quite rational basis for anti-Turkish feeling: a gift to anti-inoculators.) Advocates for inoculation found it practicable to defend scientific advance, but not the female and oriental origins of the new process: these could only be concealed. This makes it hard to assess the part played by Princess Caroline and Lady Mary; but the practice would probably not have become naturalized without them.

The same year, 1721, saw a parallel smallpox epidemic in Boston, Massachusetts. Inoculation was launched in Boston, but it failed to take. The city fathers outlawed it, in a ruling backed by calculated untruths about the numbers of Bostonians dead of smallpox. Boston differed from London in many ways; one crucial distinction was that there the practical experience backing the printed Royal Society reports came from black slaves instead of from Lady Mary. But perhaps equally crucial was Boston's lack of an informed, élite, non-professional pressure group.

In England monarchical and other institutional authority was also mobilized. George I, impelled by his daughter-in-law, acted like a properly constitutional ruler and referred the legality of the Newgate experiment to the Attorney-General and Solicitor-General (both of them new brooms appointed since the South Sea scandal). Through June 1721, with occasional

boasting and of pushing inoculation for personal gain (1723: 3–4). Timoni's Royal Society report was reprinted by *The Weekly Journal: or British Gazetteer*, 19 Aug. 1721.

[33] *E&P* 35–6; Hunter 1831, ii. 322 n.   [34] Cf. Wilson 1990a: 29.

lapses into incredulity and denial, the papers reported the Newgate plan's progress towards realization. In early July, Philippe Néricault Destouches reported it too, mentioning Lady Mary's example. He noted that Lord Townsend (more properly his wife, Dorothy or Dolly) was following suit; so were almost all the fathers and mothers in England. Such hyperbole was the style of the moment. Pope told his friend and collaborator Broome (who was planning a verse tribute to Lady Mary) that immortality would be no more than 'a due reward' for her benefaction to 'all posterity'.[35] On 9 August, surrounded by official observers, Maitland inoculated six convicts, three of each sex.[36] All (except one who turned out to have had smallpox already) followed the pattern of brief, mild illness and rapid recovery. They were then duly pardoned.

Even after the experiment was pronounced successful, on 25 August, controversy and vituperation continued to boost newspaper sales. Further experiments were eagerly reported and debated. Upper-class inoculees were tantalizingly almost identified: the 'Eldest Son of a Noble Duke in Hanover Square'.[37] Richard Mead tried out on a girl in Newgate the Chinese method of inoculating by stuffing infected matter up her nostrils.[38] One of the released Newgate guinea-pigs was sent to Maitland's Hertford practice, where smallpox was rife, to test her acquired immunity by sharing a bed with a sufferer.[39]

Every newspaper selected a tone to take about this radical issue. The *St James's Evening Post*, a court paper, reassuringly cited persons 'of known Credit and Reputation, who have seen this Practice in Turky'.[40] The *Post-Boy* and *Applebee's Weekly Journal* could not see credit or reputation in anyone supporting the practice. A child's death in November 1721 was attributed by the *St James's Evening Post* to natural smallpox but by the *Post Man* to inoculation.[41] Princess Caroline proposed to inoculate 'all the Orphan Children belonging to the Parish of St. James's, Westminster'; but the plan hung fire for months and finally covered only half a dozen children.

[35] Wade 1931: 41; Pope, *Corr.* ii 77. Destouches's English visit has been ranked with those of Voltaire, Montesquieu, and Prévost (Bonno 1949: 11).

[36] *St James's Evening Post*, 10 Aug. One of the women under sentence of death was Anne Tompion, wife of the famous watchmaker.

[37] *London Mercury*, 16 Sept. 1721.

[38] The girl was Ruth Jones (*Daily Post*, 23 Aug.). Mead, one of MWM's doctors, noted that it was inoculation which first revealed smallpox to be contagious (MacMichael 1968: 63).

[39] Sloane 'joined purses' with another royal physician, John George Steighertahl, for this (*Post-Boy*, 22 Aug., 9 Sept. 1721; *London Journal*, 26 Aug.; *London Mercury*, 16 Sept.; Sloane 1756: 517).

[40] 26, 31 Aug. 1721. A report of a Turkish lady visiting London (surely not possible as fact) may allude in some way to MWM (*Applebee's* and *London Mercury*, 14 Oct.).

[41] 7 Dec. and 2 Dec. respectively.

Reports of deaths from natural smallpox ran neck and neck all winter with reports of the spread of inoculation. Inoculated children were even advertised as available for inspection at various London addresses. Maitland published his *Account of Inoculating the Small Pox* (preface dated 13 February 1722) after four months' delay. He had been waiting vainly for the charity children experiment—perhaps for a more favourable climate of opinion.[42]

Caution was in every way advisable for professionals. August members of the Royal Society gave the matter their careful attention; shortly after Maitland drafted his preface, James Jurin, Secretary to the Society, pronounced, 'We are all convinced here, yt ye true legitimate Small Pox may be given by inoculation.' Sloane had his grandchildren inoculated, but would not take the responsibility of advising Princess Caroline to do the same for the royal children. She caught him out by asking whether he would advise *against*: that, he said, he could not conscientiously do. That was enough. Caroline had Maitland inoculate her two still unpoxed daughters, with the king's consent but medically at her own risk.[43] This was a major victory; but it was closely followed by the first major setback.

With the risk of natural smallpox always pressing, not all parents had waited for the results of official experiment. Though newspapers or pamphlets might depict them as gambling with their children's lives, those who had watched a child going through smallpox, let alone dying of it, tended to think like Dr Keith. The parents who acted earliest (before newspaper coverage hit its stride) are mostly unidentified, though they included Dorothy, Lady Townshend. Those we know of tend to have two things in common: some bereavement by smallpox; and personal acquaintance with Lady Mary, or with the Princess of Wales. It seems they did not have to be close to Lady Mary, or even to like her; they did have to know her. Her circle, of course, overlapped with Caroline's. For instance, several of her friends the Molesworth clan, who formed a kind of inoculation network, worked for the princess.

Having gained ground slowly during the year between Lady Mary's inoculation of her daughter and Caroline's of hers, the practice now spread like wildfire. Lady Mary's relations, her closest girlhood friends, and members of her current circle, all included early inoculators. Only Lady

---

[42] *London Gazette*, 10, 27 Mar. 1722; Sloane 1756: 518; Maitland 1722: 6. Later this year Dr John Arbuthnot (who as music lover and friend of Pope had much in common with MWM) pub. a brilliant, angry vindication of Maitland. He noted the 'bloody attempts' of Boston anti-inoculators against Cotton Mather's life (61). Cf. Shuttleton 1995.

[43] Jurin 1996: 88; BL Sloane MS 403. 23. Caroline's sons waited another one and two years respectively, either because of their constitutional importance or because one was an infant and one in Hanover.

Gower held out against her sister's persuasion. She may have felt surfeited with medical procedures, since her second son, William, had been born with defective legs (Lady Mary said they were 'backward'), 'and they were forced to break his legs to make them straight'. Fate was pitiless: two years later this boy's elder brother died of smallpox.[44]

Caroline's daughters were inoculated on 17 April 1722. Two days later Lord Sunderland, head of the government, died suddenly. This meant a seismic shift in politics. For Lord Mar it was the cutting of a supply-line, or lifeline. Edward Wortley Montagu was invited to name his own price for future support of Walpole. (He refused.)[45] For the moment the newspapers forgot inoculation for coverage of this startling event. But not for long. A couple of weeks before the princesses, Sunderland's fifth and youngest son had been inoculated by Claude Amyand, royal surgeon and Twickenham resident. Two days after Sunderland's death, while his former mother-in-law, Sarah, Duchess of Marlborough, still raged at the government's seizure of his confidential papers,[46] his little son died too. First reports said this toddler ('Willy' in his father's letters, 'the Honourable Mr. William Spencer' in the papers) died of 'Convulsion Fits'. Later reports said he died of smallpox; *Applebee's* said, 'of the Innoculations, a new kind of Distemper not known in former Days, and an unhappy Experiment to this young Nobleman, who might in all Probability have liv'd many Years'. *Applebee's* issue of 28 April 1722 was crammed with references to this death, and with anti-inoculation comment.

It was almost certainly not inoculation that killed little William Spencer. He lived nineteen days after it; his pustules had dried up and he was just about recovered. The post-mortem found that he died of fits from other causes; relatives on both sides of his family remained keen inoculators. But his death certificate (signed by surgeons, not doctors) was a hostage to prolonged hostile publicity,[47] which also fastened on the recently inoculated princesses. The operation on another noble child, already prepared, was reported to be 'suspended'. Even supportive papers foretold that the practice would now 'lose ground', and their fears intensified with a second death: that of a young servant of Lord Bathurst.[48] The six Bathurst children did well after inoculation; it was probably natural smallpox from contact with them

---

[44] Egmont 1920–3: ii. 188; *CL* ii. 26.   [45] Gregg 1982: 109; Sedgwick 1970.

[46] One of two peers overseeing this was MWM's father.

[47] Arbuthnot printed the death certificate ([Arbuthnot] 1722: 49–50; Howgrave 1724: 53). Sunderland's career, his three marriages, various children, pregnant widow, were good copy. It was said a dead daughter would be exhumed and reinterred with him and her brother.

[48] *London Mercury*, 5 May; *Whitehall Evening Post*, 19 May; *St James's Evening Post*, 28 Apr. 1722; most papers, 26 May.

which killed the young man.[49] But confidence was shaken: from now on there were reasonable grounds to look on inoculators with mistrust.

Vituperation sharpened, and pamphleteers locked horns as fiercely as reporters. Among many published attacks on the new practice, the two most outrageous appeared during the wet and miserable summer of 1722: by the Revd Edmund Massey and William Wagstaffe. Massey's anti-inoculation sermon, preached on 8 July, followed his earlier sensation-sermon on the plague as a judgement on sin. Court Whigs saw him as 'a fanatick Priest, bigotted to Party Tenets'; he had clashed swords with Whiston.[50] From Sacheverell's pulpit at St Andrew's, Holborn, he preached on the text: 'So went Satan forth from the Presence of the Lord, and smote *Job* with sore Boils . . .' It was a theological coup to locate a scripture example of Satan inflicting a disease plausibly similar to inoculation, and doing so in order to weaken dependence on God.[51] Extreme as he was, Massey represented the orthodox theological case against inoculation: that it negates the two spiritual functions of disease, divine punishment, and divine testing. (Fear of smallpox is therefore 'an *happy Restraint*', without which people would be '*less Righteous*').[52]

This theological heavyweight recommended from the pulpit a medical heavyweight: William Wagstaffe arguing by pamphlet that inoculation was both unreliable and dangerous. Wagstaffe rested his case on superiority and exclusivity. He was for physicians of the College, against apothecaries, surgeons, nurses, and 'private People'. He was, in today's terms, racist, antifeminist, and orientalist. He positively bristled at a medical procedure 'cry'd up' by non-physicians, stemming from a country inferior in 'the Nature of the Climate, [and] the Capacity of the Inhabitants'. He could hardly believe 'that an Experiment practiced only by a few *Ignorant Women*, amongst an illiterate and unthinking People, shou'd on a sudden . . . so far obtain in one of the Politest Nations in the World, as to be receiv'd into the *Royal Palace*'. He speculated ghoulishly about inoculation as a vehicle for poison, an '*artful way of depopulating a Country*'. Sometimes he seemed to have Lady Mary in his sights as 'some *sanguine* Traveller from *Turkey*'.[53]

---

[49] *London Journal*, 26 May 1722. Lady Bathurst was pregnant: she bore a daughter on 24 May (*Applebee's*, 16 May). Her husband remained MWM's friend.

[50] Massey had hit the headlines with a political sermon of 8 Dec. 1721, which was quickly pub. Wagstaffe's pamphlet was dated before the anti-inoculation sermon (12 June), but pub. later (advertised 2 Aug.). Wet weather slowed up printing.

[51] As Massey observed, no medical hypothesis could explain inoculation any *more* convincingly than this scriptural interpretation.

[52] Massey 1722: 10, 24, 26, 15, 22. He has stylistic affinities with Richardson's parson Brand in *Clarissa*.

[53] Wagstaffe 1722: 5–6, 8–9, 35–6, 39, 45, 50, 57–8, 68–9.

Most telling among many voices on the other side were Maitland (the doyen in practical experience, operator on the Wortley Montagus, the convicts, and the princesses), Arbuthnot (almost the only Tory physician to espouse inoculation), and Jurin. Maitland's narrative about Lady Mary's children put her name into the public arena (presumably with her consent). He wielded the authority of Sloane (his dedicatee) and the royal example. He and Arbuthnot used facts, dates, testimonies, scrupulous politeness, and ostentatious rationality. Arbuthnot noted that the other side smacked of witchcraft and '*Satanick Possession*'. Jurin pioneered the use of statistics in furthering inoculation; he also promulgated the ideal of honourable, selfless, gentlemanly service as the medical norm. He addressed his first work on inoculation statistics to the leading physician Caleb Cotesworth, who came from Durham and had a relation in Wortley's employ.[54]

Each side deplored the other's violent tone. The rhetoric of Massey and Wagstaffe sought to promote hysteria and paranoia, while that of Maitland, Jurin, and their allies privileged the use of reason.[55] Many of the public's medical doubts were not unreasonable: might inoculation communicate other unlooked-for diseases? how dangerous was it? did it really confer immunity? But fears also lurked of Turkish or female influence, financial exploitation (inoculators as South Sea directors), a secret weapon in unscrupulous hands, wicked step-parents or guardians doing away with infant heirs.[56] Each side had a stake in vilifying the other.

Lady Mary, who was far from idle in this second phase of the debate, held a position unique among the warring factions. Her one identified contribution in print, 'A Plain Account of the Innoculating of the Small Pox', in the *Flying-Post* of 13 September 1722, begins by vilifying doctors: something one expects from the anti- but not from the pro-inoculators. As a laywoman she saw most doctors not as incorruptible professionals or heroic reformers, but as diehards protecting their income and prestige, or as opportunists seizing a new niche in the market. She felt that inoculation was too important to be left to doctors. She was also convinced that the Turkish way was best: that a needle-prick, the tiniest possible quantity of smallpox matter, and no preparation or follow-up beyond common-sense moderation, were safe in the hands even of lay operatives, even of women. Conversely she judged that a more macho or heroic intervention—introducing large quantities of

---

[54] [Arbuthnot] 1722: 1–2, 4, 47, 51–61, 64; Jurin 1723; parallel reports for the next three successive years; Lillias E. Cotesworth n.d.: 46.

[55] Crawford 1722; letter from Yorkshire inoculator Thomas Nettleton to Jurin, 16 June 1722, printed in [Arbuthnot] 1722; Williams 1725.

[56] Howgrave 1724: 58; Massey 1723: 3–4, 17; *New Practice*, 1722, 34, 37, 39.

infected matter into 'Gashes' in the flesh of patients weakened by purging and bleeding—was irresponsible and dangerous. Her Turkish discovery had been corrupted and spoiled in the hands of her compatriates.[57]

These beliefs, vigorously and angrily expressed in her published essay, were hers alone. Most of the doctors who pioneered inoculation in the west were proponents of a comparatively mild approach. They argued at bedsides and in print for moderating the amount of vomits, purgatives, fasting, and bleeding that patients should undergo. But none of them was so eccentric as to advocate doing entirely without these aids to recovery. In this, of course, the laywoman was right and current medical wisdom was wrong. But little good it did her. In every generation until vaccination took over from variolation, the leading professional inoculators argued for *some* de-escalation of purging, etc. In every generation they presented this as an unprecedented reform. Even after James Carrick Moore in 1815 noted the superiority of 'Byzantine practice' (which, he said, had began to be corrupted and inflated as early as Charles Maitland), nobody remembered Montagu's fierce and despairing plea against such inflation. As a medical innovator she was locked in interdependence with the professionals; in professionalizing her discovery they spoiled it. She won her battle but lost her campaign. The war was won at last, but not in her lifetime.[58]

After the *Flying-Post* essay (which she may or may not have published deliberately) it seems she wrote no more on inoculation. Her energies went into networking among individuals. This spanned a wide spectrum. Scores of inoculations were brought about by women of her own age (many of them with literary interests) and men of her father's. The first big wave had passed in the spring of 1722: children of Princess Caroline, of Lady Mary's old friend Charlotte Amelia Tichborne, of Tichborne's sister-in-law Lady Sunderland, of Lord Bathurst, and of Lady Dorset. The recently married and formerly 'giddy-headed' Lady De La Warr inoculated her first baby.[59]

Spring 1723 brought premature claims that the battle was won; that May saw the inoculation of Margaret Rolle (barely a teenager, but soon to marry

---

[57] As 'a Turkey Merchant' (*E&P* 95–7). An experiment at St Thomas's Hospital used 'two vastly large Incisions, and an immoderate Quantity of the Matter apply'd' ([Arbuthnot] 1722: 24).

[58] Moore 1815: 234. Eventually Peter Razzell attributed early inoculation deaths to 'the very severe technique' used in England (1965: 317; Razzell 1977: 4–8, 12–16).

[59] As Bedchamber Woman, the widowed Charlotte Amelia (Mary Monck's sister), chatted to the princess while serving her supper. Her other sister-in-law inoculated her family later. De La Warr's baby was falsely reported to be 'dangerously ill under the modish Experiment' (HMC 1913: viii. 272; Egmont 1920–3: ii. 288; *London Journal*, 26 May 1722).

Robert Walpole's eldest son), and that June the nephew and niece of Griselda Murray. Lady Mary affected to be so run off her feet with medical visiting that she fled to Twickenham 'to hide my selfe'.[60] Twice more the spring brought an annual wave of upper-class inoculation (though newspapers had campaigned all winter against it): two young dukes and their siblings,[61] Walpole's youngest son Horace, Princess Caroline's latest daughter (at under five months), children of Wortley's cousin Sandwich, of the Austrian ambassador (an old Vienna acquaintance of Lady Mary), and many more. Boys at Westminster School were set to debate for and against 'the Physicians'.[62] In March 1725 Lady Mary's father, to whom she had written about 'Smallpox' from Turkey, inoculated his grandson and heir and the elder daughter of his second marriage. The snowball effect rode over another setback in April 1725, when three-year-old George Perceval recovered from inoculation and then went down with what *looked* like a case of natural smallpox.[63]

Inoculation spread far as well as fast. Lady Mary's influence reached to Wallingford in Berkshire—if it was really the apothecary Cudworth Bruch who engaged with her in an 'Epistolary Correspondence' about her discovery and later celebrated it in quirky, brilliant allegory.[64] How many more unsung scientists, one wonders, boasted direct contact with her? Her influence was felt at Worcester through the medium of Bishop John Hough.[65]

In Salisbury, too, she may have influenced a wave of inoculations in 1722–3 (duly reported to Jurin), which included those of the family of the future novelists Henry and Sarah Fielding: cousins of Lady Mary and of Lady Hester Feilding who had died of smallpox two years before. The Salisbury surgeon, William Goldwyre, also 'did' Fielding's future wife (Charlotte Cradock) and her two sisters, and Fielding's future friend James Harris and many of his family. Lady Mary's direct involvement is not demonstrable. But she struck up a warm and enduring friendship with Katy Harris (later Lady Knatchbull), who was eighteen when she was inoculated, and Katy apparently provided some pedagogical help to Mary Wortley Montagu

---

[60] *Whitehall Journal*, 2 Apr. 1723; *Applebee's Journal*, 1 June 1723; *CL* ii. 25–6.

[61] Bedford and Rutland: newspapers, 30 May 1724, 6 Apr. 1725.

[62] e.g. *British Journal*, 3 Oct. 1724; *Flying-Post: or, Post-Master*, 24 Oct. 1724; *Whitehall Evening Post*, 7 May, 25 Apr. 1725; *St James's Evening Post*, 1 May, 22 Apr. 1725.

[63] Jurin pub. the case, with the mother's blow-by-blow diary, in 1726: 36–53. Cf. Rusnock 1995: 297–8.

[64] *Triumph of Inoculation*, 1767: Bodleian copy (the only one known) Vet M2 d 1 (14).

[65] Wilmot 1812: 321–2. Hough was a correspondent of Addison, a protégé of Lady Oxford, an admirer of Elizabeth Rowe (x, 219, 272). His successor founded the Worcester Infirmary in conjunction with Dr James Mackenzie, who wrote on inoculation and has been called a friend of MWM's son and perhaps of MWM (Goodridge 1995: 150; *DNB*; Mackenzie 1760; Nichols 1812: iv. 640).

(then aged five).[66] This at least suggests that Lady Mary visited Salisbury (so handy to West Dean) as a publicist, with young Mary as usual her prime teaching aid.

Throughout the 1720s her friends, relatives, distant connections, continued to fall in with the new practice: her cousin Lord Chesterfield (father of the famous one); her friends Walpole, Hervey, and the Duchess of Montagu; a Tyneside colliery family.[67] Inoculees in 1726 included the children of Elizabeth West (who had corresponded with Lady Mary on the embassy), and of George Montagu, 2nd Earl of Halifax, whose earlier smallpox bereavements had caused Lady Mary anxiety about delayed contagion. In 1728 Henrietta, Duchess of Marlborough, had her daughter by Congreve done.[68]

Lady Mary herself said she was very 'much pull'd about and solicited to visit' inoculated patients. Family tradition later said that 'all who could make or claim the slightest acquaintance' with her 'used to beg for her advice and superintendence'. For years she struggled with regrets about her 'great' or 'patriotic' undertaking; she said she 'never would have attempted it, could she have foreseen the vexation, and even persecution, it was to bring on her'. Her little daughter, taken along to prove her immunity, later remembered 'the significant shrugs . . . the looks of dislike' of nurses and servants and the open hostility of 'aunts and grandmothers' quoting their traditional authority-figures at her. No doubt she also remembered the jeering 'common people'.[69]

All this took place as Lady Mary was writing her surviving letters to her sister Mar: letters whose familiar tone suggests there was nothing at all that Mary could not say to Frances. But to compare the letters with the later tradition reveals that much was unsayable. In her letters Lady Mary sounds wholly focused at the date of her daughter's inoculation on her troubles with Rémond; she sounds complacent about inoculation just as it received a serious setback with the death of Sunderland's son; the month of Massey's sermon she calls a 'Dead Season' hopelessly lacking in news; and as her uninoculated nephew lay dying she voiced airy contempt for the anti-inoculators as if their power were negligible. Perhaps political implications kept her mute: a topic with a royal-family angle might be taboo for fear of snooping by spies. None the less one suspects that either the letter genre or

[66] *CL* iii. 158–9; Grundy 1993*b*. Lady Louisa also mentions MWM's particular friendship for Katy and her husband (*E&P* 60).

[67] Slare in Williams 1725: 30, 33; BL Sloane MS 406b. 79, 85, 89; Miller 1957: 110.

[68] This little girl was a naughty patient (BL Sloane MS 406b. 42–4). An undated note from Henrietta, effusively thanking MWM and hoping to see her, may relate to this (*CL* ii. 70).

[69] *CL* ii. 26; *E&P*, 35–6; Hunter 1831: ii. 322 n.

her relationship with her sister could not cope with an account, written to the moment, of such ungenteel struggle.

The most explicit part of her smallpox notoriety was praise, not blame, but even this may have been less than welcome. It came in three very different forms: gallant flattery, strident pamphlets,[70] and the mocking, paradoxical, near-sacrilegious Voltaire. The first, so adept in its praise of beauty or wit, faltered when it tried to praise a female for medical nous or social courage. It was not designed for that. William Broome's intended tribute to Lady Mary cannot be traced. Cudworth Bruch (if it was he) waited till she was dead.[71] Richard Savage waxed effusive on her and on inoculation, but separately. Aaron Hill's *Plain Dealer*, praising her *as* inoculator in prose and verse, does so in the stock terms of gallant flattery.[72] Hill printed her name in full: a noble lady's name looked right in the title of a poem, as it did not in pamphlet polemic. He explicitly praised the good done by women to mankind. Yet still he was a dubious champion. His essay exhibits casual racism, views healthy children as a national economic resource, and locates hostility to inoculation not among professional men but among crones and spinsters who envy beauty. It presents Lady Mary as preserving mainly beauty, male scientists as preserving *life*. In the poem, the Muses beg Apollo to bestow the art of inoculation on her as a gift. This neatly reduces her from agent to object or figurehead, in the familiar role of presiding over beauty or wit.[73]

This *Plain Dealer*, the initial apogee of Lady Mary's inoculation fame, came at a moment when her relish for praise may have been shadowed by anxiety for her sister. Voltaire's celebration in his *Letters Concerning the English* came in 1733 (a year before the work in its French version), when her life had moved into a new and gruelling phase.[74] He takes a riddling, paradoxical tone, not so much praising England for itself as sniping at priest-ridden and benighted France. When he calls the Turks a sensible people, he implies a

[70] *CL* ii. 19; pamphlets e.g. by Slare, who was reluctant to set his own name to his inoculation statement (Williams 1725: 26), and Colman (1722: 5).

[71] In July 1721, before the Newgate experiment, Pope had commended Broome's plan to write MWM into immortality (Pope, *Corr.* ii. 77). For Bruch see next page.

[72] No. 30, 3 July 1724; MWM's copy H MS 80. 135. Hill bridged the worlds of gentility and Grub Street; his friends included Edward Young and Eliza Haywood; he was helped on the *Plain Dealer* by William Bond (Martha Fowke Sansom's 'Strephon'). MWM scorned Hill's writing on Turkey as inaccurate (*CL* i. 405–6). Pope (flattered in the same essay) may be implicated in the flattery of her. The poem reappeared in Richard Savage's *Miscellanies*, 1726, and in Hill's *Works*, 1753. John Dussinger thinks it not by Hill (private communication).

[73] The line 'Charm'd, into *Love*, of what eclips'd their [obscures my] Fame', present both in the *Plain Dealer* essay and in Astell's Embassy Letters preface, made Paston suppose that Astell wrote the essay too. But Astell is quoting Hill in order to combat the idea that envy is a female trait.

[74] Written during his London stay, 1726–9: later *Letters philosophiques*.

contrast with his countrymen. He showers paradoxes: that the Circassians value female education, but only for a career in the sex trade; that good girls and bad girls are socially constructed. He attributes inoculation, a giant step for humankind, directly to Lady Mary and Princess Caroline—partly in order to anatomize the reasons why France cannot produce women like them. Even so he sees them as acting out of mother-love and self-interest, less noble motives than disinterested public spirit. Though he gets a few details wrong (he thinks Lady Mary's son was born in Turkey), he seems to have read her relevant Embassy Letter, if not the whole work. His praise carried the germ of immortality; but it was not such as to raise Lady Mary's reputation in England in 1733.

In the 1750s, when she was far distant from England, new-wave inoculators knew from the Sloane MSS that it was she and not her husband who enquired into inoculation in Turkey and initiated it at home. James Burgess and James Kirkpatrick used her name and her daughter's with panache for advertising purposes. After her death came Bruch's *Triumph of Inoculation*. Its dreamer-narrator watches the evil goddess Variola routed by the 'new Divinity' Inoculatio and her benevolent, Circassian-garbed 'Conductress'; he awakes 'in a transport of joy, with the sound of *Montagu! Montagu!*' ringing in his ears.[75] In 1789 one of her great-nieces placed a monument to her achievement in Lichfield cathedral; James Moore's *History of Smallpox* gave her, on balance, more credit than it gave Maitland.[76] Yet in 1980, when the World Health Organization celebrated eradication of smallpox, Genevieve Miller gave the presidential address to the American Society for the History of Science under the title, 'Putting Lady Mary in her Place'. It is hard indeed to be accepted as a medical pioneer if you are also a society lady.

[75] [?Bruch] 1767, does not say *when* he corresponded with MWM (preface, 20).
[76] Moore 1815: 228, 233, 234, 247, 253, 255.

14

January 1721–December 1724

᷾᷾

Vers de société: 'Nor can a Woman's Arguments prevail'[1]

INOCULATION did not absorb all Lady Mary's energy. No matter what her efforts for public health, no matter what her contempt for the 'Grand Monde' or her pleasure in country retirement, she spun with gusto in the London social whirl. In January 1721, before people began dying of small-pox, her sister Mar ended a six-month stay in England. She had 'obtain'd leave' to return to her husband in Paris. The reason cited was his health;[2] uncited were the facts that he was now accepting secret British government pay-outs and that the Duke of Kingston had failed in strenuous efforts to reclaim the forfeited Mar estates for his daughter.[3] Rémond had tried to divide the sisters by telling Lady Mary that Frances talked against her behind her back. Now that damage was repaired.[4] For the next several years they corresponded regularly, and despite Jacobite spies and Hanoverian spies many letters got through.[5] Lady Mary's staple topic (once the Rémond affair had been laid to rest) was society gossip.

She appears at her most flippant and brittle in her letters to Lady Mar: sounding rather as Wortley had dreaded before their marriage. Since her

---

[1] *E&P* 230.

[2] She left on 9 Jan. (*Post-Boy*, 9 Jan. 1721, *St James's Post*, 11 Jan., *Weekly Journal or Saturday's-Post*, 14 Jan.). Her stepson followed her in early July (*Whitehall Evening-Post*, 4 July).

[3] One of Mar's links to Walpole was Sutton, who had replaced EWM in Turkey. In 1722 Mar used his wife as cover for visits from Col. Charles Churchill, who was actually investigating his conduct on Walpole's behalf (Atterbury 1869: ii. 10, 46).

[4] *CL* ii. 3.

[5] Originals of all but those about Rémond are in the Bute MSS. Many have addresses, showing they were actually sent. In transcripts in H MSS 77, apparent ciphers replace names in the bodies of letters, and blank covers of letters bear 'cipher' lists of those named inside. The handwriting of the 'cipher' letters (not of the copies themselves) *might* be either MWM's or Lady Mar's. The same hand has added year-dates to many letters which lacked them. Lady Lansdowne is L.B.; Stair is S.A.; Lady Mar is D.S. ('Dear Sister'); Lord and Lady Gower are G.D. and G.F.; MWM's father and stepmother are K.A. and K.B.; Wortley is W.K.; Twickenham is T.A.; and so on. The system is not mere indexing. But it is imperfect (the Duchess of Montagu is both M.A. and M.F.; Griselda Murray, too, is M.A.) and hard to explain.

sister meanwhile was sliding gradually towards clinical depression, her jokiness may look like a serious error of judgement, an attempt at jollying along which must surely have been counter-productive. Her motives are impossible to read. Perhaps she wanted to expose for Lady Mar the risible pettiness and back-stabbing of the Whig social world which she had lost. Perhaps Frances shared Mary's relish for satire. Though she had been liable to depression since her teens, the impression she made as a mature woman, on her husband as well as on friends, was one of unfailing poise amid the vagaries of others.[6] Perhaps Mary never plumbed the full frightfulness of Frances's life in Paris. Lady Mar lived under siege from creditors, while her turncoat husband (still scheming incessantly) was now shunned by his erstwhile associates. Letters from France would have had to observe even greater secrecy than letters from England. Lady Mar often failed to write at all; perhaps the flavour of her Paris existence remained uncommunicated. Lady Mary often talked of visiting her, but apparently never did so. It may have presented political difficulties. For more than two years, it seems, she entertained thoughts of taking a 'superfluous' diamond or diamonds to Paris to sell. She may have had a semi-illicit need for cash, or have been acting for someone else—or have thought trafficking in diamonds a non-controversial reason to assign for a projected visit. Sister Mar scotched the diamond plan by telling her that prices were high in Paris, money scarce, and buyers non-existent.[7]

The sisters' relationship was a social one. In 1721 they had close friends in common: Griselda Murray and Lady Stafford. After six months of separation Lady Mary wrote, 'I wish to see you, Dear Sister, more than ever I did in my Life. A thousand things pass before my Eyes that would afford me infinite pleasure in your Conversation and that are lost for want of such a Freind to talk 'em over.' Her letters are candid in their 'regular accounts of all your Acquaintance' (which Frances at first was eager for); they are semi-candid about the more rackety aspects of her own—like her letters to Rémond, which, though 'very innocent in the main, yet may admit of ill constructions'.[8]

---

[6] Mar's 'Legacie to my dear son Thomas, Lord Erskine', written in 1726 while still hoping for a Stuart restoration, recalls the young man's obligations to his stepmother: 'though she has not a way of making a show of her concern for anybody, she has been as much so about you, and realie kind as if she had born you ... That mariage has proved happie to me. It gave me a virtuous woman of very good sense, and admirable good equall temper.' He further praised her courage in adversity, her behaving 'as became my wife', and her universally admired prudence and discretion. He said she 'never likt or inclined to medle in politicks' (Mar 1896: 176–7).

[7] *CL* ii. 19, 42, 43 and n. 1, 66, 76, 83. In autumn 1721 Mar had planned to invade Britain at election-time; by spring 1722 he was 'this hired traitor and spy' to his own side (Bennett 1975: 233; Atterbury 1869: i. 376 n.).

[8] *CL* ii. 8, 3, 5–6.

Their correspondence flourished on errands and commissions. Lady Mary asked her sister at various times to buy her porcelain from St Cloud, lutestring (matt taffeta), and a ready-made nightgown or negligée 'à la mode', which Lady Mar was to wear for a day so that it could be truly described as used. Lace from France was a must for Lady Stafford (as a Frenchwoman settled in England), for Griselda Murray, even for the three-year-old Mary, 'who is very much your Humble servant, and grows a little Woman'.[9] Mutual friends, many of them with ulterior reasons for travel between London and Paris, were pressed into service as go-betweens and couriers.[10] From the time the girls were seven and ten, Lady Mary kept up a flow of messages from her daughter to her niece Lady Frances Erskine.[11]

Lady Mary had probably already embarked on her next important friendship. According to Lady Louisa Stuart, she met Maria or Molly Skerrett, then about eighteen, in 1720.[12] In August 1721 her *almost* perfectly pleasing solitude at Twickenham was enlivened by a 'fair Companion', a 'little thread satin Beauty', who often reminded her of her young days with sister Frances. It sounds as if Molly may have begun as nothing more or less than a humble companion; but if so then service must have grown rapidly into friendship. 'We read and walk together, and I am more happy in her than any thing else could make me except your conversation.' Lady Mary later recalled 'contracting an intimacy with a girl in a village, as the most distant thing on earth from power and politics', only to find her friend tossed into power and politics by 'the force of destiny'.[13]

By September Molly was staying in her house, sharing in her invitations, and feeding the musical element in her life. Their time 'melted away . . . in allmost perpetual Consorts'. The composer Giovanni Buononcini or Bononcini said Molly's voice was the finest he had heard in England.[14] Professionals were at hand as well. Two leading singers were lodging in

---

[9] *CL* ii. 6, 8–9, 10–11, 19, 21, 22, 25, 46. 'Muslins' (not mentioned) was Jacobite code for money raised in England and transmitted abroad (Atterbury 1869: i. 331 ff).

[10] This motley group included 'travelling ladies', fops, servants, intellectuals like Anne-Claude, comte de Caylus (friend of Conti and former traveller to Turkey), and politicians like Horatio Walpole, diplomat, and Charles Churchill (Marlborough's illegitimate nephew and Robert Walpole's private investigator). Lady Lansdowne (whose husband the poet was, with Mar, one of the Jacobite leaders in Paris) was co-opted by Churchill in 1722 to work for the other side (Atterbury 1869: ii. 65; Pope, *Corr.* ii. 117 n. 3).

[11] *CL* ii. 54 ff.: perhaps to counteract the correspondence which her niece had begun with her half-brother Lord Erskine (Mar MSS GD 124/15/1235).

[12] Molly was born on 5 Oct. 1702 (Plumb 1960: 112 n. 2).

[13] *CL* ii. 12, 13, 182–3; Pope, *Corr.* ii. 82. Lady Mar's later mention of her own 'Miss Skerritt' suggests the companion role (H MS 77. 114–15).

[14] Pope and MWM (and EWM for 5 copies) subscribed to his *Cantate*, 1721.

Twickenham, both altos: Anastasia Robinson and the top castrato Senesino. Robinson moved in Lady Mary's social circle: Lady Darlington patronized her, and she was soon to be secretly married to Lord Peterborough, with the future Lady Oxford as witness. Senesino was, like Buononcini, newly arrived in England: Handel had imported him as linchpin in the grandiose plans of the Royal Academy of Music to naturalize the newfangled Italian opera. Lady Mary secured both singers frequently to supper. All her life she took a passionate delight in music; she had a good ear, but not, to her grief, a voice to match.[15] Musical life at this date was conducted not in public halls but private houses. Lady Mary held regular concerts. She approached Pope about borrowing his harpsichord; he would not move it, since it was his landlord's, but he offered her both it and the gallery it stood in for her regular use.[16]

This was her summer of 1721: idyllic but for her simmering concern over Rémond and over the dawn of public interest in inoculation. In the autumn—probably about the time that, somehow or other, Edward Wortley Montagu learned the whole sorry Rémond story—another scandal burst on the public. Griselda Murray, a relation of Bishop Burnet and a friend of Lady Mary and her sister, suffered an apparent rape attempt. She was separated from her husband, childless, and lived in her parents' London house. In the early hours of Sunday, 15 October,[17] one of her brother-in-law's servants entered her bedroom, carrying weapons. The first newspaper account, out by midweek, was breathless and circumstantial:

he . . . forc'd the Door open, Arm'd with a Case of Pistols, and a drawn Sword . . . The Lady being either awake, or disturb'd by the Noise, sat up in her Bed, and ask'd him what he wanted that he came in such a manner? He told her he must Lye with her, and made some Advances toward it; but she reason'd with him, and told him the Danger and Mischief of it, and kept him near half an hour in Parley; assuring him that if he would retire and desist from so horrid a Purpose, she wou'd forgive him, and keep it a secret: But this wou'd not satisfy him, for having laid the Sword down, he went to lay his Hand on her; upon which finding her opportunity, she laid hold of that Hand which held the Pistol, and struggling with him threw him backward, got the Pistol from him, Cry'd out, Rung a Bell and allarm'd the Family. The

---

[15] *CL* ii. 13; *E&P* 155. MWM's 'Sing Gentle Maid, reform my breast' *might* describe Molly diverting her mind from Rémond, though it probably dates from later (*E&P* 286). I assume the 'fair Companion' or 'thread satin Beauty' is Molly. For Senesino's importance see Heriot 1956: 67, 91; Larue 1995: 3–4, 80, 125–6. Years later his relations with Handel soured.

[16] Pope, *Corr*. ii. 82. She was an assiduous opera-goer. In 1722 her protégé Buononcini supplied music for the funeral of the Duke of Marlborough, for whom she wrote an elegy. Later she felt he had been rather taken over by the young Duchess of Marlborough (who paid him a salary from spring 1723). But she went on attending the duchess's concerts (*CL* ii. 47, 48, 52).

[17] The day after the news item about a travelling Turkish lady (see p. 213 n. 40).

Villain then retreated down Stairs, and before he cou'd be seiz'd got out of Doors; but being pursu'd he was taken . . .'[18]

The surprising wealth of detail includes the locked door, precise movements and motives, and the gist of what was said. All this must have come from some family spokesperson: no lady would speak to the press about such matters. Next day another paper filled in more names (not all correct) and details, all tending to emphasize Mrs Murray's resistance and Gray's dangerous character. The report concludes that 'this Ladys Name will be celebrated for this signal and resolute defence of her Chastity'.[19]

Two days later came further elaboration: what the servant, Arthur Gray, had done with the candle he was carrying; and considerably extended dialogue, in which Gray declared his love, and incidentally made the point that until recently Mrs Murray had been sleeping in a room from which any noise would have been audible. This account said Mrs Murray had kept Gray talking 'above an Hour'. It further choreographed the succeeding flurry of action: he grabbed the bedclothes with his 'Pistol-Hand'; she parried 'the Sword with one Hand, and with the other struck down the Pistol'. She physically overcame him, though she was hurt in the process. It expanded the aftermath, too: Gray at first said he was after one of the maids, but once in Newgate he wrote to Mrs Murray pleading that 'his Fault was only a Fault of raging Love'. Mrs Murray herself and a 'certain great foreign Lady of Quality' were further deployed to present his love as fine and as deserving pity. An appended poem hailed this 'bright Example of true Chastity' in a lewd age full of shamefully immoral gentlewomen. Bards, it said, should 'record her Story, | And with fam'd *Lucrece* let her vye in Glory.'[20]

These narratives performed complex negotiations around the 'rape myths'[21] of the period. They catered, of course, to readers' pleasure in scandal and disruption. But also they reassuringly insisted that proper defences were in place and that only exceptional determination could have breached them. Readers were encouraged to feel good about their society, by learning that Gray was a basically good man driven mad by romantic passion, while Mrs Murray was a heroine of chastity. Masculine desire was celebrated; so too was female or ladylike purity.

On 7 December the story resumed, when a jury found Gray 'guilty of Felony and Burglary'. He was sentenced to death but admitted to bail.[22] His demeanour in prison was ostentatiously pious. The Baillie-Murray family

---

[18] *The St James's Post*, 18 Oct. 1721.
[19] *The St James's Evening Post*, 19 Oct.   [20] Several newspapers, 21 Oct.
[21] A modern term for a long-lived set of stereotypical beliefs.   [22] Newspapers, 8 Dec.

made strenuous efforts to get him a pardon, and succeeded three days before Christmas, when the 'Dead Warrant' had already come for him. He was transported instead.

Into all the dubious elaboration of the incident stepped Montagu the poet. Seizing the report of Gray's letter from Newgate,[23] she spun for him an Ovidian effusion of passion and of despair over the injustice of his social position. An idealist contemptuous of his upper-class rivals, he is driven to transgress by the erotic tableau that meets his eyes when, in the course of his duties, he brings Mrs Murray early tea in bed. 'Your Nightgown fastned with a single pin,' wrote Montagu, echoing her own 'Tuesday': 'Fancy improv'd the wondrous charms within, | I fix'd my Eyes upon that heaving Breast | And hardly, hardly, I forbore the rest.' She elides the rape attempt ('Too well you know the fatal following Night') and passes quickly to the prospect of death. Her Gray, a true courtly lover, is content to die if only his mistress will pity him.

Montagu's 'Epistle' was not the only serious poetic treatment of the incident, or the only one to take epistolary form.[24] Hers, however, achieved wide circulation in manuscript. (It took some time to reach Griselda Murray.) Most critical response has centred on Montagu's feat of imaginative empathy across class and gender lines. She has been read as presenting a common servant as aspiring and oppressed, as criticizing the penal code and the class system of her day. As far as I know the poem has not been examined by feminist critics in the light of present-day debates about rape. In this context her glorification of Gray might be less welcomed.

Even more regrettable by these criteria is Montagu's other—presumed—comment on the event. She never admitted having written the anonymous, mocking, very funny broadside ballad *Virtue in Danger*; but Griselda Murray came to believe it was hers, and so did others in her circle.[25] At the opposite pole from the sentimental 'Epistle', it ostensibly showcases an almost bar-room style of rape myth. The pistol becomes jauntily Freudian. Newspaper detail is converted gleefully into innuendo. 'It never came into her head | To lock her Chamber door.'

> His Pistol hand she held fast clos'd,
> As She remembers well;

---

[23] But writing apparently in Dec., after the death sentence.

[24] *E&P* 221–4. Since MWM kept a copy of the other 'Epistle from Arthur Gray' (broadly similar in approach) she may have been writing in collusion or rivalry with someone else (H MS 81. 16–17; BL Harley MS 7316. 139–40).

[25] Murray sent a copy of *Virtue in Danger* to her friend Lady Mar before Gray's trial; she did not yet ascribe it to MWM (Suffolk 1824: i. 84–5; Walpole, *Corr.* xxxiv. 256).

> But how the other was dispos'd
> There's none alive can tell.

Facing rape, the lady cries, 'I thought this fellow was a Fool, | But there's some Sense in this.' She makes all the running, and is careful not to 'bawl' until he gets safely away. In the final stanza irony reaches outward from the protagonist to embrace the commentators:

> This Lady's fame shall ever last
>   And live in British Song:
> For She was like Lucretia chast,
>   And eke was much more strong.[26]

This is an odd way for one woman to write about the narrow escape of another—a friend too—from rape. Some ink has been expended to justify or to explain such heartlessness. But beside or behind the story of a rapist foiled lies a different story: Arthur Gray's own version. This makes him no rapist, even in intent, and a victim not of love but of the class system. At the trial he finally got a chance to set his story against the newspaper one: 'his Plea was that he had gott in drink and had a mind to see if Mr Burnet ... was not in bed with her, and he knew he would use him roughly if he was there and therefore he took pistol—it was prov'd by all the Servants that he often staid till Morn. and then one of the Servants was called to lett him out.'[27]

Gray's story about the Revd Gilbert Burnet was not believed; no newspaper carried it. But if it was true, then he never fell in love with Mrs Murray, and never thought of raping her. What he aimed at was the voyeuristic and insubordinate thrill of seeing her in bed with an illicit lover of her own class—perhaps, too, at some kind of hush money. If his story was true, then Burnet was an unnamed participant in the resulting fracas.

Gray had by then had time to concoct a defence. But testimony from 'all the Servants' supported him as regards Griselda Murray's affair with Burnet. If his highly plausible tale is true, he was sacrificed to save a lady's honour. Then the avid reporting of the case must be seen as a smokescreen fostered by the family to conceal her lapse, and the collusions or corruptions which permitted it. Mrs Murray's brother-in-law (Gray's employer) was Lord Binning, heir to an earldom.[28] Her parents, George Baillie of

---

[26] *Virtue in Danger, A Lamentable Story how a vertuous Lady had like to have been Ravished by her Sister's Footman*, To the Tune of The Children in the Wood (*E&P* 216–21, which follows the text of Lord Oxford's MS copy).

[27] John Thomlinson, 24 Dec., BL Add. MS 22560. 30.

[28] Coincidentally, MWM reported Burnet in 1723 to be engaged in an adulterous love-triangle with Elizabeth West (sister of Griselda Murray's alleged lover) and another Scottish peer (*CL* ii. 31).

Jerviswood and Lady Grizell née Hume, were godly though not unworldly. They belonged to the Scottish Whig élite; their parents had been persecuted as Covenanters. George Baillie was a Lord of the Treasury. Lady Grizell as a girl had performed feats both of outdoor heroism and domestic virtue. She was later a song-writer who strictly subordinated her art to household duties, according to affectionate and dutiful *Memoirs* of her by her daughter Griselda.[29] She was not above censorious gossip herself: about Lady Mary's friendship with Pope, for instance. She and her husband were friends and supporters of Lord Mar, though politically opposed to his rebellion. With their close-knit sense of family values, they could scarcely admit that their daughter was having an affair.

Lady Mary was well placed to know the true version. The alleged lover was her old mentor's son; she had written to his sister from Turkey and been celebrated in verse by his brother Thomas; she was a Twickenham neighbour of his cousin James Johnstone.[30] When he died, five years after this, she remarked tartly on Griselda Murray's failure to grieve.[31] If Gray's version was the one she believed, then what she was doing in her two poems was exaggerating and parodying, each in turn, the two complementary newspaper fictions: that of yearning lover, that of chaste exemplar. She was not sympathizing with the proletarian lover, but mocking him as an improbable fiction; she did not blame a rape victim but mocked and goaded a false claimant to chastity.

⁓⁂⁓

This society fostered hypocrisy. Marriages were made by parents on financial grounds; remnants lingered of a libertine code (chiefly for males); the pursuit of pleasure was the business of the rich; yet the moral imperatives of Christian marriage were officially unchallenged. Most public discourse wielded a powerful rhetoric of family honour and female purity. Some long-term extramarital liaisons, like Henrietta Marlborough's with Congreve, were widely but ever so discreetly accepted: even this one elicited fierce disapproval from Sarah Marlborough and oblique comment from Lady Mary.[32]

To her sister Lady Mary adopted a tolerant, worldly tone about other people's sexual peccadilloes, while implicitly claiming to stand above such

---

[29] See Ramsay 1724; Murray 1822; Baillie 1911.

[30] *Virtue in Danger* says Mrs Murray expected the approach of '*his* Grace'; Horace Walpole guessed this was the Duke of Atholl (*E&P* 217 and n.). She may have had, or been rumoured to have, two lovers. MWM did not accuse her to Lady Mar, but said the affair proved how even groundless charges can hurt a woman (*CL* ii. 14).

[31] *CL* ii. 70.   [32] Harris 1991: 102, 258–9; *CL* ii. 30.

sordid goings-on herself. 'Your acquaintance D. Rodrigue has had a small accident befalln him', she writes, 'Mr Annesley found him in bed with his Wife.' Of the resulting divorce proceedings she comments, 'Those Things grow more fashionable every day.' She thinks the best solution 'would be a genneral Act of Divorceing all the people of England'. Any who wished could re-enact their marriages, and many reputations would be saved.[33] A decline in morals is one of her frequent themes; but her moralist stance is always spiked with irony. Gallantry or raking, she says, is no longer a male preserve: it is 'no Scandal' now to allude—not bluntly, but transparently— to the pregnancies of unmarried girls of good family. 'Honnour, Virtue, Reputation etc., which we used to hear of in our Nursery, is as much laid aside and forgotten as crumple'd Riband.' In such libertine times 'the forlorn state of Matrimony' is despised and outmoded: 'we marry'd Women look very silly', and fall back for excuse on phrases fitter for sexual frailty: 'twas done a great while ago and we were very young when we did it.' Her comments on personal conduct routinely parody, and so de-authorize, political or legal discourse.[34]

A fine instance of her moral ambivalence is her extravaganza on the topic of 'the Schemers' (a rakes' club which was arousing hysterical newspaper attention). She addressed this account to Lady Mar only just before the latter set out for England in 1724, and before the Schemers had made the papers. She says these '20 very pritty fellows', headed by the notorious Duke of Wharton, are dedicated to 'that branch of Happyness which the vulgar call Whoring'. With elaborate parody of ecclesiastical and civil ceremony, they gather together, masked, with their masked ladies. Their code states that these women must not be prostitutes, but members of respectable society with their identities carefully concealed.

The Schemers set out to breach society's rigorous barriers between chaste and unchaste women: they flout an 'Authority . . . built on grosse impositions upon Mankind'. Lady Mary's professions here—libertarian allegiance to them, disdain for their enemies—are ironic. Yet she seems to have enjoyed relaxed relations with them: they 'got hold of' her spoof celebration and she had trouble getting it back.[35]

---

[33] *CL* ii. 51–2.

[34] *CL* ii. 32. Hervey sent a similar flight of fancy to Griselda Murray. If the recent rush of marriages is no 'accidental Epidemical Madness', then perhaps the 'declining Institution' may survive; it will not after all become the mode to enquire politely after a birth 'whose Child it was' (18 May 1725, Mellerstain MSS). Cf. MWM's alleged comments on Mary Edwards (p. 318).

[35] [Mar.–Apr. 1724], *CL* ii. 38–40. The *Universal Journal* reported the Schemers' 'Master-Piece of Impiety', their unmentionable 'Designs against Women', on 6 June 1724.

Irony about the Schemers implies that her own real values are not theirs; but she herself is not exempt from her own irony. 'We wild Girls allways make your prudent Wives and mothers.' There is an edge to her pen as she mentions alleged liaisons of Griselda Murray and others. A notoriously promiscuous woman marrying a peer is, she says, an invitation to others 'to be as infamous as possible in order to make their fortunes'. When a widow, by remarrying, 'renounces the care of her Children', Lady Mary tells a friend she feels 'heartily asham'd of my Petticoats'; but to Frances she expresses only amusement.³⁶ The target of her satire is less infidelity or promiscuity as such, than discrepancy between preaching and practice. She likes to sound shocking—'There is but three pretty Men in England and they are all in love with me at this present writeing'—she knows Frances will not be shocked. But neither her pleasure in outrage nor her pleasure in counteracting sermonizing ensures candour about any aberrations of her own. Fig-leaves, she later believed, 'are as necessary for our Minds as our Bodies'.³⁷

Lady Mary told her sister that she saw Pope very little, at a time when Mrs Murray's mother Lady Grizell thought they 'keep so close yonder that they are a talk to the whole town'. He was just perfecting his grotto, so the 'town' may have been reading his love-verses to Lady Mary on that occasion.³⁸ This relationship, which she plays down, seems innocuous indeed compared with the scandals of other people (including friends) which she light-heartedly disseminates. During 1722–3 these included a stabbing by a prostitute whose every action was public news.³⁹ But they also included alleged extramarital liaisons of Lady Bristol ('Cardelia'), Lady Rich, and Margaret Pulteney,⁴⁰ the long-running, on-again-off-again courtships of the Duke of Rutland's sisters, the proposed marriage of the nearly seventy-year-old Lord Pembroke to a woman very much younger, and an incident in which a young married woman found herself benighted far down the Thames on a private yacht, in terror of her husband's reaction. (Her gallant escorts took the story—as a jest—straight to the king's ear.)⁴¹

---

³⁶ *CL* ii. 57, 46, 33–4, 37.
³⁷ *CL* ii. 69; iii. 97. Since she did not confide the full story of her inoculation work, she was hardly likely to confide either her real feelings about other people's love-lives, or the details of her own, if any.
³⁸ 14 July 1722, Mellerstain MSS; *CL* ii. 15; *E&P* 247.
³⁹ Sally Salisbury stabbed her lover, John Finch (not fatally), when she thought he meant to seduce her sister; she died in prison during her one-year sentence (*CL* ii. 15, 20 and nn.).
⁴⁰ *CL* ii. 17, 23, 24. MWM had corresponded with the first two during the embassy; the third belonged to the Molesworth-Tichborne family network.
⁴¹ *CL* ii. 24, 26, 79–80, 17–18. Pembroke, a man of learning, was impressed by MWM's Embassy Letters (which he read in MS) and her classical learning; he visited her to discuss the Sigean inscription (H MS 77. 208–11).

During the cold, wet summer of 1722, Griselda Murray's mother was clearly furious with Lady Mary. With a pious disclaimer ('let not us introduce scandal'), she relayed at second-hand scandal 'of her using Mr. Wortley like a dog'.[42] But any anger of Griselda's own remained unvoiced until 1725, nearly four years after the provocation. In the interim Lady Mary had commented in verse on a not dissimilar story: another gaffe involving sex, class, and one of sister Mar's friends. The story went that Jane Lowther had been told a man was waiting to see her: someone who 'dyed' for her (i.e. recoloured old fabrics). She had misconstrued this as 'died', and expected to receive a hyperbolical lover. The poem pokes predictable fun at a woman past her prime and desperate for a man.[43]

Lady Mary may have written, in spring 1723, a far riskier, untraced ballad satire. It was, she says, variously ascribed to either her or Pope. This must be a joke, for it dealt with a topic on which her views and his would be conspicuously different: the Jacobite invasion plot which Lord Mar had planned back in 1721, then partly uncovered when bribed by Charles Churchill to change sides. Pope's friend Francis Atterbury was now, in May 1723, being tried by the House of Lords for agency in this plot; Pope, after agonies of terror, had performed creditably as a witness. From this were to spring Atterbury's exile, his unmasking of Mar's duplicity, and Mar's final disgrace as a Jacobite.[44] Lady Mary's loyalty lay with the Whig government, but she was alert to the crassness of government in general (exemplified by this trial, with its ridiculous harping on details like a gift of a lap-dog). It would be like her to versify her ambivalence about this situation, with its grotesquely disparate side-effects for her sister Mar and her friend Pope—and like her too to cover her tracks.[45]

Still, comfortably off in England, she may probably have underestimated sister Mar's troubles. English newspapers were avid for news of the Mars; but the items they printed gave no notion of what exiled life was like.[46] Lady

---

[42] *Post Man*, 7 June; *Baker's News*, 24 July; Lady Grizel, 14 July, Mellerstain MSS. This may reflect a rumour about Rémond; Griselda Murray seems to have been to some extent a confidante (*CL* ii. 4).

[43] Lady Grizel Baillie found 'Malice' even in trivia—MWM's hinting that the Baillie/Murray family were at home when they said they were out. She *implied* that MWM was a social pariah (Mellerstain MS, 14 July). The would-be youthful Jane Lowther was sister of the Lord Lonsdale who, Horace Walpole thought, had courted MWM (*CL* ii. 23; *E&P* 225–7).

[44] Mack 1985: 392–402; *London Journal*, 19 May 1722; Bennett 1975: 247–51, 255–6, 277–9, Gregg 1982: 109 ff.

[45] MWM was also well acquainted with Atterbury's ally Wharton, who later planned the *next* invasion project (Bennett 1975: 272, 287, 281). Ballads on the plot appeared in newspapers of 23 and 27 Apr. 1723; others in Foxon 1975 (W344, C440, C421, A192, K53). From now on Pope was Walpole's enemy. Some time this spring MWM was seriously ill.

[46] *Post-Man*, 2 Nov. 1723; *St James's Evening Post*, 26 Dec. 1723.

Mary often complained of Frances's failure to answer her letters. Once she affected to blame this on her involvement in 'the pleasures of Paris', though soon afterwards she acknowledged her 'Complaints of uneasyness, which I wish with all my soul I was capable of releiving'. Even so, she sounded loath to admit that her sister had a harsher lot than hers: in England many people were sick, or had died, and 'Time but dully lingers on.' She blamed the prevailing stupidity on 'this Vile Climate', and envied the 'Serene Air' and other supposed advantages of Paris. She sought to enliven her sister: with a letter 'piping hot' from the Prince of Wales's birthday, full of 'fine Cloths, fine Gentlemen, brisk Tunes and lively dances'; with the notion that 'people are grown . . . extravagantly ugly' since she and Frances were young; with a lengthy disquisition on the 'damnable Sin' of hypocrisy, and England's rapid progress towards sinlessness in this respect. She offered to detail her personal situation, but only if Lady Mar should ask.[47]

A year later, another dozen letters having gone unanswered, she wrote to complain of the waste of her precious time and wit, to charge Lady Mar with 'utter Indifference for all things on this side the Water'—and to offer another virtuoso epistolary performance. This letter is a fantasia on topical sex scandals, escalating from the conquests of the man who was to carry the letter, through a public row between her two ex-protégés Senesino and Anastasia Robinson, to the scandalous society of Schemers.

Very shortly after this worldly letter she found exhibited in public, as 'said to be written by the Lady *W—y M—e*', her earnest little poem of 1712, 'While Thirst of Power'. Aaron Hill's *Plain Dealer* printed it, as 'The Resolve', with a frame story around it. A 'young gentleman' pulls a copy of it from his pocket in mixed company and reads it out to '*loud . . . Commendation*'. But even more '*extravagant*' praise greets the verse reply which another anonymous gentleman—Hill himself—composes on the spot, 'with an Oath' that '*He would not be behind-Hand with the SEX in Modesty*'. The story appears to be driven by sincere admiration; the poem expresses a horror of rakes which Lady Mary often expressed herself. Still, she may have felt she had been set up to be trumped by a member of the opposite sex. Another reply was going the rounds in manuscript; much later when it appeared in print she said it was by the Schemer Sir William Yonge.[48]

❧

---

[47] *CL* ii. 22, 25, 26, 29–30 (31 Oct. [1723]).
[48] *CL* ii. 36–40; *Plain Dealer*, no. xi, 27 Apr. 1724; *E&P* 179; Grundy 1971: 334. MWM identified Yonge in Dodsley's *Collection* (Grundy 1982: 32).

In Paris meanwhile, the dutiful wife Lady Mar was enmeshed in Jacobite life if not in Jacobite dreams. She had corresponded with the Chevalier or Pretender and made her moral support available to his young bride, Clementina Sobieska, since 1719. James reassured her that the anti-Whig backbiting against her cut no ice with him; and he munificently added an Irish dukedom to the Scottish one already conferred on Mar.[49]

Now, in 1724, developments in Lord Mar's fortunes or misfortunes made it expedient for Lady Mar to visit England again. After vain and repeated pleas to the Crown for pardon or restoration of his forfeited estates, his next hope had been for his brother, Lord Grange, to purchase the estates. This signalled another round in the combat between Grange and the Duke of Kingston. Grange stood for the law and customs of Scotland, and the cause of his brother Mar and his nephew Lord Erskine. Kingston stood for the law and customs of England, and the cause of Lady Mar and his grandchild.[50] *(Lady Frances)* Lady Mar was the football, or the tug-of-war rope, between these two. She must have known in the autumn of 1723 (while she was frantic for cash, and failing to answer Lady Mary's letters)[51] that a visit home would involve her in a reprise of many themes played and replayed since 1715.

In 1719 a decree had been given in favour of her stepson Erskine. Kingston had considered appeal, and national, hostile prejudice had escalated on each side.[52] Grange kept Kingston informed when, by November 1723, he and his kinsman Erskine of Dun took over a whole tariff of debts borne by the estates. Next spring (while Lady Mary was writing about the Schemers) they assumed responsibility for Lady Mar's annual £1,000 and Lady Frances Erskine's interest on £10,000.[53] At the last moment the estate sale nearly foundered on derogatory rumours about Grange, who of course blamed Kingston.

Nevertheless, the deal went through.[54] Grange and Erskine of Dun became legal owners of the Mar estates. And on 19 May, having forewarned her sister in 'a delightfull letter', Lady Mar arrived in London with her

---

[49] Mar MSS GD 124/15/1188, 1212, 1230, 1265; HMC 1904: 258; Gregg 1982: 191. Lady Mary never called her sister a duchess.

[50] This was a new threat of seeing his grandchildren beggars (see p. 35).

[51] Raitt to Grange, 2 Sept. 1723 (Mar MSS GD 124/15/1237); Grange, 31 Oct. 1719 (Mar MSS GD 124/15/1190).

[52] Mar MSS GD 124/15/1196, 15/1193/2, 15/1197/1. Lord Loudoun (whose wife was later hostile to MWM) seems to have advised both sides (15/1195). Grange said he heard Kingston misleading Walpole about the sale (to Lady Mar, 18 Aug. 1724: Mar MSS GD 124/15/1246/10).

[53] Mar MSS GD 124/15/1241, 2/200/1–7. Grange had adjudicated a case in 1722 between the notorious Francis Charteris and Lord Hyndford (GD 124/6/198). (Among those advancing Mar money were Charteris and many Scottish gentlewomen.)

[54] 13 May 1724, BL Eg. MS 3531. 102–4.

nearly-nine-year-old daughter.[55] She brought a detailed agenda from her husband about what she was to accomplish.[56] He wanted her by hook or by crook to squeeze some cash out of the estates, though he must have known this was almost impossible. She was to negotiate with Grange (although Mar omitted to tell Grange either the full extent of their Paris debts, or that he had promised the creditors that his wife would not fail to bring money at her return). He may even have hoped, as did more guileless Jacobites, that she could manage to negotiate his long-sought pardon. Finally he voiced a hope that she might find 'a fitt match for Tom [Erskine], which might clear all'.[57] She had her work cut out.

Lady Mar probably visited Lady Mary before moving in early June into a house in Soho Square lent by her friends Lord and Lady Bateman, who were in France.[58] During her visit letters flew back and forth between Grange in Scotland and three English correspondents: herself, her father, and the agent Raitt.[59] The dossier gives fitful, vivid impressions of the power struggle being waged through her. Behind Grange lay the estates of Alloa, encumbered with debt, even their coal-mines confessedly run down and mismanaged. Behind Kingston lay large swathes of Nottinghamshire, Wiltshire, Shropshire, and half a dozen other rich English counties, mostly enclosed and improved, or coal-producing; also the Pierrepont pride of birth and his own personal standing at court. To him it was unthinkable that his descendants should have to settle for less than the sums clearly and elaborately set out in the Mar marriage contract. Grange, at the top of his profession of the law, had a matching quota of family and national pride; to him it was equally unthinkable that such sums should be demanded in present circumstances. He saw Kingston (and Lady Mar) as spoiled and unrealistic. Kingston saw him as a dinosaur.

On 13 June Grange sent Lady Mar details of the estate purchase (on which

---

[55] 13 June 1724, *CL* ii. 40. Lady Lansdowne probably travelled with them (*Evening Post*, 23 May, 21 May 1724). Lady Stafford, meanwhile, was just off to spend some time in Paris (*Whitehall Evening Post*, 7 May, *British Journal*, 13 June).

[56] Atterbury 1869: ii. 33. His political affairs were in turmoil. At a 'painful interview' with Atterbury in May he had surrendered papers which damned him as a traitor. By August his posts with 'James III' had fallen to Atterbury and John Hay (McLynn 1989: 4).

[57] Gregg 1982: 192; Lord Mar to Lady Mar, 25/14 July 1724 (Mar MSS GD 124/15/1247/10). He did not say what an heiress might see in Erskine.

[58] *Applebee's*, 6 June 1724 (the day that Jane Smith, the former Hermenesilda, became governess to the royal children, and the *Weekly Journal or Saturdays-Post* reprinted 'In Beauty or Wit', entitled 'Upon the Learned Lady M—y W—y' and ascribed as usual to Pope). William Bateman was son of a South Sea Director; Lady Ann Bateman was granddaughter of Sarah Marlborough, daughter of the late Lord Sunderland, much older half-sister of the ill-fated Willy Spencer. MWM commented on a love-affair of hers in 1725 (*CL* ii. 48).

[59] GD 124/15/1246, 1247, 1250.

Raitt duly offered congratulation). Lady Frances Erskine (Fanny to her English relations, Frannie to her Scots ones), as an only daughter, had £10,000 under the marriage settlement; this was now reduced to £7,000. Grange thought this generous; Kingston thought it unacceptable.[60] Grange was keen to get Lady Mar away from her father and back to 'those who understand these affairs and have just thoughts of them'. On 20 June he sent Raitt a bill of credit for her journey, but having no idea of the real circumstances he did not send enough.

Lady Mar was by now not at all unwilling to leave—but not without cash in hand. Her husband, much as he wished her back 'where you are so much wanted and long'd for', reminded her of the consequences of appearing empty-handed.[61] Raitt reported her as readying herself to leave as soon as Grange provided more credit. At the end of June she made a farewell visit to Lady Mary, who had Skerrett staying for the summer at 'Twittinham'. (It was just before *The Plain Dealer*'s inoculation number.) Lady Mar was then unexpectedly delayed; Griselda Murray went down with a dangerous fever at her parents' country house at Barnet, and her friend spent a week ministering to her. Raitt became anxious: she would be making a farewell visit to Kingston too, and further delay would incommode Grange.[62]

Getting away was tactically difficult for Lady Mar, whatever it may have been emotionally. She besought Grange to send her £3,000. A postscript added: 'My Daughter presents her duty to you, and begs you'll make haste to let us go to her Papa.' Grange replied, two weeks later, not as an uncle but as a lawyer. Scottish tenants, he informed her, by custom paid in arrears, in instalments, and in kind, probably grain. If the grain should come to hand by, say, Candlemas (2 February) it would have to be sold to a corn-merchant who would bargain to pay at Whitsun, or Lammas, or Michaelmas—more than a year away. It is easy to see, adds Grange with gloomy relish, that Kingston is 'not accustom'd to business of this sort': the only way to raise cash is by a 'convoyance' of Lady Frances's fortune.[63]

This suggestion was like a red rag to Kingston: his daughter diplomatically reported him 'surpriz'd' at it.[64] By now, mid-July, Lady Mar's correspondence with Grange was growing more and more tense and frigid, though Grange assured Raitt that the letter he sent her was much gentler

---

[60] Grange added a homily about young ladies marrying foolishly, to please their 'eye' (which Lady Mar had not done). He presumably wished to suggest the general financial incompetence of women and the unreliability of Lady Frannie as an investment (Mar MSS GD 124/15/1246/1, 1247/1, 2).

[61] Mar MSS GD 124/15/1247/2, 1247/7, 1247/10. [62] Mar MSS GD 124/15/1247/3; *CL* ii. 41.

[63] Lady Mar, 30 June, Grange, 14 July: Mar MSS GD 124/15/1246/4, 1246/5.

[64] Lady Mar, 18 July 1724 (Mar MSS GD 124/15/1246/6).

than his first draft. Everything angered him: the Mars' concealments (now discovered), the amount Lady Mar was spending even now, 'her needless continuance at London', the refusal of her and her father to 'assign', and especially their apparent belief that they could compel him to advance money before it came to hand. He began to dwell on the trouble all this was costing him in 'drudgery of business', to the possible detriment of 'my own poor Family'. He contrasted human ingratitude with the approval he counted on from 'the great judge of all'.[65]

Raitt informed Grange that Lady Mar was so 'anxtious' to be gone that she would negotiate behind her father's back. But then she made two visits to Acton. Kingston was still in the game; but his imminent departure for Thoresby provided a deadline. Raitt now risked his employer's wrath by a moving appeal on Lady Mar's behalf. He had gone so far as to tell Kingston that Grange and Erskine of Dun would borrow money to bail her out. Lord Mar, like Raitt, expected Grange to manage the feat of borrowing in Scotland, 'this being so absoluitly necessary'.[66]

Lady Mar's time in England dragged on through August (while Marjory Hay, another Jacobite's wife on an errand parallel to hers, was arrested on Lord Mar's information). Grange justified himself and blamed Kingston's 'scruples' and ignorance, Lady Mar's bad management: the 'opulent' and 'exorbitant' English. To her plea that ever since her marriage she had denied herself everything for the sake of 'my Lord and his children', Grange opposed his own self-sacrifice and overwork. He cited corroborative opinion from fellow-Scots, and remained tight-lipped and pharisaical. 'I assure your Ladyship it is not at all agreeable to me to be making these remonstrances.'[67]

On 11 August Raitt (now almost openly siding with Lady Mar against Grange) expressed a fear that she would 'freat her Self into a fitt of sickness'. He hoped to travel to Scotland and collect Kingston's signature *en route* (he thought Thoresby 'almost half way to Scotland'); but Lady Mar dreaded his leaving her.[68] That day Grange authorized the Edinburgh banker Alexander Tait to pay her an advance of up to £2,000 sterling; but he kept writing

---

[65] Grange to Raitt, 14 July 1724 (Mar MSS GD 124/15/1247/7). He was corresponding with Isaac Watts over this period (GD 124/15/1253).

[66] Raitt to Grange, 21, 23 July (draft), Lord Mar to Lady Mar, 25/11 July 1724, copy (Mar MSS GD 124/15/1247/8, 1247/9, 1247/10).

[67] Grange, 15, 22 Aug., Lady Mar, 18 Aug. (GD 124/15/1246/9, 1246/10, 1246/11); Atterbury 1869: ii. 56–7. Lord Mar used a softer style: 'I have often observed that it is pritty hard to give an English lawier a right notion, or to comprehend Severall of the forms and ways of business in Scotland' (GD 124/15/1247/10).

[68] 11 Aug., Mar MSS 124/15/1247/11.

wounding letters. At last, after some flurried removing and visiting, Lady Mar left London.[69] With her daughter and three servants, she seized the tide with a 3 a.m. sailing from Dover, and landed at Calais on the first of September. As she took up again the weary business of trying to pacify creditors with small sums and large promises, and her father and brother-in-law pursued their tug of war over her daughter's fortune, *Applebee's* assured the British public that her family lived 'in the utmost Splendor and Magnificence'.[70]

These struggles left no trace in the famous and brilliant letters of Lady Mar's sister. But some subtle shift of tone may be detected in those letters after Lady Mar's time in England. She took to opening regularly on concern for Lady Mar's health and spirits; she hinted at ageing and disillusion. But in condoling over her sister's financial and emotional troubles, Lady Mary sturdily refused to admit them as excuses for silence: 'what ever keeps one at home naturally enclines one to write, especially when you can give a Freind so much pleasure as your Letters allways do me.' This was shortly after her sister left. Inoculation fever was still high. Maitland's *Account* was in its second edition (with a vindication by Arbuthnot). Lady Mary ignored this and much else in her letter, filling it with other quarrels, ballad news, social news; and she half-promised to visit Paris at Christmas.[71]

Her poetry, too, took a new direction in 1724: into two poems of 'feminist' anger which may have drawn on her feelings about sister Frances. Each seizes on a topical occasion for a trenchant critique of marriage as an institution; she wrote them to contest the received view of a divorce (that of Mary Yonge) and a death (that of Eleanor Bowes). But many of her lines on these 'Oppress'd and Injur'd' women would apply equally well to Lady Mar: she too was compelled to impossible fortitude; she too trusted and was deceived.[72] At least Frances's wrongs coincided with Mary's anger, however the two were related.

In June 1724, as the Scots and English lords tightened their grip on Lady Mar, a case was brought in the House of Lords by William Yonge for damages from the lover of his estranged wife, Mary née Heathcote. Yonge was one of those people whom everyone dislikes (Hervey's pen-portrait in his

[69] Raitt told Grange this with effusive thanks for his noble self-sacrifice in offering to raise £2,000 (15 Aug. 1724, GD 124/15/1247/12).

[70] Raitt to Grange, 15 Aug., 20 Aug. 1724 (GD 124/15/1247/12, 13); GD 124/15/1250; English newspapers, 5 Sept. 1724). In Nov. more documents were drawn up. A 'Scheme of account, showing the amount of debts on the estate of Mar' says she and her daughter had had £8,356 and odd shillings advanced them.

[71] *CL* ii. 41–2; advert., *Weekly Journal: or Saturday's-Post*, 7 Nov. 1724.

[72] *E&P* 230. MWM was not always so 'feminist'. On a widow's foolish remarriage she felt ashamed for her sex, afraid men might be right to say 'nothing hinders Women from playing the Fool but not having it in their power' (*CL* ii. 34).

Memoirs is particularly damning). He had probably just impinged on Lady Mary's writing life with an answer to her early poem 'While Thirst of Power'. He had married a City banker's daughter, whose family (though they wrote her warmly loving letters) had apparently judged that his status as heir to a baronetcy warranted receiving her hand in marriage and her impressive portion. He was now legally separated from his wife though not from most of her money. When he caught her in a love-affair he seized his chance of further profit. He was awarded £1,500 damages, with costs; he then divorced her and married a noblewoman.

Some might set Mary Yonge's liaison on a par with that of Griselda Murray with the Revd Gilbert Burnet: not Lady Mary. Perhaps on the hint of Mary Yonge's love-letters, which were read out in open court, she composed an 'Epistle from Mrs Yonge to her Husband'. This inveighs against Yonge and his political climbing: his toadying to his patron, his plans for a second and even more advantageous match. It attacks the sexual double standard (he was a leading Schemer; everyone knew of his promiscuity and infidelity), and individual males known as seducers. Most remarkably, it broadens out from this particular case to general advocacy for ill-used wives, 'To daily Racks condemn'd, and to eternal Chains'. Since women are created with passions just like those of men; how can society treat them so differently? Since women's weakness is a cliché parrotted by 'every Prattling Fop', how can society demand and get from women a fortitude beyond the reach even of male heroes like Cato? This, the strongest social protest among Montagu's poems, remained unpublished till 1972.[73]

In December (as the king signed Yonge's divorce papers and the newspapers rehashed old inoculation debates) came another occasion. George Bowes (from a Tyneside mining family with which Wortley had dealings) had married the fourteen-year-old Eleanor Verney, a Twickenham girl who was a precocious poet. Within eleven weeks of the wedding she was dead. She was buried 'with great Funeral Pomp and Solemnity' in Henry VIII's chapel in Westminster Abbey. But her death was controversial. Montagu put her views in verse; so did Mary Astell. Montagu wrote her poem at a crowded social gathering the very day Eleanor Bowes died; it was likely there that Astell wrote hers on the opposite side of the same sheet of paper. The two women shared a single outrageous perception: marriage was so awful that this young bride was better off dead.

---

[73] See p. 229; *E&P* 230–2; Grundy 1972a: 417–28. Among the rakes MWM names is her frequent target Sir George Oxenden (H MS 255. 28). The tone in which Mrs Yonge was condemned (hearings, from newspapers) is staggering today.

There the resemblance between them ends. For Astell, any sexual pleasure in marriage is gross, vulgar, and poisonous, well exchanged for the joys of Heaven. If this pushes orthodox Christian belief to extremes, it may be responding to an extreme case. Eleanor Bowes 'was said to die of the violence of the Bridegroom's embraces'. (Just clumsy violence? or sadistic? There is no way to tell.) Male poets likened her to Danaë or Semele, struck dead by Jove's superhuman potency. For Montagu, sex in marriage is nature's gift, a 'Rapture' which heaven is unlikely to match (she does not think, like Astell, of Christ as bridegroom); but marriage in its social aspect is bound to bring betrayal and tyranny in the end. No wife escapes—except by dying young.

As in her poem for Mary Yonge, Lady Mary's feminist anger sounds solidly heterosexual. It was also scandalous: comparing a man to lustful Jove was acceptable; celebrating a woman's pleasure was not. While Astell's poem remained unknown, hers was published with her initials a week after Eleanor Bowes died, and circulated busily in print and manuscript.[74] Most copies annexed to it some reproving or scurrilous reply. Again she attracted the notice of the Schemers: the libertine Philip, Duke of Wharton, answered repressively, 'In ev'ry line your wanton soul appears.' His reply also launched the improbable fiction of her affair with the sultan.[75]

Montagu's 'Mrs Bowes' offended many. But it did not offend Astell; it contradicted her views on sexuality but not on society. It may have brought the two women close, for Astell wrote most of her probably unsolicited preface to the Embassy Letters only four days after Eleanor Bowes died. Lady Mary had responded to her enquiries with the loan of her albums. When Astell returned them she had added into the manuscript travel book her manuscript preface. From now on, anyone reading the original text would read with it her vigorous, feminist celebration of it.[76]

Astell was a powerful ally and advocate; she records in her preface her

[74] *E&P* 233. Besides the probable original (Daly MS, Hampshire Record Office, 5m 50/2237), MWM's appeared in H MS 256. 7, 17 (her own album); Portland MS (Longleat) xx. 112; Cornell MSS; Leeds University Library, MS Lt 12; Osborn Collection (Yale) P. B. X/82, U/13, c. 188, p. 21; BL Add. MS 5384, Add. MS 28095, Add. MS 32463, Eg. MS 2560; and Weston Hall MS, Northants. Pub. in *The Weekly Journal or Saturdays-Post*, 26 Dec. 1724; *A Collection of Epigrams*, 1727, 2nd edn. 1735-7, etc.

[75] Wharton in *New Foundling Hospital*, 1784, i. 229-30. In the Daly MS MWM's poem and Astell's is each in her own hand; the Weston Hall copy has the two poems back to back in an unknown hand. Astell was from Newcastle, like George Bowes. Lady Anne Coventry and Philippa née Mundy saved poems on this death (MWM's and others); young Eleanor's poems were saved too (Badminton MSS, Fm T/B1/4/4; 2MM/b/11/5/39; Portland MSS, xvii. 23).

[76] Astell put two dates on her preface (18 Dec. 1724, 31 May 1725), with her initials—which, by the time the letters reached print, no one remembered or identified (*CL* i. 466-8). She acted in similar spirit when she filled a book of MWM's with indignant marginalia (see pp. 193-4).

view that the work ought to be published. It was fifteen years since she herself had published anything new. Clearly, this friendship reminded her that she was an author as well as a public-spirited private gentlewoman. To her reading of Montagu's Embassy Letters she brought a robust late seventeenth-century view of literature as a contest between individuals and between the sexes. She bids readers notice 'to how much better purpose the LADYS Travel than their LORDS'. She quotes from and implies rebuke to the recent *Plain Dealer* verses on Lady Mary (in which the Muses envy her). For her part she abjures envy of writing which 'obscures my *Fame*'; instead she is '*Charm'd into Love*' of it. Her solidarity with this younger author rejects the temptation to rivalry. Having failed to persuade her to publish at once, she still hopes the work will 'appear hereafter, when I am in my Grave'. Lady Mary, old and sick and homeward bound in 1761, taking pains to set this MS on the road to print, may have felt she was keeping a promise made to Astell.

15

1725–March 1728

⁓⊹⁓

Some Losses: 'Joys . . . made imperfect by fears of the Future'[1]

MONTAGU wrote more poems in 1725 whose muse was Astell. When she wrote a verse rejection of an amorous male ('Fond Wishes you persue in vain'), Astell wrote a companion piece on the occasion, and headed it 'The Anti-Song'. Lady Mary carefully kept it together with her own poem. It seems that having been propositioned, she sat down with her older friend—Ruth Perry imagines them over tea—to discuss the propositioner and to draft their different versions of the same message to him, translatable as 'Get lost!'

Those two poems are firmly linked by the disposition of manuscripts. A more tenuous linkage connects Astell with Montagu's weightiest effort in this genre: 'Answer to a Love Letter in Verse'. This repulses a suitor-in-verse with special outrage since he is recently married. Indeed, he may well have been Edward Thompson, whose wife Montagu later mourned in verse when she fell victim to the double standard (seduced by Oxenden, whom Montagu denounced in other poems as well.[2] Her 'Answer' moves from particular to general, to analyse the social attitudes which condone such advances. If the verse love-letter which provoked it is one which Lady Mary kept, it bore the same date with which Astell closed her Embassy Letters preface. This may be coincidence; but it may not. Perhaps the wooer had the bad luck to present his lines to Lady Mary just as she received Astell's praise of 'the Beautys of her Mind', and another tea-table session produced her 'Answer'. Possibly a single such session (with or without tea) produced all three replies: Montagu's 'Answer' and 'Fond Wishes', and Astell's 'Anti-Song'. All three would make quite a barrage.

[1] *CL* ii. 44.
[2] *E&P* 259, 277–8, 292, 298; H MS 255. 11 (MWM's hand); loose leaf (Astell's hand, the only such extrinsic leaf bound into 255).

Lady Mary's disgust at this suitor (his rush to marital infidelity, his self-seeking, his destructiveness), perhaps fed her reaction against predatory males in general. Her essay refuting Rochefoucauld calls such libertine seduction anti-knight-errantry, not rescuing but ruining maidens.[3] In the 'Answer' she likens it to extortion by threat of violence. The most fitting punishment she can imagine is that after his fabricated passion this man should at length love truly and unrequitedly.

The 'Answer' tells a story about Lady Mary's own past experience, parallel to what she says in her 'Epistle to Lord Bathurst' of an incurable wound in her heart. 'Once, and but Once, that Devil charm'd my Mind,' says the 'Answer':[4]

> To Reason deaf, to Observation blind,
> I Idly hop'd (what cannot Love persuade?)
> My Fondness equall'd, and my Truth repaid,
> Slow to Distrust, and willing to believe,
> Long hush'd my Doubts, and would my selfe deceive;
> But Oh too soon—this Tale would ever last,
> Sleep, sleep my wrongs and let me think 'em past.

If this has an actual referent, he can hardly be her husband. Perhaps there was someone more recent than the shadowy lost lover of her courtship days.

The same month Lady Mary received the verse love-letter which *may* have provoked her 'Answer', she wrote that she was distracted, expecting to be locked up as a madwoman.[5] This sounds quite plausibly like rage and upset over an unwanted proposition with aggravating circumstances. Or it sounds, as I shall suggest below, plausibly like falling in love. Or it could have a dozen other explanations. During these years her antagonisms with men are open and obvious, her softer feelings (if any) secret and unseen. The two men she invokes here (the rejected wooer, the 'Devil' who spurned her love) are not certainly identifiable, even if not fictional. Her 'Answer to a Love Letter' powerfully constructs man as destroyer, woman as victim. But the victim has an analysis for her situation; she extracts from her suffering a potential antidote to protect other potential victims.

In December 1724 Lady Mary made her second unmistakable mention of the young Duke of Wharton, who in 1722 had taken Craggs's former house in Twickenham. Her links with this unstable and scandalous character are

---

[3] *E&P* 163.

[4] 'Answer', *E&P* 244–6; epistle to MWM dated 31 May 1725, H MS 81. 121; Perry 1986: 21. Other copies of her 'Answer' name the versifying suitor as 'Mr. T.' or 'Mr. T——n'. Thompson m. in 1725 (Cornell MS E. 6004; Osborn collection f. c. 51; see p. 319).

[5] *CL* ii. 51. 'Epistle to Lord Bathurst' probably belongs to 1725, too (*E&P* 242–4).

tenuous. Her father had been a crony of his father; she had crossed swords with his mother over Dolly Walpole; she was a friend of his sister Lady Jane.[6] No more is known beyond exchanges of verse. His reply to her 'Mrs Bowes' is not friendly. She wrote at least two poems for him: one an epilogue for a play he was writing (but never finished), the other an inscription in a book he gave her (a copy of *Paradise Lost*), which she gave in turn to Skerrett. Her poems deal respectively with women who desire power instead of love (Elizabeth I versus Mary, Queen of Scots), and with male infidelity (traced back to Adam). Her epilogue indicates that she and Wharton were spinning literary schemes together. Both her poems reflect a sparring relationship: chiefly on topics of gender, though Wharton's fluently expressed Jacobitism offered another potential arena for debate.[7] The slightly shaky identification of 'Sophia' as a code name for Wharton would extend their relationship to include 'an immortal Quarrel' about authorship of a ballad, for which Lady Mary was 'persecut[ed]'.[8]

One more detail signals that this was not a close friendship. Lady Mary reported flippantly how an Irish officer in the French service had been humiliatingly disarmed in a duel. She called him 'My poor Love Mr. Cook . . . born to conquer nothing in England' (either ladies or gentlemen). In fact Cook's duelling partner, Stapylton, was the single Whig in a rowdy party of Jacobites. Wharton took the lead in goading Stapylton; Stapylton challenged Wharton; Wharton ducked the challenge and Cook took it up. In her jesting sympathy for Cook (who was left wounded by the encounter), Lady Mary does not much sound like Wharton's friend.[9]

Lady Mary had already joked to her sister about their having been replaced by a new (and inferior) generation. At thirty-five she increasingly laments the passing of time: 'the Damn'd, damn'd Quality of growing older and older every day, and my present Joys are made imperfect by fears of the Future.' She says her present, chosen way of life could keep her happy for

---

[6] He associated with Yonge. MWM's father had been one of his guardians and introduced him in the House of Lords in 1719. She had noted his leadership of the Schemers; she now noted his return from 'other Women' to the wife he had married, nearly ten years back, as another 15 year old (Blackett-Ord 1982: 22, 45–6, 86, 88 and *passim*; Blackett-Ord and Halsband, *TLS* 1983: 907, 1044; *CL* ii. 11, 44; see p. 22).

[7] Wharton was the only peer to attend Atterbury when he left the Tower, 18 June 1723 (*Flying-Post: or, Post-Master*, 25 June). 'Paston' assumes his notorious cowardice made him ascribe many of his potentially offensive lampoons to MWM (1907: 309).

[8] MWM said 'Sophia' palmed off a libellous ballad as hers in Nov. 1724, quarrelled with her on and off till June 1725, then went to Aix-la-Chapelle. Wharton too went there about then. In ciphers on copies of MWM letters, 'W.A.' stands for both Wharton and 'Sophia'. But some other sets of initials apply to two people. Lists of Jacobite ciphers do not include 'Sophia' for Wharton; Lady Mar wrote of MWM's 'Sophia' as 'she' (see p. 223 n. 5; *E&P* 240–1; *CL* ii. 44, 42, 53; Royal Archives, Windsor; H MS 77. 1–111, 114–15).

[9] *CL* ii. 46. John Lekeux reported the affair to John Molesworth, concluding, 'The Court don't mind much what the Duke of Wharton says or does' (15 Feb. 1725, HMC 1913: viii. 385).

two or three centuries; but then she swerves into melodrama, borrowing words from Dryden's Virgil and Pope's Homer to invoke 'Dullness and wrinkles and disease . . . Age and Death's irrevocable Doom'. Now she prays 'that what relates to my selfe may ever be exactly as it is now'; now she confesses, 'I dont know how—I would fain be 10 years younger.'[10]

With this theme comes a note of disillusion or disgust. In February 1725 she wrote: 'All our Acquaintance are run mad; they do such things, such monstrous and stupendous things!' She still says she enjoys the social round—assemblies, court, operas, masquerades—and even its follies: 'With Youth and Money 'tis certainly possible to be very well diverted in spite of Malice and ill Nature.' Sister Mar had heard Lady Mary say rather this kind of thing before (except, perhaps, for the reference to money). But the next sentiment was startling: 'For my part, as it is my establish'd Opinion That this Globe of ours is no better than a Holland Cheese and the Walkers about in it Mites, I possess my Mind in patience, let what will happen, and should feel tolerably easy thô a great Rat came and eat halfe of it up.' This sounds downright alienated. Next month Lady Mary says she has stopped participating. She speaks to almost nobody, 'thô I walk about every where'.[11]

Speculation over the causes of her alienation has free play, since evidence is, as usual, lacking. Was it sympathy for her sister's troubles? (Around this time she says, 'I wish you here ev'ry day . . . If my Letters could be any Consolation to you I should think my time best spent in writing.' 'Dear Sister, I would give the World to converse with you.') Was it her various pamphlet and ballad battles? Or the newly roused resentment of Griselda Murray, who had begun cutting her dead in public? (Lady Mar's offered 'good offices' apparently failed to heal the breach.) Or does her expressed wish for men to be entertaining but *not* lovable suggest that her trouble was a love-affair, either suppressed or indulged?

It was just after this that she wrote the passage mentioned above as perhaps suggesting a love-affair.

I have such a complication of things both in my Head and Heart that I do not very well know what I do; and if I can't settle my Brains, your next News of me will be that I am lock'd up by my Relations . . . I know not whither to laugh or cry . . . I am glad and sorry, smiling and sad . . . I give my selfe sometimes admirable advice but I am incapable of taking it.[12]

---

[10] *CL* ii. 31, 44, 45, 65, 52; Dryden, *Georgic* iii. 108–9, Pope, *Iliad*, xii. 391–2.
[11] *CL* ii. 45–6, 48. She completes the picture by citing a poem by Prior on lives of inanity and futility.
[12] *CL* ii. 48–50, 53, 51.

This *could* be the voice of a woman in love—plausibly, not conclusively.

A year later, however, she made an unequivocal though not an unironical assertion of her own chastity. After recording the usual bulletin of infidelities and *mésalliances*, she comments,

'Tis a strange thing that Women can't converse with a Lawyer, a parson, nor a man midwife without putting them all to the same use, as if one could not sign a deed, say one's prayers, or take physic without doing you know what after it. This Instinct is so odd, I am sometimes apt to think we were made to no other end. If that's true, Lord ha' mercy upon me; to be sure, I shall broil in the next world for living in the neglect of a known duty in this.

This is devious; it is intellectually mercurial. It pokes fun at the orthodox doctrine that Woman was designed for the comfort and solace of Man. Yet Lady Mary *is* saying (as she said to Molly Skerrett in 'The Lover. A Ballad') that she lives without doing 'you know what'.[13]

Other shifts in attitude may have stemmed either from her sister's visit, or her own embattled situation, or the mere passage of time. Instead of glorying in her solitude as in the early 1720s, she now, in 1725, assured Frances that she resisted 'solitary Amusements' as 'a Temptation of Satan'. She wanted now to enjoy the world, not bring on wrinkles by despising it. Since she now named Skerrett and Stafford as part of her sociability, when she formerly called them part of her solitude, she may have been recasting her opinions according to what she saw as healthiest for Lady Mar. But the shift is clearly legible. Even as optimism about Lady Mar was becoming harder, she adjured her to therapeutic busy-ness. 'My cure for lowness of Spirits is not drinking nasty Water but galloping all day, and a moderate Glass of Champagne at Night in good Company.' Her single rule for 'Health of Body and Mind' was activity.

As soon as you wake in the morning, lift up your Eyes and consider seriously what will best divert you that Day. Your Imagination being then refresh'd by sleep will certainly put in your mind some party of pleasure, which if you execute with prudence will disperse those melancholy vapours which are the foundation of all Distempers.

Lady Mar was not comforted.[14] After one long silence she tried to account for her baffling lapse. She feared 'a time will come when I Shall neither write

---

[13] Years later she said she was nothing like those girls who say that if they had been male they would have been rakes, 'which is owning they have strong Inclinations to Wh—ing and drinking' (*CL* ii. 59; iii. 98; *E&P* 236).

[14] *CL* ii. 53–4, 76, 82. Lord Mar was by now almost an outcast in his own party; some thought him literally, temperamentally incapable of sincerity.

nor see any body'. She wished 'forgetfullness cou'd steal upon me to Soften and asswage the pain of thinking'. She said she wanted Lady Mary to visit; yet she sounds more warning than enticing. It would be a visit to a depressive recluse, whose 'house cou'd be no entertainment to you', besides her diamond-selling project being a non-starter.[15] Lady Mary chose to answer in terms not of planning or emotions, but rather of ideology. Her philosophy, she said, was 'not altogether so Lugubre as yours'. Nature had kindly provided fools, she argued, as 'preservatives against the Spleen'. Her 'vast delight' in their folly could encompass the various antics of people she knew, like Lord Bathurst. By insisting on amusement instead of regret as a response to trouble, she perhaps hoped to give Frances some distance from her husband's ruined career and fortunes. She saw her sister's depression as something to deny. When she had painful news to impart—the gambling debts and suicide attempt of their old friend Lady Lechmere, née Howard, the death of their 'past play fellow' Sarah Chiswell—she moved on quickly (although, she said, touched to the heart). Like the theatre managers of her day, she thought it her business to supply a farce to dispel the suffering a tragedy caused.[16]

·⁓ఴ⁓·

Another playfellow, Molly Skerrett, was a summer fixture in Lady Mary's house at Twickenham. It seems Molly's father was rich enough to leave her £14,000 (though a sleasy publication, *Tell-tale Cupids*, later called her a gold-digger).[17] By 1724 in any case, since she was in her early twenties, it was high time for her to find a husband and a secure station in life. Instead, she did something less understandable. She became mistress to Robert Walpole: Secretary of State, *bête noire* of Edward Wortley Montagu, in Jacobite code 'the Pilot'. This year saw him at a peak of success, marked by the new title of Prime Minister, the nickname of 'the Great Man', and rapid progress on his private palace at Houghton Hall.

Walpole's attraction is not easy to perceive. He was, of course, married. He was every inch a squire: stoutly built, with a gross belly, broad face, heavy black eyebrows, and Norfolk accent. Printed attacks, spawned by his power, said he looked more like a ploughman or porter than a gentleman. He was a jovial drinking companion, famous for talking bawdy (which he said was a great leveller, enabling everyone to join in the—obviously all-male—conversation). He had boundless energy and gargantuan appetites: for food and drink, power, wealth, and Italian paintings; presumably for sex

---

[15] [?Nov. 1725], H MS 77. 114–15; see p. 224.   [16] *CL* ii. 82, 56–9, 67.
[17] Plumb 1960: 112; *Tell-tale Cupids*, 1735: 33; Hervey 1931: i. 86 n.

but not, it seemed, for sexual conquests. After knowing him for years, Lady Mary felt surprise at hearing 'Robin' accused of paranoia, rapacity, and treachery: she noted his unchanged 'lively eyes and rosy hue', his 'chearfull Smile and open honest Look', his good sense and popularity as host and guest, and especially his domestic virtues as the 'tender Father and th'Indulgent Spouse'.[18]

She had known him first as loving brother to his wild sister Dolly. He was a complaisant husband to a notoriously unfaithful wife. Their youngest son, Horace, was said to be sired not by Walpole but by Carr, Lord Hervey, elder brother of Lady Mary's friend. But Walpole treated him with fatherly fondness. He said he went 'his own way, and let madam go hers'; but promiscuity was not his way. He was a faithful lover to Maria Skerrett, twenty-six years his junior. In 1734 Hervey could summon him from her arms at a moment of political crisis by quoting Dryden on Antony and Cleopatra.[19] When, four years later again, Walpole's wife died, he waited very few months to marry Skerrett and bring her fully into his family. He pressured Queen Caroline to overlook her past and formally receive her at court, to the scandal of Pope and other self-appointed guardians of public morality. He had a family portrait painted with the two of them at its centre. They had two daughters, one of whom died young; when Maria died after fourteen years with him, she was again pregnant.[20]

Still, he was not an obviously desirable suitor. In the 1720s Molly received from Lady Mary several cautionary poems about the choice of a lover: they obviously imply that Walpole is ineligible. 'A Man in Love' (a non-existent creature, the French subtitle insists) would forget himself, forget society, and pine for solitude. 'When thus your absent Swain can do | Molly; you may believe him true.' In 'The Lover' Lady Mary writes, again to Molly, like a celibate promulgating celibacy in her hearer:

> I am not as cold as a Virgin in Lead
> Nor is Sunday's Sermon so strong in my Head,
> I know but too well how Time flys along,
> That we live but few Years and yet fewer are young.
> But I hate to be cheated, and never will buy
> Long years of Repentance for moments of Joy.

This poem imagines the delicious pleasure of a love-meeting 'with Champaign and a Chicken at last' after hours of public distance. Yet it concludes

---

[18] *Tell-tale Cupids*, 1735: 50; *E&P* 276–7 (probably written 1734). Hervey was surprised to find such a powerful man so warm in personal affection (1931: i. 18–19).

[19] *E&P* 25–6; Hervey 1931: 172.   [20] See p. 382 f.

that until men become quite different from what they are in present society, 'As I have long have liv'd Chaste I will keep my selfe so.' The 'nice Virgin' (i.e., presumably, Molly) would be well advised to imitate the nymphs in Ovid's *Metamorphoses*, who harden into trees or chill into rivers.[21]

But Molly was not cold to the Prime Minister. Hervey alleged that he paid her £5,000 'entrance money'. *Tell-Tale Cupids* gave a nastier turn: she spurned him at first, but financial motives made her set aside her 'Aversion', her 'Trembling and . . . Fear'. It said her family needed the money—though it may have said this purely to highlight the public money which she and they had later had from Walpole.[22] (Lady Mary's poems to her advise against commitment without mentioning mercenary marriage, which she so often attacked.)

Whatever Molly's initial hesitation, by autumn 1724 she had succumbed. Her daughter, christened Maria like herself, was born in 1725. Apparently, though, she spent a last summer with Lady Mary at Twickenham before Walpole fitted up Old Lodge, Richmond Park, for her.[23] If the early 1720s poems are true to the feelings of the time, Lady Mary was far from throwing her two friends into each other's arms. Nor was she, at the time, publicly mentioned as doing so. But while she chalked up Molly's rise to 'destiny'— even while she perhaps tried to prevent it—young Horace Walpole blamed her. Though he was later painted standing close to Molly, he did not accept his mother's successor.[24]

꙳

January 1726 brought heavy snow and rain. In March, as floods receded and spring green appeared, it fell to Lady Mary to relay to her sister an undreamed-of blow: their father's death. She had duly transmitted other birth-and-death news: the arrival of Leveson-Gower nieces and nephews, the deaths of uncle William Feilding ('prodigiously' regretted),[25] and of

---

[21] *E&P* 233–6. One copy of 'The Lover' explicitly said it was 'as wrote from Miss Skerrett to Sir Robert Walpole.' MWM said she wrote it to a tune, 'My Time o ye Muses'. I now think the companion poem (a rake's specifications for a woman who could keep him faithful) unlikely to be hers (Grundy 1982: 27, 29; Grundy 1971: 438; Osborn MS f.c. 51; *E&P* 236–8).

[22] Hervey 1931: i. 86. The satire claims, improbably, that Walpole then meanly cut her allowance by £500 a year. In fact his generosity meant that by July 1730 she had £6,000 in Bank of England stock, plus £260 in bank notes and further sums in foreign coin. Her father had opposed the liaison (Plumb 1960: 79, 81, 113–14 n. 2; *Tell-Tale Cupids*, 1735: 33, 51; Houghton MS R.B. 1.54).

[23] Old Lodge, renovated in 1726 for £14,000, is now demolished (Plumb 1960: ii. 90, 113). Maria was also much at Walpole's Chelsea house.

[24] *CL* ii. 182–3; see p. 417. Wharton said the Whig hanger-on Philip Lloyd or Floyd was 'Walpole's Ferret | To hunt out poor Miss Molly Skerret' (BL Harl. 7318. 51; H MS 255. 13). Mahaffey supposes MWM was heartbroken at Molly's defection to Walpole (1963: 198).

[25] Clayton letters, Victoria and Albert, F. 48 E 14. 47; Pope, *Corr.* ii. 369; *CL* ii. 31.

their sister-in-law. This was different: their father had been a force in both their lives, and they had expected him to remain so. Lady Mary, the prodigal daughter, was present at his deathbed; at the end he 'realy express'd a great deal of kindness to me', and *even* a 'desire of talking to me, which my Lady Dutchess would not permit'. Lady Mary found neither aunt Cheyne nor sister Gower (who was seven months pregnant) would back her up, 'and Mama and I were in an actual scold when my poor Father expir'd'. So she was denied any final contact with him, and left to replay in isolation her now useless emotions, familiar and unfamiliar: fear, resentment, admiration, and loss. As for sister Mar, she was already so ill when the news came that her husband concealed it from her for quite a time.

The Duke of Kingston's death was a big event: public, financial, and dynastic. An autopsy was conducted and a messenger despatched, riding post, to Nottinghamshire. The Garter King at Arms was consulted about the funeral and rewarded with a present of wine.[26] Newspapers published long obituaries. Kingston's will (made exactly a year before he died, on the day after his grandson's inoculation) carefully provided for sons he might have:

first Second Third and All and every other his Sons lawfully to be begotten Severally Successively and in Remainder One after another as they and every of them shall be in Priority of Birth and to the Severall respective Heires Male of the Body and Bodies of all and every Such Son and Sons Lawfully Issuing Every Elder of such Sons and the Heires Male of his Body being alwaies preferred and to take before a Younger of them and the Heires Male of his Body.

All this was now academic. His second wife was left a 'passable rich Widow', with two young daughters to think of.[27] She had sound Hobbesian reasons for hostility towards Lady Mary (whose lack of a dowry she probably thought well deserved). Lady Mary found her 'hardness of Heart upon this Occasion' almost incredible; the gentler Lady Gower said she 'has behaved very oddly'. The duke's will left the duchess guardian of her daughters, but not of the orphan grandchildren (the young duke, and Lady Frances Pierrepont). Their custody was vested in the executors and trustees;[28] the

---

[26] *CL* ii. 61–2, 63, 65; Manvers MS 4349. 49, 59.

[27] Her jointure, with allowances to support each daughter, came to about £3,800 p.a.; she got the Acton house. People linked her name, said MWM, 'with variety of young Husbands', but ill health would probably keep her single (*CL* ii. 63). She worried a lot over her own and her daughters' health (BL Sloane MS 4075. 356–7, 358–9). They would each have £15,000 at marriage or majority. Their mother later sued for possession of library books 'of great Vallue' and her bridal silver plate—now owned by the new duke (BL Eg. MS 3531. 37–8).

[28] *CL* ii. 63. The trustees were Lord Cheyne, Sir John Monson (later Lord Monson: a relation of Cheyne by marriage), and Thomas Bennett. Lord Carlisle would have been one of them, had he not been 'dedicated to Retirement'—a pity, MWM thought (*CL* iii. 162).

widow challenged it, but lost. The new duke turned fourteen within a month of his grandfather's death, and was then legally able to confirm the will. It was settled that aunt Cheyne would bring up his sister.

The will meticulously specified estates to provide income for each of the old duke's three elder daughters. Each got £200 cash, too, to fit herself out with mourning. Lady Mar received income from Lincolnshire, Wiltshire, and Hampshire, in trust for her heirs. But she had first to discharge £20,000 paid for her as portion; and heirs who were Roman Catholics or resident outside *England* were excluded: the tug of war went on. Lady Mary received income from Yorkshire and Derbyshire estates, in trust for her heirs, plus income from £6,000, not paralleled in her sisters' shares and so probably seen as replacing her forfeited dowry.[29]

Lady Mary sent off a short letter to Paris at once, mentioning her state of shock, and the family's 'surprizing management'; she also broke the news that there was no 'considerable Legacy' to Lady Mar, who of course desperately needed one. When she received her sister's outpourings of grief, she reacted as usual by minimizing her own emotion and commenting sardonically on other things: on her aunt's and sister Gower's spineless behaviour. She was 'very sorry' for Lady Mar's distress, but still could not see 'why filial piety should exceed fatherly fondness'. To go over every detail, she said, 'would be tedious in a Letter'; Lady Gower said it would be 'only renewing our grief'.[30]

The duke died leaving his library catalogue half-printed, new woods half-planted, and a room half-fitted up 'in Imitation of Marble'. He had just been sitting for several portraits. The week before he died he took delivery of Tillemans's view of him in Thoresby Park. The executors had to pay for this, for finishing his other projects, and for portraits done as gifts for his elder daughters. Lady Mary got a painting by Dahl, while Lady Gower and Lady Mar got works by Aikman: respectively a copy of the Dahl, and a drawing.[31]

The aftermath played itself out. The trustees of the will busied themselves over goods and chattels. They also paid the duke's debts, which included bonds drawn in 1725 of £80 to the late Lord Pierrepont's cook, and

---

[29] Copies of the will (Prerogative Court of Canterbury, Romney, fo. 90) include MSS El 10638, 10667, Huntington Library; Mar MSS GD 124/3/86 (incomplete); BL Eg. MS 3531. 3–18 (the Thoresby copy: MWM on fos. 5–6, 9). The original and Thoresby copy inexplicably call Lady Mar 'Catherine'. MWM was to receive the interest on her £6,000 'Whether she shall be Sole or Covert and Notwithstanding her Coverture'; it was to be inherited by her daughter(s) before son(s), with any younger sons preceding the eldest. A lawyer pronounced on how she might invest it (BL Eg. MS 3531. 99–100; see p. 277).

[30] *CL* ii. 62–3.

[31] Manvers MS 4883. 39; BL Eg. MS 3531. 110. MWM and Lady Gower received their pictures framed.

£600 to 'the Lady Diana and Frances Feilding' (the latter a particular friend of Lady Mary). It seems Kingston had been supplying financial aid to his first wife's relations.[32]

The mourning was of stunning formality. After the funeral at Holme Pierrepont, an exclusively male affair,[33] came the female ceremony. The widow had to see company—exactly as a new bride had to, except that it was condolences, not felicitations, which *had* to be offered in person by 'every lady on her grace's visiting list'. Lady Louisa Stuart describes it from her mother's memory:

the apartments, the staircase, and all that could be seen of the house, were hung with black cloth; the Duchess, closely veiled with crape, sate upright in her state-bed under a high black canopy; and at the foot of the bed stood ranged, like a row of mutes in a tragedy, the grandchildren of the deceased Duke—Lady Frances Pierrepont, Miss Wortley herself, and Lady Gower's daughters. Profound silence reigned: the room had no light but from a single wax-taper; and the condoling visiters, who curtseyed in and out of it, approached the bed on tiptoe; if relations, all, down to the hundredth cousin, in black-glove-mourning for the occasion.[34]

Lady Mary seems not to have mentioned to her sister the death, soon after their father's, of Lady Townshend. The former Dolly Walpole was not yet forty; she had borne eleven children and lost four; she died of smallpox after inoculating her family.[35] Deflecting her feeling, Lady Mary turned in her next letter to complaint about Griselda Murray's latest offences. These were, specifically, three. At a masquerade she had given a loud and lengthy tongue-lashing both to Lady Mary and to her escort ('a very slight acquaintance', to whom Murray implied inside knowledge of 'some very notorious' and current affair of Lady Mary's). Two days later, when bearded at an assembly about this tirade, she had repeated the general gist.

She did worst at the posthumous sale of Sir Godfrey Kneller's paintings. These included the fine full-length of Lady Mar which Kneller had painted in 1715 but for which there had clearly not been money to pay (Pl. 4). Mrs Murray wanted to buy the portrait for Lady Mar, but first she civilly offered Lady Gower not to bid against her if *she* wanted to do this. ('You know', wrote Lady Mary, 'Crimp and Quadrille incapacitate that poor Soul from ever buying any thing.') Murray made no such offer to Lady Mary, but

---

[32] Monson MSS 28B/12/4/8, 28B/12/3/8; Manvers MS 4349. 57, 59.

[33] The corpse set out northwards on 14 Mar.; the funeral cost £1,475 plus the mourning expenses (*St James's Evening Post*; Beckett 1986, 345).

[34] *E&P* 31.

[35] On 29 Mar. in London (*Applebee's Journal*, 9 Apr. 1726). Another child died just after her; three of her nine stepchildren were also dead (Rosenheim 1989: 8).

instead 'with all possible spite bid up the picture' for another ten guineas after everyone else dropped out. Lady Mary kept bidding and secured it anyway, triumphantly assuring her sister that it was now 'at your service if you please to have it'. Her account of all this ends by abjuring revenge.[36]

Family affairs came to absorb more and more of her letters. She found herself 'embourbé' in issues surrounding the orphans, 'my ever-dear Brother's children'. The boy duke was packed off on the Grand Tour; his trustees prepared to manage the estates properly during his minority, before he could start leaching money out. The result was a massive accumulation of capital (which the duke, once he came of age, immediately set about squandering). Lady Mary, who had supervised her nephew's inoculation only two years before, saw that his education so far had been deplorable, and that although he had spirit he lacked his father's good sense. 'As young Noblemen go', she still hoped he might pass muster. Perhaps she overestimated the norm: Evelyn Pierrepont, 2nd Duke of Kingston, proved 'as great a rake as any in England'.[37]

His sister Lady Frances, three years younger, posed problems of a different kind. She had £400 a year allocated for her maintenance, plus £200 for her clothes and £20 as her guardian's 'salary'. This, said Lady Mary, ensured the activation of 'the consciences of halfe her Relations'—all except herself—to take on the charge. Their squabbles, 'Lyes, Twattles, and contrivances about this affair are innumerable'. The Cheynes had the girl, but needed the trustees' permission to let her spend the summer in the   country with the Gowers; one trustee thought the matter should be submitted to Chancery. Lady Mary was approached out of the blue by a cousin, the widowed Anne (Pierrepont) Newport, Baroness Torrington, to abet her in displacing Lady Cheyne.[38] This must have given her a wry smile, but, although she feared 'My dear Aunt Cheyne' was in it purely for the money, she sought to remain uninvolved. She thought her niece impervious to the full drawbacks of her situation, in short a fool; her daughter, who loved her cousin, was to pronounce Lady Mary quite mistaken about her character, which was bashful not sullen, and inexpressive not insensitive.[39] Misreading her was later to cost Lady Mary something.

---

[36] *CL* ii. 63–5. The picture (now at the Scottish NPG, with its companion piece of Lord Mar and his son) was sold on 20 Apr. (Stewart 1971: 78).

[37] *CL* ii. 69; iii. 138; ii. 49, 65; *Hastings Wheler*, 1935: 144–5. For his trustees' management, see Mingay 1952, and 1963: 67–71; for his Grand Tour, see Mingay 1963: 138–40. Reports from his tutor, Peter Platel, and physician, Nathan Hickman, are Huntington Library MSS El 10824–10858 and Monson MSS. In 1752 the duke spent £2,000 in two weeks at Thoresby; his debts had already topped £66,000, despite his selling a good deal of land.

[38] Monson MSS, vols. xlv, cx; BL Eg. MS 3530. 34.

[39] *CL* ii. 69, 77–8; MWM 1861: i. 509 n. 2.

At the moment there was real pain to cloak behind acerbity about the family's sordidness and behind swagger about her social triumphs. 'That young Rake my Son', 'My blessed offspring', had kicked over the traces, perhaps not for the first time. He 'took to his Heels' and ran away from Westminster School to Oxford, 'being in his own opinion thoroughly qualify'd for the university'. After a long search his parents 'found and reduc'd him much against his Will to the humble condition of a School boy'.[40]

Edward Wortley Montagu, junior (last heard of as a mutinous five year old in Turkey), was now thirteen, a year younger than his rich cousin Kingston. His mother obviously construed the Oxford escapade as further mutiny against humble schoolboy status. He was short for his age, taking after her; but his fresh colour, 'grey Eyes, lightish brown Hair' were his father's. She thought him 'extream handsome', while his sister was sober, discreet—and ugly. But while his sister's rowdy games or grown-up civilities are a staple of Lady Mary's letters, he (so frequently written about as a baby) never appears there until he begins to rebel. Perhaps this was because he was away at school; perhaps it was because Lady Mar had no son; perhaps his mother was already uneasy about him. In his young teenage she calls him 'rake'—as his grandfather and his cousin Kingston were, but his father and his loved-and-lost uncle were not. In old age Lady Mary wrote, 'Never was nor lov'd a Rake.'[41] But her anguish at her son's early escapades makes it clear that she did still love him.

She does not even say specifically whether he was present when in March 1727 her sister Gower 'dragg'd' her to the theatre 'en famille in the most literal Sense . . . in Company of all our children with Lady F. Pierrepont at their Head'. Lady Frances was younger than Lady Mary's son, but with her courtesy title she might head the parade even if he was there. But this cheerful event, a year after the first duke's death, may well have arisen from the mourning purgatory shared by granddaughters only. Even if there were two Wortley Montagus present as well as one Pierrepont, Leveson-Gowers would still have handily outnumbered the rest. Lady Mary commented warmly on the beauty of one of them, Jane or 'Miss Jenny'. (For her *own* daughter's perfections, she referred her sister to the more disinterested testimony of Lady Stafford, who much to her regret had just left for France.)

---

[40] *CL* ii. 69–70. Curling says this was the fourth time he had run away, that he took to Oxford two books MWM had brought from Turkey, and lived with a woman of 20 (1954: 38). The Revd John Forster said he was found by chance after his first escapade, crying fish for sale in Blackwall, East London (*Scots Magazine*, 1777: 39. 625–6).

[41] *CL* ii. 70; iii. 227; newspaper advertisement, 5, 9 Sept. 1727. Years later she claimed he had *always* had a marked 'wildness' in his eyes (*CL* ii. 285); but she did not mention it yet.

In her friend's absence Lady Mary felt 'more stupid then I can describe', driven back on banal maxims about the fleetingness of worldly joys. She was finding her sister's sad letters 'very monstrous and shocking. I wonder with what Conscience you can talk to me of your being an old Woman; I beg I may hear no more on't.' She had written quite similarly of her own ageing; indeed Hervey rebuked her for it soon afterwards very much as she rebuked Lady Mar.[42] It seems she was combating in Frances a mood which she feared in herself.

For two more months at least she worked at keeping up her sister's spirits. (She had discovered Mme de Sévigné's letters recently, and was setting herself to outdo them.) She proffered a Phaedra-and-Hippolytus story enacted on the fringes of the royal family: the sixtyish Duchess of Cleveland, married to a bastard son of Charles II, was besottedly in love with another, twenty-five-year-old descendant of Charles by a different mistress. Lady Mary concluded, 'Lord ha' mercy upon us; see what we may all come to!' She proffered a story of Rémond of uncherished memory, who had acquired a socially inferior fiancée. She offered to send a ballad (not by her) about *Gulliver's Travels*; she advised champagne, galloping, 'Air, Exercise and Company' as 'the best med'cines'.[43]

She composed one of her funniest efforts on the theme of illicit love. In this story two lovers keep an unwanted guest occupied by repeated requests to keep on playing the harpsichord during their dalliance in another room. A row ensues; the tale gets out; and 'poor Edgcombe met with nothing where ever he went but complements about his third Tune, which is reckon'd very handsome in a Lover past forty'.

This episode occurred in the house of Lady Sunderland, whose child had died after inoculation years before, and who had since remarried none other than Sir Robert Sutton, Wortley's replacement as peace negotiator. Lady Mary may have been using her outrageous humour to combat unhappy associations with Sutton, for news of George I's death had just reached England, and Wortley seized the opportunity of a new monarch to raise the matter of his embassy losses. George II spoke 'very graciously' about it, but did nothing.[44] Wortley may have blamed this on Walpole, who had unexpectedly weathered the succession without losing his power.

But another blow was in store. The Edgecombe letter was written but not yet sealed when Lady Mary was 'intterupted by a summons to my sister

---

[42] *CL* ii. 72–6, 87–8.

[43] Apr.–June 1727, *CL* ii. 74–7. Lady Stafford, who told her about Rémond, had seen Lady Mar, but was living at some distance from her (H MS 77. 246–7).

[44] *CL* ii. 78–80; Halsband MSS.

Gower's, whom I never left since. She lasted from Friday till Tuesday, and dy'd about 8 o'clock, in such a manner as has made an Impression on me not easily shaken off. We are now but two in the World, and it ought to endear us to one another.' She vowed to do what she could to 'serve my poor Nieces and Nephews'. The last-born, Diana, was not quite a month old; it was only three months since the family theatre party. For once Lady Mary could genuinely feel for her aunt Cheyne. She ended her brief letter, 'I hope you will not let melancholy hurt your own Health, which is truly dear to your affectionate sister.'

She followed an established pattern over this loss. On receiving Lady Mar's expression of grief she recoiled into tight-lipped style. Whereas her first letter had voiced concern for Lord Gower's feelings, her second poked fun at him for compromising his Tory principles by court attendance on the new king. 'I desire you would not continue greiving your selfe,' she told her sister. 'Of all sorrows those we pay to the Dead are most vain, and as I have no good Opinion of Sorrow in general, I think no sort of it worth cherrishing.'[45]

She was to argue almost precisely the opposite a decade later in a general context: 'I look upon tenderness and Greife as the Excrescencies of Virtue. They are only to be found in the Humane and Honest mind . . . when the expressions of our Love can never reach their knowledge they can only proceed from a Heart truly touch'd . . . How aimable appears to me a Heart capable of such an attachment!'[46] But such sentiments were inadmissible to Frances. Lady Mary's vehemence and deflection give no reason to suppose that she herself ceased thinking about sister Evelyn: who loved playing cards, who had borne eleven children but could not stand up to her stepmother, who after the birth of her sixth daughter a couple of years back had been 'as merry as if nothing had happen'd'. Years later Lady Mary was to fear her 'poor Sister Gower' had 'shorten'd her Life by fretting at the disagreable prospect of a numerous Family slenderly provided for'. Meanwhile she assured Frances, her dear *only* sister, that 'There can be no situation in Life' in which her company would not bring some comfort.[47]

She was in renewed need of comfort on account of her son. A fortnight after his aunt's death he ran away from Westminster School again. This time

---

[45] *CL* ii. 80, 81. One of the nieces (later Lady Wrottesley) was a Mary, probably MWM's god-daughter. It was her daughter who placed the memorial to MWM in Lichfield Cathedral (see p. 222). EWM was busy just now with parliament, which began a brief sitting on the day Lady Gower died. Elections were coming, and following George I's death *everyone* would be in mourning.

[46] *Nonsense of Common-Sense*, no. 5, 17 Jan. 1738 (*E&P* 128).

[47] *CL* ii. 46, 83; iii. 154. Lady Stafford, who had not much valued Lady Gower, thought her passion for quadrille had killed her—presumably by taking her out too soon after childbed (H MS 77. 242).

he had done some planning. He sold books to raise cash. He walked east-wards, changed clothes with a poor boy in Whitechapel, and headed for the river. (It seems he had asked his parents to be allowed to go to sea.) He picked out a troopship and 'Accosted Boatmen to take him aboard'. There he spun a yarn well tailored to his borrowed clothes: that he worked at the lime-pits, the son of a widow with ten children. He was added in some capacity to the ship's crew before she sailed.

After a while he began to find his situation unpleasant. It was not so much the physical labour and spartan living, though both must have come as a shock. The trouble was that he failed to keep up his story: under some provocation or other he mentioned his real identity, and let himself in for unmerciful teasing. At every turn it was 'My Lord do this or you Duke of Montagu do that'. At last he was miserable enough to go to the captain (whose daughter long afterwards provided the details of their encounter).

Interviewed in the captain's cabin, the boy 'said his name was Edward Wortley Montagu and that he was the son of etc—and had run away from Westminster School—had sold his Books and could not see either Master or parents'. This was something outside the captain's experience. He expressed scepticism. The boy replied, 'Ask me any question in Greek or Latin.' This was no use: the captain knew neither. He asked, instead, the name of the boy's master at Westminster. Edward gave it, and added that he was the 'first that was Inoculated and shew'd his Arm'. This was probably too odd to dis-count. When the ship reached Gibraltar the captain spoke to the Admiral of the Mediterranean Fleet. The admiral had seen newspaper advertisements for the boy (which mentioned his inoculation scars as identifying marks). He 'took him under his care'.[48] In December 1727, five months after running away, Edward boarded a London-bound naval vessel; he reached home in the new year.

For his mother the months without news were very long. Lady Stafford expressed more sympathy now for her cruel suspense—worse than actual bereavement, she said—than when Lady Gower died. Lady Mary tried at first to keep this latest blow from sister Frances. The letter which begged her not to grieve, and which ended by advising a daily 'party of pleasure', said nothing more explicit than, 'My Girl gives me a great prospect of satisfaction, but my young Rogue of a Son is the most ungovernable little Rake that ever plaid Truant.' Her next letter said more.

[48] Wh MS 439/21, 'Information respecting E. W. M. given me by Mr. J. Wright Esq 26 New Bond Street.' This conflicts with Forster's version: that on his second flight he worked his passage to Oporto and earned his living at labouring jobs for 'two or three years' before recapture; and that the third time he ran not from Westminster but from Forster's care (*Scots Magazine*, 1777: 39. 626). Stories Forster had from his pupil are suspect.

I am vex'd to the blood by my young Rogue of a Son, who has contriv'd at his age to make himselfe the Talk of the whole Nation. He is gone Knight Erranting God knows where, and hitherto 'tis impossible to find him. You may judge of my uneasyness by what your own would be if dear Lady Fanny was lost. Nothing that ever happen'd to me has touch'd me so much. I can hardly speak or write of it with tolerable temper.[49]

Efforts to find him were proceeding. They probably picked up the Whitechapel lad who had exchanged clothes, because when they advertised for Edward they said he had hired himself either to a tradesman or labourer or to a ship's crew. They offered a reward of £20 for information. If he would 'return of himself', the advertisements assured him, 'he shall be kindly received, and put to Sea, if he desires it'.[50]

In early September, two months after his disappearance, there was still no word. Lady Mary had a bout of dangerous illness.[51] She was upset enough to begin a letter to Frances with an outburst against the 'vile World', without regard to Lady Mar's fragile state of mind. She spun a tissue of words around her disgust: she was furious with the world and her fellow humans, with 'Fool and Knave', with laws and customs. Perhaps, she said, this world was Hell and she justly condemned to it for sins committed 'in some prae-existent state'. Or perhaps it was only Purgatory, and 'after whining and grunting here a certain number of years I shall be translated to some more happy sphere'. This was a new twist to the shared imagery from courtship days. She added a tender recollection of herself and Frances sharing their misery in the little parlour; how they had looked to marriage to make them happy; 'then came being with Child etc., and you see what comes of being with Child.'

Still she clung to her belief that 'one should pluck up a Spirit'. 'I run about thô I have 5,000 pins and needles running into my Heart.'[52] This was setting herself deliberately against the practice of her sister, who soon after this sent her a deeply dispiriting letter. Lady Mar had just begged and borrowed money to pay some of the family's debts when a devaluation of the French coinage had left them worse off than ever. Lady Stafford, though in France, was inaccessible; another old friend had 'grown very old and very Stupid'.

---

[49] *CL* ii. 82–3. Lady Stafford's sympathy came tardily because she had heard a report that Edward was already found (18/7 Sept., H MS 77. 244–5).

[50] Newspapers, 18 Aug., 19 Aug., 9 Sept. 1727. The latter two dates fell one each side of EWM senior's trouble-free re-election for Huntingdon.

[51] *Daily Journal*, 5 Sept. 1727; *Whitehall Evening Post*, 7 Sept.

[52] *CL* ii. 83–4. Lady Gower d. from 'being with Child'. Hervey was grieving, too, for his favourite sister, d. 3 Sept. 1727 ('Verses to the Memory of my dearest Sister the Lady Elizabeth Mansel', Hervey MSS 941/53/1).

'Lazyness, Stupidity and ill humour', said Lady Mar, 'have taken such hold upon me that I write to nobody nor have Spirrits to go any where.' But she added, 'Perhaps a letter from you may contribute to my Cure.'[53] It was Mary's part to give consolation rather than to receive it. In October, still waiting for news, Lady Mary sent spirited accounts to Lady Mar and Lord Hervey of George II's coronation.[54]

The year had one last family event in store. On 9 November Sidney Wortley Montagu died at Wharncliffe. He left behind him five successive versions of, or codicils to, his will.[55] His son, now his heir, as he duly read these and endorsed them in his usual business-like style, could see just how his father's intentions had shifted. Sidney had not believed, any more than Edward, in the eldest son getting everything. His earliest will, 1721, gave Edward a legacy of £1,000 and half the personal estate; it gave his surviving brother, John, half the collieries. A codicil of 1722, after brother John's death, arranged to leave his half in trust, presumably for his son.

Sidney remade his will in 1724 and again, almost for the last time, on 2 April 1726. He thought of everything: repaying a large debt incurred by his father-in-law Sir Francis, tying the loose ends of complex property deals, arranging tenancies, doling out legacies to business associates, nephews, and servants, with £400 for the poor of Peterborough and Huntingdon. His son Edward was to receive (besides the entailed Wortley estates, Wortley Hall, and some church patronage) just the Barnsley collieries. The surplus of the personal estate (half of it allotted to Edward in 1724) and the Northumberland and Durham mines were now all to go to the executors: these mines were in trust for Edward's nephew John, till he reached twenty-two. The elder John's widow and daughters were to have annuities.[56] Finally, if Edward should contest the will, everything left to him would also revert to his nephew or nieces.

A final version performed some fine-tuning. It provided legacies of £1,000 apiece for Edward, for his late brother John (presumably an oversight), for Edward's son, and for each living child of John: that is, for every one of Sidney's grandchildren *except* Edward's eight-year-old daughter.

Edward's endorsements throw no light on the problematic aspects of all this. He was not an executor; he had to wait for his share. Having inventoried his father's goods and chattels at Wharncliffe Lodge, he paid the executors £157. 5s. 3d. for the whole lot on 1 March 1728. (This inventory contrasts strikingly with the one recently taken of the opulence of Evelyn, Duke of

---

[53] 10 Nov. [1727], H MS 77. 112–13.
[54] *London Journal*, 9 Jan. 1728; Stafford, H MS 77. 252; *CL* ii. 86–7.
[55] Wh MS D 246 a–e.   [56] They were Agnes, Catherine, and Anne.

Kingston.) A separate inventory for Wortley Hall marks everything of value as 'carried to [Wharncliffe] Lodge': the Hall, left by Sidney to 'fall down', was now to be rebuilt. John Platt of Rotherham set to work on the west wing in 1728.[57]

Tradition later said that on Sidney's death 'it was proposed that they should reside upon the family estate'—that is, obviously, that Wortley proposed this to Lady Mary. She replied that neither the ruined Hall nor the tiny Lodge was possible, but that she would be 'content' to live at St Ellen's Well, in the elegant house with its busts of goddesses where Sidney had kept his mistress. Her husband in turn 'could not endure' *that* house, so the matter was closed. Wortley had St Ellen's Well pulled down.[58]

Lady Mary's household accounts for the last four years before Sidney's death (kept meticulously in her own handwriting) suggest a comfortable yet frugal style of living. The annual outgoings hover around the thousand-pound mark. Too much should not be read into individual items. A payment of seven pounds for 'my Saddle' (1726) might presumably have come at any time, though £22. 7s. to a jeweller in the same year looks like splurging. The figure for 'my pocket' stays just above £60 until 1727, when it drops by a third; 'my Cloaths' were £145. 9s. 7d. in 1724, but never again reached a hundred pounds. (Was Lady Mar's presence an incentive to shopping? The same year Lady Mary spent £13. 10s.—her highest figure—on her garden, and £6. 17s. 8d. on 'odd things for the house'.) The amount she spent on herself therefore hovered between a half and two-thirds of the pin-money that would have been hers if she had married Clotworthy Skeffington. The 'children's expence', about £62 in 1724 and 1725, rose to more than twice that by 1727; meanwhile spending on operas dropped steadily over the years from three guineas to half a guinea. Sidney's death made little difference to this lifestyle.[59]

❧

Lady Mary had more of a life outside her family than most women of her class. She was acknowledged as a wit, both in talk and in writing:

> In Masquerades I go well drest
> And talk so very pretty
> That by the crowd I am confest
> Like Lady Mary witty.[60]

[57] Wh MSS M 126, 58. 17; Hunter, 1831, ii. 323.   [58] Hunter 1831: 323, 395.
[59] Wh MS M 508; see p. 304. Expenditure ran from £849. 3s. 6½d (1725) to £1140. 12s. 8d. (1727).
[60] 'What thô I am a London Lass', among 'poems addressed to Lady Anne Coventry', Badminton MSS Fm T/B1/4/4.

One of her famous *bon mots* dates from 1724, just before her sister's stressful visit and around the Schemers period. The Duke of Newcastle (whose political capacity she had sketched for Wortley ten years before) became Secretary of State. Someone expressed surprise at Walpole's choosing so 'insignificant' a man. 'Oh, said Lady Mary, I can account for it. If I was a Country Gentlewoman and came suddenly to a great fortune and set up my Coach, I should like to show it in the neighbouring village—but I woud not carry you with me, for people might doubt whether it was your Coach or mine—but if you woud let me carry your Cat with me, I woud; for Nobody woud think it was the Cat's Coach.'[61]

After her sister's departure she went to Bath, and attended Steele's *Conscious Lovers* (which was having a wild success there) no less than four times. According to Lady Lechmere (who agreed with her in disliking the play), she said it 'was like so many doses of physic. She declared that the reason why she had submitted was obedience to Mr. Wortley, whose friend Sir Richard was.' She may have been riled less by the play's uplifting sentimental ideology in general than by its extreme endorsement of paternal authority over children's marriage choices. She was by no means intolerant of sentiment, for she later maintained that 'whoever did not cry at George Barnwell must deserve to be hanged'.[62]

Careerism was a favourite target of her wit. Late in the unhappy year 1727, Lord Pomfret became Master of the Horse to Caroline when she became queen; the story went that he had 'bought' the post from Charlotte Clayton

for a pair of diamond ear-rings, of £1400 value. One day that she wore them at a visit at old Marlbor's [*sic*], as soon as she was gone, the Duchess said to Lady Mary Wortley, 'how can that woman have the impudence to go about in that bribe?' 'Madam,' said Lady Mary, 'how would you have people know where wine is to be sold, unless there is a sign hung out?'[63]

This was not the furthest her wicked tongue would go. Her granddaughter told a story of her impatience with her old friend Lady Rich, who as 'a decayed beauty' was affecting a more and more juvenile style. Lady Rich affected to have no idea who was Master of the Rolls (a high legal

<hr/>

[61] Newcastle's appointment was 2 Apr. 1724 (Horace Walpole, 'Book of Materials 1771', vol. 2. 73, told by Lord John Cavendish). Hervey agreed as to Walpole's motives (1931: 6–7).

[62] Lady Lechmere to Sarah Marlborough in Reid 1915: 444; *E&P* 52. MWM ranked an emotive scene in Dryden's *Don Sebastian* as a touchstone equal to Lillo's Barnwell. Since Sarah Fielding draws the same moral point from the same two plays (*David Simple*, Bk. I, ch. ii), the two cousins may have exchanged opinions. A letter from a lady at Bath to a 'Lady Mary——' (*British Journal*, 6 June 1724) is probably not to MWM.

[63] Horace Walpole (who had it from his father) to Mann, 7 Jan. 1742 (*Corr.* xvii. 276–7).

position held by Sir Joseph Jekyll). Lady Mary proposed the most unlikely candidate she could think of, and got the company's laugh on her side. Lady Rich persisted: 'I dare say I ask a mighty silly question; but, pray now, what is it to be Master of the Rolls?' Lady Mary could not resist: 'Why, madam, he superintends all the French rolls that are baked in London; and without him you would have no bread and butter for your breakfast.' Lady Rich was reduced to flirting her fan and complaining prettily about Lady Mary's '*wit*'. Lady Mary moved in for the kill. Pretending to be fifteen, she said, was quite all right: '*that* every body must approve of; it is quite fair: but, indeed, indeed, one need not be five years old.'[64]

She was an active literary patron as well as a conversationalist. She read a draft of a verse-tragedy, *The Brothers*, by Addison's protégé Edward Young, and proposed a more active role for its heroine. Young responded with a contorted expression of hope that the weaknesses she had spotted might escape the general public. He then decided to take Holy Orders, and left his tragedy unstaged for thirty years.[65] It seems that, unlike Addison years before, he resented Lady Mary's criticism (though he stayed in touch, since he saw enough of her daughter as a girl to form a high opinion of her). He put a female critic into *The Universal Passion*, satire vi, on women. He calls her Daphne; but since she sits with 'legs tost high on her Sophee' she must be *the* female critic who had been in Turkey. Young mocks her dogmatic pronouncements about literature, which are listened to only because of her beauty.[66] Lady Mary left no known comment on this poem. She was later unenthusiastic about another of Young's tragedies, *The Revenge*. He for his part grew even more censorious of her. The scholar Edmond Malone reported that he kept till shortly before his death 'a great number' of letters from her; he then destroyed them, as 'too *indelicate* for public inspection'.[67]

She offered patronage, too, to Richard Savage, who is famous today less for his poetry than for his claim to be the rejected bastard of a peeress and a peer, and for Samuel Johnson's life of him. There were several possible channels between him and Lady Mary. His alleged mother lived at Twickenham. His patron the Duke of Rutland was Lady Mary's friend and distant cousin. His later patron, Lord Tyrconnel, had married that Nelly Brownlow who had hobnobbed over the garden wall with the child Mary Pierrepont. Savage's associates Young and Aaron Hill were known to Lady Mary; he had endless help from Hill with *Miscellaneous Poems*, the edited volume

---

[64] *E&P* 44–5. [65] *CL* ii. 34–5. Young seems to have asked Pope too for advice (Pope, *Corr.* ii. 171).
[66] Pub. 1727; coll. as *The Love of Fame*, 1730.
[67] MWM thought *The Revenge* not up to Otway (Young 1971: 233, 511; *CL* ii. 400–1; Prior 1860: 456).

(mainly written by others) which he dedicated to her.[68] He was perhaps the first to use inoculation as metaphor, in an odd poem entitled 'The Animal-cule', in which the germ of patronage passes from one body to another like a virus, from Maecenas to Rutland. Knowing his methods, one may suspect that its own germ was a pre-existing desire to please Lady Mary.

Savage had his eye on Tyrconnel as a patron from 1724, when his collection was already in press. When it reached print, in handsome large-paper format with title-page in black and red, it contained his first outspoken public attack on his supposed mother, and his effusive dedication to Lady Mary. For this—which, in Johnson's words, 'flatters without reserve, and . . . with very little art'—Lady Mary sent him a few guineas via Young. Her aunt Cheyne and sister Gower subscribed too.[69]

Among Savage's burgeoning relations with patrons and proxy mothers, this one did not go far, for various reasons. *Miscellaneous Poems* aimed a second compliment at Lady Mary: in a poem to Hill's wife, Miranda, Savage says she has Martha Fowke Sansom's poetic talent—and Lady Mary's soul. Savage obviously spoke truth when he said he did not know her personally: it was not good tactics to lump her together with bourgeois women (one of them less than respectable) in praise not of her writing but theirs. And though she would have approved his chiding the 'loud *Pamphleteers*' against inoculation, she would not have approved his overriding allegiance to Pope or his helping hand in compiling the *Dunciad Variorum*.[70] Savage went on to praise 'Fair *Wortley*'s angel-Accent, Eyes, and Mind' in *The Wanderer*, an ambitious poem dedicated to Tyrconnel;[71] but this time she seems not to have rewarded him.

Early in 1727 she began helping a more congenial young author. Her second cousin Henry Fielding, one of a family whose inoculations she had probably forwarded, approached her with three acts of a MS comedy entitled *Love in Several Masques*. She read them, and was impressed. That autumn he first appeared in print; he also finished his play. Her influence secured it a hearing at Drury Lane, where it opened on 16 February 1728, shortly after the premiere of the smash-hit *Beggar's Opera*. Lady Mary

[68] Savage himself wrote only fourteen poems in the volume. Hill drummed up many of its subscribers; his name might have been more appropriate for its title-page than Savage's (Brewster 1913: 154).

[69] Johnson 1905: ii. 343. MWM's library in 1739 included two copies of the *Miscellaneous Poems*, probably the form suppressed at Tyrconnel's wish, and the revised version with controversial items dropped: Feb. and Sept. 1726. The later edition revises the dedication and includes Ladies Gower and Cheyne among subscribers brought in by the *Plain Dealer*'s efforts. I have not found the 1728 edn. mentioned by Tracy (1963: 75, 77–8; Holmes 1993: 92–3; Wh MS M 135).

[70] Tracy 1963: 66, 75–6; Savage 1962: 63, 70; *Authors of the Town*, 1725 (not in *Miscellaneous Poems*); TE v, pp. xxv–xxvii.

[71] Savage 1962: 139.

'gamely' attended two of the four performances of *Love in Several Masques*. Fielding printed it at once, dedicated to her. Unlike Savage, he knew how to praise. He enthused about the learning which she had managed to amass in 'those short Intervals You can be supposed to have had to yourself, amid the Importunities of all the polite Admirers and Professors of Wit and Learning'.[72]

Her social and intellectual life extended beyond her own nation. In 1726, both before and after her father's death, she corresponded with the poet Jean Baptiste Rousseau, whom she knew from Vienna in 1716 and probably from his London visit which began in December 1722. She regaled him with English politics in terms which permitted him to take an anti-court, pro-independent line in response. He relayed news of her Vienna acquaintance the duc d'Aremberg and of the opera singer Faustina Bordoni, thanked her for introducing him to Mary Anne Cantillon, and sent her a mini-fable about the genealogy of Wisdom.[73] The next year she may have met a Swiss medical student named Théodore Tronchin. While in England he visited Pope at Twickenham, and observed the practice of inoculation; he was to become the leading inoculator on the Continent.[74]

Still more important was her meeting with Voltaire, who came to England as an exile in May 1726 with a letter of introduction from Horatio Walpole to Newcastle. After a spell in retirement at Wandsworth, south of London, brushing up his English, he began making intellectual and social contacts. He met people important to Lady Mary (like Sloane, Congreve, Samuel Clarke, and Hervey), people she disliked (like Swift), and some who *had* been her friends (like Pope and Gay). His epic *Henriade* benefited from Sir Robert Walpole's personal help with its subscription list, and was floridly dedicated to Queen Caroline. His tour of country houses in the summer of 1727 included those of Peterborough, Hervey, and Sarah, Duchess of Marlborough. Since Voltaire was pursuing an interest in Islam and the orient, he had reason to seek out Lady Mary. She subscribed for two copies of the *Henriade*; he read her verse epistle 'To [William Feilding]'.[75]

---

[72] Battestins 1989: 56–7, 59–60, 61, 63; *CL* iii. 312. Fielding's letter to MWM pub. as written in [Feb. 1732] about *The Modern Husband* was probably written in autumn 1727 about *Love in Several Masques* (*CL* ii. 96; Battestin 1989: 'Dating Fielding's Letters', 246–8).

[73] *CL* ii. 59–60, 67–8; Wade 1931: 44.

[74] He also met and learned from Mead (Tronchin 1906: 4–7; Janssens 1981: 248).

[75] Voltaire got on better with Gay than with Pope. He later kept up his friendship with Hervey (Barling 1968: 13–27; Pomeau 1953: 67–76; Pomeau 1985–95: 176–9, 186–7, 226, 399–400; André-Michel Rousseau 1976: 145–7). MWM was pressingly invited by Sarah to Blenheim this year (Pierpont Morgan MS). She shared the *Henriade*'s anticlericalism. Voltaire probably read her poem in MS rather than in Hammond's six-year-old *Miscellany*.

In the summer of 1728, as Lady Mary battled her way through the horrors
of her sister's custody case, Voltaire was back at Wandsworth drafting his
praise of Lady Mary and Caroline, as the mothers of inoculation, in the work
which became *Letters concerning the English Nation*.[76] A further anecdote
about Lady Mary and Voltaire, told by Sir James Caldwell twenty years later,
invites some scepticism. Caldwell addressed his somewhat ham-fisted French
to Montesquieu, whom he saw as a rival of Voltaire, and willing to hear ill of
him. If his account is true, then Voltaire's admiration for Lady Mary survived
some rough critical handling (something he usually took badly). Sir James
said Voltaire took her the Milton section of his English-language *Essays on
Epic Poetry* for her opinion. After reading a few pages she told him she could
hardly believe he had written it: the English was too good to be his own but
too poor to be by 'une personne distinguee'. On the other hand, she said, it
was like his other works in being 'affroyable'. This might be a play on words:
Voltaire's frighteningly bad English matched his frightening ideas.[77]

Lady Mary's meeting with Montesquieu is sadly undocumented: his
grandson burned his journal of his visit to England (November 1729 to
1731). But he must have met her as an author, since he made extracts from her
works and wrote in his notebook an analysis of her Rochefoucauld essay. It
may have been at his behest that she subscribed to Pierre Coste's splendid
edition of Montaigne's *Essais*, the first in French since the Papal Index listed
the work in 1676.[78]

⁓⁂⁓

The last of Lady Mary's letters to sister Mar was the one about George II's
coronation, in October 1727. Lady Mar's situation was then much as before.
Grange was still keeping her posted on his badgering of Walpole—whom he
trusted less and less—about pardoning her husband. The Mars were in dire
financial straits, pathetically reporting to Grange how they knew 'money
is hard to be got' but had 'nothing to live on, and had not the Banker
Mr. Allexander been so kind to advance us, we must have starv'd'. The
house in Whitehall was too run down to let, and they could not afford
repairs. Lord Erskine had taken to gambling. Lord Mar was suffering as
never before from 'Maladie Du Pays': 'this winter is like to be the most
disagreeable to him he ever yet pass'd a broad.'

---

[76] See pp. 221–2.
[77] Caldwell says she knew Voltaire well and disliked him. This passage immediately precedes two pages
torn out (1746, Bagshawe MSS B 3/7/1).
[78] Shackleton 1988: 159; Shackleton 1961: 133; see p. 472; Montaigne, London, 1724: not the edn. she later
owned (Wh MS M 135).

Then it appeared that Lady Mar had a 'Journey propos'd for her' to England. Mar consulted Grange on whether she should go, and when, and how much it would benefit their affairs. He doubted whether she could go, but only because of money, not health. He wished 'her friend' (probably her father) were 'still in being', and he consoled himself with hopes of her going in the spring. Lady Mar's last surviving letter to Lady Mary was the despairing one about laziness and stupidity, writing to no one and going nowhere. But she said more about money troubles than emotional ones.[79]

During the winter that followed, reports began to emanate from Englishmen abroad, like Atterbury and Horatio Walpole, that she was in a dangerous and lamentable state. Lord Mar was later said to have 'tried the physicians there but to no purpose'. Grange assured the Paris banker Alexander Alexander of his great concern at her indisposition, and after conferring with Erskine of Dun he issued instructions, if necessary, to advance money to persons in charge of her rather than to herself.[80] Having visited London, he reported that her distress (probably emotional rather than financial) was common talk there at the end of the year.

By 10 January 1728 Alexander Raitt, having travelled from Scotland to London, was ready to leave for Paris to bring her 'home'.[81] Six weeks later she was judged a little better, but there were still fears of a relapse. It was decided that she should set out with Raitt as soon as she was well enough. She arrived in England on 9 March, but 'so disorder'd in her Head, that it is believed she'll scarce ever recover her Senses'.[82]

[79] Mar MSS GD 15/1315/2, 15/1317, 15/1321; H MS 77. 112–13 (Nov. 1727).
[80] Atterbury 1869: ii. 107, 244; petition for lunacy commission, Halsband MSS; Mar MSS GD 124/2/203/1–7. Years of trouble flowed from a promissory note for £1,000 issued by 'Mar/F. Mar' to Alexander Alexander on 22 Aug. 1727 (Mar MSS GD 124/2/228).
[81] An advance of £100 more from Alexander Tait, Edinburgh merchant, followed on the 16th (2/203/8).
[82] *London Evening Post*, 5 Mar., *Whitehall Evening Post*, 12 Mar. 1728.

16

1728

༈

Lady Mar, Pope: 'Scenes of Sorrow'

THIS year marked a low point for Lady Mary. Her sister Mar descended into madness; Pope delivered his first jabs or pinpricks. These two matters became connected, for it was in Lady Mary's family relationships (with her sister and her son) that Pope found a twist of the peculiar and individual for his otherwise hoarily generic charges that she was dirty, promiscuous, and vain—or in other words a true specimen of the learned lady famed in song and story. The title of this chapter is the way Montagu summed up life in this 'World below' when she commemorated Congreve (a man from the lost age of honour) and praised him as the very opposite of Pope.[1]

The retrieval of young Edward opened the year, duly delivered up to his family by the navy.[2] What was done with him next is unclear. Lady Mary said he has 'place'd' at sea (as the advertisements had promised) but 'deserted it'. By the time she wrote this, twelve years later, she felt her husband had been too lenient: the boy should have been 'forc'd' to stay with what he had chosen. According to Forster, it was decided to send him abroad; 'the West Indies were chosen as the place of retreat'; there he was to 'renew his classical studies'. Forster says they stayed there several years, Curling that they returned in 1730. Nothing more is heard of young Edward's childhood: very soon he was married.[3]

Pope's accusations of promiscuity renew a question already raised: did Lady Mary have lovers? Popularly this becomes a leading question: 'Did she have a great many lovers?' The popular answer is, 'Dozens . . . How can you

---

[1] Congreve d. Jan. 1729. MWM's elegy fuses the personal and the generic. She deleted praise of his keen critical 'sight', which was mournfully ironic: he had gone blind (*E&P* 246–7).

[2] A posthumous account says his parents 'received him with the joy equal to that of the father of the prodigal son in the gospel' (*The Weekly Magazine, or Edinburgh Amusement*, 1776: 32. 341).

[3] *CL* ii. 250; *The Scots Magazine*, 1777: 39. 625–6; Curling 1954: 44 ff. For the choice of the Caribbean see p. 302.

doubt it?' This reflects, as often, the answerer's preference.[4] Not a scrap of solid evidence remains. By the time of Horace Walpole's later but similar charges, Lady Mary had indeed been madly, intoxicatedly, and documentedly in love—once. Not that Walpole knew about this: he, like Pope, was thinking generically.

Before 1728 hints of an adulterous love-life are very slim. Lady Mary's letters to her sister are the only source; as yet 'the world' was not talking against her, though it had raised its eyebrows at some of her poems. Hints amount to a generally sexualized tone and a few oblique references to unspecified emotional turmoil. Lady Mary mentions 'the Things one can't do and the Things one must not do'. She confesses that she has a less voracious appetite for diversions than formerly, and that she might come in time to feed on butcher's meat rather than wild game; but this should probably be read as referring to the satirist's pursuit of 'Folly as it flies', which is a regular theme in her letters.[5] Her episode of 'Distraction' in May 1725 has already been noted. If this sounds like love, what it does *not* sound like is a woman in love for whom this is a regular and frequent occurrence.

There is, of course, another possibility besides men. Lois Kathleen Mahaffey speculates that Lady Mary and Maria Skerrett were secretly lovers, and that plumbing this secret was what shocked Pope beyond recovery, causing him to pillory Lady Mary at once and prepare to pillory Maria in 1738 in 'the triumph of Vice'. But again evidence is lacking; none of Pope's lines on either woman suggests such a thing. Quite possibly Lady Mary *was* covertly accused in print of being a lesbian; but that was after Pope's entirely different charges had made her fair game.[6] She did keep copies of a couple of lesbian poems, one of them by Hervey; they seem to refer to specific persons, but not Skerrett.[7] Any evidence was burned by Skerrett before her marriage. But Montagu's known poems to her turn on their shared discussion of men in general and of Skerrett's lover the Prime Minister in particular. They give no hint of an erotic relationship. When Lady Mary fell for Algarotti, it was only a couple of months before she broached the idea of their living together, revolutionizing her life entirely to do so. There is no sign of any such upheaval in the 1720s or early 1730s.

[4] Novel by Virginia Gay, 1992, 1995: 160: question asked by a woman and answered by a man at MWM's Belgrade Village villa during the 19th century.

[5] *CL* ii. 30, 44; Pope, *Essay on Man*, 1733–4, i. 13.

[6] Pope, *Epilogue to the Satires*, Dialogue I, 141–70; Mahaffey 1963; see pp. 345–6. In 1726, when Pope was on dining terms with the Prime Minister, he anxiously besought Fortescue to repair any damage done by the reporting of an innocent word indiscreetly dropped. This might be *something* about Molly; it could hardly be that MWM was her lover (*Corr*. ii. 368).

[7] H MS 255. 39–41, 60. She compared Molly with Venus in a poem of her own, and kept a poem ascribed to Philip Floyd, which does the same (*E&P* 238–9; H MS 255. 60–1).

That leaves in play, as regards Pope's hatred, the questions 'Why?' and 'When?' The second is at least slightly more open to investigation, and may throw some possible lights on the first.

Their friendship was problematic even in its earliest phase, 1715–18; and Pope's eager manœuvring to procure both her neighbourhood and her portrait in 1719–20 may well have left him feeling he had less control over her than he would have liked. Emotional attraction and turbulence remained between them, as is clear from his undatable, confessedly agitated note which assures her, 'Indeed I truly Esteem you, and Trust in you.'[8]

He had managed, apparently, to juggle his relationships with her and with the Blount sisters. But as early as 1722 he had met a younger and more compliant 'Kinswoman in Apollo': Judith Cowper, later Madan, who promised to fit more snugly into the slot in his life once filled by Lady Mary. In 1717 he had seen in Lady Mary the 'gentleness and serenity' of the moon. By October 1722 he had praised Cowper in verse as the mild and sober moon whose (reflected) light will endure beyond the sunset of the glaring, 'sprightly Sappho', who *forces* love and praise. (He probably knew of Lady Mary's personal devotion to Scudéry's 'Sapho'.)[9] Pope contrasts the two women, charges Montagu with the grave *literary* fault of gender transgression, and redirects towards Cowper the very same tropes in which he had expressed his former homage. Next month he recast the lines of unrequited love which he had written for 'Wortley' that spring, and sent Cowper the new version. Next year he urged Cowper to write 'something in the descriptive way . . . mixd with Vision & Moral'—to rival, perhaps, Montagu's poem of this kind written at Constantinople.[10]

By that year, 1722, a similar sketch of Lady Mary's aggressive attractions had been drawn, not by Pope but by Peterborough, who had succeeded to Jervas as the friend providing Pope's regular base in London. Peterborough, at about sixty-five, had secretly married Lady Mary's protégée Anastasia Robinson, but was making political, pseudo-gallant court to Henrietta Howard. In its best-known versions his jaunty ballad, 'I said to my Heart, between sleeping & waking', compliments Howard by selecting her

---

[8] *Corr.* ii. 62: the assigned date of 1721 is doubtful. He named her as proof that women have brains in 'Sandys's Ghost'; this might have almost any date between 1717 and 1727. In her copy MWM struck out the stanza mentioning her, and the next (TE vi. 173 and n.; Pierpont Morgan MS).

[9] *Corr.* i. 439–40; ii. 138–9; Battestins 1989: 71. Henry Fielding praised MWM as 'Sappho' in 1728; for her devotion see pp. 17–18.

[10] To each in turn he mentioned 'stealing' her picture, and her spoiling him for other company (*Corr.* ii. 142–3, 202). Rumbold notes that he writes to Cowper of melancholy rather than love (1989: 147). Whether or not MWM was in the know, she took an interest in Cowper. She wrote a poem for *her* voice about *her* unsatisfactory lover—apparently Martin Madan, whom she married in Dec. 1723. This both quotes Cowper's work and likens her to Sappho (*E&P* 227–30).

from among other women rejected for this or that imperfection. The spirit and fire of Lady Mary ('our Sappho') *force* admiration in Peterborough's ballad just as in Pope's lines to Cowper that year, while Howard's artless gentility and modest reason arouse unforced love.

Lady Mary kept a copy of this ballad (labelled as Peterborough's) *without* the compliment to Mrs Howard; and she answered it with a quatrain concluding, 'who but a Bawd will design on Threescore?' But she also kept a maddeningly rough, partly illegible draft of a related, longer ballad in Pope's handwriting. This parallels Peterborough's in structure, but differs from it in apparently complimenting Lady Mary herself. It rejects five or more women for 'a Nymph that sate hard by the King' in St James's Chapel, in whom 'Not a Grace, not a Muse, not a Virtue is wanting'. The rough state of Pope's version leaves the reader to guess the identity of 'this Goddess'. Its mutilated last line *might* easily have read '[Lady Mary] I'm sure, won't imagine tis She.'[11]

This *may* have been the source of Peterborough's poem, and it *may* plausibly be the poem which Pope allegedly later circulated in a reworked version which cancelled Lady Mary to compliment Mrs Howard. Horace Walpole (not an ideal witness because of his dates and his prejudice) said that this transfer of a compliment was the germ of the famous quarrel: when Lady Mary saw the new version praising Howard she confronted Pope by sending him 'the original copy in his own handwriting'.[12] Pope's ballad, the twin of Peterborough's, does not survive in complete and final form. But it looks a quite plausible first cause of offence. It had several offspring among Pope's works; and each of these, like Peterborough's version, rebukes assertive women.[13] If this *was* the germ, it was trivial, but perfectly indicative of what was to follow.

The year 1723 brought Atterbury's trial and Bolingbroke's first return to England from banishment: both events to remind Pope and Lady Mary of their deep and serious political differences. She supported Walpole, out of conviction and personal loyalty; to Pope, Walpole became an emblem of bad government and personal evil. Pope's outpourings of love and admiration to the exiled Atterbury (in which he reused imagery prototyped on Lady Mary's 'exile' of 1716) cited the heroic statesman Lord Clarendon—who, in her historiography, was an apologist for the wrong side. Bolingbroke became a fixture in Pope's world, his 'guide, philosopher, and friend', when

[11] Grundy 1969: 461–8; *E&P* 225; Hervey MS 941/69/16.
[12] Walpole, *Corr.* xiv. 243. This parallels Pope's diversion of praise from MWM to Cowper and his matching Kneller's MWM with Jervas's Howard (p. 202).
[13] 'Sylvia. A Fragment' (TE vi. 286–8); *Epistle to a Lady*, 45 ff, 59 ff.

he settled at Dawley in 1725. To Lady Mary he was 'a vile man': contemptible, endlessly treacherous, like a cheap copy of Milton's Satan, his name 'blotted by Cowardice and murder'.[14] She felt similarly about Swift, who was over from Ireland in 1726 visiting Pope at Twickenham. When *Gulliver's Travels* appeared that year, Lady Mary's tartness about it suggested no very friendly feelings for 'the first poet of the Age', whom she believed to share in its authorship with Swift and Arbuthnot. Next year the Pope–Swift *Miscellanies* included in 'Memoirs of P.P.' a send-up of her mentor Burnet, and in *Peri Bathous* gibes at her friends Walpole, Cadogan, and Steele.[15]

Lady Mary and her husband subscribed handsomely to Pope's *Odyssey*. Wortley put his name down for five copies; this was generous, especially if he did not claim all the copies subscribed for. But this commitment may have been made early; Pope had thought of publishing proposals in 1722.[16] The Wortley Montagus ignored his edition of Shakespeare, for which newspapers solicited subscribers in November 1724.[17]

The forms of friendship survived several Twickenham years. In 1723 Lady Mary dashed off a request to Pope for a book, and an offer to call—if he was not well enough to come to her—'having something particular to say to You'. Pope left undated a note in which he asked to bring his mother to visit her, and to beg a favour.[18] In 1724 he apologized to Bathurst for neglecting Lady Mary; although he professed to find her indecipherable, he promised to 'endeavour (for Your sake) to know more of her, than perhaps I might otherwise do'. This sounds uneasy, but not estranged. As late as 1726 Lady Mary was painted by Pope's close friend Jonathan Richardson, and Pope reprinted his 'Epistle to Jervas' with the compliment to '*Wortley's* Eyes' still intact. If this was merely oversight, that was unusual for him. Yet by this time their once close social lives had diverged. Only Bathurst and Congreve remained friends of both.[19]

---

[14] Pope, *Corr.* ii. 167; *Essay on Man*, iv. 390; Spence 1966: 755; note in Guillim 121.

[15] *CL* ii. 71–2; iii. 63. *Peri Bathous* probably does not (as recently suggested) malign MWM's 'Roxana' (Pope 1986: ii. 197–271 *passim*, 268).

[16] Foxon and McLaverty 1991: 91, 99–100.

[17] This was not from allegiance to Pope's editing rival, Lewis Theobald, protégé of MWM's close friend Lady De La Warr: he launched his subscription only in 1730. Lady De La Warr's immense efforts for this subscription contrast with the smaller-scale help (with selling donated 'stationery ware') which she offered a female author, Elizabeth Thomas (Seary 1990: 122; HMC 1901: vi. 29).

[18] *CL* ii. 27–8; *N&Q* 1987: 34. 338. In 1759 MWM jotted 'remarkable Letter' on an apparently quite *un*remarkable note among her papers, concerning Henrietta Marlborough and arrangements to meet. The oddity *may* be Pope's amicable tone, since the hand looks like his (H MS 79. 280–1).

[19] See p. 301. MWM mocked Bathurst's short attention-span in her 'Epistle' to him, but gently; Pope seems to have suggested to him in 1724 that her poem was more fictional than need be. Congreve was hardy enough to remind Pope in May 1727 of the story of Curll's emetic (Pope, *Corr.* ii. 258, 434). *Miscellany Poems*, 5th edn., 1726, included Buckingham's 'Election of a Poet Laureat In 1719', which linked 'the fam'd Lady *Mary*' and Swift as candidates (167, 223).

Lady Mary (she said later) had been warned against Pope by Addison: that is, before 1719. Addison thought Pope's 'appetite to satire' would sooner or later play her 'some devilish trick'. She paid no heed. After their enmity was established fact, various rumours sprang up of her playing tricks on him. One says that when he showed her his epigram on a woman with lovely looks and an ugly mind, Lady Mary retorted thus:

> Had Pope a person equall to his Mind
>   How fatal wou'd he be to Womankind
> But Nature which doth all things well ordain
>   Defac'd the Image and inrich'd the Brain.[20]

Another story has her making a ribald retort when he set up in Twickenham church a memorial to his old nurse, Mary Beach, and her lifelong nurturing care: 'No wonder that he's so stout and so strong, | Since he lugg'd and he tugg'd at the bubby so long.'[21] This would have been less forgiveable than the other. But neither story holds water; and stories emanating from closer to the centre are not much more convincing.

Many suggested causes for their quarrel (whether romantic or literary) are trivial: lamely advanced in default of better. Furthermore, both parties agreed that Pope had dropped the friendship *before* serious offence was given or taken.[22] But his own writings demonstrate that, once roused, his negative feelings about her went immeasurably beyond his other enmities, apparently into real, almost obsessive hatred in the guise of judicial condemnation. Nor was she behindhand in rage. In such a context, every pin-prick was a fresh and grievous offence.[23]

Lady Mary told Spence that on her second attempt to find out (through Arbuthnot) 'why he had left off visiting me', Pope said that she and Hervey 'had pressed him once together . . . to write a satire on some certain persons'; that he refused; that they took offence. This she rejected as false on the grounds that she, Pope, and Hervey were never all together 'in our lives'. This seems to turn on a technicality. But Pope may really have felt her friendship with Hervey as an affront to his masculinity.[24]

---

[20] Spence 1966: 748. One source says Pope's lovely, brainless woman was the Duchess of Queensberry; but his authorship, like MWM's, is dubious (TE vi. 443–4).

[21] Mary Beach d. 5 Nov. 1725. *GM* 1784 first mentioned this couplet as written on the tombstone 'with a piece of chalk' (875).

[22] Pope, *Corr.* iii. 53; Spence 1966: 751. Besides citing the Henrietta Howard poem as cause of the quarrel, Horace Walpole put forward a different one: MWM borrowed a pair of Pope's sheets and returned them unlaundered (*Corr.* xxxiv. 255). This sounds like back-formation from the trope of woman-as-dirt.

[23] *The Rape of the Lock* opened prophetically: 'What dire offence from amorous causes springs, | What mighty contests rise from trivial things.'

[24] Spence 1966: 751; Pope, *Letter to a Noble Lord*, 1733; see p. 335 ff. Mahaffey guesses Griselda Murray as the person Pope was asked to satirize (1963: 160); but Murray remained Hervey's friend.

Alternatively, Lady Mary told Lady Pomfret that Pope was jealous of her friendship with Wharton. Her family, years after her death, believed that her 'own account' declared he had made her an ill-timed '*declaration*' and been met with 'an immoderate fit of laughter'. This cruel snub is implausible. Whether or not *she* was capable of it, Pope was far too self-protective to risk such a declaration; besides, he seems to have nourished romantic feelings in her absence rather than in her presence, which he found unsettlingly independent and assertive. It *is* possible that this romantic story of love rejected is a Chinese-whispers version of something uglier and more complicated: of Lady Mary turning savagely on what she felt as sexual harassment by innuendo. Its outline was undeniably anticipated in an anonymous squib of 1732 which carried no authority at all.[25]

More probably Pope's first printed accusation voices, more or less, the truth: that sexual issues inflamed a quarrel based in authorship issues; that she was desirable and unattainable, and made him feel humiliated; that he felt her poetic creativity trespassed on the prerogative of his.

✼

Pope's first accusation appeared in the Pope–Swift *Miscellanies*, volume iii, on 8 March 1728, in a poem entitled 'The Capon's Tale: To a Lady who father'd her Lampoons upon her Acquaintance'. Lady Mary is represented twice over in this piece: as a Yorkshire yeoman's wife (the right county!) who keeps poultry, and as the sexiest of her hens, 'With Eyes so piercing, yet so pleasant, | You would have sworn this Hen a Pheasant.' The hen is besieged by cocks—'Lord! what a Brustling up of Feathers! . . . such Flutt'ring, Chuckling, Crowing'—and hatches 'more Chicks than she could rear'. The farmer's wife therefore selects a capon as her 'Dupe', gets him drunk, makes his rump itch by applying nettles, and palms the chicks on, or under, him as his own.

The moral is plain: 'Such, Lady *Mary*, are your Tricks; | But since you hatch, pray own your Chicks.' So are many of the implications. 'And not a Cock but would be treading'; 'Nor like your Capons, serve your Cocks.' Lady Mary is a society coquette, says the first line; the second might be a gibe at her entertaining castrato singers, or it might be an offensive reference to Hervey. The fable also implies that females need fertilization by males for literary production as for reproduction. Lady Mary kept an undated draft of this poem written in Pope's hand. It is headed 'To Lady Mary Wortley', and purports to be the work of two cocks (himself and Gay?). No example springs

<hr>

[25] *E&P* 37; see p. 333.

to mind of her writing a poem and palming it off as someone else's, since the *Court Poems*. As a squib in MS, part of a wit's life of warfare upon earth, 'To Lady Mary Wortley' might be taken as friendly raillery. As a printed statement for all the world to read, 'The Capon's Tale' was a slap in the face.[26]

But Lady Mary may not have taken much notice. When this volume appeared, she can be assumed to have regained her equanimity after her son's return and after the news (not deeply upsetting) of her stepmother's death in Paris in February.[27] But her sister Mar was newly arrived from France, in a condition Lady Mary had never seen her in before.

Nothing in the surviving papers about Lady Mar's madness explains what form it took. She had long been subject to depression; presumably this was something more. But whether she saw visions or heard voices, whether she was silent or raving, suicidal or amnesiac or apathetic, is not recorded. The issue of whether she had lucid intervals became hopelessly enmeshed in the issue of whether, during such intervals, she had expressed a wish to live in Scotland.[28] Lady Mary came to believe that

Madness is as much a corporal Distemper as the Gout or Asthma, never occasion'd by affliction, or to be cur'd by the Enjoyment of their extravagant wishes. Passion may indeed bring on a Fit, but the Disease is lodg'd in the Blood, and it is not more ridiculous to attempt to releive the Gout by an embrodier'd Slipper than to restore Reason by the Gratification of wild Desires.

Placement in an asylum was all that could be done for such persons.[29]

She wrote this about Richardson's mad heroine Clementina, but she must surely have had her sister in mind. It seems odd of her to deny the apparently obvious link between Lady Mar's afflictions and her madness. If the disease expressed itself in wild desires, what may they have been? Her husband's pardon, or the restoration of his estates, or the dissolution of her marriage, or the return from the grave of her father or her sister Gower? To wish for the cancellation of some part of her experience since her marriage, though not rational, might surely have been natural. Her husband admitted that living on the Continent had proved 'inconvenient' to her. Later he admitted he had been criticized for letting her travel to England 'in the Condition she was'; but he said that no man 'of tollerable good Nature . . . could have done Otherwise'.[30] This sounds as if her material circumstances had at least aggravated her illness.

---

[26] Griffith 1922–7; Mack 1985: 456; TE vi. 256–8; Mahaffey 1963: 78, who notes that the draft was originally among MWM's papers.

[27] She d. 23 Feb. 1728, OS (BL MS Eg. 3526), and was buried at Holme Pierrepont on 3 May.

[28] 12 July 1728, PRO C211/8/16.   [29] *CL* iii. 96.

[30] Copy, 16 Dec. 1729, from Antwerp, where Mar had fled from his Paris creditors (GD 124/15/1362).

In any case, Lady Mary was discovering what she had never thought to see: a condition of life in which her sister's company could be no consolation to her, but only a grief and a burden. However painful in itself, Lady Mar's condition caused further pain by its entanglement with her husband's financial and political straits. He hoped that her being in England would help him to follow. Raitt, bringing Lady Mar back from France, carried a letter from Mar to Horatio Walpole (brother of Lady Mary's friend Sir Robert). Mar expatiated, no doubt sincerely, on his distress at his wife's illness and his grief at being unable to travel with her and care for her in 'Britain'. He defended the decision to send her over as likely to 'contribute greatly to the recovery of her perfect hailth'. He excused himself for failing to give the king or the government advance notice of her journey, insisted that she had never meddled in politics, and renewed his request for leave to return. He had no ambitious motives, he said, but only wanted to attend to his ruined fortune and his long-neglected gardens. Implicit here is his desire to win some advantage from his wife's illness, without being seen to do so. The month of Lady Mar's arrival, Grange kept up his pressure on Sir Robert Walpole for Mar's pardon.[31]

At this time when Lady Mar's 'distress' was widely known in London, and 'all Physicians' agreed that her native air might help, Lady Mary tried by letter to influence 'the Pilot's brother' (i.e. Horatio Walpole) against Mar's return. Mar's son, Lord Erskine, is the witness here (not a disinterested witness, but then nobody *was* disinterested). Erskine wrote from Scotland that Lady Mary 'exclaim'd against' Mar's ill treatment and unkindness as being to blame for his wife's condition. (He also alleged that she had wanted her sister not brought to England, but intercepted and turned back.) Horatio Walpole, said Erskine, reported all this most politely to 'the man he met 'twixt Calais and Paris' (Mar), 'and bid him make what use of it he pleased'. Mar, said Erskine, had written forgivingly to Lady Mary, who did not deserve such forbearance.[32]

Lady Mar was re-entering an all too familiar wasteland between the entrenched battle-lines of the English and the Scots sides of her family. She did not stay with her sister, but in lodgings in Marlborough Street. Her dilapidated house in the Privy Gardens, Whitehall, was vacated by a tenant on Lady Day—25 March—and a start was made on plastering and painting it.[33] By the time the bill for all this had come in, Erskine had torn himself

---

[31] March (copy), Mar MSS GD 124/15/1330; 23 Mar. 1728, GD 124/15/1329.
[32] Erskine to Grange, 4 Apr. 1728, Mar MSS GD 124/15/1331.
[33] On 5 Apr., for £14. 15s. (GD 124/17/647/2, 124/16/47/1).

away from Scottish politics and galloped south, with some delay from flooded roads. He reached London on 4 April and 'went as soon as I could get my boots off to the Sollicitor's'.[34] He reported that Lady Mary was 'working with all her might', in 'the most oddest and most unexpected manner', to get her sister's jointure placed in the hands of a third party ('whom I suppose she intends to be herself'), for the sole use of Lady and not Lord Mar. To this end she had 'already begun to tamper with Lawyers'.[35] Erskine justly feared that if Lady Mar were to begin absorbing all her own money, it would mean 'utter ruin' for his father and himself.

In this emergency fellow Scots (Lord Loudoun and the Baillie family, presumably including Griselda Murray) offered Mar's camp at least moral support. Nevertheless Erskine urgently summoned his uncle Grange to London. Grange had sickness in his family, and was fighting off a political smear campaign: he did not reach London till early June. These were eventful months for Lady Mary. She had not yet received her father's legacy: now legal opinion ruled against her putting it into a mortgage on Wortley's estate, i.e. lending her or her children's money to the husband and father.[36] This ruling (pointing the contrast between her own financially protected situation and her sister's) was handed down on 18 May 1728. That same day came Pope's next mention of her, in the *Dunciad*, version one.

Whereas 'The Capon's Tale' had flaunted her name and fame, the *Dunciad* at least pretended to conceal its reference. The goddess Dulness is advising her son always to lay the blame on other people. Bawds, she says, retail their human wares under the names of great ladies, so that any aggrieved, infected customer—say a 'hapless Monsieur' in Paris—will blame his wrongs not on their whores but on 'Duchesses and Lady Mary's'.[37] Logically, therefore, some nameless plebeians have committed the crimes for which the Monsieur rails at noblewomen. But poetic effect does not work by logic: reading, Lady Mary must have been startled at the implied evocation of Rémond's complaints. Logically, the *Dunciad* presents the complaints as misdirected, but it jarringly recalls that they were made, and

[34] Grange had joined the Whig opposition and was running Erskine for Stirling, against Lord Ilay's candidate. With 51 voters and skulduggery on each side, Erskine lost by 5 votes. The Solicitor-General, Charles Talbot, later Baron Talbot (uncle to the writer Catherine Talbot), was 'an especial foe to professional chicane' and 'sought, perhaps rashly, to infuse a little reason into equity' (*DNB*).

[35] 4 Apr. 1728. EWM had just been made by the Speaker to 'ask pardon of the House' for stirring up trouble: he urged Pulteney to challenge Robert Walpole to a duel (Sedgwick 1970).

[36] GD 124/15/1331, 15/1337 (Grange, on oath); Grange 1843: xiv; Thomas Lutwyche, 18 May 1728, BL Eg. MS 3531. 99–100; see p. 252.

[37] *Dunciad*, i. 127–8. The *Dunciad* had been years in writing. A draft further used MWM as 'W—', an unkempt would-be poet, oddly linked with the successful middle-class dramatist Mary Pix (TE v. 112, 162; Rumbold 1989: 155–6). 'Duchesses' was common slang for whores.

that they linked her name with those of 'batter'd jades'. Pope knew her well enough to know what would hurt. She had been upset when her son made himself 'the Talk of the whole Nation'.[38] Her sister was filling that slot at the moment. She would soon be filling it herself.

Printed response to *The Dunciad* began ten days later, with Curll's *Compleat Key* to it. That does not mention Lady Mary; but her name was not long absent from the paper wars which dogged Pope for the rest of his life. He very soon became convinced that she had taken revenge—in *A Popp upon Pope*, published on the first of June.[39] This wickedly funny prose squib purports to relate how the poet, while strolling in Ham Walks (across the Thames from Twickenham), suffered a 'horrid and barbarous Whipping' by two gentlemen in revenge for lampooning them. Named characters in the story include Dr Arbuthnot and Martha Blount, who rescues Pope by carrying him in her apron like a baby. This miniaturizing is in tune with Lady Mary's later methods; so is the pretended concern for Catholics, as fellow Christians who ought not to be persecuted. The story of brutal physical chastisement and the victim's consequent madness owes much to Pope's literary treatment of Curll in 1716; the phrase 'horrid and barbarous' is an echo. All in all, it is not impossible that Lady Mary wrote this pamphlet. But if she did, what can one make of its reference to 'the learned Dr. *Hale*, of *Lincoln's-Inn-Fields* . . . who doubts not (God willing) but to restore the poor Man to his Senses'? Richard Hale, a respected and progressive 'mad doctor', was soon to have Lady Mar under his care, if indeed he had not already.

Exposure of Lady Mary's name continued. Her initials appeared that month in a list of those abused by Pope and Swift: it begins with GOD ALMIGHTY and names no other female except the queen.[40] But again more serious matters were claiming her attention: Grange had arrived in London. His first port of call was Lord Gower; but Gower had left London for the summer. His next was Lady Cheyne; but her husband had died on 26 May and she said she could see no one.[41] There was nowhere to go next but Lady Mary; and she, said Grange, 'was pleas'd to be so very angry and to raill so heartily' against Lord Mar that he resolved not to visit her again. His legal deposition setting forth all this was carefully calculated to justify his proceedings later in June; nevertheless it sounds plausible so far. Lady Mary must have sorely needed the relief of railing.

Grange explained that he next consulted 'his Friends and such as wish'd

---

[38] *CL* ii. 82.

[39] Guerinot 1969: 114–16. Pope complained to Robert Walpole of this as MWM's work (*Corr.* iii. 53).

[40] *A Popp*, 6–7; *A Compleat Collection* . . ., 1728: 51–2; Guerinot 1969: 116–22.

[41] GEC. His death is wrongly dated in several sources.

well to my Lady Mar and had been long intimate with her'—that is, Mrs Murray and her parents. They advised that both her health and 'Estate' would benefit from being at 'Alloa in Scotland, an Ancient and fine Seat of her Husband's Family'. Here she would 'live in great Respect, be carefully attended, and have the advice and direction of very skillfull Physicians'. Finally, Lady Mar 'her self was mighty well pleas'd to go to Alloa, and was very desireous to set out soon' in order to travel with Griselda Murray and the Baillies, who were to leave soon for Scotland.

The source of all information about Lady Mar's departure/abduction is Grange's affidavit.[42] On this, its second page, he did a good deal of editing. He inserted the detail that Alloa was 'in a healthfull air' and deleted the statement that Lady Mar 'testifyed no uneasyness but a little at the length of the journy'. He deleted reference to affidavits by Lady Grizel Baillie, Griselda Murray, and Alexander Raitt, and added that the journey was designed to be 'in every point . . . most commodious and decent for my Lady and most for her Satisfaction', that she spoke with pleasure of it, and that her daughter and stepson were eventually to join her at Alloa.

On Thursday, 20 June, the journey began. Lady Mar was conducted from her lodgings by Lady Grizell, Mrs Murray, Raitt, Erskine, and her daughter Lady Frances, now nearly thirteen. Grange, having stood by till she was about to enter the coach, followed the party later to Barnet, eleven miles north of London, where they all spent the night. Next morning at breakfast, said Grange, 'my Lady was well and easy, and talk'd . . . about several passt things and with good Memmory and judgement'. He returned to London confident that she and her 'jointure' payments would remain hence forth at Alloa.

But at Stevenage, twenty miles further on, the coach party was overtaken by a group on horseback: Lady Mary, attended by a tipstaff employed by the Lord Chief Justice, Lord Raymond,[43] flourishing a warrant to bring her sister back to London. Grange claimed she had secured her warrant by falsely swearing that her lunatic sister had been carried off 'by she knew not whom nor whither but suppos'd to Scotland', and that she had deliberately misrepresented a group of caring friends and relatives as 'Strangers'. The journey, said Grange, had not been clandestine, but had been spoken of as openly as was 'discreet'. He sharpened his case in revision, asserting in the margin that Lady Mary had known of the intended journey for nearly a week, and instead of objecting straight away had 'thought fit to take a harsher method and more disturbing to her sister'.

[42] Mar MS GD 124/15/1337.
[43] The *DNB* credits Raymond (a Tory appointed in 1725) with 'great learning' and 'strict, impartial, and painstaking administration of justice'.

The rest of the day was not to be any less harsh or disturbing. After the long haul back to London, Lady Mary took her sister not to her Marlborough Street lodgings but to her own house in Covent Garden (or 'the House of her Husband Mr Wortley Mountague', as Grange accurately calls it). Grange maintained that Lady Mary 'would not allow' Lady Mar's own servants to wait on her, and put Raitt out of the house.

Meanwhile Grange had had time to verify the terms of the warrant, and finding it 'was to put My Lady Mar in Statu quo', he at once prepared to go with official backing and get her returned to her own lodgings. Lady Mary *may* have tried to throw him off the scent; in any case Lady Mar was soon moved back to her former lodgings, and Grange, Lady Grizell, and Lady Grizell's other daughter Lady Binning were all sitting there with her.

To them entered Lady Mary, who, reported Grange, 'said things which he conceiv'd could not but be very grievous and disturbing to her Sister'. Grange remarked that it was too bad, after upsetting her poor sister all day, to go on doing so at night, and persuaded Lady Mary 'to walk into another Room', where she 'was pleas'd to treat him still more uncivilly and rudely' than before.[44]

Grange's self-righteousness seems to rise straight off his page, along with Lady Mary's rage and frustration. No parallel self-justification of hers survives. There can be no doubt that she acted disturbingly for her sister; on the other hand it is hardly credible that Lady Mar really wanted to go to Alloa. To some extent Lady Mary had inherited their father's role in her sister's life: caring for her material interests as distinct from those of her stepson and her husband (who made no distinction between his interests and hers, or between his love for her and his need for her income). It seems that Lady Mary sometimes let her sister's emotional well-being come second to practical arrangements; it is certain that she sometimes threatened that well-being by failing to control her temper. But she cared more, and needed the money less, than did the other side.

Midsummer had come. Lord Monson named Monday, 24 June, as the date 'when her Ladyship was put under the Guardianship of Lady Mary Wortley her sister'. Monson, who had declined Lady Mary's request to act as trustee for Lady Mar, found himself concerned in her affairs anyway as a trustee of her father's will.[45] He drew up a careful accounting between Lady Mar and her stepson Erskine for the previous four years, and concluded that Erskine owed her almost £400. This, however, was just the beginning. Of a further seventeen items of Erskine's expenses charged to her during that time

---

[44] Grange, Mar MS GD 124/15/1337.   [45] 14 July [1728], *CL* ii. 88; Monson MSS 10/3/9.

(totalling £5767. 13s. 3d.), Monson queried six items, or more than a third. Beside one sum after another stand the notes of his dogged insistence that these expenses had nothing to do with Lady Mar and ought not to be charged to her. With the silent eloquence of the bottom line, Monson's accounts explain why Grange and Erskine objected to Lady Mary as her sister's guardian.[46]

Lady Mary's next move was to petition for a commission of lunacy to rule on whether her sister was insane. The petition was heard on 3 July 1728 at the Lord Chancellor's house.[47] It was recorded that Lord Mar had sent his wife into the hands of Grange and Erskine, but that her sister Lady Mary 'had in some measure the care of her'; that Grange and Erskine had attempted to take her to Scotland without Lady Mary's 'privity or knowledge', and that Lady Mary 'now petitions the court that a commission of lunacy may issue'.

Those acting for Grange (including Talbot, Solicitor-General) 'admitted ... that she was not fit to have the sole care of herself'. But they 'insisted that it was more proper for her to go to Scotland', and claimed that she herself desired this in 'some of' her 'lucid intervals'. Since she was married to a Scot, albeit an attainted one, they argued that she was 'to be considered as a Scotch person'; no commission of lunacy could be granted, nor could the king's 'custody of the body of an idiot' apply. Instead, she must be found a guardian under Scots law: a 'tutor a (pretra) datus' appointed by the Court of Exchequer in Scotland. A final argument for her being in Scotland was that her government grant—her sole support—emanated from her husband's Scottish estates. The subtext of this is that with Lady Mar at Alloa the whole problem of squeezing cash out of Scottish rents would vanish.

These arguments take up most of the shorthand report. They had some weight with Lord Chancellor King, since he would not give a ruling without consulting the Master of the Rolls (Jekyll) and two judges. Lady Mary's case was presented by the Attorney-General, a personal friend of Talbot.[48] His arguments, and the fact that Lady Mar after all had the house in Whitehall appointed by the Crown for her use, decided Talbot against the arguments of his own side. The commission of lunacy 'was ordered in a manner by consent'—a walkover for Lady Mary.[49]

In a sort of entr'acte, she and her husband submitted to the Lord Chancellor a 'Petition and complaint' on behalf of young Lady Frances Erskine,

[46] Similar records and similar queries for 1732–6 are Monson 28B/12/8/5.

[47] Dudley Ryder made a shorthand transcript of it (copy made by Lord Harrowby: Halsband MSS 53, from Library of Lincoln's Inn). The Lord Chancellor was Wortley's old and close friend Sir Peter King.

[48] Sir Philip Yorke, later Lord Hardwicke, a strong supporter of Walpole's government. The *DNB* praises his vigilance and moderation.

[49] Halsband MSS 53.

to make Grange divulge the value of her entitlement on the Mar estate and of deeds in her favour, and to make him pay her arrears of interest, so that she might be educated in England by her mother's relations (that is, no doubt, by Lady Mary).[50]

Next came the lunacy commission itself, held with authority of the Great Seal of Great Britain, at the Braunds Head Tavern in the parish of St George's, Hanover Square, on 12 July 1728. This event is recorded in a vast intimidating Latin parchment.[51] Sixteen good men and true took their oath on the Sacrament to establish the truth about the condition of 'Domina Francisca Erskine vulgo vocat Domina Mar'. They concluded that 'Lunatica est et non Compos mentis sua', that she had been in that state for four months and had no lucid intervals. They could not say what had caused her illness: presumably it was a visitation of God. Shortly afterwards the Court of Chancery awarded her custody to Lady Mary.[52]

It was all over bar the shouting. Lady Mary's 'atorny', Hutton Perkins, submitted a bill for £83. 2s. 4d. (including three affidavits at seven shillings each and five guineas for the jury); it was paid almost a year later, one-third by Lady Mary and two-thirds by Grange. Lady Mary demanded not less than £500 annually for her sister's maintenance, and that Grange should provide City of London security for it. But she was content to allow Lord Mar the other £500 which had also been assigned to his wife. Every February and every August for eight years Lady Mary signed receipts for £250; later Grange packeted up the bundle of receipts and endorsed it, 'L. Mary Wortley's £4000 St.'[53] Pope wrote 'She turns her very Sister to a Job', and later 'Who starves a Sister'.[54]

Lady Mary still had anxieties in store. She placed her sister in the care of Dr Richard Hale, FRS, member of the College of Physicians, and physician to Bethlehem Hospital or Bedlam since 1708. He had provided an affidavit about Lady Mar's condition for the inquisition of lunacy; she was perhaps living at his Hampstead house (site of his private practice) when on 10 August 1728 *Applebee's* reported her as 'upon the Recovery at Kentish Town'.

Private madhouses had an evil reputation. They were open at a price, wrote Eliza Haywood, 'as well for those whom it was necessary, for the

---

[50] 6 July 1728, GD 124/6/209.   [51] PRO C211/8/16.   [52] Newspapers, 23 July 1728.

[53] GD 124/16/48/1, 16/48/3, 15/1339, 16/51 (Grange, 'Memorial of . . . Ld Mar's Affair', 18 Sept. 1728). Cf. the child Lady Frances *Pierrepont*'s annual £600, plus £20 salary for her guardian.

[54] *Sober Advice from Horace*, 1734: 21; *Epilogue to the Satires*, 1738: I. 112. James Prior related, hedged round with misinformation, a story of Lady Mar's whole daily rations being served in a single helping, to save trouble (1860: 150). Dr Cheyne held that mental patients should be fed 'the *lightest* and the *least* food' (1742: 90, 95).

Interest of their Friends, to be made Mad, as for those who were so in reality'.[55] Hale has been faulted recently for lack of special expertise and for making a fortune (chiefly from private patients). But Lady Mary had good reasons for her choice. He apparently favoured sociability rather than solitude as a cure; he took a gentle, non-punitive approach; though he did not publish, he was of a scholarly turn, friendly with men like Mead, Mattaire, and Wanley. Jurin the monitor of inoculation was his neighbour; Jonathan Richardson painted him. He was blunt, but erudite and benevolent.

On 25 September 1728, however, Hale suffered an apoplectic fit, and despite the efforts of Mead and other eminent physicians, he died next day. Obituaries celebrated his 'indefatigable Care . . . sound Learning and Skill in his Profession', and the fame which, they said, 'conducted to him innumerable Patients of that most Miserable and Bewilder'd sort' who were seeking 'the Recovery of their lost Reason'. Rumour said Hale's death would bring Lord Mar to England. Mar besought Lady Mary to tell him the name of his wife's new doctor; her answer does not survive. It may have been either Richard Tyson of St Bartholomew's, who had married Hale's niece and was Hale's choice to succeed him at Bedlam, or James Monro, his actual successor, who with his descendants ruled Bedlam for over a century. Hale's death was followed in November by that of Alexander Raitt, Lady Mar's sympathizer and supporter.[56]

～✺～

Lord Mar's discontent, his quest for pardon and for an end to his exile, rumbled on for months and years. A memorial in French explains his grievances: Lady Mary had taken against him on frivolous and unreasonable grounds; she had got possession of his wife's person, Wortley of his wife's goods; anything saved from her maintenance money would go to her heirs, not his; he stood deprived of all the rights and privileges which husbands normally possess over their wives' persons and goods. He reiterated these points in a letter to Cardinal Fleury: his aim was to reclaim the possession and direction of his wife and family which were due by right to a husband.[57] These documents in French are a powerful aid to understanding the sources of Lady Mary's rage.

---

[55] Defoe wrote against them in *Augusta Triumphans*, 1728; Haywood's novel *The Distress'd Orphan, or Love in a Mad-House*, 1726, shows how the moment a woman is declared mad (by her uncle-guardian), any treatment is believed (e.g. by the servants) to be for her own good. It takes a strong hero to rescue her.

[56] Scull 1993: 20 n. 54, 180; Andrews 1990: 170–1, 173, 176–84, 191; *Post-Boy*, 28 Sept. 1728; Mar MS GD. 124/16/81.

[57] 'Memoire pour Le C—te de M—r', 28/30 Aug. 1728 OS, GD 124/15/1340/2; Mar to Fleury, 23 Sept. 1728, GD 124/15/1340/4.

To facilitate Mar's receipt of his annual £500, she was willing for him to be pardoned, but not for him to return home. She wanted any pardon 'clog'd' with the condition of exile, enabling him to transact business in Britain 'in his own name (tho not in person)'. Such conditional pardon was rumoured to be forthcoming in September 1728—to Mar's discontent. While stories circulated of his implacable enmity to Lady Mary, he enlisted her aid (and Ilay's) in England as he enlisted Fleury's in France. He drew up another memorial, which Grange conveyed to the French ambassador in England. It argued that Mar would be able to manage more cheaply and efficiently on his home ground, and that the annual payment to Lady Mary made him '£500 sterl. yearly poorer than he was'. He said he needed an extra £300 a year to manage. (His £12,000 expenditure in the first ten months of 1729 was far lower than in 1728.)[58] If £300 a year could not be transferred from Lady Mary (that is, from his wife's maintenance) to himself, he hoped the British government might allot him a pension (George I had formerly paid him one of £2,000 'on no other Condition but not to medle in business'), or if not a pension then 'some small helps'. But if only he might come home, he would not mind Lady Mary's getting £500.[59]

Mar blatantly insisted on his entitlement to his wife's money (and her body). His contemporaries saw nothing unusual in this language, nothing to contradict the affection which he also professed. But when Lady Mary too (or those fighting the legal battle for her) used the language of legal entitlement, this was held to disprove any motive of sisterly affection.

Mar was never to return home. Even when, in October 1728, a full pardon *without* return had been promised and was daily expected, he and Grange were thrown into panic by news that the Prime Minister 'has Chang'd his mind and said he medled no more in the affair'. Rumour said that Mar had shown no proper gratitude. Mar was sure that someone, 'out of ill Nature or mistaken Notions', had 'spoke to' Walpole against him. Besides lamenting his own ruin, he added that this would 'Likewise be most Inconvenient to Lady Mary Wortley', since the lack of a full pardon would hinder Grange from paying the 'mantinence'. 'It grieves me to think too how poor Lady Mar, in her Disstres, may be Neglected and neither in my power or my Brother's to prevent it.' Grange, still in London, did his bit by visiting the

---

[58] He had spent freely while his wife was with him. During Dec. 1727–Oct. 1728 he paid a maitre d'hotel or steward at least £500 a month; payments were made to a physician, perhaps for Lady Mar, of £480 and to a periwig-maker of £140. Lady Frances's clothes cost £284, her dancing master £89, and eight months of London newspapers £126. 16s. 3d. (Mar MS GD 124/16/62).

[59] Atterbury said Mar claimed to have plotting letters of MWM's which he could produce to her detriment (1869: ii. 197, 302–3; Ilay to Grange, 10 Sept. 1728, GD 124/15/1338; 'Memorial of . . . Ld Mar's affair', 18 Sept. 1728, GD 124/15/1339).

court at Windsor, trying to find out what they wanted from his brother, and enlisting the aid of Lady Mary's former friend Charlotte Clayton.[60]

Mar needed support from his wife's sister, but was ready to blame any setback on her. He expounded her crimes to his son ('by all thats sacred I tel you truth') in a letter enclosing for her ('the great Lady') a respectful, nonhostile entreaty that she and Wortley should use their best endeavours for him.[61] In February 1729 she told Ilay she wanted 'no more' than £500 per annum; Articles of Agreement in June confirmed this amount.[62] The next bone of contention was the Whitehall house, whose repair and leasing kept Grange and others in dispute throughout 1729–31—the period that Grange's family correspondence shows him busy arranging the abduction of his own wife to St Kilda.[63]

Meanwhile there was an end of Lady Mary's letters to her sister, of wishes for her company, and of efforts to cheer and divert her. She may have felt that she was now but one in the world; and in Pope she faced an enemy whose particular virulence increased as the general war around him hotted up following his pre-emptive strike in *The Dunciad*. Lady Mary's name was becoming an indispensable missile for fighters in this war, rather as her sister's was in family financial skirmishes.

The gruelling summer of 1728 saw a sequence of pamphlet detonations, none of them coming close to Lady Mary yet each using her name in a manner compromising to her dignity and status—a manner unthinkable a couple of years before. Jonathan Smedley's *The Metamorphosis*, a 'thoroughly unpleasant' attack on Pope and Swift, images them as dogs addicted to dirt, and their opponents as concocting against them a potion made from bad poetry. Lady Mary is mentioned by name as one poet not to use: her work is too good, and would destroy the potion. A doggerell 'New Metamorphosis' (one of six items comprised in *The Female Dunciad*) mentions changing 'a snarling POPE to a smooth Lady MARY'. Although this is puzzling and ill expressed, other details in this work might well make Pope suspect that she

---

[60] To supply the maintenance money, Mar told Horatio Walpole, would take 'a sentance of the proper Court in Scotland'; Scots judges would probably be 'picqet at the Chancery's Medling within their province' (27 Oct. 1728, copy, GD 124/15/1342; Mar to Clayton, 19 and 29 Oct., BL Add. MS 20102. 151, 20103. 152–3). Walpole rejected, together, applications for pardon from Mar and from MWM's old friend Wharton (Bennett 1975: 299).

[61] Mar to Erskine and to Lady Mary, 19/8 Nov. 1728 (GD 124/15/1343; *CL* ii. 89–90). He also wrote to George II (GD 124/15/1346).

[62] *CL* ii. 90. Grange and Ilay (who had already differed over who should sit for Stirling) were to fall out finally by Aug. 1733 (GD 124/15/1415).

[63] Grange, 2 Sept. 1729–20 Apr. 1731 (GD 124/15/1357; 15/1372–80). Mar complained in Dec. 1729 that MWM had let the house for ten years, thereby preventing him from selling it. He then needed £4,500 to clear his Paris debts, from which he had fled to Antwerp (copy, 16 Dec. 1729, GD 124/15/1362).

had some hand in it. *Characters of the Times*, including her in a roster of those attacked by Pope, fulsomely defends her as 'Renown'd for Wit, Beauty, and Politeness, long admir'd at Court; Author of many pretty Poems scatter'd abroad in Manuscript; a Patroness of Men of Wit and Genius . . . a Woman of Merit and Quality'. These three works exemplify the kind of context in which to be mentioned at all, even admiringly, was damaging.[64]

Lady Mary was still, it seems, not too overwhelmed by scandal directed at herself to take an interest in the lives of her neighbours and her family.[65] Wortley's surviving sister was married in August 1728. He seems to have arranged an annuity for her: on a sum of £5,000 she was to be paid interest at 5 per cent, declining to $4\frac{1}{2}$ per cent, on condition that 'the Clauses relating to Children are added in the Settlement'. The interest was duly paid until 1730; there is no record of any children of the marriage.[66]

Whatever happened around her, however, Lady Mary must have felt, as the year 1728 closed, that the landscape of her life had shattered into new and unknown shapes.

[64] *Metamorphosis*, 18 July 1728; *Female Dunciad*, 8 Aug. (the 'New Metamorphosis' discusses Ovid, Addison, and Pope's sound-effects); *Characters*, 29 Aug. (Guerinot 1969: 133–4, 142–4, 151–3).

[65] She or EWM kept letters on other people's scandals: one to the widow of Samuel Molyneux (astronomer and butt of ballads by Pope) at Kew, 1728, about suspicions regarding her husband's death, and an undated one to Anne, Lady Blount, of Twickenham, who lived apart from her husband 1729–35, and wrote to MWM as a widow (H MS 79. 194–5, 192–3; *CL* iii. 235).

[66] Catherine Wortley Montagu m. John Orme of Northants., naval officer (*CL* i. 7 n. 2; Wh MS M D 252; newspapers, 3 Sept.).

17

1729–1732

❧

Past Forty: 'this various Scene with equal Eyes'[1]

IN spring 1729 Lady Mary turned forty. Her husband was fifty-one. While her friend Hervey visited Italy for his health that summer, Wortley visited Tunbridge Wells. There he amused himself by composing 'Maxims after the manner of Mr. de la Rochefoucault', of which numbers 11 and 12 read:

We are apt to fall in Love with those whose professions, we are persuaded, will make us secure of their affections; but when we think we have the desired security we are apt to lose the Passion.

As hard as it may be to cure a Strong Passion without Success; it is far more difficult to preserve one long for a Person to whom there is a Constant and Easy Access.

Number 21 asserts the rarity of 'delicious' marriages among 'persons of Distinction in Great Cities'. This is a gloss on La Rochefoucauld's maxim that marriage may be convenient, but never 'délicieux': the very maxim that Lady Mary wrote an essay to confute. It is at least possible that here, in one of her most famous texts, she was engaging as of old in debate with her husband on a topic they had in common.[2]

From Newcastle that July he wrote to her about his partners' 'gaietys', his 'good deal of difficulty to get them to settle to business', and the great fortunes of eligible girls in County Durham. She too wrote regularly, but it seems he did not keep her letters. For the next several years, almost none of hers survives. Her doings left abundant traces, but mostly fragmentary and puzzling.[3] She continued to build her life between her family and her friends,

---

[1] *E&P* 258.   [2] P. 295; H MS 80. 137–8; *E&P* 157–64.
[3] *CL* ii. 90–1. She was still a busy correspondent. Her letter on young Lord Sunderland's death, in Sept. 1729, brought some comfort to his bereaved grandmother, Sarah, Duchess of Marlborough. None survives from a whole series of 'very clever and rather *paw*' or *risqué* letters to Anne (Sebright) Buck, whose husband,

her social and literary activities. But she had a source of unease and dissatisfaction which left no area untouched. In practice she now lived in two
modes: that of her own activity in her various roles, and that of public
printed discourse in which Pope's unresting enmity was building an almost
free-standing mythical version of her. Though these two modes interacted,
I shall look at them separately.

Of the world she lived and acted in, Lady Mary's family was still the
centre, especially the rising generation—who, with her brother dead and
her surviving sister incapacitated, became more and more her responsibility.
For several of them, coming of age involved some fairly radical assertions of
independence.

The daughter who had been 'everything that I like' was growing up fast.
Her father was glad to find she looked like his dead sister Anne. Years later
Lady Mary told her of the pleasure she used to take in young Mary's company, and of the affection which was all the stronger for being concentrated
on a single daughter. The younger Mary would never have her mother's
beauty, but she was gifted: during the next few years she developed talents
for singing, acting, and writing poetry. The Armenian nurse was long since
gone. Young Mary was now waited on by a woman of 'excellent' character,
with a passion for Scudéry romances, who was to stay in her service till her
own children were grown up.[4] In later years Lady Mary almost apologized
to her daughter for not giving her a scholarly education; but she probably
supplied that familiarity with English literature which shows in the latter's
adolescent writings.[5] By her mid-teens, too, young Mary's rapidly maturing
handwriting was very like her mother's. (Her brother Edward developed a
hand running to curlicues, nothing like that of either parent.)

The daughter later told an anecdote which nicely illustrates her relationship with her mother. She came running—'with *"Mamma, only think!"*'—
to tell her how a young heiress, Miss Furnese, had declined acquaintance
with her: she had said she knew she was dull, and the clever Miss Wortley
would naturally despise and ridicule her. Lady Mary was not amused; instead
she became unusually thoughtful. 'After a pause', she lectured her daughter
on the important lesson just imparted. Dull people, she said, *always* 'view
people cleverer than themselves as natural-born enemies . . . if ever you feel

---

Sir Charles Buck of Hamby Grange, Lincs., was first cousin of MWM's early admirer Edward Vernon.
MWM gave Lady Buck her portrait (probably the half-length by Jonathan Richardson), and kept a song
addressed to her. Their long, close friendship ended in 'a violent quarrel' (Marlborough, 25 Sept. [1729], H
MS 77. 183–4; Lady Louisa Stuart to Lord Wharncliffe, 30 Dec. 1833, Wh MS 439/42; Grundy 1982: 34).

   [4] *CL* ii. 84; iii. 154; *E&P* 13; MWM 1861: i. 55–6.
   [5] Wh MS M 506 (see p. 310 ff.); 'The History of Aphaestaea and Altena, by Miss Wortley Mountagu' (H
MS 80. 266–9).

any complacency in the reputation of superiority, recollect that to be the object of suspicion and secret ill-will, is the sure price you must pay for it'.[6]

Young Edward, whatever his abilities, became steadily more and more ungovernable. In 1730, the year he turned seventeen, he married 'a woman of very low degree, considerably older than himself'. She was named Sally; she may have been a washerwoman. His motives on this occasion are as impenetrable as any of his mother's on any occasion whatever. Sally was clearly not the only woman he was involved with during his adolescence. Did he marry her, as later report had it, 'in a frolic'?[7] Did he love her? It is hard to see what charm she might have had for him; besides, he left her almost at once. Did she or her family ensnare him for his father's money? The submissiveness of her one surviving letter makes this hard to credit. Did he marry to spite his parents? If so, he succeeded. They kept the marriage a secret, but they had to find some support for his abandoned wife. His father—who was going through a turbulent period in the coal trade—consulted lawyers about breaking the Wortley entail to disinherit him.[8]

They sent him abroad again: this time to Europe, under the tutelage of a Scot named John Anderson. He was Anderson's first travelling pupil. Lady Mary corresponded with him and received Anderson's reports. In June 1732 young Edward was settled at Troyes in Champagne.[9] Anderson's chief concern seemed to be with his pupil's health: he had a bad cough, but his colour was good, and so would his appetite be 'were he allow'd to eat according to his inclination'. Apparently he was thought to be tubercular. His behaviour was erratic: he took a religious turn during which he would pray 'for 4 or 5 hours together'. Anderson was hard put to it to prevent his turning Catholic and entering a monastery. Later that summer he was said to be in perfect health and—at least 'at present'—cured of his drinking. Anderson saved this piece of good news for a sweetener after admitting that he was not cured of his 'old intriguing disposition'. Whether this meant keeping a mistress or frequenting brothels, Anderson thought it a 'very considerable failing in a young Gentleman'. Edward's studies were suffering, and Anderson proposed, 'with much submission', that the parents 'wou'd Judge it proper to

---

[6] Hunter 1831: ii. 323 n. 1; cf. *E&P* 43–4.

[7] MWM 1861: i. 111; *Scots Magazine*, 1777: 39. 626; Sedgwick 1970; *Anecdote Library* [1822]: 399–400.

[8] The coalmasters were in conflict with each other and with the dealers over combining and price fixing. In the early 1730s EWM stood outside a 'Regulation' aimed at closing redundant pits. In Feb. 1731 he was for keeping prices up, but within a few weeks was pressing to lower them, though concerned to prevent Bowes taking the lead in this (Hughes 1952: 225, 228, 242–6).

[9] She *may* have visited him in France: one of her books bears her only partly legible note: '. . . Blois 6 . . . 1732' (*Nouveau Recueil de Contes de Fées*, 1731, at Sandon). Blois was where Mary Anne Cantillon spent her summers.

remove us to some other Town'. He counted on Lady Mary to arrange this, in her 'own prudent way', concealing his own hand in it. Edward later made something like a Grand Tour in Italy, while Anderson reported with muted optimism on his delicate health and his response to what he saw. Then or later Edward visited many places where his mother later followed him: Genoa, Geneva, Bergamo, Brescia, Milan, and Venice. In most he left debts behind.[10]

Since no comment of Lady Mary's on all this survives, it might seem she dealt with this wound, as she had dealt with others, by avoiding mention of it. But this may be a false impression, since 100 or 200 letters which the parents exchanged about their errant son were later destroyed.[11] Clearly he was a sore subject, not for years but for decades. At the end of her life Lady Mary said Edward had broken her heart.

Meanwhile the older generation of her family was almost extinct: in June 1732 Lady Catherine Jones reported that 'Good Lady [Cheyne] declines apace'; on the 19th she died. She bequeathed £12,000 to Lady Gower's younger children.[12] The care of Lady Frances Pierrepont devolved on Lady Mary, the only member of the family who had not wanted it. She had buried reasons to feel negative about this girl, whose mother she had always disliked and resented, and whose father's untimely death had followed her birth so closely as to leave a lasting association with it.

Nor could Lady Mary forget the unhappy condition of her sister Mar: she signed twice a year for the money (usually some months in arrears), visited her (not often enough, said Lady Mar's friends), monitored the visits of others (who required 'an order from the Chancelor'), supervised the use of remedies like Spa water (which did not help), and tried to ensure the 'Quiet and Regularity' which she believed her sister to need.

Wortley shared the business responsibilities: he, with Lady Mary, signed and sealed 'Articles of Agreement' with Grange on 9 June 1729. These laid down that Grange would hand over annually half the £1,000. (After Lord Mar's death it seems the half conceded to him still went towards his debts.)[13]

---

[10] Wh MS 439/14; Huntington MS Mo 8 (EWM jr to Edward Montagu, 3 Oct. 1742); H MS 77. 150–3, 78. 20–1 (Anderson to MWM, Troyes, 17/6 June, 29/18 Aug. 1732; Gibson to EWM, 14 June [?1733]); *CL* ii. 249; see pp. 403, 442. Edward addressed to Anderson a highflown essay on friendship. By 1749 he was recounting a romantic tale of how he had lived by casual jobs in many different countries: as postillion, ploughman, ship's cook, etc. (Curling 1954: 46–9; *Scots Magazine*, 1777: 39. 399; Luynes 1860: ix. 505).

[11] In the early 19th century by the 1st Marquess of Bute, their eldest legitimate grandson, to protect the family from scandal.

[12] To Lady Betty Hastings (*Hastings Wheler*, 1935: 106); GEC. Her residual legatee was a relation and companion who killed herself five weeks later for grief.

[13] Mar MSS GD 124/8/89, 2/233; Lady Loudoun to her husband, 13 Feb. [1731] (copy), Bute MSS. The agreement said payment would be made at the Common Dining Hall of Lincoln's Inn; in practice a messenger would chase around London and Twickenham looking for MWM to pay her in person.

Even after the rent and taxes on the Whitehall house were all arranged, running it still made work. In 1733 an unsatisfactory tenant had to be pursued to Greenwich for an 'ejectment' to be served. Lawyers shuttled around London between Lady Mar's daughter (then visiting near Grosvenor Square), Lady Mary, Erskine, and Grange; the whole business took months. When painters worked there, there was debate as to who should pay. Estimates of family and estate debts continued to rise. One contrivance was for Lady Fanny or Frannie to sue her father's 'vassals' for non-payment. The Paris banker Alexander Alexander moved against the family for non-payment to him of nearly £2,000.[14]

On the emotional side there were plenty of mischief-makers (from Lady Mary's viewpoint) to side with Lord Mar against her. They were not all of them Scots. Lady Lechmere met Mar at Spa in the winter of 1730–1, and was primed with messages to relay to Britain: his devotion to his promising young daughter, his love and anxiety for his wife, his suspicion that Lady Mary treated her harshly, hindering both her recovery and her correspondence with himself. He said his main reason for seeking a pardon was to get her away from her sister. Griselda Murray (now Lady Murray), duly made party to all this by Lady Lechmere, went off to visit Lady Mar. She also passed on Mar's account to Lady Loudoun; Lady Loudoun sent it on, slightly embellished, to her husband. All deplored Lady Mary's 'barbarous' treatment of a sister who was 'as much in her sences as ever she was in her life', although stuck in 'a poor little house with scarse cloth's to her back or any thing that was fit for her'.[15]

Although her stepson reported in February 1730 that 'poor Lady Mar' 's health had not improved,[16] his uncle Grange preferred to rely on tales—emanating from Ladies Murray and Loudoun—that she was mentally normal and unhappy in her sister's care. In April 1731 he arrived in London for one last try at getting the lunacy verdict quashed and his sister-in-law's person conveyed to Scotland 'for the advantage of the family'.[17] He got Lady Hervey and even Dr Arbuthnot to testify to her sanity; the former and Lady Murray spread the news in court society. Between them they brought Lady Mar to profess willingness to go and live in Scotland; but

[14] *CL* ii. 95; Mar MSS GD 124/16/47/3, 16/51/19, 2/240 (joint bill of complaint by the Advocate-General and Lady Frances Erskine, draft).

[15] Lady Lechmere to Lady Murray, 20/9 Dec. 1730, Mellerstain MSS; Lady Loudoun to her husband, 13 Feb., 1–2 Mar. 1731, Bute MSS. Mrs Pelling too, who had once carried gifts between the two sisters, now joined in the chorus, and told Lady Cheyne lies about Lady Mar's daughter's visit.

[16] Erskine reported at second hand, 21 Feb. 1730 (Mar MS 124/17/647/5).

[17] *Spalding Club*, 1846: iii. 4–8; Wodrow 1842–3: iv. 227.

a visit from Lady Mary changed her mind again. Grange's version of this was that Lady Mary 'went in rage to her poor sister, and so swagered and frighted her, that she relapsed'.[18] Lady Mary's version was that her sister could not be moved without 'down right Force' and that even trying to persuade her to move ruffled her. Grange withdrew, tacitly admitting defeat, having found on his last visit that Lady Mar was consumed by 'fancies which now perplext her brain . . . like the clouds, fleeting, inconstant, and sometimes in monstrous shapes'. A few months later Lady Mar was again able to write to her daughter (who was in France with Lord Mar)—which is *almost* what Lady Lechmere said Lady Mary would not allow.

At the end of the year 1731 Lady Mary, too, wrote a guardedly polite letter to this sixteen-year-old niece: defending her conduct, sympathizing with Lord Mar's difficulties, and, as she used to do more casually years before, sending messages from her daughter. On the very same day Lady Frances ('your poor little girle') wrote her one surviving letter to 'My Dear Dear Mama'. She lamented 'the melancholy life you lead', hoped for an answer to her prayers on this subject, and reminded her mother that they must wait patiently like good Christians. She feared her mother was too much alone and working too hard with her needle; she hoped they would both write often in future. She could 'not forbear' sending a New Year's present, which she said was trifling but suitable because 'Amathist is say'd to denote constancy'. It is a moving document.[19]

Lord Mar by now was ill with what was to be his final sickness. His next move was to write emotionally to Lady Loudoun, one of his staunchest allies. Her husband had recently died. He extolled the ancient friendship between their families, hoped it would continue into the next generation, and hinted that his daughter would make a good wife for her son, now Lord Loudoun. He said nothing of the transfusions of Lady Frances's money into Mar debts (which Lady Mary and her supporters sought to staunch), but he noted that she would come into another £3,000 a year if her cousin Kingston, 'yet unmaried and on his travels' should die 'without heirs of his body'. If he did not himself find a husband for her, he said, Lady Mary 'would sell the girle like a horse in a market'. Lady Loudoun declined this chance to put her son among those who stood to gain by prizing Lady Mar loose from her sister. She passed him Mar's letter without comment. But both she and he adopted Mar's terms about 'that unaccountable mad avaritious woman Lady

---

[18] Grange even feared his wife might make contact with MWM (*Spalding Club*, 1846: iii. 17; Halsband 1956: 138).

[19] MWM 11 Dec. 1731 (*CL* ii. 94–6); Lady Frances, 22/11 Dec. (Mar MS GD 124/15/1396).

M—y W—y', and her presumed oppression and exploitation of her sister and niece.[20]

Somebody else was worse oppressed. In January 1732 Grange had his wife kidnapped and imprisoned, and announced her death. She remained a non-person for about eight years. Lady Loudoun received from Mar one last letter fulminating against Lady Mary, and wishing to get his wife out of her hands. She had not time to respond: next month Mar was dead. Lady Mary sent her condolences to Lady Frances Erskine.[21]

Now her sister was a widow. Wortley (since many of his financial arrangements with Grange expired with Lord Mar) next year refused to endorse papers about Lady Mar until the Attorney-General was called in. The first 1733 instalment of her allowance did not come to hand until 26 May (Lady Mary backdated her receipt to 20 February). The second payment this year was also in arrears: received on 15 September.

The orphaned Lady Frances can be tracked through the careful accounting of the Monson MSS. She seems at once to have supplied a 'Bond of Provision' to Lords Grange and Dun (purchasers of the Mar estates) for £10,000 at £500 annual interest. After settling her father's affairs abroad, she visited Scotland for the first time, from November 1732 to August 1733. The latter was the month in which she turned eighteen, the age of majority under Scottish law. She moved the Sheriff Court in Edinburgh to appoint 'curators' for her 'against her nearest-of-kin'; the court did so on her birthday, 8 August. She then returned to London, a journey for which hire of horses cost her £21 and Grange £49.[22]

Grange was now in London more or less permanently. He and his nephew Erskine had joined the Opposition; he favoured impeaching his erstwhile ally Lord Ilay. His niece, a young woman to be reckoned with, was as keen as he was to get her mother out of Lady Mary's hands, but she was much more careful of Lady Mar's own welfare. She had been twelve when to all intents and purposes she lost her mother, who went to England on a journey designed to effect her own cure and Lord Mar's pardon, but failed at both and never returned. Lady Frannie's attitude to Lady Mary was coloured by her father's; she may have felt the discrepancy between her own wealth (on paper only) and her family's ruinous debts. For the present she waited until she should come of age by English law too, at twenty-one, and she kept her alliances in good repair. Though siding with her father's relations, she was

[20] Lady Loudoun to her son, 22 Mar. 1732, Mar to her, 11 Mar. and 1 Apr. NS, Bute MS.
[21] Mar wrote on 21 Apr. and d. in May. Summary of MWM's lost letter (*CL* ii. 96).
[22] Mar MS GD 124/16/51/14, 51/16; Monson MSS 28B/12/8/2. In London her expenses included lodgings, purchases, and a surgeon (8 Aug. 1733, GD 124/3/92).

careful not to lose touch with her Pierrepont ones: she corresponded with
her cousins or aunts Gertrude Leveson-Gower, Lady Frances and Lady
Caroline Pierrepont, and the younger Mary Wortley Montagu.[23]

❧

In September 1730 (the year of her son's marriage) Lady Mary fell 'dangerously ill'. She was attended by Arbuthnot, who had so strongly backed inoculation but signally failed to back her against Pope or Grange. At her bedside,
he began to speak of the financial provision he had made for his children:
possibly a lead-in towards good advice about young Edward. She reportedly
'cried out, "God damn your Children and mine, mind my illness" '.[24]

At this time a well-meaning female friend turned on her some well-worn
advice which, as it happens, she herself had recently addressed to Hervey: to
give less time to social life, more to the moral satisfactions of retirement.
(Could the friend have been Astell? She was now near the end of her life, and
had always been inclined to worry that Lady Mary mixed with people who
were too brittle and shallow for her.) Lady Mary replied in verse, with an
off-the-cuff claim to the moral high ground. 'You little know the Heart that
you advise,' she wrote: 'In crouded Court I find my selfe alone, | And pay
my Worship to a nobler Throne.' More unequivocally than anywhere else,
she here stated her belief in, and submission to, God: 'That sole Being, Mer-
cifull and Just.'[25]

This idealism might be dismissed as a temporary effect of illness. When
Pope heard from Bathurst of the latter's concern and unaltered friendship for
her, he rejoined that now she was better she 'cares not a pin for you, or any
Man of honour in Christendom'. But her high-minded self-portrait finds
support from an unexpected quarter. Sarah, Duchess of Marlborough, had
contrasted Lady Mary, probably in 1727, with fickle town ladies, and credited
her with 'one advantage that few of our sex has in an equal degree, which is,
that you can bee alone, and entertain your self at least as well as any company
can do it'. Sarah said her own old age had given her a taste for 'solitary
contemplative ways of living . . . spent in reflexion and emprovement of the
mind': it was this shared taste which endeared Lady Mary to her.[26]

[23] Mar MSS GD 124/15/1400, 15/1462, 15/1446/1 (1733–6).

[24] Sherburn 1938: 487.

[25] *Grub Street Journal*, 17 Sept. 1730; 'An Answer to a Lady Advising me to Retirement', *E&P* 258–9. Mary
Pendarves (later Delany) found the poem *'pretty'*, but added 'how *ill* her *actions* and *her words agree!*' (11
Mar. 1732: 1860–1: i. 339). Hervey had a different worry about her associates: too many were stupid (to
MWM, 31 Dec. OS 1739, Hervey MS 474/2. 81). Julia Evelyn and Frances Boscawen, including this among
11 MWM poems in a commonplace-book, called her adviser 'Mrs.——' (Osborn MS fc 51. 142).

[26] Pope, *Corr.* iii. 134, 137; Marlborough, 12 Mar. [?1727], Pierpont Morgan MSS). Consultants say
MWM's mature handwriting shows her to be self-contained and private, controlled and straightforward,

Yet Lady Mary also issued advice of diametrically opposite tendency. Probably just about the time that her husband, in parliament, deplored the ridiculing of serious things, she was doing this with gusto. Addressing the widowed Lady Irwin, whom she had known years before as Lady Anne Howard, she debunked the idea of deep mourning for a spouse whom 'Long ago the Worms have eat'. She declared herself, reported Lady Irwin, to be 'inspired for my service', and insisted that constancy was unnatural, a lapse into irrationality that needed curing with a daily 'dose' of flattery from a witty young fellow. It is true Lord Irwin sounds not worth mourning. Just before his wedding he wrote to his brother about 'my Doxy' and the 'little Nymth' whom he meant to 'swive' before his brother could do the same to his 'hore'. Even *if* the 'Nymth' is his noble bride, his letter remains equally offensive and swaggering. Still, this was ancient history. Lady Mary clearly delighted in tailoring her arguments to the debate of the moment; it would be foolish to seek in *any* of her occasional poems for serious long-term opinions.[27]

At least one of her prose works raises similar questions about its opinions: seriously held or rhetorically assumed? Her essay on marriage, written in French to refute La Rochefoucauld's maxim that marriage may be convenient but not delightful, became one of her best-known works during her lifetime, which she was proud to display. The language chosen suggests that Lady Stafford as well as La Rochefoucauld and Wortley may have been in the writer's sights; and she had probably written it before Charles de Montesquieu left England in spring 1731, since he read her manuscript and later transcribed part of it.[28]

In this essay she presumes to speak for both sexes, both as a woman and as if she were a man. She acknowledges her boldness in taking on such a celebrated antagonist in her zeal for truth. Marriage, she says, despite the vulgar jokes against it, is really the highest pleasure Nature offers: that of living with one's lover without the exploitation and deceit that spoil unmarried relationships. Marriage consoles a women in her petty daily tasks, and a man in his struggles with the world. It mitigates sorrows by sharing them, and

not respectful of social convention but observant of it, readier to discuss ideas than feelings (which they say made her prefer men's company to women's). They find her strongly attached to her family and to the past, acerbic but not aggressive or given to confrontation: 'too clever and too flexible to prove obstinate'. They say she sought variety and stimulation but not attention or praise, and had a firm, and justified, belief in her own ability and originality (Graphology Business, 21 Apr. 1995).

[27] *E&P* 257–8; Irwin quoted in Smith 1990: 187. Elsewhere MWM had written, 'Constancy is nature too' (see p. 149).

[28] 'Sur la Maxime de Mr de Rochefoûcault. Qu'il y a des marriages commodes, mais point des *Delicieux*', *E&P* 157–64; Montesquieu, 'Spicilège', 576, 1951: ii. 1373–4. Delarivier Manley had put this Rochefoucauld maxim (misattributed) into the mouth of a seducer in *The New Atalantis*, ii. 601.

multiplies love through the bringing up of children. It is Paradise, which
Adam and Eve had not the experience to appreciate. To close her essay,
Montagu draws on her Turkish experience (otherwise one might suspect it
dated from the time of her idealistic courtship letters). The Turks look on a
male seducer with the horror which Europeans reserve for an unchaste
woman. Turkish women do not run to dissipation and sexual pleasure like
those of Europe. Happy marriages are rare, she concludes, because they
require each party to renounce the customary games of sexual pleasure and
power. Though this last sentiment echoes Astell and other turn-of-the-
century feminists, the essay as a whole is conservative, particularly in its
clear division of male and female roles.

In late 1729 came an event which highlighted the disparity between ideal
marriage and actual marriage practices, a reprise of Mary Yonge's story and
one which Lady Mary might be expected to write on. Katherine, Lady
Abergavenny, was exposed as an adulteress by her husband—who, Hervey
believed, had connived at her infidelity as long he could make money out of
it. The husband now, in another money-making move, set 'her Steward and
her Butler' to catch her 'en flagrant Delit'. He sued her lover, Richard Liddell (whose family were coal-owning associates of Wortley's), and packed
off his wife post-haste to London 'with orders to the Servants, if her Father
would not recieve her, to sett her down in the Street'. She was heavily pregnant; she bore her child and died two weeks later. As Goldsmith later had it,
dying was the only action that could have restored her to public sympathy.[29]

Hervey told his friend and lover Stephen Fox that the lady ought to be
whipped. Yet in verse he lauded her as a kind of martyr to love. At least half
a dozen poems greeted her death.[30] Hervey congratulated Lady Mary on the
authorship of two of these: one demanding, 'What breast does not a soft
Compassion feel | Whose ev'ry thought's not tip'd with harden'd steel?'
and another generally ascribed to Charles Beckingham (*Epistle from Calista
to Altamont*). Someone else ascribed to her another elegy, which links Lady
Abergavenny's death with those of Dido and Cleopatra, Monimia and
Calista, Sophia Howe in 1726, and Lady Mary's own sister-in-law in 1722.

---

[29] Hervey to his mother, Hervey MSS 474/2. 237; Goldsmith, 'When lovely woman stoops to folly', *The Vicar of Wakefield*, 1766, ch. 24; Black 1994: 153–9. The jury may have intended the damages of £10,000 to put Liddell in debtors' prison for life; but his career quickly recovered (Stone 1991: 273). About now Col. Francis Charteris, convicted of raping a servant, received royal pardon (Hillhouse 1928: 228–9).

[30] Hervey MS 47/4. 88–90 (written at Bath); Bod. MS Rawl. poet. 207. 157 (collected by Judith Cowper Madan); BL Add. MS 32463. 116; BL Harl. MS 7318. 128–9; Longleat MS xx. 105, 116; various published poems of 1729 (see Foxon 1975; *Grub Street Journal*, 16 Apr. 1730; *Whitehall Evening Post*, 14 May 1730; Hanbury Williams 1822: i. 119–21; Pope 1776: i. 155–6). There was a printed *Account* of the trial, a lampoon on it as epilogue to Charles Johnson's *Medea*, Dec. 1730, and an opera (*Calista*, Apr. 1731).

For the last two this writer's Muse has shed a tear.[31] *If* this verse-copyist was right, Lady Mary authored a whole series of elegies on fatally seduced women. But if she wrote them, must she not have been implicated in their failure to survive? This is one of several moments in her life when she comes close to the role of feminist heroine; but close is as far as she comes.

What she seems to have done apropos Lady Abergavenny was to encourage a response by a younger, male writer. Her cousin Henry Fielding used this case (especially) as source-material for a hard-hitting problem play called *The Modern Husband*. He submitted his draft of this work to Lady Mary for criticism on 4 September 1730, very anxious to know if she would think it as good as 'my lighter Productions'.[32] When he followed his manuscript to Twickenham 'to receive my Sentence', he was proud to find it favourable. (Lady Mary approved of his Lady Charlotte Gaywit, a flighty coquette sympathetically portrayed, which was some consolation when the lower-class part of the theatre audience objected to her as unnatural.) *The Modern Husband* was read in MS by others about this time; but it took nearly another year to reach rehearsal at Drury Lane.[33] The delay *may* have had to do with its potential shock value.

Lady Mary had qualifications as a theatre patron. She was a keen playgoer with catholic tastes (Lillo as well as Dryden). She wielded some power behind the scenes: Montesquieu appealed to her to use it on behalf of the innovative ballet dancer Marie Sallé, whom Lady Stafford also patronized.[34]

The Modern Husband finally opened on St Valentine's Day 1732. Fielding's biographer judges it the 'masterpiece' of his dramatic career. It achieved fourteen performances (including four welcome author's-benefit nights): the longest run by a straight play for four years. When it was published, a week after opening night, it was dedicated to Walpole. Readers would have laughed at this as a joke against a well-known complaisant husband; yet the implied preference of complaisance to brutality is not *merely* comic. This bold *exposé*, which if not feminist is firmly anti-antifeminist, owes a good deal directly and indirectly to Lady Mary's influence. When Drury

---

[31] 21, 29 Dec. 1729 (Hervey MSS 47/2. 51–2, 26–7); Grundy 1971: 683–4, 765; 'Upon the Death of Lady Abergavenny by Lady Mary Wortley Mountague', Osborn MS (P.B. IV/169).

[32] Real life offered parallel cases; so did Eliza Haywood's *A Wife to be Lett*, 1723; but Lady Abergavenny was the spur. This year Fielding produced the light-hearted *Author's Farce* (patronized by 'Ladies of Quality' and Robert Walpole) and *Rape upon Rape* (which, albeit comically, stigmatized the notorious rapist Charteris).

[33] *E&P* 52. Drury Lane, a pro-government theatre, had just drawn Fielding back after the Haymarket closed. *The Modern Husband* was blamed as 'indelicate, even pornographic' (Cleary 1984: 56; Battestin 1989: 123–4; *CL* ii. 93, 94; Dédéyan 1990).

[34] See p. 262 n. 62. Sallé spent several seasons in London, choreographing her own ballets. Her simple costumes and expressive, athletic movements were new. Her benefit, after a deficit in 1727, netted £195 in 1730.

Lane reopened at the end of the summer, it did so, by the express command
of Queen Caroline, with a Fielding work: *The Mock Doctor*, adapted from
Molière, which he printed in 1732 with a dedication to Lady Mary.[35]

In deploying her almost-family connection with the Prime Minister for the
benefit of her cousin the playwright, Lady Mary could almost be seen as an
undutiful wife. Her husband had allied himself with the dissident Whigs,
who were more of a threat to Walpole than the Tories. By anti-Walpole
speeches in the House of Commons[36] and by anti-Walpole electioneering in
Yorkshire, he worked for a political agenda the opposite of hers. They seem
to have managed this broad area of disagreement between them with courteous distance.[37] From the time of his father's death Wortley had been
increasingly involved in Yorkshire matters. In every department of Lady
Mary's life, Pope's blasting of her name would come to be felt more and
more; her husband must have hated this, but his responses are not recorded.

   The chief witness about the Wortley Montagu marital relationship during
the 1730s was a hostile one: Mrs Verney, whose fourteen-year-old daughter's death Lady Mary had ironically celebrated. Eleanor Verney remained
friendly with her daughter's widower, George Bowes, whose colliery interests kept him constantly associated with, and sometimes at loggerheads
with, Wortley. To him she addressed from Whitton near Twickenham a
steady stream of innuendo-ridden gossip. In 1730, for instance, she twice
hinted that Lady Mary had recently been pregnant.

   After eighteen years married and twelve without bearing a child, any
pregnancy of Lady Mary's would have gossip value (whether the gossip
thought she was having sex with her husband or betraying him). Mrs Verney's
practice was to begin with gossip about him, then turn her sights to his
lady. In August 1730 she reported that he had developed a sudden taste for
playing cards, in October that he was frequenting card parties and that Lady
Mary planned to indulge him with a weekly assembly at their Twickenham
house, then in November that this plan had lapsed and that he was back up
north. The rumours about his wife are bizarrely linked to the cards saga: in
August Lady Mary has 'returned to him [apparently to Twickenham], rid of

---

[35] Battestins 1989: 91, 99, 124, 127–32; Molière, *Select Comedies*, 1732: vi. A pamphlet by Aaron Hill said
(improbably) that Fielding made nearly £1,000 on the *Modern Husband*, only to lose it gambling.

[36] He attacked Walpole on 23 Feb. 1731 for abuse of power: using the king's name to bring pressure on the
House. This was an issue on which MWM's principles might be expected to put her on the pro-parliament,
anti-monarchy side; but her loyalty to Walpole was personal.

[37] MWM maintained some literary acquaintance with Opposition luminaries like Chesterfield and Lyttelton (the latter an inoculee); she collected a good deal of their poetry (H MSS 81 and 255).

all her swellings and incumbrances but him'; three months later she 'now appears at Church again, says she did not come all the summer because she was ashamed to appear in a Sack'. Eleanor Verney takes this as tantamount to confessing that her 'shape all that time would not admit of any other' less concealing dress.[38]

What should one make of this? Perfect discretion might leave it unmentioned; whole-hog indiscretion might hazard some names of possible lovers, preferably high-profile ones. Verney was not the only person to comment on the sack as Lady Mary's chosen wear. At this date the sack was still fairly informal dress, perhaps unorthodoxly casual; but it was just about to become the dress of choice even at balls and assemblies.[39]

It was a fact that this summer was exceptionally hot;[40] Lady Mary was not a keen churchgoer. Her own quip about her shape—in the form that Eleanor Verney reports it—clearly hints at pregnancy; and Verney had alluded to 'swellings' months before this. Yet Lady Mary's words also recall the way her early letters had purveyed outrageous rumours, trusting her correspondent to know what not to believe.

It was not impossible for her to have been pregnant. She was forty-one, her husband fifty-two. Hervey, to reassure her that she was still young, had recently cited the pleasure it would give a man to undress her. Several of her friends had children by men who were not their husbands.[41] She had remarked on society's newly blasé view of extramarital pregnancy, and had strongly defended at least one unfaithful wife. She was interested in sexual *mores*. To the eminently respectable Catherine Secker, wife of a rising churchman, Lady Mary was an ideal audience for a story about 'keeping': of an exquisite girl of about fifteen seen sitting on a dust-cart in the street, all 'rags and Dirt', who was soon afterwards nicely set up as mistress to Edward Walpole, the Prime Minister's eldest son.[42]

But in Lady Mary's own life, if she was pregnant could Eleanor Verney have been the sole witness? Quite apart from her own statements about her confidential closeness with her daughter, Pope would surely have known,

---

[38] Sir C. Sharpe's copies (10 Aug., 24 Oct., 20 Nov. 1730, Wh MS M 439/13–14). MWM's illness in Sept. occurred at the wrong time to fit this narrative as either a birth or a miscarriage (see p. 294).

[39] From resembling the loose-fitting 'nightgown' which MWM had ordered in the 1720s, it developed a more fitted front, with open pleats only behind. It no longer looked like concealing a pregnancy; by 1741 it was *de rigueur* for married women even among the more formally dressed French; yet it still provoked jokes about pregnancy (see p. 316; Buck 1979: 26, 36, 40–1; *Freeholder's Journal*, 13 Apr. 1723; Walpole, *Corr.* xxxvii. 334).

[40] See newspapers, e.g. *Whitehall Evening Post*, 16 July 1730.

[41] Molly Skerrett; Henrietta, Duchess of Marlborough; perhaps Henrietta's sister, Mary, Duchess of Montagu (see p. 316).

[42] *CL* iii. 213.

and would surely not have missed such a handle against her. And Edward Wortley Montagu was a proud man with a steady, unresting sense of what was due to himself. If he had found his wife to be pregnant by another man, he might perhaps have chosen the Walpole-like tactic of keeping his head in the sand about it; but he could surely not have retained his trust in her good judgement, or have continued to consult and to rely on her as he did. Most probably the rumour's sources are all non-factual: Verney's unmistakable hostility, Lady Mary's irresponsible joking, her style of dress, and her ease and outspokenness in male company. In short, the rumour of Wortley's passion for cards and that of his wife's pregnancy may be equally flimsy.

The question to ponder is, why did her style attract the repressive censure she so often complained of? Apparently she cracked jokes about forbidden subjects, and chose or wore her clothes in a manner to give offence. This wilful outrageousness was probably a factor even in Pope's outrage.

On New Year's Day 1730 Lady Mary stood godmother at St Martin-in-the-Fields to St George Molesworth, the third son (by his second wife, Sarah Maria) of an old family friend, army officer Walter Molesworth.[43] The size of this baby's family over two generations almost guaranteed his relative poverty.[44] When he was nearly two (and his mother a couple of months pregnant with his next brother), his father wrote to tell Lady Mary about a necklace and pair of earrings of his wife's, which they hoped to sell to her. This was to be their first step towards clearing 'a load of Debt' left by some 'untoward business'. Walter appealed to Lady Mary's 'Benevolence' and 'sagacity' to find some way of bailing his family out. If she could not, he professed himself willing to 'sacrifice to Justice the gayeties of this life' and to pull through by economizing alone.[45] In short, he appealed to her as financial adviser and mother-confessor.

Whether Lady Mary was to buy these jewels for herself, or as agent for someone else, does not appear. Nor does it appear whether she should be praised for Christian charity or criticized for encouraging fecklessness (or even for exploiting people in difficulties). Walter was probably the Mr Molesworth to whom she presented a copy of her Embassy Letters: the only

---

[43] Walter was 5th son of 1st Viscount Molesworth (a leading Old Whig). For his sisters known to MWM, see pp. 24, 218 and n. 59 Walter's first wife had stayed at Twickenham in 1722 (HMC 1913: viii. 345, 388).

[44] Walter had at least one daughter by his first wife; he and Sarah Maria baptized another son in 1732 and a daughter in 1740.

[45] The necklace, bought some years before, had been improved with better stones; Sarah Maria thought it and the earrings (a gift from her first husband) had cost £500 (York Buildings, 29 Nov. 1731, H MS 77. 200–1). MWM had discussed buying and selling jewels before (H MS 77. 220–2; see pp. 161, 224).

copy known to survive besides her own. But it seems she gave the sumptuous full-length portrait of herself by Jonathan Richardson (dated 1726) to her godson 'the Rev. and Hon. Mr Molesworth'—that is, to little St George.[46]

This portrait, the finest ever painted of Lady Mary, is an extraordinary gift to a child (St George Molesworth was only nine when Lady Mary left England in 1739). It gives the lie to the notion that Richardson was a boring or unimaginative artist. Himself a poet of talent and feeling, he became a kind of court painter to Pope, incorporating in painting after painting ingenious allusions to literary greatness. His two portraits of Lady Mary, full-length and three-quarter-length, both featuring her favourite backdrop of the Constantinople skyline, contrast markedly with each other. In each her Turkish dress is modified, its generally western outline revealing oriental detail on closer scrutiny. The smaller picture, understatedly elegant, shows her wearing deep rose colour.[47] In the full-length she dazzles in gold. Here the full Turkish costume can be enumerated: anteri, wide trousers looking at first glance like a petticoat or skirt, talpoche with standing spray, ermine-lined curdee, broad jewelled belt.

One element in the full-length is first a shock, then a puzzle: a young black boy in red livery, wearing a silver collar, who stands in shade which contrasts with her light, and holds a parasol less over her than over himself. A modern student of Lady Mary, seeing her juxtaposed with a black slave, might think first of the 1721 smallpox epidemic which brought inoculation to London and Boston: on the testimony of Lady Mary in the capital and of African slaves in the colony.[48] Clearly, however, the painter did not intend this boy as any kind of collaborator (though that was more or less the role of Onesiphorus, slave to Cotton Mather); presumably he did not intend him as a symbolic attribute (like the mosques of Constantinople) signalling her far-reaching medical effectiveness.

---

[46] H MS 259; the Revd George Ashby in *GM* 1809: 79: [202]. Walter had sought patronage from Henrietta Howard. He had connoisseur friends (Suffolk 1824: i. 245–7; HMC 1913: viii. 345). St George became Vicar of Northfleet in Kent (his father wangled it through William Pitt), and was said to be the worst type of absentee incumbent (*GM* 1763: 99; 8 Sept. 1758, PRO Chatham papers 30/8; Cooke [1960]: 40–2). On his death, MWM's nephew-in-law the Duke of Bedford bought the picture; it and the Molesworth MS now owned by Lord Harrowby.

[47] J. Nicholls identified the Molesworth painting as the full-length (Sandon exhibitions file; thanks to Jane Waley); a note at the NPG makes it the ¾-length. Cf. Pointon 1993: 48. The full-length (see Frontispiece) was shown in 'Manners and Morals', Tate Gallery, 1987–8. The ¾-length is now at Sheffield Central Art Gallery. MWM's descendant C. Stuart copied the head of the full-length. The ¾-length was engraved for MWM's *Works*, 1803, by Caroline Watson, there dated 1719. It is related to two pictures in the National Gallery of Ireland, attributed to Jervas. Paintings of men (Richard Pococke; Lord Sandwich) used the buildings of Constantinople in this way (Ribeiro 1984: plates 223, 62).

[48] See p. 212; Grundy 1994c: 21–3. Richardson was a close friend of several medical men involved in the inoculation wars.

A more likely theory is that the boy was a studio prop—an inauthentic one in the Turkish ambience. The child slaves in Turkish households were whites from Circassia and such places; the only black slaves were adult males employed in harems.[49] The parasol is equally un-Turkish. Lady Mary knew these things, though other English people might not. Van Dyck and other artists had juxtaposed, for effect, some tall white beauty with a smaller black figure gazing admiringly upwards. Black children holding parasols had appeared in exotic orientalized representations done in England, with reckless disregard for authenticity.[50] If the black boy here belongs to that tradition, it seems that someone other than Lady Mary, someone entertaining their own fictional concept of Turkey, must have influenced what Richardson painted.[51]

The final theory is that this is a slave belonging to Lady Mary[52]—that is, that like all her possessions he was owned by her husband. There are some arguments against this idea. Blacks were generally seen as signs of an affluence which was beyond Wortley in 1726, and of an ostentation which was alien to him and to Lady Mary;[53] ladies' black slaves often attracted comment, while the flood of comment on Lady Mary never mentions one; and I have traced nothing Caribbean among Wortley's business interests. On the other side, a slave might represent an investment, or might have come as a gift; slaves were sold at the kind of auction which Lady Mary loved to attend; her close friend the Duchess of Montagu was painted with a black page; sugar-producers in general depended on coal-producers; and Walter Molesworth had financial dealings with a Governor of Jamaica.[54] Lady Mary might have been a slave-holder, for all her enlightenment. Slave-owning was a given in her milieu.

---

[49] Davis 1986: 7, 100. *Later* western painters of harems often included black female slaves (e.g. Charles-Amadée-Philippe Van Loo, 1774, Jean-Léon Gérôme, 1885, both in Croutier 1989).

[50] Turkish dress was worn with black boy and parasol in portraits of Lucy, Duchess of Wharton, and of Sarah Marlborough's granddaughter Anne (Egerton), Duchess of Bedford, then Countess of Jersey (in Blackett-Ord 1982, and Marlborough 1943). Anne Bracegirdle as Dryden's Indian Queen wore feathers with attendant black putti (painted by ?J. Smith, engraved by W. Vincent: Harvard Theatre Collection, Barranger 1984—thanks to Shirin Emmanuel for this reference).

[51] Gilman notes the sexualizing effect of blacks in portraits of whites (1985: 209).

[52] Gerzina 1995 (142), and others assume this.

[53] Dabydeen 1984: 34–50; Pointon 1992: 51–2. Black slaves were unpaid; but the cost of purchase is to be set against servants' very low wages. MWM's father left a life-annuity—£40—to his 'black', John Bever (Gerzina 1995: 55, 142; BL Eg. MS 3531).

[54] *CL* i. 324; ii. 159; Gerzina (1995: 54–9: on the Duchess of Queensberry and Julius Soubise); Duchess of Montagu picture by ?Enoch Seeman, owned by Duke of Buccleugh and Queensberry. Molesworth lent £3,000 in 1735 to Henry Cunningham, Governor of Jamaica, a Walpole supporter and an opponent of Grange and Erskine (NLS MSS 16594. 168–74, 17490. 127–33, 17492. 77, 96; Sedgwick 1970; Cundall 1937: 166–70). MWM's son supposedly spent three years in the West Indies, after Richardson's picture was painted.

She might have followed the fashion in using this human accessory, although her trademark use of Turkish dress seems to have led rather than followed fashion. English dressmakers made free with their concept of oriental style, as is seen in the 1730s costumes at Sandon Hall. If these were really Lady Mary's, they reinforce what the portraits suggest about her preferred colours.[55] In their glass cases they stand as traces of her slender, elegant figure, witnesses to her taste and style and pleasure in fine things.

The year 1731, in which she was *perhaps* willing to expend something like £500 on jewels, *perhaps* for the benefit of friends in financial straits, is another for which her household accounts survive: listed under twenty-five headings by T[homas] K[ent], who was her husband's secretary.[56] By Lady Mary's addition the figures totalled £1,472. 14s. 9½d. Kent corrected her total upwards by £63. 9s. 4d.[57] Many items were listed month by month, a saddle (as in her earlier accounts) in May, opera tickets in January, February, and July—each suggesting some faint relaxation of stringency since the 1720s. The smallest amount listed was the year's porterage at £2. 9s. 6d., the largest the blanket 'Houskeeping' at over £300. But a penny farthing, was worth listing under housekeeping, and small amounts were carefully listed for candles, coal, beer, and wine. The apothecary was paid in seven of the twelve months, his receipts mounting up to twenty pounds and twopence.[58]

These columns of figures offer food for thought. Whereas the children were formerly listed as a single item, Edward is now absent, transferred to some other account. His sister seems to be there as 'Girl', accounting for £52. 12s. 11d.—much more than what she cost a few years before, but little enough compared with the hundreds allocated annually to her girl cousins and her young aunts.[59] Other items remain opaque, like 'Mr W asking', which accounted for a sum of £2. 14s. 1d. in April. Wages were paid in every month but July, and board wages (for servants who were merely house-sitting in their employers' absence) in every month but February, presumably marking the simultaneous upkeep of London and Twickenham households. The total wages bill was just over £232.

[55] Gown of deep pink silk embroidered with gold; gown of gold and silver brocaded on yellow silk; open robe and petticoat of maroon and silver brocaded French silk, all 1730s; short-sleeved lady's coat, embroidered with gold on white, possibly from 1717–18 (notes by Victoria and Albert Museum staff).

[56] Halsband MSS; *CL* ii. 141.

[57] A calculator used to arbitrate between them makes the total higher still.

[58] By contrast, EWM's housekeeping expenses at Wharncliffe Lodge in 1730 totalled 7s. 4d. (excluding coal or brewing). 1728 was similar, 1729 a pound more. Even a penny for soap was recorded (Wh MS M 141).

[59] Figures for the Leveson-Gowers (many daughters of a baron) might not be high. For the rest (all ranking as earls' daughters) the annual figures range from £400 to £1,000 p.a.

Early in September 1731 the Wortley Montagus left Covent Garden (where a new theatre was going up, and the bohemian encroaching on the fashionable) for Cavendish Square, an exclusive new area which Lady Oxford's husband was developing on land she had brought him in her dowry. Lady Mary wrote it 'Candish'.[60] Her accounts this year list rent for both addresses, as well as 'Taxes'. Payments of £36 for 'Plate', and for three or four times that much for repairs and for furniture, may also have stemmed from the move.

A total of £17. 3s. 7d. and a halfpenny was listed for Lady Mary's 'Pocket': a sum actually much lower than in the 1720s, and quite out of kilter with £500 for the Molesworth jewels or the cost of having a portrait painted. The accounts mention no books, which must therefore have come out of Lady Mary's slender 'Pocket' or out of 'Several expences'. But a number of other individual items reflect personal expenditure on pleasure or mobility, like 'Chair hire' at £21. 6s. 11d., 'Waterman' at £10. 16s. 4d. The sum for 'Garden', at £38. 7s. 3d. and a farthing, is higher than during the 1720s. The coachmaker received £35. 3s. 4d. (paid in April, May, June, July, November, and December), which seems too much for repairs. Did their new address cause them to set up a new—or even their first—coach? In the light of Wortley's already enormous colliery holdings, the overall outlay is astonishingly slim.

On 20 July 1731, a couple of months before they moved, Lady Mary and her husband attended to a huge volume of business. Among documents they signed and sealed that day were leases of property to tenants including Wortley's sister-in-law Agnes Wortley alias Montagu of Exeter, and a mortgage of property held in trust for Agnes's two daughters. It looks as if Wortley was dealing with all his family responsibilities at once. The most interesting document assigns Lady Mary future compensation for her presently resigning her notional right to 'dower'. Dower, which was fast becoming obsolete, entitled a widow to one-third of her husband's estate. Now, by her hand and seal, she 'Barred herself of her dower'. In 'Sufficient Recompence' to her for 'all and singular the said Lands Tenements Hereditaments and premisses' due to her under the old system, she assisted in the levying of a 'Fine'. By this token payment of five pounds, Thomas Bennett and Lord Monson (the eagle-eyed checker of Lady Mar's accounts) entered into possession of the lands etc., and bound themselves and their 'Executors Administrators and Assignes' to extract from them for her benefit, in

---

[60] Cavendish Square was not *necessarily* an exclusive address: Samuel Johnson and his wife lived there early in their London years (Orrell 1992: 144–54; *CL* ii. 99; Kaminski 1987: 175–6).

case she survived her husband, the money equivalent of what she now surrendered.[61] She too attended to her financial affairs this month, reinvesting her father's legacy more profitably, and settling a mortgage on property in Surrey.[62]

[61] Her sister Mar's marriage contract had renounced her 'thirds' (Mar MSS GD 123/3/83. 11, 25; see pp. 73–4).

[62] Wh MS D 257–62.

18

1732–August 1736

✦

As Aunt and Mother: 'A Mother only knows a Mother's fondness'[1]

HER days of exotic journeys must have seemed far away. Now her trips were short and sober. In the London area she visited Lord Ilay's Kenwood House, with Lady Oxford, and the spa at Islington, with young Mary. There they attended regularly, and saw it grow from a secluded spot to a fashionable and crowded one.[2] Mary Anne Cantillon invited her to Paris, with banter about Englishwomen's wit and England's weather. She still felt the pull of foreign parts. She sought out diplomats and other visiting foreigners. (Some of Mary Anne's letters came with English travellers, others with Voltaire's friend Thieriot or Montesquieu's friend Francis Bulkeley.)[3] But Lady Mary herself was a traveller no longer.

Her heroic battle for inoculation surfaced in memory from time to time, often with pain and regret, when some child died after the operation. Lady Mary was firmly committed to the gentle methods which she had seen practised in Turkey, and opposed to the more draconian English approach; she would not have accepted guilt or responsibility for such deaths, but would blame them on doctors' unwarranted escalation of what could have been safe. Still it must have both hurt and angered her when her past intentions and competence came under public questioning and sharp reproof.[4]

---

[1] *CL* iii. 15.   [2] *CL* ii. 438, 488.

[3] Messengers included Giuseppe Osorio-Alarcon of Sardinia (*CL* iii. 204), and Mme Hewer or Huerse, who *may* be MWM's old friend Frances Hewet. Mary Anne, left in a convent by her husband while he visited Spa in 1733, confided to MWM her views on 'les Prêtres, et la prêtraille', and imagined Bulkeley—later her second husband—prancing on horseback at Twickenham (to MWM, 1732, 1733, H MS 77. 158–67; Murphy 1988: 201).

[4] The 11-week heir of Lord Essex died on 16 Apr. 1728, and the 5-year-old heir of the Duke of Bridgewater on 2 May 1731; each was a recent inoculee; each was the child of a 2nd wife whose predecessor MWM had known well.

The family deaths of the 1720s were succeeded in the 1730s by deaths of friends. Not Sarah Marlborough: she seemed everlasting. She kept Lady Mary up to date on the eternal making and remaking of her will, and debated the remarriage of Lady Blandford (widow of her senior grandson).[5] But Mary Astell developed breast cancer, underwent a mastectomy, and died two months later, in May 1731. She had needed courage. There was, of course, no anaesthesia; and the standard surgical procedure was a circular incision, so that when the breast was off a huge round wound was left, without skin, to be dressed with lint until it scabbed.[6] She and Lady Mary often discussed death and futurity, the one expressing her modern uncertainties, the other asserting, 'very eagerly', her Christian faith in 'the bliss of another world'. Astell felt that her friend, 'tho' no unbeliever, thought too little, and too lightly on the chief concern of mortal beings'. A few weeks before her death, when she finally confided the truth about her 'mortal disease', she made 'a solemn promise' to prove her point, if this should be permitted, by visiting from beyond the grave. But after she died Lady Mary waited in vain.[7]

Many of Lady Mary's friends had their own worries, sometimes bizarre ones. In summer 1732 Hervey was in bad odour with the royal family after trying to sabotage the Prince of Wales's affair with his own former mistress Anne Vane. Lady Mary, who pulled no punches with Hervey, wrote a ballad representing the prince as a puppy with a cracked bottle (Miss Vane) tied to his tail, and her friend as a well-meaning bystander who tries to disengage the bottle and gets soundly bitten.[8] Personal lampoon was the chosen literary mode of the 1730s. Lady Mary's sallies on other fronts went hand in hand with the continued pro- and anti-Pope campaigns (see next chapter), as well as with her continued exercise of her powers as a wit.

Early in the year 1733 Lord William Hamilton, a peer's son about to be married, apparently caught the eye of Lady Hertford, who was married already, thirtyish, literary, and high-minded. She addressed to him (so it was said in Lady Mary's circle) a love-poem beginning 'Dear Colin, prevent my warm blushes, | For how can I speak without pain?' This gave great merriment to Lady Mary and Lady De La Warr, both veterans of the occasional-poetry scene. Lord William made no response, and Lady De La Warr begged Lady Mary to 'say something on behalf of a poor man who had

---

[5] *CL* iii. 134; Sarah to her granddaughter the Duchess of Bedford, 9 June 1734 (Bedford Office). Sarah supported the young woman; MWM thought she was throwing away her liberty.

[6] First to recommend a 'longitudinal' incision was Henry Fearon, 1784.

[7] From notes of Lady Louisa's anecdotes by Joseph Hunter, BL Add. MS 24483. 401–6; *E&P* 34–5.

[8] As a 9 year old at Hanover the prince had delighted her (Halsband 1973: 135–6; *E&P* 261–3; *CL* i. 286).

nothing to say for himself'. Lady Mary obliged, ruthlessly and entirely without feminist solidarity. She wrote for Lord William words in which to reject Lady Hertford, concluding: 'the Fruit that can fall without shakeing | Indeed is too mellow for me.'[9]

This unsisterliness was later to backfire against her. But at round about this time she twice used poetry to defend women, in her favourite reactive mode: in answers to poems by men. Young Lord Lyttelton, a friend of Fielding, published a poem which instructs his 'Belinda' how to be decorous, subdued, *not* like other women. Woman's *only* business, he says, is love; the intoxicating power of wit is too much for her feeble brain. He thus decouples the beauty and wit which in Lady Mary's youth had been seen as a natural pair. She responded by boiling down his advice (and that of a hundred future conduct books) to 'Be plain in Dress and sober in your Diet; | In short my Dearee, kiss me, and be quiet.'[10]

She also composed[11] a more serious *Answer* to James Hammond, who held the same rank as Lady De La Warr's among her poetical friends, though politics had divided him from his former friend Hervey. Hammond had addressed his Delia in a love-elegy, in which (like Strephon in 'Wednesday') he professes willingness to rest content with friendship only, but then swings back to declarations of passion and accusations of coldness. Delia was said to have declined his proposal of marriage 'on *prudential* reasons'; others as well as her suitor had very likely criticized her as heartless.[12] Lady Mary's answer repeats arguments she had made in 'Wednesday' and in answers to other love-addresses. Women risk more in love or marriage than men do, she argues; men lure women into commitment, but share none of the burdens which it brings. Hammond would be happy either to seduce Delia (so ruining her), or marry her (so involving her in poverty which will certainly destroy his love). Either way it would go badly with her. Wise virgins in this day and age are those

> Who *Hospitals* and *Bedlams* would explore,
> To find the Rich, and only dread the Poor;
> Who *legal Prostitutes* for Interest's sake,

---

[9] *E&P* 263. The first poem appeared in *The Cupid*, 1736 (9); MWM's is ascribed to Lord William's sister in NLS MS 3784. 63.

[10] *Advice to a Lady*, pub. 12 Mar. 1733 (MWM could have answered it before it was printed); *E&P* 264.

[11] Almost certainly hers, though no MS survives. Hervey kept a printed copy, but the sentiments are not his. One copy was annotated, 'Lady Mary Wortley—but the poem is printed as Lord Hervey's' (BL 1346 m. 34; *E&P* 270–2).

[12] The attribution to Hammond was not made till 1755; his Delia was Catherine Dashwood, later a friend of MWM's daughter. She was also close to Mary Delany, and thus to Lady De La Warr, the Tichbornes and the Molesworths—all MWM's friends (Delany 1861–2: i. 4, 100, 108, 117, 125, 136).

> *Clodios* and *Timons* to their Bosom take
>
> .   .   .   .
>
> Those, *Titles*, *Deeds*, and *Rent-Rolls* only wed,
> Whilst the best Bidder mounts their venal Bed

Delia, in Lady Mary's ventriloquizing of her, cannot bear to demote Hammond from lover to friend; but she will 'tho' I like the Lover quit the Love'. This poem, published on 29 March 1733, is the strongest of all Montagu's attacks on mercenary marriage: in blaming the 'grave *Aunt* and formal *Sire*' she may have in mind her own, twenty years before.[13]

Such repartee was fun to compose, even though anger (absent from the jokes at Lyttelton and Lady Hertford) animates the answer to Hammond. To the same period belongs Montagu's angriest poem, also an answer: *Verses to the Imitator of Horace*, the ultimate weapon which she and Hervey swung at Pope. Spring 1733 was a time of battles. In March and April Walpole and Hervey were fighting for their political lives as a result of Walpole's proposed Excise Bill, which proved the most unpopular taxation scheme ever put forward. The City presented a petition against it; in parliament, Edward Wortley Montagu spoke against it and Hervey defended it. At last Walpole, his majority having plummetted from seventy to seventeen, decided to 'postpone' the scheme.[14]

❧

Only her poetry, with distant reminders of travel and of inoculation, now distinguished Lady Mary's life at all from those led by others of her age and rank. Her summer 1733 was consumed by family matters. She had a responsibility to the new generation growing up around her (chiefly for getting the girls safely married); the young people, meanwhile, were as literary-romantic as she had once been. This phase of Lady Mary's experience as mother and aunt was fraught with difficulty. She saw her daughter's companions as a giddy gang, and implies that family pressure (to permit young Mary a lively social life) overruled her own views on how to bring up a daughter. The gang appears as a lively, attractive group of children in a painting done a few years before this: the second Duke of Kingston, his sister Lady Frances Pierrepont, and aunts (younger than his sister) Lady Caroline and Lady Anne Pierrepont.[15] With the young duke and Lady Mary's son (as well as

---

[13] Delia distinguishes herself from other women—as MWM did in 'While Thirst of Power' (see pp. 63–4); not quite as Lyttelton wished Belinda to.

[14] Walpole proposed to tax wine and tobacco; rumour said he was to tax food, clothing, and other necessities (Halsband 1973; 133, 146; Hervey 1931: i. 133, 146–7, 160–5, 273–4).

[15] Picture formerly at Thoresby, illustrated as by Vanderbank in Beattie and Stanley 1964, 1978.

Lady Frances *Erskine*) now abroad for much of their time, the younger generation was a female one: the three girls in the picture and Mary Wortley
Montagu.[16] In 1732 Ladies Caroline and Anne, at about sixteen and eleven,
were listed as subscribers to Elizabeth Boyd's unusual fiction, *The Happy-
Unfortunate, or the Female Page: A Novel.*[17]

Young Mary had her share of giddiness. One of her friends was Lady
Margaret Cavendish Harley, daughter of her mother's friend Lady Oxford.
Mary sometimes teased her mother about her friend's mother: 'Dear mama!
how can you be so fond of that stupid woman?' This, said family tradition,
'never failed to bring upon her a sharp reprimand, and a lecture against
rash judgements, ending with, "Lady Oxford is not shining, but she has
much more in her than such giddy things as you and your companions can
discern." '[18]

By 1734 young Mary (as 'Sylvia') and Lady Frances Pierrepont (as
'Melantha') were writing up their giddy lives in songs and verse, some of it
jointly composed.[19] Others who joined in the game called themselves
Evadne, Timandra, and Eurilla (the two young aunts and Lady Frances
Erskine). Their untitled album with its invented names invites comparison
with Lady Mary's own juvenile volumes. It does not, like those, imitate a
printed book. Its ambience is more social, less literary (though not *unliter-
ary*). The most frequent handwriting is that of 'Sylvia', the future Lady
Bute, the youngest but one of the group but evidently a natural leader. These
poems testify to her intelligence, which Lady Mary as mother recognized,
and also of that of 'Melantha', which Lady Mary as aunt denied.[20]

It would be hard to say which was the more promising fifteen-year-old
poet: Lady Mary or her daughter. But where Lady Mary based her early
work closely on the literary concerns of seventeenth-century poets like
Cowley and Waller, Behn and Philips, her young relatives write more like
the fashionable, occasional poets of her own circle, those whose poems she
kept in manuscript. They write about their own social lives.

In their poems, adolescent girls ogle 'teddy Lad[s]'. (A marginal note

[16] Their Leveson-Gower cousins were less close.

[17] Boyd, who wrote to support herself and her mother, had already shown high literary originality. She
had 134 women among 332 subscribers (including Elizabeth Carter and Lady Hertford), and the Duke of
Argyll as patron.

[18] *E&P* 39.

[19] Wh MS M 506. Sylvia may signify a lover of woods and groves; Melantha *may* come from a coquette in
Eliza Haywood's *Love in Excess*, 1719, who 'had the good Fortune not to be suspected by her Husband
though she brought him a Child in Seven Months after the Wedding' (*Love in Excess*, end of part 2).

[20] Mar MSS GD 124/15/1446/1; see p. 16 ff.; Isobel Grundy, 'Two generations of Mary Wortley
Montagu', in book on manuscript culture, ed. Nathan Tinker, forthcoming; *CL* ii. 427; MWM 1861. i. 509 n.
2. Two (later) notes in the volume wrongly interpret some of the names.

explains that 'teddy' means clever; it clearly means desirable too.)[21] The girls are rowed on the river, their steersman a charming young duke. They play a game which involves random pairing of male and female names; they dance till five in the morning. They go hunting in T[horesby] Park, where the Duke of K[ingsto]n flirts with the Duchess of N[orfol]k, whose husband meanwhile ogles Lady M[ar]y.[22] Their poems describe in sharp-eyed detail the love-affairs and jiltings of their friends. Like Pamela or like Boswell (neither of whom had yet written), 'Sylvia' and 'Melantha' write to the moment, and they seem to live to write. On the occasion of a visit to the opera, which they hope (like Lady Mary twenty years before) to use as a rendezvous, each dashes off one stanza beforehand and another afterwards to express her anxious feelings.

The poetry volume has a strong story-line: Melantha's courtship. It opens with her, at or near the fictional-heroine age of eighteen, defending love, while the younger Sylvia spurns it. Sylvia prefers friendship or even 'Cold Indifference';[23] Melantha already loves 'Melanthus' (whose fictional name shows that the young poets believe he is meant for her), while her brother wants her to marry Clitophon. (Lady Mary before her marriage would have called Melanthus her Paradise, Clitophon her Hell.) Some poems relate how Sylvia falls in love (for the first time) with 'Sylvander'; but she discovers his shortcomings, exerts all her strength of mind, and drops him. Sylvia is not the heroine here.

In real life Melanthus was Philip Meadows, who pursued Lady Frances Pierrepont perseveringly and eloped with her the day after she turned twenty-one. The poems occasionally call him Phil. The despised Clitophon was Sarah, Duchess of Marlborough's one-time favourite grandson, the Honourable John Spencer.[24] Lady Mary appears recognizably in the volume only once, flirting on horseback. But older women in general—'old Matrons as grave as a cat'—are these younger women's enemies.

> Lett beldames visit in their Coaches
>   And Delight in telling Lye's.
> When age has furrow'd every feature
> Then like them we'll vent our Satyr.
> We've time enough for growing wise.[25]

---

[21] Presumably this derives from someone named Edward; 'Sylvia''s scapegrace brother seems unlikely.

[22] Edward Howard, a Jacobite, succeeded his brother as 14th Duke of Norfolk in Dec. 1732 and was first received at court in Jan. He had a mansion at nearby Worksop and had married five years before. He was well known as silent or tongue-tied (GEC). Hervey wrote on Norfolk House, 1738, concluding 'Bad is it's Head, but ten Times worse it's Heart!' (Halsband MSS 48).

[23] She anticipates Frances Greville's famous 'Prayer for Indifference'.

[24] Brother of Lady Mar's friend Lady Bateman, half-brother of the unfortunate Willy.

[25] Wh MS M 506, 3–4.

A wheel had come full circle: Lady Mary, whose poetry once lamented her chastisement by her elders for meddling with 'love and wit', is now seen as an enemy of Melantha's 'equall flame'.

Lady Mary is not the volume's chief oppressor; that role is played by Lady Frances Pierrepont/Melantha's brother, Kingston, who had arrived at majority and ducal power on 3 April 1733. Lady Mary was not likely to favour Spencer when even his once doting grandmother Sarah had become disenchanted with him.[26] But she was no more likely to favour Meadows.

Years later Lady Mary still had painful feelings about this episode, and about the rashness of 'undertaking the management of another's child'. She told herself she had done her duty by her 'ever-dear Brother's children'; it was not her fault she could not counteract Lady Frances's 'nice' and pious notions imbibed from 'sillily good' people—that is from Lady Cheyne.[27] Lady Frances during her Melantha phase may not strike us as pious. If she took a high moral tone in rejecting Spencer she was only following in her aunt's footsteps. The romantic idealism she showed in eloping with Meadows may *seem* to follow in those footsteps too. But she did not assess, or debate, or agonize as her aunt had done.

Lady Mary, who had official charge of this young heiress, knew that Phil/Melanthus was in the picture, and saw him as a fortune-hunter.[28] She had written often and hotly against mercenary marriage, especially when it was the man who was mercenary. Spencer needed to marry money; he was going through it fast. In June 1733 Lady Frances's uncle Lord Gower thought her marriage treaty with Spencer would 'soon be concluded'; by early August it was known that her resistance had killed it. Gower reported that the 'censorious part of the town says she has declared she will never marry any man but Phil Meadows', and Lady Strafford that her love-affair with him had 'gon to farr to be prevented'. Lady Mary may have hoped to divert her niece's mind by taking her to the races at Lichfield in Staffordshire; but, if gossip can be believed, Lady Frances had a public fainting-fit at a ball and missed the races.[29]

She was, however, well enough to go on with Lady Mary (and the elder Leveson-Gower girls and a whole party of others) from the races to Gower's nearby estate at Trentham. Gower had intended to be elsewhere (he was planning to marry again, as he did within a couple of months); but he wrote

---

[26] He had contracted venereal disease (Harris 1991: 283–6).   [27] *CL* iii. 31, 138; ii. 459, 452.

[28] Hervey had reported in 1731 a rumour of his marrying a widow (Ilchester 1950: 105).

[29] Gower to Essex, 7 Aug. 1733 (BL Add. MS 27732. 218); Lady Strafford and someone else to Lady Huntingdon, 26 Aug., 23 Sept. (HMC 1934: 17, 18). Another cousin, Lady Frances Erskine, was about now trying Scots law against her English relatives.

hastily to his steward to bespeak a late dinner (between 5 and 6 p.m.) and 'a seven dish table'.[30] From Trentham Lady Mary went on to Thoresby, to discuss the Meadows problem with Kingston. She took her niece and daughter with her. While she retained a rosy memory of 'what the Duke of K. was at Thorsby', the young women wrote of this visit satirically.

It seems that at this date Lady Mary and Kingston mutually respected each other. She consulted him about his sister; Whig politicians worried about her political influence over him. It seems she helped to deter him from accepting a proffered court post; but this may not have been hard to do. Kingston was hardly promising political material. While on his Grand Tour he had evidently identified France as the land of pleasure, and later this year he headed back there, having turned doen not merely this post but also any part in election politics. For Lady Mary, her brother's son, as well as her own, was turning out a disappointment.[31]

Before leaving, Kingston wrote to ask Edward Wortley Montagu if his sister might again live with Lady Mary while he was away. Lady Mary, typically, had referred the matter to her husband, who presumably confirmed that the arrangement would 'not be disagreable or inconvenient'. Lady Mary still had charge of the heiress. Soon afterwards Gower remarried. It seems certain that Lady Mary was unhappy about this from the delicate way his daughter Gertrude Leveson-Gower broke the news, stressing that he had not sought to conceal the marriage (though he left it so late to notify Lady Mary that it was done before she heard), that the first Lady Gower's children were all in favour, that everyone had the highest possible value for Lady Mary, and that Lady Frances Pierrepont was invited for 'walking at the wedding'.[32]

It was a season of weddings. Spencer/Clitophon had his in February 1734. In March Princess Anne was attended to the altar by ten train-bearers 'all dressed in white habits', including Ladies Caroline and Frances Pierrepont.[33] Lady Frances/Melantha was not daunted by this close-up view of an unpalatable royal wedding. She turned twenty-one on 22 April. Next day she and Mary/Sylvia (whose father was probably away wooing

[30] Gower to Thomas Gregory, [1733], 1971 catalogue (Halsband MSS 53).

[31] *CL* iii. 159; Wh MS M 509; Thomas Bennett, 24, 28 Sept., 22 Oct. 1733, BL Add. MS 32688. 382–1, 413–14, 554–5; Bennett, BL Add. MS 32686. 554; George Gregory, BL Add. MS 32688. 131–2, 313–4; Kingston to the Duke of Devonshire, Chatsworth, MS 217.0.

[32] Kingston, 30 Oct. 1733; Gertrude Leveson-Gower to MWM, 1 Nov. (Halsband MSS; H MS 77. 176–7).

[33] Spencer m. Georgiana Carteret on 14 Feb. The Prince of Orange m. Princess Anne on 17 Mar.; MWM's rank entitled her to a place in a special gallery but not in the procession. The prince was so deformed that when the bride's mother saw 'ce monstre' ready for the marriage bed she nearly fainted (Harris 1991: 296; Delany 1861–2: i. 439; Hervey 1731: i. 268, 270, 271–2).

the voters of Peterborough) again attended the opera in Lincoln's Inn Fields; Phil/Melanthus was there too, in another box. The young ladies went out after the first act, saying Lady Frances felt ill; after a discreet pause, Meadows 'marched off', while Mary returned to her seat after fifteen minutes. Mary Pendarves (later Delany), who was sitting just behind Meadows, said '[m]ost people guessed what they were about'. The wedding did not follow for a couple more weeks. Lady Frances was probably already pregnant: she bore a daughter about seven months later.[34]

Young Mary's help in this courtship perhaps began the tensions between her and her mother which were to fester for more than a decade. Lady Frances received a worse press for eloping than Lady Mary had done. Delany remarked that she was right to seize her chance 'if she could not live without a husband, for nobody else would have cared for her notwithstanding her twenty thousand pounds'. Hervey wrote that Meadows 'is welcome to her for me; she has a sly, and at the same time a determin'd look, that would have made me dislike her more for a Wife than any Woman I know.'[35]

'Sylvia' was left to face a Twickenham summer without company of her own age. 'How Tedious is Life now Melantha is gone', she wrote, and added anxious hopes for her married happiness. She was able to conclude her album on a hopeful note. Lady Frances Meadows sent poems vibrant with love, joy, and reassurance that her husband fully deserved her heroic fidelity.

The piety and nicety which Lady Mary disliked in her niece can be glimpsed in the poems she wrote as a bride, about love in a cottage. They apparently drew from Lady Mary two unforgiving verse comments.[36] For one she minimally adapted a seventeenth-century epigram, spoken by a rejected suitor to the man who got the girl. Her fictional Spencer-equivalent advises his rival not to boast of his prize:

> No wonder that her Heart was lost
> Whose senses first were gone
>
> .   .   .   .   .   .
>
> Her loving thee is not the Cause;
> But Sign that she is mad.

---

[34] A marriage settlement was drawn up (BL Eg. MS 3660. 95). The wedding was noted by Hervey and *The Corn-Cutter's Journal*, 14 May, the birth as 14 Dec. by GEC and as 17 Dec. by *The Weekly Register: Or, Universal Journal*, 21 Dec. A later *canard* that Lady Frances had been married, with children, *before* marrying Meadows, may have been propagated with the intention of barring the Meadows children from the Pierrepont succession (GEC).

[35] Delany to Ann Granville, 27 Apr. (1861–2: i. 461–2); Hervey to Henry Fox, 11 May 1734, BL Add. MS 51410.

[36] As so often, attribution is probable, not certain.

Her other comment was a parody of a parody: from Nicholas Rowe's popular 'Colin's Complaint', filtered through another version called 'Melinda's Complaint', of which she kept a copy. It seems that Lady Mary wrote 'Melantha's Complaint' for her niece, appropriating the private nickname. She makes Melantha sorry for her foolish elopement and her loss of town pleasures, already disappointed in her dear Phil: 'Whatever a Lover may boast | A Husband is what one may hate.'[37]

Lady Mary's cynicism, if premature, was not entirely disproportionate. Lady Frances had five more children. During the 1740s and 1750s her family lived largely in dependence on the Duke of Kingston, sharing a household at Thoresby or in London with his various mistresses.[38] By then Lady Mary ostensibly pitied her niece for the 'mean Compliances' forced on her by financial need; but a hint of 'I told you so' sounds in her expressed wonderment that all Lady Frances's nicety and piety 'would end in being the Humble Companion' of a kept mistress. The Meadows family had, of course, powerful motives for believing that Kingston's notorious marriage to Elizabeth Chudleigh was bigamous; after his death they expended much effort and money to establish this as fact.[39] They succeeded: Lady Frances's second son became Earl Manvers and inherited the Pierrepont fortune.

❧

It is impossible to know just how deeply Lady Mary felt her niece's defection. She had been publicly fooled; her daughter had sided against her. But as usual she had other things on her mind: combat was in full swing between Pope on one side and herself and Hervey on the other; her biting, indecent, very funny verse attack on Swift had recently appeared in print. Her husband had been returned with a comfortable majority for his father's old constituency of Peterborough and was about to begin campaigning for another in Yorkshire.

Elected for Peterborough in April 1734 (three days after his niece's elopement), Wortley agreed to step in as a last-minute candidate for Yorkshire purely in order to help a Tory in his bid to squeeze out the two government

---

[37] MWM, 'Supposed to be wrote from J[ohn] Sp[encer] to Ph[ilip] M[eadows] on his marriage' and its original (H MS 255. 77; GEC, under 1st Duke of Montagu); 'Melinda's Complaint' (H MS 255. 58–9 and other copies); Rowe's poem (whose Colin, said Horace Walpole, was the man MWM's stepmother jilted to marry her father) and the 'Melantha' version (H MS 81. 55, 168–9; Walpole, *Corr.* xiv. 243). H MS 81's complete copy of the Melantha poem is in Lady Bute's hand, incomplete in MWM's, but surely only MWM would thus snub Lady Frances. This poem *may* have been excised from the end of Wh MS M 506. Printed as MWM's in 1803 (v. 220–3), it is omitted from *E&P*.

[38] Marie Thérèse de La Touche; Elizabeth Chudleigh; Frances Anne, née Hawes, Lady Vane—not the same as Miss Anne Vane (Egmont 1920–3: ii. 381).

[39] *CL* ii. 459; Rizzo 1994: 61–82.

Whig candidates. This county election brought tumult to York; a frenzied influx of voters into the city included the elderly and infirm, rousted out and conveyed by those who needed their votes. 'The great Mr Wortley', a key figure in Yorkshire's anti-Walpole thrust, dispensed free food and drink, rode in a 'cavilcade', and entertained gentlemen to dinner at Wharncliffe.[40]

The result was declared on 21 May 1734, the day after Wortley's official appointment as Deputy Lieutenant of the West Riding. He had a majority in his home region, but came bottom of the poll overall. No matter: he was 'vastly carest by the gentlemen'. He had been instrumental in keeping out one of the ministerial candidates—who at once levelled charges of mob intimidation and 'foul artifices', which dragged on for eighteen months. If not a famous victory, Wortley's Yorkshire campaign ranked as effective harassment of Walpole. He took his duties as Deputy Lieutenant with typical seriousness, set to work to study local issues (especially the cloth trade), and accumulated notes and papers on every possible related topic. He was also by now keeping detailed notes about the management of fish ponds and the sale of wood from his Yorkshire estates.[41]

Lady Mary's reactions to these political ventures were ambivalent. In January 1734, as the Yorkshire campaign hotted up, she dropped in on Lady Strafford, whose husband was on Wortley's side in Yorkshire and receiving a flood of letters praising his performance. Though Lady Mary walked from her house in Cavendish Square to St James's Square (about three-quarters of a mile), wearing a sack dress 'and all her jewells', her hostess was not impressed: 'she had no news [presumably of the election], and I was sadly tired of her before she went.' The two women moved in the same circles: Lord Strafford owned a house at Twickenham; his Great Dane was the 'Eldest-born' puppy of Pope's Bounce. But as a convinced Tory who had slandered Dolly Walpole on principle in 1713, Lady Strafford was not a real friend. Lady Mary was apparently attempting tactical friendship for her husband's sake; apparently her attempt was spurned.[42]

In private she flung off an extempore squib on this year's elections: 'Epigram 1734', adapted from something in her old favourite, *Poems on Affairs of State*. Her version runs,

[40] Cartwright 1883: 489–94, 496, 503–5. EWM had become an assiduous anti-government speaker (Egmont, *Diary*, i. 185; ii. 125–6).

[41] Collyer 1952: 53–83; Cartwright 1883: 511–13. EWM's notes cover the election, the Leeds economy, fulling mills, West Riding cloth production 1725–30, and the effects of a recent Act for regulating it (Wh MS M 117, 107, 121–2, D 265).

[42] Cartwright 1883: 321, 501. Lady Strafford had inoculated her children in 1723. The sack was not slovenly wear, cf. p. 299 and n. 39. MWM later wrote to Lord Strafford about help for one Elizabeth White (*CL* ii. 102–3).

Born to be slaves, our Fathers freedom sought,
And with their blood the valu'd treasure bought,
We their mean offspring our own bondage plot,
And born to Freedom, for our chains we vote.

She must be locating past freedom-fighting in the Civil War. In a related poem she ridicules Wortley's Opposition friends as emulating a low moment in Old Testament history by setting up the Prince of Wales (Prince Frederick) as a golden calf.[43] Neither of these would have pleased the writer's husband—especially if they were contributed to public debate at some gathering of those who thought like the Straffords.

Lady Mary sounds opposed to her husband's Opposition. Yet she was not, like her friend Hervey, a straighforward supporter of the court and government. It may well have been now that she wrote her 'Expedient to put a stop to the spreading Vice of Corruption'. This ironical effusion sees parliament as a gang of bullies who run up debts with no intention of paying, who 'cant Liberty and promote Slavery, talk pertly of the King and sell the Subject'. They, not the Prime Minister, foster the corruption which poisons personal integrity, learning, and domestic virtues. Abolishing parliament, says Montagu, would reform morals and substitute finer goals for 'the great End of acquiring Money'. Walpole 'is as Honest as his present post gives him leave to be': let him and the king rule without parliament. (This from one who elsewhere sided with seventeenth-century anti-monarchists!) Her irony is not disciplined or partisan but anarchic and disaffected. She wrote to please herself alone.[44]

On 14 January 1735 Wortley took his seat in the new parliament, with eighty-two more Opposition Whigs. He also sat on a Place Bill committee to push a reform he had favoured since 1710, of government handouts of jobs or 'places' to party hacks. Other reforms were in the air too: to the theatre licensing system, and to the system whereby the 154 Scottish peers elected sixteen of their number to represent them at Westminster. Walpole had the selection of Scottish peers sewn up. They were a key element in his trusty House of Lords majority, and the men who managed it were the brothers Argyll and Ilay.

Place Bill reformers and 'Scotch-Petition' reformers (including Wortley) had Walpole in their sights. Theatre reformers, on the other hand, included among their targets a gadfly critic of Walpole: Henry Fielding.[45]

---

[43] *E&P* 278–9.

[44] *E&P* 100–4. There is perhaps an element of feminist disaffection from systems which excluded women's contribution.

[45] Fielding married in Nov. 1734. His friendship with MWM is ill documented aside from literature: but

Lady Mary, with allegiances pulling her several ways, was reported as approaching this knot of issues with paradox, in talk as in writing. She 'declares a loud for a Reformation' of the theatres; 'but then she sais the Parliament shou'd have first began [*sic*] with Westminster Hall [that is, the law] and the Church.' She suggested, that is, that abuses in those two most patriarchal institutions massively outweighed anything wrong in the theatre system (and perhaps in the parliamentary system too). To reform the theatre without the law and the church 'is of no more use than the saving and [*sic*] Old pair of Bellows when a House is on fire'. And if it was futile to attempt controlling Fielding, it must be equally so to try, as her husband was doing, to control Walpole.[46]

Lady Mary's wit on political subjects was a byword: people needing an epigram turned to her. Some of her verse is known today only from fragments that got quoted. She also turned her wit on social targets. Soon after this Mary Anne Cantillon, recently widowed, was suspected of an affair with a man who had just returned to Paris leaving her in England. The queen asked her (in what could have been either a *gaffe* or a sneer) why she did not 'follow her husband'. Lady Hervey replied archly, 'Madam she has none.' The queen extricated herself graciously; but Lady Mary later suggested that Mary Anne ought to have *assumed* that her late husband was meant, not her alleged current lover, and 'made answer, what Madam doe you take me for an Indian wife? Must I have burnt my self with my husband?'[47]

Probably some time after 1734, Lady Mary wrote in her diary about a lady boasting of having kept a man as a sex-object. She quoted the boast: 'I am not such a Fooll as to make him Master of my Fortune—I have only settled upon him £1,000 a Year for Life, for the temporary use of his beautifull Person.' Lady Mary made believe to admire: 'all the Women in England should join to erect a statue in honor of that one of the sex who first proclaimed her Disregard of the shackles which Man had for so Many Ages imposed upon Women.' In fact, though her great-nephew Erskine of Mar garbled the names, this heroine must be Mary Edwards, an heiress who did in fact marry, at the Fleet Chapel. When she found her husband likely to leave not a penny of her fortune unspent, she boldly erased her marriage record and altered that of her son's baptism, calling herself a spinster.[48]

Meanwhile, beyond the end of summer 1734 (which her daughter had

she was godmother to his first child (b. Apr. 1736). She knew his sister Sarah well; her daughter got to know his wife; Lord Bute nominated his son Allen to Charterhouse School (Battestin 1989: 177, 618).

[46] Lady Betty Finch [Apr. 1735], Devonshire MS 230. 8.

[47] Probably the love-affair was apocryphal, and Mary Anne already living with a different man, Bulkeley (Lady Betty Finch, 3 June 1735, Devonshire MSS 230. 8; Murphy 1988: 203).

[48] See Uglow 1997: 364–5.

dreaded as a lonely one), Lady Mary lingered at Twickenham. Europe was at war; Walpole and Hervey were striving to keep England out of it. In October she read in the papers of the death of Arabella Thompson, another frail and victimized wife, apparently a friend of Skerrett. She had commented at the time on Mrs Thompson's marriage, and (more than once) on the vices of Sir George Oxenden, her brother-in-law and seducer. The husband, Oxenden's intimate friend and perhaps a pursuer of Lady Mary herself, seems to have repudiated Arabella more than once, taking her back between times. Mrs Thompson died in childbirth (a fact the papers left out) while 'on the Road from France to London'. Hervey observed darkly that Oxenden was 'suspected of having a greater share in her catastrophe than merely having got the child'.

Montagu wrote for her a poignantly felt elegy. 'Tho' short thy day and transient like the Wind, | How far more blessed than those yet left behind! | Safe in the grave with thee thy griefes remain . . .' She finds no defence for the dead woman's behaviour, as she had for the living Mary Yonge; she even uses her fate as a warning to other 'tender Nymphs in lawless passions gay, | Who heedless down the paths of pleasure stray'. What she mourns is beauty and short-lived pleasure. All her Muse can compass is a sigh, a tear, a veil drawn over 'faults she can't commend'; all the consolation she offers is that scandal and malice will soon move on to their next victim. It would not have surprised her when this poem, like that on Mrs Bowes, attracted censorious replies. Though it focuses entirely on Arabella, it can perhaps be fully tasted only in light of the author's own situation as regards scandal and malice as she wrote it.[49]

Lady Mary could not remain wistful for long. It was probably this year that she wrote an amused, energetic verse letter to Hervey on 30 October, the king's birthday, to capture in words this ritual of pomp and ceremony, as she had done twenty years before for Philippa Mundy. She was glad to miss it; Hervey, as Vice-Chamberlain of the Royal Household, was bound to attend it.[50] She pictured her friend Sir Robert in brocade ('the Potent Knight whose Belly goes | At least a Yard before his Nose'), the queen in pink ('Superior to her waiting Nymphs, | As Lobster to attendant Shrimps'), and the 'new batch of Lords' fresh from the Grand Tour.[51]

---

[49] *E&P* 277–8; MS R.B. 1. 53 at Houghton Hall, Norfolk (information from archivist); *Daily Post-Boy*, 21 Oct.; Hervey 1931: ii. 741–2; Tickell 1931: 131; see p. 244. Lady Oxford's daughter had a copy of MWM's poem by Nov. She kept with it one of the reproving replies (Delany 1861–2: i. 522; Portland MSS xx. 31, xix. 323; *GM* June 1755: 327).

[50] She and Hervey seem to have had a long-running joke about her liking for, and his dislike of, the rural colour green (Hervey to MWM, 2/13 Nov. 1739, Hervey MS 474/2. 77; cf. *Spectator*, no. 387).

[51] *CL* ii. 98–99.

A satirist happy to be on the sidelines, she wrote of the young lords as colts whose human mothers have not the sense of equine ones. But crisis was coming in each of her own maternal relationships. Her negotiating of it was reported by a hostile witness, Eleanor Verney.

Edward Wortley Montagu the younger turned twenty-one in May 1734. This was the moment for him to claim his legacy of £1,000 from his grandfather Sidney, and in his view to succeed to some part of the Wortley estates.[52] Public opinion, as reported by Verney, felt he had right on his side on both points; it is not clear whether or not Wortley's legal steps to disinherit him had taken effect. In the autumn (some months after Pope had alleged his parents would be glad of his death) he turned up in England, leaving John Anderson and some debts behind him at Troyes. (Wortley held Anderson responsible for this, and refused to see him for years.) Wortley was in the north. Lady Mary was at Twickenham; her daughter had a role in Nathaniel Lee's *Theodosius*, which 'the young ladies of Twittenham' were to perform on 18 November at Orleans House. (They may have included Lady Frances Erskine, who was a friend of the Johnstones.) When her son appeared on the doorstep Lady Mary refused to see him, saying she was forbidden 'to let him come into her house'. He went on to visit a friend, while she decamped in haste to London.

There he caught up with her. He was handsome in appearance, charming in manner, voluble in speech. But the interview was tense and unhappy. He accused her of blocking a reconciliation with his father. Either now or on his next London visit, three years later, there occurred two episodes which she long remembered. He had an outburst of rage against her (what she called being 'hot headed') at a periwig-maker's shop just off the Haymarket; and when she suggested that he might redeem his reputation by serving as a volunteer officer in the Austrian emperor's army, he replied 'He suppose'd I wish'd him kill'd out of the Way.' She did not, she said, lose her temper in return, but used a gift or bribe of £50 to get him to return abroad. But Verney reported, 'they say he has left orders with his lawyer to get the Estate in dispute'. She also wrote, 'Lady Mary now owns her son is married.' It can have been little comfort to Lady Mary that her daughter performed her stage role as Athenais 'exceeding well'.[53]

The mother did what she had done after the crisis with Edward in 1727

---

[52] Wh MS M D 246e.

[53] Verney, 7 Nov., 19 Nov. 1734, Wh MS M 439/14; *CL* ii. 257, 273, 275; EWM jr. to Gibson, 7/18 May 1742, and to Edward Montagu, 3 Oct. 1742, Huntington MS MO 7, 8. MWM thought Pope had set her son against her through the tutor Forster. This *may* also have been the time, when Edward was 'persuing his Ruin in the worst manner', that John Gibson pressed her, as her Christian duty, to 'set a gloss' on his actions when speaking to EWM; she made him 'very angry' by answering that 'I thought the first Duty was Truth' (*CL* ii. 204–5).

and perhaps in 1730: she fell sick. Newspapers reported her as seriously ill on 9 December 1734; Hervey said she was dying.[54] It was not a good moment for weakness. The year ended and 1735 began with a succession of hammer-blows from Pope. Early in February Lady De La Warr died. Maria Skerrett was dangerously ill with pleurisy that spring.[55]

Young Mary was still writing to her cousins. In January she told Lady Frances Erskine from London that it was 'realy quite odious of you to Stay so Long at Twick'. She urged her to come to town in time for the new opera. She herself had been opera-going (she was 'quite charm'd with Farenelli') and at court for the Prince of Wales's birthday. She kept up the old kind of secret language, and had news to report of two of Lady Frances Erskine's 'Husbands'—presumably suitors.[56]

Lady Mary later wrote that she 'in every point perform'd' her duty to her daughter. She had her presented at court, and felt intense anxiety, followed by pleasure at hearing her 'universally commended'. She treated her, she said, 'with a tenderness and Freindship that is not commonly found . . . even from her Infancy I have made her a Companion and Wittness of my Actions'. This treatment, she felt, deserved in return 'not only the regard due to a Parent' but the esteem and gratitude due to 'a valuable Freind'. She wrote this, in anger and self-justification, to her husband; but she took the same tone to Lady Bute herself. Her insistence on her own blamelessness suggests that she felt she might be blamed.[57] But if her conduct towards her marriageable daughter was culpable, it seems she sinned less in oppressing her child than in failing to resist her husband.

Her writing took a new departure about now, probably fostered by young Mary's theatrical interests and courtship prospects. In the autumn of 1734 a French company visited Fielding's Little Theatre in the Haymarket and gave several performances of *Le Jeu de l'amour et du hasard* by Pierre de Marivaux. Montagu wrote her own free version of this comedy, in which the heroine tests her suitor by changing clothes with her maid, not knowing that he has done the same with his valet. She thought well enough of her version (which she called *Simplicity*) to keep a fair copy.[58]

---

[54] Newspapers, 9 Dec. 1734; Ilchester 1950: 213–14.

[55] De La Warr (whom MWM imagined in elysium with 'Ovid, Congreve, Sappho') had borne a son (at least her fifth child) in 1733. In summer 1734 she was gravely ill and neglected by her husband (*CL* ii. 113; Hervey 1931: ii. 420; Collins, *Peerage*; Hervey to Henry Fox, 10 Feb., BL Add. MS 51410; Harris 1991: 303).

[56] 'Melantha', met once by chance, did not look well, though her baby was 'the prettyest creature that ever was seen' (transcript, 22 Jan. [1735], GD 124/15/1446, endorsed 'From Evadne [*sic*] and Silvia').

[57] *CL* ii. 168–9; iii. 142. To tell her husband about a constant witness of her own actions may have served another purpose of self-justification.

[58] *E&P* 315 ff. By 1739 MWM owned three novels by Marivaux (Wh MS M 139; Yale, no. 1523 in *Tinker* 1959).

In her hands the formally elegant French piece becomes more homely and down to earth. A stage direction says the two girls, mistress and maid, 'run out jumping'. When her heroine, Bellinda, thinks her sexuality has betrayed her into loving a footman, she says 'I hate every body, I hate my selfe, I could tear the whole world to pieces.' It also becomes soft-centred in a manner unusual for comedy and unusual for the writer Montagu. A benevolent father and brother, who desire nothing but the heroine's happiness, keep watch over her bid for autonomous choice. Montagu has been read as wishfully reversing her own past experience of paternal tyranny; but from the date she is more likely thinking of the present experience of her daughter. *Simplicity* perhaps reflects its author's motherhood, too, in its sympathetic depiction of the heroine's anguish when she thinks she is shaming herself by inappropriate love. Some years before, Lady Mary had flippantly imagined her daughter doing just this; in real life it would have poisoned the self-esteem of a nicely-brought-up girl. When Bellinda finds it is a gentleman and not a footman she loves, she cries, 'My Life is sav'd.'[59]

Simplicity does indeed read well as a fantasy of free-but-protected choice of partner, but as a maternal, not a first-person fantasy. It lightly evades the threat of paternal tyranny, and rather less lightly the threat of loving the wrong man. Lady Mary later said she had felt compelled to stay in London all summer in 1735, on her daughter's account, to avoid a Twickenham social life dominated by Lady Vane's 'Balls and partys of pleasure'. This shady lady had spent an earlier summer, during her marriage to Lord William Hamilton, 'in a variety of pleasures and parties', mostly got up by Hamilton's sister and Maria Skerrett. Now she was widowed, advantageously remarried, and even more notorious. Probably not yet involved with Lady Mary's nephew Kingston, she was just now ostentatiously in love with Sewallis Shirley. Shirley's famously pious mother, Lady Ferrers, permitted her brood of daughters to attend Lady Vane's parties. Lady Mary denied hers this indulgence, despite the Skerrett connection. She had other motives too for keeping Mary in Cavendish Square.[60] Twickenham was developing drawbacks. Its proximity to Pope, to the Johnstones (recently hosts to Lady Frances Erskine), and to Argyll and Ilay, uncles of the young Earl of Bute, were all in various ways undesirable for the mother if not for the daughter.

Soon after the Johnstone theatricals of November 1734, Elizabeth Robinson sought confirmation from the Duchess of Portland 'that Lord Percival is

[59] *E&P* 323, 356, 357.
[60] MWM says she had no acquaintance with Lady Vane (*CL* iii. 3; 'Memoirs of a Lady of Quality': Smollett 1964: 443, 452, 459, 467–9).

to be married to Miss Wortley'.[61] The rumour was premature, but not wholly invented. Perceval's father, Lord Egmont, dated the serious negotiation from 12 July 1735. By then he had asked his lawyer to wait on Wortley, and was ready to sup with Lady Mary and tell her the details. Lady Mary 'replied, that she was but one of three': herself, her husband, her daughter.

Three suitors were in the ring besides Perceval: Lords Cornbury, Sunbury, and Holdernesse.[62] Lady Mary preferred Perceval, and thought she might bring her husband to prefer him too, although his property lay in Ireland. But her seventeen-year-old daughter, when consulted, refused everyone named; she 'cried, and desired she might not marry at all'. Lady Mary wrote fluently to Egmont of the young men's various qualifications (financial and other), and of the 'very settled affection' which their daughter had earned from both her parents. There was substance under her flourishes. She concluded that 'Mr. Montague's estate was all in his power [i.e. free from entail], and her daughter would indeed be a great fortune.' She countermanded Egmont's lawyer, 'for she would herself carry the matter on, if it would bear'.[63]

'Sylvia' was now in her cousin 'Melantha''s former position: a marital jackpot waiting for her elders to dispose of her. Lady Mary knew that Wortley 'design'd [her] his Heiresse', but had been instructed not to tell her daughter so; she was not even to tell her that she would have her grandfather Kingston's legacy some day.[64] Gossip, however, took note of her brother's disgrace and put her portion at £20,000.[65] When Lady Mary reported to Wortley her negotiation with Perceval, 'he did not give any encouragement, saying it was no great catch for his daughter, to whom he designed to give 100,000*l*'. His coal-trade wealth was growing fast. According to a pamphlet of 1739, the Grand Alliance of which he was a member had been pursuing a policy of price-cutting to drive out any owners outside its ranks. Having achieved this by 1732, they reduced the measure or selling unit of coal by

---

[61] 6 Dec. 1734 (Huntington MS MO 249). The writer was later famous as Mrs Montagu; the duchess became the closest friend of MWM's daughter.

[62] Holdernesse had been an earl at 4; his mother's remarriage had scandalized MWM. Cornbury was heir to Lord Clarendon, Sunbury (an early inoculee) to Lord Halifax. Cornbury was already an MP, the others still undergraduates at Cambridge. None married for six more years. A poem allegedly written at Tunbridge Wells by the 14-year-old Mary on the 15-year-old Holdernesse expresses desire ('When he kiss'd me, I long'd for the Book | The Parson, and something else more') but some mistrust (Osborn MS c 360/1. 251).

[63] Egmont 1920–3: ii. 185–6, 187.

[64] *CL* iii. 267. MWM later criticized the error of parents who try not to let their daughters know they are beautiful; she apparently connived at EWM trying not to let theirs know she would be rich.

[65] Just the sum which EWM, as a suitor, had pronounced 'a very trifle' for a rich family to provide (*CL* i. 68). Egmont's respect for MWM may have dated from the inoculation of his younger son, George Perceval, in 1724.

'a sixteenth part or more'. In 1736 they raised prices again, and scrapped a traditional small payment to London dealers. Their holdings both by lease and ownership continued to grow before and after the pamphlet appeared.[66] Wortley was riding high.

In his Rochefoucauldian maxims he had written, 'The Profuse are seldom Generous, commonly dishonest, always Vain. Frugality is the Daughter of Prudence and the Mother of Generosity.'[67] His generosity to his daughter, however, was to take the form of inheritance after his death, not an immediate portion. Suitors' demands ran at £20,000; he offered only £10,000. Yet he was well into dynasty-building. Of the field so far, he favoured Sunbury, 'being of his own name and family'. But next week he thought of a better candidate: Lord Gower's eldest surviving son. This choice was founded not on family sentiment but on the huge Gower estates. In the background lay the lure of the Duke of Kingston's as well. If he were to die without issue, his property would be divided between the heirs of his two non-Jacobite aunts. (Wortley thought nothing of any Meadows claim.) In that case, a marriage of Mr William Leveson-Gower[68] and Miss Mary Wortley Montagu would add the reunited Kingston fortune to the massive Gower and Wortley Montagu fortunes. By the end of the month Wortley was more than ever set on Leveson-Gower, although three sessions with the young man's father had produced no agreement as to figures.

Lady Mary at this stage believed Perceval the man most likely to make her daughter happy. Both Marys were set against young cousin Granville; Lady Mary cited the old problem with his legs. She confessed to Perceval that her husband had 'the foible of loving money'.[69] The unhappy daughter 'said she would do what her parents direct her'; but it seemed that, like those of Jane Austen's Elizabeth Bennet, they might direct her in different directions. Lady Mary couched her choice of Perceval in romance terms; and she went so far as to let him make his proposal directly to her daughter, in her presence. After that meeting she secured a promise from her husband 'not to force his daughter . . . nor to marry her against her own consent', and told

---

[66] A new agreement, signed in autumn 1737, consolidated their gains. Though parliament was petitioned in Apr. 1738 against the 'late advance of the price of coal', the owners' regulations probably survived another decade (*An Enquiry into the Reasons of the Advance of the Price of Coals*, 1739, quoted in Sweezy 1938: 27–9; Flinn and Stoker 1984: 41; Buxton 1978: 37–8).

[67] H MS 80. 173–8.

[68] He died in 1739. Sunbury later added the surname Dunk to Montagu.

[69] Leniently as this is stated, it is the nearest thing to criticism of him which survives from her pen since her reproaches for lack of paternal feeling, back in 1718 (Egmont 1920–3: ii. 228). Perceval married a fortune of £20,000 in Feb. 1737; he became a strong opponent of Walpole.

Egmont she hoped 'to be able to give him a more final answer' in early August 1735. (Did she still hope to persuade her daughter?) Egmont and his son were left hanging.[70]

Young Mary's heart had already been touched, more than a year before, by 'Sylvander'. But the 'teddy Lad' whom she loved and contrived to marry was John Stuart, 3rd Earl of Bute. He was probably not Sylvander. Lady Mary may or may not have known he was in the running during the time of her active support for Perceval. It *seems* that some time between the summer of 1735 and the summer of 1736 she came to approve or at least accept Bute instead.

Bute was a handsome young man with politically powerful uncles (Wortley's opponents). His father was dead, and his estate in his own hands. But it was in Scotland, and therefore unequal to supporting its owner in the cash economy of the south, as Lady Mar had learned. Since boyhood Bute had been not in Scotland but at Eton. He spent his holidays near Twickenham, at his uncles' estates: Argyll at Whitton (the village where Eleanor Verney also lived) and Ilay at Hounslow Heath.[71] This must be how he got to know young Mary. It is telling that her gift for acting (which was a passion with him) had just emerged.

Egmont, recording the courtship of his son Perceval, left Mary's feelings unreported. Perceval said he was drawn by love, not just money. He was certainly persevering; he presumably saw Mary a good deal in London during 1735. In January 1736 Lady Mary was invited to Egmont's house in Pall Mall to watch the grand funeral procession of the Duke of Buckingham. But that April, after a courtship of some eighteen months, Perceval withdrew. He gave no hint that the lady, as well as her father, preferred another. He told his father he had done everything possible to reach agreement with Edward Wortley Montagu; to offer more would be inconsistent with his honour. This outcome (notified to Lady Mary, not her husband) cannot have come as a surprise.[72]

By then Bute was probably a declared suitor; but he must have known he could hardly hope to make an acceptable offer where Perceval had failed. Since Lady Mary had supported Perceval she must have thought that she could win Wortley round to offer him *some* dowry. For Bute, Wortley was prepared to offer nothing at all. According to Eleanor Verney, he told Bute's

---

[70] Egmont 1920–3: ii. 187–8, 189–90. In the 1720s in her circle parentally sanctioned lovers were left alone together all day (*CL* ii. 22).

[71] The uncles co-operated politically, though they had not been on speaking terms since a quarrel years before (Hervey 1931: i. 297).

[72] Egmont's friendship with MWM survived (1920–3: ii.257, 419).

uncle Argyll this when Argyll 'waited on' him on behalf of his nephew. Argyll would give nothing himself in response to nothing: that would be to encourage improvidence. Ilay, too, said he 'would have made a settlement' if only Wortley had given 'a handsome fortune down'.[73] But as it was, nothing at all would be forthcoming to support the marriage, beyond what supported Bute as a bachelor.

Lady Mary's self-justifying account of the matter years later reflects emotional pain and unease. She claimed she had recognized Bute's integrity (that is, she knew he was no Phil Meadows), and therefore consented easily (that is, more easily than Wortley?) to the match. Still, she saw it as her maternal duty to lay before her daughter, 'in the strongest manner', a view of 'all the hazards attending Matrimony', especially the solitude and relative poverty that awaited her in the Isle of Bute. She seemed to think young Mary would have been happiest in 'a single Life';[74] only her father wanted her married and her 'many near Relations'—the gang—influenced her to want the same. Lady Mary even gave Bute's beloved a disquisition on the faults she discerned in his character—and patiently bore the resulting anger, since she felt her to be 'blinded with a passion'.[75]

Presumably all this took place after Lady Mary knew that marrying Bute would be marrying into (relative) poverty, less because of his circumstances than because of Wortley's—and therefore his uncles'—intransigence. She knew they would all have to live with her husband's decision; she knew her daughter would be poorer than she had been; whatever she thought of Bute (his politics, his nationality, his personality) she did not believe one could be happy with love on a crust. Her letters imply that any support she offered her daughter was grudging at best. Yet two people, Horace Walpole and her own son, later claimed that she was instrumental in bringing about the Bute marriage. Each gave the story a nasty twist; a modern reader may feel that a kernel of truth in it would be to Lady Mary's credit.[76]

Wortley's feelings are equally hidden: the easiest interpretation is that he did indeed, as Pope maintained, care for nothing but money. Or he may have held politics against Bute as well;[77] he may have held his daughter's

[73] Wh MS M 439/13.

[74] This surprising sentiment is the clearest hint that she was thinking of, and identified her daughter with, her own younger self.

[75] *CL* ii. 290, 481; iii. 24. Bute claimed descent from Banquo and Robert the Bruce; his assets fell below his birth. Chesterfield, who found him dry, sullen, and proud, noted that he never looked at the person he was speaking to (1990: 474). Later on MWM was readier than EWM to see their son disinherited for the Butes' children.

[76] Walpole, *Corr.* xiii. 244; *CL* iii. 255. During his courtship Bute became a candidate for selection as a Scottish Representative Peer.

[77] Ironically, Argyll was soon to differ from his brother and join the anti-Walpole faction.

self-assertiveness against her. He cannot be read, charitably, as defending her from a fortune-hunter or as driven by an affectionate, possessive reluctance to see her married at all. Having failed to use her as a bargaining chip, he jibbed at helping her to marry Bute. We today may feel he behaved even more like an unfeeling brute than his father-in-law. Yet he kept his wife's respect and his daughter's love and duty.

He did, unlike Lady Mary's father, permit the wedding. On the third of August (not four months from Perceval's withdrawal) Eleanor Verney reported, 'Miss Wortley is going to be married to Ld Bute the Duke of Argyle's nephew. The father and mother suffer him to visit but will give no fortune with her.' They were married on the evening of 13 August 1736, in the parish of Marylebone. The earliest newspaper paragraphs (before the ceremony) thought Wortley was a baronet and his daughter had 'a plentiful Fortune', even the £100,000 first suggested. (The fortune was as nonexistent as the baronetage.) Verney wrote that the parents were present: Wortley gave the bride away. It is only from this that we know Lady Mary heard her daughter pronounce the 'words of mystery' (as she later called them)[78] of the Anglican marriage service. Verney adds that the father 'would not stay to give them a dinner on Friday.—How can People be such wretches to their children?'[79]

Lady Mary made several visits to Argyll's house, sometimes as a dinner guest. He was a heavy father, whose four daughters were mostly silent in his presence. Ironically in the circumstances, she was drawn to the youngest and cheekiest, later Lady Mary Coke.[80]

Some time after the wedding Verney was still riveted. She mentioned that Lady Mary had attended a Sunday dinner at Ilay's together with the young couple, who had then 'drank coffee with her Papa at Twitnam'. (Her phrasing suggests that Wortley was not at the dinner.) She wondered at the parents' harshness. 'Wortley has acted according to [? their ? usual][81] way, given no fortune—and so the new married couple retire into Scotland next week.' She added a report on the money negotiations: Bute, she said, 'has shewed himself a man of Honour' in standing by his choice when he learned she would have no dowry. (Perceval, on the contrary, had pleaded his honour in withdrawing.) Bute had 'said he liked the young Lady and if she would be content to live in Scotland he would marry her. She said, any where rather then stay with her Mother.'[82]

---

[78] Or 'paroles mysterieuses' ('Docile', *RW* 132, 231).   [79] Wh MS M 439/13.

[80] *CL* iii. 161.   [81] Uncertain MS reading.

[82] On 25 Sept. she noted 'Wortleys son is where he was in Holland, and fares no better for his sister having no fortune' (Wh MS M 439/14).

Eleanor Verney would have pop psychology on her side in blaming the family conflict on mother-daughter tensions. One can imagine this kind of thing being said in Twickenham, where Lady Mary must have stood out among the card-playing or pious matrons of her daughter's poetry, as different from either. Verney's letters present both Wortley Montagus as eccentrics, and both as equally empowered to give or withhold a fortune.[83]

So far so good. Lady Bute chose her mother as godmother to her first child. But it seems these courtship events had inflicted some slow-acting strain on their relationship. Over the next few years Lady Mary did indeed come to feel that her daughter was guilty of vaguely defined offences against her: that her maternal care had been ill repaid. Did Lady Bute perhaps show some dissatisfaction with her mother's behaviour? Or did she show an anger against her father which her mother could not tolerate? This would set Lady Mary in a very non-feminist light.

Their quarrel (still to come) was painful and unexplained. But one point is worth remembering. Mary Wortley Montagu junior married her Paradise, and she did not have to elope to do it. Neither her mother, nor her aunts,[84] nor her cousin Lady Frances Meadows could say the same.

---

[83] It may appear that I credit Verney's disparagement of EWM but not of MWM. It is rather that I assume her accurate on the parties' positions about money, but not on psychological interpretation.

[84] Except Lady Caroline Pierrepont, who m. at 32.

1. Thoresby Hall, Nottinghamshire, where Lady Mary grew up from 1699. From a decoration in her father's printed catalogue of his library, 1726. Evelyn Pierrepont, *Bibliothecae Kingston-iae*, M1 verso. Reproduced by permission of the Bodleian library, University of Oxford (Caps.9.14)

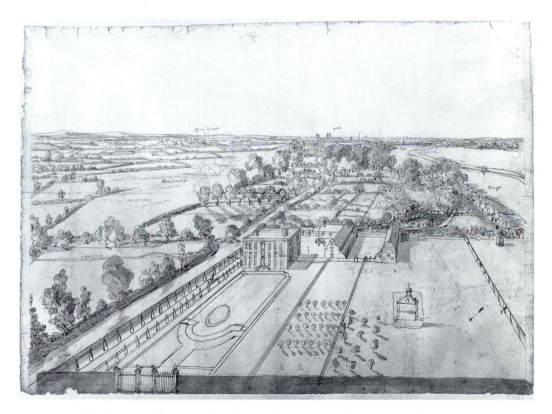

2. Middlethorpe Hall, near York, where Lady Mary Wortley Montagu lived in 1713–14. Reproduced by permission of City of York Libraries. York Reference Library

3. Lady Mary's father, Evelyn Pierrepont, first Duke of Kingston, by John Vanderbank, painted after 1715. In private hands

4. Lady Mary's sister Frances (Pierrepont) Erskine, Countess of Mar, painted by Sir Godfrey Kneller, 1715. Reproduced by permission of the Scottish National Portrait Gallery

5. Alexander Pope, painted in 1715 (the time of his closest friendship with Lady Mary) by their shared friend Charles Jervas. Reproduced by permission of the National Portrait Gallery, London

6. Lady Mary's friend Maria Skerrett, later Lady Walpole, painted by Jean-Baptiste van Loo, Houghton Hall. Reproduced by permission of the Bridgeman Art Library, London

7. Lady Mary's friend Lord Hervey, by Bouchardon, at Ickworth, Suffolk. Reproduced by permission of the National Trust.

8. Lady Mary's idol Francesco Algarotti, drawn by Jonathan Richardson, 19 August 1736.
Reproduced by permission of the Victoria and Albert Museum

9. The Regatta at Venice which Lady Mary attended in 1740, by Canaletto. Reproduced by permission of the National Gallery, London

19

1729–June 1735

❦

Pope, Round Two: 'Universal Rancour'[1]

THE years that saw the departure of Lady Mary's children were also those of Pope's sustained vilification. Behind his attacks lay, no doubt, his sneaking attraction towards those qualities of brilliance and assertiveness which he officially condemned (and probably feared) in females. Behind it too lay a whole complex of political attitudes. These were the years of Bolingbroke's pseudonymous writings in the *Craftsman*, aimed at undermining Lady Mary's friend Walpole. She hated Bolingbroke before she hated Pope, and since Bolingbroke was a member of high society her hatred did not go un-expressed, if only in conversation. Political differences may seem a feeble motive for such intense antagonism. But she had a personal loyalty to Walpole, as Pope had a personal reverence for Bolingbroke;[2] these alliances must have had their effect. More basically though, as Valerie Rumbold has noted, it would be a mistake to read Pope's rancour as an objective response to any presumed actions of Lady Mary. She became his image of the Bad Woman: dirty, degraded, and unnatural, driven by perverted, rapacious appetites. This rhetoric had its own force and its own logic, impelling it to ever more shocking extremes.[3]

Just how Lady Mary felt at various stages of this campaign against her can only be surmised. Her diary would surely have told us, if it had survived. It might have omitted or glossed over her sister's mental state, her daughter's marriage, her own middle-aged love-affair, and yet been candid about her

---

[1] A quality ascribed to Pope in *Verses to the Imitator of Horace* (*E&P* 267).

[2] See Hammond 1984. MWM's views on Bolingbroke *may* have reached print: the anonymous *Epistle From the late Lord Bo——ke to the D. of W——n*, 1730, has close—though inconclusive—parallels with her words.

[3] It is hard to shake. Sherbo, for instance, reviewing Halsband 1956, thought it 'almost universally accepted' that she was dirty (1958: 127).

ongoing pamphlet battles. Here her forcefulness was unsapped by any feeling that she herself might be to blame.[4]

Having opened hostilities against a swarm of literary and political enemies in the *Dunciad*, Pope consolidated his ground in April 1729 with a *Variorum* version: the original poem, revised and elaborated with spoof pedantic footnotes. This softened nothing in its handling of Lady Mary, though at least one insult he coined in his draft never reached print.[5]

That summer or autumn she apparently decided to retaliate. In July her husband was first at Tunbridge Wells, writing his bitter maxims, then in Newcastle, complaining of the 'gaietys' of his business partners. Hervey had been absent from England for a year, travelling for his health with Stephen Fox. Lady Mary assured him in a verse-letter that he was still in her thoughts; and when he announced that he would return to retirement, abjuring ambition and public life, she replied with an accurate prophecy that his 'firm resolves' would melt away once he got home.[6]

Meanwhile Henry Fielding, who for a year had been studying on and off at the University of Leyden, finally abandoned his studies in April 1729 (leaving debts and impounded possessions behind him). By September, in time for the theatre season, he was in London. He said that dire need would make of him either 'a Hackney Writer or a Hackney Coachman'; really he was looking around for some way to extract a living from his considerable talents and ambition. His next play, *The Temple Beau*, was the first new piece to open (January 1730) at the marginal theatre of Goodman's Fields. Lady Mary was soon doing her best for her young cousin: his next two plays, *The Author's Farce* and *Tom Thumb*, were given as a double bill (his benefit night) on 13 May at 'the particular Desire of several Ladies of Quality', and *Tom Thumb* caught Walpole's attention.[7]

Lady Mary must have confided in Fielding some of her feelings about the *Dunciad*. Somehow the two decided to take Pope on with his own weapons. They would pillory him and his circle in mock-epic poems borrowing the form and the mythology of his.[8]

---

[4] Though her own poetry is allusive in just Pope's style, she noted in her copy of his *Works*, 1717, now at Sandon, the authors of lines which she felt he had stolen, including Spenser, Dryden, Buckingham, Addison, Lansdowne, Prior, Parnell, 'Rag' Smith—and herself.

[5] See pp. 277–8.

[6] H MS 80. 137–8; *CL* ii. 91; *E&P* 255–7. The earlier of these poems mentions, enigmatically, the tortures she endures from 'the rage of Bosom-War', and her visionary hopes of joy (possibly of love?), quickly snuffed out by reason. For Hervey's delectation she also 'cook'd up' a speech for the Duchess of Marlborough (probably Henrietta, not Sarah).

[7] Battestins 1989: 63, 66, 73, 76–8, 80, 87; *CL* iii. 66. The Lord Mayor of London tried to close down Goodman's Fields in Apr. 1730.

[8] Perhaps on the analogy of William Bond's *Progress of Dulness*, 15 June 1728 (Guerinot 1969: 122–4; Battestins 1989: 78–80).

The *Dunciad*'s story-line concerns the expansionist ambitions of the goddess Dulness. She represents the power of inertia or anti-intellect, who was dethroned from her realm of 'Chaos and eternal Night' when God created the world.[9] Now, says Pope, she hopes to repossess her dominions; and she begins by leading an invasion force of stupid hack writers from their low-life haunts in the crass, commercial City of London, westwards towards the lawcourts, the theatres, the publishing district, and the court.

As his King of the Dunces, right-hand man of Dulness, Pope had chosen the scholar Lewis Theobald, who had adversely criticized his editing of Shakespeare. Theobald was a friend of Fielding and protégé of Lady Mary's intimate friend Lady De La Warr. By November 1729 he had *his* revenge planned: an edition of Shakespeare to show up and replace Pope's. Lady De La Warr, 'drumming up support among the nobility', came up with 'such a list of Quality as were well worth waiting for'. In the spring of 1730, when Theobald's edition was publicly announced, she was his 'Arbitratress of Termes', negotiating with the publisher Jacob Tonson the younger, whose family held the copyright of Shakespeare. Tonson, who was Pope's friend as well as his publisher, proved difficult; that year brought no agreement. But in late October 1731 Tonson was finally brought to sign a contract which was advantageous for Theobald—and which he owed, says his biographer, to Lady De La Warr's skilful management.[10] For Lady Mary, Theobald's disrespect for Pope may have been a recommendation. For Pope, who would know well both the business issues involved and the friendship between the two women, Lady Mary was probably guilty by association.

Meanwhile Lady Mary and Fielding recast the Dulness myth for their own ends in parallel but related poems. She gave the goddess a headquarters underground, in Pope's own grotto,[11] and timed her reign to coincide with that of Queen Anne, the political regime of Lords Oxford and Bolingbroke. To challenge Dulness on behalf of intellect and culture she appointed Congreve and Addison (supported by others she admired: Sir Isaac Newton, Anne Dacier, Thomas Tickell, John Tillotson). Dulness's champion against them was, of course, Pope himself, whose early poems she represents as a mishmash of lewdness, tedium, and impiety, fit offerings to the goddess. Montagu includes a vignette of Bolingbroke (whose recent return from Jacobite exile must have riled her) transacting political business with a crippling hangover. With Bolingbroke's French connections in mind, she bases

---

[9] *Dunciad*, i. 10.   [10] Battestins 1989: 151; Seary 1990: 122–4.
[11] Montagu's two untitled, mock-epic anti-Pope fragments (*E&P* 247–55). His grotto originated in the need for access to most of his garden, which was cut off from the house by the main London–Hampton Court road. It was a glorified tunnel or underpass.

this scene on one in Boileau's *Le Lutrin*. Her message is, 'The Consequence of Sense is Liberty | And if Men think aright they will be free.'[12]

For his part Fielding produced, some time between June 1729 and January 1730,[13] three cantos with the same theme and style. He set Dulness's reign even further back in time: to pre-Enlightenment, pre-Reformation 'Monkish days! those glorious Days of Rhime!' He eulogizes the Hanover family as 'Wit's brightest Patrons', endorses Montagu's literary models (Congreve, Newton, and Addison), and attacks the opposition paper *The Craftsman*. He gives mock-classical names to Pope's friends and makes Swiftian fun of their physical size.[14] Lady Mary kept his heavily corrected drafts, like her own, among her papers: she wrote on them 'H.F.' She must have been the driving force behind this literary stratagem; but her intentions are not clear: to make a single work of their respective contributions? to publish it? to bring it to Pope's notice in manuscript? Equally unclear is how she felt about it: did she abandon these drafts in frustration, or did she hug to herself the feeling of having a weapon primed and ready against Pope?

Some rumour of its priming may have reached him, for he told Fortescue she had libelled him—for no better reason than his 'leaving off her conversation when I found it dangerous'. He complained to Walpole, and advised him to watch out: he might be her next victim.[15] He continued to batter her in his unresting fight with the 'dunces'. In turn, his libels—and other offences against her—entered the repertoire of accusations levelled at him.[16]

A standard pattern was for some attack on Pope to accuse him of mistreating Lady Mary, and for him therefore to suspect she must have written or had a hand in it. For instance, this charge was repeated in *One Epistle To Mr. A. Pope*, a verse satire which was doing the rounds, unpublished, throughout 1729.[17] During this furtive stage in its existence Pope maintained that it must be by Lady Mary because he had seen a copy in her handwriting. Arbuthnot tipped her off about Pope's suspicion—which, she said, came as a complete surprise to her. She begged Arbuthnot '(as an act of Justice), to

---

[12] *E&P* 253. Smithers mistakenly reads Dulness's view of Addison as MWM's own (1968: 223–4).

[13] Battestins 1989: 78–9; Grundy 1972*b*.

[14] Cleary sees Fielding as making an unambiguous plea for Walpole's patronage (1984: 19–25); Goldgar notes that he soon afterwards addressed two facetious epistles to Walpole, perhaps through MWM, positioning himself as jauntily independent (1976: 100).

[15] 13 Sept. 1729, *Corr.* iii. 53.

[16] e.g. *Pope Alexander's Supremacy . . . Examin'd*, 13 May 1729, says he lampooned 'exalted Characters' and also 'a Lady of Quality, whose Wit is equal her Beauty'. The *Court Eclogues* are probably meant. Pope saw in this the hand of Thomas Burnet, who might well be alert to MWM's grievances (Guerinot 1969: 166, 169).

[17] Apparently written by Leonard Welsted and James Moore Smythe, with perhaps some input from Richard Savage (Guerinot 1969: 188–93).

endeavour to set the Truth in an open Light'. She told him she thought Pope knew she had *not* written the poem, and was affecting suspicion as 'a contrivance . . . to blast the Reputation of one who never injur'd him'. She may have weakened Arbuthnot's sympathy by letting him see the full force of her anger: if Pope was forging her handwriting, she said, she hoped he would be hanged for it. When *One Epistle* reached print in April 1730, the *Grub Street Journal* (a Pope-related paper) said she had 'some hand' in it. The same number said she 'confidently reported He once was whipt': a turn of phrase which as good as asserted her authorship of *A Popp upon Pope* as well.[18]

After Pope's fictional miser Timon was (damagingly to his reputation) identified as his patron the Duke of Chandos, he relieved his feelings in a prose squib which he never published. This rididuled the idea that Timon was Chandos, and complained that he was being slandered not only by pathetic scribblers but by his social 'Betters'. Among others he singled out 'Lord Fanny' (Hervey) and 'Lady De-la-Wit'. The latter sounds more like Lady Mary's friend Lady De La Warr than like Lady Mary herself; but this makes little difference, since the two were poetic collaborators and conspirators.[19] Pope's temper was rising.

In the same year, 1732, scandal against Lady Mary found some new angles in an anonymous pamphlet, *Mr. Taste, the Poetical Fop*. Among a wide range of targets this presents Pope as Alexander Taste, a deformed, incompetent poet and translator 'imprudently' pursuing the 'whimsical' Lady Airy. This is the debut of the story that he proposed himself to her and was rejected. It makes her a widow: either camouflage or a gibe at her marriage. It gives her a friend called Phrodita ('An Heiress, very masculine . . . in love with her Maid'), and a sister, Lady Addle, who has been driven mad by her husband's 'barbarous Usage, tho' she brought him a large fortune'. The last must really have twisted the knife.[20]

Next year escalation reached new levels. On 15 January 1733 Pope published his *Epistle* to Lady Mary's old friend Bathurst, which attacks her not through her sister but through her husband. (The use of people close to her, chosen with an insider's knowledge, became a favoured technique.) This year the Tyneside cartel allocated more than one-sixth of national coal production to Wortley's mines. At the same date they precipitated a crisis by

---

[18] *CL* ii. 91–2; see p. 278; *Grub Street Journal*, 21 May. Its editor and chief writer was the non-juror Richard Russel (Battestins 1989: 135).

[19] Neither MWM not Lady Delorain (the usual suspects) is so likely as Lady De La Warr (*A Master Key to Popery*, 1732, Pope 1986: ii, 411, 423; TE III. ii. 176–88; Mack 1985: 557).

[20] Alluding to Lady Stafford (probably) and Lady Mar: 5 Apr. 1732 (reissued with an updated title-page 17 Apr. 1733), in the form of a play, possibly by Eliza Haywood (Guerinot 1969: 217–20; Halsband 1956: 139–40). The name 'Taste' followed Pope through further pamphlets (Guerinot 1969: 233–8).

selling 'mixed coal as best coal'; customers began looking elsewhere and price war ensued.[21] Pope transformed the coal magnate Wortley into Worldly, or Shylock, 'crying coals from street to street, | Whom with a wig so wild, and mien so mazed, | Pity mistakes for some poor tradesman crased.' His attached note drives the point home: 'Some misers of great wealth, proprietors of the coal-mines, had entered at this time into an association to keep up coals to an extravagant price, whereby the poor were reduced almost to starve, till one of them taking the advantage of underselling the rest, defeated the design. One of these Misers was *worth ten thousand*, another *seven thousand* a year.' In draft, Pope had toyed with the idea of further insults: that Worldly's wife wanted him dead; that she and her friend Skerrett were heaping 'monstrous' wealth against future inflation in the price of a man.[22]

Pope was pouring out a rush of new poems: at least one a month during early 1733.[23] In February he launched a new poem-series: 'imitations' of the Roman poet Horace, designed to reshape ancient satire to present-day contexts, present-day scandals. First in the new series came *The First Satire of the Second Book of Horace*—hardly a catchy title, but a striking one to any classically educated gentleman. It is cast in a dialogue between the poet (a rigorously ethical critic of corrupt society) and his smooth-tongued lawyer friend, who favours a low profile and letting sleeping jackals lie. Pope drew this figure from Fortescue, with whom Lady Mary had shared laughter and good fellowship in 1715. The poem gives Hervey a glancing blow (he is effeminate and lacks talent) but Lady Mary a crueller cut. All noxious animals, it argues, use whatever offensive weapons they naturally possess: 'furious *Sappho*' has two weapons at her disposal, and leaves people either 'p—x'd by her Love, or libell'd by her Hate'.[24]

This was the lowest blow yet. Its second charge, that Lady Mary was a libeller, paled into insignificance beside its first: overtly, that she gave her lovers syphilis; covertly, that the inoculation she sponsored was a killer

---

[21] Sweezy 1938: 24–8; Buxton 1978: 36–7.

[22] Line 62 and n; Rumbold 1989: 156. MWM was 'Lesbia' here, a variant of Sappho. This was one of a composite series, *Epistles to Several Persons* (later called *Moral Essays*), addressed to Lords Burlington, Cobham, and Bathurst, and (anonymously) to Martha Blount.

[23] This although he had been having a terrible year. His own health was as bad as usual, his mobility steadily declining. Gay had died in 1732; his mother, on whom he was in constant attendance, was to die in July 1733.

[24] Pub. 15 Feb. 1733; line 84 (TE iv. 13; Foxon and McLaverty 1991: 122). MWM had already tried to get Walpole to get Fortescue to get Pope to cancel the couplet—which an undated, anonymous poem, *The Satirists*, calls 'this gross, this shocking Line' (Guerinot 1969: 242–3). In an earlier version it was clearly the poet who might be poxed or libelled (Mack 1984: 169). Pope's aspiration to 'vindicate the ways of God to Man' followed, anonymously, five days later (*Essay on Man*, i. 16).

rather than a cure. She had indeed [small]poxed people; she had done it for their good.[25]

Something had to be done. Lady Mary first visited Peterborough, hoping to enlist him as an ally in silencing Pope. He proved even less ready to help than Arbuthnot had been. Whatever he said to her in person, he sent after her a thoroughly mean and brazen letter, probably ghost-written by Pope. This repeated Peterborough's spoken refusal to act for her, but told her Pope had happened to call 'the moment you went away' (as if he was hiding somewhere during their interview, like a lover in farce). Pope had assured Peterborough that Lady Mary was imagining the whole thing. He was at a loss to understand how she could suppose *herself* alluded to under Sappho's name. (This was particularly rich as channelled through Peterborough, whose poem 'I said to my heart' had first, ten years before, publicly called her Sappho.) Peterborough now relayed Pope's word of honour that in naming Sappho he had never thought of Lady Mary, only of 'some noted common woeman', someone low born, unconnected, dabbling in the dirt of the literary market-place. Everyone knew that such female scribblers had 'given very unfortunate favours to their Friends'; how could Lady Mary possibly link herself with them?[26]

The forms of civility had failed. Lady Mary made one more effort at persuasion, through the Prime Minister;[27] but before she knew whether this would produce any result, it seems she turned to tactics much closer to those of the female scribblers abused by Pope. Perhaps remembering her experience of working in tandem with Henry Fielding, she enlisted Hervey's aid. (Her much graver injury from Pope leaves little doubt that she was the moving spirit in their alliance.) They were close friends, with similar political views; they had each written political and personal lampoons, and poems on what we should now call gender issues; the persistent rumours that she was active in politics as well as in literature *may* even indicate that she had some involvement in his highly effective career as a pamphleteer.

John, Lord Hervey, is a figure who resists interpretation, even after Robert Halsband's biography. His friendship with Lady Mary, one of the most important she had, is equally enigmatic. Her well-known *mot* 'that this

---

[25] This surely makes nonsense of Maynard Mack's view of her hatred of Pope as 'increasingly psychotic' (1985: 555).

[26] *CL* ii. 97; Pope, *Corr*. iii. 352. The women named were Behn, Centlivre, Haywood, and Manley (who, MWM had long since observed, would function as a scarecrow to frighten other women off writing). MWM had much on her mind just now. On 20 Feb. she had received her sister's allowance as usual; but a week later Wortley reportedly refused to sign for it without consulting the Attorney-General. They signed at last on 26 May (Mar MSS GM 124/16/51/14–16).

[27] Pope, Corr. iii. 354; Mack 1985: 588; Goldgar 1976: 130.

world consisted of men, women, and Herveys' may glance at other members
of his family besides himself, and other eccentricities besides the sexual.
Still, his sexual character deeply affected his dealings in the world. His gift
for repartee was said to come from his mother, who was first a butt of Lady
Mary's satire (in 'Thursday'), then a correspondent on the embassy. Lady
Mary was an amused, only partly sympathetic observer of John Hervey's
early marital bliss; for his part, at that date he thought her an 'incomprehensible' verse plagiarist. She was at odds with his wife, who was intellectually
minded as well as beautiful. The Herveys inoculated their eldest son in 1725;
but long afterwards Lady Hervey mentioned that some incident 'between
her and Lady Mary'—almost certainly her support for Lord Grange—
'made any renewal of their acquaintance impossible'.[28]

Lady Mary's close friendship with Lord Hervey probably developed after
he became a Robert Walpole supporter, on George II's accession. Holding a
court post and lodged in Lady Darlington's old rooms, Hervey saw a good
deal of Lady Stafford. Lady Mary often met him at Heidegger's masquerades, finding him instantly recognizable through all disguises.[29] But their
relations centred on writing. Hervey voiced comic complaint about Lady
Mary's talking—'so fast, so incessantly, and so loud'—yet he named her,
with Lady Stafford, and Queen Caroline, as exemplars of civilized conversation.[30] In his own flippant style he took her seriously as an author, praising
her work to Algarotti and others. They corresponded for years, and Lady
Mary kept some passages of verse she wrote him, though she destroyed
the letters containing them.[31] Only Skerrett seems to have been more her
confidante.

Each kept large, heterogeneous collections of MS poetry in which the
other's work is jumbled in with the rest. They shared some favourite genres:
political squibs and ballads, racy occasional verses, compliment and its
reverse, and the Ovidian epistle adapted to the unideal love-affairs of their
own set. Each had a strong poetic interest in gender issues. Lady Mary's

---

[28] 'Men, women and Herveys' was much echoed (often expanded to include the words 'three sexes . . .');
MWM was named as its originator by Horace Walpole and Lady Louisa Stuart (Walpole, Corr. xvii. 274 n.
31; E&P 39, 41; Amyand to Jurin, 6 Feb. 1725, Royal Society Inoculation Papers, courtesy of Andrea
Rusnock).

[29] Hervey MSS 47/2 147, 137; Sundon 1847: ii. 227–8.

[30] Dec. 1731, 18 June 1737 (Ilchester 1950: 127; Hervey MS 47/2. 53). MWM was vocal only among
intimates; Lady Bute remembered her 'as by no means a great talker, but rather silent in mixed society,
unless the conversation took an interesting turn' (BL Add. MS 24483. 405).

[31] CL ii. 98–9, 122–13, 238–9; E&P 301, 305–6. In an undated letter Hervey refers to a past misunderstanding with her (13 Dec. [?], Hervey MS 47/2. 17). 140 of his letters to her are extant among his papers
(1729–43: Hervey MSS), besides others elsewhere. It was about this date that he began his Memoirs of
George II's reign.

poems on female victims of seduction are not without pathos, and Hervey's are not wholly without anger. His 'Monimia to Philocles' (which Lady Mary transcribed) was the best known of all those written on the unfortunate Sophia Howe. He also wrote on Lady Abergavenny; and Lady Mary *may* have written on Howe and Abergavenny as well as on Arabella Thompson.[32]

Other Hervey poems she kept are compliments or dramatized invitations to pleasure. In his own voice he celebrated the Duchess of Richmond as modern avatar of Venus;[33] through any number of fictional speakers he pressed some absent or wavering love-object for reciprocation of love.[34] 'To Molly on Easter Eve' is jaunty rather than supplicating. While priests prepare to dispense the sacrament (thereby proving they are either blockheads or hypocrites), the speaker begs Molly to retire with him 'tete à tete, to your dressing room Fire | With Champaign, and a snug little Supper'. After sitting up till the small hours with 'singing and chat', they will 'crown every Wish, give a loose to desire | And alternately quench and rekindle the Fire'. This *may* have been written as from Hervey's patron Walpole to Maria Skerrett; its metre, and its motif of the erotic champagne supper, link it with Montagu's 'The Lover'. Lady Mary kept two copies of it. *Fog's Weekly Journal*, printing a garbled version of it with another poem (which quotes her unpublished 'Wednesday'), *may* have been making public some verse exchange between her and Hervey.[35]

Hervey wrote another poem in this vein as by one woman to another: Lady Mary's copy calls it 'The Countess of——to Miss——'. The speaker is fifty, coarse of complexion and rugged of feature, but crowned with laurel and myrtle, Sappho's worthy successor; in her youth she was praised by St-Evremond (who died in 1703). This might easily be Lady Stafford. Amid proper names veiled by dashes, the girl she woos is called Sophia. Typically, Hervey blends *risqué* touches ('With my warm Lip to dry the modest Tear') with anticlericalism: priests preach chastity as cover for their own sins. Among the advantages of lesbianism his countess numbers the fact that it is 'unprolific': 'Still shall thy Shape its taper form retain, | Eve shall have

[32] See pp. 296–7; H MSS 81, 255; also see p. 319; most of Hervey's poems also in Hervey MS 491/53/1.

[33] 'What do Scholars, and bards, and Astrologers wise', given as by Chesterfield in his *Works*, 1927 (19) and Badminton MSS (which also include Hervey and MWM: Fm T/B1/4/4, Fm S/b4/25); as Hervey's in Hervey MS 941/53/1 (implicitly), BL Harley MS 7318 (108), Pope 1776 (i. 149–50), and H MS 255 (Lady Mary's album, where she altered 'Chesterfield' to 'Hervey').

[34] 'Verses sent To——' (H MS 255; H MS 81. 141 in Hervey's hand); 'Epistle to——' (H MS 255), otherwise 'A Love Letter' (Hervey MSS 941/53/1; *London Magazine*, Feb. 1750: 89; Dodsley, *Collection*, 1775: iv. 106–8).

[35] H MS 255, H MS 81. 148. 'A.B.' in *Fog's Weekly Journal*, 7 Nov. 1730, presents these as versions (somewhat distant) of Horace's ode 3.28. As partners in the game of literature, Hervey and MWM produced riddles on her two surnames: he on Wortley, she on Montagu (*E&P* 382).

sinn'd, and thou been curs'd in vain | Admitted to the Joy, exempted from the Pain.'[36]

When Hervey died and his eldest son returned Lady Mary's letters to her, unread, she destroyed them: almost twenty years-worth of jokes and confidences. She then told the son that reading then would have shown him 'the possibility of a long and steady friendship subsisting between two persons of different sexes without the least mixture of love'.[37] And this friend was, no doubt about it, of the opposite sex from herself. Although he kept his deepest feelings for men (thus confirming the suspicion aroused by his girlish looks), he also engaged in sexual relationships with women both inside and outside marriage. His letters to Lady Mary, especially the early ones, carry a burden of those mechanically gallant compliments (assuming her goddess status and his worshipper role) which made friendship between the sexes so problematic. In later years at least, his compliments targeted her mind ('For Wit and Science still Maria's Name | Should deck our Island in Athenian Fame'), while his wit became more fluent and playful.

For her part she promised, in a verse-letter, to 'disclose to you alone | Such thoughts as n'ere were thought upon'. This is not to be taken literally; but it suggests a real intimacy of mind. Hervey said there were few people he liked or trusted; Lady Mary was one of the few. His last letter to her ends on a benediction; fifteen years later she numbered his 'Gentle Shade' among those few who had been dear to her.[38]

Nothing can be certainly substantiated about these two people's most ungentle partnership, the notorious *Verses Address'd to the Imitator of Horace*. It *seems*, however, that she was the mover and he the associate in composing the most outrageous as well as the most poetically forceful of all the attacks on Pope.[39] Its style has some hallmarks of each. Hervey assumed authorial rights in tinkering with the text as if for a revised edition (arguably spoiling rather than improving it). No evidence now survives to prove a link with Montagu, despite long-lived rumours of a manuscript in which she asserted authorship.[40] But contemporaries almost unanimously ascribed the poem to her: partisans pro and anti Pope, Pope himself (at first, before he began to

[36] H MS 255. It has at least one unsavoury detail: the countess is wooing the daughter of a former lover whom she calls 'the hag your mother'.

[37] *E&P* 40. Such return of letters was standard practice.

[38] *CL* ii. 99, 306; iii. 150; see pp. 459, 562; Hervey MS 941/53/1; Hervey, 2/13 Nov. 1739, 17/28 June 1740 (Hervey MS 47/2. 77; Murray MS).

[39] See Grundy 1977: 96–119. Later Oxford posited a third collaborator: William Windham, whose new wife, Lady Delorain, Pope had also attacked.

[40] Hervey tinkered twice (once as 'the Author'); neither printed version wholly agrees with his wishes (Grundy 1971: 506–7, 511). MWM's MS mentioned by her editors Wharncliffe and Thomas, and (a better authority) Paston (Grundy 1971: 506).

hedge), and anonymous annotators of manuscript and printed copies.[41] *The Answer to the foregoing Elegy* (see pp. 308–9) was published by Roberts as 'By a Lady, Author of the Verses to the Imitator of Horace'. Swift thought it was Montagu's. So did Lord Oxford, Theobald, and Voltaire (who corresponded with Hervey). So, a little later, did Elizabeth Montagu, John Wilkes, Lady Mary's son, and reviewers of her *Poetical Works*, 1768.[42]

This controversial text was purveyed to consumers within three weeks of Pope's act of provocation, by methods carefully concealed. Two *very* slightly different versions of it appeared on 8 March 1733: as *Verses to the Imitator* . . . through Anne Dodd, and as *To the Imitator* . . . through James Roberts. Dodd and Roberts were mere fronts, regularly chosen by authors or publishers who had something to hide. (Once when Roberts printed a satire as Pope's, Pope had talked of forcing him to divulge the real author.) Lady Mary had links to each of them; but so had Hervey. It was not a case of each poet working through their own publisher: nothing so simple.[43]

The *Verses* retain undiminished their power to awake outrage, exhilaration, and fierce debate. They begin by attacking Pope as traducer of Horace; they touch on his low birth; they utter veiled threats of physical punishment; but (like many of his attackers) they home in with gusto, no holds barred, on his physical disabilities. He is a travesty or caricature of the human: a bristling porcupine, a stinging wasp, 'One over-match'd by every Blast of Wind'. He is impervious to beauty and enraged by greatness or generosity; he hates the entire human race. 'To Thee 'tis Provocation to exist.' Most crucially, his crooked body is the accurate, God-given sign of his inner nature. The poem's concluding curse conflates him with Cain, the first murderer: 'with the Emblem of thy crooked Mind | Marked on thy Back, like *Cain*, by God's own Hand, | Wander like him, accursed through the Land.'[44]

---

[41] Pope, *Corr* iii. 362. Even someone who thought Pope wrong to praise MWM in the first place agreed that 'No Title Page the Lady needs express | Where every Line displays the Poetess' ('On Lady Mary Worteley's Verses to Mr. Pope', Badminton MSS, Fm T/B1/4/4). Pope later called the *Verses* a 'witty fornication', whose mother was Hervey and whose absconded father was MWM.

[42] Voltaire requested them from his friend Thieriot (whom Mary Anne Cantillon had introduced to MWM) as a work by 'mylady Mary Montaigu' (1963–93: i. 382, ref. misunderstood in note; Jones 1919: 313; Elizabeth Montagu 1923: ii. 157; Curling 1954: 208; H MS 77. 162–3a). Wilkes transcribed the *Verses* (as MWM's) into a copy of Pope 1751, in marking it up as the basis of a new edn. (viii. after 280; BL G.12850–8).

[43] Each was a leader in their line: Roberts as a 'trade publisher', Dodd as a 'mercury' buying from trade publishers and selling to hawkers (Treadwell 1982: 110–11, 117–25). The two editions were advertised as rivals throughout Mar. 1733. Dodd issued two different states of her first edn., a revised edn. on 20 Mar., then 5th and 6th edns. An undated 8vo repr. was probably printed in Edinburgh, designed for binding up with Pope's major satires (Harry Ransom Center, University of Texas). This month was advertised *Sappho to Adonis, after the manner of Ovid*, untraced (Guerinot 1969: 325).

[44] *E&P* 265–70. Lady Louisa Stuart thought the sneer at Pope's birth 'most illiberal and what people themselves of high birth should have disdained to utter' (to Lord Wharncliffe, 9 Nov. 1836, Wh MS M 507/37).

The *Verses* relate interestingly to a poem by Henry Fielding of about this date, just as Montagu's *Dunciad* imitations parallel his. Again she may have been the driving force behind his work. He says he is provoked to verse by 'injur'd Sappho's Wrongs'; he presents her as a champion of her sex, to whom 'Man, proud Man', has listened with submission. Only Pope is unmoved by 'thy Sex, thy Birth, thy Wit, thy Eyes'. Fielding provides a reasoned account of what satire should and should not do. True satire, he says, is like the work of reformers; personal lampoon is like that of military conquerors. Any acclaim accorded the lampooning satirist (even Pope) is undeserved. Despite this high-mindedness, Fielding brings together sexual and animal imagery in one of the most shocking ideas in the anti-Pope dossier: "Twere capital to suffer thy Embrace, | For thou art Surely not of human Race.' He ends by imaging Pope as a snarling cur, himself as the 'gen'rous Mastiff' guarding his lady and flinging the cur in the gutter.[45]

Fielding's poem remained prudently unknown; it would be unknown still if Lady Mary had not kept a copy. But the *Verses* were often reprinted (at Dublin and Edinburgh as well as London), and made a lasting mark on literary consciousness. In writing (or part-writing) this scorching assault, Lady Mary stepped outside the sheltered enclosure of high rank and gender chivalry. Its publication slammed the gates of the garden behind her, committing her to a wilderness inhabited by warring tribes of pamphleteers. But this was by no means certainly her own act. It may have been Hervey's. Or it may have been Pope's.

That final possibility, at first glance so unlikely, has been persuasively argued by James McLaverty.[46] He points out that Pope, although hurt in his reputation by the poem's circulation in manuscript (especially at court), had nothing to lose from its printing. Indeed, he stood to gain. If it appeared that Lady Mary had *published* such a cruel attack, she would lose her moral and social advantage. Pope would appear amply justified in attacking her for libels if not for pox—and justified too in equating her with the deplorable tradition of Behn and Manley. Secretly, Pope could relish having stolen her agency in her own work, leaving her tricked but with no avenue of complaint. If she had prided herself on the *Verses*' artistry she could say with a former woman poet, 'What ought t'have brought me Honour brought me shame!'[47]

---

[45] A flourish of irony: Pope kept a mastiff, partly for protection (Fielding, 'Epistle to Mr Lyttleton occasioned by two Lines in Mr Pope's Paraphrase on the first Satire of the 2d Book of Horace', in Grundy 1972*b*: 245; Battestins 1989: 165–6). Fielding addresses Lyttleton, whom MWM had recently mocked, but praises Theobald, whom she supported.

[46] McLaverty 1995: 42, 55; McLaverty forthcoming.

[47] 'Upon the Saying that my Verses were made by another' (Killigrew [1685]: 45).

This exchange of fire opened a pamphlet vendetta between Pope and Hervey. From now on Lady Mary's name too appeared more frequently and more prominently as a missile hurled by both pro- and anti-Pope factions. She became a rallying point for Pope's enemies, a natural choice as dedicatee or protector for works written against him.

Pamphlet wars, unlike the real thing, tended to die down in summer, since many potential buyers were out of town. But for weeks from the end of March 1733, a series of reciprocal counter-offensives hammered away. First Bezaleel Morrice dedicated his slashing, anonymous *On the English Translations of Homer* to Lady Mary, as a 'deliberate affront' to Pope. Next a more effectively masked 'Gentleman' on the other side supported Pope by turning the machete on Lady Mary as Sappho. Then a 'Gentlewoman', also calling her Sappho and aiming at a more balanced stance, invited her to admit her unfair treatment of Pope, to reform, and be reconciled with him. A general attack on women cited 'good lady M—y' as a vintage example of marital wrong-doing; the *Gentleman's Magazine* championed her by name as author of the *Verses*.[48]

In May (as Lady Mary expected Lady Stafford's return to Twickenham) Giles Jacob presented her with a copy of *The Mirrour*, a letter-collection which offers support to (male) fellow victims of Popean satire, and ends with a trial of Pope for satire and dullness. Jacob thanked Lady Mary for her favourable reception of this somewhat humdrum offering; she probably gave not only approval but a cash gift as well. (Did she charge it to 'Pocket' or to 'Several expenses'?) Jacob solicited her contribution, too, to a second edition.[49] At the end of that month came another conciliatory work, cheaply produced. The 'Lady' who wrote *The Neuter: Or, A Modest Satire on the Poets of the Age*, and dedicated it with high praise to Lady Mary, cannot have thought she was addressing the author of *Verses to the Imitator*. She judged good breeding (not the *Verses*' forte) a requisite for satire, and reproved Pope's enemies at much greater length and in stronger terms than Pope himself.[50]

Before the summer lull in hostilities, Pope had published three of the four epistles which made up his new high-serious venture, *An Essay on Man*.[51]

---

[48] Morrice, 31 Mar. 1733, recast from a work of a dozen years before (Guerinot 1969: 228–9); *A Proper Reply to a Lady*, 3 Apr.; *Advice to Sappho*, 13 Apr. (Guerinot 1969: 329); *Woman of Taste*, 2nd edn., 1733: 10. Claudia Thomas thinks the Gentlewoman may be Elizabeth Boyd (1994: 269; *GM*, Apr.: 206).

[49] Lady Stafford, H MS 77. 254; Jacob to MWM, 11 June 1733, H MS 77. 178; *The Mirrour*, 10 May 1733. No 2nd edn. appeared (Guerinot 1969: 229–33; *CL* ii. 97–8).

[50] She is especially hard on Haywood. She does criticize Pope for mocking James Moore Smythe's ungainly body—a crime in which the *Verses* easily outdoes him (Guerinot 1969: 235–6).

[51] He sought to deflect hostile reaction by publishing them anonymously; MWM shows in her verse satire on Swift that she was in the know.

After the lull Lady Mary found herself abused as 'the *Saphian* Muse' in an evening newspaper's tribute to him.[52] He for his part resumed his campaign against Hervey, putting him in his first imitation of John Donne as an impudent courtier with 'half his Nose . . . in his Patron's Ear'. It was probably by chance that someone, a week later, printed a private verse-letter of Hervey's containing a tirade against Pope; but Hervey said he was delighted to have put Pope in a fury. Pope sent Arbuthnot round to lean on Hervey, and Hervey told him that Pope had begun it all and deserved as good as he got; if he felt any regret at the publicizing of his private letter, that was only because 'Paper-War' with such an adversary was below him.

Below him or not, he was in it. He fenced with Pope for a while in scurrilous newspaper advertisements; Pope printed but kept unpublished a devastating prose attack on him. This does not name Lady Mary, but assumes her joint authorship of the *Verses*, revives the accusation of satire falsely and damagingly passed off as Pope's, and denies that 'Sappho' could mean anyone but a lewd and 'infamous Creature'. In December 1733 an anonymous, anti-Hervey pamphlet called *Tit for Tat* dragged Lady Mary's name back into the fray.[53] In January and February 1734 there appeared in different guises, with variant titles and sometimes with extra items attached, *A* [or *The*] *Tryall of Skill* between Hervey and Pope. An unidentified Mr Gerard announced, in an *Epistle to the Egregious Mr. Pope*, that Lady Mary was a victim of Pope's ingratitude, one of those penalized for treating him generously. He called her Sappho and added that she 'assisted *Pope* in his Subscription'.[54]

Generosity was certainly not 'Sappho' 's only crime. A week earlier had appeared in print a handsome, anonymous folio, *The Dean's Provocation for Writing the Lady's Dressing-Room. A Poem*. Lady Mary's draft and fair copy of this work clearly mark her as its author, though its topic and style caused her to exclude it from the album of acknowledged work which she regularly showed around. The draft, vigorously altered and re-altered, gives unusual insight into her methods of composition; it shows that the family story that she wrote easily and never revised does not apply to her poems. Her fair

---

[52] 'To Mr. Pope', *Whitehall Evening-Post*, 16 Oct. 1733, accuses 'Sapho' of using 'scurril Taunt, and low Abuse' in *Sarah, The Quaker, to Lothario*, an attack on Spencer Cowper, actually by Charles Beckingham.

[53] *An Epistle from a Nobleman to a Doctor of Divinity*, 10 Nov. 1733; Halsband 1973: 162–5; Pope, *Letter to a Noble Lord*, 30 Nov.; *Tit for Tat*, 4 Dec.; several times reissued (Pope 1986: ii. 444–7; Guerinot 1969: 339–40). *Tit for Tat* (which was withdrawn for sale while 8 lines on the queen were deleted) has Hervey writing lampoons *on*, not with, MWM (Ilchester 1950: 195).

[54] Pub. 14 Feb. 1734 (John Spencer's wedding day): 4 (Guerinot 1969: 245–6). This year MWM *may* have been glanced at as the 'female firebrand' Hecatilla in James Forrester, *The Polite Philosopher* (Grundy 1980: 409).

copy—entitled 'The Reasons that Induce'd Dr S[wift] to write a Poem call'd the Lady's Dressing room'[55]—is on the whole *less* like the printed text than her draft was. This makes it doubtful whether she or someone else arranged its printing: through the untraceable medium of Thomas Cooper, who like Roberts was a leading trade publisher.

Swift's *Lady's Dressing-Room* had appeared four years before. It debunks (as Lady Mary had herself done in a letter) the delusion of 'litterally think-ing fine Ladys compos'd of Lillys and Roses'. It shows Strephon peeping illicitly into his beloved's inner sanctum and repelled by the squalor in which she lives, by scurf and snot and finally by the chamber-pot which hideously reveals that '*Celia, Celia, Celia* shits!'[56] The official line on this poem some years later was that it was not misogynist: no woman 'of real sense or clean-liness' would be offended; she would apply the satire to other women, but not to herself.[57] Lady Mary had often been prone (for instance, in her courtship letters) to deal with male criticism of women by claiming that *she* was an exception. Now, however, she took offence on her sex's behalf, and sallied forth to retaliate. Again, as in her *Dunciad* imitations, she appropri-ated the attacker's style in which to return his blow. She parodied unpub-lished as well as published lines by Swift: somehow she had access to privileged material.[58] Her 'Reasons', or *Provocation*, deliciously depicts 'The Doctor in a clean starch'd band, | His Golden Snuff box in his hand', going to visit a whore—and succumbing to impotence. 'The Reverend Lover with surprize | Peeps in her Bubbys, and her Eyes, | And kisses both, and trys—and trys.' She ingeniously presents Swift's misogynist poem as a bid to sabotage the livelihood of the woman who has shamed him.

Like many of her writings, this poem turns tradition to highly original use. Swift's Celia is (like all his fictional whores) wholly and disgustingly physical; his male protagonist is (even ludicrously) overinvested in the spiritual and non-physical. Montagu's whore is a sharp businesswoman who remains as capable of 'Blushing Grace' as a gently reared virgin. In the last line she admits, with perfect composure, that she too shits; her admirer's poems will come in handy as toilet paper. He meanwhile, despite his ecclesi-astical rank, is made unregenerately physical, comically ill assorted with the narrator's digression into Swiftian moral philosophy. Montagu follows Rochester and Behn in her treatment of impotence. Like Rochester she uses

[55] Pub. 8 Feb. 1734; *E&P* 237–6. '*Reasons that* [or *which*] *Induced* . . .' was a popular formula for titles of political pamphlets: both Curll and Addison had used it. MWM thus demotes Swift from literature to scandal.

[56] *CL* ii. 56; Swift 1937: ii. 524–30.   [57] Pope 1776: i, p. ix.

[58] Her lines 35 ff. echo Swift's 'Day of Judgement' (1937: ii. 576–9).

it for bleak comedy; like Behn uses it to reverse traditional male satire on
female materiality. (She did something similar in her epigram on Charles
Churchill.)[59]

The day her anti-Swift poem appeared, Hervey sent Henry Fox some
unattributed verses which jovially regret that he, Hervey, was immune from
criticism. 'Sapho who might have answer'd thee,' it says, 'But smiles at all
thy ribaldry'; Centlivre, Haywood, Swift, are none of them censorious, only
amused. Whoever wrote this was perhaps in the secret of Montagu's rebuke
to Swift, and was certainly independent minded in citing Centlivre and
Haywood with approval.[60]

That day, too, Hervey passed on Pope's briefest but perhaps most effective attack. It calls him a 'Pimp or Flaterer', Lady Mary a 'flagrant Whore'.
Nevertheless it moves to an almost caressing conclusion: 'I answer thus—
poor Sapho you grow grey, | And sweet Adonis—you have lost a tooth.'
Hervey took this and other equally vicious attacks with a sang-froid which
Lady Mary probably could not match.[61] His political career gave him plenty
of enemies, some of them eager to exploit his quarrel with Pope; but he was
battle hardened.

Pope seems to have meant to keep the Sappho/Adonis lines to himself.
His public attacks on Lady Mary wielded the knife, but kept it at least partly
under the cloak. Privately he coupled her with Hervey as a 'Dirty pair'; publicly, in imitating Horace's satire II. ii, he spotlighted not her but her husband. Yet her supporting role is crucial. This Horatian satire is about food:
moral questions of temperance, luxury, hospitality, self-sufficiency. Horace
calls Avidienus, the quintessential miser, a dog—which perhaps gave Pope
the hint[62] for his full-length double portrait.

> *Avidien* or his Wife (no matter which,
> For him you'll call a dog, and her a bitch)
> Sell their presented Partridges, and Fruits,
> And humbly live on rabbits and on roots:
> One half-pint bottle serves them both to dine,
> And is at once their vinegar and wine.
> But on some lucky day (as when they found
> A lost Bank-bill, or heard their Son was drown'd),

---

[59] See p. 380.   [60] 'Horace to Barine, imitated to Ld. Hervey. Book 2. Ode 8' (Ilchester 1950: 297).
[61] Hervey had hardly a tooth left. He was a ministerial hero just now for a speech in the House of Lords.
He told Henry Fox of Pope's squib on 8 Feb. 1734; his false teeth were admired in late 1736 (Halsband 1973:
165–6; TE vi. 357). Another attack was the anonymous *Epistle from a Gentleman at Twickenham* [Pope] *To a
Nobleman at St James's* [Hervey], pub. 14 Mar. 1734.
[62] I owe this point to James McLaverty.

on such a red-letter day (a birthday in Horace's original) they splurge—and 'sowse the Cabbidge with a bounteous heart'.

Among this rush of details the most wounding flirts with credibility (might they really have been glad if their son had died?), but most are demonstrably inaccurate. Wortley had just been praised for lavish spending on voters; he regularly *gave* presents of game from his estates, rather than selling presents received; his favourite luxury was Tokay wine. But the underlying charge—that he was tight with his money—and the unstated charge—that he was married to Lady Mary—were both undeniably true. He was recognized in these lines, and the name Avidien stuck.[63]

This year *The Plain Dealer* appeared in volume form, recirculating admiring notice of Lady Mary as poet and as medical pioneer. On the other hand she may have found herself implicated in a new area of sleaze: in an anonymous work by Erasmus Jones called *Pretty Doings in a Protestant Nation*. Though this purports to be driven by zeal for moral reform, its blend of titillation and pious outrage is highly suspect. It touches on the perils of female apprentices; on the frightful spectacle of public prayers for a patron whom everyone knows to be 'at that very Instant in Bed between a Brace of Harlots'; on the '*new Vice*' of women keeping '*Fellows*' just as men keep women. It then plagiarizes from William Walsh's anonymous *Dialogue Concerning Women*, 1691, on the topic of lesbians. Walsh had noted a new invention in lust made by the ancient wit Sappho: 'Not content with our Sex, she begins Amours with her own, and teaches us a new sort of Sin, that . . . is practis'd frequently in *Turkey* at this day.' Prurient curiosity about lesbians had intensified in the last forty years.[64] Jones, otherwise copying Walsh exactly, names the sin as 'the *Flats*' and adds '*Twickenham*' to Turkey.[65]

Lady Mary was closely associated with these two places; yet Jones *may* not have been aiming at her. Walsh's mention of seraglio lesbians had a source, which he named though Jones did not: it was one of those generic travellers' clichés which Lady Mary despised. In adding 'Twickenham', Jones may have targeted Lady Newburgh, who was soon to be lambasted as

[63] *Second Satire of the Second Book of Horace*, 49 ff., pub. 4 July 1734 (TE iv. 57–9). For EWM's parsimony at Wharncliffe see p. 303 n. 58.

[64] In 1717 John Thomlinson had mentioned lesbianism (ascribed to MWM's childhood friend Nelly Brownlow) quite matter-of-factly (BL Add. MS 22560. 43).

[65] [Walsh], 34–5 (he defends women overall; but one of his speakers is typically misogynist); [Jones], *Pretty Doings in a Protestant Nation. Being A View of the Present State of Fornication, Whorecraft and Adultery*, 1734: 9, 17, 20, 23–4. Dedicated to London whores, this poses as coming from the French of 'Father Poussin', whose name is a dirty joke. It plagiarizes also from Bernard Mandeville's *Modern Defence of Publick Stews*, 1724. Next year (probably) Jones pub. *Luxury, Pride, and Vanity, The Bane of the British Nation*, whose fulminations include only oblique reference to lesbians.

a lesbian in William King's *The Toast*, 1736.[66] But Lady Mary *could* have been meant as well: a dubious allusion would be safer than a certain one.

Today it would be risky in a different way either to chastise or admire Lady Mary as a lesbian: her orientation towards men seems well established. But there was still life in the Restoration tradition of sexual innuendo as the primary mode of printed attack. Public debate about Hervey's sexuality was raging hot and strong; through recent developments in Pope's paper wars Lady Mary was universally known as an ally of Hervey. If readers of *Pretty Doings* did assume that Turkey and Twickenham pointed at her,[67] she was being sucked into a subworld of semi-pornographic texts which propagated by cannibalizing each other. *Pretty Doings* supplied some pages to *A Trip through the Town*, 1735; it was recycled entire in *Satan's Harvest Home*, 1749.[68]

Pornographic publishing overlapped with that of literary-libellous publishing. The *St James's Register*, 1736, a collection of sex-scandal texts, lists on its title-page an epistle called 'Woman convinc'd', which is said 'to be written by a certain . . . *little, diminutive, Very Great Poet*' (Pope) and dedicated to 'a *very pretty Lady*', 'an *intolerable* Wit!' (probably Lady Mary), whose husband has tried to prevent its publication. This is a mere advertiser's come-on; nothing in the book's actual contents corresponds to it.[69] But it exemplifies the gap opening up between Lady Mary as she was seen by herself, her family, and her friends, and the grotesque myth which the media of her day were making of her. Maynard Mack remarks that Pope, as a writer dependent on his public, 'had to give as much consideration to what he was perceived to be as to what he was'. An exactly similar point was regularly made, straight-faced, in advice addressed to women: how you are perceived matters as much as what you are.

Yet still perceptions of Lady Mary had not reached their nadir. Long before the *St James's Register*, Pope had consummated a marriage between exploitative scandal-pornography and his own poetic art. At the very end of 1734, not long after the three new departures represented by his *Essay on Man*, his *Epistles to Several Persons*, and his imitations of Horace, he launched another genre which was new for him. For this one he not only

---

[66] Myra, bisexually lustful protagonist of this anonymous satire, is Lady Newburgh; her aunt, Lady Westmorland, was MWM's next-door neighbour (*CL* ii. 76; note in BL copy of *The Toast*, 1466. k.21). Cf. Nussbaum 1995: 142–3.

[67] It includes personal allusions: e.g. to the 'late *Col. Chart—s*' and Secretary '*H—ry St. J—n*' (4, 40, 57–8).

[68] *Trip*, 5th edn., 1735: 41–6; *Pretty Doings*, 6–16 (not the Turkey and Twickenham section). These texts are bound up together with *The St James's Register* in the Bodleian copy. *Satan's Harvest Home: or the Present State of Whorecraft . . . And the Game of Flatts . . .* 1749, reprints *Pretty Doings*. It adds tirades on sodomy and male effeminacy, and a story (from 'Busbequius's Travels into Turkey') about a woman punished with death for lesbianism (60–1). Cf. Nussbaum 1995: 142–3.

[69] *St James's Register: or, Taste A-la-Mode*, 1736.

chose anonymity, but confused the trail by a title-page that read 'Imitated in the Manner of Mr. Pope', and a dedication to 'Alexander Pope, Esq.' This made it plausible that an 'unknown' poet should pick on so many of Pope's favourite targets.

The new poem was Horatian again, but instead of being soberly titled with book and poem number it was called *Sober Advice from Horace*; and it was misogynist in a manner that Horace is not. Its theme is sex: not amorous or erotic but grotesque, comic, often brutal—as is, so Pope insists, the modern way. It has spoof footnotes ascribed to the scholar Richard Bentley: these dwell insistently on matters which the real Bentley had politely ignored, flagging every mention of female genitals and male homosexuality. 'Bentley' 's very first note complains about the poet using female equivalents for originally male characters, like Horace's Fufidius: this highlights the most extended treatment of Lady Mary. But she appears, or half-appears, again and again and again. She is unmistakable under her own name in line 2, as Fufidia in lines 17–18, and unnamed in an allegation about Rémond (53–4). She may be suspected with Hervey in 'Sweet *Moll* and *Jack* are Civet-Cat and Boar' (30), as the undressed 'Lady M—' (125), and as '*Angel! Goddess! Montague!*' (166).[70]

Pope's first target is the incongruity of high society's deep mourning for the stage star Anne Oldfield. She had specialized in playing ladies of quality; Pope (wrongly, but in common with many others) assumed that she was wildly promiscuous. Here Lady Mary makes her first appearance (with Hervey) as representative of vicious high society.[71] Sketches of two notorious kept women follow, then a kindred portrait, given in detail:

> With all a Woman's Virtues but the p—x,
> *Fufidia* thrives in Money, Land, and Stocks;
> For Int'rest, ten *per Cent*. her constant Rate is;
> Her Body? hopeful Heirs may have it *gratis*.
> She turns her very Sister to a Job,
> And, in the Happy Minute, picks your Fob
> Yet starves herself, so little her own Friend,
> And thirsts and hungers only at one End:
> A Self-Tormentor, worse than (in the Play)
> The Wretch, whose Av'rice drove his *Son* away.

[70] 28 Dec. 1734 (TE iv. 74–89). Though Moll has been identified as Hervey's wife, she did not attract such opprobrium; Lord Oxford thought Lady M—was Lady Mohun; cf. Williams 1973–4: 56–8. But Pope could not have written these names without thinking of MWM; she could not read them unmoved.

[71] Whig notables turned out for Oldfield's funeral, on 27 Oct. 1730. Hervey was a pallbearer (with Lord De La Warr) and executor (with John Hedges). Newspapers printed as an epitaph on Oldfield lines from a poem which Dallaway gives as MWM's on the Duke of Marlborough (19 Jan. 1731; *E&P* 224–5).

This repeats several old charges, in a brilliant blend of the undeniably true (Lady Mary's dealing in stocks), partly true (her son), distortedly factual (her sister), and implausibly monstrous (nymphomania, self-starvation). To say she *hasn't* got the pox comments ironically on her anguished, private denials of 'p—x'd by her Love' nearly two years before; the 'you' who has his pocket picked in the act of sex is based on Rémond, who is to reappear later. As if Pope had learned from the commercial pornographers, he now uses her as an emblem of corrupt sexuality. The way she is framed and placed in *Sober Advice* suggests real sexual hatred.

But it did not satiate his appetite for attack. Five days later came one of his best-known poems, *An Epistle to Dr. Arbuthnot*, published not surreptitiously but with his name as part of its title. Its inevitable allusions to Lady Mary take a precise, near-accurate form. Arbuthnot is made to intervene now and again in the poem, like Fortescue in the *First Satire of the Second Book*, vainly urging Pope to be cautious. As if belatedly acting on Lady Mary's pleas of 1729, he first breaks in to hush some allegation by Pope about 'Sapho'. 'Hold! for God-sake—you'll offend: | 'No names—be calm—learn Prudence of a Friend: | I too could write, and I am twice as tall...' This paints Lady Mary as a user of physical violence, and serves as pretext for the intrepid poet to refuse to be silenced.

The second allusion to Lady Mary in *Arbuthnot* is not to Pope's present attacks but to his former love. 'Yet soft by Nature, more a Dupe than Wit, | *Sapho* can tell you how this Man was bit [i.e. tricked]'. This was probably, by now, the way Pope really saw his former friendship with her. He had been soft and gullible; he had idolized her; she had turned out hard and unfeminine. His early draft of this couplet admits to past liking, even to present regret: 'Once, and but once, his heedless youth was bit, | And lik'd that dang'rous thing, a female wit.' His published version diminishes liking to softness; both versions name her treachery and apply to her the nickname which boded no good, but which by now made her instantly recognizable to every member of the reading public.[72]

Arbuthnot's casual, damning references to Lady Mary were outshone by its fully developed, elaborate caricature of Hervey. On first appearance the portrait was called 'Paris'; thereafter it was 'Sporus' (a castrated youth whom the emperor Nero 'married'). Today, when the concept of homophobia is generally current, it may be hard to realize just how powerfully the disgust and moral outrage of this portrait resonated to readers of Pope's own day or of, say the 1970s. The structure of the passage suggests that it was

---

[72] *An Epistle to Dr. Arbuthnot*, 2 Jan 1735, TE iv. 91–127, lines 101–3, 368–9.

Hervey's bisexuality which goaded Pope beyond endurance. Everything else in the portrait follows from that: on the one hand the effeminate looks, magnetism for women, and career in political manipulation which indeed belonged to the actual, historical Hervey; on the other the dirt, impotence, and intellectual vacuity which were his very opposite. The phrase 'at the Ear of *Eve*' brackets Milton's Satan in the garden with Hervey at Queen Caroline's court; it also alleges that Hervey has perverted Lady Mary, who had been memorably nicknamed the second Eve.[73] Hervey, Whig manager and spokesman, sexual but not masculine, was anathema to the poet who went straight on to boast of himself that 'if he pleas'd he pleas'd by manly ways'.[74]

So Hervey was transmuted into Sporus, in a poem which has become one of Pope's most admired and most studied works, and in lines so well known as to be almost hackneyed. It is less often noticed that the terms of the Sporus portrait are lifted from the *Verses to the Imitator of Horace*.[75] If Lady Mary was indeed the leading spirit in that attack, Pope had wrested away her weapon and turned it on her ally. He addressed this latest work to Arbuthnot, whom Lady Mary had known as a friend and associate in the fight for inoculation (though she had found him a broken reed since then). He was now failing in health: Pope, who had long ago promised to honour him with a poem one day, had rushed this one into shape and into print for his sick friend's sake as well as to meet the deadline for his projected *Works*, volume II.

Arbuthnot must have wondered about 'his' poem's probable effect on Lady Mary, since he apparently assured her *before* it was printed that he could see no reason to identify its 'Sapho' with her. It is hard to see how anyone could expect her to swallow this disingenuous argument, which had already sickened her in Peterborough's use of it. Yet she hastened, the very day after publication, to assure Arbuthnot that she too could see nothing of herself in Sappho's character or circumstances. (It must have hurt to say this, since the name was still current coin for honouring female poets.) The trouble was, she said, 'the Town (except you who know better)' believed that Pope meant her by Sappho. Arbuthnot—who in fact knew better than to believe the lie they were mutually pretending to accept—must surely have felt some shame in reading her letter. But that did not help her.

---

[73] Allegedly by Pope himself: 'In Beauty or Wit'.

[74] *Epistle to Arbuthnot*, 305–33, 337. Hervey had reached his acme of court favour between the *Verses to the Imitator* and *Epistle to Arbuthnot* (1931: ii. 348–9). Camille Paglia 'dredges up' (her phrase) from Hervey's *Memoirs* a clutch of shaky psychoanalytical diagnoses: that he longed to be a woman because his mother had coddled him; that his refusal to revere the ancient Romans is deeply suspect; that he was willing to 'sully himself' in a way Pope was not. Mack finds the Sporus portrait an index of Walpole's success in lowering the political moral tone. Halsband acutely calls it 'the culmination of Hervey's career as a satiric object' (Paglia 1773: 348–71; Mack 1985: 647–8; Halsband 1973: 176).

[75] Grundy 1977: 117–18.

She wanted him to show her letter to Pope; she had designed it to hurt him. Pope needed malice to sell his poems, she said, since nobody would buy them otherwise; he had abused the dead who could no longer defend themselves; Congreve had despised him and his work. She admitted that his parents were 'honest' (a favourite word of the upper classes about the lower); indeed, she said, she had always judged his mother, though very old, 'to have much better sense than himselfe'. Most importantly, in this letter she denied authorship of the *Verses to the Imitator of Horace*: 'they were wrote (without my knowledge) by a Gentleman of great merit, whom I very much esteem, who he will never guess, and who, if he did know, he durst not attack.' (This did not describe Hervey, when Pope had just incontrovertibly proved that he did dare attack him.) Lady Mary praised the *Verses*: she named them as the cause of Pope's 'terrible malice' against 'Sappho'; she even said she was glad they had been written, but she denied that she did it.[76]

This letter did not ask Arbuthnot to *do* anything for her. It did not ask him to believe her, but only to pretend, as she pretended she believed him. This game of masks fooled nobody. The *Verses* were reissued through Anne Dodd's mercury firm on 16 January 1735 with a title-page that said 'The Fifth Edition Corrected'. Changes were minimal, but included a couple of new footnotes pointing to the *Epistle to Arbuthnot*. Lord Oxford, husband of Lady Mary's friend, thought it was 'a sham of the Booksellers', to dispose of unsold copies on the coat-tails of Pope's new poem; but he was wrong. Either Lady Mary, or Hervey, or Pope, or someone lower down the print chain, may have arranged the new edition. Newspapers advertised it as 'by a Lady'; it was probably the 'very satyrical poem on *Pope* by a lady' which Catharine Cockburn read in Aberdeen before the end of the year.[77]

Meanwhile Pope (with the deadline approaching for his new *Works*) was turning out new poems so fast that answerers lagged behind. The next new work to support Lady Mary against him, *An Epistle to Alexander Pope, Esq; Occasion'd by some of his Late Writings*, came too soon after *Arbuthnot* to address it. She had had at least *some* part in this, since she wrote on the title-page of her copy, 'not by me except a Correction or two, M.' Her disclaimer arouses more suspicions than it quiets. This poem of 140 lines depicts Pope as a Jacobite, a hanger-on of Bolingbroke, plotting ineffectual treason in his grotto; it contrasts his appearance with Hervey's, and advises him to stick to non-political lyric poetry. These are all points which Lady Mary made elsewhere. It reproves him for drawing her 'in a gay Idiot's Dress', and more

[76] *CL* ii. 99–101.
[77] Cockburn, 8 Nov. (1751: ii. 279); Oxford's copy Bod. M. 3. Art (18). A 'Sixth Edition' is undated.

pertinently for suppressing her knowledge and expertise about the East, for calling her 'homebred'. This seems an odd point for anyone *except* her to take up. Her 'Correction or two' may have been fairly crucial.[78]

If she had judged it useless to appeal to Pope through Arbuthnot, she was right. In less than a month Arbuthnot was dead, and ten days after his death Pope published another poem which showcased his Lady Mary image, though here he called it—for the moment—not Sappho but Flavia (once her own name for herself). This poem too has become one of his most famous: *An Epistle to a Lady, Of the Characters of Women*. Flavia embodies not lust or avarice, but another indispensable feature of the stock learned lady: dirt. Pope contrasts '*Flavia*'s diamonds with her dirty smock; | Or *Flavia*'s self in glue (her rising task) | And issuing fragrant to an ev'ning Mask.' Sententiously he adds, 'So morning Insects that in Muck begun, | Shine, buzz, and fly-blow, in the setting-sun.' This is not the poem's only gibe at Lady Mary: she is mutely present again to be reproved and rejected in the closing compliment to Martha Blount. Martha is the sober, virgin moon whose soft radiance pleases when the glaring, tiring sun—who else but Lady Mary?—declines, and nobody cares to watch.[79]

Before this could be answered, Thomas Bentley, nephew to the scholar Pope had caricatured some months before, took up the cudgels in *A Letter to Mr. Pope, Occasioned by Sober Advice from Horace*. He defended his uncle and blasted Pope's obscenity, taking a few hints from *Verses to the Imitator*.[80] He also sought to redress the balance by a striking counter-portrait of Lady Mary, derived, he said, from common knowledge. She 'has a great deal of Wit and Learning . . . she is Mr. Pope's very own Sister in Poetry, and writes almost as well as himself; not *inferior* to the *Grecian* Sappho in Spirit and Delicacy.'[81]

This may have provided balm, but not for long. To rehabilitate the name of Sappho was a lost cause. In April Pope 'brought out with considerable pomp and circumstance'[82] his *Works* in folio and quarto formats—a second volume designed to go with the one which he had published in 1717 and sent

---

[78] 4 Jan. 1735 (Guerinot 1969: 249–51; copy in Osborn Collection, Yale).

[79] *Epistle to a Lady, of the Characters of Women*, 8 Feb. 1735, TE iii. 2. 46–74, lines 24–8, 253–6 (text of first version; Rumbold 1989: 195, 277). It has not been noticed how 'setting-sun' ties these two passages together.

[80] He writes of razor and wedge, the *Verses* of razor and oyster-knife; he writes of 'a little Creature, scarce four Foot high', the *Verses* of 'One over-match'd by ev'ry Blast of Wind'; both describe onlookers laughing (Bentley 1735: 4, 17; *Verses*, 25–7, 81–2).

[81] Pub. 4 Mar. 1735: 7 (Guerinot 1969: 251–4).

[82] Mack 1985: 652. He published 18 new pieces this year, and 68 books, either new or reprinted (Griffith 1962: 267). Hervey was this month 'up to the Elbows in . . . the Sinking-Fund', staying every day at the House until 5 or 6 p.m., which was seen as a quite abnormal workload (Halsband 1973: 180).

to Lady Mary in Turkey. The new volume glanced at her in several revisions of earlier poems. In 'The Second Satire of Dr. John Donne' he now observed that 'other whores' are nothing to anyone 'who knows Sapho'. In the 'Epistle to a Lady' he altered Flavia (a private allusion) to Sappho (a public one). In the 'Epistle to Jervas' he cancelled, at last, the compliment to Wortley's eyes, giving it to Lady Worsley instead. He added to the *Dunciad*'s lines on Rémond a riddling footnote connecting it *not* with 'a famous Lady who cheated a French wit of 5000 pounds in the South-Sea year' but with 'all bragging Travellers, and . . . all Whores and Cheats under the name of Ladies'. This redoubles the clues linking the passage to Lady Mary, concealing further insult under apparent disavowal.[83]

The next move in this bout came from an old player: Edmund Curll. In May 1735 he achieved what he no doubt felt to be the coup of publishing some of Pope's letters. He included some to Lady Mary in Turkey: without her name, though in one case the designation 'Lady M.' gave a hint. In fact Pope had outplotted Curll, even 'bitten' him into pirating these letters. He thus achieved various aims. He hoped to get Curll punished for breach of privilege (printing letters written by peers); he did get serious questions about copyright raised in parliament; and he was able to issue his letters in an authorized edition (after protracted negotiations with Swift) without appearing vain or egotistical.

In 1735, as Curll's Pope letters went through one printing after another, those to Lady Mary seem hardly to have been noticed amid the uproar. But *she* must have noticed—if nothing else, the comment on what a fine sight the unnamed 'Lady Abroad' would be if she were naked. The authorized edition, two years later, was to produce worse.[84]

Meanwhile Curll retaliated by using *his* natural weapons. As well as more volumes of letters, he printed the tale of how he had been tricked. He published, too, a dialogue called *The Poet finish'd in Prose*. Its author (probably one of his regular hacks) achieved a brilliant, irresponsible, anarchic humour. Of its two speakers, A. dislikes Pope and B. defends him, but B.'s remarks are much the more damaging. It uses Lady Mary as a lever against Pope with no regard whatever for her own preferences or sensibilities. A. hints at the notorious 'P—x'd by her Love' line (though he does not quote it) and at the poet's evident terror of 'that Lady'. B. hastens to *explain* the 'extravagant Aversion' which Pope has to her: it comes from 'a Suspicion he

---

[83] *Works*, 24 Apr. 1735 (Griffith 1962: 370; Foxon and McLaverty 1991: 121); TE iv. 133; v. 112; liii, *Dunciad*, i. 127–8 and note.

[84] See p. 368. *Mr. Pope's Literary Correspondence. Volume the Second*, 14 July 1735, included 'In Beauty or Wit', addressed to MWM by name (Griffith 1962: 308–10).

had that she intended to ravish him'. This comic reversal of gender roles around the idea of rape is played to the hilt. B. feels sure Pope's charge must have some substance; otherwise 'a Man of strict Virtue . . . could never have been guilty of so vile an Insinuation'. If she is indeed a would-be rapist, no punishment can be too bad for her, 'for nothing can be imagin'd more terrible than a Rape, to a Gentleman who has not the least Passion for the Sex'. He then excuses Pope's alleged deviance: 'no doubt he has found out some other Amusement, equally entertaining to him in his Solitude.'[85]

Lady Mary was still writing against Pope; but her last and arguably most telling attack never got into print. She must have written or drafted her 'P[ope] to Bolingbroke' by this time, before Bolingbroke again left the country in June 1735. She was not the only person to feel that Pope damaged his credibility by choosing for his 'guide, philosopher, and friend' this notorious sensualist and serial turncoat, who seemed always ready to switch allegiance to snatch at the will-o'-the-wisp of power.[86] She makes Bolingbroke an egoist who feeds his 'self-content' by contrasting his own flawless perfection with the 'Sensual, Passionate and blind' human norm. His pursuit of power leaves a trail of victims; his 'glorious schemes' of demagoguery encompass plunging his country in civil war. Her Pope here is a sycophant eaten up with envy of high life: he plays to the gallery, cheats his publisher, and has 'Whisper'd the Husband to correct the Wife'.

Some of these unpublished charges are undeniable. Bolingbroke did indeed leave the Catalan allies in the lurch; did he also boast of the easy forgiveness accorded him by a court he had betrayed? (Either the Hanoverian court or that of 'James III' might fit the bill.) Pope had indeed 'defam'd' at least one of his subscribers: Lady Mary herself. 'And when detected never was asham'd' is fair comment on his response when she got Peterborough and Arbuthnot to remonstrate. The hard bargains he drove with publishers were fact; did he therefore also boast of sexual 'joys I ne'er obtain'd' with Judith Cowper? Did he whisper to Wortley that Lady Mary ought to be corrected? Again the unknown is full of intriguing possibilities.

But even if some of her accusations were apt, she deliberately mingled them with fantasy. She ends with nostalgia for the reign of Henry VIII, when Pope would have been flogged and Bolingbroke beheaded. The lines she drafted but excluded contain (as well as the reference to Cowper) a vignette

---

[85] Pub. 26 June 1735 (Guerinot 1969: 254–8). Advertising in *The Poet finisd'd*, 'E. CURLL, TERROR PAPAE', boasts '*the Hunt's up! a Poet is the Game.*'

[86] *Essay on Man*, iv. 390; Dickinson 1970: 5. The poem is one of only two in her album not in her hand; Claudia Thomas, contradicting Mack, thinks it the most successful of her attacks on Pope (H MS 256; Thomas 1994: 128).

of poet and mentor scouring 'dirty Lanes' for whores: 'Even there superior, there it often happ'd | My Lord was pox'd, when I was only clapp'd.'[87] Over this poem, as over her attack on Swift, Montagu took a lot of trouble. She kept two rough drafts which have little but a first paragraph in common; and at a late date she had a fair copy made in her authorized album of poems. She freely admitted readers to this volume; accordingly its version of 'Pope to Bolingbroke' omits Pope's whispering to a husband and getting the clap.[88]

To have written 'pox'd' (even in draft) might surely have made her recognize some parallel between what Pope endured and what he dished out. The wrongs he enumerated in *To Arbuthnot*—the 'Tale reviv'd, the Lye so oft o'erthrown . . . Abuse on all he lov'd, or lov'd him, spread'—were exactly her own wrongs from him. But as he did not see this, neither did she.

Their feud must have functioned in her life like the deep, unseen, secret wound (of a different, erotic kind) which she wrote of in her 'Epistle to Bathurst'. Among her male friends, Arbuthnot and Peterborough had sided with her enemy against her. Her bitterness about Pope rankled for years, in many contexts. She came to believe that all his friendships with those of higher rank were mercenary: he had been legacy-hunting from many friends who were also hers (Buckingham, Peterborough, Congreve). When her son blamed his troubles on her, or found supporters against his father, she supposed that Pope was at the bottom of it.

Her friendships among women, however, those in or near her own class, were probably unaffected. On moving to Cavendish Square in 1731 she became a neighbour of one of her earliest friends, Henrietta Cavendish Holles, now Lady Oxford. Lady Mary's enmity with Pope seems actually to have reinforced the bond between these two. Although Lord Oxford was one of Pope's chief patrons and supporters, his wife 'adored Lady Mary and hated Pope'—as she hated 'most of the wits who surrounded her husband'. Lady Mary's wit was different: Lady Oxford admired that 'with all her might; pretty much as the parish-clerk reverences the rector for his Greek and Hebrew.' On her side Lady Mary, 'though in general not over tolerant to her inferiors in capacity, appears upon the whole to have loved nobody so well'. Lady Oxford guarded carefully against such a gross insult to Lady Mary as setting her up for a dinner-table encounter with Pope. Sooner than permit such a thing, said her daughter later, 'she would have put her hand in the fire'.[89]

---

[87] No doubt this was inspired by Pope's saying, first that she gave her lovers the pox, then that she had every virtue *except* that.

[88] H MS 81. 22–4, 44–5; H MS 256 (after 1755). She had certainly read *An Epistle from the late Lord Bo—ke to the Duke of W—n*, 1730—unless, indeed, she had written it.

[89] Johnson wrote that MWM 'infested' Oxford's table, and could not be restrained from crossing Pope in

These are strong words; they describe a situation that goes far to explain Lady Mary's depth of appreciation for the dull Lady Oxford. But no matter how tactfully handled, the situation must have caused her pain. She was drawn to Oxford's London houses not only as a dinner guest but also by his collections. She was an assiduous borrower and punctual re-deliverer of items such as a 'very finely illuminated' manuscript which she and the Duchess of Montagu pored over together. She noted, critically, Oxford's carelessness about his priceless possessions.[90] Probably before each such visit she took steps to ascertain that the coast would be clear of Pope; years later Pope's name sprang to her pen as she wrote of her use of the Harleian MSS. Her intellectual pleasures were pursued in the shadow of his enmity. It was impossible for her to forget about him.

conversation 'till . . . the one or the other quitted the house'. Lady Bute, on the Duchess of Portland's authority, flatly denied this (*E&P* 38–9; *CL* ii. 249, 257; iii. 58; Johnson 1905: iii. 202.

[90] *CL* ii. 354. Later the MSS stayed in Oxford's Dover St. house when the books (at his Cavendish Square house) were sold (Kaminski 1987: 175).

20

March 1736–March 1738

~❧~

Algarotti: 'This Youth (Delightfull Vision of a day!)'[1]

LADY MARY the publishing guerrilla was not the whole Lady Mary, any more than was Lady Mary the mother. The month Lord Perceval abandoned his hopes of her daughter was that of her first known letter to Francesco Algarotti, a young Italian who had arrived in London in March 1736. The month of the Butes' marriage was that of Algarotti's decision to leave England—a decision that plunged Lady Mary into emotional turmoil and despair.

Algarotti, of a wealthy middle-class Paduan-Venetian family, had high ability and unbounded ambition and charm. On his version of the Grand Tour, the people he sought out were not potentates and diplomats but practitioners of the arts and sciences, luminaries of Enlightenment. He had made a great hit with Voltaire and his brilliant life partner, the marquise du Châtelet. He was working on an Italian popularization of Sir Isaac Newton's *Optics*—not translated but loosely adapted—on the model of Fontenelle's influential *Pluralité des mondes*. This project recalled Addison's *Spectator* design of bringing 'Philosophy out of Closets and Libraries, Schools and Colleges, to dwell in Clubs and Assemblies, at Tea-Tables and in Coffee-Houses'.[2] It was bound to appeal to Lady Mary.

Algarotti was, in time, to acquire a name as a cultural theorist. Lady Mary found him—at about the age of her unsatisfactory son—teeming with new ideas on manuscripts, poetry, *objets d'art*, conversation, and wine. He was seeing the world, soaking up ideas and experiences, making friends in high places, having the time of his life. 'Europe he saw, and Europe saw him too.'[3]

---

[1] *E&P* 306. [2] *Spectator* 10, 12 Mar. 1711.

[3] *CL* ii. 237; *Dunciad*, 1742: iv. 294. MWM was later quoted as saying 'that women see men with their ears' (Stuart 1899: 4).

Voltaire had commissioned him to show Queen Caroline a panegyric he had written on her;[4] Emilie du Châtelet pursued him with letters. In London on the first of April he attended a meeting of the Royal Society; a week later he was nominated to a Fellowship. In late May he was elected to the Society of Antiquaries, following a debate as to whether 'Foreigners of Eminent Note and Learning' were eligible. Algarotti, with Anders Celsius the Swedish astronomer and Scipione Maffei the Veronese savant, was one of the first three such members.[5]

Voltaire recommended Algarotti to Hervey; Hervey introduced him to Lady Mary. Algarotti may well have heard her name first from Voltaire, who quoted her poetry about this time. The recommendation to Hervey was a success, for sexual orientation gave the two men an instant rapport. Hervey, indeed, proved almost as susceptible as Lady Mary.[6] Algarotti may have brought his new acquaintance Maffei to the Wortley Montagus' to inspect the inscription they had collected at Sigeum in 1718. He and Maffei each paid homage to Pope at Twickenham.[7]

Lady Mary's first note to Algarotti runs the gamut of themes which were to thread their relationship. 'My Lady Stafford and my selfe waited for you three Hours', she wrote. 'Three Hours of expectation is no small Tryal of Patience, and I believe some of your Martyrs have been canoniz'd for suffering less.' To obtain absolution, she said, he must visit her next evening. This plays with conventional gallant attitudes (divine lady, suppliant male; male sinner, female priest), hints at libertine or sceptical debate (she had bantered Conti about 'your' Catholic saints)[8]—and unwittingly anticipates the months and years she was to spend waiting vainly for Algarotti. The physical or emotional dimension of her love for him has tended to obscure its intellectual element; but this relationship took 'wit' as its aphrodisiac.

In less than two weeks Lady Mary was wildly in love. She wrote and kept

---

[4] In the preface to *Alʒire*, an epistle to du Châtelet—who hoped next year to travel to England, under Algarotti's conduct, to meet the queen herself (André-Michel Rousseau 1976: 166, 168).

[5] Halsband 1956: 154; debate on 20 May 1736 (Evans 1956: 87). Algarotti had studied science as well as *belles lettres* at Bologna.

[6] Treat 1913: 69–70; Bosisio 1959; Voltaire 1963–93: i. 671. Hervey was busy both professionally (with the Prince of Wales's marriage and vital parliamentary business) and personally. The end of March saw the birth of his youngest child, the wedding of his lover Stephen Fox, and the death of his mistress Miss Vane (Hervey 1931: ii. 530–6; Halsband 1973: 192–7).

[7] Algarotti to Agostino Paradisi, 4 Oct. 1759 (MS sold at Basle, 19 Sept. 1992, Erasmushaus Haus der Bücher: thanks to Jim May and John Grundy). Maffei left Paris on 8 May for England: he met Pope and saw Lord Oxford's library, but wrote few surviving letters. Conti probably recommended him to MWM; he met her daughter too (Marchi 1992: 127–8, 138; *CL* iii. 84).

[8] *CL* ii. 101; i. 376. MWM subscribed this year to Le Courayer's French translation of Paolo Sarpi's *History of the Council of Trent*, a work of theological learning and Protestant history. Samuel Johnson worked long but abortively on an English version (Kaminsky 1987: 67 ff.).

a number of poems of love and desire, many of them unfinished or in rough draft, which probably reflect her feelings for Algarotti.[9] Of the poems of hers which he kept, in her handwriting or his own, several are not original but extemporary adaptations, either from others or from herself. This does not mean that he sapped her originality but that she was thinking and writing on the spur of the moment, as she often did in topical writing. Now she was mediating for him the English poetic tradition. Among other things this was a tutor–pupil relationship, with the woman, unusually, as tutor. Algarotti kept the erotic addresses, from woman to man *and* from man to woman, which she crafted out of Lansdowne or Addison (who in turn was just then drawing on Horace). He also kept a political epigram which she had already adapted and updated, and a dramatic speech she wrote for Brutus, justifying his murder of Caesar.[10]

Lady Mary's discovery of Algarotti coincided with her loss of her daughter (emotionally in marriage; physically, some time that autumn, on the long journey to the Isle of Bute) and of her sister. When Lady Frances Erskine turned twenty-one that August she at once sought full custody of her mother. The day after the Butes' marriage, Grange's agent was wondering whether he should pay Lady Mar's allowance to Lady Mary or to someone else. It went to Lady Frances. There must have been further legal wrangling, for on 6 November Wortley, up north on business, urged his wife to relinquish custody of her sister once and for all. The terms in which he did so were not endearing. If Lady Frances should do anything wrong, 'you cannot be blamed . . . you are justified to the world, whatever happens to your sister and your niece'. Even if Lady Mary wanted to share in the care of her sister's person, he insisted on being set 'free from the care of her estate'. He wanted it all settled as soon as he got back to London. Lady Mary capitulated.[11]

Lady Frances's victory was cause of rejoicing to her cousin Gertrude Leveson-Gower, who remarked that Lady Mary's 'behaviour upon her Daughter's marriage is quite consistent with the rest of her actions', and fantasized as to how she might eventually leave 'all her Riches'. It is remarkable that a young woman of her class (whose own mother used always to be short of cash) should be so out of touch with the financial facts of life: if she did not know that Lady Mary had no marriage settlement, she might at least have known that all married women's property belonged by law to the husband. Later, after making a rich marriage herself, Gertrude was able to

    [9] *E&P* 286–91, 295–6, 304–6, 381–2; H MS 81. 153.
    [10] *E&P* 304–5, 295, 296, 279, 150–2; see p. 317. Political thinking about Bolingbroke went into her Brutus speech. Other writers she knew (like Buckingham and Conti) reworked the story of Brutus and Caesar.
    [11] Mar MS GD 124/16/51/26; H MS 74. 146–7.

provide Lady Frances and her mother with a house to live in.[12] In 1751
Horace Walpole (who believed Lady Mar had been mistreated by her sister
while out of her senses) admitted that she was 'not entirely recovered'.[13] So
far as is known she never went to Scotland.

During his months in England Algarotti was finishing his version of
Newton's *Optics* (published at Milan, late 1737). Lady Mary (an experienced
collaborator) and Hervey listened, praised, and offered linguistic and other
finishing touches.[14] Algarotti set the scientist-narrator's dialogues with his
noble, brilliant, and beautiful female pupil in an arbour or private Parnassus,
which reflects both Lady Mary's Twickenham garden and Voltaire's Cirey.
The pupil is a marchesa (Emilie du Châtelet's title). She speaks strongly
against war, and is called a citizen of the world (as Lady Mary called herself).[15] Early in volume ii comes a more unmistakable allusion. To prove the
utility of science to women, the narrator cites inoculation, which now pre-
serves the charms of English as well as of Circassian beauties.

On the scale of tributes to Lady Mary's inoculation work, this ranks
somewhere between *The Plain Dealer*'s gallantry and Voltaire's heroiniz-
ing. Algarotti does not name her; he stresses the saving of beauty, not of
life; and he takes no note of her engagement in social struggle. However, his
treatise won from her a commendatory poem which he placed first in the
volume when the *Newtonanismo* was reprinted at Naples, 1739.

Lady Mary, who preached prudence to her daughter, was embarking on
perilous waters. By mid-August Algarotti, having completed his book, was
planning to leave for Italy to arrange its publication.[16] For writing to him she
had switched to French, the language of passion. Although he was so flighty,
she said, and she had once been so rational, her love was forever. The philosophical indifference she used to live by had vanished: at a note from him, a
suggestion of meeting, she was ready to faint away. She thought of his departure with terror—and she knew that unless he loved as fervently as she did,
he would find her letters intolerable.[17]

---

[12] Gertrude to Lady Frances Erskine, 13 Sept. 1736, sending 'Respects' to her aunt Mar (Mar MSS GD
124/15/1462). Her father, Gower, had sympathized with MWM on 11 Sept. about young Mary's having 'fixt
upon an husband that had not your approbation', and on her troubles with Lady Frances Erskine. Frances
had given her own version to Gertrude—whose husband, the Duke of Bedford, later became both a
financial prop and a scapegoat for the Erskines (H MS 77. 174–5; Mar MS GD 124/2/281/5, 2/284).

[13] *Corr.* xx. 281 (to Mann, 14 Oct. 1751).   [14] Treat 1913: 70.

[15] 'Voi siete . . . o Madama, Cittadina del Mondo' (*Newtonianismo*, Naples, 1739: 173). MWM may have
applied the phrase to herself in allusion to Algarotti's book; it was used of him too (*CL* iii. 141; Thomas
Hollis, 13 Sept. 1763: Hollis 1992: 263).

[16] Hervey had expected his departure two months earlier, when he wrote his praise to Voltaire (June
1736, Halsband MSS 46; Barling 1968: 24–5).

[17] *CL* ii. 103–7. The Graphology Business claim her feelings were previously undeveloped, therefore
liable to sudden outburst (3 May 1995).

On 19 August, six days after her daughter's wedding, he sat to the pencil of Jonathan Richardson, who had so splendidly painted Lady Mary. The results (probably done for one of his other admirers) seem to depict a split personality: full-face he is smiling, debonair, with waving curls like some innocent in pastoral; in profile his sharply beaked nose gives him the air of a bird of prey.[18]

Algarotti had supper with Lady Mary on 5 September, his last day in England; he told Hervey he spent the evening with someone else.[19] The two friends had become rivals for this young man's love. But not in the same way. Hervey had no illusions; Lady Mary knew that she had entered into wilful self-deception.[20] Moreover, Hervey knew she was in love, and she did not know that he was. In letters she sought to charm Algarotti by her learning (deploying a range of reference: Virgil, Horace, Montaigne, Fénelon) and by a would-be amusing clear-sightedness. She called herself the Dido to his 'little Aeneas', and admitted she had thrown herself at his head. But her love, she said, was as pure as—no, more pure than—that of devotees of the Virgin: it had no hope of return.[21]

In this letter, the first after he left, she wrote that she could have stopped him going, but that false delicacy held her back. This can mean only one thing: she knew she could have kept him with her by offering money.[22] She also lamented her gender: if she had been male she could have travelled with him. (Perhaps she was thinking of Hervey and Stephen Fox.)

Algarotti had promised to write from Calais; he did not. He wrote to Hervey, however, and Hervey (who now knew that Lady Mary, not he, had been chosen for Algarotti's last evening) took care to let her know it. Hervey wrote assiduously to Algarotti, but he confided his feelings of loneliness and loss not to him but to Henry Fox (whom he asked to burn his letter). Lady Mary was less guarded; in the fortnight after Algarotti left she sent him four letters, all open avowals. According to Hervey she even boasted of her conquest.[23]

These weeks with no word made her desperate enough to think seriously

---

[18] See Pl. 9; interpretation is Robert Halsband's (cf. 1973: 192).

[19] Martin Folkes, FRS, whom Algarotti had first met in Rome.

[20] Hervey to Algarotti, 9/20 Sept. 1736, Murray MSS. Years later she wrote, 'no Man ever was in Love with a Woman of 40 [7 years less than she was now], since the Deluge. A Boy may be so, but that blaze of straw only lasts till he is old enough to distinguish between Youth and Age' (*CL* iii. 98).

[21] *CL* ii. 104–5, 107, 109. Algarotti kept a verse epistle which *may* be by MWM, likening her to the abandoned Dido or Sappho (BL Eg. MS 23. 239).

[22] Later she implied that she *had* helped finance his departure (*CL* ii. 134). Perhaps it would have cost more to finance his stay.

[23] To Algarotti, 9/20 Sept., Murray MS. Hervey calls Algarotti a true son of Adam, damned for tasting in MWM the apple of knowledge.

of pumping Hervey: to learn, at least, whether Algarotti had reached Paris safely. Algarotti in due course received two divergent accounts of what followed. Lady Mary said that she sent to tell Hervey she wished to see him, and 'with his politeness' she did not have to wait long. He for his part said he evaded a meeting until he ran into her at Lady Stafford's and there was no polite way to escape her 'Summons'. She said he then offered to call on her, but she preferred to call on him. He said that having offered to call he then sent an excuse, whereupon she turned up. She arrived at seven on Tuesday evening, 21 September, called for supper at eleven, and stayed till òne a.m. On Saturday they met again. Lady Mary when she wrote to Algarotti ran the two encounters into one.

At first she could not bring herself to pose a bald question; Hervey told her with surely malicious courtliness that 'after so much neglect as [she] had shewn him he could not fancy [she] would honnour him with a message'— unless it was a matter of life or death. This made it impossible for her to con- fess her desperation by asking anything. He sardonically reported her vainly employing 'thousands of different ways to make me talk of you' while vainly trying to hide her feelings. He said she told him 'a thousand deliberate lies & a thousand accidental truths'. She had sworn him to secrecy, so he would not pass on what she had said. But he found her so changed that he wondered who this unknown person could be: she 'was as drunk before as wine can make one, & you have added *Gin*'. Hervey was a faithful friend at least in what he declined to say; but, as his biographer remarks, he did not match her generosity. He made fun of her to Algarotti (even of her peculiar style of curtseying), and contrasted her instability with his own solid, unswerving commitment.[24]

At one of these meetings their 'dispute whether Absence ended Love' took a literary turn. Lady Mary wrote down an epigram, 'extempore', about the violence of her love. She drew a line across the sheet of paper after her three couplets; but Hervey took the paper from her and contradicted her in couplets of his own, borrowing an argument from Dryden's Cleopatra. Lady Mary in turn replied; and the dialogue continued in their alternate handwritings. Most amazingly of all, they seem then to have turned the paper over and versified the earlier stages of the conversation, with Hervey questioning and Lady Mary unable to tell but asking him to guess. In this way, the paper going back and forth, they wove a philosophical dialogue

---

[24] [*c*.29 Sept. 1736], *CL* ii. 108. Hervey had warned Algarotti that Lady Stafford was not in the secret (Halsband 1973: 200–1; Hervey MS 47/2, 15, 69–71). He said MWM visited him accompanied by 'the little ugly singer'. This sounds like Lady Bute, but she would have been a surprising companion, and had prob- ably left for Scotland (*CL* ii. 108; Halsband 1973: 201; Murray MS, trans. from French).

about secrecy, trust, love, and its possible cure. Lady Mary asserted that her love was all-consuming, unique, and enduring; Hervey alleged that it was appetitive, typically human, and temporary. The pain would not last, he said: 'Nature who made the Wound, will give the Cure.' He added a comparison with letters written on sand, which time erases. This was the very simile that Lady Mary had used in her poem to Bathurst, to contrast *his* fickle heart with her constant one. She would not accept it as applicable to herself. At last Hervey wrote, 'I'm tired of all this fine poetic Stuff; | Now call for Supper, we have writ enough.' She crossed this out with some violence; but she accepted supper.[25]

This situation repeats but reverses one from earlier in her life. Before she eloped, Lady Mary expended much ink trying to convince Edward Wortley Montagu that she was acting not out of passion but out of reason and high principle. Both parties to that correspondence seem to have equated passion with appetite, something involuntary and irrational. Wortley acknowledged *his* passion and his inability to control it; he felt that gave him certain entitlements in return. Lady Mary asserted her worth by denying her capacity for passion. Twenty-five years later Hervey too equated passion with appetite; Lady Mary denied his equation while confessing her passion: it was, she said, an aspect of her higher and idealistic nature.

Such debate had literary if not real-life precedents. In the third act of Dryden's *Aureng-Zebe* (pub. 1676), which the young Lady Mary often quoted, Indamora and Arimant debate a love-situation in rather this manner and with some of the same imagery. Outside tragic drama such debate remains extraordinary, and for Lady Mary it must surely have been humiliating. Hervey assured her he would not abuse her trust. But while he kept his promise and withheld the details from Algarotti, he shared with him the amusement which lurked behind his façade of sympathetic concern. Lady Mary herself viewed her feelings wryly; she owned to Algarotti that Hervey must have thought her 'very near if not quite distracted'.

Within a few more days she received at last a letter from Algarotti, 'in very good time to save the small remains of my understanding'. While Hervey was busy with politics (the controversial Gin Act came into effect on 29 September), she withdrew to out-of-season Twickenham, where there was nobody to distract her from introspection. 'I chuse to see nothing but trees since I cannot see the only Object dear to my Heart and Lovely to my Eyes.' She kept up the flow of letters and verses towards her absent ideal, and she set about having her picture painted to send him—illogically,

[25] *E&P* 287–9; Grundy 1981: 244–9.

she admitted, since her heart or soul would better represent her than her ageing face.[26]

Hervey was, as usual, preoccupied with royal family management. Queen Caroline showed signs of openly resenting her husband's new German mistress, Madame von Wallmoden, for whose sake he had even remained in Hanover beyond his birthday on 30 October. Watchful as ever, Hervey alerted Walpole to reason with the queen. She accepted advice, wrote submissively to the king at Hanover, prepared to welcome Mme von Wallmoden to England, and was rewarded (as her English advisers had promised she would be) by her husband's effusive gratitude, and his return alone. Lady Mary attended court (at Kensington) shortly before the skimpy birthday celebration, chiefly in order to see and again to question Hervey.[27] Later that autumn she must have felt mortified when her nephew Kingston, head of the Pierrepont family, returned from France with a married woman whom he had seduced. Her banker father had some of Kingston's servants arrested: an odd response, Lady Betty Finch observed, to 'the loss and infamy of his daughter'.[28]

But love kept Lady Mary mostly solitary and musing: a powerful stimulus to her writing. Her letters, straight from the heart, nevertheless bear the impress of a genre she knew well: the sentimental-erotic missives found in fiction from the immensely popular *Lettres portugaises*, 1669, to the novels of Aphra Behn and Eliza Haywood.[29] Like their fictional heroines, Lady Mary found self-expression, perhaps self-realization, in expressing a passion which was self-abasing as well as idealizing. After the caution and propriety of her long-past courtship letters, and the sardonic reports of love-affairs which she sent her sister, there is release and freedom in these artful outpourings. She even adapted to her use the bargaining element of more routine courtships, seeking to convince Algarotti by argument of the points in her favour: without the obvious attractions of youth, she offered higher currency in her ability and devotion. She argued, passionately, that she was worth loving for reasons other than passion.

She poured out poems as well as prose. A stanza about the power of singing to tame 'the Lions, and the Tygers' in her bosom may come from this

---

[26] *CL* ii. 108–9. Hervey joked that Algarotti was lucky to be away: Lady Mary's face could not now spoil the allure of her wit (Halsband 1973: 199–200).

[27] 20 or 21 Oct. 1736 (*CL* ii. 110; Hervey MS 47/4 597–606; Halsband 1973: 203–4; Hervey 1931: ii. 621).

[28] 13 Nov. 1736 (Hervey to Henry Fox, BL Add. MS 51410; Devonshire MSS, Chatsworth, 230.10). Marie-Thérèse de La Touche (ten years married, three children) met Kingston in good society in Paris. It was said she later suffered deeply from guilt (*Chudleigh* 1776: 36–7, 41, 79, 124–7; Ilchester 1950: 256, 258).

[29] [G. J. Guilleragues], *Lettres portugaises*, 1669, had ten reprints in English by 1740 (Day 1966: 32).

painful time.[30] One quarter-sheet of paper received on one side a much-altered draft of an outpouring in Sappho's manner—'My Heart beats thick, my senses fail'—and on the other side a neatly written rejection of excess: 'Come cool Indifference and calm my Breast.' In these two poems she seems to span both sides of her debate with Hervey. Another, in French, combines both sides in itself, in a highly reasoned dismissal of Reason.

Perhaps the finest poem produced by this love-affair is her 'Hymn to the Moon'. In aurally delicious liquids and sibilants it establishes the lofty serenity of the moon, which then suddenly becomes the goddess Cynthia or Diana, drawn down from her 'amazing height' by the 'Charms of young Endimion'. Though she stoops, the goddess retains her poise; this poem makes something delicate and dream-like from the confused turmoil of reality. (Years later Algarotti quoted it in full in print, praising its 'atteggiamento greco'.)[31]

She must have addressed either him or Hervey in the most celebrated poem of this group. She headed it with the momentous year date, '1736'; it begins 'With toilsome steps'. This again combines philosophy with sensibility, or anguish. The speaker likens herself to a packhorse drudging on life's 'dirty Journey', and wondering what comes next. Is there heaven? Or will there be annihilation, or reincarnation? Reading philosophy brings no conviction; nor does the exercise of reason. Only death holds the answer to this conundrum. She had already mentioned to Algarotti the charm of suicide. Now she asks,

> Why then not hasten that decisive Hour,
> Still in my view, and ever in my power?
>
> .   .   .   .
>
> In chains and darkness wherefore should I stay
> And mourn in Prison while I keep the Key?[32]

In her storms of emotion she wrote to the moment. By night, the candle wasting beside her, she exclaimed: 'He comes!—'twas nothing but the rustling Wind, | He has forgot, is faithless, is unkind— | While expectation rends my labouring mind.' Can any prospective pleasure, she wonders, recompense her for 'the long sighing of this tedious day?' The implied answer is no. She invokes Reason like a lapsed votary who cannot expect the

---

[30] *E&P* 286; see p. 226 n. 5. Her daughter may have been the singer.   [31] *E&P* 382, 304–5, 300.

[32] *E&P* 290–1. Hervey was not opposed to suicide. Either now or later MWM voiced her desire for death in lines which echo his 'Monimia to Philocles', and convey her fervent thanks for his sympathy (Ilchester 1950: 94; *E&P* 305–6). This poem may be the reason why Wrenn 1920 ascribes to her *The Fair Suicide*, 1720, a folio pamphlet containing two poems: self-justification from a jilted woman about to kill herself, and feminist endorsement of her action.

divinity to answer. Again she just hints at a death-wish: 'And thou fond Heart, go beat thy selfe to rest.'[33] But one thing is constant in all these poems: love is an affliction; it is the classical, divinely inflicted madness, a punishment for which she is singled out. 'If Age and Sickness, poverty, and Pain, | Should each assault me with Alternate Plagues,' she wrote, she could adopt a Christian stoicism; like a pious farmer whose crop is blighted, she would submit devoutly. 'But ('spite of Sermons) Farmers would blaspheme | If a Star fell to set their Thatch on Flame.'

Despite the ring of finality to this poem (in stanzas), when she showed it to Hervey he continued it. Again he turned her own imagery against her, maintaining that her case was not, like the farmer's, portentous. Algarotti may be a cataclysm in nature, he wrote, but plenty of people have learned to live with, even to harness, such forces. Lady Mary began a riposte, which does not argue her uniqueness but strays to a topic which Hervey had not broached: 'This sensibillity which oft you praise | Serves but to plague me in unusual ways.' She always felt her exceptional, enduring sensitivity spelled nothing but trouble. She seldom showed or shared it, and this made for emotional isolation. (But, she later wrote, 'Fig leaves are as necessary for our Minds as our Bodies, and tis as indecent to shew all we think as all we have.') This second poetic debate petered out here. Hervey sent Algarotti one of 'Sapho''s poems (together with one he had written to her). He thought hers admirable, though heavily influenced by Prior.[34]

In December 1736 repeated storms swept the country, and brought rumours that George II (returning from his mistress in Hanover) was in grave danger of shipwreck in the Channel. The Prince of Wales strutted about like Shakespeare's Prince Hal trying on the crown. Hervey worked hard at reassuring the queen; but until the king arrived in the New Year he saw his own career and Walpole's as hanging in the balance. Lady Mary meanwhile had just got ready her portrait ('wrapp'd up in poetry without Fiction') to send to Algarotti—a connoisseur who was later to make a living selecting pictures for others as well as collecting them himself.

Lady Mary's portrait does not appear in the sale catalogue of Algarotti's pictures (which is posthumous and incomplete). Since it showed her at the height of her beauty—'This once was me, thus my complexion fair'—it may perhaps have been based on the Kneller of 1715 (as, it seems, was Zincke's miniature of 1738). It may, too, have used attributes to make visible

---

[33] *E&P* 295.
[34] *E&P* 289–90; Hervey to Algarotti, 30 Oct. 1736, 27/16 Jan. 1737, Murray MS, Hervey MS 47/4. 597–606; *CL* iii. 97. When in later years she let people read this poem, she passed it off as written on her daughter's wedding. Lady Hertford wondered why this event should cause such surprise.

her activities and achievements (like Vertue's engraving from Zincke in 1739). Algarotti was familiar with a portrait of Madame du Châtelet which employs such attributes. It is tempting to imagine Lady Mary finding visual means (in the picture as in the poem she sent with it) to maintain that her other qualities could outweigh the loss of her beauty. 'Look on my Heart, and you'll forget my Face.'[35]

In this letter, despite her mistrust of doctors, she supplied Algarotti with information about surgery for cataract, which he needed for the sake of an elderly relation. She also told him her thoughts of him exceeded 'the strongest Panegyric that the vainest Man upon Earth ever wish'd to hear made of him selfe'. But Algarotti, reading, may have disregarded her flattery for one riveting sentence: 'If you seriously wish to see me, it will certainly happen; if your affairs do not permit your return to England, mine shall be arrang'd in such a manner as I may come to Italy.'

Back in Italy at the very end of 1736,[36] he must surely have quailed at this—if, that is, he took it seriously. He was twenty-four, and elderly people persisted in falling in love with him. He probably connived at this. He clearly found it useful, perhaps enjoyable. When Hervey repeatedly urged him to revisit England, he could enjoy the flattery and keep the power of decision in his own hands. Just then he requested both Hervey and Emilie du Châtelet not to write so often: he was too busy working on his book. Lady Mary's arrival in his native city could hardly have been a welcome prospect. But there is no indication that he took any steps to temper her passion, except by sloth in replying.

Untempered, her passion continued to make the background to everything she did and everything she saw. The Prince of Wales opened a new season of political strife by demanding that his Civil List allowance should be doubled (to £100,000) and freed from his father's control. Again Walpole and Hervey applied themselves first to personal negotiation, then to parliamentary and pamphlet rhetoric. They carried the day; in late February 1737 both Houses rejected—for the moment—the motion for the prince's rise. Between the House of Commons and the House of Lords debates Lady Mary wrote to Algarotti complaining that 'Faction and Nonsense' were trying to drive out the 'soft remembrances' of her love. In fact, she said, political 'epidemic madness' was as prevalent as the effects of the 'watry climate', which she was inclined to blame for her present toothache. But she

---

[35] *E&P* 381; *CL* ii. 110; Haskell 1980: 347–60; *Catalogo dei quadri dei disegni e dei libri . . . del fu Sig. Conte Algarotti* n.d. (with thanks to David Parker); see pp. 000–0.
[36] *CL* ii. 110–11; Haskell 1980: 349.

had hopes of Algarotti's coming to England that spring. She closed on an invocation to him as the Apollo of her verse.[37]

❧

It would be wrong, though, to suppose that she had no time for anything but love. In summer 1736 she wittily adapted a Horatian dialogue between bickering lovers to make it fit a tentative *rapprochement* between Walpole (now allied with Henry Pelham) and Pulteney (now compromising himself with Bolingbroke). In early 1737 the irregular anti-ministerial *Craftsman*, a paper dominated by Bolingbroke, gave way to a venture of Chesterfield and Lyttelton: *Common Sense; or, The Englishman's Journal*.[38] 'Common sense' then meant something less like 'mother wit' than like 'the consensus of humanity'; to the Enlightenment it implied a universalist faith in the sway of reason. As a political title, it conveyed—offensively to Lady Mary and to Hervey—that anti-Walpole sentiment was both right and unanimous. Hervey soon hit back at one of its essays, with a slim, sprightly pamphlet: *A Letter to the Author of Common-Sense . . . of Saturday, 16 April*. Lady Mary hit back somewhat later.

This year Lord Bute was chosen one of those Scottish representative peers who were needed by Walpole, disapproved by Wortley, and mar-shalled by Bute's uncles. They were central in a controversy just gathering. At issue was the punishment to be meted out for the Porteous riots of the year before, when soldiers had fired into a demonstrating crowd in Edinburgh, and the citizens had taken the law into their own hands and hanged the officer in command. This had caused alarm south of the border about mob outrages. Opposition policy was to needle the government into inflicting draconian punishment, not for ethical reasons but in hope that the Scottish peers would defect from Walpole.

All this not only raised the level of faction and nonsense; presumably it also brought both the Butes to London. It was probably there that Lady Mary's daughter became pregnant with her first child, born early in 1738. But no record remains of the relations of mother and daughter at this time.

That spring, 1737, the Opposition moved to attack Walpole over the national debt. Sir John Barnard (who had attracted notice when Walpole's excise scheme went down) promulgated a plan for converting the debt. Wortley spoke in support of Barnard and sat on a parliamentary committee

---

[37] Debates of 22, 25 Feb. 1737 (Halsband 1973: 207–10); 24 Feb. [?1737], *SL* 233–5, redated from *CL* ii. 114–15.

[38] *E&P* 284–5. *Common Sense* began on 5 Feb. 1737. Fielding was rumoured to have supplied its germ (*Daily Gazetteer*, 14 Apr., quoted in Battestin 1989: 222).

convened with the object of pushing through the plan. Walpole won this round by effecting its defeat.[39] The affair re-emphasized the gulf dividing Lady Mary's husband from her own views, friends, and sympathies.

In May, 'the warmest Season that any body now alive remembers to have felt', came the carefully planted, 'authentic' edition of Pope's letters. This exposed in public, more fully than Curll's edition had done, Pope's romantic, heavily sexualized admiration for an unnamed female traveller. Indeed, its tightrope act between exposure and concealment must have made anxious reading for Lady Mary. The printed letters exposed Pope's fantasy about a beautiful body being freed for every indulgence by its Islamic loss of a soul; they censored the companion fantasy about the male traveller being circumcised. Lady Mary began an indignant response, in the form of a letter to Pope: meant not to send, but to publish. She made two accusations: he had forged some letters printed as his friends' (how could Atterbury have approved his satire on Addison, for instance?), and he had printed as addressed to Buckingham and to 'poor dead Gay' some letters which were actually versions of ones she had herself received. But apparently she could find no terms for public mention of the insistent letters of adoration. She left her comments unfinished and unprinted.[40]

In June Hervey spent some weeks in the country with his father, who had been ill. Lady Mary's 'Faction' faculty was lively enough to send him satirical descriptions which he relished, as well as praise of her rural Twickenham retreat (good for the imagination, she said). This he found provoking, and he demanded how she could 'talk so like a canting Seneca'. Just at the end of the parliamentary session their mutual friend John Hedges died. Lady Mary sent some elegiac lines to Hervey. Again Hervey wrote a reply, arguing (as she had for Mrs Bowes) that death was not to be lamented if the best of life was over. This he sent to Algarotti, wishing he had hers by him to send with it.[41]

Algarotti spent the summer in Milan working on his book. Hervey pressed him for letters, fearing that Lady Mary might now be more favoured than himself: 'Sometimes she says she hears from you, sometimes that she

---

[39] The plan was to lower interest on the sinking fund from 4% to 3%. *The Freeholders Journal* (a government paper) had called Barnard 'busy, furious, clamorous and loquacious' (9 Apr. 1722). He became Lord Mayor of London later in 1737; Pope's friend Cobham set up a bust of him in his pantheon of patriot worthies. EWM was running a wire works at Wortley, and selling timber patiently, small amount by small amount (Wh MS M 118, 122).

[40] Badminton MS Fm T/B1/4/4; Pope, *Corr.* i. 352–3, 368–9; *E&P* 98–9. Ilay raised in the House of Lords the matter of publishing peers' letters (Mack 1985: 653; McLaverty 1980).

[41] *CL* ii. 111–13; Halsband 1973: 212; 28/27 Sept. 1737, Murray MS. This exchange recalls their long-running town–country debate. Hedges, son of a wealthy London merchant (Christie 1995: 61), had joined the Opposition.

does not; which is true I know not.'[42] None of her London friends or enemies seems to have had an inkling of her infatuation. But it was a matter of comment to French or French-connected circles, apparently through Mary Anne Cantillon, who had married Francis Bulkeley in 1736. On 20/9 May 1737 the Bulkeleys were in England and Francis wrote, partly on his wife's behalf, to urge Montesquieu to join them. As an inducement he suggested that Montesquieu might succeed Algarotti in Lady Mary's affections. The two exchanged banter about her in several letters. Montesquieu was somewhat more polite than Bulkeley: he wrote that Algarotti's conquest was matter for congratulation, and sent admiring and respectful messages for Lady Mary—who would surely, however, have been much displeased at this jesting.[43]

One event that summer closely concerned a dearer friend than Mary Anne: the death of Catherine Walpole, the Prime Minister's estranged wife. Speculation began at once as to whether and when Molly Skerrett would succeed her. Anne, Lady Irwin, reported on 30 November that the couple were married: other reports gave later dates. Maria's new stepson Horace wrote later that on their marriage 'Sir Robert made her burn a whole trunk of Lady Mary's letters and verses'. Sir Robert needed her silence, if not about the friendship itself then about its surrounding climate of gossip and ballad-mongering.[44] Satirists were less busy with Maria than one might expect; but they did not ignore her, and her anomalous position in society was hard to negotiate. A candidate for a bishopric was seen as having ruined his chances by being too publicly attentive to her.[45] Walpole's haste to regularize their relationship shows a spirit very different from that of his rakish friends and associates (many of whom Lady Mary had lampooned in verse for their treatment of women);[46] public opinion knew better where it stood with an average rake than with him.

Speculation had not long to concentrate on the Prime Minister's private

---

[42] 29/18 July 1737 (Halsband 1973: 223).

[43] Pomeau 1982: 248–52 (mistaken about the Bulkeley marriage).

[44] Catherine Walpole d. 20 Aug. 1737. On 3 Mar. 1738 Walpole made his second marriage public (although the government was then under heavy attack). That day he secured Molly's presentation at court, which caused more outrage than the marriage itself (Sedgwick 1970; Hervey MS 47/4; Horace Walpole, *Corr.* xxxiv. 256; Egmont 1920–3: ii. 469). Lady Louisa Stuart thought MWM herself destroyed her letters to Maria (*E&P* 40).

[45] Egmont 1920–3: ii. 250. She was often excused either as a passive victim or as sincerely in love, even in attacks on Walpole as villain or tyrant (e.g. on stage in 1731, John Bancroft's *Fall of Mortimore* and Fielding's *Welsh Opera*, later *The Grub-Street Opera*; the government took steps against each). Fielding perhaps targeted her in *Don Quixote in England* 1734; the marriage brought a ballad calling her a 'public whore' (Goldgar 1976: 110; Cleary 1984: 70; Egmont 1920–3: ii. 471).

[46] e.g. in 'Miss Cooper', 'Mrs Yonge', and an untitled attack on a Walpole satellite which recycles 17th-century lampoons (*E&P* 229, 232; MWM 1803: v. 157–8; Grundy 1971: 610–11).

life. During the evening of 31 August 1737 the Princess of Wales (who was, she said, not quite eight months pregnant) went into labour at Hampton Court. The prince, hell-bent on disobeying his father's orders that his child should be born there and nowhere else, hustled her into a coach without female attendance, and 'drove full gallop' the fifteen miles to St James's Palace in central London. It fell to Lady Mary's friend Charlotte Amelia Tichborne, Woman of the Bedchamber, to wake the queen at 1.30 a.m. with the news of the princess's labour, and to convince her that in order to attend the birth she needed not merely her nightgown but also her coach. Hervey, of course, was one of those the queen summoned from bed to go with her. They arrived too late for the actual birth. After meeting her son, daughter-in-law, and newborn granddaughter, Caroline adjourned for hot chocolate in Hervey's palace lodgings (where a grumpy Walpole soon joined them) and related what Hervey later wrote up.

The royal row this caused was the most resounding yet. Hervey was somewhat consoled for its tedium and irritation by being employed to ghost-write the king's letter expelling the prince (Hervey's personal enemy) from St James's Palace. Each side put out propaganda, and people speculated as to the outcome of the next vote on the prince's allowance. Lady Mary had a 'Dispute' about this with the Opposition hopeful George Lyttelton. As she argued the imprudence of a young man running up debts and counting on paying them at his father's death, her text was Caroline's son; her subtext was her own. Edward had been in London this year, behaving badly.[47]

Worse was in store for the royal family and for Hervey. Queen Caroline was taken ill on 9 November and died eleven days later of a rupture. It need not have been fatal if she had not left it concealed and untreated in deference to her husband's horror of illness in any form. Hervey slept on a couch in the next room during her gradual and very public martyrdom; in the end he broke his promise and told the doctors her secret, but too late. He kept a diary of these days, from which he was later to write the harrowing, moving, and grimly comic account in his *Memoirs*; meanwhile he found himself unable for some time even to write to Algarotti.[48] Mary Astell's old friend Lady Catherine Jones reported that the queen had died among 'a throng of the killing profession trying their utmost skill to prolong her life in

---

[47] Caroline greeted the baby: 'Dieu vous bénisse, pauvre petite créature; vous voici arrivée dans un bien désagreable monde' (Hervey 1931: 761–3). The letter was given to the prince on 10 Sept. 1737 (Halsband 1973: 218–21; *CL* ii. 308, 481; see p. 320 for scenes made by Edward which might belong now instead of earlier).

[48] He then wrote, 'Upon my Word if I knew her, she was a thorough great, wise, good, and agreable Woman' (26/15 Jan. 1738, Halsband MS 46a).

adding more torment to it'. Pope marked the occasion with one of his most callous couplets ever.[49]

About a week after the queen's death, Henry Fox told Stephen that Hervey's 'Life is spent in talking of Her'. But that was only his private life. He at once found himself courted by Walpole's enemies to make common cause with them. He declined, but he sent the Prime Minister a very odd letter complaining of neglect yet expressing 'unshakable . . . attachment': asserting, in fact, that he was ready to put up with neglect. 'I submit to be a nothing', he wrote. At this point his *Memoirs* conclude.[50]

In December, as Algarotti's *Newtonianismo* saw the light at Milan, the journal *Common Sense* printed a piece about Nonsense—presenting it as the deity of the Walpole government and of 'the Ladies'. A week later there appeared the first number of a new journal, the *Nonsense of Common-Sense*, 'To be continued as long as the Author thinks fit, and the Publick likes it'. The title signals determination to challenge Chesterfield and Lyttelton on their own ground.

The author, unidentified till the present century, was Montagu. This was, so far as is known, an unprecedented step for her. She later said she had been, all her life, absolutely indifferent to political disputes, and believed 'that Politics and Controversie were as unbecoming to our Sex as the dress of a Prize Fighter'. The existence of her very own paper denies that claim. It even makes one wonder if she had already served an apprenticeship in political writing, whose traces are not known.

On a printed copy of the *Nonsense*, no. 1, she noted, 'all these wrote by me M.W.M. to serve an unhappy worthy man'. But whom was she serving?—Hervey? Walpole? Some editor or manager of her paper? Was this one of the 'thousand affairs that I had resolved to avoid as long as I lived', which, she said, engulfed her because of her friendship with Maria Skerrett? No answers emerge.[51] The *Nonsense* bore the deceptive imprint of James Roberts, who had issued various works by Montagu, including one form of *Verses to the Imitator of Horace*.[52] This time she dealt with him herself. Her manuscript of the first essay bears a note she later almost obliterated, making him three requests: she wanted her copy returned to her, contrary to usual

[49] Lady Catherine, Christmas Eve 1737, *Hastings Wheler* 1935: 153; Pope, 'Here lies wrapt up in forty thousand towels | The only proof that C*** had bowels' (TE vi. 390).

[50] Halsband 1973: 227–31.

[51] *Common Sense*, 10 Dec. 1737, *Nonsense*, 16 Dec.; H MS 80. 143; *E&P* 105 ff.; *CL* ii. 182–3. Cf. 'I ever thought Politics so far remov'd from my Sphere I cannot accuse my selfe of dabling in them' (*CL* iii. 140).

[52] The others (*Court Poems*, 1716, the *Letter* from Constantinople, 1719, the *Answer* to James Hammond) probably appeared against her will; Roberts had also handled the prospective reward for finding her runaway son in 1727.

practice; she wanted, it seems, her identity kept secret; and she wanted six copies of the printed paper.[53]

Montagu was not the first woman to author a periodical. Delarivier Manley at the *Examiner*, 1711, had even preceded her in running a heavy-duty political one. But it was an odd milieu for a lady of rank. In each number the essay takes up most of the paper's first leaf; but the rest, and the whole second leaf, harbour materials common to all newspapers of the day: Home News; Stocks; Casualties, Christenings, and Burials; and finally Foreign Affairs. This is a far cry from verses crowned with Apollo's laurel; this is writing under the sign of Grub Street.

The opinions expressed are, accordingly, not at all what one might expect. The first essay begins by explaining the recent perversion of the phrase *Common Sense*. Instead of the 'plain degree of understanding' of every 'reasonable Man', it now means 'a certain paper, with many flights and small reason', costing twopence but 'not worth one farthing', designed to amuse the idle, the malicious, and the ignorant, but actually baffling and enraging them. In Addisonian style, Montagu professes her aim of reaching these people at their 'coffee and tea tables', and of countering the doom and paranoia of partisan politics by praising whatever good news she can find. This is the apolitical façade of many a political moderate.

She then broaches the issue of the mourning for Queen Caroline (which Opposition peers were decrying both as undeserved, and as a heavy expense to court attenders). Nonsense, says Lady Mary: since mourning excludes lustrous fabrics like silk, it is a boon 'to the Woolen manufacture, the staple commodity of these Kingdoms'. Admitting that she favours taxing 'super-fluitys' (but without the moral posturing so common in anti-luxury rhetoric) she moves briskly on through the good effects which woollen garments produce on the male pocketbook and the female complexion, to the more crucial question of cloth-workers' earnings. Here, she says, in this vital trade, 'the utmost cruelty and oppressions are us'd against the helpless Labourer'. Workers are forbidden to combine, though owners make a point of doing so; 'the Master tradesmen without mercy grind the Faces of the poor . . . whose Familys suffer more real misery in a free Country than the slaves in Jamaica or Algiers.'[54]

The printer censored 'in a free Country', evidently thinking it inflammatory. It is typical of Lady Mary to bracket West Indian slavery with the 'Barbary' kind (the enslavement of whites by Muslims), which at this date

---

[53] *CL* ii. 114.
[54] *E&P* 105–8. For the low wages throughout the period see Porter 1982: 106–7. Knitting was a staple industry around Thoresby (Chambers 1966: 92–5), and weaving around Wortley.

aroused far more moral outrage (and charitable subscriptions). Her fervour on behalf of the underdog is surprising in a paper which she says she designed 'in defence of good nature and good breeding';[55] it harks back to her early idealism. More puzzling still is the relation of this stance to her husband's as Deputy Lieutenant of the West Riding of Yorkshire. Wortley was much concerned with the cloth trade. He had spoken on behalf of merchants, clothiers, and 'Persons interested in Fulling Mills';[56] he is not known to have considered those his wife calls 'the miserable workers'. Here was another area of disagreement between them.

The *Nonsense of Common-Sense* did not fulfil its original promise to appear every Tuesday; it soon became irregular, and ceased in March 1738, after nine numbers. Its second number (one of two with mottoes from the Old Testament)[57] combines feminist exhortation to women to study and to influence the state of society, with support for 'the real patriot scheme of reduceing of Interest'. It seems that her claim to be non-partisan was serious, for Sir John Barnard's plan for lowering interest rates was not favoured by Walpole but by the 'patriots' or Opposition. Montagu supports it, arguing that high interest damages 'a Tradeing Nation' by drawing capital into stocks, away from trade and manufacture.[58] Here she was on the same side as Wortley. But she is unique in turning for evidence to women's lives. With lower interest, she says, tradesmen who now expect their daughters to live off a small legacy will apprentice them to 'honest Trades', and they will 'in their sphere contribute to the Wealth of their Country'. If high-born ladies living on capital have to economize, fashions will become less showy and young women can attract a husband for smaller outlay.

In this essay Montagu likens politicians carrying through unpopular measures for the public good to 'a tender mother who forces necessary Physic down the Throat of a beloved Infant, thô it squalls and struggles with all its strength'. To her disgust her printer added, 'or like a Lover that, *&c.*' But she remembered her disgust, to make copy out of it.

On 3 January 1738, Handel reopened the opera season which the queen's death had cut short. Montagu celebrated with *Nonsense*, no. 3: a proposal from one Balducci, a fictitious expert in 'Statuary, Machinery, and Musick', to replace opera singers with his own patent robots.[59] This, he says, will save the country the astronomical fees paid to foreign stars. Meanwhile it

---

[55] No. 5 (*E&P* 125).   [56] EWM, 11 Feb. 1733 (Wh MS M 117).

[57] Nehemiah 5: 5, on daughters brought into bondage.

[58] No. 2 came out on 27 Dec. 1737 (*E&P* 109–13). John Law believed in lowering interest rates to stimulate economic activity (Murphy 1988: 129). John Maynard Keynes agreed.

[59] *E&P* 114–20.

provides a handle for light-hearted *doubles entendres* about the castrati and about the chastity of mechanical divas, and for tribute to Senesino and Farinelli (who had both been recently in the news, the latter as a possible cause for war with Spain). The sparks fly: gibes at the Opposition's 'Opera of the Nobillity' (which had collapsed the previous summer, dragging Handel down with it), at travel writers, at the Society of Antiquaries, and at the unlikely prospect of the Pope turning Christian.

Number 4, a week later, dealt with the topic of levées.[60] (It would be nice to think that Hogarth was acting on Montagu's direct hint to him when he depicted one of these in *Marriage à la Mode* seven years later.) She fancies how the poets Horace and Virgil might have fared at Maecenas's levée, and laments the assiduity and impudence which it takes nowadays to rise in the world. (She had expressed diametrically opposite opinions with at least equal panache to her husband twenty-four years before.) This essay was snapped up and reprinted by the *London Magazine*.

The next number is longer:[61] unusually heartfelt and scintillating. It sets out to defend Walpole from the Opposition charge of sapping the liberty of the press; one proof adduced of his not doing this is that 'the Highest Characters' *are* being freely attacked. Even if liberty of the press *is* in danger, Montagu reasons, that is not the government's fault. She recounts with relish her own experience (or that of the 'Gentleman' she impersonates) of finding printers of both political parties hostile to her moral, apolitical paper. One calls government supporters 'hirelings', but is himself a tool of Opposition. He urges her to print lies about ministers and to plagiarize some dirty jokes; he even foists one of these into her copy. What he most admires is sneering satire aimed against love, or friendship, or 'legitimate sorrow'.

Mention of such sorrow leads her into a digression. *Common Sense* had been poking fun at the public tributes of Orator Henley to his recently dead wife. (There were two contrasted political parallels: tributes to the late queen, Walpole's absence of grief for his dead wife.) Passionately, Montagu argues that grief should be inviolable: it is the only, final touchstone for the sincerity of love or friendship. Professions made to the living may be self-interested; those to the dead cannot. Just as 'tenderness and Greife' are the ultimate test of a noble soul, so ridiculing them is the ultimate depravity.[62]

In accord with her supposedly non-partisan stance, she balances her venal Opposition printer with an equally venal government one. Their views on

---

[60] 10 Jan. 1738 (*E&P* 121–4).   [61] No. 5, 17 Jan. (*E&P* 125–9).

[62] She stresses that she is discussing principles, not particular cases; still, she probably had in mind both Pope's treatment of her sister's madness, and the Opposition's treatment of the king's (and perhaps Hervey's) grief.

publishing offer free rein to her talent for dialogue: 'if you will rail at no body, nor put in no feign'd names that every body may understand, all the Bawdy in the Dunciad won't carry it off!' ' "A moral paper!" cry'd he start-ing, "and how do you expect to get money by it?" ' Here the author who had just championed workers' rights to seek higher wages refuses to extend the same rights to middlemen. It is the printing trade itself, she argues, which threatens the liberty of the press, making it 'as impossible for a man to express his thoughts to the public as it would be for one honest Fishmonger to retail Turbots in a plentiful season below the price fix'd on them by the Company'. This complaint is reinforced by a closing paragraph protesting that book- and pamphlet-shops are refusing to stock the *Nonsense*: that is, combining against a new competitor in the field. As in her first number, she attacks her husband's business principles: fishmongers keeping up the price of turbot were small fry indeed compared with the Tyneside coal cartel.

The regular week's interval elapsed before the next number. During it— on 20 January, the day after her twentieth birthday—Lady Bute bore her first child. They called her Mary, like her mother, her grandmother, and her great-grandmother. Times were changing. Lady Bute was probably attended by a male midwife; her bedroom may have been no darker during her lying-in than the season would naturally make it. Lady Mary agreed to be godmother to the baby, who was christened at about a month old. Of the feelings surrounding all this nothing, of course, is known.[63]

On 24 January the parliamentary session began; and Montagu, goaded by a casually misogynist piece in *Common Sense*, produced a rousingly feminist *Nonsense*, no. 6.[64] (She may have been spurred on by possessing a grand-daughter; or she may have written the essay before the birth.) Here she adds to her role of moralist that of 'a Freind thô I do not aspire to the character of an admirer of the Fair sex'. *Common Sense* had advised women not to attempt reason but to stick with social trivia. Such advice, says Montagu, only exposes the adviser. Though she no doubt knew perfectly well that the author was Chesterfield, she argues that internal evidence reveals him to be 'a performer in the Opera' (and therefore of dubious gender). In general, self-appointed gurus about women either know nothing about them (like academics who have never met one, except their bedmaker) or have something to gain from some woman's loss. One resents paying his sisters' portions or his mother's jointure; another wants his wife dead so that he can scoop an heiress. 'How welcome is a couplet or two in scorn of Womankind' to such men!

---

[63] The other godparents were EWM and the Duke and Duchess of Argyll (Halsband 1956: 169).
[64] 24 Jan. 1738 (*E&P* 130–4).

Anger rising audibly in her tone, Montagu draws a parallel between two disadvantaged groups, servants and women. Would a wise man tell his servants that their whole class is 'a pack of Scoundrels', incapable of sense or virtue? 'On the contrary, I would say in their presence that Birth and Money were accidents of Fortune . . . that an Honest faithfull servant was a character of more value than an Insolent corrupt Lord . . .' With women the case is still clearer. 'A Lady who has perform'd her Duty as a Daughter, a Wife, and a Mother, appears to my Eyes with as much veneration as I should look on Socrates', and far more than conquerors or politicians deserve. Montagu, perhaps remembering the *Female Tatler*'s idea of a Table of Fame for ladies,[65] proposes a picture gallery celebrating women who deserve fame for their actions, not their beauty. She concludes with a flourish: 'Begin then Ladies by paying those Authors with Scorn and contempt who with the sneer of affected Admiration would throw you below the Dignity of the Human Species.'[66]

This essay, with the one on levées, was reprinted by the *London Magazine*. But three weeks elapsed before the next *Nonsense*.[67] Perhaps Lady Mary was practising what she preached, and performing her duty as a grandmother. Her next paper, on authorship, was a vintage one, which both the *London* and the *Gentleman's Magazine* reprinted. Again she secretly savours the in-joke of her sex: 'My Acquaintance think me no more qualify'd for a writer than for a General.' Nostalgically she names some heroes of her youth: Cowley, Roscommon, Buckingham, Steele. With patrician scorn she dismisses dirty jokes which are 'calculated for the amusement of all the blind alleys' of the London slums, 'too dull and too gross to corrupt even the lowest form in a boarding School'. Authors of this kind need 'to keep a Girl that understands her trade': a mistress who can double as ghost-writer. But it would be rash to dismiss Montagu as a mere snob. She cheerfully accepts that her writings may go to line trunks and baking tins: 'yet in that shape I shall be usefull to my Country. Pies and band boxes will be the better for me.' The standards she protects are those of 'Honor, probity, and Freindship'.

Again the next paper followed in a week.[68] It returns to the topic of liberty: a shibboleth of the Opposition, who claimed that Walpole was destroying it. Montagu sees them as appealing to class hatred, and adopts her

---

[65] 1709: nos. 53, 57 ff.

[66] This echoes Makin, who hoped to persuade 'some of this abused Sex to set a right value upon themselves, according to the dignity of their Creation, that they might, with an honest pride and magnanimity, scorn to be bowed down and made to stoop to such Follies and Vanities, Trifles and Nothings, so far below them . . .' (1673: 41).

[67] No. 7, 14 Feb. (*E&P* 135–40).　　　　[68] No. 8, 21 Feb. (*E&P* 141–5).

loftiest tone (though she deleted from her draft the probably ironical view that 'the lowest of the people . . . by a shamefull prostitution of learning can generally write and read'). None but the virtuous can be free, she says, citing the slave Epictetus, whom she had once translated. 'The same pride that makes an Oyster Wench scold and a Dutchess paint makes them both miserable.' Her essay concerns chiefly the oyster wench, since it connects pride with envy, and musters against envy the argument that great wealth brings unhappiness. This was a stock position; so were the details she deploys, like the misery inflicted by expensive physicians.

Again the essay's relation to her own life is intriguing and puzzling. She writes contemptuously of men with 'so little sense as to acquire' a vast estate.[69] Such a man, she writes, sacrifices health or virtue, 'and genneraly sees the Fruit of his restless nights and toilsome days destind to foolish or ungratefull children, or children that he knows are none of his own'. 'His Hours are now past in the Mist rais'd round him by his Money', so that he can no longer distinguish friends (if any) from flatterers. Did she think of her husband as one of these? Or did he exemplify for her the rare exception that proves the rule? She concedes 'the *possibility*' that a rich man may 'be as innocent and abstinent as a poor one . . . and perhaps there may be 2 or 3 such instances in the three Kingdoms'.[70]

Her manuscript of this essay went to the publisher with a note arranging to see him; she had, she said, 'many matters to communicate'. Perhaps they had to do with ending the series: only one more number followed, after a gap of three weeks during which Lady Mary suffered from toothache and merchants petitioned for war with Spain.[71] In her last number (under an epigraph from Horace) she again attacks impudence, and the dominance of self-interest, and satiric writers who 'look on Defamation as a Branch of Trade'. Again she appeals to the past, to Cowley, Wycherley, Congreve, Addison, Dryden, and to the gender-specific virtues of courage and chastity.[72] 'I cannot help looking upon Poetry (the Mistress of my Youth) with the same Compassion and Abhorrence, the Angel in *Milton* does on *Lucifer*, How chang'd! How fall'n!' Her last paragraph is defiant enough to

---

[69] Probably later in life, she wrote, 'Misers like Hoggs good for nothing while they live but profitable at their Death' (CB 5).

[70] She adds a simile about driving a coach on the edge of a precipice: something she had done with EWM (see p. 127).

[71] No. 9, 14 Mar. 1738 (*E&P* 146–9; *CL* ii. 114). News items include announcements of Walpole's second marriage (crediting Maria with a '80,000l. Fortune'), and the birth of an heir to Mary Banks's recently remarried widower.

[72] Yet in a note she jotted 'We all mistake virtue; tis not courrage makes a Man brave, or Chastity a Woman honest' (CB 2).

'praise a *first Minister*': not Walpole, except allegorically, but Cardinal Fleury of France.

The *Nonsense of Common-Sense* is Montagu's only identified foray into the world of professional writing. She is not entirely at home there: her ideals of honour are aristocratic; she can champion the oppressed, but not the middle classes. Her essays sparkle with intellect, with the play of ideas; she is at her best when amused, either about her male disguise, or about the crazy society she depicts. Her plea for thoughtfulness in the public and integrity in public servants is heartfelt, if also backward-looking. Through the whole work runs a thread of disgust at the 'Race of Libellers'. Readers in the know, if there were any, would have perceived that the wounds made by Pope had not healed.

21

March 1738–July 1739

❧

Leaving: 'O more than Madness!'[1]

SPRING 1738 brought renewed hopes of Algarotti. His book had been listed on the Papal Index, and its author was *persona non grata* in his own country. He borrowed money from his brother to take him to England, citing, almost as collateral, his hopes from rich admirers there. He left Italy in December 1737, travelling with a new friend or lover of his own age, named Firmacon. They did not hurry. Hervey, who had been hopeful of seeing him in March, was less so in April, and was making snide remarks about Firmacon in July.[2] By then Lady Mary assumed that Algarotti had reached Paris: to her complaints of his not writing he replied complaining that *he* did not hear from *her*. This made her almost frantic, though she retained enough of her wit to tell him she not only wondered where he was, but even whether he really existed. Her feeling for him was, she said, an 'Enthusiasm' (a word generally used for dubious religiosity) nurtured on 'Human Vanity'; yet her heart would retain his indelible impression till she died. She was afraid he still did not know her, and might think her rapid capitulation to him was typical when it was the very reverse.

In June, Algarotti was still intending to come to England; but that was before he reached Paris.[3] He did not see England that year; and for Lady Mary it was an unhappy one, but not idle. To it belong her laudatory verses on his *Newtonianismo*. Her signed tribute appeared with equally flattering ones from Hervey and Voltaire, in a new edition, Naples, 1739. As well as celebrating Algarotti's paradisal blend of flowers and fruit, youthful flourish

---

[1] *E&P* 381.

[2] Haskell 1980: 349; Halsband 1973: 145. He thanked for a copy of the *Newtonianismo* on 6 Mar. (6/17 Mar., 11/22 Apr., 24/13 July 1738, Murray MSS).

[3] *CL* ii. 116–17; Algarotti to Andrew Mitchell, 17/28 June 1738 (Craigievar MSS). In July he was still in the south of France, seeking a Veronese painting for Walpole (Haskell 1980: 356 n. 4).

and mature wisdom, Montagu praises his genius as natural rather than cultivated—an unusual compliment from a woman to a man.[4]

In July 1738 the *London Magazine* printed her anti-compliment on
Charles Churchill. Reversing a hundred poems by men (including her good
friend Congreve) which voice contempt for ageing women, she describes
Churchill as superannuated but still just fluttering, 'Awake to Buz, but not
alive to Sting'.[5] That year another periodical, the *Lady's Curiosity*, printed
her 'Fifth Ode of Horace Imitated'. The speaker of this often-translated
poem rejoices that he has escaped the snares of his changeable beloved, and
pities her next victim. Montagu substitutes a fickle youth and betrayed
woman for Horace's fickle woman and betrayed man, as Behn had done
before her. If she had Algarotti in mind, it was too soon to give thanks for
escape.[6]

Her next involuntary appearance in print was quite benign. *Callistia; or
The Prize of Beauty. A Poem*, 1738, hands out some harsh judgements (on
Lady Bristol, for instance, as 'Erinnys'). But it says Sapho is renowned 'for
Verse and *Satire* keen', and for eyes as sharp as her wit and as fierce as an
eagle's. Elsewhere she was hailed by name as poet and scholar, friend to the
budding movement for the study of English literary history. Thomas
Hayward dedicated to her his ground-breaking anthology of fifteenth- and
sixteenth-century poetry, *The British Muse*. The dedication was actually
written (in March 1738) by William Oldys, who pronounced that she was 'so
nearly ally'd in genius and judgment to [the British Muse], that I could not
distinguish your name, but as another for her own'. Lady Mary gave this
tribute her sanction and kept the book.[7] Nor did she forget the moderns: the
raffish, struggling Samuel Boyse thanked her for patronage next month, in a
poem resolving to make his work worthy of her.[8]

Though her new protégés (the publisher Hayward, authors Oldys and
Boyse) were very minor writers, the first two were forwarding the progress
of knowledge. Oldys was 'a man of eager curiosity and indefatigable diligence', a pioneer in scholarship, a regular consultant on others' historical

---

[4] Fos. [a5v], [a6r], [b3v]. Her opening couplet echoes Congreve's tribute to a woman writer, Grace,
Lady Gethin (Dryden 1704: 367).

[5] She was said to have left her lines on view at the studio when she went to see the picture (within about
a year of their printing). She is a more likely author than a later claimant, David Mallet (*E&P* 294; contemporary note, Halsband MSS). The *London Magazine* had reprinted essays from her *Nonsense of Common-
Sense*, and later added many more of her poems.

[6] *E&P* 302; Behn 1992–6: i. 84–5; Bataille 1980: 87–8.

[7] Oldys 1862: 23; Wh MS M 135. James Thomson had recently called Milton the British Muse (*Winter*,
1726: line 291). EWM subscribed to *The Seasons*; Algarotti admired Thomson though Hervey despised him
(Halsband 1973: 246–7).

[8] 19 Apr. (H MS 81. 127).

works. He was Lord Oxford's literary secretary, on good terms with Lady Oxford, and familiar with their friend Pope. Lady Mary used him to hunt up old books.[9] Boyse, then about thirty, had printed mostly eulogies of patrons (including Peterborough). His best-known poem, *The Deity*, 1739, was yet to come; so were the 'low vices' and crushing poverty recorded by his friend Samuel Johnson.[10]

This year saw the foundations laid for an unexpected tribute to Lady Mary's genius and achievements. Christian Friedrich Zincke, who was now painting everyone who was anyone, did a miniature of her as a gift for Lady Oxford. It was specifically said to be 'from life'; but the result veils her age and bears a suspicious likeness in pose and costume to Kneller's first portrait of her, done in 1715. Zincke (who was said to make all his sitters look alike) was also known for producing copies or versions. Perhaps Lady Oxford wanted a memorial of their shared youth. The resulting miniature—pretty pose, unremarkable dress—is somewhat bland.[11]

As memorial of her friend in maturity, Lady Oxford had a second, more striking gift: a half-length by Carlo Francesco Rusca, painted in 1739. This is both expressive and emblematic. Lady Mary, wearing her Turkish ermine, glances up and outwards as if arrested in action: the action of reading, for her right index finger marks her place in a book. That right hand rests casually on a human skull, beside which lie a half-open rosebud, a crumpled bit of paper, and more books, piled up. In this most unusual self-image the skull projects an aura of mortality, of religion or philosophy; with it go the flower and books, beauty and learning.

Lady Mary's daughter later thought 'the gods never made anybody less poetical than Lady Oxford'. Yet Rusca's emblematizing may perhaps owe something to her as well as to its sitter. In 1739 an engraving by George Vertue took Zincke's miniature of Lady Mary and surrounded it with more luxuriant emblems or attributes. With this it grouped Zincke's similar, contemporary miniatures of Lady Oxford's daughter and son-in-law, the Duke and Duchess of Portland. The couple's portraits share their attributes; Lady Mary's has her own. The three pictures were then set side by side in a

---

[9] Oldys recommended books to Elizabeth Cooper for *The Muses' Library*. Hayward relied on him even more: to proof-read *The British Muse* and write its introduction. He and Johnson later catalogued Oxford's library ([Yeowell] 1862: xi–xiv, 1, 7, 8, 16, 20, 23, 28).

[10] He is known for sitting in bed to write: clothes pawned, arms stuck through holes cut in the blanket (Nichols 1971: 342–4). His link to MWM may have been Henry Fielding, who praised him in *Tom Jones*.

[11] One of several engravings of it adds an Eastern allusion: an attendant female figure holding a representation of pyramids (MWM 1763, repr. 1790). Zincke did some of his best work for his patron the Duke of Portland (Murdoch *et al.* 1981: 164, 168; Kerslake 1977: 190).

composite print:[12] an unusual composition, for which the most likely explanation might be that Lady Mary was godmother to the Portlands' eldest son,
William, born on 14 April 1738.

Lady Mary, the oldest and least in rank of the three, is distinguished by
highly impressive attributes. They include oak-leaves and a trumpet (both
for fame), a globe for travel, three books for literature, a caduceus[13] and
snakes for medicine, and a mahlstick for art. Her full name—married name,
birth name, Right Honourable—appears below the coat of arms which cor-
rectly gives half the shield to Pierrepont, a quarter each to Wortley and
Montagu. Below is a punning motto which the Pierreponts used to favour:
PIE REPONE TE. So the sign of her family identity is framed by her achievement as an individual. Lady Oxford perhaps blended her sense of heritage
with personal friendship and admiration.[14] But perhaps Lady Mary's wishes
were also consulted, and perhaps she had in mind the kind of fame more
readily available to her sex in Europe than England. At Cirey, home of
Voltaire and his intimate friend Emilie du Châtelet, there hung above the
gallery fireplace a portrait of the marquise painted with the emblems of her
life as an intellectual: books, compasses, sheet music, and mathematical
instruments. Madame de Graffigny found it charming; so perhaps did
Algarotti.[15]

In June 1738 Maria Skerrett, now Lady Walpole, slipped from the Prime
Minister's life as unobtrusively as she had entered it. She was said to die of a
miscarriage. Lady Catherine Jones (friend and patron of Mary Astell)
reported in detail some time later,

That last enemy called death has carried off poor Lady Walpole, who thought herself many years distance from the discharge of that certain debt, and always spoke
of [sic] a high dread of it ... Yet of her last moments she resigned with more composure and patience that [sic] could have been imagined for she had her senses to the
last and a violent purge they could not stop carried her off in two days.[16]

Maria's death was overshadowed by continuing public debate over peace or
war with Spain, and by the imminent arrival from Hanover of the new royal

---

[12] *E&P* 39. Bernard Lens did, about 1689, a similar group of miniatures of the royal family: William and
Mary, Anne and her husband (E. 435–1959, Victoria and Albert Museum: information from Elizabeth
Miller).

[13] The staff carried by Mercury or Hermes.

[14] Information from Richard Quaintance, Robin Brackenbury, and Alistair Small; copies at Princeton
University, the Victoria and Albert Museum, and archives of the borough of Marylebone, where the duke
was lord of the manor. The punning motto (meaning, irrelevantly, 'O pious one, reform thyself') is mentioned in Cussans 1893: 197. A mahlstick is used in oil painting.

[15] Frontispiece to *Institutions de physique*, 1740; Voltaire 1953–65: iii, fig. 14; de Graffigny 1985: i. 199–200.

[16] She died on 4 June (Walpole 1903: i, p. xxxv; Lady Catherine, 6 Sept., *Hastings Wheler* 1935: 164–5).

mistress, Madame von Wallmoden. (Hervey's wife was to pick out servants for her household.) Robert Walpole seemed his usual jovial self at Houghton in July; he fell ill two months later. Lady Catherine wrote that 'Sir Robert showed good concern for her in her illness and has kept up to great decency since her death which is quite out of fashion madam in the Grand Mound.' He showed, in fact, the 'tenderness and Greife' which Lady Mary in the *Nonsense of Common-Sense* had judged to be a touchstone of 'the Humane and Honest mind'. Years after she had cast aspersions on his qualifications as a lover, he proved her wrong.

Maria was 'carried down to Norfolk by five in the morning', Lady Catherine reported, 'with only two coaches following her hearse with her servants to attend her which I think perfectly right'. Any suggestion of death in childbirth was discreetly censored: Lady Catherine blamed a cold caught by 'sitting in her grotto three hours'.[17] Pamphleteers got busy in the dialogue-of-the-dead genre, with verse speeches exchanged between Walpole's first and second wives in the 'Elysian Shades'. One poem deplored 'Skirra' 's shameful triumph; a second saw her as culpable; both stressed her intellectual ability. Catherine Walpole was made to say that 'If not with Charms, you did with Sense abound' and that Maria guided Walpole's policies. Maria agreed: 'To me in ev'ry knotty Point he flew'; she, 'like sage *Mentor*, was his *Better Guide*. . . . The *Wise* of every Nation *wrote to me*.'[18] What a pity this woman is so lost to history!

Just how acutely did Lady Mary miss her? How often did they meet? How often did they write? Did Maria know about Algarotti? As usual, there are no answers. No word survives from her about Maria's death.

On 20 August she sent Algarotti a five-sentence ultimatum, its curtness probably independent of the fact that she did not really trust her messenger. That month she told Lady Pomfret that there was nobody about but 'miserable invalids' whose conversation revolved around 'infirmities and remedies'. That summer and autumn she complained of the 'fogs' of the English climate and consequent dreariness of the inhabitants; but she did so in order to entertain this new correspondent. If she was feeling that sorrow which she had recently called 'the noblest proofes of the noblest mind', this was no place to express it.[19]

---

[17] Halsband 1973: 238–9; *Hastings Wheler* 1935: 164–5. Lady Catherine went on to praise her 'genius . . . good nature and humanity to those below her'. Skerrett was linked to Astell's circle of clever, pious ladies by Orford House, Chelsea, which from 1714 was Walpole's town base (Plumb 1956: 205). MWM may have been another link. The Duchess of Portland, too, visited Maria's grotto or 'shellery' (Delany 1861–2: i. 608).

[18] *The Rival Wives*, 1738: 6; *The Rival Wives Answer'd*, 1738: 8.   [19] *CL* ii. 119–20.

After marrying Molly, Walpole had drawn her into the heart of his family by commissioning a group portrait attributed to John Wootton and Lady Mary's former friend Charles Jervas. It shows the recently married couple with their own daughter Maria, surrounded by the rest of Walpole's family: Dolly's widower, and his own children by his first wife, including two daughters who were long since dead.[20] This picture seeks to recuperate Molly, to give her a respectable, domestic niche. But a better-known representation of her is Pope's savage caricature in the passage often called 'the Triumph of Vice'. What makes Maria an emblem of vice for him is not that the Prime Minister illicitly loved her, but that he then married her and, worse, got the queen to receive her. When the poem first appeared the queen was dead, but Lady Walpole was alive; people probably read part of the passage before realizing, with a unnerving mental jolt, the presence of a real woman behind this allegorical figure to whom a whole nation grovels:

> 'Tis the *Fall* degrades her to a Whore;
> Let *Greatness* own her, and she's mean no more ...
>
> . . . .
>
> Hear her black Trumpet thro' the Land proclaim,
> That 'Not to be corrupted is the Shame' ...
>
> . . . .
>
> The Wit of Cheats, the Courage of a Whore,
> Are what ten thousand envy and adore ...
>
> . . . .
>
> 'Nothing is Sacred now but Villany.'[21]

When Pope reissued the poem in the latest volume of his *Works* a year later, he rendered visible another reference. A line which had at first read 'Who starves a Mother, or forswears a Debt?' now read 'Sister' for 'Mother': the 'Lye so oft o'erthrown' was revived.[22] He changed nothing in the lines on Molly. Whether alive or dead, her moral status as the great man's married whore was fixed.

⤳⧉⤶

Not long before Molly's death, another friendship of Lady Mary's emerges into the light. Henrietta Louisa, Countess of Pomfret, was a friend, but not an *amie choisie*. Though she was granddaughter of Judge Jeffreys, who had

---

[20] Hill 1989: 194: picture (between pp. 110–11) at Houghton Hall.
[21] 'Dialogue I' in *Epilogue to the Satires*, May 1738, lines 141–70: TE iv. 308–9. The conciliatory Friend concedes that Horace himself might 'In *Sappho* touch the *Failings of the Sex*' (line 15).
[22] 'Lye' from *Arbuthnot*, 350. He changed mother to sister again in a line in 'Dialogue II' which refers to this one (TE iv. 121, 306, 314).

passed the death sentence on so many politically inept supporters of Monmouth's Whig rebellion, she had been a devoted Lady of the Bedchamber to Queen Caroline. Lady Mary had many friends among Caroline's household, notably Lady Hertford, whom she had known for years, and Ladies Betty and Bell (Elizabeth and Isabella) Finch. The Finches' brother had married Lady Mary's favourite cousin, Lady Frances Feilding; their letters have just that playful way with words and with human folly which appealed to her.

Lady Pomfret was somewhat staider than the Finches and more conventional than Lady Stafford. She let her children act in private theatricals,[23] but she never made Lady Mary, as she did Lady Oxford, a godmother to any of them, probably for reasons of piety. Her literary interests extended to prose fiction and antiquarianism. She was a hoarder, keeping copies of letters sent, lists of letters sent and received, and exhaustive, carefully systematized, non-confidential diaries, some in tabular form. Her daughters grew up to be her amanuenses; she left several blank volumes ruled and ready for diary use. She made a roster of the 230 ladies on her visiting list, ordered by rank (duchesses first), with a note of how she met each one. Several had been on visiting terms with her mother; most were introduced at some formal occasion of congratulation or condolence. But she knew Lady Mary from 'meeting at Auctions'. Both were on tight budgets; both had an eye for fine things. (Lady Mary was proud of two large china jars which she picked up for two guineas and stood in the windows at Cavendish Square.) Lady Pomfret valued her 'Wit and Charming Conversation', used her to borrow volumes of old plays through Oldys,[24] and appreciated her keeping their friendship alive during her own preoccupation with court and family duties.

Lord Pomfret was Master of the Queen's Horse, so at the queen's death the couple lost two salaries, totalling £1,500 a year.[25] They had ten children, and while travelling in Europe in 1736—to the surprise of their friends—they had found not only that they enjoyed themselves immensely but that living was cheap. Now they decided to return abroad. Lady Pomfret took up a new diary volume to record that on 8 July 1738 she 'got up at four, dress'd breakfasted and wrote a little note to take leve of Ly My Wortley'. Then she was off. The little note was soon followed by letters from Abbeville and

---

[23] The Finches' letters in Devonshire MSS. Lady Pomfret's 'dear Friend my Lady Stafford' is not MWM's dear friend, but a relation by marriage (Finch MSS, DG7/D 3. 99, July 1736). Hogarth painted Lady Pomfret's children in 'Dryden's *Conquest of Mexico*', 1731–2.

[24] Finch MS DG7/Lit 23 i (fiction), DG7/D 1 i (letters 1738–42), DG7/D4 ii (visiting list); *CL* iii. 176; ii. 118 n. 2; George Vertue or Thomas Hayward in [Yeowell] 1862: 28.

[25] *The State of the Court of Great Britain*, 1737. For MWM's crack about the bribe which allegedly got Lord Pomfret his job, see p. 262.

Paris (where Algarotti was believed to be still loitering), and then a gift in 'a very pretty box'.[26]

Lady Mary, for her part, sent what was probably her first letter a couple of weeks after Lady Pomfret left. She wrote regularly (as the diaries duly recorded), expressing 'the warmest inclination as well as the highest esteem'. One of her opening themes is that kind of compliment which consists in self-denigration. She finds, she says, her friend's letters so delightful that she fears she can provide nothing so pleasing from stupid London. This was of course an invitation to Lady Pomfret to write of her own dullness and fear of being tedious: it did not promise a lively correspondence.

Maria's death (and Algarotti's delay) were not the only reasons for Lady Mary to be downhearted just now. She had said in the *Nonsense* that writing diverted her mind from many uneasy and troublesome thoughts. By now she was probably watching over the slow decline of Lady Stafford. This one survivor of all her close friends was near death, and her closing months were melancholy. Montesquieu had noted some years earlier her horror of growing old.[27]

Lady Mary had, too, some specific and painful quarrel with her daughter. Lady Bute, after the christening and before leaving with her baby for Scotland, had done something to convince her mother that she did not love her.[28] Lady Mary's strong feelings and tendency to self-righteousness made her very prone to quarrels, and there were plenty of issues on which she differed from her daughter: those involving Lady Frances Erskine, Lady Frances Meadows—and indeed Lord Bute, and Wortley himself. Lady Bute was pregnant again this winter, but she did not come south for the birth. She had her baby at Mount Stuart on Easter Day 1739: a son, stillborn.[29]

To Lady Pomfret abroad Lady Mary often complained about English life. She linked the damp English climate to dismal English politics: Lady Pomfret was lucky to be out of it all, about to settle near Paris in 'purer air' and more intelligent society. Lady Mary passed over without detail the evenings she spent, no doubt merrily, with Lady Pomfret's friend Lady Bell Finch. She wrote dolefully about politics, sometimes under the figure of stage performances, which may have been a device to elude the censor, but also enabled her to adopt the role of passive spectator of a boring spectacle.[30]

---

[26] Finch MSS DG7/D 4. 1; *CL* ii. 120.

[27] *Nonsense* no. 7, 14 Feb. 1738, *E&P* 137; *CL* ii. 119, 139 and n. 1.   [28] *CL* ii. 168.

[29] 22 Apr. (Bute MSS). Lord Bute was already collecting political intelligence by post (BL Add. MS 36796).

[30] *CL* ii. 127. Political life this autumn turned on Walpole's efforts to get a treaty in place with Spain before parliament reconvened in the new year, to forestall opposition cries for war (Halsband 1973: 240).

Literature lay under the same blight as politics. 'Pamphlets are the sole productions of our modern authors, and those profoundly stupid.' It must have been about now that she subscribed, at Hervey's behest, to Dr Conyers Middleton's *Life of Cicero*, which did not appear until 1741: perhaps she did this out of friendship rather than with high hopes of the book.[31]

The gossip Lady Mary sent Lady Pomfret sounded a less brilliant, less intimate echo of her letters to Lady Mar; the new generation's antics sound often saddening or shocking. Though she pitied Lady Sundon (who had cancer), and sided with those who approved of Lady Betty Finch's marrying the barrister William Murray, most illnesses and most marriages provoked her scorn.[32] The wedding of an earl's daughter to her father's aide-de-camp was, sarcastically, a 'worthy choice' of an 'amiable' partner; that of a young widow, Lady Harriet Herbert, to the opera singer John Beard drew heavier fire. Lady Mary reported the family convulsions over this *mésalliance*, her conviction that the lady was prompted by lust, and her advice to one of the family to poison the bridegroom. She reported with relish a rich widow setting out like a 'lady-errant . . . to seek adventures at Paris', attended by a lover who meant to finance other affairs out of her jointure. She made it a joke that Lady Vane (once a threat to her daughter, lately mistress to her nephew) thought fidelity 'but a narrow way of thinking' yet drew the line at foreigners.[33]

The 'lively people' whom she reported as 'play[ing] the fool with great alacrity' were mostly women. One wonders how she reconciled her ready scorn of others' follies with the consciousness of her own thraldom to Algarotti. Did she, while projecting just one side of her divided mind, imagine what would be said of herself if she finally kicked over the traces?

The risky theme of women's passion and foolishness ran in tandem with expressions of a desire to travel. She said she envied Lady Pomfret's residence in a foreign 'purer air'—like Lady Bell Finch, who had wished she could go with Lord and Lady Pomfret, as they had suggested. 'There are some moments when I have so great an inclination to converse with dear Lady Pomfret,' wrote Lady Mary, 'that I want but little of galloping to Paris.' She suggested only a magical flying visit, as a fantasy born from affection for her friend and disgust with England.

---

[31] *CL* ii. 126; Halsband 1973: 243–4, 266.

[32] In early summer 1739 she was told in confidence a story of Murray's insincerity: she duly said nothing (*CL* ii. 249). She writes satirically about both the illness and the marital relationship of Lord Townshend, stepson of the former Dolly Walpole (*CL* ii. 121–2, 131).

[33] *CL* ii. 123, 127–8, 130–4. Egmont and Lady Frances Hastings reported Lady Vane as with Kingston in Mar. 1737. She had met him in Paris through his next mistress, Madame La Touche, who renounced her Catholic faith for him the month that MWM left England. By 1741 La Touche was an Anglican and a naturalized British subject (Egmont 1920–3: ii. 381; *Hastings Wheler* 1935: 145; Manvers MSS 4098, 4099, 4100).

As she wrote these letters, in the summer and autumn of 1738, Algarotti was in Paris. By March 1739 Madame du Châtelet knew he would not after all be visiting England.[34] By then Lady Mary had probably made a counter-proposal clearer than any she had yet ventured: seriously, she told him in French, if his circumstances made it impossible for him to come to London, she would not hesitate to settle permanently near Venice—if she were once certain that that would please him. This proposition came linked with a recognition that it was stupid of her to answer his letter so promptly when he never answered hers, that all her love and tenderness were nothing but 'chimeres' or sweet illusions.[35]

It is worth a closer look at the circumstances of this offer. Lady Mary and Algarotti had lived in the same country for about four months; in the more than two years that had passed since then, his answers to her letters had always been dilatory, erratic, and disappointing. The first winter after their separation she poured out her soul to him with anguish, yet also with some exhilaration in her own eloquence; the second winter she wrote her *Nonsense* essays (vigorous, ingenious analysis of politics and society); the third she wrote, for Lady Pomfret, gossip which is sharp tongued but socially con-formist. Her gossiping letters drop a hint or two of impending radical change: apropos a marriage arranged for a fifteen-year-old royal princess she comments, 'women and priests never know where they shall eat their bread'.[36]

Hervey's letters to Algarotti discussed external events (currently the approaching publication of the *Newtonianismo* in English).[37] Lady Mary's were all inward. By now they had become short. While to Lady Pomfret she spun out her phrases and anecdotes, to him she used succinct, even clipped phrases. He was offended with her for some unexplained reason; she forgave him. She seemed to suppose that any rival she might have in Paris would be female: painted, gilded, indifferent to the love which she craved. Algarotti apparently responded to her offer of moving to Venice by insisting that he wanted to come to London, but could not afford the fare. She offered to let him draw on her jeweller. For some reason this offended him again; she had to digest his reproaches as well as to provide a bill of exchange instead.[38]

---

[34] *CL* ii. 123, 125; DG7/D 3. 7; Halsband 1973: 246.

[35] 15 Jan. [?1739] (*SL* 241; dated 15 June [1738] in *CL* ii. 115–16). It appears from a later letter that she was thinking of a country retreat in the Venetian dominions rather than living in Venice itself.

[36] *CL* ii. 124. The surviving texts are not necessarily representative.

[37] Translated by the scholar Elizabeth Carter, whose name Hervey perhaps neither knew nor cared, it was repeatedly delayed (to Alg 28 Dec. 1738/9 Jan 1739, 22 Jan./2 Feb., Murray MSS).

[38] *CL* ii. 129, 132, 134–5, 137–8. Her first offer on this occasion seems to mention having given him money before.

In March 1739, therefore, she was expecting the return of her idol. She mustered all her old brilliance in relating to Lady Pomfret how a group of Opposition ladies laid siege to the House of Lords when policy towards Spain was to be debated and visitors were excluded. The Duchess of Queensberry, 'as head of the squadron' first 'pished at' the officer barring the door, then exchanged round oaths with him. With the connivance of MPs (who were also excluded) the ladies lay in wait and then rushed the chamber, where they disrupted the debate as much as they could. Lady Mary professed to feel ashamed that she was 'ingloriously sitting over a tea-table' during this famous female victory; but of course the heroic ladies supported the war party which she opposed, and her loyalty lay with Hervey, who made a key speech justifying the peace.[39]

That month Algarotti arrived at last. He stayed briefly in the Middle Temple with Andrew Mitchell, a young lawyer and Fellow of the Royal Society, then with Hervey in St James's Palace, then with Lord Burlington at Chiswick (handy for Twickenham). What transpired between him and Lady Mary is unknown. Her one extant letter written during his visit (to Lady Pomfret) says, 'We have nothing here but clouds and perpetual rains, nor no news but deaths and sickness . . . A loss more peculiarly my own is that of poor Lady Stafford, whose last remains of life I am daily watching with a fruitless sorrow. I believe a very few months, perhaps weeks, will part us for ever.'

The prospect of this parting left Lady Mary too disordered in mind, she said, to write more. Yet she concluded her letter with hopes that Lady Pomfret would 'repair the loss' of Lady Stafford. She had already mentioned her 'great . . . inclination to see Italy once more', her 'serious thoughts of setting out the latter end of this summer', and the delight she anticipated in 'the charms of music, sculpture, painting, architecture, and even the sun itself'—as well as in seeing Lady Pomfret again. This was shortly before Algarotti left; presumably something had been settled between them.[40]

She did not now expect to meet him immediately in Venice. He had picked up another invitation: to visit St Petersburg with Lord Baltimore, on a quasi-diplomatic court mission from the Prince of Wales.[41] He set sail just before

---

[39] On 1 Mar. Sources differ as to whether Hervey was thrown off his stride by the women's 'noisy laughs and apparent contempts' (*CL* ii. 135–7; Halsband 1973: 240–1). MWM later wrote slightingly of these 'Ladies of bright parts' (*CL* iii. 157).

[40] *CL* ii. 138–9. Lady Stafford lived only a few more days. She was buried in Westminster Abbey, leaving her cousin Lord Arran her heir. Hervey too had been ill (to Algarotti, 8 Mar. 1739, Murray MS). MWM's half-sister Lady Anne died this May (of smallpox, uninoculated). So did Lord Halifax, formerly George Montagu, having gambled away the dowries of his daughters (including Lady Barbara, later the friend of novelist Sarah Scott).

[41] Halsband 1973: 247–8. He had made friends with Prince Antioch Cantemir, Russian ambassador in London, and contemplated becoming a diplomat.

Lady Stafford's funeral (on 22 May), leaving Elizabeth Carter vainly hunting him to present a copy of her newly published translation of his *New-*
tonianismo.[42] His absence very likely had Lady Mary and Hervey again
competing for letters from him. But this time, while any letters to Lady Mary
have vanished, he kept copies of those to Hervey, for publication in an epistolary travel book on Russia. He may well have learned about this genre
from Lady Mary's example; like her he edited out any truly personal
elements in making his letters into a book.[43]

Ahead of Lady Mary lay a couple of months of intense, undocumented
activity. She was making ready for a journey which she intended to be for
ever, though her goodbyes to friends were probably couched as *au revoirs*.
Wortley seems to have thought she was heading for the south of France.
When she saw Lady Irwin for the last time she thought her the 'same as I
knew her at Castle Howard' (that is, well-meaning but pretentious and
vain). During these months she went to several sales at Christopher Cock's
well-known auction rooms. This, too, was an opportunity for retrospect: the
salerooms occupied part of her own former house in Covent Garden.[44]

She had to see to the heavy luggage which was to follow her abroad once
she had decided (so the fiction ran) where to settle. Presumably she oversaw
the packing of most the thirteen 'parcels'.[45] The bulky trunks and cases were
all marked with a distinctive, stylized MWM monogram. The three boxes of
books comprised several cubic metres. The 23-page book-list specified
about 465 identifiable titles, plus 137 unparticularized 'pamphlets', 51 collections of plays, and 34 manuscript volumes.[46] Further books went into other
containers; so did 'Italian writing'.

Besides a 'hair Trunk of my Cloaths', there were listed 'a black Gawze
hood, a Laced Hat in a Box' and riding caps in black and green velvet. Her
'Work Box' went full of needlework, complete or in progress (one piece was
'drawn', presumably not yet stitched). There were hangings, backs and seats
for chairs, a screen (probably patchwork, like the one Jane Barker had
written of), a pillowcase and two quilts (one of them embroidered),

[42] Thomas Birch's inscription, Carter's note (Carter 1739: BL copy, 535 b. 10, 11).

[43] Still, the conventions of *politesse* allowed such phrases as 'Adieu, my Lord, continue to love me', and
'I embrace you, my Lord'. He wrote to Hervey from his first landfall (Elsinore) and to Mitchell on arrival at
St Petersburg (1769: i. 96, 121; 24 June 1739, Craigievar MS).

[44] Her last sale was Halifax's (*CL* ii. 151–2, 190; iii. 162).

[45] Inventory, 25 Mar. 1740, H MS 74. 117–18; Afterthoughts followed: her side-saddle and other riding
gear, a box of snuff to replace some taken by French customs (*CL* ii. 141–2, 153).

[46] Wh MS M 135. With her book-list EWM had a shorter one drawn up: 'Catalogue of Select Books
among L. Mary Wortleys, most of which were supposed to have been E.W.'s' (135/4). His meaning is
doubtful. MWM's books at Sandon include some she wrote in or signed as 'Pierrepont', though their titles
occur on his 'Select' list (Grundy 1994*a*: 5; Grundy 1994*b*).

worsteds and chintz. She packed valuables to take with her—'3 Shagreen Cases for Jewels', and 'a Box of my China'—but for the time being lodged her 'Dressing plate' at Child's Bank. This extensive deposit included many items in gilt (tray, plates, mirror, cups, salver, and saucer), a tray and cup in silver, a basin in agate, and an enamelled ewer and saucer. These were precious to her, though legally they belonged to her husband; she later became passionately keen to leave them to her daughter.

She took mementoes of her earlier travels, among them some known today from her portraits: '20 Pieces of Turkish Caffoy, formerly were Cushion cases. 1 Scarlet Cloth Turkey Dress',[47] and 'a Turkish Knife'. She took items of furniture: four chairs, 'My Bureau with papers', a little japanned cabinet full of letters,[48] and a 'small Book Case' which cannot have held all her library. The whole shipment was valued at £500 or more. To have all this packed (though not yet sent) implied at least near-certitude about transplanting her life—her personal treasures and her pursuits of reading, writing, and embroidery—to a new home.

Her obvious secret reason for this uprooting was Algarotti. But other motives (some of them canvassed by reviewers of each new issue of her letters throughout the nineteenth century, when the Algarotti story was unknown) have not lost their force. Her closest friends were recently dead, her children under her displeasure, her husband ideologically remote, her reputation mangled by Pope, and her dislike of the English climate real. Her public story was that she was travelling for her health, though no serious illness is known.[49] This sounded plausible in her circle: Hervey, who had himself gone abroad for his health, joked about the way '*every body*' was doing so.[50] Although Lady Mary's constitution was robust, this story may have been true in a particular way: her recent letters to Lady Pomfret suggest she could have been medically depressed, and this might well alarm her in view of her sister's history.

She later told Lady Pomfret that she expected Wortley to follow her abroad; probably neither intended this. Victorian reviewers often surmised that he had banished her, unable to stand the notoriety which Pope had brought on them both. Such writers often uncritically accepted Pope's (and Horace Walpole's) allegations that she was dirty, promiscuous, and socially shunned; they were unaware either how many respectable women saw her as

[47] The *OED* calls caffoy 'Some kind of fabric, imported in the 18th c.' MWM had the dressing plate in Venice in 1758: it too must have followed her.

[48] Hervey [18 Sept. 1736], Hervey MSS 47/2 15.

[49] She had given up riding as beyond her strength; she already suffered from peridontal (gum) disease (*CL* ii. 142, 460).

[50] Ilchester 1950: 187.

one of themselves, or how routinely such charges pursued *any* 'learned lady'.[51] Their speculations therefore carry little weight.

But another, more circumstantial story is worth mentioning. James Dallaway, editor of Montagu's *Works* in 1803, said 'the cause of Her going abroad was that she had a strong propensity to money speculations and had imprudently engaged in purchasing stock for time, and lost £10,000 which Mr Wortley, Her Husband, refused to pay. It was then settled that she should live abroad upon an Annuity.' Purchasing stock for time was 'essentially betting on the stock rising or falling in the market'; it might well have attracted Lady Mary, who was a veteran both of the gaming table and of the South Sea. Wortley later believed she had private sums concealed from him. If this were true it would explain her later references to involuntary exile, though it would not explain why or how the separated couple remained on such cordial terms.[52]

A few days before she left came a discovery which she took as a last reminder of Pope's enmity. Lord Cornbury (who had always treated her with flattering respect) had once brought her 'a Hat full of paper': a poem he had written and wished to publish, on which he wanted her opinion. Lady Mary, who thought him nice but not bright, 'was not so barbarous to tell him that his verses were extreme stupid (as, God knows, they were)', but mildly advised him 'that it was not the busynesss of a Man of Quality' to print his work; he had better circulate it privately in manuscript. They had parted amicably, and she thought her ruse had worked. However, he changed his mind and published his poem, on the encouragement of 'better judges'. It was badly received and only now did she learn that Cornbury believed she had engineered this opprobrium. Pope, it seemed, had told him so. It was too late now to enlighten him, so she had lost a friend.[53]

She announced her departure to Algarotti in a brief letter whose urgent rhythms echo some of her last notes to Wortley before they eloped. Again she moved into a position of command: 'I am off to find you', she wrote (in French), 'Such a proof of undying Attachment needs no embroidery of words. I appoint you a meeting in Venice.' She had, she said, thought of meeting up with him on the way (which would have taken her 'pilgrimage' overland closer to the route of 1716); but she decided otherwise.[54]

---

[51] Cf. Nussbaum 1984.

[52] Farington 1979: 2133. This kind of transaction is one in options, which were taken out (instead of shares being actually bought or sold) on long-term share prices in companies like the East India Company (information from Antoin E. Murphy, 16 Feb. 1995).

[53] *CL* iii. 36–7, 48. One would expect MWM to dislike Cornbury on political grounds. The poem must be one of his Opposition tributes, 1737; he was a Jacobite as well a new protégé of Pope.

[54] *CL* ii. 139 (my trans.). He was in fact about to leave Russia; by early August he was in Danzig.

The rest of this note is given to practicalities: he must not write to her again at London—that, in her absence, might give the game away. If he reached England after she was gone he must not stay. The afternoon before her departure there was an eclipse of the sun: the air darkened for an hour. Lady Mary's parting note returned to a lofty style: 'At last I set out tomorrow, with the Confidence of a true Believer, clear in conscience, full of faith and hope.'[55] But in equating departure with death, as Pope had in 1716, she readmits the scepticism which had informed her poem 'With toilsome steps'. The 'other world' to which she travels *may* prove to be the Elysian Fields, but only if Algarotti keeps his promises. No more doubting, she says: she will enjoy her hopes. She writes no version of the question she had asked Wortley: 'Are you sure you will love me for ever?' It was not, it seems, a question that would bear asking.

[55] *CL* ii. 140 (my trans.); *Almanack For the Year . . . 1739.*

Map 2. France and Italy 1739–61

London
Dover
Boulogne
St Omer
Rotterdam
Cologne
Würzburg
Augsberg
Innsbruck
Dijon
Geneva
Chambéry
Turin
Milan
Brescia
Venice
Padua
Genoa
Florence
Leghorn
Rome
Naples
Lyons
Avignon
Nîmes
Toulouse

1739–56
1761

22

July 1739–August 1740

❦

Venice: 'I find my selfe very well here'[1]

THE day came. She stepped up into the carriage, and the door slammed behind her. The horses leaned their weight into the traces, and she was off. Her 'woman', another Mary, travelled knee to knee with her; her manservant, William Turner, probably rode on horseback. Mary and William were married, but they had not confided this fact to their employer. The carriage, belonging to Wortley, was to be sent back from Dover; Lady Mary's baggage for the journey included clothes, jewel boxes, and two pounds of snuff.

As they threaded through the streets of London, crossed the Thames, and plodded uphill to Blackheath, she must have been thinking of that other departure, heading for Constantinople twenty-three years before. Then she travelled as the wife of His Excellency the British Ambassador; now she was 'incognito'[2] and, despite the servants, she was alone. When she reached Blackheath, however, she stopped and spent an hour with the Duchess of Montagu. Once they had laughed and cried together over the girlish happiness of the duchess's soon-to-be-married daughter; now that marriage had failed, and the daughter had recently been a butt of Lady Mary's satire. In fact her two last conversations in England—both extremely cordial— were with this duchess and her mother, Sarah, Duchess of Marlborough.[3]

Lady Mary covered fourteen miles that first day, to Dartford in Kent. The next day she did more like sixty, to Dover. As she crossed the Downs the roadside plants were white with chalk dust, like those around West Dean. She wrote a note to Wortley from Dartford to tell him he might still catch her

---

[1] *CL* ii. 155.

[2] If she made her name known in the towns she stayed in, social protocol would require her to pay and receive visits (*CL* ii. 149).

[3] It was perhaps lucky that her long-cherished friendship with Sarah never faced the test of the latter's later intimacy with Pope.

with a letter before she sailed. (He did write next day, but missed her.) She wrote again from Dover, and the day after that from Calais. What is more, she continued to average a letter a week for the rest of the year.[4]

These letters ring the changes on several themes. She expressed eagerness for news of him, especially of his health. She returned regular bulletins on her own. At Dartford she was 'less fatigued than I expected'. At Dover, 'I cannot say I am well, but I think not worse for my Journey.' At Calais she reported being 'better on ship board than I have been this six months, not in the least sick', and looked forward to taking up riding again. At Dijon (despite bad weather *en route*) she felt 'so much mended in my Health that I am surpriz'd at it'. After reaching Venice she asserted that even the fatigue of the road had 'greatly contributed to the Restoration of my Health'.

With equal regularity she justified her proceedings and especially her expenditure. She spent five guineas on a private boat, because the public packet sailed by night, and she was advised against it. She paid fourteen guineas for a chaise at Calais, having shopped around very carefully for a cheaper one before following the advice on Calais chaises given her at Dover. She went from Chalon-sur-Saône to Lyons by river, to save on horse-hire. (It proved hardly any cheaper and very disagreeable.) She haggled for the lowest possible fare over the Alps to Turin: 12 louis, or less than £3, for herself and servants. The final stage, by boat from Padua to Venice, cost only about a pound.[5]

Another regular feature is her affectation of doubt which direction she should take and where she should settle. At Laon she wrote that the 'continual cold Rains' had decided her (as if spontaneously) to head south. Alas for her later claims to constant, unfaltering truth and probity: with a rendezvous appointed in Venice, she pretended to her husband that she had in mind first Burgundy, then Dijon, then Turin, as a final destination. It was not till she reached Turin (with her health, she said, wholly restored) that she began to discuss with him the pros and cons of Venice.[6]

But already at Calais one hears an echo of the young woman who had loved travelling. She was evidently delighted by the 'very high sea', the amazingly quick crossing ('2 hours 3 quarters'), and the servants' good conduct: 'Mary not in the least afraid, but said she would be drowned very willingly with my Ladyship.' She reported enthusiastically on the prosper-

---

[4] *CL* ii. 140–1. In 1740 her average drops to half that; some letters must have been lost, owing to the imminent War of the Austrian Succession.

[5] *CL* ii. 140–3, 147, 156–8. She had an allowance of £800 p.a. from EWM and £180 p.a. interest from her father's legacy (*CL* ii. 227 n. 1).

[6] *CL* ii. 142–5, 147, 149.

ity and the law and order which Fleury's ministerial rule had brought to France since 'we pass'd through 20 year ago'. At Dijon she switched to dating her letters in the New Style used on the Continent.

She enjoyed meeting up with English friends at Boulogne, St Omer, Dijon, Lyons, and Pont Beauvoisin (just below the Alps), but was less happy to find her compatriots so plentiful: 'as to travelling incognito, I may as well walk incognito in the Pall Mall.' Arrived in Venice, she wrote, 'I have met nothing disagreable in my Journey but too much company . . . I verily beleive if one of the Pyramids of Ægypt had travell'd, it could not have been more follow'd, and if I had receiv'd all the visits that have been intended me, I should have stop'd at least a year in every Town I came through.'[7] Her pyramid comparison seems to reflect a wry sense that her age and sex made her an anomaly among travellers; but to feel herself the cynosure of *friendly* eyes was no doubt a relief after the dominance of her public reputation by the Popean myth.

She recorded her adventures *en route* in 'an exact Journal' (later burned with the rest). At Boulogne one Captain Cokely (probably an Irish mercenary officer) advised her which route to take: to avoid Paris and head southeast through Arras, Reims, and Châlons-sur-Marne. At St Omer (still in Flanders, short of the French border), she changed her English guineas, on the advice of a lady staying at the same inn, for a bill of exchange which a local banker assured her 'would be paid at sight in any Town in France'. It was, however, refused in Dijon. A banker there said he could not accept it without consulting his Paris agent, which would take at least eight days. A grand tourist, Lord Mansell, heard of her quandary from her landlord 'and without mentioning it to me, went immediately himselfe to the Banker and pass'd his word for what ever Summ I pleas'd to take up'. He then most politely begged her to take up whatever she needed. Lady Mary as politely declined, 'chuseing rather to live a few days upon Trust'. But she was delighted by this generous action, which she attributed not to Mansell's initiative but to his 'Governor', Dr John Clephane.[8]

Everywhere along the route were young Englishmen on their travels, acquiring the 'Improvements!' she had mocked some years before. At Lyons, which boasted an 'academy', she noted the good looks and manners of Lady Pomfret's eldest son, Lord Lempster, as a good topic for a letter to his mother; her own young cousin Lord Feilding was a disappointing contrast.[9]

---

[7] *CL* ii. 141–4, 148, 151.

[8] Guineas might be taxed or even impounded at the frontier; the bill was drawn on Waters of Paris, a Jacobite agent who had dealt with Mar. EWM was using him as MWM's forwarding address (*CL* ii. 142–5, 157).

[9] See pp. 319–20; *CL* ii. 99, 150. Lempster squired her to the opera.

Side by side with staid letters to her husband and Lady Pomfret, she wrote very differently to Hervey. He professed to find the tone of 'Festivity' in her first letter 'a sort of Insult', which snubbed his regret at losing her; he felt inclined to throw it on the fire 'for entring the House of Mourning in all the cherfull Aparel of the Rainbow'. Instead, 'Since all the Pray'rs of weeping Friends were vain, | To stay your hated Passage O'er the Main', he generously wished her 'Days all Luxury, your Nights all Love'. She had departed this life, taken flight for another world, with 'the Pilgrim's Staff in your Hand, and . . . Shells upon your Garment'. Her faith was to be rewarded by a 'Paridise upon Earth', where myrtle and orange-trees would grow in every hedge; having no faith himself, he saw no point in 'jolting in Post-Chaises and lying in dirty Inns'. (At these inns Lady Mary slept and ate in the same room with her maid Mary, for the sake of economy, surveillance, and the reserve which she felt 'the Decency of [her] Sex' demanded.)[10]

To Algarotti she wrote at least once, as she faced the Mont Cenis pass over the Alps, her personal Rubicon. She reminded him of the perils before her, and recommended herself to him like a worshipper to a saint or like Don Quixote to his Dulcinea. Since Dulcinea was a fraud, and not the lady-love for whom Quixote took her, it sounds as if Lady Mary, like Hervey, was prepared to play with the notion that her faith or her imagination was delusive. Still, this letter (couched in French prose and English verse) is one of her most passionate avowals. In verse she painted herself passing unseeingly among the 'pendant Rocks and ever during snow' of the Alps: 'Amidst this Chaos that around me lyes, | I only hear your voice, and see your Eyes.' To Wortley on the other hand she said she had better make the crossing quickly, 'being told that the rains very often fall in this month, which will make the passage more disagreable'.

She crossed the mountains southwards at just the same time of year she had crossed them northwards in 1718, and just two months ahead of Walpole and Gray. Their descriptions of their crossing are famous. Lady Mary no doubt put hers in her lost diary; but she had seen it all before. Now once again her chaise was taken to bits and loaded on mules; again she took her seat 'of twisted Osiers fix'd upon Poles'; again she was hoisted on the shoulders of four men; again the words *prodigious, vast, eternal, solemn* drifted through her mind, even while her body was jolted and scared and half-frozen.[11]

At Turin occurred one of her most hair-raising adventures: something

---

[10] 28/17 Aug., Hervey MSS 47/2. 73–6; *CL* ii. 145–6, 194, 281.
[11] *CL* ii. 147–8; see pp. 173–4.

she mentioned in later years only in outline, and did not mention at all to Wortley at the time. If one may, for once, believe Horace Walpole, 'she was stopped by a custom-house officer who went to strip her in search of a pound of snuff'. Probably he either saw her using snuff or saw its traces on her clothes; he was not to know her supply had been confiscated at Calais; he was apparently oblivious of her rank. She was horror-struck at the prospect of being strip-searched; but intervention first by a grand tourist and then by the British Resident prevented it. She felt they had saved her life.[12]

What she did now tell Wortley was that she meant to try Venice as a place to settle. Although, she said, she had some reservations about its being 'too cold or moist', she was advised to it by two authorities: Lord Carlisle (whom she had met at a village in the foothills) and Lady Pomfret, who (from Sienna, much further south) had written that she would move there shortly. Writing to Lady Pomfret, however, Lady Mary said it was Lord Lempster who had said his mother was heading for Venice. One suspects that she made this up. When Lady Pomfret talked of moving on it was not to Venice but Rome; and from this time Lady Mary's letters home made frequent mention of Rome's drawbacks. It now harboured the Old Pretender's court; Carlisle, she said, had warned her of its 'many little dirty Spys that write any Lye comes into their Heads'. This was true enough; but it is pretty clear that Lady Mary was busy constructing reasons for choosing Venice, besides the reason she could not tell.

The secret of her identity having got out at Turin, she had to receive visitors, though she excused herself from court attendance on grounds of 'having no Court dress' (which was as elaborate at Turin as Vienna). She was delighted with Milan, where to prove her recovered health she climbed up past the forest of gothic pinnacles to 'the very top' of the cathedral. She inspected 'several curious Manuscripts' in the Ambrosiana Library.[13] Then she was off again, her chaise bowling through the fertile lands of the Po Valley.

At Brescia, a walled medieval town with hazy glimpses of mountains to the north, the chaise broke down. She hired another to take her as far as Padua (last stop before Elysium). There she transferred into a local boat called a *burcelo*. At last the river-banks, slicing through meadows in quite the style of the Thames at Twickenham, gave way abruptly to open water with a line of posts marking the channel: a seascape of boats moving back

---

[12] They were Lord Hartington (later Duke of Devonshire) and Arthur Villettes (*CL* iii. 278, 282).
[13] *CL* ii. 148–50, 151, 154, 234. Carlisle, son of her father's old friend, brother of Lady Anne Irwin, was travelling with his son, who was gravely ill.

and forth, and there on the skyline the towers, cupolas, and masts of shipping. Venice.

⁓⁂⁓

On 14/25 September 1739, before making contact with anyone in Venice but the British consul, she wrote with consummate hypocrisy to her husband: 'I am at length happily arriv'd here, I thank God. I wish it had been my original Plan, which would have Sav'd me some money and fatigue.' She told him she would have been 'tempted to stay' at Milan if she had not arranged for letters to be sent to Venice. She asked for a bill of exchange: she was nearly at the end of her ready money, but thought herself 'a very good Huswife to come thus far' on it. Her next letter said, 'As far as I can yet Judge, this Town is likely to be the most agreable, and the quietest place I can fix in.' Referring her decision to Wortley's judgement, she asked him, if he approved, to have her heavy baggage shipped. She had heard of a British man-of-war bound directly for Venice, which would be an ideal conveyance. For one thing it need not fear the French privateers which were rumoured to be fitting out; for another, her books would not be stopped by the Inquisition if they landed at Venice, as she was told they would at any Italian port, even Leghorn.[14]

Having written home, she was free to explore a city ideally suited to her predilection for going on foot: the only horses in it were the statues. The weather felt like spring. She discovered 'a great town, very different from any other': the alleys and squares, the quays and bridges, the fountains and water-spouts, the glimpses of gardens behind high walls, the churches and palazzos that make up Venice.[15] She observed how the Grand Canal follows a serpentine line; how palaces show their fronts on canals if they can, and only public buildings like churches prefer to front on courts or piazzas for the accommodation of crowds of people; how grand portals are awash at high tide, and at low tide steps appear covered with bright green weed. Venice was a more multi-ethnic city than London. In the streets, though many identities were masked, others were flaunted. The conspicuously different costumes of Jews, Turks, and Africans (virtually all male) must have brought Constantinople vividly to her mind; the strong ecclesiastical presence showed itself in dark or gaudy vestments. From her own century she seemed to have stepped back into the Renaissance.

---

[14] *CL* ii. 157–8, 151–3. Venice was an independent republic. The consul was Neil Browne. MWM's letters from Venice, 1739–40, are trans. into Italian and annotated in Valcanover 1989.

[15] *CL* ii. 154. Did she take a look at Algarotti's family palazzo, near the lagoon edge opposite Murano, whose address she had often written?

As she learned the 'manner of living', she found that too unique and equally to her taste. Venice was an aristocratic republic: a political entity that might have been designed for her own odd blend of élitist and anti-establishment views. Giustiniana Wynne (when she was familiar with all the major European countries) called the Venetians 'the most mildly governed, and perhaps the least oppressed, of any nation whatsoever'. Despite its alleged 'political, economic, and spiritual decline' during the eighteenth century, Venice had a vital cultural life: 'bright, festive, celebratory'. Artists at work included Tiepolo, Giambattista Piazzetta (who had done the frontispiece for Algarotti's *Newtonianismo*), Canaletto, Antonio Guardi, and Rosalba Carriera. Up and down the canals, new building was in progress; so was a publishing revival. Albinoni, a patrician composer, was still producing music. Vivaldi was choirmaster at the new church of the Pietà, working with a choir of orphan girls. Hervey said Lady Mary's letters described her spiritual home: 'where Arts flourish, Sciences are cultivated, Conversation is tasted, and Wit distinguished.'[16]

Socially she fell on her feet. Pietro Grimani, whom she had known and liked in Vienna, was now one of the Procurators of St Mark, high officers of the Republic. He had 'retained a partiallity for the English Nation from the time of his Embassy in the Reign of Queen Anne'. He thought highly of Algarotti. He came to visit (scarcely changed, if 'something fatter'), spoke of Wortley with the greatest 'regard and Esteem', and offered his services to make Lady Mary's stay in Venice agreeable. He did everything that 'a tender Father or a kind Brother' could have done. He introduced her to noble Venetian ladies—usefully, since Venetians generally kept foreigners at a certain distance.[17]

Antonio Conti was another old friend eager to be reacquainted. Ambassadors from the major European powers were soon at Lady Mary's door. Diplomatic feelers were extended before she met the Spanish ambassador and his wife, because England hovered on the brink of war with Spain. War was indeed declared on 30/19 October, yet the Spanish ambassadress became one of her 'best Freinds'.[18] From knowing no one but Grimani and

[16] *CL* ii. 154–5, 167; Wynne 1785*a*: ii. 145; Martineau and Robinson 1995: 427. Hervey said MWM depicted Venice better than Canaletto (Hervey MS 47/2. 77).

[17] Grimani's palazzo in Ca'Civran Grimani, at the corner of Rio della Frescada and the Grand Canal, had a particularly fine library (picture in Vedrenne 1990). He was remarkable, said MWM, for benevolence, 'easy chearfullness of Temper', and holding power without making enemies. The French ambassador warned her that she would never achieve any intimacy with the proud native Venetians, but he was wrong (*CL* ii. 152, 184; iii. 11–12).

[18] *CL* ii. 152, 154–6, 161. She was Caterina Gravina e Gravina, Princess of Campoflorido, nearly a decade older than MWM.

Conti, Lady Mary acquired within a few weeks 'a very agreable general Acquaintance'. With one of these, Chiara Michiel, she built a friendship which lasted the rest of her life. Meanwhile she was inundated with offers— more than she wanted—to make use of the grand private boxes at La Fenice opera-house, which were a feature of Venetian life. 'Here are no English', she reported with glee and with only a hint of exaggeration.

Besides all this, Venetian 'laws and customs are so contrived purposely to avoid expences'. Tickets for the two theatres and two opera-houses (open every night) were cheap. Better still, it was the custom for 'every mortal' to go masked, leaving no need for costly sartorial display. Public life was cosmopolitan, and the ambassadors' time was not eaten up in court attendance as in a monarchy. It was not 'the fashion' for anybody outside the diplomatic corps to give dinners, so that having been received with gratifying honours at the Spanish ambassador's, she did not need to reciprocate. She told Wortley she could 'live here very genteely on my Allowance'. To Lady Pomfret, as incentives to join her, she stressed the social variety, liberty, and remarkable absence of scandal or backbiting. As the only foreign lady in the city she was 'courted, as if I was the only one in the world'. She loved 'the fashion for the greatest ladies to walk the streets, which are admirably paved; and a mask, price sixpence, with a little cloak, and the head of a domino, the genteel dress to carry you every where. The greatest equipage is a gondola, that holds eight persons, and is the price of an English [sedan] chair.'[19] The noble Venetian ladies were forbidden to converse openly with foreign diplomats (though they did so freely when wearing masks), so members of each group would check if the coast was clear before they crossed Lady Mary's threshold. By then she had found a palazzo to rent on the Grand Canal, and moved from her lodgings.[20]

<hr />

Algarotti had been on the move as she had; but not towards Venice. He had gone from St Petersburg to Potsdam, Berlin, and Rheinsberg: the last the court of Crown Prince Frederick of Prussia. The future Frederick the Great had artistic and sexual tastes perfectly in tune with the young Italian's; and he intended, when his father should die and the throne should be his, to amass a circle of intellectual giants, a new Athens of the Enlightenment. From his next stop Algarotti invoked an east wind to waft him not to Venice

[19] *CL* ii. 154–6, 159, 161–3, 165, 169. De Blainville described the contemporary gondola's central chamber as 7 or 8 foot long, tall enough to stand up in, glass-windowed (1743: 494).

[20] *CL* ii. 162 and n. 3, 169. The palazzo she rented is unidentified. It was near the Palazzo Foscari, where the Prince of Saxony lodged (Valcanova 1989, 231 n. 3, 240 n. 16). As yet she had none of her own furnishings.

but to London, and he poured out to Hervey his rapture over Frederick's character, talents, and potential as a patron. The admiration was mutual: Frederick wrote to him partly in verse, calling him the Swan of Padua.

Almost as Lady Mary reached Venice, Algarotti reached London. Hervey returned from Bath a month later, and their friendship flourished. As Lady Mary's informant he was carefully discreet. He mentioned 'Our Friend', but not how long he had been in London, and he asked her for 'Instructions' before saying anything to Algarotti of her.[21]

By mid-October Lady Mary had been at Venice long enough to receive, all at once, five letters from her husband. There had been a mix-up about forwarding, which each seemed to think the other's fault. Wortley wanted further details of her route and her spending; these she hastened to supply, with a further round of justifications, and an account of her practice about tips. He sent her carefully numbered scribal copies of papers she had left behind; she reassured him that it was all right to throw the originals away. He sent, too, the draft of a letter to their son for her to transcribe (she changed almost nothing) and send as her own. But she did not let Edward know where she was, 'least he should be extravagant enough to come to me'. She later concluded that, having visited Venice and left large debts unpaid, he would not be back. She was glad to find that 'as he kept himselfe altogether in low Company he did not pass for my Son'. Grimani supposed him a confidence trickster assuming the name of Montagu 'to get credit'. She 'was glad to have it pass over in this manner to avoid being daily dunn'd by his Creditors'.[22]

Her daughter was by now almost equally a source of pain and resentment. In December Lady Mary received a letter from Scotland which Lady Bute had sent via her father, unsealed—in order, said Lady Mary, to make him 'Wittness of the fine things she is pleas'd to say, to convince you (as she thinks) that she has never fail'd in her Respect to me, in case I had made any Complaint'. She diagnosed 'Scotch Artifice' in this procedure. 'It is rubbing a Wound to talk on this Subject', she went on, 'she has been the passion of my Life, and in a great measure the cause of all my ill Health.' When, shortly afterwards, she heard that Henry Pelham's two young sons had died, both together, she commented, 'tis long since that I have look'd upon the Hopes of continuing a Family as one of the vainest of mortal Projects'.[23]

---

[21] It sounds as if Algarotti was having an affair with Andrew Mitchell (Hervey to MWM, 13/2 Nov. 1739, 11 Jan. 1740/31 Dec. 1739, Hervey MS 47/2. 77, 81; *CL* ii. 160, 167; Halsband 1973: 250–1, 253; 30 Sept. 1739, in 1769: ii. 36; Halsband MSS).

[22] *CL* ii. 156–8, 193–4. However his parents lamented over Edward's debts, he was only doing what most of his class did: 'the eighteenth-century upper classes were net debtors, people living above their means and in constant need of credit' (Staves 1990: 206).

[23] *CL* ii. 162–3, 166.

Her holiday from all the cares of life seemed to be over. She had written to Algarotti by every route she could think of, but had no answer. (Hervey made some demur about forwarding her letters, fearing they would be opened and read *en route*.) Now Lady Pomfret, who was about to settle herself not in Venice but Florence, wanted Lady Mary to join her there. In response Lady Mary concocted a story which must have been invented, since she mentioned not a word of it to her husband: she had 'taken some pains to put the inclination for travelling into Mr. Wortley's head, and was so much afraid he should change his mind, that I hastened before him in order (at least) to secure my journey. He proposed following me in six weeks, his business requiring his presence at Newcastle.' Since then, she said, the war with Spain had intervened: she hoped he might join her in the spring; 'his inclinations . . . must govern mine.' To him, however, she wrote, 'Lady Pomfret has been stopp'd by the illness of one of her Daughters, but I expect her very soon.' By February 1740 Lady Pomfret seemed ready to take offence at her non-arrival in Florence. Lady Mary was reduced to blaming the weather, the roads, and Fate, for denying her a pleasure which she now said she ranked higher than those of Venice.[24]

Just before Christmas, meanwhile, she heard from one whose inclinations mattered more than Wortley's. Algarotti claimed not to have received her letters; he hoped she was enjoying her travels, as if she were a mere tourist. Still more astounding, he suggested meeting in Paris. This must surely have been meant as a brush-off; but Lady Mary's reply was serious, though angry. She reminded him that he had agreed to live with her in the Venetian dominions; she had arranged her life accordingly. She could not move to Paris even if she had wanted to, which she did not. She wrote like someone bargaining from a position of strength: she had given ample proof, she said, of her desire to spend her life with him, but if she could not make him happy then he could not make her so. Venice was treating her very well, and she would be perfectly happy there but for the remembrance of his unworthiness. Only at the very end did her guard slip, and she reproached him for causing her exile. Hervey knew that something was up. He mentioned Algarotti with studied carelessness, explicitly declined any mediating role, and invoked what seems to have been a shared joke: that as Lady Mary had fallen in love with Algarotti in London, she would now fall for some 'Piedmonteze' (or Sardinian) in Venice. Whether or not he had some actual candidate in mind, this was surely advice to forget Algarotti.[25]

---

[24] *CL* ii. 161–3, 165, 172–5; Hervey to Algarotti, 17/28 June 1740. Since her original letters to Lady Pomfret are missing, their text is unverified.

[25] *CL* ii. 164, 167. Piedmont-Sardinia was a political unit, its capital Turin.

Her Venetian life was in other respects delightful. She assured both Wortley and Lady Pomfret that she really went out very little. She took no steps to learn the unfamiliar playing cards in use. It was customary for ladies to visit each other at any time of day; she had a large visiting circle. But more importantly, her palazzo was a centre for literati, antiquarians, and virtuosi. In Venice, she noted, the first category included some women. Conti never missed her at-homes, and Grimani seldom. Another of her visitors was Francesco Venier, a savant who was soon to be appointed Venetian ambassador to Rome. She 'wrapt' herself up in books—though they were borrowed ones, including a Horace from Consul Browne.[26]

She was to find various places in Europe more congenial than England to her writing life. Foreign intellectuals (male) seemed readier to take her seriously than home-grown ones. Perhaps some eccentricity might be expected from an English miledi; more significantly, Venice had a tradition of female learning.[27] Its cosmopolitanism nourished hers; and foremost among its literati was Conti, a warm admirer both of her and of English culture.

Conti set out to give her European circulation. During these months he translated nine of her poems, and her French essay 'Sur la Maxime de Mr Rochefoûcault', into Italian verse. His recent editor thinks Lady Mary worked with him on his renderings. Certainly she kept manuscript copies of the translated poems, though apparently not of the translated essay. Perhaps by her wish, the poems did not appear in volume i of Conti's *Prose e poesie*, 1739 (which would have been their first exposure to print in any language), but waited till the posthumous second volume. The versified, translated essay on marriage appeared in 1739 in an appendix which Conti dedicated to Grimani. Lady Mary kept a copy of a French poem intended 'To Stand at the Head of a Translation', which praises her as 'une divine miledy' and as 'Montaigu Sapho nouvelle'.[28] She may have helped Conti with the section on oriental poetry in his 'Dissertazione sulla poesia di vari popoli'.[29] She inscribed to him her autobiographical fairy tale, 'Carabosse'. In this the

---

[26] *CL* ii. 162, 169, 223 n. 1; Jan Teding Van Berkhout, diary, 5 June 1740.

[27] For early women's lives in Venice and Italy see Patricia H. Labalme, Margaret L. King, and Paul Oskar Kristeller, all in Labalme 1980: 129–52, 66–90, 91–116.

[28] H MS 81 (loose MSS bound after MWM's death) comprises 223 leaves in English, 86 leaves mostly in French, 4 items in Latin, and 73 leaves in Italian. The French begins with the Rochefoucault essay (224–9), is interrupted by Conti's Italian translations (256–61, order somewhat shuffled), and includes 'Pour Mettre a La Tete D'une Traduction' (266–7, with a poem on freethinking and one on Mohammedanism). Conti trans. 'The Lover', 'Epistle [to Bathurst]', 'An Answer to a Lady Advising Me to Retirement', 'Tho age and sickness' (without Hervey's response), 'An Answer to a Love Letter in Verse', 'Why will Delia', 'Verses Written in a Garden', 'Hymn to the Moon', and 'Epigram 1734.' MWM 1803 includes two of his translations as hers. Conti also trans. Catullus, Horace, Pope, Buckingham, Racine, and Voltaire (1966: 77–101, 655–6).

[29] This MS was much revised. Another shared interest was the Caesar–Brutus story. Conti dealt with it in criticism and theatrical drafts; MWM wrote a speech for Brutus (see p. 358; Manin MSS 1352, 1357).

heroine's gifts—beauty, intellect, riches, health, disinterestedness—are all perverted into curses by a malevolent fairy; the last curse is that of sensibility. 'Carabosse', a delightful *jeu d'esprit*, assumes some intimacy with its auditor.[30]

Lady Mary's collection of loose papers tells a confused tale of her literary relationships. She kept two different (rival?) French versions of one of the poems which Conti translated, 'Verses Written in a Garden'. Whoever wrote these out in French also transcribed for her a large number of poems in the same language, most of them animal fables. She (or people in her circle) played at *bouts rimés* in French. The first rhyme-words to be set were 'angelique, bachique'; the player, predictably, filled in the blanks with a spirited rejection of a woman called Angelique, spoken by man who turns to drinking instead. Somebody put into French the *Plain Dealer*'s praise of Lady Mary for introducing inoculation.[31] Items among her Italian manuscripts which *may* have been written at this time (probably not by her) include Petrarchan sonnets and a translation of Sappho's Ode to Aphrodite.

❧

Venice had begun filling up by Christmas 1739; the Carnival (to run from St Stephen's Day, 26 December, until Ash Wednesday) was 'expected to be more brillant than common from the great concourse of Noble strangers'. Lady Mary could 'hardly believe it is me dressed up at balls, and stalking about at assembles'.[32] The grand tourists made her their first stop in the city; her entrée to Venetian circles put it in her power to do them social favours if she chose, and she earned paternal thanks from, for example, the Duke of Rutland. To Lady Pomfret she gave a scathing account of the young travellers. Her palazzo, she said,

> must be their refuge, the greater part of them having kept an inviolable fidelity to the languages their nurses taught them. Their whole business abroad (as far as I can perceive) being to buy new cloths, in which they shine in some obscure coffeehouse, where they are sure of meeting only one another; and, after the important conquest of some waiting gentlewoman of an opera Queen, who perhaps they remember as long as they live, return to England excellent judges of men and manners.

She likened them to one of the plagues of Egypt.[33] But she was later to enjoy

---

[30] *E&P* 153–5.

[31] H MS 74. 268, 274, 230, 288–9, 323–4, 341. The translation of the Hill poem is undatable; and though some of the poems clearly belong to this year, others as clearly were composed later.

[32] *CL* ii. 163, 182.

[33] *CL* ii. 177, 196. Did she think of herself as trapped (awaiting Algarotti) like the Israelites in Egypt?

these young men's company, even in shoals. Already a few individuals pleased her, notably Lord Bute's younger brother, James Stuart Mackenzie. Some months later she wrote of him, 'I could not wish a child of my own a more affectionate behaviour than he has shewn to me.'[34]

Some travellers were tiresome, some at least amusing. William Hewett, tutor to Lord Granby, took it badly when Lady Mary could not gain him an entrée with the Venetian ladies, who saw him as their social inferior. Some-one 'was Brute enough' publicly to strike the foolish and cowardly Sir John Rawdon. Lord Mansell tried to spirit up Rawdon to issue a challenge: 'no Gentleman could take a Box o'th' ear. Sir John answer'd with great calmness: I know that, but this was not a Box o'th'ear, it was only a slap o'th' Face.'

Next summer Mansel recrossed the Channel to England with other Venice acquaintances: the retired physician Sir John Shadwell and his family. Mansel exchanged cheerful, newsy letters with Lady Mary; but Lady Shadwell censured her. She told the young Elizabeth Robinson (later famous as 'Mrs Montagu') that Lady Mary had abjured England, where 'people were grown so stupid she could not endure their company'. The future bluestocking surmised that the 'insupportable dulness' was Wortley's, and sneered at Lady Mary's 'sprightly genius' and 'great family merit'. Such a woman, who had 'banish'd her Children', might well abandon a dull husband. 'I suppose as she cannot reach Constantinople she will limit her Ambition to an intrigue with the Pope or the Doge of Venice.' Elizabeth Robinson asked not to be quoted, since some of her friends held Lady Mary's 'Virtues in great Veneration, judging her by her words which are good, without considering how her practice follow'd her precepts'.[35]

Other nationalities were more immediately attractive than the backbiting English. The Prince de Beauvau, an early inoculee, arrived from Florence with a letter of introduction from Lady Pomfret.[36] Many 'German' visitors hailed from a ruling class which Lady Mary had admired in 1716–17. One of them lodged in the Palazzo Foscari just opposite:[37] the teenage Prince Frederick Christian of Saxony, who was on a lavish official visit with his

---

[34] *CL* ii. 194, 209. Mackenzie had taken the extra name along with an inheritance. Lewis Dutens said he possessed the most 'good qualities with the fewest faults' he had ever met (1806: i. 164–5). Mackenzie had been in Florence and, MWM told Lady Pomfret, admired the latter's daughter Sophia (*CL* ii. 198). Another of these young men, Lord Gowran, later Earl of Upper Ossory, pleased her by marrying one of her nieces (*CL* ii. 326).

[35] *CL* ii. 440, 457–8; iii. 7; Mansel to MWM, 7 July [1740], H MS 77. 181–2; Elizabeth Robinson, 22 July 1740, Huntington MS Mo. Her friendship with Lady Bute's friend the Duchess of Portland may be impli-cated here.

[36] He left for Venice on 10/21 Jan. 1740; MWM duly praised him to Lady Pomfret (DG7/D 1 i; *CL* ii. 174).

[37] Valcanover 1989: 240 n. 16.

'governor', Josef Anton Gabaleon, Count von Wackerbarth-Salmour. Lady Mary had known the mothers of both prince and tutor at the Viennese court, the one as a royal princess showing off her skill at archery, the other as an intimate friend with whom she later corresponded from Turkey. The prince paid Lady Mary marked public honour; the count developed into a close friend. He was as much confined to a spot behind the chair of his young master (who was crippled) as a nun in a convent. His English was excellent, and he welcomed Lady Mary's friendship because to her he could speak freely.[38]

Lady Mary was able to report to her husband a steady stream of honours accorded her. On Christmas Eve, anti-Catholic as she was, she attended High Mass in St Mark's. (She 'went to see the Ceremony', she explained, and was 'not oblig'd to any Act of adoration'.) The doge's niece (he being a widower) met her at the gate of the Doges' Palace and conducted her to a private gallery set aside for her and the Prince of Wolfenbüttel (nephew of the Austrian empress she had so much admired). Giustiniana Gradenigo, 'who is one of the first Ladys here', gave a 'great Supper' for her, an honour unprecedented for a foreigner. Other ladies—Venetian senators' wives, the Princess of Holstein—were offended at her enjoying a homage above her rank. Grimani seated her next to the guest of honour, the Prince of Saxony, at a Shrove Tuesday ball ('the most magnificent . . . I ever saw') to which she 'could not avoid going . . . with a set of Noble Ladys'. On the other hand she had been once only to the Ridotto, the state-sponsored gambling venue.[39]

Hobnobbing with diplomats and minor royalty, she renewed her offers both to Sir Robert Walpole and to her husband of sending intelligence reports whenever she could find a safe route. Wortley was now so anti-Walpole that this sounds like playing two opposing sides against each other, but she must have felt she could serve national rather than party interests. She later remarked that British prestige was low in Europe, but that she had always had 'the good fortune of a sort of Intimacy with the first persons in the Governments where I resided'. Politicians did not guard themselves 'against the Observations of a Woman as they would have done from those of a Man'. Walpole politely declined her services, citing insoluble problems of transmission. Wortley found a traveller he considered trustworthy, and wrote to instruct her where to send reports, not in her own writing but copied by her maid Mary or anyone with a 'merchantlike hand'. None are now known.[40]

---

[38] *CL* ii. 162, 165, 172, 193.

[39] *CL* ii. 163, 165–6, 170 (where 'Gradenigo' is spelt wrong), 172, 178. The Doge was Alvise Pisani. The supper guests included five female friends of MWM and ten senators.

[40] *CL* ii. 167–8, 195, 257, 258. Hervey mentions a report she sent Walpole. Horace Mann later told Horace

Lady Bute would not give up, but went on, in her mother's words to her father, 'troubling you concerning me'. Lady Mary told Wortley she would answer only if he required her to. 'I had rather drop the Correspondance.' Now there was no need to keep up a public front, she could no longer dissemble. 'I will say no more on this Subject, which is shocking to me and cannot be agreable to you.' He did require it, and she did write, wishing Lady Bute well with, she insisted, perfect sincerity.

Their son was agitating, in letters 'pretty much in the usual Style', to be allowed to leave Ysselstein in Holland for France, where he might demonstrate that he could now resist 'Temptation to Riot'. He also wanted Wortley to get his marriage annulled, reopening to him that favourite source of revenue for his social group: wedding an heiress. Lady Mary gave her opinion for leaving him where he was: France, she said, would instantly supply some English or Irish 'bad Councellor' to lure him back to his 'Former Follys' (gambling and women). She wrote to him 'mildly to shew him the necessity of being easy in his present situation'. Soon afterwards, on the advice of his agent John Gibson, Wortley proposed to raise Edward's allowance to £300 a year. Lady Mary demurred. By Gibson's methods, she felt, 'your Son would have run out £5 or 6,000 and been at this time just where he is'. She thought it foolish of Edward to imagine 'that your immense Riches will furnish him with all the fine things he has a fancy for', and that his marriage project was equally damning.[41]

This spring, 1740, was cold and tardy, reflecting Lady Mary's mood as the brilliant autumn had done. Even in mid-May the Venetians were still 'warming beds and sitting by fire-sides'. (She had, however, missed England's worst winter of the century, which outfroze the ice-fairs of her youth). She was now feeling unhappily compelled by a situation she had not chosen. She did her best to pacify Lady Pomfret, repeatedly assuring her that it was not Carnival 'raree-shows' that kept her in Venice, but the weather, the roads, social obligation to the Prince of Saxony, or 'the force of destiny'. From her youth on, she said, she had never been able to believe she was a free agent; accident was always overruling her wishes (among which seeing Lady Pomfret, she implied, was the first). It was ironic that she should find herself 'seated by a sovereign prince, after travelling a thousand miles to establish

Walpole that she had contacted Sir Robert to excuse or minimize the honours paid by Venice to the Young Pretender in 1737; she hoped to re-establish British–Venetian diplomatic contact, which had been suspended since then (Walpole, *Corr.* xvii. 98).

[41] *CL* ii. 168–9, 171, 172, 179, 185–6. Edward may have cast an envious eye on his cousin Kingston's grand tour, which lasted ten years at a cost of over £4,000 a year. But many English country gentlemen—not large landowners—at this date ran their households on £200 a year (Burnett 1969: 147, 149–50).

myself in the bosom of a republic, with a design to lose all memory of kings and courts'.[42]

Even Lent could not damp the festivities as long as the Prince of Saxony stayed. Operas ceased, but there were weekly concerts and thrice-weekly assemblies. Lady Mary sailed a short way in the *Bucentaur*, the splendid ceremonial barge of the Republic, when the prince inspected the Arsenal. He saw two cannon cast, 'and a Galley built and launch'd in an Hour's time'. She attended a concert which eclipsed those of 1720s London; at another concert and ball she was the only foreigner present. She told Lady Pomfret she would be staying in Venice for the feast of the Ascension, the day of the Republic's famous wedding with the Adriatic Sea, and she continued to argue that, politically speaking, Venice represented liberty and Florence slavery. She was already declining invitations to spend the summer at the country houses of Venetian ladies; in the event she was to stay in Venice almost a year from her arrival.[43]

In March she sent Algarotti a sharper, longer letter, beginning, 'Why so little Sincerity?' He had suggested replanning their shared retreat for Geneva or Holland instead of Venice. (He was probably mindful that his writing had offended the Papacy once and was likely to do so again.) This, she said, was contradicting what he had said before, in talk and by letter. Once already she had sacrificed every comfort of her life for him. Miraculously, this had worked out well for her. She was ready to do the same again, but only, she said, if she could really make him happy. They could not live in the same house, but he could lodge nearby and see her every day. At a word from him, she would return to share their idyll in some quiet French provincial town. A fortnight later she told Wortley that if privateers posed a real threat to her luggage by sea, she could move to the south of France so that it might come by land. Too late: the goods were already on board a ship, though it proved to need several weeks' repairs before sailing.[44]

The month of May opened and closed with the height of Venetian splendour: with a regatta (the first for nearly forty years, being reserved for visits of sovereign princes), and the symbolic espousal of the 'everlasting Sea'.[45] The regatta was both contest and spectacle; for the latter, vessels were

---

[42] *CL* ii. 172–5, 182–3, 187; Hughes 1952: 246. MWM imaginatively linked her love-destiny with Maria Skerrett's opposite one.

[43] *CL* ii. 178–84, 187.

[44] To EWM she suggested she had only *not* settled in France the previous autumn for fear of war. She told Lady Pomfret she had 'some thoughts of removing into Africa' for the sake of the sun (*CL* ii. 175–6, 180–1, 187, 197).

[45] Hertford–Pomfret, *Corr.* ii. 83; William Wordsworth, 'On the Extinction of the Venetian Republic', 1802.

transformed into floating masques by the Venetian nobles and any foreigners who cared to vie with their magnificence. Lady Mary was invited to watch the show from Grimani's palazzo; it stood near the floating extravaganza from which the prizes were presented, and its owner marked the day with 'a great Entertainment'. In turn she offered the almost equally fin vantage point of her own palazzo to friends who did not live on the Grand Canal. The scene is familiar from paintings. Guistiniana Wynne too describes the excitement both of the competing gondoliers and the watching crowds.[46] Lady Mary concentrated her account on the 'little Fleet' of boats adorned at a cost of between £500 and £1,000 apiece 'with all that sculpture and gilding can do to make a shineing appearance', and 'row'd by Gondoliers dress'd in rich Habits suitable to what they represent'. Some ensembles were classical, some political. One boat as the chariot of the night, drawn by seahorses, featured statues of each of the twenty-four hours; stars and a rising moon gave way to the dawn of Aurora, then the midday sun; both statues and gondoliers appeared at the three successive races in three different costumes. Another, as the chariot of Diana hunting in a forest, boasted 'trees, hounds, Stag, and Nymphs all done naturally, the Gondoliers dress'd like peasants attending the chase, and Endimion lying under a large Tree gazing on the Goddess'. Other boats represented 'Poland crowning of Saxony' and 'the Triumphs of Peace'.

Lady Mary described all this in her journal. When Wortley expressed interest, she copied her account into a letter. Later she showed it to Lady Pomfret, who passed it on to Lady Hertford. Lady Mary also attended the state 'wedding' of the Adriatic, in a gondola party consisting of Lord Mansell, two Venetians, and two Flemings. Any account she wrote of that does not survive, but the young traveller Jan Teding van Berkhout recorded it in his diary-letters home. By now she was not only a tourist but also a tourist attraction. Van Berkhout wrote of visiting her and Chiara Michiel as an aspect of his Venetian experience analagous to concerts, operas, and artists' studios. He mentioned that Lady Mary was 'd'un certain age', and noted her wit and learning, and her Turkish travels.[47]

In early June Lady Mary found she had a new, 'unforeseen, impertinent' excuse to offer Lady Pomfret, 'in vulgar English called a big belly. I hope you won't think it my own'. Her maid, Mary Turner, had just confided that

[46] Wynne: 1785: ii. 155 ff. See pl. oo for Canaletto's painting in the National Gallery, London, which probably shows this regatta: it bears Pisani's coat of arms as doge.

[47] *CL* ii. 184, 189–92; Hertford–Pomfret, *Corr.* ii. 85 ff.; Halsband 1956: 194–5. Van Berkhout calls Michiel Ambassadress to Spain: her husband had just been appointed (18 June 1740). His friends included Lord Hartington (who rescued MWM at Turin) and a M. Du Cange (a Dutch resident of Venice), to whom MWM apparently addressed verses (H MS 81. 192).

she was in the final stages of pregnancy, 'which my negligence and her loose gown has hindered me from perceiving till now; though I have been told to-day by ten visitors that all the town knew it except myself'. Lady Mary said she could not travel alone, and could not trust Italian servants, so she would have to stay in Venice another month at least. She relayed the news to her husband a couple of weeks later: Mary Turner was 'downlying', the baby still not born. To both correspondents she expressed exasperation at this sign that her servants had a life of their own. She called the birth 'a foolish Accident', a 'ridiculous detail', and called Mary 'my dear chambermaid', a 'creature' who 'was pleased to honour me' with her belated confidence. To Wortley she stressed the expense of the coming birth, to Lady Pomfret only the inconvenience. Lady Pomfret must have been showing irritation, for Lady Mary's next letter protested, 'You can't possibly suspect I have got my chambermaid with child myself for a pretence to stay here. This is a crime of which all mankind will acquit me.'[48]

With Wortley she dotted i's and crossed t's about the despatch and receipt of her allowance; but the most pressing topic was, again, their son. He persisted in his demand (backed by 'others' besides Gibson) to be allowed to leave Ysselstein. His father was set on his proving 'that he can act with more prudence than a downright Idiot'. No prudence could settle his existing debts, which might be £1,000 or £100,000: 'no one can ghess.' His allowance, even with the increase still under debate, would be £300 a year, and claims on it for 'the last Woman' and 'Menil's daughter' amounted to £160 a year. But prudence, if it could not pay his creditors off, might induce them 'to give him a licence or be able to hide himselfe from them'.

Wortley felt they must permit him to move, or he would do so without permission. The question was where he could evade arrest for debt. Wortley had consulted (for instance with a banker who knew Amsterdam); he wished his wife to consult with 'the Foreign Ministers and merchants at Venice' about their various homelands (whether Frankfurt or Aix-la-Chapelle would offer a refuge, as Avignon might if the Pope would ignore Protestant debts). He feared that after all this effort it was most likely that their son would 'again go into the hands of Sharpers, or worse'. Young Edward of course wanted his father to cut the knot by paying up; his father wanted him notified 'that he will be confined for his life if once he gets into a Jail, since no one will be weak enough to pay his Debts'. Wortley had no dealings with him directly, but only through Lady Mary or Gibson; he warned Lady Mary

---

[48] *CL* ii. 192–4, 198. It 'was not then usual to countenance the private lives of one's servants' (Rizzo 1994: 148).

that Edward 'has behaved himselfe so that no one ought to give the least Credit to what he says or writes'. Lady Mary duly consulted, but could hear of no haven for debtors. 'If he should come where I am,' she wrote, 'I know no remedy but running away my selfe. To undertake to confine him would bring me into a great deal of trouble and unavoidable Scandal.'[49]

Her fears were not groundless. On 1 August he sent her, nicely packaged in effusive protestations of gratitude, esteem, etc., a proposal to be allowed to accompany her for the three or four years that he heard she was likely to remain abroad. She 'would then be a witness of my whole conduct and I should have no occasion for any allowance att all since every thing would be att Your Ladyship's disposal'. By obeying her orders and 'searching with the greatest zele every thing that could give Your Ladyship the least pleasure', he would finally convince her 'of the sincerity of my Reformation'. The sincerity of his letter is open to doubt: less in its professions of reform than in its harping on Lady Mary's tenderness to him (which, as he often told his cousin Edward Montagu, he did not for a moment credit). He may indeed have calculated that his mother would accept almost any plan to forestall this one. She, however, believed him sincere, and used tact in writing to 'prevent his coming near me'.[50]

While the triumphs of peace were enacted on the Grand Canal, 'War seems to kindle on all sides.' England, where Hervey had just achieved his long-coveted post of Lord Privy Seal, was at war with Spain and squaring up to France; it was negotiating for the services of Hessian soldiers.[51] The year 1740 saw two royal deaths which were violently to alter the course of events in Europe: those of Frederick William of Prussia on 20/31 May, and the Emperor of Austria, Charles VI, on 9/20 October. The second of these brought about the War of the Austrian Succession; the first, which brought a leading figure to the war, was equally violent in its effect on Lady Mary's life. No eldest son in this age of inheritance had waited more eagerly for his father's death than the new Frederick II of Prussia. Now he lost no time in despatching the following summons, or billet-doux. 'Mon cher Algarotti, mon sort a changé. Je vous attends avec impatience; ne me faites point languir.' This time Algarotti, too, acted quickly. He left England for the new Athens at Berlin 'in such haste that he left some of his belongings at Hervey's house', and 'borrowed money from Lady Hervey for his journey'. He must

---

[49] *CL* ii. 188–9, 194; H MS 74. 119–20.   [50] *CL* ii. 201, 203.
[51] *CL* ii. 186; Halsband 1973: 255, 257.

have felt he had hit the jackpot. Hervey was left to give Lady Mary the news—tucked away in a postscript—of his 'great Affliction for the Loss of my Friend Algarotti'.[52]

Lady Mary, truly stuck in Venice by the other Mary's approaching delivery, wrote to an increasingly impatient Lady Pomfret of the 'atoms of attraction and repulsion' (an image from Algarotti's *Newtonianismo*) that were holding her suspended. She seems to have reacted to the news of Algarotti's jackpot in a scrappy note sent as comment on some other writing, perhaps a poem. She sounded angry, dismissing his present errand as foolery. But she still expected to see him in time; she would wait, she said, with patience and submission. Meanwhile she bombarded him with letters: Hervey, who had to forward many of them, said they were as endless as 'Sancho's Geese and Ban[qu]o's Kings'.[53] She also made determined efforts to break the chains that held her in Venice. She badgered Wortley for an overdue instalment of her allowance, and told him she was going to Florence, which would be handy for taking care of her shipment at Leghorn. She told Lady Pomfret she would come with or without Mary (who had still not given birth) and would willingly go on with her from Florence to Rome. She told Wortley that if invited to Rome she would probably refuse, but 'should be glad of your opinion of such a Journey'.

On 10 August 1740 a grand tourist in Venice added a postscript to a letter: 'There are no British here but Mr Mackenzie . . . and Lady Mary Wortly Montagew, Mr. Pope's friend, who is most exceedingly entertaining.' A very few days later Lady Mary was gone, tracing in reverse last autumn's passage between land and water. Her pleasure in travel was in abeyance: she found the Apennines 'terrible' and 'more disagreable than the Alps'. She set out although she had a 'swelled face' (as she so often did, either because of her smallpox or her dental problems). Mary Turner attended her, although she had 'lain in but sixteen days'. Nothing more is heard of this baby until (joined by a younger brother or sister) it set out with its parents for England in March 1744. From this time, in Lady Mary's later jaundiced view, both Turners began misbehaving on purpose, in hopes that she would dismiss them and thereby render herself liable for their travelling expenses home.[54]

[52] 'My dear Algarotti, my life has changed. I expect you impatiently; do not make me linger' (3 June/23 May 1740, Halsband MSS). Hervey wrote on 21/10 June (*CL* ii. 195; Halsband 1973: 259).

[53] *CL* 196, 198–9; Hervey to Algarotti 3 Oct./22 Sept. 1740, Murray MS: images from *Don Quixote* and *Macbeth*.

[54] Lord Deskford to James Ogilvy, later 6th Earl of Findlater (Seafield Muniments, Scottish Record Office, GD 248/48/1; *CL* ii. 199–203, 252, 324).

23

August 1740–March 1741

❧

Florence, Rome, Naples: 'I have yet determined nothing'[1]

FLORENCE was her first re-entry for a year into the kind of society she had left at home. It was a distraction, perhaps an annoyance; it must also have been a relief. She stayed two months with Lord and Lady Pomfret in the house they were renting. This was the Palazzo Ridolfi, a handsome building with some fine modern rooms added to those exuberantly decorated by the Medici cardinal who had owned it first. Lady Pomfret liked its historic associations: with Machiavelli and several famous women. Behind lay an eight-acre garden with a central walk of orange and lemon trees, a large and elaborate grotto, and 'marble statues, not bad' (wrote Lady Pomfret, tempering rapture with judgement).

Here Lady Mary shared the Pomfrets' domestic life, their visitors, their sightseeing (which was extensive, though medieval Florence had not yet acquired its modern drawing power).[2] The opera, she wrote to her husband, could not equal La Fenice, but the Venus de Medici lived up to his account of it. She told him much less of the Florentine society than of the Venetian: this time she did not expect to become part of it.[3]

The most detailed source for her stay is a diary in which Lady Pomfret listed 'Where and when Company' in one column and 'Incidents and Occurrences' in another.[4] The day Lady Mary arrived, 'We' visited a convent and a contessa. Next day they took the air in the nearby Cascine: pleasure-gardens beside the Arno, one of their favourite haunts, whose 'mixture of grass, wood, and water' reminded Lady Pomfret both of English landscape gardens and of

---

[1] *CL* ii. 214.
[2] Lady Pomfret was well ahead of her age in choosing to spend time in Sienna. Her Florence palazzo is now 75 via della Scala, just west of the city centre. MWM stayed from 22 Aug. to 16 Oct., having meant to stay just a month—till her goods arrived at Leghorn (Hertford–Pomfret, *Corr*. ii. 82).
[3] Finch MS DG7/D 1 i; Hertford–Pomfret, *Corr*. i. 227–31; *CL* ii. 203–4.
[4] Finch MS DG7/D 1 i. 'Incidents and Occurrences' include letters sent and received.

Arcadia.[5] They later made trips to antiquities and artists' studios, a collection of shells, a sale, a breakfast; they attended operas and concerts and walked on the Ponte Vecchio. One frequent visitor was Lady Walpole, Sir Robert's daughter-in-law, an unfaithful (now separated) wife who had caught Lady Mary's notice by her sense of humour when she was a mere girl.[6] Another was Giovanni Battista Uguccioni, Lady Pomfret's chief admirer among the Florentine nobles. Two days after Lady Mary's arrival Horace Mann, the British Resident, came with a batch of grand tourists including Horace Walpole, Thomas Gray, and Samuel Sturgis (lover of Lady Walpole).

Lady Pomfret had put off visiting the Uffizi and Pitti Palace galleries until Lady Mary arrived.[7] They then went there several times. The first time they ran into Lady Walpole; the last time they inspected mathematical and scientific instruments and a horribly graphic waxwork of plague symptoms. By the end of August Lady Mary was staking out some time for herself. Lady Pomfret and her daughter Sophia visited several convents without her; another day she 'had Company in her Apartments' while all the others 'went to take the Air'.

Enumerated but not described, the daily timetable sounds punishing, especially for someone in emotional distress. Lady Pomfret was learning the flute. They went to see a nun take the veil. Lady Mary went to a wedding with the Pomfret ladies, then off on her own to visit the Princess de Craon.[8] Lord Pomfret rode off with Sir Francis Dashwood to Vallombrosa, about 20 km away; his family were left to make visits, then pick up Lady Mary and proceed to another *conversazione*. On 30 September their 'last Conversation' (before Florentine society dispersed for its annual *villegiatura*) concluded with music and dancing until 2 a.m. Lord Pomfret had a dangerous fall from his horse, but was safe home to dinner, 'God be praised.'

At Florence as at Venice, Montagu conducted a literary life. She kept poems in Italian by a Dr A. M. Salvini of Florence.[9] Having already shown

[5] It later provided the scene about which Percy Bysshe Shelley wrote his 'Ode to the West Wind'; it now houses a race-track, tennis courts, etc.

[6] Inoculated in her youth, she corresponded with Skerrett and possibly with MWM (*CL* ii. 67; MS R.B. 1. 53 at Houghton Hall, Norfork (information from archivist); H MS 77. 260). For her life in Italy, see Salvadori 1983.

[7] She then judged that 'all the collections in the world put together could not furnish such another' (Hertford–Pomfret, *Corr.* ii. 42, 45, 93, 96).

[8] Anne-Marie de Ligneville, princesse de Craon, was mistress to the Duke of Lorraine, and kept a high-style gambling table. MWM had met and liked her son, Prince de Beauvau; her husband headed Tuscany's Council of Regency. Walpole (interested in her as a kept woman) reported that MWM, at cards with her, cheated 'horse and foot'. Her daughter Anne-Marguerite-Gabrielle, duchesse de Mirepoix, had known Lady Stafford's sister (Hertford–Pomfret, *Corr.* ii. 119–22; *CL* ii. 174; Walpole, *Corr.* xiii. 234).

[9] One is on a Hercules in the Pitti Palace (perhaps the one 'killing the Centaur' which Lady Pomfret remarked); another translates a poem by Addison (Hertford–Pomfret, *Corr.* ii. 96, 115).

Conti her writings, she now showed Lady Pomfret her Rochefoucauld essay, her description of the Venice regatta, her epistle to Bathurst, and 'With toilsome steps'. She said no one else had yet had a copy of this last, and Lady Pomfret passed it under the seal of secrecy to Lady Hertford. The latter, while much admiring the regatta account, was upset at the poem's pagan sentiments and openness to the idea of suicide. She hoped it reflected no more than 'a gloomy hour, which soon blew over', and wished one might advise Lady Mary to spend more time reading the New Testament.[10]

Another reader and transcriber of Montagu's poems, and witness to her life in Florence, was oblivious to whatever here seems cultured, earnest, or domestic. Horace Walpole, one of the Pomfrets' visitors, did not approach Lady Mary with an open mind. He already saw her as the cause of his mother's having been first betrayed and then replaced by Maria Skerrett. When he met Lady Mary he met her in company with his shameless sister-in-law. After knowing her for some weeks and having her identify for him the people and scandals behind her eclogues, he admitted she was entertaining, but no more. He judged her writings 'too womanish; I like few of her performances.'[11] (He was to change his tune after finding they were admired by some young men he respected.) His response indicates his expectation that one day her journal as well as her poems would be published. He took enough interest to complete her eclogue series with a seventh—quite unlike the rest. He also, during his second visit to Florence, wrote an epitaph for his mother's tomb. 'Great without Titles, Good without Pretence', it ran: 'She loved a private Life, Though born to shine in public, And was an Ornament to Courts, Untainted by Them.'[12] As far as one can tell, he thought this the simple truth about his mother. Lady Mary was, in his eyes, the opposite pole of a familiar binary: madonna and whore.

He clearly showed that he did not need to meet her in order to make up his mind about her. Before she reached Florence he told Richard West what he expected:

---

[10] Lady Hertford thought MWM's 'Epistle to Bathurst' written 'in early youth' (Finch MS DG7/D5.52). She sent Lady Pomfret in her turn MWM's 'Answer to a Lady Advising me to Retirement' and amused her by suggesting that MWM might yet be open to conversion (Hertford–Pomfret, *Corr.* ii. 85 ff., 116–18, 128, 153 ff., 170–1, 175–6, 200–2; iii. 5). Another poem these two shared was Elizabethan Carter's 'Dialogue between body and mind' (iii. 7–8).

[11] His relations with his father were probably shaken when Sir Robert married Maria, and when he grieved so deeply for her (*Corr.* xiii. 211 n. 19, 234; note in vol. ii of his copy of Dodsley's *Collection*, 2nd edn., BL C. 117 aa 16. He found Sarah Marlborough's memoirs 'womanish' too (xvii. 357).

[12] *Corr.* xiv. 242, 38 n. 40; 'Sunday or the Presence Chamber. A Town Eclogue' and 'Wrote at Florence, 1741' ('Poems and Other Pieces', Lewis Walpole MS 49, commonplace-book, 32–3, 38). Anne Pitt thought the inscription showed amazing ignorance of his mother's character (Lady Louisa Stuart to Lord Wharncliffe, 11 Mar. [1837], Wh M 439/57). Walpole said he wrote his eclogue 'at Florence, as a Sequel to Lady Mary Wortley's Six. She was then there, & Lady Vane was expected . . .'

a third she-meteor. Those learned luminaries the Ladies Pomfret and Walpole are to be joined by the Lady Mary Wortley Montagu. You have not been witness to the rhapsody of mystic nonsense which these two fair ones debate incessantly, and consequently cannot figure what must be the issue of this triple alliance . . . Only figure the coalition of prudery, debauchery, sentiment, history, Greek, Latin, French, Italian, and metaphysics; all, except the second, understood by halves, by quarters, or not at all. You shall have the journals of this notable academy.

To amuse West, who had been at Eton with him and Gray, Walpole constructed the antithesis of that young, male stronghold of learning: the middle-aged, female anti-academy.[13]

Years later Lady Mary took pains to defend herself, to Wortley, from any suspicion of intimacy with Lady Walpole (who, widowed at last, had then just married an ex-lover of Lady Vane). 'She made great Court to me,' she wrote. 'She has parts and a very engageing manner; her Company would have amus'd me very much.' She said she was scared off, not by 'her Galantrys, which no body trouble'd their Heads with', but by her freethinking. Lady Mary had politely refused to join her weekly assembly of theological libertines. These gatherings scandalized 'all Good Christians' and made Lady Walpole's reputation one of 'universal Horror'. Lady Mary held aloof, she told her husband, because she thought it wrong to make a public jest of religious doctrines. She held them sacred, not because she believed them but because they were 'absolutely necessary in all Civiliz'd Governments'.[14] This paragraph has the self-justifying ring so common in her letters to Wortley. Privately, she had shared with Hervey and Lady Stafford opinions very close to Lady Walpole's.

She implied to Lady Pomfret that she often argued with Lady Walpole about the latter's public flaunting of her love-life. She may have entertained conflicting or shifting attitudes to the current affair: she was *reported* as saying Lady Walpole treated 'poor Sturgis' badly and he was 'too Sensible' to love her; long afterwards she said *herself* that he treated Lady Walpole with contempt and humiliation: 'the most submissive Wife to the most Tyranic Husband that ever was born, is not such a slave.' For her part Lady Walpole, some months after meeting Lady Mary, did not sound impressed. She spoke dismissively about Lady Mary's 'The Lover. A Ballad': that fantasy admirer, so discreet and respectful, was 'so different in every article from the lover I should choose that I don't care even to read' the poem. She also disparaged Lady Mary's favourite reading (romances and novels), professing

---

[13] 31 July 1740, *Corr.* xiii. 227–8. Walpole, Gray, West, and Ashton called themselves the Quadruple Alliance; MWM had corresponded with West's mother.
[14] 20 June [1750], *CL* ii. 486.

herself baffled that anybody could find pleasure in them at all, since they had 'no imitation of nature in the characters'.[15]

Clearly Lady Walpole was here assuming a high-culture stance. Horace Walpole kept up the jest of the academy. He said it was 'all disjointed'. Lady Pomfret, having a husband and children, had retained some 'modesty and character' despite being 'a learned lady': he reported her as 'extremely scandalized with the other two dames, especially Moll Worthless, who knows no bounds'. At the Pomfrets' 'Dancing', he said, Lady Mary had competed over a young man with her fellow predator Lady Walpole: 'to get him from the mouth of her antagonist, she literally took him out to dance country dances last night at a formal ball, where there was no measure kept in laughter at her old, foul, tawdry, painted, plastered personage.'[16]

Walpole's scintillating account merits some unpacking. It recalls responses to Lady Mary's wearing sack dresses. Like that style in 1730–4, country dances had spread from informal occasions—a new fashion supported, no doubt, chiefly by the young. They were vigorous dances which drew attention to the body directly, as the sack did indirectly. Walpole (whose own taste was for men) found Lady Mary's physical energy not merely unattractive but inappropriate. In taking a man to dance (instead of allowing herself to be taken) she trespassed against rules of gender; in dancing vigorously she trespassed against rules of age. She was fifty-one. To Walpole she was an old woman, and ought to behave accordingly.

He sent a detailed portrait of her to someone related to him through his mother.

She laughs at my Lady Walpole, scolds my Lady Pomfret, and is laughed at by the whole town. Her dress, her avarice, and her impudence must amaze any one that never heard her name. She wears a foul mob, that does not cover her greasy black locks, that hang loose, never combed or curled; an old mazarine blue wrapper, that gapes open and discovers a canvas petticoat. Her face swelled violently on one side with a ——, partly covered with a plaister, and partly with white paint, which for cheapness she has bought so coarse, that you would not use it to wash a chimney.[17]

Walpole, of course, *had* heard Lady Mary's name. He owed a debt to her: he had been inoculated as a child. But her 'name' came most pertinently not

---

[15] Spence 1966: 1560, 1559; *CL* ii. 13, 488; Lady Pomfret's son Lempster, 19 Apr. [1741], Finch MS. Lady Walpole especially disparaged Marie Madeleine de La Fayette's *Princesse de Clèves*, an important text for MWM (*RW* 187).

[16] 2 Oct. 1740, *Corr.* xiii. 233–4. In Sheridan's *The Rivals* country dances mean 'run[ning] the gauntlet through a string of amorous palming puppies', unsuitably for 'a truly modest and delicate woman' (II. i).

[17] To Henry Conway, *Corr.* xxxvii. 78–9. Hervey, a friend, had once mentioned MWM's complexion as a type of the unnatural (Ilchester 1950: 84).

from his father or his stepmother but from a favourite author: Pope. The details of avarice and lewdness, of greasy uncurled hair, of unpinned, dirty linen, of cosmetics, and, most tellingly, of pox (the word shadowed here by a dash) are all found in Pope's poems.[18] They parallel what she herself said about her impatience with dress codes (with their demands in time and trouble as well as in money); but they exaggerate and demonize. Their only contribution to actual knowledge is the detail that Lady Mary had not gone grey.

From this time Walpole made her a byword. Next year he wrote a brilliant but nasty epigram on her which comes straight out of the classical misogynist tradition. His 'Anecdotes' of her and Lady Pomfret are not like those of Joseph Spence (who collected his from Lady Mary's own mouth, as he did from Pope's). Walpole recorded things which, he said, 'are known': he buried what Lady Mary 'says' or 'owns' among an avalanche of the wildly garbled. He often got things wrong inadvertently (thinking, for instance, that Lord Mar was violently *against* his wife's negotiating with Sir Robert Walpole for his pardon). But his bias, or his myth-making, went far beyond inaccuracy.[19]

His myth was posited on Lady Mary's insatiable lust and greed. Whereas it was normal for himself and other grand tourists to move on from one place to another, when Lady Mary moved on from Venice it had to be that she was 'forced' to leave. For this he adduced reasons: she 'danc[ed] all night at a public ball made for the Prince of Saxony' (which is likely enough, but hardly grounds for being run out of town); she 'persecut[ed] with her fulsome love a noble Venetian' (which seems to be pure invention). Had Walpole been challenged to name a noble Venetian, he could have found none more likely than Conti, who never missed Lady Mary's gatherings of literati. But he needed Conti in another guise: the 'two or three abbés who translated her verses into Italian', her hangers-on, the only people to tolerate her. A Conti disennobled and demasculinized by his scholarly interests and priesthood, belongs with Lady Mary; but glamorous, attractive masculinity is something she must be doomed to pursue in vain. Walpole had met and talked with this woman; but his anecdotes are of interest chiefly as they illuminate the pathology of sexual hatred. Not until nearly half a

---

[18] *British Journal*, 3 Oct. 1724; Rumbold 1989: 156–8. The canvas petticoat denotes avarice: Walpole later wrote that a shift of MWM's usual quality would cost virtually nothing (to Mann, 7 Sept. 1743, *Corr.* xviii. 306). Elizabeth Burton, believing Walpole, thinks the sore could be caused by mercury or arsenic in make-up (1967: 232).

[19] *Corr.* xiv. 242–7, including 'To the Postchaise that carries Lady Mary Wortley Montagu'. Adapting Horace's lines to a notorious whore, this turns on the joke of a nose so rotten with syphilis that a jolt might knock it off.

century on did he admit that when he saw her at Florence she was 'still graceful' in the 'decay' of her celebrated beauty.[20]

For years he went on collecting new stories: that her bedchamber at Lady Pomfret's had needed airing when she vacated it; that she had tried to get a young Italian to join her in satirizing the English in Florence and to father the result on her host Lord Pomfret; that she had made a pass at a young suitor of Lady Pomfret's daughter Charlotte. An ogling woman was said to have 'flung the broadest Wortley-eye'. Walpole bracketed an unsavoury joke about rape (aimed at Lady Mary's husband if not her son) with a vicious one about her insatiable sexual appetite.[21]

None of these stories has any independent support. Lady Pomfret reported most favourably to Lady Hertford on Lady Mary's visit, and resumed their correspondence (in reply to a lively but decorous thank-you letter) with as good a will as ever. Nobody but Walpole was scandalized; nobody but Walpole *and his friends and correspondents* laughed.

Lady Mary left Florence with no notion of how Walpole saw her. She thought 'Hory' had been 'particularly civil', and remarked complacently that 'you may beleive I know him'.[22] Walpole, meanwhile, writing of her as a man-eater, had no notion of her actual secret passion. Their knowledge of each other was pretty equally matched.

~ৡৢ~

Lady Mary's departure from Florence on 16 October 1740 took up the whole of Lady Pomfret's morning. She had let Algarotti know that while waiting to hear from him she was making a short tour. She was ready to go wherever he decided; his commands would direct her, and it was high time for her to know whither. Meanwhile she headed for Rome, taking with equanimity the 'violent transition' from Lady Pomfret's 'palace and company to be locked up all day with my chambermaid'—and the chambermaid's baby?— 'and sleep at night in a hovel'. She meant to give a solid month to the classical sights of Rome, then visit Naples. She told Wortley she expected Lord and Lady Pomfret to join her in a few days, but she said nothing of this to Lady Pomfret. She seems to have taken her friend partly into her confidence, but more likely about her troubles as a mother than as a lover. From Rome she wrote that she would be perfectly happy if only she could find the waters

---

[20] To Lady Craven (not sent), *c.*July 1786 (1978: 6–7).

[21] *Corr.* xvii. 92; xix. 72; xvii. 91, 468; Film 2533, Lewis Walpole Library, Dec. 1744 and ?Jan. 1745. Fathering her satires on another was Pope's first accusation. Walpole dismissed the proposed collaborator, Giuseppe Maria Buondelmonti, as 'a low mimic', though his poetry had some success.

[22] In 1758 (*CL* iii. 146, 184, 186). While claiming this knowledge she wondered how a poem of hers had ever 'fallen into the hands of that thing Dodsley'—in which Walpole may have been implicated.

of Lethe, but that meanwhile, like a deer with an arrow in its side, she carried 'the serpent that poisons the paradise I am in'. Lady Pomfret continued teasing her about eligible youngish men.[23]

The grand tourists had supplied her with advice about lodgings. One landlord rejected her because he preferred a young man—hoping, she told Lady Pomfret, to sell his wife's sexual favours. She found a tiny abode in the Palazzo Zuccaro: its painted ceiling outshone the Uffizi or Pitti, but its garden was no bigger than Lady Pomfret's dressing-room. This last did not matter, for the gardens of Rome proved to be one of its great pleasures. On her second or third evening she walked for two hours in that of the Villa Borghese, which had associations with Claude Lorraine; she thought it 'one of the most delightful I ever saw'. Soon she was finding a new garden for every evening. In Renaissance settings which still remembered the Roman Empire, she paced for hours in the deep shade of the long, straight alleys, under the sightless eyes of statues.[24]

For a week or more she made no contact with anybody, keeping all her time for 'the fine Buildings, paintings, and antiquitys', whose splendour surpassed all her expectations.[25] Gradually, then, the world began to impinge once more, in the form of news and plans for the future. The emperor's death was now known. He had left no son, but a daughter: Maria Theresa, known as Queen of Hungary. The great question of European politics was whether all, or any, of the carefully acquired signatories to his Pragmatic Sanction (a document making it legal for a woman to succeed) would stand by their word. Lady Mary told Wortley that the emperor's ambassador at Rome had re-presented his credentials in Maria Theresa's name, and had had them refused. She also told him about an excavated statue of Antinous for sale, which her nephew-in-law the Duke of Bedford might wish to buy. It may have been now that she commissioned an ivory copy of a sculpted province mourning under the heel of Rome, and had engraved on it the words 'O Liberty! O Virtue! O my Country!' (a line from Addison's *Cato*, of doubtful political import).[26]

In mid-November it was 'as dark and rainy as ever I saw it in England'. Florence had already had snow. Naples seemed to offer an escape from

---

[23] Hertford–Pomfret, *Corr.* ii. 134; *CL* ii. 206–8, 210, 225. EWM had been pressing her to say where he should send her next quarter's money. She reached Rome on 19 Oct. (H MS 74. 119–20; Finch MS DG7/D 1 i).

[24] *CL* ii. 207–10; Faure 1960: 51, 96–9. The 16th-century painter Federico Zuccaro had built and decorated the palace (Towers 1986: 79).

[25] John Cotton, however, told Lady Pomfret's daughter that both Roman princes and English travellers ignored her (1 Jan. 1740, Finch MS).

[26] *CL* ii. 211; Spence 1966: 757. The statue is now in the Capitoline Museum; MWM's ivory is unknown.

winter, though James Stuart Mackenzie was pressing Lady Mary to return to Venice. She told Lady Pomfret she might do this after a couple of weeks at Naples.[27] But reaching Naples proved an ordeal. Tired of hiring chaises, she bought one in Rome for

twenty-five good English pounds; and had the pleasure of being laid low in it the very second day after I set out. I had the marvellous good luck to escape with life and limbs; but my delightful chaise broke all to pieces, and I was forced to stay a whole day in a hovel, while it was tacked together in such a manner as would serve to drag me hither.

The poverty of the Papal States was 'beyond what I ever saw', the country-side 'allmost uninhabited' until she reached the 'gay and Flourishing' king-dom of the Two Sicilies (as Naples and Sicily were called). Now she was out of reach of the censors in the Roman postal system, she was able to tell her husband about the poverty and the highly inconvenient dearth of cash in cir-culation—and about her hopes that the new Pope, Benedict XIV (who had a social conscience and a legal education), might ameliorate both these economic problems.[28]

At Naples Lady Mary found herself once again in court circles, with plenty of gossip to send Lady Pomfret about people they both knew. Lady Walpole had been there in the early 'fury of her passion' for Sturgis; the British con-sul (whose in-laws she had met in Venice) relayed an anecdote of their exhib-itionist dalliance. The San Carlo opera-house (only two years old and 'far the finest in Italy') was illuminated for the young queen's birthday when Lady Mary first went there. Having been partial to Spaniards ever since her time in Vienna, she thought the Neapolitans reflected the influence of their ruler, Charles III (son of Philip V of Spain); she preferred them to the Romans or even the Florentines.[29] Despite the constraints which 'Arbitrary Courts' set on their subjects' contact with foreigners, she was visited by 'several of the principal Ladys', and by the Prince and Princess Iaci, son and daughter-in-law of that Spanish ambassador and his wife whom she had liked so well at Venice. She took against the French-born princess, as an ignorant and self-satisfied (though lovely) coquette; but she liked and admired the prince. She also found, 'in great Figure', Count James Joseph Mahony, a brother of her old friend Mary Anne Cantillon; he had been a year

---

[27] He even offered to come as far as Bologna to meet her.　　[28] *CL* ii. 211–13.
[29] *CL* ii. 213–14; Valcanover 1986: 81–4.

married to Lady Anne Clifford, 'Lady Newburgh's eldest Daughter', whom she thought Wortley might know from Twickenham.[30]

Naples had 'many pretty houses' to let. In the middle of winter there was no need for fires, though with this mildness came damp. On 5 December Lady Mary heard that her cargo of possessions had docked at Leghorn; she debated having it transported to Naples. There were reasons however, even apart from her secret ones, for hesitating. Frederick II of Prussia was about to march on Silesia (an oft-disputed territory, today mostly in Poland), which he meant to take from Maria Theresa. There was no knowing what place might become a 'Theatre of War'; Naples was a candidate, having been wrested from Austria only six years before. Besides, it had Spanish notions of what constituted a genteel appearance: '2 Coaches, 2 running footmen, 4 other footmen, a Gentleman usher, and 2 pages are as necessary here as the attendance of a single Servant is at London.' All this would be 'disagreable and incommodious', as well as expensive. Moreover, the court was 'more barbarous than any of the ancient Goths': a lovely copper statue of a vestal virgin from the new excavations at Herculaneum had been melted down to make commemorative medallions for a royal christening. Prince Iaci, a Gentleman of the Bedchamber, lived like a slave to the king, compelled to rise at dawn and tramp miles in all weathers to shoot snipe; he longed for Sunday as fervently as the poorest labourer. Lady Mary decided not to settle in Naples; but her planned two weeks there stretched out to six, chiefly because she was hoping and negotiating for a sight of the digging at Herculaneum or at least of the surviving artefacts discovered there.

The shell of the Roman town buried in volcanic lava had been recently discovered on land belonging to the Crown. The excavated passages had crumbled and become dangerous, and access was currently denied, though Walpole and Gray had looked at the site in June that year. Even to see the pictures and statues found there required 'the King's License', which was 'at present a very singular favor'. Lady Mary applied, and Prince Iaci did his best to pull strings for her; but the grant was 'delaid on various pretences' (one being that some English tourists had had art objects illicitly copied). Information was hard to come by, but Lady Mary gathered that the remains included 'a Theatre entire with all the Scenes and ancient Decorations'. She kept pressing for leave to view the underground site, hoping to send the

---

[30] This knot of people illustrates the range and variety of MWM's acquaintance. Mary Anne had married successively two Irish expatriates; her brother had married an Anglo-Irish aristocrat. Lady Newburgh had suffered from printed scandal which this suggests it was possible to ignore. Lady Pomfret's daughter Sophia, understandably confused, called Mary Anne's brother Cantillon instead of Mahony (see pp. 401, 346 n. 66; Finch MS; *CL* ii. 221 and nn., 258, 304).

report which Wortley had requested. At last, early in the new year 1741, she gave up and returned to Rome, *en route* for Leghorn.[31]

~~✦~~

Before Lady Mary left Naples, James Stuart Mackenzie in Venice had struck up a friendship with her friend Chiara Michiel; the two joined their entreaties that Lady Mary should return to them. Mackenzie, in fact, may have been a catalyst for Lady Mary's and Signora Chiara's correspondence, which lasted, with some interruption, for over twenty years. Since he was always on the best of terms with his brother Lord Bute, his liking and admiration for Lady Mary may also have had some bearing on Bute's efforts to build friendly relations with his mother-in-law. In an immensely respectful note in his 'curiously crabbed hand of extraordinary neatness', Bute informed her, on the last day of 1740, Old Style, that Lady Bute had survived a labour of 'a few days', to be 'safely deliver'd of a Son . . . Both her Self and the Infant are as well as can possibly be Expected . . . She intends to write to Your Ladyship the Minute her strength shall suffer her.' Lady Mary wrote promptly; she carefully preserved Bute's note. She was never again to sound so bitter about her daughter as she had done, though it took some years more to restore cordial relations.[32]

Though she had told Lady Pomfret on 20 January 1741 that she was only waiting for 'moon-light' to set out for Leghorn, she was still in Rome when Lord Bute's letter reached her a fortnight later. It was not the only family news. Her 'poor Sister' wrote to announce her daughter's wedding the previous autumn—to James Erskine, a son of the erstwhile Lord Grange (who, having resigned from the Scottish Bench, was now also plain James Erskine again). Lady Mary felt that sister Mar's lunacy was clearly visible in her calling this 'a Match of her making'. Though Erskine, formerly Grange, claimed to know nothing about it, she was sure he had engineered this marriage which finally liberated the Erskines of Grange from financial demands from Lady Mar and Lady Frances, by conveying their money (Pierrepont money) into Erskine hands. Lady Mary admitted she was amazed at his 'Impudence', but stoutly denied being amazed at what Lady Frances had done: 'she had allways a false cunning which generally ends in the ruin of those that have it.'

Other people made no bones about being amazed, even as they felicitated Lady Frances. Her cousin the Duchess of Bedford observed that she did not

---

[31] *CL* ii. 213–17, 220. She later expressed anxiety that her letters about Herculaneum should reach him safely, though she admitted they were 'perhaps not very satisfactory' (*CL* ii. 226, 231).

[32] *CL* ii. 217–9; Desmond 1995: 31.

know Mr Erskine, Griselda Murray that she 'little suspected when I parted with you that you had marriage in your thoughts. You are very secret.' Lady Mary judged her niece 'too like her Father for me to correspond with'. But she wrote nicely to sister Mar. As well as wishing both her and the bride 'all Happyness', she was able to report that twenty years after Lady Mar's stay at the Jacobite court at Rome she was remembered there with high regard and esteem.[33]

Lady Frances did not end in 'ruin', but she battled all her life with her husband's family's debts. (Though new demands could not now be made, Monson and the Duke of Bedford continued to press the old ones.) James Erskine the younger was not a faithful husband.[34] But Lady Frances retained her links with the old cousinhood. Lady Caroline Pierrepont, later Brand, continued the Pierrepont tradition of solicitude for the affairs both of Lady Frances Erskine and Lady Frances Meadows, coupled with scepticism about the Erskine and Meadows connections. The Duke and Duchess of Bedford provided financial support, but Lady Caroline advised against trying the duke too far. As godmother to one of the Erskine sons, Lady Caroline asked Lady Mar to be her proxy at the christening; she later returned the compliment by inviting Lady Mar to be godmother (together with the Duchesses of Bedford and Portland) to her own baby girl.[35] From these warm family exchanges Lady Mary was severed by distance and by old grudges: her half-sister Lady Caroline was later in her bad books, perhaps partly on account of her championship of the two wayward Lady Francesses.

The problem of Lady Mary's son still lay at her door: it was she who paid over his allowance from his father. He now wanted them to let him stay at Ysselstein, rather than move at his own expense. He had submitted a list of debts, guaranteed absolutely complete. This said that the 'notes of hand' (for which he might be arrested, even in Holland) came to £123. 16s. 6d.; less urgent 'Book debts' were 'about £464' and 'Other small Debts . . . about £50'. He had agreed to pay an annuity of £100 to 'Menil's daughter', but none to any other woman. Wortley, forwarding this list, noted its omissions of a £250 lump sum, of £60 a year 'to the last Woman', and of who knew what else. He judged that Edward was under the thumb of three English footpads who were milking him for money and stood to lose by his moving.

---

[33] *CL* ii. 222, 223–4; iii. 226; Mar MS GD 124/15/1517/1, 3. Lady Mar must have mentioned the young couple's financial problems, since MWM added that she wished she could help.

[34] Noted by his son James Francis Erskine (Mar MS GD 124/15/1718).

[35] The Duchess of Bedford made a point of respect and affection for Lady Mar (Mar MSS GD 124/15/1534, 1588, 1590, 1591, 1602).

He tried to prick Lady Mary's Pierrepont pride by concluding, 'I think you might tell him not to disgrace more names than one.'[36]

She had responded to all this before leaving Florence. She was glad to have Edward stay put, agreeing that if Wortley (in Edward's phrase) 'set me free from my notes of hand', he would run up as many more in six months. (She noted that his list omitted his Italian debts.) She saw no sincerity or common sense or hope of reform. She guessed he had 'again falln into plotting against himselfe' with criminal associates, either old or new; she thought him 'easily led by people that know neither you nor me'. She delivered judgement on Gibson, who she thought unconnected with the criminal element but given to 'silly flattery' and pious inanities. She had not forgiven Gibson his anger at her when she refused to co-operate in whitewashing Edward to Wortley.

Edward's new plan was that his father should get him elected to parliament. He could then come home, since MPs were immune from arrest for debt. But to 'come in' for an uncontested pocket borough might take five or six thousand pounds. Wortley had recently acquired a lease on Tintagel Castle in Cornwall which gave him control of such a borough. Lady Mary (who had written against abuse of parliamentary privilege) thought it would not be 'reasonable' to bail Edward out like this. From Rome she relayed to him in 'mild but very plain terms' Wortley's view that, while he obviously could not clear his debts, he could win respect by setting aside *something* from his allowance towards them. The parents seemed to be seeking a basis on which Edward could decently be reinstated; but Lady Mary's 'very plain terms' made Wortley and Gibson uneasy.[37]

Her second stay in Rome lengthened out, like that at Naples, to six weeks. Her apparent aimlessness probably means she was waiting to hear from Algarotti. He had been in regular correspondence with Hervey, who found him useful as a channel to, and informant about, Frederick II. His first request for advancement had been for a diplomatic mission to London (probably not something to tell Lady Mary). His non-noble birth having proved a stumbling-block, he persuaded Frederick to make him a Count. Quite in the manner of young Edward Wortley Montagu (and of young men immemorially), he took it for granted that public life could be made to serve his private ambition. Lady Mary may have tried some string-pulling to get him the plum job of Prussian ambassador to Venice.[38] This did not work out

---

[36] Edward owed money to one Warren, who with two others had robbed a Mr Wheatly; his name had come up at the trial of one Greenwood (4 Sept. 1740, with Edward's list and letter of 26 July: H MS 74. 119–20).

[37] *CL* ii. 204–5, 223; Maclean 1879: iii. 212–13; 'An Expedient to put a stop to the spreading Vice of Corruption', *E&C* 104.

[38] 20 Jan. [1741], *CL* ii. 222–3.

either. What he got was a mission to Turin. There, while posing as a private traveller, he was to sound out the court about alliance with Frederick, who was now with his army in Silesia.

Algarotti had a means of persuasion that Edward lacked: he brought Frederick round by playing hard to get, absenting himself from the king's presence. He at least, if not Frederick too, was treated this winter for sexually transmitted disease. At about the same time Voltaire (another of the Prussian Athenians) wrote a poem in jaunty bad taste about Algarotti as Socrates buggering a male partner.[39] All this was beyond Lady Mary's ken, but she presumably heard, either directly or through Hervey, enough to make her loiter in Rome during early 1741. On 18 February, when she was 'in some hurry prepareing for my Journey' to collect her cargo, she must have heard of Algarotti's arrival in Turin.

Rome had suffered severe flooding in her absence, but had now recovered. The season had brought the English flocking in, and Lady Mary, as she waited, led a far more social life than on her first visit there. She renewed acquaintance with Italian friends from Florence and Venice, and met for the first time a Genoese and a Sicilian (both male) who shared her dilemma of seeking a place to settle. 'We often talk over every town in Europe, and find some objection or other to every one of them.' As usual there was news from home of many unsuitable pairings, which Lady Mary, with or probably without a pang for herself, called 'a great heap of our sex's folly'. Sturgis was in Rome without Lady Walpole, wearing 'the very face of a lover kicked out of doors'.[40]

During her time at Rome Lady Mary 'never saw' the Old Pretender, 'James III', who had such esteem for her sister. He was by now sinking in depression and debauchery. She keenly observed his two sons at a public ball. Though they wore masks, she was able to note the 'ingenuous Countenance' of the younger (who was only fourteen), as well as his figure, his dancing, and his elder brother's jewels.[41] Once safely away from the Roman censors and the 'foolish rogues' of Jacobite spies, she reported to Wortley on the 'royal' family's splendid style of life, their apparent solvency, and stories

---

[39] Halsband 1973: 262–3, 272–3. Frederick found Algarotti infinitely superior to Maupertuis as a companion (2 Sept. 1740, Halsband MSS).

[40] *CL* ii. 222–3, 225–7. The Sicilian was brother of the Princess of Campoflorida, and so Prince Iaci's uncle; the Genoese was an abbé, possibly the abbé Durazzo whom Lady Pomfret knew in Florence, probably the man whom Walpole later represented as MWM's 'cicisbeo . . . poor man!' Lady Lechmere's widower was said to be wooing a rich widow fifteen years his senior (Walpole, 31 Jan. 1741, *Corr.* xxx. 11; Hertford–Pomfret, *Corr.* ii. 116).

[41] *CL* ii. 227–8. Laetitia Pilkington says MWM wrote a poem on a portrait of Bonnie Prince Charlie painted during the '45 rebellion (1997: 277 and n.). This must be either a joke or a canard of James Worsdale the painter, once Kneller's apprentice at Twickenham.

from their past. She gave a circumstantial account of 'great endeavors to raise up a sham plot': someone had been offered 'any Money' to lay false accusations. She also commented on the Papal court, repeating her approval of Benedict XIV and his plans for combating poverty. To Chiara Michiel she indulged in flippant comment on the Romans' extreme ugliness.

The English grand tourists in Rome were not only well behaved in general, but

all exceedingly obliging to me . . . they realy paid a regular Court to me, as if I had been their Queen, and their Governors told me that the desire of my aprobation had a very great Influence on their conduct . . . I us'd to preach to them very freely, and they all thank'd me for it.

Years later she said she had owed this influence to mere chance; but still she delighted in recalling how 'my Authority was so great it was a common Threat amongst them—I'll tell Lady M[ary] what you say.—I was judge of all their disputes, and my Decisions allwaies submitted to.' She put a stop to all the usual vices: extravagance, 'gameing, drinking, quarrelling, or keeping' mistresses. A genial Scots Roman Catholic priest told her it was her duty to stay there forever, 'for the good of my Countrymen'. To Chiara Michiel she remarked that she had outlived a prejudice against the young; since getting to know them through travel, she had found them more honourable and sincere than most older people. She was, it seems, a teacher or tutor *manquée*.[42]

These obliging and sincere young men included Lord Lincoln ('Linki' to his intimates), nephew of the politically powerful Duke of Newcastle and Henry Pelham. Both Lady Mary and Lady Pomfret approved the good looks, 'spirit and understanding' of Lincoln, who had just become the family heir on the deaths of Pelham's two small sons. He had fallen desperately in love with Lady Pomfret's eldest daughter, Sophia. Lady Mary kept up the idea of his devotion to her for a long time, while he drifted reluctantly towards obeying his uncles and marrying a rich, reputedly extremely ugly cousin, elder sister of the two who had died.[43]

Lincoln's 'governor' on his tour was the fortyish Joseph Spence, scholar and writer. He had already published on Pope and a couple of other poets, and was to become (like Algarotti) something of a cultural and aesthetic theorist. (His major task at present, however, was to prevent Lincoln from

---

[42] These young men included David Wemyss, Lord Elcho, whose sister Lady Frances Steuart later became MWM's close friend; he confirmed the popularity of MWM's and Lady Pomfret's salons for monoglot Britons (*CL* ii. 210, 227–31, 234; iii. 32; Chamley 1965: 98).

[43] Walpole, *Corr.* xxx. 64, 74; xxxvii. 114.

acting on his feelings for Lady Sophia Fermor.) He took a close and informed interest in Montagu the writer. He read and admired her Rochefoucauld essay; he collected her sayings to go with those of Pope and other literary lights, and he got a scribal copy made of seventeen poems from her album of her own work, and edited it carefully.[44]

Much of Spence's interest in Lady Mary stemmed, like other people's, from her tortured relationship with Pope. He questioned her extensively about this, and she remained good-humoured even when he declined to admit that Pope had an 'appetite to satire'. He recorded her derogatory comments on Pope (and on Swift, Gay, and Bolingbroke), and her version of Pope's relations with Addison. Pope's poetic style, she now said, was nothing but 'a knack': that very 'all tune and no meaning' which he himself despised. She showed Spence her fifty or sixty letters from Pope (mostly not now extant), to prove 'what a goddess he made of me in them'. This, however, backfired. Spence thought the letters said no more than 'what is almost necessarily said to a fine lady'. His reaction nicely illustrates the problem facing any 'fine lady' who dreamed of being taken seriously as a writer or a human being.

Pope was not Spence's only topic. He also canvassed, and recorded, Lady Mary's views on her life and travels, on Ovid, Montesquieu, the Kit-Cat wits, politics, and gender relations in Christendom and Islam. She told him that she 'travelled because she could not bear to see the distresses of her country', and of her loathing for 'those anti-knight-errants who run about only to ruin as many ladies as they can'. He reported her as seriously putting forward two proposals for reforming the institution of marriage: that no dowries should be given with brides or jointures paid to widows; and that marriages should be for a term of seven years only (the time that parliament might sit without an election), though they would be simply and automatically renewable. She said she took her ideas 'from the customs of the Turks'. The 'present marketing-way' would be reformed if women had to rely on 'their own good qualitys and merit' to find a husband. But she apparently said nothing about what women might live on if they stayed single, or were widowed, or elected to leave a marriage after seven years. Any statement about paid employment would have put her in the ranks of the feminist pioneers; but she made none.[45]

---

[44] *CL* ii. 228; Hertford–Pomfret, *Corr.* ii. 160; Spence 1975: 8–10, 361–2. Spence collected all the poems in H MS 256. 1–52 except the controversial 'Mrs Yonge'. He supplied a contents list and explanatory notes (almost exactly the same as Walpole's notes elsewhere), corrected scribal slips, but added one or two errors of fact. In 'The Lover' he altered MWM's addressee, Molly, to 'Chandler' (Cornell MS E6004; Grundy 1971: 214–17). Walpole also transcribed her epigram on Churchill, though he thought it plagiarized ('Poems and Other Pieces', Lewis Walpole Library, 49 2616. II. 39).

[45] Spence said she had written a treatise on these topics (1966: 743–65). It was some advantage to her that

The attentive Spence offered Lady Mary (as first Pope and Gay, then Henry Fielding, and lately Conti and Grimani had done) confirmation that she was genuinely an author. He was more intellectually mature than the grand tourists but just as respectful. To discuss beauty with them was to provoke a barrage of flimsy compliment; to discuss it with Spence was a stimulating exercise in which she cited Bacon and he cited Locke. (He used her Bacon citation later, in print.) Spence was dazzled by Lady Mary. He filled his letters home with her perfections—and with the wilder rumours about her. He noted acutely that travel had done two things for these conversations: it had given her 'liberty' of speech and put her socially within his reach. He probably drew on his talks with her in his *Crito*, a 'Dialogue on Beauty' written in 1752.[46] He quoted from her 'Wednesday' in his *Polymetis*, 1747—to which her husband subscribed.

But while Spence prepared to join with Walpole in getting Montagu's poems into print, Spence's pupil joined with Walpole in feeding the myth of Lady Mary's monstrosity. Lincoln wrote quite soberly to his uncle about finding her 'as extraordinary as my imagination had fancied her (which by the by is not saying a little)'. He was, he said, glad of their distant cousinship (which she had pointed out), glad 'to be mightily in [her] good graces', and happiest of all that she thought he resembled his uncle. Even here he made her attention to him into a joke: 'the Lord knows what would happen if it was not for the nearness of blood.' He must have made the same point in grosser terms to Walpole, who in reply called her blood 'poxed, foul, malicious, black'. Walpole added that when alone with her in a coach (clearly an analogue to the back seat of a car in recent times), he had 'felt as little inclination to her as if I had been *her son*. She is a better specific against lust than all the bawdy prohibitions of the Fathers.'[47]

Months later Walpole developed the blood image further; he sent Lincoln a rumour that Lady Mary's landlord at Rome 'complains he did not imagine so old a woman could have spoiled his bed with her flowers: she is most extraordinary in all her concerns.' He added a quotation from Virgil about a river of abnormal fullness and persistence.[48]

---

having given no dowry to her husband, her father had left her a bequest whose interest, though not its capital, was her own. She may have felt she earned her allowance from her husband, by her support and advice about their son.

[46] Spence 1975: 17, 356.

[47] Lincoln to Newcastle, 21 Jan. 1741 (Spence 1975: 346); Walpole to Lincoln, 31 Jan. 1741 (*Corr.* xxx. 10). MWM told Lincoln their shared love of reading derived from Wise William Pierrepont. Spence reported but did not subscribe to 'the malicious world' 's story that MWM had infiltrated the Sultan's harem and that he had chosen her for the night by 'fling[ing] a handkerchief at her'. This charge against her uses an orientalist myth which she had explicitly denied (Spence 1975: 357; Spence 1966: 760; *CL* i. 383).

[48] 3 Jan. 1741, *Corr.* xxx. 8.

Lady Mary's crime was thus not that she menstruated, as such, not even that she spoiled the bed, but that she menstruated *although so old*. Fifty-one. Perhaps she was bleeding heavily because she was approaching menopause; perhaps the whole thing is another example of that pure fantasy which holds such attraction for imaginative letter-writers. In any case, it is remarkable how far these young men were prompted to go, in their imagination, by their need to despise and mock the ageing female body.[49] Lady Mary—either by some particular act, by her free-and-easy social demeanour, by the rumours surrounding her, by travelling on her own regardless of her age and sex, or by presuming to behave to the English 'boys' as a tutor or male mentor might—had put herself beyond the normal pale of courtesy. She was no longer a person of their own rank and standing (well known to their respective father and uncles); she had become an emblem of indecently active, indecently physical older womanhood. As such, and in the privacy of pen and paper, it was no holds barred. A couple of years later, when Lincoln's mistress gave birth, and Walpole responded with a verse 'celebration of priapic power', he did not forget to perform a kind of exorcism. It was glory, not shame, to Lincoln that Walpole should describe in graphic detail his role as 'Stallion of the Age'; it was shame to Lady Mary that he should write that 'One has sung of *Wortley*'s Loves' and explain that she was 'often mention'd in Mr Pope's Works, & famous for her Wit, Poems, Intrigues, Avarice, and Dirt'. Priapic power, it seems, had an investment in abusing her.[50]

One need not conclude that the apparent respect shown her by *all* the grand tourists was equally phoney. Many of them—Jan Teding van Berkhout, James Stuart Mackenzie, Lord Deskford, and others—voiced admiration for her in private writings, just as they did face to face. Their admiration, like Spence's, was mixed with amazement. She was different, she was unique, she provoked delight or disgust, nothing in between.

❦

Lady Mary left Rome too early to hear the latest English news. On Friday, 13 February 1741, Old Style, both Houses of Parliament debated an address 'humbly to advise and beseech his majesty that he would be graciously pleased to remove the right honourable sir Robert Walpole from his presence and councils for ever'. This drama had roles for most of her male

[49] Linda A. Pollock notes that noxious humours were thought to accumulate in the female body when it could no longer purge them by menstruating (1990: 59).

[50] Walpole, 'Little Peggy A Prophetic Eclogue, In Imitation of Virgil's Pollio' ('Poems and Other Pieces', 49.2616.II, 120; Black 1994: 156–7).

acquaintance. Walpole's attackers included Wortley, Hervey's father, and Lord Carteret (a middle-aged widower who was soon to marry Lincoln's beloved); his major supporters were himself, Hervey, and Hervey's old friend Stephen Fox (along with Lincoln's uncle Henry Pelham and the egregious William Yonge). In the small hours of the morning Walpole's victory was declared; he lived to fight another day.[51] But a couple of months later Lady Mary sounded more critical of his administration (its foreign policy, that is) then ever before. Whether her views had been influenced by the Europeans she was talking to, or whether she was making some concession to Wortley's, she blamed Walpole for 'Notorious Blunders' of policy which were 'the general Jest of all the nations I have pass'd through'. British ships lying idle, she said, might have shown themselves at Naples and frightened Spain 'into a Submission to whatever terms we thought proper to impose'. Suddenly she sounded more like one of the Westminster Opposition than like a government supporter.

On the evening that Walpole stood at bay (24 February, New Style) Lady Mary reached Leghorn. There she received her quarter's allowance, reported to Wortley on the two courts at Rome, and saw to her baggage. Wortley (calculating the probable cost if he had to send everything on to Venice) had expected customs duty to be 'but a trifle' on used items not for resale, that 'no one will look into a Ladies Cloths, Furniture or Papers', and that even the Inquisition would not 'seize Books meerly for a Lady's amusement, that never meddled with Controversy'. Even if they took every book relating to the Catholic religion, he added, those 'cou'd scarce amount to the value of £2'.[52]

He was wrong: his wife did meddle in controversy. She later described with gusto her prowess in 'controversial disputes': not of her own seeking, but forced on her by self-appointed Catholic champions. She developed a technique. First she got her adversary to agree that 'the Scripture' was true and that Saints Peter and Paul knew the Christian religion. Then she listed those items of Catholic belief which are missing from the Bible and from the practice of the saints. Then she cited Bible texts—and not only those but also the three Creeds (Apostles', Nicene, Athanasian), the 'Fathers and Councils' which her antagonists would mistakenly try to use against her, the etymology of the word 'sacrament', and the history of factions within Catholicism. She forbore to answer their aspersions on Henry VIII with

[51] Lady Hertford thought Walpole's triumph that night his greatest ever, and his own speech inspired (Hertford–Pomfret, *Corr.* iii. 1–5; Halsband 1973: 263–4).

[52] *CL* ii. 233–4, 227; H MS 74. 117–18. He sent duplicate copies of his instructions, 25 Mar. and 27 May 1740.

equally scurrilous facts from 'the Lives of their Popes and Cardinals'.[53] Her books relating to religion were well thumbed.

The Inquisition, however, was not to know all this, and she got off lightly. She busied herself with her 'parcels', and the intricacies of bills of lading etc.—but not too much to write to Signora Michiel and to Lady Pomfret. To the first (along with praise of Mackenzie and of the young in general, and compliments to Grimani) she speculated as to where her wandering star might conduct her next. To the second (along with comment on some delicate matter, perhaps Lincoln's courtship of Lady Sophia) she apologized for yet another failure to connect in the same place at the same time. As soon as her goods had cleared customs, she embarked them again on a different ship: HMS *Dragon* of the British Mediterranean fleet, captain Curtis Barnett, bound for Genoa. Beyond that lay her rendezvous with Algarotti.[54]

The last leg of her journey was not easy. It was only a day's sail from Leghorn to Genoa (far shorter than by land), but it was a day of 'hard gales'. Horace Walpole's later gleanings included a tale about this sea passage, which he said she 'begged' on one of her 'jaunts'. The captain told her that a storm was coming, but would not be dangerous.

She said she was not afraid, and going into a part of the gallery, not much adapted to heroism, she wrote these lines on the side,

> 'Mistaken seaman, mark my dauntless mind,
> 'Who, wrecked on shore, am fearless of the wind.

On landing, this magnanimous dame desired the commander to accept a ring: he wore it as a fine emerald, but being over-persuaded to have it unset before his face, it proved a bit of glass.[55]

Like so many of Walpole's stories, this raises questions. The tale of the precious ring bestowed but found to be worthless is a traditional one: older than Walpole, older than Lady Mary, the kind of tale that floats in the collective mind, waiting for a magnetic name to cling to. Lady Mary had received at Leghorn the instalment of her allowance which was due to her at Christmas; there would seem to be no reason why she should not pay normally for her passage, no reason in the world why she should think of giving Barnett anything as valuable as an emerald. But the bill of exchange awaiting her at

---

[53] As non-biblical elements in Catholicism she listed 'Purgatory, Transubstantiation, invocation of Saints, adoration of the Virgin, Reliques (of which they might have had a cart Load), and observation of Lent . . . Vows of Coelibacy', the status of the Pope, and eternal damnation for millions who never heard of Christianity (*CL* iii. 91–4).

[54] *CL* ii. 227–31.

[55] To Mann, 27 Jan 1761, *Corr.* xxi. 472; Thomas Gray at once passed the story on to two friends (*Corr.* iii. 727–8, 734).

Leghorn was not 'sent payable at sight', and some months later she had 'not yet receiv'd' its value.[56] She was indeed short of cash. Might she really have paid Barnett with a ring? If so, then the myth about her would almost necessarily later represent her ring as fake.

Again, the ship's privy, as a spot for Lady Mary to write graffiti, so perfectly matches the myth as to be almost beyond belief. Nor did she compose this couplet: she was quoting (with some variations to make the couplet fit, which are more probably hers than some naval officer's) from the Restoration poet Anne Wharton.[57]

Yet the *core* of the story is unlikely to have been invented by either Walpole, Captain Barnett, or Admiral Forbes (who told it to Walpole). The boasted courage, the wry consciousness of wrecked hopes, *and* the close knowledge of undeservedly forgotten poetry: all these speak the authentic Lady Mary. At least some part of her mind had no illusions about the dream which, nevertheless, she pursued through all obstacles.

---

[56] *CL* ii. 227, 240. She used a variant of the ring story in 'Docile', where the ring the heroine leaves in place of money is so large that it is wrongly taken to be fake (*RW* 146–7). The story was told, too, of Elizabeth Chudleigh (Rizzo 1994: 66).

[57] 'On the storm between Gravesend and Dieppe', written 1681, pub. 1693 and 1695. MWM may have known it in MS; a transcript connected with the poet's friend Lady Anne (Osborne) Coke, Countess of Leicester (who later married a Walpole), remains among MSS preserved at Holkham, Norfolk (information from Germaine Greer).

24

March 1741–October 1742

❧

Turin and Elsewhere: 'the present disturb'd state of Europe'[1]

ALGAROTTI had been at Turin since the end of January. Lady Mary got there on 16 March, having left her baggage at Genoa and traversed 'very bad roads' (which she had thought 'fine' in 1718). For two months Turin held them both; then they parted, to remain out of touch for probably fifteen years.[2] That is all that is certain. The recent context of Lady Mary's waiting and of Algarotti's pursuing other goals, both sexual and careerist, might lead one to expect that he rejected her expeditiously even if not unkindly.

A newly noticed clue to their meeting is a poem lodged in Lady Mary's copy of Marie Madeleine de La Fayette's *La Princesse de Clèves*. This novel (about a married woman who heroically resists illicit love) dated from 1678, but this was a new edition, printed at Paris in 1741. Pinned inside it—*probably* by the owner—is a scrap of paper bearing fourteen lines of Italian verse in Algarotti's hand. The poem is clearly original and occasional. It essays a definition of love: learnedly, mock-scientifically, personally. It opens, 'True love is, my fair lady, if you don't know it—myself I learned it from you—the child of who knows what . . .' It ends, 'True love, Maria, is what one guesses it to be.'[3]

This conjures up a vivid, if hypothetical scene: the pair enact a medieval court of love, disputing the nature of this mysterious passion, fencing verbally as Lady Mary had done with Hervey. Like that earlier debate, this one flows into verse and on to paper; Algarotti pins his graceful but elusive verdict into a brand-new copy of La Fayette, and presents it with a graceful

---

[1] *CL* ii. 244.

[2] *CL* ii. 231. Algarotti spent these years in Prussia, Dresden, and Venice, mostly in the employ of Augustus of Saxony (Haskell 1980: 349).

[3] Now at Sandon. This poem explicitly rejects Plato's definition of love, and alludes to Virgil's in eclogue x. Translation by Helena Fracchia. MWM already owned a 1720 edn. of La Fayette's *Histoire de Madame Henriette d'Angleterre* (youngest daughter of Charles I).

flourish. Or did Lady Mary produce her book to receive his poem? Or did she place it there herself, alone? And did she do this in 1741 at Turin, or years afterwards? And was the poem indeed written at Turin, or at some other period? As usual, apparent likelihood glimmers and fades. All it leaves behind is a probability that Lady Mary connected her time at Turin with this pretty but unconsoling poem, and with La Fayette's novel of tragic love—which she later alluded to in the bitter conclusion of 'Docile'.

Whatever went on in the courts of love, other things were going on as well. Algarotti (in his own lodgings, having moved from an inn) must have been busy in court circles pursuing his diplomatic aims (which were doomed to fail) and exploring the local art world.[4] Lady Mary reported that the kingdom of Savoy and Sardinia was making 'great preparations for War'; but it declared for Maria Theresa, not for Frederick. During the same period it became clear that George II was also keen to enter the war in support of Maria Theresa. England urged Vienna to reject Frederick's terms; Frederick wavered between fighting France and fighting Britain.[5] It seemed that Lady Mary and Algarotti would soon be nationally divided by the war. Before Algarotti left Turin he would have had the news of Frederick's victory over the Austrians at Mollwitz on 10 April. It was a dramatic story: Vienna paralysed at Frederick's invasion (all except Maria Theresa herself, who was twenty-three, pregnant, and indomitable); Frederick's nerves and anxiety before the battle; his premature flight when he supposed he had lost; the victory which his father's army won without him; the desertion of Maria Theresa's allies.[6]

Lady Mary meanwhile (having perhaps had to sell more jewellery to keep herself solvent) avoided the 'trouble and expence' of attending the overdressed court of Savoy at Turin. Her apologies were decently conveyed by the British consul, Arthur Villettes: she found her high opinion of his abilities fully confirmed. Her definite views about the king ('no bright Genius, but has great natural Humanity') and his powerful and popular minister[7] were formed at second hand. There was curiosity at court about her behaviour, and some suspicion that she was in Turin as a spy.

Her time was not entirely her own. In the household which the Turners, as usual, were running for her, she had swarms of visitors. The nobility of Turin prided themselves on civility to foreigners, and she in turn found 'the people in general . . . more polite and obliging than in most parts of Italy'. She pursued her acquaintance with the savant Scipione Maffei, who had a

---

[4] Cf. Pinto 1987.   [5] *CL* ii. 234; Browning 1994: 49–50, 57.   [6] Mitford 1968: 9–10.
[7] Charles Emmanuel III and the marchese d'Ormea.

house at Turin. English travellers passed through, including Hervey's eldest
son and James Stuart Mackenzie. He brought a letter from Chiara Michiel,
and when he left he carried one to Wortley: a chance for Lady Mary to write
more freely of international politics than she could do by post. Mackenzie
stayed just a few days, getting away despite spring snow which threatened to
close the Alpine passes. He had supper with Lady Mary the night before he
left, and they drank Michiel's health. (Lady Mary was beginning to regard
the link between these two friends as something special.)[8]

Hervey's letters furnish more clues to the time which, despite what he
called 'the present, warm, intangled, turbulent State of Europe', Lady Mary
and Algarotti gave to purely private matters. Newly arrived in Turin, she
sent Hervey a festive letter, as she had when she left England eighteen
months before, rejoicing that her desire was within her grasp. Of other
letters to him (not, of course, extant), one included a paragraph written by
Algarotti ('your—*Friend*'); another was more open about her 'thoughts',
since it was personally carried by Hervey's eldest son. Algarotti let his
contact with Hervey be subsumed in Lady Mary's; he stopped writing inde-
pendently. Hervey kept writing to him, and sent 'best respects and wishes'
for 'your delightfull Companion'. At the end of her stay (probably after
Algarotti had already left) she let Hervey know that Turin had been 'a very
disagreable Epoque of [her] Life'.

Her vanished letters to Hervey, if not Algarotti's added paragraphs,
would have thrown much light. In one it seems she argued that reason and
philosophy are worse than useless—a frequent theme in her early, impassioned love-letters. As she had once sought to conjure up the distant
Algarotti in Hervey's company, so now she tried to fold him into her
correspondence with Hervey, or used the distant Hervey to triangulate her
feelings for him.[9] Hervey served the self-conscious element in her love,
which Algarotti's Italian verse reflects. Algarotti for his part used imprecise
words and contorted syntax to tell his brother that Turin had been not the
least extraordinary episode in his extraordinary life.[10]

Whether they went to bed together (either at Turin or during those
few months when they were both in England) remains an unanswerable
question. It hardly sounds as if they did. It hardly sounds as if there was a

---

[8] *CL* ii. 233–6, 255; Finch MS D. 5. 133–4.

[9] Hervey encouraged her renunciation of reason, quoting Queen Christina's words on renouncing her
crown: 'Non mi bisogna e non mi basta' ('not necessary for me, not enough for me'). She was charmed when
Hervey's son showed her the little souvenirs of his travels which he had bought for his parents (*CL* ii. 232,
240, 286; Hervey to MWM, 21 Apr./2 May, to Algarotti, 18/29 May 1741: Hervey MS 47/2. 99, Murray MS).

[10] 25 Mar. 1741; Treviso MS 1256 A. Between 11 Feb. and 8 Apr. Algarotti sent his brother eleven letters,
but they give nothing away.

solid basis, beyond fantasy, for a physical affair. Whatever there was now
came to an end—though enough remained to rebuild a flirtatious friendship
fifteen years later. It may be that this is all we can know. But Lady Mary did
write one surviving letter to Algarotti which was intended to finish their
relationship: which did not, like so many others, move from complaint into
acquiescence. From its appearance (its paper, ink, apparent quality of pen)
this letter might well belong to spring 1739, and represent an effort, determined but unsuccessful, to break off the affair before it should lead her to
break up her life. But editors have agreed in dating it on grounds of its contents, to around the time of the parting in Turin.

Lady Mary built this letter out of images from the *Newtonianismo*, of the
way a prism breaks white light into its component parts, and the way that
sight focuses on objects at various distances. Using his eyes as her prism, she
tells Algarotti, she has dissected the ideas of his soul. She has found him full
of the finest and most brilliant taste, delicacy, and imagination on all kinds of
dilettante topics. But when he directs those faculties at her, they flow
together into bland and lumpish indifference. She is calibrated wrongly, or
she stands at the wrong distance, to draw out his brilliance. She develops
these images somewhat less logically than I have done here, but with force
and passion. She knows, she says, that her letter will anger him. Never mind.
She has begun to return contempt for contempt. She refers bitterly to 'le
tems (de sotte memoire)' when she was afraid to speak so openly, because of
her 'goût effrené pour vous'. An outsider ridiculing her passion could not
have been harder on it.[11]

If she ended her dreams of love with this letter, she ended them with her
own kind of dignity: giving free rein to her pen, not so much looking the
truth squarely in the eye, as creating a new-minted parable of it. In any case,
she now freed herself from her dreams. Henceforth she would have to live
without them.

She re-traversed the very bad roads to rejoin her baggage at Genoa and to
re-confront, in changed circumstances, the issue of where to settle. Now for
the first time the option of returning home may have presented itself. But she
mentioned nothing of this to Wortley, only the likelihood of Italy being
invaded, and the need to avoid 'the disputed States'. For once she made the
easiest choice. Putting aside for the moment the claims of Venice or Geneva,
she decided to summer in Genoa. In 1718 this had been her first, delicious

---

[11] *CL* ii. 237: 'that time (of stupid memory) . . . an unbridled appetite for you'.

taste of Italy. Now she leased a most beautiful palace, charmingly situated, whose views of sea and land seemed made to inspire day-dreaming. It offered society too: the local ladies paid her 'great civilities'.

They came by sedan chair, each attended by two footmen, a page, and a gentleman usher. (Lady Mary paid about £3 a month for a chair.) A number of them were divorced: she later learned with wry amusement of the pretexts by which, under Genoese law, married couples could be 'set free, to their mutual content'. All were dressed in black, but dazzlingly bejewelled and belaced. The republic had sumptuary laws which regulated personal display within the city walls. Its many immensely rich citizens had to keep their elaborate clothes and coaches for use only in the suburbs (the city streets were in any case too narrow for coaches). There were no public assemblies or gaming-rooms, and Genoa had an international reputation for parsimony; but grand private dinners were given. Lady Mary sat down as one of ninety-six guests at a wedding dinner where she thought 'the Entertainment one of the finest I ever saw.' She was often with the Marquis di Mari and Signora Clelia Durazzo, who had been friends of Hervey and of Lady Pomfret respectively. Meanwhile Wortley had chosen the time of her sojourn in Turin with Algarotti to increase her allowance, 'As you have been travelling about.' Since the increase was only £20 a year, it probably caused no guilt feelings.[12]

Perhaps the sparkling sea beyond her windows was some balm to her hurt soul (though she told Michiel that she sometimes thought of throwing herself into it, to seek new worlds for old). Hervey made an extended visit to his father in the country this summer (following his unloved mother's death), and he revived their long-running joke about country living, telling her he was a convert to it. She responded with two passages of verse about the vanity of worldly ambition. Ostensibly she meant Hervey's political rivals by those whose 'Enjoyments never pay the chase, | But melt like Snow, within the warm Embrace'; but her words also evoke herself. She added an avowal of her undying friendship. Hervey would have her warmest thoughts, 'Where ever Fortune points my Destin'd Way, | If my Capricious Stars ordain my Stay | In Gilded Palace or in Rural Scene.'

In prose which she did not preserve, she asked his advice in her present situation—though it was a bit late, she admitted, to be making a choice of life. Along with some rather heavy compliment, he replied that not 'Solomon and Socrates together could give you any [advice] so good as what you may give your-self'. She had only her own pleasure to consider, he said:

---

[12] *CL* ii. 496, 238, 239, 247–8, 255; Howard 1971: 10; Hervey, 12/1 Sept. 1741, Hervey MS 47/2. 115.

she should consult only her 'Passions, Affections and Inclinations'. As for its being late in the day, that only made the choice more important: the less time one has left 'the more industrious one should be to manage and improve it'. As he had done five years before, he reminded her (quoting Ovid) that new love can drive out old. (He had just written to Algarotti, saying no word of Lady Mary, and concluding, 'Adieu. Busy your mind with ambition and you will never feel the Regret you give.')[13]

Hervey, who saw nothing wrong with the idea of Lady Mary's taking a new lover, stands at one extreme of opinion. Lady Pomfret and her daughter represent the middle ground: the former saw her as wandering in quest of friends, seeking 'in parcels' what most people seek in monogamy; the latter thought that if her quest failed she would return to 'old and odd Mr Wortley'.[14] At the other extreme, Horace Walpole assumed both that Lady Mary was looking for sex and that she had no right to find it. He arrived in Genoa in July (not now travelling with Gray but with Lincoln and Spence), and was irked to find her there before him: 'full of abuse on Turin, where I suppose, she was found out as well as at Florence, Rome, Naples, Venice, etc. etc. etc.'[15]

She mustered energy that summer for two long-standing interests: literature and politics. She probably renewed her talks with Spence, convincing him that 'the ladies (if they applied themselves to them) would excel the men in the practice of the finer arts'.[16] Someone, probably he or Walpole, showed her recent unpublished poems from England. She spent whole days, she told Michiel, among her dusty old books. She requested from Hervey a list of current ones which sounds uncannily like a round-up of Henry Fielding's satirical butts of the moment. She wanted Richardson's *Pamela*, Colley Cibber's *Apology* for his life, and Middleton's life of Cicero (to which she had subscribed). Off his own bat Hervey added a sexy *Pamela* spin-off: James Parry's *The True Anti-Pamela*. Hervey was attacked rather than mocked (along with *Pamela*, Cibber, and Middleton) in Fielding's recent *Shamela* and not-yet-published *Joseph Andrews*; but he had an unusual capacity for taking a joke against himself. He may have alerted Lady Mary to this group of inter-related texts. Or she may have heard of them from English newspapers or English tourists; or (a tempting, unproveable possibility) she may have heard from a nearer source, in letters from either Henry or Sarah Fielding.[17]

---

[13] *CL* ii. 251, 238–42; Murray MS.

[14] Finch MS D 5. 140. EWM increasingly loved measuring things: colliery way-leaves, optimum widths for new roads, lengths of existing roads and the cost of repairing them; and local journeys, both uphill and down, broken down into sections of so many minutes (Wh MS M 109–11).

[15] *Corr.* xvii. 91–2.   [16] Spence 1975: 397.

[17] *CL* ii. 394, 251, 241–2, 244–5. If MWM is indeed the 'Lady of a very high Rank' and intellect whom

Walpole, though silent just now about her interest in literature, was again provoked to contempt and satire when she involved herself in politics. Early in June 1741 a British warship, the *Dursley*, was lying at anchor at Genoa when its captain, Richard Hughes, went ashore to see the British consul. He left Lieutenant John Donkley in charge. Donkley saw a small rowing bark (a brigantine or xebeck) 'under Genoese colours, which having no passport made him suspect her to be a Spaniard': that is, a privateer. He fired three cannon shots (not loaded) to bring her to.

To the Republic of Genoa this constituted a breach of their cherished neutrality. When Donkley went on shore that evening he was 'Seized and sent Prisoner to the Pallace of the Duke'; the crew-members with him were imprisoned elsewhere. Captain Hughes at once, 'by way of Reprisal, made prisoners of the Bark's Crew'. For a moment it looked as if a battle would follow, but Hughes prevented this by sending a midshipman with a flag of truce. Events unrolled predictably. Each side refused to release their prisoners until the other side did so first; prisoners on each side alleged cruelty; debate raged as to whether privateers were in the area or not; the Genoese took measurements to ascertain whether the shots were fired in or into their territory. They demanded reparation; the British proposed to send the brigantine and its cargo of tuna for safe keeping to their consul at Leghorn.[18]

During all this, John Birtles, 'Consul to His Britannic Majestie in These Dominions', found himself the mediator and channel of communication between the two sides.[19] He held his post in succession to his uncle (who had been foolish enough, some years back, to lend £200 to young Edward Wortley Montagu). Walpole at first called Birtles 'as unlicked a poor cub as ever I saw' but warmed to him on hearing that his professional conduct was being impugned by Lady Mary. She thought that Genoa was right and her own country wrong. Birtles must have hated her interference; but he went on sending her the English newspapers.

Walpole, newly arrived and looking round him, was sure that Lady Mary had no more political than literary entitlement.

She was here three weeks without receiving a visit, when to get company she took it into her head to offer her mediation in this affair of the Genoese and the English

Henry quotes as saying that *David Simple*, 1744, 'could not have been written by a Man' then she probably corresponded with either sister or brother (Henry, preface to Sarah's *Familiar Letters*, 1747; Battestin 1989: 415–16). MWM had a kitten just now, whose playful claws were menacing her books (Hervey, 6 July/25 June 1741, Hervey MS 47/2. 111).

[18] Hughes, 6 June, PRO Ad. MS 1/1882. This file includes letters from Hughes up to 22 Aug., and a journal kept by Donkley. Hughes dates the event 3 June, Donkley 5 June.

[19] Hughes, 20 PRO Ad. June, MS 1/1882.

captain. Rather their defence, for she says she will have the captain broke; and accordingly has wrote her pleasure to Lord Hervey. Don't you like her taking Genoa under her protection? I don't know whether is greater her impudence in pretending an interest [i.e. political clout], or the stupidity of the Genoese in believing she has it.

Lady Mary meanwhile insisted to Chiara Michiel how non-political she was.

She had indeed written to Hervey. Before any decision about the *Dursley* had been taken in England, he assured her of his agreement with her general political analysis: 'one Map of Europe is worth all the Refinements of Tacitus, the Maxims of Machiavel and the whole Corps Diplomatique, when we are deliberating upon the Measures this Country ought to pursue.' Most people, he added strongly, were quite obtuse about politics. Three weeks later he was able to tell her that the matter—'the only Squabble in Europe of which you will soon hear of any Conclusion'—was satisfactorily settled. An English court of law had found for the Genoese. Prisoners on both sides were released; Britain acknowledged herself at fault; Lady Mary was vindicated. When she passed on to Birtles some privileged information about a coming Spanish invasion, he 'laugh'd, and answer'd it was impossible'; events vindicated her again.[20]

Walpole gathered one more intriguing story about her summer at Genoa: a young Englishman named Raper had delivered to her, from Turin, a little diamond-encrusted cross 'worth eleven thousand pounds'. Henry Raper's chief virtue for Horace Mann (the source of the story) was his having 'often dined' at Houghton Hall. He had Norfolk friends, and came from a London merchant and banking milieu similar to that of Maria Skerrett, Lady Walpole. But a possible link with the messenger does nothing to explain Lady Mary's receipt of such a precious item. Raper was exploring markets for silk, hides, and what-not, not for jewellery; and although Lady Mary had been suspected (at Turin and elsewhere) of spying, she was not in anyone's pay. The sum named as the cross's value, set against everything known of her finances, sounds mythical. It would be credible only if less costly. Had she left it behind by mistake in leaving Turin? Or had she ordered it and not picked to it up? Or won it at play? Did someone invent the story? Or just exaggerate it? If substantially true, it would show how much of Lady Mary's activity remains impenetrable to our gaze; if not, it would re-emphasize her magnetism for gossip.[21]

[20] Donkley journal, 1 Aug., PRO Ad. MS 1/1882; PRO SP 79/19; Walpole, *Corr.* xvii. 91, 103; *CL* ii. 241–2, 245, 259, 260.

[21] Walpole, *Corr.* xvii. 138. This was not Matthew Raper but his younger brother Henry, travelling in the way of trade. Though he assured his father that he avoided English company as 'very bad for a merchant to

Ripples kept reaching her of life beyond Genoa. This summer saw her old admirer Admiral Vernon's doomed attack on Cartagena on the coast of Colombia, a Franco-Prussian treaty, and Maria Theresa's gradual realization how tenuous was her support. The Spanish claim on Habsburg possessions in Italy looked increasingly likely to result in invasion. Lady Oxford's husband died on 16/27 June 1741: an alcoholic, hovering on the brink of financial ruin.[22] Lady Mary rather oddly said she was 'vex'd' (rather than sorry) at his death, for reasons which Wortley would understand. Three days later Grimani was unanimously chosen Doge of Venice. Three days later again her husband wrote with a detailed tally of letters received, asking her to supply the equivalent from her end. He urged her to take the trouble to endorse all the letters she received, with their dates and short summaries: 'it would save a great deal of time to yourselfe and me.' In fact the war was blocking most of her letters. Hervey, who wrote three times in September despite severe health problems, did not hear from her either.[23]

In August she received a letter from her son, sent care of Birtles; she denied the relationship in order to avoid being landed with his £200 debt. He still wanted his marriage dissolved. Probably he hoped to bribe witnesses to swear it had been illegal; yet just after this Lady Mary said he was laying claim to some kind of religious conversion. She thought this quite likely genuine: she judged him to be not a rogue but a fool—which, as she observed gloomily, quoting La Rochefoucauld, 'is the only incorrigible Fault'.

She advised Wortley that he must make a choice: either he must be reconciled to Edward, which would mean paying his debts, or steel himself to ignore people approaching him on his son's behalf. Anything short of paying the entire debt, Lady Mary argued, would seem to Edward 'very little'. Meanwhile, what with his good looks and manners, his habit of making 'lavish promises of Eternal Service and Freindship' to new-found acquaintances, and the endless potential supply of people to believe Pope's lies about his parents, he would always be finding someone new to badger Wortley on his behalf. And whoever was sent to Ysselstein to report on him would probably return as his partisan.

The underlying issue was the future destination of Wortley's wealth. Lady Mary claimed that she now regarded her son quite dispassionately, and

Come into because they are all upon the Expence and pleasure', he had cultured and gallant tastes. He was alert for various dangers: army deserters, and Jacobitism among Scots or Irish people (Henry to Matthew Raper, 19 June 1742; Matthew and John Raper to Henry, 23 May 1741: Raper MSS).

[22] Lord Orrery reported that 'after proper sales and right management' Lady Oxford would still be rich. She accepted £10,000 from the nation for the collection of books and MSS—a fraction of their value (Swift 1963–5: v. 206; Mack 1985: 379, 761).

[23] H MS 74. 124; *CL* ii. 243–4; Hervey MSS 47/2. 115, 117, 119.

wished his father to do the same. 'I hope and beleive I shall never know who is your Heir', she wrote (oddly, since she was eleven years her husband's junior). Yet it seems that from at least this date she kept her mind steadily fixed on the contrast between Edward's claims and those of Lady Bute, once the chosen heiress, who was now living with her husband and two children on the Isle of Bute because they could not afford London. Emphasizing her own integrity, her wifely duty, and her sense that this was 'a very nice subject for me to write on', Lady Mary advised Wortley that he too should exercise dispassionate judgement: compassion would be just as much a sign of weakness in him as anger.[24]

By mid-September the fear of Spanish invasion was enough to drive her 'out of Italy'. She decided to settle in Geneva: a small town where living should be cheap. There she anticipated (quoting Horace) a life of studious leisure, free from worldly cares. But before the familiar packing process was half-done, the Turners delivered a bombshell: they 'both declar'd that they will not pass the Alpes'. It was just over a year since the birth of their first baby. (They had another while they were in Lady Mary's service, but there is no way of knowing whether Mary was pregnant just now.) During that year they had unpacked and repacked seven times in successive cities and stayed at innumerable inns (whose level of service and honesty Lady Mary, like most English travellers, ranked extremely low). Their employer's travels had involved them in one chaise breakdown, one major mountain crossing (the Apennines), and one storm at sea, besides the normal wear and tear of the road. They had been two years away from England, which they had left expecting (probably) a quiet life in the south of France.

Now they had struck a good bargain with a Dutch ship to carry them home from Genoa. A domestic row no doubt followed their ultimatum: Lady Mary was too much upset that night to sleep. She felt she had already spent too long in fear of their leaving her, putting up with 'all their Sauciness with the Temper of Socrates', sooner than be forced upon Italians who might rob or murder her—or who at least would be less likely, in case of her death, to preserve the little, precious, personal objects which she wished to pass on to her daughter. More calmly she reasoned that while William could be easily replaced, she needed 'an English maid that I could in some measure depend on in the case of Sickness or other Accidents'. She wrote to ask her husband to despatch yet another Mary, a 'sensible and handy' woman who had been with her as housemaid in 1739, to come out and meet her at Geneva. The journey would be cheap, and could be paid for out of next

---

[24] *CL* ii. 249–50. In 1741 Bute ceased to be a Scottish Representative Peer.

month's allowance. 'If Mary will not come, I do not desire any other to be sent in her room.'

Whether Wortley carried out this request, or what Mary the housemaid thought of it, we do not know: once Lady Mary and the Turners had slept or failed to sleep on the matter, they withdrew their notice and she withdrew her request. Her story was that they 'repented their Folly, and on their Tears and promises of a better behaviour for the Future, I have forgiven them.' The packing was resumed; 'great Rains' gave way to fine weather, and Lady Mary's caravan, now augmented by the baggage from England, set out again. She stayed long enough in Turin to make contact there with Lady Pomfret's son and to write to his mother. But she said nothing about her imminent Alpine crossing (her third) or her destination. On 11 October 1741, after a long mountain journey, she arrived in Geneva.[25]

❧

This historic stronghold of Protestantism must have been a marked contrast to Lady Mary's recent Italian homes. She found its setting, on the clear blue Rhone at the foot of its crescent lake, inferior only to Naples and Genoa. (Had these European cities crowded Constantinople out of her memory?) On bright days Mont Blanc was visible a hundred kilometres off, but near at hand the streets were narrow and the town encased in medieval walls. Its style of life reversed that of Italy. Just like an English country town, it had 'no shew and a great deal of eating'. Sumptuary laws prevented the show; the eating went on in private. But prices were as high as in London because produce had to be imported (apart from the lake fish, 'large and well tasted'). She liked the local people, who were helpful and obliging, 'very desirous of attracting strangers to inhabit with them'. The 'little Republic has an air of the Simplicity of Old Rome in its earliest Age. The Magistrates toil with their own Hands, and their Wives litterally dress their Dinners against their Return from their little Senate.' After condescending at first towards these 'extreme good sort of people',[26] Lady Mary struck up a friendship with the cultured, intellectual Tronchin family.

She may have been building on a link from the past, if she had indeed met the future inoculator Théodore Tronchin back at Twickenham in 1727. Her chief contact in Geneva now was Jean-Robert Tronchin, twenty years her

---

[25] There were no English merchant ships because of the war with Spain. Before leaving MWM entrusted Birtles with a box (probably containing some kind of antiquities) to ship to Lady Oxford's daughter the Duchess of Portland (Halsband 1956: 219; *CL* ii. 252–4, 256–7, 361).

[26] *CL* ii. 256–9. Hervey found two letters from MWM at Geneva highly entertaining (5/16 Nov. 1741, Hervey MS 47/2 121). A recent visitor had spent his time there at billiards, the 'Common Room', and cricket (John Preston to Henry Raper, 8 July 1741, Raper MSS).

junior and an intimate friend of Montesquieu. He belonged to the Genevan Council of Two Hundred, and was later to follow his father as *procurateur-général*. He was about to be married. With him and his circle Lady Mary discussed some of her favourite philosophical topics: the tenuousness of free will, the heinousness of war. She kept in touch for at least a year after she left Geneva.[27]

But all these amenities could not keep her. After four months at Genoa, where she never seriously meant to stay, she put in less than one at Geneva, though she had risked losing her servants to get there. Yet one need not suspect that she went there on some mysterious assignation or that she did not mean what she said about liking the bourgeois character of Genevan society. Her arrival coincided with alarm there about the expected descent of Don Philip with a large army.[28] She also cited discontent with high prices, 'the sharpness of the Air', and terrible winds (which, she said, revived various physical complaints which she had escaped while in Italy). Perhaps most potent causes were the fear of war and the fact that she was now entirely at a loose end.

Rather than cross the Alps in November, she stayed to the west of them, and settled at Chambéry, ancient capital of the Duchy of Savoy, in its gorge at 'the door of Italy'. There she 'fix'd for this Winter in this little Obscure Town'. It was so little known that she thought it worth a detailed description. Having been too poor for improvements during the last two hundred years, it too looked like old English towns, with narrow streets miserably paved, and thick-walled, low-roofed houses. It was 'wholly inhabited by the poor Savoyard Nobillity', who were very good company and had most exalted pedigrees. 'Many of them have travell'd, and tis the Fashion to love reading; we eat together perpetually and have assemblys every night for Conversation.'

There were no English, no coaches, and no gilt paper. But the food and especially the wines (at 'a penny a Quart') were excellent; there was 'profound peace, and unbounded plenty . . . but not one rag of Money'—the latter just as in Rome. Lady Mary found herself a gourment cook 'for very small Wages', hired a sedan chair for one-third what they cost at Genoa, and bought

---

[27] The Genevan circle with whom MWM corresponded (Tronchin, Sara Franconis, the savant Michel-Louis de Lescheraine) was the one in which inoculation began a few years later (*CL* ii. 267, 278–9, 296–7; Tronchin 1895: 4; Tronchin 1906: 122; Miller 1957: 197–201; Tissot 1754: 8). Another inoculation pioneer, Tissot, was newly at Geneva as a student during her visit (Eynard 1839: 14). MWM may also have met Jacob Vernet, travel-writer and friend of Montesquieu; she made a note later about one of the '2 Vernets of Geneva' having given up medicine for theology (CB 10).

[28] Sordet 1854: 65–6. A later, probably apocryphal story had her staying a night at Vevey (the other end of Lake Geneva, quite out of her way); her son stayed just across the road; they did not meet (*Quarterly Review*, 1820: 23: 417).

a little horse to 'amble about' on the 'few tolerable rides' that the mountains offered. She abandoned her side-saddle to ride astride like the local ladies. She thought she could live well for a year in Chambéry on a week's London expenses. Though it was a fierce and snowy winter, the air was 'the best in the World'. Her health improved. Her new friends included octogenarians of both sexes who looked and behaved like forty-year-olds. When Carnival came on, there were balls twice weekly. They aspired to be Parisian, and were just as agreeable as London ones, although smaller and plainer.[29]

Her only complaint was of letters lost in the post: an effect of the war. (As she had predicted, the Spaniards had 'landed at Several Ports in Italy'.) Hervey was ill and silent this winter, and Lady Bute's letters from Scotland never got through. But Lady Mary was supplied with English news by Lady Pomfret (who had reached home in October 1741) and the widowed Lady Oxford (who, however, was not yet saving Lady Mary's letters). She also corresponded with James Stuart Mackenzie.[30]

February 1742 saw two noteworthy events in Britain. Sir Robert Walpole fell at last, leaving Hervey to wear the shell of power a little longer;[31] and Lady Mary's first grandson died of a fever and convulsions at rather over a year old. All she is known to have said about the end of Walpole's reign was about how busy her husband would now be. The Butes' loss made her both sorry and anxious. She was afraid that grief would sap the health of her daughter, who was near her time again. She recalled, no doubt, the gruelling birth of the son now lost, and that another birth would make four in four years: a rate only just below that which had killed her own mother. But she also hoped the coming child would 'repair' the other's loss. Wistfully she wrote, 'It is a great pleasure to me when I hear she is happy.' Lady Bute came south to Wortley's London house for this birth. She had a second daughter, christened her Jane, and again made her mother a godmother, this time *in absentia*. About now Lady Mary often reiterated to Wortley her pious hopes that their daughter would prove dutiful to him. Just before this distant birth came a rare flash of bitterness: 'I hope her obedience and affection for you will make your Life agreable to you. She cannot have more than I have had; I wish the success may be greater.'[32]

---

[29] *CL* ii. 259–63, 266, *SL* 292–3. (MWM's first letter to Lady Pomfret from Chambéry is the only MS extant from this correspondence.) Brocard describes the social and culinary life of Chambéry and the high status of its bourgeoisie (1992: 109, 111, 120–1).

[30] *CL* ii. 260, 282–3.

[31] He was almost offended when MWM advised him to despise ambition and power (Hervey MS 127, 19/8 Sept. 1742).

[32] EWM wrote of the dead baby: 'The Surgeons say his brains were too large and occasioned the Fits.' Eight years later MWM still feared that 'breed[ing] so fast' might impair Lady Bute's constitution (*CL* ii. 259, 264, 271, 274, 278, 455; Browning 1994: 80–1).

How did she think she had failed? At pleasing Wortley, or at making him happy? When she wrote this she was 'much mortify'd at [his] long silence'. How far back in time does her brief comment reach? It seems she had at this moment erased all memory of Algarotti. Did she remember Wortley's early dissatisfactions, or their sexual life together, or the scandal she had brought on him by means of Pope, or her hypothetical financial offences, or the failure represented by their son? All that is clear is that crucial and uncomfortable aspects of their relationship lay, most of the time, unmentioned between them.

Their son was always a worry. Lady Mary kept dutifully writing to him, though she knew he blamed her for his father's displeasure. At Chambéry someone asked her about a confidence trickster bearing her name: Edward had met this Savoyard at Genoa, told him he had just come into an annual income of £5,000 or £6,000 from a recently deceased uncle, and asked for a temporary loan. The Savoyard had refused. Lady Mary told him the would-be borrower was related to her, but not how closely. It seems that Edward had used similar tactics to wheedle money out of somebody in Ysselstein in Holland; next year further demands came in for a debt he had incurred in Champagne in 1734. Meanwhile in December 1741 (only three months after enrolling at Leyden University to study oriental languages) he left Holland and turned up in London, where his father thought he stood in danger of being hanged or at least sentenced to the pillory. He said he had moved without permission because of 'the Uneasines he was under'. Wortley called this 'the same excuse which is constantly used by all Murderers and Robbers'. To this category, it seems, he felt his son essentially belonged.[33]

Edward spent three months in England, and used them to good effect. He convinced Gibson (who duly reported to Wortley) that he had steered clear of 'the Sharpers' and learned to manage his money. He established valuable patronage links with his father's cousin Edward Montagu and with Lord Carteret. These coevals of his mother were wealthy, powerful—and heirless. Montagu,[34] MP for Huntingdon, was to marry the young Elizabeth Robinson this August. Carteret, a widower and one of the coalition which had succeeded to Walpole's power, was to marry Lady Pomfret's daughter Sophia two years later, hoping to father a son. Young Edward enlisted them both (though he dealt with Carteret chiefly through Montagu) as allies in his

---

[33] *CL* ii. 277, 257, 288 n. 1; EWM, 22 Mar.; Gibson to Edward, 12 Apr., copied by Edward to Montagu 7/18 May, MS MO 7.

[34] Names are a problem here. I shall use 'Wortley' for MWM's husband, 'Edward' for her son, and 'Montagu' for her cousin by marriage. Edward also involved the Duke of Montagu—another relation, husband of a close friend of his mother (MS MO 3774).

campaign to stay in England, to get his marriage dissolved, and to obtain an army commission. He would then make his fortune in the war. Carteret promised a commission (a gift worth something like £2,500).[35] Wortley was not certain that a military career was either his son's true object or even a desirable one. He only said 'I will not oppose his going into the Army as a volunteer.' He still suspected that Edward might be a religious enthusiast. He thought Lady Mary's influence might procure him a position in the forces of Sardinia (a British ally), 'where if he should do wrong it will be less known than if he did it in Flanders'.

As soon as Edward left London, letters began flying back and forth. Even before crossing the Channel he sent John Anderson back from Harwich with a letter to Gibson. He was not allowed to approach his father directly; Gibson's reply was really Wortley's. It reproached him for his recent visit, named Lady Mary as the most sincere and impartial judge of 'Your present condition and the best course for you to take', and instructed Edward to beg her permission 'to attend upon her at any place she pleases to appoint'. He was to come no closer, and stay no longer, than she should allow. She would propose; Wortley would agree. If her advice was for Edward to fight in Flanders, he could still get there in plenty of time. Wortley would advance his April allowance and add £20 for travelling expenses; he would ensure 'the Woman and those concern'd with her' did not molest him, although Edward's debts incurred at Leyden (doctors' bills as well as rent) still rankled.

As Gibson wrote all this out, Wortley was sharing it directly with Lady Mary. He was inclined to let his son accept a commission. Lady Mary had no doubt it would be 'pawn'd or sold in a Twelve month', but thought this would at least be instructive for his new patrons. Wortley still relied on her for a first-hand 'impartial account', and wanted mother and son to meet somewhere in southern France. He fussed over arrangements (including a promise to refund anything Lady Mary might pay to Edward) and advice: 'I hope you will try him thoroughly, speak always mildly, gently and kindly to him and keep him within a reasonable distance of you till you and I have settled what is to be done about him.'[36]

Edward, still negotiating through Gibson, forwarded copies of the entire dossier to his cousin Montagu. He reproached Gibson for 'thinking I can take no resolution of my own but that I am still in leading strings', and said he would like his father's advice better 'if I could be so happy as to receive it from himself'. He would, he said, be 'certainly inexcusable if I doubted my

---

[35] The Duke of Montagu suggested that Edward might buy a company in the guards—bearing the rank of lieutenant-colonel—for about this (Huntington MS MO 3774).

[36] 22 Mar./2 Apr. 1742, *CL* ii. 269–72, 277; H MS 74. 125–30.

Mother's capacity to advice me in my affairs and should be happy if I could have her council, but have never yet been able to obtain it but in general terms viz: to behave well'. He recalled that his father had once half-offered 'something that would be more advantageous for me than the Army', and had fully offered to fund the requisite military 'Equipage'. He argued, citing authorities, that he would need £50, not £20, to get himself and his servant to Lady Mary's vicinity. He might fall ill; 'and realy I do not like countries where I may be laid hold of by a *lettre de Cachet* and should [*sic*] up for all my life in the Bastille.' He passed effusive thanks to Wortley for dealing with 'that Woman', but said he had still not received the whole sum promised for his expenses in London and in a previous illness: 'as I promised every body payment I now cannot go from my word.' He objected to the style of Gibson's letters as unacceptable 'from any body but my Father'.

With Edward's copies of all this to cousin Montagu went reminders of Carteret's promise to get him a company, and of his father's bad record on promises. He begged his cousin would 'put my Lord Carteret in mind, that if He does not save me, You will see Lost and undone, sir, Your most humble' etc. Of Lady Mary he wrote, 'She is my Mother so my tongue is tied', but then untied it to add that she would certainly block anything that might be for his good. If Montagu should stop hearing from him, 'You may be assur'd some accident has happen'd to me or some trick been play'd me.' (He seems to have feared cloak-and-dagger violence as well as the seizing of his possessions, especially his carefully garnered book collection.)[37]

The other side of the saga was slow to cross Europe: Wortley, said Lady Mary, had failed to frank his letters. Before any of it caught up with her she was on the move again, driven from Chambéry to Lyons by rumours of an approaching French army. She stayed only a few weeks: long enough to tell Wortley she was 'very glad you have been prevail'd on to let our Son take a commission'. To refuse would have been to lay himself open to charges of keeping his son down. She did not expect Edward to rise in the world, or to 'make a tolerable Figure in any Station in Life'. She remembered how he had once taken her advice to become a soldier as a hope of getting him killed. She now feared, despite herself, that his reformation was a fiction. John Birtles, consul in Genoa, had just shown him up in a lie; she transcribed for Wortley the letter she had sent him about this, which he had not answered. 'It is very

---

[37] Edward to Montagu, 1/12 Apr., 6/17 Apr., to Gibson 1 May/20 Apr., Huntington MS MO. Montagu thought, apparently after becoming disenchanted with Edward, that his trouble was having 'too much of the rapidity of his mother's genius' (Elizabeth Montagu 1923: i. 29).

disagreable to me to converse with one from whom I do not expect to hear a word of Truth.'[38]

She accepted her brief to interview him, however, and proposed to do it at Valence, just down the Saône from Lyons, which she hoped would be free of English people. Once she was used to the idea, she felt 'not sorry to converse with my Son'. She thought she could keep calm and make an unprejudiced judgement. She would 'wish him your Heir rather than a stranger', she said. (So Lady Bute was not yet reinstated?) The truth was that she could 'see nothing but Falsehood and weakness through his whole Conduct'. Her tone of calm and balance slipped as she speculated that Carteret's interest might stem from his needing a son-in-law, a mate for 'an ugly Girl that sticks upon his hands'. But only indirectly, only to Mackenzie, did she hint the degree of her disturbance.[39]

The long-drawn-out preliminaries to this meeting were practically on a par with those of Wortley's ambassadorial days. Lady Mary wanted Edward to take the stage coach, with no servant, under 'a feign'd name': this method (quite usual for young men, even rich ones) would get him from Paris to Lyons for £5. (Wortley, through Gibson, suggested it might take a pound or two more.) Edward meanwhile said it had taken him £26 to reach Paris and he was broke. Passing as a Dutch officer was no objection (he had just visited the French court in the guise of a French officer, and sent an intelligence report to Montagu). But the prospect of travelling by 'Postwaggons, Stage coaches or diligences' and eating at the public table at inns revolted him. He told Gibson that he needed a servant in case he fell ill, and that it would dishonour his father and himself to level him with 'the meanest creature on the face of the Earth'. He told Montagu that getting him alone under a false name 'seems as a plot lay'd to play me some trick without there being any possibility of its ever coming to light'.

He had no intention of serving as a volunteer (which would take money) or depending on his parents' plans at all. He admitted with regret (to Montagu) that he was too late to be made an aide-de-camp to Stair, though he seems to have told his parents this was still possible. He wished Carteret (whose encouragement, he said, had inadvertently landed him in his present dilemma) would act quickly to save him 'from ruin'. He told Montagu he would stay on in Paris in the hope of help from Carteret, and his parents that he would stay till Lady Mary advanced him money to travel as became his rank. She thought Paris the last place he ought to be, because of his debts

---

[38] *CL* ii. 272–4, 278. The Spaniards occupied Chambéry in Dec. 1742 and stayed till 1748 (Brocard 1992: 123).

[39] A couple of days before the meeting she told Mackenzie she was 'often tir'd of being' (*CL* ii. 275, 283).

there; he argued that it was ideal for proving he could resist temptation. In Paris he transcribed for Montagu another month's-worth of correspondence with Gibson, who had sent him £10 and hinted that he ought to take the military option more seriously.[40] He told his cousin he longed 'to be service-able to my country in some shape or other' and to do honour to *their* rela-tionship; that he feared his mother (both 'as a woman set upon a young man's ruin and much more still as a woman of superior genius'); and that he dreaded their meeting would 'prove . . . a fatal interview to me'.[41]

No other offer but meeting her materialized, however. Two months after leaving London he was in the south of France: voicing to Montagu, as Lady Mary voiced to Wortley, deep scepticism about the coming encounter. Still, even when enjoying the hospitality of a local lady at Montelimar, his last stopping-place, he duly preserved his alias.

Lady Mary had moved on to Avignon, by roads 'fill'd with French troops'; they met at Orange. The meeting was not acrimonious, as others had been; they 'parted very good Freinds'. Still, Lady Mary reported to Wortley her unabated distrust and disappointment. She allowed some gleams of feeling to peep out: it pleased (and no doubt surprised) her to find her son's conversation charming and his learning wide, if superficial; it pained her that he had lost his looks and run to fat. He seemed, she said, much older than his twenty-nine years.

She took at face value his high delight at 'the prospect of going into the army' and his statement that Carteret had confirmed his promise of a com-mission; but over the two days she weighed and judged his behaviour. She found him polite and genteel, with a perfect command of colloquial French, a 'vollubility' which she did not rank as true wit, a flattering manner, and towards herself an elaborately submissive tone. She cut him short in his 'usual silly Cant' of resolving to reform. He meekly agreed with everything she said about his father's moderation and generosity, appeared to accept as a revelation the idea that he might have saved £150 a year (half his allowance) while at Ysselstein, and blamed his heavy expenses on what Gibson had thought due to 'Mr. W.'s Son'. He meekly endured her lectures, whether she dwelt on the public respect to be gained by 'Sense and Probity', or insisted that 'being allways at his last shirt and last Guinea' was something 'any Man of Spirit would be asham'd to own'. But all his submission only convinced her that he was infinitely malleable: having no judgement of his

---

[40] Gibson, 29 Apr./10 May, copied to Montagu on 7/18 May, MO 7. Long before, MWM had thought the army both noble and profitable: the perfect way for any young man to make his fortune (*CL* i. 107–8).

[41] Edward to Montagu, MS MO 2836. 3, 5, 6, 7, 12/23 Apr., 20 Apr./1 May 1742 (copying a letter to Gibson); *CL* ii. 275–6.

own, he would 'allways be led by the person he converses with, either right or wrong'. He might easily be made 'a Monk one day and a Turk three days after'.

It was he who raised the stakes of their talk. 'He ask'd me if you had settle'd your Estate.' This was the real issue: not how many hundreds Wortley might be brought to disgorge annually or occasionally, but where his hundreds of thousands would go after his death. Loyal as always, Lady Mary answered 'that I did not doubt (like all other wise men) you allways had a Will by you, but that you had certainly not put any thing out of your power to change'. Edward knew his mother had no dowry; it seemed he did not know of the agreement of 1731.[42] This was his cue to hint (careful lest he offend, drawing on every power of insinuation) that if she could make him the heir he would make her a rich widow. Lady Mary responded in the style of her priggish heroine Princess Docile. Her 'very clear and possitive answer' was that, should she be so unhappy as to outlive her husband, 'I do not beleive he will leave me in your power; but was I sure of the contrary, no Interest nor no Necessity shall ever make me act against my Honor or Conscience, and I plainly tell you that I will never persuade your Father to do any thing for you till I think you deserve it.' This left Edward no option but a reprise of promises of reform.

By mutual consent, it seems, they then set money matters aside. Gaily, Edward deployed the knowledge he had gained during his chequered existence, and showed off his command of 'most of the modern Languages'. (He said he knew Arabic and Hebrew too.) She gave him about £12 for his journey and received various promises in return. He would maintain his alias; he would write to her from Paris; he would stay only one night there and proceed for 'six posts' towards Flanders; he would await, and act on, Wortley's instructions.[43]

It was more than six weeks before he wrote, and four more before she had an address. It was Wortley who supplied the address, in a letter filled with the praises of Lord Bute.[44] It took a year or more for the next episodes in her son's story to filter to Lady Mary's ears. He had gone straight back to his Montelimar circle and related to them how Lady Mary had summoned him to Orange, how high he stood in her favour, and how 'he had another name much more considerable than that he appear'd with'. He left behind a strong impression that he must be a confidence trickster.

Later that year, after unspecified misconduct in Paris, he returned to London, at either Wortley's bidding (as he hinted to Lady Mary) or

---

[42] See pp. 304–5.   [43] *CL* ii. 278, 285–8 (MWM, 10 June [1742]).   [44] *CL* ii. 288–91.

Carteret's (as he told Montagu).[45] There he was first imprisoned for debt and then laid low by illness, so that he could not obey his father's command to leave the country. Wortley was much at Wharncliffe in the summer of 1742, and recorded his fastest time ever for the 171 miles between it and London: two days' brisk riding, amounting to twenty-eight hours in the saddle. (He was sixty-four, and did not intend to enrich any heir just yet.) He grudgingly supplied his son with £25, but refused to meet his lawyer to discuss long-term arrangements. Edward, finding cousin Montagu disappointingly occupied with his own marriage, retired to Hammersmith 'for the air' (and also to avoid re-arrest). He left Anderson to receive his letters at a coffee-house near Charing Cross. Whereas he had earlier striven to persuade reluctant relations to place him in the army, he now argued that he had a duty to comply with *their* desire to place him there. Carteret, he said, was most favourably disposed, and was consulting with the brothers Newcastle and Pelham, who advised him to stay in England until a commission materialized. He feared Wortley, who wanted him gone, would disbelieve this account.

His debts still prevented him from the usual attendance on his prospective patrons, and would effectively prevent his taking up any proffered commission. He was anxious in case his father might stop his allowance once he had the commission. He hoped his creditors would sign a 'letter of licence', and that 'that Woman' would, in exchange for £50 per annum, persuade *her* creditors to do the same, with some 'Substantial man to be bound under a Penalty that she shall contract no debt'. He hoped Wortley would be impressed at seeing him thus managing his own affairs, meting out to the woman the kind of admonishment so often given himself. He hoped, too, once the commission was in the bag, to solicit Carteret for some sinecure 'in which I should have no occasion to appear, which [might] be accepted of and executed by Mr Anderson'. This small place was to solve his financial problems *and* recompense Anderson for the penalties he had incurred by loyalty. In the event it was another year before Edward secured his commission: as cornet in the Seventh Hussars, dragoons commanded by Sir John Cope.[46]

[45] *CL* ii. 311, 314–15, 308.
[46] Wh MS 110; EWM jr. to Montagu, 3 Oct. 1742, MS Mo 2840. 8; *CL* ii. 312 n. 3.

25

May 1742–August 1746

Avignon: 'rather distant from Ostentation than in poverty'[1]

DISPLACED and unsettled, Lady Mary had been making her random sojourns briefer and briefer. In May 1742 she reached Avignon, which as part of the Papal States (not yet of France) was a sanctuary from the war.[2] Almost on her arrival she told Jean-Robert Tronchin that she might not stay for long: the lovely houses, gardens, and walks, even the good company, might not outweigh the disadvantage of the icy mistral which often blew there. Six months later she told him she was there by predestination. From Calvinist Geneva to Papal Avignon was quite a change; but, anti-Catholic as Lady Mary was, she admired Pope Benedict XIV. The town was full of Spaniards and full of Jacobites; it was French enough to draw from her a crack about French incapacity for friendship; she missed her beloved Italy—but she did not know where else to go. She found the locals, the Spaniards, and a handful of resident English ladies, all polished and conversible.[3] Even the Jacobite Duke of Ormond seemed 'quite inoffensive', though she later, privately, called him covetous and vain. She railed against the war, which had now engulfed Italy; but while she told Michiel that she was philosophically detached from her surroundings, she told Lady Pomfret that the assemblies, suppers, and comedies at Avignon were quite good. She did not really intend to stay, but as months stretched out into years she found the place pleased her more and more.[4]

She sent Wortley fewer details about Avignon than other towns she had

---

[1] *CL* ii. 319.

[2] She agreed with Hervey in the unfashionable opinion that Britain's support of Maria Theresa was misjudged and quixotic (Hervey to MWM, 31/20 May, Hervey MSS 47/2. 123).

[3] Identifiable friends she made were the duchesse de Crillon, and the marquise de Fortia, who had married into a leading local family with Spanish roots (Rigaud to MWM, 30 Apr. 1762, H MS 78. 233–4).

[4] *CL* ii. 278–84, 289–90, 296; CB 10.

stayed in, until he asked. Her house was high up in the town, next door to a convent. (She said this was the most reputatable of the town's fourteen nunneries; but proximity did nothing to improve her opinion of the religious life.)[5] She soon revised her first impression of Avignon as cheap. The climate was pleasant (except for the mistral), the wine and the mutton excellent, but other provisions poor and dear on account of the sandy delta soil. She had to do without milk or butter: the local cattle produced none, being (she thought) too badly fed.[6] There was little trade (except smuggling) or manufacture (except illicit printing of books banned elsewhere). Both France and Italy protected their own industries by prohibiting imports from Avignon. The nobility were snobbish but hospitable: several kept 'a constant open Table', relying on produce from their own estates.

Local government, Lady Mary found, was modelled on that of ancient Rome. Two consuls (one a nobleman) were elected each year in keen competition. They presided over a town council engaged in constant power struggles with the court of the Papal Vice-Legate. When Lady Mary first arrived, she ignored this ecclesiastical enclave; in 1744 a new Vice-Legate, 'Young, rich, and handsome', put a different complexion on town–court relations.[7]

During her first Avignon summer, 1742, she wrote few and short letters: they might never arrive, and she was worried about her eyesight. She wrote kindly to her daughter, but she felt sure she had lost her real affection, and wanted no dutiful pretence of it. While the war raged over Europe, Avignon seemed less given to political gossip than anywhere else she knew. During the warm evenings Lady Mary often walked up to the ancient citadel, the Rocher-des-Doms, to enjoy the 'fresh breeze and the most beautiful land prospect I ever saw'. Up there with the swifts and the jackdaws, she saw the rock-ribbed city falling steeply away from her feet. Bleached in the haze below her, the territories of Avignon, with parts of Provence, Languedoc, Venaisin, and Dauphiné, stretched to the far mountains of Auvergne; near at hand lay little chequered fields and vineyards, and 'the windings of two great Rivers', the Rhône and the Durance.[8]

In October she spent some days at Lyons, for the sake of seeing James Stuart Mackenzie, who was on his way home to catch the reconvening of parliament. With this young man she had achieved an easy intimacy. He

---

[5] *CL* ii. 320, 420. She thought convents as corrupting as an education on stage: a view supported by Casanova's hearing 'there was not a nun in Venice whom one could not have for money' (Casanova 1967: ii. 420).

[6] *CL* ii. 298, 366, 372.   [7] *CL* ii. 320–1, 331, 336. She also explained the local legal system.

[8] *CL* ii. 315, 336–7. To EWM (not to Lady Pomfret) she ranked the Wharncliffe prospect above this.

pleasantly surprised her by reporting how his brother, Lord Bute, 'frequently said amongst his companions that he was still as much in Love with his Wife as before he marry'd her'. She and Mackenzie marked their reunion by a double letter to their mutual friend Chiara Michiel. Michiel was in Spain with her husband's embassy, spectator of the last years of the mad king Philip V. Lady Mary wrote for her sketches of people she might meet there; but her share of the joint letter is chiefly compliment and high-flown political idealism—a contrast to Mackenzie's comic fantasia about her using force and violence to get him to write at all. This gleam of fun and playfulness contrasts with her either conventional or fiercely anti-militaristic messages to Wortley, Hervey, Lady Pomfret, Lady Oxford, and even Tronchin. She cherished the idea that, though she was stuck at Avignon, she might catch Michiel herself on the wing one day.[9] Her close friends were few, and were each in their way remarkable.

Winter was uneventful: November as warm as summer, December clear and cold with a single, astonishing snowfall around Christmas. Carnival was like Carnival everywhere: masked balls, amateur theatricals, and gambling (with its attendant quarrels and obsessions, which she found harder and harder to take). In February 1743 there was an epidemic of fever, not dangerous but a wretched experience. Lady Mary, who did not escape it, observed that bleeding, the doctors' remedy, merely prolonged the disease. This infection spanned the width of war-torn Europe; her daughter and elder granddaughter caught it in England. Lady Mary traced its origin to the terrible siege of Prague.

William Turner was 'struck with the Palsy' this winter: probably a stroke, it kept him bedridden for months and left one hand permanently affected. He put it down to the air (perhaps that notorious wind). Lady Mary thought the trouble was his refusal to adapt his eating and drinking habits to a hot climate which made much red meat and strong wine unhealthy, even though William did not actually get drunk. However, when she hinted this to him he took offence, thinking it a typical employer's idea that servants ought to eat and drink less.[10]

The spring brought transients to Avignon: Spanish officers (including the exiled Jacobite Duke of Berwick), and a young couple, Godfrey and Diana Bosville, whose fathers were both coal-mining associates of Wortley. They let it be known that they were on their way, war or no war, to settle at Turin. (Diana Bosville, in fact, had a lover in the British Mediterranean fleet.) Lady Mary invited them to dinner, offered them every civility, and

---

[9] *CL* ii. 293–4, 302, 304, 309, 318, 406; cf. 427.   [10] *CL* ii. 296, 298–303, 324–5.

admired Mrs Bosville's spirit in preparing for a mountain crossing (which in the end they exchanged for passage to Genoa in a man-of-war). That mountain route was well remembered; Lady Mary may have sighed as she wrote, 'tis necessary to be young and Gay for such projects; all mine terminate in Quiet'.[11]

Hervey had been an assiduous correspondent since his fall from power. Her first winter in Avignon he brought her up to date with the warfare of wits by sending her 'eight Pacquets of the most entertaining things stirring in London'. These included Pope's *New Dunciad* (in which Colley Cibber replaced Theobald as Dulness's son), *A Letter from Mr. Cibber to Mr. Pope*, and Hervey's own *Letter to Mr. C—b—r, On his Letter to Mr. P.* He was gratified when she instantly recognized his anonymous hand.[12]

That summer she had the grief of receiving his last letter—one of the last uses he made of his pen. It is a farewell full of stoic calm, opening and closing with measured dignity. 'The last stages of an infirm life are filthy roads', he began. He ended, 'May all your ways (as Solomon says of wisdom) be ways of pleasentness, and all your paths peace; and when your dissolution must come, may it be like that of your lucky workman. Adieu.' It was typical of the age to invoke the mortality of the hearer as well as the speaker; whether Hervey had in mind an actual or an ideal 'lucky workman', the analogy has a *gravitas* strongly in contrast with Pope's habit of equating the demise of his women friends with the 'death' of sexual climax.[13]

Hervey died but the world went on. George II satisfied his long-held aspirations by commanding at the battle of Dettingen (which was won, with terrible losses, because of a mistake by the enemy). A Paris–Avignon courier was murdered and robbed; bubonic plague seeped northwards through Italy, spreading terror before it. Lady Mary sent William to a nearby spa to treat his chronic localized paralysis, and received her most rational letter from her sister Mar 'since her Disorder'.[14] Lady Oxford regaled her with details of Hervey's will, especially its shocking rudeness to his wife. Edward Wortley Montagu, junior, failed to mobilize in time to fight with King George, but followed him abroad 'just a week after the news of the Battle came to London'. Elated with his new commission, he sent his mother a letter so stylish that she thought he had help with it, though his 'saying nothing has been done without him, when I know nothing he has done' struck a familiar note.

---

[11] *CL* ii. 303, 305–6.   [12] 31/20 Dec. 1742, 15/4 Apr. 1743, Hervey MSS 135, 137.

[13] 29/18 June 1743, *CL* ii. 306; Pope e.g. 'To Mrs. M.B. on her Birth-day', TE vi. 245–6.

[14] Browning 1994: 139; *CL* ii. 306–8, 324. MWM had probably written to Lady Mar about some of her old Jacobite acquaintance. A deed of 9 Oct. 1741 promising to make up arrears in her and her daughter's income mentions her 'growing Infirmitys' (Monson MSS 286/12/8/10).

Meanwhile the model youth, Mackenzie, had slipped from grace. He fell in love with the Italian dancer Barberina Campanini, pursued her to Venice, and 'tremblingly' proposed marriage to her. This time he did not stop to make contact with Lady Mary, but he wrote to enlist her support and justify his love in the kind of high-flown, idealistic terms she might have been expected to admire. She wrote back sharply, arguing that if Barberina truly loved him she would sacrifice her principles for his prospects and settle for being his mistress. Lady Mary kept his letter, and by his assertion that he was old enough to judge for himself she wrote, '*The poor boy is about nineteen.*' (He was six years older.) To Michiel she covered up the true reason for his journey, blaming it on the recent death of his uncle John, Duke of Argyll. The new duke, uncle Archibald, made it his business to separate the star-crossed, and cross-class, lovers for ever. They were forcibly moved on: she from Venice to Berlin (where she was contracted to dance), he from Berlin, when he followed her there. He fell dangerously ill; but he recovered.[15]

❧

Lady Mary continued her evening visits to Rocher-des-Doms, the acropolis of Avignon. Among its ruined buildings there remained entire only 'an ancient round tower', in use until recently. One day she remarked, in the presence of Avignon's First Consul, that if it were hers she 'would turn it into a belvedere'. The consul relayed this to the town council; at his suggestion, they voted, '*nemine contradicente*', to grant her the use and enjoyment of the tower for her lifetime. The news was brought her by both consuls together. It was more than four years since she had last had (at Twickenham) somewhere to show her fancy on her own ground, and she lost no time. Within two months she had capped her tower with a dome, thus producing 'a little rotunda'. She had her books carried up the steep path to this impromptu temple, and took to spending most of her evenings there in her 'monastic' studies. Now, failing Hervey, she sent requests for English books to her son-in-law, Bute, as well as to Wortley.[16]

An apt finishing touch for even a modest pleasure dome would be some lasting words. As her workmen patched the tower, Lady Mary amused herself 'with patching up an Inscription', though she did not seriously mean to display it. Instead of words about the view, or about the temple of Diana which had once stood on the site, she chose an epitaph: Abraham Cowley's Latin epitaph on himself. By means of a few changes—'Couleius' to 'Maria'

[15] Stuart 1899: 52–4; *CL* ii. 311–13, 318, 341; Namier and Brooke 1964.

[16] *CL* ii. 315–16, 336–7, 360, 366. A hermitage on the rock was mentioned this century (Marcel 1912: 39 f.). Today nothing remains (information from Joan and Michael Partridge).

and other gender shifts—she transformed herself into a recently dead poet, and her belvedere into a kind of tomb. The result, if Englished on the model of Addison's Englishing of Cowley, says she has been 'With decent poverty content, | Her hours of ease not idly spent'; yet 'oh! how small | A spot of earth is now her all.'

Lady Mary showed her Latin version to local acquaintances, including the Archbishop of Avignon; they took it as original, and received it admiringly. Copying it for Wortley (who must, like her, have remembered when the *Tatler* printed Addison's English version), she commented, 'You will know how I pick'd up these Verses, thô the Arch Bishop did not.' To tell her husband she was dead and buried was perhaps even odder than to tell other people so. Wortley was indeed disturbed: not by the mention of death so much as by the mention of poverty. He imagined the inscription would appear publicly on her dome, and he hated the idea. She assured him she would never have had it set up without his approval, and that the Latin word *pauperie*, in context, signified someone not poor but only unostentatious. His concern, it seemed, was not about how she felt but exclusively about what people might think.[17]

Her monastic employments included writing. To her years at Avignon belongs her graceful French-verse refusal to an impromptu love-song addressed to her by an unnamed count. She may have drafted here her major surviving fiction, 'La Princesse Docile'. At least, she indulged in philosophical speculation about the chances of life on other planets. Fontenelle had made this a common topic; but her Avignon letter about it parallels a passage (later dropped) in a draft of 'Docile'.

Another genre she tried was that of letters between the dead and living: she replied in French to a letter supposedly received from a feminist thinker of a bygone age, whom she calls only 'Mademoiselle'. She is fairly critical of her foremother's book, almost certainly Anna Maria van Schurman's Latin treatise translated into English in 1659 as *The Learned Maid; or, Whether a Maid may be a Scholar?* As one might expect, she endorses Schurman's message but finds its style outmoded. She makes believe to have received a letter from Schurman, modern and relaxed in style: she plays with the deliciously incongruous notion that Schurman in the Elysian Fields has been learning from Petronius.[18] A tempting explanation for this *jeu d'esprit* would

---

[17] *CL* ii. 315–17, 319, 331.

[18] *E&P*, 306, 165–7; to Mackenzie, *CL* ii. 268–9; *RW* 127–32, 134, 189–90. Schurman asks whether learning is '*convenient*, that is, expedient, fit, decent' for a woman, and answers, 'Whatsoever *perfects* and *adorns* the intellect of Man, that is fit and decent for a Christian woman' (1659: 1, 15). The *Satyricon* of Petronius, which turns on the anger of Priapus as the *Odyssey* turns on the anger of Poseidon, is worlds away.

be that some kindred spirit of Lady Mary's (probably a woman) had exercised her invention on a letter in Schurman's voice. But who might have done this is unknown.

In spring 1746, when Lady Mary's belvedere in the former temple of Diana was two years old and she was plunged in anxiety over the Jacobite rebellion, came an incident highlighting her local standing as a savante. The French were excavating another temple of Diana and a complete ancient site near Nîmes. Medals and other artefacts from the dig were supposed to belong to the French Crown, but many made their way to Avignon for sale. A peasant brought Lady Mary 'a very curious piece' made of some unidentified alloy, depicting 'the Figures of Justice, a Roman officer, and several other Groupes', guaranteed as coming from 'very deep amongst the ruins' of a Roman palace. She showed this illicit treasure to several people at Avignon, but none could tell what the object was designed for or what it might be worth. She meant to send it to Wortley 'by the first opertunity'; but it is not known if it arrived.[19]

Her life-after-death was not entirely placid. Next winter, 1743–4, gave her opportunities for science (tracking the progress of a brilliant comet) and renewed local political embroilment. The duchesse de Crillon persuaded her to join a party of ladies on a foray to Nîmes for a lavish entertainment which Freemasons of that town were holding for the duc de Richelieu, governor of Languedoc. There was to be a grand supper and a masked ball. Illicit Protestantism was rife in the province; a service had been raided a few days earlier, and 'their minister and about a dozen of his Congregation were seiz'd and imprison'd'. Lady Mary, a distinguished citizen of a Protestant power, 'had not been in the Town 2 hours when I was visited by two of the most considerable of the Huguenots, who came to beg of me with Tears to speak in their Favour to the Duke of Richlieu, saying none of the Catholics would do it and the Protestants durst not, and that God had sent me for their Protection'.

She was moved, willing to try and help, though not hopeful about the outcome. Perhaps she thought of her old friend Marie La Vie. She went to the ball in mask and concealing cloak instead of formal dress, to increase that freedom which her petitioners felt sure her sex, rank, and nationality would give her. She found there was no need to seek out the duke (a great-nephew of the famous cardinal): he had 'heard a great deal' about her, and made a point of seeking her. She took proper time for compliments, and then to enlist the duke's aid in securing her exemption from the *droit d'aubaine* (so

---

[19] *CL* ii. 368.

that if she were to die on French soil, her possessions and personal trinkets would not after all be forfeit to the Crown). At the right moment she made her request for freeing the Huguenots. The duke told her he was no bigot; 'he pity'd them as much as I did, but his orders from Court were to send them to the Gallys.' However, as a crowning compliment to her, he would beg their freedom himself on his return to Paris. If his later memoirs can be believed, he stage-managed his whole handling of this incident, intending clemency from the outset but putting on a fine show of rigour before securing the Protestants' pardon.[20]

This adventure had both bad and good effects for Lady Mary. When wind of it reached Avignon, she found herself regarded as a Protestant champion, and therefore by Jacobites like Marjory Hay as a spy and 'a dangerous Person'. (Hay was sister-in-law of Lord Mar's first wife, and had a kind of hereditary enmity to Lady Mary.) When Lady Mary reported her latest outrages to Lady Oxford, the latter tried to defend her, and a rare, brief coolness ensued between the two friends. Meanwhile some British people cold-shouldered Lady Mary; others set traps to make her reveal her secret political agenda.[21] This, which began as a minor annoyance, contained the seed of her terminal disgust with Avignon.

On the other side, her Nîmes adventure gave her (as well as a happy sense of self-approbation) something of value in the spying line: intelligence from Richelieu's own lips that the French government intended to back the Jacobites in invading Britain. Lady Mary must have returned from the Freemasons' party with this privileged information burning a hole in her brain. (In fact, the English government learned it, from a different source, almost on the same date.) She could not expect such information to arrive safely via the post. With Hervey dead and Sir Robert Walpole out of office, she chose her husband to receive it; but she waited nearly two months for a trustworthy messenger.

When one of these presented himself it was not in the way she would have chosen. Mary and William again gave notice. They had had enough of abroad; they were going back to Yorkshire. Lady Mary represented to them

---

[20] *CL* ii. 319, 321–3, 361. It is tempting to ascribe to MWM *The Travels and Adventures of Mademoiselle de Richelieu*, a London novel of this year, ostensibly translated from French by a Mr Erskine, with a cross-dressing, lesbian traveller-heroine (Woodward 1993: 854–5). But too much in it is alien to MWM's thinking: respect for Jesuit theology, subordination of reason to faith, padding to spin out the work, and a happy ending which rewards (unorthodox) virtue.

[21] 'Mrs Hay' (MWM ignored her Jacobite title, Lady Inverness) was a Catholic convert. Mar had allegedly plotted her husband's ruin in the 1720s; for his action in 1724 see p. 238. She was joined at Avignon in summer 1747 by her brother James Murray (now Jacobite Earl of Dunbar), who had helped her persecute Lady Mar. She was related by marriage to Lady Oxford, to whom Lady Mary always took an apolitical tone (*CL* ii. 325, 328–9, 330; Atterbury 1869: ii. 19, 56–7; Tayler 1938: 63, 83, 139).

that, with war imminent between England and France, travel costs would be artificially inflated. William replied that 'he had rather be a chimney sweeper in London than a Lord in France'; he thought, too, that his native air would restore his health. They were bent on leaving at once, before England and France became actual enemies. Neither of them mentioned that Mary was pregnant for the third time; having promised Lady Mary after their second child was born that it would never happen again, they apparently feared to confess. France did declare war a very few days after these conversations. The Turners declined Lady Mary's final offer, the very morning they were to leave. They found the journey much harder and more costly than they had expected; they waited ten days at Calais for official clearance to cross the Channel. Lady Mary had arranged for Mary to receive on arrival a £5 present out of her allowance; but by summer 1745 they were reportedly in distress.

Their mistress long remembered the experience of being 'without servants in a strange country'. But she went over (like other expatriates) to local servants, a 'man and maid'. The man, Jean François Gremaud, known as Fribourg, came to her from the service of a lawyer named Rigaud (who had seen Lady Mary in company and never forgot her). Within a couple of years she found these two servants had followed their predecessors' example. 'They are marry'd and she big with child. I find it impossible to have a Family small enough to consist of reasonable Creatures.' Still, Fribourg at least, a 'very faithfull good Servant', stayed with her till 1761.[22]

Worry about her son did not abate. He felt his fellow cornets were his social inferiors, and wanted an 'Equipage' that would mark him out. His mother advised his father to have no truck with this exorbitant desire. In spring 1744 he was back in London, where he joined the Divan or Turkish Club. Members were probably attracted to this self-consciously orientalist institution (which titled its minutes *Al-Koran*) by two libertine motives: Islam was (self-evidently) non-Christian, and it was polygamous, which to English minds meant sexual licence.[23] Edward was making some present mileage out of his childhood months in Turkey.

Most of spring and summer 1744 was cold and wet. A Jacobite invasion of Britain fizzled out. In reply to social news from home, Lady Mary wrote mostly about the European war. Avignon and Malta, she heard, were the only spots unafraid of invading troops. Even in her Avignon refuge the war

---

[22] *CL* ii. 324–5, 330–1, 338, 340, 359–60, 368, 463, iii. 148; Fribourg to MWM, 3 Nov. 1761, H MS 78. 231–2. He is called both manservant and steward. His wife (not MWM's Huguenot housekeeper Mari Anna) drops from the record; probably she died.

[23] *CL* ii. 317, 328 n. 2.

doubled food prices. Don Philip (younger son of the Spanish king, who laid claim to territories in Italy) passed through Avignon with much pomp and ceremony. The Jacobite leader Lord Marischal made a longer visit, and Lady Mary demonstrated her oft-boasted ability to rise above politics by finding that she enjoyed his company. She could respect his principles without sharing them, and find something romantic in his stubborn loyalty to a lost cause. To Michiel, she rejoiced at the renewed alliance of Britain and Venice, and imagined a world in which national quarrels might be settled by means of card-games instead of battles. Now that England and France were at war, she could no longer get English newspapers. Sailings ceased between Dover and Calais; letters had to go via Holland, and were often delayed or lost.

English correspondents still supplied some personal if not public news. Lady Pomfret's daughter Lady Sophia made a grand marriage.[24] Lady Bute gave birth to a son and heir, 'a fine thriving child'. This news was a relief, for the pregnancy had overrun its due date.[25] One of Lady Gower's daughters turned out to have made a secret marriage: the news broke when she 'fell in Labour'. Lady Oxford, who also had a new grandchild, embarked with Lady Mary's warm approval on ambitious improvements at Welbeck Abbey: this would retard the clearing of her late husband's 'Great Debts', but would ensure Welbeck's place as the primary seat of her heirs. She kept Lady Mary a stake in English life by buying her three tickets in a lottery for Joint-Stock Annuities.[26]

In August Lady Mary heard, as gossip, that Pope was dead: a piece of news which neither Wortley nor Lady Oxford had mentioned. She was curious about his will. Although he could control the use of his rented Twickenham house for only a year after his death, she badly wanted to know who would enjoy it for that year. When Lady Oxford sent her the will, copied from a newspaper, she found it 'more reasonable and less vain than I expected from him'.[27] Did the idea of returning home now present itself afresh to her? Twickenham without Pope! It might have been a tempting thought.

Early that month Chiara Michiel travelled home from Madrid to Venice.

---

[24] *CL* ii. 333; iii. 265. Her husband, the elderly Lord Carteret, held his position as Secretary of State only until the end of 1745.

[25] *CL* ii. 340, 344. She had two daughters living and had borne two sons, both dead.

[26] *CL* ii. 328–9, 331–6, 339, 345, 349. MWM's friend and her husband met this autumn, on business concerning the late Lord Oxford's MSS (342 and n. 3).

[27] Lady Oxford had supposed MWM would not want the news, 'knowing the Contempt you have for worthless People' (*CL* ii. 339 and n. 2, 345). The lease of Pope's house is unmentioned in his will (Pope 1986: ii. 506–8).

Lady Mary wanted so much to see her *en route* that she sent a note to await her arrival at Nîmes, and for some time kept a post-chaise in readiness to dash thither at a moment's notice. But no meeting materialized. Apart from simply being lonely, she had wanted to talk about Mackenzie to Michiel—who had now heard from someone the truth about the Barberina Campanini affair. These two represented the kind of intimate friendship which was the breath of life to Lady Mary, and which Avignon did not provide.

Friends, now so rare, became more and more precious. She fretted dreadfully over news that Lady Oxford was ill. 'If I am so unhappy to survive you,' she wrote, 'I shall look upon my selfe as a Widow and an Orphan, having no Freind in this World but your selfe.' She besought her with tears to take care of herself. Then, poring over Dutch newspapers in default of English ones, she learned of the death of another old friend, Sarah, Duchess of Marlborough. Again she was curious about the will, and no wonder: she had been privy to Sarah's years of restlessly unmaking and remaking it. That winter (the coldest she had known at Avignon) she learned for the first time the full story of her son's behaviour following their meeting. She wrote at once, angrily and self-righteously, to tell him such promise-breaking was unworthy of a gentleman: 'tatling and lying are Qualitys not to be forgiven even in a chambermaid.' Edward was back with his regiment in Bruges. Having no address for him, she sent her letter via Wortley, who then insisted that she keep up the correspondence.[28]

In her present mood she was ready to write her son off. Even the first spring weather of 1745 elicited from her no comments but gloomy ones. But in May there began a sequence of events, not all pleasant in themselves, which galvanized her back to life. First came the battle of Fontenoy, a terribly destructive one for the British forces. Reading about it (perhaps in Dutch), Lady Mary found 'I cannot so far forget I am a Mother as not to be under concern for my Son.' It was weeks before she saw a French list of dead and wounded, and found him mercifully absent. While she was still in suspense came news from Lady Oxford that the lottery had yielded her a prize worth £50—and from her daughter that Thoresby had been burnt to the ground. Her nephew Kingston, who was there at the time, had risen to the occasion. His papers and many possessions were saved. But the house—the scene of Lady Mary's self-education, of her first writing, her love for Hermenesilda, her adolescent angst shared with her sister—was gone. She indulged 'many Refflections on the Vanity of all Worldly Possessions'. She took some comfort in the idea of being 'entirely detach'd' in spirit from such

[28] *CL* ii. 340–1, 346–9, 350 n. 2.

concerns. She later reminded herself that Thoresby lacked the important amenity of 'prospect', and thought her nephew would do well to abandon this unlucky spot and rebuild elsewhere.[29]

She could not detach herself from family feeling. She still wanted a list of *English* casualties at Fontenoy. When, however, a letter arrived from Wortley passing on highlights from their son's account of the battle, her response was disenchanted. Edward was alive, but he was still the same Edward. His breathless narrative of his conduct under fire seemed to her typical of his 'Idle vain way of talking of himselfe'. He had received no serious injuries, but one 'shot in my cloaths' and another which tore off his shoulder-knot; he had been 'twice dismounted by the Cannon'. Lady Mary could not but wonder whether this was 'entirely invented'. Could the wind from a passing cannon ball throw a man off a horse? But at least her son had not disgraced himself, like two local French gentlemen 'who ran away while their Companys fought'.

Wortley's next communication entirely won her round. It was a package: extracts from accounts by Edward and by his commanding officer (General James Sinclair, Royal Scots), Wortley's tally of distinguished men who had commended their son's conduct, and his précis of what he wanted her to write to Edward. She was impressed, not by the great men's testimonials but by her son's improved style. Her letter written to Wortley's specifications began, 'I am very well pleas'd with the accounts I have had of your behaviour this Campaign.' It did not maintain such a generous-spirited tone, but slipped into the usual advice and warnings, even a reminder of his failure to write to her.[30]

Her anxiety was assuaged, but the war still gripped her life. The recent run of French victories had 'given them an Air of Triumph that is very difficult for an English Heart to suffer'. She had perhaps the only such English heart in Avignon, all the other Britons being devoted Jacobites. She was ceaselessly, covertly watched, 'as a very deep Polititian'. She found Avignon more and more disagreeable, and longed to return to Italy; she watched for opportunities to get away, but could not find one. As the summer wore on she was 'stunn'd here every day with a Succession of ill news'. She told Wortley this in a letter written in August 1745, when it was known that Prince Charles Edward, whose jewels she had once admired, had sailed for Scotland. After that no more survive, to Wortley or anyone else, till January 1746. Nothing is known of how she weathered the time of the Jacobite

---

[29] *CL* ii. 352–4, 359, 428. Thoresby had suffered from fire before it was completed.
[30] *CL* ii. 355–8.

rebellion. In its later stages she said she was 'as totally ignorant of all English Affairs as if I was the Inhabitant of another Planet'.[31]

The war or wars were not the only hindrance her letters faced. Wortley had left his large house in Cavendish Square; the Westminster rate-books show a hiatus of a year or more before he settled in a smaller house in the same square. Not only that: he set out for the spa of Pyrmont near Hanover on 22 July/2 August 1745, and stayed away until December. He did not tell Lady Mary this, but left her to learn it from a postal intermediary.[32]

In the days of their courtship he had gone abroad for his health, leaving her without news of him. This time too his health was his object. He found, as he explained later in another querulous memo to the English government, that at Pyrmont 'he had his health better than for several years before'. Nevertheless, when it looked as if Bonnie Prince Charlie's soldiers would reach Yorkshire, he cut short his stay and returned to offer 'his best Assistance against the Rebels'. This patriotic intention was foiled 'by an Overturn on the Road from Harwich', which left him too badly 'lamed' to travel, even by coach.[33]

Speculation as to Lady Mary's reasons for living abroad has often focused on her failure to meet up with her husband when he too crossed the Channel. A related question needs asking: did he conceal this trip from her lest (in spite of her frequent assertions that she could not get away from Avignon in wartime) she should have proposed trying to meet him?

The decisive fighting of the '1745' rebellion took place in spring 1746, well after Lady Mary, daily 'frighted with false reports' and anxiously scanning foreign newspapers, had hoped it might be all over. As the Jacobite march southward neared its furthest point (Derby), Lady Oxford chose to stand her ground at Welbeck while 'All Notts. fled with great Precipitation'. In Avignon spring brought 'the hopes of Peace', which Lady Mary hardly dared believe in. The exchange of letters with England mysteriously became easier again. Lady Bute must have been feeling more warmly towards her mother, for it was now that she began keeping the letters she received.

Lady Bute needed her mother's affection and backing, because she found herself at odds with her father. Nearly ten years married, the once vivacious 'Sylvia' had become increasingly unhappy at Mount Stuart, Isle of Bute. She was cut off in various ways from contact with her friends in London: by the

---

[31] *CL* ii. 358–9, 364, 375.

[32] Before leaving he had despatched to her (through this intermediary, the banker Henry Muilman) Sarah Fielding's *David Simple* (*CL* ii. 358–60).

[33] Immediately after this, and twenty eight years after his dismissal from Turkey, he composed his last extant detailed bill of complaint about it to officialdom (Halsband MSS, draft).

Firth of Clyde and days of difficult road travel; by a general shortage of cash; by her husband's loss of his representative parliamentary seat and her father's move from the larger house which had accommodated the family on visits. She had learned to join in Lord Bute's gardening and botanical interests; but still she was lonely. Anxiety and suspense during the Jacobite rebellion must have aggravated her situation; Lady Mary found her letters so melancholy as to be deeply upsetting.[34] (No doubt they reminded her of her sister.)

Now Lady Bute had an old Twickenham friend badgering Wortley on her behalf about financial help to bring her family south. This was Lady Frances Shirley: unmarried, fortyish, and rumoured to have had a 'romantic attachment' of some years with Lord Chesterfield.[35] She was refreshingly outspoken in her comments on Wortley, whom she thought 'pretty steady where he is to part with his money'. She sent Lady Bute a very funny account of her elaborate efforts to soften him up. Her every gambit met a monosyllabic reply. At last she wondered aloud whether he 'knew any pretty place' near Twickenham suitable for the Butes. 'No, he said. In short I had some dificulty to command my self.' Wortley went straight from her to tell somebody else 'he wonder'd every body did not like best living upon their own Estates, for his part he never was so happy as in Yorkshire'. But Lady Frances meant to renew the attack. 'I will then make Your London Scheme intirely my own and beg him to approve.'

It does not appear that Lady Mary was any more supportive now than she had been over Lady Bute's marriage. She told Wortley she was 'much mortify'd to find my Daughter has not follow'd your opinion in every thing' and that she was strongly advising her 'to consult you on all occasions as her surest and best Freind'. As before, she ascribed any filial indiscretion to 'those by whom she is directed', and referred to Wortley the question of what direction she might offer herself. She did draw the line at telling Lady Bute she had 'any way fail'd in the Duty she owes you'.

The Butes did move south this summer. They took a house in Twickenham (in Montpelier Row, east of the village), and a London house (at the low rent of £45 annually), where their next child was born. To this they won Wortley's consent, however grudging: by 20 July Lady Mary was 'exceedingly pleas'd that my Daughter's behaviour has your aprobation'. She was equally pleased—and grateful—that he had granted her request to make a

---

[34] *CL* ii. 362 and n. 2, 363, 366. Bute's father had moved the family seat 5 miles out from the town of Rothesay in order to lay out gardens.

[35] Chesterfield 1932: i. 76. MWM kept a couple of poems to Lady Frances, whose brother Sewallis she knew as lover of Lady Vane and husband of Lady Walpole (H MS 255. 62–4; see 521).

will leaving Lady Bute her jewels and silver toilet set (which were legally his, not hers). But the duc de Richelieu had not yet acted on his promise to get her exempted from *droit d'aubaine*.[36]

Edward's behaviour at this time was more acceptable than usual to his parents. In autumn 1745 he had been made aide-de-camp to the British commander-in-chief in the Low Countries. In spring Lady Mary received his latest account of his favour with his superiors, including the governor of the region, Prince Charles of Lorraine. Though she was not certain how much of this she could believe, it pleased her so much that she answered it kindly and encouragingly without even consulting her husband.

By then events had moved on. Edward's service with Prince Charles dated from before the siege of Brussels. When the city surrendered, on 4 May 1746, he was captured by the French and imprioned at Liège. This brought a new and blameless need for money: for a ransom. In this emergency he approached other sources besides his father: the Duke of Newcastle and his cousin Edward Montagu. He too must have hoped peace was coming, for he began angling for a diplomatic post.[37]

Weeks of heavy rain that spring brought on floods in Avignon. People living lower in the town than Lady Mary were trapped in their houses for two days. Since the collapse of the Jacobite invasion, the place was full of 'Scotch and Irish Rebells', 'miserable Refugees'. She thought the Vice-Legate protected them. At every social event she heard them talking treason: 'improper to be listen'd to and dangerous to contradict'. That month she set out on what she described to Wortley as a little trip for health reasons, 'into the high Languedoc'.[38] Really she was looking for somewhere else to live, somewhere with intellectual stimulation.

She found it impossible to travel incognita in France, where strict official surveillance was imposed at 'every Town of passage'. From Montpellier she took to the 'Bateau de Poste' on the great Languedoc Canal. At Toulouse the Archibishop promptly invited her to supper. It was there that she came on *Lettres amusantes et critiques*, 1743 (probably by François de La Chesnaye-Desbois), and in it, apparently, a portrait of herself. The letters are addressed to the cultivated 'Myledy W.', who has strong views on many topics, especially English literature. The discovery did not please her. 'When I print,

---

[36] *CL* ii. 361, 369 and nn., 372–3, 374; Lovat-Fraser 1919: 45.

[37] *CL* ii. 368 and n. 1, 372 and n. 3; Gibson to EWM, 26 Sept. 1745, H MS 78. 22–3. Huntington MS MO 2842.

[38] *CL* ii. 372, 373, 375, 382. One 60-year-old Irishman (unidentified) particularly incensed MWM by wooing and winning a young Englishwoman for whom she had a kindness and who, she felt, had 'flung her selfe away' (ii. 398).

I submit to be answer'd and criticis'd, but as I never did, 'tis hard to be abus'd...'[39]

These sudden, tantalizing glimpses of her mostly hidden intellectual life are always startling. An anonymous, undated, respectful letter to her, written in French some time after 1745, probably belongs to this summer. It comments on the tragi-comic state of affairs in her present domicile, and relates current gossip to episodes in the fiction of Gabrielle-Suzanne de Villeneuve (author of 'Beauty and the Beast' in its longer form). It complains about the standard of recent publications (little fairy tales, pale imitations of Crébillon *fils*), and ends by mentioning something better: witty, original, still unpublished. A certain Chevalier is to arrange for this work to appear; Lady Mary's correspondent hopes she will not object, and promises to keep her posted with further news. Could this text, one wonders, be by her? But the letter-writer also encloses some sheets of manuscript (not extant) and promises more to follow. Unless he was Lady Mary's scribe, this sounds more like a venture in patronage than in authorship.[40]

At Toulouse she met a young Irishman, Sir James Caldwell: he may have lent her the *Lettres*. He knew she was looking for somewhere to settle. He knew she had in mind (or he may even have suggested) one of the small towns near the junction of the Rivers Lot and Garonne. Of these Clairac boasted an Académie, whose librarian was the abbé Filippo Venuti, a protégé both of Pope Benedict XIV and of Lady Mary's old acquaintance Montesquieu. The latter, who often travelled the fifty kilometres up-river from Bordeaux to visit Venuti, had also interested himself in Caldwell. Twenty-five kilometres from Clairac was Nérac, bustling and picturesque, another haunt of savants and currently a site for experiments with electricity. Lady Mary, too, seems to have been attracted.[41]

Caldwell told Montesquieu that she was considering Nérac and also Albi, on the other side of Toulouse. He reported, too, that she was 'a Companion hunting', but unlikely ever to find one to please her. For great wits, as for conquerors, he concluded with a flourish, one world was not enough. The 'Companion hunting' was not merely his fantasy. He later reminded Lady Mary of a conversation about 'a Person that would be proper to Live in the

---

[39] *CL* iii. 95. She ascribed this work of 'Literary Correspondence' to Jean-Baptiste de Boyer, marquis d'Argens, but nothing in his *œuvre* meets her description. She probably missed Montpellier's smallpox epidemic that summer, in which (said Tissot, a first-year doctoral student there) 2,000 died (Tissot 1754: 16; Eynard 1839: 15).

[40] H MS 77. 239: writer probably male.

[41] Shackleton 1961: 106–7, 217–223. Venuti, of an intellectual family of Cortona in Umbria, was a founder member of the Accademia Etruscana (which still holds his portrait and MSS). He became a prior at Leghorn and published *Dissertations sur les anciens monumens de ... Bordeaux ...*, 1754.

House with as a Companion'—meaning a male, not a female person—and of her speaking to such a person at Toulouse. Whoever this person was, he was not the answer. Caldwell suggested Venuti to her as a possible candidate, although Venuti had a good job already and was soon afterwards appointed to a benefice at Bordeaux.

Lady Mary was not, as the myth might suggest, in the market for a *cicisbeo* or toy-boy. She clearly had in mind a secretary, a man of classical erudition: such a person as Dr Bartolomeo Mora, who entered her service in 1755. Whether or not she had any plans for publication, she was probably writing fiction as well as large numbers of letters (far more than those that survive). She was anxious about her eyesight, and about what would happen to her books and papers after her death. Caldwell had some standing in the world of letters: he had spent seven months in Montesquieu's Bordeaux household, and had become his friend and correspondent. He was not well qualified for Lady Mary's needs: his French was almost semi-literate, his English badly spelled, and he had yet to learn Italian. But he suggested Venuti, a man of distinction; and he next wrote to ask Montesquieu himself 'to make inquiery' on Lady Mary's behalf.

Caldwell clearly knew how to recommend himself to great wits by judicious use of flattery. He wrote more than once to Montesquieu about Lady Mary: enthusiastic mixtures of fact, rumour, and compliment. He supposed her the richest of British ladies, as well the most universal and most enlightened genius among European ones. He admired her writings, but supposed she had published many of them, naming as example a poem actually by Judith Cowper Madan. Along with Latin and all the modern languages, he supposed she knew Greek; he added that she had spent a month in the Grand Signor's seraglio. He wrote expansively of her veneration for Montesquieu: she had sent a thousand compliments; she longed to travel to Bordeaux, perhaps on foot, to see him; she said he had done honour to the whole human race. By contrast, said Caldwell (perhaps still in ingratiating mode), she thought very little of Voltaire.[42]

Caldwell later implied that Lady Mary gave him copies of a good many of her writings; two he preserved were her 'Verses wrote under General Churchill's Pictour' and 'With toilsome steps'.[43] Each of these poems has something slightly shocking about it to intensify his breathless delight at meeting the intellectually fascinating Lady Mary. Soon afterwards, while

[42] He said she admired *Zaire* and disparaged the *Henriade*; for another story see p. 266. She collected verse of Voltaire's while at Avignon (H MS 255).

[43] Caldwell to Montesquieu, 25, 26 May 1746; to Lord Newtown, 20 Sept. 1761 (Bagshawe MS 3/6/1, 3/7/1, 3/10/11 no. 595). He was with a Monsieur Meighan when he met MWM.

still at Toulouse, he told a friend that her 'Companion hunting' had met with success. He told others that he was 'now determined to go to Italy having made the Party with Lady Mary Wortly Montegue', and more excitingly still that they were to go 'to Italy and perhaps to Grand Caro'.[44]

Caldwell claimed years later that Lady Mary wrote him many letters expressing warm regard and respect. All that survives of their exchange is a tatty, undated draft of a letter from him, sent after a tour through the Pyrenees—a tour which he hoped to describe to her more fully in person. Meanwhile he ran on in flippant, confidential style, about a 'Boat stuft with Garlick' (presumably the post-boat to Toulouse), about his trials on the road and hers at Avignon, and about the English girl who had fallen for the elderly Irishman. He hoped to hear 'what you have done with the Jacobits Pristes and Gamesters of Avignon'. This reminded him of his chief reason for writing: to break the news that he could not after all go 'to Itily this autome', having gambled away much of the money intended for the trip. Besides, he had not yet studied Italian and needed the winter to do so; besides, the war looked like continuing.[45]

Airily, Caldwell proposed an alternative scheme. 'I should like retiring into a small town for part of this winter.' There he hoped to have the honour and pleasure of Lady Mary's company and conversation. If this should come to pass he promised to 'do all in my Power to be as agreable and as usfull to your Ladiship as I can'. It was here that he deployed his compliments involving Montesquieu's high opinion of Lady Mary. He even requested, with a flourish of *politesse*, a reply by return of post, and added as a sweetener that he had found her a copy of Froissart (he wrote 'the Best edition' but lost his nerve and crossed this out) and a Latin life of Henry VII.[46] It does not seem that Caldwell was proposing himself as a *cicisbeo*, though the excited tone in which he writes *about* Lady Mary is certainly sexualized. It does seem that he hoped she would contribute significantly towards his winter's expenses.

All this at least shows how seriously she intended to leave Avignon. She was back there in early June 1746 (having been entertained by another Archbishop, that of Narbonne); later that summer Caldwell wrongly believed her to have moved to Nérac. In July she had another inflammation of the eyes, so

[44] To Henry Belasyse, Lady Clifford, and others unidentified, n.d. (Bagshawe MS 3/7/1). Almost a year later he was still writing to Montesquieu of going to Egypt (Bagshawe MS 3/15/85).

[45] Bagshawe MSS 3/16/127 (draft, 1762), 3/15/104 (draft).

[46] Bagshawe MS 3/15/104 (draft). Caldwell wrote 'frosart'. Jean Froissart, a French chronicler of England, had some influence on his contemporary Chaucer. Lady Pomfret had worked on translating him (Walpole, *Corr.* xv. 60; xviii. 424). Neither book remains in MWM's library; they may have missed her when she left Avignon. Caldwell's draft, written in 1746, is the only one of its date among much later papers: he made a point of saving it.

bad that she could hardly read a letter, much less write one. As she began to recover, a way of escape presented itself. There arrived in Avignon, on diplomatic business from the court of Poland and Saxony, a man who seemed to spring from a carefree moment in her past, a man with close links to several of her good friends. He planned to travel on to northern Italy. He offered to serve as her escort.

Born between the births of Lady Mary's own children, he was thirty. His name was Count Ugolino Palazzi. Her friend Signora Pisana Mocenigo had introduced him to her in Venice six years before; she had also helped him to a job in the service of the crippled Prince of Saxony, with whom he had soon afterwards departed. Now he was Gentleman of the Bedchamber to the prince and bore a letter of reintroduction from his colleague the Count von Wackerbarth, who had then been the prince's tutor and a close friend of Lady Mary. No personal history could have induced greater confidence, or played more strongly on Lady Mary's yearning for Venice. In conversation with Palazzi, she 'lamented to him the impossibillity of my attempting a Journey to Italy'; from this sprang his offer of protection, and her acceptance. He had, however, another side to his character, which she did not yet suspect.[47]

[47] Bagshawe MS 3/15/104; *CL* ii. 374–6; 'Italian Memoir', *RW* 81–2. Foreign service was usual for mainland nobles, who were barred from Venetian state office. Palazzi's later career was in banditry. Fappani calls him and his brothers the leading violent criminals of their day (1961: 102, 105–7).

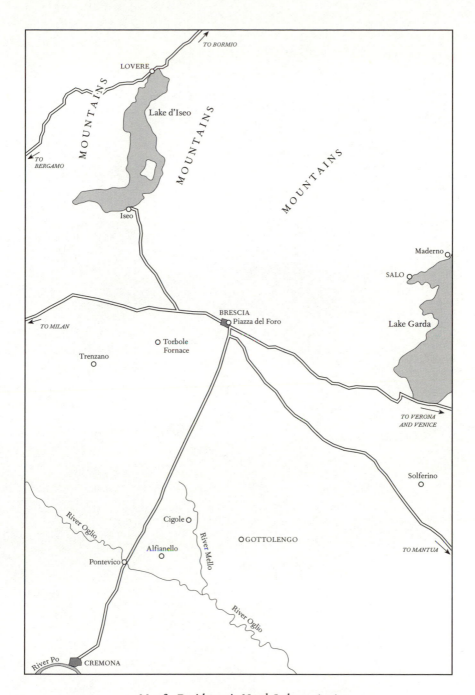

Map 3. Residence in North Italy 1746–56

26

August 1746–February 1750

❧

Gottolengo, Lovere: 'Mille perils pour me retrouver a la cara Italia'[1]

LADY MARY knew that Palazzi's motive for offering her his escort from Avignon to Brescia (where he was going to visit his mother) was to save on travelling expenses. She wondered whether she had better assume the whole of these herself. He showed her a letter from his mother expressing delight that he was now discreet enough to be chosen as escort to 'such a respectable Lady'. With duly elaborate compliment, the letter extended Lady Mary an invitation to stay with the Contessa Giulia Palazzi in Brescia.

Lady Mary then, despite a further, frightening inflammation of her eyes, paid the necessary visits of leave-taking. This time she had to pack up without the Turners; but probably she already had as her maid Mari Anna or Marianne Fromenta, a French Huguenot who stayed with her till her death. Within a few years she was so satisfied with Italian servants that she wondered how she had ever stood for being 'bought and sold' by cheeky English ones.[2]

All her books had to be carried down the steep dusty track from her belvedere. She entrusted them, and her furniture, to the Vice-Legate for forwarding later. She arranged about post-chaises. Then Palazzi suddenly began behaving like Sir James Caldwell, or indeed like her son Edward. On the eve of departure, he told her 'that he was truly mortified, but that since all his property was in his Mother's hands and since he had a very small allowance, he had been obliged to run into debt'. It was because he was broke that he was going home. To get him out of Avignon would take 300

---

[1] MWM told Michiel she had braved a thousand dangers to get back to dear Italy: for the last words she switched from French to Italian (*CL* ii. 378).

[2] 'Italian Memoir', *RW* 82; *CL* iii. 67.

sequins, which he hoped Lady Mary would supply. He 'would give me a note which his Mother would not refuse to pay upon our arrival. I had some doubts about making such a loan, and saw too that he set too high a price on the escort he proposed to give me; nonetheless, having many strong reasons to leave Avignon, I gave him the 300 sequins, and took his note.'[3] In a different sense he too no doubt took note: she was rich; she was a resource.

The journey began with an agreeable air of cloak-and-dagger adventure. First they took ship for Genoa. During their brief stay there Lady Mary lay low, passing with Palazzi's aid as a Venetian lady, for she had no passport and might be stopped if recognized. On 16 August 1746 their line of post-chaises set out. In La Bochetta, a pass in the mountains behind Genoa, they found the narrow road almost blocked with carriages and loaded mules. It was the Spanish army's baggage train, retreating 'in a very great Hurry' with 'a prodigious number of sick and wounded'. Palazzi quickly instructed his servants to tell the soldiers who questioned them that they were on an urgent mission in the same service as the questioners: that of Don Philip. This worked; they were left to battle their way onwards as best they might.

It took them till nightfall to reach their staging post, Seravalle, where to their astonishment they met a tide of troops pouring out of the little town, 'surrounding a body of Guards, in the midst of which was Don Philip in person, going a very round trot, looking down and pale as ashes. The Army was in too much Confusion to take notice of us and the night favouring us we got into the Town.' There they found every inn full of wounded Spaniards, the dark air full of cries and groans. Palazzi got the governor to provide a chamber in his own house 'for a Venetian Lady'. There was 'nothing in it but the bare Walls', for the household was even then fleeing, with their goods and furniture, to the citadel. The party spent the night without beds or supper; Lady Mary does not say if she slept.

As it was getting light the Austrian troops entered the town they had taken (though the remaining Spaniards, fallen back to the citadel, maintained a brisk cannon fire). Palazzi went off to see the commanding officers: it seemed he was charged with some message to them. He revealed Lady Mary's identity, and her old Viennese connections paid off: 'there was no sort of Honor or Civillity they did not pay me.' Food and drink of all kinds appeared, and a guard of Hussars, 'very necessary in the present disorder' was detailed to her. On the second day in Seravalle 'all the principal officers' found time to visit her and praise her heroic coolness under cannon fire.

---

[3] *RW* 82. Two sequins or *zecchini* made a pound sterling. MWM drew up the 'Memoir' (in Italian) between 1756 and 1758 to use in suing Palazzi. The Palazzis' income was below their pretensions (Fappani 1961: 102).

Lack of transport forced them to linger: the Spaniards had taken all the horses they could find, and the postmaster and his staff had fled. On the third day horses were found, and they were sent on their way with their strong escort. Palazzi had certainly proved the value of his protection. Further on, at Voghera, fresh horses were refused to them 'till the Hussars drew their Sabres'.[4]

After all this it took them only two days from Seravalle to Brescia (where Lady Mary's French chaise had broken down in 1739). The Italian country-side they passed through, 'some of the most Plentifull parts of the World', was terribly altered by the war, its people reduced to near-famine; but the province of Brescia (in the neutral Venetian territories) was flourishing. Ugolino Palazzi sent a messenger ahead, for his mother came out from the walled city of Brescia to meet Lady Mary 'in her Coach and six,[5] and it was impossible to resist her Importunity of going to her House, where she would keep me till I had found a Lodging to my likeing'. The Palazzi mansion stands in the Piazza del Foro (then Piazza del Novarino), at the north-east corner of the city: a sloping square with the remains of the Roman forum at the top end, and a steep green hillside beyond. It is structurally part of an imposing palace built in the 1660s and 1690s by a branch of the leading Brescian family of Martinenghi, who still occupied the other, larger end.[6]

Lady Mary was later to call Countess Giulia Palazzi the only friend she had in the province of Brescia. They must have become intimate quickly, because after her first months there Lady Mary saw little of her. In their early conversations the countess confided 'that her Son had ruined the Family by his extravagances in Saxony; from this I understood that she would not be inclined to pay his debts, and so I judged it would be useless to present her with the note from Avignon.' Lady Mary may have felt a sympathy based on her relations with her own son. She told Wortley, without specifying her lost £150, that the journey had been 'very expensive', but well worth making. The Venetian territories, whose doge was now her old friend Grimani, stayed out of the war. She intended soon to press on to Venice, but she had accepted the countess's suggestion that she first relax at Brescia for the rest of the summer. She met some of the local nobility, chose herself lodgings (most

---

[4] *CL* ii. 376–7.

[5] *CL* ii. 382, 378. The countess, however, had pleaded poverty in order to sell some property three years earlier (ii. 379 n. 1). Brescia occupied a rectangle enclosed by medieval walls, its tall houses dominated from one corner by a taller fortress. Its first guidebook dated from 1700 (Frati, Massa, Piovanelli, and Robecchi 1989: 115, 126).

[6] This is MWM's plural for Martinengo. The family had provided a patron and a lover to Veronica Franco, 16th-century Venetian poet and letter-writer (Rosenthal 1992: 91–6). This branch now included a pair of intellectual-minded brothers, Cesare and Marcantonio Martinengo Cesaresco. For the medievally derived power of the Martinengo, Palazzi, and Rodengo families see Ferraro 1993: 70, 95, 228–30.

likely the pleasant Villa Palazzi at nearby Torbole, pop. 531), and wrote to tell Wortley of her adventures and Michiel of her intentions.[7]

Lady Mary's bad eyes had improved on her hair-raising journey. But now, before she could move into her lodgings, she found herself immobilized by 'a malignant fever' (probably malaria), so violent that she was 'surpris'd a Woman of my Age could be capable of it'.[8] All the Brescia physicians pronounced her to be in the utmost danger; Countess Palazzi cared for her like a sister, 'and omitted no Expence or trouble to serve me'. Mari Anna's chief worry was that the countess would subject her mistress in this extremity to visits from a Catholic priest, but tact overcame piety, and this did not happen. Two weeks into her illness Lady Mary rallied enough to write again to Michiel; then she relapsed. She spent two months confined to bed, burning with fever. It must have been during this illness that she saw her reflection in a mirror and found it 'so disagreable, I resolv'd to spare my selfe such mortifications for the Future'. She was prescribed a vegetarian diet, such as she had seen Hervey relying on.[9]

From this point the story of her doings in the province of Brescia becomes hazy and sometimes contradictory. She stepped up her existing practice of putting a good face on what she reported to Wortley, at the same time that she began to experience events which could not be made to sound good without actual distortion. There was a dark side to these years which she related only in the narrative, written years later in Italian and called by scholars her 'Italian Memoir', drawn up as the basis for bringing suit against the so-helpful Count Ugolino Palazzi for extortion and fraud.

In letters to her husband and Lady Oxford dated 24 November 1746, she described her illness and said she now was able to sit 'in my great chair by the Fire side, still so weak I am not able to move farther'. She headed this 'Brescia', as if she was still at 8 Piazza del Foro with Giulia Palazzi. But she also wrote 'Brescia' on letters from elsewhere in the province; and the 'Italian Memoir' says that by 11 November she had reached the village of Gottolengo, where she was to spend most of the next ten years.

Her illness left her weak and depressed, and so readier to accept the

---

[7] *CL* ii. 478, 377–9; *RW* 82–3; CB 22; Perogalli, Sandri, and Zanella 1985: 411; Mazzoldi 1966: 166. One of those she met was a local historian, also named Conti, who recorded that she was served by ('*servita da*') Palazzi. He *may* have been hinting at a sexual relationship (Marinoni 1904: 11).

[8] Malaria was rife in Europe (north as well as south), but localized—even to particular buildings. The 18th century had it more than earlier and later ages; the Po Valley had it less than Rome, Naples, or Venice. MWM was dogged by this fever during 1746–56 (Hackett 1937: 7, 15, 61, 75–6, 97).

[9] *CL* ii. 378–9, 478; iii. 135. Even in youth she had paid little attention to the mirror. In making this gesture (as in writing 'Satturday'), she probably thought of an epigram by Prior: 'Venus, take my votive glass. | Since I am not what I was, | What from this time I must be | Venus, let me never see.' She kept her resolution (Prior 1971: i. 448; Pope, *Corr.* i. 441).

doctors' ruling 'that Country air was absolutely necessary to re-establish my health'. Palazzi offered to rent her a country house, and she 'agreed to go there, although I was so weak that I had to be carried in a Litter'. Both Palazzis went with her: either to tiny Torbole, or else to Gottolengo, a large village in the fertile Po valley, still contained in a square shape by its crumbling medieval walls. The 'Castle' at Gottolengo (so-called from its ancient predecessor on the same site) became her long-term base. In a note she said she went 'to G[ottolengo] from Torbule'; she did not say why.[10]

She found the Castle 'so run down and in such bad condition that if I had known the state it was in, I should never have gone there, but it was too late to change my mind'. It was 'not much more than the shell of a Palace', left unfinished forty years before on the builder's death. The move there put Lady Mary straight back to bed with a recurrence of fever. She was dosed with quinine, and next morning her temperature had dropped and she was able to get up and attend to her life. With 'a thousand apologies', Giulia Palazzi explained that they had to go back to Brescia on important business, which she seemed to imply would be brief. Lady Mary stayed, attended by Mari Anna and Fribourg.

Ugolino Palazzi returned alone, to assure her that she was mistress of his mother's house, and free to command him to anything he could do for her. Still intermittently fever-ridden, she responded by voicing distress at having imposed on the countess. What kind of present, she asked him, would her generous hostess like? Her question seemed to cause the count embarrassment. After some hesitation and 'much ceremony' he told her that his mother was all the prouder for her poverty, and a stickler for social forms. Any gift made her would have to be properly reciprocated, which she would find hard to do. But 'she would not make any scruple to receive cash', if paid secretly through her son. Lady Mary paid him 200 sequins, or £100, for this purpose.

So Lady Mary was established at Gottolengo. Giulia Palazzi at Brescia kept sending her son with apologies because she was not free 'to come and keep me company'. Lady Mary was still confined to her room and had therefore hardly taken the measure of 'her' house. But she was recovering fast, sitting up and receiving 'many visits from Ladies in the vicinity'. Among the swarms of Palazzi relatives, the Countess of Cigole was particularly attentive. She sent the count with an invitation 'to share the St. Martin's Goose' with a large party of family and friends at her house nearby. Lady Mary was

---

[10] *CL* ii. 378–9, 401, 403; CB 22 (where MWM struck out something before 'Torbule'). Mazzoldi says Gottolengo had 2,200 inhabitants; the parish priest told MWM he had 2,000 communicants. Its 'osteria di Casa Palazzi' employed several people (1966: 42–3, 164).

familiar with the tradition, which England shared with Italy, of a feast of goose for Martinmas, 11 November. Palazzi exerted pressure: the honour she would confer by going, the disappointment if she did not, and the urgent desire of 'the most distinguished People of the Neighbourhood' to meet her. She was afraid she might still not be up to a party; but he persuaded her. It was only a couple of miles; 'it was a beautiful day'; she could dress informally and go in a closed carriage. Lady Mary consented, wrapped herself up in a fur, and instructed Mari Anna to guard her room, since the house had no locks or keys. This raised a new difficulty. The count said it was imperative that she should take both her servants with her. Custom demanded it, and they would both be needed: her maid if she should have a bout of fever, and her man 'to serve me at table'. Lady Mary objected to leaving her room in the custody of strangers; the count replied that he would leave on guard an abolutely trustworthy manservant of his own.

Lady Mary went in her fur and her closed carriage to Cigole. She found the company exclusive and the dinner magnificent; but the dining-room 'was so grievously cold that I was obliged to leave the table and to call for my Carriage to return home'. Here again she ran up against the forms of Italian hospitality. The Countess of Cigole positively 'would not permit me to leave'. She called a doctor, who diagnosed 'a very severe fever' and advised bed. In a bed at the countess's house, nicely warmed for her, Lady Mary slept peacefully till ten next morning and awoke free from fever.[11]

Her first thought was that she had caused the countess enough trouble, and must now be off. Ugolino Palazzi had attended the dinner with one of his brothers (Alessandro, a priest). He returned to escort Lady Mary back to Gottolengo. There she 'was astonished upon entering my Room, to find many things out of their places, and to learn that the Servant who had been assigned to guard it was out Hunting'. She looked under her bed for the velvet bag containing her locked jewel-boxes, and found it gone. Palazzi, when informed of this, seemed at first incredulous. Then 'he flung himself in Tears at my feet, inconsolable, as he said, for the dishonour brought upon his House. I replied merely that he must find a way of getting them back; and the fever returned, and I went to bed again.'

Later Lady Mary observed that robbery (regarded very seriously in Italy) was accordingly rare, 'thô stealing is in daily practise'. It seems that for her, as for Johnson, 'robbery' involved an element of violence.[12]

---

[11] *CL* ii. 389; *RW* 84. Villa Cigole, now owned by the commune of Cigole, is quite a grand building (Perogalli, Sandri and Zanella 1985: 296–7).

[12] *RW* 85; *CL* iii. 46. 'To *steal* generally implies secrecy, to *rob*, either secrecy or violence' (Johnson, *Dictionary*).

Next morning Palazzi presented himself with a bulletin. He 'had searched the entire Castle without result'. For further investigation he would need money. With surprising meekness Lady Mary

counted out forty sequins for this alleged search, and so he went off on Horseback to look for the Thieves. He stayed away for three days, and then told me with Tears and sobs, that he had found no trace of them, and that if I did not take pity on him, he would be a lost Man: that he would become the disgrace of his Family, and that his Mother, who was already dissatisfied with him, would use this pretext to disinherit him.

He hinted suspicion of his brother Alessandro, for which disloyalty Lady Mary sternly reproved him. A later account says he also had the doctor searched and imprisoned for some days. The scene of high drama, with Palazzi raving hysterically of his honour (which it seemed it was up to Lady Mary to preserve) was the first of many. It did not convince her of his innocence, but if he was guilty she saw no way to prove it except to wait for the evidence to emerge. If he had taken the jewels, she supposed he would use the money to return to the court of Saxony and Poland, so that she would at least be rid of him. This, anyhow, was the rationalization she offered years later for her supineness.

Meanwhile the affair was not over. Palazzi came and went (using Lady Mary's horses, and therefore at her expense). He was still in histrionic despair, ready to interrogate the servants under torture if Lady Mary had not vetoed it. He brought another aunt to weep at her bedside: Madalena Roncadelli, his late father's widowed sister, 'a respectable elderly Lady who had lived honourably and had the reputation of a saint'. Lady Mary liked her on sight, judging her to be honourable and well disposed. Madame Roncadelli asked for a list of the stolen jewels, 'to send away to all the Jewellers of Italy'. Lady Mary thought this futile, but let herself be overruled. She was 'in no state to write' because of her high fever; the list was dictated and 'incomplete, although it did record the principal items. Madame Roncadelli had it printed, and sent round all the largest Cities.'[13]

Lady Mary apparently lived through all this before making 'the first use . . . of my Hand' since her illness, in letters to England. They made no mention of any of it. The quinine finally cured her fever; but it was too late in the season to attempt to reach Venice before the spring. On New Year's Eve, though still very weak, she wrote to promise Michiel that she would embrace her at the Feast of the Ascension—that is in May. Meanwhile her

---

[13] She called the use of her horses 'a small favour that I thought not worth the trouble of refusing'. The banishment case against Palazzi, years later, places this episode in Sept. 1748 (*RW* 85–6; Fappani 1961: 111).

hold on the outside world was tenuous. Fewer and fewer letters to or from England got through. She put this down to the war, which had now closed the port of Genoa for her purposes. But someone (presumably one of her own servants) told her something more disturbing about a letter to Michiel in Venice: that a peasant whom she had given it to take to the post office (at Brescia) had lost it, and been afraid to tell her so. 'Imagine my fury!' she wrote (in a replacement letter); but it took her a year to enunciate the deduction that her messengers were inclined to pocket the postage money she gave them and throw the letters away.[14]

Meanwhile, since she felt compelled to stay in the dilapidated house at Gottolengo, she had to come to terms with it. It stood 'on an Eminence' (an eminence for the Po Valley, if not as compared with the Rocher-des-Doms), right on the street—on the corner of two streets—in the centre of the little town. Passers-by brushed against its walls, of which the bottom layers were medieval. There was no garden, only a little stream (now dried up). It was not at all what Lady Mary had been used to. It was clearly not worth the expense of major renovations to the 'Castle' just for a few months, but there were things she had to do. The 'great chair' by her fireside was a dilapidated relic she bought for far too much: the count assured her it was the only one in the village, where chairs without arms were the norm. Lady Mary 'had locks put on the doors, and glass in the windows'. To cover the damp stone walls and beat the cold, she bought a set of old (probably Renaissance) tapestries from one of the Martinengo family. He refused to divide the set, so she was forced to buy more than she needed, but at least the walls were covered throughout the house. For this transaction too the count was the intermediary.[15]

By the end of February her health was perfectly recovered. She went riding (astride) every morning, among the flat, rich fields divided by streams and dykes, in the early light of days which were often frosty, usually sunny. She had missed the Carnival at Brescia, but now all Palazzi's numerous relations came to visit her. She was made to feel that her having her jewels stolen had brought him disgrace, and that she ought somehow to make this up to him. When she told him she was almost ready to leave, 'he began once more to enact despair, and said that I was destroying his honour, and would leave an eternal stain on his Family. His conduct appeared to me in every way so unbalanced that I ceased to suspect him of cunning, and considered him an object of pity.'[16]

A few evenings after this conversation (in which the Castle's lack of a

---

[14] *CL* ii. 379, 380, 392, 529. Among other things she lost new poetry sent by EWM (ii. 395).
[15] *CL* ii. 425; *RW* 86. Now owned by the town, the building is used for exhibitions, etc.
[16] *RW* 86; *CL* ii. 381, 383, 393.

garden had also been canvassed), he came to tell her he had discovered a way to expunge, in part, the eternal stain. An 'old dying Priest wanted to sell a little piece of land to pay his debts'; she 'could have it for a very low price if I would let him occupy the House until the end of his life . . . there was a large Garden which could be embellished to suit my own taste . . . it was near enough to the Castle to meet all my needs, and . . . in any event I should be able to sell it for a profit whenever I might wish to do so.' To put such a bargain in her way would be to make some reparation.[17]

Lady Mary wrote that she 'had these matters examined into by competent people'. She visited the place. It was, she said, on a little peninsula fifty feet above the River Oglio, with steps cut in the bank down to the water. It had fishing rights attached. There was a simple farmhouse, a vineyard of a hundred yards by about seventy, just waiting to be *ornée*, and a 200-yard avenue leading to a 100-acre wood 'cut into walks and rideings'. Lady Mary had still not decided to remain in Gottolengo: yet she put down 800 sequins in cash for this 'Spot of Ground . . . so Beautifull I am afraid you will scarce credit the Description'. With what she spent on laying out her garden, she dispensed £500 altogether: more than half a year's income.[18]

Though the 'Italian Memoir' and her letters clearly date this transaction in early 1747, she 'staid little' there that year. Spring came late: she had a fire burning on 18 May. She did not mention her purchase to any of her family.[19] She did not yet send for her heavy baggage from Avignon, but waited for peace. She was not committed to her Castle; she apparently canvassed other possibilities. But little by little the solitude of Gottolengo grew on her. To her riding she added long walks. The soil of the Po Valley was deep and sticky, excellent for farming but very heavy after rain; it did not deter her. She thought the air agreed with her. Living in a building of some importance to the little community, she found that people treated her as a patron, bringing her their troubles and ailments. 'I do what good I am able', she told Lady Oxford, 'and have had so much success that I am thought a great Physician and should be esteem'd a Saint if I went to Mass.' She gave herself up to 'rural Amusements', and forgot that 'Wits or Fine Ladys' even existed. The

---

[17] *RW* 87. Another priest who sold property to Palazzi was never paid, but was kept quiet by years of physical intimidation (Fappani 1961: 105).

[18] MWM's Dairy House is not the mansion at Seniga owned by the Fenaroli (Countess Palazzo's family); it may have been one of several sites within visiting distance of that. Nor is it 'Villa Montagu' at Costa Volpino, just outside Lovere, as Marinoni deduced from Dallaway's misinformation (MWM 1803; Marinoni 1904: 46). MWM calls it 'Legere'. She was early in the *ferme ornée* mode, perhaps following Philip Southcote's example (from mid-1730s) at Woburn Farm near Chertsey (*RW* 87; *CL* ii. 403; CB 22; *SL* 365; Brogden 1983: 41).

[19] In March, however, she alluded to Sarah Marlborough's passion for buying property (*RW* 87; CB 22; *CL* ii. 383).

down-at-heel local gentry came to call; her house was the only place where they were prepared to be civil to one another. She did not encourage them, finding their feuds tedious. She set up a poultry yard and other projects, which soon began to show a profit: if she could live for a hundred years, she said, she would be able to provide for all her grandchildren. (There were five young Stuarts when she wrote this.)[20]

Now, in her late fifties, she began to speak of herself as old. She and her still older husband exchanged tips about longevity and the preservation of health: she reported on her hearing, eyesight, memory, appetite, and sleep patterns (all satisfactory in May 1751). She said she was, fittingly, 'more and more wean'd' from the world; she quoted an Italian proverb signifying that her final hour had struck. She did not join in the social life of her own class or sex (her letters said nothing of the Palazzi tribe), or the old custom whereby the nobility and gentry went 'in troops to one anothers' houses, hunting and danceing together, a month in each Castle'. This was not now her style. Evenings at home (perforce except in summer, because the rough cobbled streets of Gottolengo were unlit) were what she now preferred. There was one snag: even when her books arrived, her eyes were no longer up to reading by candlelight. But she got to know some inmates of the local monastery, found them sympathetic, and taught them new skills. 'I play at Whist every night with some old Priests that I have taught it to, and are my only Companions.' She hastened to add that they staked 'only a penny per Corner'. She found the absolute regularity of her new life good for both her health and spirits.[21]

One of her visitors was 'an Old Priest, a learned Man, particularly esteem'd as a Mathematician', whose warm heart and quick temper reminded her of William Whiston. He was soon at her house every day, 'and talk'd of me every where with such violent praise that had we been young People, God knows what would have been said'. This friendship ultimately foundered on religious debates, in which he became heated while she stayed calm. They tried the technique which Lady Mary had practised with Astell and with Hervey, of making their debate share the same sheet of paper. She wrote out her arguments on one side, 'leaving the other for his Answer. He carry'd it with him, promising to bring it the next Day, since which time I have never seen it, thô I have often demanded it, being asham'd of my defective Italian.' Years later she had 'given over asking for it, as a desperate Debt. He still visits me, but seldom and in a cold sort of a way.'[22]

[20] *CL* ii. 388, 391, 402, 404. A recent local crop was corn, maize, or 'Turkish Wheat' (ii. 494; iii. 1).

[21] *CL* ii. 391–3, 399, 402 (1747–8), 447, 483; iii. 43.

[22] *CL* iii. 93–4. Cf. 'if the S[cripture] is true the R[oman] C[atholic] Religion is false because contrary, if the S[cripture] is false the R[oman] C[atholic] Religion is false because founded on it' (CB 6).

Before summer 1747 was over she had decided to stay. 'The Count made his House at Gottolengo over to me by a deed signed in the presence of Witnesses.'[23] She told Lady Oxford he was 'pleas'd to part with it for a Triffle'. The walls at least were perfectly sound. In the 'Memoir' she said she 'let [her]self be talked into' making improvements, but to Lady Oxford she sounded enthusiastic. The next step was to get it 'fitted up with my Furniture', left at Avignon with the Vice-Legate. Palazzi recommended as agent his family's protégé Signor Bettoni, a great Brescian merchant who was just going to Avignon. Lady Mary knew him by repute and believed him trustworthy. Her things, however, 'arrived in a terrible state. Many pieces of my furniture were missing, also some of my China and four fine snuff-boxes, one of them set with diamonds and rubies.' This produced another row with the count, who 'cursed all merchants as Thieves, and offered in all seriousness to have Signor Bettoni shot'. In the end Lady Mary laughed at the count, paid Bettoni's bill of 100 sequins, and blamed his faults on his underlings. Her books, at least, 'had all arrived safe and sound'.[24] Perhaps they were thought not worth stealing.

News from England, of old friends and their children, still occupied her. She asked especially after Lady Pomfret and her family.[25] Lady Bute bore another son in September 1747: James Archibald, the eventual inheritor of his grandfather's fortune. She had her six year old, Lady Jane, inoculated. Her intimacy with Lady Oxford's daughter (the Duchess of Portland) was growing, to the joy of both their mothers. Lady Mary took to concluding her letters with a regular 'blessing to my Grand Children' or to 'your little ones'. On 5 January [1748] she expressed the hope that Lady Bute might 'allways be as well satisfy'd with your Family as you are at present, and your children return in your age the tender care you have of their Infancy'. The implied contrast with herself was clear.[26]

That summer had brought an epoch-making event for that family. They were renting at Egham, not Twickenham—somewhat remote, since they could not afford to keep a carriage. A local apothecary offered Lord Bute a lift in his chaise to some horse-races being held at Maidenhead: it would be a small, informal meeting, but graced with the presence of the Prince and

---

[23] Significant phrasing: though MWM said she had bought the house, it later turned out to be entailed; no sale would be legal (*CL* ii. 389; *RW* 88, 104).

[24] *RW* 87–8; *CL* ii. 390.

[25] While keeping up her visiting among MWM's former circle, Lady Pomfret grew steadily more occupied with religious observance (Finch MSS DG7/D3).

[26] *CL* ii. 393, 399, 426. When Jane sailed through smallpox, she had presumably been inoculated. Lady Oxford virtually apologized to MWM that her own grandchildren were not to be inoculated; she would have wished it, but would not interfere (25 Jan. 1752, Halsband MSS).

Princess of Wales. Lord Bute accepted. It rained heavily during the afternoon, and the prince and princess, trapped under the marquee which had been erected for them, badly wanted a fourth so that they could play 'Whisk'. Someone recommended Bute, as a racegoer of a rank to sit down with royalty. They played late. Bute found that the apothecary had had to get home to attend to business, and he faced a walk of a dozen miles in the rain, for which he was no doubt unsuitably dressed. Prince Frederick graciously offered to take him back for the night to his nearby estate of Cliveden. The prince was already spending heavily on his garden; next morning he discovered that Bute knew the names of all his rare plants. Bute stayed several days at Cliveden, by royal command; the rest is history.[27]

Young Edward Wortley Montagu, meanwhile, had been set free without a ransom, in exchange for French prisoners of war. He then found a place on the staff of another cousin, John Montagu, Earl of Sandwich. In spring 1747 he visited England with Sandwich. He was still seeking patrons, this time to help him *leave* the army. Lord Chesterfield, approached for this purpose, advised against it, but became firmly persuaded that Edward was 'a very sensible clever fellow', vilified and brought low by his unkind parents. Lady Mary commented, 'I know my Son; he is a showy companion and may easily impose on any one for a short time.' That phrase, 'I know my Son', always boded disillusion. Sure enough, though he served as secretary when Sandwich became British Minister Plenipotentiary at the peace talks at Aix-la-Chapelle, the final verdict on his performance was not encouraging.[28]

There were elections in 1747, and Sandwich, after the usual horse-trading all round, secured the county of Huntingdon for Edward. (There was no other candidate.) Though Wortley had secured control of one of the notorious Cornish pocket boroughs, he evidently did not feel that his son had earned it. He stood for Bossiney himself, and on being voted in for two constituencies he assigned Bossiney not to Edward but to someone else.

At this stage Wortley thought, following Sandwich, that Edward was so far reformed that patrons would not repent of helping him. Lady Mary was less sure. After the election she hoped he had turned the corner and might now prove to be 'capable of makeing a good Figure, at least such a one as not to be a reproach to his Family'. But next spring, when he had resigned his army commission, she reverted to fearing Sandwich might be prejudiced or

---

[27] Story told by Walpole (1978: 80–1) and Sir Nathaniel Wraxall (1884: i. 318–20), endorsed by Hester Lynch Piozzi. The prince had spent hugely on plants at Kew from at least 1734; late in the 1740s he took up this interest again (Desmond 1995: 26–7).

[28] *CL* ii. 384, 397. In Sept. 1748 Edward (like his father before him) was still petitioning, with his cousin and colleague, for their 'extraordinaries' to be paid (Huntington MS MO; Curling 1954: 115 ff.).

mistaken. Edward, she thought, was metaphorically as well as literally 'capable of giving Bonds for more than he will ever be worth, in the view of any present Advantage'. She wrote this before reading in a newspaper of his appointment at Aix. The disadvantage of this post, from his parents' point of view, was that it led to further requests for money, to make an appearance fitting Edward's status not merely as secretary but the British Plenipotentiary's relation. His mother wrote to recommend, in familiar terms, that he should seek the good opinion of wise men instead of fools, by modesty, frugality, honesty, prudence, and decency, instead of 'an embrodier'd Coat or a rich Livery . . . Public Tables and rich Equipage'. She reproached him with his past wildness, and held up his father as a model of generosity and disinterestedness. This letter was more likely to please Wortley, to whom she copied it, than Edward. But perhaps Edward never received it.[29]

Though she often mentioned her solitude during these years, Lady Mary was not, of course, strictly alone. She had Mari Anna, Fribourg, a cook, and other servants who, like the maid Chechina, came and went. But, despite the visiting nobility, the parish priest, and the whist-playing monks, she *felt* alone.[30]

This perhaps contributed to her warmth of feeling for her daughter. She wrote her longer and longer letters, with a background of loving concern. Their foreground is carefully built from materials which Lady Mary could share with her: detailed comment on items of news from England;[31] vignettes from her present life, especially the picturesque, or delightful, or amusing; and meditations drawn from years of rich experience of living and reading. Any mention of her difficulties with Palazzi was excluded. To Wortley too she sent relaxed, chatty, informative letters, with some acute comment on topics of scientific or virtuoso interest, and on the copies he sent her of poetry circulating in England. When he criticized Lord and Lady Bute for abandoning their retreat and being 'much in Public', she cited the authority both of Sir Robert Walpole and (more tactfully) of Bute's surviving uncle, the new Duke of Argyll, to argue that this would have career benefits. What pleased her even more than Bute's growing favour with the Prince of Wales was Lady Bute's with the Princess (she whose first childbirth had dragged Hervey across London at a gallop). For her part she explicitly approved Lady Bute's apparent ambition, as being 'for the good of your Family'—of her children as well as her husband, whose own aspirations she

[29] *CL* ii. 383–5, 386–7, 388, 397, 410–11, 482, and nn.
[30] *CL* ii. 391, 393, 415, 425.
[31] Most interesting she found *déclassé* weddings and the prospects of her sister Gower's children (*CL* ii. 399–400).

commended too. In imagining her daughter having 'one day . . . a large share of power' she renewed a dream of her own; in confessing to Wortley her astonishment that Lord Bute should be still in love with his wife, she reflected other dreams, long dismissed.[32]

When Lady Bute remarked that society seemed to have degenerated during her absence in Scotland, her mother replied by developing one of her favourite ideas. 'I have never, in all my various Travels, seen but two sorts of people (and those very like one another); I mean Men and Women, who allways have been, and ever will be, the same.' Vices and follies, she said, change their names from age to age but not their nature. They would be still the same when her granddaughter Mary reached middle age; they could surprise only the inexperienced young. Sometimes, she said, 'the active part of Life is over before an honest Mind finds out how one ought to act in such a World as this'. Such passages can be read in two ways at once: they are 'sage literature', distillations of philosophic thought; they also carry oblique or coded comment on their author's particular circumstances.[33] She *may* have been thinking of Palazzi as an age-old character type which she ought to have recognized, and of herself as having been late to learn a lesson in human nature.

When Wortley explained the latest medical craze in England, tar-water, she replied with her views on the desire for a universal remedy, the credulity of her own nation especially, and the vast fortunes amassed by English doctors. They were, she remarked, equivalent to the 'Monks and Confessors' of Catholic countries; both played on 'the Fear and Hope which rule the actions of the Multitude'. 'We have no longer faith in Miracles and Reliques, and therefore with the same Fury run after receits and Physicians.' This sounds universalist; but she named as worst offenders 'Women and halfe witted Men'.[34]

Wortley's life was shifting its focus. An Act of Parliament had reduced the price of best coal in 1744, and from the end of the decade the Grand Alliance's stranglehold on the Tyneside coal trade was weakened by technological advance and proliferating new firms. On the other hand the Barnsley and Wortley coal-mines became *more* competitive as the River Don was made navigable by Acts of 1733 and 1751. Though the greater part of Wortley's huge income still came from the north-east, his heart was in Yorkshire. His surviving personal papers, though they hardly mention his

---

[32] *CL* ii. 397–8, 406–7, 408, 427.
[33] *CL* ii. 392–3. Cf. Samuel Johnson's essays, often seen as timeless, which yield new insights when read for topical and personal reference.
[34] *CL* ii. 397. She was consulted on tar-water in her capacity of medical expert (ii. 486–7).

collieries there, teem with detail about road improvement, iron-founding, and the management of venison, fishponds, and woods. His meticulous bookkeeping extended to enumerating every tree in his 2,200 acres of woodland.[35]

Lady Mary's first healthy winter at Gottolengo was bitterly cold in January 1748, spring-like again in February. The Christmas and Carnival season produced picturesque events to share in letters. First a party arrived unannounced at her castle: '30 Horse of Ladys and Gentlemen with their servants', who 'came with the kind Intent of staying with me at least a fortnight, thô I had never seen any of them before; but they were all Neighbours within ten mile round.' They were in time for supper. It was sheer good luck, she said, that she 'had a large Quantity of Game in the House, which with the help of my Poultry furnish'd out a plentifull Table. I sent for the Fiddles; and they were so obliging to dance all Night.' It amused her to watch a woman of her own age dancing with her even older husband, 'and I can assure you she jumps and Gallops with the best of them'. Lady Mary withdrew to bed about 1 a.m. Next day more poultry must have bitten the dust: her visitors dined with her, 'thô none of them had been in Bed, and were much disapointed I did not press them to stay'. She felt such hospitality cost too much. She left all visits unreturned, preferring if she could manage it to see the new opera at Brescia.

Her next impromptu visitors were women 'dress'd in white like Vestal Virgins, with garlands on their Heads. They came at night with Violins and Flambeaux, but did not stay more than one Dance, persuing their way to another castle some miles from hence.' She began to have some insight into North Italian society. The law vested property inalienably in families, but divided it equally among all the sons when a proprietor died: great families therefore divided and subdivided into poorer and poorer branches. The old pattern of oppressed wives and jealous husbands had been broken, she said, by time and French influence: Brescian women now enjoyed full social liberty, 'and you cannot more affront a Gentleman than to suppose him capable' of jealousy.[36]

Bad weather and bad roads prevented her opera jaunt. (In her first few years at Gottolengo she said she made only two brief visits to Brescia.)[37] But at the height of Carnival, just before Shrove Tuesday, she enjoyed an equivalent entertainment 'in low life'—equivalent, too, to the amateur theatricals

[35] Buxton 1978: 37–8; Lewis 1971: 19; Wh MS M 109–11, 118, 120, 122; Coke 1889–96: iv. 391–2.
[36] *CL* ii. 393, 395, 396, 495–6.
[37] Marinoni thought she kept an apartment at Brescia, and cultivated members of its flourishing Academy, but this seems speculative (1904: 18, 26).

which Lord Bute loved to show off in. She greatly relished it—although she had just told Lady Oxford about being 'wean'd' from the world.

During the years that the 'Castle' had stood empty, the Gottolengo villagers had been free to present their Carnival comedy in its stables. Since these were now occupied by Lady Mary's horses, the priest came to her with a petition that they might stage the show in her most formal reception room. She 'easily comply'd with their request', and was rewarded when their backdrops, done 'by a country painter', outclassed any second-rank London theatre in perspective and colouring. She liked this scenery so well that she left it up and lived with it for two months. The script was terrible, but the peasant actors displayed, she said, 'so natural a Genius for Comedy, they acted as well as if they had been brought up to nothing else'. The village tailor made the best Harlequin she had ever seen, though he had never been to a play outside Gottolengo. Finally, the three-day run cost her nothing beyond a barrel of good wine (cheaper than small beer in London) for the cast. The parish paid for music, costumes, and lighting.[38]

On 10 July 1748 she sent Lady Bute the first of several progress reports on her garden by the Oglio: she was as proud of it as a young playwright of *his* first stage success. (Was she thinking of Henry Fielding?) She called the garden 'a long mile from the Castle': in modern miles it is more like five.[39] She would nevertheless go there for the day, sometimes on foot, sometimes in a chaise, until the weather got too hot. Then she fitted up a room in the old farmhouse dubbed her 'Dairy House'. She 'strewd the floor with Rushes, cover'd the chimney with moss and branches, and adorn'd the Room with Basons of earthen ware (which is made here to great perfection) fill'd with Flowers, and put in some straw chairs and a Couch Bed, which is my whole Furniture'. Here was the 'Little Farm' of her youthful daydreams. When she had got it to her liking, she thought it 'the most Beautifull of any in this province'.[40]

She threw herself into the work. Along the existing paths in her wood she 'added 15 Bowers in different views', with turf seats and interlaced wild vines to shade them comfortably from even the noonday sun. Beside the river she made 'a camp Kitchin, that I may take the Fish, dress and eat it immediately', while she watched the cargo-boats plying between the larger towns on the well-developed system of rivers and canals. She saw the violets give way to wild strawberries; in the warm evenings she listened to the nightingales.

---

[38] *CL* ii. 399, 401–2.   [39] None of the possible spots along the Oglio is at lesser distance than this.
[40] *CL* ii. 402–4, 407–8, 428; *E&P* 206 and n.

Her wood added use to beauty by supplying her with game (every kind but deer and wild boar). Her vineyard, in becoming a garden, did not cease to be a vineyard. Its small space yielded great variety of wines and fruit; 'Cabbage, Onions, Garlick etc.' were banished to another, lower garden. She planted tea (a novelty), and found her crop a little weaker than Indian tea, but purer and fresher. She trained her vines between fruit trees, according to local custom, and 'cram[med] in' roses and jasmines in a manner all her own. In the resulting 'cover'd Gallerys of shade', she could walk comfortably even in the heat. She 'made a dineing room of Verdure, capable of holding a Table of 20 Covers' and planned to add Windsor chairs—when she could get a little model from England, for explaining their structure to the local workmen was beyond her. Her finest flowers were planted in parterres (or formal flowerbeds); the rest edged the garden paths. At the end of her 'great walk' she added two little terraces, rising twelve steps each. Yet more fruit trees studded the hedge that ringed the garden; the whole countryside was so rich in fruit that no one would steal it.

Here she lived a life as regular as that of a monastery—or a clock.

I generally rise at six, and as soon as I have breakfasted put my selfe at the head of my Weeder Women, and work with them till nine. I then inspect my Dairy and take a Turn amongst my Poultry, which is a very large enquiry. I have at present 200 chicken, besides Turkys, Geese, Ducks, and Peacocks. All things have hitherto prosper'd under my Care. My Bees and silk worms are double'd, and I am told that, without accidents, my Capital will be so in two years time. At 11 o'clock I retire to my Books. I dare not indulge my selfe in that pleasure above an hour. At 12 I constantly dine, and sleep after dinner till about 3. I then send for some of my old Priests and either play at picquet or Whist till tis cool enough to go out. One Evening I walk in my Wood where I often Sup, take the air on Horseback the next, and go on the Water the third.

A green awning sufficed to convert her fisherman's boat into a barge; he and his son rowed her, for no payment beyond their catch, which they were free to sell after supplying her with one fish dish each day.[41]

What would Hervey have said about his brilliant friend's bucolic choice of life? In relating it to her daughter, Lady Mary confessed she sometimes wished for 'a little conversation', but she shrugged this off with a moral reflection on 'the commerce of the World' as unsatisfying and unsuitable to her age. Gardening, she said, was 'certainly the next amusement to Reading'. It would 'be the plaything of [her] Age', now her eyes had grown so bad that writing and needlework were difficult. (This was premature: her daily

---

[41] *CL* ii. 402–5, 407–8.

reading, now rationed to a single hour, soon re-extended to 'many hours', without glasses and without ill effects.) Meanwhile the 'best Book of practical Gardening extant' headed her list of commissions from home now that the peace of Aix-la-Chapelle was expected to re-establish normal trade. She also wanted Colen Campbell's *Vitruvius Britannicus* (the leading work on English stately homes and gardens). She wished she could send the produce of her farming to England: wine as a gift (if only there were no duty to pay) and silk as a commodity for sale.

Sending things back and forth was a constant preoccupation. Wortley sent her political pamphlets and was to supply 'six dozen of Nottingham ale' for her neighbours; but he evidently decided at the last moment that this would not travel well, and he did not send it. Lady Mary agonized for years over the quest for 'a safe hand' to carry a 'token' to her god-daughter and eldest grandchild, Lady Mary Stuart.[42]

Optimism about the postal service turned out to be unfounded. Lady Mary (the only inhabitant of Gottolengo to send letters abroad) had already been complaining of losses in both directions. In July 1748 she thought she had found a safe route, only to relapse into near-despair. (One letter arrived opened and stamped with the seal of the Venetian Sanitary Office, charged with controlling infectious diseases.) In October 1748, confessing to 'a little peevishness' on this topic, she asked Wortley to list all the letters he *had* received; and she experimented by sending off three at once by different routes. Her life, she said, was really embittered by these losses, leaving her 'not Spirits enough to try at amuseing you'. She wanted news, and she wanted assurances of affection. If nothing could be done she would have to move, 'notwithstanding the Inconveniences attending a Winter journey'. At last, on Christmas Day, she wrote to tell Wortley she had found a Venetian merchant who should be a reliable intermediary.[43]

This winter was mild: not good news. The warm weather was blamed for a 'malignant fever' (which raged in the province but spared Gottolengo) and for the prospect of a summer without ice, 'which is as necessary as Bread'. During the 1749 Carnival fever at Brescia a young man from near Gottolengo gambled away the entire sum which his guardians had managed to accumulate while he was a minor. He could not sell his estate, which was entailed: he settled down there as 'a sort of Prisoner', to live by what Lady Mary called 'Rapine: I mean running in debt to poor people who

[42] *CL* ii. 410, 416, 427, 439, 483. The needle sounded as important as the pen. She did not take to glasses, as EWM recommended, since she could not get personally fitted (ii. 432).
[43] *CL* ii. 405–6, 408–9, 412–14, 421, 427, 428, 432.

perhaps he will never be able to pay.' She wrote this to Wortley: no doubt she thought of their son.[44]

To her this season again brought visitors. The previous summer she had travelled upwards of sixty kilometres to attend a splendid auction: that of 'the whole Furniture of the Palace of Guastalla', whose last duke had died two years before. She had watched, no doubt with pain, while pictures by 'the first masters . . . went off for a Song, and a Crucifix of Silver said to be the Work of Michael Angelo sold for little more than the Weight'. Most things, she said, 'fell into the hands of the Jews'. Palazzi had told her much about this duke's widow, Eleonore, who was about thirty. He claimed to be high in her favour and often at her court. He had warmly invited Lady Mary there in the duchess's name, but she had ignored him.

Now Eleonore appeared at her door—with most of her court: 'her Grand Master . . . the first Lady of her Bedchamber, 4 pages and a long etc. of inferior Servants, beside her Guards. She enter'd with an easy French air, and told me since I would not oblige her by comeing to her Court she was resolv'd to come to me and eat a salad of my raising, haveing heard much Fame of my Gardening.' Lady Mary's old familiarity with courts stood her in good stead. She 'gave her as good a supper as I could', though when the duchess praised her sack-posset (an English delicacy of warm milk curdled by adding sweet wine), she suspected insincerity. She graciously offered hospitality, while confessing she could not possibly 'find Beds for all her suitte'. Eleonore's reply was a relief: she was to return home later than night, after moonrise (which would be at 1 a.m.). Lady Mary sent out again for those handy local violins. The duchess's attendants danced; Lady Mary played piquet with the duchess and her Grand Master; she even found a private moment to sound out the latter about his mistress's relationship with the King of Sardinia, as reported in the Mantua newspaper. (Answer: though the king sent the duchess 'an express every day', they might be just good friends, and the matter must not be mentioned.)

Lady Mary declined an invitation to go home with her distinguished guest and stay for an indefinite period. She said that fifteen miles in the middle of a cold winter's night would be beyond her, but promised with due deference to come soon. She may have hoped her promise would be a dead letter, since the duchess was planning to return to her native Germany.[45] Lady Mary also decided against making the forty-mile trip to Parma in spring 1749 to 'assist at the entry of Don Philip', when he came to inspect the duchy which was part

[44] *CL* ii. 430–1.
[45] *CL* ii. 383, 409, 415–16. If the duchess was still at Guastalla, MWM underestimated the distance.

of his winnings under the Treaty of Aix-la-Chapelle. She was too incurious (or perhaps, she hinted later, too proud): 'peasants are as agreable to me as Princes.' Most of the local ladies went, in specially provided magnificent get-ups, only to find the court disappointingly dowdy as well as frenchified.[46]

Lady Mary did go this winter, with a party of sightseers, to the Convent of St Ursula in the duchy of Mantua, about twelve miles away.[47] It was, she said, 'the only Institution of the kind in all Italy'. The nuns were all of noble (that is, gentry) birth; they dressed in black, but almost like laywomen—no wimple, no conventional religious habit, no hiding their hair—only 'a thin cypress veil at the back of their heads'. In their large, rambling convent building (with an extensive garden), each sister had 'liberty to build her own Apartment to her Taste, which consists of as many rooms as she pleases'. Each had her own kitchen, her cook and whatever other servants she liked, and could therefore choose between eating privately or in the fine communal refectory. They were also free to go out visiting (in pairs, not alone) and to be visited by women and men. The men in Lady Mary's group were not excluded from any part of the convent tour. The nuns' most remarkable liberty, in her eyes, lay in the Order's possession of a country house three miles away. Here any four nuns together might take holidays at their own discretion; and all of them regularly spent the vintage season there. Lady Mary met there a nun from an Irish expatriate family which she knew. This was the most agreeable and well-spoken religious order she had ever seen; she ascribed these qualities unhesitatingly to its freedom. These nuns, she said, 'seem to differ from the Channonesses of Flanders only in their Vow of Celibacy'.[48] This was the Protestant religious group which had nurtured her admired Anna Maria van Schurman. Here, unexpectedly, were Italian women living out a 'feminist' dream of her youth.

This year too brought its English news items (often stale before they arrived). Wortley inherited from a cousin the highly desirable estate of Newbold Verdon in Leicestershire.[49] Lady Bute bore another daughter, Augusta, bringing her total to six children (after eight pregnancies). Her mother risked giving offence by suggesting that 'your Family is numerous enough . . . the Education and disposal of 4 Girls is employment for a whole

---

[46] *CL* ii. 418, 421–2, 423, 425; 426; iii. 223.

[47] The Ursulines were founded by St Angela Merici (*c.*1470–1540), who was born beside Lake Garda and chose her followers from 'the best families of Brescia'. She wanted them to live 'in the world without being of the world', to adapt as necessary to social change, and to do their own teaching of girls—at which they excelled (*Ursula* [1932]: 2–3).

[48] *CL* ii. 419–20.

[49] *CL* ii. 427. He later paid meticulous attention to the precise degree of fat on the venison from its park (to James Delarue, 11 Aug. 1753, Halsband MSS).

Life'. Lord Monson died, and Lady Mary wondered what would happen to her sister Mar, who had been living in his household though nominally under her daughter's care. Her *half*-sister Lady Caroline married a rich, middle-class member of parliament—a match which Lady Mary quite wrongly thought mercenary and 'absurd'. Mackenzie too got married: to his cousin Lady Betty Campbell, daughter of the late Duke of Argyll, a woman of sterling character, badly scarred by smallpox.[50] From this union Lady Mary expected happiness on both sides.

Spring 1749 was a melancholy season of rains and floods. Lady Mary was tormented by a 'Quotidian Ague'. This meant, apparently, a reactivation of the malaria lingering in her blood since her attack in 1746. Every day at the same hour her temperature shot up, her body shook and sweated. No amount of quinine could stop it. Mari Anna had already been suffering since the New Year with the tertian variety, which attacked her in the middle of every third day. Other servants too were ill, but Mari Anna was 'the most necessary Servant in my Family'. Her illness threw everything into disorder. Lady Mary remained perforce in Gottolengo, past her sixtieth birthday, past the coming of the hot weather, longing for her Dairy House. The village was full of building work. A new parish church was in hand, the old one having been demolished as 'ready to drop'. (The new one was to take fifteen more years to complete.) Lady Mary had her bumpy courtyard levelled—and found quantities of scorched bricks, indicating some past destruction by fire. She searched in vain for local sources or archives, but sent Wortley such historical accounts as she could muster, and copied for him a Roman inscription found in the pavement of the old church.[51]

She wrote to him, about now, several letters on philosophical or scientific topics. She explained the Brescian system for funding health service. Every house in the community was taxed to provide the doctor a stated income, 'on condition he neither demands nor receives any fees, nor ever refuses a visit either to rich or poor'. Lady Mary enthusiastically approved this method of outwitting quackery and human gullibility.

Unfortunately she judged Dr Giovanni Battista Cavalino, the 'medico condotto' who received such enlightened support, to be 'a grave, sober, thinking Great Fool, whose solemn appearance and deliberate way of delivering his sentiments gives them an Air of good sense, thô they are often the most injudicious that ever were pronounc'd'. His inadequacy came to her notice when a male child was born with two heads. It was born feet first

[50] *CL* ii. 421, 428, 429–30, 431–2; Stuart 1899: 51.
[51] *CL* ii. 430, 424. For this 'celebrated' stone, transferred to the new church, see Bonaglia 1985: 83; (photograph) Lucini 1988: 243.

(luckily for its mother) but died in the process. Lady Mary regretted that the doctor was not up to doing a proper autopsy or making 'nice Observations'. Her opinion of the medical profession had not improved since she had fought in its civil wars.[52]

A couple of months after she completed her structural improvements came another crisis with Palazzi. He 'arrived from Brescia with joy painted all over his face', praising God for showing him a way to make reparation. The tale he told had an air of *déjà vu*. He had an offer from one Castelli, a decrepit and childless old man from Trenzano near Brescia, 'to sell his Property for a Life Annuity of two thousand six hundred sequins per annum'. The count had had the land valued by experts at 70,000 ducats at least; he could supply written evidence that the owner was ninety. He had seen the place, 'and fallen in love with it. The poor invalid cannot live more than six months, and the profit will be all yours.' Lady Mary tried to resist. She wanted no involvement with land ownership in a foreign country, she said; she 'was not a Person greedy for Property'. This brought on the usual recriminations and shouting: Palazzi had *promised* her acceptance to Castelli, who would arrive at Gottolengo 'next morning with the deed ready for signing'. For the count to break his word would make him a laughing-stock and deeply disappoint his mother.

Castelli appeared—white-haired, bent, and shaky—bringing the deed of sale as described and a 'valuation of his Property calculated by public Appraisers'. Lady Mary thought he might be an impostor; yet she signed the deed of sale 'in the presence of the Notary of Gottolengo and of two witnesses, and paid the first annuity in advance'.[53] Nothing was ever said of her using or occupying her Trenzano property; she later found she had indeed expended more in annuity payments than it was worth. Did she at least receive rent from this third piece of Italian property?

❧

In July 1749, when both she and Mari Anna had recurrences of the ague, the doctor ordered her to Lovere, a spa village on Lago d'Iseo in the adjoining province of Bergamo. Apart from its medicinal waters, he told her that its doctor, Baglioni, was her best hope, being 'Master of several secrets'.[54] Lady

---

[52] *CL* ii. 423, 431; iii. 4–5; Mazzoldi 1966: 43. Such medical availability would be hard to arrange in England, she thought, because of the prevalence there of imaginary or psychomatic ills.

[53] *RW* 88–9, 95. Venetian gold ducats were sequins, which would make the land value about £35,000, annuity £1,300; silver ducats were worth about one-third as much (Pepys 1926: 348). Gottolengo boasted two notaries, Giovanni Battista Gorno and Antonio Passarella (Mazzoldi 1966: 43).

[54] CB 22; *CL* ii. 433, 436. The lake (Sebino to the Romans, who built villas on its shores) was renamed for a supposed temple of Isis. MWM's notes clearly say she visited Lovere in 1747; she sent her *apparently* first

Mary believed not a word of this, and felt painfully unequal to the journey. Still, she submitted to both bits of advice. She got herself to Lovere, 'almost shook to pieces' on the stony road: one of the worst she had encountered anywhere, not excepting the Alps, 'being all over precipices'. She little knew the route would become almost as familiar to her as the smooth carriage road between London and Twickenham, lined with nursery gardens.

North of Brescia the lush plains gave way to broken or hilly land where chestnut woods punctuated the barley and the vines. Cherries and walnuts were nearly ripe; grapes had further to go. Where they reached the lake, it was edged with towering cliffs in crumbling white stone. The road (once the Roman Via Valeriana) became a series of vertiginous zig-zags; the travellers chose to take to a boat, and had 'the ill luck to be surpriz'd with a storm on the Lake'. They would have sunk if they had not been 'near a little port (where I pass'd a night in a very poor Inn)'. Once in Lovere she found good lodgings with two elderly unmarried women who lived in the reflected glory of their late mother, who had attained the age of 110.[55]

Lady Mary then sought out Dr Baglioni. He prescribed for both her and Mari Anna a twelve-day course of a powder of his own invention: a secret recipe on a quinine base. It was to be taken in a small dose (this at least Lady Mary approved, on the same grounds that she had fought for gentle, non-heroic inoculation practices). Unlike other 'courses of physic', Baglioni's did not demand rest and confinement, but could be combined with a normal social life. And it worked. Lady Mary and Mari Anna were both amazingly restored. Lady Mary sang Baglioni's praises to Lady Bute, though she sounded a trifle embarrassed, expecting her daughter to echo her own former incredulity.

She later expanded her portrait of the doctor known locally as 'the Miraculous Man'. He was his own surgeon and apothecary. He had 'very little learning' but unbounded stores of experience. He was 'the 7th Doctor of his Family in a direct line', and relied in all difficult cases on the private archive left him by 'His Fore Fathers'.

His vivacity is prodigious, and he is indefatigable in his Industry, but what most distinguis[h]es him is a disinterestedness I never saw in any other. He is as regular in his attendance on the poorest peasant, from whom he never can receive one farthing, as on the richest of the Nobility, and when ever he is wanted will climb 3 or 4 mile in the mountains, in the hottest Sun or heaviest rain, where a Horse

impressions to Lady Bute in *probably* 1749 (CB 22; *SL* 336 n. 1). Lovere is *c.*25 km from Brescia as the crow flies. Its 'Steel Waters' were prescribed for post-menopausal symptoms and vapours (*CL* ii. 491).

[55] *CL* ii. 434, 466, 493.

cannot go, to arrive at a Cottage where, if their condition requires it, he does not only give them advice and med'cines Gratis, but Bread, Wine, and whatever is needfull.[56]

Lovere, once a haunt of itinerant fishermen, had become a summer haunt of Bergamese and Brescian nobility when its medicinal waters were discovered.[57] It had then been almost wiped out by a great plague. Ancient palaces in its medieval centre stood empty and ruinous, or 'degraded into Lodging Houses'. To the world outside it was 'almost unknown'; its fence of towering mountains made it seem not 'destin'd by Nature to be inhabited by Human Creatures'. Lady Mary came to see it as 'certainly one of the prettyest places in the World', actualizing 'all the delightfull Ideas of Romance'. Bit by bit she described it all to her daughter. It fronted the lake in a semi-circle, a confusion of 'Shops and Palaces, Gardens and Houses', two miles long and a mile high. Most of its streets were alleys or flights of steps, 'impassible for any wheel carriage except a Wheelbarrow' but paved with local marble in colours as various as those of 'the finest mosaic work'. Its scattered buildings reminded her of Tunbridge Wells, and its terraced gardens of Richmond Hill.[58]

The lake was sea-green as if from suspended minerals. The slopes about it, overhung by mountains like 'vast Rocks', were 'thick set with villages (and in most of them Gentlemen's seats)', threaded with delightful walks, and 'cover'd with Vines and fruit trees, mix'd with several natural Cascades, and embellish'd with variety of Beautifull prospects'. The provisions—fish from the lake, game from the mountains, fruit from the orchards—were excellent.[59]

The social life of Lovere (which flourished only during the brief annual season for drinking the waters) was a tonic in itself to Lady Mary after the company of her servants, her villagers, and her poultry (though she professed to be 'heartily weary of the Eternal Hurry'). She said that 'we' gathered regularly to take the waters at an oasis of coolness, a spring between two 'hanging Hills . . . over shadow'd with large Trees'. Dress was informal: even at social gatherings people wore the 'Vestimenta di confidenza', which at Brescia would be unthinkable in public. Ladies went

[56] *CL* ii. 436; iii. 53. A Dr Antonio Baglioni was a 'medico condotto' at Adro near Gottolengo (Mazzoldi 1966: 132).

[57] There is now no memory of these waters in the town, though Boario, just up the valley, is a flourishing spa. In mid-19th-century Lovere doctors sent patients to a spring near Pianico, outside the town. This rose between two peaks like the one MWM describes (Offredi 1963).

[58] *CL* ii. 441, 466; iii. 54. Her picture of its jumble of buildings echoes her lines on Constantinople (*E&P* 209).

[59] *CL* ii. 434, 435; iii. 53–4.

without caps (which only unmarried ones might do in winter). Instead of shirt, ruffles, coat, hat, breeches, and boots, gentlemen wore 'light night-caps, nightgowns (under which I am inform'd they wear no Breeches) and slippers'. Ladies wore 'their stays, and smock sleeves ty'd with Ribands, and a single lutestring petticoat': at least one layer less than usual on body, arms, and skirts. There was 'not a Hat or a Hoop to be seen'.[60]

Operas were staged three times a week: at 10 p.m., so that Lady Mary, having got used to early hours, was half-asleep by the end. Then came a farce, a rapturously received song (which she calls a cantata) by one of the actors, and a ball. Even without staying for the ball, she found 'it was one before I could get to bed'. But the scenery, the voices and the acting were so good that she would have been 'surpriz'd . . . if I had not remember'd I was in Italy. Several Gentlemen jump'd into the orchestre and joyn'd in the con-sort, which I suppose is one of the freedoms of the Place, for I never saw it in any great Town.'

Music, it turned out, was the soul of Lovere. Everyone assembled on the water every night, with 'Violins, Lutes, Mandolins and Flutes doux'— nothing 'so rough' as horns or trumpets. Almost every man in the place was a skilled musician, eager to augment the professionals and serenade 'the Lady of his affections'. Lady Mary despised the puppet shows, and assured Lady Bute that she had never visited the 'gameing room'; but music, she now found, was something she had been starved of.

Despite the mountains, there was even a regular courier to Brescia: a huge improvement on the private messengers she was forced to employ from Gottolengo. News from England duly arrived. Lady Oxford had built herself a new house near Welbeck, and called it by her maternal name: Cavendish Lodge. Lady Mary's nephew Kingston was occupying the kitchen wing at Thoresby (all that had survived the fire) with his mistress Madame La Touche and the whole Meadows family.[61]

Lady Bute's activities made happier news. She was on the best of terms with Wortley. She was busy with court attendance. She had as closest friend Lady Middlesex, who was 'a vast scholar', Mistress of the Robes to the Princess of Wales (and, according to Walpole, already the prince's mis-tress). Lady Bute had despatched a box of new English books—via Venice, whither Lady Mary sent a messenger in haste to see to them. The Butes had moved with their family to Kenwood House, Hampstead. Bute had owned it since 1746; Lady Bute fitted it up. Lady Mary was glad to deduce that they

---

[60] *CL* ii. 435, 437; iii. 12–13.
[61] *CL* 434–5, 437, 442. La Touche was soon to be discarded (Rizzo 1994: 68).

must be 'in no Want of Money', and deeply interested in their garden improvements and choice of furnishings. But wistfulness crept in. 'It would be a great pleasure to me to see my Grand children run about in the Gardens.'[62]

In late August Lovere's theatre closed and life slowed down. The 'Beau monde' were off to Bergamo for the famous annual fair. Lady Mary was pressed to go too, but decided at the last moment to stay put. She sent Mari Anna to hunt for bargains. She could spare her because she had just taken on an extra maid: Francesca or Chechina. She did this, she said, because Mari Anna complained that as combined chambermaid and housekeeper she was overworked: also because Chechina and her father (a leading Lovere merchant) were so keen on the arrangement. The girl was barely sixteen, but highly intelligent, unusually well educated—and amazingly beautiful. She had nice handwriting, kept immaculate accounts, and loved sewing; she never went out except to church on Sunday, and she never complained. But her arrival precipitated domestic strife. Throughout the household—and later throughout Gottolengo—the men pursued her and the women (Mari Anna especially) 'declar'd open War with her'. Lady Mary (who seems to have been hoping to acquire a secretary as well as a chambermaid) gritted her teeth and remembered *Pamela*. She was sorry but also relieved when Chechina's father sent for her home in early November. Next year Chechina was married, and her erstwhile employer probably attended.[63]

Meanwhile Lady Mary stayed one more month at Lovere, living by the kind of routine she now liked best: rising early, playing 'Whisk' for an hour or two in the afternoon, going on the water every evening, and usually landing and finding 'some new Walk amongst the Mountains'. Again the idea of buying a house presented itself. Mansions were on offer everywhere at knockdown prices: if they could only be transported, Lady Mary told Wortley, she might ship him a few to their mutual profit. She was even offered one gratis if she could find 20,000 crowns for the land around it, and she believed the owners would throw in their furniture ('allmost new') and pictures ('good', probably Renaissance).[64] Was Palazzi, one wonders, at Lovere? Or was he not the only person in North Italy who could not see an English lady without trying to sell her a palazzo?

---

[62] Kenwood had been Bute's father's, then Ilay's; MWM had seen it while Ilay owned it. MWM approved Lady Bute's choice of 'paper Hangings' and Lady Middlesex's taste for a quiet life (*CL* ii. 438–9, 442; Healey 1992: 59 n.; Walpole, *Corr.* xix. 62 n.; xx. 97 n.).

[63] CB 22; *CL* ii. 438, 441, 443–4. It was normal in this society for unmarried girls to be confined to the house (working) except on Sundays (Wynne 1785: ii. 170–1).

[64] *CL* ii. 440–1. A crown was almost a generic name for foreign coins worth around 5s., so this is about £5,000.

While Lady Mary joked with her husband about trading in palaces, he had again gone abroad without letting her know. This time he met their son in Paris. He did write to tell her (when he had been there over a month) that he and Edward were about to be presented at the court of Versailles. This was the high-water mark of Wortley's relations with his son.[65]

His letter about this event never arrived, and Lady Mary became concerned at his silence. She went home to her Castle in September 1749, greatly reinvigorated. She rode a lot, and boasted that converting from side-saddle to riding astride had made her 'a better horse Woman than ever I was in my Life'. She had ridden in, by moonlight, from a twenty-mile jaunt in company when she found Lady Bute's box of books safely arrived. It was ten at night, but she 'could not deny my selfe the pleasure of opening it, and falling upon Fielding's Works was fool enough to sit up all night reading'. She devoured both *Joseph Andrews* and *Tom Jones*, preferring the earlier work to the later, more original one. To Wortley, who had sent her Bolingbroke's *Letters, on the Spirit of Patriotism*, she replied with a detailed critique; it does not survive.

She busied herself, too, with a different kind of text: 'my receipt Book'. She brought the local arts of baking bread and making butter up to English standards, and won 'universal applause' by introducing French rolls, custards, cheesecakes, plum pudding, and mince pies, 'which were entirely unknown in these Parts'. She told Lady Bute that improvements in the art of living deserved fame as much as those in other arts (a favourite paradox), and defended her solitary pleasures—like a walk in the November sun—as more truly enjoyable than her daughter's busy social ones.[66]

This winter Lady Bute consulted her about educating her daughters. Lady Mary's response is commonsensical: don't give children prejudices; don't deceive them if you hope to keep their respect. It revolves round the value of books and of a life of retirement. 'If your Daughters are inclin'd to Love reading', she says, don't forbid them reading which is just for fun. She prescribes differently for the different situation of each sex: boys needed to read widely, for reputation, girls only for amusement or pastime. 'Let their Brothers shine, and let them content themselves with makeing their Lives easier by it.' She knew by experience, she says, the value of study, and she knew by observation how ignorance breeds vice.

She called her first advice-letter tedious, and apologized for it; but she soon followed it with another, more detailed one. This pinpoints another

---

[65] They were presented on 23 Sept. 1749 NS. The duc de Luynes found both the father's wealth and status and the son's colourful history worthy of record (1860: ix. 505).

[66] *CL* ii. 443, 444, 446–8, 485.

parental error: telling a beautiful girl either that she is plain or that beauty is worthless. This amounts to lying to her about the value of the hand dealt her in a game she needs to win.[67] Lady Mary argues that pious books, which teach 'contempt of Beauty, Riches, Greatness etc.' can seriously skew a girl's sense of reality; she cites her niece Lady Frances Pierrepont, throwing herself away on a poor man out of misplaced idealism and loyalty. One of her most original insights—later developed by the 1790s radicals—is that society's definitions of female virtue ought not to be uncritically accepted. Girls, she says, are drilled to be virtuous 'without limits or distinction', and without ever questioning what exactly virtue means. She developed these ideas in 'Docile', whose virtuous heroine first imbibes the doctrines of self-mortifying religion, then those of philosophic reason, duty, and honour, and so remains forever ignorant of the forces of power and self-interest which govern her world.

It was part of her common sense to deprecate parents who groom their daughters for a high rank which the marriage stakes are unlikely to yield them. She thought her granddaughters likely to live very private lives, to be (in a phrase she several times repeated) 'Lay Nuns'. She clearly assumed they would have no dowries. She had known, in the days before her daughter's marriage, that she was Wortley's chosen heir. Did she know that choice had been revoked and never reinstated? Perhaps she was thinking of his recent favour to Edward; perhaps his refusal to pay Lady Bute's dowry had convinced her he would offer no help towards dowries for his granddaughters. She did go so far, in 1751, as to tell him she favoured the Roman practice of dividing family property equally among males and females; any reply is not recorded.

Folded into the second of these letters on education comes a melancholy moment: advice to Lady Bute to 'moderate that fondness you have for your children': not to care less for them, but to 'prepare your selfe for Disapointments'. Though she jotted among her maxims, 'No Duty owing to a Parent meerly as a Parent', she also noted, 'Children are Creditors never paid.' Some of Lady Bute's might turn out badly; some might live to be unhappy. Their mother would suffer less in these eventualities if she had foreseen them, and schooled her imagination.[68] In Lady Mary's later letters this wistful note was to become more common.

---

[67] Not MWM's image, but related to images she uses.
[68] *CL* ii. 449–52, 487; iii. 25, 267; CB 8, 10.

27

March 1750–1753

❧

Lone Philosopher: 'to divert my solitary hours'[1]

IN early March 1750 Lady Mary wrote quite cheerfully to Lady Oxford: she was well; she would go back in summer to Lovere, which had done her such good; her only sorrow was the conduct of her nephew Kingston and niece Lady Frances Meadows.[2] She left unmentioned something nearer home: infection of the gums. She was living on soft food, applying 'the little remedys common for the Tooth ach', but her mouth was becoming steadily more painful. At last she was persuaded to let the village surgeon examine it. She trusted his honesty and skill; when she saw him turn pale she was seriously alarmed. He said nothing to her, 'but went away, and told every body he met that the Gangreen was already form'd, and he thought my recovery impossible'.

Still without consulting the patient, a neighbour 'took post Horses', and fetched from Cremona 'the most celebrated Surgeon in all these parts'. He came the seventeen or eighteen kilometres within a few hours. On his arrival Lady Mary 'heard Sentence of Death pronounce'd against me', and 'consented to let him use what Operations he pleas'd'. (How she consented she does not say: her tongue was so swollen that she could not speak.) The surgeon 'immediately apply'd red hot Irons to my Gumms'. During the ensuing agony Lady Mary remained fully conscious and rational; she did not, as the surgeon expected, run a high fever from sheer terror. Indeed, she felt less pain afterwards than before, and she 'slept very well that night'. The surgeon, surprised and delighted, announced that she might survive, for she was strong enough to undergo the second step: caustics applied to her seared gums. This went on for several days.

---

[1] *CL* iii. 19.
[2] Lady Oxford said Kingston's chief amusement was cricket (31 July 1751, Halsband MSS).

She ascribed this 'severest illness I ever had' to getting chilled on one of her long walks. She recovered 'with great difficulty and very slowly'. It was weeks before she wrote an account of her ordeal to Lady Oxford, and she told her family much less. She trusted that Lovere would complete her cure: indeed, one of Dr Baglioni's marvels was his mouthwash concocted to treat 'the Scurvy in the Teeth', or peridontal disease.[3]

Palazzi had been a less frequent visitor of late, which she was glad of because of the wear and tear he inflicted on her horses and her furniture. He came in early June, while she was still convalescent, bringing his mother's compliments and assurances 'that she would have come herself to take care of me, if her health had not been so delicate, and the roads so damaged by the excessive rain'. He was still at her house when, probably the next day, one François-Zacharie de Quinsonas Laub
erivière turned up. It is hard to resist the inference that Palazzi's expressed concern for Lady Mary's health was mere cover, and that he went to Gottolengo to forestall Lauberivière.

From this point onwards, two conflicting versions of the story each allege unprovoked violence by the other side. Lauberivière said he had brought a letter for Lady Mary from John Anderson, her son's old tutor; he also meant to offer to escort her to Venice. Before he could deliver his letter, Palazzi's servants intercepted him, surrounded and threatened him, and shut him up in a cellar for two hours; Palazzi confiscated the letter. Lady Mary said Lauberivière was a madman and an impostor; he had arrived disguised as a priest and sent in by Mari Anna an idiotic letter purporting to be from some unknown, perhaps non-existent, lady. When Lady Mary refused the letter and asked him to leave, he drew a pistol on her servants.[4]

Lauberivière was not unknown to her. She had met him at Avignon; he said (perhaps ironically?) she had had him expelled from the town. Her later account of the present fracas makes it sound as if it all took place without her knowledge. But at the time she clearly said she had communicated with him, if not actually seen him. She had no known reason to refuse a letter from Anderson (whom she was glad to see when he arrived at Gottolengo a month later) or from any lady. She *may* have guessed (probably wrongly) that this anonymously proffered letter emanated either from Algarotti or from her son.[5]

---

[3] *CL* ii. 454, 460–1, 436; *RW* 89. The surgeon from Cremona (which is nearer Gottolengo than MWM thought, even nearer than Brescia) agreed with advanced thinking in London. John Hunter, on research done before 1755, describes gums so swelled that the mouth, and the eye on the affected side, can hardly open (1778: 11). He advises incision, or caustics, for abscesses or 'Gum Boils' (which are exacerbated by exposure to cold), and scarifying for ulcerated gums, which may be linked to scurvy (29, 31, 36, 51–2, 57). He strongly favours having the tooth pulled.

[4] *RW* 89–90; Venetian Archivio di Stato, Brescia, Busta 21. 11, 14; documents in the case pub. in Fappani 1961: 113–24; MWM to Contarini, *CL* ii. 456–7.

[5] She jotted Algarotti's name and Lauberivière's side by side (CB 21).

Complications continued. Two days after Palazzi's first arrival and the day after Laubervière's brief appearance, an express came in from Brescia and the count appeared before Lady Mary 'looking very frightened'. Countess Palazzi had sent to inform them that Laubervière had laid a complaint before the Podestà or Venetian administrator of the province, Angelo Contarini. (Lady Mary enjoyed high status in Brescia because of her personal friendship with the doge, Grimani.)[6] Laubervière had complained of violence to her as well as to himself: that Palazzi was 'holding [her] Prisoner in his Castle'. Palazzi said this was all a plot by his hereditary enemies the Rodenghi;[7] he proceeded, as before, to prophesy doom and tearfully implore Lady Mary to save him. She said she was ready to testify that she was there of her own free will, and had always been treated with respect.

Two hours behind the express messenger came an official from the Podestà, 'with orders to speak with me privately'. He met no hindrance from Palazzi, and found her 'ensconced on my Couch'. He brought Contarini's written request that she should come to Brescia and clear up the affair. She said she was not well enough to travel.[8] Instead she repeated, both orally and in a personal letter to Contarini, her assurances 'that I had received nothing but courtesy from the Palazzi Family'.

The count now went off to Brescia, but he was back in two days

with a closed Carriage sent for me by his Mother, who besought me for pity's sake to come to her House, to silence all the false rumours still in circulation, which only my presence could quash. The doctor assured me that I could make the journey without risk, and I made it in such a state of weakness that my Maid had to support me in the carriage.

The count and his brother Alessandro could hardly get her to the rooms prepared for her. 'They treated me with all possible honour and respect. I slept well, and in the morning I was well enough to receive visitors.' The ladies and gentlemen of Brescia poured in, and to them Lady Mary, flanked by the Palazzi family, 'laughed at the idea that I was kept at Gottolengo by violence', and extolled retirement as a 'very natural' choice for someone of her age.[9]

She might have cited her writing as another reason for her choice. She found that cultured Italians often complimented her 'on the Books I have given the Public'. At first she would 'deny it with some Warmth', supposing

---

[6] *CL* iii. 12.

[7] Large landowners at Gottolengo (genealogical notes in Queriniana MSS).   [8] Busta 21. 16.

[9] *RW* 89–90. Signora Roncadelli was there, and a Palazzi daughter who was either then or later a nun. Laubervière wrote again from Turin, sending her good wishes from friends and urging her to leave her retreat (Busta 21. 11).

that anything else would bring on unfriendly mockery. By now she knew that no one believed her denials, and that 'the character of a learned Woman is far from being ridiculous in this Country'. Female writers and scholars were acceptable to—often members of—'the greatest Familys'. There was no danger that she would be seen as a disgrace to her name, in the way she saw her son or her nephew. Once assured of this, she 'contented my selfe with laughing' at flattery about her supposed publications.

It may have been on this visit that she made a friend of Cardinal Angelo Maria Querini, the scholarly, cultured, somewhat self-important Bishop of Brescia, who was celebrating his jubilee in his see.[10] Querini was a great benefactor of the town and diocese. He had achieved the long-delayed completion of the new cathedral, 'where he has already the comfort of seeing his own Busto finely done both within and without'. He had remodelled his bishop's palace, and set up a new college for seminarians, a monastery, a printing press, and as his *pièce de résistance* the Biblioteca Queriniana (still a notable research library).[11] He was writing his autobiography, which opened with the portents attending his birth. He had corresponded with Conti, Gilbert Burnet, and Sir Isaac Newton—and still did so with Maria Gaetana Agnesi, a female professor of mathematics at the University of Bologna. He credited Lady Mary with high status in the learned world, but did not perceive her somewhat satirical attitudes, either towards himself or to 'the Authority of the Church' (which in Italy, she said, 'can not only veil but sanctifye any absurdity or Villainy whatever').[12]

Meanwhile the Palazzi family was still not satisfied. A new Podestà was expected any day to succeed Contarini, and they besought Lady Mary to stay in town to repeat her assurances to him. He was no other than Gerolemo Gradenigo, whose wife, Giustiniana (Morosini) Gradenigo, had done her great honours in Venice ten years before.[13] Lady Mary was eager to see her, so she was happy to remain in Brescia (displayed as a living proof of Palazzi integrity) long enough to renew her friendship.

In her 'Italian Memoir' she goes no further with the story of Lauberivière's complaint. Whatever he had wanted to achieve, he must have felt himself worsted. Once away from Brescia, however, he talked. Next year Walpole heard an obscure tale of Lady Mary being held 'close prisoner' by a

[10] Valcanover notes that they might have met when Querini was in London in early 1711 (1987: 139 n. 1).

[11] A print commemorated all this (Queriniani MS F vi. 4b).

[12] *CL* iii. 13–15, 39, 58; Queriniani MSS E vi. 30, F v. 7. Querini kept an elegant copy of Conti's translation of *Eloisa to Abelard*. Agnesi, from Milan, had been picked for her post by Pope Benedict XIV; she thanked Querini for books in Sept. 1749.

[13] At a 'great Supper' and at Venice's wedding with the sea (see p. 408, 410).

young man who had been her kept lover, who vetted all her letters before letting them in or out, and who planned to marry her once she was a rich widow. He begged Mann to find out more; Mann reported that the story was generally believed, and that although she denied to Contarini being in 'durance' she had admitted it by post to Michiel. Walpole had a particular reason for curiosity: he had just borrowed and read her letters to Lady Mar, which he found spirited, vivacious—and debauched. He linked her with Lady Rachel Russell as a proof of women's writing better letters than men; but he might just as well not have read her letters for any weight he gave to her own testimony as against Pope's, about the Rémond affair or about her relationship with her sister. When Lady Mary called *men* sots and scoundrels he automatically applied her words to people of both sexes.[14]

Meanwhile, Lady Mary regained her strength after the ordeal with her gums. (She soon faced a new domestic crisis: Fribourg suddenly developed cataracts. Unexpectedly, however, he did not go blind.)[15] Palazzi went off roving the country as usual, pursuing the career of robbery and extortion of which she was presumably ignorant. He came back with news of a most beautiful palazzo and perfect garden which could be hers for a trifle. He 'begged me at least to go and look at it'. Her 'Memoir' implies that she refused this bait and 'made what haste I could to travel to Lovere'.[16] It seems that this, her first refusal of a property deal with Palazzi, was absolute. But her haste was relative. She made a brief trip with him (unmentioned in her surviving letters to England) and was back in Brescia when Anderson arrived with his tourist pupil. She thought this boy very promising and played with the notion of his falling in love with her eldest granddaughter. She gave three letters to Anderson to convey to England, and 'some little commissions' to execute, like buying books in Holland. (Probably this meant books of science or controversy, unavailable in Catholic countries.)[17] Then she made ready to leave for Lovere.

Though she had spent the previous summer there, Palazzi spoke as if it would be a novelty. He 'warned me that I should have to traverse a very dangerous Forest, and that if I had any money I should do well to leave it in the

---

[14] Walpole, *Corr.* xx. 235, 278–9. Voltaire, too, heard rumours of MWM's sexual misconduct. Walpole had her letters from Lady Frances Erskine, via her cousin the Duchess of Bedford (*Corr.* xx. 121, 281). For the market for such stories, cf. Rizzo 1994: 182.

[15] MWM ascribed this to his having himself excessively bled to cure an eye infection (*CL* ii. 463).

[16] Another advocate for Lovere was Dr Gian Francesco Guadagni, the leading physician of Brescia, whom MWM called 'elderly' though he was 15 years younger than she (*RW* 91 and n. 2).

[17] *CL* ii. 464, 476–7; iii. 11; Contarini to the Venetian Governor, 21 June and 12 July 1750, Busta 235. 1, 7. The mails were bad again, taking up to four months either way. MWM did not entrust Anderson with her 'token' for the young Lady Mary (a pearl necklace): he was making 'a long Tour' before going home (*CL* iii. 16).

hands of a Banker'. Again, as in the matter of shipping her furniture, he had someone to recommend who was a grateful protégé of the Palazzi family as well as 'a man of unblemished integrity, and of great wealth': Signor Francesco Ballini. When Lady Mary asked to meet Ballini it seemed that he was laid up with gout, and Palazzi proposed to 'take him the money and bring me back the receipt'. Lady Mary consented. She was later cagey about the sum she paid out (and never saw again); she thought it was 200 sequins. She rejected the count's escort and went on her way after receiving 'visits of leave-taking' from the ladies of Brescia.

Again Lovere healed her. She spent two months there, July to September 1750, loving both the place and (whatever she might say about it) its polite society. But public lodgings were noisy; besides, this year's fell short of her former ones with the two sisters. She lamented to Dr Baglioni that without a comfortable house to stay in she would keep her visit short, and might not return next year. She suggested that he should help her to find a house; and after long searching he told her, just before she left, that he had found a hopeful candidate among the ruined and tattered palazzi that had struck her on her first visit. Well situated above the lake, with beautiful views, it had stood empty for at least two generations. It was up for auction after the death of an owner who had never seen it. Its condition, its relatively small size, and the fact that the governor of the town 'bid for me, and no body would bid against him' meant that Lady Mary got it for 300 scudi or £100. She 'gave Dr Baglioni a note on Ballini for this sum', and he arranged the paperwork. Thus 'I am become a Citizen of Louvere, to the great Joy of the Inhabitants'—who vainly hoped she would 'attract all the travelling English'.[18]

It was typical of her growing scattiness that she left this purchase unused—and unreported to her daughter—until three years later. She then confessed ('I see you lift up your Eyes in wonder at my Indiscretion') and described her prize. It was 'founded on a rock, and the Walls so thick they will probably remain as long as the Earth'. It had a courtyard behind, and 'a very pretty Garden in Terrases down to the Water'. It lacked doors or windows, but its floors and ceilings were sound. It won Lady Mary's affection, she said, by the nobility and beauty of its 'great salon': tall and spacious, with a marble-banistered balcony opening off it. As a final sop to Lady Bute, it carried no ground rent, poor rate, or church tax.[19] For the moment, however, Lady Mary did not linger there: other places were calling.

---

[18] *RW* 91–2; *CL* iii. 54–5. Today Lovere public library has books, theses, and articles on her.

[19] Local tradition says this was among buildings pulled down to make the present Piazza XIII Martire in the town centre. MWM's accounts are slightly confusing. The 'Memoir' says Baglioni organized a

Leaving Lovere on lago d'Iseo, she made another expedition with Palazzi: to see some splendid palaces in and around Salò on lago di Garda. Perhaps this was the jaunt she had declined to take a few months earlier: at this point the minor discrepancies in her stories or her memory multiply puzzlingly. She told Lady Oxford that she was back at her Dairy House for some weeks between her visits to the two lakes; in the later 'Memoir' she said Palazzi persuaded her to travel from Iseo straight to Garda, on the improbable grounds that it was a better route back to Gottolengo. The 'Memoir' reads 'Solferino' for Salò (which there is no doubt she meant).[20]

Lady Mary's chief object on this trip was a palazzo just outside Salò. She found the count had not exaggerated its splendour. She had by now lived in a number of Renaissance palaces, but she thought this 'the finest place I ever saw': beyond anything boasted by the monarchs of France, Germany, Naples, or England. Furthermore, even the majestic interior was outshone by the gardens, which were the stuff of fairy tales.[21] She told Lady Bute that the owner (who had ruined himself by gambling and could not afford to live there) 'would be glad to let it for a Triffle'. To persuade her to rent his 'Paradise', he spent a week showing her round the western shore of Lake Garda. But in her 'Memoir' she said Palazzi had urged her to *buy* it.[22] Moreover, she casually added that she took his advice, put in her application to purchase this acme of splendour (the very opposite pole in dwellings from her humble Dairy House), and divided her time between it and Gottolengo for the next four years. Her letters, on the contrary, never mention it after her first rapturous description, but say she lived always at Gottolengo or Lovere. Other sources on the palazzo say nothing of her.

On such a large body of water as Lake Garda, there was 'allwaies some little Swell like that on the Sea'. It beat on the courtyard wall; Lady Mary enjoyed the sound. When storms blew up they were terrific; she recalled Virgil's lines in the *Georgics* about this lake, and pleased herself with the thought that his eyes had looked upon the same view.

---

house-purchase for her at Lovere in 1750; her letter of 1754 implies the purchase at auction was recent. I *assume* she bought one palace at Lovere, not two (*CL* iii. 54–5, 59; *RW* 91–2).

[20] *RW* 92; *CL* ii. 467 ff. Salò, site of the palazzos she describes, lies on Lake Garda about 20 km from Brescia; Solferino, between Salò and Mantua, is not on a lake and has no such palazzos.

[21] Built by Sforza Pallavicino in 1556, owned by the Martinengo Cesarescos, a refuge in 1585 for the woman whom MWM probably knew as John Webster's White Devil, it was converted into a fortress in 1796. Photos of its gardens are disappointing. She also saw and described the lovely Villa Gonzaga at nearby Maderno (Perogalli, Sandri, and Zanella 1985: 403–4, 411–12).

[22] Palazzi said it had been confiscated during the war by Empress Maria Theresa, and MWM must apply to the Austrian military governor. She told Lady Oxford she wanted somewhere to rent for at least part of the year, having decided Lady Oxford was right to think the air of Gottolengo was bad for her (*CL* ii. 467–71; *RW* 92; Lady Oxford, 7 Jan. 1750, 14 Oct. 1751, Halsband MSS).

An independent witness to her time at Salò is someone then living nearby: Bartolomeo Dominiceti, a blue-blooded but shady medical practitioner. Exiled soon afterwards over an affair of honour, he settled in England, where he became just the kind of self-publicizer she most disliked. He wrote that he had met her in 1749 while she was staying with his 'unfortunate friend' Palazzi. He knew her reputation and seized his opportunity to talk inoculation with her. Those talks continued at Salò.[23]

In 1750 Lady Mary stayed at Salò more than a month. She was back at Gottolengo at the end of November, when snow buried the village. It confined her indoors for two months or more, wiped out the Carnival, and made her regret the milder climate of Lake Garda. Newspapers from Holland (or anywhere outside Italy) had been banned, and she felt more than ever at the mercy of the unreliable postal service. She sent Lady Bute Italian poetry, and eagerly took up her offer of more English books. 'I thank God my Taste still continues for the Gay part of reading.' She welcomed the news that Lord Bute was now First Lord of the Bedchamber to the Prince of Wales. From a *habitué* of the Princess of Wales's home court of Saxe-Gotha she acquired matching pictures of the prince and princess, copies of those sent as a ceremonial gift to Saxe-Gotha from Britain.[24] She added them to her 'Gallery': that prince whom she had lampooned as a tormented puppy was now the prop and patron of her family. But she counselled against too heavy reliance on royal favour. To Wortley she wrote that 'You and I know enough of Courts not to be amaz'd at any Turns they may take.' To Lady Bute she wrote that Wortley's continued good health was 'the greatest Blessing that can happen to his Family'. For herself, she did not expect to live to see her grandchildren settled in marriage.[25]

She hastened to assure Lady Bute that these reflections must not be read as melancholy. 'There is a Quiet after the abandoning of Persuits, something like the rest that follows a Laborious Day. I tell you this for your Comfort. It was formerly a terrifying view to me that I should one day be an Old Woman; I now find that Nature has provided pleasures for every State.' She might deny she was melancholy; she could not deny that she was meditating on age and death. Last year's illness, present isolation (exacerbated by the

[23] *CL* iii. 32; ii. 476; Blunt 1914: 140. Dominiceti pub. on inoculation at Venice in 1770. Writing in Italian he did not mention MWM, though he claimed backing from many of her Venetian friends ([1776]: 19, 37). In English he boasted that all his facts and opinions on inoculation had received her 'strongest confirmation' (1781: 431 n.).

[24] *CL* ii. 471–3, 474, 478. Originals by Joseph Highmore, 1742 (*GM* 1780: 50: 177). Algarotti had been Saxe-Gotha's picture-buyer.

[25] *CL* ii. 472–3, 476, 477. EWM watched his health carefully, weighing himself regularly and noting the good effect of certain wines. In spring 1751 he was ill and lost nearly a stone (Halsband MSS).

snow), the shockingly sudden end of Giulia Palazzi, who had recently gone from health to death in three days: all these had turned her mind to her own mortality in a way that was new. But she was irrepressible. If 'Old Woman' was to be her next role, she would play it to the hilt.[26]

Meanwhile she was in better health than for years (the natural result of her recent serious illness, said the doctors). She sat indoors through rain and floods which followed the snow, and described for Wortley a tornado at Gottolengo, a localized 'blast of Wind' which uprooted trees and unroofed houses before their occupants had time to be scared. Then came news of a metaphorical tornado: the sudden death of the Prince of Wales. Bute's career had rested solely on his personal favour. It now seemed to be over, and her grandchildren's prospects materially diminished.

This blow perhaps turned Lady Mary's thoughts back to her sister Frances. While she spared a thought for the prince's creditors, she addressed to Lady Bute (who was four months pregnant) an earnest plea that she should not allow herself to fall into depression.[27] Powerless as humans are, she told her, one thing is *partly* in our power:

> the disposition of our own Minds. Do not give way to melancholy; seek amusements . . . Weak people only place a merit in affliction. A grateful remembrance, and what ever honor we can pay to their memory, is all that is owing to the Dead. Tears and Sorrow are no Dutys to them, and make us incapable of those we owe to the living . . . My Dear Child, endeavor to raise your Spirits, and believe this advice comes from the tenderness of your most affectionate Mother.

She probably knew her daughter pretty well. Soon Lady Bute was complaining of loneliness, and Lady Mary urged her to count her blessings: house and garden, loving husband, and 'numerous hopefull Progeny'. But while she advised her daughter to control her feelings she admitted to Wortley that she could not practise what she preached: that her tenderness and anxiety for Lady Bute were 'stronger than my philosophy'.

At once her mind began running through the political consequences of the prince's death. His thirteen-year-old son George would now have office-holders assigned him in keeping with his new status. Lady Mary thought 'his Father's Servants should have the Preference'. But she well

[26] *CL* ii. 477, 478, 484; iii. 11. Lady Oxford sent sympathy on this loss (13 May 1751, Halsband MSS).

[27] *CL* ii. 479–81. Lady Mar was said to be ill this year. Her daughter, Lady Frances Erskine, had developed evangelical leanings; like the former Lord Grange (her uncle and father-in-law), she corresponded with Philip Doddridge (Mar MS GD.124/15/1596, 15/1559; Doddridge 1829: i. 226). The Princess of Wales was 'seven months gone' with her ninth child; Walpole said 'no pity is too much' for her (*Corr.* xx. 232).

knew George II's long-cherished hatred of his son and heir; whatever *ought* to happen, Frederick's servants were now *persona non grata*. She trusted her husband to help keep up their daughter's spirits; but Wortley went abroad again this summer, travelling as far as Vienna and staying away until November.[28]

She felt another 'Concern' which she was almost ashamed of. Edward had stopped writing to her, having nothing to get from her. She felt his long-term conduct made her natural feeling for him inappropriate; it was irrational, purely instinctive—but unconquerable. In May 1751 she could no longer resist her desire for news, 'long suppress'd . . . from a beleife that if there was any thing of good to be told, you would not fail to give me the pleasure of hearing it'. She was right; there was nothing good to hear. Wortley had for once acted without consulting her in his overtures to Edward in Paris in 1749; since then he had reverted to his former policy. He may have heard in France of the British ambassador's recurrent anxieties about Edward's money sources and his contacts; or he may have made some unwelcome discovery in London. Now that Edward was an MP and immune from arrest for debt, he went freely back and forth. He was thought to be a crony of the highwayman Maclaine or McLean (who was hanged in a blaze of notoriety in late 1750) and had offered to second him in a duel. When Wortley went back to Paris in 1750, he ordered his son to leave before he arrived.[29] More sensational news was not far off.

Lady Mary tried to follow her own advice and keep up her spirits. After months of confinement by bad weather, she planned in May 1751 'some little Excursions' as soon as the roads should permit. Lord Bute was to send her china from England; she was keeping an eye out for a picture to give him in return. She was still seeking a safe way to send a pearl necklace to her elder god-daughter. She herself was, she said, 'as fond of Baubles as ever'. She had come to believe that most things classed as serious and important are trivial, while 'trivial' things like ornaments and amusements and light reading are not to be despised. She repeated her views on the high dignity of the art of cooking. She professed complete emotional indifference to the people around her in Gottolengo, but eagerness for word of friends left behind in England.[30]

[28] *CL* ii. 480–1, 483, 487, 491, 496–7.

[29] Edward was presented at Versailles again on 7 Nov. 1750 NS (Curling 1954: 120–2; de Luynes 1860: x. 366). For Maclaine see Walpole, *Corr.* xx. 99, 188, 199.

[30] Several events touched her this year: the death of her friend the Duchess of Montagu, who was blind and sad; the remarriage of the widowed Lady Walpole to Sewallis Shirley (a blow to his pious mother, MWM guessed); another pregnancy of Lady Bute's. The grandson b. Sept. 1751 was named after the late prince (*CL* ii. 487–8, 450, 491, 494).

She strove to sound indifferent as she relayed news of a high honour offered her: the first of several, all of which she declined. The people of Gottolengo, 'thinking themselves highly honnour'd and oblig'd by my resi-dence' (and mindful, too, of her friendship with the local magnate Querini), had formed a plan to set up a statue of her, book in hand, in 'the most con-spicuous Place' (presumably the market square). 'The marble was bespoke and the Sculptor bargain'd with before I knew any thing of the matter.' Indeed, the grateful townsfolk would have surprised her with a *fait accompli* if only the sculptor had not required a sitting. When the plan was disclosed, she

thank'd them very much for the Intention, but utterly refus'd complying with it, fearing it would be reported (at least in England) that I had set up my own Statue. They were so obstinate in the Design, I was forc'd to tell them my Religion would not permit it. I seriously believe it would have been worshipp'd (when I was for-gotten) under the name of some Saint or other.

The titles of saint and witch, she said, were very freely bestowed, and the sculpted book 'would have pass'd for a proofe of canonization'.[31]

Lady Mary is remembered today in Gottolengo—but not quite in the way she would be if her marble statue had now been sitting in the market-place, poring on her book while cars parked round her and stray tourists snapped her. In the English-speaking world, in bookshops and libraries and universi-ties, she is remembered in a way she never dreamed of, even as an adolescent conscious of her powers and hungry for fame. In her early sixties, when she declined to be sculpted, she had learned the incompatibility of literary fame (in England) with a lady's reputation; she had tasted the bitterness of no-toriety; she had withdrawn, first from London, then from the international society of European cities, to a remote village of 2,000 souls. Now she found herself offered, not the laurels she had once dreamed of, but what must have seemed like a mockery of them, from well-meaning people ignorant of her real gifts or achievements: a gesture which, if news of it ever reached her own world, would feed her notoriety but not her fame.

In Brescia the tradition of learned women provided a context for recogni-tion of her as intellectually eminent. Scipione Maffei, whom she had last seen in Turin in 1741, sent her 'many honourable invitations' to visit his assembly or academy at Verona. This was almost an informal private university, where every evening Maffei proposed topics for the seminar. He 'took great Delight in Instructing the young people' in historical and literary subjects,

[31] *CL* ii. 485, 494.

and required them when possible to back their arguments with evidence from his museum or library. Alas, 'some accident or other' always prevented Lady Mary from attending.[32]

Another gesture of recognition came from Querini: a gift of his portrait, an idealized likeness 'with a most pompous Inscription under it. I suppose he intended it for the Ornament of my Library.' He evidently visualized her library as very much grander than the 'closet' which she called it.[33] The next honour he offered, in 1753, was less welcome still:

here arriv'd one of his cheif chaplains, with a long complement which concluded with desiring I would send him my Works. Having dedicated one of his cases to English Books, he intended my Labours should appear in the most conspicuous place. I was struck dumb for some time with this astonishing request. When I recover'd my vexatious surprize (foreseeing the Consequence) I made answer, I was highly sensible of the Honor design'd me, but upon my word I had never printed a single line in my Life.[34]

This was not strictly true. Probably most of her writings then in print had appeared without her knowledge or consent: poems issued by Curll, Aaron Hill, and Anthony Hammond, and more recent ones of which she may not have heard. Even the *Verses to the Imitator of Horace* may have reached print not through her agency but by the hostile initiative of Pope. Others (from her *Spectator* paper and inoculation essay to the *Nonsense of Common-Sense*) she had made public herself. But most of these were quite unsuitable for Querini's library. Her single *Spectator* essay alone would have made the basis for a literary reputation, but she had kept her authorship secret. Most of her singly published poems were the very reverse of the dignified eulogies on himself that Querini loved to collect; her inoculation essay was no scientific treatise but a pseudonymous topical lampoon. Her most library-worthy works—her critique of *Cato*, her Embassy Letters, even the *Nonsense*— were virtually unknown to the world.[35]

Querini's emissary thought Lady Mary had snubbed a perfectly civil request, indeed a high honour. He

answer'd in a cold tone, his Em[inence] could send for them to England but they would be a long time coming and with some hazard, and that he had flatter'd him selfe I would not refuse him such a favor, and I need not be asham'd of seeing my

---

[32] *CL* iii. 84–6.

[33] *CL* iii. 14–15: a portrait of Querini hangs above the great staircase of the Queriniana.

[34] *CL* iii. 38–9.

[35] For the *Verses* see pp. 338–40; for *Spectator* cachet see Boswell 1934: iii. 33. The Biblioteca Queriniana had no work of hers in 1995.

Name in a collection where he admitted none but the most Eminent Authors. It was to no purpose to endeavor to convince him. He would not stay dinner, thô earnestly invited, and went away with the air of one that thought he had reason to be offended. I know his Master will have the same Sentiments, and I shall pass in his opinion for a monster of Ingratitude . . . I realy could cry for vexation.

She implies that it pained her to be taken for a real, professional author. But her account exposes different sources of pain. She goes on to enumerate the motives—or excuses—she had had for publishing. Her reputation was not non-existent, but mangled and falsified. 'I have seen Poems I never read publish'd with my Name at length, and others that were truly and singly wrote by me, printed under the names of others.'[36] She claims, as a merit, that she has 'never aim'd at the Vanity of popular Applause'; but this sounds like sour grapes (as when, her travels being ended, she affected to prefer untravelled ignorance). Her next topic, vehemently expounded, is Italy's respect for women and England's exorbitant contempt for them. Public power is best left to men, she agrees (implying that women are not so power-hungry or sadistic as to seek it); but it is unforgiveable to debar women from private study, or to penalize them if they choose it. 'We are educated in the grossest ignorance, and no art omitted to stiffle our natural reason; if some few get above their Nurses' instructions, our knowledge must rest conceal'd and be as useless to the World as Gold in the Mine.' This is not the tone of someone reconciled to a place in the shadows. She closes her letter: 'This subject is apt to run away with me.'[37]

But already, unknown to her, a niche in the canon was being assured her. It stemmed from her meetings with Walpole and Spence. In 1747 Walpole arranged to publish *Six Town Eclogues with some other Poems* by 'the Rt. Hon. Lady M. W. M.' This appeared under the imprint of the famous 'mercury' Mary Cooper. A couple of months later came Robert Dodsley's *Collection of Poems*, an anthology which quickly gained and has long maintained its place as *the* canonical sampling of Augustan poetry. Dodsley was a champion of Pope and of Pope's stand on distinguishing real authors from dunces; but his selection was 'pict out' by 'some gentlemen', chiefly Spence. This no doubt

---

[36] Neither of these clear-cut cases seems to have been at all frequent, though much in her writing life may be still unknown. The abbé Antoine Yart (probably misled by Caldwell via Montesquieu) printed as hers a French version of Judith Cowper's 'Progress of Poetry'; but his 8-vol. anthology, *L'Idée de la poesie angloise*, 1753–4, had limited circulation. Later MWM twice repeated an enigmatic note: '3 reasons for printing' (CB MS 5, 6).

[37] *CL* iii. 38–40. MWM used 'stiffle'd' of suppressing a compliment to herself (*CL* ii. 15). She cited Querini's correspondent Maria Gaetana Agnesi. She might have added Laura Maria Katharina Barsi (whose Bologna Ph.D. was noted by Lady Pomfret and in Algarotti's *Newtonianismo*) and very many Brescian learned women (Rabil 1981; Kristeller 1980).

accounts for Lady Mary's presence there: the poems Walpole printed, plus three more. In Dodsley's first edition, published in January 1748 (a slipshod affair of poor print on cheap paper), these appeared in the third volume. They were promoted to volume i in the *Collection*'s second edition, the form which gave it authority: transformed by better paper, better design, better printing, and a twenty-fold increase in printers' ornaments. In this gracious, neo-classical production, Montagu's 'poetical performances' were show-cased among those of peers and close friends of Pope, as meriting 'a longer rememberance' than the merely topical.[38]

Her presence in Dodsley's *Collection* was crucial in exposing her work to a wider circle than those who might see it in manuscript. A further step was taken in 1749, when the *London Magazine* (now part-controlled by Dodsley) began featuring her in its poetry column. The *London* was the younger brother of Edward Cave's *Gentleman's Magazine*. Whereas Cave relied on his post-office sinecure and his unique links with provincial newspapers to build a nation-wide middle-class audience, the *London* took more account of the upper classes and the capital. Its declared policy was to publish only work by geniuses 'of establish'd Character', not 'obscure Persons, or . . . Authors of no Name in the Commonwealth of Learning'.[39] Ten years from Lady Mary's leaving England, it seems she had an established character as an author—and Dodsley was its prime agent though not its originator.

This minor position in the commonwealth of learning might have been no more ostensibly welcome to her than a statue in the market-place. And for good reason: new fame bordered on old notoriety. In 1753 *The Lover's Manual* reprinted several of her pieces. In 1754 (coinciding with the exploitation of her name for advertising hype by a new generation of inoculators) John Duncombe's *Feminiad* celebrated women writers with strict, almost exclu-sive attention to morals. Duncombe repeated Pope's positioning of Lady Mary: as an anomalously upper-class daughter of Behn, a friend to Vice and foe to Virtue.[40] This lay in the future; meanwhile it seems none of Lady Mary's correspondents thought fit to mention Dodsley's *Collection* to her. When she learned of it, it came as a shock.

Her old infamy, like her poetic reputation, was still putting out fresh

---

[38] *Six Town Eclogues*, Nov. 1747; Dodsley's *Collection*, Jan. 1748, 2nd edn. Dec. 1748; Suarez 1994; Thoms 1856: 237; Dodsley 1988: 15. Hervey occupies vol. iii of the *Collection*. MWM and Elizabeth Carter are the only women.

[39] *London Magazine*, preface, 1737. Typographically superior to the *GM*, the *London* had print runs of c.7,000 (McKenzie and Ross 1968; see p. 374 ff.). It had already reprinted poems of MWM's anonymously; in June 1749 it used her name in full.

[40] Duncombe, *Feminiad*, 1754. The 13-year-old Elizabeth Ogilvy Benger, in 1791, was first to accord MWM cordial praise in a work of this kind.

shoots. One appeared this year, 1751, in a novel by John Cleland, who was already notorious for *Memoirs of a Woman of Pleasure*, better known as *Fanny Hill*. Cleland's mother had been a friend of Griselda Murray and Lady Hervey and an admirer of Bolingbroke; his father, a friend of Lords Mar and Grange, had lent Pope his initials as cover from which to snipe at enemies.[41] Their son came honestly by his prejudice against Lady Mary.

His new work was *Memoirs of a Coxcomb*; among the conquests of his egregious hero is Lady Bell Travers, an epitome of fashionable corruption. Lady Bell is clearly Lady Mary, but Lady Mary travestied. A 'daughter of one of the highest rank of our nobility', she eloped with a rich man who then ceased to love her. She is a great traveller who has 'seen most of the courts in Europe' and is 'a Seraglio in herself'; she wears an 'Armenian' or oriental dress to seduce the hero. Her effete friend Lord Tersillion is a version of Pope's version of Hervey. Her villa, however, is placed at Chiswick and given gardens down to the river, which Lady Mary's lacked. Lady Bell was married very young, and is famous for debaucheries at a villa near Rome. (This suggests Walpole as a further channel of misinformation.) Cleland likens her to Sappho: not for poetry, which she does not write, or even for wit (she has only 'a specious, fluent jargon'), but for addiction to sexual pleasure and perverse ingenuity in heightening it.

Cleland's Bell Travers episode is deeply misogynistic. It teems with casual insults to women in general: their conversation is despicable; they can *never* beat a man at cards; if they have any political knowledge it 'becomes them no better than whiskers and jack-boots would do'. Even after all this, the manner of the hero's final disillusion with Lady Bell comes as a real shock. Spying on her from her closet in the manner of Swift's Strephon, he is amazed to see her intimate with a foully decrepit foreign manservant: not coupling with him but supporting him in her arms while a properly reluctant wet-nurse is forced to suckle him, prolonging his life and his sex-object role. Dread and disgust well up in this climactic scene, where comedy of manners gives way to a kind of proto-gothic.

Lady Mary read this monstrous metamorphosis of herself. But whatever she felt, she gave nothing away. In her copy of *Memoirs of a Coxcomb* she wrote one word: 'Instructif'.[42]

❧

If Lady Mary visited Salò in 1751, she does not say so; she was at Lovere from the end of July until early November. She felt unwilling to face either the

[41] Epstein 1974: 16–21, 126.   [42] Cleland 1751; 1964: 137–58; volume now at Sandon.

mountain journey or the busy social life, but she was 'forc'd' there by her doctors when her gum disease showed signs of flaring up. She found the journey did her good rather than harm, but she said nothing this year of miraculous benefits from the place. Instead she acquired a new complaint there: deafness. Her dismay at this suggests that society was more important to her still than she admitted. If she lost her hearing, she said, her life would become 'burdensome' (a word she had just used of the blind Duchess of Montagu). It was most galling that the doctors put her deafness down to vapours, and judged that writing was bad for it. 'My Health is so often disorder'd that I begin to be as weary of it as mending old Lace; when it is patch'd in one place it breaks out in another.' She said she could 'expect nothing better at my time of Life, and will not trouble you with talking any more about it'. But she 'talked' much to Wortley of the long-lived 'old Woman of Louvere' (mother of her former landladies). She scanned her medical history for tips, although in years of minute enquiry into 'the Health and manner of Life' in many different countries, she had 'found little Difference in the length of Life'.[43]

Just before or just after this stay at Lovere, Lady Mary's presence of mind was unexpectedly tested. She was interrupted in her reading by the chambermaid of one of her nearest neighbours, Signora Laura Bono. In 'an agony of sobs and tears', the maid besought her to intervene in a fight between the brothers Bono; but when she rushed to the house, guided by 'the noise of Oaths and Execrations', she found the maid had lied from motives of discretion. Signora Laura's husband had caught her in bed with another man (or boy) and was 'standing with a drawn stilletto in his Hand, swearing she should never see to morrow's Sun'. Lady Mary kept her head, and performed splendidly as a peacemaker. She

did not endeavor a defence that seem'd to me impossible, but represented to him as well as I could the Crime of a Murder which, if he could justify before Men, was still a crying Sin before God, the disgrace he would bring on himselfe and posterity, and irreparable injury he would do his eldest Daughter (a pretty Girl of 15, that I knew he was extreme fond of).

She spent the rest of the afternoon and all the evening persuading him to swear not to harm his wife; she rightly judged she could rely on 'his Oath, knowing him to be very devout'. She and the maid kept his secret: Lady Mary had high praise for the maid's initiative, but attributed her later silence

---

[43] *CL* ii. 488–91, 493–4. The old woman's daughters confided to MWM that her new lease of life at the age of 100 had included renewed menstruation; her physician and surgeon said her age had no bearing on her accidental death.

to caution rather than virtue: a servant stepping out of line could expect violent retribution.[44]

Meanwhile Lady Bute, who by September 1751 had eight children and slim prospects, was becoming anxious, low-spirited, and painfully uncertain of the affection of her parents. Lady Mary, very much touched, thought about composing for her 'a consolatory epistle on my own Death'. She urged upon her that 'truest Wisdom' which makes the best of things and strives to be cheerful. She added, 'I can assure you I give no precepts I do not daily practise. How often do I fancy to my selfe the pleasure I should take in seeing you in the midst of your little people! And how severe do I then think my destiny, that denys me that Happiness!' She thought it wise deliberately to remind herself that separation was their only protection against quarrelling over how to bring up the children.[45]

Her deafness gave her a fright, but was gone for good in a fortnight. Back at Gottolengo for the winter, seeing nobody from the wider world, she received almost with ecstasy Lady Bute's next shipment of books. She read three of them the day the case was unpacked (one by candlelight), and finished the lot in under two weeks, reading 'night and Day'. Lady Bute, no doubt remembering how her mother had barred her from parties given by the future Lady Vane, advised her to start with Smollett's *Peregrine Pickle*, where Lady Vane's memoirs were interpolated. Lady Mary did so, and was riveted. She was distantly related to each of Lady Vane's two husbands, and knew several of her lovers. (One, Sewallis Shirley, had later married Lady Walpole.) She found the style 'clear and concise, with some Strokes of Humour': too good, surely, to be Lady Vane's own work. But she was most struck by the 'mortifications and variety of misery' endured by this woman of pleasure, and her enthusiasm for unprepossessing men. 'Her History, rightly consider'd, would be more instructive to young Women than any Sermon I know.' With these memoirs she bracketed the *Apology* of Teresia Constantia Phillips, another publicly scandalous woman. She thought Phillips the more intelligent and the less culpable: if sincerely penitent, she might yet look down from heaven on a particularly odious lover roasting in hell.[46]

That first evening Lady Mary also read *Pompey the Little*, Francis Coventry's *roman à clef* about a lapdog. She was much taken with one of its

---

[44] *CL* iii. 43–6. Brescia was a violent province: 118 murders recorded during MWM's years there (Ferraro 1993: 133, 135, 142; Fappani 1961: 105).

[45] *CL* ii. 491–2; iii. 15–16.

[46] *CL* iii. 1, 2–3, 5–6, 7. Phillips's lover was Philip Southcote the gardener, whom MWM thought 'as odious in his outside as stupid in his conversation' (*SL* 365; Morris 1872: 366).

satirical butts, a woman who believes, mistakenly, that her appetite is life-threateningly delicate.[47] Lady Mary, who had just got the better of a period of poor health and incipient hypochondria, was delighted to recognize and condemn herself. Dr Cavalino (whom she had already marked down as a fool) had had her half-convinced that her daily diet was inadequate. She enumerated it to Lady Bute, and (apart from a lack of fresh vegetables, no surprise in February) it sounds both generous and varied. She had the habit, she said, of waking around 7 a.m., drinking half a pint of warm ass's milk, and sleeping another two hours. Once she was up she drank 'milk coffee' (three cups of it) and at mid-morning a cup of 'milk chocolate'. Her dinner hour was soon after one o'clock. A typical menu would consist of 'gravy Soup with all the Bread, roots, etc. belonging to it', a capon and a veal sweetbread, and some of the fine large local chestnuts, roasted, with custard.[48] She took pains to emphasize the large quantities involved in each course. At five in the afternoon came 'another Dose of Asse's milk', and later still her supper: a further dozen chestnuts, 'one new-laid Egg, and a handsome Poringer of white Bread and milk'. The doctor (perhaps because she did not eat red meat) had tried hard to persuade her she was in danger of starving; it took *Pompey* to convince her how wrong he was.

For ass's milk, she must have acquired an ass which had recently foaled. This was a very popular remedy (for 'defluxions of the eyes' as well as for most other things). The ass was to be milked 'as near the patient as you can' and the milk drunk still warm. It was to be taken on an empty stomach, and nothing eaten for two hours afterwards. This helps to explain Lady Mary's otherwise eccentric schedule.[49]

With renewed gusto she turned back to the books with her morning ass's milk. She was scathing about some of the novels. She disliked fiction whose efforts at verisimilitude or at moralizing were crude; she especially hated unconvincing depictions of ideal virtue. (Charlotte Lennox was one of those she damned on these grounds, and she blamed as insipid Sarah Scott's first novel, which she feared might be by Sarah Fielding.) She loved fiction *à clef*, preferably about people she had known, and was disappointed if she could not 'find out' the characters. She vehemently condemned Lennox for criticizing Lady Bell Finch as a disappointing patron, and applauded Edward Kimber's praise for the Duke of Montagu.[50]

[47] She is Mrs Qualmsick, a name perhaps from *Female Tatler*, no. 16.

[48] *CL* iii. 5. A capon is a cock castrated to improve its flavour; a sweetbread, considered a delicacy, is probably the thymus gland. Chestnuts were poor people's food (Brocard 1992: 121).

[49] Nicolson and Rousseau 1968: 42–4.

[50] *CL* iii. 4, 5, 8; Lennox, *Harriot Stuart*, 1751; Scott, *Cornelia*, 1750; Kimber, *Joe Thompson*, 1750.

She loved satire and humour. *Roderick Random* pleased her: she thought it might be by Henry Fielding. But her most important discovery was Samuel Richardson's *Clarissa*. Its opening touched her, she said, 'by a near ressemblance of my Maiden Days'—not that she thought herself a Clarissa (though that heroine's stubborn idealism and moral superiority *do* recall her young self) but that she had stood in Clarissa's shoes, ruthlessly pressured by her family to marry a man she detested. Thus softened, Lady Mary 'was such an old Fool as to weep . . . like any milk maid of sixteen over the Ballad of the Ladie's Fall'. She revenged herself by pulling the novel to pieces. She had no time for either Anna or Clarissa. She thought Anna more vicious than the whore Sally Martin ('whose Crimes are owing at first to Seduction, and afterwards to necessity'). Clarissa deserved to 'be carry'd to Bridewell or Bedlam the next day' for eloping 'with a young Fellow without intending to marry him'. With this letter began a struggle which Lady Mary was to wage for years: she could not accept *Clarissa*, but she could not forget it. Much of her argument went into letters to Lady Bute; some went into 'Princess Docile'.

Meanwhile she pulled back from her literary criticism. 'I fancy you are now saying—'Tis a sad thing to grow old. What does my poor mama mean by troubling me with Criticisms on Books that no body but her selfe will ever read over?' She need not have worried. Lady Bute recognized the worth of her mother's letters. She wrote at once to say so, which freed Lady Mary to 'indulge my selfe in thinking upon paper when I write to you'. She began by allowing an anecdote from her time in Venice to lead her into comment on marriage and on attitudes to money.[51] Over the next few months she wrote about Querini, about the universal sameness of human nature, about mother love, and about the folly of war. She still never knew when she despatched a letter whether it would ever arrive; yet early next year she resumed the topic of girls' education, producing some of her best-known letters.

Her spur was the news that her eldest granddaughter, at almost fifteen, showed marked promise, particularly in mathematics. Lady Mary responded with a brief essay on how to educate a girl 'not only capable but desirous of Learning'.[52] She begins and ends her letter with self-justification: Lady Bute herself had clearly been capable of learning; but her mother had expected that as only daughter of a wealthy father she would attract 'the highest offers' in marriage, and would be a great lady with no time to read. The

[51] *CL* iii. 8–9; ii. 457–9.
[52] *CL* iii. 20 ff. MWM never writes of maths as gendered male; in Sarah Scott's *Sir George Ellison*, 1766, girls ideally educated pursue astronomy only as far as they can 'without a knowledge of mathematicks' (1985: 201).

subtext was that she had not foreseen Lady Bute's rebellion and disinheriting. She now assumed that her granddaughters would be too poor to marry. This made it all the more important to teach them well, for only the educated could be happy in domestic retirement. 'No Entertainment is so cheap as reading, nor any pleasure so lasting.' It would supply any lack of smart clothes or entertainment or company. Education, argued Lady Mary, was entirely a matter of private investment for personal satisfaction.

To achieve such satisfaction, reading must be 'extensive'; this meant learning ancient as well as modern languages. At this point her advice became controversal, for Latin and Greek were regarded as a male preserve. Lady Mary mobilized all her ingenuity to argue the contrary. It is actually easier for a girl to find the time to master those languages: because she 'cannot advance her selfe in any profession', she has more time to spare.

Lady Mary sharply distinguishes a scholarly gentlewoman from mere professionals. The former, liberally educated, knows that 'True knowledge consists in knowing things, not words.' The latter, with nothing but their pedantic grammatical expertise, are 'the most ignorant fellows upon Earth'. This may have been following Francis Bacon; it was certainly following Bathsua Makin, who insisted that gentlewomen ought rather 'to know things, than to get words', and that languages are 'only subservient' to 'the Principles of Arts and Sciences'. Lady Mary sees learned languages as ancillary: tools to unlock the precious ancient texts which are 'often corrupted and allwaies injur'd by Translations'. So much for the stock charge that classical learning turns women into pedants. She adds a point from her letter to Burnet more than forty years before: it is not real learning but mere smattering that makes for noisy overconfidence and pontificating.[53]

Two hours a morning will do, she says, to master Latin and Greek. She also advocates modern studies: history, geography, and 'Philosophy' or physical sciences. 'I beleive there are few heads capable of makeing Sir I. Newton's calculations, but the result of them is not difficult to be understood by a moderate capacity.' All this will still leave 'leisure enough beside to run over the English poetry'. She produces an ingenious gender-specific defence of literary learning, citing the story of how she herself saved a friend from imminent seduction by pointing out that her suitor's elegant verse proposition was plagiarized from a little-known Caroline poet.[54]

Lady Mary's advice both parallels and diverges from that of her more

<hr>

[53] *CL* iii. 20–4. Jocelyn Harris compares with Bacon and with *Sir Charles Grandison*, letters xi–xiii (to Robert Halsband, 22 June 1976, Halsband MSS; Makin 1673: 34; see p. 37). MWM disliked Bacon (note in Guillim).

[54] Such recycling was probably common. One Clytander took a tribute to MWM and addressed it to Mary Deverell ('In Beauty or Wit', see pp. 196–7, 27–8; Deverell 1781: 253).

conventional contemporaries. The student's reading, she says, needs to be carefully supervised—not by any authoritative male but by her mother, whose excellent judgement can ensure 'she does not mistake pert Folly for Wit and humour, or Rhyme for Poetry'. Then she must 'conceal whatever Learning she attains, with as much solicitude as she would hide crookedness or lameness'. Lady Mary probably borrowed this advice (but not her bitter comparison of learning to disability) from her admired Sapho in *Le Grand Cyrus*, who advises women to conceal their learning. It was to be echoed by novelists like Sarah Scott and moralists like Dr John Gregory. But these later writers give it a different slant. Gregory says men will condemn learning in a woman, Lady Mary that both men and women will hate its possessor because they covet her attainments. The society of Scott and Gregory condemns women's learning as an aberration; that of Scudéry (already obsolete in Lady Mary's day) had recognized it as precious and desirable, though not for display.[55]

Lady Mary did not scorn 'accomplishments'. Along with her more academic recommendations she advised that her young namesake should learn to sew, to draw, and to write a beautiful hand. Yet she must have been haunted by a sense of her own temerity, for some weeks later she penned 'a sort of Apology for my last letter, foreseeing that you will think it wrong, or at least Lord Bute will be extremely shock'd'. Most men, she said, would see a learned education for girls as 'a prophanation', just the way the clergy would see lay encroachment on their prerogative. She then reiterated her earlier arguments. Learning is a pleasure for those who have few pleasures, something to make solitude 'not only . . . tolerable but agreable'. It helps virtue to flourish and discourages vice. (This was her first recourse to the argument from morality, so prevalent in discussions of female education.) The 'search after knowledge' would be a reliable, lifelong delight. She longed to correspond with her god-daughter, to offer her advice directly.

Here as elsewhere, her more subversive suggestions appear as almost involuntary outbursts: rents in the even fabric of her argument, lapses from the tone taken by her smooth-tongued allies in the inoculation debate into an outrage which was all her own. Men, she wrote, fancy 'the improvement of our understandings would only furnish us with more art to deceive them'. She pours scorn on the dancing and good breeding which are reckoned sufficient learning for women and royalty. In other animal species, both sexes are equally intelligent: Nature would hardly give human beings a

---

[55] Scudéry 1690: x. 192–3, 233. Plaisant notes that Mmes d'Epinay and du Châtelet both recommend women to conceal learning (1987: 40).

unique inequality—'thô I am persuaded if there was a Commonwealth of rational Horses (as Doctor Swift has suppos'd) it would be an establish'd maxim amongst them that a mare could not be taught to pace. I could add a great deal on this subject . . .' But she was not addressing an ideal audience. Lady Bute seems to have replied that all this learning would be too expensive on top of the cost of dancing lessons. Lady Mary took this quietly, though her reply touches on her own past efficacy as a kind of freelance tutor to grand tourists. Whatever happened, she needed to keep on cordial terms with her daughter. She voiced the impossible wish that young Mary might visit her in Italy to seek a husband. She could, she said, have 'dispos'd . . . advantageously' of half a dozen girls in Rome.[56]

As her correspondence with Lady Bute took wings, it fulfilled the object, among others, of distracting Lady Mary from what was unsatisfactory in her life: her isolation, her confinement, her disappointments. (She cheered the unhappiness of her solitude by assuring her daughter that learned solitude could be happy!) But many of these letters, with others to Lord Bute, her granddaughter Mary, and her sister Mar, all disappeared in the void, leaving her 'quite sick with vexation'. The death in March 1752 of her friend the doge 'sincerely afflicted' her; it also removed a power in the land who was at least potentially available as her protector.

She was startled and saddened by news of her son's latest exploits. In London the card game of faro, banned the year she left, was back. It was all the rage, and faro 'bankers' for society hostesses made fortunes. Most notorious of them were Edward and his friend Theobald Taaffe, another adventurer, professional gamester, and member of parliament. These two were bankers to the French ambassador's wife, Madame de Mirepoix, daughter of Lady Mary's friend the princesse de Craon. Edward further tangled his life by bigamously marrying Miss Elizabeth Ashe, who was as far beyond the pale of respectability as himself. She was a close friend of the notorious Elizabeth Chudleigh, who was still secretly married to one of Hervey's sons, but who probably seduced Edward's cousin Kingston this year (as well as, possibly, the ageing king).[57] Edward's intellectual interests—like his newish Fellowship of the Royal Society—were less striking than his self-display. Horace

---

[56] *CL* iii. 22, 23–4, 25–7, 31–2.

[57] *CL* ii. 492–3; iii. 10–11, 33, 50; Mavor 1964: 42. Edward's wedding (which he said was 'only done that there might be something to say to the father in case of a surprise') took place on 21 July 1751; he apparently deserted his wife within six months. He was outraged years later when a court awarded her some provision for their son (Walpole, 9 Jan. 1752, *Corr.* ix. 129; Namier and Brooke 1964). He had at least three children— Edward, George, and Mary—during the 1750s, perhaps by different mothers (Curling 1954: 146).

Walpole famously reported: 'His father scarce allows him anything: yet he plays, dresses, diamonds himself '—even to different sets of diamond shoe-buckles for each costume—'and has more snuff-boxes than would suffice a Chinese idol with an hundred noses'.[58]

Having heard some of this from Wortley, Lady Mary commented that the 'Drudgery' of 'taillying at Bassette' could produce a steady income even without cheating. But, she added, 'I never knew any one persue it long and preserve a Tolerable Reputation'. This was prophetic. Edward was then, November 1751, back in Paris with his new wife and his crony Taaffe.[59] One of their victims was the hapless young Abraham Roberts, alias Payba, whom they manipulated into huge losses by adroit use of Edward's social status. Roberts accused them of swindling, and refused to pay up. Their gambling business depended on reliable debt-collection. They drove Roberts from Paris with threats of physical violence, and in his absence broke into and wrecked his lodgings, and made off with jewels and other property. Roberts came back and had his tormentors arrested (dragged out of bed in the middle of the night, said the shocked and aggrieved Edward) and sent to separate prisons to await trial. In solitary confinement they made statements which contradicted each other.

In this predicament Edward showed his skill at string-pulling. His urgent letters persuaded the British ambassador to engineer his release, on very substantial bail. The two gamesters were threatened with the galleys; appeals were brought and pamphlets published for and against them. Edward admitted being present, but denied that he had personally handled stolen property or threatened to cut Roberts's face. In August 1752 he and Taaffe were cleared and Roberts 'non suited'. Their counter-action for defamation of character was upheld: one charge against Roberts was that he had perverted the course of justice by concealing his opponents' rank. These verdicts were probably racist as well as manifestly corrupt; most reports refer to Roberts, or Payba, throughout as 'the Jew'. It is more surprising that Edward's allowance (standing at £500 a year) was at this time supplemented via Gibson by an advance of £900. Through the affair Gibson sent Wortley letters supportive and admiring of Edward. He still maintained him to be on the verge of reform.[60]

---

[58] Walpole, *Corr.* xx. 226.

[59] Taaffe later caused at least one suicide, and was imprisoned in the Bastille. Horace Mann voiced disgust at his and Edward's conduct (Sedgwick 1970; Walpole, *Corr.* xx. 294). A taste for economizing, said MWM, was 'an admirable shield against the most fatal weaknesses' as well as against financial ruin (*CL* iii. 47).

[60] Walpole, *Corr.* xx. 287–9; *Memorials* by Payba and by Edward and Taaffe, 1752; *Remarks*, 1752; Anderson to EWM, 16 Aug. 1752, H MS 78. 13–14; Gibson to EWM, Dec. 1751–Sept. 1752, H MS 78. 28–37; Curling 1954: 143, 145.

Lady Mary was out of touch and had to have the background to this story explained to her. After Edward returned to England, seeking money to defray the expenses of a new character, she advised Wortley to steel himself against being upset at anything their son might do. 'The only way to avoid disapointment is never to Indulge any Hope on his Account.' This was aimed at Gibson, whom she openly accused of unwarrantably keeping these hopes alive, and obliquely accused of making a pact with Edward to secure his inheritance from his father in consideration of a cut for himself. In other people's affairs Lady Mary's judgement was acute.[61]

In June 1752 North Italy was exceptionally, unseasonably hot. Lady Mary got a bad cold which brought on 'a troop of complaints' and a fever which raged for two weeks. She was confined to her room for a month. Then it turned horribly rainy. She says nothing this year of any trip away from Gottolengo; but this is no evidence that she made none.[62] She was much annoyed to learn that the British ambassador to Venice had left for home without her knowledge, and thus with no letters or parcels of hers. After years of lamenting the sins of the mails (which were worse than ever), she later discovered with exasperation from one of her clerical friends that her fat letters to England were assumed to contain coded comment on international affairs: 'people like your Excellenza do not use to write long letters upon Triffles . . . it was very easy to write intelligibly under feign'd names . . . in such a manner as should be almost impossible to be understood' by those not in the secret. This would account for official tampering: 'when I talk of my Grand children they are fancy'd to represent all the potentates of Europe.'

When the winter of 1752–3 set in, she even told Wortley her health might benefit from a warmer climate (hardly a description of her most likely choices, London or Venice). But this remained fancy. Whether by a lakeside or in the steamy heat of the Po Valley, whether in her Castle with cartwheels rumbling under her windows or in her Dairy House among the nightingales and the fireflies, she stayed in the homes she had created for herself, writing and writing to Lady Bute at Hampstead.[63]

She wrote satirically of Querini, wistfully of her distance from her growing grandchildren, and hopefully of the thank-you letter she might expect from young Lady Mary whenever she managed to convey her promised gift.

---

[61] *CL* iii. 10–11, 28.

[62] A young Englishman named Joshua Reynolds, homebound from Venice, was in Brescia on 21 Aug. (Leslie and Taylor 1865: i. 84–5; see pp. 620–1).

[63] *CL* ii. 459–60; iii. 13, 17, 19–20, 41–2. She had been writing seldom to EWM because he could only read large, careful writing; but his eyes now improved.

Philosophically she contrasted the rapid modern advance of 'usefull as well as speculative knowledge' (giving conveniences to modern peasants which the Roman emperors never dreamed of) with the painfully slow moral maturation of the human race, which might, 'perhaps a thousand years hence', make war appear an adolescent aberration like schoolboys' boxing. She was glad to hear that any of her English friends—Lady Rich, for instance—still remembered her. Marriages, deaths, wills, in England drew from her streams of reminiscence and meditative comment.[64]

This autumn, 1752, she mentioned another and more remarkable writing project. Introducing it as more trivial than Lady Bute's current occupation of stitching a carpet, she said she was

> writeing the History of my own Time. It has been my Fortune to have a more exact knowledge both of the Persons and Facts that have made the greatest figure in England in this Age than is common, and I take pleasure in putting together what I know, with an Impartialty that is altogether unusual. Distance of Time and place has totally blotted from my Mind all Traces either of Resentment or prejudice, and I speak with the same Indifference of the Court of G[reat] B[ritain] as I should do of that of Augustus Caesar.

This kind of history had a pedigree. Lady Mary knew the leading insider accounts of Queen Anne's court (Burnet's *History of His Own Time*, Manley's scandal-histories, and *An Account of the Conduct of the Dowager Duchess of Marlborough*, 1742). She may even have been in the secret of Hervey's *Memoirs*, which remained unpublished till a century after his death.[65] She had first-hand insider knowledge, from her stint at the courts of George I and the future George II, and from her friendships with Robert Walpole, Lady Darlington, Hervey, and Skerrett. She had talked court politics with Lyttelton, one of the new generation, just before she left England. Her surviving 'Account of the Court of George I' (a fragment of a dozen pages) sparkles with cynical wit and trenchant analysis of personal power-relations. In the system of government throughout her London years, the personalities of the leading players were the key to political action. Both her own inoculation campaign and Pope's attacks on her were deeply influenced by political loyalties and political enmities. Montagu's history of her own times would have been a treasure trove for historians and literary historians, as well as a delight for general readers.

---

[64] One of the weddings in prospect involved a John Spencer, great-grandson of Sarah Marlborough, a generation removed from his namesake who had courted Lady Frances Pierrepont (*CL* iii. 13–18, 36–8, 47–9, 50–1).

[65] She owned both vols. of Burnet, pub. ten years apart (Wh MS 135). For the genre see Goldgar 1995: 288–91. Burnet, Marlborough, and Hervey, if not Manley too, had shaped as well as recording.

This was not to be. Lady Mary hastened to reassure Lady Bute that she was not 'turning Author in my old age'; she had 'no concern beyond my own Family'. The recent episode with Querini, though it may have fed an ambition to produce a substantial work of history, had also fed her anxieties. She said she knew 'Mankind too well to think they are capable of receiving Truth, much less of applauding it. Or were it otherwise, Applause to me is as insignificant as Garlands on the Dead.' (Again, she called 'the Passion Men have for perpetuateing their Memory' a childish though a universal weakness.) So she assured her daughter, 'I regularly burn every Quire as soon as it is finish'd.'[66] Such self-erasure is surely unique. One is left with a feeble, futile hope that she might have been lying to her daughter; but in any case the history is not known to exist.

꙳

During the next few years Lady Mary sounds increasingly wistful. She imagined the mutual support that she and Lady Oxford (whose health was failing) might offer each other if only she were within reach: she called such ideas 'Castles [in the air] I must not indulge'. She told Lady Bute that her solitude was like Robinson Crusoe's. 'His Goats and kids were as much companions as any of the people I see here. My Time is wholly dedicated to the care of a decaying Body, and endeavoring (as the old Song says) to grow wiser and better as my Strength wears away.' She cultivated spiritual detachment, citing theologians of various ages and nations who believed that the pains of hell might consist of intensified attachment to the world which the soul has quitted. She implied that she was investing intellectual and emotional energy in the quest for self-knowledge, in precious, difficult 'impartial selfe-examination'.[67]

In other letters she spoke more sharply than of yore. She was still attached enough to the world to tax Lady Bute with inattention to detail: 'You should be particular in your Relations: I am as ignorant of every thing that passes at London as if I inhabited the Desarts of Africa.' The death of her half-sister Lady Caroline in June 1753 drew from her moral reflections but no grief. 'It is true she was my sister, as it were, and in some sense, but her behaviour to me never gave me any Love, nor her general conduct any esteem.' She had not forgiven what she saw as Lady Caroline's *mésalliance*, and was prompted by her death to a diatribe against the 'confounding of all Ranks and making a Jest of order', the 'Levelling Principle' which she perceived (largely from her novel-reading) as rampant in England. She was not, she

---

[66] *CL* iii. 18–19, 37.   [67] *CL* iii. 30–1, 32, 37, 48, 50.

said, 'an Enemy of the poor', but she had moved a long way from 'the silly prejudices of my Education'. She recognized the unpopularity of these views, and claimed a merit in telling Lady Bute 'my real thoughts' as proof of 'the most intimate Freindship'. Her perceptions about 'Levelling' may have been hidebound, but they were not wrong. Linda Colley notes that the upper classes were under strong attack during these years.[68]

She had cause for bile or for heavy philosophizing—which in her lay close together. The full horror of her situation with Palazzi (discussed in the next chapter) was beginning to dawn on her. Her son-in-law had lost his hopes of high office and could not provide for her beloved grandchildren. Her son had developed into the kind of character she most disliked, and she could not feel quite secure that he would not be rewarded with his father's fortune.

At this juncture, in spring 1753, the preceptor to the young Prince of Wales resigned, alleging that the prince was being exposed to Jacobite influence. Both old and new preceptors were bishops: a fact that Lady Mary deplored. But on this tricky ground Bute was to rebuild his career. The prince's mother did not trust the king's educational choices. She could not openly object, or she would swiftly have lost the care of her son. But in strictest secrecy, Bute became his tutor.[69] Lady Mary was no longer the family's educational expert.

[68] Colley 1992: 87–8.   [69] *CL* iii. 35–6, 50–1; Bullion 1991: 245–8.

28

1753–September 1756

❧

Escaping Palazzi: 'determined to go to Venice'[1]

IN 1753 the Po floods were worse than usual: cattle were drowned, but harvests were bumper. Lady Mary singled out for comment the abundant production of wine and silk; she observed with regret the prospect of perfectly good wine being thrown away, and wished she could find a merchant to share a silk-exporting enterprise. She had taken up the study of 'Simples' or herbs (perhaps inspired by her son-in-law's botanizing).[2] This summer at last she found a means to send the pearl necklace to 'our Daughter (for I think she belongs to us both)'. The younger Lady Mary duly wrote her thanks. But, alas, she did not save her grandmother's reply, and did not write again.

Lady Mary was delighted when Lady Bute praised her letters, and she reached into her memory for the two-year-old story of the adulterous Signora Bono. She added some comments on Italian life and customs: 'the great Submission of Domestics, who are sensible of their Dependance', the dreadful prevalence of murder. Even the peasants freely carried firearms and would shoot on the slightest provocation: 'they see one of their own Species lye dead before them with as little remorse as a Hare or a Partridge, and when Revenge spurs them on, with much more pleasure.'

It was now that she said robbery was rare in Brescia. Her 'Italian Memoir', on the contrary, says that about now she was scared by proliferating stories of houses broken into and occupants murdered. She had the amazing sum of £2,400 in the house, in cash and bills of exchange from England; she decided this was too risky. Retaining only a trifle for household

---

[1] 'Italian Memoir', *RW* 93.
[2] *CL* iii. 33–4. Increase in demand for silk in England was fuelling a search for new sources of supply, of which Italy was already one.

expenses, she took Palazzi's advice and lodged all the rest with the banker Ballini.[3]

She was now allowing Lady Bute more frequent glimpses of flaws in her pastoral retreat; but she gave no glimpse of her actual attempts to get away. Three times during these years, she later said, she went so far as to have 'Post-Horses brought from Brescia' to take her to Venice, at least for a visit. Each time, however, she sent them back again, because people—not Palazzi, but 'the Doctor, the Parish Priest, and all those I spoke to'—regaled her with dreadful stories of gangs of bandits, rivers in spate, or 'contagious diseases at the Inns'. In spring 1754 she intended to try again: an additional spur was provided by two boxes from England (china from Lord Bute, books from Lady Bute), which had got as far as Venice and stuck there. She had her 'Trunks packed, and was only waiting for fine weather' when Palazzi arrived on one of his periodic rent-collecting visits and became incapacitated (apparently by arthritis). He spent two months at her house, bedridden, while the fine weather delayed.[4]

In May a number of Lady Mary's previous ailments suddenly recurred. She was seized with fever, and her face swelled and produced a discharge. She thought she had stayed out too late walking, and did not at first take it seriously. She resisted the remedies of the count's doctor, who assured her she was dangerously ill, whereupon the count engaged Mari Anna on his side and sent to Lovere for the wonder-working Dr Baglioni. (Lady Mary said later that the count did this; she told Lady Bute at the time that it was 'Some of my Neighbours'.) Baglioni agreed that she was in great danger and must have change of air. 'Venice would be downright adverse to me,' he swore, but Lovere just the thing. 'The other Physician asserted positively I should die on the road.'

Lady Mary, who had 'prepar'd my selfe for Death with as much resignation as that Circumstance admits', felt it 'a matter of the utmost Indifference where we expire'. She consented to go. There was a hasty packing up. Next morning her bed was lifted into a closed litter. She was not to return to her castle for sixteen months, or ever again to feel wholly settled there. But now no one was thinking beyond the moment. Her servants followed her litter in carriages; Dr Baglioni and her cook went ahead to make ready an unoccupied nobleman's seat to receive her. She spent two nights at such empty houses, the second in the little town of Iseo. Next morning she 'was put into

[3] *CL* iii. 42–6, 49, 76. She thus had on hand three times her annual allowance (without the interest on her bequest). It was a lot to make on farming (*RW* 93 and n. 1).

[4] *RW* 92–3. She later said she left for fear that her possessions would 'be disipated by servants' if she died (*CL* iii. 127); it was probably Palazzi she really feared.

a Bark in my Litter bed'. Three hours on the water brought her to Lovere. She felt better rather than worse for the journey—which was lucky, because the first night in her 'barely habitable' palazzo came as a shock.

Dr Baglioni said she had fallen ill for lack of Lovere waters over the last few years, and 'sentence'd me to a long continuance here'. He persuaded her to bathe: a whole new physical experience for her, at sixty-five. Within three days she found herself in perfect health, 'which appear'd almost a Miracle to all that saw me'. She turned her attention to improving her latest house, and 'decided to enlarge it, so that I should no longer be obliged to lodge my Domestics elsewhere. I put my plans into the hands of a Man much renowned for his experience in building, and I had pleasure in watching them carried out.' A plasterer stuccoed the walls; a carpenter made window frames. She left to 'the sole use of the spiders that have taken possession' the hazardous great staircase, the state bedchamber, 'the Grand Cabinet and some other pieces of magnificence quite useless to me, and which would cost a great deal to make habitable'. She 'fitted up 6 rooms, with Lodgings for 5 servants', and rejoiced to think that her venture would make a nice profit if she felt like selling it.

About once a week Baglioni appeared from some mission of mercy high in the mountains: 'as dirty and tir'd as a foot post, having eat nothing all day but a roll or two that he carries in his pocket, yet blest with such a perpetual flow of Spirits, he is allwaies Gay to a degree above chearfullness.' He spoke of her recovery as a miracle, and wished Palazzi would switch to his care from 'the Ignorant people he frequented'.[5] (Could he have been speaking of Dominiceti?)

Lady Mary was not long at Lovere before her box of books from England finally reached her, via Venice and Gottolengo. She left the box of china in Venice rather than risk it 'amongst the precipices that lead hither'; since it could have got as far as Gottolengo on the flat, this confirms her belief that she would soon be at Venice herself. Yet nearly two years later she had the china sent to Gottolengo after all. Had she by then despaired of getting away?

Lovere afforded less reading time than Gottolengo: she took three days to finish Lord Orrery's *Remarks on . . . Swift*. Knowing the author, she was not surprised but highly entertained by his self-congratulatory tone. She looked forward with sardonic eagerness to his memoirs, no matter how lengthy.

---

[5] *RW* 92–34; *CL* iii. 52–3, 54–5. Hunter says discharge from an upper-jaw abscess can make its way 'through the common integuments of the face', leaving 'a disagreeable scar on the face, about half an inch from the nose' (1778: 41, 42). He recommends sea bathing for scrofulous ulcerated gums (57–8).

Meanwhile he provoked her to a tirade 'of a horrible Length' on Swift's behaviour and character. She saw Swift as deriding faith and piety, despising the very church which gave him 'large benefices and Dignitys'. He was disloyal to his patron the first Earl of Oxford; he made 'a servile Court where he had any interested views', and was 'meanly abusive when they were disapointed'. He was a modern Caligula. She stoked her anger by rehashing Pope's iniquities of old, then quieted it by a digression on the literary works of Orrery's forebears for three generations back.[6]

Within a month she had read the other books, and was ready to comment on them all, even those 'not worth speaking of'. She dealt with Bolingbroke's *Letters on History* first, in ironical 'respect to his Dignity'. She differed from him radically on every conceivable topic: on the politics of 1710–13; on style (he 'sometimes spoils a good Argument by a profusion of Words'); on the ancient Roman Atticus, whom Bolingbroke scorned as a trimmer and Lady Mary admired as one steering between two equally mistaken factions (rather like some of her ancestors in the English Civil War). For Bolingbroke's 'Reflections upon Exile' she felt some sympathy, even while discerning in it 'the most Abject Dejection under a pretended Fortitude'. All in all she had 'small regard for Lord B. as an Author, and the highest contempt for him as a Man'. He had, she felt, squandered fortune, reputation, and health 'by a wild persuit of Eminence, even in Vice and Triffles'. He probably 'never look'd into halfe the authors he quotes'. As she wrote of him, her mind turned to his confederates Pope and Swift; as she wrote of Atticus, she remembered how Pope had attacked Addison under his name. Her indignation against Pope rose afresh, both from Addison's 'own merit, and having been your Father's Freind'. Many of the new books from England opened up old battles for refighting.

For many readers today, her comments on literature are more interesting than those on behind-the-scenes history.[7] This parcel from Lady Bute contained the harvest from some amazingly fertile years: Samuel Johnson's collected *Rambler* essays, Henry Fielding's *Amelia*, Sarah Fielding's sequel to *David Simple*, Tobias Smollett's *Ferdinand Count Fathom*, Eliza Haywood's *Betsy Thoughtless*, Jane Collier's *Art of Tormenting*, Charlotte Lennox's *Female Quixote*, and the anonymous *Adventures of a Valet* and *Sir Charles Goodville*. Except the last two, every one of these is seen by *some* scholars today as canonical, still worthy the serious attention of students and general readers.

[6] *CL* iii. 55–9, 77, 100.
[7] *CL* iii. 61–5, 76. It was on history that she offered comments to EWM (iii. 69, 76–7).

Lady Mary was not to be impressed by critical orthodoxies; but in any case to her these books were light reading. Her literary opinions were far removed from those of today's academic establishment, either traditionalist or feminist. She saw in the books she read a 'servile Flock of Imitators' with a 'General Want of Invention'. In her lifetime, she complained, 'no original has appear'd' but Congreve and Henry Fielding; and Fielding had never achieved his promise, since lack of money had led him to write and publish too fast and inattentively. She thought his two occupations, writing and the law, 'when duly executed do Honor to Human nature, but when degenerated into Trades are the most contemptible ways of getting Bread'.

Although she praised his observation of life (and although she wrote in this copy of *Amelia*, 'inferior to himselfe, superior to most others'), she judged Henry Fielding a lesser moralist than Johnson. His happy endings were unrealistic and 'very mischeivous'. He made 'extravagant Passions' seem praiseworthy, and encouraged young people to believe they might evade the consequences of foolish actions through lucky breaks which in real life would be as unlikely 'as Fairy Treasures'. Sarah Fielding on the other hand, depicting good people unjustly oppressed, was conveying 'a usefull moral'. Lady Mary had subscribed to her *Familiar Letters*. It was *David Simple. Volume the Last*, which elicited these comments; but she seems to have thought of 'Sally' more as poor relation than as serious literary artist.[8]

Often she did not know whose book she was reading. She thought *The Female Quixote* was Sarah Fielding's when she casually dismissed it as 'pretty plan, ill executed'. She admired the Smollett of *Roderick Random* and *Peregrine Pickle*, despised the Smollett of *Ferdinand Count Fathom*. She found Eliza Haywood's later novels quite amusing, but did not connect them with Haywood's earlier work.

Consistent attitudes thread her impromptu criticism. She was interested in the fictionalizing of fact; she defended reading for sheer pleasure; but she condemned books that misled their readers. This particular letter concludes on the last two points. Lady Mary wanted her granddaughters, 'who are very near my Heart', left free to read as they pleased in 'Poetry, Plays or Romances'—but she wanted their mother to talk over their reading with them. Remembering her early delight in Prior's 'Henry and Emma', she now felt its heroine's self-abnegating love, set out with 'melody of Words and pomp of Sentiments', was likelier to ruin an imaginative girl (without

---

[8] *CL* iii. 66–8; copy of *Amelia* at Sandon. EWM may have subscribed in her name. He subscribed in his own for ten copies of Sarah Fielding's *Lives of Cleopatra and Octavia*, 1757. (Their son subscribed too; the Butes did not.) This action (*perhaps* related to MWM) may have already taken place: Fielding printed subscription receipts for her *Lives* in 1748 (Sabor 1997: 12).

parental guidance) than were 'the lewdest Poems extant'. These comments too may have reflected recent reading. Sarah Fielding's *Remarks on Clarissa*, 1749, includes 'Some Reflections on the Character and Behavior of Prior's Emma'. Here Prior's *hero*'s character and behaviour is praised by a male reader, trenchantly condemned by a female one. Though she condescended to 'Sally', and could not recognize her anonymous hand, Lady Mary was probably, whether she knew it or not, allying herself with her young cousin's feminist critique.[9]

As Lady Mary was finishing these books, in late July 1754, Baglioni prescribed her another month at Lovere. She took his advice, though it meant postponing once again her move to Venice. In August Palazzi turned up, still not recovered, but 'moving with difficulty, supported with Walking-sticks'. Baglioni found him a lodging near Lady Mary's house.

He came, as usual, with a story: the Duchess of Guastalla (Lady Mary's visitor of six years before) had been ordering furniture and china in England; she needed to pay for it with bills of exchange on a London banker; she had sent Palazzi to request Lady Mary to oblige. Lady Mary doubted that Palazzi was such a favourite with the duchess as he maintained, but she did not doubt the general tenor of the story. Besides, his crippled condition made her feel sorry for him; it seemed to get steadily worse, though he was 'constantly surrounded by Doctors and Surgeons'. She 'was delighted to render this small service to the Princess', and handed over 'bills of exchange to the value of two thousand sequins', or £1,000. Palazzi promised to arrange repayment of this sum 'in Venice, or wherever I might decide to spend the winter'.

By the time she had completed the two-month asses'-milk treatment recommended by Baglioni, heavy autumn rains had come on. She was 'easily' persuaded that her projected journey would be hazardous at this time of year; 'and so not knowing what better to do I stayed at Lovere. I had a stove put in my Room, I had Books brought, and I contented myself with the Conversation of those Few People who came to visit me.'[10] Among these were Aurelio and Diana Ardengo, an elderly brother and sister, much respected by their neighbours, living in a 'pretty House as neat as any in Holland'. Lady Mary now regaled Lady Bute with a long story about them.

Its heroine, Octavia, entered this story as an eight-year-old pauper taken in by Diana Ardengo to make a servant of; she had now become a countess.

[9] *CL* iii. 66–7.   [10] *RW* 94–5.

Richardson, said Lady Mary, would have spun '7 or 8 Volumes' from this real-life analogue to *Pamela*. Octavia excelled at everything she learned: 'to read, write, and cast accompts', to cook and embroider, to make confectionery and distil potions. She was 'well Bred, humble and modest', and never went out except to church. She acquired renown as a model servant and, from the age of seventeen, as a dazzling beauty. She now attracted offers of marriage from 'many honest thriving Trademen', and ogling from 'several young Gentlemen, very well powder'd'. She declined advice that she ought to marry (with the classic reply that she wished to remain single), and moved to Bergamo to better herself by working for an elderly Countess Sozzi. (The neighbours said she had been got rid of: Aurelio Ardengo fancied her.)

Soon Countess Sozzi died; her son Count Jeronimo tried to seduce Octavia—and failed, despite his good looks, his dancing, his courtly Parisian manners. She left his employ for that of an aged judge, who after three months of trying in his turn to seduce her offered her marriage. She refused, and fled back to the Ardenghi. They disapproved of her flight; but they took her in, allowed her to cook and clean, and concealed her presence when the judge came looking for her. But in early December 1754 there came for her a handsome vessel with an escort of armed and mounted servants, an old priest with Count Sozzi's summons to marriage, and a valet de chambre with a complete set of lady's laced finery.

Octavia summoned her own priestly supporter, Don Giuseppe (a young classical scholar, well known to Lady Mary). After consultation and dressing the bride, 'away they march'd, leaving the Family in a Surprize not to be describ'd'. Octavia met the count on the far shore of the lake. She insisted on their both making their confessions before the wedding ceremony and receiving communion the morning after consummation. She then reformed her husband, both spiritually and financially.

The social order tottered; all Lovere was agog. Lady Mary heard the final chapter from Aurelio Ardengo over coffee; but neither of them applauded. He feared the anger of the count's relations for aiding and abetting Octavia; Lady Mary suspected he was also jealous. For her part, her anti-levelling response was driven not only by ideology but also by anger and pain. She had only just learned the end of an analogous story in England: of the death of her friend the Duchess of Bolton (*née* Lady Anne Vaughan), and of the duke's speedy remarriage to his low-born mistress (Lavinia Fenton, better known as the original Polly in Gay's *Beggar's Opera*). The duke had now died, leaving this second wife his whole disposable estate. So 'Polly, bred in an Alehouse and produce'd on the stage', had scooped the just deserts of

Lady Mary's despised and rejected friend. Vengefully she noted that Countess Octavia was careful to keep her poor aged mother at a distance (while doling out limited charity) and had sent no message to Diana Ardengo (who had so recently been advising her to settle for a far less splendid lot). She diagnosed in Octavia 'a designing Head', which had cannily managed her gift of beauty. Her anger at the fate of the pious and gentle Lady Anne spilled out into blame, not for the system of arranged marriages but for the sexy, scheming girls who outwitted it. She was ruffled enough to be unreasonable: on the one hand it would be maternal wisdom to keep daughters locked away 'till no body cares to look on 'em'; on the other, she blamed the 'Saint-like Governess' who had kept Lady Anne innocent and ignorant.[11]

~ махайка ~

Winter 1754–5 was Lady Mary's first at Lovere. Considering the town's proximity to glaciers and (today) to ski centres, its climate was mild, because of the lake. Her daughter, too, was living in new places. After the Prince of Wales's death, Lord Bute had turned back to botany and planned to fill the Kenwood gardens with exotic trees. But by 1754 he found Hampstead too remote for the political life reactivated by his mentoring relationship with young George, the new Prince of Wales. That year he gave up Kenwood for a house in South Audley Street (in London's most newly fashionable district) and another on Kew Green (handy for the summer court at Richmond and for Kew Gardens, which were burgeoning under Bute's supervision). Leaving Kenwood served both his career and his scientific interests. For Lady Bute, it meant a reinvolvement in the court life which she had dropped out of. For Lady Mary, it meant that her daughter would never again have such leisure for letter-writing. Lady Bute explained who Smollett was; she related her daughters' progress towards womanhood; but she could never satisfy her mother's appetite for news of home.[12]

Palazzi, that familiar annoyance, spent the winter at Lovere too, and made the most of it by running a gambling assembly, from motives he had in common with Lady Mary's son. She refused his invitations to attend his basset table. 'Dr Baglioni related me a hundred good stories about him, and told me seriously that he feared he might be going mad.' Then Baglioni brought a

---

[11] *CL* iii. 70–5, 77.

[12] *CL* iii. 78, 79. Bute, 'finishing tutor' to the future George III from 1755, sold Kenwood to William Murray, later Lord Mansfield. Already corresponding with Linnaeus, Bute played a key role in building up Kew Gardens. His protégé 'Sir' John Hill (whose books MWM was reading with pleasure) implemented his plans for Kew and dedicated to him *Eden: or, A Complete Body of Gardening*, Nov. 1757 (Miller 1988: 213–39; Desmond 1995: 31, 36–8).

message. Instead of a house to sell, Palazzi had an employee to pass on. This was Dr Bartolomeo Mora or Moro, his recently acquired secretary.[13] He assured her that Mora was a man 'of great learning and integrity' (a change, said Lady Mary sardonically, from the knaves he normally employed); he 'flattered himself that I should find his conversation agreeable'. Baglioni 'added that he had recommended him because he supposed I was truly likely to kill myself with my perpetual studying'. Lady Mary laughed off this solicitude, insisting that she loved to be alone with her books, and 'did not study, but diverted myself'. Next day Mora, who was apparently as eager for the change as Palazzi, arrived to see her. She 'found him to be a Man of wit and learning, proving on experience to be gentle and sincere'.

He was also to prove loyal and steady in crisis. He transcribed the 'Italian Memoir' and others of Lady Mary's latest writings. Like Mari Anna, he worked for her for the rest of her life, including her last months in England. He was the only person to whom she left a substantial cash bequest.

One of the first tasks she gave him was to look over her contract with the ancient Castelli for the Trenzano property. She had stopped her annuity payments, suspecting they had mounted up to more than the land was worth. Palazzi, when appealed to, confessed with apparent frankness that he might have been taken in over this deal, but could offer no remedy beyond hoping 'the old Ruffian (that was his expression)' would soon die. It was mistrust merely of his judgement, not his integrity, that made Lady Mary refer the contract to her new secretary. For one who valued herself as clever it was painful to admit to having been duped; for one who valued herself as 'an uncommon kind of Creature, being an old Woman without superstition, peevishness or censoriousness', it was hard to make a fuss. Mora 'told me that indeed, as was too evident, I had been deceived, and that he had no doubt I could legitimately demand my money back'. But she does not say she did so.[14]

Other matters for sorrow or dissatisfaction clustered this winter. Lady Bute was ill, then confessed that she was pregnant again, at which her mother was 'not heartily glad'. Querini died, leaving Lady Mary truly grieved. She admired his record of channelling towards the public his great ecclesiastical revenues; she also admired the public's gratitude— the thronged and splendid funeral accorded him by the city of Brescia, the medals cast and statues erected. But the statues signalled once again the

---

[13] Eldest of six brothers, he had been a priest for years by 1737, when his father made a will leaving him 1,000 scudi, plus 500 scudi a year. He had been Palazzi's chaplain (*RW* 95–6; Archivio di Stato, Venice; Graeme to Bute, 30 Aug. 1758, Bute MSS).

[14] *RW* 95; *CL* iii. 78–9.

contrast between Querini's celebrity and her own ambivalently willed obscurity. When Maffei too died only a month later, her eulogy on him stressed his rejection of ambition for intellectual and cultural pleasures.[15]

From these months came a highly personal, highly concentrated little poem: a stoic dying fall, with echoes from the reading of Lady Mary's Restoration youth. She headed it, 'Wrote in the Year 1755 at Louvere.'

> Wisdom! slow product of experienced Years,
> The only Fruit that Life's cold Winter bears!
> Thy sacred seeds in vain in Youth we lay
> By the Fierce storms of Passion torn away;
> Should some remain in a rich Generous Soil
> They long lie hid, and must be rais'd with Toil;
> Faintly they struggle with inclement skies,
> No sooner born, than the poor Planter dyes.[16]

In prose she reminded her daughter that 'there is no real Happiness to be found or expected in this World . . . all Human endeavors after Felicity are as childish as running after Sparrows to lay salt on their tails.' She thought Lady Bute was old enough to have learned this already, but might still need to learn that liberty is as chimerical as happiness:

so many inevitable accidents thwart our Designs and limit our best laid projects, the poor efforts of our utmost prudence and political schemes appear (I fancy) in the eyes of some superior Beings like the pecking of a young Linnet to break a Wire Cage, or the climbing of a Squirrel in a Hoop. The Moral needs no explanation. Let us sing as chearfully as we can in our impenetrable Confinement and crack our Nuts with pleasure from the little Store that is allow'd us.

This is a deservedly well-known passage. Human beings treated by some superior power with the casual cruelty that they mete out to animals: this is a vision akin to that of Samuel Johnson's even more famous review of Soame Jenyns. But Montagu's gallant stoicism could hardly be more distant from Johnson's rage.[17] Readers of this passage, however, seldom notice its writer's *particular* reasons for fatalism. She had declared her belief in pre-destination often, but especially while she waited at Algarotti's beck and call. Now she re-declared it during another period when control of her own life eluded her.

---

[15] *CL* iii. 80–1, 83, 84–6. Lady Bute bore her youngest son, William, in Mar. 1755.

[16] *E&P* 306–7. Cf. 'No Love, sown in thy pros'prous Days, | Can Fruit in this cold Season raise'—in Anne Finch's lament for the ousting of James II ('The Change': 1903: 85). Soon afterwards MWM called herself 'many years dead and bury'd' (*CL* iii. 95).

[17] *CL* iii. 79–81, 84–6; Johnson's review of *A Free Inquiry into the Nature and Origin of Evil*, 1757.

She had prepared herself anew for her journey when in February Mari Anna 'fell ill, seriously as I was told'. It took her a month to recover. Then Baglioni forbade the journey 'unless I wanted to risk my life', on grounds of the severity of March weather in the mountain country. In April a renewed attempt to leave was cancelled when Lady Mary developed an intermittent diarrhoea which dragged on and on. Palazzi left Lovere before she did, travelling 80 kilometres northwards into the Alps, on doctors' orders, to the spa of Bormio. She went down to bid him a formal farewell at the lakeside, at his request, as if he expected never to see her again.

Lady Mary sang in her cage. The month she fell ill, she sent Lady Bute a letter rich in distillations of mental fight. She commented on her brother-in-law Gower's death and will, reported receiving a marriage proposal for her granddaughter Lady Mary, and lauded her husband for generosity as well as prudence. She sprinkled her aphorisms freely: 'Learning is necessary to the Happiness of Women'; to greet her new grandson, 'I am never in pain for any of that Sex'; and 'Fretting mends nothing.' This last was self-criticism: she confessed that lost letters and delayed parcels made her 'ready to break out into Alacks and allass's, with many murmurs against my cruel Destiny'. Her delight in getting letters, she said, equalled that of her eldest grand-daughter in fine clothes or her youngest in sweets. Apropos the baby she wrote that men have many roads to good fortune; women have only one, 'and that surrounded with precipices, and perhaps, after all, better miss'd than found'. There is no doubt that she meant marriage; but was she also thinking of the road out of Lovere?

When in six weeks she was finally free from diarrhoea she 'thought once again about leaving'. Again Baglioni pronounced the journey impracticable, this time because the roads were badly broken up by the thaw. He promised to procure from Bergamo a closed carriage which could negotiate steep places impassible in a chaise. 'This Carriage had left with a Great Lord for Milan, but its return to Bergamo was expected daily.' This sounds plausible enough; it does not sound like a hindrance which could extend, 'on one pretext after another, and in spite of all my efforts to leave', for an entire summer. Yet for the summer of 1755 Lady Mary, although 'firmly resolved on leaving for Venice', remained at Lovere. Palazzi was not exerting direct influence, for he was away.[18] Had her energy flagged? Or was the vivacious and friendly Baglioni also suspect?

---

[18] *RW* 96; *CL* iii. 81–4. MWM had used precipices as a metaphor for danger before she began to feel trapped at Lovere. In Sept. 1755 Palazzi was admitted to the Brescian City Council—a late and perhaps grudging admission (Fappani 1961: 102).

She did leave Lovere for the last time in autumn 1755, though the exact date looks different in two different texts. According to the 'Italian Memoir', it was September when she left (with Palazzi's encouragement) for Gottolengo, with Venice as ultimate goal; it took them about two weeks (as against two days last time) to reach Gottolengo; and further events brought the date at least to November before he told her of an opportunity of a personal courier to Lady Bute. (This was the obscure episode of the merchant Pitrovani, related below.) Yet Lady Mary exulted over this potential courier in a letter dated 20 October [1755], looking forward to first-hand news of 'how you look, how you're dress'd, and in what manner your room is furnish'd'.[19]

She was still at Lovere when she received Lady Bute's next cargo of books: Henry Fielding's *Journal of a Voyage to Lisbon*, Sarah Fielding and Jane Collier's *The Cry*, Susan Smythies's *The Stage-Coach*, Eliza Haywood's *Invisible Spy*, several novels by unknown authors, and—most epoch-making of all—Richardson's *Sir Charles Grandison*. There were some duplicates of things Lady Mary had read already, and a letter 'consisting only of 3 lines and a halfe', which probably announced Henry Fielding's recent death. Lady Bute must have thought it not worth sending a proper letter by such a slow conveyance; but her mother's reply gave a paragraph to her disappointment before moving on to criticize the books.

She began with personalities: a reminiscent sketch of Fielding and Steele, their happy-go-lucky natures 'so form'd for Happiness, it is pity they were not Immortal'. From the *Voyage to Lisbon* she picked out the single episode of a kitten rescued at sea: this was because she herself had just rescued a starving kitten. Again she homed in on personal allusion in what she read; again she was fairly scathing about several of Lady Bute's selections. In principle she favoured the popular and defended 'Trash, Trumpery etc.'— but her critical faculty never slept. She was unimpressed by the experimental structure of *The Cry*, though she liked its morality; indeed, she compared it favourably with the intellectually heavyweight works of Bolingbroke. Of *Grandison* she said little in this first letter, but that little is revealing. 'This Richardson is a strange Fellow. I heartily despise him and eagerly read him, nay, sob over his works in a most scandalous manner.'[20]

For months to come, the 'strange fellow' haunted her mind. She could not reconcile herself to him, but could not leave the idea of him alone. More than

---

[19] *RW* 97; *CL* iii. 98. The discrepancy about date is matched by discrepancy about the way she met Pitrovani, below; it casts some general doubt on the 'Memoir' 's dates.

[20] 22 Sept. [1755], *CL* iii. 86–90.

those of any other author, his views led her irresistibly into expounding her own opinions and experience. She denounced his pictures of Italian nobility and English upper classes as distortion, and his satire on activities like masquerades and collecting old china as prejudice. She hated several aspects of his pattern hero, Sir Charles, whose readiness to have his daughters educated as Roman Catholics called forth her most detailed disquisition on Papist errors and her own debating exploits as a Protestant champion. She hated Richardson's passion for weddings, and his habit of demonstrating his heroines' delicacy by 'Fits and Madness'; but she was no better pleased by the behaviour of his female rebels (Anna Howe and Charlotte Grandison), who seemed to her merely pert and ill-natured though designed as witty and spirited. She was angry that he put in the mouth of his bold and masculine Miss Barnevelt a saying of her own: that the one advantage of 'being a woman . . . is, *that she cannot be married to a WOMAN*'. (She admitted she had said this, but then a 'light thing said in Gay Company should not be call'd upon for a serious Defence, especially when it injures no body'.)[21]

Lady Mary made no mention of her intended uprooting. But along with her usual library order she put in a request for '3 of Pinchbec's watches' (handsome ones, priced when she left England at £5, while the seven volumes of *Grandison* sold for under a pound). She wanted parting presents for Baglioni and 'for 2 Priests to whom I have some obligations'. On Palazzi's return to Lovere (supposedly from Bormio) he seemed surprised to find her not yet gone. He made no demur about her now leaving Lovere, but he insisted on escorting her, against her will, on grounds of danger from footpads. A 'large party would be an insurance against being attacked'. He was no longer the protector of ten years previously, but an invalid carried in a litter. It was to suit his own convenience that he made her leave at once.[22]

He also dictated her choice of route towards Venice. He 'besought me humbly to pass through Gottolengo to take possession of the Furniture which I had practically abandoned on my sudden departure'. Mari Anna seconded this: she wanted to pack up the linen. Lady Mary accepted this brief detour; she only insisted on going via Brescia (which was the obvious if not the only route), 'in order to consult my banker, Ballini, whom I had never met'. But fate or the count circumvented this plan. They had got no further than the foot of lago d'Iseo when he announced 'with expressions of sorrow . . . that a Bridge was broken, and we should be compelled to go via Delo. There we stayed for ten days on account of the heavy rains which had flooded the Countryside.' This delay was crucial: Lady Mary did not see

---

[21] *CL* iii. 91, 94–7; cf *CL* ii. 33; CB 4.   [22] Sale 1936; 1969: 76; *CL* iii. 90; *RW* 96–7.

Ballini; when she reached Gottolengo it was (says the 'Memoir') late October. The relentless rain and quagmire roads were such that she 'allowed myself to be persuaded' that a journey to Venice was out of the question; she sent the post-horses and postilions back to Lovere. The 'Memoir', supposedly centred on her grievances, here drifts away from Palazzi's sabotaging of her purpose, towards her subsidizing of him, and the contemptuous pity (both for his declining health and for his apparent stupidity and poverty) which prevented her from standing up to him.[23]

Again preparations for European war were affecting correspondence. Again Lady Mary's safety-valve for her personal frustrations was writing to her daughter on other matters. One 'tedious miscellany of a Letter', rich in theological and literary opinions, was to travel via the merchant Pitrovani. According to a later letter, she had met him at Lovere and accepted his offer of his London correspondent, George Prescot, as a safe intermediary. But according to the 'Memoir', Palazzi out of the blue brought up Pitrovani's name, as 'a Friend of his . . . for whom he could vouch', who was about to travel to England and would act as courier.

Whatever the exact nature of the delivery route, Lady Mary trusted it enough to send 'a ring, the only one that remained to me of my jewels, because I had had it on my finger when the others were stolen'. Her hope of receiving letters from her god-daughters had by now moved down from Mary the younger to the twelve-year-old Jane. Prescot was to carry for delivery to Lady Jane 'that Bauble of a ring'. Lady Mary planned next to 'find something for Lady Anne . . . I think I have ill luck if none of my many Grandaughters have a turn for writeing. She that has will be distinguish'd by me.' She was not happy that news of the ring's delivery came (from Pitrovani) before she heard from Jane. Later 'I am very well pleas'd with Lady Jane's Letter, and wish it was longer'. Lady Mary arranged that Lady Bute should buy Anne a watch in London (to cost six times as much as the other watches) and sent, perhaps in recompense for her trouble, a necklace 'which you need not be asham'd to wear'.[24]

☙◊❧

It seems that no letters got through between 2 November 1755 and 22 March 1756 to throw light on Lady Mary's last winter at Gottolengo. From this

---

[23] *RW* 96–7. 'Delo' is not identifiable on modern maps; cf. the 'Memoir' 's use of 'Solferino'. Madame du Boccage said the mud on the Venice road out of Brescia could swallow a waggon and 6 or 8 oxen (1762: iii. 142).

[24] Pitrovani came from Valtellina (between Lovere and Bormio), so Palazzi might have contacted him that summer (*CL* iii. 98, 99–100, 104, 107, 109, 110; *RW* 97).

period she kept what seems to be an ongoing draft or summary, in Italian, of topics which she also discussed in other, normal letters to Lady Bute. Unless this was some kind of linguistic exercise for Dr Mora, it was probably an effort to combat the dislocation of her correspondence. She told her daughter that lost letters were one more item 'set down by Destiny' among her many mortifications; later she realized they were being intercepted. In this Italian 'letter' she reverts to the topic of Richardson and his pernicious heroines. She comments on husbandly authority, wifely submission, and the influence women exercise in patriarchal society (which she thought would ensure Richardson's success). Again she enquired about his identity.[25]

Richardson's heroines gave her a point of reference for an extraordinary member of Brescian high society, whose story she thought worth telling. This was the Marchesa Licinia Bentivoglio, heiress of the senior branch of the Martinenghi, for twenty years a talking point in the province for her pride and inflexibility. She had left her husband without having borne him a son, enraged her father, embittered her husband's family, quarrelled with everyone she knew, incurred excommunication, and refused to countenance her elder daughter's wedding. She now lived as a recluse, 'hateing and being hated'. In February 1756 she was seized with mysterious sickness, and her two servants died after eating some soup which she had tried and rejected. The suspicion of poisoning her for her father's money lay heavy against her estranged husband. The local ladies all defended him; several, thought Lady Mary, would be quite happy to marry him if he were free. For her own part, 'I decide nothing.'

Next month Lady Mary received the china from Lord Bute which had been languishing at Venice. 'Every thing that comes from England is precious to me,' she wrote, 'to the very Hay that is employ'd in Packing.' She at once began to worry about circumventing Venetian trade and inheritance regulations to make some suitable return: perhaps a picture, if she could get one.[26]

In April came a letter from the Duke of Portland, breaking the news that Lady Oxford had died in December 1755. She had left her friend a remembrance: a legacy of £200. Lady Mary (having scrupulously obtained permission from her husband, as the legal owner of all her belongings) eventually used this money to buy or have made a 'white brilliant diamond Ring' with her name and her friend's enamelled on it: 'Maria Henrietta'. She wrote to tell Lady Oxford's daughter that she would bequeath her this memorial, and she kept her word.[27]

[25] It is in the same hand as the 'Italian Memoir' (H MS 81. 299–302; *SL* 423–6; *RW* 98; *CL* iii. 100).
[26] *CL* iii. 100–3, 107.   [27] *CL* iii. 100, 109–10, 294.

She was deeply afflicted, and could speak of nothing but her grief. Palazzi sent 'compliments of condolence' on her loss; she had him in her house again this spring, physically prostrated, just as in 1754. In May 'he had himself carried to my Antichamber' to break to her another of his schemes. Pitrovani, his faithful friend and agent, had to make a payment in London and wanted to avoid losing money on changing *zecchini* into pounds sterling. (So says the 'Memoir'; Lady Mary told Lady Bute that Pitrovani wrote to her to ask that 'in consideration of his care and faithfull delivery of the Ring I would favor him with a Bill on the Person who was to pay it'.) Whoever put the request, it was for Pitrovani to borrow her legacy, from the Duke of Portland, and repay it to her (in sequins?) at Gottolengo. For a month she resisted Palazzi's 'continual insistence', and she wrote to Pitrovani that she 'would not draw a Negotiable Note on the Duke of Portland as on a common Banker'. Then she gave way, and sent the duke 'a respectfull Demand payable to the Bearer' for her legacy. Or for half of it; her figures are inconsistent.[28] But she caved in: either because she thought this would be the last time, or because she was now in physical fear.

As the spring wore on and she tried to push on preparations for her journey, she 'realised that I was a Prisoner. Every kind of ruse was employed to make me stay. My chaises were broken, my Horses lamed, my Maid taken ill, the rivers in flood.' The doctor (Cavalino? surely not Mora?) said that if she set out she would die on the road. She mentioned nothing of this to Lady Bute, writing instead of English politics (or their faint reflection in the newspapers), of the immense wealth of two Greek girls (daughters of a murdered tax-collector), of the earthquake hysteria provoked by the Lisbon disaster, of the books she wanted sent and of the grandchildren whose 'inside and out' she so badly wanted described. (Oddly, she thought the girls had the luck to live in an age less sentimental, and more tolerant of education for women, than her own.)[29] Yet it seems that imperceptibly she was turning away from the stoicism of Epictetus towards something a little more assertive.

She mentioned her problems only in connection with George Prescot, Pitrovani's London contact. He had declined to take on her correspondence with Lady Bute, ostensibly because the Butes had treated him discourteously when he delivered the ring. Prescot was on his way up in the world, and may have been sensitive to possible snubs from the lordly Bute

---

[28] Asking on [22 Aug. 1756] for information about the duke's payment of the money, she sounded as if she already had doubts (*CL* iii. 110). From here until the end of the chapter the primary source is the 'Italian Memoir', *RW* 98–105.

[29] *CL* iii. 104–7. She said 'prudential considerations' kept her from laughing at the processions and pilgrimages meant to appease 'divine Vengeance'.

household. One cannot help wondering, though, if it was Pitrovani whom he was declining.[30] Lady Mary was disappointed; but she gave no hint of her hopes or fears to an unexpected and welcome visitor. This was General William Graeme, a connection of Lord Bute's who had just been appointed commander-in-chief of the Venetian military forces with a brief to modernize and reform them. Lady Bute had taken fright at her mother's silence, and asked Graeme to investigate and report.[31] What he said is unknown.

Palazzi 'had had himself taken to Cremona'—perhaps because of Graeme's visit. It is not clear how long he was gone, nor why Lady Mary did not seize her chance to get away in his absence. She wrote to Lady Bute in May about human ingratitude and repayment of benefits with 'Insults, nay, perhaps abuses'. During her long life, she said, she had 'endeavor'd to purchase Freinds. Accident has put it in my power to confer great Benefits, yet I never met with any return, nor indeed any true Affection but from dear Lady Oxford, who ow'd me nothing.'[32] She must have been feeling low indeed to discount the affection of other past friends—Skerrett, Stafford, Hervey.

The count returned to find her, not indeed departed but apparently on the verge of it, 'unmoved by all the tricks he had used to make me stay in Gottolengo', or by the doctor's threats. He reinstalled himself in the Castle, and 'mounted another stratagem', grandly produced as usual. From his bed he sent a message by 'a certain Priest, his protégé, named Don Geronimo Zarza': he was in violent pain, perhaps near death, and begged to see her 'for a Moment'. She 'found him in Bed, propped up on Pillows, his face pale and distorted'. With elaborate precautions of secrecy, he told her he had discovered the whereabouts of her stolen jewels. They

had been pawned to a great Ecclesiastic, a Relative of the Pope . . . it would take twelve thousand sequins to redeem them. This story seemed to me so ridiculous that it made me laugh. I answered that I had never owned jewels worth that amount of money, that I supposed he meant to coin a few sequins by this trick, that I had long since given up the search, and that I wouldn't give a farthing for such information. I went out laughing.

She felt, however, that if this was not a fantasy it must be another stratagem for delay.

---

[30] *CL* iii. 104–9. Bute was having a hard year. Suspicious of MWM's old acquaintance Newcastle, he had thrown in his lot with Pitt; in Nov. 1755 Pitt was dismissed from government. George II opposed Bute's position of trust with the prince (McKelvey 1973: 18–19, 28, 30–1).

[31] Graeme fought through the War of the Austrian Succession in the Dutch forces. He and Bute had a brother-in-law in common (Graeme 1903: 422–30; *RW* 98).

[32] *RW* 98; *CL* iii. 107–8.

That afternoon 'he had himself carried to my Antechamber and complained to me, weeping, how little regard I had for his honour'. The familiar rhetoric flowed. The Pope's relation was a Bolognese marchesa; the money to redeem the jewels must go to her. The thief had revealed his crime in a deathbed confession. There was a monk even now in the house, 'charged with the restoration of my property' but insisting on anonymity. Palazzi begged Lady Mary to see him. 'Quite thunderstruck by this story, I agreed.' Palazzi, who was or said he was too weak to stand, 'was carried back to his Chamber' and sent in the monk. More shocks followed. From 'a case which I recognized as belonging to the Count', the monk drew out not only much of the stolen jewellery (variously spoiled and damaged), but many items which Lady Mary had last seen when they were packed up at Avignon, and which she had supposed stolen by Bettoni's agents: 'a beautiful embroidered Indian shawl', a 'diamond and ruby snuffbox', and so on. With the objects came the blinding light of comprehension. 'I knew then what I had to believe, and recognized also the danger of being in such scoundrelly hands.' Apparently the discovery had been staged for intimidation. She pretended, however, to feel nothing but naïve relief at recovering her things. She checked through them, pointed out two items which were not hers (a large cross and an episcopal-looking ring, both in emeralds) and said she would keep them till the right owners were found.

'The Monk, who kept his face hidden the whole time under his Hood, made a great deal of difficulty about leaving me my jewels, but I spoke to him in such a tone that he durst not reply, and withdrew with muttered complaints.' She behaved as if victorious, and unhesitatingly restored the cross and ring when Palazzi sent to say they were his. In the evening Zarza came back to pursue the pay-off: Palazzi, he said,

had pledged all his present and future possessions to this Marchesa of Bologna to get my jewels back, and he feared she would foreclose on him, and that I was obliged as a matter of honour to get him out of this most difficult situation, in which he had placed himself out of zeal for my service.

Lady Mary made no accusations, but, with high-flown moral sentiments about her own integrity, she denied that the marchesa could claim his property. (She must have known that by law it would be entailed on his family.)

Then, as usual spurred on rather than deterred by challenge, she took the action she had not taken in Palazzi's absence. She 'sent for the post-Horses, which arrived very late that evening'. She proposed to leave next morning, but then Palazzi distracted her by a reprise of an earlier theme. He asked for a letter to exonerate him from rumours put about by the Rodenghi 'that he was keeping me at Gottolengo by force and threats'. Lady Mary composed a letter too truthful to satisfy him but too polite for him to reject. While she was writing, the postilion disappeared from the door; Zarza told her, with apparent indigation, that he had got tired of waiting. Lady Mary turned to Mora, who 'had wit enough to understand the danger I was in, and energy enough to find a way to save me'. He ran after the postilion 'and compelled him to await my orders'.

It took until the next morning to make final preparations. She then 'found the Count in his Armchair in the Courtyard, where he had himself carried to bid me Farewell'. He ran through his strategies for delay. First 'he tried to terrify me with stories about Bandits. When he saw that this had no effect, he requested me as a last favour to call in at Signora Roncadelli's Country House', a few kilometres away at Pontevico. He pleaded his widowed aunt's trouble in advertising for the lost jewels, the ultimate success of her efforts, the warmth of her invitation, the disappointment she would feel if Lady Mary left without seeing her. Lady Mary at once promised to go there.

There was still the matter of her money—more than £2,000—left in the hands of Ballini. Palazzi wanted to organize its payment. Lady Mary 'replied that I intended to pass through Brescia and would leave . . . my own orders'. It seemed that Ballini now, like Pitrovani before him, was 'obliged to pay out a considerable sum in London'. Lady Mary could 'do him a great favour by sending him a bill of exchange for that City'. She said she would see Ballini herself. Palazzi persisted: 'my Aunt loves you too much to permit you to leave her until after several days'; this would make the bill of exchange too late. By now Lady Mary knew she was bartering for her actual safety; she gave him a note for one-tenth the sum which Ballini held.

This raised the curtain on her final departure from her Castle: her ideal retreat, where she had played Lady Bountiful, had enjoyed the reverence of peasants, clergy, and nobility alike, and had written some of her wisest, most philosophical letters. She left 'accompanied by my Maid in the Carriage, by Doctor Mora, by my old Manservant on Horseback, and my Footman, to whom the Count insisted on adding some armed Peasants, and his faithful Don Geronimo Zarza on horseback, for my protection'. *Protection* was now a word of ill-omen, signifying intimidation.

'The Postilion drove so badly, and found, or pretended to find, the roads so bad, that it was already night when we arrived at the villa of Fianello.' The whole day's travel had taken them about 10 or 12 kilometres. Fribourg was no longer with them, 'having proved easy to seduce into a Tavern'. The postilion said the road (heading for Pontevico) would get worse not better, and was reluctant to proceed at all. Zarza said he had already made arrangements for Lady Mary to sleep at a merchant's house in Alfianello; he claimed great credit for this.[33] 'The House seemed to me above suspicion; but on our entering it my Maid was seized with an attack of vomiting so violent that she was unable to wait on me. I was obliged to undress on my own.' Zarza said 'he had to leave us in the morning to attend the Fair at Brescia' and could take care of any commissions she might have there. She said he could take a letter to Ballini, and 'that if he wished to set out before daybreak I could write that evening. He begged me not to fatigue my eyes by candle-light, saying that he would wait on me at breakfast time.' But in the morning he was gone, without the unwritten letter.

Lady Mary slept very soundly, worn out by 'agitation . . . both of body and mind'. The suffering Mari Anna was elsewhere, the drunken and oblivious Fribourg in her antechamber for the latter part of the night, Mora downstairs with Zarza. On the bedroom table lay her two large leather bags, specially made to hold her jewel-cases and her sealed purse of receipts, banking correspondence, contracts, 'and in short all my important papers'. The bags were still in place next morning.

Lady Mary 'was so glad to have got out of Gottolengo that I felt myself in perfect health. I got up before any of my Servants, dressed myself, and had the others roused'. She thought nothing of Zarza's departure, but 'ordered the Horses to be harnessed. Dr Mora found one of the wheels broken. Then I realised that a plan had been laid to keep me there.' Mora, who shared this opinion, 'summoned a Master-Carpenter and had a new wheel made and attached in spite of the Postilion, who appeared displeased at this operation. It was the evening before I was able to set out'—without Palazzi's armed escort, who 'took themselves off'. The reduced caravan was a mile away from Pontevico, and the footman had just been sent ahead 'to notify Madam Roncadelli of my arrival', when they saw galloping towards them a young officer with an enormous firearm of obsolete design.

'This terrified Dr Mora, who was a few steps ahead of my Carriage; he came to its window with his eyes staring and hair on end; he confessed to me later that he thought he had come to the last moment of his life.' The officer carried a paper purporting to be the Venetian Republic's official mandate informing Palazzi of the confiscation of all his property by the Bolognese marchesa, with a covering letter from him to Mora saying that in this emergency 'he had been forced to cash in my money'. This phrase puzzled Lady Mary, since she had left him nothing but her note for Ballini, which was not

---

[33] *RW* 98–101. The Alfianello 'osteria' bore the name of the noble Cesare Martinengo; a man named Ippolito Zorza worked for him (Mazzoldi 1966: 58–9).

negotiable. The letter contained the usual rhetoric of dishonour and imminent suicide.[34] 'This last article was so ridiculous that when I had looked at
the papers I hurled them at Dr Mora and directed the Postilion to move on.
A few moments later I saw Madam Roncadelli's fine carriage approaching
with many of her Servants.' Lady Mary found her hostess waiting at the door
to receive her. She was cordially embraced and led inside to meet a gentleman friend from Cremona.

'I had my head full of the encounter with the Officer, and I naturally
related it.' To explain her mystification about what money Palazzi could
have taken, she pulled out of her bag the purse of documents—and 'found
they had been replaced with blank paper of the same size'. Roncadelli, who
'appeared just as outraged as myself', sent for her nephew, promised to
obtain redress for his infamous conduct, and begged Lady Mary 'as a favour
to stay at her House' to await him. He arrived next day, in spite of the 'real or
assumed' ailments which made him go straight to bed.

Madam Roncadelli besought me to hear his case, which I refused to do otherwise
than in her presence. She wept, and took my hand and kissed it, and led me to the
Chamber where he was. He tried to make a long speech punctuated with sobs; I cut
his oration short, and told him that I had not come to listen to his excuses, but to
demand the return of my papers. 'They are burned (he replied, weeping), and even
if they had not been, they would have been just as useless to you, because they were
all forged.' His Aunt apparently fell in a swoon, and I left the Chamber saying, 'You
are a worthless Thief.'

The truth was out. Lady Mary locked herself into her room, to think over
the grave danger of her situation. She still trusted Roncadelli, and 'believed
myself to be safe in her House. But I had to pursue my journey, and I faced a
desperate Man capable of any Crime', with villains in his employ who would
not stick at assassinating her on the road if he thought she intended to bring
legal charges. She 'resolved to keep my resentment hidden'.

Next morning she received her weeping hostess 'with the appearance of
calm' and with 'genuine pity for her grey hairs'. Roncadelli told Lady Mary
(who was in fact the older of the two) that most of her money was irrevocably lost: spent or gambled away at Turin, Milan, and elsewhere. She 'was
not rich enough to refund it', but she had a compromise to propose. Lady
Mary replied, in just the insufferably noble and selfless manner of her
own Docile, that it would in any case be 'unjust that you should pay for his
dissipations. I ask nothing from you, and will take nothing from you.'

---

[34] *RW* 101–2. Palazzi might have taken lessons from Frances Burney's Mr Harrel (*Cecilia*, books iii–v).

The compromise went like this. The note written only two days ago for Ballini was untouched, and would be returned. The Castle at Gottolengo, being entailed, did not legally belong to Lady Mary. But she 'was Mistress of it if I wished to stay there'; if not, it would be best to allow Palazzi to hide his shame in it. New deeds would be drawn up to confirm Lady Mary's owner-ship of other properties, puzzlingly named as 'Fornace and Solferino'.[35] Lady Mary accepted this, and entrusted her case wholly to Roncadelli. Nevertheless she stayed in her room and 'ate alone, from one dish only'. Perhaps she thought of the Marchesa Licinia.

There were great comings and goings of various relatives, in which I wanted no part. In the end Madam Roncadelli informed me that the Count, although much indisposed, had had a document drawn up which he implored me to sign, and that he had the money ready that was specified in the final note, which would be restored to me with the title-deeds of the properties. She brought the Notary to me, who presented me the document in the presence of the above-mentioned Gentleman of Cremona, two others whose names I have forgotten, and Dr Mora.

When I read it I found the statement, obscurely expressed, that I admitted to having lived for ten years at his expense. I tore the Paper into a thousand pieces, saying in a loud voice that they meant basely to swindle me. Dr Mora drew near me, all trembling, and said in a low voice, 'Madam, be less hot-headed; think of your danger.' I replied, raising my voice, 'I would rather die than sign such a foul lie, which would dishonour me.'

This was the second day which Lady Mary had closed by laying defiant, histrionic claim to the high moral ground. Everyone 'left in confusion, and I went to bed'. Next morning Roncadelli asked pardon, said she had not looked at the document, and would now have another drawn up. This would specify, as already agreed, that Lady Mary should receive the 400 sequins named in the note on Ballini, and the restoration of her properties (except Gottolengo). Roncadelli gave her personal word of honour that she would keep this document in her own custody, out of Palazzi's hands. Lady Mary agreed to sign, 'thinking that unless I did so I should never be permitted to leave', and pretended to have forgiven and forgotten. Palazzi did not appear in person, but 'sent to beg me as a last favour to permit him to escort me as far as Mantua, where he had Relatives'. She accepted this too, and after the fondest adieus to Signora Roncadelli she set out accompanied by Ugolino Palazzi and (on horseback) his youngest brother, Ignazio.

The rest of her journey was anticlimactic, if not precisely uneventful. She

---

[35] Solferino presumably means Saló, as it does throughout the 'Memoir'; Fornace is more than 10 km from Trenzano, but *might* mean the estate there.

presumably did not go via Brescia or see Ballini. At Mantua a letter from
Lady Bute caught up with her. Her reply, in sublime disregard of her recent
adventures, reproved her daughter for being unbusinesslike, informed her
that one cannot 'be too cautious in dealings with Mankind', justified her own
financial dealings (those which Lady Bute knew about), and casually mentioned that she was *en route* to Venice 'to try to settle our commerce in a
better manner'. She 'left the Count confined to Bed at Mantua' and was surprised to find him installed in the same inn as herself at Vicenza. She thought
it unwise to demand an explanation, and pressed on for Padua without him.
Again he turned up, a mile short of the city, and 'informed me that he had
prepared a Lodging for me'.

By this time Lady Mary had an interest in secrecy, since she was in the
place where she meant to begin a new life. Padua was a charming old city,
even though it was licking its wounds after a devastating tornado only about
a week earlier. She probably remembered it from 1739–40. She stayed two or
three days in the lodgings chosen by Palazzi, then found a convenient,
charming, inexpensive house to rent, and took water for Venice. It was early
September; she had spent ten years trying to get where she now was. She
found that Palazzi had taken lodgings for her in Venice too; again she stayed
three days before moving. She had hoped for a reunion with Chiara Michiel,
but the latter, she heard, had been rusticated ('banished into the Country for
some Weeks') for the crime of talking to a foreign ambassador, Count
Rosenberg of the Holy Roman Empire.[36]

Lady Mary returned to Padua. There she 'found the Count, who had settled himself in my House, in my Swiss servant's Room near the Door. I had
him informed that I was not running a boarding-house, and I begged him to
leave.' He did so, but he refused (either then or later) to disgorge the
promised replacement title-deeds or the name of the merchant to whom the
Duke of Portland had paid the legacy from Lady Oxford.

Over a ten-year period Palazzi had made thousands of pounds out of
Lady Mary (double those thousands in *zecchini*). The spin he put on it for
Venetian society was apparently that she had 'kept' him for sexual purposes.
John Murray, the British Resident in Venice, reported that she had been
some years in the hands of a Brescian count 'who it is said plunders her of all
her riches'. He thought this was still continuing in September 1756. For
Palazzi, sponging on a mistress would have been an unwontedly gentle
variant on his usual means of subsistence. In 1760 he and his three brothers

---

[36] *Padova* 1961: p. xxclviii; *CL* iii. 114; report by secret agent G. B. Manuzzi, 24 July 1756, quoted in
Comisso 1984: 77.

were banned from the Venetian dominions for a complicated list of violent
crimes. Palazzi was first to serve a jail sentence; five years later he was still in
prison.[37]

Though he had not cowed Lady Mary's spirit, he had finally shattered her
dream of self-sufficiency, retirement, and benevolence. It must have pained
her to know that her Castle was now the seat of his machinations and depredations. But no doubt she plucked up a spirit. General Graeme, informing
Algarotti of her return to civilization, thought she intended 'to call Count
Palazzi to account. I do not know the tenth part of her history there, but she
began to hint it to me when last here. She is more ashamed, I believe, for
passing for a dupe in the eye of the public, than she is for passing for a woman
of gallantry.'[38] She drew up her 'Memoir'; she took legal advice from
Michiel's friend Rosenberg; but she never brought her case to court. Meanwhile the sophisticated yet ordered society of Venice and Padua would be all
the sweeter. And Princess Docile, her naïve, eternally victimized heroine,
probably owes a good deal to her creator's experience of being battened on.

[37] *RW* 102–5; Murray to Henry Fox, 10 Sept., SP 99/66. Palazzi's old master, Stanislas Augustus of
Poland, wrote to the Doge in his favour, but did not assert his innocence. Even MWM's 'Memoir' may
slightly soften his crimes against her (*Enciclopedia Bresciana*; 23 Dec. 1765, Queriniani MSS; Fappani 1961:
108).
[38] Quoted in *Quarterly Review*, 1820: 23: 417.

29

November 1756–April 1758

❧

Venice and Padua: 'The active scenes are over'[1]

HER return from the wilderness gave Lady Mary some golden years. The burden of Palazzi was lifted: the suppressed anger, the drain on her self-esteem, the endless scheming and being outwitted, latterly the fear. Although approaching seventy, she enjoyed better general health in Padua and Venice than in the Po Valley. Nothing more is heard of either fever or dental troubles.[2] She was fonder now of Lady Bute and of her grandchildren (from the almost adult to the not yet born) than she had ever been; or else she found it easier now to express her feelings. She delighted in making a fresh start: setting up her new life with houses, furnishings, routines. She rediscovered old friends and acquired new ones—new correspondents, too. Some of these must have brought out her writing talents to the full; but only one new correspondence survives. Her references to the nine Muses and the daemon of poesy show she was writing other things as well: perhaps 'Docile', probably other texts now lost.

She got out an album she had had since before her marriage and resumed her habit of noting down maxims: some commonplace enough, some start-lingly original. She mixed gleanings from classical, English, and French authors with the fruits of her own thought and with Lockean observation of herself. She noted she had such good spirits she could hardly believe she was an old woman; but then 'My Verses not children but miscarriages of my Mind.' Some of her 'Memorandums' are entirely cryptic, not communica-tions but merely reminders: names of correspondents, names of authors (Epictetus, Lady Chudleigh), names from a lifetime's exchange of ideas.[3]

---

[1] *CL* iii. 134.   [2] She says nothing of long-term effects from her gums being cauterized.
[3] *CL* iii. 183, 190. 'Me a Cat' or 'Me a Cat[holic]'? Two jokes, but with different tendencies. She noted that the Renaissance scholars George Buchanan and Hugo Grotius were 'good poets' (CB 5 ff., 8, 21 ff.).

Padua, tightly penned between its walls and the River Brenta, was still regarded by many of the Venetian nobility as a good site for a second or 'country' house. Lady Mary went back and forth between Padua and Venice, between solitary study and socializing, between her foreign and English worlds. Having been largely deprived of music, she now had a choice of concerts as well as other social gatherings. She settled happily into her 'favorite' palazzo in the parish of San Massimo, Padua, which was handily situated near the river, the highway to Venice.[4]

When Chiara Michiel's exile gave way to a kind of house arrest, Lady Mary hastened to Venice to see her. She was delighted that Michiel had been studying English, and eager to lend her books; but she went on writing to her almost wholly in French, sending her just such fervent professions of affection as she had to Lady Oxford. Michiel had been having a difficult time. Her father had just died. Her bachelor uncle's ex-mistress had thereupon schemed to marry the uncle and to legitimate her son as the Bragadin heir. The mistress's plan had been foiled by a libertine protégé of the uncle: Giacomo Casanova, who had since been imprisoned. Lady Mary's arrival at Padua coincided with his sensational escape from the Leads (cells high under the roof of the Doges' Palace) and from Venice itself. Chiara Michiel's sister, Maria Eleonora Bragadin, was a nun in the Murano convent of Santa Maria degli Angeli; so was 'M.M.', a nun who partnered Casanova and many others in sizzling affairs.[5] It is possible that they were the same woman. Lady Mary probably never met Casanova personally; but the kind of Venetian life he represented was to impinge heavily on hers.

Meanwhile she thought Venice too expensive except for special occasions like Carnival. But she thoroughly approved its freedom from 'the Embarras of a Court', and the informal dress that went with masks (ubiquitous during the winter season). Since 'No Toilet can fight against Nature', it was good to be able to go the opera without 'the Mortification of shewing a wrinkled face'. If masks were not permitted, she stayed away.[6] She later spent a good deal of time at Venice, and found it best of all outside the Carnival and Ascension seasons, when the theatres and Ridotto (the state-run gambling centre) were closed. She loved the 'little assemblys' of intimates held at such seasons—consisting of seventy or eighty persons! They featured private gambling, 'concerts of Music, sometimes danceing and always a handsome

---

[4] *CL* iii. 114, 125, 170; Aymonino *et al.* 1970: fig. 152.

[5] *CL* iii. 111–12; Casanova 1967: ii. 192–4; iv. 20, 155, 161 and n., 172–3; Childs 1961: 55, 77–8.

[6] *CL* iii. 111–12, 144; Casanova 1967: iv. 139. Some old women, she observed, appeared at formal (unmasked) occasions in *décolletée* and jewels; Walpole censured her old friend the princesse de Craon for this (*Corr.* xx. 213).

Collation . . . Whoever is well acquainted with Venice must own it is the center of Pleasure, not so noisy, and in my opinion more refin'd than Paris.'[7]

Receiving the welcome news that Lord Bute was now Groom of the Stole to the Prince of Wales (with every chance to rise further), Lady Mary issued a 'short Instruction' or two.[8] Bute should remember that 'the real interest of Prince and People cannot be divided'; Lady Bute should remember a Turkish maxim: 'Carress the favorites, avoid the Unfortunate, and trust no body.' Lady Mary did not disclose the republican strain in her thinking: the private jottings which link kings with wars (and matrimony) as 'proofes of mankinds irrationality', or bracket a hereditary king and hereditary coachman, or call a king 'a large puppet'. Instead she promised to 'relinquish the motherly Prerogative I have hitherto indulg'd' of trying Lady Bute's patience with preachments. She now planned to correspond with the fourteen-year-old Lady Jane. She sent off 'play things' to Augusta, the next girl after Anne (in vain, since either storms or privateers intercepted them). Soon afterwards (having asked Wortley's permission) she sent Lady Bute the best of her newly recovered jewels: a handsome pearl necklace and 'a pair of Earrings which are not altogether worthy to accompany it'. This gift, which she thought would be useful for 'Court attendance', produced the warmest of thanks. Lady Mary's first response was a happy one: 'You have been the Passion of my Life. You need thank me for nothing.' Then a shadow fell: 'I desire you would thank your Father for the Jewels; you know I have nothing of my own.'[9]

She wrote to Lady Bute at least once a fortnight. Letters were coming to grief again as this year Europe tottered into the Seven Years' War, dragging the wider world with it. By a seismic shifting of the Old System, Britain allied itself in January 1756 with Prussia instead of Austria. In June it declared war against France; in August Frederick of Prussia invaded Saxony. In November Newcastle, unable to adjust to such changes, resigned. The way was clear for Pitt, with Bute's aid, to assume control. Their power survived a hiccup in 1757, regrouping in June that year by entering into coalition with Newcastle.[10]

Lady Mary deplored Frederick's militarism, yet she thought Britain had been mistaken in expending blood and money to right the wrongs of Maria

[7] *CL* iii. 194, 235, 243.

[8] Bute was appointed in Sept. 1758. Prince George had just come of age (at 18); he and Bute had won their contest with the king, who would have liked to impeach Bute. Rumours of Bute's love-affair with Princess Augusta, dating from 1755, were probably spread on purpose to discredit her: they were widely believed (McKelvey 1973: 35, 264; Bullion 1991: 248–9, 258, 262 n. 15).

[9] *CL* iii. 112–13, 116–17, 127, 130, 133, 200; CB 6.

[10] McKelvey 1973: 48–59. Privately MWM called the coalition 'Arlequin's Coat' (CB 6).

Theresa. She looked for the day when her country would 'see we are an Island' and put its energy into commerce instead of conquest. She took a consistently progressivist view of history, and hoped that, 'When Time has ripen'd Mankind into common Sense, the Name of Conqueror will be an odious Title.' These were not sentiments in fashion on the eve of Britain's great colonial expansion and of Bute's alliance with William Pitt, the man of imperial vision. Meanwhile when preparations for war intercepted Lady Bute's letters, Lady Mary dreaded some family calamity. She 'stiffled my Fear as much as possible, yet it cost me many a Midnight Pang'. She could generalize her own response ('My time of Life is naturally inclin'd to Fear'), but not alter it.

In return for her gifts she hoped for supplies of reading matter. She found the English newspapers and magazines full of publishers' advertisements. In April 1757 she listed fifteen titles which had caught her eye. Most were fiction; most were recent; but it was an eclectic list. She ordered Charlotte Charke's autobiography and two of Francis Noble's reprints of works from the 1720s: Defoe's *Roxana* and Mary Davys's *The Accomplished Rake*. Lady Bute also included the latest, finely produced periodical-essay collection, *The World*. Lady Mary confessed this was entertaining; but she disliked its publisher, Robert Dodsley. Her animus probably stemmed from his being a protégé of Pope (if not from his early career as a footman, notably to her acquaintance Jane Lowther). She probably did not yet know that he had been printing her poems.[11]

She added another title to her wish-list as soon as she heard of it: Horace Walpole's *Catalogue of the Royal and Noble Authors of England*. The first edition, printed at Strawberry Hill in 1758, was small and limited. Walpole was slow to despatch her a copy, and it may never have reached her. She was much exercised in case he had treated Queen Elizabeth with disrespect. If so, 'all the Women should tear him to pieces for abusing the Glory of their Sex'. Lady Mary felt Elizabeth had been 'bespatter'd because she was a woman', though she deserved the highest respect for her learning and her writings, and also for 'having never publish'd any thing'. (Walpole knew, and wrote, that she *had* published.) If Lady Mary did see his book, she would have found it properly respectful of the queen—and of her own great-great-uncle Lord Kingston, of members of her husband's family, and of her friend Hervey, whose pamphlets it praises highly. Walpole was less polite about her early favourite Lansdowne or her friends Wharton and Sarah, Duchess of Marlborough ('fourscore years of arrogance . . . so fantastic an understanding').

[11] *CL* iii. 130, 132, 140, 146; Pope, *Corr.* iii. 454; see p. 518.

There was no entry on herself; she would not expect it, having only a courtesy title. But Walpole's entry on Wharton mentioned her epilogue written for him and now printed in Dodsley's *Collection*. To be in print, and linked with Wharton, was hardly respectable; but it was not damning. Walpole could have done much worse. Her anxiety for Queen Elizabeth may have been fed by deflected anxiety for herself.[12]

Wortley, meanwhile, sent her an unctuous account of the prince's intellectual and social prowess, and of Bute's exceptional favour. He also wrote: 'I do not recollect that any letter sent me from a foreign country besides yours ever miscarried.' He expounded the system of double checks whereby he himself secured the safety of letters going abroad, thus implying, with all his old absence of tact or sensitivity, that she was either inefficient or not to be believed. Lady Mary gamely replied that this letter had 'brought me the most sensible pleasure' by its good news of the family, and that she trusted Lord Bute would properly value Wortley's advice.

As her reason to keep her letters short, she cited Lady Bute's increasing busy-ness; she might as well have cited her own. General Graeme was pleasingly attentive: throwing parties, squiring her to the opera, and losing to her at cards. He introduced her to Major William Cunningham, on his way home from Minorca with his wife and children. Cunningham had voluntarily joined the besieged British garrison at Port Mahon and contributed supplies at his own expense. He was wounded. Lady Mary eagerly took up the cause of getting such heroism rewarded. She also happened on something she thought suitable for Lord Bute to offer Prince George as a gift: a whole set of furniture in Venetian glass for sale at £400—large armchairs, table, candelabra, and a 'prodigious Looking Glass'. With all this activity, she found time to read voraciously; a year after leaving Brescia she sent Lady Bute her most energetic and developed defence of her taste for popular fiction.[13]

Her past returned to her now in the shape of Algarotti. He had retired from Frederick II's service to Venice in 1753, citing ill health, and was by now dividing his time between Bologna, Pisa, and Mirabella, a country villa about 6 kilometres from Padua. He knew Graeme, and had known Casanova. He had sent an exploratory letter to Lady Mary at Gottolengo; but she had never replied, for someone (presumably Palazzi, playing censor) had told her that Algarotti had died of a stroke shortly after writing.

---

[12] *CL* iii. 160, 185, 243; Walpole 1758: i. 23–32; ii. 35–7, 82–6, 113–15, 121–2, 129, 137, 179.

[13] *CL* iii. 113, 115–6, 118–20. She did give Lady Bute a prodigious pierglass, now in the drawing-room at Mount Stuart.

She now found he was alive, and soon he was sending her his recent writings, asking for hers, and inviting her to visit his Mirabella. In autumn 1756 someone at Padua asked the pair of them to 'manger la soup'. A third guest, Contessa Cecilia Zenobio, was rumoured to be Algarotti's latest love interest.[14]

The balance of power had shifted between them. Lady Mary was no longer emotionally nor Algarotti financially grasping. She was a self-confessed old woman, and he a scholar-critic in his early forties, retired from public life. Their minds still struck sparks. She kept up allusion to, perhaps illusion of, love between them. Her letters (his do not survive) are vividly flirtatious. She reminded herself 'to wear G[ol]d Bracelets when I see Al.'[15] She told him that Graeme was piqued at having laid siege for months to a citadel (herself) which Algarotti had once taken by storm in a fortnight. On the other hand she freely mentioned her age. She had turned soft and sentimental, she said, and was recklessly squandering her short remaining time when she enjoyed the pleasures of Carnival.

As before, she sought to charm him by her wit. The earliest of these letters, written at the end of 1756, showed off by imitating Homer (as she put it) in combining different dialects: that is, in her case, by shifting from English into Italian and thence into French. It also flattered him and sniped at his former 'Roial Patron' by exalting the wisdom of retirement and attacking the destructive, even demonic, pleasures of the military hero. She sounded and resounded this anti-war motif, playing it both for strong feeling and for airy paradox. She suggested that killing innocent beasts for sport is more culpable than killing human beings who mostly deserve no better. The butcher-hero thus becomes the hunted animals' avenger, less guilty than meat-eaters like herself.[16] She blended her Enlightenment reformism with impish play.

Though so much the elder, she sounds too quick for Algarotti. After her death he published in his *Opere* a version (perhaps tidied and formalized for print) of a compliment which he had addressed to her. It is a solemn tribute, apt for sending from one ancient university (Bologna) to another (Padua). Its climax echoes and refashions her published praise of him for combining the virtues of youth and age, spring and harvest. It says the Ancients live on

[14] 30 Oct. [1756], Murray MS. In the 1740s Tiepolo revised and repainted at Algarotti's behest a banquet of Cleopatra (to whom MWM had likened herself in writing to Algarotti). Tiepolo's Cleopatra, at first blonde, became a brunette strongly resembling Kneller's early picture of MWM (Haskell 1980: 349, 359–60, plate 61a and b; Haskell 1958: 212–13; Levey 1960: 250–7).

[15] CB 21. Gold, not jet, is the correct reading.

[16] Not a straight plea for vegetarianism, but an oblique one against war (*CL* iii. 117–18, 120–4).

in her mind, while her own writings 'the Moderns already regard as treasure, and much more so will those *Who will call this time ancient*'.

Here was the incense which Querini had tantalizingly offered, but made impossible to accept. Lady Mary replied with another virtuoso display, a mini-essay on the unappeasable human appetite for flattery. (Appetite was a theme of her meat-eating passage too.) She now pictures Algarotti as a master chef of flattery, serving up a substance so mouth-watering, though dubious and addictive, that she bolts it down (to her later regret). She then slides away to depict Voltaire as a self-flatterer, and herself as a non-flatterer: an old woman whose good qualities can be defined only by negatives. Her greatest virtue is clear-sightedness, she says—yet all her virtues may be mere figments of her unquenchable self-love.[17]

These jugglings with paradox also carry serious feeling—a feeling she now defined as 'amitié'. The notion weaves through the letters: friendship alone brings happiness; her friendship is all for Algarotti. This friendship outlived the excitement of rediscovery. Early in 1757 she wrote, 'Nous nous reverrons. Que j'aurois des choses a vous dire!'[18] Next year she paid her verbal libation to Lord Hervey's 'Gentle Shade', and added, 'I am insensible to every thing but the remembrance of those few Friends that have been dear to me.' It seems she continued to see Algarotti when they were both at Padua, though no more letters survive.[19]

⤙❧⤚

Venice was cosmopolitan, Padua academic. Its botanic garden, the earliest extant, no doubt proved a resource for Lady Mary's study of herbs. (Her interest went beyond her small garden: she offered Michiel a potion as 'the first fruits of my Laboratory'.) She became acquainted with the younger Antonio Vallisnieri, professor of natural history and a great collector.[20] She intended 'to reside the greatest part of the Year' in Padua. But she stayed on in Venice after Carnival, and finding her lodgings inconvenient she took a little second house there. It too had a garden, just large enough to walk in. Next came the fun of buying furniture (always with ready money) and 'placeing' it. She assured Lady Bute that she would make it neat and convenient, certainly not magnificent—though she added, 'I sometimes indulge my taste in Baubles.' She took on a lame gondolier whom Michiel dubbed Vulcan. On 18 April 1757 she embarked for Padua with a retinue

[17] Algarotti 1764–5: vii. 319; *CL* iii. 122–3, 141.

[18] 'We shall see each other again. What things I shall have to tell you!' (*CL* iii. 122, 301: translation modified).

[19] *CL* iii. 149–50.   [20] Schiller 1987; *CL* iii. 168, 220, 305.

consisting of Mora, Fribourg, an 'agent', and a maid called Maddalena Giulei. But she was back in Venice in May and June (still busy 'fitting and furnishing'), and again in September, perhaps for most of the winter.[21]

Although she sometimes missed her Brescian solitude, she was building a circle of new friends to augment the old. Not among the resident English-women of her own class (or near it): with them she had little in common. For a poverty-stricken Elizabeth Brown (perhaps a relation of the late consul), she acted as benefactor, and enlisted Chiara Michiel as another. She was vis-ited by a petty ruler, distantly connected with her by marriage: Charlotte Sophia, Countess von Aldenburg, who was looking for a corner of Europe to settle in. Her networking included the Papacy itself: the reforming Pope Benedict XIV sent her 'a most obliging message by his particular Order' just before his death.[22]

She met with 'much Freindship amongst the noble Venetians'—though a later story said she was unmercifully satirical, in letters, about noblewomen who for their part admired her learning and wisdom. These letters were said to contain ambiguous gossip—perhaps about politics, perhaps about love-affairs—and to mention her long-standing 'habit of reading seven hours a day'.[23] She said one of her 'best Freinds at Venice' was Antonio (Alvise V) Mocenigo, the patriarch of a patrician family. He was eighty-four when Lady Mary returned to Venice (she underestimated his age by a couple of years until he set her right): 'in perfect Health and Spirits', his outstanding good looks little changed, still a force to be reckoned with in the Senate. Years before in London, Lady Mary had purchased a Rosalba Carriera miniature of 'his Ador'd Lady', now long dead. It was perhaps this possession which set her so high in his favour; she was 'proud of being admitted into the num-ber of 7 or 8 select Freinds, near his own age, who pass the Evenings with him' in the central portion of the magnificent Palazzo Mocenigo. When, later, hostile gossip put it about that Lady Mary was in financial need after losing 'all my money at play at Avignon', he privately sent for Dr Mora to learn whether this was true, and to press on him £1,500 to be placed anonym-ously on her dressing-table.[24]

---

[21] Mari Anna must have been at Padua, unless her name was much mangled. The agent, Giuseppe Frannzese (or perhaps a Frenchman named Joseph), may or may not be the Padua concierge mentioned later (*CL* iii. 125 and n. 1, 127, 148–9, 168, 199, 267; Michiel, 19 Mar. 1762, H MS 77. 198–9).

[22] Child and Co, ledgers, 1758; *CL* iii. 129, 152–3, 162, 225. The countess's deceased husband had been half-brother to MWM's stepmother.

[23] *Quarterly Review*, 1820: 23. 416–17. *If* this is true, the letters (not extant but probably from this period) were perhaps to Graeme.

[24] Palazzo Mocenigo comprises a complex of four blocks; an 18th-century double palace inserted between two older ones. It is often said that MWM (like Byron later) lived there; but this is highly unlikely. Of its owner's intended generosity she commented: 'I don't beleive I could borrow that Sumn without good

Someone, perhaps Algarotti, introduced her to Caterina (Sagredo) Barbarigo: a great traveller, remarkable among the Venetian ladies for her intellectual interests as well as her beauty. (She patronized the inoculator Dominiceti.) Lady Mary wished she could invite her to Padua, to see her *not* surrounded by company. She attended the Barbarigos' Venetian gatherings, which amounted to a quasi-academy like that of Scipione Maffei. She wove an elaborate, mock-sentimental anecdote for Algarotti of how she had disgraced herself during a concert there. A Barbarigo daughter was singing angelically, singing to stir the soul. Her mother was ecstatic; the huge audience was transported. The man sitting by Lady Mary whispered that he had heard Lady Bute sing in London—and Lady Mary dissolved in floods of tears, and had to leave the room so as not to disrupt the concert by her sobbing.

She was not of a generation to feel that weeping in public did her any credit. Now, as when she cried over Richardson, she treated her own tears unsympathetically: 'une vieille tendre, quel Monstre!'[25] She said she would never forgive her concert neighbour's damnable politeness. He, however, was Michele Sagramoso, ambassador to Venice from the Order of the Knights of Malta, a man of learning, another traveller, who became her real friend. (He had visited England in 1750, with an introduction from Maffei to learned men like Mead; he too was a patron of Dominiceti.)[26] Lady Mary was drawn to cosmopolitans: people like an Austrian nobleman, Leopold von Talmann (who as ambassador to Turkey had been a channel between Wortley and the emperor), and the present imperial ambassador to Venice, Philipp Josef, Count von Rosenberg-Orsini. He was her own age, a member of the Casanova-John Murray circle; it was he who had recently been observed by a spy in converse with Chiara Michiel. Lady Mary had met him years before in Vienna. She now enlisted his help in preparing the case she meant to bring against Palazzi.[27]

She relied on General Graeme as a kind of representative of her absent family. Soon after her arrival she told him she had made her will, and asked

Security amongst my great Relations' (*CL* 164, 166–7, 174–5; Lauritzen and Zielcke 1978: 190–4). A Carriera miniature inscribed 'Lady Wortley Montague' (Foskett 1963: 93 and pl. 70) might be this one of Lucrezia Mocenigo.

[25] 'An old woman with feelings, what a Monster!' (Dominiceti [1776]: 44, 117–18; *CL* iii. 122–4, 302—translation modified—148).

[26] Marie Anne du Boccage thought well of him, and said he proposed himself to her as *cicisbeo* (1762: iii. 162; Maffei 1955: ii. 1272–3; Dominiceti [1776]: 37).

[27] Bernis noted his high birth, wit, and spirit of intrigue; he also noted how Venice's spy system kept it crime-free. Rosenberg was on bad terms with Murray soon after MWM arrived (BL Add. MS 61547. 139; de Bernis 1878: i. 169, 181; Murray to Pitt, 29 June 1757, SP 99/67/50; Casanova 1967: iv. 137). Graeme implied that the case was brought, but no trace has been found.

him to be an executor.[28] But Graeme's duties took him on a tour of the Venetian dominions for more than a year from the spring of 1757.

Now she was back in an international setting, however, links with home were easier to build and maintain. In summer 1757 (while Frederick of Prussia suffered dreadful military reverses) she wrote to establish contact with Wilhelmina Tichborne, whose inoculation she had supervised in 1722, and whose Molesworth aunts and uncles were many of them her friends. In her letter Lady Mary reminisced about her old friendship with the Duchess of Montagu, calling those days the happiest of her life. Wilhelmina Tichborne was not merely a link to the past, but an acquisition in the present. Lewis Dutens found her correspondence 'one of the principal comforts of my life' and called her 'the most finished model I have ever known of true, enlightened, cordial, and sincere friendship'. He thought 'no English lady ever wrote better in the epistolary style than she did. Her letters were, like her conversation; natural, lively, gay; full of reason, wit, and interest.' Lady Mary found her an ideal audience: 'I write to her with more pleasure than I ever dressd for a [royal] Birth day.'

Her first reply to Lady Mary was somewhat dominated by compliment, but she had some trenchant things to say about politics and the new fashion for political caricature. Pitt's '*Compound*' or coalition government put her in mind of a fable of a mastiff, monkey, parrot, cat, and kittens all packed up together. When the British Museum opened its doors in 1759 Lady Mary told Tichborne 'I wish to see nothing in L[ondon] but her selfe and the musaeum.' To this unmarried woman of her daughter's age she felt free to philosophize ('The World the same in all Climates and generations . . . Knowledge out of reach'), but also to indulge in 'Railery' or flights of fancy. Of these letters only the summaries survive.[29]

At the Ascension the summer travellers began, with Marie Anne Fiquet du Boccage. She was a woman of letters in a style that highlighted the different status of women in England and in Continental Europe. She was collecting memberships of academies (she achieved Lyons, Bologna, Padua, and Rome); she had had a tragedy staged in Paris; in poetry she translated Alexander Pope and praised Prince Eugene and Pope Benedict XIV. She had corresponded with Algarotti since 1749. She boasted that Lady Mary welcomed her warmly, called her 'Muse', and wished she were still young

[28] Graeme to Bute, Aug.–Sept 1758 (Bute MSS).
[29] Tichborne to MWM, 25 July 1757, H MS 77. 258–9; *CL* iii. 204, 208, 210, 212, 246. Brought up with Lady Hertford's daughter (later Duchess of Northumberland), Tichborne wrote charmingly to her grandmother at 8. The duke and duchess, like Bute and Mackenzie, patronized Dutens (HMC 1913: viii. 274, 397; Dutens 1806: iii. 267–8).

enough to travel on with her to Naples. They met several times, and talked of Constantinople, inoculation, and Lady Mary's present pastimes. Du Boccage expected to find her library full of Latin authors, and was intrigued to hear her say she read nothing now but romances, of which she offered a brief critical defence. Lady Mary showed off her portraits of Pope Benedict and Lord Bolingbroke (tactfully softening her opinion of the latter). Du Boccage went on to Bologna, where Algarotti showed her, and she much admired, Lady Mary's fine ode on death (probably this was 'With toilsome steps'). All that remains of the correspondence between these two writing women, which lasted for more than a year, is a one-word summary of a letter Lady Mary sent in August 1758: 'War.'[30]

Most of the travellers she saw were British. Colonel William Hamilton, a younger colleague of Graeme, carried to her family in London a gratifying account of her health and looks. The budding Scottish architect Robert Adam impressed her 'in one short visit' as 'a Man of Genius'; she recommended him to Lady Bute.[31] Francis Hutcheson or Hutchinson (later Sir Francis) made notes about her like a minor Spence or du Boccage.[32] He was prepared for something special by Michiel, who showed him all her letters from Lady Mary, carefully preserved and bound up into a volume. Lady Mary he found to be 'a little woman, fair complexion and well enough looking for her age'. But she made fun of her own looks. She was 'all cover'd up in [a] great Beaver Cloak' against the intense cold (there was heavy snow in Venice in 1757–8), and 'ask'd him did she not look like one of the old women that sold roasted Chesnuts at Whitehall and the Bridges in London'.

Lady Mary expressed to Hutchinson her satisfaction that her former acquaintance Lady Walpole (now Lady Orford) had outwitted the second husband who was after her money. She made a ribald joke of her grudge against Pope, Swift, and Bolingbroke. She told Hutchinson they were rascals, and 'shew'd him her Commode, with false back of books': their works. This arrangement, she said, gave her 'the satisfaction of shitting on them every day'. It sounds as if the books were pictured actually on the toilet bowl, not just on the frame or surround. One can imagine her cackling over

[30] *CL* iii. 166. Du Boccage owed her Padua Academy membership to Algarotti (1762: i. *passim*; ii, p. v; iii. 177–8; 1770: i. 162–4, 174; CB 15; Algarotti MSS, Treviso, 1258). MWM was probably writing of the British defeat at Ticonderoga and victories at Louisbourg and Fort Duquesne (now Pittsburg).

[31] It was apropos Hamilton's report that she said she had given up mirrors (*CL* iii. 135, 142–3). Hamilton was probably sending Bute intelligence from Venice (BL Add. MS 36796. 48). It was not MWM who persuaded Bute to patronize Adam; he took some years to perceive the genius of the man who later built for him Luton Park or Luton Hoo (Fleming 1962: 235, 254).

[32] Hutchinson had been in Venice in late 1756; he was back on 11 May 1757 (Inquisitori di Stati, Forestieri, Archivio di Stato, Venice).

this sudden self-association with her fictional whore, Betty, in 'The Reasons that Induced Dr Swift'.[33]

She was unimpressed by the writers Fulke and Frances Greville, whom she met in May 1757. They are known to literary history as, respectively, the patron of Charles Burney and the godmother of his daughter Frances; Frances Greville is now becoming known again for her writings. But Lady Mary suspected her of coquetry if not adultery, and says nothing of her poetry. On Fulke's *Maxims, Characters, and Reflections*, 1756, Lady Mary wrote a satirical mock-encomium: 'Past all describing, your descriptions are.' In Hutchinson's presence she complimented Fulke Greville to his face, only to make fun of him the 'moment he left the room'. (His admiration of Swift probably told against him.) He took the flattery as sincere, visited her every day, and begged her to correspond with him; she declined on grounds of poor eyesight.[34]

Then there were the travellers pursuing education. The lapse of years had done nothing to endear these young men in the mass, who herded together and had not the 'secret of introduceing themselves' into good Italian society. Individuals, however, could be likable. Lord Rosebery came to breakfast at Padua and Lady Mary fed him 'Bread and Butter of my own Manufacture, which is the admiration of all the English'. A Mr Oliver won her approval when he had 'high words' about politics with the British Resident, John Murray.[35] Andrew Archer caused a panic by wounding himself accidentally with a blunderbuss. His tutor was Lady Mary's old friend Anderson, who coped with the accident with admirable efficiency and real concern. She was glad to see Anderson, glad to employ him once more as a courier, and glad to write a letter of reference for him to her old friend Lord Lincoln. She was only sorry to contrast him with Nathan Hickman, tutor to her nephew Kingston—a learned man, but a 'Wretch' in her eyes because his pupil had turned out so badly. 'But this is a melancholy Thought, and as such ought to be suppress'd.'[36]

Many things in Venice conspired to turn her thoughts to the education of

[33] MS in Osborn Collection; Halsband 1979: 241–6; Murray to Pitt, 25 Jan. 1758, SP 99/67/97; *E&P* 276. MWM did not invent this gesture: Henry Sacheverell had appeared on chamber-pots (*Grub Street Journal*, no. 59, 18 Feb. 1731).

[34] *CL* iii. 136–7, 158; *E&P* 307–8; Hutchinson, Osborn MS. Frances's 'Ode to [or Prayer for] Indifference', probably written in 1756, was immensely popular in MS. See forthcoming life of her by Betty Rizzo.

[35] The only Englishmen she knew who made foreign friends were Hervey's eldest son and James Stuart Mackenzie. Oliver may have been Richard Oliver, b. in Antigua, raised in a counting-house, later a radical associated with John Wilkes. His tutor, Mr Law, carried a letter to Lady Bute (*CL* iii. 127, 136, 150–1, 159).

[36] Anderson still corresponded with Gibson, who still worked for EWM (*CL* iii. 128–31). Andrew Archer was in Venice 9 May–8 June 1757 (Inquisitori gli Forestieri, Archivio di Stato, Venice, where Anderson is J. Andrea).

boys. She met two Englishmen fresh from Russia, who reported the decline, both mental and physical, of the British ambassador there, her old acquaintance Sir Charles Hanbury Williams. Thinking of him as servile, 'rotten and ridiculous' (and mindful, no doubt, of the wife whom he had infected with syphilis), she exclaimed, 'How happy might that Man have been if there had been added to his natural and acquir'd Endowments a dash of Morality!' And, although she had said she never worried about boys, she did so now about Lady Bute's 'growing Sons'. She hoped money would never tempt them 'to marry Women they cannot love, or comply with Measures they do not approve'. As she sang the praises of living frugally, without the corruptions of 'silly Splendor', she thought, no doubt, of her son; she also thought of Bute's moral tutoring of the son of Prince Frederick.[37]

In Graeme's absence she became thoroughly disenchanted with Murray, the Resident. She described him as an ex-smuggler, 'always surrounded with Pimps'. The very thought of him impelled her to a strong paragraph about the low calibre of British representatives abroad these days, compared with those of the Elizabethan age. British politics gave her an underlying cause to differ from Murray: though Pitt's imperial vision was so alien to her, she supported his coalition ministry, which was in part the achievement of Bute.

Chiefly she disliked Murray's lifestyle. She visited him regularly at first, probably on account of his wife (called Lady Wentworth from a former marriage): she was a cousin of Lord Holdernesse—whom Wortley had wanted as a son-in-law, and who was now Murray's patron. Murray was an ageing rake. When Lady Mary called him the 'Sir J. Falstaffe of Venice', she did not speak as an admirer of Falstaff. Murray had done much sharing and exchanging of women with Casanova. He liked to be watched in the act of copulation. Casanova numbered among the most memorable sights of his life that of Murray making love to his mistress 'Ancilla' fifteen minutes before she died of syphilis, when her nose and half her face were eaten away. After her, Murray could always be counted on to have 'the prettiest girls in Venice'. These men were consumers of women in just the style that Lady Mary had hated in Bolingbroke.[38]

Some of Murray's friends were equally suspect to her. He conspicuously admired a Greek woman named Lady Wynne, allegedly an ex-prostitute, widow of a baronet of ancient Welsh lineage. Her daughters were wards of Holdernesse, and shared with their mother in Murray's gallantry. Lady

---

[37] *CL* iii. 131–2; *E&P* 307–8. Hanbury Williams's wife was a niece of Astell's friend Lady Catherine Jones.

[38] *CL* iii. 127–8, 244; Casanova 1967: iv. 136–7, 155–6, 174–5.

Mary said most women of rank shunned Lady Wynne's weekly assembly, where 'all the young fellows in the Town, Strangers and Natives', cast a non-marital eye on her daughters. One daughter figured (said Lady Mary) in Murray's set of miniatures of '*Ladies*' whom he had enjoyed, all painted in the same state of tousled undress. (Lady Mary used a phrase from Congreve to equate Lady Wynne's house with a brothel.) More serious still was Murray's attention to the sexual initiation of grand tourists: he took pains, said Lady Mary, to debauch them. A mentor of Casanova (without Casanova's sensibility) was not likely to appeal to her.[39]

Her dislike extended too to Murray's friend Joseph Smith, the British consul, who moved closer to Murray after his wife died in 1756.[40] He was a bon viveur, scholar, collector, and the greatest art patron of his day. He had given support to Rosalba Carriera and the young Canaletto; he had worked with Algarotti. But he was obsequious, cynical, a man whom 'no one really liked'.[41] Soon Lady Mary found herself persistently tormented by Murray and Smith for her pretensions as a writer; this feud seriously embittered her years in Venice.

Now she was an 'old woman', she began to feel the need for some male person in authority to help her with the business aspects of life as an alien in Venice. Among such persons, Graeme developed a protective (and patronizing) attitude towards her. Murray and Smith found her an irritating anomaly. They were no doubt irked by her maxims about public spirit and the virtues of sobriety; they needled her in return with sexist and ageist jokes—learned-lady jokes—and they encouraged their whole circle to do the same.

~ஜ~

On 12 August 1757 Lady Bute gave birth to another daughter, nearly twenty years after her first. She was near forty. Lord Bute made the announcement in terms implying his high opinion of Lady Mary, and she replied with 'tender esteem'. To Lady Bute she wrote, 'may she be as meritorious in your Eyes as you are in mine. I can wish nothing better to you both.' Once again she was godmother. She approved the choice of name (Louisa) because it was not susceptible of any low-life short form ('a Bess, a Peg, or a Suky').

---

[39] *CL* iii. 157–8, 179–80, 226; *SL* 451 and n. 9; Brunelli 1929: 71, 200, 227; Casanova 1967: iv. 156. Anna (Gazzini) Wynne had changed her Orthodox religion for Catholicism.

[40] MWM probably meant Smith by her dismissive 'Brokers' (*CL* iii. 127). His biographer says he was friendly with Mackenzie and not close to Murray (Vivian 1971: 49, 51); but for MWM Smith and Murray were a pair.

[41] Haskell 1980: 299–302; Vivian 1971: 51–2. Du Boccage said he imported from London everything in his house, down to the bolts on the doors. Walpole judged him ludicrously ignorant of the contents of the books he collected (du Boccage 1762: iii. 161; Walpole, *Corr.* xviii. 465).

She would have rejoiced yet more had she been able to foreknow two things: that this baby would be Lady Bute's last, and that she would be the one she herself had promised to favour, the one who loved books.

As the youngest, Lady Louisa Stuart grew up much in her mother's company. She inherited an ample portion of her grandmother's wit (so said Frances Burney), and that love of reading which was the only characteristic Lady Mary wished to hand on. But this inheritance was not smiled on. As a child, Lady Louisa 'heartily hated' the name of her grandmother, for she understood it to be her fault that whatever she wanted to learn was forbidden, for fear she should turn out a learned lady. But in her 'secret heart' she felt like a king's natural daughter in a story, whose belief in her own royalty grew stronger the oftener she heard it denied.[42]

Lady Mary wrote, 'May all your Young Ones grow up an Honor to you.' She thought Lady Bute would 'scarce think it possible those I have never seen should so much employ my thoughts'. Somebody told her that the eldest boy, John, Lord Mountstuart, now thirteen, was 'too handsome' (like her own son at the same age); this fault, she said, would 'certainly mend every day. I should be glad to hear your Daughters accus'd of the same Deffect.' In November 1757 she received a letter from Wortley describing in great detail an illness which had struck him in January and kept him at Bath and Tunbridge Wells all year. It had begun with 'a Purge and a Vomit improperly (I believe) given me', had made him 'for two days and two nights' unable to take an atom of solids or liquids, even Tokay wine; he had never told Lady Bute how bad he had been.[43]

This activated a fear underlying Lady Mary's present contentment: the fear of Wortley's death. In England Lord Bute was assumed to be his heir; but Lady Mary, who knew her husband's capacity for changing his mind, must still have feared he might settle on Edward after all. He was head of the family; he still held the reins. No one could tell what would happen when he died.

She had asked Lady Bute to have her letters enclosed in the diplomatic bag sent regularly to the Resident. Nevertheless over the winter of 1757–8 there was almost total silence. Hearing nothing between early October and early April, she could not entirely resist ascribing blame. She urged Lady

---

[42] *CL* iii. 133–4, 136; Burney 1905: iii. 123; [Stuart] 1898: ii. 94; 1903: 21–2. MWM had a proxy at the christening: Lady Mary Coke, whose youthful forwardness had pleased her (Stuart 1901: 260; *CL* iii. 144, 161).

[43] *CL* iii. 138, 155; 15 Oct. 1757, H MS 74. 141–2. EWM subscribed this year to *Letters of Henry and Frances*, by Elizabeth and Richard Griffith. Did he keep up with modern fiction, or did he do it for his daughter or his wife?

Bute (not for the first time) to use her daughters as secretaries. Once she said, 'I wish you would write to me with that openess of Heart I do to you.' Murray was now treating her with 'low malice', singling her out for ridicule. He saw her as a 'Freind' of Pitt. She was surprised when Wortley wrote that party rancour in England had eased. Hostility against her as a Pittite sounds perverse, when she wrote regularly against the war and against dreams of empire; her position was far closer to that of her contemporary Newcastle, Pitt's incongruous ally. The war was going badly; until the tide turned in 1758, a supposed Pittite was a sitting target.

Lady Mary thought Murray also envied and resented her Venetian friendships, and suspected her of setting the nobility against him. He had stopped visiting her, and did not send her the English newspapers as other diplomats had done, even when she humbled herself to ask for them. He told her that in the event of her death he would immediately 'secure' her effects; this did nothing to reassure her that they would come 'intire' to Lady Bute's hands. She reported that she dealt with him by laughing—wryly, no doubt, as she had laughed at Palazzi. But by spring 1758, feeling herself treated like an actual member of the Opposition, she was bothered enough to say that if she had not 'taken leases of my Houses, been at much pains and expence in furnishing them' and been too old for travelling, she would have moved on.[44]

Joseph Smith the consul, a recent widower aged upwards of eighty, had in 1757 abandoned an ardent courtship of Giustiniana, the eldest Wynne girl, and married Murray's sister (a match which Lady Mary derided). His ties with Murray thus strengthened, he too sniped at Lady Mary, making such a palaver about expecting her box of books from England that she requested Lady Bute to find a different channel next time. She hoped that Pitt might bring pressure to bear on this 'illustrious Groupe'. When she thought of reading in spring 1758, she thought of its power to 'restore quiet to the most trouble'd Mind'.[45]

She was then lingering in Venice—through weddings and balls and the Feast of the Ascension—waiting for Graeme and Hamilton to return from their tours of duty. She no longer much minded if bad weather spoiled the doge's wedding with the sea; she did mind when Murray headed off the

[44] *CL* iii. 135, 139–40, 141, 142, 145. Murray boasted on 12 May 1758 of the civilities shown him 'by the Nobles of the first Consequence in this Republic' (to Pitt, SP 99/67/127). Handwriting experts find MWM at this date independent and introverted, crystal clear of mind and still 'a force to be reckoned with'; but aloof, joyless, lonely, and (contrary to her own invariable self-estimate) untender (Graphology Business, 21 Apr., 3 May 1995).
[45] Wynne 1785: i. 57 ff.; *CL* iii. 144, 146–7, 156–7. Wynne says her family at this time 'exhibited a brilliant group' (i. 60). It seems both Smith's marriages served mercenary ends: the first his own, the second those of Murray (Pottle 1984: 229).

seasonal grand tourists from paying their respects to her as of yore. Francis Otway (tutor, ex-officer, and brother-in-law to one of her Feilding cousins) visited her to talk over old times; but he then left Venice hastily—in order, Lady Mary was certain, to forestall his pupil's corruption by Murray. She held serious discussions about marriage with Christopher Des Bouverie, a young man with earnest notions of right and wrong and 'a peculiar sweetness of temper'. He had been summoned home, and suspected his father must have a bride in mind for him; Lady Mary's thoughts turned as usual to her eldest granddaughter. But (owing to Murray, she said) she could find no homebound traveller to carry a present which she had ready for Lady Bute.

Graeme appeared in May, bringing her a letter from Algarotti. He then withdrew to Valdagno near Vicenza, in order to write up his report to the Venetian Senate; he told Lord Bute he found this much the hardest part of his job.[46]

[46] *CL* iii. 144, 151, 154–5, 160, 186–7; Bute MSS (*CL* iii. 144 n. 1).

30

May 1758–December 1759

❧

Friends and Foes: 'I thank God Witches are out of Fashion'[1]

THE most exciting arrivals in spring 1758 were unexpected: Sir James Steuart and his wife. This, though spelled differently, was the Butes' surname: it made Lady Mary 'fly' to call on them. She addressed her call, as social protocol prescribed, to Lady Frances Steuart. It was friendship at first sight. In Sir James, Lady Mary found a man of learning and wide European culture, who was writing an important study in political economy. He was '[a]mbitious, charming, subtle, convivial'. Perhaps more importantly, he loved 'the voices of song'; he was 'blessed with eloquence' and with 'a constant flow of cheerfulness and good humour', like Richard Steele and Henry Fielding. Lady Frances was 'more Aimable than the fairest of her Sex'. They for their part were dazzled. Lady Frances later recalled how Lady Mary 'flew to them with eagerness, and, quitting all other company, made it her sole business to administer to their consolation and entertainment'. Her friendship 'partook of all the ardour of her disposition'. Lady Frances thought it a sign of 'superior minds' like her husband's and Lady Mary's to form such a close bond so quickly. The Steuarts were poor, and travelling without servants (their maid had been 'seduced'—probably, that is, by higher-paying employers). No problem: Lady Mary found them a man with good testimonials to work as 'cook, valet de chambre, purveyor and steward'. Sir James was an invalid. No problem: Lady Mary 'entirely changed her hours of living', to fit in with his routine.

There *was* a problem, however. The Steuarts were Jacobites. Sir James had joined Bonnie Prince Charlie under mysterious cloak-and-dagger circumstances after the '45 invasion, travelled to France as his agent, and reputedly ghost-written manifestoes for him. He was now, like Lord Mar

---

[1] *CL* iii. 187–8.

before him, an exile, excluded by name from the 1747 Act of Indemnity. The couple were based at Tübingen in Germany; they had left it temporarily for the sake of Sir James's health.[2]

Lady Mary the anti-Jacobite did not care: it was true that for her some things mattered more than politics. But Murray and Smith found another stick to beat her with: she was 'in the Interest of Popery and Slavery'. The Murray cabal raked up many old stories about her, and added one about her exploiting her daughter's Armenian nurse (probably contributed by the Greek Lady Wynne). Lady Mary began to identify herself with righteous men who had been 'defam'd and vilify'd' (like her mentor Bishop Burnet) and with old women persecuted as witches. She was afraid these slanders might hurt the Butes or offend her husband. It was especially galling to her after enduring social persecution from Jacobites at Avignon (and, she might have added, upholding Protestantism far and wide) to meet such accusations now, 'when I hop'd all our Odious Divisions were forgotten'. She feared Lady Bute (and Wortley) would assume she must have done *something* to incur these attacks: ''Tis realy incredible they should be carry'd to such a height without the least provocation.' She assured her that she had always treated Murray and his family with 'the utmost Civillity'. She begged her not to 'tell your Father these foolish squabbles; it is the only thing I would keep from his knowledge.'[3]

Nevertheless, the acquisition of new intimates was a blessing. Lady Mary had the Steuarts to stay in her house in Venice. Then they moved on to Padua. (She remained to await Graeme, meaning to confide her troubles to him, but then did not do so.) Sir James probably needed the library at Padua University; he left Lady Mary a copy of his latest book to read. The friends seem to have debated as to whether the Steuarts should try the inn at Padua (which Lady Mary did not recommend) or move into her house there in her absence. They delighted her by doing the latter; her concierge wrote (in an impenetrable handwriting which Mora had to read aloud) that they had 'found the Palazzo very clean'. Before the end of May she joined them in Padua. They stayed till August and shared her life; her letters to them after they left are full of domestic intimacy and household gossip.[4]

    [2] Raynor and Skinner 1994: 756, 765; *CL* iii. 145, 148; MWM 1818: preface; Skinner 1993: 1. They had been brought together by Lady Frances's brother Lord Elcho, the only man rash enough to urge Charles after Culloden to head not for France but for 'the mountains of Lochaber and Badenoch' (Lenman 1980: 260; 'Papers of John Murray of Broughton' in Blaikie 1916: 43, 423–9). They reached Venice on 2 May 1758 (Murray to Pitt, 12 May, SP 99/67).
    [3] *CL* iii. 146, 150, 151, 157–8, 160. Murray flatly refused to receive Steuart, though he accepted that he was in Venice purely for his health (to Pitt, SP 99/67).
    [4] *CL* iii. 148–9, 150, 151, 168–9, 175; Graeme to Bute, 30 Aug. 1758 (Bute MSS). Steuart's book was *Apologie du sentiment de monsieur le chevalier Newton sur l'ancienne chronologie des Grecs*, 1757.

These friends made her summer at Padua (1758) a happy one. She enjoyed their 'pleasing and instructive' conversation and their mutual devotion. She 'almost' envied their domestic happiness, saying there were 'not many such couples'; they reminded her of her widowed friend Mocenigo. She introduced Sir James to Algarotti and Vallisnieri; but on the whole she avoided other company, and savoured 'how much happiness may be found with two amiable friends at a *leger repas*'. Besides her usual reading, writing, riding, and walking, she may have explored the locality with Sir James's analytic eye. He loved to draw information from every possible source: 'the arrangement of the kitchen gardens round Padua' later figured in his major work.[5]

Her written works, she told the Steuarts, were 'consecrated to the fire for fear of being put to more ignoble uses'. This summer she began keeping summaries of most of the letters she sent abroad.[6] Those to Michiel conveyed sympathy (Michiel was contending with illness: first her mother's, then her own) and thanks: Michiel took her part in a dispute about the rights and wrongs of her dealings with Palazzi. More cheerfully, Lady Mary passed on the news that James Stuart Mackenzie had been appointed British Envoy in Turin. This, if not exactly nearby, was close enough for her to build castles in the air about a reunion. She also hoped to make Mackenzie a conveyance for parcels.[7]

In July Padua erupted in 'illuminations, Fire works, and Assemblys', to celebrate the elevation of its bishop, Carlo Rezzonico, to the chair of St Peter as Pope Clement XIII. Lady Mary assured Lady Bute that she 'had no share in them, going to Bed at the Hour they begun'. The rejoicings in Venice lasted even longer. They included a regatta (which Lady Mary was keen to see, remembering the splendour of the 1740 one), and more fireworks at the home of the Rezzonico family, whose older generation was well known to her.[8]

Though she professed to be glad the grand tourists were avoiding her, 'Boys and Governors being commonly (not always) the worst company in the World', Lady Mary *was* visited in Padua. When young Sir Wyndham Knatchbull-Wyndham sent in his name, she read it as his father's. It was a blow to learn that his father and mother (née Katy Harris of Salisbury) were both dead; she received the son 'with Tears in my Eyes'. Her fondness for his parents brought her instantly close to Sir Wyndham. He was bound for

[5] *CL* iii. 164, 221, 268; Skinner 1993: 7–8.
[6] *CL* iii. 170; CB 15 ff. Murray noted that Aug. how irregular the post was getting (SP 99/67/141).
[7] Lady Bute assured MWM how much she would like Mackenzie's wife, who was going with him. The war caused anxiety about choice of route; in the end they went through France, leaving in Oct. 1758 and relying on diplomatic immunity (*CL* iii. 152–3, 155–6, 160–1, 162, 177; Dutens 1806: i. 166).
[8] *CL* iii. 161, 181; Murray in SP 99/67/138.

Rome, but she hoped he might return a year later and carry her gift to Lady Bute. Meanwhile she feared his falling victim to Murray's 'alurements', though she was much taken with his tutor, Louis Devismes, a future diplomat. She corresponded with Devismes after he left, deploying shock, paradox, and contrast in her most virtuoso style. She protested at the contempt meted out to women: especially learned women like Queen Elizabeth and Anne Dacier; especially old women, whose wisdom is 'as much laugh'd at as the wisdom of Solomon'. She deprecated her own education: 'was aplauded when I should have been whipp'd'. She quoted from her youthful reading in *Poems on Affairs of State*, and asked for a copy of the new literary sensation, *Tristram Shandy*. She also wrote, 'me Drunk'. This may be just another way of telling him what she told herself: 'I am a Rake in reading.' But she would not have said quite this to Lady Bute.[9]

Antonio Mocenigo, too, made a formal visit in order to present 'the Elected Husband of his Brother's great Grand Daughter'. Lady Mary rejoiced at the cordial relations between the old man and the youth, but less at their invitation to the wedding. This would necessitate lavish expenditure by guests as well as host, and she was 'unwilling to throw away money on fine cloaths, which are as improper for me as an embrodier'd Pall for a Coffin'. Though the wedding might not be for two more months, Mocenigo tried to persuade Lady Mary to return to Venice with them, and she was hard put to it to excuse herself.[10]

That same month, August, Colonel Hamilton and General Graeme came up the river to Padua. (Graeme had promised to come in June, and Lady Mary had hoped he would stay some time at her house, but pressure of business prevented this.) He now came to show her a letter from Bute which spoke of her with gratifying respect and admiration. Hamilton came bringing a letter from Lady Bute, augmented by his own account of her 'little Colony'. Lady Mary shed tears of joy (and called herself an 'old Fool' for doing so) to think of her daughter's blessings: her eminent, admirable, and loving husband and her 'numerous beautifull posterity'. But her joy was 'mix'd with Sorrow that I cannot pertake the blessing of seeing them round you'. Hamilton said that Anne (not quite twelve) was 'the Beauty of the Family'; henceforth when drinking in Lady Mary's presence he always toasted 'Lady Anne Stuart'.[11]

---

[9] *CL* iii. 158–9, 243–4; CB 9. She quoted 'Queen Bess never thought it' from an anti-Whig ballad in her *POAS* (1703–7: i. 220). Murray told Pitt he would show all possible civility to Knatchbull-Wyndham, who had been in Venice before, leaving in Sept. 1756 (SP 99/67/136; Inquisitori di Stati, Forestieri, Archivio di Stato). Smith offered *Tristram* to Algarotti in Mar. 1761 (Vivian 1971: 53).

[10] *CL* iii. 166–7.   [11] *CL* iii. 163, 173, 175, 180.

These visitors soon moved on to Vicenza; again Lady Mary had found no opportunity to confide in Graeme about Murray and Smith. No company could make up for the loss of Sir James and Lady Frances, after whose departure nature seemed to sympathize, with 'storms, tempests, pestilential blasts', the Brenta bursting its banks, and Padua cut off. She was, in fact, never to see them again, though she remained their fast friend. Now she waited in vain for a letter: they having been her guests, it was up to them to write first. At last, having ascertained from a friend that they were safely back in Tübingen and *had* written, though the letter must have been stopped, she took 'the liberty to put you in mind of one that can never forget you and the chearful hours we have passed together'. She told them she had every hope of procuring a pardon for Sir James (through Lady Bute). She told them how she and her Swiss servants (probably Mari Anna and Fribourg) were keeping themselves going in the now suffocating heat 'by hearty eating and drinking', while Mora was ill in bed and 'the poor Italians are languishing on their salads and limonade'. She indulged in 'tender' memories of drinking punch, which was as insipid as river-water without the Steuarts to share it. She hinted at her impatience with social rules and forms, and her self-identification as a poet, 'a sister of the quill', haunted 'by the Daemon of Poesie'.

When she did receive a letter, it reassured her of their affection, and brought messages too from their only child, James the younger. At about fourteen, he was already a student at Tübingen University. Lady Mary called him 'the beautiful young plant from which you may so reasonably expect honour and felicity'; and, perhaps thinking of Hamilton and her granddaughter Anne, she proposed that he 'shall be my toast from this forward, and (provided he never sees me as long as he lives) I may be his'. Next year she defended him when his parents thought he ought to be studying harder. The news that Lady Frances was low-spirited—that is, depressed—in exile elicited quick response. (Again there was the other Lady Frances, her sister, to remember.) With her sympathy she mingled opinions and medical tips. She confessed her delight that the medical authority Sydenham had demonstrated men's 'wise honourable spleen' to be no different from women's 'vapours'. It seems that her spirits soared in writing to the Steuarts, especially Sir James. She found him more receptive to 'feminist' ideas than most of the men she had known. She admitted to being happy, but tried hard not to sound *too* happy.[12]

---

[12] 4, 5 Sept. [1758], *CL* iii. 168–73, 183, 208. MWM addressed the first letter to Lady Frances, but summarized it as to Sir James.

She wrote with renewed fervour at this time to Lady Bute, telling her that age intensified her early 'tenderness', or acuteness of feeling. She felt it was a weakness 'to indulge any attachment at a Period of Life when we are sure to part with Life it selfe at a very short warning'; but indulge it she did. To her husband she wrote, not without ulterior motive, of 'the great and good Character I hear from every body of Lord Bute. It is a Satisfaction I never hop'd, to have a Son that does Honor to his Family.' She trusted that, like her, Wortley would 'rather be related to him than to any silly Duke in Christendom', and would agree that money 'in the hands of a Fool is as useless as if presented to a Monkey and will as surely be scatter'd in the Street'. If her nephew Kingston was a silly duke, her son was an outright fool. She may have looked back, too, at the rich suitors whom Wortley had favoured for their daughter, all of them now so far outshone by the man young Mary had chosen for herself. But she still could not be sure the eighty-year-old Wortley would not be swayed by old inheritance customs to reinstate Edward as his heir. Her son was now a man-about-town with a long history of shady dealing and several illegitimate children, still running up debts on the strength of expectations from his father's death; her daughter, 'generally esteem'd, and . . . commended', had eleven young ones to settle in life. Her warmth of feeling about Lady Bute and her family was tinged with anxiety.[13]

The exchange of gifts was one way to express her feelings. She wished she could find a way to send over all her jewels and her dressing-table set (though on second thoughts she thought that if she stopped wearing the jewels, Murray would spread the word that they were pawned). 'I reserve a present for the first Bride in your Family', she wrote, and added a line from Parnell: ''Tis now my Daughter's Daughters' turn to shine.' She sent young Mary a miniature to show her how different fashions were in Venice. When asked what she would like from London, she replied, 'My Dear Child, do not think of reverseing Nature by making me presents . . . As I would not new furnish an Inn I was on the point of leaving, such is this world to me.' But again she had second thoughts: what about the two large china jars she had bought for the Cavendish Square house? She was sure Wortley 'don't value them and beleive they would be of no use to you'. What about sending via Mackenzie 'a few dishes in the shape of leaves, a salad dish, and a dozen of plates of English china, and any other new fashion'd Triffle'? Wortley agreed to relinquish the jars; she said they would 'do me great Honor in this

---

[13] *CL* iii. 174, 178. Judged too notorious to stand for Huntingdonshire in 1754, Edward was offered Bossiney on condition of assent to his father's breaking the entail on his recently inherited Newbold Verdon estate (EWM jr. to John Bridger, 15 Aug 1760, MS owned by Konrad Suchanek).

Country', and she would look on them as a present from him. But they never arrived; a French privateer intervened.[14]

Lady Mary moved back to Venice in mid-September 1758. In this great town, she said, she was 'almost as solitary as in a desert'; yet tourists swirled around her. Some interested her on account of her granddaughters, or of their own families. (Lord Brudenell, for instance, was the great-grandson of Sarah, Duchess of Marlborough; his parents were friends of Wilhelmina Tichborne.) Lady Wynne and her daughters were leaving for England, since the collapse of her hopes that Giustiniana would marry consul Smith. Lady Mary assured Lady Bute that whatever the Wynnes might say, they were *not* entitled, in their assault on London society, to pose as friends of hers. She may have had a soft spot for Giustiniana, who was an avid and discriminating reader. But if there was any friendship she concealed it. From the impression the Wynnes made when they finally reached London she was wise to do so.[15]

She was now (probably without knowing it) back under the watchful eye of Graeme, who apparently felt it his duty to Bute to supervise her. Even before his long absence from Venice, he had hinted that it might be wisest for her to return to England. (She 'waved the subject', and later reminded him several times that 'the air of England never agreed with her health'.) On his visit to Padua he had thought her changed, a little deaf, even 'a good deal faild'. In August he said he 'would gladly perswade her to thinke of going home'; he was only waiting for her return to Venice 'to make another atack'.

His care and concern were real; but still his surveillance would not have been welcome. He reported to Bute on her domestic, physical, social, and financial life. He noted that her cook, two men and two maids were all 'derected by the abby Mora', whom he suspected of getting her away from Palazzi in order to exploit her himself; 'she dos what she can to hinder those about her to cheat her but it is not possible that at her time of life she can look nearrowly into all the expen[s]es of her family.' He was sure she must be 'grossly cheated', firstly because 'the honestest Italien servant is he that cheats his master with discration' and secondly because she lived so cheaply. Though she 'daly' bought baubles and trifles, he could not 'see how she can

---

[14] *CL* iii. 175–7, 185, 194, 207, 212, 213, 244. Parnell's 'Elegy, To an Old Beauty' presents a woman unwilling to relinquish her jewels to her granddaughters; MWM implicitly asserts her better sense (*CL* iii. 222).

[15] *CL* iii. 179–80, 182, 214. Having met MWM at Murray's, Giustiniana spent a morning with 'Milady'. After a life rich in scandal (a baby abandoned in Paris, an affair with Casanova), she married MWM's friend and contemporary Count Rosenberg: Michiel implied (perhaps ironically) that MWM would approve. In her essays Giustiniana sounds not unlike MWM, discussing the place of reading and study in women's lives with reference to reputation and fashionable society (Wynne 1785; Brunelli 1929: 20, 27–8, 46, 68–9, 71, 76 ff.; Casanova 1967: v. 172).

spend what she draws for' except by being cheated. He thought her 'turned fatter and looks much better' for her time at Padua. He noted that she stayed 'a good dale at home', that she exchanged formal visits with various Venetian ladies, and that 'her most intimate acquaintence' was Michiel, with Rosenberg not far behind. Since she had not yet confided her troubles to him, he was puzzled by the cessation of friendly relations with Smith, Murray, and Lady Wentworth, whom he thought 'worthy friendly people'. He had even discussed with Smith the probable value of her jewels. (He thought them worth something like £2,000, though for a time Smith persuaded him that this was too high.)[16]

Lady Mary remained unaware of this monitoring. She might sound a trifle self-pitying sometimes to Lady Bute; but to the Steuarts she exuded mental energy. When she told them 'All my pleasures are recollections of those past', she was thinking of the philosophical proposition that memory is the only reality. She wrote of her solitude and melancholy, but she did so with wit and stylistic flourish. She was to receive from Sir James a copy of his work-in-progress, *Political Economy*; she was on her mettle because she thought he read her letters like a literary critic. Whatever he said of criticizing, she had a happy sense of the value of her letters to him and his wife in their somewhat restricted existence. To Lady Bute she spoke deprecatingly of her 'old Wives' Tales' taking time from more important business. (She had been running on about English news, and about how her female Venetian friends were lobbying in the election of a new Patriarch.)[17]

It was apparently in autumn 1758 that Joseph Smith the consul lent her his set of Dodsley's *Collection of Poems* (four volumes so far, with her own work conspicuous in volume i). The loan *may* have been a friendly gesture; and Lady Mary's annotations in Smith's volumes do not suggest that she was upset by meeting herself unexpectedly in print. She wrote 'mine' beside her Eclogues, and 'I confess it' beside the footman's epistle to Griselda Murray; she made some textual corrections, named the tunes which had set her to writing a song and a ballad, and provided a more exact date for 'While Thirst of Power'. All this suggests some ease with her public role. She also noted some ascriptions of poems by other people: beside one dating from 1717 she wrote, 'I renounce and never saw till this year 1758.' The poem, by Thomas Tickell, is an epistle from a lady in love with a Jacobite. It sounds as if Lady Mary had been teased about being in love with Sir James, and saw this poem as likely to increase the teasing.[18]

---

[16] Graeme to Bute, 30 Aug.–8 Sept., 31 Dec. 1758, Bute MSS.   [17] *CL* iii. 182–3, 185.

[18] Cf. Grundy 1982. Smith's Dodsley vols. i–iv date from 1755. MWM's note to the Tickell poem gives the year she saw them. Dodsley had a quarter-share in the *London Magazine*, where more of her poems

But a related event in November upset her enough to bother Lady Bute with it. The sixth and final volume of Dodsley met her eyes, and in it a verse exchange written in 1733: an erotic invitation from an older woman to a younger man, and his crushing rejection. In fact, said Lady Mary, these poems had passed between Lady Hertford (ridiculously in love with Lord William Hamilton) and herself (impersonating the airily dismissive young man). In print they were misattributed: she was credited with the come-on, and Sir William Yonge with the brush-off, which was printed as addressed to herself.

She was 'realy sick with vexation'. 'I do not beleive either Job or Socrates ever had such a provocation.' She trusted that nobody who knew her would be taken in; but it was a gift to the enemies and scandalmongers by whom she already felt beleaguered: a gift, that is, to Smith and Murray. She knew 'silence and neglect is the best Answer to defamation'. She wrote nothing on this page of Smith's Dodsley, and resolved at first not to tell Lady Bute. But then someone advised her she had better do so. (Who? Some non-British sympathizer seems more likely than Graeme.) She expected her daughter to take some action, presumably against Dodsley. She concluded her letter, 'I thank God Witches are out of Fashion, or I should expect to have it depos'd by several credible wittnesses that I had been seen flying through the Air on a broomstick etc.' Then she fell silent for a month, claiming she had 'my Head too muddled' for writing letters.[19]

But she was not too muddled to write to the Steuarts. To them she poured out her feelings, but indirectly. She rhapsodized about witchcraft, affecting to believe that the recent relaxation of the laws against it (vehemently opposed by her old enemy Lord Grange) had caused it to proliferate in a scandalous manner. Soon there would 'not be an old woman in the nation intirely free from suspicion'. She enumerated a string of alleged recent events so contrary to nature that they must be witchcraft: Fribourg had become *cicisbeo* to 'the finest lady in Venice', Mora a highwayman, the venerable Antonio Mocenigo an opera-singer, and the rake Murray a Methodist. Duellists had clashed 'in the Place of Saint Marc for the charms of his excellent lady, and I have been seen flying in the air in the figure of

---

appeared (Dodsley 1988: 4–5, 519). There is no sign that she knew of her inclusion in Colman and Thornton's *Poems by Eminent Ladies*, 1755, where the lack of a biographical note implies respect for her rank, but the absence of 'Thursday' and 'Friday' implies belief that they were not by her.

[19] *CL* iii. 187–8, 193. Dodsley vols. v–vi were newly pub. this year, probably after she annotated vol. i. Vol. v added more of her poems; but only the misattribution in vol. vi drew her comment. Of two MS copies of the wooing poem as hers, one was made by 1739 (MSS Adv., NLS, 23-1-20. 38; CUL Add. MS 7907). Jane Collier and Sarah Fielding quoted a couplet of it in *The Cry*, 1753, unascribed (vol. i, scene v).

Julian Cox, whose history is related with so much candour and truth by the pious pen of Joseph Glanville'.[20]

Out of all those unfortunates whose persecution Glanvill recorded in his *Saducismus Triumphatus* (of which Lady Mary owned the third edition, published the year she was born), she probably chose Julian Cox for being, like herself, a woman 'aged about 70 years'. In the summer of 1663 neighbours had accused Julian of flying in the air, bewitching cattle, possessing the body of a hunted hare, magically forcing a girl to swallow pins, and conjuring up a toad between a man's legs. She denied all this, but she was executed. The account of her trial, with the learned opinions then given on it, are indeed, as Lady Mary told Sir James, 'very well worth reading but rather too long for a letter'.[21]

Lady Mary further developed her relation with Julian Cox. She had herself, she said, provided testimony to condemn herself. Had she not argued that everyone, 'even the most despicable creatures alive', had some kind of pleasure allotted to them by nature? 'Now observe this comment: who are the most despicable creatures? Certainly, Old women. What pleasure can an old woman take?—Only Witchcraft.' This syllogism would surely convince all good Christians—everyone in fact except 'such atheists as you and Lady Fanny'. 'I own all the facts, as many witches have done before me, and go every night in a public manner astride upon a black cat to a meeting where you are suspected to appear.' Commentators, she said (like those who had debated whether Julian really became a hare or only a '*Hare-like Spectre*'), were unsure whether this 'clandestine midnight correspondance' was treasonable or lewd; but all agreed 'there was something very odd and unaccountable in such sudden likings'. This last sounds as if quoted verbatim from some actual comment, probably made at John Murray's, on Lady Mary's liking for the Steuarts.

After this indecipherable 'rhapsody', her next letter addressed two topics apparently irrelevant to any witch-hunt against herself. The first was the death of the third Duke of Marlborough (soldier and spendthrift, grandson of Duchess Sarah, whose only sincere mourners would be the 'tradespeople and . . . usurers' who now would never be paid). Second came the exploits of a 'heroic', unidentified countess, Lady B., née O., who was an exploiter of men and thereby an avenger of her sex. Lady Mary's admiration for this

---

[20] *CL* iii. 188–9. In two separate notes she says, 'Methodists, Poulcats', and 'I am a Methodist, in my own Way . . . 'tis necessary to give up the temporal world for the spiritual' (CB 10, 11).

[21] [Glanvill] 1689: 387–92; *CL* iii. 189. In Henry Fielding's *Welsh Opera*, 1731, a suspected witch confesses to entering a hunted hare's body; far from being executed, she foretells or perhaps produces the magical happy ending. Sir James was interested in the occult; so, too, was Casanova.

adventuress is clearly assumed; anger and sarcasm lurk beneath her professed desire to confess her past errors and to be re-educated, by someone unprincipled and promiscuous, in the proper treatment of men. She declares herself a man-hater. All old maids hate men, she says (this much was a truism, even if not true); so do 'most women of my age'.[22] How seriously should we take this? Clearly it is not the simple truth (for one thing, her male addressee had become very dear to her). But just as clearly she crafted this whole flight of fantasy to voice her gendered rage at the gendered attacks of Murray—and perhaps, she felt, of Dodsley too.

Her next extant letter, to Lady Bute, is calmer. She was prepared now to let the Dodsley affair rest. She hoped the Wynnes might never reach London, but stay in Paris instead. She had met a visiting English couple who really appealed to her, Catherine and James Wright. They had stayed in Venice because Catherine was expecting a child, which was born dead: their care for each other at this painful time made Lady Mary think of the Butes' marriage. She enjoyed their company more than any since the Steuarts', and said she had 'reason to applaud their good Nature, who seem to forget I am an old Woman'. When they left she kept in touch with Catherine Wright by letter, offering her two touchstones of intimacy: open confession of low spirits, and a 'Burlesque account' of another of John Murray's upstart female favourites.[23]

A leitmotif for her letters this winter, 1758–9, was the desire to see Mackenzie and his wife, Lady Betty, who were now settled at Turin. She first mentioned this desire to Lady Bute as unattainable. Apart from any (unmentioned) sourness left by her parting from Algarotti there, she felt it was too long a journey and would present her with too many social obligations. But their presence in Italy, with that of the Steuarts at Tübingen, fed her wish, come spring, to take some health-giving 'little jaunt', and sometimes she thought she could manage it. She yearned for some delightful spot of ground in a valley 'encompass'd with high Mountains'. She had got a copy of Bolingbroke's works for Sir James, and assured Mackenzie she would be 'inventing Schemes' when summer came. Before she later, reluctantly, ruled out these journeys, Mackenzie had told Bute that the 'friend of Ours on this side of the Alps' had actually bought a covered carriage and engaged Hamilton as her squire ('Ecuyer') for the journey.[24]

It would be nothing odd for Lady Mary either to waver in her decision or to offer Mackenzie some hyperbole which he, now 'a Minister and a

---

[22] *CL* iii. 189–92.   [23] *CL* iii. 193–4, 263.
[24] *CL* iii. 194, 195–6, 198, 201, 219. The carriage, or berlin, seems to have been the subject of sneers from Murray's circle (*CL* iii. 198, 217).

Courtier', might fail to read aright. Her letters display no 'visible signs of dotage', though Graeme convinced Mackenzie he had discerned such signs, and Mackenzie did his best to convince Bute. Only one detail might possibly signal real confusion: Lady Mary said the Steuarts were living 'in a little Town but two days from Padoua'. The natural route to Tübingen would be through the Brenner Pass, for which Padua is well placed; but twice two days would be good going for the journey.

Still, this sounds far less like dotage than mere mistake. Even as Mackenzie was presenting her as a quixotic traveller, Lady Mary was telling Sir James she must renounce all idea of Tübingen. 'The Alps were once mole-hills in my sight when they interposed between me and the slightest inclination', she wrote with panache. But 'now age begins to freeze'; traversing precipices and staying in hovels had lost its allure. As usual she assimilated her own experience to philosophical generalization. This topic was a favourite. 'Poor human-kind! We always march blindly on; the fire of youth represents to us all our wishes possible . . . Why are our views so extensive and our power so miserably limited?' Another time she wrote to Sir James, 'I am afraid we are little better than straws upon the water; we may flatter ourselves that we swim when the current carries us along.' Now, with a brief glance at the Steuarts' son (still young enough to dream of martial or political fame), she moved on to deny free will and to denounce ambition. It sounds as if, in her browsing through Dodsley's *Collection*, she had been struck by *The Vanity of Human Wishes*. But her conclusion is very un-Johnsonian. The only real blessing, she says, the only undeniable good that human beings have at their command, is pleasure that harms nobody, 'the innocent gratification of their senses'. She would therefore 'endeavour to comfort my selfe for the cruel disappointment I find in renouncing Tübingen, by eating some fresh oysters'. She hoped that the Steuarts too would console themselves with their own local delicacies.[25]

To Lady Bute she commented on the English news. She was duly anxious when sixteen-year-old Lady Jane Stuart had measles, but more anxious that her mother would catch it (as she did). She was delighted to hear of the marriage of a granddaughter of Lady Oxford; she inspected grand tourists, always alert for likely grandsons by marriage, or suitable candidates for Lord Bute's patronage. On New Year's Eve, 1758, she wrote a letter to be carried by a gentleman 'just return'd from a very extraordinary Journey', whose account (and map) of it had impressed her. She took the opportunity

---

[25] *CL* iii. 196, 197, 198–9, 201, 215–16; Mackenzie to Bute, 13 Jan. 1759 (Bute MSS). Johnson's poem appeared in Dodsley's *Collection*, iv.

to reiterate praise for those who observed and analysed but did not publish. Next March when she heard that the Prince of Wales was to marry and have his household expanded, she put in a word for John Anderson, adding that her recommendations would be few since she saw few people as deserving.[26]

Mackenzie, too, now had patronage at his command, and Lady Mary tried to enlist him on behalf of Hamilton. The Venetian authorities had not come through with a pension to satisfy Hamilton (Murray thought he was over-valuing himself, demanding too much). One option for him was to join the army of the King of Savoy and Sardinia, at whose court Mackenzie was ambassador. Lady Mary passed on Graeme's praise of Hamilton's military abilities, coupled with her own good opinion and Lady Bute's. Her final point was Hamilton's devotion to Bute: she clearly had in mind Bute's interests as well as his. When Mackenzie insisted he was no patron but merely a personal friend, Lady Mary replied that he would 'be allwaies to me the Aimable Mr. Mackensie, however dignify'd or distinguish'd; and if you was elected Pope, I am persuaded your Freinds would find no Alteration in your Behaviour to them.' She apologized again later for the absurdity of suppos-ing that he could let the diplomat encroach on the man. She must be entering her dotage, she said—sublimely unaware that this was something else Mackenzie was capable of taking seriously.[27]

At the end of the year 1758 Graeme sent another report to Bute. Having done so he may have felt some compunction, for he ended by acknowledg-ing that Lady Mary was 'yet most delightful companie'—when 'in good humor'. He thought Rosenberg was now 'a little coold in his atention to her'. He admitted that Murray 'ought to show some more respect then he has done of late to a woman of her birth and country'. Yet he was so much in the dark about recent developments that he thought the situation was improv-ing: 'there seems to be a little more hermony twixt her and the Residents family. These things have their ups and downs you know, my Lord.' He had again cautiously broached a return home: that 'it would be a much more comfortable life for her at her age to be near her relations and served by people she could trust instead of being in the hands of those she knew had no concience to hinder them from cheating her to the utmost of their power'. She seemed to have accepted his general drift ('which is more then she condescended to say before'), but was concerned that she might reach England and find that 'the climat and air' disagreed with her. How would she then get back?

---

[26] *CL* iii. 194–6, 205–6.

[27] In flippant mood she later called Hamilton 'brave and senseless as the sword he wears'. In 1760 he was seeking his fortune at St Petersburg (*CL* iii. 196–7, 201, 203, 218, 249).

If she was stalling, it worked. Soon the moment had passed. Bute had disclosed his 'Sentiments as to that Persons return home': he wanted to prevent
it. Mackenzie, perhaps surprised, said he was glad to be in the know, 'because
the subject may in a variety of ways, be brought upon the tapis, and I shall
now be so much upon my guard, as to suit my language to what I know is
your Inclination'. There was no doubt that his brother's inclination would
prevail if need be over his friend's; it was now that he reassured Bute (probably on the authority of Signora Michiel) about Lady Mary's dotage and failing.[28] Those very men who had tried to persuade her home were now
mobilized to persuade her to stay put.

⤮

Meanwhile Carnival time had come, with Lady Mary maintaining she would
take no part in its more strenuous social pleasures. She dined at Graeme's;
she visited the Wrights at their lodgings 'in the Mouth of the Port'; she spent
evenings tête-à-tête with Michiel. But it was an even more brilliant Carnival
than most, from the recent appointment or consecration of new Procurators, new cardinals, and a new Patriarch. Lady Mary found she could not
decline the invitations of her Venetian friends; she put on her mask and
enjoyed the splendid pageantry, wishing her granddaughters could see it
too. Even at home she found herself writing a letter with 'twenty people talking round me'.[29]

In January 1759 (the warmest she had ever known, except in Naples) her
little garden felt like England in May. She told Wortley this, but said nothing
to him of her regret at his selling the Twickenham house which had held so
much of her past. In February she discovered—by accident, not from
Murray—that a ship was just about to sail for London. Quick action enabled
her to catch it, not with a letter but with a novelty present: a *scaldapiedi* or
Venetian footwarmer, as used in gondolas. In March she made a similar
last-minute discovery of a traveller leaving for England, and scribbled down
a letter while he courteously waited.[30]

In April came a fresh blow-up with Murray, who had publicly snubbed
and humiliated Knatchbull-Wyndham and Devismes 'meerly for their

---

[28] Graeme to Bute, finished on 31 Dec. 1758; Mackenzie to Bute, 17 Mar. 1759 (Bute MSS). MWM seemed
to think her return might somehow damage Lady Bute's prospects.

[29] *CL* iii. 202, 203, 205.

[30] Her messenger was a Mr Gregory. She mentioned her regret about Twickenham to Lady Bute,
making it sound purely practical. She next sent her god-daughter Mary a miniature of Venetian ladies in
informal summer wear; she could 'find no picture worthy Lord Bute'. EWM wrote rather grumpily in
January, afraid she underestimated his problems with his health and his sight (*CL* iii. 180, 199–200, 202;
H MS 74. 143).

Civillities to me'. By now Lady Mary believed that Graeme was 'fully sensible of the ill behaviour of these great people' and had remonstrated, though the only result was coldness to himself and increased rudeness to her. She thought Murray must mean either to drive her out of Venice, or else to use her somehow to further his plan for getting a more advantageous posting: he was 'every day complaining of this odious Country'. 'They do not know me', she wrote. 'I have throughout my long Life persisted in noncompliance with Hush money.'[31]

An especially painful scene occurred about now at Murray's 'court'. (Though Murray never once visited her during the years of their neighbourhood, she kept up appearances by visiting his wife.) She let several months elapse before relating this scene with angry gusto to Sir James, summarizing it as 'Dialogue at the Resident's'. Her 'wise monitors' had demanded why she persisted in 'reading or writing seven hours in a day' when she was again worried about her eyesight. Her reply—'I am happy while I read and write'—was greeted with winks and titters, as if to be happy implied something disreputable. A lady who falsely claimed to be both young and learned advised Lady Mary to use glasses; others implied, 'in the best-bred way in the world', that she must be using them already, and lying when she said she did not. There were requests to see some of her writing, and simpering references to Sir James Steuart. Lady Mary snubbed the innuendoes by confirming 'in a dry stern tone' that she was indeed honoured with his correspondence.

'This rudeness of mine', she wrote,

occasioned a profound silence for some minutes, and they fell into a good-natured discourse of the ill consequences of too much application, and remembered how many apoplexies, gouts and dropsies had happened amongst the hard students of their acquaintance. As I never studied any thing in my life, and have always (at least from 15) thought the reputation of learning a misfortune to a woman, I was resolve[d] to believe these stories were not meant at me.

Around her silence, however, the teasing resumed. She found herself led into apologetics on behalf of Lady Vane (whom others attacked) and of the Scots. A 'gaping school-boy' (no doubt a grand tourist) delivered a wisecrack. 'I confess (to my shame be it spoken), I was grieved at the triumph that appeared in the eyes of the King and Queen of the company'— or of the two queens, Murray's wife and Smith's. After Murray had withdrawn, with 'his train of courtiers . . . laughing amongst themselves as

---

[31] *CL* iii. 206–7.

they followed him', the queens 'renewed their generous endeavors to set me right'.

Lady Mary, 'graceless beast that I am', could take no more. She had been quietly holding a card over a candle-flame to blacken it: now she scribbled on it a stanza of rebuke, 'and flung down the card on the table, and myselfe out of the room in the most indecent fury'. A few minutes in her gondola 'on the cold water' made her feel foolish, but not penitent. Her verse put-down came from a song by Lord Dorset, asserting his choice of pleasure and rejecting the dullness of the 'miserably wise'. She implicitly accepted, that is, the parallel drawn by her tormentors between poetry and pleasure. Poetry, indeed, she implied, embraced not only erotic but also vengeful pleasure. She hated to think the Murray circle might be 'below satyre'.

Slander from Pope had made her reach (as he did himself) for the pen as weapon; her aggressive use of the pen had then become an item in his charge-sheet against her. The same pattern was repeated with the Murray circle. Lady Mary was painfully reminded that vengeance, like love, was 'in a peculiar manner, forbidden to us wretches who are condemned to petticoats'. She fell back on quoting to Sir James from her own 'Epistle from Mrs Yonge to Her Husband': her most trenchant statement of women's case against men. She rearranged the lines, ending with one that reads in part, 'we must sigh in silence'. In its original context this meant a wife stifling her feeling for a potential lover; now it meant herself stifling her resentment.[32]

Meanwhile she told Tichborne she had 'the Spirit of Martyrdom or contradiction'; she told Lady Bute she had the spleen. 'My Spirits in Company are false Fire; I have a Damp within.' This might, she said, be the fault of overindulging her passion for sedentary study, of being 'a Rake in Reading': precisely the fault found with her by Murray's circle. To her daughter she contrasted her fault of excess with Wortley's 'uncommon' moderation and self-control. But in a disquisition on the spleen for Sir James, she said that it could be kept in check by 'employment for the mind and exercise for the body', and that her own studies '(good for nothing as they are)' at least preserved her health and her will to live.[33]

She was glad to hear that Lady Bute had inoculated the nearly two-year-old Louisa, and that all had gone well. Writing just before her annual removal to Padua, she commented on the foolish pastimes of old age: will-making, building, getting married. Living at Gottolengo, she said, had

---

[32] *CL* iii. 216–19, 264. A jotted series of comments: 'I never look in the Glass . . . an adorn'd Old Woman, a painted Sir . . . Age never ridiculous but when it imitates Youth' shows her mulling over age, looks, and the double standard (CB 7).

[33] *CL* iii. 207, 208–9, 212.

made her naïve and rustic; she was 'oftner out of Humour' now in the busy world 'than amongst my plants and Poultry in the Country'. But Padua was balm to her spirit. Again she hoped for a visit from Graeme, if his work allowed; meanwhile she kept 'College Hours', ignoring the new opera but having, somehow or other, 'conserts at Home'. She likened herself to 'a Mouse in a Parmasan cheese'. Gambling, formerly a passion, was now anathema to her: she inveighed against it for producing unseemly familiarities on the one hand and 'pouts and Quarrels' on the other. But though she might allow herself to sound stuffy when writing to Lady Bute, she told Sir James that she avoided low spirits by keeping up 'a certain sprightly folly that (I thank God) I was born with'.[34]

In her Padua mousehole she began dictating a letter to Sir James, intending to spare her eyes. But her amanuensis ('the first that could write as fast as I talk') was not Mora but a visitor. After he left she found his writing full of mistakes. It was harder on her 'poor eyes' to correct and explain than to have written the letter in the first place, and she recklessly extended it sevenfold in her own hand. She related the memorable bad scene at Murray's, then wove one of her tissues of satire, paradox, and self-referential comment. She declared war on stylistic obscurity and then allowed a 'dab of Italian' to slide 'involuntarily' from her pen. She abused Bolingbroke (a traitor to the Jacobite cause as well as other causes), but called Steuart's fellow Jacobite James Irwin or Irvin an 'honest man', and his recent suicide an act of stoic firmness. She mocked Algarotti for careerism ('composing panegyrics on whoever is victor in this uncertain war'). She lumped together heroes with poets, 'bloody battles' with sport, Homer with Pindar, and judged all this frenzy of competition 'extremely mistaken or extremely mercenary'. She was at least consistent, holding to her scorn of heroes in 1759, a year of British victories. Her Enlightenment hedonism or epicureanism was just what she had addressed to Conti forty years before; only her manner of expression had shifted, from the smooth and elegant to the gnomic and whimsical. Her hedonism was not Murray's. 'Pl[easure] and debauchry, L[ight] and Darkness,' she noted about now, 'Never was nor lov'd a Rake.' Her pleasures centred on friendship; she concluded her letter with affectionate remembrance of the past, with love to Sir James and Lady Frances and to 'your young man because he is yours'.[35]

The summer was one of extreme heat and drought. It did Lady Mary's eyes no good; but she kept writing. To Tichborne went another richly jumbled letter full of names and citations, comparing the status of women in

---

[34] *CL* iii. 210–12, 214, 215, 223.   [35] *CL* iii. 215–21, 227.

England and Venice, comparing views on old women (as despicable, or as 'amusing to themselves'), building castles in the air. 'I would part with all the Palaces of Palladio for a Pavillion near Hers, and avoid being troublesome.' (A few months later she punctured this dream, realizing 'I should be troublesome if at London.') To Lady Bute she sent news of grand tourists, and references for those seeking employment.[36]

A society wedding drew her back to Venice in September 1759. One caller at her house gave her a shock. This was a Mr Southwell, 'Tall, fair, well shap'd', sensible, rich—and horribly disfigured. He had suffered a mouth infection which destroyed much of the lower part of his face. Lady Mary could not sleep all night for thinking about him: not with sympathy but with a kind of fury. 'I charge you not to look upon him, and to lock up your Daughters if he should visit Lord Bute . . . such a figure should not be seen by any Woman in a possibillity of Breeding.' She was jolted out of the age of sensibility back into the earlier and superficially crueller age from which she sprang; yet within a few months Southwell's politeness and conversational skills had more or less reconciled her to his appearance.[37]

In another parcel of books (via Mackenzie) she received Swift's *History of the Four Last Years of Queen Anne*. She flattered her husband, who had spent those years as an Opposition MP, by seeking his opinion of it. He had read and dismissed it as 'not worth remembring'. Either from her daughter or from someone else she received a copy of Voltaire's *Candide*—so sensationally original yet so like her own 'Docile'—in which she inscribed 'delicieux'.[38] Hearing from Lady Bute about the Wynnes' doings in London, she wished Lady Wynne had the capacity to write memoirs. (She might have enjoyed Giustiniana's *Essays*, 1785.) On the news of James Wolfe's glorious death at Quebec, she thought his mother and especially his fiancée were to be pitied, but not the hero himself. She was sorry to hear that her sister Mar had been moved to London by Lady Frances Erskine, fearing 'her deplorable Condition' would now be 'more expos'd'.[39]

After a delightful autumn, winter 1759 set in severely. Carnival suffered 'extreme wet Weather'; the solid ground of Venice seemed almost dissolved

---

[36] *CL* iii. 221–3, 227. She mentioned Graeme's brother Hugh, and Richard Dalton, whom Bute later helped to become George III's librarian. Bute was at a tricky moment: inducing Prince George to set duty and self-sacrifice above his love for Lady Sarah Lennox (McKelvey 1973: 83; Tillyard 1994: 125).

[37] *CL* iii. 224, 228; Mackenzie to Bute, 2 Apr. 1760, Bute MSS.

[38] Now at Sandon. One book sent in these years survives in the original blue wrapper, on which MWM wrote its title: *Memoirs of a Young Lady of Quality, A Platonist*, 1756. Horace Walpole, too, indignantly repudiated Swift's version of history (*Corr.* xxi. 184–5). Voltaire had sent MWM a message in 1758 by his friend Pierre-Michel Hennin (1963–93: v. 1236).

[39] *CL* iii. 226, 228.

away by water from above, water from below. Lady Mary found her garden useless, her time idle, herself 'profoundly Dull'. Graeme was ill; Hamilton was away somewhere or other. Venice, she implied, was a good place only for 'those who have money to throw away'. She commented with asperity on its gambling habit, and on the poor outlook afforded by 'the rising Generation'.[40] Another prospect seeming heavenly at a distance had proved disappointing on a nearer view.

[40] *CL* iii. 228–9.

31

January 1760–December 1761

❧

Inheriting: 'on the threshold of this dirty world'[1]

A MONTH or so into the new year Lady Mary received a couple of shocks. The first was a book package, an unusually small one. Inside was a work entitled *Reflections on the Rise and Fall of the Antient Republicks*. Its title-page bore the name of her son, who had not written to her for years. There was no covering letter now. She found the book 'very Nonsensical', though it received respectful reviews. Its celebration of republican virtues might hold some appeal for Lady Mary; its diatribes against luxury and degeneracy would hold less. She would not have missed the Opposition politics they cloak, and would have been merciless to its pompous, sententious style (not wholly unlike Bolingbroke's). It convinced her that Edward was 'still a knavish Fool', and his manner of sending it proved that he had 'private Correspondancies' in Venice or Padua. She felt harried. It was some time this year that her discarded daughter-in-law 'Had the Honour of Writing a Latter to my Lady Mary sitting [*sic*] forth the great Want I am in for Money to support my self with Meat and Drink, and all the common necessaries of Life.' Lady Mary may or may not have mustered sympathy for Sally; she could muster none for Edward.

The next blow was harder: a letter from Wortley which convinced her he was going blind. He said his 'Eyes grow weaker every year': he seldom dared to write even a short letter. At once she fell prey to the kind of fears which Graeme and Mackenzie entertained about her. She imagined her husband, up there in remote Yorkshire, falling 'into the Hands of Servants (as all blind people must necessarily do)'. She imagined Edward pressing Wortley about the inheritance, telling him lies about her own behaviour, approaching the servants with lavish promises of future reward if they could fix his father's

[1] *CL* iii. 251.

will. She had been offered such promises herself. There was no knowing who Edward might enlist on his side. Her high opinion of Wortley's integrity and ability was unwavering: but still. She imagined him being 'impos'd on'; she imagined Lady Bute and her children cut off. She did not voice this idea. 'I dare not say more; I hope I say enough to be understood.' But for the first time she wrote unguardedly of Edward to his sister: 'I have long wept the misfortune of being Mother to such an Animal.'

Her distress was extreme: she sounded suddenly ten years older. She told Lady Bute these vexations would hasten her end, 'and I shall have no regret in leaving a World I have long been weary of'—none but the thought of Lady Bute's grief and her possible financial loss. She then offered, formally if somewhat obliquely, to come home to England. She stressed that her offer was disinterested. 'My Life is so near a Conclusion that where or how I pass it (if innocently) is almost indifferent to me.' She had few friends left in London; she would find its 'Croud and Bustle' disagreeable. But 'if I could be of use either to your Father or your Family I would venture shortening the insignificant days of | your most affectionate Mother, | M. Wortley.' On the same date she placed this offer directly before her husband: 'If I could be of any Service to you on that [blindness] or any other occasion, I shall think my last remains of Life well employ'd.' She was so upset that she forgot to date her note to him, though she well knew that few things annoyed him more.[2]

These two shocks eclipsed a third potential worry: a groundless report of some kind of 'disgust' between Mackenzie and his powerful brother, Bute. As it happened Graeme, who had serious health problems and had been finding the terms of his appointment a trial, had been granted four months' leave and was about to depart overland for England. (He was ill, and his health continued to give concern until after Lady Mary left Italy.) He carried Lady Mary's anxious letters to her daughter and husband, and a calm, affectionate one for Mackenzie (who, she said, would always have a faithful friend while 'there remains a parcel of attoms call'd Me'). Lady Mary sent no presents for anyone with Graeme: she was afraid he might die on the journey. She would have liked to travel with him as far as Turin, but she said the weather was too cold.[3]

Having made her momentous offer, she wrote cheerfully to Sir James Steuart next day, and to Lady Bute a few days later. But still her fears

    [2] *CL* iii. 230–1; Sally to EWM, n.d., H MS 76. 5–6; EWM, 29 Dec. 1759, H MS 74. 144.
    [3] *CL* iii. 232. Murray reported Graeme's departure in late Feb. His plan for the army was considered after he left, and passed the Senate in Sept. (SP 99/68/13, 78).

resurfaced at intervals. She heard no word from either Graeme or her daughter till long after Venetian gossip said (wrongly) that he had reached London. By April she feared that she had overreacted to the bad news of her husband's sight, and that he would be unwarrantably disturbed—even angry?—at her offer to come home. She wrote to Lady Bute about her fears themselves as the problem. Now in old age, she said, she was giving way to tendencies she had once struggled against. Since 'Courage was the favorite Virtue in my early Youth, I study'd to seem void of Fear, and I beleive was rather esteem'd Fool-hardy. I am now grown Timerous and enclin'd to low Spirits. Whatever you may hear to the contrary, my chearfullness is like the Fire kindled in Brush wood, which makes a shew but is soon turn'd to cold Ashes.' Apparently her offer to come home had taken courage. In early May she tried to withdraw it. 'If you have not already sent my Letter to your Father,' she wrote, 'I desire you would not do it.' She felt sure it would be taken wrongly: perhaps she would be misunderstood as clamouring to come home, or as foolishly exaggerating her problems with Murray.[4]

Weeks before she wrote this Wortley had received her offer. He endorsed it; he answered it; but he gave not the faintest hint how he felt about it. Nor did she give any such hint, in her letter to him of 23 June [1760]. By then Graeme was back in Italy, and reported Wortley to be in perfect health, though the state of his eyes still required her to keep her letter short. It had all been a fuss about nothing.[5]

That short letter to Wortley (and a summary to Lady Bute) are the only traces of what Lady Mary sent home between mid-May and October 1760. She spent the summer at Padua as usual; that is all we know.[6] Apart from any personal reasons (Lady Bute's family suffered some serious illnesses this year), this silence was probably due to the Seven Years' War. Though for Britain it was a colonial war, fought in India, North America, the Caribbean, the armies of the other powers were active in Europe. Postal services suffered.

The habit of writing plaintively to her daughter was growing on Lady Mary; but she mustered her spirits—if briefly—for writing to her newer correspondents. She jogged Steuart's memory in February about sending her his *Inquiry into the Principles of Political Economy*, and wished he might tackle his health problems by coming to Venice (whose sea air would surely

---

[4] *CL* iii. 233–4, 239–40, 242.

[5] *CL* i. 231; *SL* 479. Graeme reached Turin on 13 June (Mackenzie to Bute, 18 July 1760, Bute MSS). MWM's letter to EWM is one of those purloined after his death, sold by the lawyer Silverlock to the publisher Phillips, and bought back by MWM's eldest grandson. He gave it to Dallaway, who erroneously endorsed it, 'This is the last letter by Lady MWM to her Husband' (*SL* 512).

[6] Graeme to Bute, 15 Sept. 1758, Bute MSS, Cardiff; *CL* iii. 245 n. 1; McKelvey 1973: 88. Algarotti was in Padua in Sept. (Treviso MSS 1256B); they may have met again.

do him good). She would not pressure him, she said, and indeed she wished that he and Lady Frances were free to move back to Scotland and their friends there instead. He had asked if she had seen the new histories (probably William Robertson's of Scotland, 1759, and David Hume's of England, still appearing); but she replied that she had had no books from England for a year. Her son's, clearly, did not count. She expressed generous pleasure at the progress of young James Steuart: 'it is perhaps the most pleasing employment in life to form a young mind well disposed to receive instruction. When a parent's care is returned with gratitude and compliance, there is no conqueror or legislator that receives such sincere satisfaction.' She must have been thinking partly of Bute and the Prince of Wales. But she rated Steuart highly as a potential teacher, since she recommended him for no less a post than preceptor to emperors-in-the-making at the court of Maria Theresa and Francis I in Vienna.[7]

As Carnival ended, late in February, the young men dispersed, leaving a lull that would last until the Ascension in May. It was now that Lady Mary (between talking of her life as almost over, and contrasting herself in seclusion with Tichborne in the great world) enthused about her pleasure in agreeable little evening assemblies of seventy or eighty people. She did not lack for retired pleasures either. Sir James's MS arrived, 'neatly bound and gilt', in beautiful script, with a dedication to her which, she said, 'Lord Burleigh or even Julius Caesar would have been proud of'.[8] She read through his draft (a section which later became the first two books of the *Political Economy*) and returned a highly enthusiastic review. She thought Steuart had 'explained in the best manner the most difficult subject'. His arguments must convince every thinking reader; she 'never saw a treatise which gave me so much pleasure and information'. It had the great merit of utility. She made a point of praising its style, about which Steuart was insecure. Lady Mary assured him how much she preferred his 'nervous manner' (we might say 'sinewy') to a more elaborate or florid one.[9]

She then at once sat down to a rereading and a second harvest of

---

[7] *CL* iii. 233–4. As unformed minds she cited 'our travelling young gentlemen'. Steuart's niece Anne Durham reported her recommending him. Chamley cites the parallel with Fénelon as the duc de Bourgogne's tutor and the 'Chevalier' Ramsay as Bonnie Prince Charlie's; MWM might have had reservations about each (1965: 31, 63).

[8] Steuart was influenced by Richard Cantillon. His dedication of his MS vol. i to MWM (written Aug. 1759, with that of vol. ii to Karl Friedrich, Margrave of Baden-Durlach) foreshadows the printed preface, 1767, but is more logical in construction, more spontaneous in tone, more self-revealing and politically franker (Chamley 1965: 20; Skinner 1993: 5).

[9] *CL* iii. 235, 236–7; Chamley 1965: 20, 83–6. For inferior, decorated style MWM cited Fénelon's *Télémaque*—tactfully, since Steuart and his circle favoured a project of Jean François Tabarie to translate *Télémaque* out of frivolous French into the weightier medium of Virgilian verse (Chamley 1965: 66, 57).

comment. She was increasingly struck by the originality of Steuart's analysis, and could not help feeling 'a little vain' that she had mastered his argument on issues about which she had had 'only a confused idea'. She hastened to explain that she did not see her gender as any barrier to such mastery. Indeed, the ignorance of the average girl was probably less of a handicap in grappling with new ideas than the garbled university-taught views of the average lad. She permitted herself a digression on the Lockean notions of the mind as blank paper, and of self-analysis as groundwork for the understanding of ideas in general. Truth can seldom be found in this world, she concluded; but when new truths are discovered (as in Steuart's system of economics) they will be self-evidently acceptable to any open mind. However, because open minds are rare, she thought the reading public might not be ready to accept Steuart's system, and publication might be better delayed. No doubt she was really thinking of its probable political effects: whether it might hinder his quest for a pardon. But she evidences once more the sharp distinction she made between authorship and print.

In its plain style, its modernity of interest, and in every possible way, Steuart's book was a contrast to her son's. She consulted Wortley before she wrote to thank for the *Antient Republicks*. Then, with his blessing, she no doubt said all that was proper, though her letter (which took some effort to compose) does not survive. She let slip some of her true feelings in remarking that authorship was an innocent pastime even if not useful. To Wortley she did not mince her words: 'If he can take pleasure in reading let him read what he will, t'will, at least, keep him out of harm's way.'[10]

Her letter to Edward drew a reply, written more floridly than ever. (It too came in a book-parcel: he sent her his second, revised edition, to prove his success.) He confirmed her view that he had aimed at political relevance. He besought her to advise him what to write on next; her judging him not useful had evidently rankled. He pulled out all the stops on the theme of repentance:

I had long reflected with Anguish of Soul that I was in a manner cut off as an Alien and an Outcast from my Parents, and what peirc'd still more deeply was the Consciousness that the blame lay wholly upon myself, and that I had nothing to plead in Mitigation of what I had been guilty of.

He had now 'bid a final Adieu to the hurry and dissipation of a Town life' and was labouring 'to form such a Character as I should wish to die with'. He professed himself inarticulate with gratitude for her letter—'a Joy too big

---

[10] *CL* iii. 236–9; *SL* 479.

for Utterance', far beyond his deserts—and for Wortley's giving him the rotten borough of Bossiney, and promising he could keep it. His work as an MP, he implied, was all part of his joyfully rendered duty to God, his country, his parents, and himself; no one would guess from his letter that he needed it as a haven from arrest for debt.[11] So far as is known, his mother left his letter unanswered.

This summer she liked at least one English traveller well enough to correspond with him after he had moved on to Naples, and tell him that if her health were better she would join him there. (He was not a grand tourist but a man of nearly forty travelling for health reasons.) Though she told Lady Bute that she seldom saw a newspaper, someone showed her a copy of *A Letter to Two Great Men*, by Lord Bath, the former William Pulteney. And she commented to Tichborne on the disgrace after the battle of Minden of Lord George Sackville (brother-in-law to one of the Leveson-Gower nieces), the sensational murder of a servant by Lord Ferrers (of the Twickenham family of Shirleys on whom she was so often moved to comment), and the famous, beautiful Gunning sisters, now Lady Coventry and the Duchess of Hamilton. Her summaries do not give her views on all this headline material, but they show her interest in her native land was still lively.[12]

~~≈~~

By 5 October 1760 Lady Mary was back in Venice: anxious about the Butes' health, suffering a painful eye infection, and despairing of sending the gifts she had ready, 'till it pleases Heaven to send Peace upon Earth'. Of the grand tourists, some did not want the responsibility; some were 'too Giddy and careless' to trust; most she never saw at all, owing to Murray's machinations. (She had some hopes of Lady Oxford's grandson Lord Titchfield, but he seems not to have reached Venice.) She thought it a wonder that her constitution had survived the strain placed on it by her great sensibility, had in fact 'held out to a miracle'. Lady Bute's life, she wrote, 'is far more important than mine'. For *her* to care for herself was a patriotic duty: Lord Bute's political efforts must be chiefly driven by the desire 'to make you and his Family happy'.

Graeme had evidently been talking to her about Bute's unique position as virtually the 'only constant companion and confidant' to the young heir to the throne. To Bute alone, he said, the Prince of Wales 'unbosomed his thoughts; with him the prince rode, walked, read, and conversed'. He

---

[11] *CL* iii. 240–1.
[12] *CL* iii. 243, 244, 246, 262. This Lord Ferrers was grandson to the highly philoprogenitive one. In calling Bath's pamphlet 'equal to any Composition I ever saw of his writeing' MWM meant she was not impressed (*SL* 479). Her correspondent Humphry Morice later returned to live in Naples.

probably did not mention seeing Giustiniana Wynne in London. Wynne told her absent lover in Venice how she had eagerly awaited Graeme, had run to embrace him (once for herself, again for her lover), 'and could not have enough of him. How many questions and demands did I not ply him with in a moment!' Next day he stayed with her more than three hours, though it was Easter Day and she had to skip Mass. 'At present he's my only love.'[13]

Hard on Lady Mary's talks with Graeme came momentous news: the death of George II. Bute had been on horseback with the prince as usual, somewhere near Kew, when it first reached them: one imagines him flinging his fine right leg over his horse's withers to swing down in a single movement, ending gracefully on his knees. He steadied the boy, and delivered him to the palace to hear the news officially from Pitt. George III behaved with great self-command, with the purpose and personal loyalty typical of him. (Pitt, however, edited his Accession Speech: the war which George called 'bloody and expensive' he called 'expensive, but just and necessary'.) Within two days George made Bute a Privy Counsellor, within three weeks Groom of the Stole and First Gentleman of the Bedchamber. As he embarked on these posts Lady Mary in Venice was writing to Lady Bute, 'I bless God I have liv'd to see you so well establish'd, and am ready to sing my *Nunc Dimittis* with Pleasure.'[14]

Glad as she was for her family, she was shaken by the passing of George II. He had reigned for almost half her lifetime; like Wortley, he had been getting blind, but his general health was robust and his death a shock. To Lady Mary it was a *memento mori*. She could not resist a couple of requests to Lady Bute—on behalf of John Anderson and Sir James Steuart—though she knew she would be 'sufficiently tormented by pretentions and petitions'. But then her thoughts turned wistfully towards the idea of replacing Murray (but not by promotion), and so to her motives for wishing this, and so to her fear that, if she were to die, Murray would prevent her small possessions from reaching her daughter's hands. 'General G[raeme] is extreamly infirm, and also so easily impos'd on that whatever his Intentions may be, he is incapable of protecting any body.'[15]

---

[13] *CL* iii. 245–6, 249, 275; Wraxall 1884: i. 306; Brunelli 1929: 185–6.

[14] Wraxall 1884: i. 306; Furneaux 1973: 178; *CL* iii. 247. The 'Nunc Dimittis', sung at Anglican Evensong, uses the words of the aged Simeon on recognizing the infant Messiah: 'Lord, now lettest thou thy servant depart in peace: according to thy word. For mine eyes have seen: thy salvation' (Book of Common Prayer). For MWM they aptly, if hyperbolically, look forward to death—and voice a hope of national regeneration through a young monarch (like the hope she had despised in Bolingbroke).

[15] *CL* iii. 247–8. She repeated her solicitations at intervals, and dropped a note to Sir James to keep up his hopes. In Apr. 1761 she thanked Bute for getting the Steuarts' son an army commission; but it was not his doing (*CL* iii. 267–8).

It was not in her nature to be inactive, and the proximity to power was too tempting to resist. A week later she just dropped the name of 'poor Mr. Hamilton' at St Petersburg as someone who could use a leg-up—and she sought to intervene once more in international affairs. The Venetian Senate had picked two Procurators of St Mark to bear the Republic's compliments to 'his Majesty on his accession'. They were wealthy men, eager to make a splash in London and in every way suitable to do so. (One was Angelo Contarini, who ten years before had investigated allegations about Palazzi's treatment of Lady Mary.) Venetian gossip said that the British court planned to decline this embassy, albeit graciously. Lady Mary was concerned that her native land should not violate international *politesse*. The Procurators' mission duly went ahead, though probably not because of any action by her or Lady Bute.[16]

Lady Bute must indeed have been immensely busy as she fitted herself to her husband's new prominence. But she found the time to write of her 'Health and Prosperity', and to sing the praises of the new monarch—who, thought Lady Mary, 'needs only be halfe so perfect as she describes' to be a denizen of romance and not of real life.

That autumn, 1760, Venice suffered again from torrential rain. Lady Mary was ill a lot and her eyes gave constant trouble. In January she was 'confined to my stove for many days'. But she could no sooner hold a pen than she mustered the energy for a long letter to Sir James. She disputed good-humouredly with him about the advisability of George III's unprecedented step of surrendering hereditary revenues in consideration of his 'Civil List' payment, which was fixed at £800,000 annually. She was glad to believe that a new era was coming to English politics, free from the bitterness of party strife: glad even though 'I am preparing for my last and longest journey, and stand on the threshold of this dirty world, my several infirmities like post-horses ready to hurry me away'. Just so had the post-horses waited to hurry her from Gottolengo—waited long before she finally went with them.

By now she had probably discovered a new and pressing infirmity: a lump in her breast. Lady Mary knew about breast cancer: Mary Astell had died of it, besides others known to her. She had talked about life, death, and afterlife with Astell after that gallant old woman's mastectomy and shortly before her death. Her recognition of her own disease is in doubt. It was later said that she brought it back with her to England; yet towards the end of that journey

---

[16] *CL* iii. 248–9. Another emissary replaced Contarini. *A* pro-Bute Hamilton sought election to parliament (BL 10 Jan. 1761, Add. MS 36796).

she wrote that, unusually for her age, she had 'no distemper'. If she did find and identify her tumour this winter, she kept her own counsel.[17]

She assured the Steuarts (amid their new hopes of returning home) that she had no wish to return herself—less than ever now that Bute's position would make her a target for patronage-hunters. 'If all people thought of power as I do, it would be avoided with as much eagerness as it is now sought. I never knew any person that had it who did not lament the load'— though, she added, not one of them had willingly relinquished it.[18] (Her son-in-law was to do just that, but she would not be alive to see it.)

⁓✢⁓

In February 1961 came bad news. Wortley had died.[19] Lady Mary was probably grieved; she was certainly shocked. She was more than shocked; she was half-distracted. As she began to emerge from this distraction weeks later she told Lady Bute, 'I never thought to survive your (ever honor'd) Father.' Why not? He was after all eleven years older than she was, and if he had enjoyed good health then so had she. But she also wrote, 'what I most dreaded (the greatest part of my Life) has now happen'd'. She may have been trying to say (in syntax which during these days she often found hard to marshall) not that she had never thought she might outlive her husband but that she had always resisted the idea; she had known that if she *did* outlive him she would 'see my Family torn to pieces' by forces beyond her control. Even in her absence from it, her family had been her equilibrium, and Wortley had been its dominant force.

The news of his death may have been first broken to her in casual conversation: she spoke of 'the Brutal usage I have receiv'd from Mr. Murray on this occasion' when she had 'only this minute receiv'd' Lady Bute's letter. On the other hand, this may be just one of several discrepancies and confusions arising from her deep-seated panic.[20]

Like the death of her father years before, that of Wortley had pressing financial ramifications. Close on the immediate blow came the first rumours

---

[17] *CL* iii. 249–50, 251. Lady Carlisle, whose daughters were MWM's friends, died of breast cancer (*London Journal*, 19 Oct. 1723). Astell, Lady Sundon (formerly Charlotte Clayton), and Lady Elizabeth Hastings (whom MWM also knew) all had mastectomies (Perry, 1986: 322). Untreated breast cancer, though it *can* kill quickly, generally takes two or three years to do so (Bloom, Richardson, and Harries 1962: 213).

[18] *CL* iii. 251.

[19] He d. in Cavendish Square. *The Yearly Chronicle*, abstracted from the *St James's Chronicle*, called him 'one of the oldest members of the house of commons'.

[20] *CL* iii. 252, 261. Probably now, she reminded herself to persuade Graeme that 'M[urray] ask'd me to be employ'd in my affairs; I did not ask him'. Hervey's eldest son sent a letter of condolence (*CL* iii. 271; CB 21).

that Edward was contesting his father's will—not in his own name but in his mother's. This was a scenario that she had perhaps not thought of in all her anxieties about the inheritance. Wortley had made his will in 1755, and apart from codicils had not tinkered with it since. It was (as Mackenzie remarked) an extraordinary one. He had left Lady Mary £1,200 per annum (continuing, as it were, her existing allowance), plus the jewels, silver, furniture, and books which she had always insisted were his and not her own.[21] He wrote that he *gave* her 'such sum or sums of money . . . put out on Government or other Securitys in her own or any other person's name in Trust for her and such ready money and other things she has and which were reputed hers'. Edward received £1,000 per annum, plus his existing annuity (half as much as his mother's), plus the reversion of her £1,200 after her death.[22] He did not receive the rest (which was estimated at £1,350,000). This probably surprised no one but Edward himself; but he had desperately needed that money. People guessed his debts were as high as £80,000; from one moneylender he had borrowed nearly £7,000, at 10 per cent interest, on the strength of expectations from his father's death. He had, as it were, invested in himself-as-heir; he now gave it out that the Butes were unlikely to help him to remain an MP, and that he would be compelled to 'pauperly banishment abroad'.[23]

After legacies (including £2,000 apiece to his legitimate grandchildren), Wortley left his whole 'personal Estate' to Lady Bute for her lifetime, 'wherewith her present or future husband shall not intermeddle or have any power to dispose'. This was the same style in which Lady Mary's father had left his legacy to her. It was perhaps logical for these men (who so fully endorsed the general principle that a husband is legal owner of his wife's property) to be careful about legally exempting the particular case from the general principle. This, which sounds odd today, was not odd in its time.

But after Lady Bute's death Wortley decreed that his money was to go not to her eldest boy, Lord Mountstuart, but to her second, James Archibald, now nearly fourteen. Since Wortley was hugely wealthier than Lord Bute, the younger brother would one day be wealthier than the elder. This was odd in eighteenth-century terms. Wortley's will must have left at least *two* people feeling that they had been disinherited. Mountstuart was at this time,

---

[21] P. C. C. Cheslyn, 198. Cf. Susan Staves on the question which of a wife's possessions were her husband's, and when (1990: 135, 147, 149–50).

[22] A codicil gave Edward the furniture at Newbold Verdon; he soon began selling pictures (Elizabeth Montagu 1906: ii. 249). EWM set strict limits to posthumous spending on himself: £150 on a funeral and £100 on a monument.

[23] Thomas Gray (whose estimate of the debts later fell to £50,000) 1935: iii. 727, 734; Namier and Brooke 1964.

in eldest-son fashion, abroad. The news reached him in Turin, where he was studying and visiting his uncle Mackenzie. The latter thought Wortley had 'indeed been most unkind' to the young man.[24]

Probably Wortley had nothing personal against John, Lord Mount-stuart,[25] and no special fondness for James Archibald. More likely he wanted the Wortley Montagu fortune to remain separate from the Bute title. This would be a version of the old sentiment against the privileges of elder sons, which he had expounded in the days of his own courtship. It would relate to dynastic daydreams such as he had indulged when his daughter first became marriageable (and which Lady Mary had recently warned him against).[26]

London was agog about the whole story: the amount of money, its destination, and Edward's attempt to throw a spanner in the works. Only a day or two after Wortley died, Lord Hardwicke, congratulating Bute on 'the advantages accruing to his family', probably supposed he would control the money until it passed to his eldest son; Mackenzie, telling a friend of 'the large Fortune that has *at last* fallen to my Brother's family', knew his brother was not in control.[27] By the end of the month the latest gossip was winging its way to correspondents at home and abroad. Arthur Symmer and Elizabeth Montagu concurred in thinking that the estate coming to Lady Bute would amount to about £800,000, quite apart from what was tied up in land. The latter included the coal-mines, and would yield another £20,000 (said Symmer) or £17,000 (said Elizabeth Montagu) *a year*. Symmer calculated that until Lady Bute died (and James Archibald took over) her family would be £50,000 a year richer than they had been.

He also related how Edward had couched his challenge: by a 'caveat' against the will on grounds that, since Lady Mary had had no marriage settlement, she was entitled to her thirds under the old tradition of dower: that is, to one-third of her husband's landed property, coal-mines and all. Walpole for one (convinced as he was of Lady Mary's avarice) assumed that since the thirds of 'such a fortune' would come to far more than what the will provided, 'to be sure she will not accept' the will.[28] In short, gossip said that

[24] Mackenzie to Bute, 25 Feb. 1761, Bute MSS. At some unknown date MWM noted 'Younger Brothers the favorites of Heaven, vide Abel, Jacob, Joseph, David etc.' (CB 10). Her nephew Kingston chose his sister's 2nd son as heir.

[25] The eldest son was to turn out badly, but this was not yet evident.

[26] The Butes' first son (after the stillborn one) had been christened Edward; EWM was probably his godfather. If he had survived infancy, would this have made any difference to his grandfather's decision?

[27] Hardwicke, 23 Jan. 1761, BL Add. MS 36796; Mackenzie to ?Andrew Mitchell, 22 Apr. 1761, Add. MS 6830. 17.

[28] Symmer to Mitchell, Add. MS 6839. 207, 210; Elizabeth Montagu 1923: i. 14; Walpole to Mann, 27 Jan., *Corr.* xxi. 472.; cf. Staves 1990: 111–12. Mitchell, now British Envoy in Berlin, may have been specially curious about MWM, since he had very close knowledge of Algarotti (and Frederick the Great).

Edward would succeed in cracking the will on the basis that his father had been mean to his mother.

By mid-February the coming legal battle was big news. In Venice Lady Mary could not sleep. Her eyes were bad. Graeme (who at the best of times was prone to take Murray's word against hers) had now been in bed for several days, 'in a very bad state of Health . . . alwaies surrounded by Murray's imps'. It took him a long time to recover. Murray (perhaps not unprovoked) had said his diplomatic instructions did not require him to be civil to Lady Mary. She had just learned that the inoffensive John Udney had replaced Smith as consul. Having received her last several letters 'aukardly, palpaply open'd', and being sure that Edward had his sources of intelligence in Venice, she was keen to get her letters from England rerouted to Udney. She told Mackenzie that Murray's behaviour was driving her almost mad. 'I write every post to my Daughter but so distracted I hardly know what I say.'[29]

Indeed, several of her letters this spring sound a little unhinged. She was sure they were being opened and stopped; some of her servants were spying on her; others were receiving threats. She even accused Lady Bute of unspecified ill-treatment, as well as someone unnamed (probably Graeme) of outrageous insults. She had been told (and at first had believed) that 'the young People understand one another and have a mind to get rid of an Old Woman'. She told Lady Bute she was cut to the heart. Lady Bute may have wondered where this paranoia came from, and Lady Mary later blamed it on something that Edward had written to her.[30] But it would have been a natural speculation that Wortley's children might sink their differences in a joint attempt to overturn the will.[31] Lady Mary clearly and explicitly wanted the will to stand. Any fear she may have felt for her £1,200 a year was probably unnecessary (like her reiterated anxiety about the books, jewels, and silver plate which the will had made legally her own at last); but it was not wholly irrational. She sent another somewhat incoherent note to Lord Bute to

[29] *CL* iii. 252–3, 256, 267; newspapers, 14 Feb. 1761; Graeme, Smith, and Murray to Pitt, 27, 29 Oct. 1760, 6 Feb. 1761: SP 99/68. Smith, who had lost money on account of the war, had apparently hoped to use MWM as intermediary in selling his art collection to Bute. Graeme wrote to Smith about this on 26 Nov. 1760 (Vivian 1971: 56), but MWM says nothing of it.

[30] *CL* iii. 253–4, 256, 266, 269–70. She said combining against her would be like Sarah Marlborough's Spencer grandsons. Sarah may have popped into her mind because she too had left everything not covered by entail to a younger brother, John Spencer. He and his elder (later 3rd Duke of Marlborough), both massively in debt, had allied against Sarah, who called it 'necessary for me to dye to support' the heir (Harris 1991: 326–7, 302).

[31] Soon afterwards Lady Bute did try to transfer the money from her own hands to her husband's. This was acting like a dutiful wife, and as her mother might very likely have acted herself; but the trustees of her second son sued to prevent it, and the Lord Chancellor and House of Lords backed them on appeal (Eden 1818: ii. 87–107).

disavow 'those infamous libels my son has produce'd in my name'. She also
confided to him that Edward's 'Agents' had convinced Wortley that she,
Lady Mary, had 'sold' her daughter to Bute—that is, accepted some kind of
bribe to make sure he got the girl.[32]

By the end of February she had a copy of the will, forwarded by Mackenzie, and had at least begun reading it. Soon she felt equal to writing to
Edward. She began, 'Son, | I know not how to write to you and scarcely
what to say.' Yet in contrast to her recent incoherent notes to Lord and Lady
Bute, this one is hard-hitting and crystal clear. His conduct was now more
infamous than ever, she said: if he could not live on £1,600 a year he did not
deserve to live at all. She concluded, 'You have shorten'd your Father's days
and will perhaps have the Glory to break your mother's Heart—I will not
curse you—God give you a real not affected Repentance.' She also wrote
Anderson a letter designed to be shown to Edward, so that he might see how
she expressed, to a third person, her 'affliction and sorrow' both for his
father's death and for his dishonourable practices. (She particularly stressed
wrongdoing with Italian connections.)[33]

She tried to pull herself together and repair any emotional damage done.
She assured Lady Bute that she would do nothing against her family's
interest; she would not co-operate with Edward and she trusted them not to
do so either. Her heart was 'as clear to you as it has ever been', she wrote,
'God send us a happy meeting.' She later came a little closer to apology for
her unjust suspicions. 'I hope there never will be any misunderstanding
between us. I am persuaded my Late Letters (wrote with a confus'd Head
and trembling hand) may want some explanation. I hardly remember what
is in them. I am now (I thank God) more settled in my Mind.' She began corresponding with 'our' Lord Mountstuart in Turin. She even considered writing to Bute's lawyer, Alexander Wedderburn (a future Lord Chancellor).
Joseph Smith thought her a model of philosophic calm. It seems to have been
a help to realize that action was called for. She told Mackenzie, 'I entirely
acquiesce to the Will you wot off.' (Mackenzie understood the legal force of
this and copied her letter to Bute.) And she sent Lady Bute 'a sketch of
the Entail to serve in her unhappy Law suit'. Her sketch explained that
Wortley's family inheritance (that which could be subject to entail) was very
small, and that 'All the rest are acquire'd by him by true and lawfull
Purchase'—giving him the right to leave them to whom he pleased. She
adjured Lady Bute, 'Never make an infamous concession.' A little later

---

[32] She calls Graeme to witness this; but her state of mind was so fraught that she sounds less than wholly
credible (*CL* iii. 255).

[33] *CL* iii. 256, 257, 261–2.

she asked for 'some account' of the lucky heir, 'Mr. J[ames] W[ortley] S[tuart]'.[34]

Still, she was not the woman she had been. She could not recover her appetite or her sleep pattern. She was still obsessed with Murray's persecutions, and wished Lady Bute would call on Catherine Wright, to hear a disinterested, truthful account of 'the usage I have receiv'd from Murray and his Confederates'. It was April before she was able to read the will with a calm mind and full attention. She was then unpleasantly struck by Wortley's supposition that she had 'sumns of Money conceal'd', and told her daughter she had nothing whatever beyond her father's legacy. (Presumably the farming profits from her Dairy House had vanished; perhaps, too, the £50 joint-stock annuity won for her by Lady Oxford?)[35]

She told Mackenzie in March, 'I am still in the state of halfe-witted, that is to say, halfe out of my Wits.' He for his part was concerned and baffled at her conduct, which he duly kept Bute apprised of. 'She says nothing of what she intends to do, and . . . does not seem to know herself . . . she is so undetermin'd about everything she makes fifty resolutions every day, and changes them before night.' He supposed that Bute would wish her to stay in Venice, and therefore planned how he might induce her to do so. But he waited to hear for certain what Bute wanted: for his brother's sake (rather than for hers) he was even willing to get leave to go to Venice and see her.[36] While she feared losing her family's full attention, while she feared hostile spying, she really was being spied on by her concerned family.

In England meanwhile, lower guesses were made at the income that Wortley's landed estate would produce: perhaps £7,000, or a third of what had been said earlier.[37] It appeared after all that, although her 'thirds' would give Lady Mary more than the will had, they would not give *much* more. Nobody seemed to remember the document she had signed in 1731, waiving her right of dower.[38] And as time went on, though her first object was to support the Butes, she began to be concerned about her own interests too.

[34] *CL* iii. 255, 256, 259, 265, 266, 271; Wh MS M 513; BL Add. MS 36796. 14. James Archibald (who took the name of Wortley only when his mother died) somewhat recalled his uncle Edward. As a student at Edinburgh University he secretly got married and was sent abroad with a 'governor'; he became a drinker and gambler. His sister Louisa thought he became 'much gentler' after the death of a beloved small daughter in 1786.

[35] *CL* iii. 259, 272; see pp. 466, 493.

[36] *CL* iii. 260 (MWM to Mackenzie, 6 Mar. 1761), 266–7, 272; Mackenzie to Bute, 7 Mar. 14 Mar., Bute MSS.

[37] Symmer to Mitchell, 3 Feb. 1761, BL Add. MS 6839. 210.

[38] Back in 1717 John Thomlinson had noted that a woman was bound only by a settlement made before marriage; if it was made afterwards 'she may chuse whether she will stand to it, or have her thirds, which may be much more, if they have purchased or improv'd any Lands or ground' (BL Add. MS 22560. 61).

She worried about her legacy from her father, which Wortley had handled but had not mentioned. Although she thought the will 'mistaken in some points', she would acquiesce in every part 'that does not injure the just demand I have of what my Father left me. I do not beleive he intended I should be depriv'd of it.' In digging out the catalogue of her books and other paraphernalia, she recalled 'some other writings' which she had had. Perhaps this was a vague memory of the dower waiver. Lady Bute would surely not advise her, she wrote, 'to authen[t]icate the Will in such a manner as to deprive me of the Benefit, thô perhaps they are of little use, the Wittnesses being (it may be) all dead'.[39]

But to challenge her husband's will on her own account would have gone against Lady Mary's lifelong policy of submission. She told Lady Bute she would write to Edward on Wortley's orders: 'I never disobey'd him in my Life and will not now begin.' But if she could not control, she wanted to observe. At first she meant to 'set out for England as soon as the Weather and my Health permits'. Although short of cash, she thought she would leave Venice before the Alpine passes were open, traverse Italy (to see Mackenzie and his wife, and make the acquaintance of Mountstuart), and take the Mont Cenis crossing into France. But France was at war with Britain and getting a passport was not easy, as Lawrence Sterne was to discover. In the end she chose the Brenner Pass and the little states of Germany (many of them recently conquered by Britain's glorious ally Frederick the Great). Visiting the Steuarts thus replaced Turin as the hoped-for high spot of a daunting journey. The trip to Tübingen which Lady Mary had thought too much for her two years before would now be merely her first stage.[40]

Readying herself for the journey took time; by April she thought the realistic date for setting out would be September, before the passes closed. In late April Mackenzie told her he was coming to Venice as Ambassador Extraordinary. He had known for some time of this possibility, and wanted it partly because of his friends in Venice; but he kept it from Lady Mary in case she should leak it—and in case he needed it later as inducement to dissuade her from going home. Once she knew, she told Lady Bute she would stay long enough to 'put my little affairs here into his hands' before she set out. But she

[39] *CL* iii. 261, 263–4. She received only the interest on the legacy, which was to go to Lady Bute at her death. Lord Monson and Thomas Bennett had bound 'their Executors Administrators and Assignes' to see that this was done. Bennett was alive: Monson had been succeeded by his son.

[40] *CL* iii. 253, 259, 265, 273. She wrongly said that EWM's last surviving letter had told her to write to their son (16 Dec. 1760, H MS 74. 145, ?draft). She was glad Mountstuart was not bound for Venice and the corrupting Murray (*CL* iii. 266). MWM's drive to get home seems puzzling; but people expected it as soon as EWM died (e.g. Montagu 1906: ii. 230; *CL* iii. 259). She may have hoped to lodge with the Steuarts the MS of her Embassy Letters, which she later left in Rotterdam.

told Sir James Steuart she might not go to England after all, to exchange her 'solitude and reading' for 'crouds and bustle', to miss her lost old friends, and to feel her disconnection from present London society. For him she tapped her philosophic vein once more, writing of her delight in Bute's elevation, her anxiety as to whether it would last, her further fear that her anxiety itself might be all part of 'the worst effects of Age'—and, finally, her confidence that 'the privileges of friendship' permitted her to burden him with these fears.[41]

On the whole she remained convinced that Lady Bute needed her in England: needed her testimony to defeat Edward. She promised not to see him unless she was 'forc'd to it by some unavoidable Distress', and vowed she would not be 'brib'd, Flatter'd or bully'd'. She made her will in early April: consulted no lawyer, but wrote it out herself, carefully avoiding ambiguity, and rounded up a batch of grand tourists to witness it. She sealed it up and stamped the wax with her seal; then she put it away in a little ornamental cabinet which she knew Lady Bute remembered. If she were to die suddenly, she did not intend her daughter to be swindled. She thought her anxiety feeble, but there it was. She thought the Butes were too generous to Edward; but she did not cavil as he received Wortley's last purchase before his death (an estate of £8,000), a series of cash payments, and re-election for Bossiney.[42]

She was frequently diverted from her packing and organizing by further unwelcome news. Her sister Mar died in March, taking from her the dream of seeing her again and 'giveing her some comfort'. She heard again from Edward, 'utterly denying' that the caveat to Wortley's will was his, and ascribing it to a presumably fictional 'J. Jones'. Much that he said was incomprehensible to his mother. This time she did not answer, but handed the problem over to Anderson to deal with. Anderson promptly offered to travel to Venice to escort her home. She was touched, but she declined.[43] She had Dr Mora and Mari Anna. She also feared that her health might yet prevent her going at all (which sounds as if she *did* know she had breast cancer).

She was anxious about getting her things through customs and about where to live when she got to London. (She did not even know Wortley's address; on his instructions, she had sent letters care of his banker.) Then the Duke of Argyll (formerly Lord Ilay) died. This was a blow to Bute, who

---

[41] *CL* iii. 265, 268–70; Mackenzie, 7 Mar., Bute MSS; Dutens 1806: i. 234.

[42] *CL* iii.264–5, 266–7, 269, 271–2; Coutts and Co. MSS; Curling 1954: 159. This will seems not to survive.

[43] *CL* iii. 266, 274, 275–6, 278. Lady Mar had no money to leave. A sad little note asked that at her death her two servants might have a year's wages, and one of them her Bible and prayer book. 'I desire my Daughter may do this also if she is able and forgive the Trouble I have been to her. Frances Mar.' MWM said her sister 'was realy honest, and lov'd me' (Mar MS GD 124/3/95).

depended on his uncle's political management of Scotland. Feeling he had no one so able and trustworthy as his brother to take over this function, he countermanded Mackenzie's mission to Venice. Lady Mary, who had no idea why Mackenzie was recalled, was upset as well as disappointed. Having heard from Mackenzie himself, with warm anticipation, of his coming, she was humiliated before her Venetian friends when his recall was known first to Murray's intimates and last to her. After she knew he had been promoted, she tried once more to get him to travel home via Venice: she began 'Your Excellency is dead, but . . . I do not doubt it is only a removal to a better Life.' He was soon drawing a £2,000 pension for managing Scotland; by September he was a Privy Counsellor.[44]

Meanwhile Lady Mary suffered another hiatus in letters from Lady Bute. In late July she wrote to Sir James Steuart, 'The notable plan of our great politician is to make me surrender my little castle; I, with the true spirit of old Whiggism, resolve to keep my ground.' This sounds oddly from a woman who was trying to evacuate both her 'castles'. Murray may have been trying to dictate the date she vacated one house or the other. Or he may have tried to persuade her to sell the Venetian house (the only one she owned), whereas she left it a going concern, as if expecting to return. The wages of her gardener there continued till after she died.[45]

Most of her servants elected to go with her to England. But Fribourg wanted to go back to Avignon and join the Vice-Legate's Swiss Guard. Lady Mary arranged to pay him an annual pension of five guineas or ten *zecchini*. He reached Avignon in October, found shelter with his former master, Rigaud, and wrote to beg for the fifty ecus (about £11) which he found a Guard's place would cost.[46] He supposed Lady Mary would be already in England, but he underestimated the difficulties.

Lady Mary packed. She had, at least in her head, an efficient grand plan. She made notes—inside the cover of *Sir Charles Grandison*, volume ii, she wrote: 'Books No. 1 | my Bureau no. 4.[47] She meant to leave some things behind, fostering the dream of return. She left two boxes with Smith; but the obvious person to entrust valuables to was Chiara Michiel. She, however, was in bad health, and as a widow had no home of her own. (Her situation was not unlike Lady Mar's of old. Her son and daughter-in-law wanted to get her out of their house but not to hand over funds she was entitled to: 'mon bien'. Without that, her own mother said she could not afford to take her in.)

[44] Murdoch 1988: 117–46; *CL* iii. 272–4.
[45] *CL* iii. 277; Antonio Fachini to MWM, 9 July 1762, Michiel to MWM (H MS 77. 170–1, 198–9).
[46] Fribourg to MWM, 3 Nov. 1761; Rigaud to MWM, 30 Apr. 1762 (H MS 77. 231–4).
[47] At Sandon.

She had no storage space for a friend's needs. She suggested someone who did have space: her sister-in-law, the Murano nun who *may* have been Casanova's M. M. Lady Mary left in store at the convent a chest or coffer and three silver pieces in an envelope.

This last-minute operation was bungled in various ways. Lady Mary had not packed the chest herself, but left it to Mora and Mari Anna, and to Michiel's exasperation it came without either key or inventory, though Lady Mary had provided sealed instructions to the nuns. Nobody knew what was inside. When Michiel took the things to Murano, the nuns would not take them without an inventory, especially since the lock on the chest looked fragile. Luckily Lady Mary had given Michiel, as keepsake, a ring bearing the same Pierrepont arms with which her instructions were sealed. Michiel covered the hopeless lock with paper and sealed it impressively with this ring. Thus fortified, it was accepted by the nuns. Michiel's sister-in-law provided a receipt for Lady Mary, and they shut her small chest in one of their huge safes, where (said Michiel later) the air itself could barely penetrate.[48]

~~❧~~

Lady Mary was delayed once more by a severe 'fluxion' on her eyes in mid-August, when she had hoped to be on the road. Her last extant letter from Venice was to Lady Bute: 'a sort of Codicil to my Will'. She implied she had managed to dispense penalties as well as rewards. But it is hard to see what she meant, or even whether she was certain herself.[49] She must have left not long afterwards. France and Spain had just signed the 'Family Compact', whose secret clause set a date for Spain to enter the war against Britain; in London the Cabinet went into long-term crisis. In mid-September Bute lost his appeal against the Chancery decree confirming Wortley's will. Lady Mary was not at all sure she would be able to get through her journey, but 'said that when she was tired, she would winter at some place on the road'.[50] She left no account of this last and hardest travelling: whether it lifted her spirits once again.

Again her path was beset by war, though the theatre of struggle lay to the north, towards Hanover. Christopher Des Bouverie (also known as

[48] De Moser de Ailseek to MWM, 9 Apr. 1962, Michiel to MWM, 1 May, 10 July 1762, H MS 77. 172–3, 194–7.

[49] *CL* iii. 277–8. She recommended Arthur Villettes, the diplomat who had rescued her from the Turin customs twenty years before, and commended Mackenzie and Anderson. Perhaps she then intended legacies to them all

[50] Furneaux 1973: 186–8; Caldwell to Lord Newtown, 20 Sept. 1761 (Bagshawe MSS B 3/10/11. 595); Mann to Walpole, 31 Oct. 1761 (*Corr.* xxi. 545).

Hervey), following a similar route some weeks behind her, took just a month
from Trento in Tyrol to Rotterdam. Even he was unnerved by the looks of
soldiers in the inns; and he was arrested while crossing the Rhine. But he was
young, healthy, and male; for him the journey held no terrors.[51]

For Lady Mary it was different. Chiara Michiel, left behind to suffer
panics and palpitations on her account, was astonished at her courage. It was
Mari Anna who found herself unequal to 'the frights and fatigues' of the road.
Lady Mary, 'dragging [her] ragged remnant of life to England', remained
unbowed.[52] She probably knew before she set out that the Steuarts had left
Tübingen. Her journey would contain no convivial interlude with them. She
was soon, in all probability, the only member of her little party to speak a
word of the local language. They followed the valleys of the Brenta and the
Adige uphill through the Dolomites to a miserable inn at the Brenner Pass.
Then the River Inn led them downhill to Innsbruck, where a Hungarian passport had to be procured from surly officers of Maria Theresa. From
Augsburg Lady Mary sent a note after the Steuarts.[53] Having sought advice
on what route to take next—and having found some means or other to cope
with the Bavarian roads, which were too narrow to take a standard carriage—
she pressed on via Würtzburg to Frankfurt, where there was a French garrison. Next came the Rhine valley: past Cologne (now strongly garrisoned),
where in another lifetime Lady Mary had flirted with a young Jesuit.

By November, as her 'well-beloved cousin' Lord Granby retreated with
exhausted troops, then doggedly counter-attacked, she was close to home.
She had, she said, 'scrambled through more dangers' than Granby himself,
or even Frederick the Great.[54] The point she made for was Amsterdam,
where she looked in vain for the Steuarts. From there she went south to
Rotterdam, another place vividly remembered from her embassy journey. It
was a hard winter; but still she hoped to 'make one jump more' to see the
Steuarts at Antwerp; she thought Sir James, who had the gout, less fit to
travel than herself.[55]

As it turned out, she spent two months at Rotterdam, getting back in
touch with the world. She wrote to Lady Bute and the Steuarts. She began

[51] Christopher Hervey 1785: iii. 476–528.

[52] To MWM, 10, 19 Mar. 1762, H MS 78. 192–3, 198–9; *CL* iii. 279, 280.

[53] Hervey 1785: 476, 486–7, 491; MWM to Steuarts, 1 Oct. (*CL* iii. 279). She did not yet know they were
in Antwerp, close to the English Channel. Lady Pomfret had crossed the Brenner twenty years before
(Finch MS DG7/D5. 291).

[54] Hervey 1785: 496. Granby was prominent in the German campaign in early Nov. (Savory 1966:
350–3). On 15 Nov. Bute received an anonymous recommendation of Mr Samuel Johnson for a pension
(BL Add. MS 36796).

[55] *CL* iii. 280.

receiving patronage requests: from Sir James Caldwell for one, channelled through a Mrs Pratt.[56] It seemed a miracle that she had got so far; she felt no more certain of reaching England alive than she had felt at Venice. For a while Mari Anna was seriously ill, and when she recovered her mistress had still to struggle with a 'great snow, weak sight, trouble of mind and a feeble body'. She wanted to find a vessel that would bring her right up the Thames to the Port of London. She was afraid of going through customs. She was also afraid of meeting her daughter. Her mind dwelt on the lies her son had put about to divide them—and perhaps, though she did not say so, on the anger and bitterness with which they had parted. Her role as loving mother and doting grandmother had rested entirely on letters. Face-to-face contact must have been a daunting as well as an alluring prospect. She warned Lady Bute of 'the many weaknesses you will see in your most affectionate Mother'.

She was also aware that this return was expected to be final. Had she told her daughter about her cancer? 'I heartily wish you may close my Eyes,' she wrote from Rotterdam, 'but to say truth I would not have it happen immediately.' If she saw the end coming, she resisted it. She looked forward to seeing her granddaughters happily married.[57] She looked forward to seeing the house that Lady Bute had taken for her in Great George Street, south of Hanover Square and not far from her own in South Audley Street. But she hoped it was taken for one year only, so that if the air disagreed with her she might move. Meanwhile she wrote, 'God send us a happy meeting', and 'I think I know your Heart; I shall without reserve tell you what is in mine.'[58]

She had previously noted Rotterdam's Calvinist tradition; it now fitted her own fatalist mood. It had been a centre of the Huguenot *république des lettres*; it was a centre for inoculation; it had a flourishing British merchant colony.[59] But Lady Mary found 'neither amusement nor conversation', and feared that if she had to stay long she would be reduced to 'smoking and drinking like the natives'. But she must have thought somewhat better of the British Presbyterian minister, the Revd Benjamin Sowden, an evangelical pupil of the famous Philip Doddridge.[60] On 11 December 1761, about to set

[56] Mrs Pratt to Caldwell, 24 Nov. 1761 (Bagshawe MSS 3/10/2 no. 77).

[57] *CL* iii. 279–82. The eldest granddaughter, Lady Mary, had in Sept. 1761 married Sir James, later Lord, Lowther, Wortley's successor as 'the richest commoner in England'. Before the wedding Lady Bute dwelt on his love and solicitude; but he proved a tyrannical husband (Suffolk 1824: ii. 259; Brady 1984: 344 ff.). None of the others married till after MWM's death.

[58] *CL* iii. 281–2. In 1762 another Great George Street resident, John Wilkes, attacked Bute in the *North Briton* and parodied Pope in his pornographic *Essay on Woman*.

[59] Janssens 1981: 249; Klein 1984.

[60] *CL* iii. 284. Sowden, d. 1778, had held this post for years (Steven 1832: 229, 335, 342). He later reviewed for the *Monthly Review*, together with the Revd Archibald Maclaine, brother of the highwayman formerly linked with MWM's son—a probably meaningless coincidence (Nangle 1955: 64–5).

out for London, she pulled from her baggage the two MS volumes of her Embassy Letters, with Astell's preface and someone else's prefatory poem. She inscribed them with her 'will and design' that they should be 'dispos'd of as [Sowden] thinks proper'. Then she handed them over. Undoubtedly her wish (for which Walpole said she 'expressed great anxiety' on her deathbed) was that these at least, among all her works, should reach print; and after a chapter of accidents they did so.[61] It is just possible that she made other, similar deposits.[62]

The day after this transaction came 'a hard impenetrable frost'. No boats could sail; Lady Mary was suspended 'in the disagreeable state of uncertainty'. Hoping every day for a thaw, she never got round to travelling to Amsterdam. By Christmas the weather had gone grey and dull, but no longer freezing; she hoped to leave soon. She had met a young Jacobite on his way to London in hopes of an Act of Grace to quash old sentences of political exile, and she thought again of Sir James and Lady Frances. How could she wish them a merry Christmas while their state of uncertainty was even worse than her own? In every letter she reiterated her hopes that Lady Bute's influence would enable her to secure their return home.[63]

---

[61] *CL* i. xvii; Walpole, *Corr.* xxii. 84. MWM expected publication to benefit Sowden. But he told Lord Bute of the MS, surrendered it, and pocketed £200 for his trouble—not a bribe, his daughter later insisted (Sowden 1805: 254–6). He had, however, let two English travellers borrow it overnight; it was transcribed and published (see pp. 625–6).

[62] Some sisters named Wilkinson (known to Samuel Johnson) had letters of MWM 'consigned to their care' in Paris (n.d., Phillipina, Lady Knight, in Hill 1897: ii. 174–5). They *may* have had some link with Henry Wilkinson, Rotterdam merchant (Klein 1984: 125 and n. 28).

[63] *CL* iii. 283–6.

32

1762

❦

Back in London: 'inclement skies'[1]

AT New Year 1762 Lady Mary embarked on a trading vessel, but at Hellevoetsluis they met 'mountains' of ice and the captain turned back. He held out hopes that if the thaw lasted they could sail soon. Crowds of army officers were heading for England too, though peace negotiations to end the Seven Years' War were still only a gleam in the offing. They may have exacerbated Lady Mary's difficulties, for it was not until the British ambassador at the Hague allotted a packet boat for her personal use that she was able to sail. He did this on 15 January 1762. It was not till the 27th that she arrived in her Great George Street house; probably this means she stayed a few days first with Lady Bute in South Audley Street.[2]

After the choppy Channel, after the misty levels along the Thames, came the Pool of London crowded with masts of shipping. Then came the momentous meeting of mother and daughter, each marked by the changes of more than twenty years. Did Lady Mary look to her daughter like an old woman selling chestnuts? Did Lady Bute show the forbidding exterior which was noted in her later? Did she fear being dragged into quarrels of her mother's? (She had already been warned by a close friend, Lady Hervey, that *she* could never speak to Lady Mary again.)[3] In any case, it was an encounter to shake Lady Mary's emotional equanimity. She met also with Lord Bute, transformed from a sceptically regarded suitor to the most powerful man in the kingdom—and according to his youngest daughter, 'the most insufferable proser'.[4] She met the oft-imagined grandchildren, from the recent bride to the four-year-old Louisa. She met the servant who had been with Lady Bute since before her marriage. The only missing family member

[1] *E&P* 307.   [2] *CL* iii. 285, 286.   [3] See p. 336; Burney 1905: iii. 123; *E&P* 41.
[4] Stuart 1903: 254.

was Edward: he had left England shortly after his father died, never to return.[5] Once in her own house she turned to her pen as to a refuge, to tell Chiara Michiel that she was shattered—*accablée*, *excedée*—and to gesture longingly towards beloved Venice and her Horatian retirement.

She suffered from culture shock, as she never had beside the Bosphorus or lago d'Iseo. She complained of the babel of different languages around her,[6] though she must surely have known worse in other places. Perhaps the number of voices rather than of languages was the trouble. Lady Mary had known the limelight before, but nothing like this. She found herself a sight, a lion, in a society avid for nine days' wonders. By some she was remembered for herself—for her travels, for inoculation,[7] for her poems in print, and especially, of course, for Pope's vilification. But to many more she was known as a supporting actor in more recent dramas: the furore over Wortley's will, her granddaughter's splendid wedding, Lord Bute's precarious political eminence (Walpole said Lady Mary was receiving homage as Queen Mother), and especially the scandal linking Bute with the former Princess of Wales.

Bute had become Prime Minister while Lady Mary was on her way home. He had been better than anyone at finding common ground between the Pittite imperialists and the peace party. But he owed his office largely to indefatigable power-broking by Newcastle (on whom Lady Mary had commented half-disparagingly almost fifty years before). Once Bute was in place, he surprised Newcastle with his professionalism: he saw to business himself instead of delegating it, and was at his office at nine each morning.

Britain and Spain had gone to war as Lady Mary was on the last leg of her journey. In April Bute was to face a crisis in Cabinet about financing the war.[8] But every day he faced a 'tidal wave of media hostility'. The London press had changed little since Robert Walpole's day; it was still virulent in words and even more so in cartoons. The climate of opinion, however, had changed beyond recognition. The media now saw marriage as sacrosanct: sexual infringements were met less with open salacious enjoyment, than with horrified condemnation. (It was about now that Restoration plays ceased to be acceptable in the theatre.) By 1762, 400 caricatures had guyed Bute as the

---

[5] MWM 1861: i. 55. The three middle grandsons were at Winchester (Baker 1931: 147). EWM junior left London for Venice (taking his daughter Mary with him) more or less as MWM left Venice for London. He perhaps hoped her Venetian friends would provide some pickings. It was said he had tried to blackmail the Butes into handing over half EWM's fortune, by threats 'to circulate a scurrilous story about his mother, involving his own legitimacy . . . He even forged his mother's signature to some document to give credence' to this (Curling 1954: 155, 158).

[6] *CL* iii. 286.   [7] Her name had been bandied about during the 1750s inoculation wave (see p. 222).

[8] *CL* i. 216–17; Schweizer 1988a: 6, 41–55; Furneaux 1973: 191; Schweizer 1992: 175–85.

lover of Augusta the Queen Mother.[9] This was a story with innumerable historical analogues, a gift to political satirists. The relationship of these two people had been in a sense illicit ever since Bute had moved in on the education of Prince George against the wishes of the old king.[10] Whatever she thought of Bute's classic good looks, the beleaguered Princess Augusta had relied on him for support. Since then, his Scottish background and court career, contrasted with the parliamentary charisma of Pitt, had made him the people's bugbear; and the more he was publicly hated the more he tried to conceal his personal, domestic contact with the royal family. That there was almost certainly no sexual relationship meant little; the world believed there was. Even Walpole, who respected Lady Bute as much as he despised her mother, supposed her husband had climbed to power by making the princess his mistress.

Lady Bute, then, was living as closely and painfully with scandal as her mother had done in the 1730s. That mother's return—as if from the dead, as if directly from the more raffish society of Queen Anne or even of the Restoration—must have presented itself as a public and political problem, no matter what it meant to her in emotional terms. (Her husband, we remember, had tried to prevent it happening.) It was a situation fraught with turbulence, with intense private feelings and delicate social dilemmas. Lady Mary probably found it harder than she had anticipated to tell her heart without reserve. There was an edge to her hyperbole as she told Michiel that a knock at her door heralded the arrival of her daughter with five or six *dozen* 'satellites' who had to be received and entertained.[11]

By Venetian standards Lady Mary's house was cramped and dark. She called it 'harpsichord-shaped', and told a visitor 'I am most handsomely lodged . . . I have two very decent closets and a cupboard on each floor.' It was inadequate to the influx of people—for which Walpole was at first quite ready to blame his hostess: 'she receives all the world . . . and crams them into this kennel.'[12] Early among her visitors were others she had known abroad: Mackenzie (though he was harassed and hag-ridden with political management), Hervey's son Bristol, and Sir James Caldwell (who claimed she had promised him that 'there was nothing in her power, that she would not do, for him, or for anybody, that belong'd to him'). Elizabeth Montagu came,

---

[9] Furneaux 1973: 191; Bullion 1991; O'Gorman 1988; Schweizer 1988*b*: 86.

[10] Bullion 1991: 245–8.

[11] *CL* iii. 286; McKelvey 1973: 35. One of the satellites was probably Walpole, who saw MWM that day (*Corr.* xxii. 3). Lady Bute may have chosen a house for MWM too far off to witness the anti-Bute crowds who often mobbed her own house and broke her windows (Stuart Wortley [1948]: 99).

[12] *E&P* 53–4; *Corr.* xxii. 4.

out of curiosity: she hardly knew Lady Mary, but had, with her husband, tried to forward young Edward's career. She thought her scarcely aged since 1739, having 'more than the vivacity of fifteen; and a memory, which perhaps is unique'. Others concurred about Lady Mary's lively and racy talk, her youthfully vigorous mind, and her originality: she 'neither thinks, speaks, acts, or dresses, like any body else'. Her exotic household was 'made of all nations, and when you get into her drawing-room you imagine you are in the first story of the Tower of Babel. An Hungarian servant takes your name at the door; he gives it to an Italian, who delivers it to a Frenchman; the Frenchman to a Swiss, and the Swiss to a Polander.'[13]

Few of Lady Mary's old friends were alive to greet her; but there was an endless flow of new friends, and old friends' children (and grandchildren), and the merely curious, who annoyed her. Her most socially prominent nephew and niece (the Duke of Kingston and the Duchess of Bedford, whose husband was a leader of the peace party) extended invitations. At the duchess's 'Routte', it even seemed to a twenty-year-old grandson of sister Mar that 'a Beauty and Wit of the two last preceeding Ages had arisen from The Dead', eclipsing modern wits and beauties.[14] It would be nice to know what Lady Mary thought of Kingston's new and sumptuous interior decor, in a fantasy oriental style chosen by Elizabeth Chudleigh. Once the edge of Walpole's hostility was blunted he would surely have brought to visit her his sister, Maria Skerrett's daughter (now Lady Mary Churchill), to whom he was closer than to many other members of his family. One hopes that Wilhelmina Tichborne came, as a valued friend in her own right as well as a member of the Molesworth clan. Apparently Sir Joshua Reynolds came.

Though Lady Mary wrote to Michiel of the horrors of receiving ten thousand visitors, she went out visiting herself. She was full of curiosity about the novelties which London presented. Within a few weeks of arriving she made a lengthy call on Lady Pomfret's second daughter (now Lady Charlotte Finch). Lady Charlotte was a diarist like her mother: she recorded, 'she . . . was Vastly entertaining, very oddly dressed, but retains a great deal of beauty especially in her eyes'.[15]

Walpole actually softened towards her. Before her arrival he was implacable, suggesting that she must be made to 'perform quarantine for her own dirt'. After his first call he sent Mann a virtuoso description of her appearance and behaviour quite in his old style, presenting her as a kind of flirtatious crone, who had reacted to his flattery by boxing his ears. Her

[13] Mrs Pratt to Caldwell, 24 Nov. 1761 (Bagshawe MS 3/10/2 no. 77); Doran 1873; 129–30.
[14] John Francis Erskine of Mar to Richard Phillips, publisher [1804], Mar MS GD/124/15/1716/5.
[15] _CL_ iii. 287; see pp. 620–1; Finch 1901: i. 311).

oddity of dress was of course an issue once again. As she had made herself conspicuous in the Turkish style in the 1720s and 1730s, so now she clung to Venetian manners which were too relaxed for London. Walpole shared a joke with a passing duchess that 'she has left *all* her clothes in Venice'. Before meeting Dr Mora he guessed that he would be some kind of toy-boy. He pitied Lady Bute. To George Montagu he summarized: 'I think her avarice, her dirt, and her vivacity are all increased.'[16] By late March his attitude was shifting. He had seen her at a great party at the Duchess of Bedford's, 'dressed in yellow velvet and sables, with a decent laced head and a black hood, almost like a veil, over her face. She is much more discreet than I expected, and meddles with nothing.' He still found something to criticize: 'she is woefully tedious in her narrations.' In July, when he knew she was dying of cancer, he was finally able to praise her fortitude.[17]

For the moment Lady Mary was far from giving up. The plea of her old servant Fribourg reached her from Avignon; she sent the money to set him up in an assured job. In reply came his promise of perpetual prayers for her, and a letter from Rigaud the lawyer deferentially recalling her former brilliance in both the world of fashion and the 'république des letters'.[18] Her second letter to Venice voiced a faint hope of mustering strength to return and take refuge in Michiel's house. Michiel (who had been ill, and was virtually homeless) took this seriously. For one thing, the gondolier Vulcan was spreading rumours that Lady Mary would soon be back. Michiel opposed this plan. Though she recognized that in the end Lady Mary would do as she wished, she enlisted Mora's aid to dissuade her. Soon Lady Mary wrote about forwarding the things she had left at Murano. She had evidently accepted London as her fate, and Michiel must have breathed a sigh of relief. Their friendship was precious to both women during this difficult year. Michiel repeatedly said she felt for Lady Mary like a daughter. She remained angelically patient (as Lady Mary herself recognized) throughout confusions over the baggage at Murano; and she wrote wonderfully warm and supportive letters, lightened with jokes about Mackenzie. In return Lady Mary praised her style and sympathized with her family troubles.

The things stored at Murano caused a lot of bother. The nuns, or rather the abbess, felt they had been clearly instructed not to release the chest or the envelope of silver pieces without two documents: the receipt which Michiel's sister-in-law had given Lady Mary, and explicit instructions under her Pierrepont seal. A letter in French to Michiel was no help: they could not

16 8 Oct. 1761, 29 Jan., 2 Feb. 1762: *Corr.* xxi. 540; xxii. 3, 4; x. 5.
17 To Mann, 29 Jan., 22 Mar., 31 July, to G. Montagu, 28 July 1762, *Corr.* xxii. 17, 56; x. 36.
18 30 Apr. 1762, H MS 77. 233–4.

read it. Nor did Michiel want to pass the things onwards for shipping without an inventory; she feared pilfering.[19] Lady Mary probably had no inventory and had very likely lost the receipt. Reading between the lines of her next letters, of 18 May and 11 June, Michiel saw clearly that she was ill and unhappy. She said no more to her of business, but addressed a screed to Mora on that topic (with hopes for Lady Mary's speedy recovery) and filled her letter to her friend with nothing but love and concern.[20]

Meanwhile Lady Mary did her best to keep the reins of her life in her own hands. She 'concealed' her cancer. She must have decided to steer clear of surgery (perhaps remembering Astell) and of unconventional prescriptions like Richard Guy's cauterizing. All other treatments (ointments and opiates) were merely palliative.[21] She sent the new Lord Monson a business like letter about the rate of interest on her father's legacy (which ought to have been higher in current conditions), and after some delay Monson acted on her instructions. She tried to find a suitable mode of despatch for her goods from Venice. She entertained literary admirers. One John Lane effusively praised 'With toilsome steps'), sent a rejoinder, stirred in flattery of Lord Bute, and copied an up-to-the-minute epigram into the album she had been filling for fifty years. She kept reminding Lady Bute about Sir James Steuart's pardon.[22]

Her most persistent client was Sir James Caldwell. He had recently been seeking an Irish peerage (one of those which Lady Mary had described as sold like second-hand clothes) on grounds of service to the government: he had raised a regiment of horse at his own expense, to serve either in the war or against seditious Irish Catholics. He was visiting London when his 'old friend' Lady Mary arrived. He had the sense to devote his first visit to literary topics, and found her 'extramly well and in good Spirits'. Knowing 'she writes a great deal and has many Excellent performances by her', he pressed her to publish something. But his *idée fixe* was not forgotten. Lady Mary seemed at least as good a bet for an Irish peerage as any of the clutch of peers he had already thought of.[23]

---

[19] *CL* iii. 287, 289, 291–4. Michiel, still in her son's house, could only find time to write late at night, in bed (10 Mar., 19 Mar., 1 May, H MS 77. 192–3, 196–8). MWM's family knew that had she lived she would probably 'have gone abroad again' (*E&P* 53).

[20] *CL* iii. 292–4; Michiel to MWM and to Mora, 10 July 1762, H MS 77. 190–1, 194–5. One Antonio Fachini made payments for her in Venice, including the gardener (H MS 77. 170–1).

[21] Richard Guy, *An Essay on Scirrhous tumours, and cancers,* 1759, *Practical Observations on Cancers and Disorders of the Breasts,* [1762]; Bloom, Richardson, and Harries 1962: 215. In Astell's day prescriptions included the 'chestnuts' from a horse's foreleg boiled in wine, or an ointment of mutton suet, beeswax, and flax-seed (Perry 1986: 319).

[22] Walpole, *Corr.* xxii. 56; Lane to MWM, 1 June, H MS 77. 179–80; H MS 255. 81; *CL* iii. 290–1.

[23] In 1761 her husband's cousin George Montagu Dunk, Lord Halifax, took over as Lord Lieutenant from her nephew-by-marriage the Duke of Bedford.

Caldwell's accounts of Lady Mary in 1746 give no high idea of his accuracy, even where his own interest was not involved. And his account of his transactions with her in 1762 is unsupported by other witnesses (though Mrs Pratt had assured him of Lady Mary's goodwill in November 1761). In trying later to justify his conduct to Lady Bute, he said that Lady Mary had herself taken the initiative by mentioning him warmly to her, and had *then* asked him if he had anything in particular to solicit. He confided his desire for a peerage; she promised to take upon herself the *whole* business of procuring it, but not so soon after her reunion with her daughter. Caldwell was to leave it all to her, keep it secret, and go back to Ireland; after a few months he could return with some papers in support of his claim.

He had, he said, carried out her instructions to the letter. On his second visit to London that year he handed her the papers, and delicately mentioned that 'transactions of this Kind frequently depend for dispatch upon those who can have no inducement to exert themselves but a pecuniary gratuity'. Someone, in short, might have to be bribed. Caldwell said this did not bother Lady Mary: she declared herself willing to lay out money as needed and be reimbursed later. He could not allow this, and pressed her to take a thousand guineas—which he happened to have 'lying by me'—to meet any necessary expenditure. She 'at length though with some reluctance consented' to this, saying she would not do the same for anyone else. Again she advised him to go back to Ireland and wait: there were 'civil commotions' in which he could prove his zeal for the government in action against 'those White-Boys'. She arranged a kind of cipher for summoning him at a moment's notice without alerting post-office spies. There things rested some time.[24]

In May 1762—a cold May—Lady Mary was ill, but only with some germ which was laying low everyone in London. Mora had it; Mari Anna had it even worse; Lady Mary's nephew Kingston had to cancel a grand dinner because he had not enough servants on their feet to wait on the guests. In her last surviving letter to Michiel, some weeks later, Lady Mary complained of heaviness of spirit. She blamed the English climate, and said nothing of cancer; but she ended with a word she had not been using lately: Adieu.[25]

According to Walpole, her tumour 'burst' in late May. This meant that open ulcers appeared. The news was out—though, according to Elizabeth

[24] Bagshawe MSS B 3/10/11, 3/22/1–28, 3/6/198, 3/16/127. The last is a draft of a long letter to Lady Bute after MWM's death.

[25] 11 June 1762, *CL* iii. 294. Michiel's reply ends, 'Adieu ma respectée, et respectable Dame. Adieu. Adieu' (10 July, H MS 77. 190–1).

Montagu, Lady Mary still *looked* remarkably well in June. She was under the care of a man named Middleton, who had 'the highest obligations' to Lord and Lady Bute: probably the king's Principal Surgeon, David Middleton. Her door-knocker kept on announcing visitors: but now many of them were thinking in terms of bidding farewell. Among these was one she had never met: a young army officer, James Steuart, son of her still-exiled friends. Lady Mary responded *en grande dame*: she had the room cleared of Lord and Lady Bute and all her other visitors. 'My dear young friend has come to see me before I die, and I wish to be alone with him.' If she had been healthy, Walpole would have made a smutty joke of this; but Walpole wrote to Mann, 'there are no hopes of her. She behaves with great fortitude, and says she has lived long enough.'[26]

By then she had made her will. She wrote it out twice over in her own hand, dating it 'this 23rd of June 1762'. The literary John Lane was one of her witnesses. It was a simple will, as far as possible from the legal repetitions and circumlocutions of Wortley's. After a few legacies, her 'dear daughter Mary Countess of Bute' was to have 'whatever I am possess'd of'. Edward was to have 'one Guinea, his Father having amply provided for him'. (His brother-in-law was providing for him too: dollops of cash amounting to almost £5,000 over the four years from Edward's leaving England.) Lady Mary bequeathed few legacies. To the Duchess of Portland she left the ring she had bought or had made with her own legacy from the duchess's mother, Lady Oxford: 'a white brilliant diamond Ring with this motto enamell'd: Maria Henrietta'. To Chiara Michiel she left her choice among her other rings. To Mackenzie she left a 'large Gold Octogon Snuff Box'. To Dr Mora she left a legacy of £500: a sum which clearly marked him as a professional rather than a servant. To each of her servants she left a year's wages (around £8 for men and £4 for women), and to the foreigners among them the expenses to take them home 'to their own Country'. Mari Anna got a year's wages (perhaps about £25), her travelling expenses home, ten guineas more, and 'all my wearing Apparel either made or not made and all my Linnen either for the Bed, Table, or my person'.[27]

As well as the valuable objects named in the will, it seems she bestowed, less officially, some of the 'baubles' which she had so enjoyed collecting. In 1953 Christie's of London sold a butterfly ring, engraved: 'MARY WORTLEY

---

[26] Walpole to Mann, 31 July 1762, *Corr.* xxii. 56; Bloom, Richardson, and Harries 1962: 219; Elizabeth Montagu 1923: i. 35; Bagshawe MS 3/16/127; MWM 1818: v. As well as young James Steuart, MWM probably received about now his cousin Anne Durham: daughter of Sir James's writer sister, Margaret Calderwood (Chamley 1965: 31).

[27] A housekeeper in a great house might get £28 (Burnett 1969: 144).

MONTAGU TO JOSHUA REYNOLDS SIC TRANSIT GLORIA MUNDI 1762'. It sounds an enchanting piece: 'the wings studded with diamonds and fancy-cut rubies, the body with emeralds, the hoop engraved and chased with poppy leaves, buds and flowers, the petals set with amethysts, quartz, topaz' and a diamond for the stamen. But it would not have been worth very much. Lady Mary's link with Reynolds comes as a surprise. She *might* have met him very briefly in Brescia in 1752; she had little enough time to meet him in London in 1762. But the evidence of the inscription seems incontrovertible.[28]

Her suffering was eased by opium or hemlock. Elizabeth Montagu, who called her cancer 'the most virulent . . . I ever heard of', said she was 'very placid and easy tho' she sees her end approach'. About a week after making her will, she wrote her last known letter: to Lady Frances Steuart. 'Dear Madam, I have been ill a long time, and am now so bad I am little capable of writing, but I would not pass in your opinion as either stupid or ungrateful. My heart is always warm in your service . . .' As a leave-taking it has a quiet dignity and expressiveness that matches Hervey's to her.[29]

※

But she was not to die without further scandal: murky transactions such as society would not approve. At 'the latter end of July' (as Lord Bute laboured on a political pamphlet and received Johnson's thanks for his first pension payment), a letter arrived at Castle Caldwell from Caldwell's sister-in-law in England, which casually mentioned that 'Lady Mary was given over by her physicians.' Caldwell thought of his peerage; he thought of his guineas; he 'took post horses that moment and on the fourth day arrived in London'. By a stroke of luck he was a friend of Lady Mary's doctor, to whom he applied for a meeting, insisting 'that I had the honour to be greatly esteemed by Lady Mary'. Middleton said she was very weak, but promised to 'do all in his power to procure me an Interview'. Lady Mary, said Caldwell, let him know 'that she had neither forgott nor neglected my affair'; when she could see anybody she would see him, and hoped she might feel well enough within a few days.

Caldwell had set out 'without leave from the Government' and was 'obleged to post back again that very day'. First he confided the whole affair

---

[28] Scarisbrick 1994: 295; sale 20 May 1953; further information from Diana Scarisbrick and Jeremy Rex-Parkes.

[29] *CL* iii. 294–6; Elizabeth Montagu 1923: i. 25, 35–6. Fearon, the surgeon who revolutionized mastectomy (see p. 370 n. 6), advised alternating liberal doses of opium with cicuta (1784: 74); Richard Guy warned against hemlock ([1762]: e.g. 48–9). The Steuarts' son said MWM's efforts were a factor in his father's pardon, granted early the next year (Steuart 1805: vi. 373).

to Middleton; Middleton pondered the trust reposed in him. His opinion of Lady Mary's 'principal Domesticks' was low. When she died, which might happen any day, he feared they would 'unlawfully get possession of' Caldwell's money. He therefore took it upon himself to stop the payment of the bank-bill and to arrange for anyone presenting it to be arrested.

Caldwell, hearing this in Ireland, knew it was a dreadful mistake. Even losing a thousand guineas would not be so bad as for the 'circumstances of my transaction with Lady Mary' to become known. (He presented this as concern for her reputation rather than his.) He wrote a countermanding order to the bank, sending it 'by Express to Dublin in order to overtake the Packet, with directions to a Friend there, if the Packet should be sailed from thence to hire a Vessel to take them to Holy head, and there to take out a Post Office order for an Express to proceed with them directly to London'.[30]

❧

While this frenetic activity unrolled on both sides of the Irish Channel, it was very quiet in the Great George Street house. In late July Elizabeth Montagu said Lady Mary had rallied; her correspondent replied that it could not be for long.[31] The visitors—those who cared, as well as those who had something to gain or lose—dropped away. No one recorded her loss of appetite, her loss of weight, her pain. No one recorded the nursing care of her servants, of Lady Bute, of (perhaps) her elder granddaughters. No one recorded her thoughts, or caught her last words.[32]

Her last days were haunted, just like her adolescence, by the desire to be an author. Lady Louisa Stuart implied that when she perceived the end was near she presented her 'voluminous' journal to Lady Bute. But Lady Louisa did not *say* this in so many words: only that the journal then came into Lady Bute's hands. John Erskine of Mar (the great-nephew who had seen Lady Mary at a ball and thought her beautiful) believed that on her deathbed she bestowed 'the Memoires of her own not very common life' on the shady character Philip Thicknesse, on his promise to publish them unabridged within a year of her death. This may be contaminated by the story of the volumes left with Sowden, which she worried about at the end. The gift to Thicknesse cannot be fact, for when he *did* try to blackmail Bute with a threat to publish some of her letters (which he said were 'uncommonly

---

[30] Bagshawe MS 3/16/127. Lady Falmouth had been denied a court job, years before, for blatantly pressing a handfull of bank-bills on Charlotte Clayton (Sundon letters 41, Forster Collection).

[31] Lord Bath (formerly William Pulteney), 30 July (Elizabeth Montagu 1923: i. 29–30).

[32] Iris Barry imagines her saying *to herself* 'it has all been very interesting' (1928: 328); this has entered last-word lore as actually spoken.

severe' about Wortley), he claimed to have had them from a Mrs Forrester, a long-time correspondent of Lady Mary.[33]

Might these 'Memoires' have been Lady Mary's diaries? or the 'History of [her] own Time' which she had said she burned? Erskine of Mar does not inspire confidence; nor does his story. Thicknesse mentioned letters and poems, not memoirs, and contradicted Erskine's version of the way he acquired them.[34] But Erskine's story is enough to cast a faint shadow over the transmission of the diary. Maternal bequest, or blackmail attempt? Did people tiptoe about, arranging, disposing, while Lady Mary still lived? Did Lady Bute receive the diary in circumstances of embarrassment and shame? The rumour-mill which had gripped Lady Mary in life did not relinquish her in death. The event behind the rumours is typically enigmatic. Perhaps Lady Mary the secret writer communicated her private text for her daughter's eyes alone; perhaps Montagu the author made a last-ditch effort to secure a public voice. Or perhaps she lay passive while chance and fate played around her bed.

By whatever means, Lady Bute received the diary. There it was, a record going back to Lady Mary's marriage, whose fiftieth anniversary was just days away. Half a century of sharp-eyed observation and doubtless satiric comment lay compacted in those travel-stained volumes. Lady Bute—the only reader, it seems, that most of it ever had—had once been the satiric 'Sylvia'. She treasured her mother's journal (while keeping it under lock and key like a guilty secret) for many private rereadings. She eventually allowed her youngest, unmarried daughter the privilege of reading it too: but only the most safely distant volumes (ending in 1718), and with copying or note-taking expressly prohibited.[35]

Lady Mary had been face to face with death before: at other people's deathbeds, in storms at sea, in various painful illnesses, even in fleeting thoughts of suicide. This time she had long hours for thinking, and no doubt she thought of the past. It held many of her words, many speaking selves, that *might* now have come back to haunt her. There was the girl scaring herself with questions: 'What's death, that at the name Wee are Dismay'd, | Why shrinks my soul, and why am I affraid? | Trembling wee stand, and when wee plunge wee fear, | And goe to unknown worlds wee know not where.' There were moods of serene belief: 'unconcern'd my Future Fate

---

[33] Erskine of Mar to Phillips [1804], Mar MS GD/124/15/1716/5; Grundy 1980. In 1795 the *GM* printed a supposed letter from MWM in Avignon to a Mrs Forster, which *might* be genuine (MWM 1861: ii. 123–4).
[34] Thicknesse 1766. [35] *E&P* 18–19, 55.

I trust; | To that sole Being, Mercifull and Just.' There were moments of despair: 'Whence this misterious bearing to exist, | When every Joy is lost, and every Hope dismist?' There were moments of decision: 'I leave my friends weeping my loss, and boldly take the leap for another world.' There were moments of recognition that wisdom is 'No sooner born, than the poor Planter dyes.'[36] She died on 21 August 1762.

❦

There was no ceremonial. Lady Bute had her mother buried the day after she died, in the vault of Grosvenor Chapel, South Audley Street.[37] Absence of fuss was best, both for a lady of letters and for a Prime Minister's mother-in-law, in a climate that mixed new female decorums with old appetite for scandal. It seems that Mora and Mari Anna again proved honester than Britons would give them credit for, for Caldwell's bank-bill remained in place. Lady Bute found it, and had to engage in damage limitation with Caldwell.[38] No matter how she grieved, she must have been giving the largest share of her attention to her husband's career. His correspondence this month teemed with anxious voices expatiating on elections, on hostile rumbling from the City of London, and on the army. Lady Mary's death coincided with those of nearly six thousand British troops (mostly not in battle but of disease) expended to capture Havana.[39]

The only obituary worthy of the name came from Walpole: 'She had parts, and had seen much.' But curiosity for her posthumous works, which had been at the forefront of Hervey's mind when he thought she might die, came second with Walpole to curiosity about her will. (He was sorry it did not reveal how much she had left.)[40] Only after that did he wonder about the fate of her 'twenty-one large volumes in prose and verse in manuscript'. He expected them, in any case, to amount to nothing more than 'an olio of lies and scandal'. Nothing in Lady Bute's hands, he knew full well, would 'see the light in haste'. But he also knew of the manuscript left at Rotterdam. 'Her family are in terrors', he reported, before Sowden agreed to give up the

---

[36] Grundy 1971: 292; *E&P* 259, 291, 307; *CL* ii. 140 (translation adapted). It was asserted that she wrote, 'towards the latter end of her life', a verse address to Plato which maintains 'That Virtue opens Heaven, to Mortal Race, | Life's but a trial,—Death a change of place'. This appeared in an obscure, proto-feminist Dublin periodical, *The Parlour Window*—titled from the place where Montaigne feared his work might end up (Eustace 1795: no. 3, 83).

[37] Register Book of Burials, St George's, Hanover Square (the parish containing the Chapel), 13. She was later joined there by her erstwhile neighbour John Wilkes.

[38] Caldwell to Lady Bute (draft written for him by Dr John Hawkesworth), Bagshawe MS 3/16/127; Windham 1930: 83 (saying Caldwell used a bill written by a third party); Abbott 1982: 128. Caldwell never got his peerage.

[39] BL Add. MS 36796; Furneaux 1973: 197.   [40] Walpole, *Corr.* xxii. 72; Ilchester 1950: 213–14.

volumes. Although Walpole had read a good deal of Montagu's poetry, and although he credited her with wit, ingenuity, and even some delicacy, he still expected her prose to be something in the line of courtesan memoirs.[41]

~⋙⋘~

Her various circles provided matter for a dozen epilogues. Sir James Steuart was pardoned, published, and achieved a degree of fame. Michiel lived with her mother but continued to regret the days of living with her husband, or even with her son. Lord Bute chose to spend more time with his family. There was probably nothing in Horace Walpole's story that Bute honoured his mother-in-law by converting an existing statue into that of a coroneted muse.[42]

Lady Bute kept the love and respect of all her children, though several of them turned out badly. They mostly married well, however, spreading Lady Mary's genes widely among the nobility. Lady Louisa Stuart, the youngest daughter who never married, left many writings which are a joy to read, and despite her lifelong horror of print she put immense care and effort into the worthy publishing of her grandmother's works. Edward Wortley Montagu the younger became a devout and stringently misogynist Muslim. When he heard a report (false, as it turned out) of his legal wife's death, he tried to cut his nephews out by advertising for a pregnant woman to marry. Soon afterwards he himself died, 'repeating to his son, Fortunatus, in Arabic: "Elhamdulillah—May God be praised." '[43] Fortunatus, formerly Massoud (Lady Mary's putative black grandchild), lived a short, unfortunate life.[44]

But the only epilogue of consequence is that which concerns Montagu's works.[45] On 7 May 1763 Becket and De Hondt printed *Letters of the Right Honourable Lady M—y W—y M—e, written during her travels in Europe, Asia, and Africa, to persons of distinction, men of letters, &c., in different parts*

---

[41] Walpole, *Corr*. xxii. 72, 84–6, 138–41; Ilchester 1950: 213–14. The rumoured total of her volumes fluctuated wildly. Walpole adds a story of her giving away another 17, for publication, two days before she died, and of the Butes buying them back. Today 15 vols. are known (12 in the Harrowby MSS Trust, one at the University of Sydney, one in the New York Public Library, one among the Bute MSS). Hervey's death had aroused similar rumour (Lady Burlington, 3 Sept. 1743, Chatsworth MSS).

[42] This probably mangled a story about the column Bute set up (now at Mount Stuart) to record his undying devotion to the recently deceased Princess Augusta (*Corr*. xxxii. 91 and n. 29). MWM's monument in Lichfield Cathedral (see p. 222) is fact.

[43] *The Weekly Magazine, or Edinburgh Amusement*, 1776: 32: 341–2; biographical note in Montagu-Lewis Collection, Stanford University Library.

[44] Described as 'lively, quick, inclined to be expansive', he may or may not have been Edward's biological son. He d. in England, 1787, aged 25. MWM may have Italian descendants. Jane Waldie met one in Rome: an otherwise unrecorded daughter of Edward, since Mary had become a nun (Curling 1954: 235, 237; Waldie 1820: iii. 256).

[45] See Grundy 1998.

of Europe. Which contain, among other curious relations, accounts of the policy and manners of the Turks, drawn from sources that have been inaccessible to other travellers. They were a hit, a talking-point, a spur to orientalist debate about Turkey and medical debate about inoculation.[46] There was newspaper excerpting and a rapid 'second edition'. Walpole found the letters entertaining, with 'certain marks of originallity', but not up to Lady Mary's other works (presumably, that is, her poems). What he wanted from her was not curious relations or policy, but 'personal history'. He took it for granted that the Embassy Letters would be unreliable, that she 'had little partiality' for truth.[47] Edward Wortley Montagu was 'very impatient to see' his mother's letters, and wrote for them from Rosetta in Egypt, where he was 'studying the Arab Root and Branch'.[48] Voltaire reviewed them for the *Gazette littéraire*, expanding the praise he had already distilled in a letter. They were all the rage, though some doubted that Lady Mary had really written them.[49]

Meanwhile Thicknesse offered to Bute, for publication, the letters and poems which he said Lady Mary had left with Mrs Forrester. He must have known Bute would not co-operate: if he *had* given any undertaking to Lady Mary (as Erskine of Mar believed) he was breaking it. Erskine said Thicknesse sold the manuscripts for £2,700 and the promise of 'Preferment'. Thicknesse, in a pamphlet calculated to embarrass the Butes, said he got nothing.[50]

The later publishing story is one of ironies and inaccuracies. Shortly before her own death, Lady Bute had Lady Mary's diary burnt, which she said the diarist must have 'forgotten or neglected' to do, since to publish it would be exposing her spontaneous, even involuntary feelings. That is, much as she admired the diary, she chose to see her mother as a non-author: expressing, not deliberately composing. *Her* daughter, Lady Louisa, entreated Lady Bute to preserve the diary, but once her mother was facing death she would have been willing to let it go, 'had it [been] the finest work in the world'. That is, she too subordinated literary value to personal feelings.[51]

The 1763 *Letters* were closely followed by a stylish piracy, allegedly

---

[46] Woodville 1796: i. 72–5.   [47] To Mann, 10 May 1763 (*Corr.* xx. 141 and n.).

[48] Letter written for him by Nathaniel Davison, Alexandria, 5 Apr. 1764 (Beattie Collection, Swiss Cottage, B 826.51 W.B. 86).

[49] e.g. *Annual Register*, 1763: 290–307, probably by Burke. Voltaire lauds MWM's knowledge (*science*), taste, and style: she is an antidote to prejudice; she is for all nations (*Gazette*, 4 Apr. 1764; to the comte and comtesse d'Argental, 21 Sept. 1763, 1963–93: vii. 378).

[50] Erskine's source was his younger brother, whom Thicknesse used as a channel to Bute (Mar MS GD/124/15/1716/5; Thicknesse 1766: 26–7).

[51] *E&P* 18–19.

printed by A. Homer and P. Milton for a publisher in St Paul's Churchyard, London. It fitted the existing Embassy Letters into one volume, and appended as afterthought a slim volume ii, occupied mainly by five alleged extra letters. These, it later emerged, resulted from a bet made at a convivial gathering, as to whether Lady Mary's style was or was not inimitable.[52] The epic poets' edition (probably emanating from Edinburgh) had a smallish circulation; but in 1767 Becket and De Hondt picked up the spurious letters for an *Additional Volume* to their edition. These forgeries held their place in reprints of the 1763 *Letters* as part of Montagu's canon, which in 1768 was expanded by a volume of *Poetical Works*.[53]

In 1803 James Dallaway brought out his bumbling edition of her *Works*, with much fanfare about its endorsement by her family. The first Marquess of Bute (the grandson who had missed out on Wortley's fortune) had in fact enlisted Dallaway after facing down a publication scheme of the printing entrepreneur Richard Phillips: a scheme born when Phillips was offered 200 letters purloined by a crooked lawyer after Wortley's death. Bute exchanged less objectionable letters, for Dallaway to use, against the purloined ones, which he burned. (Their most scandalous titbits concerned Edward.) He tried to persuade his cousins the Erskines to burn the letters to Lady Mar in their possession.[54] He rejected a proposal from Sir James Steuart's son that they might join forces to publish the letters they each owned: Steuart went ahead on his own in 1818 with Lady Mary's letters to his parents. John Francis Erskine, in whom the attainted Mar title was soon to be restored, acted much like his cousin Bute in turning down a proposal from the publisher Constable to print Lady Mary's letters to her sister. By 1826 Lady Louisa Stuart, who had not been consulted in 1803, was planning an improved edition.[55]

Despite the honest efforts that her family put into the edition of 1837 and the professional skill of W. Moy Thomas in 1861, no halfway decent edition of Montagu's writings appeared before those of Robert Halsband, more than a century later on. Her rank and gender were against her; and the deficiencies of Thomas's edition could only be discovered by going back to the original manuscripts, as 'George Paston' did for her biography of 1907. It is the feminist movement and the consequent rewriting of women's literary

---

[52] *Monthly Review, or, Literary Journal*, 1795: 70. 575.
[53] Poems already in print, collected by Isaac Reed (Nichols 1971: 7).
[54] Bute to John Erskine, 8 Apr. 1803, Mar MS GD/124/15/1716/3.
[55] Wh MS M 439/38. Lady Louisa, for instance, insisted on including MWM's letters about Rémond, though Lord Wharncliffe kept them segregated in an appendix. Charles Kirkpatrick Sharpe had hoped to print them and/or the letters to Algarotti (to David Laing, MS at Edinburgh University Library).

history that have given Lady Mary the audience she commands today. Yet she remains no less anomalous as a feminist than she was as a great lady or a writer of fiction. Habits of thought at the close of the twentieth century accommodate her no more comfortably than did those of the eighteenth. Though she called Congreve and Fielding the only originals to appear in her lifetime, their originality pales beside her own. Her surviving writings—a fraction of the whole—are enough to ensure than she 'cannot bee forgot'.

LADY MARY WORTLEY MONTAGU: SIMPLIFIED FAMILY TREE

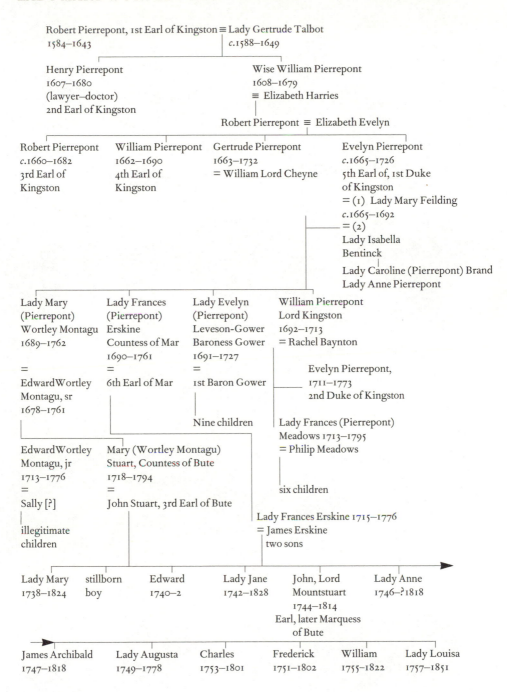

BIBLIOGRAPHY

UNPUBLISHED SOURCES

Admiralty MSS, Public Record Office, Kew.

Badminton MSS, Badminton House.

Bagshawe MSS, John Rylands Library, Manchester.

Bute MSS, Mount Stuart, Isle of Bute; Cardiff; Aberystwyth (copies among Halsband MSS).

Cambridge University Library.

Cornell University MSS.

Craigievar MSS (copies among Halsband MSS).

Daly MSS, Hampshire Record Office.

Devonshire MSS, Chatsworth House.

Egerton MSS, British Library.

Finch MSS, Leicestershire Record Office.

H MSS (Harrowby MSS).

Halsband MSS, Columbia University, New York.

Hervey MSS, Suffolk Record Office, Bury St Edmunds.

Huntington MSS, Huntington Library, San Marino, California.

Manin MSS, Biblioteca civica, Udine, Italy.

Manvers MSS, University of Nottingham.

Mar and Kellie MSS, Scottish Record Office.

Mellerstain MSS, Mellerstain House, Berwickshire.

Monson MSS, Lincoln Record Office.

Mundy MSS, Lincoln Record Office.

Murray MSS (copies among Halsband MSS).

J. M. Osborn Collection, Yale University Library.

Panshanger MSS, Hertfordshire Record Office.

Pierpont Morgan MSS, Pierpont Morgan Library, New York.

Portland MSS, Longleat House.

Portland MSS, University of Nottingham.

Treviso MSS.

Wharncliffe MSS, Sheffield Central Library.

PUBLISHED WORKS

ABBOTT, JOHN LAWRENCE (1982), *John Hawkesworth.*

ADDISON, JOSEPH (1720), *Scating. A Poem.*

—— [1803], *Addisoniana.*

—— (1914), *Miscellaneous Works*, ed. A. C. Guthkelch.

—— (1941), *Letters*, ed. Walter Graham.

Advice to Sappho (1733), By a Gentlewoman.

ALDERSON, A. D. (1956), *Structure of the Ottoman Dynasty.*

ALGAROTTI, FRANCESCO (1737; 1739; 1752), *Il Newtonianismo per le dame, ovvero dialoghi sopra la luce, i colori, e l'attrazione* (Milan; Naples; Naples).

—— (1764–5), *Opere* (Leghorn).

—— (1769), *Letters . . . to Lord Hervey and the Marquis Scipio Maffei, containing the state of . . . the Russian Empire*, trans.

ANDREWS, JONATHAN (1990), 'A Respectable Mad-Doctor? Dr Richard Hale, F. R. S. (1670–1728)', *Notes and Records of the Royal Society of London*, 44: 169–203.

Anecdote Library [1822].

ARAVAMUDAN, SRINIVAS (1995), 'Lady Mary Wortley Montagu in the *Hammam*: Masquerade, Womanliness, and Levantinization', *English Literary History*, 62: 69–104.

[ARBUTHNOT, JOHN] (1722), *Mr. Maitland's Account of Inoculating the Small Pox Vindicated from Dr. Wagstaffe's Misrepresentations*, 2nd edn.

[ASTELL, MARY] (1694; 1697), *A Serious Proposal to the Ladies . . .*

—— (1709), *Bart'lemy Fair.*

ATTERBURY, FRANCIS (1869), *Memoirs and Correspondence*, ed. Folkestone Williams.

AVERY, E. L. (1960) (ed.), *The London Stage, Part 2, 1700–29.*

AYMONINO, CARLO, *et al.* (1970), *La città di Padova* (Padua).

BADALONI, NICOLA (1968), *Antonio Conti, un abato libero pensatore tra Newton e Voltaire* (Milan).

BAGEHOT, WALTER (1965–86), *Collected Works*, ed. Norman St John Stevas.

BAGFORD, JOHN (1861), 'London Libraries', *Notes and Queries*, 2nd ser. 11: 381–464 passim.

BAILLIE, Lady GRIZEL (1911), *Household Book*, ed. R. Scott Moncrieff.

BAKER, JOHN (1931), *Diary*, ed. Philip C. Yorke.

BARKER, G. F. RUSSELL, and STENNING, ALAN H. (1928), *The Record of Old Westminsters.*

BARLING, T. J. (1968), 'Voltaire's Correspondence with Lord Hervey: Three New Letters', *Studies on Voltaire and the Eighteenth Century*, 62: 13–27.

BARRANGER, MILLY S. (1984), *Theatre Past and Present: An Introduction*.

BARRY, IRIS (1928), *Portrait of Lady Mary*.

BATAILLE, ROBERT R. (1980), 'The Dating of *The Lady's Curiosity* and Lady Montagu's [*sic*] "The Fifth Ode of Horace Imitated" ', *American Notes and Queries*, 18: 87–8.

BATTESTIN, MARTIN C. (1989), 'Dating Fielding's Letters to Lady Mary Wortley Montagu', *Studies in Bibliography*, 42: 246–8.

—— with BATTESTIN, RUTHE R. (1989), *Henry Fielding, A Life*.

BEATTIE, ALEXANDER, and STANLEY, C. W. N. (1964), *Thoresby Hall*.

BECKETT, J. V. (1986), *The Aristocracy in England 1660–1914*.

BEHN, APHRA (1992–6), *Works*, ed. Janet Todd.

BENGER, ELIZABETH OGILVY (1791), *The Female Geniad*.

BENNETT, G. V. (1975), *The Tory Crisis in Church and State 1688–1730: The Career of Francis Atterbury Bishop of Rochester*.

BENTLEY, THOMAS (1735), *A Letter to Mr. Pope, Occasioned by Sober Advice from Horace*.

BERNIS, FRANÇOIS-JOACHIM DE PIERRE DE (1878), *Mémoires et lettres* (Paris).

Betley Hall: A Catalogue of the ... Library (19 Apr. 1723).

BIONDI, GIOVANNI FRANCESCO (1624), *Eromena, or Love and Revenge*, trans. James Hayward (1632), copy at Sandon Hall.

BLACK, JEREMY (1985), *British Foreign Policy in the Age of Walpole*.

—— (1992), 'Non-Walpolean Manuscripts in the Lewis Walpole Library', *Yale University Library Gazette*, 67.

—— (1994), 'The Language of Licentiousness', *Scriblerian*, 26: 156–7.

BLACKETT-ORD, MARK (1982), *Hell-Fire Duke: The Life of the Duke of Wharton*.

BLAIKIE, WALTER BIGGAR (1916) (ed.), *Origins of the 'Forty-Five, and other Papers Relating to that Rising*.

BLAINVILLE, Monsieur DE (1743), *Travels through ... especially Italy*, trans. George Turnbull and William Guthrie.

BLOOM, H. J. G., RICHARDSON, W. W., and HARRIES, E. J. (1962), 'Natural History of Untreated Breast Cancer (1805–1933): Comparison of Untreated and Treated Cases According to Histological Grade of Malignancy', *British Medical Journal: The Journal of the British Medical Association*, 28 July: 213–21.

BLUNT, REGINALD (1906), *Paradise Row, or A Broken Piece of Old Chelsea*.

—— (1914), *In Cheyne Walk*.

BOCCAGE, MARIE ANNE FIQUET DU (1762), *Recueil des œuvres* (Lyons).

—— (1770), *Letters concerning England, Holland and Italy*.

BOHLS, ELIZABETH A. (1994), 'Aesthetics and Orientalism in Lady Mary Wortley Montagu's Letters', *Studies in Eighteenth-Century Culture*, 23, ed. Carla H. Hay and Syndy M. Conger.

BONAGLIA, ANGELO (1985), *Gottolengo dalle origini neolitiche all'età dei Comuni* (Brescia).

BOND, RICHMOND P. (1964), 'Mr Bickerstaffe and Mr Wortley', in Charles Henderson, Jr. (ed.), *Classical, Mediaeval and Renaissance Studies in Honor of Berthold Louis Ullman*, ii. 491–504.

BONNO, G. (1948), *La Culture et la civilisation britannique devant l'opinion française de la paix d'Utrecht aux Lettres Philosophiques (1713–1734)* (Philadelphia).

BOSISIO, ACHILLE (1959), 'Veneziani nel mondo: Francesco Algarotti', *Giornale economico della Camera di Commercio di Venezia*, Aug.: 3–20.

BOSWELL, JAMES (1791; 1934), *The Life of Samuel Johnson*, ed. G. B. Hill and L. F. Powell.

BRACKENBURY, ROBIN (1992), *Brothers At War: The Story of the Pierrepont Family in the Civil War* (Radcliffe-on-Trent).

BRADY, FRANK (1984), *James Boswell: The Later Years, 1769–1795*.

BRAUDE, BENJAMIN, and LEWIS BERNARD (1982) (eds.), *Christians and Jews in the Ottoman Empire: The Functioning of a Plural Society*.

BREWSTER, DOROTHY (1913), *Aaron Hill, Poet, Dramatist, Projector*.

BROCARD, MICHÈLE (1992), 'Dans l'orbite des Lumières (1713–1792)', in Christian Sorrel (ed.), *Histoire de Chambéry*.

BROGDEN, WILLIAM A. (1983), 'The *Ferme Ornée* and Changing Attitudes to Agricultural Improvement', *Eighteenth-Century Life*, NS 8.

BROWN, F. C. (1910), *Elkanah Settle: His Life and Works*.

BROWN, HARCOURT (1967), 'The Composition of the *Letters concerning the English Nation*', in *The Age of the Enlightenment: Studies Presented to Theodore Besterman*.

BROWNING, REED (1975), *The Duke of Newcastle*.

—— (1994), *The War of the Austrian Succession*.

[?BRUCH, CUDWORTH] (1767), *The Triumph of Inoculation; A Dream*.

BRUNELLI, BRUNO (1929), *Casanova Loved Her*.

BUCHOLZ, R. O. (1993), *The Augustan Court: Queen Anne and the Decline of Court Culture*.

BUCK, ANNE (1979), *Dress in Eighteenth-Century England*.

BUFFON, GEORGE LOUIS LECLERC DE (1749–67), *Histoire naturelle* (Paris).

BULLION, JOHN L. (1991), 'The Origins and Significance of Gossip about Princess Augusta and Lord Bute, 1755–1756', *Studies in Eighteenth-Century Culture*, ed. Patricia Craddock and Carla Hay, 21: 245–65.

BURNET, GILBERT (1724–34; 1897–1900), *History of His Own Time*, ed. Osmund Airy.

BURNET, THOMAS (1914), *Letters*, ed. David Nichol Smith.

BURNETT, JOHN (1969), *A History of the Cost of Living*.

BURNEY, FRANCES (1905), *Diary and Letters*, ed. Charlotte Barrett and Austin Dobson.

—— (1782; 1988), *Cecilia, or Memoirs of an Heiress*, ed. Margaret Ann Doody and Peter Sabor.

BURTON, ELIZABETH (1967), *The Georgians at Home, 1714–1830*.

BUXTON, NEIL K. (1978), *The Economic Development of the British Coal Industry*.

CAMPBELL, JILL (1994), 'Lady Mary Wortley Montagu and the Historical Machinery of Female Identity', in Beth Fowkes Tobin (ed.), *History, Gender & Eighteenth-Century Literature*.

CARLETON, JOHN D. (1965), *Westminster School: A History*.

CARSWELL, JOHN (1960; 1993), *The South Sea Bubble*, 2nd edn. rev. Alan Sutton.

CARTER, ELIZABETH (1739), *Sir Isaac Newton's Philosophy Explain'd*.

CARTWRIGHT, JAMES J. (1883) (ed.), *The Wentworth Papers, 1705–1739*.

CASANOVA, GIACOMO, Chevalier DE SEINGALT (1967), *History of my Life*, trans. Willard R. Trask.

CHABER, LOIS A. (1996), '"This Affecting Subject": An "Interested" Reading of Childbearing in Two Novels by Samuel Richardson', *Eighteenth-Century Fiction*, 8/2: 193–250.

CHAMBERS, J. D. (1932; 1966), *Nottinghamshire in the Eighteenth Century: A Study of Life and Labour under the Squirearchy*.

CHAMLEY, PAUL (1965), *Documents relatifs a Sir James Steuart* (Paris).

CHESTERFIELD, PHILIP STANHOPE, Earl of (1927), *Poetical Works*.

—— (1932), *Letters*, ed. Bonamy Dobrée.

—— (1778; 1990), *Characters*.

CHEYNE, GEORGE (1742), *The Natural Method of Cureing [sic] the Diseases of the Body, and the Disorders of the Mind Depending on the Body*.

CHILDS, J. RIVES (1961), *Casanova: A Biography Based on New Documents*.

CHRISTIE, IAN R. (1995), *British Non-Élite MPs 1715–1820*.

Chudleigh (1776), *Les Avantures trop amoureuses ou Elisabeth Chudleigh*.

CLARENDON, HENRY HYDE, Earl of (1702; 1888), *History of the Rebellion and Civil Wars in England*, ed. William Dunn Macray.

CLARK, Sir GEORGE (1964), *A History of the Royal College of Physicians of London*.

CLARK, RUTH (1921), *Anthony Hamilton (Author of Memoirs of Count Grammont): His Life and Works and his Family*.

CLARKE, T. E. S., and FOXCROFT, H. C. (1907), *A Life of Gilbert Burnet, Bishop of Salisbury* (Cambridge).

CLAVERING, JAMES (1967), *Correspondence*, ed. H. T. Dickinson.

CLEARY, THOMAS (1984), *Henry Fielding: Political Writer*.

CLELAND, JOHN (1751; 1964), *Memoirs of a Coxcomb*, ed. P. R. A. Lingham.

COCKBURN, CATHARINE (Trotter) (1751), *Works*, ed. Thomas Birch.

C[OKAYNE], G. E. (1910–59), *Complete Peerage*, ed. Vicany Gibbs *et al*.

COKE, Lady MARY (1889–96), *Letters and Journals*, ed. I. A. Home.

Collection of Epigrams, A (1727; 2nd edn. 1735–7).

COLLEY, LINDA (1992), *Britons: Forging the Nation 1707–1837* (New Haven, Conn.)

COLLIER, JEREMY (1698), *A Short View of the Immorality and Profaneness of the English Stage.*

COLLYER, C. (1952), 'The Yorkshire Election of 1734', *Proceedings of the Leeds Historical Society,* 7: 53–83.

COLMAN, BENJAMIN (1722), *A Narrative of the Method and Success of Inoculating the Small Pox in New England.*

COLMAN, GEORGE, and THORNTON, BONNELL (1755) (eds.), *Poems by Eminent Ladies.*

COMISSO, GIOVANNI (1984) (ed.), *Agenti Segreti di Venezia 1705–1797* (Venice).

Compleat Collection Of all the Verses, Essays, Letters and Advertisements, Which Have been occasioned by the Publication of Three Volumes of Miscellanies, by Pope and Company, A (1728).

CONTI, ANTONIO (1739, 1756), *Prose e Poesie,* i, ii (Venice).

—— (1966), *Versioni poetiche,* ed. Giovanna Gronda (Bari).

COOKE, S. H. [1960], *A History of Northfleet and its Parish Church.*

COTESWORTH, LILLIAS E. (n.d.), *Records of the Cotesworths of Egglesburne.*

COWPER, Lady MARY (1864), *Diary.*

CRAVEN, Lady ELIZABETH (1789), *Journey through the Crimea to Constantinople.*

CRAWFORD, J. (1722), *The Case of Inoculating The Small-Pox Consider'd, And its Advantages Asserted; In a Review of Dr. Wagstaffe's Letter.*

CRAWFORD, PATRICIA (1990), 'The Construction and Experience of Maternity', in Fildes 1990.

CROUTIER, ALEO LYTLE (1989), *Harem: The World Behind the Veil* (New York).

CUNDALL, FRANK (1937), *The Governors of Jamaica in the First Half of the Eighteenth Century.*

Cupid: A Collection of Love Songs, The (1736).

CURLING, JONATHAN (1954), *Edward Wortley Montagu 1713–1776: The Man in the Iron Wig.*

CUSSANS, JOHN E. (1893), *Handbook of Heraldry.*

CUST, Lady ELIZABETH (1898), *Records of the Cust Family.*

DABYDEEN, DAVID (1984), *Hogarth's Blacks: Images of Blacks in Eighteenth-Century English Art.*

DALLAWAY, JAMES (1797), *Constantinople Ancient and Modern.*

DAVID, DEIRDRE (1987), *Intellectual Women and Victorian Patriarchy.*

DAVIS, FANNY (1986), *The Ottoman Lady: A Social History from 1718 to 1918.*

DAY, ROBERT ADAMS (1966), *Told in Letters: Epistolary Fiction before Richardson.*

DÉDÉYAN, CHARLES (1990), *Montesquieu ou les Lumières d'Albion* (Paris).

DeJean, Joan (1991), *Tender Geographies: Women and the Origins of the Novel in France*.

Delany, Mary (1861–2), *Autobiography and Correspondence*, ed. Lady Llanover.

DelPlato, Joan (1988), 'An English "Feminist" in the Turkish Harem: A Portrait of Lady Mary Wortley Montagu', in Frederick M. Keener and Susan E. Lorsch (eds.), *Eighteenth-Century Women and the Arts* (Greenwood, Ill.), 163–78.

Desmaizeaux, Pierre (1720) (ed.), *Recueil de diverses pièces sur la philosophie, la religion naturelle, l'histoire, les mathematiques etc. de Samuel Clarke, Gottfried Wilhelm von Leibnitz, Isaac Newton etc.*

Desmond, Ray (1995), *Kew: The History of the Royal Botanic Gardens*.

Deverell, Mary (1781), *Miscellanies in Prose and Verse, mostly written in the Epistolary Style, chiefly upon Moral Subjects, And particularly calculated for the Improvement of Younger Minds*.

Dickinson, H. T. (1970), *Bolingbroke*.

Doddridge, Philip (1829), *Correspondence and Diary*, ed. John Doddridge Humphreys.

Dodsley, Robert (1988), *Correspondence 1733–1764*, ed. James E. Tierney.

Dominiceti, Bartolomeo [1776], *Memorie Mediche*.

—— (1781), *Medical Anecdotes, of the last Thirty Years*.

Doran, John (1873), *A Lady of the Last Century (Mrs. Elizabeth Montagu)*.

[Dryden, John, and others] (1704), *Poetical Miscellanies: The Fifth Part*.

Dumont, Jean (1705), *A New Voyage to the Levant*, 4th edn.

Duncombe, John (1754), *The Feminiad: A Poem*.

Durant, David N. (1977), *Bess of Hardwick: Portrait of an Elizabethan Dynast* (Derby).

Dutens, Lewis (1806), *Memoirs of a Traveller*.

Eden, R. H. (1818) (ed.), *Reports of Cases . . . in the High Court of Chancery 1757 to 1766*.

Egmont, John Perceval, Earl of, *Diary*, HMC 1920–3.

Elias, Norbert (1978), *The Civilizing Process*.

Encyclopaedia of Islam (1995), new edn. (Leiden).

Epstein, William H. (1974), *John Cleland: Images of a Life*.

Equiano, Olaudo (1789), *The Interesting Narrative of the Life of Olaudo Equiano, or Gustavus Vassa, the African*, in Henry Louis Gates (ed.), *The Classic Slave Narratives* (1987).

Ettinghausen, Richard (1976), 'The Man-made Setting', in Lewis 1976.

Eustace, Mrs, and her sister (1795), *The Parlour Window* (Dublin).

Evans, Joan (1956), *A History of the Society of Antiquaries*.

Evans, Robert Rees (1991), *Pantheisticon: The Career of John Toland*.

Evelyn, John (1661), trans. ['Interpreted'] Gabriel Naudé, *Instructions Concerning Erecting of a Library*.

EVELYN, JOHN (1955), *Diary*, ed. E. S. de Beer.

EYNARD, CHARLES (1839), *Essai sur la Vie de Tissot* (Lausanne).

Fair Suicide, The: Being An Epistle From a Young Lady, To The Person who was the Cause of her Death (1733).

FAPPANI, ANTONIO (1961), 'Lady Montagu ed il co: Ugolino Palazzi', *Commentari dell'ateneo di Brescia*, 97–130.

FARINGTON, JOSEPH (1979), *Diary*, vi, ed. Kenneth Garlick and Angus Macintyre.

FAURE, GABRIEL (1960), *Gardens of Rome*.

FEARON, HENRY (1784), *A Treatise on Cancers, with A New and Successful Method of Operating, Particularly in Cancers of the Breast and Testis*.

FERNEA, ELIZABETH WARNOCK (1981), 'An Early Ethnographer of Middle Eastern Women: Lady Mary Wortley Montagu (1689–1762)', *Journal of Near Eastern Studies*, 40: 329–38.

FERRARO, JOANNE M. (1993), *Family and Public Life in Brescia, 1580–1650: The Foundations of Power in the Venetian State*.

FIELD, JOHN (1987), *The King's Nurseries: The Story of Westminster School*.

FILDES, VALERIE (1990) (ed.), *Women as Mothers in Pre-Industrial England: Essays in Memory of Dorothy McLaren*.

FINCH, ANNE (1903), *Poems*, ed. Myra Reynolds.

FINCH, PEARL (1901), *History of Burley-on-the-Hill*.

FLEMING, JOHN (1962), *Robert Adam and His Circle*.

FLINN, MICHAEL W., with STOKER, DAVID (1984), *The History of the British Coal Industry*, ii.

FOSKETT, DAPHNE (1963), *British Portrait Miniatures*.

FOXON, DAVID (1975), *English Verse 1701–1750: A Catalogue of Separately Printed Poems with Notes on Contemporary Collected Editions*.

—— and MCLAVERTY, JAMES (1991), *Alexander Pope and the Early Eighteenth-Century Book Trade*.

FRATI, V., MASSA, R., PIOVANELLI, G., and ROBECCHI, F. (1989), *Brescia*.

FURNEAUX, RUPERT (1973), *The Seven Years War*.

GAY, JOHN (1720), *Poems on Several Occasions*.

—— (1966), *Letters*, ed. C. F. Burgess.

—— (1974), *Poetry and Prose*, ed. Vinton A. Dearing and Charles E. Beckwith.

GAY, VIRGINIA (1992; 1995), *Penelope and Adelina*.

GERZINA, GRETCHEN (1995), *Black England: Life Before Emancipation*.

GILMAN, SANDER L. (1985), 'Black Bodies, White Bodies: Toward an Iconography of Female Sexuality in Late Nineteenth-Century Art, Medicine and Literature', *Critical Inquiry*, 112.

[GLANVILL, JOSEPH] (1689), *Saducismus Triumphatus: or, Full and Plain Evidence Concerning Witches and Apparitions*, 3rd edn.

GÖÇEK, FATMA MÜGE (1987), *East Encounters West, France and the Ottoman Empire in the Eighteenth Century*.

GOLDGAR, BERTRAND A. (1976), *Walpole and the Wits: The Relation of Politics to Literature, 1722–1742*.

—— (1995), 'Fielding on Fiction and History', *Eighteenth-Century Fiction*, 7.

GOODRIDGE, JOHN (1995), *Rural Life in Eighteenth-Century English Poetry*.

GRAFFIGNY, FRANÇOISE DE (1985), *Correspondance*, ed. English Showalter.

GRAEME, LOUISA G. (1903), *Or and Sable: A Book of the Graemes and Grahams*.

GRANGE, JAMES ERSKINE, Lord (1843), *Extracts from the Diary of a Senator of the College of Justice*.

GRAY, THOMAS (1935), *Correspondence*, ed. Paget Toynbee and Leonard Whibley.

GREGG, EDWARD (1982), 'The Jacobite Career of John, Earl of Mar', in Eveline Cruickshanks (ed.), *Ideology and Conspiracy: Aspects of Jacobitism, 1689–1759*.

GRIFFITH, REGINALD HARVEY (1922–7), *Alexander Pope: A Bibliography*, i (Austin, Tex.); ii (London).

GRONDA, GIOVANNA (1964), 'Antonio Conti e l'Inghilterra', *English Miscellany: A Symposium of History, Literature and the Arts*, ed. Mario Praz and Giorgio Melchiori (Rome), 15: 135–74.

GRUNDY, ISOBEL (1969), 'Pope, Peterborough, and the Characters of Women', *Review of English Studies*, 461–8.

—— (1971), 'The Verse of Lady Mary Wortley Montagu', D.Phil. thesis, University of Oxford.

—— (1972a), 'Ovid and Eighteenth-Century Divorce: An Unpublished Poem by Lady Mary Wortley Montagu', *Review of English Studies*, 23: 417–28.

—— (1972b), 'New Verse by Henry Fielding', *PMLA* 87: 213–45.

—— (1977), 'A Skirmish Between Pope and Some Persons of Rank and Fortune: Verses to the Imitator of Horace', *Studies in Bibliography*, 30: 96–119.

—— (1980), 'A "Spurious" Poem by Lady Mary Wortley Montagu', *Notes and Queries*, 27: 407–10.

—— (1981), ' "New" Verse by Lady Mary Wortley Montagu', *Bodleian Library Record*, 10: 237–49.

—— (1982), 'The Politics of Female Authorship: Lady Mary Wortley Montagu's Reaction to the Printing of her Poems', *The Book Collector*, 31: 19–37.

—— (1993a), ' "The barbarous character we give them": White Women Travellers Report on Other Races', *Studies in Eighteenth-Century Culture*, ed. Patricia Craddock, 23: 73–86.

—— (1993b), 'Inoculation in Salisbury', *Scriblerian*, 26/1: 63–5.

—— (1993c), ' "Trash, Trumpery, and Idle Time": Lady Mary Wortley Montagu and Fiction', *Eighteenth-Century Fiction*, 5/4: 293–310.

GRUNDY, ISOBEL (1994*a*), 'Books and the Woman: An Eighteenth-Century Owner and Her Libraries', *English Studies in Canada*, 20/1: 1–22.

—— (1994*b*), 'Books and the Woman: Postscript', *Eighteenth Century Studies*, 20/4: 373–6.

—— (1994*c*), 'Medical Advance and Female Fame; Inoculation and its After-Effects', *Lumen*, 13.

—— (1998) 'Editing Lady Mary Wortley Montagu', in Ann Hutchison (ed.), *Editing Women* (Toronto)

GUERINOT, J. V. (1969), *Pamphlet Attacks on Alexander Pope 1711–1744: A Descriptive Bibliography*.

GUY, RICHARD (1759), *An Essay on Scirrhous Tumours, and Cancers*.

—— [1762], *Practical Observations on Cancers and Disorders of the Breasts*.

GYÖRGY, GÖMÖRI (1994), *Angol és skót utazók a régi Magyarországon (1542–1737)* (Budapest).

HACKETT, L. W. (1937), *Malaria in Europe: An Ecological Study*.

HAEN, ANTONIO DE (1759), *Refutation de L'Inoculation*.

HALSBAND, ROBERT (1953), 'Pope, Lady Mary, and the *Court Poems* (1716)', *PMLA* 68: 237–50.

—— (1956), *The Life of Lady Mary Wortley Montagu*.

—— (1956–7), 'Lady Mary Wortley Montagu as a Friend of Continental Writers', *Bulletin of the John Rylands Library*, 39: 57.

—— (1967), 'Virtue in Danger: The Case of Griselda Murray', *History Today*, 692–700.

—— (1973), *Lord Hervey: Eighteenth-Century Courtier*.

—— (1979), 'New Anecdotes of Lady Mary Wortley Montagu (1757)', in René Welleck (ed.),

HAMILTON, ANTHONY (1713; 1772), *Memoires de la vie du comte de Grammont* (Strawberry Hill).

HAMILTON, Sir DAVID (1975), *Diary 1709–1714*, ed. Philip Roberts.

[HAMMOND, ANTHONY (ed.)] (1720), *A New Miscellany of Original Poems, Translations and Imitations*, By the most Eminent Hands.

HAMMOND, BREAN (1984), *Pope and Bolingbroke: A Study of Friendship and Influence*.

[HAMMOND, JAMES] (1733), *An Elegy to a Young Lady . . . With an Answer*, By a Lady, Author of the Verses to the Imitator of Horace.

HAMMOND, PAUL (1993), 'Anonymity in Restoration Poetry', *Seventeenth Century*, 8.

HANBURY WILLIAMS, Sir CHARLES (1822), *Works*.

HARRIS, FRANCES (1991), *A Passion for Government: The Life of Sarah Duchess of Marlborough*.

HARRIS, JOHN (1961; 1963), 'Thoresby House, Notts', *Architectural History*, 4: 11–19; 6: 103–5.

HARRIS, WALTER (1722), *A Description of Inoculating the Small Pox.*

HASKELL, FRANCIS (1958), 'Algarotti and Tiepolo's "Banquet of Cleopatra" ', *Burlington Magazine*, 212–13.

—— (1980), *Patrons and Painters: A Study in the Relations Between Italian Art and Society in the Age of the Baroque*, rev. edn.

Hastings Wheler Family Letters 1704–1739 (1935).

HATTON, RAGNILD (1978), *George I, Elector and King.*

[HAYWOOD, HAYWOOD] (1724), *A Spy upon the Conjurer.*

HEALEY, EDNA (1992), *Coutts & Co 1692–1992: The Portrait of a Private Bank.*

HENDERSON, G. D. (1934) (ed.), *Mystics of the North-East including . . . Letters of James Keith.*

HENNING, BASIL DUKE (1983) (ed.), *History of Parliament: The House of Commons 1660–1690.*

HERIOT, ANGUS (1956), *The Castrati in Opera.*

HERVEY, CHRISTOPHER (1785), *Letters from Portugal, Spain, Italy and Germany, in the years 1759, 1760, and 1761.*

HERVEY, JOHN, Lord (1931), *Some Materials Towards Memoirs of the Reign of King George II*, ed. Romney Sedgwick.

HIGGINBOTTOM, MIKE (1987), *Country Houses of Nottinghamshire* (Newark).

HILL, AARON (1709), *A Full and Just Account of the Present State of the Ottoman Empire.*

—— (1724–5) (ed.), *The Plain Dealer.*

HILL, BRIAN W. (1989), *Sir Robert Walpole, 'Sole and Prime Minister'.*

HILL, G. B. (1897) (ed.), *Johnsonian Miscellanies.*

HILL, J. W. F. (1952) (ed.), *Letters and Papers of the Banks Family 1704–1760*, Lincoln Record Society, xlv.

HILLHOUSE, JAMES T. (1928), *The Grub-Street Journal.*

HMC (1872), *Third Report.*

—— (1887), *Eleventh Report.*

—— (1934), *Hastings MSS*, iii.

—— (1899, 1901), *Portland MSS*, v. vi.

—— (1904), *Report on MSS of the Earls of Mar and Kellie*, i.

—— (1923), *Stuart Papers*, vii.

—— (1913), *Various Collections*, viii.

HOBHOUSE, JOHN CAM (1813), *A Journey through Albania . . . to Constantinople, during the years 1809 and 1810*, 2nd edn.

HODGART, M. J. C. (1954), 'The Eighth Volume of the *Spectator*', *Review of English Studies*, NS 5: 367–87.

HOLLIS, GEORGE TRUETT (1992), 'Count Francesco Algarotti and the Society', in D. G. C. Allan and John L. Abbott (eds.), *The Virtuoso Tribe of Arts and Sciences: Studies in the Eighteenth-Century Work and Membership of the London Society of Arts, Manufacture and Commerce*.

HOLMES, GEOFFREY, and SPECK W. A. (1967), *The Divided Society: Parties and Politics in England, 1694–1716*.

HOLMES, RICHARD (1993), *Dr Johnson and Mr Savage*.

HORWATH, PETER (1987), 'Lady Mary Wortley Montagu: Passage "over the [battle] feilds of Carlowitz" ', *Notes and Queries*, 232: 342–3.

—— (1988), 'Identifying Place Names in Hungary used by Lady Mary Wortley Montagu', *English Language Notes*, 25: 36–9.

—— (1991), 'Name and Location of Lady Mary Wortley Montagu's "Rascian Town" ', *Notes and Queries*, 236: 189.

—— (1992), 'Why did the Turks Meet the Wortley Montagus at "Betsko" (1717)?', *English Language Notes*, 29: 24–6.

HOURANI, ALBERT (1991), *Islam in European Thought*.

HOWARD, EDMUND (1971), *Genoa: History and Art in an Old Seaport*.

HOWGRAVE, FRANCIS (1724), *Reasons Against the Inoculation of the Small-Pox. In a Letter to Dr. Jurin*.

HUDSON, NICHOLAS (1996), 'From "Nation" to "Race": The Origin of Racial Classification in Eighteenth-Century Thought', *Eighteenth Century Studies*, 29: 247–64.

HUGHES, EDWARD (1949), 'The Eighteenth-Century Agent', in H. A. Croune, T. W. Moody, and D. B. Quinn (eds.), *Essays in British and Irish History in Honour of James Eddie Todd*.

—— (1952), *North Country Life in the Eighteenth Century: The North-East, 1700–1750*.

HUGHES, HELEN SARD (1940), *The Gentle Hertford: Her Life and Letters*.

HUNTER, JOHN (1778), *A Practical Treatise on the Diseases of the Teeth*, part 2 of *The Natural History of the Human Teeth*.

HUNTER, JOSEPH (1831), *South Yorkshire: The History and Topography of the Deanery of Doncaster, in the Diocese and County of York*.

—— (1869), *Hallamshire: The History and Topography of . . . Sheffield*, rev. and enlarged Alfred Gatty.

ILCHESTER, Earl of (1950), *Lord Hervey and his Friends, 1726–38, Based on letters from Holland House, Melbury, and Ickworth*.

IRVING, W. H. (1940), *John Gay, Favorite of the Wits*.

JACOB, MARGARET (1981), *The Radical Enlightenment: Pantheists, Freemasons and Republicans*.

JANSSENS, UTA (1981), 'Matthieu Maty and the Adoption of the Inoculation for Smallpox in Holland', *Bulletin of the History of Medicine*, 55.

JERVAS, CHARLES [1740], *Catalogue of the . . . pictures, prints and drawings late of C. Jarvis.*

JOHNSON, SAMUEL (1905), *Lives of the English Poets*, ed. G. B. Hill and L. F. Powell.

[JONES, ERASMUS] (1734), *Pretty Doings in a Protestant Nation. Being A View of the Present State of Fornication, Whorecraft and Adultery, in Great-Britain, and the Territories and Dependencies thereunto belonging . . .*

[———] [?1735], *Luxury, Pride, and Vanity, The Bane of the British Nation.*

JONES, R. F. (1919), *Lewis Theobald.*

JURIN, JAMES (1723), *A Letter to the Learned Caleb Cotesworth . . . Containing, A Comparison between the Mortality of the Natural Small Pox, And that Given by Inoculation.*

——— (1726), *Account . . . for the year 1725.*

——— (1996), *Correspondence*, ed. Andrea A. Rusnock.

KAMINSKI, THOMAS (1987), *The Early Career of Samuel Johnson.*

KERSLAKE, JOHN (1977), *Early Georgian Portraits.*

KILLIGREW, ANNE [1685], *Poems.*

KLEBS, ARNOLD C. (1913), 'The Historic Evolution of Variolation', *Bulletin of the Johns Hopkins Hospital*, 24: 265.

KLEIN, P. W. (1984), ' "Little London": British Merchants in Rotterdam during the Seventeenth and Eighteenth Centuries', in D. C. Coleman and Peter Mathias (eds.), *Enterprise and History: Essays in Honour of Charles Wilson.*

KNEPLER, GEORG (1994), *Wolfgang Amadé Mozart*, trans. J. Bradford Robinson.

KRISTELLER, PAUL OSKAR (1980), 'Learned Women of Early Modern Italy: Humanists and University Scholars', in Labalme 1980: 91–116.

LABALME, PATRICIA H. (1980) (ed.), *Beyond their Sex: Learned Women of the European Past.*

LA GRANGE, HENRY-LOUIS DE (1990), *Vienne, Histoire Musicale 1100–1848.*

LA MOTTRAYE, AUBRY DE (1723, 1732), *Travels through Europe, Asia, and into Part of Africa*, i and ii, iii.

LANGLEY, BATTY (1728), *New Principles of Gardening.*

LARUE, C. STEVEN (1995), *Handel and his Singers: The Creation of the Royal Academy of Operas, 1720–1728.*

LAUGERO, GREG (1995), 'Infrastructures of Enlightenment: Road-making, the Public Sphere, and the Emergence of Literature', *Eighteenth Century Studies*, 29: 1.

LAURITZEN, PETER, and ZIELCKE, ALEXANDER (1978), *Palaces of Venice.*

LAWSON-TANCRED, T. S. (1937), *Records of a Yorkshire Manor.*

LEEKS, WENDY (1986), 'Ingres Other-Wise', *Oxford Art Journal*, 9.

LENMAN, BRUCE (1980), *The Jacobite Risings in Britain 1689–1746.*

LESLIE, CHARLES ROBERT, and TAYLOR, TOM (1865), *Life and Times of Sir Joshua Reynolds.*

LEVEY, MICHAEL (1960), 'Two Paintings by Tiepolo from the Algarotti Collection', *Burlington Magazine*, 250–7.

LEVINE, JOSEPH M. (1977), *Dr. Woodward's Shield: History, Science, and Satire in Augustan England*.

LEVTZION, NEHEMIAH, and VOLL, JOHN O. (1987) (eds.), *Eighteenth-Century Renewal and Reform in Islam*.

LEW, JOSEPH W. (1991), 'Lady Mary's Portable Seraglio', *Eighteenth Century Studies*, 24.

LEWIS, BERNARD (1963), *Istanbul and the Civilization of the Ottoman Empire* (Oklahoma).

—— (1968), *The Middle East and the West*.

—— (1976) (ed.), *The World of Islam*.

—— (1982), *The Muslim Discovery of Europe*.

LEWIS, BRIAN (1971), *Coal Mining in the Eighteenth and Nineteenth Centuries*.

LOCKE, A. A. (1916), *The Hanbury Family*.

LONG, EDWARD (1774), *History of Jamaica*.

LOVAT-FRASER, J. A. (1919), *John Stuart Earl of Bute*.

LOW, D. M. (1916), 'The Eighteenth Century in Classical Verse', *Classical Review*, Feb.

LUCINI, PIERO (1988), *Gottolengo* (Brescia).

LUTTRELL, NARCISSUS (1857), *A Brief Historical Relation of State Affairs from September 1678 to April 1714*.

LUYNES, CHARLES-PHILLIPPE D'ALBERT, duc de (1860), *Mémoires . . . sur la cour de Louis XV (1735–1758)* (Paris).

McDOWALL, DAVID (1994), *Richmond Park: The Walker's Historical Guide*.

McGOVERN, BARBARA (1992), *Anne Finch and Her Poetry: A Critical Biography*.

McGUIGAN, HUGH A. (1937), 'Medical Thermometry', *Annals of Medical History*, NS 9.

MACK, MAYNARD (1969), *The Garden and the City: Retirement and Politics in the Later Poetry of Pope, 1731–1743*.

—— (1984) (ed.), *The Last and Greatest Art: Some Unpublished Manuscripts of Alexander Pope*.

—— (1985), *Alexander Pope, A Life*.

McKAY, DEREK (1977), *Prince Eugene of Savoy*.

McKELVEY, JAMES LEE (1973), *George III and Lord Bute: The Leicester House Years*.

McKENZIE, D. F., and ROSS, J. C. (1968) (eds.), *A Ledger of Charles Ackers, Printer of the London Magazine*.

MACKENZIE, E., and ROSS, M. (1825), *An Historical, Topographical, and Descriptive View of the County of Northumberland*.

—— and—— (1834), *An Historical . . . View of . . . Durham*.

MACKENZIE, JAMES (1758; 1760), *The History of Health, and the Art of Preserving it*, 3rd edn.

MACKY, JOHN (1733), *Memoirs of the Secret Services*.

McLAVERTY, JAMES (1980), 'The First Printing and Publication of Pope's Letters', *The Library*, 6th ser. 2: 264–80.

—— (1995), 'Pope in the Private and Public Spheres: Annotations in the Second Earl of Oxford's Volume of Folio Poems, 1731–1736', *Studies in Bibliography*, 48.

—— (forthcoming), ' "Of which being publick the Publick judge": Pope and the Publication of *Verses Address'd to the Imitator of Horace*', *Studies in Bibliography*.

MACLEAN, Sir JOHN (1879), *Trigg Major*.

McLYNN, PAULINE (1989), *Factionalism among the Exiles in France: The Case of Chevalier Ramsay and Bishop Atterbury*.

MacMICHAEL, WILLIAM (1827; 1968), *The Gold-Headed Cane*.

MAFFEI, SCIPIONE (1955), *Epistolario (1700–1755)*, ed. Celestino Garibotto (Milan).

MAHAFFEY, LOIS KATHLEEN (1963), 'Alexander Pope and His Sappho: Pope's Relationship with Lady Mary Wortley Montagu and its Influence on his Work', Ph.D. thesis, University of Texas.

—— (1970), 'Pope's "Artimesia" and "Phryne" as Personal Satire', *Review of English Studies*, 21: 466–71.

MAITLAND, CHARLES (1722), *Mr. Maitland's Account of Inoculating the Small Pox*.

MAKIN, BATHSUA (1673), *An Essay To Revive the Antient Education of Gentlewomen*.

MANTRAN, ROBERT (1982), 'Foreign Merchants and the Minorities in Istanbul during the Sixteenth and Seventeenth Centuries', in Braude and Lewis 1982.

MAR, JOHN ERSKINE, Earl of (1896), *The Earl of Mar's Legacies to Scotland and to his Son*, ed. Stuart Erskine.

MARCEL, ADRIEN (1912), 'Le Rocher des doms', *Annuaire Société des amis du Palais des Papes et des monuments d'Avignon*.

MARCHI, GIAN PAOLO (1992), *Un Italiano in Europa, Scipione Maffei tra passione antiquaria e impegno civile* (Verona).

MARINONI, C. L. P. (1904), *Lady Montagu Wortley e la sua decennale dimora alle rive del Lago d'Iseo* (Lovere).

MARLBOROUGH, SARAH CHURCHILL, Duchess of (1943), *Letters of a Grandmother 1732–1735*, ed. Gladys Scott Thomson.

MARTIN, PETER (1984), *Pursuing Innocent Pleasures: The Gardening World of Alexander Pope*.

MARTINEAU, JANE, and ROBINSON, ANDREW (1995), *The Glory of Venice: Venetian Art in the Eighteenth Century*.

MASSEY, EDMUND (1721), *The Signs of the Times*.

—— (1722), *A Sermon against the Dangerous and Sinful Practice of Inoculation*.

MASSEY, ISAAC (1723), *A Short and Plain Account of Inoculation. With some Remarks on the main Arguments made Use of to recommend that Practice*, 2nd edn.

MATHER, INCREASE (1721), *Some Further Account*, 2nd edn. (Boston).

MAVOR, ELIZABETH (1964), *The Virgin Mistress, A Study in Survival: The Life of the Duchess of Kingston*.

MAZZOLDI, LEONARDI (1966), *L'Estimo mercantorio del territorio 1750* (Brescia).

MELMAN, BILLIE (1992), *Women's Orients: English Women and the Middle East (1718–1918)*.

MESSENGER, ANN (1986), 'Town Eclogues', in *His and Hers: Essays in Restoration and Eighteenth-Century Literature*.

MICHAEL, WOLFGANG (1896; 1936), *England under George I: The Beginnings of the Hanoverian Dynasty*, trans.

MICHAUD, J. F. [1870–3], *Biographie universelle* (Paris).

MILLER, DAVID P. (1988), ' "My favourite studdys": Lord Bute as Naturalist', in Schweitzer 1988c: 213–39.

MILLER, GENEVIEVE (1957), *The Adoption of Inoculation for Smallpox in England and France*.

MINGAY, G. E. (1952), 'The Duke of Kingston and his Estates', BA thesis, University of Nottingham.

—— (1963), *English Landed Society in the Eighteenth Century*, 67–71.

MITFORD, NANCY (1968), 'Tam and Fritz: Carlyle and Frederick the Great', *History Today*, 18: 1968, 3–13.

MONCK, MARY (1716), *Marinda: Poems and Translations Upon Several Occasions*.

MONOD, PAUL KLÉBER (1989), *Jacobitism and the English People, 1688–1788*.

MONOD-CASSIDY, HÉLÈNE (1941), *Un Voyager-Philosophe au XVIIIe siècle: l'abbé Jean-Bernard Le Blanc* (Cambridge, Mass.).

MONTAGU, EDWARD WORTLEY, and TAAFFE, THEOBALD [1752], *A Memorial, or Humble Petition presented To the Judge in the High Court of the Tournelle, in Paris . . . against Abraham Payba alias James Roberts and Louis Pierre, jeweller, appealing from sentence given in favour of those two on 14 June 1752*, trans. from French.

MONTAGU, ELIZABETH (1906), *The Queen of the Blue-Stockings: Her Correspondence from 1720 to 1761*, ed. Emily J. Climenson.

—— (1923), *Mrs. Montagu 'Queen of the Blues': Her Letters and Friendships from 1762 to 1800*, ed. Reginald Blunt.

MONTAGU, Lady MARY WORTLEY (1763, repr. 1790), *Letters . . . Written during her Travels in Europe, Asia, and Africa . . .*

—— (1803), *Works*, ed. James Dallaway.

—— (1818), *Original Letters . . . to Sir James and Lady Frances Steuart; also, Memoirs and Anecdotes of those Distinguished Persons* (Greenock).

—— (1837), *Letters and Works*, ed. Lord Wharncliffe.

—— (1861), *Letters and Works*, ed. W. Moy Thomas.

—— (1965–7), *Complete Letters*, ed. Robert Halsband (Oxford).

—— (1977*a*), *Court Eclogs Written in the Year 1716: Alexander Pope's Autograph Manuscript of Poems by Lady Mary Wortley Montagu*, ed. Robert Halsband.

—— (1977*b*; 1993), *Essays and Poems and Simplicity a Comedy*, ed. Robert Halsband and Isobel Grundy (Oxford).

MONTESQUIEU, CHARLES DE SECONDAT DE (1949–51), *Œuvres complètes*, ed. Roger Callois (Paris).

MOORE, JAMES CARRICK (1815), *The History of the Small Pox*.

MORRIS, JOHN (1872), *Troubles of our Catholic Forefathers*.

MURDOCH, ALEXANDER (1988), 'Lord Bute, James Stuart Mackenzie, and the Government of Scotland', in Schweizer 1988*c*: 117–46.

MURDOCH, JOHN, *et al.* (1981), *The English Miniature*.

MURPHY, ANTOIN E. (1986; 1988), *Richard Cantillon: Entrepreneur and Economist*.

MURRAY, Lady GRISELDA (1822), *Memoirs of the Lives and Characters of George Baillie and of Lady Grisell Baillie*.

NAMIER, Sir LEWIS, and BROOKE, JOHN (1964), *History of Parliament: The House of Commons 1754–1790*.

NANGLE, BENJAMIN CHRISTIE (1955), *The Monthly Review Second Series, 1790–1815, Indexes of Contributors and Articles*.

New Foundling Hospital for Wit, The (1784).

New Practice of Inoculating the Small-Pox Consider'd, The (1722).

Newcastle upon Tyne, An Impartial History of the Town and County of (1801).

NICHOL, DONALD W., and LARKIN, JACOB (1995), 'Wilkes & Editorial Liberty: Attacks on Warburton as Pope's Editor', in Donald W. Nichol, Iona Bulgin, Sandra Hannaford, and David Wilson (eds.), *TransAtlantic Crossings: Eighteenth-Century Explorations* (St John's, Newfoundland), 49–58.

NICHOLS, JOHN (1812), *Literary Anecdotes of the Eighteenth Century*.

—— (1971), *Minor Lives: A Collection of Biographies*, ed. Edward L. Hart.

NICOLSON, MARJORIE, and ROUSSEAU, G. S. (1968), *'This Long Disease, My Life': Alexander Pope and the Sciences*.

NOKES, DAVID (1995), *John Gay: A Profession of Friendship*.

NUGENT, THOMAS (1778), *The Grand Tour*, 3rd edn.

NUSSBAUM, FELICITY (1984), *'The Brink of All We Hate': English Satires on Women, 1660–1750*.

—— (1995), *Torrid Zones: Maternity, Sexuality, and Empire in Eighteenth-Century English Narratives*.

OFFREDI, GIOVANNI (1963), in *Giornale di Bergamo*, 11 May.

O'GORMAN, FRANK (1988), 'The Myth of Lord Bute's Secret Influence', in Schweizer 1988*c*.

OLDHAM, JOHN (1987), *Poems*, ed. Harold F. Brooks.

OLDYS, WILLIAM (1862), *Memoir . . . with his Diary*.

OLIVIER, EDITH (1951), *Wiltshire*.

ORR, BRIDGET (1994),' "The Only Free People in the Empire": Gender Difference in Colonial Discourse', in Chris Tiffin and Alan Lawson (eds.), *De-Scribing Empire, Post-colonialism and Textuality*.

ORRELL, JOHN (1992), 'The Lincoln's Inn Fields Playhouse in 1731', *Theatre Notebook*, 46.

Padova: Guida (1961).

PAGLIA, CAMILLE (1773), 'Lord Hervey and Pope', *Eighteenth Century Studies*, 6: 348–71.

PARNELL, J. T. (1994), 'Swift, Sterne, and the Skeptical Tradition', *Studies in Eighteenth-Century Culture*, 23.

'PASTON, GEORGE' [Emily Morse Symonds] (1907), *Lady Mary Wortley Montagu and Her Times*.

[PAYBA, ABRAHAM] (1752), *The Memorial Presented to The High Court of La Tourelle at Paris, in favour of Abraham Payba, Jew, A Native of London; against E—d W—y M—u, Esq; and T—d T—e, Esq; The*, trans. from French.

PEIRCE, LESLIE P. (1993), *The Imperial Harem: Women and Sovereignty in the Ottoman Empire*.

PEPYS, SAMUEL (1926), *Private Correspondence and Miscellaneous Papers*, ed. J. R. Tanner.

PEROGALLI, CARLO, SANDRI, MARIA GRAZIA, and ZANELLA, VANNI (1985), *Ville della Provincia di Brescia* (Milan).

PERRY, RUTH (1986), *The Celebrated Mary Astell: An Early English Feminist*.

PEVSNER, NIKOLAUS (1951), *Nottinghamshire*.

PIERREPONT, Lady MARY (1994), *Indamora to Lindamira*, ed. Isobel Grundy (Edmonton, Alberta).

PILKINGTON, LAETITIA (1748–54; 1997), *Memoirs*, ed. A. C. Elias, Jr.

PINTO, SANDRA (1987) (ed.), *Arte di corte a Torino da Carlo Emanuele III a Carlo Felice*.

PIOZZI, HESTER LYNCH (1989), *Letters*, ed. Edward A. and Lillian D. Bloom, i.

PIX, MARY (1700), *The Beau Defeated: or, The Lucky Younger Brother*.

PLAISANT, MICHÈLE (1987), 'Lady Mary Wortley Montagu: Paradoxes et strategies du savoir', in Alain Morvan (ed.), *Savoir et violence en Angleterre du xvie au xixe siècle* (Lille).

PLUMB, J. H. (1956; 1960), *Sir Robert Walpole: The Making of a Statesman; The King's Minister*.

POINTON, MARCIA (1992), 'Killing Pictures', in John Barrell (ed.), *Painting and the Politics of Culture: New Essays on British Art 1700–1850*, 39–72.

—— (1993), *Hanging the Head: Portraiture and Social Formation in Eighteenth Century England*.

POLLARD, GRAHAM, and EHRMAN, A. (1965), *The Distribution of Books by Catalogue . . . to A.D. 1800*.

POLLNITZ, CHARLES-LEWIS (1739), *Memoirs*, 2nd edn.

POLLOCK, LINDA A. (1990), 'Embarking on a Rough Passage: The Experience of Pregnancy in Early-Modern Society', in Fildes 1990.

POMEAU, RENÉ (1953), 'Voltaire en Angleterre', *Annales publiées par la faculté de lettres de Toulouse: Littéraires*.

—— (1982), 'Une correspondance inédite de Montesquieu', *Revue d'histoire littéraire de la France*, 186–262.

—— (1985), *D'Arouet à Voltaire 1694–1734*.

—— (1985–95), *Voltaire en son temps*, new revised edn.

POPE, ALEXANDER (1735), *Mr. Pope's Literary Correspondence. Volume the Second*.

—— (1751), *Works*, ed. William Warburton.

—— (1776), *Additions to the Works of*.

—— (1797), *Works*, ed. Thomas Warton.

—— (1939–64), *Poems*, Twickenham Edition (London and New Haven).

—— (1986), *Prose Works*, ii. *The Major Works, 1725–1744*, ed. Rosemary Cowler.

PORTER, ROY (1982), *English Society in the Eighteenth Century*.

—— (1995) (ed.), *Medicine in the Enlightenment*.

—— and ROUSSEAU, G. S. (1987), *Sexual Underworlds of the Enlightenment*.

POTTLE, FREDERICK A. (1984), *James Boswell: The Earlier Years, 1740–1769*.

PRICE, F. G. H. (1875), *Temple Bar, or Some Account of 'ye Marygold', No. I, Fleet Street*.

PRIOR, JAMES (1860), *Life of Malone*.

PRIOR, MATTHEW (1718; 1941), *Poems on Several Occasions*, facs.

—— (1959; 1971), *Literary Works*, ed. H. B. Wright and M. K. Spears.

RABIL, ALBERT, Jr. (1981), *Laureta Cereta: Quattrocento Humanist*.

RAMSAY, ALLAN (1724), *The Tea Table*.

RAYNOR, DAVID, and SKINNER, ANDREW (1994), 'Sir James Steuart: Nine Letters on the American Conflict, 1775–1778', *William and Mary Quarterly*, 3rd ser. 2.

RAZZELL, PETER (1965), 'Population Change in Eighteenth-Century England: A Re-Interpretation', *Economic History Review*, 2nd ser. 18: 312–32.

—— (1977), *The Conquest of Smallpox: The Impact of Inoculation on Smallpox Mortality in Eighteenth Century Britain* (Firle, Sussex).

REID, STUART J. (1915), *John and Sarah Duke and Duchess of Marlborough 1660–1744*.

Remarks on the Sentence Given in Favour of E—W—M—, and T—T—, Esqs; by the L—t C—l at Paris (1752).

RÉMOND DE SAINT-MARD (1721), *Lettres Galantes et Philosophiques de Madame de ***(Paris)*.

RIBEIRO, AILEEN (1984), *The Dress Worn at Masquerades in England, 1730 to 1790, and its Relation to Fancy Dress in Portraiture*.

RIBEIRO, ALVARO, and BASKER JAMES G. (1996) (eds.), *Tradition in Transition: Women Writers, Marginal Texts, and the Eighteenth-Century Canon*.

RICHARDS, ERIC (1973), *The Leviathan of Wealth: The Sutherland Fortune in the Industrial Revolution*.

RICHARDSON, SAMUEL (1753–4; 1972), *Sir Charles Grandison*, ed. Jocelyn Harris.

Richelieu: The Travels and Adventures of Mademoiselle de Richelieu. Cousin to the present Duke of that Name. Who made the Tour of Europe, dressed in Men's Cloaths . . . Now done into English from the Lady's own Manuscript (1744), trans. 'Mr Erskine'.

Rival Wives, The: Or, the Greeting of Clarissa to Skirra in the Elysian Shades (1738).

Rival Wives Answer'd, The: Or, Skirra to Clarissa (1738).

RIZZO, BETTY (1994), *Companions Without Vows: Relationships Among Eighteenth-Century British Women*.

ROBINSON, FRANCIS (1982), *Atlas of the Islamic World since 1500*.

ROGERS, PAT (1993), 'Book Dedications in Britain, 1700–1799: A Preliminary Survey', *British Journal for Eighteenth-Century Studies*, 16: 216.

ROSENHEIM, JAMES M. (1989), *The Townshends of Raynham: Nobility in Transition in Restoration and Early Hanoverian England* (Middletown, Conn.).

ROSENTHAL, MARGARET F. (1992), *The Honest Courtesan: Veronica Franco, Citizen and Writer in Sixteenth-Century Venice*.

ROUSSEAU, ANDRÉ-MICHEL (1976), *L'Angleterre et Voltaire*.

ROUSSEAU, G. S. (1987), '"Wicked Whiston" and the Scriblerians: Another Ancients-Moderns Controversy', *Studies in Eighteenth-Century Culture*, 17, ed. John Yolton and Leslie Ellen Brown.

—— and PORTER, ROY (1990), *Exoticism in the Enlightenment*.

ROUSSEAU, JEAN BAPTISTE (1712), *Œuvres* (Rotterdam).

Royal Society (1665–), *Philosophical Transactions Giving Some Account of the . . . Studies and Labours of the Ingenious In Many Considerable Parts of the World*.

RUMBOLD, VALERIE (1989), *Women's Place in Pope's World*.

RUSNOCK, ANDREA A. (1995), 'The Weight of Evidence and the Burden of Authority: Case Histories, Medical Statistics and Smallpox Inoculation', in Porter 1995.

RUSSELL, ALEXANDER (1794), *The Natural History of Aleppo*, 2nd edn. by Patrick Russell.

SABOR, PETER (1997), in *The Female Spectator*, 2 Feb. (Mountain View, Calif.).

SAID, EDWARD (1978), *Orientalism*.

SALE, WILLIAM MERRITT, Jr. (1936; 1969), *Samuel Richardson: A Bibliographical Record of his Literary Career with Historical Notes*.

SALMON, CHRISTINE (1991), 'Representations of the Female Self in Familiar Letters 1650–1780', Ph.D. thesis, University of London.

SALVADORI, FABIA BORRONI (1983), 'Personaggi inglesi inseriti nella vita fiorentina del '700: Lady Walpole e il suo ambiente', *Mitteilungen des Kunsthistorischen Institutes in Florenz*, 27: 83–123.

SANSOM, MARTHA FOWKE (1752), *Clio: Or, A Secret History of the Life and Amours of the Late Celebrated Mrs. S-n-m.*

Satan's Harvest Home: or the Present State of Whorecraft, Adultery, Fornication, Procuring, Pimping, Sodomy, And the Game of Flatts (1749).

SAVAGE, RICHARD (1725), *Authors of the Town: A Satire.*

—— (1726) (ed.), *Miscellaneous Poems and Translations*, By several Hands.

—— (1729), *The Wanderer.*

—— (1962), *Poetical Works*, ed. Clarence Tracy.

SAVORY, REGINALD (1966), *His Britannic Majesty's Army in Germany during the Seven Years War.*

SCARISBRICK, DIANA (1994), *Jewellery in Britain 1066–1837: A Documentary, Social, Literary and Artistic Survey* (Norwich).

SCHEFER, CHARLES (1894), *Mémoire historique sur l'ambassade de France a Constantinople Par le marquis de Bonnac* (Paris).

SCHILLER, PETER (1987), *Der Botanische Garten in Padua | L'Orto botanico di Padova* (Venice).

SCHURMAN, ANNA MARIA VAN (1659), *The Learned Maid; or, Whether a Maid may be a Scholar?*, trans. Clement Barksdale.

SCHWEIZER, KARL W. (1988*a*), 'Lord Bute, William Pitt, and the Peace Negotiations with France, April–September 1761', in Schweizer 1988*c*, 41–55.

—— (1988*b*), 'Lord Bute and the Press: The Origins of the Press War of 1762 Reconsidered' in Schweizer 1988*c*, 83–98.

—— (1988*c*) (ed.), *Lord Bute, Essays in Re-interpretation.*

—— (1992), 'The Vote of Credit Controversy, 1762', *British Journal for Eighteenth-Century Studies*, 15: 175–85.

SCODEL, JOSHUA (1991), *The English Poetic Epitaph: Commemoration and Conflict from Jonson to Wordsworth.*

SCOTT, SARAH (1766; 1985), *The History of Sir George Ellison*, ed. Betty Rizzo.

SCOTT, WILLIAM ROBERT (1912), *The Constitution . . . of . . . Joint-Stock Companies* (Lexington, Ky.).

SCUDÉRY, MADELEINE DE (1690), *Artamenes; or, The Grand Cyrus*, trans.

SCULL, ANDREW T. (1993), *The Most Solitary of Afflictions: Madness and Society in Britain, 1700–1900.*

SEARY, PETER (1990), *Lewis Theobald and the Editing of Shakespeare.*

SEDGWICK, ROMNEY (1970), *History of Parliament: The House of Commons 1715–1754.*

SEWELL, GEORGE (1719), *Poems on Several Occasions.*

SHACKLETON, ROBERT (1961), *Montesquieu: A Critical Biography.*

SHACKLETON, ROBERT (1988), *Essays on Montesquieu and the Enlightenment*, ed. David Gilson and Martin Smith (Oxford).

SHERBO, ARTHUR (1958), review of Halsband 1956, *Modern Language Notes*, 73.

SHERBURN, GEORGE (1934), *The Early Career of Alexander Pope*.

—— (1938), 'Walpole's Marginalia', *Huntington Library Quarterly*, 1.

SHUTTLETON, DAVID E. (1995), ' "A Modest Examination": John Arbuthnot and the Scottish Newtonians', *British Journal for Eighteenth-Century Studies*, 18: 47–62.

SKINNER, ANDREW W. (1993), 'Sir James Steuart: The Market and the State', *History of Economic Ideas*, 1/1: 1–42.

SLOANE, Sir HANS (1756), 'An Account of Inoculation' (communicated 1736), Royal Society *Transactions*, 516–20.

SMITH, CHARLES SAUMAREZ (1990), *The Building of Castle Howard*.

—— (1993), *Eighteenth-Century Decoration: Design and the Domestic Interior in England*.

SMITHERS, PETER (1954; 1968), *The Life of Joseph Addison*.

SMOLLETT, TOBIAS (1751; 1964), *The Adventures of Peregrine Pickle*, ed. James L. Clifford.

Sofia, A Guide to (1960) (Sofia).

SOMERSET, ANNE (1984), *Ladies in Waiting, from the Tudors to the Present Day*.

SORDET, L. (1854), *Histoire des résidents de France a Genève* (Geneva).

SOWDEN, HANNAH (1805), letter, 31 Jan. 1804, *Edinburgh Review*, 4: 254–6.

SÖZEN, METIN (1987), *The Evolution of Turkish Art and Architecture*.

SPACKS, PATRICIA MEYER (1984), 'Imaginations Warm and Tender: Pope and Lady Mary', *South Atlantic Quarterly*, 83: 207–15.

—— (1988), 'Female Rhetorics', in Shari Benstock (ed.), *The Private Self: Theory and Practice of Women's Autobiographical Writings*.

Spalding Club, Miscellanies of the (1846).

SPELLMAN, W. M. (1993), *The Latitudinarians and the Church of England, 1660–1700*.

SPENCE, JOSEPH (1747), *Polymetis: Or, An Enquiry concerning the Agreement between the Works of the Roman Poets, and the Remains of the Antient Artists*.

—— (1966), *Observations, Anecdotes, and Characters of Books and Men Collected from Conversation*, ed. James M. Osborn.

—— (1975), *Letters from the Grand Tour*, ed. Slava Klima.

STAVES, SUSAN (1990), *Married Women's Separate Property, 1660–1832*.

STEELE, RICHARD (1714) (ed.), *Poetical Miscellanies . . . By the best Hands*.

—— (1941), *Correspondence*, ed. Rae Blanchard.

—— (1944), *Tracts and Pamphlets*, ed. Rae Blanchard.

—— *et al.* (1987), *The Tatler*, 1709–11, ed. Donald F. Bond (Oxford).

STEUART, Sir JAMES (1805), *Works, Political, Metaphysical, and Chronological*, ed. James Steuart.

STEVEN, WILLIAM (1832), *History of the Scottish Church, Rotterdam.*

STEWART, J. DOUGLAS (1971), *Sir Godfrey Kneller.*

STONE, LAURENCE (1991), *The Road to Divorce: England 1530–1987.*

STRAUS, RALPH (1927), *The Unspeakable Curll.*

[STUART, Lady LOUISA] (1898), *Gleanings from an Old Portfolio*, ed. Mrs Godfrey Clark, privately printed for David Douglas (Edinburgh).

—— (1899), *Selections from her Manuscripts*, ed. James A. Home (Edinburgh).

—— (1901, 1903), *Letters to Miss Louisa Clinton*, ed. Hon. James Home, i, ii (Edinburgh).

STUART WORTLEY, VIOLET (1925), *A Prime Minister and His Son, from the correspondence of the third Earl of Bute and of Lt.-General the Hon. Sir Charles Stuart, K.B.*

—— [1948], *Magic in the Distance: A Chronicle of Five Generations.*

SUAREZ, MICHAEL F. (1994), 'Dodsley's *Collection of Poems* and the Ghost of Pope: The Politics of Literary Reputation', *Papers of the Bibliographical Society of America*, 88: 189–206.

—— (1996), 'Trafficking in the Muse: Dodsley's *Collection of Poems* and the Question of Canon', in Ribeiro and Basker 1996: 297–313.

SUFFOLK, HENRIETTA [HOWARD], Countess of (1824), *Letters to and from . . . 1712 to 1767* [ed. J. W. Croker].

SUNDON, Viscountess (1847), *Memoirs of Viscountess Sundon, Mistress of the Robes to Queen Caroline.*

SUTTON, Sir ROBERT (1953), *Despatches*, ed. Akdes Nimet Kurat.

SWEEZY, PAUL M. (1938), *Monopoly and Competition in the English Coal Trade 1550–1850.*

SWIFT, JONATHAN (1937), *Poems*, ed. Harold Williams.

—— (1948), *Journal to Stella*, ed. Harold Williams.

—— (1963–5), *Correspondence*, ed. Harold Williams.

SYDENHAM, THOMAS (1669), *The Whole Works*, trans. from Latin by John Pechy.

TAYLER, HENRIETTA (1938), *The Jacobite Court at Rome in 1719.*

Tell-tale Cupids Lately discover'd in the Eyes of a certain Court Lady (1735).

THICKNESSE, PHILIP (1766), *A Narrative . . . Relative to the Publication of some Original Letters and Poetry of Lady Mary Wortley Montague's.*

THOMAS, CLAUDIA N. (1994), *Alexander Pope and His Eighteenth-Century Women Readers.*

THOMS, WILLIAM J. (1856), 'Curll Papers, Stray Notes on the Life and Publications of Edmund Curll', *Notes and Queries*, 1.

THRUPP, G. A. (1877), *The History of Coaches.*

TICKELL, R. E. (1931), *Thomas Tickell.*

TILLYARD, STELLA (1994), *Aristocrats: Caroline, Emily, Louisa and Sarah Lennox 1740–1832.*

TINKER, C. B. (1959), *The Tinker Library: A Bibliographical Catalogue of the Books and Manuscripts collected by Chauncy B. Tinker (1876–1963)* (New Haven).

TISSOT, S. A. A. D. (1754), *L'Inoculation justifiée* (Lausanne).

TOLLET, ELIZABETH (1724), *Poems on Several Occasions.*

TOTT, FRANÇOIS DE (1784), *Mémoires sur les Turcs et les Tartares* (Amsterdam).

TOWERS, ERIC (1986), *Dashwood: The Man and the Myth.*

TRACY, CLARENCE (1963), *The Artificial Bastard: A Biography of Richard Savage.*

TREADWELL, MICHAEL (1982), 'London Trade Publishers 1675–1750', *The Library*, 6th ser. 4: 110–25.

TREAT, IDA (1913), *Francesco Algarotti.*

TREGLOWN, G. L., and MORTIMER, M. C. F. (1981), 'Elegant and Elusive: Wine-glasses of the Kit-Cat Club', *Country Life*, 170: 46–8.

TRONCHIN, HENRY (1895), *Le Conseilleur François Tronchin et ses amis, Voltaire, Diderot, Grimm etc. d'après des documents inédits* (Geneva).

—— (1906), *Un Médicin du xviiie siècle: Théodore Tronchin (1709–1781) daprès des documents inédite* (Geneva).

TYERS, THOMAS (1782), *A Historical Rhapsody on Mr. Pope.*

UGLOW, JENNY (1997), *Hogarth: A Life and a World.*

Ursula, The Order of St [1932].

VALCANOVER, ANNA FRANCESCA (1986), 'Le lettere da Napoli di Lady Mary Wortley Montagu', *Esperienze Letterarie*, ed. Mario Santori, 81–4.

—— (1987), in *Studi Veneziani.*

—— (1989), 'Le Lettere da Venezia . . . 1739–40', *Studi Veneziani.*

VAN LUTTERVELT, R. (1958), *De 'Turkes' Schilderijen Van J. B. Vanmour* (Istanbul).

VEDRENNE, ELIZABETH (1990), *Living in Venice.*

[VERVILLE, F. BEROALDE DE] (1610), *L'Histoire veritable, ou le voyage des princes fortunez.*

VIVIAN, FRANCES (1971), *Il console Smith mercante e collezionista* (Vicenza).

VOLTAIRE (1953–65), *Correspondence*, ed. Theodore Besterman (Oxford).

—— (1963–93), *Correspondance*, ed. Theodore Besterman (Paris).

WADE, IRA O. (1931), 'Destouches in England', *Modern Philology*, 29.

WAGSTAFFE, WILLIAM (1722), *A Letter to Dr. Freind; shewing The Danger and Uncertainty of Inoculating the Small Pox.*

WALDIE, JANE (1820), *Sketches descriptive of Italy in the years 1816 and 1817.*

WALPOLE, HORACE (1758), *A Catalogue of the Royal and Noble Authors of England, With Lists of their Works* (Strawberry Hill).

—— (1903), *Letters*, ed. Mrs Paget Toynbee.

—— (1937–83), *Correspondence*, ed. W. S. Lewis *et al.*

—— (1978), *Miscellany 1786–1795*, ed. Lars E. Troide.

WEAMYS, ANNA (1651; 1994), *Continuation of Sir Philip Sidney's Arcadia*, ed. Patrick Colborn Cullen.

WELLEK, RENÉ, and RIBEIRO, ALVARO (1979) (eds.), *Evidence in Literary Scholarship: Essays in Memory of James Marshall Osborn* (Oxford).

WIEDEMANN, THEODOR (1883), *Geschichte der Frauenklöster St. Laurenz & Maria Magdalena*.

WILLIAMS, AUBREY (1973–4), 'The "Angel, Goddess, Montague" of Pope's *Sober Advice from Horace*', *Modern Philology*, 71.

WILLIAMS, PERROTT (1725), *Some Remarks upon Dr. Wagstaff's Letter against Inoculating the Small-Pox*, with appendix by F[rederick] Slare.

WILMOT, JOHN (1812), *The Life of the Rev. John Hough*.

WILSON, ADRIAN (1990a), 'The Politics of Medical Improvement in Early Hanoverian London', in Andrew Cunningham and Roger French (eds.), *The Medical Enlightenment of the Eighteenth Century*, 4–59.

—— (1990b), 'The Ceremony of Childbirth, and its Interpretation', in Fildes 1990.

—— (1995), *The Making of Man-Midwifery, Childbirth in England 1660–1770*.

WINCHILSEA, Lady, *see* Finch.

WINDHAM, WILLIAM (1930), *Early Life and Diaries*, ed. Robert Ketton-Cremer.

WODROW, ROBERT (1842–3), *Analecta*.

WOOD, A. C. (1925), 'The English Embassy at Constantinople, 1660–1762', *English Historical Review*, 40.

WOODVILLE, WILLIAM (1796), *History of the Inoculation of the Small-Pox in Great Britain*.

WOODWARD, CAROLYN (1993), ' "My Heart So Wrapt": Lesbian Disruptions in Eighteenth-Century British Fiction', *Signs*, Summer: 838–65.

WOOLF, VIRGINIA (1928), *Orlando* (repr. 1978).

—— (1929), *A Room of One's Own* (New York).

WORDIE, J. R. (1982), *Estate Management in Eighteenth-Century England*.

WORSLEY, GILES (1985), 'Middlethorpe Hall, Yorkshire', *Country Life*, 12 Dec.

WRAXALL, Sir NATHANIEL WILLIAM (1815; 1884), *Historical and . . . Posthumous Memoirs . . . 1772–1784*, ed. Henry B. Wheatley.

WRENN, HAROLD B. (1920), *A Catalogue of the Library of the late John Henry Wrenn*, ed. Thomas J. Wise (Austin, Tex.).

WYNNE, GIUSTINIANA (1785a), *Moral and Sentimental Essays on Various Subjects*.

—— (1785b), *Pieces morales et sentimentales*.

[YEOWELL, J.] (1862), *A Literary Antiquary: Memoir of William Oldys*.

YOUNG, EDWARD (1727), *The Universal Passion*, v.

—— (1971), *Correspondence*, ed. H. Pettit.

ZIPES, JACK (1989) (trans. and introd.), *Beauties, Beasts and Enchantment: Classic French Fairy Tales*.

INDEX